FURTHER PRAISE FOR Dissent in America

"This is a wonderfully rich collection of voices of courage and resistance through all of our national history. These are the true heroes of our country, not the presidents and generals and industrialists, but those who spoke truth to power, and their words not only instruct us about our history, but inspire us at a time when dissenters are so needed."

—Howard Zinn, author of *A People's History of the United States*

"A treasure trove of American voices across the centuries, well-edited and richly varied. *Dissent in America* opens windows into our history that have been too long kept shut. Of value to students and lay readers alike."

—Michael Parenti, author of *The Culture Struggle* and *Superpatriotism*

"There's something to offend everyone in these [pages]: The founding fathers being denounced by British loyalists as traitors and wastrels, and by Indians as cheats and scoundrels; abolitionists denounce southern despots and civil libertarians denounce Lincoln's tyranny; women denounce men and workers denounce capitalists; and the latter groups respond to their critics with equal vituperation. This offensive book, in short, is a primer on American democracy, which is not about waving the flag, but about taking ideas seriously and debating them intensely. It couldn't come at a better time."

—Mark C. Carnes, Executive Secretary, Society of American Historians and author of *The American Nation*

"As a nation of practiced dissenters, born of dissent and nurtured by fulsome dissenters, all Americans, including those who today call themselves 'conservatives,' will see the value and virtue in retracing the perpetual challenges to the established order that Ralph Young has so expertly organized in this single, incredibly constructive and informative volume. Indispensable to students of American politics and social movements, this book belongs on the shelves of all who contemplate change and the forces of change within American culture."

—James W. Hilty, Professor of History and Dean, Ambler College, Temple University, and author of *Robert Kennedy: Brother Protector*

"*Dissent in America* puts in [people's] heads—and hopefully in their minds—the words of those we usually read *about* but so rarely read. From Native Americans on the other side of 'progress' to ecoterrorists today, [this volume] allow[s] voices to speak that challenge and enrich our monotonic national narrative."

—James W. Loewen, author of *Lies My Teacher Told Me: Everything Your High School History Textbook Got Wrong*

Dissent in America

The Voices That Shaped a Nation

RALPH F. YOUNG

PEARSON
Longman

New York   San Francisco   Boston
London   Toronto   Sydney   Tokyo   Singapore   Madrid
Mexico City   Munich   Paris   Cape Town   Hong Kong   Montreal

Printer and Binder: Courier Corporation/Westford
Cover Printer: Coral Graphic Services

Visit us at www.ablongman.com

ISBN 0-321-44297-0

1 2 3 4 5 6 7 8 9 10—CRW—09 08 07 06

For Pat

CONTENTS

What Is Dissent?   XXI

PART ONE

Pre-Revolutionary Roots, 1607–1760   1

Introduction: The Long Roots of Modern Dissent   1

Roger Williams (c. 1603–1683)   5
The Bloudy Tenent of Persecution, 1644   6

Anne Hutchinson (1591–1643)   12
The Trial of Anne Hutchinson, 1637   12

Alice Tilly (1594–c. 1660)   18
Petitions for the Release of Alice Tilly, 1649   18

William Dyer (1609–1672) and Mary Dyer (c. 1611–1660)   21
Petitions and Letters, 1660   22

Nathaniel Bacon (1647–1676)   27
Declaration in the Name of the People, July 30, 1676   28

Quaker Antislavery Petition   30
A Minute Against Slavery, 1688   31

Letter from an Anonymous Slave   33
Releese Us Out of This Cruell Bondegg, 1723   33

Native American Voices (1609–1752)   34
Powhatan, Speech to John Smith, 1609   34
Garangula, Speech to Governor La Barre of New France, 1684   35
Stung Serpent, Reply to Antoine Simon Le Page du Pratz, 1723   37
Loron Sauguaarum, Negotiations for the Casco Bay Treaty, 1727   38
Lenni Lenape, Grievance Against the "Walking Purchase," 1740   40
Atiwaneto, Remarks to Phineas Stevens, 1752   42
Mashpee, Petition to the Massachusetts General Court, 1752   43

John Peter Zenger (1697–1746)   44
   Articles from *The New York Weekly Journal*, 1733   45

Eighteenth-Century Runaway Women   48
   Advertisements from the *Pennsylvania Gazette*, 1742–1748   49

PART TWO
───────

Revolution and the Birth of a Nation, 1760–1820   51

Introduction: The Republic Takes Shape   51

John Woolman (1720–1772)   53
   "Considerations on Keeping Negroes, Part Second," 1762   54

John Killbuck (1737–1811)   58
   Speech to the Governors of Pennsylvania, Maryland, and Virginia,
      December 4, 1771   58

Samuel Adams (1722–1803)   59
   The Rights of the Colonists, November 20, 1772   60

Revolutionary Women   64
   Hannah Griffiths, Poem, 1768   65
   Ladies of Edenton, North Carolina, Agreement, 1774–1775   66

The Second Continental Congress   67
   A Declaration by the Representatives of the United Colonies, 1775   67

Thomas Paine (1737–1809)   72
   Common Sense, 1776   72

Abigail Adams (1744–1818) and John Adams (1735–1826)   79
   Letters, 1776   80

Thomas Hutchinson (1711–1780)   83
   A Loyalist Critique of the Declaration of Independence, 1776   84

Slave Petition   95
   Petition for Gradual Emancipation, 1777   95

Joseph Brant (1742–1807)   96
   Speech to Governor Haldimand at Quebec, May 21, 1783   96

Alexander McGillivray (c. 1759–1793)   *98*
   Speech to the Governor of Florida, 1785   99

United Indian Nations   *100*
   Protest to the United States Congress, 1786   101

Shays's Rebellion, 1786–1787   *103*
   Statement of Grievances, 1786   104

George Mason (1725–1792)   *104*
   Objections to This Constitution of Government, 1787   105

Judith Sargent Murray (1751–1820)   *106*
   "On the Equality of the Sexes," 1790   107

Shawnee, Miami, Ottawa, and Seneca Proposal   *115*
   Proposal to Maintain Indian Lands, 1793   115

Protest Against the Alien and Sedition Acts   *117*
   The Virginia Resolutions, 1798   117
   The Kentucky Resolutions, 1799   119

Tecumseh (1768–1813)   *120*
   Letter to Governor William Henry Harrison, 1810   121
   Speech to the Southern Tribes, 1811   122

Congressmen Protest the War of 1812   *124*
   Federalist Protest, 1812   124

Hartford Convention   *125*
   Proposals, 1814–1815   126

Free Blacks of Philadelphia   *127*
   Protest Against Colonization Policy, 1817   128

PART THREE

Questioning the Nation, 1820–1860   129

Introduction: The Reforming Impulse   *129*

Theodore Frelinghuysen (1787–1862)   *132*
   Speech Protesting the Indian Removal Bill, April 9, 1830   133

Cherokee Chief John Ross (1790–1866)   *135*
    Letter Protesting the Treaty of New Echota, 1836   136

Sylvia Dubois (1788–1889)   *137*
    Reminiscences from *Sylvia Dubois, a Biografy of the Slav Who Whipt Her
        Mistress and Gand Her Fredom*, 1883   138

David Walker (1785–1830)   *141*
    Appeal to the Coloured Citizens of the World, 1830   141

William Lloyd Garrison (1805–1879)   *150*
    The Liberator, Vol. I, No. I, January 1, 1831   151

William Apess (1798–1839)   *153*
    "An Indian's Looking-Glass for the White Man," 1833   153

Laborers of Boston   *158*
    Ten-Hour Circular, 1835   159

Angelina Grimké (1805–1879) and Sarah Grimké (1792–1873)   *161*
    Appeal to the Christian Women of the South, 1836   162
    "The Original Equality of Woman," 1837   169

Wendell Phillips (1811–1884)   *172*
    On the Murder of Lovejoy, December 8, 1837   172

Ralph Waldo Emerson (1803–1882)   *176*
    "Self-Reliance," 1841   177
    Address to the Citizens of Concord, 1851   185

Margaret Fuller (1810–1850)   *187*
    Woman in the Nineteenth Century, Part 3, 1844   188

Lowell Mills Girls   *192*
    Lowell Female Labor Reform Association, 1846   193
    Lowell Female Industrial Reform and Mutual Aid Society, 1847   195

Elizabeth Cady Stanton (1815–1902)   *197*
    Speech at Seneca Falls, July 19, 1848   198
    Declaration of Sentiments, 1848   200

Sojourner Truth (c. 1797–1883)   *204*
    Ain't I A Woman?, 1851   204

Frederick Douglass (1818–1895)   *205*
    The North Star, July 28, 1848   206
    What to the Slave Is the Fourth of July?, July 5, 1852   207

Henry David Thoreau (1817–1862)   *211*
   "On Resistance to Civil Government," 1849   213

Lucy Stone (1818–1893)   *228*
   Statement on Marriage, 1855   228

The Know-Nothings   *229*
   American Party Platform, Philadelphia, February 21, 1856   230

John Brown (1800–1859)   *231*
   Address to the Virginia Court at Charles Town, Virginia,
     November 2, 1859   232

PART FOUR

Civil War and Reconstruction, 1860–1877   235

Introduction: A Divided Nation   *235*

Clement L. Vallandigham (1820–1871)   *238*
   Response to Lincoln's Address to Congress, July 10, 1861   239

William Brownlow (1805–1877)   *245*
   Knoxville *Whig* Antisecession Letters and Editorial, May 1861   245

The Arkansas Peace Society   *250*
   Arkansas Peace Society Documents, 1861   250

Joseph E. Brown (1821–1894)   *258*
   Letter to Alexander H. Stephens, 1862   259
   Message to the Legislature, March 10, 1864   260

Cyrus Pringle (1838–1911)   *265*
   The Record of a Quaker Conscience, 1863   266

African American Soldiers of the Union Army   *277*
   Correspondence Protesting Unequal Pay, 1863–1864   279

Frederick Douglass (1818–1895)   *289*
   What the Black Man Wants, April 1865   289

Zion Presbyterian Church   *294*
   Petition to the United States Congress, November 24, 1865   294

American Equal Rights Association   *295*
   National Convention Resolutions, New York, May 1867   296

Susan B. Anthony (1820–1906)   *297*
    From an Account of the Trial of Susan B. Anthony, July 3, 1873   298
    Is It a Crime for a U.S. Citizen to Vote?, 1873   299

Robert B. Elliott (1842–1884)   *305*
    Speech in Congress on the Civil Rights Bill, January 6, 1874   306

PART FIVE

Industry and Reform, 1877–1912   313

Introduction: Progress and Discontent   *313*

Terence Powderly (1849–1924)   *317*
    Preamble to the Constitution of the Knights of Labor,
        January 3, 1878   318
    "Eight Hours," by I. G. Blanchard and Jesse Jones, 1880s   319

Chief Joseph (1840–1904)   *321*
    Appeal to the Hayes Administration, 1879   322

Mary Elizabeth Lease (1850–1933)   *324*
    Speech to the WCTU, 1890   324

The People's Party   *328*
    The Omaha Platform, July 1892   329

Jane Addams (1860–1935)   *332*
    The Subjective Necessity of Social Settlements, 1892   333

Frances E. Willard (1839–1898)   *334*
    Speech to the World's Woman's Christian Temperance
        Union, 1893   335

Booker T. Washington (1856–1915)   *341*
    Cast Down Your Bucket Where You Are, 1895   342

W. E. B. DuBois (1868–1963)   *344*
    "Of Mr. Booker T. Washington and Others," 1903   345
    Address to the Niagara Conference, Harpers Ferry,
        West Virginia, 1906   353

Ida B. Wells-Barnett (1862–1931)   *355*
    Lynch Law in Georgia, June 20, 1899   356
    "Tortured and Burned Alive," 1899   357

Carl Schurz (1829–1906)   *360*
  Address at the University of Chicago Denouncing U.S. Imperialism,
    January 4, 1899   360

William Jennings Bryan (1860–1925)   *363*
  The Paralyzing Influence of Imperialism, July 1900   363

Mother Jones (1830–1930)   *369*
  "The March of the Mill Children," 1903   370

John Muir (1838–1914)   *374*
  "The Hetch Hetchy Valley," January 1908   375
  "Save the Redwoods," January 1920   381

Emma Goldman (1869–1940)   *383*
  "Marriage and Love," 1911   384

Walter Rauschenbusch (1861–1918)   *390*
  Christianizing the Social Order, 1912   390

The Socialist Party   *391*
  Socialist Party Platform, May 12, 1912   392

PART SIX

Conflict and Depression, 1912–1945   397

Introduction: Becoming a World Power   *397*

Joe Hill (1879–1915)   *401*
  "We Will Sing One Song," 1913   402
  "The Preacher and the Slave Girl," 1913   403

Robert M. LaFollette (1855–1925)   *404*
  Antiwar Speech, April 4, 1917   405
  Defense of Free Speech, October 6, 1917   407

Eugene V. Debs (1855–1926)   *410*
  Antiwar Speech, Canton, Ohio, June 1918   411

Randolph Bourne (1886–1918)   *416*
  "War Is the Health of the State," 1918   417

A. Philip Randolph (1889–1979)   *429*
  "On Socialism," 1919   430

Marcus Garvey (1887–1940)   *431*
  Speech to the Universal Negro Improvement Association,
    Philadelphia, 1919   432
  Appeal to the Soul of White America, 1923   434

Margaret Sanger (1879–1966)   *434*
  "Legislating Woman's Morals," 1920   435
  "The Goal," 1920   440

H. L. Mencken (1880–1956)   *443*
  "On Being an American," 1922   444
  "Last Words," 1926   446
  "Mencken's Creed"   449

Langston Hughes (1902–1967)   *449*
  "I, Too, Sing America," 1925   450

Father Charles Coughlin (1891–1979)   *450*
  National Radio Address, November 1934   451
  National Radio Address, June 1936   453

Huey Long (1893–1935)   *455*
  Speech in the U.S. Senate, February 5, 1934   456
  Radio Address, January 1935   461

Emma Goldman (1869–1940)   *464*
  The Individual, Society and the State, 1936   464

Woody Guthrie (1912–1967)   *473*
  "The Ballad of Pretty Boy Floyd," 1939   475
  "Jesus Christ," 1940   476

J. Saunders Redding (1906–1988) and Charles F. Wilson (Unknown)   *477*
  J. Saunders Redding, "A Negro Looks at This War," 1942   477
  Charles F. Wilson, Letter to President Roosevelt, 1944   479

David Dellinger (1915–2004)   *481*
  Why I Refused to Register in the October 1940 Draft and a Little
    of What It Led To   481

Minoru Yasui (1916–1986)   *490*
  Reflections on Executive Order 9066   491
  Resistance   492
  Statement upon Sentencing, 1942   494
  Letters from Jail to His Sister Yuka Yasui, 1942–1943   495

Henry Miller (1891–1980) 497
  Murder the Murderer, 1944 498

PART SEVEN
─────────

The Affluent Society, 1945–1966 513

Introduction: The Crack in the Picture Window 513

John Howard Lawson (1894–1977) 519
  Testimony Before the House Committee on Un-American
    Activities, 1947 520
  Lawson's Statement That Was Excluded from the Public Record,
    1947 522

Margaret Chase Smith (1897–1995) 525
  Declaration of Conscience, 1950 525

Paul Robeson (1898–1976) 529
  Testimony Before the House Committee on Un-American Activities,
    June 12, 1956 530

Harry Hay (1912–2002) 537
  Speech at the Gay Spirit Visions Conference, Highlands, North Carolina,
    November 1990 538

Allen Ginsberg (1926–1997) 542
  "America," 1956 543

Songs of the Civil Rights Movement 546
  Pete Seeger, "I Ain't Scared of Your Jail," 1963 547
  Carver Neblett, "If You Miss Me at the Back of the Bus," 1960 547
  Bob Dylan, "Only a Pawn in Their Game," 1963 548

Martin Luther King Jr. (1929–1968) 549
  Letter from a Birmingham Jail, April 16, 1963 550

Fannie Lou Hamer (1917–1977) 563
  Testimony Before the Credentials Committee of the Democratic
    National Convention, 1964 564

Malcolm X (1925–1965) 566
  The Black Revolution, 1964 566

Stokely Carmichael (1941–1998)   567
    Berkeley Speech, October 1966   568

The Black Panther Party   577
    Black Panther Party Platform, 1966   578

Students for a Democratic Society   580
    The Port Huron Statement, 1962   580

Betty Friedan (1921–2006)   585
    The Feminine Mystique, 1963   585

Protest Music I   589
    Phil Ochs, "I Ain't Marching Anymore," 1965   590
    Malvina Reynolds, "Little Boxes," 1962   591
    Bob Dylan, "The Times They Are A-Changin'," 1963   592
    Bob Dylan, "It's Alright Ma (I'm Only Bleeding)," 1965   593

PART EIGHT

Mobilization: Vietnam and the Counterculture, 1964–1975   597

Introduction: The Movement   597

Mario Savio (1942–1996)   604
    Speech at the University of California at Berkeley,
        December 2, 1964   604

Carl Oglesby (1935–)   606
    Speech Denouncing the War in Vietnam, Washington, DC,
        November 27, 1965   606

The Weather Underground   612
    You Don't Need a Weatherman to Know Which Way
        the Wind Blows, 1969   613

John Kerry (1943–)   614
    Statement to the Senate Committee on Foreign Relations,
        April 23, 1971   614

Timothy Leary (1920–1996)   617
    Using LSD to Imprint the Tibetan-Buddhist
        Experience, 1964   618

Herbert Marcuse (1898–1979)   624
    Political Preface, *Eros and Civilization*, 1966   625

Abbie Hoffman (1936–1989)   627
    Introduction, *Steal This Book*, 1970   628

Ram Dass (1931–)   631
    Be Here Now, 1971   632

Protest Music II   637
    Pete Seeger, "Waist Deep in the Big Muddy," 1967   638
    Country Joe McDonald, "I Feel-Like-I'm-Fixin'-to-Die Rag," 1965   639
    Buffy Sainte-Marie, "My Country 'Tis of Thy People You're
        Dying," 1965   641
    John Fogerty, Creedence Clearwater Revival, "Fortunate Son," 1969   643

Redstockings   643
    The Redstockings Manifesto, 1969   644

S.C.U.M. (Society for Cutting Up Men)   646
    S.C.U.M. Manifesto, 1968   646

Gloria Steinem (1934–)   649
    "'Women's Liberation' Aims to Free Men, Too," June 7, 1970   649

Stonewall   654
    Stonewall Documents, 1969   654

César Chávez (1927–1993)   656
    Interview with César Chávez, Apostle of Non-Violence, May 1970   656

The American Indian Movement   660
    A Proclamation: To the Great White Father and All His People, 1969   661
    American Indian Movement 20 Point Proposal, October 1972,
        Minneapolis, Minnesota   663

PART NINE

Contemporary Dissent, 1975–Present   669

Introduction: Crossing the Threshold into the New Millennium—
    Globalization vs. Jihad   669

Edward Abbey (1927–1989)   674
    Desert Solitaire, 1968   676

Paul Weyrich (1941–)   677
  "A Conservative's Lament: After Iran, We Need to Change
    Our System and Grand Strategy," March 8, 1987   678

ACT UP   679
  ACT UP Activist Aldyn McKean Explains Civil Disobedience, 1987   681
  Vito Russo, "Why We Fight," 1988   683

Jeff Paterson (1968–)   686
  Interview with Jeff Paterson, January 2001   687

Gay Liberation   694
  Statement of Ernest Dillon, 1994   694
  Statement of Daniel Miller, 1994   695
  Statement of Nancy McDonald, 1994   697
  Statement of Phill Wilson, Director of Public Policy, AIDS Project, Los
    Angeles, 1994   699
  Statement of Letitia Gomez, Executive Director, Latino/a Lesbian and Gay
    Organization, 1994   700

The Michigan Militia   703
  Statement of Purpose and Mission, 1995   704
  In Defense of Liberty II, 1995   704

Theodore Kaczynski (1942–)   706
  The Unabomber Manifesto, 1996   707
  Interview with Theodore Kaczynski, June 1999   709

Ralph Nader (1934–)   711
  It's Time to End Corporate Welfare As We Know It, 1996   712
  Green Party Platform, 2000   715

Michael Moore (1953–)   718
  Introduction, *Stupid White Men*, 2001   719

Ani DiFranco (1970–)   725
  "self evident," 2001   726

Protest Music III   731
  Rage Against the Machine, "Know Your Enemy," 1992   731
  Mos Def, "Mathematics," 1999   733
  Mos Def, "New World Water," 1999   735
  Public Enemy, "Son of a Bush," 2002   737
  Immortal Technique, "The 4th Branch," 2003   739
  Steve Earle, "Rich Man's War," 2004   741

Amnesty International   742
    Amnesty International's Concerns Regarding Post–September 11
        Detentions in the U.S.A., March 14, 2002   742

Earth Liberation Front   745
    Written Testimony Supplied to the U.S. House of Representatives
        for the February 12, 2002, Hearing on "Ecoterrorism"   746
    Press Release, September 3, 2002   751

Not in Our Name   752
    Statement of Conscience, 2003   752

Veterans Against the Iraq War   755
    Call to Conscience from Veterans to Active Duty Troops
        and Reservists, 2003   755
    Message to the Troops: Resist!, October 11, 2002   757
    Defending My Freedom, March 21, 2003   758

The American Civil Liberties Union   760
    Freedom Under Fire: Dissent in Post-9/11 America,
        May 2003   760

MoveOn.org   765
    The Many Faces of the Media, 2004   766
    The Power of Connecting, 2004   767

Michael Berg (1945–)   769
    "George Bush Never Looked Into Nick's Eyes," May 21, 2004   769
    Transcript of Oklahoma City Speech (Given at a Church),
        May 5, 2005   771

Cindy Sheehan (1957–)   773
    Not Worth My Son's Sacrifice, February 7, 2005   774
    A Lie of Historic Proportions, August 8, 2005   776
    Carly's Poem—A Nation Rocked to Sleep, August 15, 2005   778

    Author's Note   781

    Acknowledgments   782

    About the Documents   784

    Text and Photo Credits   785

    Index   789

WHAT IS DISSENT?

Cautious, careful people, always casting about to preserve their reputation and social standing, never can bring about a reform. Those who are really in earnest must be willing to be anything or nothing in the world's estimation, and publicly and privately, in season and out, avow their sympathy with despised and persecuted ideas and their advocates, and bear the consequences.

—Susan B. Anthony

All we say to America is to be true to what you said on paper. . . . Somewhere I read [pause] of the freedom of assembly. Somewhere I read [pause] of the freedom of speech. Somewhere I read [pause] of the freedom of press. Somewhere I read [pause] that the greatness of America is the right to protest for right.

—Martin Luther King Jr.

In February 2003, hundreds of thousands of Americans took to the streets of New York, Washington, Philadelphia, San Francisco, and a host of other cities around the nation to protest the planned invasion of Iraq. At the same time, other groups organized counter-demonstrations to protest against the protestors who they saw as unpatriotic and disloyal. Regardless of their political views, however, both demonstrators and counter-demonstrators were exercising their fundamental right to openly express their opinions—opinions that would never have been heard without the United States' commitment, written into the Constitution, guaranteeing freedom of conscience, freedom of speech, and as Martin Luther King Jr. put it in his last speech, "the right to protest for right."

Most Americans have expressed dissent at one time or another. From grumbling about a law we feel has a negative impact upon our lives or our businesses, to voting to replace a legislator, to writing letters to the editor of a newspaper or to a member of congress, we express our disapproval of the status quo. Sometimes we sign petitions. Sometimes we become more active and join a protest march or go so far as to commit an act of civil disobedience or are even tempted to take up a brick or a stone and smash a window. However we express our dissent, we are simply part of a long American tradition of democracy.

Dissent is central to American history. Not a decade has passed without voices being raised in protest against policies and decisions made by legislators, governors, and presidents. Even before the United States was established, there was dissent. During the seventeenth century, religious dissent played a significant role in establishing the English colonies as Puritans, Quakers, and others left behind their home country in protest of religious constraints. In the eighteenth century, political dissent in the thirteen colonies eventually led to the open rebellion that resulted in the American Revolution and the creation of the United States. In the nineteenth century, dissenters demanded the abolition of slavery, suffrage for women, and fair treatment of Native Americans, while others opposed the War of 1812, the Mexican War, the Civil War (on both sides), and the Spanish-American War. In the twentieth century, dissenters not only demanded rights for workers, women, African Americans, Chicanos, gays, and the disabled, they also protested against every war (declared and undeclared) fought by the United States, and they demanded regulations to safeguard the environment. In the twenty-first century, dissenters continue to protest against NAFTA and the Free Trade Area of the Americas, globalization and the World Bank, the Iraq War, and the Patriot Act.

Who are the dissenters? *What* is dissent? Is dissent unpatriotic or deeply patriotic? Is dissent reserved for those with moral grievances whose chief desire is to persuade the United States to live up to its ideals and to ensure that the nation is truly a land where "all men are created equal," or can dissent be used for more selfish purposes? Are both Susan B. Anthony and Timothy McVeigh equally dissenters? Does dissent ever become treason? Does dissent ultimately change society by offering new ideas, new perspectives, or does dissent merely confirm the status quo by providing a relatively harmless way of letting off steam?

Simply put, dissenters are those who go against the grain, disagreeing (rightly or wrongly) with the majority view. Historically, they were often marginalized people who lacked power and who had a legitimate grievance against the way things were. Although most American dissenters have criticized the United States from the left, dissent can come from both ends of the political spectrum. There were those who sought more equality, such as feminist Elizabeth Cady Stanton, workers' advocate Mother Jones, and gay rights militant Harry Hay; those who sought more moral rectitude, such as temperance campaigner Frances E. Willard, social gospel exponent Walter Rauschenbusch, and the Christian Coalition of America; and those who sought more freedom, such as abolitionist Frederick Douglass and civil rights activist Fannie Lou Hamer.

Some, however, were not political but social and cultural dissenters who criticized societal values and attitudes, among them reproductive rights advocate Margaret Sanger, literary artist Henry Miller, poet Allen Ginsberg, LSD guru Timothy Leary, spiritual sage Ram Dass, and Christian morality crusader Reverend Jerry Falwell. There have also been those who simply strove to gain political power through dissent as well as reactionaries who resisted change and wanted to maintain the privileges and supremacy of their class, race, or gender. For example, when abolitionists demanded the end of slavery, anti-abolitionists argued vehemently to preserve the institution. Similarly, when feminists sought suffrage and equality for women, antifeminists sought to preserve male dominance and the subjugation of women. Some dissenters who were vilified by their contemporaries are now esteemed as visionaries. Yet others, no matter how hard we try to understand their point of view, are still dismissed as crackpots.

American dissenters have achieved different levels of success, inviting various types of trouble, from angry debates to arrest to beatings and even death, as a result of their views. Despite those threats, they kept hammering away at the powers-that-be until those powers began to listen. Public opinion was swayed. Laws were made. Slavery was abolished. Unions were organized. Women got the vote. The Jim Crow laws were invalidated. And today many of those who were demonized in their time have now been consecrated by history.

Ultimately, the definition of dissent has to be somewhat fluid, because the political, social, cultural, and ideological mainstream of America has been fluid. Dissenters are not always responding to the same mainstream. Dissent against Puritanism is different from dissent against McCarthyism (despite the interesting parallels that historians have drawn between the two with respect to the theme of persecution and unfounded accusations). Anti-Puritan dissenters, such as Anne Hutchinson, were dissenting against the mainstream Puritan (religious/theological/theocratic) regimen. Anti-McCarthy spokespeople, such as Margaret Chase Smith, were dissenting against a politically intolerant mainstream. Hutchinson was protesting against the mainstream of her time, just as Senator Smith protested against the mainstream of hers and Martin Luther King Jr. fought against the racial mainstream of his. This fluid view of dissent (i.e., the expression of anti-mainstream sentiments) means that such diverse groups as the Know-Nothings, who vehemently opposed the rising tide of immigration; the Temperance crusaders and anti-abortion militants; as well as such dissimilar individuals as John Brown, who took his antislavery position so far as to kill those who would stand in his way; Emma Goldman, who was deported for her anarchist and communist views; Father Charles Coughlin, whose plausible criticism of the New Deal metamorphosed into anti-Semitic demagoguery; and Pat Robertson, who became an outspoken leader of the Christian Right, are all anti-mainstream dissenters. They all have moralistic goals even though not everyone shares the same moral values and even though very few of these dissenters would ever see eye to eye. Dissenters, therefore, can be right-wing, left-wing, or even no-wing moderates. If they are anti-mainstream, they are dissenters. Political persuasion does not define dissent.

However we define it, dissent has been the fuel for the engine of American progress. If we keep in mind the importance and, indeed, centrality of dissent and protest in the history of the United States, we begin to have a clearer view of our nation as it continues to define itself and of how that process has affected each of us individually.

In a century that is less than a decade old, we cannot foresee the scope and extent of future protest movements, but if the history of the past four hundred years has taught us anything, it has taught us that dissent and protest in all its numerous forms will continue to shape the United States. The direction of our nation will no doubt be informed by our past, and the book you are holding represents the brave convictions of all those whose beliefs were stronger than their fears. This is their story, in their own words.

It is *your* story as well.

PART ONE

Pre-Revolutionary Roots, 1607–1760

Anne Hutchinson, 1637.
In the nineteenth century, artist Edwin Austin Abbey painted this stylized rendition of the trial of Anne Hutchinson. Notice how the artist casts more light on the embattled Hutchinson than on the authoritarian ministers and magistrates interrogating her.

INTRODUCTION: THE LONG ROOTS OF MODERN DISSENT

An argument could be made that the history of the United States began in 1502, when Arthur Tudor, Prince of Wales, died at the age of 15. Or in 1517, when Luther tacked his Ninety-five Theses to the door of Wittenberg Cathedral. Or in 1553, when Mary Tudor began her reign by restoring the Catholic faith to England and initiating the martyrdom of the heretics. In a sense these sixteenth-century developments would eventually have a powerful impact on the founding of English colonies in the New World, for these events led to a critical elevation of dissenting voices in the mother country and the eventual decision of many people, believing their differences were not being adequately addressed at home, to remove themselves to the American wilderness.

So dissent was endemic and pivotal in the political and intellectual history of the United States even before the idea of an independent nation in the New World had begun to take shape. Of course, a primary motive that propelled many colonists to leave their homelands and venture out into the unknown was economic. Enclosure, population growth, and increasing poverty had a huge impact. The economic motive cannot be in any way minimized, but understanding the complex texture and nuances of American history requires understanding the significant role dissent played. And it is important to appreciate the ironic fact that often those who raised voices of dissent and as a consequence were either demonized in their time as menaces to society or ignored as pathetic eccentrics became, to later generations, heroes and icons.

After Henry VII defeated Richard III at Bosworth Field in 1485 and consolidated the Tudor hold on the throne of England, he sought an alliance with one of England's chief rivals on the continent, Spain. To create this alliance, a marriage was arranged between Henry's son Arthur, the Prince of Wales, and Catherine of Aragon, the daughter of Ferdinand and Isabella. Within the year, at the age of 15, the ailing Arthur had died, and the accord with Spain was in jeopardy. After a good deal of diplomatic maneuvering, Henry VII convinced Pope Julius II to grant a special dispensation dissolving the marriage so that Catherine could be married off to Arthur's younger brother, Henry. When the marriage took place, the alliance with Spain became a reality. And it was Catherine of Aragon who was Henry VIII's queen when he succeeded his father in 1509.

On the continent, during the early sixteenth century, a young priest in Wittenberg, Martin Luther, began questioning many practices of the church. To help pay for the construction and artistic embellishment of St. Peter's Basilica and the Sistine Chapel, the pope had authorized the sale of indulgences, pluralism (by which a bishop could profit from holding more than one benefice), and other corrupt practices. To Luther, the sale of indulgences, which purportedly minimized the time a purchaser would have to spend in purgatory, gave the impression that believers could buy their way into heaven and that salvation came with a price. And so in 1517, after much prayer and contemplation, he tacked his Ninety-five Theses to the door of the cathedral in an effort to stimulate a debate that he hoped would lead the church to correct these abuses. Debate was not exactly what he got. The ensuing uproar got him excommunicated. He and his followers eventually formed the Lutheran church, and the Protestant Reformation was thereby launched. The primary problem these "protestors" presented to the church had to do with one of the central tenets of Luther's beliefs: that the only source of God's truth was Holy Scripture and therefore the Bible had authority, not the church hierarchy of pope, cardinals, archbishops, bishops, and priests. This undermining of the hierarchical structure of the church could not be allowed to go unchallenged. Luther, after his excommunication, was protected by numerous German princes who saw the political and economic advantages of emancipating themselves and their principalities from the strictures of the Vatican.

At first, one of the pope's most significant allies in his quarrel with Luther was England's Henry VIII. In fact, Henry issued a pamphlet, ghostwritten by

Thomas More, that so vehemently attacked the Lutheran heresy that a grateful pope bestowed upon Henry and his successors the title "Defender of the Faith." To this day, the English monarch retains this title, although it is now a different faith that is defended.

In the decade of the 1520s, the plot thickened, and a veritable soap opera emerged. Henry VIII, increasingly distraught that Catherine had not produced a male heir, began to question the legality and sanctity of his marriage to his brother's widow. Henry was concerned that if he died without a male heir, England would be plunged back into the chaos that it had known during the Wars of the Roses and that as a result another dynasty would attempt to place a male on the throne. Seeking to free himself of Catherine, he requested a dispensation from Pope Clement VII to dissolve the marriage. Normally, this would not pose any significant problem for the pope, but one of Clement VII's staunchest allies in the struggle against Lutheranism was Holy Roman Emperor Charles V—Catherine's nephew. Not wishing to alienate Charles V, the pope rejected Henry's request. Henry's response was to have Cardinal Wolsey, the archbishop of Canterbury, grant a divorce. Henry divorced Catherine and married Anne Boleyn, whereupon Clement VII excommunicated Henry and Cardinal Wolsey. England, because of Henry's actions, moved into the Protestant camp.

When in 1533 Anne gave birth to a daughter, Henry was nearly beside himself. He made the decision to get rid of Anne and take yet another wife, who would presumably bear him a son. (Never, during any of this, did Henry consider *he* might be at fault! To him, it was the woman's fault, coupled with the fact that God was punishing him for having married his brother's widow.) Not wishing to go through another divorce, he had Anne tried on false charges of adultery. Found guilty of adultery (and therefore of treason), Anne was condemned to death. No sooner was she beheaded than Henry married Jane Seymour. His third wife eventually bore the desired son in 1538, but the infant Edward was sickly, and Jane died of complications from childbirth. Henry, not very good at being alone, went through another three wives (Anne of Cleves, divorced; Catherine Howard, beheaded; Catherine Paar, survived) before his death in 1547. His 9-year-old son succeeded him as Edward VI.

Under Edward's short reign, the Reformation in England was consolidated. Archbishop of Canterbury Thomas Cranmer introduced the *Book of Common Prayer* and established the requirements for the polity of the Church of England. However, upon Edward's death at the age of 16 in 1553, the new monarch, Mary Tudor, the Catholic daughter of Catherine of Aragon, restored Roman Catholicism as the true, rightful church of England. Under Mary, many Protestants, Thomas Cranmer included, were burnt at the stake for heresy. Thousands fled England for the safety of the continent, especially to such Protestant enclaves as Frankfurt and John Calvin's Geneva. When "Bloody" Mary died in 1558, she was succeeded by her half sister, Anne Boleyn's daughter, Elizabeth I. With the Elizabethan settlement, restoring Protestantism to England, many of the Marian exiles returned home. Their experience on the continent with Calvinism had radicalized them, and they soon demanded that Elizabeth purify the Church of England of its popish practices: vestments, crucifixes, and reading of prayers. Elizabeth turned a deaf ear to these "puritans," and thus throughout her long reign, radical religious dissenters and sects flourished.

In the early seventeenth century, with the Stuart accession, first of James I and then of Charles I, a number of these dissenters, discontented with the state of the church and despairing of ever accomplishing the total reformation they desired in England, began to abandon their homes and migrate first to Holland and eventually to Plymouth and Massachusetts Bay Colony. The "pilgrims" who settled in Plymouth in 1620 (after a sojourn of 12 years in Holland) were known as "separatists." They no longer wished to be associated with the Church of England, preferring instead complete separation. Those who settled in Massachusetts Bay Colony in the 1630s, however, were a different variety of Puritan. Although they were Independents ("non-separating puritans" according to scholar Perry Miller) who believed that each congregation was independent and should have complete authority to choose its own members and ministers, they had no intention of separating from the Church of England. To them, it was the true church. They believed that if they set up congregational churches in the New World, their brethren back home would use their example as a model to reform the Church of England. Governor John Winthrop's "citty upon a hill" would thus be a "beacon unto the world."

Many of those who left for New England had high hopes of bettering themselves both socially and economically, but pursuing the fruition of Reformation was what prompted many of the first settlers to risk crossing the Atlantic. What is confusing to the modern mind is that these Puritans, seeking toleration for their beliefs, seeking to create the ideal society, and seeking to set up the pure church, seemed to become themselves, in their new wilderness home, zealously intolerant of others. Remember, however, that they were products of their own age who never believed that all faiths should be tolerated, only *their* faith, which they deeply believed was the only true one. They were not seeking tolerance in the New World; they were seeking to practice what they knew in their hearts to be the true faith and polity. In Massachusetts Bay Colony, intolerance of opinions that undermined the basis of Congregational beliefs was perceived as absolutely necessary for the survival of the Holy Commonwealth, which such dissenters as Roger Williams, Anne Hutchinson, and Mary Dyer quickly discovered.

Colonies in which the economic motive took precedence over the religious also experienced outbreaks of dissent. In Virginia, Bacon's Rebellion in 1676 grew out of the grievances of settlers in the Piedmont region toward the colonial government in Williamsburg. Because such a large number of those who rose up in arms were indentured servants, the rebellion created so much anxiety about relying on indentured servants to solve the labor shortage in the colony that it added momentum to the growth of slavery in the Chesapeake region and established that slavery in the English colonies would be forever based on race.

In Pennsylvania, the strong Quaker element led some to question the treatment of the Indians. William Penn himself insisted that Native Americans be dealt with fairly and that settlers had no right to take their land without compensation. Yet Penn's heirs moved away from his benevolent stance and allowed their hunger for land to dictate a far less humane relationship with the Indians. All throughout the colonies, Native Americans encountering the newcomers attempted with limited success to protest their treatment. Slaves, too, whose masters kept them illiterate and ignorant of such Enlightenment values as natural rights and liberty, tried as best they could to articulate their discontent. Women also were not afraid to struggle against the confines of a male-dominated society and to strive for more liberty than men were willing to concede. And 40 years before the American Revolution, a fledgling newspaper in New York that was brought to trial for libeling corrupt politicians argued successfully for freedom of the press in one of the most momentous court cases of the colonial period.

Roger Williams (c. 1603–1683)

From the moment Roger Williams arrived in the colonies, he ran headlong into the Massachusetts Bay authorities. He served for a time as teacher of the Salem church (many churches in New England had two ministers: the pastor and the teacher), but his form of Puritanism was considered too radical by the ministers and magistrates of the colony. Williams called for the complete separation of the New England churches from the Church of England. He also challenged the king's authority to grant a charter to the colonists and, in effect, to usurp Indian land. Finally, he argued for complete religious toleration. These views led to his banishment from the colony in 1635, whereupon he sought refuge among the Narragansett Indians. Eventually he purchased land from the Narragansetts and, in 1636, founded the colony of Providence in Rhode Island.

    In 1644 he sailed to England to secure a charter for the colony that would permit him to form a government. While in England, Williams published The Bloudy Tenent of Persecution *in which he called for religious toleration of all faiths—including Jews and atheists—and the complete separation of church and state. The book is set up as a dialogue between the position of such Puritans as John Cotton and John Winthrop (Truth) and Williams's own view (Peace). He claimed that magistrates had no right to become involved in religious affairs, nor did they have the power to punish breaches of the Ten Commandments.*

The Bloudy Tenent of Persecution: For the Cause of Conscience, Discussed in a Conference Between Truth and Peace, 1644

First, that the blood of so many hundred thousand souls of Protestants and Papists, spilt in the wars of present and former ages, for their respective consciences, is not required nor accepted by Jesus Christ the Prince of Peace.

Secondly, pregnant scriptures and arguments are throughout the work proposed against the doctrine of persecution for cause of conscience.

Thirdly, satisfactory answers are given to scriptures, and objections produced by Mr. Calvin, Beza, Mr. Cotton, and the ministers of the New English churches and others former and later, tending to prove the doctrine of persecution for cause of conscience.

Fourthly, the doctrine of persecution for cause of conscience is proved guilty of all the blood of the souls crying for vengeance under the altar.

Fifthly, all civil states with their officers of justice in their respective constitutions and administrations are proved essentially civil, and therefore not judges, governors, or defenders of the spiritual or Christian state and worship.

Sixthly, it is the will and command of God that (since the coming of his Son the Lord Jesus) a permission of the most paganish, Jewish, Turkish, or antichristian consciences and worships, be granted to all men in all nations and countries; and they are only to be fought against with that sword which is only (in soul matters) able to conquer, to wit, the sword of God's Spirit, the Word of God.

Seventhly, the state of the Land of Israel, the kings and people thereof in peace and war, is proved figurative and ceremonial, and no pattern nor president for any kingdom or civil state in the world to follow.

Eighthly, God requireth not a uniformity of religion to be enacted and enforced in any civil state; which enforced uniformity (sooner or later) is the greatest occasion of civil war, ravishing of conscience, persecution of Christ Jesus in his servants, and of the hypocrisy and destruction of millions of souls.

Ninthly, in holding an enforced uniformity of religion in a civil state, we must necessarily disclaim our desires and hopes of the Jew's conversion to Christ.

Tenthly, an enforced uniformity of religion throughout a nation or civil state, confounds the civil and religious, denies the principles of Christianity and civility, and that Jesus Christ is come in the flesh.

Eleventhly, the permission of other consciences and worships than a state professeth only can (according to God) procure a firm and lasting peace (good

SOURCE: Roger Williams, *The Bloudy Tenent of Persecution* (Providence, RI: Narragansett Club Publications, 1867), vol. III, 3–4, 58–59, 63, 138–139, 148, 170–171, 201, 247–250, 372–373, 424–425.

assurance being taken according to the wisdom of the civil state for uniformity of civil obedience from all forts).

Twelfthly, lastly, true civility and Christianity may both flourish in a state or kingdom, notwithstanding the permission of divers and contrary consciences, either of Jew or Gentile. . . .

TRUTH. I acknowledge that to molest any person, Jew or Gentile, for either professing doctrine, or practicing worship merely religious or spiritual, it is to persecute him, and such a person (whatever his doctrine or practice be, true or false) suffereth persecution for conscience.

But withal I desire it may be well observed that this distinction is not full and complete: for beside this that a man may be persecuted because he holds or practices what he believes in conscience to be a truth (as Daniel did, for which he was cast into the lions' den, Dan. 6), and many thousands of Christians, because they durst not cease to preach and practice what they believed was by God commanded, as the Apostles answered (Acts 4 & 5), I say besides this a man may also be persecuted, because he dares not be constrained to yield obedience to such doctrines and worships as are by men invented and appointed. . . .

Dear TRUTH, I have two sad complaints:

First, the most sober of the witnesses, that dare to plead thy cause, how are they charged to be mine enemies, contentious, turbulent, seditious?

Secondly, thine enemies, though they speak and rail against thee, though they outrageously pursue, imprison, banish, kill thy faithful witnesses, yet how is all vermilion'd o'er for justice against the heretics? Yea, if they kindle coals, and blow the flames of devouring wars, that leave neither spiritual nor civil state, but burn up branch and root, yet how do all pretend an holy war? He that kills, and he that's killed, they both cry out: "It is for God, and for their conscience."

'Tis true, nor one nor other seldom dare to plead the mighty Prince Christ Jesus for their author, yet (both Protestant and Papist) pretend they have spoke with Moses and the Prophets who all, say they (before Christ came), allowed such holy persecutions, holy wars against the enemies of holy church.

TRUTH. Dear PEACE (to ease thy first complaint), 'tis true, thy dearest sons, most like their mother, peacekeeping, peacemaking sons of God, have borne and still must bear the blurs of troublers of Israel, and turners of the world upside down. And 'tis true again, what Solomon once spake: "The beginning of strife is as when one letteth out water, therefore (saith he) leave off contention before it be meddled with. This caveat should keep the banks and sluices firm and strong, that strife, like a breach of waters, break not in upon the sons of men."

Yet strife must be distinguished: It is necessary or unnecessary, godly or ungodly, Christian or unchristian, etc.

It is unnecessary, unlawful, dishonorable, ungodly, unchristian, in most cases in the world, for there is a possibility of keeping sweet peace in most cases, and, if it be possible, it is the express command of God that peace be kept (Rom. 13).

Again, it is necessary, honorable, godly, etc., with civil and earthly weapons to defend the innocent and to rescue the oppressed from the violent paws and jaws of oppressing persecuting Nimrods (Psal. 73; Job 29).

It is as necessary, yea more honorable, godly, and Christian, to fight the fight of faith, with religious and spiritual artillery, and to contend earnestly for the faith of Jesus, once delivered to the saints against all opposers, and the gates of earth and hell, men or devils, yea against Paul himself, or an angel from heaven, if he bring any other faith or doctrine. . . .

PEACE. I add that a civil sword (as woeful experience in all ages has proved) is so far from bringing or helping forward an opposite in religion to repentance that magistrates sin grievously against the work of God and blood of souls by such proceedings. Because as (commonly) the sufferings of false and antichristian teachers harden their followers, who being blind, by this means are occasioned to tumble into the ditch of hell after their blind leaders, with more inflamed zeal of lying confidence. So, secondly, violence and a sword of steel begets such an impression in the sufferers that certainly they conclude (as indeed that religion cannot be true which needs such instruments of violence to uphold it so) that persecutors are far from soft and gentle commiseration of the blindness of others. . . .

For (to keep to the similitude which the Spirit useth, for instance) to batter down a stronghold, high wall, fort, tower, or castle, men bring not a first and second admonition, and after obstinacy, excommunication, which are spiritual weapons concerning them that be in the church: nor exhortation to repent and be baptized, to believe in the Lord Jesus, etc., which are proper weapons to them that be without, etc. But to take a stronghold, men bring cannons, culverins, saker, bullets, powder, muskets, swords, pikes, etc., and these to this end are weapons effectual and proportionable.

On the other side, to batter down idolatry, false worship, heresy, schism, blindness, hardness, out of the soul and spirit, it is vain, improper, and unsuitable to bring those weapons which are used by persecutors, stocks, whips, prisons, swords, gibbets, stakes, etc. (where these seem to prevail with some cities or kingdoms, a stronger force sets up again, what a weaker pull'd down), but against these spiritual strongholds in the souls of men, spiritual artillery and weapons are proper, which are mighty through God to subdue and bring under the very thought to obedience, or else to bind fast the soul with chains of darkness, and lock it up in the prison of unbelief and hardness to eternity. . . .

PEACE. I pray descend now to the second evil which you observe in the answerer's position, viz., that it would be evil to tolerate notorious evildoers, seducing teachers, etc.

TRUTH. I say the evil is that he most improperly and confusedly joins and couples seducing teachers with scandalous livers.

PEACE. But is it not true that the world is full of seducing teachers, and is it not true that seducing teachers are notorious evildoers?

TRUTH. I answer, far be it from me to deny either, and yet in two things I shall discover the great evil of this joining and coupling seducing teachers, and scandalous livers as one adequate or proper object of the magistrate's care and work to suppress and punish.

First, it is not an homogeneal [homogeneous] (as we speak) but an heterge-neal [heterogeneous] commixture or joining together of things most different in kinds and natures, as if they were both of one consideration. . . .

TRUTH. I answer, in granting with Brentius [Lutheran theologian Johann Brenz] that man hath not power to make laws to bind conscience, he overthrows such his tenent and practice as restrain men from their worship, according to their conscience and belief, and constrain them to such worships (though it be out of a pretense that they are convinced) which their own souls tell them they have no satisfaction nor faith in.

Secondly, whereas he affirms that men may make laws to see the laws of God observed.

I answer, God needeth not the help of a material sword of steel to assist the sword of the Spirit in the affairs of conscience, to those men, those magistrates, yea that commonwealth which makes such magistrates, must needs have power and authority from Christ Jesus to fit judge and to determine in all the great controversies concerning doctrine, discipline, government, etc.

And then I ask whether upon this ground it must not evidently follow that:

Either there is no lawful common earth nor civil state of men in the world, which is not qualified with this spiritual discerning (and then also that the very commonweal hath more light concerning the church of Christ than the church itself).

Or, that the commonweal and magistrates thereof must judge and punish as they are persuaded in their own belief and conscience (be their conscience paganish, Turkish, or antichristian) what is this but to confound heaven and earth together, and not only to take away the being of Christianity out of the world, but to take away all civility, and the world out of the world, and to lay all upon heaps of confusion? . . .

PEACE. The fourth head is the proper means of both these powers to attain their ends.

First, the proper means whereby the civil power may and should attain its end are only political, and principally these five.

First, the erecting and establishing what form of civil government may seem in wisdom most meet, according to general rules of the world, and state of the people.

Secondly, the making, publishing, and establishing of wholesome civil laws, not only such as concern civil justice, but also the free passage of true religion; for outward civil peace ariseth and is maintained from them both, from the latter as well as from the former.

Civil peace cannot stand entire, where religion is corrupted (2 Chron. 15. 3. 5. 6; and Judges 8). And yet such laws, though conversant about religion, may still be counted civil laws, as, on the contrary, an oath cloth still remain religious though conversant about civil matters.

Thirdly, election and appointment of civil officers to see execution to those laws.

Fourthly, civil punishments and rewards of transgressors and observers of these laws.

Fifthly, taking up arms against the enemies of civil peace.

Secondly, the means whereby the church may and should attain her ends are only ecclesiastical, which are chiefly five.

First, setting up that form of church government only of which Christ hath given them a pattern in his Word.

Secondly, acknowledging and admitting of no lawgiver in the church but Christ and the publishing of His laws.

Thirdly, electing and ordaining of such officers only, as Christ hath appointed in his Word.

Fourthly, to receive into their fellowship them that are approved and inflicting spiritual censures against them that offend.

Fifthly, prayer and patience in suffering any evil from them that be without, who disturb their peace.

So that magistrates, as magistrates, have no power of setting up the form of church government, electing church officers, punishing with church censures, but to see that the church does her duty herein. And on the other side, the churches as churches, have no power (though as members of the commonweal they may have power) of erecting or altering forms of civil government, electing of civil officers, inflicting civil punishments (no not on persons excommunicate) as by deposing magistrates from their civil authority, or withdrawing the hearts of the people against them, to their laws, no more than to discharge wives, or children, or servants, from due obedience to their husbands, parents, or masters; or by taking up arms against their magistrates, though he persecute them for conscience: for though members of churches who are public officers also of the civil state may suppress by force the violence of usurpers, as Iehoiada did Athaliah, yet this they do not as members of the church but as officers of the civil state.

TRUTH. Here are divers considerable passages which I shall briefly examine, so far as concerns our controversy.

First, whereas they say that the civil power may erect and establish what form of civil government may seem in wisdom most meet, I acknowledge the proposition to be most true, both in itself and also considered with the end of it, that a civil government is an ordinance of God, to conserve the civil peace of people, so far as concerns their bodies and goods, as formerly hath been said.

But from this grant I infer (as before hath been touched) that the sovereign, original, and foundation of civil power lies in the people (whom they must needs mean by the civil power distinct from the government set up). And, if so, that a people may erect and establish what form of government seems to them most meet for their civil condition; it is evident that such governments as are by them erected and established have no more power, nor for no longer time, than the civil power or people consenting and agreeing shall betrust them with. This is clear not only in reason but in the experience of all commonweals, where the people are not deprived of their natural freedom by the power of tyrants.

And, if so, that the magistrates receive their power of governing the church from the people, undeniably it follows that a people, as a people, naturally consider (of what nature or nation soever in Europe, Asia, Africa, or America), have fundamentally and originally, as men, a power to govern the church, to see her do her duty, to correct her, to redress, reform, establish, etc. And if this be not to pull God and Christ and Spirit out of heaven, and subject them unto natural, sinful, inconstant men, and so consequently to Satan himself, by whom all peoples naturally are guided, let heaven and earth judge. . . .

PEACE. Some will here ask: What may the magistrate then lawfully do with his civil horn or power in matters of religion?

TRUTH. His horn not being the horn of that unicorn or rhinoceros, the power of the Lord Jesus in spiritual cases, his sword not the two-edged sword of the spirit, the word of God (hanging not about the loins or side, but at the lips, and proceeding out of the mouth of his ministers) but of an humane and civil nature and constitution, it must consequently be of a humane and civil operation, for who knows not that operation follows constitution; And therefore I shall end this passage with this consideration:

The civil magistrate either respecteth that religion and worship which his conscience is persuaded is true, and upon which he ventures his soul; or else that and those which he is persuaded are false.

Concerning the first, if that which the magistrate believeth to be true, be true, I say he owes a threefold duty unto it:

First, approbation and countenance, a reverent esteem and honorable testimony, according to Isa. 49, and Revel. 21, with a tender respect of truth, and the professors of it.

Secondly, personal submission of his own soul to the power of the Lord Jesus in that spiritual government and kingdom, according to Matt. 18 and 1 Cor. 5.

Thirdly, protection of such true professors of Christ, whether apart, or met together, as also of their estates from violence and injury, according to Rom. 13.

Now, secondly, if it be a false religion (unto which the civil magistrate dare not adjoin, yet) he owes:

First, permission (for approbation he owes not what is evil) and this according to Matthew 13.30 for public peace and quiet's sake.

Secondly, he owes protection to the persons of his subjects (though of a false worship), that no injury be offered either to the persons or goods of any. . . .

The God of Peace, the God of Truth will shortly seal this truth, and confirm this witness, and make it evident to the whole world, that the doctrine of persecution for cause of conscience, is most evidently and lamentably contrary to the doctrine of Christ Jesus the Prince of Peace. Amen.

Anne Hutchinson (1591–1643)

Anne Hutchinson is one of the most controversial figures in colonial American history. She was an extraordinary woman who led weekly in-depth discussions about the sermons delivered the previous Sunday by Boston ministers John Cotton and John Wilson. Partly because she had stepped out of the submissive role of her gender and partly because she began accusing John Wilson of preaching the "popish" doctrine of a covenant of works (salvation could be achieved through individual effort and not through faith alone), she was brought to trial. During the trial, she asserted that she was in direct communication with God. To Puritans, who believed that only scripture reveals God's truth, this was the heresy of antinomianism. If the final authority of scripture was supplanted by direct communication with God, then what was to prevent any individual, even a murderer, from saying that he was only carrying out God's command? This would lead to the breakdown of law. As a result, Anne Hutchinson was banished.

THE TRIAL OF ANNE HUTCHINSON, 1637

MR. WINTHROP, GOVERNOR: Mrs. Hutchinson, you are called here as one of those that have troubled the peace of the commonwealth and the churches here; you are known to be a woman that hath had a great share in the promoting and divulging of those opinions that are causes of this trouble, and . . . you have spoken divers things as we have been informed very prejudicial to the honour of the churches and ministers thereof, and you have maintained a meeting and an assembly in your house that hath been condemned by the general assembly as a thing not tolerable nor comely in the sight of God nor fitting for your sex, and notwithstanding that was cried down you have continued the same, therefore we have thought good to send for you to understand how things are, that if you be in an erroneous way we may reduce you that so you may become a profitable member here among us, otherwise if you be obstinate in your course that then the court may take such course that you may trouble us no further, therefore I would intreat you to express whether you do not hold and assent in practice to those opinions and factions that have been handled in court already, that is to say, whether you do not justify Mr. Wheelwright's sermon and the petition.

MRS. HUTCHINSON: I am called here to answer before you but I hear no things laid to my charge.

SOURCE: Thomas Hutchinson, *History of the Colony and Province of Massachusetts* (Boston, 1767).

Gov: I have told you some already and more I can tell you.

Mrs. H: Name one Sir.

Gov: Have I not named some already?

Mrs. H: What have I said or done?

Gov: Why for your doings, this you did harbour and countenance those that are parties in this faction that you have heard of.

Mrs. H: That's matter of conscience, Sir.

Gov: Your conscience you must keep or it must be kept for you.

Mrs. H: Must not I then entertain the saints because I must keep my conscience.

Gov: Say that one brother should commit felony or treason and come to his other brother's house, if he knows him guilty and conceals him he is guilty of the same. It is his conscience to entertain him, but if his conscience comes into act in giving countenance and entertainment to him that hath broken the law he is guilty too. So if you do countenance those that are transgressors of the law you are in the same fact.

Mrs. H: What law do they transgress?

Gov: The law of God and of the state.

Mrs. H: In what particular?

Gov: Why in this among the rest, whereas the Lord doth say honour thy father and thy mother.

Mrs. H: Ey Sir in the Lord.

Gov: This honour you have broke in giving countenance to them.

Mrs. H: In entertaining those did I entertain them against any act (for there is the thing) or what God hath appointed?

Gov: You knew that Mr. Wheelwright did preach this sermon and those that countenance him in this do break a law.

Mrs. H: What law have I broken?

Gov: Why the fifth commandment.

Mrs. H: I deny that for he saith in the Lord. . . .

Gov: You have councelled them.

Mrs. H: Wherein?

Gov: Why in entertaining them.

Mrs. H: What breach of law is that Sir?

Gov: Why dishonouring of parents.

Mrs. H: But put the case Sir that I do fear the Lord and my parents, may not I entertain them that fear the Lord because my parents will not give me leave?

Gov: If they be the fathers of the commonwealth, and they of another religion, if you entertain them then you dishonour your parents and are justly punishable.

Mrs. H: If I entertain them, as they have dishonoured their parents I do.

Gov: No but you by countenancing them above others put honor upon them.

Mrs. H: I may put honor upon them as the children of God and as they do honor the Lord.

Gov: We do not mean to discourse with those of your sex but only this; you do adhere unto them and do endeavour to set forward this faction and so you do dishonour us.

MRS. H: I do acknowledge no such thing neither do I think that I ever put any dishonour upon you.

Gov: Why do you keep such a meeting at your house as you do every week upon a set day?

MRS. H: It is lawful for me so to do, as it is all your practices and can you find a warrant for yourself and condemn me for the same thing? The ground of my taking it up was, when I first came to this land because I did not go to such meetings as those were, it was presently reported that I did not allow of such meetings but held them unlawful and therefore in that regard they said I was proud and did despise all ordinances, upon that a friend came unto me and told me of it and I to prevent such aspersions took it up, but it was in practice before I came therefore I was not the first.

Gov: For this, that you appeal to our practice you need no confutation. If your meeting had answered to the former it had not been offensive, but I will say that there was no meeting of women alone, but your meeting is of another sort for there are sometimes men among you.

MRS. H: There was never any man with us.

Gov: Well, admit there was no man at your meeting and that you was sorry for it, there is no warrant for your doings, and by what warrant do you continue such a course?

MRS. H: I conceive there lies a clear rule in Titus, that the elder women should instruct the younger [Titus 2:3–5] and then I must have a time wherein I must do it. . . .

Gov: But suppose that a hundred men come unto you to be instructed will you forbear to instruct them?

MRS. H: As far as I conceive I cross a rule in it.

Gov: Very well and do you not so here?

MRS. H: No Sir for my ground is they are men.

Gov: Men and women all is one for that, but suppose that a man should come and say Mrs. Hutchinson I hear that you are a woman that God hath given his grace unto and you have knowledge in the word of God I pray instruct me a little, ought you not to instruct this man?

MRS. H: I think I may—Do you think it not lawful for me to teach women and why do you call me to teach the court?

Gov: We do not call you to teach the court but to lay open yourself. . . .

Gov: Your course is not to be suffered for, besides that we find such a course as this to be greatly prejudicial to the state, besides the occasion that it is to seduce many honest persons that are called to those meetings and your opinions being known to be different from the word of God may seduce many simple souls that resort unto you, besides that the occasion which hath come of late hath come from none but such as have frequented your meetings, so that now they are flown off from magistrates and ministers and this since they have come to you, and besides that it will not well stand with the Commonwealth that families should be neglected for so many neighbours and dames and so much time spent, we see no rule of God for this, we see not that any should have authority to set up any other exercises besides what authority hath already set up and so what hurt comes of this you will be guilty of and we for suffering you.

MRS. H: Sir I do not believe that to be so.

GOV: Well, we see how it is we must therefore put it away from you, or restrain you from maintaining this course.

MRS. H: If you have a rule for it from God's word you may.

GOV: We are your judges, and not you ours and we must compel you to it.

MRS. H: If it please you by authority to put it down I will freely let you for I am subject to your authority. . . .

MR. DUDLEY, DEP. GOV: Here hath been much spoken concerning Mrs. Hutchinson's meetings and among other answers she saith that men come not there, I would ask you this one question then, whether never any man was at your meeting?

GOV: There are two meetings kept at their house.

DEP. GOV: How is there two meetings?

MRS. H: Ey Sir, I shall I not equivocate, there is a meeting of men and women and there is a meeting only for women.

DEP. GOV: Are they both constant?

MRS. H: No, but upon occasions they are deferred.

MR. ENDICOT: Who teaches in the men's meetings none but men, do not women sometimes?

MRS. H: Never as I heard, not one.

DEP. GOV: I would go a little higher with Mrs. Hutchinson. About three years ago we were all in peace. Mrs. Hutchinson from that time she came hath made a disturbance, and some that came over with her in the ship did inform me what she was as soon as she was landed. I being then in place dealt with the pastor and teacher of Boston and desired them to enquire of her, and then I was satisfied that she held nothing different from us, but within half a year after, she had vented divers of her strange opinions and had made parties in the country, and at length it comes that Mr. Cotton and Mr. Vane were of her judgment, but Mr. Cotton cleared himself that he was not of that mind, but now it appears by this woman's meeting that Mrs. Hutchinson hath so forestalled the minds of many by their resort to her meeting that now she hath a potent party in the country. Now if all these things have endangered us as from that foundation and if she in particular hath disparaged all our ministers in the land that they have preached a covenant of works, and only Mr. Cotton a covenant of grace, why this is not to be suffered, and therefore being driven to the foundation and it being found that Mrs. Hutchinson is she that hath depraved all the ministers and hath been the cause of what is fallen out, why we must take away the foundation and the building will fall.

MRS. H: I pray Sir prove it that I said they preached nothing but a covenant of works.

DEP. GOV: Nothing but a covenant of works, why a Jesuit may preach truth sometimes.

MRS. H: Did I ever say they preached a covenant of works then?

DEP. GOV: If they do not preach a covenant of grace clearly, then they preach a covenant of works.

MRS. H: No Sir, one may preach a covenant of grace more clearly than another, so I said. . . .

D. GOV: I will make it plain that you did say that the ministers did preach a covenant of works.

MRS. H: I deny that. . . .

D. GOV: What do I do charging of you if you deny what is so fully proved.

GOV: Here are six undeniable ministers who say it is true and yet you deny that you did say that they did preach a covenant of works and that they were not able ministers of the gospel, and it appears plainly that you have spoken it, and whereas you say that it was drawn from you in a way of friendship, you did profess then that it was out of conscience that you spake and said. The fear of man is a snare wherefore should I be afraid, I will speak plainly and freely.

MRS. H: That I absolutely deny, for the first question was thus answered by me to them. They thought that I did conceive there was a difference between them and Mr. Cotton. At the first I was somewhat reserved, then said Mr. Peters I pray answer the question directly as fully and as plainly as you desire we should tell you our minds. Mrs. Hutchinson we come for plain dealing and telling you our hearts. Then I said I would deal as plainly as I could, and whereas they say I said they were under a covenant of works and in the state of the apostles why these two speeches cross one another. I might say they might preach a covenant of works as did the apostles, but to preach a covenant of works and to be under a covenant of works is another business.

DEP. GOV: There have been six witnesses to prove this and yet you deny it.

MRS. H: I deny that these were the first words that were spoken.

GOV: You make the case worse, for you clearly shew that the ground of your opening your mind was not to satisfy them but to satisfy your own conscience. . . .

MRS. H: I acknowledge using the words of the apostle to the Corinthians unto him, that they that were ministers of the letter and not the spirit did preach a covenant of works. . . .

GOV: Let us state the case and then we may know what to do. That which is laid to Mrs. Hutchinson's charge is this, that she hath traduced the magistrates and ministers of this jurisdiction, that she hath said the ministers preached a covenant of works and Mr. Cotton a covenant of grace, and that they were not able ministers of the gospel, and she excuses it that she made it a private conference and with a promise of secrecy, &c. now this is charged upon her, and they therefore sent for her seeing she made it her table talk, and then she said the fear of man was a snare and therefore she would not be affeared of them. . . .

Mrs. H: If you please to give me leave I shall give you the ground of what I know to be true. Being much troubled to see the falseness of the constitution of the church of England, I had like to have turned separatist; whereupon I kept a day of solemn humiliation and pondering of the thing; this scripture was brought unto me—he that denies Jesus Christ to be come in the flesh is antichrist—This I considered of and in considering found that the papists did not deny him to be come in the flesh nor we did not deny him—who then was antichrist? . . . The Lord knows that I could not open scripture; he must by his prophetical office open it unto me. . . . I bless the Lord, he hath let me see which was the clear ministry and which the wrong. Since that time I confess I have been more choice and he hath let me to distinguish between the voice of my beloved and the voice of Moses, the voice of John Baptist and the voice of antichrist, for all those voices are spoken of in scripture. Now if you do condemn me for speaking what in my conscience I know to be truth I must commit myself unto the Lord.

Mr. Nowell: How do you know that that was the spirit?

Mrs. H: How did Abraham know that it was God that bid him offer his son, being a breach of the sixth commandment?

Dep. Gov: By an immediate voice.

Mrs. H: So to me by an immediate revelation.

Dep. Gov: How! an immediate revelation.

Mrs. H: By the voice of his own spirit to my soul. I will give you another scripture, Jer. 46. 27, 28—out of which the Lord shewed me what he would do for me and the rest of his servants—But after he was pleased to reveal himself to me. . . . Ever since that time I have been confident of what he hath revealed unto me. . . . Therefore I desire you to look to it, for you see this scripture fulfilled this day and therefore I desire you that as you tender the Lord and the church and commonwealth to consider and look what you do. You have power over my body but the Lord Jesus hath power over my body and soul, and assure yourselves thus much, you do as much as in you lies to put the Lord Jesus Christ from you, and if you go on in this course you begin you will bring a curse upon you and your posterity, and the mouth of the Lord hath spoken it. . . .

Gov: The court hath already declared themselves satisfied concerning the things you hear, and concerning the troublesomeness of her spirit and the danger of her course amongst us, which is not to be suffered. Therefore if it be the mind of the court that Mrs. Hutchinson for these things that appear before us is unfit for our society, and if it be the mind of the court that she shall be banished out of our liberties and imprisoned till she be sent away, let them hold up their hands. . . .

Gov: Mrs. Hutchinson, the sentence of the court you hear is that you are banished from out of our jurisdiction as being a woman not fit for our society, and are to be imprisoned till the court shall send you away.

Mrs. H: I desire to know wherefore I am banished?

Gov: Say no more, the court knows wherefore and is satisfied.

Alice Tilly (1594–c. 1660)

Petitions in colonial Massachusetts were not happily received by those in authority, and there are even cases on record in which petitioners were penalized for having submitted their complaints. Still, people did petition the General Court when they felt they wanted to protest a decision that had been handed down. When John Wheelwright was banished, a group of men petitioned the General Court; others protested Governor John Winthrop's role in resolving the Hingham militia election by signing a petition. In 1649, when midwife Alice Tilly was convicted, a group of nearly 300 women (and some men) filed a total of six petitions protesting her sentence. The court records are no longer extant, and it is not known precisely what Alice Tilly's offense was, but we do have the petitions, and we do know that the petitioners were successful in their effort to secure Alice Tilly's release so that she could continue to perform her midwife services in the colony. This is the earliest known example of collective political action by women in the English colonies and indicates that reproductive issues were significant long before Margaret Sanger's twentieth-century birth control movement.

PETITIONS FOR THE RELEASE OF ALICE TILLY, 1649

PETITION 3: FROM THE WOMEN OF DORCHESTER, CIRCA EARLY MAY 1649

Alice Tilly the wife of William Tilly a professed servant of Jesus Christ both in old england and new: as we have heard and by experience doe finde that shee hath ben a woeman of singular use in the place from whence shee came {and here allso} and wee bless the Lord for her life and for the experience wee have had of her not in ordynary cases but in extraordynary cases: but wee have ben informed here of late that she hath ben a hard hearted woeman and that many woemen and children doe die under her hands which doth much redound to her discreddit and the disheateninge of our woemen amongst us—and we have heard that shee is much oppressed by the reports that goe about on her but wee whose names are her under Written with the consent of a greate many more doe earnestly pray unto god to undertake for her in a way of his owne: to cleare her name that she {may} have free passage in her callinge to the good of us and of our children from Dorchester.

SOURCE: Mary Beth Norton, " 'The Ablest Midwife That Wee Knowe in the Land': Mistress Alice Tilly and the Women of Boston and Dorchester, 1649–1650," *William and Mary Quarterly*, Third Series, 55, 1 (Jan. 1998), 105–134.

PETITION 4: TO THE COURT OF ASSISTANTS FROM BOSTON WOMEN, CIRCA MID-MAY 1649

To the honored Maiistrates Now assembled at Boston & elcewhere the humble Petition of us whose names are hereunto subscribed as alsoe in the name & with the Consent of many others Humbly sheweth.

That whereas wee yor Worships humble Petitioners did put up a petition unto your Worships in the behalfe of our approued midwife namely Mrs Tilly wee which are but fewe of many, whoe if need require; shall come and speake in her halfe; whoe hath through the goodnes of God bin carried through such difficulties in her calling that none of those whoe are her accusers could Doe but have either sent for her or left the work undone.

And as the honored Deputie Governor namely Mr Dudly Esquire did say tht shee was the ablest midwife inthe land; and as wee conceiue all the rest of the honored Maijstrats consented thereunto being silent in the thing; But whereas the honord Magistrates arfd many men more can speake but by hearesay; wee and many more of us can speake by experience and some by hearesay and whoe have bin eyewitnesses tht have bin with her in times of distrese.

Therefore our humble Petition unto yor Worships with one consent of us whose names are hereunto subscribed and in the behalfe of many others is that your Worships would bee pleased so farre to Grattify yor Worships most humble Petitioners as to vouchsafe unto us the liberty of our midwife for whome wee are bound in conscience to supplycate knowing the present need tht some of us have of her and alsoe knowing the sad events tht haue falne out both before her liberty was detained and since where she hath not had to doe and some of us heare and some of us know which make us affrayd to putt our selves into the hands of any besides our midwife tht wee haue had experience of, and of the blesseing of god uppon her endeauors and to say plainely wee realy in or conscience doe Judg her to bee the ablest midwife {that wee knowe} in the land and wee think wee canne make it appeare if {need} require.

Now the lord Guid yor worships tht you may heare the cryes of mothers, and of children yet unborne tht soe yor worships may bee moued thereby to Grant unto us yor Humble petitioners the liberty of our midwife for otherwise wee are like to Doe without seing her her husband hath inioyned her that shee should not goe forth to any uppon bayle only to a few whome shee was ingaged unto before hee went.

And Soe Humbly expecting a gratious Answere which if you grant wee shall for euer bee bound to bee thankfull to God and remaine yors in the Lord.

PETITION 5: TO THE GENERAL COURT FROM THE WOMEN OF DORCHESTER, CIRCA MAY 1650

To our honored Gouernour Deputie Gouernor And to the rest of the magistrates or any other whom it may concerne.

The humble petition of those whose names are vnder written.

Whereas Mris Tillie now of Boston a woman well knowne to be of good use in the Countrey amonge women in that practice she is often Called unto & imployed aboute yet nothwithstanding hath had great Discoragments of late tymes in that practice & her husband also for wch Cause he thinks and we doe heare & are informed, to remove himselfe & her also, unto the place whereunto he belongs, unless {her} innocencie may be cleared her Discoragments are well knowne we are informed that we feare most, is her removall, which if it should soe bee, yor poore petitioners shall be verie much grieved, & sadded, in our spirits, haveinge had such good experience of her, both of her skills, & redines, & payn-fulnes, helpfulnes, & Courage, and all this through the blessings of god on her indeavours that yor poore Petitioners may blesse god that ever we knewe her & have bine partakers of her help {as some of us have} even in such tymes as in the eye of sence or reason nothinge but Death was to be expected some of us have had Experience of her a longe tyme & all of us in tymes of our needs & therefore we doe Judge her able & fitt for that place & Callinge.

May it therefor please yor Honored selves whom it may concerne to take her cause into yor greate wise & Juditious considerations that soe if possiblie may be Innocencie may be cleared that neyther her husband nor her selfe may be grieved & may not have such thoughts of removinge but be willinge to give up to this worke of god amongst which wilbe heart reioycing unto us & many more in the Country about us and as sad her removall from us this not doubtinge of yor wisedomes care about the accomplishinge of our humble desires herein we shall humbly pray for yor worships prosperitie & remaine thankfully obliged unto your worships.

PETITION 6: TO THE GENERAL COURT FROM THE WOMEN OF BOSTON, BEFORE MAY 22, 1650

To the right worpll John Endicott Esq Governour, Tho: Dudley Esq Deputy Governor with the rest of the worpll Court. .

The humble Petition of divers women in Boston.

Humbly sheweth, tht whereas yor Petitioners having had manifolde experi-ences of the skill & ability (through the good hand of God) of an usefull instru-ment, who by providence is become a prisoner to yor Worpps (namely Alice Tilly wife to Wm Tilly) by hauing the black side of her actions presented to yor Worpps, & therein seuerall crimes written on her forehead, wch peradven-ture God nor her owne conscience may lay to her charge, further then this speaking dispensation, to take her off an ouer-much selfe conceitednes in what shee hath received, tht shee may remember tht shee hath all upon the accompt of receipt, wch yr Petitioners hope shall bee, as pray itt may bee the effect thereof.

Wherefore yor humble Petitioners though in all humility, yett in childlike boldnes, to & wth yor worpps, whose care wee believe, is as for our good, so for the posterity to succeede out of wch care (wee as hope so) desire tht yor Worpps will please to comiserate the condition of so many of yor poore trembling Petitioners, whose burdens wee doubt nott, butt will move yor compassions, as in answering some who have gone before us in this way of petitioning; so to orselues wth as much fauour as clemency may afford, ouerlooking the line of justice, so farre as will stand wth good conscience & Honor, wherein wee dare nott assume aboue or line to direct, butt leave the composure thereof to God & the wisedome given of God to you, who wee doubt nott butt will direct yor worpps therein, so as tht his owne honour may bee preserved, the security of yor children, yea those of the weakest sexe provided for, & the humble requests of yor poore petitioners granted, in opening the door of free liberty to or wonted way of instrumentall helpfullnes by her, of whom or expereinces are greatt, & necessityes greater.

Yor fauours herein given forth will more oblige yor Petitioners, who shall how euer count themselues bound to pray for you, & all of God sett ouer us, while wee shall remaine (though weake yett) true hearted well wishers, & endeauourers of the publick good of those churches & Comon wealth God hath cast us in.

William Dyer (1609–1672) and Mary Dyer (c. 1611–1660)

Mary Dyer was a follower of Anne Hutchinson during the Antinomian controversy. When Hutchinson was banished, Mary Dyer went with her to Rhode Island. Later, in the 1650s, Dyer went back to England, where she became a Quaker. Returning to Boston in 1657, she began proselytizing for Quakerism. She was imprisoned in 1657 and then again in 1659. When she was released, she was banished from Massachusetts Bay Colony and told that she would be executed if she ever returned. In October 1659 she did go back, was sentenced to death, and, while awaiting her turn on the gallows as two Quaker men (Marmaduke Stephenson and William Robinson) were hanged at her side, she was reprieved and again banished. In May 1660 she visited Boston a final time, knowing exactly what lay in store for her. She was hanged on June first.

Following are two letters from William Dyer pleading for his wife's release, as well as two prison letters of Mary Dyer's.

Petitions and Letters, 1660

WILLIAM DYER'S LETTER TO THE BOSTON MAGISTRATES, 1659

Gentlemen:

Having received some letters from my wife, I am given to understand of her commitment to close prison to a place (according to description) not unlike Bishop Bonner's rooms. . . . It is a sad condition, in executing such cruelties towards their fellow creatures and sufferers. . . . Had you no commiseration of a tender soul that being wett to the skin, you cause her to thrust into a room whereon was nothing to sitt or lye down upon but dust. . . . had your dogg been wett you would have offered it the liberty of a chimney corner to dry itself, or had your hoggs been pend in a sty, you would have offered them some dry straw, or else you would have wanted mercy to your beast, but alas Christians now with you are used worse [than] hoggs or doggs . . . oh merciless cruelties.

You have done more in persecution in one year than the worst bishops did in seven, and now to add more towards a tender woman . . . that gave you no just cause against her for did she come to your meeting to disturb them as you call itt, or did she come to reprehend the magistrates? [She] only came to visit her friends in prison and when dispatching that her intent of returning to her family as she declared in her [statement] the next day to the Governor, therefore it is you that disturbed her, else why was she not let alone. [What] house entered she to molest or what did she, that like a malefactor she must be hauled to [prison] or what law did she transgress? She was about a business justifiable before God and all good men.

The worst of men, the bishops themselves, denied not the visitation and release of friends to their prisoners, which myself hath often experienced by visiting Mr. Prine, Mr. Smart and other eminent [men] yea when he was commanded close in the towne, I had resort once or twice a week and [I was] never fetched before authority to ask me wherefore I came to the towne, or Kings bench, or Gatehouse . . . had there not been more adventurours tender hearted professors than yo'selves many of them you call godly ministers and others might have perished . . . if that course you take had been in use with them, as to send for a person and ask them whe'fore they came thither. What hath not people in America the same liberty as beasts and birds to pass the land or air without examination?

Have you a law that says the light in M. Dyre is not M. Dyre's rule, if you have for that or any the fornamed a law, she may be made a transfresso', for words and your mittimus hold good, but if not, then have you imprisoned her

---

SOURCE: Horatio Rogers, *Mary Dyer of Rhode Island The Quaker Martyr That Was Hanged on Boston Common, June 1, 1660* (Norwood, MA, 1896).

and punisht her without law and against the Law of god and man . . . behold my wife without law and against Law is imprison' and punished and so higly condemned for saying the light is the Rule! It is not your light within your rule by which you make and act such lawes for ye have no rule of Gods word in the Bible to make a law titled Quakers nor have you any order from the Supreme State of England to make such lawes. Therefore, it must be your light within you is your rule and you walk by. . . . Remember what Jesus Christ said, 'if the light that be in you is darkness, how great is that darkness.'

[illegible] . . . conscience, the first and next words after appearance is 'You are a Quaker' see the steppes you follow and let their misry be your warning; and then if answer be not made according to the ruling will; away with them to the Cobhole or new Prison, or House of Correction. . . . And now Gentlemen consider their ends, and believe it, itt was certaine the Bishops ruine suddenly followed after their hott persuanes of some godly people by them called Puritans . . . especially when they proceeded to suck the blood of Mr. Prine, Mr. Burton and Dr. Bostwicks eares, only them three and butt three, and they were as odious to them as the Quakers are to you.

What witness or legal testimony was taken that my wife Mary Dyre was a Quaker, if not before God and man how can you clear yourselves and seat of justice, from cruelty persecution ye as so fair as in you lies murder as to her and to myself and family oppression and tiranny. The God of trust knows all this. The God of truth knows all this. This is the sum and totals of a law title Quakers: that she is guilty of a breach of a tittled Quakers is as strange, that she is lawfully convicted of 2 witnesses is not hear of, that she must be banished by law tittled Quakers being not convicted by law but considered by surmise and condemned to close prison by Mr. Bellingham's suggestion is so absurd and ridiculous, the meanest pupil in law will hiss at such proceeds in Old Lawyers . . . is your law tittled Quakers Felony or Treason, that vehement suspicion render them capable of suffering. . . . If you be men I suppose your fundamental lawes is that noe person shall be imprisoned or molested but upon the breach of a law, yett behold my wife without law and against law is imprisoned and punished.

My wife writes me word and information, ye she had been above a fortnight and had not trode on the ground, but saw it out your window; what inhumanity is this, had you never wives of your own, or ever any tender affection to a woman, deal so with a woman, what has nature forgotten if refreshment be debarred?

I have written thus plainly to you, being exceedingly sensible of the unjust molestations and detaining of my deare yokefellow, mine and my familyes want of her will crye loud in yo' eares together with her sufferings of your part but I questions not mercy favor and comfort from the most high of her owne soule, that at present my self and family bea by you deprived of the comfort and refreshment we might have enjoyed by her [presence].

her husband
W. Dyre
Newport this 30 August 1659

MARY DYER'S FIRST LETTER WRITTEN FROM PRISON, 1659

Whereas I am by many charged with the Guiltiness of my own Blood: if you mean in my Coming to Boston, I am therein clear, and justified by the Lord, in whose Will I came, who will require my Blood of you, be sure, who have made a Law to take away the Lives of the Innocent Servants of God, if they come among you who are called by you, 'Cursed Quakers,' altho I say, and am a Living Witness for them and the Lord, that he hath blessed them, and sent them unto you: Therefore, be not found Fighters against God, but let my Counsel and Request be accepted with you, To repeal all such Laws, that the Truth and Servants of the Lord, may have free Passage among you and you be kept from shedding innocent Blood, which I know there are many among you would not do, if they knew it so to be: Nor can the Enemy that stirreth you up thus to destroy this holy Seed, in any Measure contervail, the great Damage that you will by thus doing procure: Therefeore, seeing the Lord hath not hid it from me, it lyeth upon me, in Love to your Souls, thus to persuade you: I have no Self Ends, the Lord knoweth, for if my Life were freely granted by you, it would not avail me, nor could I expect it of you, so long as I shall daily hear and see, of the Sufferings of these People, my dear Brethren and Seed, with whom my Life is bound up, as I have done these two Years, and not it is like to increase, even unto Death, for no evil Doing, but Coming among you: Was ever the like laws heard of, among a People that profess Christ come in the Flesh? And have such no other Weapons, but such Laws, to fight with against spiritual Wickedness with all, as you call it? Wo is me for you! Of whom take you Counsel! Search with the light of Christ in you, and it will show you of whom, as it hath done me, and many more, who have been disobedient and deceived, as now you are, which Light, as you come into, and obey what is made manifest to you therein, you will not repent, that you were kept from shedding Blood, tho be a Woman: It's not my own Life I seek (for I chose rather to suffer with the People of God, than to enjoy the Pleasures of Egypt) but the Life of the Seed, which I know the Lord hath blessed, and therefore seeks the Enemy thus vehemently the Life thereof to destroy, as in all ages he ever did: Oh! hearken not unto him, I beseech you, for the Seed's Sake, which is One in all, and is dear in the Sight of God; which they that touch, Touch the Apple of his Eye, and cannot escape his Wrath; whereof I having felt, cannot but persuade all men that I have to do withal, especially you who name the Name of Christ, to depart from such Iniquity, as shedding BLOOD, even of the SAINTS of the Most High. Therefore let my Request have as much Acceptance with you, if you be Christians as Esther had with Ahasuerus whose relation is short of that that's between Christians and my Request is the same that her's was: and he said not, that he had made a Law, and it would be dishonourable for him to revoke it: but when he understood that these People were so prized by her, and so nearly concerned her (as in Truth these are to me) as you may see what he did for her: Therefore I leave these Lines with you, appealing to the faithful and true Witness of God, which is One in all Consciences, before whom we must all appear; with whom I shall eternally rest, in Everlasting Joy and

Peace, whether you will hear or forebear: With him is my Reward, with whom to live is my Joy, and to die is my Gain, tho' I had not had your forty-eight Hours Warning, for the Preparation of the Death of Mary Dyar.

And know this also, that if through the Enmity you shall declare yourselves worse than Ahasueras, and confirm your Law, tho' it were but the taking away the Life of one of us, That the Lord will overthrow both your Law and you, by his righteous Judgments and Plagues poured justly upon you who now whilst you are warned thereof, and tenderly sought unto, may avoid the one, by removing the other; If you neither hear nor obey the Lord nor his Servants, yet will he send more of his Servants among you, so that your End shall be frustrated, that think to restrain them, you call 'Cursed Quakers' from coming among you, by any Thing you can do to them; yea, verily, he hath a Seed here among you, for whom we have suffered all this while, and yet suffer: whom the Lord of the Harvest will send forth more Labourers to gather (out of the Mouths of the Devourers of all sorts) into his Fold, where he will lead them into fresh Pastures, even the Paths of Righteousness, for his Name's Sake: Oh! let non of you put this Day far from you, which verily in the light of the Lord I see approaching, even to many in and about Boston, which is the bitterest and darkest professing Place, and so to continue as long as you have done, that ever I heard of; let the time past therefore suffice, for such a Profession as bring forth such Fruits as these Laws are, In Love and in the Spirit of Meekness, I again beseech you, for I have no Enmity to the Persons of any; but you shall know, that God will not be mocked, but what you sow, that shall you reap from him, that will render to everyone according to the Deeds done in the Body, whether Good or Evil, Even so be it, saith

Mary Dyar

MARY DYER'S SECOND LETTER WRITTEN FROM PRISON, 1659, AFTER THE HANGING OF STEPHENSON & ROBINSON

Once more the General Court, Assembled in Boston, speaks Mary Dyar, even as before: My life is not accepted, neither availeth me, in Comparison of the Lives and Liberty of the Truth and Servants of the Living God, for which in the Bowels of Love and Meekness I sought you; yet nevertheless, with wicked Hands have you put two of them to Death, which makes me to feel, that the Mercies of the Wicked is Cruelty. I rather chuse to die than to live, as from you, as Guilty of their innocent Blood. Therefore, seeing my Request is hindered, I leave you to the Righteous Judge and Searcher of all Hearts, who, with the pure measure of Light he hath given to every Man to profit withal, will in his due time let you see whose Servants you are, and of whom you have taken Counsel, which desire you to search into: But all his counsel hath been slighted, and, you would none of his reproofs. Read your Portion, Prov. 1:24 to 32. 'For verily the Night cometh on you apace, wherein no Man can Work, in which you shall assuredly fall to your own Master, in Obedience to the Lord, whom I serve with my Spirit, and to pity to your Souls, which you neither know nor pity: I can do no less than once more to warn you, to put away the Evil of your Doings, and Kiss the Son, the Light in you before his wrath be kindled in you; for where it is, nothing without you can help or deliver you out of his hand at all; and if these things be not so, then say, There hath been no prophet from the Lord sent amongst you: yet it is his Pleasure, by Things that are not, to bring to naught Things that are.'

When I heard your last Order read, it was a disturbance unto me, that was so freely Offering up my life to him that give it me, and sent me hither to do, which Obedience being his own Work, he gloriously accompanied with his Presence, and Peace, and Love in me, in which I rested from my labour, till by your Order, and the People, I was so far disturbed, that I could not retain anymore of the words thereof, than that I should return to Prison, and there remain Forty and Eight hours; to which I submitted, finding nothing from the Lord to the contrary, that I may know what his Pleasure and Counsel is concerning me, on whom I wait therefore, for he is my Life, and the length of my Days, and as I said before, I came at his command, and go at His command.

Mary Dyar

WILLIAM DYER'S LETTER PETITIONING THE BOSTON MAGISTRATES TO SPARE MARY DYER'S LIFE

Honor S',

It is not little greif of mind, and sadness of hart that I am necessitated to be so bold as to supplicate you' Honor self w' the Honorable Assembly of yo' Generall Courte to extend yo' mercy and favo' once agen to me and my children, little did I dream that I shuld have had occasion to petition you in a matter of this nature, but so it is that throw the devine prouidence and yo' benignity my sonn obtayned so much pitty and mercy att yo' hands as to enjoy the life of his mother, now my supplication yo' Hono' is to begg affectioinately, the life of my deare wife, tis true I have not seen her aboue this half yeare and therefor cannot tell how in the frame of her spiritt she was moved thus againe to runn so great a Hazard to herself, and perplexity to me and mine and all her friends and well wishers; so itt is from Shelter Island about by Pequid Marragansett and to the Towne of Prouidence she secrettly and speedyly journyed, and as secretly from thence came to yo' jurisdiction, unhappy journy may I say, and woe to theat generatcon say I that gives occasion thus of grief and troble (to those that desire to be quiett) by helping one another (as I may say) to Hazard their lives for I know not watt end or to what purpose; If her zeale be so greatt as thus to adventure, oh lett your favoure and pitty surmount itt and save her life. Let not yo' forwanted Compassion bee conquared by her inconsiderate maddnesse, and how greatly will yo' renowne be spread if by so conquering yo' become victorious, what shall I say more, I know yo' are all sensible of my condition, and lett the reflect bee, and you will see whatt my peticon is and what will give me and mine peace, oh Lett mercies wings once more sore above justice ballance, and then whilst I live shall I exalt yo' goodness butt other wayes twill be a languishing sorrow, yea so great that I shuld gladly suffer thie blow att once much rather: I shall forebear to troble yo' Hn' with words neythe am I in capacity to expatiate myself at present; I only say that yo'selves have been and are or may bee husbands to wife or wiues, so am I: yea to once most dearely beloved: oh do not you deprive me of her, but I pray give her me once agen and I shall bee so much obleiged for ever, that I shall endeavor continually to utter my thanks and render you Love and Honor most renowned: pitty me, I begg itt with teares, and rest you.

Most humbly suppliant
W. Dyre
Portsmouth 27 of [May] 1660

Nathaniel Bacon (1647–1676)

Bacon's Rebellion in 1676 was the result of a series of economic problems and the rising costs of real estate in colonial Virginia. New settlers arriving in the colony and servants finishing their indentures could not afford the more desirable plots of land in the settled areas. As a result, they began moving to the backcountry, where they came into conflict with the Indians. A number of frontiersmen, under the leadership of Nathaniel Bacon, began wantonly attacking Indians. When the governor, Sir William Berkeley, attempting to restore peace, reprimanded Bacon for his attacks on the Indians, many settlers took Bacon's side and became critical of the governor. To them, it appeared that Berkeley was siding with the Indians. In July, Bacon and his followers marched on the colonial capital at Jamestown, where he demanded to be given a commission, granting him official authority to fight the Indians. Berkeley relented and, in essence, abdicated power. On July 30, Bacon issued a "Declaration in the Name of the People" in which he cataloged his grievances. For the next two months, Bacon held power in the capital, but when Berkeley tried to regain control, Bacon, on September 19, burned Jamestown to the ground. In October, Bacon suddenly became ill with dysentery and died. The rebellion was over.

In the past, many historians viewed Bacon's Rebellion as a precursor to the American Revolution. More recently, historians have emphasized the power struggle between the Virginia tidewater elite and the backcountry people.

Declaration in the Name of the People, July 30, 1676

THE DECLARACON OF THE PEOPLE

1. For haveing upon specious pretences of publiqe works raised greate unjust taxes upon the Comonality for the advancement of private favorites and other sinister ends, but noe visible effects in any measure adequate, For not haveing dureing this long time of his Gouvernement in any measure advanced this hopefull Colony either by fortificacons Townes or Trade.

2. For haveing abused and rendred contemptable the Magistrates of Justice, by advanceing to places of Judicature, scandalous and Ignorant favorites.

3. For haveing wronged his Majesties prerogative and interest, by assumeing Monopoly of the Beaver trade, and for haveing in that unjust gaine betrayed and sold his Majesties Country and the lives of his loyall subjects, to the barbarous heathen.

4. For haveing, protected, favoured, and Imboldned the Indians against his Majesties loyall subjects, never contriveing, requireing, or appointing any due

Nathaniel Bacon and William Berkeley: Bacon's Rebellion, 1676. Nathaniel Bacon led a revolt of indentured servants against the Virginia government in an effort to force Governor William Berkeley to open up Indian land for white settlement. It is doubtful that Bacon and Berkeley actually fought face-to-face as this embellished nineteenth-century image suggests.

SOURCE: Nathaniel Bacon, "The declaration of the people against Sir William Berkeley, and present governors of Virginia," 1676. In Edward D. Neill, *Virginia Carolorum: The Colony Under the Rule of Charles the First and Second, A.D. 1625–1685* (Albany, NY: 1886), 361–365.

or proper meanes of sattisfaction for theire many Invasions, robberies, and murthers comitted upon us.

5. For haveing when the Army of English, was just upon the track of those Indians, who now in all places burne, spoyle, murther and when we might with ease have distroyed them: who then were in open hostillity, for then haveing expressly countermanded, and sent back our Army, by passing his word for the peaceable demeanour of the said Indians, who imediately prosecuted theire evill intentions, comitting horred murthers and robberies in all places, being pro-tected by the said ingagement and word past of him the said Sir William Berkeley, haveing ruined and laid desolate a greate part of his Majesties Coun-try, and have now drawne themselves into such obscure and remote places, and are by theire success soe imboldned and confirmed, by theire confederacy soe strengthned that the cryes of blood are in all places, and the terror, and consti-mation of the people soe greate, are now become, not onely a difficult, but a very formidable enimy, who might att first with ease have beene distroyed.

6. And lately when upon the loud outcryes of blood the Assembly had with all care raised and framed an Army for the preventing of further mischeife and safeguard of this his Majesties Colony.

7. For haveing with only the privacy of some few favorites, without acquainting the people, onely by the alteracon of a figure, forged a Comission, by we know not what hand, not onely without, but even against the consent of the people, for the raiseing and effecting civill warr and distruction, which being happily and without blood shed prevented, for haveing the second time attempted the same, thereby calling downe our forces from the defence of the fronteeres and most weekely exposed places.

8. For the prevencon of civill mischeife and ruin amongst ourselves, whilst the barbarous enimy in all places did invade, murther and spoyle us, his majesties most faithfull subjects.

Of this and the aforesaid Articles we accuse Sir William Berkeley as guilty of each and every one of the same, and as one who hath traiterously attempted, violated and Injured his Majesties interest here, by a loss of a greate part of this his Colony and many of his faithfull loyall subjects, by him betrayed and in a barbarous and shamefull manner exposed to the Incursions and murther of the heathen,

And we doe further declare these the ensueing persons in this list, to have beene his wicked and pernicious councellours Confederates, aiders, and assis-ters against the Comonality in these our Civill comotions.

Sir Henry Chichley	William Claiburne Junior
Lieut. Coll. Christopher Wormeley	Thomas Hawkins
William Sherwood	Phillip Ludwell
John Page Clerke	Robert Beverley
John Cluffe Clerke	Richard Lee
John West	Thomas Ballard

Hubert Farrell   William Cole
Thomas Reade   Richard Whitacre
Matthew Kempe   Nicholas Spencer
Joseph Bridger

And we doe further demand that the said Sir William Berkeley with all the persons in this list be forthwith delivered up or surrender themselves within fower days after the notice hereof, Or otherwise we declare as followeth.

That in whatsoever place, howse, or ship, any of the said persons shall reside, be hidd, or protected, we declaire the owners, Masters or Inhabitants of the said places, to be confederates and trayters to the people and the estates of them is alsoe of all the aforesaid persons to be confiscated, and this we the Comons of Virginia doe declare, desiering a firme union amongst our selves that we may joyntly and with one accord defend our selves against the common Enimy, and lett not the faults of the guilty be the reproach of the inocent, or the faults or crimes of the oppressours devide and separate us who have suffered by theire oppressions.

These are therefore in his majesties name to command you forthwith to seize the persons above mentioned as Trayters to the King and Country and them to bring to Midle plantacon, and there to secure them untill further order, and in case of opposition, if you want any further assistance you are forthwith to demand itt in the name of the people in all the Counties of Virginia.

Nathaniel Bacon
Generall by Consent of the people.

Quaker Antislavery Petition

The earliest significant antislavery document from the colonial period is this seventeenth-century petition issued by the Germantown Quaker Meeting. The chief author of the petition was the Meeting's founder, Francis Daniel Pastorius, who reveals that even before slavery was deeply ensconced in the colonies, some Quakers had already adopted a strong antislavery position. The petition was passed along to the Monthly Quaker Meeting and then to the Quarterly and Yearly Quaker Meetings, but since not all Pennsylvania Quakers were as committed to an antislavery stance as those who signed the petition, nothing came of it.

Notice that when Pastorius writes, "In Europe there are many oppressed for conscience sake; and here there are those oppressed who are of a black colour," he is, in effect, equating the physical attribute of skin color with the deeply personal faculty of an individual's conscience. Racial discrimination and oppression, to Pastorius, is thus equivalent to religious persecution and oppression. Also notice that the Monthly, Quarterly, and Yearly Meetings simply "pass the buck" and take no action on the petition.

A Minute Against Slavery, 1688

ADDRESSED TO GERMANTOWN MONTHLY MEETING

This is to ye Monthly Meeting held at Richard Worrell's.

These are the reasons why we are against the traffick of men-body, as foloweth. Is there any that would be done or handled at this manner? viz., to be sold or made a slave for all the time of his life? How fearful and faint-hearted are many on sea, when they see a strange vessel,—being afraid it should be a Turk, and they should be taken, and sold for slaves into Turkey. Now what is this better done, as Turks doe? Yea, rather it is worse for them, which say they are Christians; for we hear that ye most part of such negers are brought hither against their will and consent, and that many of them are stolen. Now, tho they are black, we can not conceive there is more liberty to have them slaves, as it is to have other white ones. There is a saying that we shall doe to all men like as we will be done ourselves; making no difference of what generation, descent or colour they are. And those who steal or robb men, and those who buy or purchase them, are they not all alike? Here is liberty of conscience wch is right and reasonable; here ought to be liberty of ye body, except of evil-doers, wch is an other case. But to bring men hither, or to rob and sell them against their will, we stand against. In Europe there are many oppressed for conscience sake; and here there are those oppressed wh are of a black colour. And we who know that men must not comitt adultery,—some do committ adultery, in separating wives from their husbands and giving them to others; and some sell the children of these poor creatures to other men. Ah! doe consider well this thing, you who doe it, if you would be done at this manner? And if it is done according to Christianity? You surpass Holland and Germany in this thing. This makes an ill report in all those countries of Europe, where they hear of, that ye Quakers doe here handel men as they handel there ye cattle. And for that reason some have no mind or inclination to come hither. And who shall maintain this your cause, or pleid for it. Truly we can not do so, except you shall inform us better hereof, viz., that Christians have liberty to practise these things. Pray, what thing in the world can be done worse towards us, than if men should rob or steal us away, and sell us for slaves to strange countries; separating husbands from their wives and children. Being now that this is not done in the manner we would be done at therefore we contradict and are against this traffic of men-body. And we who profess that it is not lawful to steal, must, likewise, avoid to purchase such things as are stolen, but rather help to stop this robbing and

SOURCE: Retrieved on 4/6/2006 from http://members.fortunecity.com/robertjshea/germusa/protest3.htm.

stealing if possible. And such men ought to be delivered out of ye hands of ye robbers, and set free as well as in Europe. Then is Pennsylvania to have a good report, instead it hath now a bad one for this sake in other countries. Especially whereas ye Europeans are desirous to know in what manner ye Quakers doe rule in their province;—and most of them doe look upon us with an envious eye. But if this is done well, what shall we say is done evil?

If once these slaves (wch they say are so wicked and stubbern men) should join themselves,—fight for their freedom,—and handel their masters and mastrisses as they did handel them before; will these masters and mastrisses take the sword at hand and warr against these poor slaves, licke, we are able to believe, some will not refuse to doe; or have these negers not as much right to fight for their freedom, as you have to keep them slaves?

Now consider well this thing, if it is good or bad? And in case you find it to be good to handle these blacks at that manner, we desire and require you hereby lovingly, that you may inform us herein, which at this time never was done, viz., that Christians have such a liberty to do so. To the end we shall be satisfied in this point, and satisfie likewise our good friends and acquaintances in our natif country, to whose it is a terror, or fairful thing, that men should be handeld so in Pennsylvania.

This is from our meeting at Germantown, held ye 18 of the 2 month, 1688, to be delivered to the Monthly Meeting at Richard Worrell's.

Garret henderich
derick up de graeff
Francis daniell Pastorius
Abraham up Den graef.

MONTHLY MEETING RESPONSE:

At our Monthly Meeting at Dublin, ye 30 – 2 mo., 1688, we have inspected ye matter, above mentioned, and considered of it, we find it so weighty that we think it not expedient for us to meddle with it here, but do rather commit it to ye consideration of ye Quarterly Meeting; ye tenor of it being nearly related to ye Truth. On behalf of ye Monthly Meeting,

Signed, P. Jo. Hart.

QUARTERLY MEETING RESPONSE:

This, above mentioned, was read in our Quarterly Meeting at Philadelphia, the 4 of ye 4th mo. '88, and was from thence recommended to the Yearly Meeting, and the above said Derick, and the other two mentioned therein, to present the same to ye above said meeting, it being a thing of too great a weight for this meeting to determine.

Signed by order of ye meeting,
Anthony Morris.

YEARLY MEETING RESPONSE:

At a Yearly Meeting held at Burlington the 5th day of the 7th month, 1688.

A Paper being here presented by some German Friends Concerning the Lawfulness and Unlawfulness of Buying and keeping Negroes, It was adjusted not to be so proper for this Meeting to give a Positive Judgment in the case, It having so General a Relation to many other Parts, and therefore at present they forbear It.

Letter from an Anonymous Slave

This recently discovered letter by an anonymous slave is a petition to the Bishop of London to influence King George I to grant freedom. Though the letter failed to receive a response from the bishop, it is an important early example of the efforts made by some slaves to protest their condition by appealing to the powers that be.

RELEESE US OUT OF THIS CRUELL BONDEGG, 1723

AUGUST THE FORTH, 1723

to the Right Raverrand father in god my Lord arch Bishop of Lonnd. . . .

this coms to sattesfie your honoour that there is in this Land of verjennia a Sort of people that is Calld molatters which are Baptised and brouaht up in the way of the Christian faith and followes the ways and Rulles of the Chrch of England and sum of them has white fathars and sum white mothers and there is in this Land a Law or act which keeps and makes them and there seed Slaves forever. . . .

wee your humbell and poore partishinners doo begg Sir your aid and assisttancce in this one thing . . . which is that your honour will by the help of our Sufvering Lord King George and the Rest of the Rullers will Releese us out of this Cruell Bondegg. . . .

wee are commandded to keep holey the Sabbath day and wee doo hardly know when it comes for our task mastrs are has hard with us as the Egypttions was with the Chilldann of Issarall. . . . wee are kept out of the Church and matrimony is deenied us and to be plain they doo Look no more upon us then if wee ware dogs which I hope when these Strange lines comes to your Lord Ships hands will be Looket in to. . . .

SOURCE: Thomas N. Ingersoll, "'Releese Us Out of This Cruell Bondegg': An Appeal from Virginia in 1723," *William and Mary Quarterly*, Third Series, 51 (October 1994), 776–782.

And Sir wee your humble perticners do humblly beg . . . that our childarn may be broatt up in the way of the Christtian faith and our desire is that they may be Larnd the Lords prayer the creed and the ten commandments and that they may appeare Every Lord's day att Church before the Curatt to bee Exammond for our desire is that godllines Shoulld be abbound amongs us and wee desire that our Childarn be putt to Scool and Larnd to Reed through the Bybell.

My Riting is varfy bad. . . . I am but a poore Slave that writt itt and has no other time butt Sunday and hardly that att Sumtimes. . . . wee dare nott Subscribe any mans name to this for feare of our masters for if they knew that wee have sent home to your honour wee Should goo neare to Swing upon the gallass tree.

Native American Voices, 1609–1752

The indigenous people of the New World faced a grave crisis with European settlement. From their first encounters with Columbus and the Spanish, their culture was profoundly threatened. The Indian population dropped so precipitously through disease and murderous onslaughts that the results might as well be labeled genocide, although not all that befell them was intentional. The term dissent does not adequately describe Native American resistance or the valiant attempt to preserve their disappearing way of life. Though they expressed their grievances against the conquerors in petitions and speeches, few such documents have survived. The reason for this is twofold: Much of their resistance and protest took the form of warfare, and the Indian tradition is primarily an oral one. Few of their speeches or petitions, especially in the sixteenth through nineteenth centuries, were written down. Those that were often were transcribed by Europeans who rarely understood the nuances and subtleties of the Indian perspective or who intentionally distorted what the Indians wanted to express. Furthermore, many of the documents that have survived were written down years and even decades after the event and so must be read with additional skepticism. Yet documents from the colonial period do exist and shed some light on the Native American point of view.

POWHATAN

One of the most familiar tales about colonial America is the story that the Jamestown settlers would never have survived the winter of 1607–1608 without the aid of the Powhatan Indians. Even with that help, only half the settlers were still alive by the spring of 1608. But deep-seated English distrust and belligerence toward the Indians elicited distrust of the settlers from the Powhatan tribe. By 1609, tensions between the two groups

*erupted into open warfare. In 1612, after his return to England, Captain
John Smith published an account of the Jamestown colony in which he
recorded the following speech by the Indian chief Powhatan.*

Speech to John Smith, 1609

Captaine Smith, you may understand that I having seene the death of all my
people thrice, and not any one living of these three generations but my selfe; I
know the difference of Peace and Warre better than any in my Country. But now
I am old and ere long must die, my brethren, namely Opitchapam, Opechan-
canough, and Kekataugh, my two sisters, and their two daughters, are distinctly
each other successors. I wish their experience no lesse then mine, and your love
to them no lesse then mine to you. But this bruit from Nandsamund, that you
are come to destroy my Country, so much affrighteth all my people as they dare
not visit you. What will it availe you to take that by force you may quickly have
by love, or to destroy them that provide you food. What can you get by warre,
when we can hide our provisions and fly to the woods? Whereby you must fam-
ish by wronging us your friends. And why are you thus jealous of our loves seeing us unarmed, and both doe, and are willing still to feede you, with that you
cannot get but by our labours? Thinke you I am so simple, not to know it is better to eate good meate, lye well, and sleepe quietly with my women and children,
laugh and be merry with you, have copper, hatchets, or what I want being your
friend: then be forced to flie from all, to lie cold in the woods, feede upon
Acornes, rootes, and such trash, and be so hunted by you, that I can neither rest,
eate, nor sleepe; but my tyred men must watch, and if a twig but breake, every
one cryeth there commeth Captaine Smith: then must I fly I know not whether:
and thus with miserable feare, end my miserable life leaving my pleasures to
such youths as you, which through your rash unadvisednesse may quickly as
miserably end, for want of that, you never know where to finde. Let this therefore assure you of our loves, and every yeare our friendly trade shall furnish you
with Corne; and now also, if you would come in friendly manner to see us, and
not thus with your guns and swords as to invade your foes.

GARANGULA

*Garangula, an Onondaga, met with the governor of New France in 1684
on the shores of Lake Ontario, and after listening to the Frenchman's
bullying attempt to coerce his people, replied in a fashion that made it
clear that the Five Nations of the Iroquois were not to be intimidated.*

Source: Philip L. Barbour, ed., *The Complete Works of Captain John Smith* (Chapel Hill:
University of North Carolina Press, 1986), vol. I, 247.

Garangula's eloquent comments reveal both his pride in the Iroquois and his scathing contempt for the French and the English. The result was a reversal for the French; Governor La Barre and he signed a treaty obliging the French to leave the next day.

Speech to Governor La Barre of New France, 1684

Yonnondio [La Barre], I Honour you, and the Warriors that are with me all likewise honour you. Your interpreter has finished your Speech; I now begin mine. My words make haste to reach your Ears; hearken to them.

Yonnondio, You must have believed, when you left Quebeck, that the Sun had burnt up all the Forests which render our Country Unaccessible to the French, or that the Lakes had so far overflown the Banks that they had surrounded our Castles, and that it was impossible for us to get out of them. Yes, Yonnondio, surely you must have thought so, and the Curiosity of seeing so great a Country burnt up, or under Water, has brought you so far. Now you are undeceived, since that I and my Warriors are come to assure you that the Sennekas, Cayugas, Onnondagas, Oneydoes and Mohawks are yet alive. I thank you, in their Name, for bringing back into their Country the Calumet which your Predecessor received from their hands. It was happy for you that you left under ground that Murdering Hatchet which has been so often dyed in the Blood of the French. Hear Yonnondio, I do not Sleep, I have my eyes Open, and the Sun which enlightens me discovers to me a great Captain at the head of a Company of Soldiers, who speaks as if he were Dreaming. He says that he only came to the Lake to smoke on the great Calumet with the Onnondagas. But Garangula says that he sees the Contrary, that it was to knock them on the head, if Sickness had not weakned the Arms of the French.

I see Yonnondio Raving in a Camp of sick men, whose lives the Great Spirit has saved by Inflicting this Sickness on them. Hear Yonnondio, Our Women had taken their Clubs, our Children and Old Men had carried their Bows and Arrows into the heart of your Camp, if our Warriors had not disarmed them, and retained them when your Messenger, Ohguesse appeared in our Castle. It is done, and I have said it.

Hear, Yonnondio, we plundered none of the French but those that carried Guns, Powder and Ball to the Twihtwies [The Miami] and Chictaghicks [The Illinois], because those Arms might have cost us our Lives. Herein we follow the example of the Jesuits, who stove all the Barrels of Rum brought to our Castle, lest the Drunken Indians should knock them on the Head. Our Warriors have

Source: Cadwallader Colden, *History of the Five Indian Nations*, part 1 (London, 1727), 53–55.

not Bevers enough to pay for all those Arms that they have taken, and our Old Men are not afraid of the War. *This Belt Preserves my Words.*

We carried the English into our Lakes to traffick there with the Utawawas [The Ottawa] and Quatoghies [The Huron] as the Adirondacks [The Algonkin] brought the French to our Castles to carry on a Trade which the English say is theirs. We are born free. We neither depend on Yonnondio nor Corlaer [the Governor of New York].

We may go where we please, and carry with us whom we please, and buy and sell what we please. If your Allies be your Slaves, use them as such. Command them to receive no other but your people. *This Belt Preserves my Words.*

We knockt the Twihtwies and Chictaghicks on the head because they had cut down the Trees of Peace which were the Limits of our Country. They had hunted Bever on our Lands. They have acted contrary to the Custom of all Indians; for they left none of the Bevers alive, they kill'd both Male and Female. They brought the Satanas [The Shawnees] into their Country to take part with them, and Arm'd them, after they had concerted ill Designs against us. We have done less than either the English or French, that have usurp'd the Lands of so many Indian Nations, and chased them from their own Country. *This Belt Preserves my Words.*

Hear Yonnondio, What I say is the Voice of all the Five Nations. Hear what they Answer, Open your Ears to what they Speak. The Sennekas, Cayugas, Onnondagas, Oneydoes, and Mohawks say, That when they buried the Hatchet at Cadarackui (in the presence of your Predecessor) in the middle of the Fort, they planted the Tree of Peace in the same place, to be there carefully preserved, that in a place of a Retreat for Soldiers, that Fort might be a Rendevouze of Merchants; that in place of Arms and Munitions of War, Bevers and Merchandize should only enter there.

Hear, Yonnondio, Take care for the future, that so great a Number of Soldiers as appear here do not choak the Tree of Peace planted in so small a Fort. It will be a great Loss, if after it had so easily taken root, you should stop its growth and prevent its covering your Country and ours with its Branches. I assure you, in the Name of the Five Nations, That our Warriors shall dance to the Calumet of Peace under its leaves, and shall remain quiet on their Mats, and shall never dig up the Hatchet till their Brethren, Yonnondio, or Corlaer, shall, either joyntly or separately endeavour to attack the Country which the Great Spirit has given to our Ancestors. *This Belt preserves my Words; and this other, the Authority which the Five Nations have given me.*

STUNG SERPENT

In 1723, war broke out in Mississippi between the French and the Natchez. One of the Indians, Stung Serpent, suddenly ended his friendship with Antoine Simon Le Page du Pratz, a Frenchman who had been living among the Natchez for 5 years. Disconcerted, du Pratz wanted to know the reason Stung Serpent had suddenly turned on him. The Indian's response, recorded by Le Page du Pratz years later in his History of Louisiana, *was probably a sentiment shared by many Native Americans in the eighteenth century.*

REPLY TO ANTOINE SIMON LE PAGE DU PRATZ, 1723

"Why," continued he, with an air of displeasure, "did the French come into our country? We did not go to seek them: they asked for land of us, because their country was too little for all the men that were in it. We told them they might take land where they pleased, there was enough for them and for us; that it was good the same sun should enlighten us both, and that we would walk as friends in the same path; and that we would give them of our provisions, assist them to build, and to labour in their fields. We have done so; is not this true? What occasion then had we for Frenchmen? Before they came, did not live better than we do, seeing we deprive ourselves of a part of our corn, our game, and fish, to give a part to them? In what respect, then, had we occasion for them? Was it for their guns? The bows and arrows which we used, were sufficient to make us live well. Was it for their white, blue, and red blankets? We can do well enough with buffalo skins, which are warmer; our women wrought feather-blankets for the winter, and mulberry-mantles for the summer; which indeed were not so beautiful; but our women were more laborious and less vain than they are now. In fine, before the arrival of the French, we lived like men who can be satisfied with what they have; whereas at this day we are like slaves, who are not suffered to do as they please."

LORON SAUGUAARUM

The following is a rare narrative, from the Indian point of view, of the negotiations that led to the Casco Bay Treaty of 1727, in which the British claimed the Indians had relinquished their sovereignty. Loron Sauguaarum, a Penobscot, was one of the delegates negotiating with the English.

NEGOTIATIONS FOR THE CASCO BAY TREATY, 1727

I, Panaouamskeyen, do inform ye—ye who are scattered all over the earth take notice—of what has passed between me and the English in negotiating the peace that I have just concluded with them. It is from the bottom of my heart that I inform you; and, as a proof that I tell you nothing but the truth, I wish to speak to you in my own tongue.

My reason for informing you, myself, is the diversity and contrariety of the interpretations I receive of the English writing in which the articles of Peace are drawn up that we have just mutually agreed to. These writings appear to contain things that are not, so that the Englishman himself disavows them in my presence, when he reads and interprets them to me himself.

SOURCE: Le Page du Pratz, *The History of Louisiana* (London, 1774), reprinted by J. S. W. Harmanson (New Orleans, 1947), 41.
SOURCE: E. B. O'Callaghan, ed., *Documents Relative to the Colonial History of the State of New York*, 15 vols. (Albany: Weed, Parsons & Co., 1855), vol. 9, 966–967.

I begin then by informing you; and shall speak to you only of the principal and most important matter.

First, that I did not commence the negotiation for a peace, or settlement, but he, it was, who first spoke to me on the subject, and I did not give him any answer until he addressed me a third time. I first went to Fort St. George to hear his propositions, and afterwards to Boston, whither he invited me on the same business.

We were two that went Boston: I, Laurance Sagouarrab, and John Ehennek-ouit. On arriving there I did indeed salute him in the usual mode at the first interview, but I was not the first to speak to him. I only answered what he said to me, and such was the course I observed throughout the whole of our interview.

He began by asking me, what brought me hither? I did not give him for answer—I am come to ask your pardon; nor, I come to acknowledge you as my conqueror; nor, I come to make my submission to you; nor, I come to receive your commands. All the answer I made was that I was come on his invitation to me to hear the propositions for a settlement that he wished to submit to me.

Wherefore do we kill one another? he again asked me. 'Tis true that, in reply, I said to him—You are right. But I did not say to him, I acknowledge myself the cause of it, nor I condemn myself for having made war on him.

He next said to me—Propose what must be done to make us friends. 'Tis true that thereupon I answered him—It is rather for you to do that. And my reason for giving him that answer is, that having himself spoken to me of an arrangement, I did not doubt but he would make me some advantageous proposals. But I did not tell him that I would submit in every respect to his orders.

Thereupon, he said to me—Let us observe the treaties concluded by our Fathers, and renew the ancient friendship which existed between us. I made him no answer thereunto; much less, I repeat, did I, become his subject, or give him my land, or acknowledge his King as my King. This I never did, and he never proposed it to me. I say, he never said to me—Give thyself and thy land to me, nor acknowledge my King for thy King, as thy ancestors formerly did.

He again said to me—But do you not recognize the King of England as King over all his states? To which I answered—Yes, I recognize him King of all his lands; but I rejoined, do not hence infer that I acknowledge thy King as my King, and King of my lands. Here lies my distinction—my Indian distinction. God hath willed that I have no King, and that I be master of my lands in common.

He again asked me—Do you not admit that I am at least master of the lands I have purchased? I answered him thereupon, that I admit nothing, and that I knew not what he had reference to.

He again said to me—If, hereafter, any one desire to disturb the negotiation of the peace we are at present engaged about, we will join together to arrest him. I again consented to that. But I did not say to him, and do not understand that he said to me, that we should go in company to attack such person, or that we should form a joint league, offensive and defensive, or that I should unite my Brethren to his. I said to him only, and I understand him to say to me, that if any one wished to disturb our negotiation of Peace, we would both endeavor to pacify him by fair words, and to that end would direct all our efforts.

He again said to me—In order that the peace we would negotiate be permanent, should any private quarrel arise hereafter between Indians and Englishmen, they must not take justice into their own hands, nor do any thing, the one to the other. It shall be the business of us Chiefs to decide. I again agreed with him on that article, but I did not understand that he alone should be judge. I understood only that he should judge his people, and that I would judge mine.

Finally he said to me—There's our peace concluded; we have regulated every thing.

I replied that nothing had been yet concluded, and that it was necessary that our acts should be approved in a general assembly. For the present, an armistice is sufficient. I again said to him—I now go to inform all my relatives of what has passed between us, and will afterwards come and report to you what they'll say to me. Then he agreed in opinion with me.

Such was my negotiation on my first visit to Boston.

As for any act of grace, or amnesty, accorded to me by the Englishman, on the part of his King, it is what I have no knowledge of, and what the Englishman never spoke to me about, and what I never asked him for.

On my second visit to Boston we were four: I, Laurence Sagourrab, Alexis, Francois Xavier and Migounambe. I went there merely to tell the English that all my nation approved the cessation of hostilities, and the negotiation of peace, and even then we agreed on the time and place of meeting to discuss it. That place was Caskebay, and the time after Corpus Christi.

Two conferences were held at Caskebay. Nothing was done at these two conferences except to read the articles above reported. Every thing I agreed to was approved and ratified, and on these conditions was the peace concluded. One point only did I regulate at Caskebay. This was to permit the Englishman to keep a store at St. Georges; but a store only, and not to build any other house, nor erect a fort there, and I did not give him the land.

These are the principal matters that I wished to communicate to you who are spread all over the earth. What I tell you now is the truth. If, then, any one should produce any writing that makes me speak otherwise, pay no attention to it, for I know not what I am made to say in another language, but I know well what I say in my own. And in testimony that I say things as they are, I have signed the present minute which I wish to be authentic and to remain for ever.

LENNI LENAPE

Although William Penn strove at all times to deal fairly with the Lenni Lenape (Delaware) Indians, even paying the large sum of £1200 for title to the land on which he built his colony, his descendants did not share the same ethical principles. In the 1730s, his son Thomas produced a 1686 deed, purportedly drawn up between his father and several Delaware chiefs, giving the colonists the rights to all the land "as far as a man can go

in a day and a half" and from there to the Delaware River and along its
length. To prepare for the implementation of this "treaty," the colonists
cleared a trail. Instead of having one man walk as far as he could in a day
and a half, three runners set out on the expedition. At the point where the
third runner fell exhausted (65 miles distant), the colonists marked their
new boundary, in effect taking from the Indians most of the territory of
eastern Pennsylvania up to the Lehigh Valley.

 In 1740, several Delaware chiefs petitioned the magistrates of
Pennsylvania to remove the colonists who had settled on these lands.
Notice how the Indians have adopted a method of framing a petition
along lines that would easily be understood by the English.

GRIEVANCE AGAINST THE "WALKING PURCHASE," 1740

TO MR. JEREMIAH LANGHORNE, 1740

To Mr. Jeremiah Langhorne & all Magistrates of Pennsilvania:

We pray that You would take Notice of the Great Wrong We Receive in Our Lands, here are about 100 families Settled On it for what Reason they Cant tell. They tell them *that Thomas Penn has sold them the Land Which We think must be Very Strange that T. Penn Should Sell him that which was never his for We never Sold him this Land.* The Case was this. That When We Were With Penn to treat as usual with his Father, He keep begging & plagueing us to Give him some Land & Never gives us leave to treat upon any thing till he Wearies us Out of Our Lives but What should We give Penn any Land for We never had any thing from him but honest Dealings & Civility. If he lets us alone We will let him alone. The Lands we do Own to be Ours, Begin, at the Mouth of Tohickon Runs up along the said Branch to the Head Springs thence up With a strait line [to] Patquating thence with a strait Line to the Blew Mountain thence to a Place called Mohaining thence along a Mountain called Neshameek thence along the Great Swamp to a Branch of Delaware River So along Delaware River to the Place where it first began. All this is Our own Land Except Some tracts We have disposed off. The Tract of Durham The tract of Nicholas Depuis The Tract of Old Weiser. We have Sold *But for the Rest We have Never sold & We Desire Thomas Penn Would take these People off from their Land in Peace that we May not be at the trouble to drive them off for the Land WE Will hold fast With both Our hands not in privately but in Open View of all the Countrey & all Our Friends & Relations That is the Eastern Indians & Our Uncles the five Nations & the Mohikkons & the Twitways Shawanahs Shawekelou Tuskeroroes & the Takkesaw the last. These all shall be by & hear us Speak & We Shall Stand at Our Uncles Breast When We Shall Speak.* Now Gentlemen & all others We Desire some

---

SOURCE: Donald H. Kent, ed., *Pennsylvania Indian Treaties, 1737–1756* (Frederick, MD: University Publications of America, 1984), 24, 45–46.

of Your Assistance in this Affair for We have lived in Brotherly Friend Ship So We
Desire to Continue the same if So be We can be Righted any Manner of Ways So
We Remainz

Your Friends

ATIWANETO

*In 1752, Phineas Stevens attempted to negotiate a treaty between the colony
of Massachusetts and the Abenaki. At a conference in Montreal, the Abenaki
spokesman Atiwaneto made it clear that his people did not trust the colonists
and that they would resist any further pressure to give up their land.*

REMARKS TO PHINEAS STEVENS, 1752

Propositions of the Abenakis of St. Francis to Captain Phineas Stevents, delegate
from the Governor of Boston, in presence of the Baron de Longueuil. Governor
of Montreal, Commandant of Canada and of the Iroquois of the Sault Saint
Louis and of the Lake of the Two Mountains, 5th of July, 1752.

Brother, We speak to you as if we spoke to your Governor of Boston. We
hear on all sides that this Governor and the Bostonians say that the Abenakis are
bad people. 'Tis in vain that we are taxed with having a bad heart; it is you,
brother, that always attack us; your mouth is of sugar but your heart of gall; in
truth, the moment you begin we are on our guard.

Brothers, We tell you that we seek not war, we ask nothing better than to be
quiet, and it depends, Brothers, only on you English, to have peace with us.

We have not yet sold the lands we inhabit, we wish to keep the possession of
them. Our elders have been willing to tolerate you, brothers Englishmen, on the
seaboard as far as Sawakwato, as that has been so decided, we wish it to be so.

But we will not cede one single inch of the lands we inhabit beyond what
has been decided formerly by our fathers.

You have the sea for your share from the place where you reside; you can
trade there. But we expressly forbid you to kill a single beaver, or to take a single
stick of timber on the lands we inhabit. If you want timber we'll sell you some,
but you shall not take it without our permission.

Brothers, Who hath authorized you to have those lands surveyed? We request
our brother, the Governor of Boston, to have these Surveyors punished, as we cannot imagine that they have acted by his authority.

Brother, You are therefore masters of the peace that we are to have with you.
On condition that you will not encroach on those lands we will be at peace, as
the King of France is with the King of Great Britain.

SOURCE: E. B. O'Callaghan, ed., *Documents Relative to the Colonial History of the State of
New York*, 15 vols. (Albany: Weed, Parsons & Co., 1853–1887), vol. 10, 252–254.

By a Belt. I repeat to you, Brothers, by this Belt, that it depends on yourselves to be at peace with the Abenakis.

Our Father who is here present has nothing to do with what we say to you; we speak to you of our own accord, and in the name of all our allies. We regard our Father, in this instance, only as a witness of our words.

We acknowledge no other boundaries of yours than your settlements whereon you have built, and we will not, under any pretext whatsoever, that you pass beyond them. The lands we possess have been given us by the Master of Life. We acknowledge to hold only from him.

We are entirely free. We are allies of the King of France, from whom we have received the Faith and all sorts of assistance in our necessities. We love that monarch, and we are strongly attached to his interests.

Let us have an answer to the propositions we address you, as soon as possible. Take this message in writing to give to your Governor. We also shall keep a copy of it to use in case of need.

Without stirring a step it is easy for your Governor to transmit his answer to us; he will have merely to address it to our Father who will have the goodness to send it to us.

MASHPEE

This petition is an example of an attempt by Indians to protest their treatment at the hands of English colonists. The petition did result in the Mashpee (who had converted to Christianity) being granted self-government, and for several years they were satisfied that their grievance had been heard. However, their satisfaction was short-lived, for when the American Revolution came to an end, their right to self-government was rescinded.

PETITION TO THE MASSACHUSETTS GENERAL COURT, 1752

Barnstable, June 11, 1752

Oh! Our honorable gentlemen and kind gentlemen in Boston in Massachusetts Bay, here in New England, the great ones who oversee the colony in Boston, gentlemen. Oh!, Oh!, gentlemen, hear us now, Oh! ye, us poor Indians. We do not clearly have thorough understanding and wisdom. Therefore we now beseech you, Oh!, Boston gentlemen. Oh! Hear our weeping, and hear our beseeching of you, Oh!, and answer this beseeching of you by us, Oh!, gentlemen of Boston, us poor Indians in Mashpee in Barnstable County.

SOURCE: Ives Goddard and Kathleen J. Bragdon, *Native Writings in Massachusetts* (Philadelphia: American Philosophical Society, 1988), 373.

Now we beseech you, what can we do with regard to our land, which was conveyed to you by these former sachems of ours. What they conveyed to you was this piece of land. This was conveyed to us by Indian sachems. Our former Indian sachems were called Sachem Wuttammohkin and Sachem Quettatsett, in Barnstable County, the Mashpee Indian place. This Indian land, this was conveyed to us by these former sachems of ours. We shall not give it away, nor shall it be sold, nor shall it be lent, but we shall always use it as long as we live, we together with all our children, and our children's children, and our descendants, and together with all their descendants. They shall always use it as long as Christian Indians live. We shall use it forever and ever. Unless we all peacefully agree to give it away or to sell it. But as of now not one of all of us Indians has yet agreed to give away, or sell, or lend this Indian land, or marsh, or wood. Fairly, then, it is this: we state frankly we have never conveyed them away.

But now clearly we Indians say this to all you gentlemen of ours in Boston: We poor Indians in Mashpee, in Barnstable County, we truly are much troubled by these English neighbors of ours being on this land of ours, and in our marsh and trees. Against our will these Englishmen take away from us what was our land. They parcel it out to each other, and the marsh along with it, against our will. And as for our streams, they do not allow us peacefully to be when we peacefully go fishing. They beat us greatly, and they have houses on our land against our will. Truly we think it is this: We poor Indians soon shall not have any place to reside, together with our poor children, because these Englishmen trouble us very much in this place of ours in Mashpee, Barnstable County.

Therefore now, Oh! you kind gentlemen in Boston, in Massachusetts Bay, now we beseech you: defend us, and they would not trouble us any more on our land.

John Peter Zenger (1697–1746)

John Peter Zenger began publishing one of the first newspapers in New York in 1733. The New York Weekly Journal, edited by James Alexander, was very critical of Governor William Cosby, a notoriously corrupt appointee of the Crown. It was common knowledge that Cosby had rigged elections, bribed judges and legislators, and dipped into the public treasury. When The Journal *ran several articles calling for freedom of the press and condemning the governor's actions, Cosby seized the newspaper and had Zenger arrested for libel. In the eighteenth century, all that had to be proved at the trial to convict Zenger of libel was that he had published the articles. Even though the articles dealt with facts, truth—according to British law—was not considered a defense against libel. Philadelphia lawyer Andrew Hamilton, however, argued that truth was a defense: "If libel is understood in the unlimited sense urged by the attorney general,*

*there is scarce a writing I know that may not be called a libel or scarce a
person safe from being called to account as a libeler. Moses, meek as he
was, libeled Cain—and who is it that not libeled the devil?" Zenger's
acquittal was a precedent-setting victory for freedom of the press.*

The following articles appeared in The Journal *in November 1733
and led to Zenger's eventual arrest and trial. Much of the argument
echoes John Locke's* Second Treatise of Government, *one of the
philosophical cornerstones for the revolution to come.*

ARTICLES FROM THE NEW YORK WEEKLY JOURNAL, 1733

NOVEMBER 12, 1733

The liberty of the press is a subject of the greatest importance, and in which
every individual is as much concerned as he is in any other part of liberty:
Therefore it will not be improper to communicate to the public the sentiments
of a late excellent writer upon this point. Such is the elegance and perspicuity of
his writings, such the inimitable force of his reasoning, that it will be difficult to
say anything new that he has not said, or not to say that much worse which he
has said.

There are two sorts of monarchies, an absolute and a limited one. In the
first, the liberty of the press can never be maintained, it is inconsistent with it;
for what absolute monarch would suffer any subject to animadvert on his
actions when it is in his power to declare the crime and to nominate the punishment? This would make it very dangerous to exercise such a liberty. Besides the
object against which those pens must be directed is their sovereign, the sole
supreme magistrate; for there being no law in those monarchies but the will of
the prince, it makes it necessary for his ministers to consult his pleasure before
anything, can be undertaken: He is therefore properly chargeable with the grievances of his subjects, and what the minister there acts being in obedience to the
prince, he ought not to incur the hatred of the people; for it would be hard to
impute that to him for a crime which is the fruit of his allegiance, and for
refusing which he might incur the penalties of treason. Besides, in an absolute
monarchy, the will of the prince being the law, a liberty of the press to complain
of grievances would be complaining against the law and the constitution, to
which they have submitted or have been obliged to submit; and therefore, in one
sense, may be said to deserve punishment; so that under an absolute monarchy,
I say, such a liberty is inconsistent with the constitution, having no proper subject to politics on which it might be exercised, and if exercised would incur a
certain penalty.

SOURCE: *The New York Weekly Journal,* November 12 and 19, 1733.

But in a limited monarchy, as England is, our laws are known, fixed, and established. They are the straight rule and sure guide to direct the king, the ministers, and other his subjects: And therefore an offense against the laws is such an offense against the constitution as ought to receive a proper adequate punishment; the several constituents of the government, the ministry, and all subordinate magistrates, having their certain, known, and limited sphere in which they move; one part may certainly err, misbehave, and become criminal, without involving the rest or any of them in the crime or punishment.

But some of these may be criminal, yet above punishment, which surely cannot be denied, since most reigns have furnished us with too many instances of powerful and wicked ministers, some of whom by their power have absolutely escaped punishment, and the rest, who met their fate, are likewise instances of this power as much to the purpose; for it was manifest in them that their power had long protected them, their crimes having, often long preceded their much desired and deserved punishment and reward.

That might overcomes right, or which is the same thing, that might preserves and defends men from punishment, is a proverb established and confirmed by time and experience, the surest discoverers of truth and certainty. It is this therefore which makes the liberty of the press in a limited monarchy and in all its colonies and plantations proper, convenient, and necessary, or indeed it is rather incorporated and interwoven with our very constitution; for if such an overgrown criminal, or an impudent monster in iniquity, cannot immediately be come at by ordinary Justice, let him yet receive the lash of satire, let the glaring truths of his ill administration, if possible, awaken his conscience, and if he has no conscience, rouse his fear by showing him his deserts, sting him with the dread of punishment, cover him with shame, and render his actions odious to all honest minds. These methods may in time, and by watching and exposing his actions, make him at least more cautious, and perhaps at last bring down the great haughty and secure criminal within the reach and grasp of ordinary justice. This advantage therefore of exposing the exorbitant crimes of wicked ministers under a limited monarchy makes the liberty of the press not only consistent with, but a necessary part of, the constitution itself.

It is indeed urged that the liberty of the press ought to be restrained because not only the actions of evil ministers may be exposed, but the character of good ones traduced. Admit it in the strongest light that calumny and lies would prevail and blast the character of a great and good minister; yet that is a less evil than the advantages we reap from the liberty of the press, as it is a curb, a bridle, a terror, a shame, and restraint to evil ministers; and it may be the only punishment, especially for a time. But when did calumnies and lies ever destroy the character of one good minister? Their benign influences are known, tasted, and felt by everybody: Or if their characters have been clouded for a time, yet they have generally shined forth in greater luster: Truth will always prevail over falsehood.

The facts exposed are not to be believed because said or published; but it draws people's attention, directs their view, and fixes the eye in a proper position that everyone may judge for himself whether those facts are true or not. People will recollect, enquire and search, before they condemn; and therefore very few good ministers can be hurt by falsehood, but many wicked ones by seasonable truth: But however the mischief that a few may possibly, but improbably, suffer by the freedom of the press is not to be put in competition with the danger which the KING and the people may suffer by a shameful, cowardly silence under the tyranny of an insolent, rapacious, infamous minister.

NOVEMBER 19, 1733 (THE REMAINDER OF THE LETTER CONCERNING THE LIBERTY OF THE PRESS BEGUN IN OUR LAST [ISSUE].)

Inconveniences are rather to be endured than that we should suffer an entire and total destruction. Who would not lose a leg to save his neck? And who would not endanger his hand to guard his heart? The loss of liberty in general would soon follow the suppression of the liberty of the press; for as it is an essential branch of liberty, so perhaps it is the best preservation of the whole. Even a restraint of the press would have a fatal influence. No nation ancient or modern ever lost the liberty of freely speaking, writing, or publishing their sentiments but forthwith lost their liberty in general and became slaves. LIBERTY and SLAVERY! how amiable is one! how odious and abominable the other! Liberty is universal redemption, joy, and happiness; but servitude is absolute reprobation and everlasting perdition in politics.

All the venal supporters of wicked ministers are aware of the great use of the liberty of the press in a limited free monarchy: They know how vain it would be to attack it openly, and therefore endeavor to puzzle the case with words, inconsistencies, and nonsense; but if the opinion of the most numerous, unprejudiced and impartial part of mankind is an argument of truth, the liberty of the press has that as well as reason on its side. I believe every honest Briton of whatever denomination, who loves his country, if left to his own free and unbiased judgment is a friend to the liberty of the press and an enemy to any restraint upon it. Surely all the independent whigs, to a man, are of this opinion. By an Independent Whig, I mean one whose principles lead him to be firmly attached to the present happy establishment, both in church and state, and whose fidelity to the royal family is so staunch and riveted as not to be called in question, tho' his mind is not overswayed, or rather necessitated, by the extraordinary weight of lucrative posts or pensions. The dread of infamy hath certainly been of great use to the cause of virtue, and is a stronger curb upon the passions and appetites of some men than any other consideration moral or religious. Whenever, therefore, the talent of satire is made use of to restrain men by the fear of shame from immoral actions, which either do or do not fall under the cognizance of the law, it is properly, and justly, and commendably applied: On the contrary, to condemn all satire is in effect the same thing as countenancing vice by screening it from reproach and the just indignation of mankind. The use of satire was of great service to the patriot whigs in the reign of King Charles and King James the second, as well as in that of Queen Anne. They asserted the freedom of writing against wicked ministers; and tho' they knew it would signify nothing to accuse them publicly whilst they were in the zenith of their power, they made use of satire to prepare the way and alarm the people against their designs. If men in power were always men of integrity, we might venture to trust them with the direction of the press, and there would be no occasion to plead against the restraint of it; but as they have vices like their fellows, so it very often happens that the best intended and the most valuable writings are the objects of their resentment, because opposite to their own tempers or designs. In short, I think, every man of common sense will judge that he is an enemy to his king and country who pleads for any restraint upon the press; but by the press, when nonsense, inconsistencies, or personal reflections are writ, if despised, they die of course; if truth, solid arguments, and elegant, just sentiments are published, they should meet with applause rather than censure; if sense and nonsense are blended, then, by the free use of the press, which is open to all, the inconsistencies of the writer may be made apparent; but to grant a liberty only for praise, flattery, and panegyric, with a restraint on everything which happens to be offensive and disagreeable to those who are at any time in power, is absurd, servile, and ridiculous; upon which, I beg leave to quote one observation of the ingenious Mr. Gordon, in his excellent discourses upon Tacitus. "In truth," says he, where no liberty is allowed to speak of governors besides that of praising them, their praises will be little believed; their tenderness and aversion to have their conduct examined will be apt to prompt people to think their conduct guilty or weak, to suspect their management and designs to be worse perhaps than they are, and to become turbulent and seditious, rather than be forced to be silent. . . .

Eighteenth–Century Runaway Women

According to English law, married women were femes covert; that is, their identity was "covered" by their husbands. Legally they did not exist.[1] *Their property (including whatever wages they might earn and even the clothes they wore) belonged to their husbands, and it was their duty to serve and obey them. Husbands had complete control over their wives. They had the legal right to beat them, when necessary, to enforce that*

[1] Women could not legally make contracts. If there was a divorce, husbands had automatic custody over the children. If a wife was injured and the husband sued the responsible party to recover money damages, the recovery belonged to him, not to her.

control. It was illegal for women to run away, but, because it was virtually impossible to obtain a divorce, many wives did just that.

These advertisements, published in the Pennsylvania Gazette in the mid-eighteenth century, are an intriguing glimpse into marital relations in colonial America. Husbands who advertised that they would not pay their runaway wives' debts were hoping to starve their wives into submission, shame them for unfeminine behavior, or finally be rid of them. Abused women, however, frequently asserted themselves and presented their own side by responding with advertisements of their own in the same paper, thus revealing that women were far from the submissive, docile creatures that many scholars have assumed them to be. And so it seems that feminist stirrings were already brewing in the pre-Revolutionary period.

Advertisements from the Pennsylvania Gazette, 1742–1748

March 25, 1742:

Whereas ELIZABETH DUNLAP, Wife of JAMES DUNLAP of Piles Grove, Salem County in the Province of New-Jersey, hath lately eloped from the said James Dunlap her Husband. These are therefore to forwarn and forbid any Person to trust said Elizabeth for any Goods or other things whatsoever for that her said Husband will pay no Debt or Debts contracted by her after the Date hereof. . . .

June 17, 1742:

Whereas JAMES DUNLAP, of Piles Grove, in the County of Salem, in the province of New-Jersey, by an advertisement lately inserted in the American Weekly Mercury and in the Pennsylvania Gazette, did publish the elopement of ELIZABETH DUNLAP his Wife, and forewarned all Persons to trust her for any goods or other things, etc.

These are therefore to certify all Persons whom it may concern, that the contents of the said advertisement as to the elopement of the said Elizabeth is utterly false, for the said Elizabeth never eloped from the said James Dunlap her Husband, but was obliged in safety of her life to leave her said Husband because of his threats and cruel abuse for several years past repeatedly offered and done to her, and that she went no farther than to her Father's House in said county, where she has resided ever since her departure from her said Husband, and still continues to reside. And the same James Dunlap having a considerable estate in lands in said county, which the said Elizabeth is informed he intends to sell as

SOURCE: *Runaway Women: Elopements and Other Miscreant Deeds As Advertised in the* Pennsylvania Gazette, *1728–1789 (Together with a Few Abused Wives and Unfortunate Children)*, compiled by Judith Ann Highley Meier (Apollo, PA: Closson Press, 1993), 5, 6, 11, 13.

soon as he can, she therefore thought proper to give this notice to any Person or Persons that may offer to buy, that she will not join in the sale of any part of said lands, but that she intends to claim her thirds (or right of dower) of and in all the lands the said James Dunlap has been seized and possessed of since their intermarriage, whosoever may purchase the same.

Elizabeth Dunlap.

July 31, 1746:

Whereas MARY, the Wife of JOHN FENBY, Porter, hath eloped from her said Husband without any cause; this is to forwarn all Persons not to trust her on his Account; for he will pay no Debts she shall contract from the Date hereof.

August 7, 1746:

Whereas JOHN, the Husband of MARY FENBY, hath advertis'd her in this Paper, as eloped from him, &c., tho' 'tis well known, they parted by Consent, and agreed to divide their Goods in a Manner which he has not yet been so just as fully to comply with, but detains her Bed and Wedding Ring: And as she neither has, nor desires to run him in Debt, believing her own Credit to be full as good as his; so she desires no one would trust him on her Account, for neither will she pay any Debts of his contracting.

MARY FENBY

June 9, 1748:

Whereas JANE, the wife of PETER HENRY DORSIUS, of Philadelphia county, the daugher of DERRICK HOGELAND of Bucks county, hath eloped from her said husband; this is to desire all persons not to trust her on his account, for he will pay no debts of her contracting, from the date hereof.

June 16, 1748:

Whereas PETER HENRY DORSIUS hath in the last Gazette advertised his wife JANE, as eloped from him, &c. This is to certify whom it may concern, that after a long series of ill usage patiently borne by the said Jane, and after a course of intemperance and extravagance, for which he has been suspended the exercise of his ministerial office in the Dutch Congregation in Southampton; when he had squandered most of his substance, sold and spent great part of his houshold goods, and was about to sell the remainder; tho' he had before in his sober hours, by Direction of a Magistrate made them over for the use of his Family; when he had for several Days abandoned his Dwelling, and left his wife and their children nothing to subsist on, her father found himself at length under a necessity to take her and them into his care and protection, and accordingly fetch'd them home to his own house, which he would not otherwise have done, having besides a large Family of his own to provide for.

DERRICK HOGELAND

PART TWO

Revolution and the Birth of a Nation, 1760–1820

The BLOODY MASSACRE perpetrated in King—t Street BOSTON on March 5th 1770 by a party of the 29th REGT

Unhappy Boston! see thy Sons deplore,
Thy hallow'd Walks besmear'd with guiltless Gore.
While faithless P—n and his savage Bands,
With murd'rous Rancour stretch their bloody Hands,
Like fierce Barbarians grinning o'er their Prey,
Approve the Carnage and enjoy the Day.

If scalding drops from Rage from Anguish Wrung
If speechless Sorrows lab'ring for a Tongue,
Or if a weeping World can ought appease
The plaintive Ghosts of Victims such as these;
The Patriot's copious Tears for each are shed,
A glorious Tribute which embalms the Dead.

But know Fate summons to that awful Goal,
Where Justice strips the Murd'rer of his Soul:
Should venal C—ts the scandal of the Land,
Snatch the relentless Villain from her Hand,
Keen Execrations on this Plate inscrib'd,
Shall reach a Judge who never can be brib'd.

The unhappy Sufferers were Mess.rs Sam.l Gray Sam.l Maverick, Jam.s Caldwell, Crispus Attucks & Pat.k Carr
Killed. Six wounded; two of them (Christ.r Monk & John Clark) Mortally

Engraved Printed & Sold by Paul Revere Boston

Boston Massacre, 1770.
This is Paul Revere's original 1770 print of the Boston Massacre that was disseminated throughout the colonies by the Sons of Liberty in an effort to drum up support to resist British "tyranny."

INTRODUCTION: THE REPUBLIC TAKES SHAPE

The history of the seventeenth century is a history of settlement, diversification, expansion, and conflict, the impact of which led to unanticipated repercussions by the eighteenth century. As English settlers expanded farther into what they saw as a wilderness, there were increasing and deadly confrontations between them and the native peoples who encountered them. But clashes also intensified between the nations that were struggling for control of the North American continent. Conflicts between the French and the British were contested on both sides of the Atlantic, and because of their global context, these wars, in a sense, can be viewed as the first world wars. In the 1690s, King William's War (War of the League of

51

Augsburg in Europe) was a struggle between the British and French. From 1702 to 1713, Queen Anne's War (War of the Spanish Succession in Europe, where the French were allied with the Spanish) was fought; in the colonies, it was simply a continuation of the previous conflict between the English and French for control of the Hudson River, Acadia, and New Brunswick. The struggle resumed in the 1740s as King George's War (War of the Austrian Succession in Europe, where the Prussians joined with the British, and the Austrians and Spanish with the French). In the 1750s, deeply entrenched tensions were further exacerbated when the French began to expand into the Ohio River valley and built Fort Duquesne at the confluence of the Monongahela and Allegheny rivers. In 1754, the young Virginia militia captain, George Washington, was sent to dislodge the French from this fort. The resulting skirmish, leading to Washington's hasty retreat, marked the outbreak of the French and Indian War (Seven Years' War in Europe). This war was truly a world war, and when the Peace of Paris was finally signed in 1763, the world had changed irrevocably. France relinquished all its possessions in continental North America; Britain had emerged as the most powerful nation in Europe, with its empire extending from North America to India; and the throne of England was occupied by the first English-speaking Hanoverian, *our* last king, George III.

During this volatile period, the writings of John Locke, David Hume, Montesquieu, Voltaire, and other Enlightenment philosophers were spreading rapidly through the Western world. In the American colonies, educated people increasingly discussed the notions of natural rights and the nature of government. Locke's ideas especially found fertile soil in a society that had begun to think of the government in London after the Glorious Revolution as a distant and negligent institution out of touch with its colonial subjects. But it was at the end of the French and Indian War, as Parliament and the new king, in an effort to recoup the costs of the war and reestablish London's control over the American colonies, that these ideas about the nature of freedom and equality took hold in a way that was simply unimaginable to British subjects at midcentury.

The colonists' protests against the new taxes imposed by Parliament led, in little more than a decade, directly to the American Revolution. The Sons of Liberty, Committees of Correspondence, the Boston Massacre, the Boston Tea Party, and the Intolerable Acts had their impact on the eventual separation of the colonies from the mother country. Loyalists, on the other hand, facing increasing discrimination and violence against themselves and their property, raised their voices in defense of the Crown. The words *liberty* and *equality* were so bandied about, so popularized, and so contagious that even groups to whom the words had never been applied also began to yearn for their attainment. When southern planters resisted the "slavery" they believed Parliament was trying to impose on them, their bondsmen were inspired to hope that freedom from tyranny might belong to them, too. Even before Jefferson wrote "all men are created equal," many women had begun to question their subordination.

When the Revolution ended, although slavery was abolished in several northern states and women's educational opportunities expanded, little else was accomplished for women and poor white men, and nothing at all for slaves in the South. And as far as the Indian people were concerned, the impact of the Revolution was devastating. No longer were the English a force to slow down the westward expansion of the settlers, nor were the French and Spanish available as allies. The American Revolution might rightfully be regarded as phase one of an uncompleted revolution. The subsequent history of the United States has arguably been the gradual (and often violently disputed) unfolding of the Jeffersonian concept, so that today it encompasses far more people than it did in 1776. Although equality is central to the American canon, in reality we are still struggling to defend that principle. The Revolution is an ongoing process that has still not come to fruition.

Even as the American nation took shape in the ensuing decades, many people and groups dissented against the authority of the new powers that be. Women arguing for their rights, Quakers like Anthony Benezet and John Woolman as well as countless slaves demanding abolition, free blacks protesting racism and segregation in the north, Indians petitioning the government for fair treatment, the Shaysite rebellion against the taxes imposed by the Massachusetts legislature, Anti-Federalists deeply distrustful of a strong central government, farmers in western Pennsylvania denouncing the excise tax, Republicans condemning the Alien and Sedition Acts, New Englanders and pro-British Federalists vehemently protesting the U.S. entry into the War of 1812, Philadelphia blacks protesting the underlying racism of the American Colonization Society's strategy of emancipating the slaves and sending them back to Africa—all were dissenting voices raised during this critical era in American history.

John Woolman (1720–1772)

John Woolman lived his Quaker ideals to the fullest. He believed that all living beings were interconnected, that there was divinity in all, and that it was necessary for all people to be aware of this connection. "I was convinced in my mind," he wrote in his Journal, *"that true religion consisted in an inward life, wherein the heart doth love and reverence God the Creator, and learns to exercise true justice and goodness, not only toward all men, but also toward the brute creatures." Such a philosophy convinced him that slavery was wrong, and during his brief life he was not afraid to express this view even to his fellow Quakers, many of whom owned slaves. As he went about the country, he never let up in arguing against slavery, both in speeches and in print. Eventually his influence led the Society of Friends in Philadelphia to deny membership to anyone who owned slaves.*

The following excerpts are from "Considerations on Keeping Negroes, Part Second," one of the several essays he wrote on the subject. Much of the essay is a demolition of the biblical argument slaveholders used to defend slavery: God's curse on Ham and his descendants and the familiar injunction that servants should obey their masters.

"Considerations on Keeping Negroes, Part Second," 1762

As some in most religious Societies amongst the English are concerned in importing or purchasing the inhabitants of Africa as slaves, and as the professors of Christianity of several other nations do the like, the circumstances tend to make people less apt to examine the practice so closely as they would if such a thing had not been, but was now proposed to be entered upon. It is, however, our duty and what concerns us individually as creatures accountable to our Creator, to employ rightly the understanding which he hath given us in humbly endevouring to be aquainted with his will concerning us and with the nature and tendency of those things which we practice. For as justice remains to be justice, so many people of reputation in the world joining with wrong things do not excuse others in joining with them nor make the consequence of their proceedings less dreadful in the final issue than it would be otherwise.

It looks to me that the slave trade was founded and hath generally been carried on in a wrong spirit, that the effects of it are detrimental to the real prosperity of our country, and will be more so except we cease from the common motives of keeping them and treat them in future agreeable to Truth and pure justice.

Negroes may be imported who, for their cruelty to their countrymen and the evil disposition of their minds, may be unfit at liberty; and if we, as lovers of righteousness, undertake the management of them, we should have a full and clear knowledge of their crimes and those circumstances which might operate in their favor; but the difficulty of obtaining this is so great that we have great reason to be cautious therein. But should it plainly appear that absolute subjection were a condition the most proper for the person who is purchased, yet the innocent children ought not to be made slaves because their parents sinned.

Placing on men the ignominious title SLAVE, dressing them in uncomely garments, keeping them to servile labour in which they are often dirty tends gradually to fix a notion in the mind that they are a sort of people below us in nature, and leads us to consider them as such in all our conclusions about them. And, moreover, a person which in our esteem is mean and contemptible, if their language or behavior toward us is unseemly or disrespectful, it excites wrath more powerfully than the like conduct in one we accounted our equal or superior, and where this happens to be the case it disqualifies for candid judgement; for it is unfit for a person to sit as judge in a case where his own personal resentments

SOURCE: Phillips P. Moulton, ed., *The Journal and Major Essays of John Woolman* (New York: Oxford University Press, 1971), 211–237 passim.

are stirred up, and as members of society in a well-framed government we are mutually dependent. Present interest incites to duty and makes each man attentive to the convenience of others; but he whose wants are supplied without feeling any obligation to make equal returns to his benefactor, his irregular appetites find as open field for motion, and he is in danger of growing hard and inattentive to their convenience who labour for his support, and so loses that disposition in which alone men are fit to govern.

The English government hath been commended by candid foreigners for the disuse of racks and tortures, so much practiced in some states; but this multiplying slaves now leads to it. For where people exact hard labour of others without a suitable reward and are resolved to continue in that way, severity to such who oppose them becomes the consequence; and several Negro criminals among the English in America have been executed in a lingering, painful way, very terrifying to others.

It is a happy case to set out right and persevere in the same way. A wrong beginning leads into many difficulties, for to support one evil, another becomes customary. Two produces more, and the further men proceed in this way the greater their dangers, their doubts and fears, and the more painful and perplexing are their circumstances, so that such who are true friends to the real and lasting interest of our country and candidly consider the tendency of things cannot but feel some concern on this account. . . .

Seed sown with the tears of a confined oppressed people, harvest cut down by an overborne discontented reaper, makes bread less sweet to the taste of an honest man, than that which is the produce or just reward of such voluntary action which is one proper part of the business of human creatures. . . .

He who reverently observes that goodness manifested by our gracious Creator toward the various species of beings in this world, will see that in our frame and constitution is clearly shown that innocent men capable to manage for themselves were not intended to be slaves.

A person lately travelling amongst the Negroes near Senegal hath this remark: "Which way soever I turned my eyes on this pleasant spot, I beheld a perfect image of pure nature: an agreeable solitude bounded on every side by charming landscapes, the rural situation of cottages in the midst of trees, the ease and indolence of the Negroes reclined under the shade of their spreading foliage, the simplicity of their dress and manners—the whole revived in my mind the idea of our first parents, and I seemed to contemplate the world in its primitive state"—M. Adanson, page 55.

Some Negroes in these parts who have had an agreeable education have manifested a brightness of understanding equal to many of us. A remark of this kind we find in Bosman, page 328: "The Negroes of Fida," saith he, "are so accurately quick in their merchandise accounts that they easily reckon as justly and quickly in their heads only, as we with the assistance of pen and ink, though the sum amounts to several thousands."

Through the force of long custom it appears needful to speak in relation to colour. Suppose a white child born of parents of the meanest sort who died and left him an infant falls into the hands of a person who endeavours to keep him a slave. Some men would account him an unjust man in doing so, who yet appear easy while many black people of honest lives and good abilities are enslaved in a manner more shocking than the case here supposed. This is owing chiefly to the idea of slavery being connected with the black colour and liberty with the white. And where false ideas are twisted into our minds, it is with difficulty we get fairly disentangled. . . .

Selfishness being indulged clouds the understanding; and where selfish men for a long time proceed on their way without opposition, the deceivableness of unrighteousness gets so rooted in their intellects that a candid examination of things relating to self-interest is prevented; and in this circumstance some who would not agree to make a slave of a person whose colour is like their own, appear easy in making slaves of others of a different colour, though their understandings and morals are equal to the generality of men of their own colour.

The colour of a man avails nothing in matters of right and equity. Consider colour in relation to treaties. By such, disputes betwixt nations are sometimes settled. And should the Father of us all so dispose things that treaties with black men should sometimes be necessary, how then would it appear amongst the princes and ambassadors to insist on the prerogative of the white colour? Whence is it that men who believe in a righteous Omnipotent Being, to whom all nations stand equally related and are equally accountable, remain so easy in it, but for that the ideas of Negroes and slaves are so interwoven in the mind that they do not discuss this matter with that candour and freedom of thought which the case justly calls for? . . .

Many are desirous of purchasing and keeping slaves that they may live in some measure comfortable to those customs of the times which have in them a tincture of luxury; for when we in the least degree depart from that use of the creatures which the Creator of all things intended for them, there luxury begins.

And if we consider this way of life seriously, we shall see there is nothing in it sufficient to induce a wise man to choose it before a plain, simple way of living. If we examine stately buildings and equipage, delicious foods, superfine clothes, silks, and linens; if we consider the splendor of choice metal fastened upon raiment, and the most showy inventions of men; it will yet appear that the humble-minded man who is contented with the true use of houses, food, and garments, and cheerfully exerciseth himself agreeable to his station in civil society to earn them, acts more reasonably and discovers more soundness of understanding in his conduct than such who lay heavy burdens on others to support themselves in a luxurious way of living. . . .

Should we consider ourselves present as spectators when cruel Negroes privately catch innocent children who are employed in the fields, hear their lamentable cries under the most terrifying apprehensions, or should we look upon it as happening in our own families—having our children carried off by savages—we must needs own that such proceedings are contrary to the nature of Christianity. Should we meditate on the wars which are greatly increased by this trade and on that affliction which many thousands live in, through apprehensions of being taken or slain; on the terror and amazement that villages are in when surrounded by these troops of enterprisers; on the great pain and misery of groaning, dying men who get wounded in those skirmishes; we shall necessarily see that it is impossible to be parties in such a trade on the motives of gain and retain our innocence.

Should we consider the case of multitudes of those people who in a fruitful soil and hot climate with a little labour raise grain, roots, and pulse to eat, spin and weave cotton, and fasten together the large feathers of fowls to cover their nakedness, many of whom in much simplicity live inoffensive in their cottages and take great comfort in raising up children; should we contemplate on their circumstances when suddenly attacked and labour to understand their inexpressible anguish of soul who survive the conflict; should we think of inoffensive women who fled at the alarm and at their return saw that village, in which they and their acquaintance were raised up and had pleasantly spent their youthful days, now lying in gloomy desolation, some shocked at finding the mangled bodies of their near friends amongst the slain, others bemoaning the absence of a brother, a sister, a child, or a whole family of children, who by cruel men are bound and carried to market, to be sold without the least hopes of seeing them again; add to this the afflicted condition of these poor captives who are separated from family connections and all the comforts arising from friendship and acquaintance, carried amongst a people of a strange language, to be parted from their fellow captives, put to labour in a manner more servile and wearisome than what they were used to, with many sorrowful circumstances attending their slavery—and we must necessarily see that it belongs not to the followers of Christ to be parties in such a trade on the motives of outward gain.

Though there were wars and desolations among the Negroes before the Europeans began to trade there for slaves, yet now the calamities are greatly increased, so many thousands being annually brought from thence and we by purchasing them with views of self-interest are become parties with them and accessory to that increase.

In this case, we are not joining against an enemy who is fomenting discords on our continent and using all possible means to make slaves of us and our children, but against a people who have not injured us. If those who were spoiled and wronged should at length make slaves of their oppressors and continue slavery to their posterity, it would look rigorous to candid men. But to act that part toward a people when neither they nor their fathers have injured us, hath something in it extraordinary, and requires our serious attention. . . .

Negroes are our fellow creatures and their present condition amongst us requires our serious consideration. We know not the time when those scales in which mountains are weighed may turn. The parent of mankind is gracious. His care is over his smallest creatures, and a multitude of men escape not his notice; and though many of them are trodden down and despised, yet he remembers them. He seeth their affliction and looketh upon the spreading, increasing exaltation of the oppressor. He turns the channels of power, humbles the most haughty people, and gives deliverance to the oppressed at such periods as are consistent with his infinite justice and goodness. And wherever gain is preferred to equity and wrong things publicly encouraged, to that degree that wickedness takes root and spreads wide amongst the inhabitants of a country, there is real cause for sorrow to all such whose love to mankind stands on a true principle and wisely consider the end and event of things.

John Killbuck (1737–1811)

After the French and Indian War, the British, in an effort to prevent war from breaking out again, issued the Proclamation Line of 1763. This line followed the crest of the Appalachian Mountains dividing the colonies on the east from Indian territory on the west. If the colonists, it was reasoned, were prevented from trespassing on and taking over Indian lands, peace would be stabilized, and England would then not have to defend the colonists in another costly war. However, the Proclamation Line did nothing to impede the continual westward expansion of the colonists. In 1768, the Fort Stanwix Treaty shifted the line farther west to the bank of the Ohio River. In 1771, chiefs from several tribes met with the governors of Virginia, Maryland, and Pennsylvania, and one of the Delaware chieftains, Gelelemend, also known as John Killbuck, gave the following speech in which he expressed their deep alarm at white encroachment. Once again, we see that Native Americans have learned enough about European institutions that they appeal to the governors to use their authority and implement the laws governing the settlers.

Speech to the Governors of Pennsylvania, Maryland, and Virginia, December 4, 1771

Brethren, in former times our forefathers and yours lived in great friendship together and often met to strengthen the chain of their friendship. As your people grew numerous we made room for them and came over the Great Mountains to Ohio. And some time ago when you were at war with the French your soldiers came into this country, drove the French away and built forts. Soon after a number of your people came over the Great Mountains and settled on our lands. We complained of their encroachments into our country, and,

Source: Public Record Office, C.O. 5/90:5; also Library of Congress transcript; reprinted in K.G. Davies, ed., *Documents of the American Revolution* (Shannon: Irish University Press, 1977–1981), 3:254–255.

brethren, you either could not or would not remove them. As we did not choose to have any disputes with our brethren, the English, we agreed to make a line and the Six Nations at Fort Stanwix three years ago sold the King all the lands on the east side of the Ohio down to the Cherokee River, which lands were the property of our confederacy, and gave a deed to Sir William Johnson as he desired. Since that time great numbers more of your people have come over the Great Mountains and settled throughout this country. And we are sorry to tell you that several quarrels have happened between your people and ours, in which people have been killed on both sides, and that we now see the nations round us and your people ready to embroil in a quarrel, which gives our nation great concern, as we on our parts want to live in friendship with you, as you have always told us you have laws to govern your people by (but we do not see that you have). Therefore, brethren, unless you can fall upon some method of governing your people who live between the Great Mountains and the Ohio River and who are now very numerous, it will be out of the Indians' power to govern their young men, for we assure you the black clouds begin to gather fast in this country. And if something is not soon done those clouds will deprive us of seeing the sun. We desire you to give the greatest attention to what we now tell you as it comes from our hearts and a desire we have to live in peace and friendship with our brethren the English. And therefore it grieves us to see some of the nations about us and your people ready to strike each other. We find your people are very fond of our rich land. We see them quarrelling every day about land and burning one another's houses. So that we do not know how soon they may come over the River Ohio and drive us from our villages, nor do we see you brethren take any care to stop them. It's now several years since we have met together in council, which all nations are surprised and concerned at. What is the reason you kindled a fire at Ohio for us to meet you (which we did and talked friendly together) that you have let your fire go out for some years past? This makes all nations jealous about us as we also frequently hear of our brethren the English meeting with Cherokees and with the Six Nations to strengthen their friendship, which gives us cause to think you are forming some bad designs against us who lives between the Ohio and Lakes. I have now told you everything that is in my heart and desire you will write what I have said and send it to the Great King. A belt. Killbuck, speaker.

Samuel Adams (1722–1803)

Samuel Adams, a failure at almost every business venture he ever attempted, was elected to the Massachusetts General Court in 1765, and from this point on he became one of the boldest of the political propagandists opposing Parliament's colonial policies during the decade leading up to the

American Revolution. He was a member of the Sons of Liberty and
organized Committees of Correspondence to disseminate news of British
"atrocities" like the Boston Massacre throughout all 13 colonies. Though the
British soldiers who fired on the unruly mob in March 1770 were acting in
self-defense, Adams spread news throughout the land that it was an
unprovoked massacre. Two years later, Samuel Adams issued a report of the
Committee of Correspondence enumerating the rights of the colonists.

The Rights of the Colonists—The Report of the Committee of Correspondence to the Boston Town Meeting, November 20, 1772

. . . 1ST. NATURAL RIGHTS OF THE COLONISTS AS MEN

Among the natural rights of the Colonists are these: First, a right to Life; Secondly, to Liberty; Thirdly, to Property; together with the right to support and defend them in the best manner they can. These are evident branches of, rather than deductions from, the duty of self-preservation, commonly called the first law of nature.

All men have a right to remain in a state of nature as long as they please; and in case of intolerable oppression, civil or religious, to leave the society they belong to, and enter into another.

When men enter into society, it is by voluntary consent; and they have a right to demand and insist upon the performance of such conditions and previous limitations as form an equitable original compact.

Every natural right not expressly given up, or, from the nature of a social compact, necessarily ceded, remains.

All positive and civil laws should conform, as far as possible, to the law of natural reason and equity.

As neither reason requires nor religion permits the contrary, every man living in or out of a state of civil society has a right peaceably and quietly to worship God according to the dictates of his conscience.

"Just and true liberty, equal and impartial liberty," in matters spiritual and temporal, is a thing that all men are clearly entitled to by the eternal and immutable laws of God and nature, as well as by the law of nations and all well-grounded municipal laws, which must have their foundation in the former.

In regard to religion, mutual toleration in the different professions thereof is what all good and candid minds in all ages have ever practised, and, both by precept and example, inculcated on mankind. And it is now generally agreed

SOURCE: Harry Alonzo Cushing, ed., *The Writings of Samuel Adams* (New York: G. P. Putnam's Sons, 1906), vol. II, 350–359. Some punctuation and capitalization have been modernized.

among Christians that this spirit of toleration, in the fullest extent consistent with the being of civil society, is the chief characteristical mark of the Church. Insomuch that Mr. Locke has asserted and proved, beyond the possibility of contradiction on any solid ground, that such toleration ought to be extended to all whose doctrines are not subversive of society. The only sects which he thinks ought to be, and which by all wise laws are excluded from such toleration, are those who teach doctrines subversive of the civil government under which they live. The Roman Catholics or Papists are excluded by reason of such doctrines as these, that princes excommunicated may be deposed, and those that they call heretics may be destroyed without mercy; besides their recognizing the Pope in so absolute a manner, in subversion of government, by introducing, as far as possible into the states under whose protection they enjoy life, liberty, and property, that solecism in politics, imperium in imperio, leading directly to the worst anarchy and confusion, civil discord, war, and bloodshed.

The natural liberty of man, by entering into society, is abridged or restrained, so far only as is necessary for the great end of society, the best good of the whole.

In the state of nature every man is, under God, judge and sole judge of his own rights and of the injuries done him. By entering into society he agrees to an arbiter or indifferent judge between him and his neighbors; but he no more renounces his original right than by taking a cause out of the ordinary course of law, and leaving the decision to referees or indifferent arbitrators. In the last case, he must pay the referees for time and trouble. He should also be willing to pay his just quota for the support of government, the law, and the constitution; the end of which is to furnish indifferent and impartial judges in all cases that may happen, whether civil, ecclesiastical, marine, or military.

"The natural liberty of man is to be free from any superior power on earth, and not to be under the will or legislative authority of man, but only to have the law of nature for his rule."

In the state of nature men may, as the patriarchs did, employ hired servants for the defence of their lives, liberties, and property; and they should pay them reasonable wages. Government was instituted for the purposes of common defence, and those who hold the reins of government have an equitable, natural right to an honorable support from the same principle that "the laborer is worthy of his hire." But then the same community which they serve ought to be the assessors of their pay. Governors have no right to seek and take what they please; by this, instead of being content with the station assigned them, that of honorable servants of the society, they would soon become absolute masters, despots, and tyrants. Hence, as a private man has a right to say what wages he will give in his private affairs, so has a community to determine what they will give and grant of their substance for the administration of public affairs. And, in both cases, more are ready to offer their service at the proposed and stipulated price than are able and willing to perform their duty.

In short, it is the greatest absurdity to suppose it in the power of one, or any number of men, at the entering into society, to renounce their essential natural rights, or the means of preserving those rights; when the grand end of civil government, from the very nature of its institution, is for the support, protection, and defence of those very rights; the principal of which, as is before observed, are Life, Liberty, and Property. If men, through fear, fraud, or mistake, should in terms renounce or give up any essential natural right, the eternal law of reason and the grand end of society would absolutely vacate such renunciation. The right to freedom being the gift of God Almighty, it is not in the power of man to alienate this gift and voluntarily become a slave.

2ᴰ THE RIGHTS OF THE COLONISTS AS CHRISTIANS

These may be best understood by reading and carefully studying the institutes of the great Law Giver and Head of the Christian Church, which are to be found clearly written and promulgated in the New Testament.

By the act of the British Parliament, commonly called the Toleration Act, every subject in England, except Papists, &c., was restored to, and re-established in, his natural right to worship God according to the dictates of his own conscience. And, by the charter of this Province, it is granted, ordained, and established (that is, declared as an original right) that there shall be liberty of conscience allowed in the worship of God to all Christians, except Papists, inhabiting, or which shall inhabit or be resident within, such Province or Territory. Magna Charta itself is in substance but a constrained declaration or proclamation and promulgation in the name of the King, Lords, and Commons, of the sense the latter had of their original, inherent, indefeasible natural rights, as also those of free citizens equally perdurable with the other. That great author, that great jurist, and even that court writer, Mr. Justice Blackstone, holds that this recognition was justly obtained of King John, sword in hand. And peradventure it must be one day, sword in hand, again rescued and preserved from total destruction and oblivion.

3ᴰ THE RIGHTS OF THE COLONISTS AS SUBJECTS

A commonwealth or state is a body politic, or civil society of men, united together to promote their mutual safety and prosperity by means of their union.

The absolute rights of Englishmen and all freemen, in or out of civil society, are principally personal security, personal liberty, and private property.

All persons born in the British American Colonies are, by the laws of God and nature and by the common law of England, exclusive of all charters from the Crown, well entitled, and by acts of the British Parliament are declared to be entitled, to all the natural, essential, inherent, and inseparable rights, liberties, and privileges of subjects born in Great Britain or within the realm. Among those rights are the following, which no man, or body of men, consistently with their own rights as men and citizens, or members of society, can for themselves give up or take away from others.

First, "The first fundamental, positive law of all common wealths or states is the establishing the legislative power. As the first fundamental natural law, also, which is to govern even the legislative power itself, is the preservation of the society."

Secondly, The Legislative has no right to absolute, arbitrary power over the lives and fortunes of the people; nor can mortals assume a prerogative not only too high for men, but for angels, and therefore reserved for the exercise of the Deity alone.

"The Legislative cannot justly assume to itself a power to rule by extempore arbitrary decrees; but it is bound to see that justice is dispensed, and that the rights of the subjects be decided by promulgated, standing, and known laws, and authorized independent judges"; that is, independent, as far as possible, of Prince and people. "There should be one rule of justice for rich and poor, for the favorite at court, and the countryman at the plough."

Thirdly, The supreme power cannot justly take from any man any part of his property, without his consent in person or by his representative.

These are some of the first principles of natural law and justice, and the great barriers of all free states and of the British Constitution in particular. It is utterly irreconcilable to these principles and to many other fundamental maxims of the common law, common sense, and reason that a British House of Commons should have a right at pleasure to give and grant the property of the Colonists. (That the Colonists are well entitled to all the essential rights, liberties, and privileges of men and freemen born in Britain is manifest not only from the Colony charters in general, but acts of the British Parliament.) The statute of the 13th of Geo. 2, C. 7, naturalizes even foreigners after seven years' residence. The words of the Massachusetts charter are these: "And further, our will and pleasure is, and we do hereby for us, our heirs, and successors, grant, establish, and ordain, that all and every of the subjects of us, our heirs, and successors, which shall go to, and inhabit within our said Province or Territory, and every of their children, which shall happen to be born there or on the seas in going thither or returning from thence, shall have and enjoy all liberties and immunities of free and natural subjects within any of the dominions of us, our heirs, and successors, to all intents, constructions, and purposes whatsoever as if they and every one of them were born within this our realm of England." Now what liberty can there be where property is taken away without consent? Can it be said with any color of truth and justice, that this continent of three thousand miles in length, and of a breadth as yet unexplored, in which, however, it is supposed there are five millions of people, has the least voice, vote, or influence in the British Parliament? Have they all together any more weight or power to return a single member to that House of Commons who have not inadvertently, but deliberately, assumed a power to dispose of their lives, liberties, and properties, than to choose an Emperor of China? Had the Colonists a right to return members to the British Parliament, it would only be hurtful; as, from their local situation and circumstances, it is impossible they should ever be truly and properly represented there. The inhabitants of this country, in all probability, in a few years, will be more numerous than those of Great Britain and Ireland together; yet it is absurdly expected by the promoters of the present measures that these, with their posterity to all generations, should be easy, while their property shall be disposed of by a House of Commons at three thousand miles' distance from them, and who cannot be supposed to have the least care or concern for their real interest; who have not only no natural care for their interest, but must be in effect bribed against it, as every burden they lay on the Colonists is so much saved or gained to themselves. Hitherto, many of the Colonists have been free from quit rents; but if the breath of a British House of Commons can originate an act for taking away all our money, our lands will go next, or be subject to rack rents from haughty and relentless landlords, who will ride at ease, while we are trodden in the dirt. The Colonists have been branded with the odious names of traitors and rebels only for complaining of their grievances. How long such treatment will or ought to be borne, is submitted.

Revolutionary Women

Women in the period before the Revolution were often just as forceful as men in their protests against London's policies. In 1768, Hannah Griffiths published a poem in which she proclaimed that women were ready to boycott British goods and wear only clothing made out of American homespun cloth to protest the taxes that British prime ministers George Grenville and Charles Townshend levied on sugar, tea, paint, and glass.

A few years later, after the December 1773 Boston Tea Party, Parliament passed the Coercive Acts (dubbed the Intolerable Acts by the colonists), which, among other penalties, closed the port of Boston. Response was swift and vocal. Around the colonies, people showed their solidarity with Boston through demonstrations and protests. Once again, women were not shy about making their dissenting voices heard. In Edenton, North Carolina, in October 1774, 51 women signed a pledge not to drink tea or wear English-made clothing: "We, the Ladys of Edenton, do hereby solemnly engage not to conform to the Pernicious Custom of Drinking Tea" and "We, the aforesaid Ladys will not promote ye wear of any manufacturer from England until such time that all acts which tend to enslave our Native country shall be repealed."

HANNAH GRIFFITHS, POEM, 1768

THE FEMALE PATRIOTS. ADDRESS'D TO THE DAUGHTERS OF LIBERTY IN AMERICA. BY THE SAME, 1768

Since the Men from a Party, or fear of a Frown,
Are kept by a Sugar-Plumb, quietly down.
Supinely asleep, & depriv'd of their Sight
Are strip'd of their Freedom, & rob'd of their Right.
If the Sons (so degenerate) the Blessing despise,
Let the Daugthers of Liberty, nobly arise,
And tho' we've no Voice, but a negative here.
The use of the Taxables, let us forebear,
(Then Merchants import till yr. Stores are all full
May the Buyers be few & yr. Traffick be dull.)
Stand firmly resolved & bid Grenville to see
That rather than Freedom, we'll part with our Tea
And well as we love the dear Draught when a dry,
As American Patriots,—our Taste we deny,
Sylvania's, gay Meadows, can richly afford,
To pamper our Fancy, or furnish our Board,
And Paper sufficient (at home) still we have,
To assure the Wise-acre, we will not sign Slave.
When this Homespun shall fail, to remonstrate our Grief
We can speak with the Tongue or scratch on a Leaf.
    Refuse all their Colours, tho richest of Dye,
The juice of a Berry—our Paint can supply,
To humour our Fancy—& as for our Houses,
They'll do without painting as well as our Spouses,
While to keep out the Cold of a keen winter Morn
We can screen the Northwest, with a well polish'd Horn,
And trust me a Woman by honest Invention
Might give this State Doctor a Dose of Prevention.
Join mutual in this, & but small as it seems
We may Jostle a Grenville & puzzle his Schemes
But a motive more worthy our patriot Pen,
Thus acting—we point out their Duty to Men,
And should the bound Pensioners, tell us to hush
We can throw back the Satire by biding them blush.

by Hannah Griffiths

SOURCE: Catherine La Courreye Blecki and Karin A. Wulf, eds. *Milcah Martha Moore's Book, A Commonplace Book from Revolutionary America*, (University Park: Pennsylvania State University Press, 1997), 172–173.

Ladies of Edenton, North Carolina, Agreement, 1774–1775

MORNING CHRONICLE AND LONDON ADVERTISER, JANUARY 16, 1775

The provincial deputies of North Carolina having resolved not to drink any more tea nor wear any more British cloth, etc., many ladies of this province have determined to give a memorable proof of their patriotism, and have accordingly entered into the following honorable and spirited association. I send it to you to show your fair countrywomen how zealously and faithfully American ladies follow the laudable example of their husbands, and what opposition your *matchless* ministers may expect to receive from a people, thus firmly united against them:

EDENTON, NORTH CAROLINA, OCTOBER 25 (1774)

As we cannot be indifferent on any occasion that appears nearly to affect the peace and happiness of our country, and as it has been thought necessary, for the public good, to enter into several particular resolves by a meeting of members deputed from the whole province, it is a duty which we owe, not only to our near and dear connections, who have concurred in them, but to ourselves, who are essentially interested in their welfare, to do everything, as far as lies in our power, to testify our sincere adherence to the same; and we do therefore accordingly subscribe this paper as a witness of our fixed intention and solemn determination to do so:

Abagail Charlton,	Sarah Beasley,	Sarah Valentine,
Elizabeth Creacy,	Grace Clayton,	Mary Bonner,
Anne Johnstone,	Mary Jones,	Mary Ramsey,
Mary Woolard,	Mary Creacy,	Lydia Bennett,
Jean Blair,	Anne Hall,	Tresia Cunningham,
Frances Hall,	Sarah Littlejohn,	Anne Haughton,
Mary Creacy,	Sarah Hoskins,	Elizabeth Roberts,
Mary Blount,	M. Payne,	Ruth Benbury,
Margaret Cathcart,	Elizabeth Cricket,	Penelope Barker,
Jane Wellwood,	Lydia Bonner,	Mary Littledle,
Penelope Dawson,	Anne Horniblow,	Elizabeth Johnstone,
Susanna Vail,	Marion Wells,	Elizabeth Green,
Elizabeth Vail,	Sarah Mathews,	Sarah Howe,
Elizabeth Vail,	Elizabeth Roberts,	Mary Hunter,
J. Johnstone,	Rebecca Bondfield,	Anne Anderson,
Elizabeth Patterson	Sarah Howcott,	Elizabeth Bearsley,
Margaret Pearson,	Elizabeth P. Ormond,	Elizabeth Roberts.

SOURCE: Richard Dillard, *The Historic Tea Party of Edenton, October 25, 1774* (Raleigh: Capital Printing, 1901).

The Second Continental Congress

*In response to the Coercive Acts, delegates from 12 of the colonies met in
Philadelphia in September 1774 to set a course of action. Radicals called
for resistance, moderates for reconciliation. After much debate they
implemented a policy of nonimportation of goods from England. When
they adjourned they agreed to meet again the following year. By the time
they reassembled in May 1775, hostilities had broken out at Lexington
and Concord. The delegates therefore found it necessary to shift their
focus from their original purpose and discuss the question of war. Though
still not wishing to break irrevocably with the mother country, they issued
a declaration justifying the colonists' resort to arms.*

A DECLARATION BY THE REPRESENTATIVES OF THE UNITED COLONIES OF NORTH AMERICA, NOW MET IN GENERAL CONGRESS AT PHILADELPHIA, SETTING FORTH THE CAUSES AND NECESSITY OF THEIR TAKING UP ARMS, 1775

If it was possible for men, who exercise their reason, to believe, that the Divine
Author of our existence intended a part of the human race to hold an absolute
property in, and an unbounded power over others, marked out by his infinite
goodness and wisdom, as the objects of a legal domination never rightfully
resistible, however severe and oppressive, the inhabitants of these colonies might
at least require from the Parliament of Great Britain some evidence that this
dreadful authority over them has been granted to that body. But a reverence for
our great Creator, principles of humanity, and the dictates of common sense
must convince all those who reflect upon the subject that government was instituted to promote the welfare of mankind and ought to be administered for the
attainment of that end. The legislature of Great Britain, however, stimulated by
an inordinate passion for a power, not only unjustifiable, but which they know to
be peculiarly reprobated by the very constitution of that kingdom, and desperate
of success in any mode of contest, where regard should be had to truth, law, or
right, have at length, deserting those, attempted to effect their cruel and impolitic
purpose of enslaving these colonies by violence, and have thereby rendered it
necessary for us to close with their last appeal from reason to arms.

Yet, however blinded that assembly may be, by their intemperate rage for
unlimited domination, so to slight justice and the opinion of mankind, we

SOURCE: *Journals of the Continental Congress, 1774–1789*, II, 140–157.

esteem ourselves bound, by obligations of respect to the rest of the world, to make known the justice of our cause.

Our forefathers, inhabitants of the island of Great Britain, left their native land to seek on these shores a residence for civil and religious freedom. At the expense of their blood, at the hazard of their fortunes, without the least charge to the country from which they removed, by unceasing labor, and an unconquerable spirit, they effected settlements in the distant and inhospitable wilds of America, then filled with numerous and warlike nations of barbarians. Societies or governments, vested with perfect legislatures, were formed under charters from the crown, and a harmonious intercourse was established between the colonies and the kingdom from which they derived their origin. The mutual benefits of this union became in a short time so extraordinary as to excite astonishment. It is universally confessed that the amazing increase of the wealth, strength, and navigation of the realm arose from this source; and the minister, who so wisely and successfully directed the measures of Great Britain in the late war, publicly declared that these colonies enabled her to triumph over her enemies.

Toward the conclusion of that war, it pleased our sovereign to make a change in his counsels. From that fatal moment, the affairs of the British Empire began to fall into confusion, and gradually sliding from the summit of glorious prosperity, to which they had been advanced by the virtues and abilities of one man, are at length distracted by the convulsions that now shake it to its deepest foundations. The new ministry finding the brave foes of Britain, though frequently defeated, yet still contending, took up the unfortunate idea of granting them a hasty peace and of then subduing her faithful friends.

These devoted colonies were judged to be in such a state, as to present victories without bloodshed, and all the easy emoluments of statutable plunder. The uninterrupted tenor of their peaceable and respectful behavior from the beginning of colonization, their dutiful, zealous, and useful services during the war, though so recently and amply acknowledged in the most honorable manner by His Majesty, by the late king, and by Parliament, could not save them from the meditated innovations.

Parliament was influenced to adopt the pernicious project, and assuming a new power over them, have, in the course of eleven years, given such decisive specimens of the spirit and consequences attending this power, as to leave no doubt concerning the effects of acquiescence under it. They have undertaken to give and grant our money without our consent, though we have ever exercised an exclusive right to dispose of our own property; statutes have been passed for extending the jurisdiction of courts of admiralty and vice-admiralty beyond their ancient limits; for depriving us of the accustomed and inestimable privilege of trial by jury, in cases affecting both life and property; for suspending the legislature of one of the colonies; for interdicting all commerce to the capital of another; and for altering fundamentally the form of government established by charter and secured by acts of its own legislature solemnly confirmed by the crown; for exempting the "murderers" of colonists from legal trial and, in effect, from punishment; for erecting in a neighboring province, acquired by the joint arms of Great Britain and America, a despotism dangerous to our very existence; and for quartering soldiers upon the colonists in time of profound peace. It has also been resolved in Parliament that colonists charged with committing certain offenses shall be transported to England to be tried.

But why should we enumerate our injuries in detail? By one statute it is declared, that Parliament can "of right make laws to bind us IN ALL CASES WHATSOEVER." What is to defend us against so enormous, so unlimited a power? Not a single man of those who assume it is chosen by us or is subject to our control or influence; but, on the contrary, they are all of them exempt from the operation of such laws, and an American revenue, if not diverted from the ostensible purposes for which it is raised, would actually lighten their own burdens in proportion as they increase ours. We saw the misery to which such despotism would reduce us. We for ten years incessantly and ineffectually besieged the throne as supplicants; we reasoned, we remonstrated with Parliament, in the most mild and decent language. But administration, sensible that we should regard these oppressive measures as freemen ought to do, sent over fleets and armies to enforce them. The indignation of the Americans was roused, it is true; but it was the indignation of a virtuous, loyal, and affectionate people. A Congress of Delegates from the United Colonies was assembled at Philadelphia, on the fifth day of last September. We resolved again to offer a humble and dutiful petition to the king, and also addressed our fellow-subjects of Great Britain. We have pursued every temperate, every respectful, measure: we have even proceeded to break off our commercial intercourse with our fellow-subjects, as the last peaceable admonition, that our attachment to no nation upon earth should supplant our attachment to liberty. This, we flattered ourselves, was the ultimate step of the controversy. But subsequent events have shown how vain was this hope of finding moderation in our enemies.

Several threatening expressions against the colonies were inserted in His Majesty's speech; our petition, though we were told it was a decent one, and that His Majesty had been pleased to receive it graciously, and to promise laying it before his Parliament, was huddled into both houses amongst a bundle of American papers, and there neglected. The Lords and Commons in their address, in the month of February, said, that "a rebellion at that time actually existed within the province of Massachusetts Bay; and that those concerned in it, had been countenanced and encouraged by unlawful combinations and engagements, entered into by His Majesty's subjects in several of the other colonies; and therefore they besought His Majesty, that he would take the most effectual measures to enforce due obedience to the laws and authority of the supreme legislature."

Soon after, the commercial intercourse of whole colonies, with foreign countries, and with each other, was cut off by an act of Parliament; by another, several of them were entirely prohibited from the fisheries in the seas near their coasts, on which they always depended for their sustenance; and large reinforcements of ships and troops were immediately sent over to General Gage.

Fruitless were all the entreaties, arguments, and eloquence of an illustrious band of the most distinguished Peers, and Commoners, who nobly and strenuously asserted the justice of our cause, to stay, or even to mitigate the heedless fury with which these accumulated and unexampled outrages were hurried on. Equally fruitless was the interference of the city of London, of Bristol, and many other respectable towns in our favor. Parliament adopted an insidious maneuver calculated to divide us, to establish a perpetual auction of taxations where colony should bid against colony, all of them uninformed what ransom would redeem their lives; and thus to extort from us, at the point of the bayonet, the unknown sums that should be sufficient to gratify, if possible to gratify, ministerial rapacity, with the miserable indulgence left to us of raising, in our own mode, the prescribed tribute. What terms more rigid and humiliating could have been dictated by remorseless victors to conquered enemies? In our circumstances to accept them would be to deserve them.

Soon after the intelligence of these proceedings arrived on this continent, General Gage, who in the course of the last year had taken possession of the town of Boston, in the province of Massachusetts Bay, and still occupied it as a garrison, on the 19th day of April, sent out from that place a large detachment of his army, who made an unprovoked assault on the inhabitants of the said province, at the town of Lexington, as appears by the affidavits of a great number of persons, some of whom were officers and soldiers of that detachment, murdered eight of the inhabitants, and wounded many others. From thence the troops proceeded in warlike array to the town of Concord, where they set upon another party of the inhabitants of the same province, killing several and wounding more, until compelled to retreat by the country people suddenly assembled to repel this cruel aggression. Hostilities, thus commenced by the British troops, have been since prosecuted by them without regard to faith or reputation. The inhabitants of Boston being confined within that town by the General, their Governor, and having, in order to procure their dismission, entered into a treaty with him, it was stipulated that the said inhabitants, having deposited their arms with their own magistrates, should have liberty to depart, taking with them their other effects. They accordingly delivered up their arms, but in open violation of honor, in defiance of the obligation of treaties, which even savage nations esteemed sacred, the Governor ordered the arms deposited as aforesaid, that they might be preserved for their owners, to be seized by a body of soldiers; detained the greatest part of the inhabitants in the town, and compelled the few who were permitted to retire to leave their most valuable effects behind.

By this perfidy wives are separated from their husbands, children from their parents, the aged and the sick from their relations and friends, who wish to attend and comfort them; and those who have been used to live in plenty and even elegance are reduced to deplorable distress.

The General, further emulating his ministerial masters, by a proclamation bearing date on the 12th day of June, after venting the grossest falsehoods and calumnies against the good people of these colonies, proceeds to "declare them all, either by name or description, to be rebels and traitors, to supersede the course of the common law, and instead thereof to publish and order the use and exercise of the law martial." His troops have butchered our countrymen, have wantonly burned Charles-Town, besides a considerable number of houses in other places; our ships and vessels are seized; the necessary supplies of provisions are intercepted, and he is exerting his utmost power to spread destruction and devastation around him.

We have received certain intelligence that General Carleton, the Governor of Canada, is instigating the people of that province and the Indians to fall upon us; and we have but too much reason to apprehend that schemes have been formed to excite domestic enemies against us. In brief, a part of these colonies now feels, and all of them are sure of feeling, as far as the vengeance of administration can inflict them, the complicated calamities of fire, sword, and famine. We are reduced to the alternative of choosing an unconditional submission to the tyranny of irritated ministers, or resistance by force. The latter is our choice. We have counted the cost of this contest and find nothing so dreadful as voluntary slavery. Honor, justice, and humanity forbid us tamely to surrender that freedom which we received from our gallant ancestors, and which our innocent posterity have a right to receive from us. We cannot endure the infamy and guilt of resigning succeeding generations to that wretchedness which inevitably awaits them, if we basely entail hereditary bondage upon them.

Our cause is just. Our union is perfect. Our internal resources are great, and, if necessary, foreign assistance is undoubtedly attainable. We gratefully acknowledge, as signal instances of the Divine favor toward us, that his Providence would not permit us to be called into this severe controversy, until we were grown up to our present strength, had been previously exercised in warlike operation, and possessed of the means of defending ourselves. With hearts fortified with these animating reflections, we most solemnly, before God and the world, declare that, exerting the utmost energy of those powers which our beneficent Creator hath graciously bestowed upon us, the arms we have been compelled by our enemies to assume we will, in defiance of every hazard, with unabating firmness and perseverance, employ for the preservation of our liberties; being with our [one] mind resolved to die free men rather than live slaves.

Lest this declaration should disquiet the minds of our friends and fellow-subjects in any part of the Empire, we assure them that we mean not to dissolve that union which has so long and so happily subsisted between us, and which we sincerely wish to see restored. Necessity has not yet driven us into that desperate measure, or induced us to excite any other nation to war against them. We have not raised armies with ambitious designs of separating from Great Britain establishing independent states. We fight not for glory or for conquest. We exhibit to mankind the remarkable spectacle of a people attacked by unprovoked enemies, without any imputation or even suspicion of offense. They boast of their privileges and civilization and yet proffer no milder conditions than servitude or death.

In our own native land, in defense of the freedom that is our birthright, and which we ever enjoyed till the late violation of it—for the protection of our property, acquired solely by the honest industry of our forefathers and ourselves, against violence actually offered, we have taken up arms. We shall lay them down when hostilities shall cease on the part of the aggressors, and all danger of their being renewed shall be removed, and not before.

With a humble confidence in the mercies of the supreme and impartial Judge and Ruler of the universe, we most devoutly implore his divine goodness to protect us happily through this great conflict, to dispose our adversaries to reconciliation on reasonable terms, and thereby to relieve the Empire from the calamities of civil war.

By order of Congress,

JOHN HANCOCK,
President

Attested,

CHARLES THOMSON,
Secretary

PHILADELPHIA, July 6th, 1775

Thomas Paine (1737–1809)

After only a year in the colonies, radical thinker Thomas Paine was dismayed and irritated that the colonists had not formally declared their independence from Great Britain, even after hostilities had broken out in April 1775 at Lexington and Concord. In January 1776, Paine published Common Sense, *in which he urged the colonists that the only sensible thing to do was to separate entirely from the mother country. This brief pamphlet (selling 120,000 copies in its first 3 months) had an enormous impact on colonial opinion, and by July the Second Continental Congress had issued the Declaration of Independence.*

COMMON SENSE, 1776

In the following pages I offer nothing more than simple facts, plain arguments, and common sense; and have no other preliminaries to settle with the reader, than that he will divest himself of prejudice and prepossession, and suffer his reason and his feelings to determine for themselves; that he will put on, or rather that he will not put off, the true character of a man, and generously enlarge his views beyond the present day.

SOURCE: [Thomas Paine] *Common Sense, Addressed to the Inhabitants of America* (Philadelphia, 1776), 29–60, passim.

Volumes have been written on the subject of the struggle between England and America. Men of all ranks have embarked in the controversy, from different motives, and with various designs; but all have been ineffectual, and the period of debate is closed. Arms, as the last resource, decide the contest; the appeal was the choice of the king, and the continent hath accepted the challenge. . . .

The sun never shined on a cause of greater worth. 'Tis not the affair of a city, a country, a province, or a kingdom, but of a continent of at least one eighth part of the habitable globe. 'Tis not the concern of a day, a year, or an age; posterity are virtually involved in the contest, and will be more or less affected, even to the end of time, by the proceedings now. Now is the seed time of continental union, faith and honor. The least fracture now will be like a name engraved with the point of a pin on the tender rind of a young oak; The wound will enlarge with the tree, and posterity read it in full grown characters.

By referring the matter from argument to arms, a new area for politics is struck; a new method of thinking hath arisen. All plans, proposals, &c. prior to the nineteenth of April, i. e. to the commencement of hostilities, are like the almanacs of the last year; which, though proper then, are superseded and useless now. Whatever was advanced by the advocates on either side of the question then, terminated in one and the same point, viz. a union with Great Britain; the only difference between the parties was the method of effecting it; the one proposing force, the other friendship; but it hath so far happened that the first hath failed, and the second hath withdrawn her influence.

As much hath been said of the advantages of reconciliation, which, like an agreeable dream, hath passed away and left us as we were, it is but right, that we should examine the contrary side of the argument, and inquire into some of the many material injuries which these colonies sustain, and always will sustain, by being connected with, and dependant on Great Britain. To examine that connection and dependance, on the principles of nature and common sense, to see what we have to trust to, if separated, and what we are to expect, if dependant.

I have heard it asserted by some, that as America hath flourished under her former connection with Great Britain, that the same connection is necessary towards her future happiness, and will always have the same effect. Nothing can be more fallacious than this kind of argument. We may as well assert, that because a child has thrived upon milk, that it is never to have meat; or that the first twenty years of our lives is to become a precedent for the next twenty. But even this is admitting more than is true, for I answer roundly, that America would have flourished as much, and probably much more, had no European power had any thing to do with her. The commerce by which she hath enriched herself are the necessaries of life, and will always have a market while eating is the custom of Europe.

But she has protected us, say some. That she hath engrossed us is true, and defended the continent at our expense as well as her own is admitted, and she would have defended Turkey from the same motive, viz. the sake of trade and dominion.

Alas, we have been long led away by ancient prejudices and made large sacrifices to superstition. We have boasted the protection of Great Britain, without considering, that her motive was interest not attachment; that she did not protect us from our enemies on our account, but from her enemies on her own account, from those who had no quarrel with us on any other account, and who will always be our enemies on the same account. Let Britain wave her pretensions to the continent, or the continent throw off the dependance, and we should be at peace with France and Spain were they at war with Britain. The miseries of Hanover last war ought to warn us against connections. It hath lately been asserted in parliament, that the colonies have no relation to each other but through the parent country, i. e. that Pennsylvania and the Jerseys, and so on for the rest, are sister colonies by the way of England; this is certainly a very roundabout way of proving relationship, but it is the nearest and only true way of proving enemyship, if I may so call it. France and Spain never were, nor perhaps ever will be our enemies as Americans, but as our being the subjects of Great Britain.

But Britain is the parent country, say some. Then the more shame upon her conduct. Even brutes do not devour their young; nor savages make war upon their families; wherefore the assertion, if true, turns to her reproach; but it happens not to be true, or only partly so, and the phrase Parent or mother country hath been jesuitically adopted by the king and his parasites, with a low papistical design of gaining an unfair bias on the credulous weakness of our minds. Europe, and not England, is the parent country of America. This new world hath been the asylum for the persecuted lovers of civil and religious liberty from every part of Europe. Hither have they fled, not from the tender embraces of the mother, but from the cruelty of the monster; and it is so far true of England, that the same tyranny which drove the first emigrants from home pursues their descendants still. . . .

Much hath been said of the united strength of Britain and the colonies, that in conjunction they might bid defiance to the world. But this is mere presumption; the fate of war is uncertain, neither do the expressions mean anything; for this continent would never suffer itself to be drained of inhabitants to support the British arms in either Asia, Africa, or Europe.

Besides, what have we to do with setting the world at defiance? Our plan is commerce, and that, well attended to, will secure us the peace and friendship of all Europe; because it is the interest of all Europe to have America a free port. Her trade will always be a protection, and her barrenness of gold and silver secure her from invaders.

I challenge the warmest advocate for reconciliation, to show, a single advantage that this continent can reap, by being connected with Great Britain. I repeat the challenge, not a single advantage is derived. Our corn will fetch its price in any market in Europe, and our imported goods must be paid for buy them where we will.

But the injuries and disadvantages we sustain by that connection, are without number; and our duty to mankind at large, as well as to ourselves, instruct us to renounce the alliance: Because, any submission to, or dependance on Great Britain, tends directly to involve this continent in European wars and quarrels; and sets us at variance with nations, who would otherwise seek our friendship, and against whom, we have neither anger nor complaint. As Europe is our market for trade, we ought to form no partial connection with any part of it. It is the true interest of America to steer clear of European contentions, which she never can do, while by her dependance on Britain, she is made the make-weight in the scale of British politics.

Europe is too thickly planted with kingdoms to be long at peace, and whenever a war breaks out between England and any foreign power, the trade of America goes to ruin, because of her connection with Britain. The next war may not turn out like the past, and should it not, the advocates for reconciliation now will be wishing for separation then, because, neutrality in that case, would be a safer convoy than a man of war. Every thing that is right or natural pleads for separation. The blood of the slain, the weeping voice of nature cries, 'TIS TIME TO PART. Even the distance at which the Almighty hath placed England and America, is a strong and natural proof, that the authority of the one, over the other, was never the design of Heaven. The time likewise at which the continent was discovered, adds weight to the argument, and the manner in which it was peopled increases the force of it. The reformation was preceded by the discovery of America, as if the Almighty graciously meant to open a sanctuary to the persecuted in future years, when home should afford neither friendship nor safety.

The authority of Great Britain over this continent, is a form of government, which sooner or later must have an end: And a serious mind can draw no true pleasure by looking forward, under the painful and positive conviction, that what he calls the present constitution is merely temporary. As parents, we can have no joy, knowing that this government is not sufficiently lasting to ensure any thing which we may bequeath to posterity: And by a plain method of argument, as we are running the next generation into debt, we ought to do the work of it, otherwise we use them meanly and pitifully. In order to discover the line of our duty rightly, we should take our children in our hand, and fix our station a few years farther into life; that eminence will present a prospect, which a few present fears and prejudices conceal from our sight.

Though I would carefully avoid giving unnecessary offence, yet I am inclined to believe, that all those who espouse the doctrine of reconciliation, may be included within the following descriptions. Interested men, who are not to be trusted; weak men who cannot see; prejudiced men who will not see; and a certain set of moderate men, who think better of the European world than it deserves; and this last class by an ill-judged deliberation, will be the cause of more calamities to this continent than all the other three.

It is the good fortune of many to live distant from the scene of sorrow; the evil is not sufficiently brought to their doors to make them feel the precarious-ness with which all American property is possessed. But let our imaginations transport us for a few moments to Boston, that seat of wretchedness will teach us wisdom, and instruct us for ever to renounce a power in whom we can have no trust. The inhabitants of that unfortunate city, who but a few months ago were in ease and affluence, have now no other alternative than to stay and starve, or turn out to beg. Endangered by the fire of their friends if they continue within the city, and plundered by the soldiery if they leave it. In their present condition they are prisoners without the hope of redemption, and in a general attack for their relief, they would be exposed to the fury of both armies.

Men of passive tempers look somewhat lightly over the offenses of Britain, and, still hoping for the best, are apt to call out, 'Come we shall be friends again for all this.' But examine the passions and feelings of mankind. Bring the doctrine of reconciliation to the touchstone of nature, and then tell me, whether you can hereafter love, honor, and faithfully serve the power that hath carried fire and sword into your land? If you cannot do all these, then are you only deceiving yourselves, and by your delay bringing ruin upon posterity. Your future connection with Britain, whom you can neither love nor honor, will be forced and unnatural, and being formed only on the plan of present convenience, will in a little time fall into a relapse more wretched than the first. But if you say, you can still pass the violations over, then I ask, Hath your house been burnt? Hath your property been destroyed before your face? Are your wife and children destitute of a bed to lie on, or bread to live on? Have you lost a parent or a child by their hands, and yourself the ruined and wretched survivor? If you have not, then are you not a judge of those who have. But if you have, and can still shake hands with the murderers, then are you unworthy the name of husband, father, friend, or lover, and whatever may be your rank or title in life, you have the heart of a coward, and the spirit of a sycophant.

This is not infaming or exaggerating matters, but trying them by those feelings and affections which nature justifies, and without which, we should be incapable of discharging the social duties of life, or enjoying the felicities of it. I mean not to exhibit horror for the purpose of provoking revenge, but to awaken us from fatal and unmanly slumbers, that we may pursue determinately some fixed object. It is not in the power of Britain or of Europe to conquer America, if she do not conquer herself by delay and timidity. The present winter is worth an age if rightly employed, but if lost or neglected, the whole continent will partake of the misfortune; and there is no punishment which that man will not deserve, be he who, or what, or where he will, that may be the means of sacrificing a season so precious and useful.

It is repugnant to reason, to the universal order of things, to all examples from the former ages, to suppose, that this continent can longer remain subject to any external power. The most sanguine in Britain does not think so. The utmost stretch of human wisdom cannot, at this time compass a plan short of separation, which can promise the continent even a year's security. Reconciliation is now a fallacious dream. Nature hath deserted the connection, and Art cannot supply her place. For, as Milton wisely expresses, 'never can true reconcilement grow where wounds of deadly hate have pierced so deep.'

Every quiet method for peace hath been ineffectual. Our prayers have been rejected with disdain; and only tended to convince us, that nothing flatters vanity, or confirms obstinacy in Kings more than repeated petitioning and nothing hath contributed more than that very measure to make the Kings of Europe absolute: Witness Denmark and Sweden. Wherefore since nothing but blows will do, for God's sake, let us come to a final separation, and not leave the next generation to be cutting throats, under the violated unmeaning names of parent and child. . . .

Small islands not capable of protecting themselves, are the proper objects for kingdoms to take under their care; but there is something very absurd, in supposing a continent to be perpetually governed by an island. In no instance hath nature made the satellite larger than its primary planet, and as England and America, with respect to each Other, reverses the common order of nature, it is evident they belong to different systems: England to Europe, America to itself. . . .

As Britain hath not manifested the least inclination towards a compromise, we may be assured that no terms can be obtained worthy the acceptance of the continent, or any ways equal to the expense of blood and treasure we have been already put to.

The object contended for, ought always to bear some just proportion to the expense. The removal of N[orth], or the whole detestable junto, is a matter unworthy the millions we have expended. A temporary stoppage of trade, was an inconvenience, which would have sufficiently balanced the repeal of all the acts complained of, had such repeals been obtained; but if the whole continent must take up arms, if every man must be a soldier, it is scarcely worth our while to fight against a contemptible ministry only. Dearly, dearly, do we pay for the repeal of the acts, if that is all we fight for; for in a just estimation, it is as great a folly to pay a Bunker Hill price for law, as for land. As I have always considered the independency of this continent, as an event, which sooner or later must arrive, so from the late rapid progress of the continent to maturity, the event could not be far off. Wherefore, on the breaking out of hostilities, it was not worth the while to have disputed a matter, which time would have finally redressed, unless we meant to be in earnest; otherwise, it is like wasting an estate of a suit at law, to regulate the trespasses of a tenant, whose lease is just expiring. No man was a warmer wisher for reconciliation than myself, before the fatal nineteenth of April 1775 [Lexington and Concord], but the moment the event of that day was made known, I rejected the hardened, sullen tempered Pharaoh of England [George III] for ever; and disdain the wretch, that with the pretended title of FATHER OF HIS PEOPLE can unfeelingly hear of their slaughter, and composedly sleep with their blood upon his soul.

But admitting that matters were now made up, what would be the event? I answer, the ruin of the continent. And that for several reasons.

First. The powers of governing still remaining in the hands of the king, he will have a negative over the whole legislation of this continent. And as he hath shown himself such an inveterate enemy to liberty, and discovered such a thirst for arbitrary power; is he, or is he not, a proper man to say to these colonies, 'You shall make no laws but what I please.' And is there any inhabitants in

America so ignorant, as not to know, that according to what is called the present constitution, that this continent can make no laws but what the king gives leave to; and is there any man so unwise, as not to see, that (considering what has happened) he will suffer no Law to be made here, but such as suit his purpose. We may be as effectually enslaved by the want of laws in America, as by submitting to laws made for us in England. After matters are made up (as it is called) can there be any doubt but the whole power of the crown will be exerted, to keep this continent as low and humble as possible? Instead of going forward we shall go backward, or be perpetually quarrelling or ridiculously petitioning. We are already greater than the king wishes us to be, and will he not hereafter endeavor to make us less? To bring the matter to one point. Is the power who is jealous of our prosperity, a proper power to govern us? Whoever says No to this question is an independent, for independency means no more, than, whether we shall make our own laws, or whether the king, the greatest enemy this continent hath, or can have, shall tell us 'there shall be no laws but such as I like.'

But the king you will say has a negative in England; the people there can make no laws without his consent. in point of right and good order, there is something very ridiculous, that a youth of twenty-one (which hath often happened) shall say to several millions of people, older and wiser than himself, I forbid this or that act of yours to be law. But in this place I decline this sort of reply, tho' I will never cease to expose the absurdity of it, and only answer, that England being the king's residence, and America not so, make quite another case. The king's negative here is ten times more dangerous and fatal than it can be in England, for there he will scarcely refuse his consent to a bill for putting England into as strong a state of defence as possible, and in America he would never suffer such a bill to be passed.

America is only a secondary object in the system of British politics. England consults the good of this country, no farther than it answers her own purpose. Wherefore, her own interest leads her to suppress the growth of ours in every case which doth not promote her advantage, or in the least interfere with it. A pretty state we should soon be in under such a second-hand government, considering what has happened! Men do not change from enemies to friends by the alteration of a name: And in order to show that reconciliation now is a dangerous doctrine, I affirm, that it would be policy in the kingdom at this time, to repeal the acts for the sake of reinstating himself in the government of the provinces; in order, that HE MAY ACCOMPLISH BY CRAFT AND SUBTILTY, IN THE LONG RUN, WHAT HE CANNOT DO BY FORCE AND VIOLENCE IN THE SHORT ONE. Reconciliation and ruin are nearly related.

Secondly. That as even the best terms, which we can expect to obtain, can amount to no more than a temporary expedient, or a kind of government by guardianship, which can last no longer than till the colonies come of age, so the general face and state of things, in the interim, will be unsettled and unpromising. Emigrants of property will not choose to come to a country whose form of government hangs but by a thread, and who is every day tottering on the brink of commotion and disturbance; and numbers of the present inhabitants would lay hold of the interval, to dispose of their effects, and quit the continent.

But the most powerful of all arguments, is, that nothing but independence, i. e. a continental form of government, can keep the peace of the continent and preserve it inviolate from civil wars. I dread the event of a reconciliation with Britain now, as it is more than probable, that it will be followed by a revolt somewhere or other, the consequences of which may be far more fatal than all the malice of Britain. . . .

A government of our own is our natural right: And when a man seriously reflects on the precariousness of human affairs, he will become convinced, that it is infinitely wiser and safer, to form a constitution of our own in a cool deliberate manner, while we have it in our power, than to trust such an interesting event to time and chance. . . .

Ye that tell us of harmony and reconciliation, can ye restore to us the time that is past? Can ye give to prostitution its former innocence? Neither can ye reconcile Britain and America. The last cord now is broken, the people of England are presenting addresses against us. There are injuries which nature cannot forgive; she would cease to be nature if she did. As well can the lover forgive the ravisher of his mistress, as the continent forgive the murders of Britain. The Almighty hath implanted in us these inextinguishable feelings for good and wise purposes. They are the guardians of his image in our hearts. They distinguish us from the herd of common animals. The social compact would dissolve, and justice be extirpated from the earth, or have only a casual existence were we callous to the touches of affection. The robber and the murderer, would often escape unpunished, did not the injuries which our tempers sustain, provoke us into justice.

O ye that love mankind! Ye that dare oppose, not only the tyranny, but the tyrant, stand forth! Every spot of the old world is overrun with oppression. Freedom hath been hunted round the globe. Asia, and Africa, have long expelled her. Europe regards her like a stranger, and England hath given her warning to depart. O! receive the fugitive, and prepare in time an asylum for mankind.

Abigail Adams (1744–1818) and John Adams (1735–1826)

Abigail Adams, wife of Founding Father John Adams, is often regarded as one of the earliest American feminists. She was extraordinarily intelligent, read widely, expressed her deeply held antislavery views openly, and supported equal education for girls and the rights of women. While her husband was in Philadelphia as a Massachusetts delegate to the Second Continental Congress in 1776, Abigail penned her famous, oft-quoted letter reminding him not to "forget the ladies" as he and the other delegates were debating the issues of independence and the creation of a new government.

John Adams, though he protested and revolted against the English Crown, did not extend his radical views to support women's rights, as his correspondence with Abigail suggests.

The four letters that follow are an intriguing glimpse into this issue. First, we have Abigail Adams's challenge to her husband; then we have his response and her reply. In the fourth letter, from John Adams to James Sullivan, Adams reveals what he thinks about his wife's opinions.

LETTERS, 1776

ABIGAIL ADAMS TO JOHN ADAMS, MARCH 31, 1776

I long to hear that you have declared an independency—and by the way, in the new Code of Laws which I suppose it will be necessary for you to make, I desire you would Remember the Ladies, and be more generous and favorable to them than your ancestors. Do not put such unlimited power into the hands of the Husbands. Remember, all Men would be tyrants if they could. If particular care and attention is not paid to the Ladies we are determined to foment a Rebellion,

Abigail Adams.
A portrait of Abigail Adams after a painting by Benjamin Blythe, circa 1775. "Do not put such unlimited power," Abigail Adams warned her husband John in 1776, "into the hands of the Husbands. If particular care and attention is not paid to the Ladies we are determined to foment a Rebellion. . . ."

SOURCE: L. H. Butterfield, ed., *Adams Family Correspondence* (Cambridge, MA: Harvard University Press, 1963).

and will not hold ourselves bound by any Laws in which we have no voice, or Representation.

That your Sex are Naturally Tyrannical is a Truth so thoroughly established as to admit of no dispute, but such of you as wish to be happy willingly give up the harsh title of Master for the more tender and endearing one of Friend. Why then, not put it out of the power of the vicious and the Lawless to use us with cruelty and indignity with impunity? Men of Sense in all Ages abhor those customs which treat us only as the vassals of your Sex. Regard us then as Being placed by Providence under your protection, and in imitation of the Supreme Being make use of that power only for our happiness.

JOHN ADAMS TO ABIGAIL ADAMS, APRIL 14, 1776

As to Declarations of Independency, be patient. Read our Privateering Laws, and our Commercial Laws. What signifies a Word.

As to your extraordinary Code of Laws, I cannot but laugh. We have been told that our Struggle has loosened the bands of Government everywhere. That Children and Apprentices were disobedient—that schools and Colleges were grown turbulent—that Indians slighted their Guardians and Negroes grew insolent to their Masters. But your Letter was the first Intimation that another Tribe more numerous and powerful than all the rest, were grown discontented.—This is rather too coarse a Compliment, but you are so saucy, I won't blot it out.

Depend upon it, We know better than to repeal our Masculine systems. Altho they are in full Force, you know they are little more than Theory. We dare not exert our Power in its full Latitude. We are obliged to go fair, and softly, and, in Practice, you know We are the subjects. We have only the Name of Masters, and rather than give up this, which would completely subject Us to the Despotism of the Petticoat, I hope General Washington, and all our brave Heroes would fight. I am sure every good Politician would plot, as long as he would against Despotism, Empire, Monarchy, Aristocracy, Oligarchy, or Ochlocracy.

ABIGAIL ADAMS TO JOHN ADAMS, MAY 7, 1776

I can not say that I think you are very generous to the Ladies, for whilst you are proclaiming peace and good will to Men, Emancipating all Nations, you insist upon retaining an absolute power over Wives. But you must remember that Arbitrary power is like most other things which are very hard, very liable to be broken—and notwithstanding all your wise Laws and Maxims we have it in our power not only to free ourselves but to subdue our Masters, and without violence, throw both your natural and legal authority at our feet.

JOHN ADAMS TO JAMES SULLIVAN, MAY 26, 1776

. . . It is certain in Theory, that the only moral Foundation of Government is the Consent of the People. But to what an Extent Shall We carry this Principle? Shall

We Say, that every Individual of the Community, old and young, male and female, as well as rich and poor, must consent, expressly to every Act of Legislation? No, you will Say. This is impossible. How then does the Right arise in the Majority to govern the Minority, against their Will? Whence arises the Right of the Men to govern Women, without their Consent? Whence the Right of the old to bind the Young, without theirs.

But let us first Suppose, that the whole Community of every Age, Rank, Sex, and Condition, has a Right to vote. This Community, is assembled—a Motion is made and carried by a Majority of one Voice. The Minority will not agree to this. Whence arises the Right of the Majority to govern, and the Obligation of the Minority to obey? from Necessity, you will Say, because there can be no other Rule. But why exclude Women? You will Say, because their Delicacy renders them unfit for Practice and Experience, in the great Business of Life, and the hardy Enterprizes of War, as well as the arduous Cares of State. Besides, their attention is So much engaged with the necessary Nurture of their Children, that Nature has made them fittest for domestic Cares. And Children have not Judgment or Will of their own. True. But will not these Reasons apply to others? Is it not equally true, that Men in general in every Society, who are wholly destitute of Property, are also too little acquainted with public Affairs to form a Right Judgment, and too dependent upon other Men to have a Will of their own? If this is a Fact, if you give to every Man, who has no Property, a Vote, will you not make a fine encouraging provision for Corruption by your fundamental Law? Such is the Frailty of the human Heart, that very few Men, who have no Property, have any Judgment of their own. They talk and vote as they are directed by Some Man of Property, who has attached their Minds to his Interest. . . .

Harrington has Shewn that Power always follows Property. This I believe to be as infallible a Maxim, in Politicks, as, that Action and Re-action are equal, is in Mechanicks. Nay I believe We may advance one Step farther and affirm that the Ballance of Power in a Society, accompanies the Ballance of Property in Land. The only possible Way then of preserving the Ballance of Power on the side of equal Liberty and public Virtue, is to make the Acquisition of Land easy to every Member of Society: to make a Division of the Land into Small Quantities, So that the Multitude may be possessed of landed Estates. If the Multitude is possessed of the Ballance of real Estate, the Multitude will have the Ballance of Power, and in that Case the Multitude will take Care of the Liberty, Virtue, and Interest of the Multitude in all Acts of Government.

I believe these Principles have been felt, if not understood in the Massachusetts Bay, from the Beginning: And therefore I Should think that Wisdom and Policy would dictate in these Times, to be very cautious of making Alterations. Our people have never been very rigid in Scrutinizing into the Qualifications of Voters, and I presume they will not now begin to be so. But I would not advise them to make any alteration in the Laws, at present, respecting the Qualifications of Voters.

SOURCE: Robert J. Taylor, ed., *Papers of John Adams* (Cambridge, MA: Harvard University Press, 1979), Volume 4, 208–212.

Your Idea, that those Laws, which affect the Lives and personal Liberty of all, or which inflict corporal Punishment, affect those, who are not qualified to vote, as well as those who are, is just. But, So they do Women, as well as Men, Children as well as Adults. What Reason Should there be, for excluding a Man of Twenty years, Eleven Months and twenty-seven days old, from a Vote when you admit one, who is twenty one? The Reason is, you must fix upon Some Period in Life, when the Understanding and Will of Men in general is fit to be trusted by the Public. Will not the Same Reason justify the State in fixing upon Some certain Quantity of Property, as a Qualification.

The Same Reasoning, which will induce you to admit all Men, who have no Property, to vote, with those who have, for those Laws, which affect the Person will prove that you ought to admit Women and Children: for generally Speaking, Women and Children, have as good Judgment, and as Independent Minds as those Men who are wholly destitute of Property: these last being to all Intents and Purposes as much dependent upon others, who will please to feed, cloath, and employ them, as Women are upon their Husbands, or Children on their Parents. . . .

Depend upon it, sir, it is dangerous to open So fruitfull a Source of Controversy and Altercation, as would be opened by attempting to alter the Qualifications of Voters. There will be no End of it. New Claims will arise. Women will demand a Vote. Lads from 12 to 21 will think their Rights not enough attended to, and every Man, who has not a Farthing, will demand an equal Voice with any other in all Acts of State. It tends to confound and destroy all Distinctions, and prostrate all Ranks, to one common Levell.

Thomas Hutchinson (1711–1780)

Perhaps the most famous Loyalist during the Revolutionary era was Thomas Hutchinson. He was active during the Stamp Act crisis, during which time his house was destroyed by a mob of anti–Stamp Tax protestors. When the Boston Massacre took place, he was acting governor of Massachusetts; later, at the time of the Boston Tea Party, he was governor. As an appointee of the Crown, Hutchinson had little sympathy for the agitators who insisted on breaking with the mother country. Like most colonists, he considered himself, above all, an Englishman who lived in the American colonies. His comment that "It is better to submit to some abridgement of our rights, than to break off our connection with our protector, England" earned him the hatred of the rebels. He fell quickly from his position as a member of the power structure to the status of persona non grata.

In 1776, Hutchinson published Strictures upon the Declaration of the Congress at Philadelphia, *in which he vehemently protests and takes apart, point by point, each of the arguments set forth in the Declaration of Independence.*

A Loyalist Critique of the Declaration of Independence, 1776

STRICTURES UPON THE DECLARATION OF THE CONGRESS AT PHILADELPHIA, 1776

My Lord,

The last time I had the honour of being in your Lordships company, you observed that you was utterly at a loss to what facts many parts of the Declaration of Independence published by the Philadelphia Congress referred, and that you wished they had been more particularly mentioned, that you might better judge of the grievances, alleged as special causes of the separation of the Colonies from the other parts of the Empire. This hint from your Lordship induced me to attempt a few Strictures upon the Declaration. Upon my first reading it, I thought there would have been more policy in leaving the World altogether ignorant of the motives to this Rebellion, than in offering such false and frivolous reasons in support of it; and I flatter myself, that before I have finished this letter, your Lordship will be of the same mind. But I beg leave, first to make a few remarks upon its rise and progress.

I have often heard men, (who I believe were free from party influence) express their wishes, that the claims of the Colonies to an exemption from the authority of Parliament in imposing Taxes had been conceded; because they had no doubts that America would have submitted in all other cases; and so this unhappy Rebellion, which has already proved fatal to many hundreds of the Subjects of the Empire, and probably will to many thousands more, might have been prevented.

The Acts for imposing Duties and Taxes may have accelerated the Rebellion, and if this could have been foreseen, perhaps, it might have been good policy to have omitted or deferred them; but I am of opinion, that if no Taxes or Duties had been laid upon the Colonies, other pretences would have been found for exception to the authority of Parliament. The body of the people in the Colonies, I know, were easy and quiet. They felt no burdens. They were attached, indeed, in every Colony to their own particular Constitutions, but the Supremacy of Parliament over the whole gave them no concern. They had been happy under it for an hundred years past: They feared no imaginary evils for an hundred years to come. But there were men in each of the principal Colonies, who had Independence in view, before any of those Taxes were laid, or proposed, which have since

SOURCE: Thomas Hutchinson, *Strictures upon the Declaration of the Congress of Philadelphia, in a Letter to a Noble Lord, &'c.* (London, 1776), 3–32, passim.

been the ostensible cause of resisting the execution of Acts of Parliament. Those men have conducted the Rebellion in the several stages of it, until they have removed the constitutional powers of Government in each Colony, and have assumed to themselves, with others, a supreme authority over the whole. . . .

It does not, however, appear that there was any regular plan formed for attaining to Independence, any further than that every fresh incident which could be made to serve the purpose, by alienating the affections of the Colonie from the Kingdom, should be improved accordingly. One of these incidents happened in the year 1764. This was the Act of Parliament for granting certain duties on goods in the British Colonies, for the support of Government, &c. At the same time a proposal was made in Parliament, to lay a stamp duty upon certain writings in the Colonies; but this was deferred until the next Session, that the Agents of the Colonies might notify the several Assemblies in order to their proposing any way, to them more eligible, for raising a sum for the same purpose with that intended by a stamp duty. The Colony of Massachuset's Bay was more affected by the Act for granting duties, than any other Colony. More molasses, the principal article from which any duty could arise, was distilled into spirits in that Colony than in all the rest. The Assembly of Massachuset's Bay, therefore, was the first that took any publick notice of the Act, and the first which ever took exception to the right of Parliament to impose Duties or Taxes on the Colonies, whilst they had no representatives in the House of Commons. This they did in a letter to their Agent in the summer of 1764, which they took care to print and publish before it was possible for him to receive it. And in this letter they recommend to him a pamphlet, wrote by one of their members, in which there are proposals for admitting representatives from the Colonies to sit in the House of Commons.

I have this special reason, my Lord, for taking notice of this Act of the Massachuset's Assembly; that though an American representation is thrown out as an expedient which might obviate the objections to Taxes upon the Colonies, yet it was only intended to amuse the authority in England; and as soon as it was known to have its advocates here, it was renounced by the Colonies, and even by the Assembly of the Colony which first proposed it, as utterly impracticable. In every stage of the Revolt, the same disposition has always appeared. No precise, unequivocal terms of submission to the authority of Parliament in any case, have ever been offered by any Assembly. A concession has only produced a further demand, and I verily believe if every thing had been granted short of absolute Independence, they would not have been contented; for this was the object from the beginning. One of the most noted among the American clergy, prophesied eight years ago, that within eight years from that time, the Colonies would be formed into three distinct independent Republics, Northern, Middle and Southern. I could give your Lordship many irrefragable proofs of this determined design, but I reserve them for a future letter, the subject of which shall be the rite and progress of the Rebellion in each of the Colonies. . . .

It will cause greater prolixity to analize the various parts of this Declaration, than to recite the whole. I will therefore present it to your Lordship's view in distinct paragraphs, with my remarks, in order as the paragraphs are published.

In Congress, July 4, 1776.

A Declaration by the Representatives of the United States of America in General Congress assembled.

When in the course of human events it becomes necessary for one People to dissolve the political bands which have connected them with another, and to assume among the Powers of the earth, the separate and equal station to which the laws of nature and of nature's God entitle them, a decent respect to the opinions of mankind requires that they should declare the causes which impel them to the separation.

We hold these truths to be self evident—That all men are created equal, that they are endowed by their Creator with certain unalienable rights, that among these are life, liberty and the pursuit of happiness, that to secure these rights, governments are instituted among men, deriving their just powers from the consent of the governed; and whenever any form of government becomes destructive of these ends, it is the right of the people to alter or abolish it, and to institute new government, laying its foundation on such principles, and organizing its powers in such form as to them shall seem most likely to effect their safety and happiness. Prudence indeed will dictate that governments long established, should not be changed for light and transient causes; and accordingly all experience hath shewn that mankind are more disposed to suffer while evils are sufferable, than to right themselves by abolishing the forms to which they are accustomed. But when a long train of abuses and usurpations pursuing invariably the same objects, evinces a design to reduce them under absolute despotism, it is their right, it is their duty to throw off such government, and to provide new guards for their future security. Such has been the patient sufferance of these Colonies, and such is now the necessity which constrains them to alter their former systems of Government. The history of the present King of Great Britain is a history of repeated injuries and usurpations, all having its direct object, the establishment of an absolute tyranny over these States. To prove this, let facts be submitted to a candid world.

They begin, my Lord, with a false hypothesis. That the Colonies are one *distinct people,* and the kingdom another, connected by *political* bands. The Colonies, *politically* considered, never were a *distinct* people from the kingdom. There never has been but one *political* band, and that was just the same before the first Colonists emigrated as it has been ever since, the Supreme Legislative Authority, which hath essential right, and is indispensably bound to keep all parts of the Empire entire, until there may be a separation consistent with the general good of the Empire, of which good, from the nature of government, this authority must be the sole judge. I should therefore be impertinent, if I attempted to shew in what case a *whole people* may be justified in rising up in oppugnation to the powers of government, altering or abolishing them, and substituting, in whole or in part, new powers in their stead; or in what sense all men are created equal; or how far life, liberty, and the *pursuit of happiness* may be said to be unalienable; only I could wish to ask the Delegates of Maryland, Virginia, and the Carolinas, how their Constituents justify the depriving more than an hundred thousand Africans of their rights to liberty, and *the pursuit of happiness,* and in some degree to their lives, if these rights are so absolutely unalienable; nor shall I attempt to confute the absurd notions of government, or to expose the equivocal or inconclusive expressions contained in this Declaration; but rather to shew the false representation made of the facts which are alledged to be the evidence of injuries and usurpations, and the special motives to Rebellion. There are many of them, with design, left obscure; for as soon as they are developed, instead of justifying, they rather aggravate the criminality of this Revolt.

The first in order, *He has refused his assent to laws the most wholesome and necessary for the public good;* is of so general a nature, that it is not possible to conjecture to what laws or to what Colonies it refers. I remember no laws which any Colony has been restrained from passing, so as to cause any complaint of grievance, except those for issuing a fraudulent paper currency, and making it a legal tender; but this is a restraint which for many years past has been laid on Assemblies by an act of Parliament, since which such laws cannot have been offered to the King for his allowance. I therefore believe this to be a general charge, without any particulars to support it; fit enough to be placed at the head of a list of imaginary grievances.

The laws of England are or ought to be the laws of its Colonies. To prevent a deviation further than the local circumstances of any Colony may make necessary, all Colony laws are to be laid before the King; and if disallowed, they then become of no force. Rhode-Island, and Connecticut, claim by Charters, an exemption from this rule, and as their laws are never presented to the King, they are out of the question. Now if the King is to approve of all laws, or which is the same thing, of all which the people judge for the public good, for we are to presume they pass no other, this reserve in all Charters and Commissions is futile. This charge is still more inexcusable, because I am well informed, the disallowance of Colony laws has been much more frequent in preceding reigns, than in the present. . . .

He has called together legislative bodies at places unusual, uncomfortable, and distant from the depository of their public records, for the sole purpose of fatiguing them into a compliance with his measures.

To the same Colony this article also has respect. Your Lordship must remember the riotous, violent opposition to Government in the Town of Boston, which alarmed the whole Kingdom, in the year 1768. Four Regiments of the King's forces were ordered to that Town, to be aiding to the Civil Magistrate in restoring and preserving peace and order. The House of Representatives, which was then sitting in the Town, remonstrated to the Governor against posting Troops there, as being an invasion of their rights. He thought proper to adjourn them to Cambridge, where the House had frequently sat at their own desire, when they had been alarmed with fear of the small pox in Boston; the place therefore was not unusual. The public rooms of the College, were convenient for the Assembly to sit in, and the private houses of the inhabitants for the Members to lodge in; it therefore was not *uncomfortable.* It was within four miles of the Town of Boston, and less *distant* than any other Town fit for the purpose.

When this step, taken by the Governor, was known in England, it was approved, and conditional instructions were given to continue the Assembly at Cambridge. The House of Representatives raised the most frivolous objections against the authority of the Governor to remove the Assembly from Boston, but proceeded, nevertheless, to the business of the Session as they used to do. In the next Session, without any new cause, the Assembly refused to do any business unless removed to Boston. This was making themselves judges of the place, and by the same reason, of the time of holding the Assembly, instead of the Governor, who thereupon was instructed not to remove them to Boston, so long as they continued to deny his authority to carry them to any other place.

They *fatigued* the Governor by adjourning from day to day, and refusing to do business one Session after another, while he gave his constant attendance to no purpose; and this they make the King's *fatiguing* them to compel them to comply with his measures.

A brief narrative of this unimportant dispute between an American Governor and his Assembly, needs an apology to your Lordship; how ridiculous then do those men make themselves, who offer it to the world as a ground to justify Rebellion?

He has dissolved Representatives Houses repeatedly for opposing with manly firmness his Invasions on the Rights of the People.

Contentions between Governors and their Assemblies have caused dissolutions of such Assemblies, I suppose, in all the Colonies, in former as well as later times. I recollect but one instance of the dissolution of an Assembly by special order from the King, and that was in Massachuset's Bay. In 1768, the House of Representatives passed a vote or resolve, in prosecution of the plan of Independence, imcompatible with the subordination of the Colonies to the supreme authority of the Empire; and directed their Speaker to send a copy of it in circular letters to the Assemblies of the other Colonies, inviting them to avow the principles of the resolve, and to join in supporting them. No Government can long subsist, which admits of combinations of the subordinate powers against the supreme. This proceeding was therefore, justly deemed highly unwarrantable; and indeed it was the beginning of that unlawful confederacy, which has gone on until it has caused at least a temporary Revolt of all the Colonies which joined in it.

The Governor was instructed to require the House of Representatives, in their next Session to rescind or disavow this resolve, and if they refused, to dissolve them, as the only way to prevent their prosecuting the plan of Rebellion. They delayed a definitive answer, and he indulged them, until they had finished all the business of the Province, and then appeared this *manly firmness* in a rude answer and a peremptory refusal to comply with the King's demand. Thus, my Lord, the regular use of the prerogative in suppressing a Revolt, is urged as a grievance to justify the Revolt.

He has refused for a long time after such dissolutions to cause others to be erected whereby the legislative powers, incapable of annihilation, have returned to the people at large for their exercise; the state remaining in the mean time exposed to all the dangers of invasions from without and convulsions within.

This is connected with the last preceding article, and must relate to the same Colony only; for no other ever presumed, until the year 1774, when the general dissolution of the established government in all the Colonies was taking place, to convene an Assembly, without the Governor, by the meer act of the People.

In less than three months after the Governor had dissolved the Assembly of Massachuset's Bay, the town of Boston, the first mover in all affairs of this nature, applied to him to call another Assembly. The Governor thought he was the judge of the proper time for calling an Assembly, and refused. The town, without delay, chose their former members, whom they called a *Committee*, instead of Representatives; and they sent circular letters to all the other towns in the Province inviting them to chuse *Committees* also; and all these *Committees* met in what they called a *Convention*, and chose the Speaker of the last house their *Chairman*. Here was a House of Representatives in every thing but name; and they were proceeding upon business in the town of Boston, but were interrupted by the arrival of two or three regiments and a spirited message from the Governor, and in two or three days returned to their homes.

This vacation of three months was the *long time* the people waited before they exercised their unalienable powers; the *Invasions from without* were the arrival or expectation of three or four regiments sent by the King to aid the Civil Magistrate in preserving the peace; and the *Convulsions within* were the tumults, riots and acts of violence which this Convention was called, not to suppress but to encourage. . . .

He has kept among us, in times of peace, standing armies, without the consent of our legislatures.

This is too nugatory to deserve any remark. He has kept no armies among them without the consent of the Supreme Legislature. It is begging the question, to suppose that this authority was not sufficient without the aid of their own Legislatures.

He has affected to render the Military independent of, and superior to, the Civil Power.

When the subordinate Civil Powers of the Empire became Aiders of the people in acts of Rebellion, the King, as well he might, has employed the Military Power to reduce those rebellious Civil Powers to their constitutional subjection to the Supreme Civil Power. In no other sense has he ever *affected* to render the Military independent of, and superior to, the Civil Power.

He has combined with others to subject us to a jurisdiction foreign to our Constitution and unacknowledged by our Laws; giving his assent to their pretended Acts of Legislation.

This is a strange way of defining the part which the Kings of England take in conjunction with the Lords and Commons in passing Acts of Parliament. But why is our present Sovereign to be distinguished from all his predecessors since Charles the Second? Even the Republic which they affect to copy after, and Oliver, their favourite, because an Usurper, *combined* against them also. And then, how can a jurisdiction submitted to for more than a century be *foreign* to their constitution?

And is it not the grossest prevarication to say this jurisdiction is *unacknowledged* by their laws, when all Acts of Parliament which respect them, have at all times been their rule of law in all their judicial proceedings? If this is not enough; their own subordinate legislatures have repeatedly in addresses, and resolves, in the most express terms *acknowledged* the supremacy of Parliament; and so late as 1764, before the conductors of this Rebellion had settled their plan, the House of Representatives of the leading Colony made a public declaration in an address to their Governor, that, although they humbly apprehended they might propose their objections, to the late Act of Parliament for granting certain duties in the British Colonies and Plantations in America, yet they at the same time, *acknowledged* that it was their duty to yield obedience to it while it continued unrepealed.

If the jurisdiction of Parliament is foreign to their Constitution, what need of specifying instances, in which they have been subjected to it? Every Act must be an usurpation and injury. They must then be mentioned, my Lord, to shew, hypothetically, that even if Parliament had jurisdiction, such Acts would be a partial and injurious use of it. I will consider them, to know whether they are so or not.

For quartering large bodies of armed troops among us.

When troops were employed in America, in the last reign, to protect the Colonies against French invasion, it was necessary to provide against mutiny and desertion, and to secure proper quarters. Temporary Acts of Parliament were passed for that purpose, and submitted to in the Colonies. Upon the peace, raised ideas took place in the Colonies, of their own importance, and caused a reluctance against Parliamentary authority, and an opposition to the Acts for quartering troops, not because the provision made was in itself unjust or unequal, but because they were Acts of a Parliament whose authority was denied. The provision was as similar to that in England as the state of the Colonies would admit.

For protecting them by a mock trial from punishment, for any murder which they should commit on the Inhabitants of these States.

It is beyond human wisdom to form a system of laws so perfect as to be adapted to all cases. It is happy for a state, that there can be an interposition of legislative power in those cases, where an adherence to established rules would cause injustice. To try men before a biassed and pre-determined Jury would be *a mock trial.* To prevent this, the Act of Parliament, complained of, was passed. Surely, if in any case Parliament may interpose and alter the general rule of law, it may in this. America has not been distinguished from other parts of the Empire. Indeed, the removal of trials for the sake of unprejudiced disinterested Juries, is altogether consistent with the spirit of our laws, and the practice of courts in changing the venue from one county to another.

For cutting off our trade with all parts of the world.

Certainly, my Lord, this could not be a *cause* of Revolt. The Colonies had revolted from the Supreme Authority, to which, by their constitutions, they were subject, before the Act passed. A Congress had assumed an authority over the whole, and had rebelliously prohibited all commerce with the rest of the

Empire. This act, therefore, will be considered by the *candid world*, as a proof of the reluctance in government against what is the dernier resort in every state, and as a milder measure to bring the Colonies to a re-union with the rest of the Empire.

For imposing taxes on us without our consent.

How often has your Lordship heard it said, that the Americans are willing to submit to the authority of Parliament in all cases except that of taxes? Here we have a declaration made to the world of the causes which have impelled to a separation. We are to presume that it contains all which they that publish it are able to say in support of a separation, and that if any one cause was distinguished from another, special notice would be taken of it. That of taxes seems to have been in danger of being forgot. It comes in late, and in as slight a manner as is possible. And, I know, my Lord, that these men, in the early days of their opposition to Parliament, have acknowledged that they pitched upon this subject of taxes, because it was most alarming to the people, every man perceiving immediately that he is personally affected by it; and it has, therefore, in all communities, always been a subject more dangerous to government than any other, to make innovation in; but as their friends in England had fell in with the idea that Parliament could have no right to tax them because not represented, they thought it best it should be believed they were willing to submit to other acts of legislation until this point of taxes could be gained; owning at the same time, that they could find no fundamentals in the English Constitution, which made representation more necessary in acts for taxes, than acts for any other purpose; and that the world must have a mean opinion of their understanding, if they should rebel rather than pay a duty of three-pence *per* pound on tea, and yet be content to submit to an act which restrained them from making a nail to shoe their own horses. Some of them, my Lord, imagine they are as well acquainted with the nature of government, and with the constitution and history of England, as many of their partisans in the kingdom; and they will sometimes laugh at the doctrine of fundamentals from which even Parliament itself can never deviate; and they say it has been often held and denied merely to serve the cause of party, and that it must be so until these unalterable fundamentals shall be ascertained; that the great Patriots in the reign of King Charles the Second, Lord Russell, Hampden, Maynard, &c. whose memories they reverence, declared their opinions, that there were no bounds to the power of Parliament by any fundamentals whatever, and that even the hereditary succession to the Crown might be, as it since has been, altered by Act of Parliament; whereas they who call themselves Patriots in the present day have held it to be a fundamental, that there can be no taxation without representation, and that Parliament cannot alter it.

But as this doctrine was held by their friends, and was of service to their cause until they were prepared for a total independence, they appeared to approve it: As they have now no further occasion for it, they take no more notice of an act for imposing taxes than of many other acts; for a distinction in the authority of Parliament in any particular case, cannot serve their claim to a general exemption, which they are now preparing to assert.

For depriving us, in many cases, of the benefit of a trial by jury.

Offences against the Excise Laws, and against one or more late Acts of Trade, are determined without a Jury in England. It appears by the law books of some of the Colonies, that offences against their Laws of Excise, and some other Laws, are also determined without a Jury; and civil actions, under a sum limited, are determined by a Justice of Peace, I recollect no cases in which trials by Juries are taken away in America, by Acts of Parliament, except such as are tried in the Courts of Admiralty, and these are either for breaches of the Acts of trade, or trespasses upon the King's woods. I take no notice of the Stamp Act, because it was repealed soon after it was designed to take place.

I am sorry, my Lord, that I am obliged to say, there could not be impartial trials by Juries in either of these cases. All regulation of commerce must cease, and the King must be deprived of all the trees reserved for the Royal Navy, if no trials can be had but by Jury. The necessity of the case justified the departure from the general rule; and in the reign of King William the Third, jurisdiction, in both these cases, was given to the Admiralty by Acts of Parliament; and it has ever since been part of the constitution of the Colonies; and it may be said, to the honour of those Courts, that there have been very few instances of complaint of injury from their decrees. Strange that in the reign of King George the Third, this jurisdiction should suddenly become an usurpation and ground of Revolt. . . .

For taking away our Charters, abolishing our most valuable laws, altering fundamentally the forms of our Governments.

For suspending our own legislatures and declaring themselves vested with power, to legislate for us in all cases whatsoever.

These two articles are so much of the same nature, that I consider them together. There has been no Colony Charter altered except that of Massachuset's Bay, and that in no respect, that I recollect, except that the appointment and power of the council are made to conform to that of the Council of the other Royal Governments, and the laws which relate to grand and petit juries are made to conform to the general laws of the Realm.

The only instance of the suspension of any legislative power is that of the Province of New York, for refusing to comply with an Act of Parliament for quartering the King's troops posted there for its protection and defence against the French and Indian enemies. . . .

He has abdicated Government here, by declaring us out of his protection and waging War against us.

He has plundered our Seas, ravaged our Coasts, burnt our Towns and destroyed the Lives of our People.

He is at this time, transporting large Armies of foreign mercenaries to compleat the works of death, desolation and tyranny, already begun with circumstances of cruelty and perfidy scarcely paralleled in the most barbarous ages, and totally unworthy the head of a civilized Nation.

He has constrained our fellow Citizens, taken captive on the high Seas, to bear arms against their Country, to become the executioners of their Friends and Brethren, or to fall themselves by their hands.

He has excited domestick insurrections amongst us and has endeavoured to bring on the Inhabitants of our frontiers the merciless Indian Savages, whose known rule of warfare, is an undistinguished destruction of all ages, sexes and conditions.

These, my Lord, would be weighty charges from a *loyal and dutiful* people against an *unprovoked* Sovereign: They are more than the people of England pretended to bring against King James the Second, in order to justify the Revolution. Never was there an instance of more consummate effrontery. The Acts of a *justly incensed* Sovereign for suppressing a most *unnatural, unprovoked* Rebellion, are here assigned as the *causes* of this Rebellion. It is immaterial whether they are true or false. They are all short of the penalty of the laws which had been violated. Before the date of any one of them, the Colonists had as effectually renounced their allegiance by their deeds as they have since done by their words. They had displaced the civil and military officers appointed by the King's authority and set up others in their stead. They had new modelled their civil governments, and appointed a general government, independent of the King, over the whole. They had taken up arms, and made a public declaration of their resolution to defend themselves, against the forces employed to support his legal authority over them. To subjects, who had forfeited their lives by acts of Rebellion, every act of the Sovereign against them, which falls short of the forfeiture, is an act of favour. A most ungrateful return has been made for this favour. It has been improved to strengthen and confirm the Rebellion against him. . . .

A Prince, whose character is thus marked, by every act which defines the tyrant, is unfit to be the ruler of a free people.

Indignant resentment must seize the breast of every loyal subject. A tyrant, in modern language, means, not merely an absolute and arbitrary, but a cruel, merciless Sovereign. Have these men given an instance of any one Act in which the King has exceeded the just Powers of the Crown as limited by the English Constitution? Has he ever departed from known established laws, and substituted his own will as the rule of his actions? Has there ever been a Prince by whom subjects in rebellion, have been treated with less severity, or with longer forbearance?

Nor have we been wanting in attention to our British Brethren. We have warned them from time to time of attempts by their legislature, to extend an unwarrantable jurisdiction over us. We have reminded them of the circumstances of our emigration and settlement here. We have appealed to their native justice and magnanimity, and we have conjured them by the ties of our common kindred to disavow those usurpations which would inevitably interrupt our connections and correspondence. They too have been deaf to the voice of justice and consanguinity. We must therefore acquiesce in the necessity which denounces our separation and hold them as we hold the rest of mankind, Enemies in War, in Peace, Friends.

We therefore, the Representatives of the United States of America, in General Congress assembled, appealing to the Supreme Judge of the World, for the rectitude of our intentions, do in the name and by the authority of the good People of these Colonies, solemnly publish and declare, That these United Colonies, are, and ought to be, Free and Independent States, and that they are absolved from all allegiance to the British Crown, and that all political connection between them and the State of Great Britain, is and ought to be totally dissolved, and that as free and Independent States they have full power to levy War, conclude Peace, contract Alliances, establish Commerce, and to do all other Acts and things which Independent States may of right do. And for the support of this Declaration, with a firm reliance on the protection of Divine Providence, we mutually pledge to each other, our Lives, our Fortunes and our sacred Honour. Signed by order and in behalf of the Congress.

JOHN HANCOCK, President.

They have, my Lord, in their late address to the people of Great Britain, fully avowed these principles of Independence, by declaring they will pay no obedience to the laws of the Supreme Legislature; they have also pretended, that these laws were the mandates or edicts of the Ministers, not the acts of a constitutional legislative power, and have endeavoured to persuade, such as they called their British Brethren, to justify the Rebellion begun in America; and from thence they expected a general convulsion in the Kingdom, and that measures to compel a submission would in this way be obstructed. These expectations failing, after they had gone too far in acts of Rebellion to hope for impunity, they were under the *necessity* of a separation, and of involving themselves, and all over whom they had usurped authority, in the distresses and horrors of war against that power from which they revolted, and against all who continued in their subjection and fidelity to it.

Gratitude, I am sensible, is seldom to be found in a community, but so sudden a revolt from the rest of the Empire, which had incurred so immense a debt, and with which it remains burdened, for the protection and defence of the Colonies, and at their most importunate request, is an instance of ingratitude no where to be paralleled.

Suffer me, my Lord, before I close this Letter, to observe, that though the professed reason for publishing the Declaration was a decent respect to the opinions of mankind, yet the real design was to reconcile the people of America to that Independence, which always before, they had been made to believe was not intended. This design has too well succeeded. The people have not observed the fallacy in reasoning from the *whole* to *part;* nor the absurdity of making the *governed* to be *governors.* From a disposition to receive willingly complaints against Rulers, facts misrepresented have passed without examining. Discerning men have concealed their sentiments, because under the present *free* government in America, no man may, by writing or speaking, contradict any part of this Declaration, without being deemed an enemy to his country, and exposed to the rage and fury of the populace.

I have the honour to be,

MY LORD,

Your Lordship's most humble,

And most obedient servant.

To the Right Honourable
the E_____ of _____

London, October, 15th. 1776.

Slave Petition

The notions of "freedom" and "liberty" that were echoing throughout the colonies in the 1770s sufficiently encouraged slaves that they began petitioning colonial legislatures for their own freedom. A few petitions were requests to be sent back to Africa, but most argued for either immediate or gradual emancipation. This 1777 petition to the Massachusetts Bay Colony legislature was an appeal for gradual emancipation. Notice that the writers are apparently familiar with the Declaration of Independence.

PETITION FOR GRADUAL EMANCIPATION, 1777

TO THE HONORABLE LEGISLATURE OF THE STATE OF MASSACHUSETTS BAY, JANUARY 13, 1777

The petition of a great number of blacks detained in a state of slavery in the bowels of a free & Christian country humbly sheweth that your petitioners apprehend we have in common with all other men a natural and unalienable right to that freedom which the Great Parent of the Universe hath bestowed equally on all mankind, and which they have never forfeited by any compact or agreement whatever. But they were unjustly dragged by the hand of cruel power from their dearest friends and some of them even torn from the embraces of their tender parents—from a populous, pleasant, and plentiful country and in violation of laws of nature and nations—and, in defiance of all the tender feelings of humanity, brought here to be sold like beasts of burthen & like them condemned to slavery for life among a people professing the mild religion of Jesus—a people not insensible of the secrets of rational beings nor without spirit to resent the unjust endeavours of others to reduce them to a state of bondage and subjection. Your honours need not to be informed that a life of slavery like that of your petitioners, deprived of every social privilege, of every thing requisite to render life tolerable, is far worse than nonexistence.

In imitation of the laudable example of the good people of these states, your petitioners have long and patiently waited the event of petition after petition by them presented to the legislative body of this state and cannot but with grief reflect that their success hath been but too similar. They cannot but express their astonishment that it has never been considered that every principle from which Americans have acted in the course of their unhappy difficulties with Great Britain pleads stronger than a thousand arguments in favour of your petitioners. They therefore humbly beseech your honours to give this petition its due weight & consideration & cause an act of the legislature to be passed

SOURCE: Massachusetts Historical Society, *Collections*, 5th ser., vol. 3 (Boston, 1877), 436–437.

whereby they may be restored to the enjoyments of that which is the natural right of all men—and their children who were born in this land of liberty may not be held as slaves after they arrive at the age of twenty one years. So may the inhabitants of this state, no longer chargeable with the inconsistency of acting themselves the part which they condemn and oppose in others, be prospered in their present glorious struggle for liberty and have those blessings to them, &c.

Lancaster Hill
Peter Bess
Brister Slenser
Prince Hall
Jack Pierpont
Nero Funelo
Newport Sumner
Job Look

Joseph Brant (1742–1807)

Joseph Brant was a Mohawk Indian who helped create an alliance between his people and the British during the Revolution. In 1776, he sailed to London, where he met George III and assured him that the Mohawks would be loyal subjects in the fight against the colonists. When the British, as part of the settlement of the Peace of Paris in 1783, ceded to the victorious Americans the territory between the Appalachians and the Mississippi River, their Indian allies were enraged. Joseph Brant vehemently protested to Frederick Haldimand, the governor of Quebec, and criticized the British for ignoring the rights of the native peoples.

Speech to Governor Haldimand at Quebec, May 21, 1783

Brother Asharekowa and Representatives of the King, the sachems and War Chieftains of the Six United Nations of Indians and their Allies have heard that the King, their Father, has made peace with his children the Bostonians. The Indians distinguish by Bostonians, the Americans in Rebellion, as it first began in Boston, and when they heard of it, they found that they were forgot and no

---

Source: Charles M. Johnston, ed., *The Valley of the Six Nations: A Collection of Documents on the Indian Lands of the Grand River* (Toronto: Champlain Society, 1964), 38–41.

mention made of them in said Peace, wherefore they have now sent me to inform themselves before you of the real truth, whether it is so or not, that they are not partakers of that Peace with the King and the Bostonians.

Brother, listen with great attention to our words, we were greatly alarmed and cast down when we heard that news, and it occasions great discontent and surprise with our People; wherefore tell us the real truth from your heart, and we beg that the King will be put in mind by you and recollect what we have been when his people first saw us, and what we have since done for him and his subjects.

Brother, we, the Mohawks, were the first Indian Nation that took you by the hand like friends and brothers, and invited you to live amongst us, treating you with kindness upon your debarkation in small parties. The Oneidas, our neighbors, were equally well disposed towards you and as a mark of our sincerity and love towards you we fastened your ship to a great mountain at Onondaga, the Center of our Confederacy, the rest of the Five Nations approving of it. We were then a great people, conquering all Indian Nations round about us, and you in a manner but a handfull, after which you increased by degrees and we continued your friends and allies, joining you from time to time against your enemies, sacrificing numbers of our people and leaving their bones scattered in your enemies country. At last we assisted you in conquering all Canada, and then again, for joining you so firmly and faithfully, you renewed your assurances of protecting and defending ourselves, lands and possessions against any encroachment whatsoever, procuring for us the enjoyment of fair and plentiful trade of your people, and sat contented under the shade of the Tree of Peace, tasting the favour and friendship of a great Nation bound to us by Treaty, and able to protect us against all the world.

Brother, you have books and records of our mutual Treaties and Engagements, which will confirm the truth of what I have been telling, and as we are unacquainted with the art of writing, we keep it fresh in our memory by Belts of Wampum deposited in our Council House at Onondaga. We have also received an ornament for the Head, i.e. a crown, from her late Majesty, Queen Ann, as a token of her mutual and unalterable friendship and alliance with us and our Confederacy. Wherefore, we on our side have maintained an uninterrupted attachment towards you, in confidence and expectation of a Reciprocity, and to establish a Perpetual Friendship and Alliance between us, of which we can give you several instances, to wit, when a few years after the Conquest of Canada, your people in this country thought themselves confined on account of their numbers with regard to a Scarcity of Land, we were applied to for giving up some of ours, and fix a line or mark between them and Us. We considered upon it, and relinquished a great Territory to the King for the use of his Subjects, for a Trifling consideration, merely as a Confirmation of said Act, and as a proof of our sincere Regard towards them. This happened so late as the year 1768 at Fort Stanwix, and was gratefully Accepted and Ratified by the different Governors and Great men of the respective Colonies on the Sea Side, in presence of our Late Worthy Friend and Superintendent, Sir William Johnson, when we expected a Permanent, Brotherly Love and Amity, would be the Consequence, but in vain. The insatiable thirst for Power and the next Object of dissatisfaction to the King's Subjects on the Sea Coast, and they to blind our Eyes, Sent Priests from New England amongst us, whom we took for Messengers of Peace, but we were Surprisingly undeceived when we found soon after, that they came to sow the Seeds of discord among our People, in order to alienate our ancient attachments and Alliance from the King our Father, and join them in Rebellion against him, and when they stood up against him, they first endeavored to ensnare us, the Mohawks, and the Indians of the Six Nations living on the Susquehanna River, and the Oneidas, by which division they imagined the remainder of the Confederacy would soon follow, but to not the Least effect.

About this Sad Period we lost our Greatest Friend, Sir William Johnson, notwithstanding we were unalterably determined to stick to our Ancient Treaties with the Crown of England and when the Rebels attempted to insult the Families and Descendents of our late Superintendent, on whom the management of our affairs devolved, we stuck to them and Protected them as much as in our Power, conducting them to Canada with a determined Resolution inviolably to adhere to our Alliance at the Risque of our Lives Families and Property, the rest of the Six Nations finding the Firmness and Steadiness of us, the Mohawks, and Aughuagos, followed our Example and espoused the King's cause to this Present Instant.

It is as I tell you, Brother, and would be too tedious to repeat on this Pressing Occasion the many Proofs of Fidelity we have given the King our Father.

Wherefore Brother, I am now Sent in behalf of all the King's Indian Allies to receive a decisive answer from you, and to know whether they are included in the Treaty with the Americans, as faithful Allies should be or not, and whether those Lands which the Great Being above has pointed out for Our Ancestors, and their descendants, and Placed them there from the beginning and where the Bones of our forefathers are laid, is secure to them, or whether the Blood of their Grand Children is to be mingled with their Bones, thro' the means of Our Allies for whom we have often so freely Bled.

Alexander McGillivray (c. 1759–1793)

Alexander McGillivray, the son of a Creek-French mother and a Scots father, fought on the British side during the American Revolution. Unhappy with the result of the war, McGillivray became an influential Creek diplomat who helped to establish relations between the Creeks and the Spanish in Florida as a way to secure some protection against American aggression. In this 1785 speech to the governor of Florida, Arturo O'Neill, McGillivray denounces American claims to the lands of the Creek, Cherokee, and Chickasaw peoples.

SPEECH TO THE GOVERNOR OF FLORIDA, 1785

MCGILLIVRAY FOR THE CHIEFS OF THE CREEK, CHICKASAW, AND CHEROKEE NATIONS, JULY 10, 1785

WHEREAS We the Cheifs and Warriors of the Creek Chickesaw and Cherokee Nations having received information that an Envoy has been appointed by his Most Catholic Majesty the King of Spain for the purpose of settling the boundarys of his territorys and those of the States of America, and as we have reason to Apprehend that the American Congress in those important matters will endeavour to avail themselves of the Late treaty of peace between them & the British Nation and that they will aim at getting his Majesty the King of Spain to confirm to them that Extensive Territory the Lines of which are drawn by the Said treaty and which includes the whole of our hunting Grounds to our Great injury and ruin—It behoves us therefore to object to, and We Cheifs and Warriors of the Creek Chickesaw and Cherokee Nations, do hereby in the most solemn manner protest against any title claim or demand the American Congress may set up for or against our lands, Settlements, and hunting Grounds in Consequence of the Said treaty of peace between the King of Great Britain and the States of America declaring that as we were not partys, so we are determined to pay no attention to the Manner in which the British Negotiators has drawn out the Lines of the Lands in question Ceded to the States of America—it being a Notorious fact known to the Americans, known to every person who is in any ways conversant in, or acquainted with American affairs, that his Brittannick Majesty was never possessed either by session purchase or by right of Conquest of our Territorys and which the Said treaty gives away. On the contrary it is well known that from the first Settlement of the English colonys of Carolina and Georgia up to the date of the Said treaty no title has ever been or pretended to be made by his Brittanic Majesty to our lands except what was obtained by free Gift or by purchase for good and valuable Considerations.

We can urge in Evidence upon this occasion the Cessions of Lands made to the Carolinians and Georgians by us at different periods and one so late as June 1773 of the Lands lying on the bank of the River OGeechee for which we were paid a Sum not less than one hundred and twenty thousand pounds Stg. nor has any treaty been held by us Since that period for the purpose of granting any land to any people whatever nor did we the Nations of Creeks, Chickesaws and Cherokees do any act to forfeit our Independance and natural Rights to the Said King of Great Britain that could invest him with the power of giving our property away unless fighting by the side of his soldiers in the day of battle and Spilling our best blood in the Service of his Nation can be deemed so.

The Americans altho' sensible of the Injustice done to us on this occasion in consequence of this pretended claim have divided our territorys into countys and

SOURCE: John Walton Caughey, *McGillivray of the Creeks* (Norman: University of Oklahoma Press, 1938), 90–93.

Sate themselves down on our land, as if they were their own. Witness the Large Settlement called Cumberland and others on the Mississippi which with the Late attempts on the Occonnee Lands are all encroachments on our hunting Grounds.

We have repeatedly warned the States of Carolina and Georgia to desist from these Encroachments and to confine themselves within the Lands [granted] to Brittain in the Year 1773. To these remonstrances we have received friendly talks and replys it is true but while they are addressing us by the flattering appellations of Friends and Brothers they are Stripping us of our natural rights by depriving us of that inheritance which belonged to our ancestors and hath descended from them to us Since the beginning of time.

As His most Gracious Majesty was pleased to Express his favorable disposition toward all those Nations of Indians who implored his favor and protection and which we the Cheifs and Warriors of the Nations aforesaid did do in General Congress, held at Pensacola in June 1784 receiving at the same time his Gracious assurances of protection to us, our respective propertys and Hunting Grounds—Relying thereupon and having the greatest Confidence in the Good faith, humanity and Justice of His Most Gracious Majesty the King of Spain we trust that he will enter into no terms with the American States that may Strengthen their claims or that may tend to deprive us of our Just inheritance.

And we request that your Excellency will have the Goodness to forward this Memorial and representation so that it may reach the foot of his Majestys throne. Humbly entreating that he will be pleased to take the same into his Royal consideration and that he will give his Said Envoy at the Americans Congress such orders respecting the premises as he in his great wisdom and Goodness may think fitte.

We conclude with the Sincerest assurances of our firmest attachment to Him and Gratitude for any favor His Most Gracious Majesty may procure us on this occasion.

Done at Little Tallassie in the Upper Creek Nation
This 10th July 1785
by order and in behalf of the Said Indian Nations

United Indian Nations

As Americans continued to encroach upon Indian lands, the native people decided to take a page out of the newborn republic's history book. The only hope to resist American expansion was for the Indian nations to unite, just as the 13 states had united, and so, in 1786, representatives of the Shawnee, Delaware, Huron, Cherokee, Wabash, Chippewa, Ottawa, Pottawatomie, and Miami formed the United Indian Nations. They issued a message to the U.S. Congress in which they insisted that the Ohio River remain the boundary between the United States and Indian territory and that any further agreements, treaties, or sales of land had to have the unanimous consent of the United Indian Nations.

PROTEST TO THE UNITED STATES CONGRESS, 1786

SPEECH AT THE CONFEDERATE COUNCIL, NOVEMBER 28 AND DECEMBER 18, 1786

Present:—The Five Nations, the Hurons, Delawares, Shawanese, Ottawas, Chippewas, Powtewattimies, Twichtwees, Cherokees, and the Wabash confederates

To the Congress of the United States of America:

Brethren of the United States of America: It is now more than three years since peace was made between the King of Great Britain and you, but we, the Indians, were disappointed, finding ourselves not included in that peace, according to our expectations: for we thought that its conclusion would have promoted a friendship between the United States and Indians, and that we might enjoy that happiness that formerly subsisted between us and our elder brethren. We have received two very agreeable messages from the thirteen United States. We also received a message from the King, whose war we were engaged in, desiring us to remain quiet, which we accordingly complied with. During the time of this tranquillity, we were deliberating the best method we could to form a lasting reconciliation with the thirteen United States. Pleased at the same time, we thought we were entering upon a reconciliation and friendship with a set of people born on the same continent with ourselves, certain that the quarrel between us was not of our own making. In the course of our councils, we imagined we hit upon an expedient that would promote a lasting peace between us.

Brothers: We still are of the same opinion as to the means which may tend to reconcile us to each other; and we are sorry to find, although we had the best thoughts in our minds, during the beforementioned period, mischief has, nevertheless, happened between you and us. We are still anxious of putting our plan of accommodation into execution, and we shall briefly inform you of the means that seem most probable to us of effecting a firm and lasting peace and reconciliation: the first step towards which should, in our opinion, be, that all treaties carried on with the United States, on our parts, should be with the general voice of the whole confederacy, and carried on in the most open manner, without any restraint on either side; and especially as landed matters are often the subject of our councils with you, a matter of the greatest importance and of general

SOURCE: *American State Papers, Class II: Indian Affairs* (Washington, 1832), 1:8–9.

concern to us, in this case we hold it indispensably necessary that any cession of our lands should be made in the most public manner, and by the united voice of the confederacy; holding all partial treaties as void and of no effect.

Brothers: We think it is owing to you that the tranquillity which, since the peace between us, has not lasted, and that that essential good has been followed by mischief and confusion, having managed every thing respecting us your own way. You kindled your council fires where you thought proper, without consulting us, at which you held separate treaties, and have entirely neglected our plan of having a general conference with the different nations of the confederacy. Had this happened, we have reason to believe every thing would now have been settled between us in a most friendly manner. We did every thing in our power, at the treaty of fort Stanwix, to induce you to follow this plan, as our real intentions were, at that very time, to promote peace and concord between us, and that we might look upon each other as friends, having given you no cause or provocation to be otherwise.

Brothers: Notwithstanding the mischief that has happened, we are still sincere in our wishes to have peace and tranquillity established between us, earnestly hoping to find the same inclination in you. We wish, therefore, you would take it into serious consideration, and let us speak to you in the manner we proposed. Let us have a treaty with you early in the spring; let us pursue reasonable steps; let us meet half ways, for our mutual convenience; we shall then bring [bury] in oblivion the misfortunes that have happened, and meet each other on a footing of friendship.

Brothers: We say let us meet half way, and let us pursue such steps as become upright and honest men. We beg that you will prevent your surveyors and other people from coming upon our side the Ohio river. We have told you before, we wished to pursue just steps, and we are determined they shall appear just and reasonable in the eyes of the world. This is the determination of all the chiefs of our confederacy now assembled here, notwithstanding the accidents that have happened in our villages, even when in council, where several innocent chiefs were killed when absolutely engaged in promoting a peace with you, the thirteen United States.

Although then interrupted, the chiefs here present still wish to meet you in the spring, for the beforementioned good purpose, when we hope to speak to each other without either haughtiness or menaces.

Brothers: We again request of you, in the most earnest manner, to order your surveyors and others, that mark out lands, to cease from crossing the Ohio, until we shall have spoken to you, because the mischief that has recently happened has originated in that quarter; we shall likewise prevent our people from going over until that time.

Brothers: It shall not be our faults if the plans which we have suggested to you should not be carried into execution; in that case the event will be very precarious, and if fresh ruptures ensue, we hope to be able to exculpate ourselves, and shall most assuredly, with our united force, be obliged to defend those rights and privileges which have been transmitted to us by our ancestors; and if we should be thereby reduced to misfortunes, the world will pity us when they think of the amicable proposals we now make to prevent the unnecessary effusion of blood. These are our thoughts and firm resolves, and we earnestly desire that you will transmit to us, as soon as possible, your answer, be it what it may.

Done at our Confederated Council Fire, at the Huron village, near the mouth of the Detroit river, December 18th, 1786.

The Five Nations,
Hurons, Ottawas, Twichtwees, Shawanese,
Chippewas, Cherokees, Delawares,
Powtewatimies, The Wabash Confederates.

Shays's Rebellion, 1786–1787

In 1786, western Massachusetts farmers had fallen on hard times, which they blamed on the bankers and merchants of Boston. They petitioned the state legislature to ease their financial distress by lowering taxes, issuing paper money, and putting a moratorium on farm foreclosures. When their pleas were disregarded, Daniel Shays led a group of farmers into Springfield, where they occupied the court house in August 1786. Shays spearheaded a subsequent attack on the Springfield Arsenal in January, but state militiamen repelled this attack and, after several days of pursuing the rebels, finally arrested Shays and the other leaders of the rebellion. Though Shays and 14 others were convicted and sentenced to death, they were later pardoned by Governor John Hancock.

Shays's Rebellion is considered one of the major factors that convinced American political leaders to call for a Constitutional Convention later that year in order to form a more efficient government to replace the Articles of Confederation. It was this rebellion that prompted Thomas Jefferson to write: "I hold it that a little rebellion now and then is a good thing, and as necessary in the political world as storms in the physical. Unsuccessful rebellions, indeed, generally establish the encroachments on the rights of the people which have produced them. An observation of this truth should render honest republican governors so mild in their punishment of rebellions as not to discourage them too much. It is a medicine necessary for the sound health of the government."

One of the Shaysites, Daniel Gray, wrote this statement of their grievances.

STATEMENT OF GRIEVANCES, 1786

AN ADDRESS TO THE PEOPLE OF THE SEVERAL TOWNS IN THE COUNTY OF HAMPSHIRE, NOW AT ARMS

Gentlemen,

We have thought proper to inform you of some of the principal causes of the late risings of the people, and also of their present movement, viz.

1ˢᵗ. The present expensive mode of collecting debts, which, by reason of the great scarcity of cash, will of necessity fill our gaols with unhappy debtors, and thereby a reputable body of people rendered incapable of being serviceable either to themselves or the community.

2ᵈ. The monies raised by impost and excise being appropriated to discharge the interest of governmental securities, and not the foreign debt, when these securities are not subject to taxation.

3ᵈ. A suspension of the writ of *Habeas corpus*, by which those persons who have stepped forth to assert and maintain the rights of the people, are liable to be taken and conveyed even to the most distant part of the Commonwealth, and thereby subjected to an unjust punishment.

4ᵗʰ. The unlimited power granted to Justices of the Peace and Sheriffs, Deputy Sheriffs, and Constables, by the Riot Act, indemnifying them to the prosecution thereof; when perhaps, wholly actuated from a principle of revenge, hatred and envy.

Furthermore, Be assured, that this body, now at arms, despise the idea of being instigated by British emissaries, which is so strenuously propagated by the enemies of our liberties: And also wish the most proper and speedy measures may be taken, to discharge both our foreign and domestic debt.

Per Order,
Daniel Gray, *Chairman of the Committee, for the above purpose.*

George Mason (1725–1792)

George Mason was one of the most vocal participants at the Constitutional Convention in 1787. Because of his strong stand on states' rights, he refused to sign the Constitution when it was completed; in his eyes, it gave too much power to the federal government. Returning to Virginia, he

SOURCE: George Richards Minot, ed., *History of the Insurrection in Massachusetts in 1786 and of the Rebellion Consequent Thereon,* (New York: Da Capo Press, 1971), 83.

campaigned against ratification of the Constitution and published one of the most influential Anti-Federalist pamphlets, Objections to This Constitution of Government. *Mason echoed one of the chief Anti-Federalist criticisms, that the Constitution contained no declaration (or bill) of rights, and he specifically deplored the absence of guarantees for freedom of the press and trial by jury. Such objections to the Constitution had the meritorious effect of convincing the Federalists to consent to the addition of the Bill of Rights.*

Objections to This Constitution of Government, 1787

There is no Declaration of Rights, and the laws of the general government being paramount to the laws and constitution of the several States, the Declarations of Rights in the separate States are no security. Nor are the people secured even in the enjoyment of the benefit of the common law. . . .

The Judiciary of the United States is so constructed and extended, as to absorb and destroy the judiciaries of the several States; thereby rendering law as tedious, intricate and expensive, and justice as unattainable, by a great part of the community, as in England, and enabling the rich to oppress and ruin the poor.

The President of the United States has no Constitutional Council, a thing unknown in any safe and regular government. He will therefore be unsupported by proper information and advice, and will generally be directed by minions and favorites; or he will become a tool to the Senate—or a Council of State will grow out of the principal officers of the great departments; the worst and most dangerous of all ingredients for such a Council in a free country. . . . From this fatal defect has arisen the improper power of the Senate in the appointment of public officers, and the alarming dependence and connection between that branch of the legislature and the supreme Executive.

Hence also sprung that unnecessary officer the Vice-President, who for want of other employment is made president of the Senate, thereby dangerously blending the executive and legislative powers, besides always giving to some one of the States an unnecessary and unjust pre-eminence over the others.

The President of the United States has the unrestrained power of granting pardons for treason, which may be sometimes exercise to screen from punishment those whom he had secretly instigated to commit the crime, and thereby prevent a discovery of his own guilt.

SOURCE: Kate Mason Rowland, *The Life of George Mason, 1725–1792* (New York: Russell & Russell, 1964), vol. II, 387–390.

By declaring all treaties supreme laws of the land, the Executive and the Senate have, in many cases, an exclusive power of legislation; which might have been avoided by proper distinctions with respect to treaties, and requiring the assent of the House of Representatives, where it could be done with safety.

By requiring only a majority to make all commercial and navigation laws, the five Southern States, whose produce and circumstances are totally different from that of the eight Northern and Eastern States, may be ruined, for such rigid and premature regulations may be made as will enable the merchants of the Northern and Eastern States not only to demand an exhorbitant freight, but to monopolize the purchase of the commodities at their own price, for many years, to the great injury of the landed interest, and impoverishment of the people; and the danger is the greater as the gain on one side will be in proportion to the loss on the other. Whereas requiring two-thirds of the members present in both Houses would have produced mutual moderation, promoted the general interest, and removed an insuperable objection to the adoption of this government.

Under their own construction of the general clause, at the end of the enumerated powers, the Congress may grant monopolies in trade and commerce, constitute new crimes, inflict unusual and severe punishments, and extend their powers as far as they shall think proper; so that the State legislatures have no security for the powers now presumed to remain to them, or the people for their rights.

There is no declaration of any kind, for preserving the liberty of the press, or the trial by jury in civil causes; nor against the danger of standing armies in time of peace. . . .

This government will set out a moderate aristocracy: it is at present impossible to foresee whether it will, in its operation, produce a monarchy, or a corrupt, tyrannical aristocracy; it will most probably vibrate some years between the two, and then terminate in the one or the other.

Judith Sargent Murray (1751–1820)

Although her name is not widely known today, Judith Sargent Murray was one of the first Enlightenment thinkers to write an eloquent argument in favor of the equality of women. Her "On the Equality of the Sexes" (appearing two years before Mary Wollstonecraft published A Vindication of the Rights of Woman*) establishes her as one of the first feminists. Although she was disparaged by her contemporaries, she influenced many of those who followed her. Denied a formal education because of her sex, she was tutored by her brother in Latin, Greek, and literature. This experience led her to believe that an important means for women to secure equal rights was universal female education.*

Judith Sargent Murray.
*A portrait of Judith Sargent Murray
(1751–1820) by John Singleton
Copley, circa 1772, painted 18 years
before the publication of her "On the
Equality of the Sexes." This landmark
essay, calling for equal educational
opportunities for all women, had a
profound influence on the early
women's movement.*

"On the Equality of the Sexes," 1790

*That minds are not alike, full well I know,
This truth each day's experience will show;
To heights surprising some great spirits soar,
With inborn strength mysterious depths explore;
Their eager gaze surveys the path of light,
Confest it stood to Newton's piercing sight.
Deep science, like a bashful maid retires,
And but the ardent breast her worth inspires;
By perseverance the coy fair is won.
And Genius, led by Study, wears the crown.
But some there are who wish not to improve,
Who never can the path of knowledge love,
Whose souls almost with the dull body one,
With anxious care each mental pleasure shun;
Weak is the level'd, enervated mind,
And but while here to vegetate design'd.
The torpid spirit mingling with its clod,*

SOURCE: Sharon M. Harris, ed., *Selected Writings of Judith Sargent Murray* (New York: Oxford University Press, 1995), 3–14.

Can scarcely boast its origin from God;
Stupidly dull—they move progressing on—
They eat, and drink, and all their work is done.
While others, emulous of sweet applause,
Industrious seek for each event a cause,
Tracing the hidden springs whence knowledge flows,
Which nature all in beauteous order shows.
Yet cannot I their sentiments imbibe,
Who this distinction to the sex ascribe,
As if a woman's form must needs enrol,
A weak, a servile, an inferior soul;
And that the guise of man must still proclaim,
Greatness of mind, and him, to be the same:
Yet as the hours revolve fair proofs arise,
Which the bright wreath of growing fame supplies;
And in past times some men have sunk so low,
That female records nothing less can show.
But imbecility is still confin'd,
And by the lordly sex to us consign'd;
They rob us of the power t'improve,
And then declare we only trifles love;
Yet haste the era, when the world shall know,
That such distinctions only dwell below;
The soul unfetter'd, to no sex confin'd,
Was for the abodes of cloudless day design'd.
Mean time we emulate their manly fires,
Though erudition all their thoughts inspires,
Yet nature with equality imparts,
And noble passions, swell e'en female hearts.

Is it upon mature consideration we adopt the idea, that nature is thus partial in her distributions? Is it indeed a fact, that she hath yielded to one half of the human species so unquestionable a mental superiority? I know that to both sexes elevated understandings, and the reverse, are common. But, suffer me to ask, in what the minds of females are so notoriously deficient, or unequal. May not the intellectual powers be ranged under these four heads—imagination, reason, memory and judgment. The province of imagination hath long since been surrendered up to us, and we have been crowned undoubted sovereigns of the regions of fancy. Invention is perhaps the most arduous effort of the mind; this branch of imagination hath been particularly ceded to us, and we have been time out of mind invested with that creative faculty. Observe the variety of fashions (here I bar the contemptuous smile) which distinguish and adorn the female world; how continually are they changing, insomuch that they almost render the whole man's assertion problematical, and we are ready to say, *there is something new under the sun.* Now, what a playfulness, what an exuberance of fancy, what strength of inventive imagination, doth this continual variation discover? Again, it hath been observed, that if the turpitude of the conduct of our sex, hath been ever so enormous, so extremely ready are we, that the very first thought presents us with an apology, so plausible, as to produce our actions even in an amiable light. Another instance of our creative powers, is our talent for slander; how ingenious are we at inventive scandal? what a formidable story can we in a moment fabricate merely from the force of a prolifick imagination? how many reputations, in the fertile brain of a female, have been utterly despoiled? how industrious are we at improving a hint? suspicion how easily do we convert into conviction, and conviction, embellished by the power of eloquence, stalks abroad to the surprise and confusion of unsuspecting innocence. Perhaps it will be asked if I furnish these facts as instances of excellency in our sex. Certainly not; but as proofs of a creative faculty, of a lively imagination. Assuredly great activity of mind is thereby discovered, and was this activity properly directed, what beneficial effects would follow. Is the needle and kitchen sufficient to employ the operations of a soul thus organized? I should conceive not. Nay, it is a truth that those very departments leave the intelligent principle vacant, and at liberty for speculation. Are we deficient in reason? we can only reason from what we know, and if opportunity of acquiring knowledge hath been denied us, the inferiority of our sex cannot fairly be deduced from thence. Memory, I believe, will be allowed us in common, since every one's experience must testify, that a loquacious old woman is as frequently met with, as a communicative old man; their subjects are alike drawn from the fund of other times and the transactions of their youth, or of maturer life, entertain, or perhaps fatigue you, in the evening of their lives. "But our judgement is not so strong—we do not distinguish so well."—Yet it may be questioned, from what doth this superiority, in this determining faculty of the soul, proceed. May we not trace its source in the difference of education, and continued advantages? Will it be said that the judgment of a male of two years old, is more sage than that of a female's of the same age? I believe the reverse is generally observed to be true. But from that period what partiality! how is the one exalted and the other depressed, by the contrary modes of education which are adopted! the one is taught to aspire, and the other is early confined and limited. As their years increase, the sister must be wholly domesticated, while the brother is led by the hand through all the flowery paths of science. Grant that their minds are by nature equal, yet who shall wonder at the *apparent* superiority, if indeed custom becomes *second nature*; nay if it taketh place of nature, and that it doth the experience of each day will evince. At length arrived at womanhood, the uncultivated fair one feels a void, which the employments allotted her are by no means capable of filling. What can she do? to books she may not apply; or if she doth, *to those only of the novel kind*, lest she merit the appellation of a *learned lady*; and what ideas have been affixed to this term, the observation of many can testify. Fashion, scandal, and sometimes what is still more reprehensible, are then called in to her relief; and who can say to what lengths the liberties she takes may proceed. Meantime she herself is most unhappy; she feels the want of a cultivated mind. Is she single, she in vain seeks to fill up time from sexual employments or amusements. Is she united to a person whose soul nature made equal to her own, education hath set him so far above her, that in those entertainments which are productive of such rational felicity, she is not qualified to accompany him. She experiences a mortifying consciousness of inferiority, which embitters every enjoyment. Doth the person to whom her adverse fate hath consigned her, possess a mind incapable of improvement, she is equally wretched, in being so closely connected with an individual whom she cannot but despise. Now, was she permitted the same instructors as her brother, (with an eye however to their particular departments) for the employment of a rational mind an ample field would be opened. In astronomy she might catch a glimpse of the immensity of the Deity, and thence she would form amazing conceptions of the august and supreme Intelligence. In geography she would admire Jehova in the midst of his benevolence; thus adapting this globe to the various wants and amusements of its inhabitants. In natural philosophy she would adore the infinite majesty of heaven, clothed in condescension; and as she traversed the reptile world, she would hail the goodness of a creating God. A mind, thus filled, would have little room for the trifles with which our sex are, with too much justice, accused of amusing themselves, and they would thus be rendered fit companions for those, who should one day wear them as their crown. Fashions, in their variety, would then give place to conjectures, which might perhaps conduce to the improvement of the literary world; and there would be no leisure for slander or detraction. Reputation would not then be blasted, but serious speculations would occupy the lively imaginations of the sex. Unnecessary visits would be precluded, and that custom would only be indulged by way of relaxation, or to answer the demands of consanguinity and friendship. Females would become discreet, their judgements would be invigorated, and their partners for life being circumspectly chosen, an unhappy Hymen would then be as rare, as is now the reverse.

Will it be urged that those acquirements would supersede our domestick duties. I answer that every requisite in female economy is easily attained; and, with truth I can add, that when once attained, they require no further *mental attention*. Nay, while we are pursuing the needle, or the superintendency of the family, I repeat, that our minds are at full liberty for reflection; that imagination may exert itself in full vigour; and that if a just foundation is early laid, our ideas will then be worthy of rational beings. If we were industrious we might easily find time to arrange them upon paper, or should avocations press too hard for such an indulgence, the hours allotted for conversation would at least become more refined and rational. Should it still be vociferated, "Your domestick employments are sufficient"—I would calmly ask, is it reasonable, that a candidate for immortality, for the joys of heaven, an intelligent being, who is to spend an eternity in contemplating the works of Deity, should at present be so degraded, as to be allowed no other ideas, than those which are suggested by the mechanism of a pudding, or the sewing [of] the seams of a garment? Pity that all such censurers of female improvement do not go one step further, and deny their future existence; to be consistent they surely ought.

Yes, ye lordly, ye haughty sex, our souls are by nature *equal* to yours; the same breath of God animates, enlivens, and invigorates us; and that we are not fallen lower than yourselves, let those witness who have greatly towered above the various discouragements by which they have been so heavily oppressed; and though I am unacquainted with the list of celebrated characters on either side, yet from the observations I have made in the contracted circle in which I have moved, I dare confidently believe, that from the commencement of time to the present day, there hath been as many females, as males, who, by the *mere force of natural powers*, have merited the crown of applause; who, *thus assisted*, have seized the wreath of fame. I know there are [those] who assert, that as the animal powers of the one sex are superiour, of course their mental faculties also must be stronger; thus attributing strength of mind to the transient organization of this earth born tenement. But if this reasoning is just, man must be content to yield the palm to many of the brute creation, since by not a few of his brethren of the field, he is far surpassed in bodily strength. Moreover, was this argument admitted, it would prove too much, for occular demonstration evinceth, that there are many robust masculine ladies, and effeminate gentlemen. Yet I fancy that Mr. Pope, though clogged with an enervated body, and distinguished by a diminutive stature, could nevertheless lay claim to greatness of soul; and perhaps there are many other instances which might be adduced to combat so unphilosophical an opinion. Do we not often see, that when the clay built tabernacle is well nigh dissolved, when it is just ready to mingle with the parent soil, the immortal inhabitant aspires to, and even attaineth heights the most sublime, and which were before wholly unexplored. Besides, were we to grant that animal strength proved any thing, taking into consideration the accustomed impartiality of nature, we should be induced to imagine, that she had invested the female mind with superiour strength as an equivalent for the bodily powers of man. But waving this however palpable advantage, for *equality only*, we wish to contend.

. . .

I AM aware that there are many passages in the sacred oracles which seem to give the advantage to the other sex; but I consider all these as wholly metaphorical. Thus David was a man after God's own heart, yet see him enervated by his licentious passions! behold him following Uriah to the death, and shew me wherein could consist the immaculate Being's complacency. Listen to the curses which Job bestoweth upon the day of his nativity, and tell me where is his perfection, where his patience—*literally* it existed not. David and Job were types of him who was to come; and the superiority of man, as exhibited in scripture, being also emblematical, all arguments deduced from thence, of course fall to the ground. The exquisite delicacy of the female mind proclaimeth the exactness of its texture, while its nice sense of honour announceth its innate, its native grandeur. And indeed, in one respect, the preeminence seems to be tacitly allowed us; for after an education which limits and confines, and employments and recreations which naturally tend to enervate the body, and debilitate the mind; after we have from our early youth been adorned with ribbons, and other gewgaws, dressed out like the ancient victims previous to a sacrifice, being taught by the care of our parents in collecting the most showy materials that the ornamenting our exteriour ought to be the principal object of our attention; after, I say, fifteen years thus spent, we are introduced into the world, amid the united adulation of every beholder. Praise is sweet to the soul; we are immediately intoxicated by large draughts of flattery, which being plentifully administered, is to the pride of our hearts the most acceptable incense. It is expected that with the other sex we should commence immediate war, and that we should triumph over the machinations of the most artful. We must be constantly upon our guard; prudence and discretion must be our characteristicks; and we must rise superiour to, and obtain a complete victory over those who have been long adding to the native strength of their minds, by an unremitted study of men and books, and who have, moreover, conceived from the loose characters which they have seen portrayed in the extensive variety of their reading, a most contemptible opinion of the sex. Thus unequal, we are, notwithstanding, forced to the combat, and the infamy which is consequent upon the smallest deviation in our conduct, proclaims the high idea which was formed of our native strength; and thus, indirectly at least, is the preference acknowledged to be our due. And if we are allowed an equality of acquirement, let serious studies equally employ our minds, and we will bid our souls arise to equal strength. We will meet upon every ground, the despot man; we will rush with alacrity to the combat, and, crowned by success, we shall then answer the exalted expectations which are formed. Though sensibility, soft compassion, and gentle commiseration, are inmates in the female bosom, yet against every deep laid art, altogether fearless of the event, we will set them in array; for assuredly the wreath of victory will encircle the spotless brow. If we meet an equal, a sensible friend, we will reward him with the hand of amity, and through life we will be assiduous to promote his happiness; but from every deep laid scheme for our ruin, retiring into ourselves, amid the flowery paths of science, we will indulge in all the refined and sentimental pleasures of contemplation. And should it still be urged, that the studies thus insisted upon would interfere with our more peculiar department, I must further reply, that *early hours*, and close application, will do wonders; and to her who is from the first dawn of reason taught to fill up time rationally, both the requisites will be easy. I grant that niggard fortune is too generally unfriendly to the mind; and that much of that valuable treasure, time, is necessarily expended upon the wants of the body; but it should be remembered, that in embarrassed circumstances our companions have as little leisure for literary improvement, as is afforded to us; for most certainly their provident care is at least as requisite as our exertions. Nay, we have even more leisure for sedentary pleasures, as our avocations are more retired, much less laborious, and, as hath been observed, by no means require that avidity of attention which is proper to the employments of the other sex. In high life, or, in other words, where the parties are in possession of affluence, the objection respecting time is wholly obviated, and of course falls to the ground; and it may also be repeated, that many of those hours which are at present swallowed up in fashion and scandal, might be redeemed, were we habituated to useful reflections. But in one respect, O ye arbiters of our fate! we confess that the superiority is indubitably yours; you are by nature formed for our protectors; we pretend not to vie with you in bodily strength; upon this point we will never contend for victory. Shield us then, we beseech you, from external evils, and in return *we* will transact *your* domestick affairs. Yes, *your*, for are you not equally interested in those matters with ourselves? Is not the elegancy of neatness as agreeable to your sight as to ours; is not the well savoured viand equally delightful to your taste; and doth not your sense of hearing suffer as much, from the discordant sounds prevalent in an ill regulated family, produced by the voices of children and many *et ceteras*?

CONSTANTIA

By way of supplement to the foregoing pages, I subjoin the following extract from a letter, wrote to a friend in the December of 1780.

And now assist me, O thou genius of my sex, while I undertake the ardous task of endeavouring to combat that vulgar, that almost universal errour, which hath, it seems, enlisted even Mr. P— under its banners. The superiority of your sex hath, I grant, been time out of mind esteemed a truth incontrovertible; in consequence of which persuasion, every plan of education hath been calculated to establish this favourite tenet. Not long since, weak and presuming as I was, I amused myself with selecting some arguments from nature, reason, and experience, against this so generally received idea. I confess that to sacred testimonies I had not recourse. I held them to be merely metaphorical, and thus regarding them, I could not persuade myself that there was any propriety in bringing them to decide in this *very important debate*. However, as you, sir, confine yourself entirely to the sacred oracles, I mean to bend the whole of my artillery against those supposed proofs, which you have from thence provided, and from which you have formed an intrenchment *apparently* so invulnerable. And first, to begin with our great progenitors; but here, suffer me to premise, that it is for mental strength I mean to contend, for with respect to animal powers, I yield them undisputed to that sex, which enjoys them in common with the lion, the tyger, and many other beasts of prey; therefore your observations respecting the *rib under the arm, at a distance from the head*, &c.&c. in no sort mitigate against my view. Well, but the woman was first in the transgression. Strange how blind *self love* renders you men; were you not wholly absorbed in a partial admiration of your own abilities, you would long since have acknowledged the force of what I am now going to urge. It is true some ignoramuses have absurdly enough informed us, that the beauteous fair of paradise, was seduced from her obedience, by a malignant demon, *in the guise of a baleful serpent*; but we, who are better informed, know that the fallen spirit presented himself to her view, *a shining angel still*; for thus, saith the criticks in the Hebrew tongue, ought the word to be rendered. Let us examine her motive—Hark! the seraph declares that she shall attain a perfection of knowledge; for is there aught which is not comprehended under one or other of the terms *good* and *evil*. It doth not appear that she was governed by any one sensual appetite; but merely by a desire of adorning her mind; a laudable ambition fired her soul, and a thirst for knowledge impelled the predilection so fatal in its consequences. Adam could not plead the same deception; assuredly he was not deceived; nor ought we to admire his superiour strength, or wonder at his sagacity, when we so often confess that example is much more influential than precept. His gentle partner stood before him, a melancholy instance of the direful effects of disobedience; he saw her not possessed of that wisdom which she had fondly hoped to obtain, but he beheld the once blooming female, disrobed of that innocence, which had heretofore rendered her so lovely. To him then deception became impossible, as he had proof positive of the fallacy of the argument, which the deceiver had suggested. What then could be his inducement to burst the barriers, and to fly directly in the face of that command, which *immediately* from the mouth of deity *he* had received, since, I say, he could not plead that fascinating stimulus, the accumulation of knowledge, as indisputable conviction was so visibly portrayed before him. What mighty cause impelled him to sacrifice myriads of beings yet unborn, and by one impious act, which *he saw* would be productive of such fatal effects, entail undistinguished ruin upon a race of beings, which he was yet to produce. Blush, ye vaunters of fortitude; ye boasters of resolution; ye haughty lords of the creation; blush when ye remember, that he was influenced by no other motive than a bare pusillanimous attachment to a woman! by sentiments so exquisitely soft, that all his sons have, from that period, when they have designed to degrade them, described as highly feminine. Thus it should seem, that all the arts of the grand deceiver (since means adequate to the purpose are, I conceive, invariably pursued) were requisite to mislead our general mother, while the father of mankind forfeited his own, and relinquished the happiness of posterity, merely in compliance with the blandishments of a female. The subsequent subjection the apostle Paul explains as a figure; after enlarging upon the subject, he adds, *"This is a great mystery; but I speak concerning Christ and the church."* Now we know with what consummate wisdom the unerring father of eternity hath formed his plans; all the types which he hath displayed, he hath permitted *materially* to fail, in the very virtue for which *they* were famed. The reason for this is obvious, we might otherwise mistake his economy, and render that honour to the creature, which is due only to the creator. I know that Adam was a figure of him who was to come. The grace contained in this figure, is the reason of my rejoicing, and while I am very far from prostrating before the shadow, I yield joyfully in all things the preeminence to the second federal head. Confiding faith is prefigured by Abraham, yet he exhibits a contrast to affiance, when he says of his fair companion, she is my sister. Gentleness was the characteristick of Moses, yet he hesitated not to reply to Jehovah himself, which unsaintlike tongue he murmured at the waters of strife, and with rash hands he break the tables, which were inscribed by the finger of divinity. David, dignified with the title of the man after God's own heart, and yet how stained was his life. Solomon was celebrated for wisdom, but folly is wrote in legible characters upon his almost every action. Lastly, let us turn our eyes to man in the aggregate. He is manifested as the figure of strength, but that we may not regard him as anything more than a figure, his soul is formed in no sort superiour, but every way equal to the mind of her, who is the emblem of weakness, and whom he hails the gentle companion of his better days.

Shawnee, Miami, Ottawa, and Seneca Proposal

During the presidency of George Washington, a number of Indian nations in the old northwest banded together in a confederacy to resist further American encroachment into the lands north of the Ohio River. After the Indians, under Little Turtle and Blue Jacket, had defeated an army led by the governor of the Northwest Territory, Arthur St. Clair, American envoys met with tribal representatives to work out some sort of settlement. During the meeting, the Indians criticized the American government for failing to enforce previous treaties.

PROPOSAL TO MAINTAIN INDIAN LANDS, 1793

Brothers;—

Money, to us, is of no value, & to most of us unknown, and as no consideration whatever can induce us to sell the lands on which we get sustenance for our women and children; we hope we may be allowed to point out a mode by which your settlers may be easily removed, and peace thereby obtained.

Brothers;—

We know that these settlers are poor, or they would never have ventured to live in a country which have been in continual trouble ever since they crossed the Ohio; divide therefore this large sum of money which you have offered to us, among these people, give to each also a portion of what you say you would give us annually over and above this very large sum of money, and we are persuaded they would most readily accept of it in lieu of the lands you sold to them, if you add also the great sums you must expend in raising and paying Armies, with a view to force us to yield you our Country, you will certainly have more than sufficient for the purposes of repaying these settlers for all their labor and improvements.

SOURCE: E. A. Cruikshank, ed., *The Correspondence of Lieut. Governor John Graves Simcoe*, 5 vols. (Toronto: Ontario Historical Society, 1923–1931), vol. 2, 17–19.

Brothers;—

You have talked to us about concessions. It appears strange that you should expect any from us, who have only been defending our just Rights against your invasion; We want Peace; Restore to us our Country and we shall be Enemies no longer.

Brothers;—

You make one concession to us, by offering us your money, and another by having agreed to do us justice, after having long and injuriously withheld it. We mean in the acknowledgement you have now made, that the King of England never did, nor ever had a right, to give you our Country, by the Treaty of peace, and you want to make this act of Common Justice, a great part of your concessions, and seem to expect that because you have at last acknowledged our independence, we should for such a favor surrender to you our Country.

Brothers;—

You have talked also a great deal about pre-emption and your exclusive right to purchase Indian lands, as ceded to you by the King at the Treaty of peace.

Brothers;—

We never made any agreement with the King, nor with any other Nation that we would give to either the exclusive right of purchasing our lands. And we declare to you that we consider ourselves free to make any bargain or cession of lands, whenever & to whomsoever we please, if the white people as you say, made a treaty that none of them but the King should purchase of us, and that he has given that right to the U. States, it is an affair which concerns you & him & not us. We have never parted with such a power.

Brothers;—

At our General Council held at the Glaize last Fall, we agreed to meet Commissioners from the U. States, for the purpose of restoring Peace, provided they consented to acknowledge and confirm our boundary line to be the Ohio; and we determined not to meet you until you gave us satisfaction on that point; that is the reason we have never met.

We desire you to consider Brothers, that our only demand, is the peaceable possession of a small part of our once great Country. Look back and view the lands from whence we have been driven to this spot, we can retreat no further, because the country behind hardly affords food for its present inhabitants. And we have therefore resolved, to leave our bones in this small space, to which we are now confined.

Brothers;—

We shall be persuaded that you mean to do us justice if you agree, that the Ohio, shall remain the boundary line between us, if you will not consent thereto, our meeting will be altogether unnecessary.

Protest Against the Alien and Sedition Acts

Passed by the Federalist majority in Congress, the Alien Act was designed to limit immigration, and the Sedition Act to make illegal written and spoken criticism of the government. Both of these acts were aimed at the Jeffersonian Republican opposition, and the Sedition Act in particular, which equated political criticism with sedition, especially infuriated the Jeffersonians. Claiming that the Sedition Act nullified the First Amendment, Thomas Jefferson and James Madison wrote eloquent attacks on the Federalist attempt to limit free speech and, simultaneously, made a strong case for states' rights and for limiting the federal government. The Virginia State Legislature adopted Madison's text as the Virginia Resolutions, and Jefferson's was adopted by the Kentucky State Legislature as the Kentucky Resolutions. The other states refused to approve the resolutions, and therefore they had no effect at the time. Decades later, they surfaced again to be used to support the southern position on secession and nullification.

THE VIRGINIA RESOLUTIONS, 1798

RESOLVED, That the General Assembly of Virginia, doth unequivocally express a firm resolution to maintain and defend the Constitution of the United States, and the Constitution of this State, against every aggression either foreign or domestic, and that they will support the government of the United States in all measures warranted by the former.

That this assembly most solemnly declares a warm attachment to the Union of the States, to maintain which it pledges all its powers; and that for this end, it is their duty to watch over and oppose every infraction of those principles which constitute the only basis of that Union, because a faithful observance of them, can alone secure it's existence and the public happiness.

That this Assembly doth explicitly and peremptorily declare, that it views the powers of the federal government, as resulting from the compact, to which the states are parties; as limited by the plain sense and intention of the instrument constituting the compact; as no further valid that they are authorized by the grants enumerated in that compact; and that in case of a deliberate, palpable, and dangerous exercise of other powers, not granted by the said compact, the states who are parties thereto, have the right, and are in duty bound, to interpose for arresting the progress of the evil, and for maintaining within their respective limits, the authorities, rights and liberties appertaining to them. . . .

SOURCE: Jonathan Elliot, ed., *The Debates in the Several State Conventions on the Adoption of the Federal Constitution*, vol. 4 (1836; New York: Burt Franklin Reprints, 1974).

That the General Assembly doth also express its deep regret, that a spirit has in sundry instances, been manifested by the federal government, to enlarge its powers by forced constructions of the constitutional charter which defines them; and that implications have appeared of a design to expound certain general phrases (which having been copied from the very limited grant of power, in the former articles of confederation were the less liable to be misconstrued) so as to destroy the meaning and effect, of the particular enumeration which necessarily explains and limits the general phrases; and so as to consolidate the states by degrees, into one sovereignty, the obvious tendency and inevitable consequence of which would be, to transform the present republican system of the United States, into an absolute, or at best a mixed monarchy.

That the General Assembly doth particularly protest against the palpable and alarming infractions of the Constitution, in the two late cases of the "Alien and Sedition Acts" passed at the last session of Congress; the first of which exercises a power no where delegated to the federal government, and which by uniting legislative and judicial powers to those of executive, subverts the general principles of free government; as well as the particular organization, and positive provisions of the federal constitution; and the other of which acts, exercises in like manner, a power not delegated by the constitution, but on the contrary, expressly and positively forbidden by one of the amendments thereto; a power, which more than any other, ought to produce universal alarm, because it is levelled against that right of freely examining public characters and measures, and of free communication among the people thereon, which has ever been justly deemed, the only effectual guardian of every other right.

That this state having by its Convention, which ratified the federal Constitution, expressly declared, that among other essential rights, "the Liberty of Conscience and of the Press cannot be cancelled, abridged, restrained, or modified by any authority of the United States," and from its extreme anxiety to guard these rights from every possible attack of sophistry or ambition, having with other states, recommended an amendment for that purpose, which amendment was, in due time, annexed to the Constitution; it would mark a reproachable inconsistency, and criminal degeneracy, if an indifference were now shewn, to the most palpable violation of one of the Rights, thus declared and secured; and to the establishment of a precedent which may be fatal to the other.

That the good people of this commonwealth, having ever felt, and continuing to feel, the most sincere affection for their brethren of the other states; the truest anxiety for establishing and perpetuating the union of all; and the most scrupulous fidelity to that constitution, which is the pledge of mutual friendship, and the instrument of mutual happiness; the General Assembly doth solemnly appeal to the like dispositions of the other states, in confidence that they will concur with this commonwealth in declaring, as it does hereby declare, that the acts aforesaid, are unconstitutional; and that the necessary and proper measures will be taken by each, for co-operating with this state, in maintaining the Authorities, Rights, and Liberties, referred to the States respectively, or to the people. . . .

Agreed to by the Senate, December 24, 1798.

The Kentucky Resolutions, 1799

THE representatives of the good people of this commonwealth in general assembly convened, having maturely considered the answers of sundry states in the Union, to their resolutions passed at the last session, respecting certain unconstitutional laws of Congress, commonly called the alien and sedition laws, would be faithless indeed to themselves, and to those they represent, were they silently to acquiesce in principles and doctrines attempted to be maintained in all those answers, that of Virginia only excepted. To again enter the field of argument, and attempt more fully or forcibly to expose the unconstitutionality of those obnoxious laws, would, it is apprehended be as unnecessary as unavailing.

We cannot however but lament, that in the discussion of those interesting subjects, by sundry of the legislatures of our sister states, unfounded suggestions, and uncandid insinuations, derogatory of the true character and principles of the good people of this commonwealth, have been substituted in place of fair reasoning and sound argument. Our opinions of those alarming measures of the general government, together with our reasons for those opinions, were detailed with decency and with temper, and submitted to the discussion and judgment of our fellow citizens throughout the Union. Whether the decency and temper have been observed in the answers of most of those states who have denied or attempted to obviate the great truths contained in those resolutions, we have now only to submit to a candid world. Faithful to the true principles of the federal union, unconscious of any designs to disturb the harmony of that Union, and anxious only to escape the fangs of despotism, the good people of this commonwealth are regardless of censure or calumniation.

Least however the silence of this commonwealth should be construed into an acquiescence in the doctrines and principles advanced and attempted to be maintained by the said answers, or least those of our fellow citizens throughout the Union, who so widely differ from us on those important subjects, should be deluded by the expectation, that we shall be deterred from what we conceive our duty; or shrink from the principles contained in those resolutions: therefore.

RESOLVED, That this commonwealth considers the federal union, upon the terms and for the purposes specified in the late compact, as conducive to the liberty and happiness of the several states: That it does now unequivocally declare its attachment to the Union, and to that compact, agreeable to its obvious and real intention, and will be among the last to seek its dissolution: That if those who administer the general government be permitted to transgress the limits fixed by that compact, by a total disregard to the special delegations of power therein contained, annihilation of the state governments, and the erection upon their ruins, of a general consolidated government, will be the inevitable consequence: That the principle and construction contended for by sundry of the state legislatures, that the general government is the exclusive judge of the extent of the powers delegated to it, stop nothing short of despotism; since the discretion of those who administer the government, and not the constitution, would be the measure of their powers: That the several states who

formed that instrument, being sovereign and independent, have the unquestionable right to judge of its infraction; and that a nullification, by those sovereignties, of all unauthorized acts done under colour of that instrument, is the
rightful remedy: That this commonwealth does upon the most deliberate
reconsideration declare, that the said alien and sedition laws, are in their opinion, palpable violations of the said constitution; and however cheerfully it may
be disposed to surrender its opinion to a majority of its sister states in matters of
ordinary or doubtful policy; yet, in momentous regulations like the present,
which so vitally wound the best rights of the citizen, it would consider a silent
acquiescence as highly criminal: That although this commonwealth as a party to
the federal compact; will bow to the laws of the Union, yet it does at the same
time declare, that it will not now, nor ever hereafter, cease to oppose in a constitutional manner, every attempt from what quarter soever offered, to violate that
compact:

AND FINALLY, in order that no pretexts or arguments may be drawn from
a supposed acquiescence on the part of this commonwealth in the constitutionality of those laws, and be thereby used as precedents for similar future violations of federal compact; this commonwealth does now enter against them, its
SOLEMN PROTEST.

Approved December 3rd, 1799.

Tecumseh (1768–1813)

*The Indian alliance led by Little Turtle in the aftermath of the American
Revolution had disintegrated by the 1790s during George Washington's
administration. In the early nineteenth century, a Shawnee chief, Tecumseh,
set about resurrecting the alliance. Tecumseh believed that an alliance of the
Indians north of the Ohio River would not be sufficient to resist American
encroachment, and so, for several years, he traveled in an attempt to
convince the southern tribes (the Cherokee, Chickasaw, Choctaw, and
Creek) to unite with the northern tribes (the Miami, Shawnee, Potawatomi,
and others) in order to present a united front. In 1809, while Tecumseh was
undertaking his diplomatic mission, William Henry Harrison, the governor
of Indiana Territory, negotiated a treaty with several of the Ohio tribes to
purchase 3 million acres of land in southern Indiana. Outraged, Tecumseh
wrote a letter to Harrison in which he vehemently protested this purchase,
which had not been unanimously endorsed by the United Indian Nations.
In November 1811, while Tecumseh was again in the South and trying to
negotiate an Indian alliance, American forces under William Henry
Harrison attacked the northern Indians at their encampment on
Tippecanoe Creek. Although the battle was a stalemate, the Indians*

withdrew the following day, and Harrison declared a victory. By the following year, the United States was at war with England, and Tecumseh went to Canada, where he became a brigadier general in the British Army. In 1813, at the Battle of the Thames, Tecumseh was killed.

The first text is from Tecumseh's letter to Governor Harrison, in which he expresses his view that all the Indian nations of North America are linked together by blood and that the land belongs to them by birthright. The second document is a speech Tecumseh delivered to the southern tribes in an attempt to persuade them to make common cause with the northern tribes in resisting white encroachment.

Letter to Governor William Henry Harrison, 1810

It is true I am a Shawnee. My forefathers were warriors. Their son is a warrior. From them I take only my existence; from my tribe I take nothing. I am the maker of my own fortune; and oh! that I could make of my own fortune; and oh! that I could make that of my red people, and of my country, as great as the conceptions of my mind, when I think of the Spirit that rules the universe. I would not then come to Governor Harrison to ask him to tear the treaty and to obliterate the landmark; but I would say to him: "Sir, you have liberty to return to your own country."

The being within, communing with past ages, tells me that once, nor until lately, there was no white man on this continent; that it then all belonged to red men, children of the same parents, placed on it by the Great Spirit that made them, to keep it, to traverse it, to enjoy its productions, and to fill it with the same race, once a happy race, since made miserable by the white people, who are never contented but always encroaching. The way, and the only way, to check and to stop this evil, is for all the red men to unite in claiming a common and equal right in the land, as it was at first, and should be yet; for it never was divided, but belongs to all for the use of each. For no part has a right to sell, even to each other, much less to strangers—those who want all, and will not do with less.

The white people have no right to take the land from the Indians, because they had it first; it is theirs. They may sell, but all must join. Any sale not made by all is not valid. The late sale is bad. It was made by a part only. Part do not know how to sell. All red men have equal rights to the unoccupied land. The right of occupancy is as good in one place as in another. There can not be two occupations in the same place. The first excludes all others. It is not so in hunting or traveling; for there the same ground will serve many, as they may follow each other all day; but the camp is stationary, and that is occupancy. It belongs to the first who sits down on his blanket or skins which he has thrown upon the ground; and till he leaves it no other has a right.

SOURCE: C. M. Depew, ed., *The Library of Oratory* (New York, 1902), vol. 4, 363–364.

Speech to the Southern Tribes, 1811

SLEEP NOT LONGER, O CHOCTAWS AND CHICKASAWS

... [H]ave we not courage enough remaining to defend our country and maintain our ancient independence? Will we calmly suffer the white intruders and tyrants to enslave us? Shall it be said of our race that we knew not how to extricate ourselves from the three most dreadful calamities—folly, inactivity and cowardice? But what need is there to speak of the past? It speaks for itself and asks, Where today is the Pequod? Where the Narragansetts, the Mohawks, Pocanokets, and many other once powerful tribes of our race? They have vanished before the avarice and oppression of the white men, as snow before a summer sun. In the vain hope of alone defending their ancient possessions, they have fallen in the wars with the white men. Look abroad over their once beautiful country, and what see you now? Naught but the ravages of the paleface destroyers meet our eyes. So it will be with you Choctaws and Chickasaws! Soon your mighty forest trees, under the shade of whose wide spreading branches you have played in infancy, sported in boyhood, and now rest your wearied limbs after the fatigue of the chase, will be cut down to fence in the land which the white intruders dare to call their own. Soon their broad roads will pass over the grave of your fathers, and the place of their rest will be blotted out forever. The annihilation of our race is at hand unless we unite in one common cause against the common foe. Think not, brave Choctaws and Chickasaws, that you can remain passive and indifferent to the common danger, and thus escape the common fate. Your people, too, will soon be as falling leaves and scattering clouds before their blighting breath. You, too, will be driven away from your native land and ancient domains as leaves are driven before the wintry storms.

Sleep not longer, O Choctaws and Chickasaws, in false security and delusive hopes. Our broad domains are fast escaping from our grasp. Every year our white intruders become more greedy, exacting, oppressive and overbearing. Every year contentions spring up between them and our people and when blood is shed we have to make atonement whether right or wrong, at the cost of the lives of our greatest chiefs, and the yielding up of large tracts of our lands. Before the palefaces came among us, we enjoyed the happiness of unbounded freedom, and were acquainted with neither riches, wants nor oppression. How is it now? Wants and oppression are our lot; for are we not controlled in everything, and dare we move without asking, by your leave? Are we not being stripped day by day of the little that remains of our ancient liberty? Do they not even kick and strike us as they do their blackfaces? How long will it be before they will tie us to a post and whip us, and make us work for them in their cornfields as they do them? Shall we wait for that moment or shall we die fighting before submitting to such ignominy?

Source: W. C. Vanderwerth, *Indian Oratory: Famous Speeches by Noted Indian Chieftains* (Norman: University of Oklahoma Press, 1971), 62–65.

Have we not for years had before our eyes a sample of their designs, and are they not sufficient harbingers of their future determinations? Will we not soon be driven from our respective countries and the graves of our ancestors? Will not the bones of our dead be plowed up, and their graves be turned into fields? Shall we calmly wait until they become so numerous that we will no longer be able to resist oppression? Will we wait to be destroyed in our turn, without making an effort worthy of our race? Shall we give up our homes, our country, bequeathed to us by the Great Spirit, the graves of our dead, and everything that is dear and sacred to us, without a struggle? I know you will cry with me: Never! Never! Then let us by unity of action destroy them all, which we now can do, or drive them back whence they came. War or extermination is now our only choice. Which do you choose? I know your answer. Therefore, I now call on you, brave Choctaws and Chickasaws, to assist in the just cause of liberating our race from the grasp of our faithless invaders and heartless oppressors. The white usurpation in our common country must be stopped, or we, its rightful owners, be forever destroyed and wiped out as a race of people. I am now at the head of many warriors backed by the strong arm of English soldiers. Choctaws and Chickasaws, you have too long borne with grievous usurpation inflicted by the arrogant Americans. Be no longer their dupes. If there be one here tonight who believes that his rights will not sooner or later be taken from him by the avaricious American palefaces, his ignorance ought to excite pity, for he knows little of the character of our common foe.

And if there be one among you mad enough to undervalue the growing power of the white race among us, let him tremble in considering the fearful woes he will bring down upon our entire race, if by his criminal indifference he assists the designs of our common enemy against our common country. Then listen to the voice of duty, of honor, of nature and of your endangered country. Let us form one body, one heart, and defend to the last warrior our country, our homes, our liberty, and the graves of our fathers.

Choctaws and Chickasaws, you are among the few of our race who sit indolently at ease. You have indeed enjoyed the reputation of being brave, but will you be indebted for it more from report than fact? Will you let the whites encroach upon your domains even to your very door before you will assert your rights in resistance? Let no one in this council imagine that I speak more from malice against the paleface Americans than just grounds of complaint. Complaint is just toward friends who have failed in their duty; accusation is against enemies guilty of injustice. And surely, if any people ever had, we have good and just reasons to believe we have ample grounds to accuse the Americans of injustice; especially when such great acts of injustice have been committed by them upon our race, of which they seem to have no manner of regard, or even to reflect. They are a people fond of innovations, quick to contrive and quick to put their schemes into effectual execution no matter how great the wrong and injury to us; while we are content to preserve what we already have. Their designs are to enlarge their possessions by taking yours in turn; and will you, can you longer dally, O Choctaws and Chickasaws?

Do you imagine that that people will not continue longest in the enjoyment of peace who timely prepare to vindicate themselves, and manifest a determined resolution to do themselves right whenever they are wronged? Far otherwise. Then haste to the relief of our common cause, as by consanguinity of blood you are bound; lest the day be not far distant when you will be left single-handed and alone to the cruel mercy of our most inveterate foe.

Congressmen Protest the War of 1812

During the animated debate in Congress over the issue of going to war against Great Britain, a group of fervent antiwar Federalist congressmen, led by Josiah Quincy, released a statement denouncing the "war hawks" (led by Henry Clay and John C. Calhoun) and President James Madison's resolve to ally the United States with France. These pro-British Federalists also opposed the war because they perceived it as an imperial venture that would add more territory, from which additional states would be carved and into which southern planters could expand the cotton kingdom.

FEDERALIST PROTEST, 1812

If our ills were of a nature that war would remedy, if war would compensate any of our losses or remove any of our complaints, there might be some alleviation of the suffering in the charm of the prospect. But how will war upon the land protect commerce upon the ocean? What balm has Canada for wounded honor? How are our mariners benefited by a war which exposes those who are free, without promising release to those who are impressed?

But it is said that war is demanded by honor. Is national honor a principle which thirsts after vengeance, and is appeased only by blood? . . . If honor demands a war with England, what opiate lulls that honor to sleep over the wrongs done us by France? On land, robberies, seizures, imprisonments, by French authority; at sea, pillage, sinkings, burnings, under French orders. These are notorious. Are they unfelt because they are French? . . .

It would be some relief to our anxiety if amends were likely to be made for the weakness and wildness of the project by the prudence of the preparation. But in no aspect of this anomalous affair can we trace the great and distinctive properties of wisdom. There is seen a headlong rushing into difficulties, with little calculation about the means, and little concern about the consequences.

SOURCE: *Annals of Congress*, 12th Congress, 1st session, Volume 2, columns 2219–2221.

With a navy comparatively nominal, we are about to enter into the lists against the greatest marine [power] on the globe. With a commerce unprotected and spread over every ocean, we propose to make a profit by privateering, and for this endanger the wealth of which we are honest proprietors. An invasion is threatened of the colonies of a power which, without putting a new ship into commission, or taking another soldier into pay, can spread alarm or desolation along the extensive range of our seaboard. . . .

The undersigned can not refrain from asking, what are the United States to gain by this war? Will the gratification of some privateersmen compensate the nation for that sweep of our legitimate commerce by the extended marine of our enemy which this desperate act invites? Will Canada compensate the Middle states for New York; or the Western states for New Orleans?

Let us not be deceived. A war of invasion may invite a retort of invasion. When we visit the peaceable, and as to us innocent, colonies of Great Britain with the horrors of war, can we be assured that our own coast will not be visited with like horrors? At a crisis of the world such as the present, and under impressions such as these, the undersigned could not consider the war, in which the United States have in secret been precipitated, as necessary, or required by any moral duty, or any political expediency.

Hartford Convention

One of the remarkable episodes in the ongoing controversy over states' rights took place not in the South, but in New England, during the War of 1812. New England Federalists were very much opposed to "Mr. Madison's War" (as they called it), primarily because the British embargo was devastating to the New England economy and their tax dollars were being used to fight battles elsewhere. New Englanders also were fearful that one of the outcomes of the war would be the addition of new states that would effectively dilute New England's power in Congress. Federalists held a convention at Hartford, Connecticut, during which they openly discussed the issue of secession. Moderate delegates, however, prevailed, and the resolutions that were passed did not openly call for secession but instead proposed several new constitutional amendments that would offset the Three-fifths Clause, which they felt had given the South inequitable political power. Unfortunately for the Federalists, news of Andrew Jackson's unexpected victory at New Orleans, and the signing of the Treaty of Ghent that ended the war, made the resolutions irrelevant, and tainted the party as treasonous. The Hartford Convention was the death knell of the Federalist Party and had the long-term effect of boosting the states' rights issue during the antebellum period.

Proposals, 1814–1815

Therefore resolved, That it be and hereby is recommended to the Legislatures of the several states represented in this Convention to adopt all such measures as may be necessary effectually to protect the citizens of said states from the operation and effects of all acts which have been or may be passed by the Congress of the United States, which shall contain provisions, subjecting the militia or other citizens to forcible drafts, conscriptions, or impressments, not authorized by the Constitution of the United States.

Resolved, That it be and hereby is recommended to the said Legislatures, to authorize an immediate and earnest application to be made to the Government of the United States, requesting their consent to some arrangement, whereby the said states may, separately or in concert, be empowered to assume upon themselves the defense of their territory against the enemy, and a reasonable portion of the taxes, collected within said states, may be paid into the respective treasuries thereof, and appropriated to the payment of the balance due said states, and to the future defense of the same. The amount so paid into the said treasuries to be credited, and the disbursements made as aforesaid to be charged to the United States.

Resolved, That it be, and it hereby is, recommended to the Legislatures of the aforesaid states, to pass laws (where it has not already been done) authorizing the Governors or Commanders-in-Chief of their militia to make detachments from the same, or to form voluntary corps, as shall be most convenient and conformable to their Constitutions, and to cause the same to be well armed equipped and disciplined, and held in readiness for service; and upon the request of the Governor of either of the other states, to employ the whole of such detachment or corps, as well as the regular forces of the state, or such part thereof as may be required and can be spared consistently with the safety of the state, in assisting the state, making such request to repel any invasion thereof which shall be made or attempted by the public enemy.

Resolved, That the following amendments of the Constitution of the United States, be recommended to the states. . . .

First. Representatives and direct taxes shall be apportioned among the several states which may be included within this union, according to their respective numbers of free persons, including those bound to serve for a term of years, and excluding Indians not taxed, and all other persons. [This is an attack on the Three-fifths Clause which allowed slave states to count slaves as three-fifths of a person in determining representation in Congress.]

Second. No new state shall be admitted into the union by Congress in virtue of the power granted by the Constitution, without the concurrence of two-thirds of both Houses.

SOURCE: Timothy Dwight, *History of the Hartford Convention* (1833), 377–378.

Third. Congress shall not have power to lay any embargo on the ships or vessels of the citizens of the United States, in the ports or harbors thereof, for more than sixty days.

Fourth. Congress shall not have power, without the concurrence of two-thirds of both Houses, to interdict the commercial intercourse between the United States and any foreign nation or the dependencies thereof.

Fifth. Congress shall not make or declare war, or authorize acts of hostility against any foreign nation, without the concurrence of two-thirds of both Houses, except such acts of hostility be in defense of the territories of the United States when actually invaded.

Sixth. No person who shall hereafter be naturalized, shall be eligible as a member of the Senate or House of Representatives of the United States, nor capable of holding any civil office under the authority of the United States.

Seventh. The same person shall not be elected President of the United States a second time; nor shall the President be elected from the same state two terms in succession.

Resolved, That if the application of these states to the government of the United States, recommended in a foregoing Resolution, should be unsuccessful, and peace should not be concluded and the defense of these states should be neglected, as it has been since the commencement of the war, it will in the opinion of this Convention be expedient for the Legislatures of the several states to appoint Delegates to another Convention, to meet at Boston . . . with such powers and instructions as the exigency of a crisis so momentous may require. [A not-so-veiled hint at secession.]

Free Blacks of Philadelphia

The American Colonization Society was founded in 1817 by northern and southern abolitionists who wanted to eliminate slavery gradually. Although the society loathed slavery, its members considered blacks to be an inferior race. Emancipation therefore posed another difficult question: What should be done with the freed slaves? The answer was colonization. Send them back to Africa. Indeed, during James Monroe's presidency, the colony of Liberia was founded (its capital named Monrovia in honor of the American president) with the express purpose of providing a home to emancipated slaves. Free blacks throughout the United States were painfully aware of the racism of American society, and they wanted to see slavery ended. However, they had no desire whatsoever to "return" to Africa. They were, after all, Americans. Shortly after the founding of the American Colonization Society, free blacks in Philadelphia sent their congressman this protest against the colonization policy.

Protest Against Colonization Policy, 1817

WHEREAS OUR ANCESTORS

Whereas our ancestors (not of choice) were the first successful cultivators of the wilds of America, we their descendants feel ourselves entitled to participate in the blessings of her luxuriant soil, which their blood and sweat manured; and that any measure or system of measures, having a tendency to banish us from her bosom, would not only be cruel, but in direct violation of those principles, which have been the boast of this republic.

Resolved, That we view with deep abhorrence the unmerited stigma attempted to be cast upon the reputation of the free people of color, by the promoters of this measure, "that they are a dangerous and useless part of the community," when in the state of disfranchisement in which they live, in the hour of danger they ceased to remember their wrongs, and rallied around the standard of their country.

Resolved, That we never will separate ourselves voluntarily from the slave population in this country; they are our brethren by the ties of consanguinity, of suffering, and of wrong; and we feel that there is more virtue in suffering privations with them, than fancied advantages for a season.

Resolved, That without arts, without science, without a proper knowledge of government, to cast into the savage wilds of Africa the free people of color, seems to us the circuitous route through which they must return to perpetual bondage.

Resolved, That having the strongest confidence in the justice of God, and philanthropy of the free states, we cheerfully submit our destinies to the guidance of Him who suffers not a sparrow to fall, without his special providence.

Resolved, That a committee of eleven persons be appointed to open a correspondence with the honorable Joseph Hopkinson, member of Congress from this city, and likewise to inform him of the sentiments of this meeting, when they in their judgment may deem it proper.

SOURCE: Herbert Aptheker, ed., *A Documentary History of the Negro People in the United States: From Colonial Times Through the Civil War* (Secaucus, NJ: Citadel Press, 1973), 71–72.

PART THREE

Questioning the Nation, 1820–1860

Henry David Thoreau.
A daguerreotype taken around the
time of Thoreau's experiment at
Walden Pond.

INTRODUCTION: THE REFORMING IMPULSE

During the administrations of the first five presidents, a rapidly growing number of Americans were extraordinarily proud of their young republic. An emergent sense of nationalism was at work as the United States strove to set itself apart from Europe by glorifying its brief history and by creating and reinforcing its myths, unconcerned with facts or evidence. Parson Weems's popular biography of George Washington was the source of the charming fiction of the chopped-down cherry tree and little George's inability to tell a lie, which elevated the first president into a messianic stratosphere. Noah Webster actively promoted American spelling standards to separate the American language from the King's English. Washington Irving's Sleepy Hollow tales were widely read and helped create a distinctively American literature.

Nevertheless, pervasive regionalism and divisive forces of sectionalism threatened this evolving yet fragile national identity. In 1819, there were 22 states in the Union—11 slave states, 11 free. This meant that each section had 22 senators. When Missouri applied that year to enter the Union as a slave state, Northerners were alarmed that slaveholding interests would control the Senate. A crisis was averted when the county of York, Massachusetts, was admitted as the free state of Maine simultaneously with the admission of Missouri as a slave state. It was also agreed that any future states carved out of the Louisiana Purchase north of the 36° 30′ parallel would be free and that those south of that line would be slave. The Missouri Compromise ensured that, for the time being at least, the balance of power in the Senate would be preserved. However, far from being a solution, the compromise served only to sweep under the rug the "serpent that was coiled under the table" at the Constitutional Convention—the unresolved issue of slavery.

The antebellum period—roughly from 1820 to 1860—was therefore a time when sectionalism threatened to tear apart the new nation. As more settlers moved west, the issue of slavery continued to fester. Settlers from the North carved new free states out of the western territories. Those from the South, seeking new lands for the cultivation of the country's most lucrative crop, cotton, took their slaves with them into northern Mexico. By 1836, enough slaveholding Americans had moved into the Mexican province of Tejas to instigate a rebellion that secured independence for the Lone Star Republic. Though the urge for expansion was becoming more and more intoxicating, many Northerners were filled with moral indignation over the fact that most settlers in Texas were from the South and appeared to be conspiring to acquire new land for slaveholding. From such new territories, new states would be carved, and this would increase Southern dominance in Congress. To Northerners who already felt that Southerners controlled the Union—all but three of the first ten presidents were from the South, and the three Northern presidents served only one term each—this apparent "conspiracy" to extend slavery was a Southern plot to take over the nation. Still, in 1845, as a fervor swept over the land that it was the United States's "manifest destiny" to conquer the entire North American continent, Texas was admitted to the Union as a slave state. The following year, as Southerners thirsting to spread the cotton kingdom fixed their eyes on the lands of the Southwest and California, the United States went to war with Mexico. By the end of 1848, with Mexico defeated, the United States took the territory that later would be carved into the states of California, Nevada, Utah, Arizona, and New Mexico. It is ironic that the expansion of the nation, which appealed to strong nationalist sentiments, widened the gulf between North and South and thrust the explosive issue of slavery, already being stirred up by a burgeoning abolitionist movement, into the foremost place in the nation's consciousness. Manifest destiny led, seemingly inevitably, to disunion.

For Native Americans, of course, manifest destiny meant disaster. No Indian nation had adapted to and accepted the white man's ways more fully than the Cherokee of Georgia, and yet their ancestral lands were unceremoniously appropriated by President Andrew Jackson against the ruling of the Supreme Court. In spite of their determined resistance, they were forced along the Trail of Tears to a bleak reservation west of the Mississippi. Other tribes, like the Winnebago, and the Sauk and Fox, also attempted to defend themselves from white encroachment, to no avail.

The antebellum period also witnessed a flood of reform movements. Many people, believing in the principles of American democracy, protested against injustice by promoting change. In a sense, this was actually influenced by the intensity of nationalistic sentiment that was particularly highlighted during the events of 1826. As Americans celebrated the fiftieth anniversary of the Declaration of Independence, congratulating themselves on the wonders of democracy, a number of people became acutely aware that their own circumstances, as well as those of others, were preventing them from achieving the equal opportunity that the new American nation had promised. Workers agitated for better wages, a 10-hour day, and universal manhood suffrage, by which all adult white men would be granted the vote without having to meet a property qualification. After William Lloyd Garrison began publishing *The Liberator* in 1831, and Nat Turner's Rebellion later that year, sentiments for and against slavery intensified rapidly. Within another two years, the American Anti-Slavery Society was founded, with tens of thousands of members. By the time of the Mexican War, abolitionists were in a position to exert an enormous influence on the debate over the extension of slavery.

Female abolitionists and their male supporters, recognizing that slaves were not the only people held in subjugation, and infuriated that since the American Revolution women had actually lost ground, began agitating for women's suffrage and equal rights. Many within the abolitionist crusade and the women's movement also raised their dissenting voices against other social problems. They worked for prison and asylum reform, universal education to enable workers and immigrants to assimilate more easily into middle-class society (ironically strengthening class differences), and the temperance crusade to limit alcohol consumption and the concomitant vices of spousal abuse, unemployment, poverty, and crime.

The Romantic Movement and its offspring transcendentalism also had a powerful impact on the strivings for reform, especially in the North, where there were serious attempts to erect utopian communities, like Brooke Farm in Massachusetts, New Harmony in Indiana, and the Oneida Community in New York. Each of these utopian experiments sought to rectify the ills of society and to expand notions of democracy by making America more inclusive.

Shortly after the Mexican War had come to an end, gold was discovered at Sutter's Mill, California. The resulting rush of forty-niners into California swelled the population so rapidly that the territory was ready for admission to the Union before the year was out. Its application to join the Union as a free state would tip the balance in the Senate, and so in 1850 the crisis over the slavery issue again reared its head. By the summer, Congress had worked out the Compromise of 1850: California would be admitted as a free state; other states to be carved out of the Mexican territories would decide for themselves whether they would be slave or free; the slave trade in the District of Columbia would be abolished (but not slavery in the district); and the Fugitive Slave Law would be vigorously enforced, thereby ensuring that Northern states would return escaped slaves to their masters. Again, the basic issue of slavery remained unresolved.

Events began to move rapidly. Senator Stephen A. Douglas, passionate to secure a Northern route for the proposed Transcontinental Railroad through the territory of Kansas, thereby guaranteeing the development of Chicago as a major railroad hub, proposed the Kansas-Nebraska Act to organize those territories under the principle of "popular sovereignty." Recognizing that nothing sounded more agreeable to the American ear than championing the people's right to choose for themselves, Douglas pushed the notion that settlers in the territories should make their own decisions on the issue of slavery when forming a state constitution. Because both Kansas and Nebraska were north of the Missouri Compromise line prohibiting slavery, however, abolitionists immediately and vehemently denounced the proposed act as a devious scheme to extend slavery. Opposition to the act led directly to the founding of the Republican Party, while proslavery and antislavery forces sent settlers to Kansas to gain a majority to elect delegates to a convention to write a state constitution. In 1856, after abolitionist John Brown murdered several proslavery settlers, brutal guerrilla warfare that would last a decade broke out. "Bleeding Kansas" thus became the harbinger of the Civil War.

Other events in the 1850s hastened the country toward civil war. The 1852 publication of Harriet Beecher Stowe's heartrending *Uncle Tom's Cabin* opened the eyes of many Americans to the evils of slavery as it angered Southerners. Senator Charles Sumner's blistering speech on "The Crime Against Kansas" in 1856 led to his being beaten nearly to death in the Senate chamber by an enraged congressman from South Carolina. The Supreme Court's ruling in the Dred Scott case in 1857 declared the Missouri Compromise unconstitutional and ruled that African Americans had "no rights which the white man was bound to respect." And in 1859 John Brown's raid on Harper's Ferry, an abortive attempt to lead a slave insurrection, was the final factor convincing both North and South that compromise was no longer possible.

Disunion seemed inescapable.

Theodore Frelinghuysen (1787–1862)

Theodore Frelinghuysen, U.S. senator from New Jersey, vice-presidential running mate of Henry Clay in the 1844 election, and later president of Rutgers University, is remembered mostly for his passionate speech to the Senate arguing against the removal of the Cherokee in 1830. Despite

*Frelinghuysen's efforts, Congress passed the Indian Removal Bill that
forced the Cherokee, at bayonet point, from their lands in Georgia and
relocated them to a reservation in present-day Oklahoma. It has been
estimated that as many as 15,000 of the 60,000 Indians died on the Trail
of Tears.*

Speech Protesting the Indian Removal Bill, April 9, 1830

... I now proceed to the discussion of those principles which, in my humble
judgment, fully and clearly sustain the claims of the Indians to all their political
and civil rights, as by them asserted. And here, I insist that, by immemorial possession, as the original tenants of the soil, they hold a title beyond and superior
to the British Crown and her colonies, and to all adverse pretensions of our confederation and subsequent Union. God, in his providence, planted these tribes
on this Western continent, so far as we know, before Great Britain herself had a
political existence. I believe, sir, it is not now seriously denied that the Indians
are men, endowed with kindred faculties and powers with ourselves: that they
have a place in human sympathy, and are justly entitled to a share in the common bounties of a benignant Providence. And, with this conceded, I ask in what
code of the law of nations, or by what process of abstract deduction, their rights
have been extinguished? ...

In the light of natural law, can a reason for a distinction exist in the mode of
enjoying that which is my own? If I use it for hunting, may another take it
because he needs it for agriculture? I am aware that some writers have, by a system of artificial reasoning, endeavored to justify, or rather excuse the encroachments made upon Indian territory; and they denominate these abstractions the
law of nations, and, in this ready way, the question is despatched. Sir, as we trace
the sources of this law, we find its authority to depend either upon the conventions or common consent of nations. And when, permit me to inquire, were the
Indian tribes ever consulted on the establishment of such a law? Whoever represented them or their interests in any Congress of nations, to confer upon the
public rules of intercourse, and the proper foundations of dominion and property? The plain matter of fact is, that all these partial doctrines have resulted
from the selfish plans and pursuits of more enlightened nations; and it is not
matter for any great wonder, that they should so largely partake of a mercenary
and exclusive spirit toward the claims of the Indians. ...

Our ancestors found these people, far removed from the commotions of
Europe, exercising all the rights, and enjoying the privileges, of free and independent sovereigns of this new world. They were not a wild and lawless horde of

Source: *Register of Debates in Congress*, 21st Congress, 1st session, vol. 6, part 1, April 9,
1830, 311, 312, 318.

banditti, but lived under the restraints of government, patriarchal in its character, and energetic in its influence. They had chiefs, head men, and councils. The white men, the authors of all their wrongs, approached them as friends—they extended the olive branch; and, being then a feeble colony and at the mercy of the native tenants of the soil, by presents and professions, propitiated their good will. The Indian yielded a slow, but substantial confidence; granted to the colonists an abiding place; and suffered them to grow up to man's estate beside him. He never raised the claim of elder title: as the white man's wants increased, he opened the hand of his bounty wider and wider. By and by, conditions are changed. His people melt away; his lands are constantly coveted; millions after millions are ceded. The Indian bears it all meekly; he complains, indeed, as well he may; but suffers on: and now he finds that this neighbor, whom his kindness had nourished, has spread an adverse title over the last remains of his patrimony, barely adequate to his wants, and turns upon him, and says, "away we cannot endure you so near us! These forests and rivers, these groves of your fathers, these firesides and hunting grounds, are ours by the right of power, and the force of numbers." Sir, let every treaty be blotted from our records, and in the judgment of natural and unchangeable truth and justice, I ask, who is the injured, and who is the aggressor? Let conscience answer, and I fear not the result. . . . Do the obligations of justice change with the color of the skin? Is it one of the prerogatives of the white man, that he may disregard the dictates of moral principles, when an Indian shall be concerned? No, sir . . . , if the contending parties were to exchange positions, place the white man where the Indian stands, load him with all these wrongs, and what path would his outraged feelings strike out for his career? . . . A few pence of duty on tea, that invaded no fireside, excited no fears, disturbed no substantial interest whatever, awakened in the American colonies a spirit of firm resistance; and how was the tea tax met, sir? Just as it should be. There was lurking beneath this trifling imposition of duty, a covert assumption of authority, that led directly to oppressive exactions. "No taxation without representation," became our motto. We would neither pay the tax nor drink the tea. Our fathers buckled on their armor, and, from the water's edge, repelled the encroachments of a misguided cabinet. We successfully and triumphantly contended for the very rights and privileges that our Indian neighbors now implore us to protect and preserve to them. Sir, this thought invests the subject under debate with most singular and momentous interest. We, whom God has exalted to the very summit of prosperity—whose brief career forms the brightest page in history; the wonder and praise of the world; freedom's hope, and her consolation; we, about to turn traitors to our principles and our fame—about to become the oppressors of the feeble, and to cast away our birthright! Sir, I hope for better things. . . .

The end, however, is to justify the means. "The removal of the Indian tribes to the west of the Mississippi is demanded by the dictates of humanity." This is a word of conciliating import. But it often makes its way to the heart under very doubtful titles, and its present claims deserve to be rigidly questioned. Who urges this plea? They who covet the Indian lands—who wish to rid themselves of a neighbor that they despise, and whose State pride is enlisted in rounding off their territories.

Chief John Ross, circa 1843. John Ross (Kooweskoowe), chief of the Cherokee Nation, could not convince Congress to permit the Cherokee to remain on their native lands despite his protests. In 1838, the Cherokee were forcibly removed to a reservation in Oklahoma. Their journey and the route they followed is known as the Trail of Tears.

Cherokee Chief John Ross (1790–1866)

Although Senator Theodore Frelinghuysen strongly opposed Andrew Jackson's Indian Removal Bill that stipulated sending the Cherokee from their native Georgia to Indian Territory (present-day Oklahoma), the bill passed both houses of Congress in 1830. The Cherokee themselves were not silent in standing up for their rights and made a strong effort first to challenge the law and then to forestall enforcement of it. Their case made it all the way to the Supreme Court. In Cherokee Nation v. Georgia *and in* Worcester v. Georgia, *Chief Justice John Marshall ruled in the Cherokee's favor. Unfortunately, a contingent of Cherokee, without the authorization of the Cherokee nation, met with representatives of the U.S. Government at New Echota, Georgia, and signed a removal treaty. Once the Senate ratified the Treaty of New Echota, President Jackson had the authority he needed to force the removal.*

In 1836, in protest, Cherokee Chief John Ross wrote a letter to
Congress denouncing the Treaty of New Echota. His protest was to no
avail, and in 1838 the Cherokee began the thousand-mile march along
the infamous Trail of Tears.

LETTER PROTESTING THE TREATY OF
NEW ECHOTA, 1836

TO THE SENATE AND HOUSE OF REPRESENTATIVES, RED CLAY COUNCIL GROUND, CHEROKEE NATION, SEPTEMBER 28, 1836

It is well known that for a number of years past we have been harassed by a series of vexations, which it is deemed unnecessary to recite in detail, but the evidence of which our delegation will be prepared to furnish. With a view to bringing our troubles to a close, a delegation was appointed on the 23rd of October, 1835, by the General Council of the nation, clothed with full powers to enter into arrangements with the Government of the United States, for the final adjustment of all our existing difficulties. The delegation failing to effect an arrangement with the United States commissioner, then in the nation, proceeded, agreeably to their instructions in that case, to Washington City, for the purpose of negotiating a treaty with the authorities of the United States.

After the departure of the Delegation, a contract was made by the Rev. John F. Schermerhorn, and certain individual Cherokees, purporting to be a "treaty, concluded at New Echota, in the State of Georgia, on the 29th day of December, 1835, by General William Carroll and John F. Schermerhorn, commissioners on the part of the United States, and the chiefs, headmen, and people of the Cherokee tribes of Indians." A spurious Delegation, in violation of a special injunction of the general council of the nation, proceeded to Washington City with this pretended treaty, and by false and fraudulent representations supplanted in the favor of the Government the legal and accredited Delegation of the Cherokee people, and obtained for this instrument, after making important alterations in its provisions, the recognition of the United States Government. And now it is presented to us as a treaty, ratified by the Senate, and approved by the President [Andrew Jackson], and our acquiescence in its requirements demanded, under the sanction of the displeasure of the United States, and the threat of summary compulsion, in case of refusal. It comes to us, not through our legitimate authorities, the known and usual medium of communication between the Government of the United States and our nation, but through the agency of a complication of powers, civil and military.

SOURCE: Gary E. Moulton, ed., *The Papers of Chief John Ross*, vol. 1, 1807–1839 (Norman: University of Oklahoma Press, 1985).

By the stipulations of this instrument, we are despoiled of our private possessions, the indefeasible property of individuals. We are stripped of every attribute of freedom and eligibility for legal self-defence. Our property may be plundered before our eyes; violence may be committed on our persons; even our lives may be taken away, and there is none to regard our complaints. We are denationalized; we are disfranchised. We are deprived of membership in the human family! We have neither land nor home, nor resting place that can be called our own. And this is effected by the provisions of a compact which assumes the venerated, the sacred appellation of treaty.

We are overwhelmed! Our hearts are sickened, our utterance is paralized, when we reflect on the condition in which we are placed, by the audacious practices of unprincipled men, who have managed their stratagems with so much dexterity as to impose on the Government of the United States, in the face of our earnest, solemn, and reiterated protestations.

The instrument in question is not the act of our Nation; we are not parties to its covenants; it has not received the sanction of our people. The makers of it sustain no office nor appointment in our Nation, under the designation of Chiefs, Head men, or any other title, by which they hold, or could acquire, authority to assume the reins of Government, and to make bargain and sale of our rights, our possessions, and our common country. And we are constrained solemnly to declare, that we cannot but contemplate the enforcement of the stipulations of this instrument on us, against our consent, as an act of injustice and oppression, which, we are well persuaded, can never knowingly be countenanced by the Government and people of the United States; nor can we believe it to be the design of these honorable and highminded individuals, who stand at the head of the Govt., to bind a whole Nation, by the acts of a few unauthorized individuals. And, therefore, we, the parties to be affected by the result, appeal with confidence to the justice, the magnanimity, the compassion, of your honorable bodies, against the enforcement, on us, of the provisions of a compact, in the formation of which we have had no agency.

Sylvia Dubois (1788–1889)

Sylvia Dubois spent most of her life as a slave. In 1883, when she was in her 90s, she related her life story to C. W. Larison, who published it under the title Silvia Dubois, a Biografy of the Slav Who Whipt Her Mistress and Gand Her Fredom. *The following excerpt, although it was recounted decades after the event took place and should therefore be regarded as a blend of folklore and fact, does suggest that slaves did not completely acquiesce to the South's "peculiar institution" and that many were not afraid to resist their masters.*

Reminiscences from Sylvia Dubois, a Biografy of the Slav Who Whipt Her Mistress and Gand Her Fredom, 1883

"Well, your mistress was always kind to you, wasn't she?"

"Kind to me? Why, she was the very devil himself. Why, she'd level me with anything she could get hold of—club, stick of wood, tongs, fire-shovel, knife, axe, hatchet, anything that was handiest—and then she was so damned quick about it too. I tell you, if I intended to sauce her, I made sure to be off always."

"Well, did she ever hit you?"

"Yes, often. Once she knocked me till I was so stiff that she thought I was dead. Once after that, because I was a little saucy, she leveled me with the fire-shovel and broke my pate. She thought I was dead then, but I wasn't."

"Broke your pate?"

"Yes, broke my skull. You can put your fingers here, in the place where the break was, in the side of my head, yet. She smashed it right in—she didn't do things to the halves."

(Hereupon I examined Sylvia's head and found that at some time long ago the skull had been broken and depressed for a space not less than three inches, that the deepest fragment had not been elevated as surgeons now do, and that in consequence there is to this day a depression in which I can bury a large part of the index finger.)

"Well, Sylvia, what did your master say about such as was done by your mistress?"

"Say? Why, he knew how passionate she was. He saw her kick me in the stomach one day so badly that he interfered. I was not grown up then; I was too young to stand such. He didn't tell her so when I was by, but I have heard him tell her when they thought I was not listening that she was too severe—that such work would not do—she'd kill me next."

"Well, did his remonstrating with her make her any better?"

"Not a bit—made her worse. Just put the devil in her. And then, just as soon as he was out of the way, if I was a little saucy, or a little neglectful, I'd catch hell again. But I fixed her. I paid her up for all her spunk. I made up my mind that when I grew up I would do it, and when I had a good chance, when some of her grand company was around, I fixed her."

"Well, what did you do?"

"I knocked her down and blamed near killed her."

"Well, where and how did that happen?"

"It happened in the barroom. There was some grand folks stopping there, and she wanted things to look pretty stylish, and so she set me to scrubbing up the barroom. I felt a little glum and didn't do it to suit her. She scolded me about

SOURCE: C. W. Larison, *Silvia Dubois, a Biografy of the Slav Who Whipt Her Mistress and Gand Her Fredom*, edited by Jared C. Lobdell (New York: Oxford University Press, 1988), 63–70.

it and I sauced her. She struck me with her hand. Thinks I, it's a good time now to dress you out, and damned if I won't do it. I set down my tools and squared for a fight. The first whack, I struck her a hell of a blow with my fist. I didn't knock her entirely through the panels of the door, but her landing against the door made a terrible smash, and I hurt her so badly that all were frightened out of their wits, and I didn't know myself but that I'd killed the old devil."

"Were there anyone in the barroom then?"

"It was full of folks. Some of them were Jersey folks who were going from the Lake Countries home to visit their friends. Some were drovers on their way to the west. And some were hunters and boatmen staying a while to rest."

"What did they do when they saw you knock your mistress down?"

"Do? Why they were going to take her part, of course. But I just sat down the slop bucket and straightened up, and smacked my fists at 'em, and told 'em to wade in if they dared and I'd thrash every devil of 'em, and there wasn't a damned a one that dared to come."

"Well, what next?"

"Then I got out and pretty quick too. I knew it wouldn't do to stay there, so I went down to Chenang Point and there went to work."

"Where was your master during this fracas?"

"He? He was gone to tend court at Wilkes-Barre. He was a grand jury man and had to be gone a good many days. He often served as grand jury man, and then he was always gone a week or two. Things would have gone better if he had been home."

"When he came home what did he do?"

"He sent for me to come back."

"Did you go?"

"Of course I did; I had to go. I was a slave, and if I didn't go, he would have brought me, and in a hurry too. In those days the masters made the niggers mind, and when he spoke I knew I must obey.

"Them old masters, when they got mad, had no mercy on a nigger—they'd cut a nigger all up in a hurry—cut 'em all up into strings, just leave the life, that's all. I've seen 'em do it, many a time."

"Well, what did your master say when you came back?"

"He didn't scold me much. He told me that as my mistress and I got along so badly, if I would take my child and go to New Jersey and stay there, he would give me free. I told him I would go. It was late at night; he wrote me a pass, gave it to me, and early the next morning I set out for Flagtown, New Jersey."

"It seems that you got along with your master much better than you did with your mistress?"

"Yes, I got along with him first rate. He was a good man and a great man too; all the grand folks liked Minical Dubois. When the great men had their meetings, Minical Dubois was always invited to be with 'em, and he always went, too. He was away from home a great deal; he had a great deal of business and he was known all over the country. I liked my master and everybody liked him."

"He never whipped me unless he was sure that I deserved it. He used to let me go to frolics and balls and to have good times away from home, with other black folks, whenever I wanted to. He was a good man and a good master. But when he told me I must come home from a ball at a certain time, when the time came, the jib was out. I knew I must go; it wouldn't do to disappoint Minical Dubois. . . .

"How did you go to Flagtown?"

"On foot, to be sure. I came right down through the Beech Woods, all alone, excepting my young one in my arms. Sometimes I didn't see a person for half a day; sometimes I didn't get half enough to eat, and never had any bed to sleep in; I just slept anywhere. My baby was about a year and a half old, and I had to carry it all the way. The wood was full of panthers, bears, wildcats, and wolves; I often saw 'em in the daytime, and always heard 'em howling in the night. O! that old panther—when he howled it made the hair stand up all over my head.

"At Easton, I went on board of a raft to go down the Delaware. A man by the name of Brink had his wife and family on board of a raft, bound for Philadelphia. I went on board to help the wife, for my passage. They were nice folks and I had a good time; I left the raft not far from Trenton, but I do not know exactly where—there was no town at the place at which I got off the raft.

"Then I proceeded directly to Flagtown, to see my mother. I did not find her there—she had moved to New Brunswick. On my way, a man called to me, asking me 'Whose nigger are you?' I replied 'I'm no man's nigger—I belong to God—I belong to no man.'

"He then said 'Where are you going?' I replied 'That's none of your business. I'm free. I go where I please.'

"He came toward me. I sat down my young one, showed him my fist, and looked at him; and I guess he saw 't was no use. He moseyed off, telling me that he would have me arrested as soon as he could find a magistrate.

"You see that in those days the negroes were all slaves, and they were sent nowhere, nor allowed to go anywhere without a pass; and when anyone met a negro who was not with his master, he had a right to demand of him whose negro he was; and if the negro did not show his pass, or did not give good evidence whose he was, he was arrested at once and kept until his master came for him, paid whatever charges were made, and took him away. You see, in those days anybody had authority to arrest vagrant negroes. They got paid for arresting them and charges for their keeping till their master redeemed them. But he didn't arrest me—not a bit.

"When I got to New Brunswick, I found my mother. Soon after I went to work, and remained in New Brunswick several years. From New Brunswick I went to Princeton to work for Victor Tulane. I remained in his family a long while; I worked for him when Paul Tulane was a child; I worked there when he was born. Victor Tulane was a great man and a good man, and he used his servants well. And Paul was a nice boy and Madam Tulane was a good woman; and I liked 'em all, and all the servants liked 'em.

"After a long while, I visited my grandfather, Harry Compton, who lived at the forks of the road, near this place. He was then an old man; they say he was more than a hundred years old, and I guess he was. But he was yet quite active; he wanted me to stay with him and take of him and I stayed; and at his death I inherited his property. I lived on the old homestead until a few years ago, when them damned

Democrats set fire to my house, and burned up my home and all that I had. Since that time I have lived at this place, with my youngest daughter."

David Walker (1785–1830)

David Walker was a free North Carolina black who became an ardent and outspoken abolitionist. By the 1820s he had moved to Boston, opened a clothing store, and enjoyed a reputation as a leader of the city's black community of about 1500 people. He helped form the Massachusetts General Colored Association and became a distributor of the first national black newspaper in the United States, Freedom's Journal. Then, in 1829, he published his Appeal to the Coloured Citizens of the World, *which uncompromisingly condemned both the institution of slavery and racism. If whites would not emancipate the slaves, he argued, then the slaves should rise up in revolt: Kill or be killed. Abolitionists worked hard to disseminate thousands of copies of this incendiary pamphlet to slaves throughout the South, and Southerners worked equally hard to prevent its distribution. So outraged were slaveholders that rumors began circulating that the South had put a price on Walker's head, and in June 1830 David Walker was found dead. Historians have established that he probably died of a respiratory disease, but, at the time, it was widely supposed that he had been poisoned.*

Walker's Appeal *is very significant because it marks the transition from the rather mild-mannered antislavery protests of Quakers and moderates to the more zealous and inflammatory antislavery protests of William Lloyd Garrison (who began publication of* The Liberator *in 1831), Theodore Weld, Elijah Lovejoy, Frederick Douglass, and eventually John Brown. When Nat Turner's Rebellion occurred in 1831, Southerners had no doubt that Walker's* Appeal *had instigated it. And so, as the abolitionist crusade became more radical, so, too, did the Southern defense of its peculiar institution.*

This excerpt from the Appeal *is taken from the 1830 edition.*

APPEAL TO THE COLOURED CITIZENS OF THE WORLD, 1830

PREAMBLE

My dearly beloved Brethren and Fellow Citizens.

Having traveled over a considerable portion of these United States, and having, in the course of my travels, taken the most accurate observations of things as

SOURCE: Charles M. Wiltse, ed., *David Walker's Appeal in Four Articles; Together with a Preamble, to the Coloured Citizens of the World* (New York: Hill and Wang, 1965), 1–18.

they exist—the result of my observations has warranted the full and unshaken conviction, that we, (coloured people of these United States,) are the most degraded, wretched, and abject set of beings that ever lived since the world began; and I pray God that none like us ever may live again until time shall be no more. They tell us of the Israelites in Egypt, the Helots in Sparta, and of the Roman Slaves, which last were made up from almost every nation under heaven, whose sufferings under those ancient and heathen nations, were, in comparison with ours, under this enlightened and Christian nation, no more than a cypher—or, in other words, those heathen nations of antiquity, had but little more among them than the name and form of slavery; while wretchedness and endless miseries were reserved, apparently in a phial, to be poured out upon our fathers, ourselves and our children, by Christian Americans!

These positions I shall endeavour, by the help of the Lord, to demonstrate in the course of this Appeal, to the satisfaction of the most incredulous mind—and may God Almighty, who is the Father of our Lord Jesus Christ, open your hearts to understand and believe the truth.

The causes, my brethren, which produce our wretchedness and miseries, are so very numerous and aggravating, that I believe the pen only of a Josephus or a Plutarch, can well enumerate and explain them. Upon subjects, then, of such incomprehensible magnitude, so impenetrable, and so notorious, I shall be obliged to omit a large class of, and content myself with giving you an exposition of a few of those, which do indeed rage to such an alarming pitch, that they cannot but be a perpetual source of terror and dismay to every reflecting mind.

I am fully aware, in making this appeal to my much afflicted and suffering brethren, that I shall not only be assailed by those whose greatest earthly desires are, to keep us in abject ignorance and wretchedness, and who are of the firm conviction that Heaven has designed us and our children to be slaves and beasts of burden to them and their children. I say, I do not only expect to be held up to the public as an ignorant, impudent and restless disturber of the public peace, by such avaricious creatures, as well as a mover of insubordination—and perhaps put in prison or to death, for giving a superficial exposition of our miseries, and exposing tyrants. But I am persuaded, that many of my brethren, particularly those who are ignorantly in league with slaveholders or tyrants, who acquire their daily bread by the blood and sweat of their more ignorant brethren—and not a few of those too, who are too ignorant to see an inch beyond their noses, will rise up and call me cursed—Yea, the jealous ones among us will perhaps use more abject subtlety, by affirming that this work is not worth perusing, that we are well situated, and there is no use in trying to better our condition, for we cannot. I will ask one question here.—Can our condition be any worse?—Can it be more mean and abject? If there are any changes, will they not be for the better though they may appear for the worst at first? Can they get us any lower? Where can they get us? They are afraid to treat us worse, for they know well, the day they do it they are gone. But against all accusations which may or can be preferred against me, I appeal to Heaven for my motive in writing—who knows what my object is, if possible, to awaken in the breasts of my afflicted, degraded and slumbering brethren, a spirit of inquiry and investigation respecting our miseries and wretchedness in this Republican Land of Liberty!!!!!!

The sources from which our miseries are derived, and on which I shall comment, I shall not combine in one, but shall put them under distinct heads and expose them in their turn; in doing which, keeping truth on my side, and not departing from the strictest rules of morality, I shall endeavour to penetrate, search out, and lay them open for your inspection. If you cannot or will not profit by them, I shall have done my duty to you, my country and my God.

And as the inhuman system of slavery, is the source from which most of our miseries proceed, I shall begin with that curse to nations, which has spread terror and devastation through so many nations of antiquity, and which is raging to such a pitch at the present day in Spain and in Portugal. It had one tug in England, in France, and in the United States of America; yet the inhabitants thereof, do not learn wisdom, and erase it entirely from their dwellings and from all with whom they have to do. The fact is, the labour of slaves comes so cheap to the avaricious usurpers, and is (as they think) of such great utility to the country where it exists, that those who are actuated by sordid avarice only, overlook the evils, which will as sure as the Lord lives, follow after the good. In fact, they are so happy to keep in ignorance and degradation, and to receive the homage and the labour of the slaves, they forget that God rules in the armies of heaven and among the inhabitants of the earth, having his ears continually open to the cries, tears and groans of his oppressed people; and being a just and holy Being will at one day appear fully in behalf of the oppressed, and arrest the progress of the avaricious oppressors; for although the destruction of the oppressors God may not effect by the oppressed, yet the Lord our God will bring other destructions upon them—for not unfrequently will he cause them to rise up one against another, to be split and divided, and to oppress each other, and sometimes to open hostilities with sword in hand. Some may ask, what is the matter with this united and happy people?—Some say it is the cause of political usurpers, tyrants, oppressors, But has not the Lord an oppressed and suffering people among them? Does the Lord condescend to hear their cries and see their tears in consequence of oppression? Will he let the oppressors rest comfortably and happy always? Will he not cause the very children of the oppressors to rise up against them, and oftimes put them to death? "God works in many ways his wonders to perform." . . .

All persons who are acquainted with history, and particularly the Bible, who are not blinded by the God of this world, and are not actuated solely by avarice—who are able to lay aside prejudice long enough to view candidly and impartially, things as they were, are, and probably will be—who are willing to admit that God made man to serve Him alone, and that man should have no other Lord or Lords but Himself—that God Almighty is the sole proprietor or master of the WHOLE human family, and will not on any consideration admit of a colleague, being unwilling to divide his glory with another—and who can dispense with prejudice long enough to admit that we are men, notwithstanding our improminent noses and woolly heads, and believe that we feel for our fathers, mothers, wives and children, as well as the whites do for theirs.—I say, all who are permitted to see and believe these things, can easily recognize the judgments of God among the Spaniards. Though others may lay the cause of the fierceness with which they cut each other's throats, to some other circumstance, yet they who believe that God is a God of justice, will believe that SLAVERY is the principal cause.

While the Spaniards are running about upon the field of battle cutting each other's throats, has not the Lord an afflicted and suffering people in the midst of them, whose cries and groans in consequence of oppression are continually pouring into the ears of the God of justice? Would they not cease to cut each other's throats, if they could? But how can they? The very support which they draw from government to aid them in perpetrating such enormities, does it not arise in a great degree from the wretched victims of oppression among them? And yet they are calling for Peace!—Peace!! Will any peace be given unto them? Their destruction may indeed be procrastinated awhile, but can it continue long, while they are oppressing the Lord's people? Has He not the hearts of all men in His hand? Will he suffer one part of his creatures to go on oppressing another like brutes always, with impunity? And yet, those avaricious wretches are calling for Peace!!!! I declare, it does appear to me, as though some nations think God is asleep, or that he made the Africans for nothing else but to dig their mines and work their farms, or they cannot believe history, sacred or profane. I ask every man who has a heart, and is blessed with the privilege of believing—Is not God a God of justice to all his creatures? Do you say he is? Then if he gives peace and tranquillity to tyrants, and permits them to keep our fathers, our mothers, ourselves and our children in eternal ignorance and wretchedness, to support them and their families, would he be to us a God of justice? I ask, O ye Christians!!! who hold us and our children in the most abject ignorance and degradation, that ever a people were afflicted with since the world began—I say, if God gives you peace and tranquillity, and suffers you thus to go on afflicting us, and our children, who have never given you the least provocation—would he be to us a God of justice? If you will allow that we are MEN, who feel for each other, does not the blood of our fathers and of us their children, cry aloud to the Lord of Sabaoth against you, for the cruelties and murders with which you have, and do continue to afflict us. But it is time for me to close my remarks on the suburbs, just to enter more fully into the interior of this system of cruelty and oppression.

ARTICLE I. OUR WRETCHEDNESS IN CONSEQUENCE OF SLAVERY

My beloved brethren:—The Indians of North and of South America—the Greeks—the Irish, subjected under the king of Great Britain—the Jews, that ancient people of the Lord—the inhabitants of the islands of the sea—in fine, all the inhabitants of the earth, (except however, the sons of Africa) are called men, and of course are, and ought to be free. But we, (coloured people) and our children are brutes!! and of course are, and ought to be SLAVES to the American people and their children forever!! to dig their mines and work their farms; and thus go on enriching them, from one generation to another with our blood and our tears!!!!

I promised in a preceding page to demonstrate to the satisfaction of the most incredulous, that we, (coloured people of these United States of America) are the most wretched, degraded and abject set of beings that ever lived since the world began, and that the white Americans having reduced us to the wretched state of slavery, treat us in that condition more cruel (they being an enlightened and Christian people,) than any heathen nation did any people whom it had reduced to our condition. These affirmations are so well confirmed in the minds of all unprejudiced men, who have taken the trouble to read histories, that they need no elucidation from me. But to put them beyond all doubt, I refer you in the first place to the children of Jacob, or of Israel in Egypt, under Pharaoh and his people. Some of my brethren do not know who Pharaoh and the Egyptians were—I know it to be a fact, that some of them take the Egyptians to have been a gang of devils, not knowing any better, and that they (Egyptians) having got possession of the Lord's people, treated them nearly as cruel as Christian Americans do us, at the present day. For the information of such, I would only mention that the Egyptians, were Africans or coloured people, such as we are— some of them yellow and others dark—a mixture of Ethiopians and the natives of Egypt—about the same as you see the coloured people of the United States at the present day.—I say, I call your attention then, to the children of Jacob, while I point out particularly to you his son, among the rest, in Egypt.

"And Pharaoh, said unto Joseph, . . . thou shalt be over my house, and according unto thy word shall all my people be ruled: only in the throne will I be greater than thou."

"And Pharaoh said unto Joseph, see, I have set thee over all the land of Egypt."

"And Pharaoh said unto Joseph, I am Pharaoh, and without thee shall no man lift up his hand or foot in all the land of Egypt."

Now I appeal to heaven and to earth, and particularly to the American people themselves, who cease not to declare that our condition is not hard, and that we are comparatively satisfied to rest in wretchedness and misery, under them and their children. Not, indeed, to show me a coloured President, a Governor, a Legislator, a Senator, a Mayor, or an Attorney at the Bar.—But to show me a man of colour, who holds the low office of Constable, or one who sits in a Juror Box, even on a case of one of his wretched brethren, throughout this great Republic!!—But let us pass Joseph the son of Israel a little farther in review, as he existed with that heathen nation.

"And Pharaoh called Joseph's name Zaphnathpaaneah; and he gave him to wife Asenath the daughter of Potipherah priest of On. And Joseph went out over all the land of Egypt."

Compare the above, with the American institutions. Do they not institute laws to prohibit us from marrying among the whites? I would wish, candidly, however, before the Lord, to be understood, that I would not give a pinch of snuff to be married to any white person I ever saw in all the days of my life. And I do say it, that the black man, or man of colour, who will leave his own colour (provided he can get one, who is good for any thing) and marry a white woman, to be a double slave to her, just because she is white, ought to be treated by her as he surely will be, viz: as a NIGGER!!!! It is not, indeed, what I care about inter-marriages with the whites, which induced me to pass this subject in review; for the Lord knows, that there is a day coming when they will be glad enough to get into the company of the blacks, notwithstanding, we are, in this generation, lev-elled by them, almost on a level with the brute creation: and some of us they treat even worse than they do the brutes that perish. I only made this extract to show how much lower we are held, and how much more cruel we are treated by the Americans, than were the children of Jacob, by the Egyptians.—We will notice the sufferings of Israel some further, under heathen Pharaoh, compared with ours under the enlightened Christians of America.

"And Pharaoh spoke unto Joseph, saying, thy father and thy brethren are come unto thee:

"The land of Egypt is before thee: in the best of the land make thy father and brethren to dwell; in the land of Goshen let them dwell: and if thou knowest any men of activity among them, then make them rulers over my cattle."

I ask those people who treat us so well, Oh! I ask them, where is the most barren spot of land which they have given unto us? Israel had the most fertile land in all Egypt. Need I mention the very notorious fact, that I have known a poor man of colour, who laboured night and day, to acquire a little money, and having acquired it, he vested it in a small piece of land, and got him a house erected thereon, and having paid for the whole, he moved his family into it, where he was suffered to remain but nine months, when he was cheated out of his property by a white man, and driven out of door! And is not this the case generally? Can a man of colour buy a piece of land and keep it peaceably? Will not some white man try to get it from him, even if it is in a mud hole? I need not comment any farther on a subject, which all both black and white, will readily admit. But I must, really, observe that in this very city, when a man of colour dies, if he owned any real estate it most generally falls into the hands of some white person. The wife and children of the deceased may weep and lament if they please, but the estate will be kept snug enough by its white possessor.

But to prove farther that the condition of the Israelites was better under the Egyptians than ours is under the whites. I call upon the professing Christians, I call upon the philanthropist, I call upon the very tyrant himself, to show me a page of history, either sacred or profane, on which a verse can be found, which main-tains, that the Egyptians heaped the insupportable insult upon the children of Israel, by telling them that they were not of the human family. Can the whites deny this charge? Have they not, after having reduced us to the deplorable condition of slaves under their feet, held us up as descending originally from the tribes of Mon-keys or Orang-Outangs? O! my God! I appeal to every man of feeling—is not this insupportable? Is it not heaping the most gross insult upon our miseries, because they have got us under their feet and we cannot help ourselves? Oh! pity us we pray thee, Lord Jesus, Master.—Has Mr. Jefferson declared to the world, that we are inferior to the whites, both in the endowments of our bodies and our minds? It is indeed surprising, that a man of such great learning, combined with such excellent natural parts, should speak so of a set of men in chains. I do not know what to compare it to, unless, like putting one wild deer in an iron cage, where it will be secured, and hold another by the side of the same, then let it go, and expect the one in the cage to run as fast as the one at liberty. So far, my brethren, were the Egyptians from heaping these insults upon their slaves, that Pharaoh's daughter took Moses, a son of Israel for her own, as will appear by the following.

"And Pharaoh's daughter said unto her, [Moses' mother] take this child away, and nurse it for me, and I will pay thee thy wages. And the woman took the child and nursed it.

"And the child grew, and she brought him unto Pharaoh's daughter and he became her son. And she called his name Moses: and she said because I drew him out of the water."

In all probability, Moses would have become Prince Regent to the throne, and no doubt, in process of time but he would have been seated on the throne of Egypt. But he had rather suffer shame, with the people of God, than to enjoy pleasures with that wicked people for a season. O! that the coloured people were long since of Moses' excellent disposition, instead of courting favour with, and telling news and lies to our natural enemies, against each other—aiding them to keep their hellish chains of slavery upon us. Would we not long before this time, have been respectable men, instead of such wretched victims of oppression as we are? Would they be able to drag our mothers, our fathers, our wives, our children and ourselves, around the world in chains and handcuffs as they do, to dig up gold and silver for them and theirs? This question, my brethren, I leave for you to digest: and may God Almighty force it home to your hearts. Remember that unless you are united, keeping your tongues within your teeth, you will be afraid to trust your secrets to each other, and thus perpetuate our miseries under the Christians!!!!

ADDITION.—Remember, also to lay humble at the feet of our Lord and Master Jesus Christ, with prayers and fastings. Let our enemies go on with their butcheries, and at once fill up their cup. Never make an attempt to gain our freedom or natural right, from under our cruel oppressor, and murderers, until you see your way clear—when that hour arrives and you move, be not afraid or dismayed; for be you assured that Jesus Christ the King of heaven and of earth who is the God of justice and of armies, will surely go before you. And those enemies who have for hundreds of years stolen our rights, and kept us ignorant of Him and His divine worship, he will remove. Millions of whom, are this day, so ignorant and avaricious, that they cannot conceive how God can have an attribute of justice, and show mercy to us because it pleased Him to make us black—which colour, Mr. Jefferson calls unfortunate!!!!!! As though we are not as thankful to our God, for having made us as it pleased himself, as they, (the whites,) are for having made them white. They think because they hold us in their infernal chains of slavery, that we wish to be white, or of their color—but they are dreadfully deceived—we wish to be just as it pleased our Creator to have made us, and no avaricious and unmerciful wretches, have any business to make slaves of, or hold us in slavery. How would they like for us to make slaves of, and hold them in cruel slavery, and murder them as they do us?—But is Mr. Jefferson's assertions true? viz. "that it is unfortunate for us that our Creator has been pleased to make us black." We will not take his say so, for the fact. The world will have an opportunity to see whether it is unfortunate for us, that our Creator has made us darker than the whites. . . .

I have been for years troubling the pages of historians, to find out what our fathers have done to the white Christians of America, to merit such condign punishment as they have inflicted on them, and do continue to inflict on us their children. But I must aver, that my researches have hitherto been to no effect. I have therefore, come to the immoveable conclusion, that they (Americans) have, and do continue to punish us for nothing else, but for enriching them and their country. For I cannot conceive of anything else. Nor will I ever believe otherwise, until the Lord shall convince me.

The world knows, that slavery as it existed among the Romans, (which was the primary cause of their destruction) was, comparatively speaking, no more than a cypher, when compared with ours under the Americans. Indeed I should not have noticed the Roman slaves, had not the very learned and penetrating Mr. Jefferson said, "when a master was murdered, all his slaves in the same house, or within hearing, were condemned to death."—Here let me ask Mr. Jefferson, (but he is gone to answer at the bar of God, for the deeds done in his body while living,) I therefore ask the whole American people, had I not rather die, or be put to death, than to be a slave to any tyrant, who takes not only my own, but my wife and children's lives by the inches? Yea, would I meet death with avidity far! far!! in preference to such servile submission to the murderous hands of tyrants. Mr. Jefferson's very severe remarks on us have been so extensively argued upon by men whose attainments in literature, I shall never be able to reach, that I would not have meddled with it, were it not to solicit each of my brethren, who has the spirit of a man, to buy a copy of Mr. Jefferson's "Notes on Virginia," and put it in the hand of his son. For let no one of us suppose that the refutations which have been written by our white friends are enough—they are whites—we are blacks. We, and the world wish to see the charges of Mr. Jefferson refuted by the blacks themselves, according to their chance; for we must remember that what the whites have written respecting this subject, is other men's labours, and did not emanate from the blacks. I know well, that there are some talents and learning among the coloured people of this country, which we have not a chance to develope, in consequence of oppression; but our oppression ought not to hinder us from acquiring all we can. For we will have a chance to develope them by and by. God will not suffer us, always to be oppressed. Our sufferings will come to an end, in spite of all the Americans this side of eternity. Then we will want all the learning and talents among ourselves, and perhaps more, to govern ourselves.—"Every dog must have its day," the American's is coming to an end.

But let us review Mr. Jefferson's remarks respecting us some further. Comparing our miserable fathers, with the learned philosophers of Greece, he says: "Yet notwithstanding these and other discouraging circumstances among the Romans, their slaves were often their rarest artists. They excelled too, in science, insomuch as to be usually employed as tutors to their master's children; Epictetus, Terence and Phaedrus, were slaves,—but they were of the race of whites. It is not their condition then, but nature, which has produced the distinction." See this, my brethren!! Do you believe that this assertion is swallowed by millions of the whites? Do you know that Mr. Jefferson was one of as great characters as ever lived among the whites? See his writings for the world, and public labours for the United States of America. Do you believe that the assertions of such a man, will pass away into oblivion unobserved by this people and the world? If you do you are much mistaken—See how the American people treat us—have we souls in our bodies? Are we men who have any spirits at all? I know that there are many swell-bellied fellows among us, whose greatest object is to fill their stomachs. Such I do not mean—I am after those who know and feel, that we are MEN, as well as other people; to them, I say, that unless we try to refute Mr. Jefferson's arguments respecting us, we will only establish them.

But the slaves among the Romans. Every body who has read history, knows, that as soon as a slave among the Romans obtained his freedom, he could rise to the greatest eminence in the State, and there was no law instituted to hinder a slave from buying his freedom. Have not the Americans instituted laws to hinder us from obtaining our freedom? Do any deny this charge? Read the laws of Virginia, North Carolina, etc. Further: have not the Americans instituted laws to prohibit a man of colour from obtaining and holding any office whatever, under the government of the United States of America? Now, Mr. Jefferson tells us, that our condition is not so hard, as the slaves were under the Romans!!!!!!

It is time for me to bring this article to a close. But before I close it, I must observe to my brethren that at the close of the first Revolution in this country, with Great Britain, there were but thirteen States in the Union, now there are twenty four, most of which are slave-holding States, and the whites are dragging us around in chains and in handcuffs, to their new States and Territories to work their mines and farms, to enrich them and their children—and millions of them believing firmly that we being a little darker than they, were made by our Creator to be an inheritance to them and their children for ever—the same as a parcel of brutes.

Are we MEN!!—I ask you, O my brethren! are we MEN? Did our Creator make us to be slaves to dust and ashes like ourselves? Are they not dying worms as well as we? Have they not to make their appearance before the tribunal of Heaven, to answer for the deeds done in the body, as well as we? Have we any other Master but Jesus Christ alone? Is he not their Master as well as ours?—What right then, have we to obey and call any other Master, but Himself? How we could be so submissive to a gang of men, whom we cannot tell whether they are as good as ourselves or not, I never could conceive. However, this is shut up with the Lord, and we cannot precisely tell—but I declare, we judge men by their works.

The whites have always been an unjust, jealous, unmerciful, avaricious and blood-thirsty set of beings, always seeking after power and authority.—We view them all over the confederacy of Greece, where they were first known to be any thing, (in consequence of education) we see them there, cutting each other's throats—trying to subject each other to wretchedness and misery—to effect which, they used all kinds of deceitful, unfair, and unmerciful means. We view them next in Rome, where the spirit of tyranny and deceit raged still higher. We view them in Gaul, Spain, and in Britain.—In fine, we view them all over Europe, together with what were scattered about in Asia and Africa, as heathens, and we see them acting more like devils than accountable men. But some may ask, did not the blacks of Africa, and the mulattoes of Asia, go on in the same way as did the whites of Europe. I answer, no—they never were half so avaricious, deceitful and unmerciful as the whites, according to their knowledge.

But we will leave the whites or Europeans as heathens, and take a view of them as Christians, in which capacity we see them as cruel, if not more so than ever. In fact, take them as a body, they are ten times more cruel, avaricious and unmerciful than ever they were; for while they were heathens, they were bad enough it is true, but it is positively a fact that they were not quite so audacious as to go and take vessel loads of men, women and children, and in cold blood, and through devilishness, throw them into the sea, and murder them in all kind of ways. While they were heathens, they were too ignorant for such barbarity. But being Christians, enlightened and sensible, they are completely prepared for such hellish cruelties. Now suppose God were to give them more sense, what would they do? If it were possible, would they not dethrone Jehovah and seat themselves upon his throne? I therefore, in the name and fear of the Lord God of Heaven and of earth, divested of prejudice either on the side of my colour or that of the whites, advance my suspicion of them, whether they are as good by nature as we are or not. Their actions, since they were known as a people, have been the reverse, I do indeed suspect them, but this, as I before observed, is shut up with the Lord, we cannot exactly tell, it will be proved in succeeding generations.— The whites have had the essence of the gospel as it was preached by my master and his apostles—the Ethiopians have not, who are to have it in its meridian splendor—the Lord will give it to them to their satisfaction. I hope and pray my God, that they will make good use of it, that it may be well with them.

William Lloyd Garrison (1805–1879)

In the years after the American Revolution, Northern states gradually eliminated slavery. By the 1820s, antislavery people were arguing for the gradual emancipation of all slaves through a process whereby the federal government would compensate slaveholders for their property and the freedmen would be relocated to Africa. Indeed, during James Monroe's presidency, several thousand freed slaves were sent to the newly established nation of Liberia in West Africa. At this time William Lloyd Garrison was in Baltimore writing for the Genius of Universal Emancipation, *a gradualist antislavery newspaper published by Quaker William Lundy. By 1830, however, Garrison no longer viewed gradualism as a viable strategy to eliminate slavery. He moved to Boston and in January 1831 began publishing his own newspaper,* The Liberator. *In the first issue, he condemned the gradualist approach in no uncertain terms and advocated the* immediate *abolition of slavery. The intensity of his views and the uncompromising nature of his language alarmed and distressed Southern slaveholders so thoroughly that they began more earnestly defending slavery. By 1832, Garrison had founded the New England Anti-Slavery Society and in 1833 the American Anti-Slavery Society. The state of Georgia offered a $5000 reward for Garrison's capture, trial, and conviction. In 1835, he was rescued from a proslavery mob that had dragged him through the streets of Boston with a rope around his neck when the mayor intervened and put him in jail. While incarcerated, Garrison wrote on the wall of his cell, "Wm. Lloyd Garrison was put into this cell Wednesday afternoon, October 21, 1835, to save him from the violence of a 'respectable and influential' mob, who sought to destroy him for preaching the abominable and dangerous doctrine that 'all men are created equal. . . .'"*

Never afraid to challenge the powers that be, Garrison became increasingly radical in the 1840s and 1850s. One of his most controversial acts was the public burning of a copy of the U.S. Constitution on July 4, 1854. To Garrison, the Constitution, because it acquiesced in the institution of slavery, was "an agreement with death and a covenant with hell." By this time the debate over slavery had become so intense that many Americans began to believe that the only resolution would be through civil war.

THE LIBERATOR, VOL. I, NO. I, JANUARY I, 1831

To the Public

In the month of August, I issued proposals for publishing "*The Liberator*" in Washington City; but the enterprise, though hailed in different sections of the country, was palsied by public indifference. Since that time, the removal of the *Genius of Universal Emancipation* to the Seat of Government has rendered less imperious the establishment of a similar periodical in that quarter.

During my recent tour for the purpose of exciting the minds of the people by a series of discourses on the subject of slavery, every place that I visited gave

SOURCE: *The Liberator* (Boston), January 1, 1831.

fresh evidencĕ of the fact, that a greater revolution in public sentiment was to be effected in the free states—*and particularly in New England*—than at the south. I found contempt more bitter, opposition more active, detraction more relentless, prejudice more stubborn, and apathy more frozen, than among slave owners themselves. Of course, there were individual exceptions to the contrary. This state of things afflicted, but did not dishearten me. I determined, at every hazard, to lift up the standard of emancipation in the eyes of the nation, *within sight of Bunker Hill and in the birth place of liberty*. That standard is now unfurled; and long may it float, unhurt by the spoliations of time or the missiles of a desperate foe—yea, till every chain be broken, and every bondman set free! Let Southern oppressors tremble—let their secret abettors tremble—let their Northern apologists tremble—let all the enemies of the persecuted blacks tremble.

I deem the publication of my original Prospectus unnecessary, as it has obtained a wide circulation. The principles therein inculcated will be steadily pursued in this paper, excepting that I shall not array myself as the political partisan of any man. In defending the great cause of human rights, I wish to derive the assistance of all religions and of all parties.

Assenting to the "self evident truth" maintained in the American Declaration of Independence, "that all men are created equal, and endowed by their Creator with certain inalienable rights—among which are life, liberty and the pursuit of happiness," I shall strenuously contend for the immediate enfranchisement of our slave population. In Park-Street Church, on the Fourth of July, 1829, in an address on slavery, I unreflectingly assented to the popular but pernicious doctrine of *gradual* abolition. I seize this opportunity to make a full and unequivocal recantation, and thus publicly to ask pardon of my God, of my country, and of my brethren the poor slaves, for having uttered a sentiment so full of timidity, injustice and absurdity. A similar recantation, from my pen, was published in the *Genius of Universal Emancipation* at Baltimore, in September, 1829. My conscience is now satisfied.

I am aware, that many object to the severity of my language; but is there not cause for severity? I *will be* as harsh as truth, and as uncompromising as justice. On this subject, I do not wish to think, or speak, or write, with moderation. No! No! Tell a man whose house is on fire, to give a moderate alarm; tell him to moderately rescue his wife from the hands of the ravisher; tell the mother to gradually extricate her babe from the fire into which it has fallen;—but urge me not to use moderation in a cause like the present. I am in earnest—I will not equivocate—I will not excuse—I will not retreat a single inch—**AND I *WILL BE HEARD***. The apathy of the people is enough to make every statue leap from its pedestal, and to hasten the resurrection of the dead.

It is pretended, that I am retarding the cause of emancipation by the coarseness of my invective, and the precipitancy of my measures. *The charge is not true.* On this question my influence,—humble as it is,—is felt at this moment to a considerable extent, and shall be felt in coming years—not perniciously, but beneficially—not as a curse, but as a blessing; and posterity will bear testimony that I was right. I desire to thank God, that he enables me to disregard "the fear of man which bringeth a snare," and to speak his truth in its simplicity and power. . . .

William Lloyd Garrison.

William Apess (1798–1839)

William Apess, a Pequot Indian, was "bound out" (like many other homeless children in the early nineteenth century) to a white family in Massachusetts. By the time he was 15, he had lived with several different white families and had adapted reasonably well to white society. After a stint in the army during the War of 1812, he returned to Connecticut in 1817 and became a lay preacher for several years until his official ordination as a Methodist minister in 1829. In that same year he published A Son of the Forest *(the first autobiography ever written by an Indian) and then, four years later, a second personal memoir,* The Experiences of Five Christian Indians of the Pequod Tribe. *In this book, his essay "An Indian's Looking-Glass for the White Man" is a strong indictment, from a Christian perspective, of the whites' treatment of the Indians. Effectively using the Bible to condemn racism, Apess became one of the most articulate nineteenth-century Indian protest voices. While continuing to work for Indian rights in the 1830s, he published two more important protest works:* Indian Nullification of the Unconstitutional Laws of Massachusetts, Relative to the Marshpee [sic] Tribe *(1835) and* Eulogy on King Philip *(1836). But after this last book was published, he seems to have dropped out of sight, and very little is known about the rest of his life.*

"An Indian's Looking-Glass for the White Man," 1833

Having a desire to place a few things before my fellow creatures who are traveling with me to the grave, and to that God who is the maker and preserver both of the white man and the Indian, whose abilities are the same and who are to be judged by one God, who will show no favor to outward appearances but will judge righteousness. Now I ask if degradation has not been heaped long enough upon the Indians? And if so, can there not be a compromise? Is it right to hold and

Source: Barry O'Connell, ed., *On Our Own Ground: The Complete Writings of William Apess, A Pequot* (Amherst: University of Massachusetts Press, 1992), 155–161.

promote prejudices? If not, why not put them all away? I mean here, among those who are civilized. It may be that many are ignorant of the situation of many of my brethren with the limits of New England. Let me for a few moments turn your attention to the reservations in the different states of New England, and, with but few exceptions, who shall find them as follows: the most mean, abject, miserable race of beings in the world—a complete place of prodigality and prostitution.

Let a gentleman and lady of integrity and respectability visit these places, and they would be surprised; as they wandered from one hut to the other they would view, with the females who are left alone, children half-starved and some almost as naked as they came into the world. And it is a fact that I have seen them as much so—while the females are left without protection, and are seduced by white men, and are finally left to be common prostitutes for them and to be destroyed by that burning, fiery curse, that has swept millions, both of red and white men, into the grave with sorrow and disgrace—rum. One reason why they are left so is because their most sensible and active men are absent at sea. Another reason is because they are made to believe they are minors and have not the abilities given them from God to take care of themselves, without it is to see to a few little articles, such as baskets and brooms. Their land is in common stock, and they have nothing to make them enterprising.

Another reason is because those men who are Agents, many of them are unfaithful and care not whether the Indians live or die; they are much imposed upon by their neighbors, who have no principle. They would think it no crime to go upon Indian lands and cut and carry off their most valuable timber, or anything else they chose; and I doubt not but they think it clear gain. Another reason is because they have no education to take care of themselves; if they had, I would risk them to take care of their own property.

Now I will ask if the Indians are not called the most ingenious people among us. And are they not said to be men of talents? And I would ask: Could there be a more efficient way to distress and murder them by inches than the way they have taken? And there is no people in the world but who may be destroyed in the same way. Now, if these people are what they are held up in our view to be, I would take the liberty to ask why they are not brought forward and pains taken to educate them, to give them all a common education, and those of the brightest and first-rate talents put forward and held up to office. Perhaps some unholy, unprincipled men would cry out, "The skin was not good enough"; but stop, friends—I am not talking about the skin but about principles. I would ask if there cannot be as good feelings and principles under a red skin as there can be under a white. And let me ask: Is it not on the account of a bad principle that we who are red children have had to suffer so much as we have? And let me ask: Did not this bad principle proceed from the whites or their forefathers? And I would ask: Is it worthwhile to nourish it any longer? If not then let us have a change, although some men no doubt will spout their corrupt principles against it, that are in the halls of legislation and elsewhere. But I presume this kind of talk will seem surprising and horrible. I do not see why it should so long as they (the whites) say that they think as much of us as they do of themselves.

This I have heard repeatedly, from the most respectable gentlemen and ladies—and having heard so much precept, I should now wish to see the example. And I would ask who has a better right to look for these things than the naturalist himself—the candid man would say none.

I know that many say they are willing, perhaps the majority of the people, that we should enjoy our rights and privileges as they do. If so, I would ask, Why are not we protected in our persons and property throughout the Union? Is it not because there reigns in the breast of many who are leaders a most unrighteous, unbecoming, and impure black principle, and as corrupt and unholy as it can be—while these very same unfeeling, self-esteemed characters pretend to take the skin as a pretext to keep us from our unalienable and lawful rights? I would ask you if you would like to be disfranchised from all your rights, merely because your skin is white, and for no other crime. I'll venture to say, these very characters who hold the skin to be such a barrier in the way would be the first to cry out, "Injustice! awful injustice!"

But, reader, I acknowledge that this is a confused world, and I am not seeking for office, but merely placing before you the black inconsistency that you place before me—which is ten times blacker than any skin that you will find in the universe. And now let me exhort you to do away with that principle, as it appears ten times worse in the sight of God and candid men than skins of color—more disgraceful than all the skins that Jehovah ever made. If black or red skins or any other skin of color is disgraceful to God, it appears that he has disgraced himself a great deal—for he has made fifteen colored people to one white and placed them here upon this earth.

Now let me ask you, white man, if it is a disgrace for to eat, drink, and sleep with the image of God, or sit, or walk and talk with them. Or have you the folly to think that the white man, being one in fifteen or sixteen, are the only beloved images of God? Assemble all nations together in your imagination, and then let the whites be seated among them, and then let us look for the whites, and I doubt not it would be hard finding them; for to the rest of the nations, they are still but a handful. Now suppose these skins were put together, and each skin has its national crimes written upon it—which skin do you think would have the greatest? I will ask one question more. Can you charge the Indians with robbing a nation almost of their whole continent, and murdering their women and children, and then depriving the remainder of their lawful rights, that nature and God require them to have? And to cap the climax, rob another nation to till their grounds and welter out their days under the lash with hunger and fatigue under the scorching rays of a burning sun? I should look at all the skins, and I know that when I cast my eye upon that white skin, and if I saw those crimes written upon it, I should enter my protest against it immediately and cleave to that which is more honorable. And I can tell you that I am satisfied with the manner of my creation, fully—whether others are or not.

But we will strive to penetrate more fully into the conduct of those who profess to have pure principles and who tell us to follow Jesus Christ and imitate him and have his Spirit. Let us see if they come anywhere near him and his ancient disciples. The first thing we are to look at are his precepts, of which we will mention a few. "Thou shalt love the Lord thy God with all thy heart, with all thy soul, with all thy mind, and with all thy strength. The second is like unto it. Thou shalt love thy neighbor as thyself. On these two precepts hang all the law and the prophets" (Matt. 22:37, 38, 39, 40). "By this shall all men know that they are my disciples, if ye have love one to another" (John 13:35). Our Lord left this special command with his followers, that they should love one another.

Again, John in his Epistles says, "He who loveth God loveth his brother also" (1 John 4:21). "Let us not love in word but in deed" (1 John 3: 18). "Let your love be without dissimulation. See that ye love one another with a pure heart fervently" (1 Peter 1:22). "If any man say, I love God, and hateth his brother, he is a liar" (1 John 4:20). "Whosoever hateth his brother is a murderer, and no murderer hath eternal life abiding in him" (1 John 3:15). The first thing that takes our attention is the saying of Jesus, "Thou shalt love," etc. The first question I would ask my brethren in the ministry, as well as that of the membership: What is love, or its effects? Now, if they who teach are not essentially affected with pure love, the love of God, how can they teach as they ought? Again, the holy teachers of old said, "Now if any man have not the spirit of Christ, he is none of his" (Rom. 8:9). Now, my brethren in the ministry, let me ask you a few sincere questions. Did you ever hear or read of Christ teaching his disciples that they ought to despise one because his skin was different from theirs? Jesus Christ being a Jew, and those of his Apostles certainly were not whites—and did not he who completed the plan of salvation complete it for the whites as well as for the Jews, and others? And were not the whites the most degraded people on the earth at that time? And none were more so, for they sacrificed their children to dumb idols! And did not St. Paul labor more abundantly for building up a Christian nation among you than any of the Apostles? And you know as well as I that you are not indebted to a principle beneath a white skin for your religious services but to a colored one.

What then is the matter now? Is not religion the same now under a colored skin as it ever was? If so, I would ask, why is not a man of color respected? You may say, as many say, we have white men enough. But was this the spirit of Christ and his Apostles? If it had been, there would not have been one white preacher in the world—for Jesus Christ never would have imparted his grace or word to them, for he could forever have withheld it from them. But we find that Jesus Christ and his Apostles never looked at the outward appearances. Jesus in particular looked at the hearts, and his Apostles through him, being discerners of the spirit, looked at their fruit without any regard to the skin, color, or nations; as St. Paul himself speaks, "Where there is neither Greek nor Jew, circumcision nor uncircumcision, Barbarian nor Scythian, bond nor free—but Christ is all, and in all" (Col. 3: 11). If you can find a sprit like Jesus Christ and his Apostles prevailing now in any of the white congregations, I should like to know it. I ask: Is it not the case that everybody that is not white is treated with contempt and counted as barbarians? And I ask if the word of God justifies the white man in so doing. When the prophets prophesied, of whom did they speak? When they spoke of heathens, was it not the whites and others who were counted Gentiles? And I ask if all nations with the exception of the Jews were not counted heathens. And according to the writings of some, it could not mean the Indians, for they are counted Jews. And now I would ask: Why is all this distinction made among these Christian societies? I would ask: What is all this ado about missionary societies, if it be not to Christianize those who are not Christians? And what is it for? To degrade them worse, to bring them into society where they must welter out their days in disgrace merely because their skin is of a different complexion. What folly it is to try to make the state of human society worse than it is. How astonished some may be at this—but let me ask: Is it not so? Let me refer you to the churches only. And, my brethren, is there any agreement? Do brethren and sisters love one another? Do they not rather hate one another? Outward forms and ceremonies, the lusts of the flesh, the lusts of the eye, and pride of life is of more value to many professors than the love of God shed abroad in their hearts, or an attachment to his altar, to his ordinances, or to his children. But you may ask: Who are the children of God? Perhaps you may say, none but white. If so, the word of the Lord is not true.

I will refer you to St. Peter's precepts (Acts 10): "God is no respecter of persons," etc. Now if this is the case, my white brother, what better are you than God? And if no better, why do you, who profess his Gospel and to have his spirit, act so contrary to it? Let me ask why the men of a different skin are so despised. Why are not they educated and placed in your pulpits? I ask if his services well performed are not as good as if a white man performed them. I ask if a marriage or a funeral ceremony or the ordinance of the Lord's house would not be as acceptable in the sight of God as though he was white. And if so, why is it not to you? I ask again: Why is it not as acceptable to have men to exercise their office in one place as well as in another? Perhaps you will say that if we admit you to all of these privileges you will want more. I expect that I can guess what that is—Why, say you, there would be intermarriages. How that would be I am not able to say—and if it should be, it would be nothing strange or new to me; for I can assure you that I know a great many that have intermarried, both of the whites and the Indians—and many are their sons and daughters and people, too, of the first respectability. And I could point to some in the famous city of Boston and elsewhere. You may look now at the disgraceful act in the state law passed by the legislature of Massachusetts, and behold the fifty-pound fine levied upon any clergyman or justice of the peace that dare to encourage the laws of God and nature by a legitimate union in holy wedlock between the Indians and whites. I would ask how this looks to your lawmakers. I would ask if this corresponds with your sayings—that you think as much of the Indians as you do of the whites. I do not wonder that you blush, many of you, while you read; for many have broken the ill-fated laws made by man to hedge up the laws of God and nature. I would ask if they who have made the law have not broken it—but there is no other state in New England that has this law but Massachusetts; and I think, as many of you do not, that you have done yourselves no credit.

But as I am not looking for a wife, having one of the finest cast, as you no doubt would understand while you read her experience and travail of soul in the way to heaven, you will see that it is not my object. And if I had none, I should not want anyone to take my right from me and choose a wife for me; for I think that I or any of my brethren have a right to choose a wife for themselves as well as the whites—and as the whites have taken the liberty to choose my brethren, the Indians, hundreds and thousands of them, as partners in life, I believe the Indians have as much right to choose their partners among the whites if they wish. I would ask you if you can see anything inconsistent in your conduct and talk about the Indians. And if you do, I hope you will try to become more consistent. Now, if the Lord Jesus Christ, who is counted by all to be a Jew—and it is well known that the Jews are a colored people, especially those living in the East, where Christ was born—and if he should appear among us, would he not be shut out of doors by many, very quickly? And by those too who profess religion?

By what you read, you may learn how deep your principles are. I should say they were skin-deep. I should not wonder if some of the most selfish and ignorant would spout a charge of their principles now and then at me. But I would ask: How are you to love your neighbors as yourself? Is it to cheat them? Is it to wrong them in anything? Now, to cheat them out of any of their rights is robbery. And I ask: Can you deny that you are not robbing the Indians daily, and many others? But at last you may think I am what is called a hard and uncharitable man. But not so. I believe there are many who would not hesitate to advocate our cause; and those too who are men of fame and respectability—as well as ladies of honor and virtue. There is a Webster, and Everett, and a Wirt, and many others who are distinguished characters—besides a host of my fellow citizens, who advocate our cause daily. And how I congratulate such noble spirits—how they are to be prized and valued; for they are well calculated to promote the happiness of mankind. They well know that man was made for society, and not for hissing-stocks and outcasts. And when such a principle as this lies within the hearts of men, how much it is like its God—and how it honors its Maker—and how it imitates the feelings of the Good Samaritan, that had his wounds bound up, who had been among thieves and robbers.

Do not get tired, ye noble-hearted—only think how many poor Indians want their wounds done up daily; the Lord will reward you, and pray you stop not till this tree of distinction shall be leveled to the earth, and the mantle of prejudice torn from every American heart—then shall peace pervade the Union.

Laborers of Boston

Although many contemporaries, as well as later historians, have called the Jacksonian era the Age of the Common Man because of the elimination of property qualifications for white men's right to vote and because of President Jackson's assault on the moneyed interests of the Northeast, it was a time of considerable inequality and exploitation of the

lower classes. Many workers, including the Lowell Mill girls (in 1834),
began agitating against exploitive employers and sought to improve their
working conditions, wages, and hours. In 1835, in Boston, after three
strikes had vainly sought to reduce the work day from 13 hours to 10, a
group of carpenters, masons, and stonecutters issued a circular in which
they once again articulated their position.

TEN-HOUR CIRCULAR, 1835

. . . In the name of the Carpenters, Masons, and Stone Cutters, [we] do respectfully represent—

That we are now engaged in a cause, which is not only of vital importance
to ourselves, our families, and our children, but is equally interesting and
equally important to every Mechanic in the United States and the whole world.
We are contending for the recognition of the Natural Right to dispose of our
own time in such quantities as we deem and believe to be most conducive to our
own happiness, and the welfare of all those engaged in Manual Labor.

The work in which we are now engaged is neither more nor less than a contest between Money and Labor: Capital, which can only be made productive by
labor, is endeavoring to crush labor the only source of all wealth.

We have been too long subjected to the odious, cruel, unjust, and tyrannical
system which compels the operative Mechanic to exhaust his physical and mental powers by excessive toil, until he has no desire but to eat and sleep, and in
many cases he has no power to do either from extreme debility.

We contend that no man or body of men, have a right to require of us that
we should toil as we have hitherto done under the old system of labor.

We go further. No man or body of men who require such excessive labor
can be friends to the country or the Rights of Man. We also say, that we have
rights, and we have duties to perform as American Citizens and members of
society, which forbid us to dispose of more than Ten Hours for a day's work.

We cannot, we will not, longer be mere slaves to inhuman, insatiable and
unpitying avarice. We have taken a firm and decided stand, to obtain the
acknowledgment of those rights to enable us to perform those duties to God,
our Country and ourselves.

Our opponents have no arguments to adduce against our determination.
We have invited them to the contest in a fair and honorable manner, but they
have declined. They have used trickery, obloquy and abuse instead of reasoning. We warn all brother Mechanics, especially Carpenters, Masons and Stone
Cutters, to beware of advertisements for hands. Be assured in all cases from this
time, now, henceforth and forever, that whenever a Carpenter, Mason or Stone
Cutter, advertises for a large number of hands as wanted in Boston or any other

SOURCE: Irving Mark and E. I. Schwaab, *The Faith of Our Fathers* (New York: Alfred A.
Knopf, Inc., 1952), 342–343.

city or town, that it is a mere trick, to deceive and oppress you. They never guarantee to you one single day's work, and you will, as in all similar cases, get only your labor for your pains. There are men enough now in this city who are skillful, able, and willing to work on an equitable and just method, and the advertisements for hands are only traps to "Catch Gulls." In no instance, in no part of the United States have such calls for hands been designed for any other purpose, than the most unjustifiable and wicked deception.

Beware also of the offers of high wages. We have not asked for an increase of wages, but are willing that demand and supply should govern the price as it does that of all other disposable property. To induce you to assist them to form shackles and fetters for your own limbs and your own minds, they offer you an increase of wages. Will you be deceived by this old and shallow artifice? We believe you will not—we know you will not.

When you understand that we are contending for your rights, for the rights of your families and your children as well as our own, we feel full confidence that you will make no movement to retard the accomplishment of the glorious and holy enterprise, both yours and ours. It is for the rights of humanity we contend. Our cause is the cause of philanthropy. Our opposers resort to the most degrading obloquy to injure us. Not degrading to us, but to the authors of such unmerited opprobrium which they attempt to cast upon us. They tell us "We shall spend all our hours of leisure in Drunkenness and Debauchery if the hours of labor are reduced."

We hurl from us the base, ungenerous, ungrateful, detestable, cruel, malicious slander, with scorn and indignation.

We assert and challenge the world to controvert the position that excessive labor has been the immediate cause of more intemperance than all other causes combined. Physical exhaustion craves and will have excitement of some kind, and the cause of Temperance never will prevail until slavery among Mechanics shall cease from the land.

We are friends to temperance "in all things," but any man who requires of us excessive labor is intemperate; if he is not actuated by ardent spirits, he is controlled by a spirit of inhumanity equally fatal to human happiness.

It is not a long period since some of our opposers made it a rule to furnish a half pint of ardent spirits to each man, every day, for no other purpose than to urge the physical powers to excessive exertion; thank God, those days have passed away, but they will ever remain a foul blot on the pages of History. Now we are told that excessive labor is the only security against intemperance.

To show the utter fallacy of their idiotic reasoning, if reasoning it may be called, we have only to say, they employ us about eight months in the year during the longest and the hottest days, and in short days, hundreds of us remain idle for want of work, for three or four months, when our expenses must of course be the heaviest during winter. When the long days again appear, our guardians set us to work as they say, "to keep us from getting drunk." No fear has ever been expressed by these benevolent employers respecting our morals while we are idle in short days, through their avarice. We would not be too severe on our employers, they are slaves to the Capitalists, as we are to them. "The power behind" their "throne is greater than the throne itself." But we cannot bear to be the servant of servants and slaves to oppression, let the source be where it may. We will be so no longer, for it is rank injustice. Further, they threaten to starve us into submission to their will. Starve us to prevent us from getting drunk! Wonderful Wisdom! Refined Benevolence! Exalted Philanthropy!

The property holders in this city are dependent night and day upon the Mechanics, to man their Fire Engines; good policy might seem to dictate to them the expediency of providing a new set of firemen, before they starve the present ones or drive them to the extremity of leaving their Engine Houses desolate unto them. We are willing to bear our portion of the burthens, and perform our part of the services of social life, if we can be treated as men and not as beasts of burthen. We claim by the blood of our fathers, shed on our battle-fields in the War of the Revolution, the rights of American Freemen, and no earthly power shall resist our righteous claims with impunity. When we hear men, not only Employers, but "highminded" and honorable Merchants and Capitalists, as they are called, who are not only dependent on us for the protection of their property, but for a safe night's rest. When we hear such men say that we shall all become drunkards, and they intend to starve us into submission to their high will, we pity their infatuation and have painful apprehensions for the safety of the social Fabric. But the public mind is with us. The glorious work goes nobly on. Many employers have acceded to our reasonable demands, and in a few days we sincerely hope and believe that the victory over old prejudices and antiquated customs will be triumphantly complete.

Mechanics of Boston—stand firm—Be true to your selves. Now is the time to enroll your names on the scroll of history as the undaunted enemies of oppression, as the enemies of mental, moral and physical degradation, as the friends of the human race.

The God of the Universe has given us time, health and strength. We utterly deny the right of any man to dictate to us how much of it we shall sell. Brethren in the City, Towns and Country, our cause is yours, the cause of Liberty, the cause of God. . . .

Angelina Grimké (1805–1879) and Sarah Grimké (1792–1873)

Angelina and Sarah Grimké, daughters of a South Carolina slaveholder, disapproved of slavery all their lives. In the 1820s, the sisters moved to Philadelphia, where they became Quakers and eventually prominent abolitionists and feminists. In the 1830s, William Lloyd Garrison published one of Angelina's letters in his newspaper The Liberator, *and shortly thereafter both sisters began traveling to speak at antislavery meetings. In 1836, Angelina published her first pamphlet, an appeal to Southern women to join the abolition crusade, not only because the institution was evil but also because slave owners were fathering children with their slaves. Slavery, thus, was destroying the sanctity of marriage and driving white women deeper into subjection. This pamphlet caused quite a furor among a population that was horrified that a woman should be so outspoken—especially about such a volatile issue. As both sisters continued to speak publicly and publish impassioned indictments of slavery, they were increasingly attacked, even by other abolitionists, because of their gender. The attacks convinced the sisters that they had to become feminists as well as abolitionists.*

In the following excerpts from Angelina Grimké's Appeal to the Christian Women of the South *and Sarah Grimké's "The Original Equality of Woman," the sisters tackle the popular arguments that made use of the Bible to validate the institution of slavery and the subjugation of women.*

APPEAL TO THE CHRISTIAN WOMEN OF THE SOUTH, 1836

RESPECTED FRIENDS,

. . . All that sophistry of argument which has been employed to prove, that although it is sinful to send to Africa to procure men and women as slaves, who have never been in slavery, that still, it is not sinful to keep those in bondage who have come down by inheritance, will be utterly overthrown. We must come back to the good old doctrine of our forefathers who declared to the world, "this self evident truth that *all* men are created equal, and that they have certain *inalienable* rights among which are life, *liberty*, and the pursuit of happiness." It is even a greater absurdity to suppose a man can be legally born a slave under *our free Republican* Government, than under the petty despotisms of barbarian Africa. If then, we have no right to enslave an African, surely we can have none to enslave an American; if it is a self evident truth that *all* men, every where and of every color are born equal, and have an *inalienable right to liberty*, then it is equally true that *no* man can be born a slave, and no man can ever *rightfully* be reduced to *involuntary* bondage and held as a slave, however fair may be the claim of his master or mistress through wills and title-deeds.

But after all, it may be said, our fathers were certainly mistaken, for the Bible sanctions Slavery, and that is the highest authority. Now the Bible is my ultimate appeal on all matters of faith and practice, and it is to *this test* I am anxious to

SOURCE: Angelina E. Grimké, *Appeal to the Christian Women of the South* (New York: New York Anti-Slavery Society, 1836), 4–67 passim.

bring the subject at issue between us. Let us then begin with Adam and examine the charter of privileges which was given to him. "Have dominion over the fish of the sea, and over the fowl of the air, and over every living thing that moveth upon the earth." In the eighth Psalm we have a still fuller description of this charter which through Adam was given to all mankind. "Thou madest him to have dominion over the works of thy hands; thou hast put all things under his feet. All sheep and oxen, yea, and the beasts of the field, the fowl of the air, the fish of the sea, and whatsoever passeth through the paths of the seas." And after the flood when this charter of human rights was renewed, we find *no additional* power vested in man. "And the fear of you and the dread of you shall be upon every beast of the earth, and upon all the fishes of the sea, into your hand are they delivered." In this charter, although the different kinds of *irrational* beings are so particularly enumerated, and supreme dominion over *all of them* is granted, yet *man* is *never* vested with this dominion *over his fellow man;* he was never told that any of the human species were put *under his feet;* it was only all *things*, and man, who was created in the image of his Maker, *never* can properly be termed a *thing*, though the laws of Slave States do call him "a chattel personal;" *Man*, then I assert *never* was put *under the feet of man*, by that first charter of human rights which was given by God, to the Fathers of the Antediluvian and Postdiluvian worlds, therefore this doctrine of equality is based on the Bible.

But it may be argued, that in the very chapter of Genesis from which I have last quoted, will be found the curse pronounced upon Canaan, by which his posterity was consigned to servitude under his brothers Shem and Japheth. I know this prophecy was uttered, was most fearfully and wonderfully fulfilled, through the immediate descendants of Canaan, i.e. the Canaanites, and I do not know but that it has been through all the children of Ham, but I do know that prophecy does *not* tell us what *ought to be*, but what actually does take place, ages after it has been delivered, and that if we justify America for enslaving the children of Africa, we must also justify Egypt for reducing the children of Israel to bondage, for the latter was foretold as explicitly as the former. I am well aware that prophecy has often been urged as an excuse for Slavery, but be not deceived, the fulfilment of prophecy will *not cover one sin* in the awful day of account. Hear what our Saviour says on this subject; "it must needs be that offences come, but *woe unto that man through whom they come*"—Witness some fulfilment of this declaration in the tremendous destruction of Jerusalem, occasioned by that most nefarious of all crimes the crucifixion of the Son of God. Did the fact of that event having been foretold, exculpate the Jews from sin in perpetuating it; No—for hear what the Apostle Peter says to them on this subject, "Him being delivered by the determinate counsel and foreknowledge of God, ye have taken, and by *wicked* hands have crucified and slain." Other striking instances might be adduced, but these will suffice. . . .

But I shall be told, God sanctioned Slavery, yea commanded Slavery under the Jewish Dispensation. Let us examine this subject calmly and prayerfully. I admit that a species of *servitude* was permitted to the Jews, but in studying the subject I have been struck with wonder and admiration at perceiving how carefully the servant was guarded from violence, injustice and wrong. I will first inform you how these servants became servants, for I think this a very important part of our subject. From consulting Horne, Calmet, and the Bible, I find there were six different ways by which the Hebrews became servants legally.

1. If reduced to extreme poverty, a Hebrew might sell himself, i.e. his services, for six years, in which case *he* received the purchase money *himself*. Lev. xxv, 39.
2. A father might sell his children as servants, i.e. his *daughters*, in which circumstance it was understood the daughter was to be the wife or daughter-in-law of the man who bought her, and the *father* received the price. In other words, Jewish women were sold as *white women* were in the first settlement of Virginia—as *wives, not* as slaves. Ex. xxi, 7.
3. Insolvent debtors might be delivered to their creditors as servants. 2 Kings iv, 1.
4. Thieves not able to make restitution for their thefts, were sold for the benefit of the injured person. Ex. xxii, 3.
5. They might be born in servitude. Ex. xxi, 4.
6. If a Hebrew had sold himself to a rich Gentile, he might be redeemed by one of his brethren at any time the money was offered; and he who redeemed him, was *not* to take advantage of the favor thus conferred, and rule over him with rigor. Lev. xxv, 47-55.

Before going into an examination of the laws by which these servants were protected, I would just ask whether American slaves have become slaves in any of the ways in which the Hebrews became servants. Did they sell themselves into slavery and receive the purchase money into their own hands? No! Did they become insolvent, and by their own imprudence subject themselves to be sold as slaves? No! Did they steal the property of another, and were they sold to make restitution for their crimes? No! Did their present masters, as an act of kindness, redeem them from some heathen tyrant to whom *they had sold themselves* in the dark hour of adversity? No! Were they born in slavery? No! No! not according to *Jewish Law*, for the servants who were born in servitude among them, were born of parents who had *sold themselves* for six years: Ex. xxi, 4. Were the female slaves of the South sold by their fathers? How shall I answer this question? Thousands and tens of thousands never were, *their* fathers *never* have received the poor compensation of silver or gold for the tears and toils, the suffering, the anguish, and hopeless bondage of *their* daughters. They labor day by day, and year by year, side by side, in the same field, if haply their daughters are permitted to remain on the same plantation with them, instead of being as they often are, separated from their parents and sold into distant states, never again to meet on earth. But do the *fathers of the South ever sell their daughters?* My heart beats, and my hand trembles, as I write the awful affirmative, Yes! The fathers of this Christian land often sell their daughters, *not* as Jewish parents did, to be the wives and daughters-in-law of the man who buys them, but to be the abject slaves of petty tyrants and irresponsible masters. Is it not so, my friends? I leave it to your own candor to corroborate my assertion. Southern slaves then have *not* become slaves in any of the six different ways in which Hebrews became servants, and I hesitate not to say that American masters *cannot* according to *Jewish law* substantiate their claim to the men, women, or children they now hold in bondage. . . .

Where, then, I would ask, is the warrant, the justification, or the palliation of American slavery from Hebrew servitude? How many of the southern slaves would now be in bondage according to the laws of Moses; Not one. You may observe that I have carefully avoided using the term *slavery* when speaking of Jewish servitude; and simply for this reason, that *no such thing* existed among that people; the word translated servant does *not* mean *slave*, it is the same that is applied to Abraham, to Moses, to Elisha and the prophets generally. *Slavery* then *never* existed under the Jewish Dispensation at all, and I cannot but regard it as an aspersion on the character of Him who is "glorious in Holiness" for any one to assert that "*God sanctioned, yea commanded slavery* under the old dispensation." I would fain lift my feeble voice to vindicate Jehovah's character from so foul a slander. If slaveholders are determined to hold slaves as long as they can, let them not dare to say that the God of mercy and of truth *ever* sanctioned such a system of cruelty and wrong. It is blasphemy against Him. . . .

The Ladies Anti-Slavery Society of Boston was called last fall, to a severe trial of their faith and constancy. They were mobbed by "the gentlemen of property and standing," in that city at their anniversary meeting, and their lives were jeoparded by an infuriated crowd; but their conduct on that occasion did credit to our sex, and affords a full assurance that they will *never* abandon the cause of the slave. The pamphlet, Right or Wrong in Boston, issued by them in which a particular account is given of that "mob of broad cloth in broad day," does equal credit to the head and the heart of her who wrote it. I wish my Southern sisters could read it; they would then understand that the women of the North have engaged in this work from a sense of *religious duty*, and that nothing will ever induce them to take their hands from it until it is fully accomplished. They feel no hostility to you, no bitterness or wrath; they rather sympathize in your trials and difficulties; but they well know that the first thing to be done to help you, is to pour in the light of truth on your minds, to urge you to reflect on, and pray over the subject. This is all *they* can do for you, *you* must work out your own deliverance with fear and trembling, and with the direction and blessing of God, *you can do it*. Northern women may labor to produce a correct public opinion at the North, but if Southern women sit down in listless indifference and criminal idleness, public opinion cannot be rectified and purified at the South. It is manifest to every reflecting mind, that slavery must be abolished; the era in which we live, and the light which is overspreading the whole world on this subject, clearly show that the time cannot be distant when it will be done. Now there are only two ways in which it can be effected, by moral power or physical force, and it is for *you* to choose which you prefer. Slavery always has, and always will produce insurrections, wherever it exists, because it is a violation of the natural order of things, and no human power can much longer perpetuate it. The opposers of abolitionists fully believe this; one of them remarked to me not long since, there is no doubt there will be a most terrible overturning at the South in a few years, such cruelty and wrong, must be visited with divine vengeance soon. Abolitionists believe, too, that this must inevitably be the case if you do not repent, and they are not willing to leave you to perish without entreating you, to save yourselves from destruction; well may they say with the apostle, "am I then your enemy because I tell you the truth," and warn you to flee from impending judgments.

But why, my dear friends, have I thus been endeavoring to lead you through the history of more than three thousand years, and to point you to that great cloud of witnesses who have gone before, "from works to rewards?" Have I been seeking to magnify the sufferings, and exalt the character of woman, that she "might have praise of men?" No! no! my object has been to arouse *you*, as the wives and mothers, the daughters and sisters, of the South, to a sense of your duty as *women*, and as Christian women, on that great subject, which has already shaken our country, from the St. Lawrence and the lakes, to the Gulf of Mexico, and from the Mississippi to the shores of the Atlantic; *and will continue mightily to shake it*, until the polluted temple of slavery fall and crumble into ruin. I would say unto each one of you, "what meanest thou, O sleeper! arise and call upon thy God, if so be that God will think upon us that we perish not." Perceive you not that dark cloud of vengeance which hangs over our boasting Republic? Saw you not the lightnings of Heaven's wrath, in the flame which leaped from the Indian's torch to the roof of yonder dwelling, and lighted with its horrid glare the darkness of midnight? Heard you not the thunders of Divine anger, as the distant roar of the cannon came rolling onward, from the Texian country, where Protestant American Rebels are fighting with Mexican Republicans—for what? For the reestablishment of *slavery;* yes! of American slavery in the bosom of a Catholic Republic, where that system of robbery, violence, and wrong, had been legally abolished for twelve years. Yes! citizens of the United States, after plundering Mexico of her land, are now engaged in deadly conflict, for the privilege of fastening chains, and collars, and manacles—upon whom? upon the subjects of some foreign prince? No! upon native born American Republican citizens, although the fathers of these very men declared to the whole world, while struggling to free themselves from the three penny taxes of an English king, that they believed it to be a *self-evident* truth that *all men* were created equal, and had an *unalienable right to liberty.* . . .

The *women of the South can overthrow* this horrible system of oppression and cruelty, licentiousness and wrong. Such appeals to your legislatures would be irresistible, for there is something in the heart of man which *will bend under moral suasion.* There is a swift witness for truth in his bosom, which *will respond to truth* when it is uttered with calmness and dignity. If you could obtain but six signatures to such a petition in only one state, I would say, send up that petition, and be not in the least discouraged by the scoffs and jeers of the heartless, or the resolution of the house to lay it on the table. It will be a great thing if the subject can be introduced into your legislatures in any way, even by *women*, and *they* will be the most likely to introduce it there in the best possible manner, as a matter of *morals* and *religion*, not of expediency or politics. You may petition, too, the different ecclesiastical bodies of the slave states. Slavery must be attacked with the whole power of truth and the sword of the spirit. You must take it up on *Christian* ground, and fight against it with Christian weapons, whilst your feet are shod with the preparation of the gospel of peace. And *you are now* loudly called upon by the cries of the widow and the orphan, to arise and gird yourselves for this great moral conflict, with the whole armour of righteousness upon the right hand and on the left. . . .

But I will now say a few words on the subject of Abolitionism. Doubtless you have all heard Anti-Slavery societies denounced as insurrectionary and mischievious, fanatical and dangerous. It has been said they publish the most abominable untruths, and that they are endeavoring to excite rebellions at the South. Have you believed these reports, my friends? Have *you* also been deceived by these false assertions? Listen to me, then, whilst I endeavor to wipe from the fair character of Abolitionism such unfounded accusations. You know that *I* am a Southerner; you know that my dearest relatives are now in a slave State. Can you for a moment believe I would prove so recreant to the feelings of a daughter and a sister, as to join a society which was seeking to overthrow slavery by falsehood, bloodshed, and murder? I appeal to you who have known and loved me in days that are passed, can *you* believe it? No! my friends. As a Carolinian, I was peculiarly jealous of any movements on this subject; and before I would join an Anti-Slavery Society, I took the precaution of becoming acquainted with some of the leading Abolitionists, of reading their publications and attending their meetings, at which I heard addresses both from colored and white men; and it was not until I was fully convinced that their principles were *entirely pacific*, and their efforts *only moral*, that I gave my name as a member to the Female Anti-Slavery Society of Philadelphia. Since that time, I have regularly taken the Liberator, and read many Anti-Slavery pamphlets and papers and books, and can assure you I *never* have seen a single insurrectionary paragraph, and never read any account of cruelty which I could not believe. Southerners may deny the truth of these accounts, but why do they not *prove* them to be false. Their violent expressions of horror at such accounts being believed, *may* deceive some, but they cannot deceive *me*, for I lived too long in the midst of slavery, not to know what slavery is. When *I* speak of this system "I speak that I do know," and I am not at all afraid to assert, that Anti-Slavery publications have *not* overdrawn the monstrous features of slavery at all. And many a Southerner *knows* this as well as I do. A lady in North Carolina remarked to a friend of mine, about eighteen months since, "Northerners know nothing at all about slavery; they think it is perpetual bondage only; but of the *depth of degradation* that word involves, they have no conception; if they had, *they would never cease* their efforts until so *horrible* a system was overthrown." She did not know how faithfully some Northern men and Northern women had studied this subject; how diligently they had searched out the cause of "him who had none to help him," and how fearlessly they had told the story of the negro's wrongs. Yes, Northerners know *every* thing about slavery now. This monster of iniquity has been unveiled to the world, her frightful features unmasked, and soon, very soon will she be regarded with no more complacency by the American republic than is the idol of Juggernaut, rolling its bloody wheels over the crushed bodies of its prostrate victims.

But you will probably ask, if Anti-Slavery societies are not insurrectionary, who do Northerners tell us they are? Why, I would ask you in return, did Northern senators and Northern representatives give their votes, at the last sitting of congress, to the admission of Arkansas Territory as a state? Take those men, one by one, and ask them in their parlours, do you *approve of slavery*? Ask them on *Northern* ground, where they will speak the truth, and I doubt not *every man* of them will tell you, *no*! Why then, I ask, did *they* give their votes to enlarge the mouth of that grave which has already destroyed its tens of thousands? All our enemies tell *us* they are as much anti-slavery as we are. Yes, my friends, thousands who are helping you to bind the fetters of slavery on the negro, despise you in their hearts for doing it; they rejoice that such an institution has not been entailed upon them. Why then, I would ask, do *they* lend you their help? I will tell you, "they love *the praise of men more* than the praise of God." The Abolition cause has not yet become so popular as to induce them to believe, that by advocating it in congress, they shall sit still more securely in their seats there, and like the *chief rulers* of the days of our Saviour, though *many* believed on him, yet they did *not* confess him, lest they should be *put out of the synagogue*; John xii, 42, 43. Or perhaps like Pilate, thinking they could prevail nothing, and fearing a tumult, they determined to release Barabbas and surrender the just man, the poor innocent slave to be stripped of his rights and scourged. In vain will such men try to wash their hands, and say, with the Roman governor, "I am innocent of the blood of this just person." Northern American statesmen are no more innocent of the crime of slavery, than Pilate was of the murder of Jesus, or Saul of that of Stephen. These are high charges, but I appeal to *their hearts;* I appeal to public opinion ten years from now. Slavery then is a national sin.

But you will say, a great many other Northerners tell us so, who can have no political motives. The interests of the North, you must know, my friends, are very closely combined with those of the South. The Northern merchants and manufacturers are making *their* fortunes out of the *produce of slave labor;* the grocer is selling your rice and sugar; how then can these men bear a testimony against slavery without condemning themselves? But there is another reason, the North is most dreadfully afraid of Amalgamation. She is alarmed at the very idea of a thing so monstrous, as she thinks. And lest this consequence *might* flow from emancipation, she is determined to resist all efforts at emancipation without expatriation. It is not because *she approves of slavery*, or believes it to be "corner stone of our republic," for she is as much *anti-slavery* as we are; but amalgamation is too horrible to think of. Now I would ask *you*, is it right, is it generous, to refuse the colored people in this country the advantages of education and the privilege, or rather the *right*, to follow honest trades and callings merely because they are colored? The same prejudice exists here against our colored brethren that existed against the Gentiles in Judea. Great numbers cannot bear the idea of equality, and fearing lest, if they had the same advantages we enjoy, they would become as intelligent, as moral, as religious, and as respectable and wealthy, they are determined to keep them as low as they possibly can. Is this doing as they would be done by? Is this loving their neighbor as *themselves*? Oh! that *such* opposers of Abolitionism would put their souls in the stead of the free colored man's and obey the apostolic injunction, to "remember them that are in bonds *as bound with them.*" I will leave you to judge whether the fear of amalgamation ought to induce men to oppose anti-slavery efforts, when *they* believe *slavery* to be *sinful.* Prejudice against color, is the most powerful enemy we have to fight with at the North.

You need not be surprised, then, at all, at what is said *against* Abolitionists by the North, for they are wielding a two-edged sword, which even here, cuts through the *cords of caste,* on the one side and the *bonds of interest* on the other. They are only sharing the fate of other reformers, abused and reviled whilst they are in the minority; but they are neither angry nor discouraged by the invective which has been heaped upon them by slaveholders at the South and their apologists at the North. . . .

There is nothing to fear from immediate Emancipation, but *every thing* from the consequences of slavery. . . .

"The Original Equality of Woman," 1837

LETTER TO MARY S. PARKER, PRESIDENT OF THE BOSTON FEMALE ANTI-SLAVERY SOCIETY

Amesbury, 7th Mo., 11th, 1837

My Dear Friend,

In attempting to comply with thy request to give my views on the Province of Woman, I feel that I am venturing on nearly untrodden ground, and that I shall advance arguments in opposition to a corrupt public opinion, and to the perverted interpretation of Holy Writ, which has so universally obtained. But I am in search of truth; and no obstacle shall prevent my prosecuting that search, because I believe the welfare of the world will be materially advanced by every new discovery we make of the designs of Jehovah in the creation of woman. It is impossible that we can answer the purpose of our being, unless we understand that purpose. It is impossible that we should fulfill our duties, unless we comprehend them or live up to our privileges, unless we know what they are.

In examining this important subject, I shall depend solely on the bible to designate the sphere of woman, because I believe almost every thing that has been written on this subject, has been the result of a misconception of the simple truths revealed in the Scriptures, in consequence of the false translation of many passages of Holy Writ. My mind is entirely delivered from the superstitious reverence which is attached to the English version of the Bible. King James's translators

SOURCE: Sarah Grimké, *Letters on the Equality of the Sexes and the Condition of Woman, Addressed to Mary S. Parker, President of the Boston Female Anti-Slavery Society,* 1838; Larry Ceplair, ed., *The Public Years of Sarah and Angelina Grimké: Selected Writings 1835–1839* (New York: Columbia University Press, 1989), 205–207.

certainly were not inspired. I therefore claim the original as my standard, *believing that to have been inspired*, and I also claim to judge for myself what is the meaning of the inspired writers, because I believe it to be the solemn duty of every individual to search the Scriptures for themselves, with the aid of the Holy Spirit, and not be governed by the views of any man, or set of men.

We must first view woman at the period of her creation. "And God said, Let us make man in our own image, after our likeness; and let them have dominion over the fish of the sea, and over the fowl of the air, and over the cattle, and over all the earth. So God created man in his own image, in the image of God created he him, male and female, created he them." [Gen. 1:26-27]. In all this sublime description of the creation of man, (which is a generic term including man and woman), there is not one particle of difference intimated as existing between them. They were both made in the image of God; dominion was given to both over every other creature, but not over each other. Created in perfect equality, they were expected to exercise the vicegerence intrusted to them by their Maker, in harmony and love.

Let us pass on now to the recapitulation of the creation of man—"The Lord God formed man of the dust of the ground, and breathed into his nostrils the breath of life; and man became a living soul. And the Lord God said, it is not good that man should be alone, I will make him an help meet for him" [Gen. 2:7-18]. All creation swarmed with animated beings capable of natural affection, as we know they still are; it was not, therefore, merely to give man a creature susceptible of loving, obeying, and looking up to him, for all that the animals could do and did do. It was to give him a companion, *in all respects his equal;* one who was like himself a *free agent*, gifted with intellect and endowed with immortality; not a partaker merely of his animal gratifications, but able to enter into all his feelings as a moral and responsible being. If this had not been the case, how could she have been an help meet for him? I understand this as applying not only to the parties entering into the marriage contract, but to all men and women, because I believe God designed woman to be an help meet for man in every good and perfect work. She was a part of himself, as if Jehovah designed to make the oneness and identity of man and woman perfect and complete; and when the glorious work of their creation was finished, "the morning stars stand together, and all the sons of God shouted for joy" [Job 38:7].

This blissful condition was not long enjoyed by our first parents. Eve, it would seem from the history, was wandering alone amid the bowers of Paradise, when the serpent met with her. From her reply to Satan, it is evident that the command not to eat "of the tree that is in the midst of the garden," was given to both, although the term man was used when the prohibition was issued by God. "And the woman said unto the serpent, WE may eat of the fruit of the trees of the garden, but of the fruit of the tree which is in the midst of the garden, God hath said, YE shall not eat of it, neither shall YE touch it, lest YE die" [Gen. 3:3]. Here the woman was exposed to temptation from a being with whom she was unacquainted. She had been accustomed to associate with her believed partner, and to hold communion with God and with angels; but of satanic intelligence, she was in all probability entirely ignorant. Through the subtlety of the serpent, she was beguiled. And "when she saw that the tree was good for food, and that it was pleasant to the eyes, and a tree to be desired to make one wise, she took the fruit thereof and did eat" [Gen. 3:6].

We next find Adam involved in the same sin, not through the instrumental-ity of a supernatural agent, but through that of his equal, a being whom he must have known was liable to transgress the divine command, because he must have felt that he was himself a free agent, and that he was restrained from disobedi-ence only by the exercise of faith and love towards his Creator. Had Adam ten-derly reproved his wife, and endeavored to lead her to repentance instead of sharing in her guilt, I should be much more ready to accord to man that superi-ority which he claims; but as the facts stand disclosed by the sacred historian, it appears to me that to say the least, there was as much weakness exhibited by Adam as by Eve. They both fell from innocence, and consequently from happi-ness, *but not from equality*.

Let us next examine the conduct of this fallen pair, when Jehovah interro-gated them respecting their fault. they both frankly confessed their guilt. "The man said, the woman whom thou gavest to be with me, she gave me of the tree and I did eat. And the woman said, the serpent beguiled me and I did eat." [Gen. 3:12]. And the Lord God said unto the woman, "Thou wilt be subject unto thy husband, he will rule over thee" [Gen 3:16]. That this did not allude to the sub-jection of woman to man is manifest, because the same mode of expression is used in speaking to Cain of Abel [Gen. 4:10-12]. The truth is that the curse, as it is termed, which was pronounced by Jehovah upon woman, is a simple prophecy. The Hebrew, like the French language, uses the same word to express shall and will. Our translators having been accustomed to exercise lordship over their wives, and seeing only through the medium of a perverted judgment, very naturally, though I think not very learnedly or very kindly, translated it *shall* instead of *will*, and thus converted a prediction to Eve into a command to Adam; for observe, it is addressed to the woman and not to the man. The conse-quence of the fall was an immediate struggle for dominion, and Jehovah fore-told which would gain the ascendancy; but as he created them in his image, as that image manifestly was not lost by the fall, because it is urged in Gen. 9:6, as an argument why the life of man should not be taken by his fellow man, there is no reason to suppose that sin produced any distinction between them as moral, intellectual and responsible beings. Man might just as well have endeavored by hard labor to fulfil the prophecy, thorns and thistles will the earth bring forth to thee, as to pretend to accomplish the other, "he will rule over thee," by asserting dominion over his wife.

> *Authority usurped from God, not given.*
> *He gave him only over beast, flesh, and fowl,*
> *Dominion absolute: that right he holds*
> *By God's donation: but man o'er woman*
> *He made not Lord, such title to himself*
> *Reserving, human left from human free.*

Here then I plant myself. God created us equal;—he created us free agents;—he is our Lawgiver, our King, and our Judge, and to him alone is woman bound to be in subjection, and to him alone is she accountable for the use of those talents with which her Heavenly Father has entrusted her. One is her Master even Christ.

Thine for the oppressed in the bonds of womanhood,
Sarah M. Grimké

Wendell Phillips (1811–1884)

Many people in the United States were stunned when, in 1837, abolitionist newspaper editor Elijah P. Lovejoy was murdered by a proslavery mob in Alton, Illinois. That a white man had been killed because of his opposition to slavery caused a lively debate in many Northern states. At a meeting in Faneuil Hall, Boston, several people gave speeches about Lovejoy's murder. Massachusetts Attorney General James Austin declared that Lovejoy deserved exactly what he got. When Austin finished, an unknown young man, Wendell Phillips, rose to his feet and passionately condemned Austin's view. The speech launched Phillips's career as one of the leading abolitionists in the nation.

On the Murder of Lovejoy, December 8, 1837

. . . A comparison has been drawn between the events of the Revolution and the tragedy at Alton. We have heard it asserted here, in Faneuil Hall, that Great Britain had a right to tax the Colonies, and we have heard the mob at Alton, the drunken murderers of Lovejoy, compared to those patriot fathers who threw the tea overboard! [*Great applause.*] Fellow-citizens, is this Faneuil Hall doctrine? [*"No, no."*] The mob at Alton were met to wrest from a citizen his just rights,—met to resist the laws. We have been told that our fathers did the same; and the glorious mantle of Revolutionary precedent has been thrown over the mobs of our day.

To make out their title to such defence, the gentleman says that the British Parliament had a *right* to tax these Colonies. It is manifest that, without this, his parallel falls to the ground; for Lovejoy had stationed himself within constitutional bulwarks. He was not only defending the freedom of the press, but he was under his own roof, in arms with the sanction of the civil authority. The men

SOURCE: Wendell Phillips, *Speeches, Lectures, and Letters* (Boston: James Redpath, 1863), 1–10.

who assailed him went against and over the laws. The *mob*, as the gentleman terms it,—mob, forsooth! certainly we sons of the tea-spillers are a marvellously patient generation!—the "orderly mob" which assembled in the Old South [Church] to destroy the tea were met to resist, not the laws, but illegal exactions.

Shame on the American who calls the tea-tax and stamp-act *laws*! Our fathers resisted, not the King's prerogative, but the King's usurpation. To find any other account, you must read our Revolutionary history upside down. Our State archives are loaded with arguments of John Adams to prove the taxes laid by the British Parliament unconstitutional,—beyond its power. It was not till this was made out that the men of New England rushed to arms. The arguments of the Council Chamber and the House of Representatives preceded and sanctioned the contest. To draw the conduct of our ancestors into a precedent for mobs, for a right to resist laws we ourselves have enacted, is an insult to their memory. The difference between the excitements of those days and our own which the gentleman in kindness to the latter has overlooked, is simply this: the men of that day went for the right, as secured by the laws. They were the people rising to sustain the laws and constitution of the Province. The rioters of our day go for their own wills, right or wrong....

I must find some fault with the statement which has been made of the events at Alton. It has been asked why Lovejoy and his friends did not appeal to the executive,—trust their defence to the police of the city. It has been hinted that, from hasty and ill-judged excitement, the men within the building provoked a quarrel, and that he fell in the course of it, one mob resisting another.

Recollect, Sir, that they did act with the approbation and sanction of the Mayor. In strict truth, there was no executive to appeal to for protection. The Mayor acknowledged that he could not protect them. They asked him if it was lawful for them to defend themselves. He told them it was, and sanctioned their assembling in arms to do so. They were not, then, a mob; they were not merely citizens defending their own property; they were in some sense the *posse comitatus*, adopted for the occasion into the police of the city, acting under the order of a magistrate. It was civil authority resisting lawless violence.

Where, then, was the imprudence? Is the doctrine to be sustained here that it is *imprudent* for men to aid magistrates in executing the laws?

Men are continually asking each other, Had Lovejoy a right to resist? Sir, I protest against the question, instead of answering it. Lovejoy did not resist, in the sense they mean. He did not throw himself back on the natural right of self-defence. He did not cry anarchy, and let slip the dogs of civil war, careless of the horrors which would follow.

Sir, as I understand this affair, it was not an individual protecting his property; it was not one body of armed men resisting another, and making the streets of a peaceful city run blood with their contentions. It did not bring back the scenes in some old Italian cities, where family met family, and faction met faction, and mutually trampled the laws under foot.

No; the men in that house were regularly *enrolled*, under the sanction of the Mayor. There being no militia in Alton, about seventy men were enrolled with the approbation of the Mayor. These relieved each other every other night.

About thirty men were in arms on the night of the sixth, when the press was landed. The next evening, it was not thought necessary to summon more than half that number; among these was Lovejoy. It was, therefore, you perceive, Sir, the police of the city resisting rioters,—civil government breasting itself to the shock of lawless men.

Here is no question about the right of self-defence. It is in fact simply this: Has the civil magistrate a *right* to put down a riot?

Some persons seem to imagine that anarchy existed at Alton from the commencement of these disputes. Not at all. "No one of us," says an eyewitness and a comrade of Lovejoy, "has taken up arms during these disturbances but at the command of the Mayor."

Anarchy did not settle down on that devoted city till Lovejoy breathed his last. Till then the law, represented in his person, sustained itself against its foes. When he fell, civil authority was trampled under foot. He had "planted himself on his constitutional rights,"—appealed to the laws,—claimed the protection of the civil authority,—taken refuge under "the broad shield of the Constitution. When through that he was pierced and fell, he fell but one sufferer in a common catastrophe." He took refuge under the banner of liberty,—amid its folds; and when he fell, its glorious stars and stripes, the emblem of free institutions, around which cluster so many heart-stirring memories, were blotted out in the martyr's blood.

It has been stated, perhaps inadvertently, that Lovejoy or his comrades fired first. This is denied by those who have the best means of knowing. Guns were first fired by the mob. After being twice fired on, those within the building consulted together and deliberately returned the fire.

But suppose they did fire first. They had a right so to do; not only the right which every citizen has to defend himself, but the further right which every civil officer has to resist violence. Even if Lovejoy fired the first gun, it would not lessen his claim to our sympathy, or destroy his title to be considered a martyr in defence of a free press.

The question now is, Did he act within the Constitution and the laws? The men who fell in State Street on the 5th of March 1770, did more than Lovejoy is charged with. They were the *first* assailants. Upon some slight quarrel they pelted the troops with every missile within reach. Did this bate one jot of the eulogy with which Hancock and Warren hallowed their memory, hailing them as the first martyrs in the cause of American liberty?

If, Sir, I had adopted what are called Peace principles, I might lament the circumstances of this case. But all you who believe, as I do, in the right and duty of magistrates to execute the laws, join with me and brand as base hypocrisy the conduct of those who assemble year after year on the 4th of July, to fight over the battles of the Revolution and yet "damn with faint praise," or load with obloquy, the memory of this man, who shed his blood in defence of life, liberty, property, and the freedom of the press!

Throughout that terrible night I find nothing to regret but this, that within the limits of our country, civil authority should have been so prostrated as to oblige a citizen to arm in his own defence, and to arm in vain.

The gentleman says Lovejoy was presumptuous and imprudent,—he "died as a fool dieth." And a reverend clergyman of the city tells us that no citizen has a right to publish opinions disagreeable to the community! If any mob follows such publication, on *him* rests its guilt! He must wait, forsooth, till the people come up to it and agree with him!

This libel on liberty goes on to say that the want of right to speak as we think is an evil inseparable from republican institutions! If this be, what are they worth? Welcome the despotism of the Sultan, where one knows what he may publish and what he may not, rather than the tyranny of this many-headed monster, the mob, where we know not what we may do or say, till some fellow-citizen has tried it, and paid for the lesson with his life.

This clerical absurdity chooses as a check for the abuses of the press, not the *law*, but the dread of a mob. By so doing, it deprives not only the individual and the minority of their rights, but the majority also, since the expression of *their* opinion may sometimes provoke disturbance from the minority. A few men may make a mob as well as many. The majority, then, have no right, as Christian men, to utter their sentiments, if by any possibility it may lead to a mob! Shades of Hugh Peters and John Cotton, save us from such pulpits!

Imprudent to defend the liberty of the press! Why? Because the defence was unsuccessful? Does success gild crime into patriotism, and the want of it change heroic self-devotion to imprudence? . . .

Presumptuous to assert the freedom of the press on American ground! Is the assertion of such freedom before the age? So much before the age as to leave one no right to make it because it displeases the community? Who invents this libel on his country? It is this very thing which entitles Lovejoy to greater praise. The disputed right which provoked the Revolution— taxation without representation—is far beneath that for which he died. [Here there was a strong and general expression of disapprobation.]

One word, gentlemen. As much as *thought* is better than money, so much is the cause in which Lovejoy died nobler than a mere question of taxes. James Otis thundered in this Hall when the King did but touch his *pocket*. Imagine, if you can, his indignant eloquence, had England offered to put a gag upon his lips. [Great applause.]

The question that stirred the Revolution touched our civil interests. *This* concerns us not only as citizens, but as immortal beings. Wrapped up in its fate, saved or lost with it, are not only the voice of the statesman, but the instructions of the pulpit, and the progress of our faith. . . .

Mr. Chairman, from the bottom of my heart I thank that brave little band at Alton for resisting. We must remember that Lovejoy had fled from city to city,—suffered the destruction of three presses patiently. At length he took counsel with friends, men of character, of tried integrity, of wide views, of Christian principle. They thought the crisis had come: it was full time to assert the laws. They saw around them, not a community like our own, of fixed habits, of char-acter moulded and settled, but one "in the gristle, not yet hardened into the bone of manhood." The people there, children of our older States, seem to have forgotten the blood-tried principles of their fathers the moment they lost sight of our New England hills. Something was to be done to show them the priceless value of the freedom of the press, to bring back and set right their wandering and confused ideas.

He and his advisers looked out on a community, staggering like a drunken man, indifferent to their rights and confused in their feelings. Deaf to argument, haply they might be stunned into sobriety. They saw that of which we cannot judge, the *necessity* of resistance. Insulted law called for it. Public opinion, fast hastening on the downward course, must be arrested.

Does not the event show they judged rightly? Absorbed in a thousand trifles, how has the nation all at once come to a stand? Men begin, as in 1776 and 1640, to discuss principles, to weigh characters, to find out where they are. Haply we may awake before we are borne over the precipice. . . .

Ralph Waldo Emerson (1803–1882)

Transcendentalists Ralph Waldo Emerson, Henry David Thoreau, and Margaret Fuller had an enormous impact on thinking in the first half of the nineteenth century. Transcendental philosophy grew out of the romantic movement, which, in rejecting the Enlightenment's veneration of reason, had emphasized the ineffable beauty of nature and spirit. Going a step further, transcendentalists urged individuals to transcend the confines of book learning and formal knowledge and cultivate instead the innate ability of each person to know beauty and truth. Each of us must become aware of our original connection to the universe, to nature, to life. We must learn who we are and become conscious that there is a spark of divinity within each individual. Our souls are part of the "Oversoul." And in this sense, each individual is interconnected with all of nature. But this does not mean that we are to be concerned only with ourselves. We must also be engaged in the world, for we are a part of the world. Since we are all part of the godhead, there is no fundamental difference between humans. Masculine and feminine principles exist in each individual, and it is through the union of the masculine and the feminine that humankind can discover the path to a truly new utopian humanity. The soul, the spirit, and the mind, therefore, favor no gender, no class, and no race. It is not surprising that transcendentalists were among the most outspoken advocates of abolitionism and feminism.

The title of Emerson's "Essay on Self-Reliance" is self-explanatory. Each person, according to Emerson, in order to live a full, meaningful life, must not conform to society but instead cultivate self-reliance. The speech Emerson gave at Concord, Massachusetts (the beginning of which is excerpted here), in May 1851 to oppose the Fugitive Slave Law makes it quite clear that his emphasis on self-reliance does not preclude commitment to political action.

"Self-Reliance," 1841

. . . To believe your own thought, to believe that what is true for you in your private heart is true for all men,—that is genius. . . . A man should learn to detect and watch that gleam of light which flashes across his mind from within, more than the lustre of the firmament of bards and sages. Yet he dismisses without notice his thought, because it is his. In every work of genius we recognize our own rejected thoughts: they come back to us with a certain alienated majesty. Great works of art have no more affecting lesson for us than this. They teach us to abide by our spontaneous impression with good-humored inflexibility then most when the whole cry of voices is on the other side. Else, to-morrow a stranger will say with masterly good sense precisely what we have thought and felt all the time, and we shall be forced to take with shame our own opinion from another.

There is a time in every man's education when he arrives at the conviction that envy is ignorance; that imitation is suicide; that he must take himself for better, for worse, as his portion; that though the wide universe is full of good, no kernel of nourishing corn can come to him but through his toil bestowed on that plot of ground which is given to him to till. The power which resides in him is new in nature, and none but he knows what that is which he can do, nor does he know until he has tried. . . .

Trust thyself: every heart vibrates to that iron string. Accept the place the divine providence has found for you, the society of your contemporaries, the connection of events. Great men have always done so, and confided themselves childlike to the genius of their age, betraying their perception that the absolutely trustworthy was seated at their heart, working through their hands, predominating in all their being. And we are now men, and must accept in the highest mind the same transcendent destiny; and not minors and invalids in a protected corner, not cowards fleeing before a revolution, but guides, redeemers, and benefactors, obeying the Almighty effort, and advancing on Chaos and the Dark.

. . . Society everywhere is in conspiracy against the manhood of every one of its members. Society is a joint-stock company, in which the members agree, for the better securing of his bread to each shareholder, to surrender the liberty and culture of the eater. The virtue in most request is conformity. Self-reliance is its aversion. It loves not realities and creators, but names and customs.

SOURCE: Ralph Waldo Emerson, *The Essay on Self-Reliance* (East Aurora, NY: Roycroft Press, 1908), 1–59, passim.

Whoso would be a man must be a nonconformist. He who would gather immortal palms must not be hindered by the name of goodness, but must explore if it be goodness.

Nothing is at last sacred but the integrity of your own mind. Absolve you to yourself, and you shall have the suffrage of the world. I remember an answer which when quite young I was prompted to make to a valued adviser, who was wont to importune me with the dear old doctrines of the church. On my saying, What have I to do with the sacredness of traditions, if I live wholly from within? my friend suggested,—"But these impulses may be from below, not from above." I replied, "They do not seem to me to be such; but if I am the Devil's child, I will live then from the Devil." No law can be sacred to me but that of my nature. Good and bad are but names very readily transferable to that or this; the only right is what is after my constitution, the only wrong what is against it. A man is to carry himself in the presence of all opposition, as if every thing were titular and ephemeral but he. I am ashamed to think how easily we capitulate to badges and names, to large societies and dead institutions. Every decent and well-spoken individual affects and sways me more than is right. I ought to go upright and vital, and speak the rude truth in all ways. . . .

Virtues are, in the popular estimate, rather the exception than the rule. There is the man and his virtues. Men do what is called a good action, as some piece of courage or charity, much as they would pay a fine in expiation of daily non-appearance on parade. Their works are done as an apology or extenuation of their living in the world,—as invalids and the insane pay a high board. Their virtues are penances. I do not wish to expiate, but to live. My life is for itself and not for a spectacle. I much prefer that it should be of a lower strain, so it be genuine and equal, than that it should be glittering and unsteady. I wish it to be sound and sweet, and not to need diet and bleeding. I ask primary evidence that you are a man, and refuse this appeal from the man to his actions. I know that for myself it makes no difference whether I do or forbear those actions which are reckoned excellent. I cannot consent to pay for a privilege where I have intrinsic right. Few and mean as my gifts may be, I actually am, and do not need for my own assurance or the assurance of my fellows any secondary testimony.

What I must do is all that concerns me, not what the people think. This rule, equally arduous in actual and in intellectual life, may serve for the whole distinction between greatness and meanness. It is the harder, because you will always find those who think they know what is your duty better than you know it. It is easy in the world to live after the world's opinion; it is easy in solitude to live after our own; but the great man is he who in the midst of the crowd keeps with perfect sweetness the independence of solitude.

The objection to conforming to usages that have become dead to you is, that it scatters your force. It loses your time and blurs the impression of your character. If you maintain a dead church, contribute to a dead Bible-society, vote with a great party either for the government or against it, spread your table like base housekeepers,—under all these screens I have difficulty to detect the precise man you are. And, of course, so much force is withdrawn from your proper life. But do your work, and I shall know you. Do your work, and you shall reinforce yourself. A man must consider what a blindman's-buff is this game of conformity. If I know your sect, I anticipate your argument. I hear a preacher announce for his text and topic the expediency of one of the institutions of his church. Do I not know beforehand that not possibly can he say a new and spontaneous word? Do I not know that, with all this ostentation of examining the grounds of the institution, he will do no such thing? Do I not know that he is pledged to himself not to look but at one side,—the permitted side, not as a man, but as a parish minister? He is a retained attorney, and these airs of the bench are the emptiest affectation. Well, most men have bound their eyes with one or another handkerchief, and attached themselves to some one of these communities of opinion. This conformity makes them not false in a few particulars, authors of a few lies, but false in all particulars. Their every truth is not quite true. Their two is not the real two, their four not the real four; so that every word they say chagrins us, and we know not where to begin to set them right. Meantime nature is not slow to equip us in the prison-uniform of the party to which we adhere. We come to wear one cut of face and figure, and acquire by degrees the gentlest asinine expression. There is a mortifying experience in particular, which does not fail to wreak itself also in the general history; I mean "the foolish face of praise," the forced smile which we put on in company where we do not feel at ease in answer to conversation which does not interest us. The muscles, not spontaneously moved, but moved by a low usurping wilfulness, grow tight about the outline of the face with the most disagreeable sensation.

For nonconformity the world whips you with its displeasure. And therefore a man must know how to estimate a sour face. The by-standers look askance on him in the public street or in the friend's parlour. If this aversation had its origin in contempt and resistance like his own, he might well go home with a sad countenance; but the sour faces of the multitude, like their sweet faces, have no deep cause, but are put on and off as the wind blows and a newspaper directs. Yet is the discontent of the multitude more formidable than that of the senate and the college. It is easy enough for a firm man who knows the world to brook the rage of the cultivated classes. Their rage is decorous and prudent, for they are timid as being very vulnerable themselves. But when to their feminine rage the indignation of the people is added, when the ignorant and the poor are aroused, when the unintelligent brute force that lies at the bottom of society is made to growl and mow, it needs the habit of magnanimity and religion to treat it godlike as a trifle of no concernment.

The other terror that scares us from self-trust is our consistency; a reverence for our past act or word, because the eyes of others have no other data for computing our orbit than our past acts, and we are loath to disappoint them.

But why should you keep your head over your shoulder? Why drag about this corpse of your memory, lest you contradict somewhat you have stated in this or that public place? Suppose you should contradict yourself; what then? It seems to be a rule of wisdom never to rely on your memory alone, scarcely even in acts of pure memory, but to bring the past for judgment into the thousand-eyed present, and live ever in a new day. In your metaphysics you have denied personality to the Deity: yet when the devout motions of the soul come, yield to them heart and life, though they should clothe God with shape and color. Leave your theory, as Joseph his coat in the hand of the harlot, and flee.

A foolish consistency is the hobgoblin of little minds, adored by little statesmen and philosophers and divines. With consistency a great soul has simply nothing to do. He may as well concern himself with his shadow on the wall. Speak what you think now in hard words, and to-morrow speak what to-morrow thinks in hard words again, though it contradict every thing you said to-day.—'Ah, so you shall be sure to be misunderstood.'—Is it so bad, then, to be misunderstood? Pythagoras was misunderstood, and Socrates, and Jesus, and Luther, and Copernicus, and Galileo, and Newton, and every pure and wise spirit that ever took flesh. To be great is to be misunderstood.

I suppose no man can violate his nature. All the sallies of his will are rounded in by the law of his being, as the inequalities of Andes and Himmaleh are insignificant in the curve of the sphere. Nor does it matter how you gauge and try him. A character is like an acrostic or Alexandrian stanza;—read it forward, backward, or across, it still spells the same thing. In this pleasing, contrite wood-life which God allows me, let me record day by day my honest thought without prospect or retrospect, and, I cannot doubt, it will be found symmetrical, though I mean it not, and see it not. My book should smell of pines and resound with the hum of insects. The swallow over my window should interweave that thread or straw he carries in his bill into my web also. We pass for what we are. Character teaches above our wills. Men imagine that they communicate their virtue or vice only by overt actions, and do not see that virtue or vice emit a breath every moment. . . .

I hope in these days we have heard the last of conformity and consistency. Let the words be gazetted and ridiculous henceforward. Instead of the gong for dinner, let us hear a whistle from the Spartan fife. Let us never bow and apologize more. A great man is coming to eat at my house. I do not wish to please him; I wish that he should wish to please me. I will stand here for humanity, and though I would make it kind, I would make it true. Let us affront and reprimand the smooth mediocrity and squalid contentment of the times, and hurl in the face of custom, and trade, and office, the fact which is the upshot of all history, that there is a great responsible Thinker and Actor working wherever a man works; that a true man belongs to no other time or place, but is the centre of things. Where he is, there is nature. He measures you, and all men, and all events. Ordinarily, every body in society reminds us of somewhat else, or of some other person. Character, reality, reminds you of nothing else; it takes place of the whole creation. The man must be so much, that he must make all circumstances indifferent. Every true man is a cause, a country, and an age; requires infinite spaces and numbers and time fully to accomplish his design;—and posterity seem to follow his steps as a train of clients. A man Caesar is born, and for ages after we have a Roman Empire. Christ is born, and millions of minds so grow and cleave to his genius, that he is confounded with virtue and the possible of man. An institution is the lengthened shadow of one man. . . .

Let a man then know his worth, and keep things under his feet. Let him not peep or steal, or skulk up and down with the air of a charity-boy, a bastard, or an interloper, in the world which exists for him. But the man in the street, finding no worth in himself which corresponds to the force which built a tower or sculptured a marble god, feels poor when he looks on these. To him a palace, a statue, or a costly book have an alien and forbidding air, much like a gay equipage, and seem to say like that, 'Who are you, Sir?' Yet they all are his, suitors for his notice, petitioners to his faculties that they will come out and take possession. The picture waits for my verdict: it is not to command me, but I am to settle its claims to praise. That popular fable of the sot who was picked up dead drunk in the street, carried to the duke's house, washed and dressed and laid in the duke's bed, and, on his waking, treated with all obsequious ceremony like the duke, and assured that he had been insane, owes its popularity to the fact, that it symbolizes so well the state of man, who is in the world a sort of sot, but now and then wakes up, exercises his reason, and finds himself a true prince. . . .

The relations of the soul to the divine spirit are so pure, that it is profane to seek to interpose helps. It must be that when God speaketh he should communicate, not one thing, but all things; should fill the world with his voice; should scatter forth light, nature, time, souls, from the centre of the present thought; and new date and new create the whole. Whenever a mind is simple, and receives a divine wisdom, old things pass away,—means, teachers, texts, temples fall; it lives now, and absorbs past and future into the present hour. All things are made sacred by relation to it,—one as much as another. All things are dissolved to their centre by their cause, and, in the universal miracle, petty and particular miracles disappear. If, therefore, a man claims to know and speak of God, and carries you backward to the phraseology of some old mouldered nation in another country, in another world, believe him not. Is the acorn better than the oak which is its fulness and completion? Is the parent better than the child into whom he has cast his ripened being? Whence, then, this worship of the past? The centuries are conspirators against the sanity and authority of the soul. Time and space are but physiological colors which the eye makes, but the soul is light; where it is, is day; where it was, is night; and history is an impertinence and an injury, if it be any thing more than a cheerful apologue or parable of my being and becoming.

Man is timid and apologetic; he is no longer upright; he dares not say 'I think,' 'I am,' but quotes some saint or sage. He is ashamed before the blade of grass or the blowing rose. These roses under my window make no reference to former roses or to better ones; they are for what they are; they exist with God to-day. There is no time to them. There is simply the rose; it is perfect in every moment of its existence. Before a leaf-bud has burst, its whole life acts; in the full-blown flower there is no more; in the leafless root there is no less. Its nature is satisfied, and it satisfies nature, in all moments alike. But man postpones or remembers; he does not live in the present, but with reverted eye laments the past, or, heedless of the riches that surround him, stands on tiptoe to foresee the future. He cannot be happy and strong until he too lives with nature in the present, above time.

. . . If we live truly, we shall see truly. It is as easy for the strong man to be strong, as it is for the weak to be weak. When we have new perception, we shall gladly disburden the memory of its hoarded treasures as old rubbish. When a man lives with God, his voice shall be as sweet as the murmur of the brook and the rustle of the corn.

And now at last the highest truth on this subject remains unsaid; probably cannot be said; for all that we say is the far-off remembering of the intuition. That thought, by what I can now nearest approach to say it, is this. When good is near you, when you have life in yourself, it is not by any known or accustomed way; you shall not discern the foot-prints of any other; you shall not see the face of man; you shall not hear any name;—the way, the thought, the good, shall be wholly strange and new. It shall exclude example and experience. You take the way from man, not to man. All persons that ever existed are its forgotten ministers. Fear and hope are alike beneath it. There is somewhat low even in hope. In the hour of vision, there is nothing that can be called gratitude, nor properly joy. The soul raised over passion beholds identity and eternal causation, perceives the self-existence of Truth and Right, and calms itself with knowing that all things go well. Vast spaces of nature, the Atlantic Ocean, the South Sea,—long intervals of time, years, centuries,—are of no account. This which I think and feel underlay every former state of life and circumstances, as it does underlie my present, and what is called life, and what is called death.

Life only avails, not the having lived. Power ceases in the instant of repose; it resides in the moment of transition from a past to a new state, in the shooting of the gulf, in the darting to an aim. This one fact the world hates, that the soul becomes; for that for ever degrades the past, turns all riches to poverty, all reputation to a shame, confounds the saint with the rogue, shoves Jesus and Judas equally aside. Why, then, do we prate of self-reliance? Inasmuch as the soul is present, there will be power not confident but agent. To talk of reliance is a poor external way of speaking. Speak rather of that which relies, because it works and is. Who has more obedience than I masters me, though he should not raise his finger. Round him I must revolve by the gravitation of spirits. We fancy it rhetoric, when we speak of eminent virtue. We do not yet see that virtue is Height, and that a man or a company of men, plastic and permeable to principles, by the law of nature must overpower and ride all cities, nations, kings, rich men, poets, who are not.

This is the ultimate fact which we so quickly reach on this, as on every topic, the resolution of all into the ever-blessed ONE. Self-existence is the attribute of the Supreme Cause, and it constitutes the measure of good by the degree in which it enters into all lower forms. All things real are so by so much virtue as they contain. Commerce, husbandry, hunting, whaling, war, eloquence, personal weight, are somewhat, and engage my respect as examples of its presence and impure action. I see the same law working in nature for conservation and growth. Power is in nature the essential measure of right. Nature suffers nothing to remain in her kingdoms which cannot help itself. The genesis and maturation of a planet, its poise and orbit, the bended tree recovering itself from the strong wind, the vital resources of every animal and vegetable, are demonstrations of the self-sufficing, and therefore self-relying soul. . . .

But now we are a mob. Man does not stand in awe of man, nor is his genius admonished to stay at home, to put itself in communication with the internal ocean, but it goes abroad to beg a cup of water of the urns of other men. We must go alone. I like the silent church before the service begins, better than any preaching. How far off, how cool, how chaste the persons look, begirt each one with a precinct or sanctuary! So let us always sit. Why should we assume the faults of our friend, or wife, or father, or child, because they sit around our hearth, or are said to have the same blood? All men have my blood, and I have all men's. Not for that will I adopt their petulance or folly, even to the extent of being ashamed of it. But your isolation must not be mechanical, but spiritual, that is, must be elevation. At times the whole world seems to be in conspiracy to importune you with emphatic trifles. Friend, client, child, sickness, fear, want, charity, all knock at once at thy closet door, and say,—"Come out unto us." But keep thy state; come not into their confusion. The power men possess to annoy me, I give them by a weak curiosity. No man can come near me but through my act. "What we love that we have, but by desire we bereave ourselves of the love." . . .

If any man consider the present aspects of what is called by distinction society, he will see the need of these ethics. The sinew and heart of man seem to be drawn out, and we are become timorous, desponding whimperers. We are afraid of truth, afraid of fortune, afraid of death, and afraid of each other. Our age yields no great and perfect persons. We want men and women who shall renovate life and our social state, but we see that most natures are insolvent, cannot satisfy their own wants, have an ambition out of all proportion to their practical force, and do lean and beg day and night continually. Our housekeeping is mendicant, our arts, our occupations, our marriages, our religion, we have not chosen, but society has chosen for us. We are parlour soldiers. We shun the rugged battle of fate, where strength is born. . . .

Insist on yourself; never imitate. Your own gift you can present every moment with the cumulative force of a whole life's cultivation; but of the adopted talent of another, you have only an extemporaneous, half possession. That which each can do best, none but his Maker can teach him. No man yet knows what it is, nor can, till that person has exhibited it. Where is the master who could have taught Shakspeare? Where is the master who could have instructed Franklin, or Washington, or Bacon, or Newton? Every great man is a unique. The Scipionism of Scipio is precisely that part he could not borrow. Shakspeare will never be made by the study of Shakspeare. Do that which is assigned you, and you cannot hope too much or dare too much. . . .

The civilized man has built a coach, but has lost the use of his feet. He is supported on crutches, but lacks so much support of muscle. He has a fine Geneva watch, but he fails of the skill to tell the hour by the sun. A Greenwich nautical almanac he has, and so being sure of the information when he wants it, the man in the street does not know a star in the sky. The solstice he does not observe; the equinox he knows as little; and the whole bright calendar of the year is without a dial in his mind. His note-books impair his memory; his libraries overload his wit; the insurance-office increases the number of accidents; and it may be a question whether machinery does not encumber; whether we have not lost by refinement some energy, by a Christianity entrenched in establishments and forms, some vigor of wild virtue. For every Stoic was a Stoic; but in Christendom where is the Christian? . . .

Society is a wave. The wave moves onward, but the water of which it is composed does not. The same particle does not rise from the valley to the ridge. Its unity is only phenomenal. The persons who make up a nation to-day, next year die, and their experience with them.

And so the reliance on Property, including the reliance on governments which protect it, is the want of self-reliance. Men have looked away from themselves and at things so long, that they have come to esteem the religious, learned, and civil institutions as guards of property, and they deprecate assaults on these, because they feel them to be assaults on property. They measure their esteem of each other by what each has, and not by what each is. But a cultivated man becomes ashamed of his property, out of new respect for his nature. Especially he hates what he has, if he see that it is accidental,—came to him by inheritance, or gift, or crime; then he feels that it is not having; it does not belong to him, has no root in him, and merely lies there, because no revolution or no robber takes it away. But that which a man is does always by necessity acquire, and what the man acquires is living property, which does not wait the beck of rulers, or mobs, or revolutions, or fire, or storm, or bankruptcies, but perpetually renews itself wherever the man breathes. "Thy lot or portion of life," said the Caliph Ali, "is seeking after thee; therefore be at rest from seeking after it." Our dependence on these foreign goods leads us to our slavish respect for numbers. The political parties meet in numerous conventions; the greater the concourse, and with each new uproar of announcement, The delegation from Essex! The Democrats from New Hampshire! The Whigs of Maine! the young patriot feels himself stronger than before by a new thousand of eyes and arms. In like manner the reformers summon conventions, and vote and resolve in multitude. Not so, O friends! will the God deign to enter and inhabit you, but by a method precisely the reverse. It is only as a man puts off all foreign support, and stands alone, that I see him to be strong and to prevail. He is weaker by every recruit to his banner. Is not a man better than a town? Ask nothing of men, and in the endless mutation, thou only firm column must presently appear the upholder of all that surrounds thee. He who knows that power is inborn, that he is weak because he has looked for good out of him and elsewhere, and so perceiving, throws himself unhesitatingly on his thought, instantly rights himself, stands in the erect position, commands his limbs, works miracles; just as a man who stands on his feet is stronger than a man who stands on his head.

So use all that is called Fortune. Most men gamble with her, and gain all, and lose all, as her wheel rolls. But do thou leave as unlawful these winnings, and deal with Cause and Effect, the chancellors of God. In the Will work and acquire, and thou hast chained the wheel of Chance, and shalt sit hereafter out of fear from her rotations. A political victory, a rise of rents, the recovery of your sick, or the return of your absent friend, or some other favorable event, raises your spirits, and you think good days are preparing for you. Do not believe it. Nothing can bring you peace but yourself. Nothing can bring you peace but the triumph of principles.

Address to the Citizens of Concord, 1851

ON THE FUGITIVE SLAVE LAW, MAY 3, 1851

. . . I accepted your invitation to speak to you on the great question of these days in the very moment it came to me, with very little consideration of what I might have to offer; for there seems to be no option. The last year has forced us all into politics, and made it a paramount duty to seek what it is often a duty to shun.

We do not breathe well. There is infamy in the air. I have a new experience. I wake in the morning with a painful sensation, which I carry about all day, & which, when traced home, is the odious remembrance of that ignominy that has fallen on Massachusetts, that robs the landscape of beauty, & takes the sunshine out of every hour. I have lived all my life in this state, and never had any experience of personal inconvenience from the laws. They never came near me to my discomfort before. I find the same sensibility in my neighbours. And in that class who take no interest in the ordinary questions of party politics. There are men who are as sure indexes of the equity of legislation & of the sane state of public feeling, as the barometer is of the weight of the air, and it is a bad sign if they are discontented. For though they snuff oppression & dishonour at a distance in the air, it is because they are more impressionable; the whole population will in a short time be as painfully affected.

Every hour brings us from distant quarters of the Union the natural expression of mortification at the late events in Massachusetts and the behaviour of Boston. The tameness was indeed shocking. Boston, of whose fame for spirit & character, we have all been so proud. . . .

The levity of the public mind has been shown, in the past year, by the most extravagant actions. Who could have believed it, if foretold, that a hundred guns would be fired in Boston, on the passage of the Fugitive-slave-bill? Nothing proves the want of all thought, the absence of standard in men's minds, more than the dominion of party. Here are humane people who have tears for misery, an open purse for want, who should have been the defenders of the poor man, are found his embittered enemies, rejoicing in his rendition,—merely from party ties. I thought none that was not ready to go on all fours would back this law. And yet here are upright men, *compotes mentis*, husbands, fathers, trustees, friends, open, generous, brave, who can see nothing in this claim for bare humanity, & the

SOURCE: Ralph Waldo Emerson, *Emerson's Antislavery Writings*, ed. by Len Gougeon and Joel Myerson (New Haven: Yale University Press, 1995), 53–58.

health & honor of their native state, but canting, fanaticism, sedition, & "one idea." Because of this preoccupied mind, the whole wealth & power of Boston 200,000 souls & 180 millions of money, are thrown into the scale of crime; and the poor black boy, whom the fame of Boston had reached, in the recesses of a rice swamp, or in the alleys of Savannah, on arriving here, finds all this force employed to catch him. The famous town of Boston is his master's hound. The learning of the universities, the culture of elegant society, the acumen of lawyers, majesty of the Bench, the eloquence of the Christian pulpit, the stoutness of Democracy, the respectability of the Whig Party are all combined to kidnap him.

The crisis is interesting, as it shows the selfprotecting nature of the world, & of the divine laws. It is the law of the world, as much immorality as there is, so much misery. The greatest prosperity will in vain escape the greatest calamity. You borrow the succour of the devil, & he must have his fee. He was never known to abate a penny of his rents. In every nation all the immorality that exists breeds plagues. Out of the corrupt society that exists, we have never been able to combine any pure prosperity. There is always something in the very advantages of a condition which hurts it. Africa has its malformation, England has its Ireland, Germany its hatred of classes, France, its love of gunpowder, Italy, its pope; and America, the most prosperous country in the universe, has the greatest calamity in the universe, negro slavery. . . .

By the sentiment of Duty. An immoral law makes it a man's duty to break it, at every hazard. For Virtue is the very self of every man. It is, therefore, a principle of law, that an immoral contract is void, and that an immoral statute is void, for, as laws do not make right, but are simply declaratory of a right which already existed, it is not to be presumed that they can so stultify themselves, as to command injustice.

It is remarkable how rare, even in the history of the worst tyrants, is an immoral law. Some colour, some indirection, was always used. If you take up the volumes of the Universal History, you will find it difficult searching. The precedents are few. It is not easy to parallel the wickedness of this American law. And that is the head & body of this discontent, that the law is immoral; that you have ordained a crime. Here is a statute which enacts the crime of kidnapping,—a crime on one footing with arson and murder. A man's right to liberty, is as inalienable as his right to life.

Pains seem to have been taken to give us in this statute a wrong pure from any mixture of right. If our resistance to this law, is not right, there is no right. This is not meddling with other people's affairs: This is hindering other people from meddling with us. This is not going crusading into Virginia & Georgia after slaves, who, it is alleged, are very comfortable where they are:—that amiable argument falls to the ground: But this is befriending in our own state, on our own farms, a man who has taken the risk of being shot, or burned alive, or cast into the sea, or starved to death, or suffocated in a wooden box, to get away from his driver; and this man, who has run this gauntlet of a thousand miles for his freedom, the statute says, you men of Massachusetts shall hunt, & catch, & send back again to the dog-hutch he fled from. . . .

Margaret Fuller.
A daguerreotype of transcendentalist philosopher Margaret Fuller from the 1840s. "There is no wholly masculine man, no purely feminine woman," Fuller wrote in 1844, "I would have Woman lay aside all thought, such as she habitually cherishes, of being taught and led by men."

Margaret Fuller (1810–1850)

During the 1830s, Margaret Fuller lived in Cambridge, Massachusetts, where she was part of Ralph Waldo Emerson and Henry David Thoreau's transcendentalist circle. In 1840, Fuller and Emerson founded a literary journal, The Dial, *which Fuller edited until 1844, when she accepted Horace Greeley's offer to become the book review editor of the* New York Tribune. *In 1846, she moved to Europe as the* Tribune's *foreign correspondent, and in 1848 she became involved in the Italian revolution. Returning to the United States in 1850, she drowned when her ship sank during a hurricane within sight of land at Fire Island, New York.*

Despite her short life, Margaret Fuller was an influential transcendentalist and feminist. Her ardent plea for women's rights, "The Great Lawsuit: Man versus Men, Woman versus Women," was published in The Dial *in 1843, and then in 1845 it was incorporated in her book* Woman in the Nineteenth Century. *Like Emerson and Thoreau, Margaret Fuller argued that the United States was a land of hypocrisy that did not live up to its self-proclaimed ideals and that the path to equality and liberty was through self-reliance and personal enlightenment. She argued also that women must gain economic independence in order to achieve equality.*

Woman in the Nineteenth Century, Part 3, 1844

... In our own country, women are, in many respects, better situated than men. Good books are allowed, with more time to read them. They are not so early forced into the bustle of life, nor so weighed down by demands for outward success. The perpetual changes, incident to our society, make the blood circulate freely through the body politic, and, if not favorable at present to the grace and bloom of life, they are so to activity, resource, and would be to reflection, but for a low materialist tendency, from which the women are generally exempt in themselves, though its existence, among the men, has a tendency to repress their impulses and make them doubt their instincts, thus often paralyzing their action during the best years.

But they have time to think, and no traditions chain them, and few conventionalities, compared with what must be met in other nations. There is no reason why they should not discover that the secrets of nature are open, the revelations of the spirit waiting, for whoever will seek them. When the mind is once awakened to this consciousness, it will not be restrained by the habits of the past, but fly to seek the deeds of a heavenly future.

Their employments are more favorable to meditation than those of men.

Woman is not addressed religiously here more than elsewhere. She is told that she should be worthy to be the mother of a Washington, or the companion of some good man. But in many, many instances, she has already learned that all bribes have the same flaw; that truth and good are to be sought solely for their own sakes. And, already, an ideal sweetness floats over many forms, shines in many eyes.

Already deep questions are put by young girls on the great theme: What shall I do to enter upon the eternal life?

Men are very courteous to them. They praise them often, check them seldom. There is chivalry in the feeling toward "the ladies," which gives them the best seats in the stage-coach, frequent admission, not only to lectures of all sorts, but to courts of justice, balls of legislature, reform conventions. The newspaper editor "would be better pleased that the Lady's Book should be filled up exclusively by ladies. It would then, indeed, be a true gem, worthy to be presented by young men to the mistress of their affections." Can gallantry go further?

In this country is venerated, wherever seen, the character which Goethe spoke of as an Ideal, which he saw actualized in his friend and patroness, the Grand Duchess Amelia: "The excellent woman is she, who, if the husband dies, can be a father to the children." And this, if read aright, tells a great deal.

Women who speak in public, if they have a moral power, such as has been felt from Angelina Grimké and Abby Kelly,—that is, if they speak for conscience' sake, to serve a cause which they hold sacred,—invariably subdue the prejudices of their hearers, and excite an interest proportionate to the aversion with which it had been the purpose to regard them.

Source: Margaret Fuller, *Woman in the Nineteenth Century*, (New York: Greeley and McElrath, 1845), 96–107.

A passage in a private letter so happily illustrates this, that it must be inserted here. Abby Kelly in the Town-House of_____.

"The scene was not unheroic—to see that woman, true to humanity and her own nature, a centre of rude eyes and tongues, even gentlemen feeling licensed to make part of a species of mob around a female out of her sphere. As she took her seat in the desk amid the great noise, and in the throng, full, like a wave, of something to ensue, I saw her humanity in a gentleness and unpretension, tenderly open to the sphere around her, and, had she not been supported by the power of the will of genuineness and principle, she would have failed. It led her to prayer, which, in Woman especially, is childlike; sensibility and will going to the side of God and looking up to him; and humanity was poured out in aspiration.

"She acted like a gentle hero, with her mild decision and womanly calmness. All heroism is mild, and quiet, and gentle, for it is life and possession; and combativeness and firmness show a want of actualness. She is as earnest, fresh and simple, as when she first entered the crusade. I think she did much good, more than the men in her place could do, for Woman feels more as being and reproducing—this brings the subject more into home relations. Men speak through, and mostly from intellect, and this addresses itself to that in others which is combative."

Not easily shall we find elsewhere, or before this time, any written observations on the same subject, so delicate and profound.

The late Dr. Channing, whose enlarged and tender and religious nature shared every onward impulse of his time, though his thoughts followed his wishes with a deliberative caution which belonged to his habits and temperament, was greatly interested in these expectations for women. His own treatment of them was absolutely and thoroughly religious. He regarded them as souls, each of which had a destiny of its own, incalculable to other minds, and whose leading it must follow, guided by the light of a private conscience. He had sentiment, delicacy, kindness, taste; but they were all pervaded and ruled by this one thought, that all beings had souls, and must vindicate their own inheritance. Thus all beings were treated by him with an equal, and sweet, though solemn, courtesy. The young and unknown, the woman and the child, all felt themselves regarded with an infinite expectation, from which there was no reaction to vulgar prejudice. He demanded of all he met, to use his favorite phrase, "great truths."

His memory, every way dear and reverend, is, by many, especially cherished for this intercourse of unbroken respect.

At one time, when the progress of Harriet Martineau through this country, Angelina Grimké's appearance in public, and the visit of Mrs. Jameson, had turned his thoughts to this subject, he expressed high hopes as to what the coming era would bring to Woman. He had been much pleased with the dignified courage of Mrs. Jameson in taking up the defence of her sex in a way from which women usually shrink, because, if they express themselves on such subjects with sufficient force and clearness to do any good, they are exposed to assaults whose vulgarity makes them painful. In intercourse with such a woman, he had shared her indignation at the base injustice, in many respects, and in many regions, done to the sex; and been led to think of it far more than ever before. He seemed to think that he might some time write upon the subject. That his aid is withdrawn from the cause is a subject of great regret; for, on this question as on others, he would have known how to sum up the evidence, and take, in the noblest spirit, middle ground. He always furnished a platform on which opposing parties could stand and look at one another under the influence of his mildness and enlightened candor.

Two younger thinkers, men both, have uttered noble prophecies, auspicious for Woman. Kinmont, all whose thoughts tended towards the establishment of the reign of love and peace, thought that the inevitable means of this would be an increased predominance given to the idea of Woman. Had he lived longer, to see the growth of the Peace Party, the reforms in life and medical practice which seek to substitute water for wine and drugs, pulse for animal food, he would have been confirmed in his view of the way in which the desired changes are to be effected.

In this connection I must mention Shelley, who, like all men of genius, shared the feminine development, and, unlike many, knew it. His life was one of the first pulse-beats in the present reform-growth. He, too, abhorred blood and heat, and, by his system and his song, tended to reinstate a plant-like gentleness in the development of energy. In harmony with this, his ideas of marriage were lofty, and, of course, no less so of Woman, her nature, and destiny.

For Woman, if, by a sympathy as to outward condition, she is led to aid the enfranchisement of the slave, must be no less so, by inward tendency, to favor measures which promise to bring the world more thoroughly and deeply into harmony with her nature. When the lamb takes place of the lion as the emblem of nations, both women and men will be as children of one spirit, perpetual learners of the word and doers thereof, not hearers only.

A writer in the New York Pathfinder, in two articles headed "Femality," has uttered a still more pregnant word than any we have named. He views Woman truly from the soul, and not from society, and the depth and leading of his thoughts are proportionably remarkable. He views the feminine nature as a harmonizer of the vehement elements, and this has often been hinted elsewhere; but what he expresses most forcibly is the lyrical, the inspiring and inspired apprehensiveness of her being.

This view being identical with what I have before attempted to indicate, as to her superior susceptibility to magnetic or electric influence, I will now try to express myself more fully.

There are two aspects of Woman's nature, represented by the ancients as Muse and Minerva. It is the former to which the writer in the Pathfinder looks. It is the latter which Wordsworth has in mind, when he says,

"With a placid brow,
Which woman ne'er should forfeit, keep thy vow."

The especial genius of Woman I believe to be electrical in movement, intuitive in function, spiritual in tendency. She excels not so easily in classification, or recreation, as in an instinctive seizure of causes, and a simple breathing out of what she receives, that has the singleness of life, rather than the selecting and energizing of art.

More native is it to her to be the living model of the artist than to set apart from herself any one form in objective reality; more native to inspire and receive the poem, than to create it. In so far as soul is in her completely developed, all soul is the same; but in so far as it is modified in her as Woman, it flows, it breathes, it sings, rather than deposits soil, or finishes work; and that which is especially feminine flushes, in blossom, the face of earth, and pervades, like air and water, all this seeming solid globe, daily renewing and purifying its life. Such may be the especially feminine element spoken of as Femality. But it is no more the order of nature that it should be incarnated pure in any form, than that the masculine energy should exist unmingled with it in any form.

Male and female represent the two sides of the great radical dualism. But, in fact, they are perpetually passing into one another. Fluid hardens to solid, solid rushes to fluid. There is no wholly masculine man, no purely feminine woman.

. . . Yet sight comes first, and of this sight of the world of causes, this approximation to the region of primitive motions, women I hold to be especially capable. Even without equal freedom with the other sex, they have already shown themselves so; and should these faculties have free play, I believe they will open new, deeper and purer sources of joyous inspiration than have as yet refreshed the earth.

Let us be wise, and not impede the soul. Let her work as she will. Let us have one creative energy, one incessant revelation. Let it take what form it will, and let us not bind it by the past to man or woman, black or white. . . .

Every relation, every gradation of nature is incalculably precious, but only to the soul which is poised upon itself, and to whom no loss, no change, can bring dull discord, for it is in harmony with the central soul.

If any individual live too much in relations, so that he becomes a stranger to the resources of his own nature, he falls, after a while, into a distraction, or imbecility, from which he can only be cured by a time of isolation, which gives the renovating fountains time to rise up. With a society it is the same. Many minds, deprived of the traditionary or instinctive means of passing a cheerful existence, must find help in self-impulse, or perish. It is therefore that, while any elevation, in the view of union, is to be hailed with joy, we shall not decline celibacy as the great fact of the time. It is one from which no vow, no arrangement, can at present save a thinking mind. For now the rowers are pausing on their oars; they wait a change before they can pull together. All tends to illustrate the thought of a wise contemporary. Union is only possible to those who are units. To be fit for relations in time, souls, whether of Man or Woman, must be able to do without them in the spirit.

It is therefore that I would have Woman lay aside all thought, such as she habitually cherishes, of being taught and led by men. I would have her, like the Indian girl, dedicate herself to the Sun, the Sun of Truth, and go nowhere if his beams did not make clear the path. I would have her free from compromise, from complaisance, from helplessness, because I would have her good enough and strong enough to love one and all beings, from the fulness, not the poverty of being.

Men, as at present instructed, will not help this work, because they also are under the slavery of habit. . . .

Lowell Mill Girls.
Four young Lowell Mill girls, circa
1850, taking time off work to pose
for the photographer.

Lowell Mill Girls

*In the early 1830s, in an effort to increase production, textile mills in
Lowell, Massachusetts, began an experiment in which young farm
women were hired in large numbers. At a time when the idea of young,
unmarried women working and living away from home was scandalous,
the mill provided a safe and secure environment. The girls resided in
supervised housing, were given boarding house–style meals, followed a
strict dress and behavior code, and were expected to attend educational
lectures and expand their minds by using the library. This uncommon
opportunity for women to leave home and earn money in a secure setting
created a great deal of camaraderie among them, and the Lowell Mills
thrived. However, in 1834, when increasing competition forced the mills
to cut wages, the tight-knit Lowell Mill girls decided to strike. The strike
was unsuccessful, as was a second strike in 1836, but the workers showed
that they had a strong sense of their own interests and were not timid
about attempting to organize. In 1846, they struck again, and this time
they were partially successful. One of the Lowell employees, Sarah Bagley,
founded the Lowell Female Labor Association in 1844 and became a
staunch labor reformer who helped to guide the Lowell Mill girls as they
called for a 10-hour workday and increased wages. Thus, although
women were a minority in the workforce of the nineteenth century, some*

*of the earliest attempts at labor organization were spearheaded by
working women.*

*In 1846, Sarah Bagley and others wrote a constitution for their union,
and in 1847, after they changed their name to Lowell Female Industrial
Reform and Mutual Aid Society, they wrote a second constitution.*

LOWELL FEMALE LABOR REFORM ASSOCIATION, 1846

Whereas we, the Operatives of Lowell, believing that in the present age of
improvement, nothing can escape the searching glances of reform; and when men
begin to inquire why the Laborer does not hold that place in the social, moral and
intellectual world, which a bountiful Creator designed him to occupy, the *reason* is
obvious. He is a slave to a false and debasing state of society. Our merciful Father
in his infinite wisdom surely, has not bestowed all his blessings, both mental and
moral on a few, on whom also he has showered all of pecuniary gifts. No! to us *all*
has he given minds capable of eternal progression and improvement!

It now only remains for us to throw off the shackles which are binding us in
ignorance and servitude and which prevent us from rising to that scale of being
for which God designed us.

But how shall this be done? How shall the mass become educated? With the
present system of labor it is impossible. There must be reasonable hours for
manual labor, and a just portion of time allowed for the cultivation of the mental and moral faculties and no other way *can* the great work be accomplished.

We know no employment is respectable only as long as these employed are
such, and no farther than they are intelligent and moral, can they merit the
companionship and esteem of their fellow-beings. It is evident, that with the
present system of labor, the minds of the mass *must* remain uncultivated, their
morals unimproved and our country be flooded with vice and misery!

Shall we, Operatives of America, the land where Democracy claims to be
the principle by which we live and by which we are governed, see the evil daily
increasing which separates more widely and more effectually the favored few
and the unfortunate many, without one exertion to stay the progress?—God
forbid! Let the daughters of New England kindle the spark of philanthropy on
every heart till its brightness shall *fill* the whole earth!

In consideration of which we adopt the following Constitution:

ART. 1st. This Association shall be called the Lowell Female Labor Reform
Association.

SOURCE: Retrieved on 10/26/2003 from http://irw.rutgers.edu/research/ugresearch/
birthplaces/preamble.html and http://irw.rutgers.edu/research/ugresearch/birthplaces/
lowellconstitution.html.

ART. 2d. This Association shall be governed by the following officers: President, two Vice Presidents, a Secretary, Treasurer and board of Directors, consisting of eight in number.

ART. 3d. It shall be the duty of the President to preside at the meetings of the Association and board of Directors, and call especial meetings whenever any three members of the same shall request it.

ART. 4th. It shall be the duty of the Vice Presidents to preside in case of the absence of the President.

ART. 5th. It shall be the duty of the Secretary to be present at all meetings of the Association, and be prepared to read the proceedings of the last meeting, if requested. Also, to keep a correct account of the business of the Association.

ART. 6th. It shall be the duty of the Treasurer to receive all money paid into the treasury, and keep a correct account of the same also, to pay all bills presented by the Association, and signed by the President and Secretary.

ART. 7th. It shall be the duty of the Directors to present all plans of operation to the Association, and to assist in all labors of the same.

ART. 8th. Any person signing this Constitution, shall literally pledge herself to labor *actively* for Reform in the present system of labor.

ART. 9th. The members of this Association disapprove of all hostile measures, strikes and turn outs until all pacific measures prove abortive, and then that is the imperious duty of every one to assert and maintain that independence which our brave ancestors bequeathed to us, and sealed with their blood.

ART. 10th. This Constitution may be altered and amended by a vote of two thirds of the members present, provided the amendment be proposed at a previous meeting. It shall be the duty of the Board of Directors to revise the Constitution at the time of the Annual meeting for choosing Officers, which shall be holden on the first Tuesday of January.

The following Officers were chosen Jan. 1846.

SARAH G. BAGLEY, *President*
HANNAH C. TARLTON, *Vice Pres.*

MARY EMERSON,
HULDAH J. STONE, *Rec'g. Sec'y.*
SARAH A. YOUNG, *Cor. Sec'y.*
MARY A. K. TARLTON, *Treasurer.*
CLIMENA BUTLER
MISS GILMAN
ABBEY KEMP

CATHERINE MAXEY

Directors
MARY J. ROBINSON
ELIZA SIMPSON
ELIZABETH L. TRUE
ELMIRA B. STONE

Voice of Industry, February 27, 1846.

Lowell Female Industrial Reform and Mutual Aid Society, 1847

The following Preamble and Constitution having been adopted, we would most strongly urge upon every female operative, as well as others who are compelled by necessity to support themselves of this opportunity to help us in this humane enterprise: Let us unite together and protect each other. In health and prosperity we can enjoy each other's society from week to week—in sickness and despondency share in and kindly relieve each other's distresses. The young and defenceless female, far away from home and loving hearts, can here find true sympathy and aid. We do hope and confidently believe that many of our toiling sisters will come in next Tuesday, sign the Constitution, and engage heart and hand in this benevolent cause.

Our meetings will be holden every Tuesday evening, at eight o'clock, at the Reading Room, 76 Central street. The officers for the coming year will be chosen Jan. 12. Let there be full attendance. Now is the time for ACTION.

H. J. Stone, Sec'y.

PREAMBLE

The time having come when the claims of Industry and the Rights of all, are engrossing the deep attention, the profoundest thought and energetic action of the wisest and best in this and other lands—when the worthy toiling millions of earth are waking from the deathlike stupor which has so long held them in ignorance and degredation, to a sense of their true dignity and worth as God's free men and women, destined to eternal progression and ultimate perfection, we, females of Lowell, feel that *we* also have a *work* to accomplish—a high and holy destiny to achieve. We deem it a privelage and also a *duty* we owe to ourselves and our race, to lend a helping hand, feeble though it may be, to assist in carrying forward the great "Industrial Reform" already commenced, and which is progressing with such unlooked for success, in the Old and New World. To assist in scattering light and knowledge among the people—to encourage in every good word and work, those who are devoting themselves, and all that they have, to the cause of human elevation and human happiness.

We feel that by our mutual, *united* action, and with the blessing of high heaven, we can accomplish much, which shall tell for the progress of Industrial Reform—the elevation and cultivation of mind and morals, in our midst—the comfort and relief of destitute and friendless females in this busy city.

With this high aim and these noble objects in view, we most solemnly pledge ourselves to labor actively, energetically and unitedly, to bring about a better state of society. In order the more successfully to accomplish these objects, we adopt the following

CONSTITUTION

ART. I. This Association shall be called the LOWELL FEMALE INDUS-TRIAL REFORM AND MUTUAL AID SOCIETY.

ART. II. The objects of this Society shall be the diffusion of correct principles and useful practical knowledge among its members—the rendering of Industry honorable and attractive—the relieving and aiding of all who may be sick, or in want of the comforts and necessaries of life, or standing in need of the counsels and sympathies of true and benevolent hearts. Also to encourage and assist each other in self-culture, intellectual and moral, that we may be fitted for and occupy that station in society, which the truly good and useful ever should. That we may know and respect our own individual rights and privileges as females, and be prepared, understandingly, to maintain and enjoy them, irrespective of concentrated wealth or aristocratic usages of an anti-republican state of society.

ART. III. Any female can become a member by signing the Constitution and paying an initiation fee of fifty cents.

ART. IV. The officers of this society shall consist of a President, two Vice Presidents, Secretary, Treasurer and Board of Directors, four in number, all of which officers shall be members, ex-officio, of the Board.

ART. V. It shall be the duty of the President to preside at all meetings of the Society, and in case of absence, the Vice President shall fill the chair.

ART. VI. It shall be the duty of the Secretary to be present at all meetings, and prepared to read the minutes of the previous meeting, if requested.

ART. VII. It shall be the duty of the Treasurer to receive all money paid into the Treasury, and to pay all bills presented by the Society and signed by the President and Secretary; also to keep a correct amount of the same.

ART. VIII. It shall be the duty of the Board to appoint a Charitable Committee the first Tuesday of each month, or oftener if necessary.

ART. IX. That Committee shall be styled the Sisters of Charity. It shall be their duty to ascertain who is needy or sick in the Society, and report the same at each meeting, that their wants may be attended to faithfully, their hearts cheered by the voice of sympathy and love. It shall also be their duty to furnish watchers for the sick so long as deemed necessary.

ART. X. Every member shall deposit not less than six cents weekly in the hands of the Treasurer, which sum, with the initiation fee and fines, shall go to make up a sick fund, which shall be appropriated no other way, except by vote of two thirds of the Board.

ART. XI. No member shall draw from this fund until she has contributed to the same three months the amount specified in article tenth; and then not less than two nor over five dollars a week, or longer than four weeks, unless the Board see fit to order otherwise.

ART. XII. Any member who shall absent herself from the meetings three weeks in succession, without a reasonable excuse, shall be subjected to a fine of thirty-seven and a half cents per week. If at the end of three months said member does not come in and pay up her fines, she shall not be entitled to any of the benefits of the sick fund.

ART. XIII. The officers of this Society shall be chosen on the first Tuesdays of January and July, two weeks notice being previously given.

ART. XIV. This Constitution may be altered or amended by a vote of two thirds of the members present, provided it be proposed at a previous meeting.

Voice of Industry, January 8, 1847

Elizabeth Cady Stanton (1815–1902)

Elizabeth Cady Stanton, an abolitionist and an advocate of women's rights, sailed with her husband to London in 1840 to attend the World Anti-Slavery Convention. After making the arduous voyage, she was dismayed and angered to discover that women were not allowed to speak at the convention. In a sense, this was an epiphany for her, a revelation that the fight for women's rights was at least as important as the fight against slavery. At the convention, she met Lucretia Mott, and the two women resolved that they would arrange a women's rights convention in the United States. In July 1848, 300 women and 40 men gathered in Seneca Falls, New York, to "discuss the social, civil, and religious condition and rights of women." The

principal outcome of this convention was the "Declaration of Sentiments."
Modeling the manifesto on the Declaration of Independence and the Bill of
Rights, Stanton called not only for women's suffrage but also for complete
social and economic equality and a restructuring of societal stereotypes
about the roles of the two sexes. Though the Seneca Falls declaration kicked
off the modern women's movement, the struggle for women's rights
remained in the background during the 1850s, as the crusade against slavery
took center stage. At the end of the Civil War, Stanton and Mott, along with
Susan B. Anthony, Lucy Stone, and many others, focused their considerable
energies on women's rights.

SPEECH AT SENECA FALLS, JULY 19, 1848

We have met here today to discuss our rights and wrongs, civil and political, and
not, as some have supposed, to go into the detail of social life alone. We do not
propose to petition the legislature to make our husbands just, generous, and
courteous, to seat every man at the head of a cradle, and to clothe every woman
in male attire. None of these points, however important they may be considered
by leading men, will be touched in this convention. As to their costume, the gentlemen need feel no fear of our imitating that, for we think it in violation of
every principle of taste, beauty, and dignity; notwithstanding all the contempt
cast upon our loose, flowing garments, we still admire the graceful folds, and
consider our costume far more artistic than theirs. Many of the nobler sex seem
to agree with us in this opinion, for the bishops, priests, judges, barristers, and
lord mayors of the first nation on the globe, and the Pope of Rome, with his
cardinals, too, all wear the loose flowing robes, thus tacity acknowledging that
the male attire is neither dignified nor imposing. No, we shall not molest you
in your philosophical experiments with stocks, pants, high-heeled boots, and
Russian belts. Yours be the glory to discover, by personal experience, how long
the kneepan can resist the terrible strapping down which you impose, in how
short time the well-developed muscles of the throat can be reduced to mere
threads by the constant pressure of the stock, how high the heel of a boot must
be to make a short man tall, and how tight the Russian belt may be drawn and
yet have wind enough left to sustain life.

But we are assembled to protest against a form of government existing without the consent of the governed—to declare our right to be free as man is free,
to be represented in the government which we are taxed to support, to have such
disgraceful laws as give man the power to chastise and imprison his wife, to take
the wages which she earns, the property which she inherits, and, in case of separation, the children of her love; laws which make her the mere dependent on his

SOURCE: Ellen Carol Dubois, ed. *The Elizabeth Cady Stanton-Susan B. Anthony Reader:*
Correspondence, Writings, Speeches (Boston: Northeastern University Press, 1992) 27–35.

bounty. It is to protest against such unjust laws as these that we are assembled today, and to have them, if possible, forever erased from our statute books, deeming them a shame and a disgrace to a Christian republic in the nineteenth century. We have met to uplift woman's fallen divinity upon an even pedestal with man's.

And, strange as it may seem to many, we now demand our right to vote according to the declaration of the government under which we live. This right no one pretends to deny. We need not prove ourselves equal to Daniel Webster to enjoy this privilege, for the ignorant Irishman in the ditch has all the civil rights he has. We need not prove our muscular power equal to this same Irishman to enjoy this privilege, for the most tiny, weak, ill-shaped stripling of twenty-one has all the civil rights of the Irishman. We have no objection to discuss the question of equality, for we feel that the weight of argument lies wholly with us, but we wish the question of equality kept distinct from the question of rights, for the proof of the one does not determine the truth of the other. All white men in this country have the same rights, however they may differ in mind, body, or estate.

The right is ours. The question now is: how shall we get possession of what rightfully belongs to us? We should not feel so sorely grieved if no man who had not attained the full stature of a Webster, Clay, Van Buren, or Gerrit Smith could claim the right of the elective franchise. But to have drunkards, idiots, horse-racing, rum-selling rowdies, ignorant foreigners, and silly boys fully recognized, while we ourselves are thrust out from all the rights that belong to citizens, it is too grossly insulting to the dignity of woman to be longer quietly submitted to. The right is ours. Have it, we must. Use it, we will. The pens, the tongues, the fortunes, the indomitable wills of many women are already pledged to secure this right. The great truth that no just government can be formed without the consent of the governed we shall echo and re-echo in the ears of the unjust judge, until by continual coming we shall weary him.

There seems now to be a kind of moral stagnation in our midst. Philanthropists have done their utmost to rouse the nation to a sense of its sins. War, slavery, drunkenness, licentiousness, gluttony, have been dragged naked before the people, and all their abominations and deformities fully brought to light, yet with idiotic laugh we hug those monsters to our breasts and rush on to destruction. Our churches are multiplying on all sides, our missionary societies, Sunday schools, and prayer meetings and innumerable charitable and reform organizations are all in operation, but still the tide of vice is swelling, and threatens the destruction of everything, and the battlements of righteousness are weak against the raging elements of sin and death. Verily, the world waits the coming of some new element, some purifying power, some spirit of mercy and love. The voice of woman has been silenced in the state, the church, and the home, but man cannot fulfill his destiny alone, he cannot redeem his race unaided. There are deep and tender chords of sympathy and love in the hearts of the downfallen and oppressed that woman can touch more skillfully than man.

The world has never yet seen a truly great and virtuous nation, because in the degradation of woman the very fountains of life are poisoned at their source. It is vain to look for silver and gold from mines of copper and lead. It is the wise mother that has the wise son. So long as your women are slaves you may throw your colleges and churches to the winds. You can't have scholars and saints so long as your mothers are ground to powder between the upper and nether millstone of tyranny and lust. How seldom, now, is a father's pride gratified, his fond hopes realized, in the budding genius of his son! The wife is degraded, made the mere creature of caprice, and the foolish son is heaviness to his heart. Truly are the sins of the fathers visited upon the children to the third and fourth generation. God, in His wisdom, has so linked the whole human family together that any violence done at one end of the chain is felt throughout its length, and here, too, is the law of restoration, as in woman all have fallen, so in her elevation shall the race be recreated.

"Voices" were the visitors and advisers of Joan of Arc. Do not "voices" come to us daily from the haunts of poverty, sorrow, degradation, and despair, already too long unheeded. Now is the time for the women of this country, if they would save our free institutions, to defend the right, to buckle on the armor that can best resist the keenest weapons of the enemy—contempt and ridicule. The same religious enthusiasm that nerved Joan of Arc to her work nerves us to ours. In every generation God calls some men and women for the utterance of truth, a heroic action, and our work today is the fulfilling of what has long since been foretold by the Prophet—Joel 2:28: "And it shall come to pass afterward, that I will pour out my spirit upon all flesh; and your sons and your daughters shall prophesy." We do not expect our path will be strewn with the flowers of popular applause, but over the thorns of bigotry and prejudice will be our way, and on our banners will beat the dark storm clouds of opposition from those who have entrenched themselves behind the stormy bulwarks of custom and authority, and who have fortified their position by every means, holy and unholy. But we will steadfastly abide the result. Unmoved we will bear it aloft. Undauntedly we will unfurl it to the gale, for we know that the storm cannot rend from it a shred, that the electric flash will but more clearly show to us the glorious words inscribed upon it, "Equality of Rights."

DECLARATION OF SENTIMENTS, 1848

When, in the course of human events, it becomes necessary for one portion of the family of man to assume among the people of the earth a position different from that which they have hitherto occupied, but one to which the laws of nature and of nature's God entitle them, a decent respect to the opinions of mankind requires that they should declare the causes that impel them to such a course.

We hold these truths to be self-evident: that all men and women are created equal; that they are endowed by their Creator with certain inalienable rights; that among these are life, liberty, and the pursuit of happiness; that to secure

SOURCE: Elizabeth Cady Stanton, Susan B. Anthony, and Matilda Joslyn Gage, eds., *History of Woman Suffrage*, vol. I (1881; New York: Arno Press and the New York Times, 1969), 70–72.

these rights governments are instituted, deriving their just powers from the consent of the governed. Whenever any form of government becomes destructive of these ends, it is the right of those who suffer from it to refuse allegiance to it, and to insist upon the institution of a new government, laying its foundation on such principles, and organizing its powers in such form, as to them shall seem most likely to effect their safety and happiness. Prudence, indeed, will dictate that governments long established should not be changed for light and transient causes; and accordingly all experience hath shown that mankind are more disposed to suffer, while evils are sufferable, than to right themselves by abolishing the forms to which they are accustomed. But when a long train of abuses and usurpations, pursuing invariably the same object, evinces a design to reduce them under absolute despotism, it is their duty to throw off such government, and to provide new guards for their future security. Such has been the patient sufferance of the women under this government, and such is now the necessity which constrains them to demand the equal station to which they are entitled. The history of mankind is a history of repeated injuries and usurpations on the part of man toward woman, having in direct object the establishment of an absolute tyranny over her. To prove this, let facts be submitted to a candid world.

He has never permitted her to exercise her inalienable right to the elective franchise.

He has compelled her to submit to laws, in the formation of which she had no voice.

He has withheld from her rights which are given to the most ignorant and degraded men—both natives and foreigners.

Having deprived her of this first right of a citizen, the elective franchise, thereby leaving her with but representation in the halls of legislation, he has oppressed her on all sides.

He has made her, if married, in the eye of the law, civilly dead. He has taken from her all right in property. even to the wages she earns.

He has made her, morally, an irresponsible being, as she can commit many crimes with impunity, provided they be done in the presence of her husband.

In the covenant of marriage, she is compelled to promise obedience to her husband, he becoming, to all intents and purposes, her master—the law giving him power to deprive her of her liberty. and to administer chastisement.

He has so framed the laws of divorce, as to what shall be the proper causes, and in case of separation, to whom the guardianship of the children shall be given, as to be wholly regardless of the happiness of women—the law, in all cases, going upon a false supposition of the supremacy of man, and giving all power into his hands.

After depriving her of all rights as a married woman, if single, and the owner of property, he has taxed her to support a government which recognizes her only when her property can be made profitable to it.

He has monopolized nearly all the profitable employments, and from those she is permitted to follow, she receives but a scanty remuneration. He closes against her all the avenues to wealth and distinction which he considers most honorable to himself. As a teacher of theology, medicine, or law, she is not known.

He has denied her the facilities for obtaining a thorough education, all colleges being closed against her.

He allows her in Church, as well as State, but a subordinate position, claiming Apostolic authority for her exclusion from the ministry, and, with some exceptions, from any public participation in the affairs of the Church.

He has created a false public sentiment by giving to the world a different code of morals for men and women, by which moral delinquencies which exclude women from society, are not only tolerated, but deemed of little account in man.

He has usurped the prerogative of Jehovah himself, claiming it as his right to assign for her a sphere of action, when that belongs to her conscience and to her God.

He has endeavored, in every way that he could, to destroy her confidence in her own powers, to lessen her self-respect and to make her willing to lead a dependent and abject life.

Now, in view of this entire disfranchisement of one-half the people of this country, their social and religious degradation—in view of the unjust laws above mentioned, and because women do feel themselves aggrieved, oppressed, and fraudulently deprived of their most sacred rights, we insist that they have immediate admission to all the rights and privileges which belong to them as citizens of the United States.

In entering upon the great work before us, we anticipate no small amount of misconception, misrepresentation, and ridicule; but we shall use every instrumentality within our power to effect our object. We shall employ agents, circulate tracts, petition the State and National legislatures, and endeavor to enlist the pulpit and the press in our behalf. We hope this Convention will be followed by a series of Conventions embracing every part of the country.

RESOLUTIONS

WHEREAS, The great precept of nature is conceded to be, that "man shall pursue his own true and substantial happiness." Blackstone in his Commentaries remarks, that this law of Nature being coeval with mankind, and dictated by God himself, is of course superior in obligation to any other. It is binding over all the globe, in all countries and at all times; no human laws are of any validity if contrary to this. and such of them as are valid, derive all their force, and all their validity, and all their authority, mediately and immediately, from this original; therefore,

Resolved, That such laws as conflict, in any way with the true and substantial happiness of woman, are contrary to the great precept of nature and of no validity, for this is "superior in obligation to any other."

Resolved, That all laws which prevent woman from occupying such a station in society as her conscience shall dictate, or which place her in a position inferior to that of man, are contrary to the great precept of nature, and therefore of no force or authority.

Resolved, That woman is man's equal—was intended to be so by the Creator, and the highest good of the race demands that she should be recognized as such.

Resolved, That the women of this country ought to be enlightened in regard to the laws under which they live, that they may no longer publish their degradation by declaring themselves satisfied with their present position, nor their ignorance, by asserting that they have all the rights they want.

Resolved, That inasmuch as man, while claiming for himself intellectual superiority, does accord to woman moral superiority, it is pre-eminently his duty to encourage her to speak and teach, as she has an opportunity, in all religious assemblies.

Resolved, That the same amount of virtue, delicacy, and refinement of behavior that is required of woman in the social state, should also be required of man, and the same transgressions should be visited with equal severity on both man and woman.

Resolved, That the objection of indelicacy and impropriety, which is so often brought against woman when she addresses a public audience, comes with a very ill-grace from those who encourage, by their attendance, her appearance on the stage, in the concert. Or in feats of the circus.

Resolved, That woman has too long rested satisfied in the circumscribed limits which corrupt customs and a perverted application of the Scriptures have marked out for her, and that it is time she should move in the enlarged sphere which her great Creator has assigned her.

Resolved, That it is the duty of the women of this country to secure to themselves their sacred right to the elective franchise.

Resolved, That the equality of human rights results necessarily from the fact of the identity of the race in capabilities and responsibilities.

Resolved, therefore. That, being invested by the creator with the same capabilities, and the same consciousness of responsibility for their exercise, it is demonstrably the right and duty of woman, equally with man, to promote every righteous cause by every righteous means; and especially in regard to the great subjects of morals and religion, it is self-evidently her right to participate with her brother in teaching them, both in private and in public, by writing and by speaking, by any instrumentalities proper to be used, and in any assemblies proper to be held; and this being a self evident truth growing out of the divinely implanted principles of human nature, any custom or authority adverse to it, whether modern or wearing the hoary sanction of antiquity, is to be regarded as a self- evident falsehood, and at war with mankind.

Resolved, That the speedy success of our cause depends upon the zealous and untiring efforts of both men and women, for the overthrow of the monopoly of the pulpit, and for the securing to women an equal participation with men in the various trades, professions. and commerce.

Sojourner Truth.
Evangelist, abolitionist, and suffragist
Sojourner Truth traveled throughout
the country mesmerizing audiences
with her demands for women's
equality and the abolition of slavery.

Sojourner Truth (c. 1797–1883)

Isabella Baumfree is a legendary figure in American history. After escaping
from slavery, she dedicated herself equally to the causes of abolition and
feminism. Proclaiming that she would travel the nation speaking nothing
but the truth, she changed her name to Sojourner Truth. Uneducated and
untrained in grammatical niceties, she was nevertheless an extraordinary
speaker who invariably mesmerized audiences wherever she went. Her most
famous speech was given at the 1851 Women's Rights Convention in Akron,
Ohio. There is some dispute about her exact words because the written
version (transcribed some 12 years after the event by Frances Gage, the
president of the convention) differs from a contemporary newspaper account
of the speech. In any case, the speech enthralled her audience and still
resonates today as a compelling example of nineteenth-century feminism.

AIN'T I A WOMAN?, 1851

Well, children, where there is so much racket there must be something out of
kilter. I think that 'twixt the negroes of the South and the women at the North,

SOURCE: Elizabeth Cady Stanton, Susan B. Anthony, and Matilda J. Gage, eds., *History of
Woman Suffrage* (Rochester: Charles Mann, 1881), vol. I, 403–404.

all talking about rights, the white men will be in a fix pretty soon. But what's all this here talking about? That man over there says that women need to be helped into carriages, and lifted over ditches, and to have the best place everywhere. Nobody ever helps me into carriages, or over mud-puddles, or gives me any best place! And ain't I a woman? Look at me! Look at my arm! I have ploughed and planted, and gathered into barns, and no man could head me! And ain't I a woman? I could work as much and eat as much as a man—when I could get it— and bear the lash as well! And ain't I a woman? I have borne thirteen children, and seen most all sold off to slavery, and when I cried out with my mother's grief, none but Jesus heard me! And ain't I a woman?

Then they talk about this thing in the head; what's this they call it? [a member of the audience calls out, "intellect"] That's it, honey. What's that got to do with women's rights or negroes' rights? If my cup won't hold but a pint, and yours holds a quart, wouldn't you be mean not to let me have my little half measure full?

Then that little man in black there, he says women can't have as much rights as men, 'cause Christ wasn't a woman! Where did your Christ come from? Where did your Christ come from? From God and a woman! Man had nothing to do with Him. If the first woman God ever made was strong enough to turn the world upside down all alone, these women together ought to be able to turn it back, and get it right side up again! And now they is asking to do it, the men better let them.

Obliged to you for hearing me, and now old Sojourner ain't got nothing more to say.

Frederick Douglass (1818–1895)

Frederick Douglass was perhaps the most articulate and influential black abolitionist during the antebellum period. After his escape from slavery in 1838, he surfaced in Massachusetts, where he met William Lloyd Garrison. Soon thereafter he became an ardent and tireless campaigner for abolition. The story is often repeated of Garrison introducing Douglass as a speaker at a Nantucket antislavery meeting in 1841. When Douglass spoke, he eloquently confessed that he was a "thief," for he had stolen his limbs, his head, and his body from his master by running away. He gave speeches around the country and in England, he wrote an autobiography, and he published an abolitionist newspaper, The North Star. *Not only was Frederick Douglass committed to the campaign against slavery but also he fought for complete civil and political rights for African Americans and allied himself to the women's rights movement.*

Shortly after the Seneca Falls convention, he reported on the event in The North Star. *Perhaps Frederick Douglass's most powerful (and*

acerbic) speech is the one he delivered at the 1852 Fourth of July
celebration in Rochester, New York.

THE NORTH STAR, JULY 28, 1848

One of the most interesting events of the past week, was the holding of what is technically styled a Woman's Rights Convention at Seneca Falls. The speaking, addresses, and resolutions of this extraordinary meeting was wholly conducted by women; and although they evidently felt themselves in a novel position, it is but simple justice to say that their whole proceedings were characterized by marked ability and dignity. No one present, we think, however much he might be disposed to differ from the views advanced by the leading speakers on that occasion, will fail to give them credit for brilliant talents and excellent dispositions. In this meeting, as in other deliberative assemblies, there were frequent differences of opinion and animated discussion; but in no case was there the slightest absence of good feeling and decorum. Several interesting documents setting forth the rights as well as the grievances of women were read. Among these was a Declaration of Sentiments, to be regarded as the basis of a grand movement for attaining the civil, social, political, and religious rights of women. We should not do justice to our own convictions, or to the excellent persons connected with this infant movement, if we did not in this connection offer a few remarks on the general subject which the Convention met to consider and the objects they seek to attain. In doing so, we are not insensible that the bare mention of this truly important subject in any other than terms of contemptuous ridicule and scornful disfavor, is likely to excite against us the fury of bigotry and the folly of prejudice. A discussion of the rights of animals would be regarded with far more complacency by many of what are called the "wise" and the "good" of our land, than would a discussion of the rights of women. It is, in their estimation to be guilty of evil thoughts, to think that woman is entitled to equal rights with man. Many who have at last made the discovery that the negroes have some rights as well as other members of the human family, have yet to be convinced that women are entitled to any. Eight years ago a number of persons of this description actually abandoned the anti-slavery cause, lest by giving their influence in that direction they might possibly be giving countenance to the dangerous heresy that woman, in respect to rights, stands on an equal footing with man. In the judgment of such persons the American slave system, with all its concomitant horrors, is less to be deplored than this "wicked" idea. It is perhaps needless to say, that we cherish little sympathy for such sentiments or respect for such prejudices. Standing as we do up on the watch-tower of human freedom, we cannot be deterred from an expression of

SOURCE: Philip S. Foner, ed., *Frederick Douglass on Women's Rights* (New York: Da Capo Press, 1992), 49–51.

our approbation of any movement, however humble, to improve and elevate the character of any members of the human family. While it is impossible for us to go into this subject at length, and dispose of the various objections which are often urged against such a doctrine as that of female equality, we are free to say that in respect to political rights, we hold woman to be justly entitled to all we claim for man. We go farther, and express our conviction that all political rights which it is expedient for man to exercise, it is equally for woman. All that distinguishes man as an intelligent and accountable being, is equally true of woman, and if that government only is just which governs by the free consent of the governed, there can be no reason in the world for denying to woman the exercise of the elective franchise, or a hand in making and administering the laws of the land. Our doctrine is that "right is of no sex." We therefore bid the women engaged in this movement our humble Godspeed.

What to the Slave Is the Fourth of July?, July 5, 1852

Mr. President, Friends and Fellow Citizens: He who could address this audience without a quailing sensation, has stronger nerves than I have. I do not remember ever to have appeared as a speaker before any assembly more shrinkingly, nor with greater distrust of my ability, than I do this day. A feeling has crept over me, quite unfavorable to the exercise of my limited powers of speech. The task before me is one which requires much previous thought and study for its proper performance. I know that apologies of this sort are generally considered flat and unmeaning. I trust, however, that mine will not be so considered. Should I seem at ease, my appearance would much misrepresent me. The little experience I have had in addressing public meetings, in country school houses, avails me nothing on the present occasion.

The papers and placards say, that I am to deliver a 4th [of] July oration. This certainly sounds large, and out of the common way, for it is true that I have often had the privilege to speak in this beautiful Hall, and to address many who now honor me with their presence. But neither their familiar faces, nor the perfect gage I think I have of Corinthian Hall, seems to free me from embarrassment.

The fact is, ladies and gentlemen, the distance between this platform and the slave plantation, from which I escaped, is considerable—and the difficulties to be overcome in getting from the latter to the former, are by no means slight. That I am here to-day is, to me, a matter of astonishment as well as of gratitude. You will not, therefore, be surprised, if in what I have to say I evince no elaborate preparation, nor grace my speech with any high sounding exordium. With little

SOURCE: John W. Blassingame, ed., *The Frederick Douglass Papers: Series One: Speeches, Debates, and Interviews, 1847–1854* (New Haven: Yale University Press, 1982), vol. 2, 359–371, 386–387.

experience and with less learning, I have been able to throw my thoughts hastily and imperfectly together; and trusting to your patient and generous indulgence, I will proceed to lay them before you. . . .

This, for the purpose of this celebration, is the 4th of July. It is the birthday of your National Independence, and of your political freedom. This, to you, is what the Passover was to the emancipated people of God. It carries your minds back to the day, and to the act of your great deliverance; and to the signs, and to the wonders, associated with that act, and that day. This celebration also marks the beginning of another year of your national life; and reminds you that the Republic of America is now 76 years old. . . .

Fellow Citizens, I am not wanting in respect for the fathers of this republic. The signers of the Declaration of Independence were brave men. They were great men, too, great enough to give frame to a great age. It does not often happen to a nation to raise, at one time, such a number of truly great men. The point from which I am compelled to view them is not, certainly, the most favorable; and yet I cannot contemplate their great deeds with less than admiration. They were statesmen, patriots and heroes, and for the good they did, and the principles they contended for, I will unite with you to honor their memory. . . .

Fellow-citizens, pardon me, allow me to ask, why am I called upon to speak here to-day? What have I, or those I represent, to do with your national independence? Are the great principles of political freedom and of natural justice, embodied in that Declaration of Independence, extended to us? and am I, therefore, called upon to bring our humble offering to the national altar, and to confess the benefits and express devout gratitude for the blessings resulting from your independence to us?

Would to God, both for your sakes and ours, that an affirmative answer could be truthfully returned to these questions! Then would my task be light, and my burden easy and delightful. For who is there so cold, that a nation's sympathy could not warm him? Who so obdurate and dead to the claims of gratitude, that would not thankfully acknowledge such priceless benefits? Who so stolid and selfish, that would not give his voice to swell the hallelujahs of a nation's jubilee, when the chains of servitude had been torn from his limbs? I am not that man. In a case like that, the dumb might eloquently speak, and the "lame man leap as an hart."

But such is not the state of the case. I say it with a sad sense of the disparity between us. I am not included within the pale of glorious anniversary! Your high independence only reveals the immeasurable distance between us. The blessings in which you, this day, rejoice, are not enjoyed in common. The rich inheritance of justice, liberty, prosperity and independence, bequeathed by your fathers, is shared by you, not by me. The sunlight that brought light and healing to you, has brought stripes and death to me. This Fourth July is yours, not mine. You may rejoice, I must mourn. To drag a man in fetters into the grand illuminated temple of liberty, and call upon him to join you in joyous anthems, were inhuman mockery and sacrilegious irony. Do you mean, citizens, to mock me, by asking me to speak to-day? If so, there is a parallel to your conduct. And let me warn you that it is dangerous to copy the example of a nation whose crimes, towering up to heaven, were thrown down by the breath of the Almighty, burying that nation in irrevocable ruin! I can to-day take up the plaintive lament of a peeled and woe-smitten people!

"By the rivers of Babylon, there we sat down. Yea! we wept when we remembered Zion. We hanged our harps upon the willows in the midst thereof. For there, they that carried us away captive, required of us a song; and they who wasted us required of us mirth, saying, Sing us one of the songs of Zion. How can we sing the Lord's song in a strange land? If I forget thee, O Jerusalem, let my right hand forget her cunning. If I do not remember thee, let my tongue cleave to the roof of my mouth."

Fellow-citizens, above your national, tumultuous joy, I hear the mournful wail of millions! whose chains, heavy and grievous yesterday, are, to-day, rendered more intolerable by the jubilee shouts that reach them. If I do forget, if I do not faithfully remember those bleeding children of sorrow this day, "may my right hand forget her cunning, and may my tongue cleave to the roof of my mouth!" To forget them, to pass lightly over their wrongs, and to chime in with the popular theme, would be treason most scandalous and shocking, and would make me a reproach before God and the world.

My subject, then, fellow-citizens, is American slavery. I shall see this day and its popular characteristics from the slave's point of view. Standing there identified with the American bondman, making his wrongs mine, I do not hesitate to declare, with all my soul, that the character and conduct of this nation never looked blacker to me than on this 4th of July!

Whether we turn to the declarations of the past, or to the professions of the present, the conduct of the nation seems equally hideous and revolting. America is false to the past, false to the present, and solemnly binds herself to be false to the future. Standing with God and the crushed and bleeding slave on this occasion, I will, in the name of humanity which is outraged, in the name of liberty which is fettered, in the name of the constitution and the Bible which are disregarded and trampled upon, dare to call in question and to denounce, with all the emphasis I can command, everything that serves to perpetuate slavery—the great sin and shame of America! "I will not equivocate; I will not excuse"; I will use the severest language I can command; and yet not one word shall escape me that any man, whose judgment is not blinded by prejudice, or who is not at heart a slaveholder, shall not confess to be right and just.

But I fancy I hear some one of my audience say, "It is just in this circumstance that you and your brother abolitionists fail to make a favorable impression on the public mind. Would you argue more, and denounce less; would you persuade more, and rebuke less; your cause would be much more likely to succeed."

But, I submit, where all is plain there is nothing to be argued. What point in the anti-slavery creed would you have me argue? On what branch of the subject do the people of this country need light? Must I undertake to prove that the slave is a man? That point is conceded already. Nobody doubts it. The slaveholders themselves acknowledge it in the enactment of laws for their government. They acknowledge it when they punish disobedience on the part of the slave.

There are seventy-two crimes in the State of Virginia which, if committed by a black man (no matter how ignorant he be), subject him to the punishment of death; while only two of the same crimes will subject a white man to the like punishment. What is this but the acknowledgment that the slave is a moral, intellectual, and responsible being? The manhood of the slave is conceded. It is admitted in the fact that Southern statute books are covered with enactments forbidding, under severe fines and penalties, the teaching of the slave to read or to write. When you can point to any such laws in reference to the beasts of the field, then I may consent to argue the manhood of the slave. When the dogs in your streets, when the fowls of the air, when the cattle on your hills, when the fish of the sea, and the reptiles that crawl, shall be unable to distinguish the slave from a brute, then will I argue with you that the slave is a man!

For the present, it is enough to affirm the equal manhood of the Negro race. Is it not astonishing that, while we are ploughing, planting, and reaping, using all kinds of mechanical tools, erecting houses, constructing bridges, building ships, working in metals of brass, iron, copper, silver and gold; that, while we are reading, writing and ciphering, acting as clerks, merchants and secretaries, having among us lawyers, doctors, ministers, poets, authors, editors, orators and teachers; that, while we are engaged in all manner of enterprises common to other men, digging gold in California, capturing the whale in the Pacific, feeding sheep and cattle on the hill-side, living, moving, acting, thinking, planning, living in families as husbands, wives and children, and, above all, confessing and worshipping the Christian's God, and looking hopefully for life and immortality beyond the grave, we are called upon to prove that we are men!

Would you have me argue that man is entitled to liberty? that he is the rightful owner of his own body? You have already declared it. Must I argue the wrongfulness of slavery? Is that a question for Republicans? Is it to be settled by the rules of logic and argumentation, as a matter beset with great difficulty, involving a doubtful application of the principle of justice, hard to be understood? How should I look today, in the presence of Americans, dividing, and subdividing a discourse, to show that men have a natural right to freedom? speaking of it relatively and positively, negatively and affirmatively. To do so, would be to make myself ridiculous, and to offer an insult to your understanding. There is not a man beneath the canopy of heaven that does not know that slavery is wrong for him.

What, am I to argue that it is wrong to make men brutes, to rob them of their liberty, to work them without wages, to keep them ignorant of their relations to their fellow men, to beat them with sticks, to flay their flesh with the lash, to load their limbs with irons, to hunt them with dogs, to sell them at auction, to sunder their families, to knock out their teeth, to burn their flesh, to starve them into obedience and submission to their masters? Must I argue that a system thus marked with blood, and stained with pollution, is wrong? No! I will not. I have better employment for my time and strength than such arguments would imply.

What, then, remains to be argued? Is it that slavery is not divine; that God did not establish it; that our doctors of divinity are mistaken? There is blasphemy in the thought. That which is inhuman, cannot be divine! Who can reason on such a proposition? They that can, may; I cannot. The time for such argument is passed.

At a time like this, scorching irony, not convincing argument, is needed. O! had I the ability, and could reach the nation's ear, I would, to-day, pour out a fiery stream of biting ridicule, blasting reproach, withering sarcasm, and stern rebuke. For it is not light that is needed, but fire; it is not the gentle shower, but thunder. We need the storm, the whirlwind, and the earthquake. The feeling of the nation must be quickened; the conscience of the nation must be roused; the propriety of the nation must be startled; the hypocrisy of the nation must be exposed; and its crimes against God and man must be proclaimed and denounced.

What, to the American slave, is your 4th of July? I answer; a day that reveals to him, more than all other days in the year, the gross injustice and cruelty to which he is the constant victim. To him, your celebration is a sham; your boasted liberty, an unholy license; your national greatness, swelling vanity; your sounds of rejoicing are empty and heartless; your denunciation of tyrants, brass fronted impudence; your shouts of liberty and equality, hollow mockery; your prayers and hymns, your sermons and thanksgivings, with all your religious parade and solemnity, are, to Him, mere bombast, fraud, deception, impiety, and hypocrisy—a thin veil to cover up crimes which would disgrace a nation of savages. There is not a nation on the earth guilty of practices more shocking and bloody than are the people of the United States, at this very hour.

Go where you may, search where you will, roam through all the monarchies and despotisms of the Old World, travel through South America, search out every abuse, and when you have found the last, lay your facts by the side of the everyday practices of this nation, and you will say with me, that, for revolting barbarity and shameless hypocrisy, America reigns without a rival. . . .

Allow me to say, in conclusion, notwithstanding the dark picture I have this day presented, of the state of the nation, I do not despair of this country. There are forces in operation which must inevitably work the downfall of slavery. "The arm of the Lord is not shortened," and the doom of slavery is certain. I, therefore, leave off where I began, with hope. While drawing encouragement from "the Declaration of Independence," the great principles it contains, and the genius of American Institutions, my spirit is also cheered by the obvious tendencies of the age. . . .

Henry David Thoreau (1817–1862)

When hostilities with Mexico broke out in 1846, there was little doubt in anyone's mind that the war was going to be a war for expansion. Many Northerners were aware that the South had set its sights on the northern provinces of Mexico as suitable territory into which slavery could be expanded and out of which new slave states could be carved. But, on the *whole, there was widespread enthusiasm and patriotic fervor in favor of war. Two hundred thousand men volunteered for the army, while politicians and newspapers claimed that the war would be a blessing for Mexico by bestowing the American benefits of liberty and equality. Abolitionists and some clergymen and politicians, however, raised their voices in opposition to a war that would expand slavery. William Lloyd Garrison staunchly condemned the war. So, too, did Theodore Parker, Henry Clay, and David Wilmot. A little-known one-term congressman from Illinois, responding to President Polk's statement that "American blood had been spilled on American soil," introduced the "Spot Resolution" to Congress, which demanded that the president reveal the exact spot on which American blood had been spilled. Abraham Lincoln's resolution, however, was defeated, and war was declared. Eventually, enthusiasm for the war began to wane, especially after reports out of Mexico revealed that tens of thousands of American soldiers were dying of dysentery and other diseases, hundreds were deserting, and atrocities were being perpetrated against the civilian population.*

The most famous dissenter against the Mexican War was Henry David Thoreau. Thoreau, like his close friend Ralph Waldo Emerson, was a transcendentalist. In the summer of 1846, Thoreau was in the midst of his experiment in living life simply and deliberately at Walden Pond. He believed that most men were living lives of "quiet desperation" because they were unable to connect with their own spirits. "However mean your life is," Thoreau wrote, "meet it and live it; do not shun it and call it hard names." In July 1846, after refusing to pay his poll tax because he refused to support a government that was undertaking a war to expand slavery, Thoreau was arrested and put in jail. Though he spent only one night in the cell (against his wishes, his aunt paid the tax for him), the experience led him to write one of the most influential essays in American literature. In "On Resistance to Civil Government" (also referred to as "On the Duty of Civil Disobedience"), Thoreau argued that when there is injustice, it is the duty of every just man to oppose that injustice. If a law is unjust—as any law supporting the institution of slavery was—then it is the duty of every just person to break that law and pay the consequences. In this way, enough pressure would be put on the government so that the authorities would have no recourse but to change the law. The story (perhaps apocryphal) has been told that Emerson, scandalized that his friend had been locked up, visited Thoreau that night and asked, "Henry, what are you doing in there?" Thoreau, looking back through the bars, without hesitation replied, "Ralph, what are you doing out there!"

"Civil Disobedience" would go on to have a far wider impact than perhaps Thoreau himself could have foreseen. Later in the century a young law student in London read it and spent the rest of his life using Thoreau's principles to fight apartheid in South Africa and British imperialism in his native India. This, of course, was Mohandas K. Gandhi. In the 1940s, a

young theology student at Morehouse College who had been following Gandhi's career also fell under the spell of "Civil Disobedience" and put its ideas to the test after he became a minister in Montgomery, Alabama, and led the Montgomery bus boycott in 1955. Eight years later, in 1963, the Rev. Martin Luther King Jr. wrote "Letter from Birmingham Jail," in which he, too, echoing Thoreau, made a distinction between just laws and unjust laws.

Though Thoreau pointed out repeatedly that individuals must strive for self-realization, he did not lose sight of the fact that individuals must operate within society and that they have an obligation to do what is right. "I learned this, at least, by my experiment," Thoreau wrote at the end of Walden, *"that if one advances confidently in the direction of his dreams, and endeavors to live the life which he has imagined, he will meet with a success unexpected in common hours."*

"On Resistance to Civil Government," 1849

I heartily accept the motto, "That government is best which governs least"; and I should like to see it acted up to more rapidly and systematically. Carried out, it finally amounts to this, which also I believe—"That government is best which governs not at all"; and when men are prepared for it, that will be the kind of government which they will have. Government is at best but an expedient; but most governments are usually, and all governments are sometimes, inexpedient. The objections which have been brought against a standing army, and they are many and weighty, and deserve to prevail, may also at last be brought against a standing government. The standing army is only an arm of the standing government. The government itself, which is only the mode which the people have chosen to execute their will, is equally liable to be abused and perverted before the people can act through it. Witness the present Mexican war, the work of comparatively a few individuals using the standing government as their tool; for in the outset, the people would not have consented to this measure.

This American government—what is it but a tradition, though a recent one, endeavoring to transmit itself unimpaired to posterity, but each instant losing some of its integrity? It has not the vitality and force of a single living man; for a single man can bend it to his will. It is a sort of wooden gun to the people themselves. But it is not the less necessary for this; for the people must have some complicated machinery or other, and hear its din, to satisfy that idea of government which they have. Governments show thus how successfully men can be imposed upon, even impose on themselves, for their own advantage. It is excellent, we must all allow. Yet this government never of itself furthered any enterprise, but by the alacrity with which it got out of its way. It does not keep the country free. It does not settle the West. It does not educate. The character

SOURCE: Henry David Thoreau, *Walden and Resistance to Civil Government*, ed. by William Rossi (New York: W. W. Norton, 1992), 226–245.

inherent in the American people has done all that has been accomplished; and it would have done somewhat more, if the government had not sometimes got in its way. For government is an expedient, by which men would fain succeed in letting one another alone; and, as has been said, when it is most expedient, the governed are most let alone by it. Trade and commerce, if they were not made of india-rubber, would never manage to bounce over obstacles which legislators are continually putting in their way; and if one were to judge these men wholly by the effects of their actions and not partly by their intentions, they would deserve to be classed and punished with those mischievious persons who put obstructions on the railroads.

But, to speak practically and as a citizen, unlike those who call themselves no-government men, I ask for, not at once no government, but at once a better government. Let every man make known what kind of government would command his respect, and that will be one step toward obtaining it.

After all, the practical reason why, when the power is once in the hands of the people, a majority are permitted, and for a long period continue, to rule is not because they are most likely to be in the right, nor because this seems fairest to the minority, but because they are physically the strongest. But a government in which the majority rule in all cases can not be based on justice, even as far as men understand it. Can there not be a government in which the majorities do not virtually decide right and wrong, but conscience?—in which majorities decide only those questions to which the rule of expediency is applicable? Must the citizen ever for a moment, or in the least degree, resign his conscience to the legislator? Why has every man a conscience then? I think that we should be men first, and subjects afterward. It is not desirable to cultivate a respect for the law, so much as for the right. The only obligation which I have a right to assume is to do at any time what I think right. It is truly enough said that a corporation has no conscience; but a corporation of conscientious men is a corporation with a conscience. Law never made men a whit more just; and, by means of their respect for it, even the well-disposed are daily made the agents of injustice. A common and natural result of an undue respect for the law is, that you may see a file of soldiers, colonel, captain, corporal, privates, powder-monkeys, and all, marching in admirable order over hill and dale to the wars, against their wills, ay, against their common sense and consciences, which makes it very steep marching indeed, and produces a palpitation of the heart. They have no doubt that it is a damnable business in which they are concerned; they are all peaceably inclined. Now, what are they? Men at all? or small movable forts and magazines, at the service of some unscrupulous man in power? Visit the Navy Yard, and behold a marine, such a man as an American government can make, or such as it can make a man with its black arts—a mere shadow and reminiscence of humanity, a man laid out alive and standing, and already, as one may say, buried under arms with funeral accompaniment, though it may be,

"Not a drum was heard, not a funeral note,
    As his corse to the rampart we hurried;

Not a soldier discharged his farewell shot
  O'er the grave where our hero was buried."

The mass of men serve the state thus, not as men mainly, but as machines, with their bodies. They are the standing army, and the militia, jailers, constables, posse comitatus, etc. In most cases there is no free exercise whatever of the judgement or of the moral sense; but they put themselves on a level with wood and earth and stones; and wooden men can perhaps be manufactured that will serve the purpose as well. Such command no more respect than men of straw or a lump of dirt. They have the same sort of worth only as horses and dogs. Yet such as these even are commonly esteemed good citizens. Others—as most legislators, politicians, lawyers, ministers, and office-holders—serve the state chiefly with their heads; and, as they rarely make any moral distinctions, they are as likely to serve the devil, without intending it, as God. A very few—as heroes, patriots, martyrs, reformers in the great sense, and men—serve the state with their consciences also, and so necessarily resist it for the most part; and they are commonly treated as enemies by it. A wise man will only be useful as a man, and will not submit to be "clay," and "stop a hole to keep the wind away," but leave that office to his dust at least:

"I am too high born to be propertied,
To be a second at control,
Or useful serving-man and instrument
To any sovereign state throughout the world."

He who gives himself entirely to his fellow men appears to them useless and selfish; but he who gives himself partially to them is pronounced a benefactor and philanthropist.

How does it become a man to behave toward the American government today? I answer, that he cannot without disgrace be associated with it. I cannot for an instant recognize that political organization as my government which is the slave's government also.

All men recognize the right of revolution; that is, the right to refuse allegiance to, and to resist, the government, when its tyranny or its inefficiency are great and unendurable. But almost all say that such is not the case now. But such was the case, they think, in the Revolution of '75. If one were to tell me that this was a bad government because it taxed certain foreign commodities brought to its ports, it is most probable that I should not make an ado about it, for I can do without them. All machines have their friction; and possibly this does enough good to counter-balance the evil. At any rate, it is a great evil to make a stir about it. But when the friction comes to have its machine, and oppression and robbery are organized, I say, let us not have such a machine any longer. In other words, when a sixth of the population of a nation which has undertaken to be the refuge of liberty are slaves, and a whole country is unjustly overrun and conquered by a foreign army, and subjected to military law, I think that it is not too soon for honest men to rebel and revolutionize. What makes this duty the more urgent is the fact that the country so overrun is not our own, but ours is the invading army.

Paley, a common authority with many on moral questions, in his chapter on the "Duty of Submission to Civil Government," resolves all civil obligation into expediency; and he proceeds to say that "so long as the interest of the whole society requires it, that it, so long as the established government cannot be resisted or changed without public inconveniencey, it is the will of God . . . that the established government be obeyed—and no longer. This principle being admitted, the justice of every particular case of resistance is reduced to a computation of the quantity of the danger and grievance on the one side, and of the probability and expense of redressing it on the other." Of this, he says, every man shall judge for himself. But Paley appears never to have contemplated those cases to which the rule of expediency does not apply, in which a people, as well as an individual, must do justice, cost what it may. If I have unjustly wrested a plank from a drowning man, I must restore it to him though I drown myself. This, according to Paley, would be inconvenient. But he that would save his life, in such a case, shall lose it. This people must cease to hold slaves, and to make war on Mexico, though it cost them their existence as a people.

In their practice, nations agree with Paley; but does anyone think that Massachusetts does exactly what is right at the present crisis?

"*A drab of state, a cloth-o'-silver slut,*
To have her train borne up, and her soul trail in the dirt."

Practically speaking, the opponents to a reform in Massachusetts are not a hundred thousand politicians at the South, but a hundred thousand merchants and farmers here, who are more interested in commerce and agriculture than they are in humanity, and are not prepared to do justice to the slave and to Mexico, cost what it may. I quarrel not with far-off foes, but with those who, near at home, co-operate with, and do the bidding of, those far away, and without whom the latter would be harmless. We are accustomed to say, that the mass of men are unprepared; but improvement is slow, because the few are not as materially wiser or better than the many. It is not so important that many should be good as you, as that there be some absolute goodness somewhere; for that will leaven the whole lump. There are thousands who are in opinion opposed to slavery and to the war, who yet in effect do nothing to put an end to them; who, esteeming themselves children of Washington and Franklin, sit down with their hands in their pockets, and say that they know not what to do, and do nothing; who even postpone the question of freedom to the question of free trade, and quietly read the prices-current along with the latest advices from Mexico, after dinner, and, it may be, fall asleep over them both. What is the price-current of an honest man and patriot today? They hesitate, and they regret, and sometimes they petition; but they do nothing in earnest and with effect. They will wait, well disposed, for others to remedy the evil, that they may no longer have it to regret. At most, they give up only a cheap vote, and a feeble countenance and Godspeed, to the right, as it goes by them. There are nine hundred and ninety-nine patrons of virtue to one virtuous man. But it is easier to deal with the real possessor of a thing than with the temporary guardian of it.

All voting is a sort of gaming, like checkers or backgammon, with a slight moral tinge to it, a playing with right and wrong, with moral questions; and betting naturally accompanies it. The character of the voters is not staked. I cast my vote, perchance, as I think right; but I am not vitally concerned that that right should prevail. I am willing to leave it to the majority. Its obligation, therefore, never exceeds that of expediency. Even voting for the right is doing nothing for it. It is only expressing to men feebly your desire that it should prevail. A wise man will not leave the right to the mercy of chance, nor wish it to prevail through the power of the majority. There is but little virtue in the action of masses of men. When the majority shall at length vote for the abolition of slavery, it will be because they are indifferent to slavery, or because there is but little slavery left to be abolished by their vote. They will then be the only slaves. Only his vote can hasten the abolition of slavery who asserts his own freedom by his vote.

I hear of a convention to be held at Baltimore, or elsewhere, for the selection of a candidate for the Presidency, made up chiefly of editors, and men who are politicians by profession; but I think, what is it to any independent, intelligent, and respectable man what decision they may come to? Shall we not have the advantage of this wisdom and honesty, nevertheless? Can we not count upon some independent votes? Are there not many individuals in the country who do not attend conventions? But no: I find that the respectable man, so called, has immediately drifted from his position, and despairs of his country, when his country has more reasons to despair of him. He forthwith adopts one of the candidates thus selected as the only available one, thus proving that he is himself available for any purposes of the demagogue. His vote is of no more worth than that of any unprincipled foreigner or hireling native, who may have been bought. O for a man who is a man, and, as my neighbor says, has a bone is his back which you cannot pass your hand through! Our statistics are at fault: the population has been returned too large. How many men are there to a square thousand miles in the country? Hardly one. Does not America offer any inducement for men to settle here? The American has dwindled into an Odd Fellow—one who may be known by the development of his organ of gregariousness, and a manifest lack of intellect and cheerful self-reliance; whose first and chief concern, on coming into the world, is to see that the almshouses are in good repair; and, before yet he has lawfully donned the virile garb, to collect a fund to the support of the widows and orphans that may be; who, in short, ventures to live only by the aid of the Mutual Insurance company, which has promised to bury him decently.

It is not a man's duty, as a matter of course, to devote himself to the eradication of any, even to most enormous, wrong; he may still properly have other concerns to engage him; but it is his duty, at least, to wash his hands of it, and, if he gives it no thought longer, not to give it practically his support. If I devote myself to other pursuits and contemplations, I must first see, at least, that I do not pursue them sitting upon another man's shoulders. I must get off him first, that he may pursue his contemplations too. See what gross inconsistency is tolerated. I have heard some of my townsmen say, "I should like to have them order me out to help put down an insurrection of the slaves, or to march to Mexico—see if I would go"; and yet these very men have each, directly by their allegiance, and so indirectly, at least, by their money, furnished a substitute. The soldier is applauded who refuses to serve in an unjust war by those who do not refuse to sustain the unjust government which makes the war; is applauded by those whose own act and authority he disregards and sets at naught; as if the state were penitent to that degree that it hired one to scourge it while it sinned, but not to that degree that it left off sinning for a moment. Thus, under the name of Order and Civil Government, we are all made at last to pay homage to and support our own meanness. After the first blush of sin comes its indifference; and from immoral it becomes, as it were, unmoral, and not quite unnecessary to that life which we have made.

The broadest and most prevalent error requires the most disinterested virtue to sustain it. The slight reproach to which the virtue of patriotism is commonly liable, the noble are most likely to incur. Those who, while they disapprove of the character and measures of a government, yield to it their allegiance and support are undoubtedly its most conscientious supporters, and so frequently the most serious obstacles to reform. Some are petitioning the State to dissolve the Union, to disregard the requisitions of the President. Why do they not dissolve it themselves—the union between themselves and the State—and refuse to pay their quota into its treasury? Do not they stand in the same relation to the State that the State does to the Union? And have not the same reasons prevented the State from resisting the Union which have prevented them from resisting the State?

How can a man be satisfied to entertain an opinion merely, and enjoy it? Is there any enjoyment in it, if his opinion is that he is aggrieved? If you are cheated out of a single dollar by your neighbor, you do not rest satisfied with knowing you are cheated, or with saying that you are cheated, or even with petitioning him to pay you your due; but you take effectual steps at once to obtain the full amount, and see to it that you are never cheated again. Action from principle, the perception and the performance of right, changes things and relations; it is essentially revolutionary, and does not consist wholly with anything which was. It not only divided States and churches, it divides families; ay, it divides the individual, separating the diabolical in him from the divine.

Unjust laws exist: shall we be content to obey them, or shall we endeavor to amend them, and obey them until we have succeeded, or shall we transgress them at once? Men, generally, under such a government as this, think that they ought to wait until they have persuaded the majority to alter them. They think that, if they should resist, the remedy would be worse than the evil. But it is the fault of the government itself that the remedy is worse than the evil. It makes it worse. Why is it not more apt to anticipate and provide for reform? Why does it not cherish its wise minority? Why does it cry and resist before it is hurt? Why does it not encourage its citizens to put out its faults, and do better than it would have them? Why does it always crucify Christ and excommunicate Copernicus and Luther, and pronounce Washington and Franklin rebels?

One would think, that a deliberate and practical denial of its authority was the only offense never contemplated by its government; else, why has it not assigned its definite, its suitable and proportionate, penalty? If a man who has no property refuses but once to earn nine shillings for the State, he is put in prison for a period unlimited by any law that I know, and determined only by the discretion of those who put him there; but if he should steal ninety times nine shillings from the State, he is soon permitted to go at large again.

If the injustice is part of the necessary friction of the machine of government, let it go, let it go: perchance it will wear smooth—certainly the machine will wear out. If the injustice has a spring, or a pulley, or a rope, or a crank, exclusively for itself, then perhaps you may consider whether the remedy will not be worse than the evil; but if it is of such a nature that it requires you to be the agent of injustice to another, then I say, break the law. Let your life be a counter-friction to stop the machine. What I have to do is to see, at any rate, that I do not lend myself to the wrong which I condemn.

As for adopting the ways which the State has provided for remedying the evil, I know not of such ways. They take too much time, and a man's life will be gone. I have other affairs to attend to. I came into this world, not chiefly to make this a good place to live in, but to live in it, be it good or bad. A man has not everything to do, but something; and because he cannot do everything, it is not necessary that he should be petitioning the Governor or the Legislature any more than it is theirs to petition me; and if they should not hear my petition, what should I do then? But in this case the State has provided no way: its very Constitution is the evil. This may seem to be harsh and stubborn and unconciliatory; but it is to treat with the utmost kindness and consideration the only spirit that can appreciate or deserves it. So is all change for the better, like birth and death, which convulse the body.

I do not hesitate to say, that those who call themselves Abolitionists should at once effectually withdraw their support, both in person and property, from the government of Massachusetts, and not wait till they constitute a majority of one, before they suffer the right to prevail through them. I think that it is enough if they have God on their side, without waiting for that other one. Moreover, any man more right than his neighbors constitutes a majority of one already.

I meet this American government, or its representative, the State government, directly, and face to face, once a year—no more—in the person of its tax-gatherer; this is the only mode in which a man situated as I am necessarily meets it; and it then says distinctly, Recognize me; and the simplest, the most effectual, and, in the present posture of affairs, the indispensablest mode of treating with it on this head, of expressing your little satisfaction with and love for it, is to deny it then. My civil neighbor, the tax-gatherer, is the very man I have to deal with—for it is, after all, with men and not with parchment that I quarrel—and he has voluntarily chosen to be an agent of the government. How shall he ever know well that he is and does as an officer of the government, or as a man, until he is obliged to consider whether he will treat me, his neighbor, for whom he has respect, as a neighbor and well-disposed man, or as a maniac and disturber of the peace, and see if he can get over this obstruction to his neighborliness without a ruder and more impetuous thought or speech corresponding with his action. I know this well, that if one thousand, if one hundred, if ten men whom I could name—if ten honest men only—ay, if one HONEST man, in this State of Massachusetts, ceasing to hold slaves, were actually to withdraw from this co-partnership, and be locked up in the county jail therefor, it would be the abolition of slavery in America. For it matters not how small the beginning may seem to be: what is once well done is done forever. But we love better to talk about it: that we say is our mission. Reform keeps many scores of newspapers in its service, but not one man. If my esteemed neighbor, the State's ambassador, who will devote his days to the settlement of the question of human rights in the Council Chamber, instead of being threatened with the prisons of Carolina, were to sit down the prisoner of Massachusetts, that State which is so anxious to foist the sin of slavery upon her sister—though at present she can discover only an act of inhospitality to be the ground of a quarrel with her—the Legislature would not wholly waive the subject of the following winter.

Under a government which imprisons unjustly, the true place for a just man is also a prison. The proper place today, the only place which Massachusetts has provided for her freer and less despondent spirits, is in her prisons, to be put out and locked out of the State by her own act, as they have already put themselves out by their principles. It is there that the fugitive slave, and the Mexican prisoner on parole, and the Indian come to plead the wrongs of his race should find them; on that separate but more free and honorable ground, where the State places those who are not with her, but against her—the only house in a slave State in which a free man can abide with honor. If any think that their influence would be lost there, and their voices no longer afflict the ear of the State, that they would not be as an enemy within its walls, they do not know by how much truth is stronger than error, nor how much more eloquently and effectively he can combat injustice who has experienced a little in his own person. Cast your whole vote, not a strip of paper merely, but your whole influence. A minority is powerless while it conforms to the majority; it is not even a minority then; but it is irresistible when it clogs by its whole weight. If the alternative is to keep all just men in prison, or give up war and slavery, the State will not hesitate which to choose. If a thousand men were not to pay their tax bills this year, that would not be a violent and bloody measure, as it would be to pay them, and enable the State to commit violence and shed innocent blood. This is, in fact, the definition of a peaceable revolution, if any such is possible. If the tax-gatherer, or any other public officer, asks me, as one has done, "But what shall I do?" my answer is, "If you really wish to do anything, resign your office." When the subject has refused allegiance, and the officer has resigned from office, then the revolution is accomplished. But even suppose blood shed when the conscience is wounded? Through this wound a man's real manhood and immortality flow out, and he bleeds to an everlasting death. I see this blood flowing now.

I have contemplated the imprisonment of the offender, rather than the seizure of his goods—though both will serve the same purpose—because they who assert the purest right, and consequently are most dangerous to a corrupt State, commonly have not spent much time in accumulating property. To such the State renders comparatively small service, and a slight tax is wont to appear exorbitant, particularly if they are obliged to earn it by special labor with their hands. If there were one who lived wholly without the use of money, the State itself would hesitate to demand it of him. But the rich man—not to make any invidious comparison—is always sold to the institution which makes him rich. Absolutely speaking, the more money, the less virtue; for money comes between a man and his objects, and obtains them for him; it was certainly no great virtue to obtain it. It puts to rest many questions which he would otherwise be taxed to answer; while the only new question which it puts is the hard but superfluous one, how to spend it. Thus his moral ground is taken from under his feet. The opportunities of living are diminished in proportion as that are called the "means" are increased. The best thing a man can do for his culture when he is rich is to endeavor to carry out those schemes which he entertained when he was poor. Christ answered the Herodians according to their condition. "Show me the tribute-money," said he—and one took a penny out of his pocket—if you use money which has the image of Caesar on it, and which he has made current and valuable, that is, if you are men of the State, and gladly enjoy the advantages of Caesar's government, then pay him back some of his own when he demands it. "Render therefore to Caesar that which is Caesar's and to God those things which are God's"—leaving them no wiser than before as to which was which; for they did not wish to know.

When I converse with the freest of my neighbors, I perceive that, whatever they may say about the magnitude and seriousness of the question, and their regard for the public tranquillity, the long and the short of the matter is, that they cannot spare the protection of the existing government, and they dread the consequences to their property and families of disobedience to it. For my own part, I should not like to think that I ever rely on the protection of the State. But, if I deny the authority of the State when it presents its tax bill, it will soon take and waste all my property, and so harass me and my children without end. This is hard. This makes it impossible for a man to live honestly, and at the same time comfortably, in outward respects. It will not be worth the while to accumulate property; that would be sure to go again. You must hire or squat somewhere, and raise but a small crop, and eat that soon. You must live within yourself, and depend upon yourself always tucked up and ready for a start, and not have many affairs. A man may grow rich in Turkey even, if he will be in all respects a good subject of the Turkish government. Confucius said: "If a state is governed by the principles of reason, poverty and misery are subjects of shame; if a state is not governed by the principles of reason, riches and honors are subjects of shame." No: until I want the protection of Massachusetts to be extended to me in some distant Southern port, where my liberty is endangered, or until I am bent solely on building up an estate at home by peaceful enterprise, I can afford to refuse allegiance to Massachusetts, and her right to my property and life. It costs me less in every sense to incur the penalty of disobedience to the State than it would to obey. I should feel as if I were worth less in that case.

Some years ago, the State met me in behalf of the Church, and commanded me to pay a certain sum toward the support of a clergyman whose preaching my father attended, but never I myself. "Pay," it said, "or be locked up in the jail." I declined to pay. But, unfortunately, another man saw fit to pay it. I did not see why the schoolmaster should be taxed to support the priest, and not the priest the schoolmaster; for I was not the State's schoolmaster, but I supported myself by voluntary subscription. I did not see why the lyceum should not present its tax bill, and have the State to back its demand, as well as the Church. However, as the request of the selectmen, I condescended to make some such statement as this in writing: "Know all men by these presents, that I, Henry Thoreau, do not wish to be regarded as a member of any society which I have not joined." This I gave to the town clerk; and he has it. The State, having thus learned that I did not wish to be regarded as a member of that church, has never made a like demand on me since; though it said that it must adhere to its original presumption that time. If I had known how to name them, I should then have signed off in detail from all the societies which I never signed on to; but I did not know where to find such a complete list.

I have paid no poll tax for six years. I was put into a jail once on this account, for one night; and, as I stood considering the walls of solid stone, two or three feet thick, the door of wood and iron, a foot thick, and the iron grating which strained the light, I could not help being struck with the foolishness of that institution which treated me as if I were mere flesh and blood and bones, to be locked up. I wondered that it should have concluded at length that this was the best use it could put me to, and had never thought to avail itself of my services in some way. I saw that, if there was a wall of stone between me and my townsmen, there was a still more difficult one to climb or break through before they could get to be as free as I was. I did not for a moment feel confined, and the walls seemed a great waste of stone and mortar. I felt as if I alone of all my townsmen had paid my tax. They plainly did not know how to treat me, but behaved like persons who are underbred. In every threat and in every compliment there was a blunder; for they thought that my chief desire was to stand the other side of that stone wall. I could not but smile to see how industriously they locked the door on my meditations, which followed them out again without let or hindrance, and they were really all that was dangerous. As they could not reach me, they had resolved to punish my body; just as boys, if they cannot come at some person against whom they have a spite, will abuse his dog. I saw that the State was half-witted, that it was timid as a lone woman with her silver spoons, and that it did not know its friends from its foes, and I lost all my remaining respect for it, and pitied it.

Thus the state never intentionally confronts a man's sense, intellectual or moral, but only his body, his senses. It is not armed with superior wit or honesty, but with superior physical strength. I was not born to be forced. I will breathe after my own fashion. Let us see who is the strongest. What force has a multitude? They only can force me who obey a higher law than I. They force me to become like themselves. I do not hear of men being forced to live this way or that by masses of men. What sort of life were that to live? When I meet a government which says to me, "Your money or your life," why should I be in haste to give it my money? It may be in a great strait, and not know what to do: I cannot help that. It must help itself; do as I do. It is not worth the while to snivel about it. I am not responsible for the successful working of the machinery of society. I am not the son of the engineer. I perceive that, when an acorn and a chestnut fall side by side, the one does not remain inert to make way for the other, but both obey their own laws, and spring and grow and flourish as best they can, till one, perchance, overshadows and destroys the other. If a plant cannot live according to nature, it dies; and so a man.

The night in prison was novel and interesting enough. The prisoners in their shirtsleeves were enjoying a chat and the evening air in the doorway, when I entered. But the jailer said, "Come, boys, it is time to lock up"; and so they dispersed, and I heard the sound of their steps returning into the hollow apartments. My room-mate was introduced to me by the jailer as "a first-rate fellow and clever man." When the door was locked, he showed me where to hang my hat, and how he managed matters there. The rooms were whitewashed once a month; and this one, at least, was the whitest, most simply furnished, and probably neatest apartment in town. He naturally wanted to know where I came from, and what brought me there; and, when I had told him, I asked him in my turn how he came there, presuming him to be an honest man, of course; and as the world goes, I believe he was. "Why," said he, "they accuse me of burning a barn; but I never did it." As near as I could discover, he had probably gone to bed in a barn when drunk, and smoked his pipe there; and so a barn was burnt. He had the reputation of being a clever man, had been there some three months waiting for his trial to come on, and would have to wait as much longer; but he was quite domesticated and contented, since he got his board for nothing, and thought that he was well treated.

He occupied one window, and I the other; and I saw that if one stayed there long, his principal business would be to look out the window. I had soon read all the tracts that were left there, and examined where former prisoners had broken out, and where a grate had been sawed off, and heard the history of the various occupants of that room; for I found that even there there was a history and a gossip which never circulated beyond the walls of the jail. Probably this is the only house in the town where verses are composed, which are afterward printed in a circular form, but not published. I was shown quite a long list of young men who had been detected in an attempt to escape, who avenged themselves by singing them.

I pumped my fellow-prisoner as dry as I could, for fear I should never see him again; but at length he showed me which was my bed, and left me to blow out the lamp.

It was like travelling into a far country, such as I had never expected to behold, to lie there for one night. It seemed to me that I never had heard the town clock strike before, nor the evening sounds of the village; for we slept with the windows open, which were inside the grating. It was to see my native village in the light of the Middle Ages, and our Concord was turned into a Rhine stream, and visions of knights and castles passed before me. They were the voices of old burghers that I heard in the streets. I was an involuntary spectator and auditor of whatever was done and said in the kitchen of the adjacent village inn—a wholly new and rare experience to me. It was a closer view of my native town. I was fairly inside of it. I never had seen its institutions before. This is one of its peculiar institutions; for it is a shire town. I began to comprehend what its inhabitants were about.

In the morning, our breakfasts were put through the hole in the door, in small oblong-square tin pans, made to fit, and holding a pint of chocolate, with brown bread, and an iron spoon. When they called for the vessels again, I was green enough to return what bread I had left, but my comrade seized it, and said that I should lay that up for lunch or dinner. Soon after he was let out to work at haying in a neighboring field, whither he went every day, and would not be back till noon; so he bade me good day, saying that he doubted if he should see me again.

When I came out of prison—for some one interfered, and paid that tax—I did not perceive that great changes had taken place on the common, such as he observed who went in a youth and emerged a gray-headed man; and yet a change had come to my eyes come over the scene—the town, and State, and country, greater than any that mere time could effect. I saw yet more distinctly the State in which I lived. I saw to what extent the people among whom I lived could be trusted as good neighbors and friends; that their friendship was for summer weather only; that they did not greatly propose to do right; that they were a distinct race from me by their prejudices and superstitions, as the Chinamen and Malays are that in their sacrifices to humanity they ran no risks, not even to their property; that after all they were not so noble but they treated the thief as he had treated them, and hoped, by a certain outward observance and a few prayers, and by walking in a particular straight though useless path from time to time, to save their souls. This may be to judge my neighbors harshly; for I believe that many of them are not aware that they have such an institution as the jail in their village.

It was formerly the custom in our village, when a poor debtor came out of jail, for his acquaintances to salute him, looking through their fingers, which were crossed to represent the jail window, "How do ye do?" My neighbors did not thus salute me, but first looked at me, and then at one another, as if I had returned from a long journey. I was put into jail as I was going to the shoemaker's to get a shoe which was mended. When I was let out the next morning, I proceeded to finish my errand, and, having put on my mended shoe, joined a huckleberry party, who were impatient to put themselves under my conduct; and in half an hour—for the horse was soon tackled—was in the midst of a huckleberry field, on one of our highest hills, two miles off, and then the State was nowhere to be seen.

This is the whole history of "My Prisons."

I have never declined paying the highway tax, because I am as desirous of being a good neighbor as I am of being a bad subject; and as for supporting schools, I am doing my part to educate my fellow countrymen now. It is for no particular item in the tax bill that I refuse to pay it. I simply wish to refuse allegiance to the State, to withdraw and stand aloof from it effectually. I do not care to trace the course of my dollar, if I could, till it buys a man a musket to shoot one with—the dollar is innocent—but I am concerned to trace the effects of my allegiance. In fact, I quietly declare war with the State, after my fashion, though I will still make use and get what advantages of her I can, as is usual in such cases.

If others pay the tax which is demanded of me, from a sympathy with the State, they do but what they have already done in their own case, or rather they abet injustice to a greater extent than the State requires. If they pay the tax from a mistaken interest in the individual taxed, to save his property, or prevent his going to jail, it is because they have not considered wisely how far they let their private feelings interfere with the public good.

This, then is my position at present. But one cannot be too much on his guard in such a case, lest his actions be biased by obstinacy or an undue regard for the opinions of men. Let him see that he does only what belongs to himself and to the hour.

I think sometimes, Why, this people mean well, they are only ignorant; they would do better if they knew how: why give your neighbors this pain to treat you as they are not inclined to? But I think again, This is no reason why I should do as they do, or permit others to suffer much greater pain of a different kind. Again, I sometimes say to myself, When many millions of men, without heat, without ill will, without personal feelings of any kind, demand of you a few shillings only, without the possibility, such is their constitution, of retracting or altering their present demand, and without the possibility, on your side, of appeal to any other millions, why expose yourself to this overwhelming brute force? You do not resist cold and hunger, the winds and the waves, thus obstinately; you quietly submit to a thousand similar necessities. You do not put your head into the fire. But just in proportion as I regard this as not wholly a brute force, but partly a human force, and consider that I have relations to those millions as to so many millions of men, and not of mere brute or inanimate things, I see that appeal is possible, first and instantaneously, from them to the Maker of them, and, secondly, from them to themselves. But if I put my head deliberately into the fire, there is no appeal to fire or to the Maker for fire, and I have only myself to blame. If I could convince myself that I have any right to be satisfied with men as they are, and to treat them accordingly, and not according, in some respects, to my requisitions and expectations of what they and I ought to be, then, like a good Mussulman and fatalist, I should endeavor to be satisfied with things as they are, and say it is the will of God. And, above all, there is this difference between resisting this and a purely brute or natural force, that I can resist this with some effect; but I cannot expect, like Orpheus, to change the nature of the rocks and trees and beasts.

I do not wish to quarrel with any man or nation. I do not wish to split hairs, to make fine distinctions, or set myself up as better than my neighbors. I seek rather, I may say, even an excuse for conforming to the laws of the land. I am but too ready to conform to them. Indeed, I have reason to suspect myself on this head; and each year, as the tax-gatherer comes round, I find myself disposed to review the acts and position of the general and State governments, and the spirit of the people to discover a pretext for conformity.

> "We must affect our country as our parents,
> And if at any time we alienate
> Our love or industry from doing it honor,
> We must respect effects and teach the soul
> Matter of conscience and religion,
> And not desire of rule or benefit."

I believe that the State will soon be able to take all my work of this sort out of my hands, and then I shall be no better patriot than my fellow-countrymen. Seen from a lower point of view, the Constitution, with all its faults, is very good; the law and the courts are very respectable; even this State and this American government are, in many respects, very admirable, and rare things, to be thankful for, such as a great many have described them; but seen from a point of view a little higher, they are what I have described them; seen from a higher still, and the highest, who shall say what they are, or that they are worth looking at or thinking of at all?

However, the government does not concern me much, and I shall bestow the fewest possible thoughts on it. It is not many moments that I live under a government, even in this world. If a man is thought-free, fancy-free, imagination-free, that which is not never for a long time appearing to be to him, unwise rulers or reformers cannot fatally interrupt him.

I know that most men think differently from myself; but those whose lives are by profession devoted to the study of these or kindred subjects content me as little as any. Statesmen and legislators, standing so completely within the institution, never distinctly and nakedly behold it. They speak of moving society, but have no resting-place without it. They may be men of a certain experience and discrimination, and have no doubt invented ingenious and even useful systems, for which we sincerely thank them; but all their wit and usefulness lie within certain not very wide limits. They are wont to forget that the world is not governed by policy and expediency. [Daniel] Webster never goes behind government, and so cannot speak with authority about it. His words are wisdom to those legislators who contemplate no essential reform in the existing government; but for thinkers, and those who legislate for all time, he never once glances at the subject. I know of those whose serene and wise speculations on this theme would soon reveal the limits of his mind's range and hospitality. Yet, compared with the cheap professions of most reformers, and the still cheaper wisdom and eloquence of politicians in general, his are almost the only sensible and valuable words, and we thank Heaven for him. Comparatively, he is always strong, original, and, above all, practical. Still, his quality is not wisdom, but prudence. The lawyer's truth is not Truth, but consistency or a consistent expediency. Truth is always in harmony with herself, and is not concerned chiefly to reveal the justice that may consist with wrong-doing. He well deserves to be called, as he has been called, the Defender of the Constitution. There are really no blows to be given him but defensive ones. He is not a leader, but a follower. His leaders are the men of '87. "I have never made an effort," he says, "and never propose to make an effort; I have never countenanced an effort, and never mean to countenance an effort, to disturb the arrangement as originally made, by which various States came into the Union." Still thinking of the sanction which the Constitution gives to slavery, he says, "Because it was part of the original compact—let it stand." Notwithstanding his special acuteness and ability, he is unable to take a fact out of its merely political relations, and behold it as it lies absolutely to be disposed of by the intellect—what, for instance, it behooves a man to do here in America today with regard to slavery—but ventures, or is driven, to make some such desperate answer to the following, while professing to speak absolutely, and as a private man—from which what new and singular of social duties might be inferred? "The manner," says he, "in which the governments of the States where slavery exists are to regulate it is for their own consideration, under the responsibility to their constituents, to the general laws of propriety, humanity, and justice, and to God. Associations formed elsewhere, springing from a feeling of humanity, or any other cause, have nothing whatever to do with it. They have never received any encouragement from me and they never will. [These extracts have been inserted since the lecture was read -HDT]

They who know of no purer sources of truth, who have traced up its stream no higher, stand, and wisely stand, by the Bible and the Constitution, and drink at it there with reverence and humanity; but they who behold where it comes trickling into this lake or that pool, gird up their loins once more, and continue their pilgrimage toward its fountainhead.

No man with a genius for legislation has appeared in America. They are rare in the history of the world. There are orators, politicians, and eloquent men, by the thousand; but the speaker has not yet opened his mouth to speak who is capable of settling the much-vexed questions of the day. We love eloquence for its own sake, and not for any truth which it may utter, or any heroism it may inspire. Our legislators have not yet learned the comparative value of free trade and of freedom, of union, and of rectitude, to a nation. They have no genius or talent for comparatively humble questions of taxation and finance, commerce and manufactures and agriculture. If we were left solely to the wordy wit of legislators in Congress for our guidance, uncorrected by the seasonable experience and the effectual complaints of the people, America would not long retain her rank among the nations. For eighteen hundred years, though perchance I have no right to say it, the New Testament has been written; yet where is the legislator who has wisdom and practical talent enough to avail himself of the light which it sheds on the science of legislation.

The authority of government, even such as I am willing to submit to—for I will cheerfully obey those who know and can do better than I, and in many things even those who neither know nor can do so well—is still an impure one:

to be strictly just, it must have the sanction and consent of the governed. It can have no pure right over my person and property but what I concede to it. The progress from an absolute to a limited monarchy, from a limited monarchy to a democracy, is a progress toward a true respect for the individual. Even the Chinese philosopher was wise enough to regard the individual as the basis of the empire. Is a democracy, such as we know it, the last improvement possible in government? Is it not possible to take a step further towards recognizing and organizing the rights of man? There will never be a really free and enlightened State until the State comes to recognize the individual as a higher and independent power, from which all its own power and authority are derived, and treats him accordingly. I please myself with imagining a State at last which can afford to be just to all men, and to treat the individual with respect as a neighbor; which even would not think it inconsistent with its own repose if a few were to live aloof from it, not meddling with it, nor embraced by it, who fulfilled all the duties of neighbors and fellow men. A State which bore this kind of fruit, and suffered it to drop off as fast as it ripened, would prepare the way for a still more perfect and glorious State, which I have also imagined, but not yet anywhere seen.

Lucy Stone (1818–1893)

A graduate of Oberlin College, Lucy Stone spent most of her life as an influential abolitionist and feminist. When she married Henry B. Blackwell in 1855, she not only kept her maiden name but also used the marriage ceremony to issue a protest statement in which she (and her husband) deplored the subjugation of women.

STATEMENT ON MARRIAGE, 1855

While acknowledging our mutual affection by publicly assuming the relationship of husband and wife, yet in justice to ourselves and a great principle, we deem it a duty to declare that this act on our part implies no sanction of, nor promise of voluntary obedience to such of the present laws of marriage, as refuse to recognize the wife as an independent, rational being, while they confer upon the husband an injurious and unnatural superiority, investing him with legal powers which no honorable man would exercise, and which no man should possess. We protest especially against the laws which give to the husband:

SOURCE: Elizabeth Cady Stanton, Susan B. Anthony, and Matilda Joslyn Gage, eds., *History of Woman Suffrage*, vol. 1, (1881; New York: Arno Press and the *New York Times*, 1969), 260–261.

1. The custody of the wife's person.
2. The exclusive control and guardianship of their children.
3. The sole ownership of her personal, and use of her real estate, unless previously settled upon her, or placed in the hands of trustees, as in the case of minors, lunatics, and idiots.
4. The absolute right to the product of her industry.
5. Also against laws which give to the widower so much larger and more permanent interest in the property of his deceased wife, than they give to the widow in that of the deceased husband.
6. Finally, against the whole system by which "the legal existence of the wife is suspended during marriage," so that in most States, she neither has a legal part in the choice of her residence, nor can she make a will, nor sue or be sued in her own name, nor inherit property.

We believe that personal independence and equal human rights can never be forfeited, except for crime; that marriage should be an equal and permanent partnership, and so recognized by law; that until it is so recognized, married partners should provide against the radical injustice of present laws, by every means in their power.

We believe that where domestic difficulties arise, no appeal should be made to legal tribunals under existing laws, but that all difficulties should be submitted to the equitable adjustment of arbitrators mutually chosen.

Thus reverencing law, we enter our protest against rules and customs which are unworthy of the name, since they violate justice, the essence of law.

[Signed]
Henry B. Blackwell
Lucy Stone

The Know-Nothings

As the issue of slavery was rapidly consuming party politics during the 1840s and 1850s, a growing number of people began to believe that the real threat to the United States was not slavery but immigration, especially the immigration of Roman Catholics from Ireland and Germany. Believing that the United States would be undermined by the influx of these immigrants, who would presumably put their loyalty to the pope over the Constitution, old-stock Americans began to espouse nativism and joined various secret antiforeigner organizations. Eventually, these nativist groups formed the American Party to keep "America for Americans" and to ensure that Protestantism remained the dominant religion. Popularly called the Know-Nothings (because they usually responded, "I know nothing" when outsiders questioned them about the party), they met in Philadelphia in 1856, drew up a platform, and nominated former president Millard Fillmore as their candidate. The party received 21 percent of the popular vote in the election, but by the election of 1860, the slavery issue so dominated the nation that the Know-Nothings' political influence had dissipated.

AMERICAN PARTY PLATFORM, PHILADELPHIA, FEBRUARY 21, 1856

1. An humble acknowledgement to the Supreme Being, for his protecting care vouchsafed to our fathers in their successful Revolutionary struggle, and hitherto manifested to us, their descendants, in the preservation of the liberties, the independence and the union of these States.

2. The perpetuation of the Federal Union and Constitution, as the palladium of our civil and religious liberties, and the only sure bulwarks of American Independence.

3. *Americans must rule America*, and to this end *native*-born citizens should be selected for all State, Federal, and municipal offices of government employment, in preference to all others. *Nevertheless*,

4. Persons born of American parents residing temporarily abroad, should be entitled to all the rights of native-born citizens.

5. No person should be selected for political station (whether of native or foreign birth), who recognizes any allegiance or obligation of any description to any foreign prince, potentate or power, or who refuses to recognize the Federal and State Constitution (each within its sphere) as paramount to all other laws, as rules of political action.

6. The unequalled recognition and maintenance of the reserved rights of the several States, and the cultivation of harmony and fraternal good will between the citizens of the several States, and to this end, non-interference by Congress with questions appertaining solely to the individual States, and non-intervention by each State with the affairs of any other State.

7. The recognition of the right of native-born and naturalized citizens of the United States, permanently residing in any Territory thereof, to frame their constitution and laws, and to regulate their domestic and social affairs in their own mode, subject only to the provisions of the Federal Constitution, with the privilege of admission into the Union whenever they have the requisite population for one Representative in Congress: *Provided, always*, that none but those who are citizens of the United States, under the Constitution and laws thereof, and who have a fixed residence in any such territory, ought to participate in the formation of the Constitution, or in the enactment of laws for said Territory or State.

SOURCE: Thomas V. Cooper and Hector T. Fenton, *American Politics from the Beginning to Date* (Chicago: Charles R. Brodix, 1882), 35–36.

8. An enforcement of the principles that no State or Territory ought to admit others than citizens to the right of suffrage, or of holding political offices of the United States.

9. A change in the laws of naturalization, making a continued residence of twenty-one years, of all not heretofore provided for, an indispensable requisite for citizenship hereafter, and excluding all paupers, and persons convicted of crime, from landing upon our shores; but no interference with the vested rights of foreigners.

10. Opposition to any union between Church and State; no interference with religious faith or worship, and no test oaths for office.

11. Free and thorough investigation into any and all alleged abuses of public functionaries, and a strict economy in public expenditures.

12. The maintenance and enforcement of all laws constitutionally enacted until said laws shall be repealed, or shall be declared null and void by competent judicial authority.

13. Opposition to the reckless and unwise policy of the present Administration in the general management of our national affairs, and more especially as shown in removing "Americans" (by designation) and Conservatives in principle, from office, and placing foreigners and Ultraists in their places; as shown in a truckling subserviency to the stronger, and an insolent and cowardly bravado towards the weaker powers; as shown in re-opening sectional agitation; by the repeal of the Missouri Compromise; as shown in granting to unnaturalized foreigners the right of suffrage in Kansas and Nebraska question; as shown in the corruptions which pervade some of the Departments of the Government; as shown in disgracing meritorious naval officers through prejudice or caprice; and as shown in the blundering mismanagement of our foreign relations.

14. Therefore, to remedy existing evils, and prevent the disastrous consequences otherwise resulting therefrom, we would build up the "American Party" upon the principles hereinbefore stated.

15. That each State Council shall have authority to amend their several Constitutions, so as to abolish the several degrees and substitute a pledge of honor, instead of other obligations, for fellowship and admission into the party.

16. A free and open discussion of all political principles embraced in our platform.

John Brown (1800–1859)

One of the most famous and controversial figures in American history is the radical abolitionist John Brown. As with William Lloyd Garrison, there was very little "give" in John Brown. He held to his beliefs with a passion bordering on fanaticism. However, Brown was willing to go much further than Garrison, who had always held pacifist views. In 1856, he murdered five proslavery settlers in Pottawatomie, Kansas, by hacking them to death, thus plunging Bleeding Kansas into a guerrilla war that did not let up for more than a decade. On October 16, 1859, he led a band of 21 men (16 whites, 5 blacks) into Harpers Ferry, Virginia, where he hoped to seize the federal armory there. He intended to arm slaves and lead them into the Shenandoah Valley, where he believed other slaves would rally to the cause of armed insurrection. But the strategy failed. Enraged townspeople besieged Brown until several companies of U.S. marines and cavalry (one company under the command of Colonel Robert E. Lee) arrived. On October 18, Lee issued a demand for Brown to surrender. Brown rejected the offer, and in the ensuing shoot-out, 12 of Brown's men were killed and Brown himself, severely wounded, was captured. The event was regarded then—and is still so regarded by historians—as the final straw leading to the Civil War. To Northerners, the martyred Brown was a great hero. To Southerners, he was the devil incarnate, who would instigate the slaves to rise up and cut their masters' throats. The Southerners' conviction that Brown was representative of all Northerners led many slave states over the next several months to expand their state militias.

At his trial, Brown acknowledged that he was guilty of trying to free the slaves but not that he was guilty of a crime and that if he had "interfered on behalf of the rich" instead of the slaves, he would not have been brought to trial. He was found guilty of treason, and on December 2, 1859, he was hanged. He handed a note to a soldier as he mounted the scaffold: "I, John Brown am now quite certain that the crimes of this guilty land will never be purged away, but with Blood. I had, as I now think vainly, flattered myself that without very much bloodshed, it might be done."

Address to the Virginia Court at Charles Town, Virginia, November 2, 1859

I have, may it please the court, a few words to say.

In the first place, I deny everything but what I have all along admitted,—the design on my part to free slaves. I intended certainly to have made a clean thing of that matter, as I did last winter, when I went into Missouri and took slaves without the snapping of a gun on either side, moved them through the country, and finally left them in Canada. I designed to do the same thing again, on a larger scale. That was all I intended. I never did intend murder, or treason, or the destruction of property, or to excite or incite slaves to rebellion, or to make insurrection.

SOURCE: Louis Ruchames, ed., *A John Brown Reader* (London: Abelard-Schuman, 1959), 125–127.

I have another objection; and that is, it is unjust that I should suffer such a penalty. Had I interfered in the manner which I admit, and which I admit has been fairly proved (for I admire the truthfulness and candor of the greater portion of the witnesses who have testified in this case),—had I so interfered in behalf of the rich, the powerful, the intelligent, the so-called great, or in behalf of any of their friends—either father, mother, sister, wife, or children, or any of that class—and suffered and sacrificed what I have in this interference, it would have been all right; and every man in this court would have deemed it an act worthy of reward rather than punishment.

The court acknowledges, as I suppose, the validity of the law of God. I see a book kissed here which I suppose to be the Bible, or at least the New Testament. That teaches me that all things whatsoever I would that men should do to me, I should do even so to them. It teaches me further to "remember them that are in bonds, as bound with them." I endeavored to act up to that instruction. I say, I am too young to understand that God is any respecter of persons. I believe that to have interfered as I have done—as I have always freely admitted I have done—in behalf of His despised poor, was not wrong, but right. Now if it is deemed necessary that I should forfeit my life for the furtherance of the ends of justice, and mingle my blood further with the blood of my children and with the blood of millions in this slave country whose rights are disregarded by wicked, cruel, and unjust enactments.—I submit; so let it be done!

Let me say one word further.

I feel entirely satisfied with the treatment I have received on my trial. Considering all the circumstances, it has been more generous than I expected. I feel no consciousness of my guilt. I have stated from the first what was my intention, and what was not. I never had any design against the life of any person, nor any disposition to commit treason, or excite slaves to rebel, or make any general insurrection. I never encouraged any man to do so, but always discouraged any idea of any kind.

Let me say also, a word in regard to the statements made by some to those connected with me. I hear it has been said by some of them that I have induced them to join me. But the contrary is true. I do not say this to injure them, but as regretting their weakness. There is not one of them but joined me of his own accord, and the greater part of them at their own expense. A number of them I never saw, and never had a word of conversation with, till the day they came to me; and that was for the purpose I have stated.

Now I have done.

PART FOUR

Civil War and Reconstruction, 1860–1877

New York Draft Riots, July 11–15, 1863.
After the conscription act of 1863 went into effect, thousands of angry men, many of whom were Irish immigrants, took to the streets in protest. The rioting continued until exhausted troops could be rushed from Gettysburg to New York City to quell the violence.

ANDREWS OF VIRGINIA & OTHER RINGLEADERS

0004199   NEW YORK: DRAFT RIOTS 1863.
Credit: The Granger Collection, New York

INTRODUCTION: A DIVIDED NATION

Abraham Lincoln's election in November 1860 precipitated the secession crisis. Before the year was out, South Carolina, convinced that the results of the election meant the death knell of slavery, seceded from the Union. By the time Lincoln took the presidential oath to preserve and protect the Union on Inauguration

Day, March 4, 1861, Florida, Alabama, Mississippi, Louisiana, Georgia, and Texas had all followed suit. The Civil War broke out on April 12, when Confederate batteries opened fire on Fort Sumter in Charleston harbor. With Lincoln's call for troops to put down the rebellion, Virginia, Tennessee, Arkansas, and North Carolina seceded and joined the Confederacy. Although anger and rage led many Americans to march eagerly off to make war on one another, their opinions were not unanimous. Thousands of citizens in both sections of the country did not go along with the patriotic fervor permeating North and South, and, in varying degrees, many of these people raised their voices in protest against the war. The nation was divided, but in that divide were further divisions.

At the outset, one of President Lincoln's primary concerns was to prevent the four remaining slave states from joining the Confederacy. Lincoln felt that if Maryland, Delaware, Kentucky, and Missouri all seceded, the "game would be up" and he would be unable to fulfill his presidential oath. The Union would be dissolved. When the governor and legislature of Maryland made noises about seceding, Abraham Lincoln wasted little time. Under the "writ of habeas corpus," it is unconstitutional to keep defendants imprisoned without filing charges against them; nevertheless, Lincoln, suspending the writ, had the 31 Maryland legislators with secessionist leanings incarcerated. It was necessary, he explained, to bend the Constitution temporarily in order to preserve it. Naturally, this action met with a great deal of opposition, especially among "Peace Democrats," who opposed the war and were willing to let the South go if a compromise could not be negotiated. Ohio Congressman Clement L. Vallandigham was the most vocal member of the radical wing of the so-called Peace Democrats, the Copperheads.

In the South, too, there was opposition to the war. Southern dissenters were primarily those who lived in the mountain regions, where slavery had never been profitable, and who therefore did not own slaves. These mountain folk were not abolitionists (meaning they did not care one iota about black rights), but they deeply resented the economic and political power that slavery brought the lowland elite, and they were not willing to break up the Union to preserve slavery.

Both President Lincoln and President Jefferson Davis were hampered by enormous opposition to their policies and military strategy. In the Confederacy, as in the United States, there were scores of congressmen and generals in the army who believed they knew far more than their commanders-in-chief. Lincoln and Davis faced a barrage of savage criticism not only from them but also from their own cabinets and from the press.

Laws establishing conscription were resented by citizens in both the North and the South. Especially infuriating to many was the clause that allowed conscripts to pay substitutes to take their places. Above and below the Mason-Dixon line, people cynically complained that it was a "rich man's war and a poor man's fight." Some were sufficiently incensed that they did everything they could to avoid being drafted; some even encouraged men in the army to desert. The New York City draft riots of July 11–15, 1863, were a vivid and violent testimony to the fact that the North was not fully unified behind the effort to save the Union. A Pennsylvania newspaper quoted one anticonscription protestor as saying he'd fight for Uncle Sam "but not for Uncle Sambo." Many Northern workers, fearing job competition from freed blacks, viewed the Civil War as a no-win situation. For them, it made no sense to fight and die to free blacks, who would then compete with them in the labor market. For several days, thousands of protesting workers, many of them Irish immigrants, took to the streets and targeted the homes of the rich as well as the black neighborhoods of New York City. When the frenzied rioting ended (quelled only after exhausted Union troops arrived from Gettysburg), 105 people lay dead—many of them free blacks who had been strung up on lampposts and burned to death.

There were, however, people who dissented nonviolently. Quakers like Cyrus Pringle refused to fight on grounds of conscience and moral principles. Black soldiers in the Union army challenged their unequal treatment, especially with respect to the War Department's policy of paying them less than white soldiers, by engaging in an effective protest campaign of refusing all money until their salaries equaled that of their white comrades in arms.

At the end of the war, as Congress began dealing with the problem of reconstructing the Union, many of those who had fought against slavery now took up the cause of the rights of the freedmen. Civil rights, citizenship, and suffrage all became significant issues. Women, who had championed abolition and black rights, began to lobby more vigorously for women's suffrage and engaged energetically in the debate over the Fifteenth Amendment. There were high hopes that the amendment guaranteeing the right to vote would include *all* citizens. But when the Fifteenth Amendment extended the suffrage only to black men, the women's movement split into moderates who supported the amendment and radicals who denounced it and heatedly agitated against its ratification. For the next 50 years, women like Susan B. Anthony and Elizabeth Cady Stanton, leading the National Woman's Suffrage Association; and Lucy Stone, leading the more moderate American Woman's Suffrage Association, carried on the struggle for suffrage.

During the 1870s, the issue of former slaves' civil and political rights began fading from public awareness. The fact that African American men now had the right to vote seemed to convince even the most ardent former abolitionists and advocates of civil rights that nothing more needed to be done to ease the transition of freedmen into the mainstream. Slaves were now free, black men could vote—what more was necessary? The nation's reply seemed to be "nothing." The presidential election of 1876 settled the issue. Although the Democratic candidate, New York Governor Samuel J. Tilden, won 51 percent of the popular vote, his 184 electoral votes were one shy of the majority he needed to be declared the victor. Twenty electoral votes from Florida, South Carolina, Louisiana, and Oregon were disputed, and those states submitted two sets of returns. From November 1876 to March 1877, an electoral commission debated how to resolve the issue. Democrats finally agreed, a few days before inauguration day, to acquiesce in granting all twenty of the disputed electoral votes to the Republican candidate, Rutherford B. Hayes. In return, Republicans agreed to several conditions, among which was the withdrawal of the remaining federal troops stationed in the South. This in effect ended Reconstruction. It removed the freedmen from the protection of the U.S. Army, put their fate into the hands of local politicians, and put conservative Southern Democrats back in power in the South. Southern state officials lost no time in establishing literacy tests and poll taxes to prevent freedmen from voting. They also set up Jim Crow apartheid, imposing the second-class citizenship on African Americans that would last for nearly a century.

In the aftermath of the Civil War, many Americans began moving west. The Homestead Act of 1862 and the completion of the Transcontinental Railroad in 1869 were two factors that made the West enormously attractive to many who sought to improve their lives after the tumult and dislocation of the Civil War. But as settlers poured into the Great Plains, erecting homesteads and wantonly killing the buffalo herds, the lives and livelihoods of Native Americans were so disrupted that Indian grievances and protests against white encroachment boiled over. In the Fort Laramie Treaty of 1868, the United States promised—in exchange for Sioux assurances not to attack whites traveling through the Great Plains—that the Black Hills would forever belong to the Sioux. Sitting Bull and Crazy Horse, believing that whites could not be trusted, refused to abide by any treaty. In 1873, Sioux warriors loyal to Sitting Bull and Crazy Horse violated the treaty by hunting on lands off the Sioux reservation and by attacking survey parties belonging to the Northern Pacific Railroad. Lieutenant Colonel George Armstrong Custer skirmished twice with these Indians while escorting Northern Pacific Railroad personnel, and because of this, the U.S. government sent him the following year to survey the Black Hills. The encroachment of Custer's Seventh Cavalry Regiment in the Black Hills deeply angered the Sioux, while simultaneously the Grant administration, eager to make the Black Hills safe for gold hunters, issued an ultimatum to all non-treaty Sioux to report to their agencies during the winter of 1875–1876. In March 1876, after a U.S. Army column attacked a Cheyenne camp, the Cheyenne joined up with Crazy Horse and Sitting Bull. The Arapaho also joined the Lakota and Cheyenne once the war had begun. The greatest Indian victory of the plains wars took place in June 1876 on the banks of the Greasy Grass in eastern Montana— whites called it the Little Big Horn—when Custer and his entire command were wiped out by Sitting Bull and Crazy Horse's confederation. But Custer's Last Stand was, in reality, one of the final blows for Indian hopes to maintain their way of life. Washington cracked down so severely that in spite of the Nez Perce's heroic run for freedom in 1877 and continued skirmishes with the Cheyenne and the Apache well into the 1880s, Indian resistance was effectively subdued.

Clement L. Vallandigham (1820–1871)

When the Civil War broke out, there was a great deal of antiwar dissent in the North. Northern Democrats divided into two factions: War

Democrats favored a war (if necessary) to preserve the Union but not to abolish slavery. Peace Democrats were unwilling to go to war even if it meant the dissolution of the Union; if negotiations could save the Union, fine, but if not, then so be it. The most radical faction of the Peace Democrats, irrevocably opposed to war, were derisively labeled Copperheads by Republicans. By equating them with poisonous snakes, the Republicans were declaring that the Peace Democrat stance was unmistakably treasonous.

The most notorious Copperhead was Ohio Congressman Clement L. Vallandigham, who, from the moment Lincoln was inaugurated on March 4, opposed the administration's policies that, he was convinced, would lead only to war. Vallandigham wanted to preserve the Union but not through war. He argued that compromise and negotiation would work and that the Union would prevail. Once war broke out, he became particularly concerned with Lincoln's policies for stifling secessionist and antiwar sentiment, policies, Vallandigham believed, that would destroy the civil liberties guaranteed by the Constitution. Throughout the Civil War, Vallandigham was a thorn in the side of the Lincoln administration. In 1863, after Vallandigham declared in a fiery speech that Lincoln's agenda was not to save the Union but merely to free the blacks and enslave the whites, he was arrested, tried, and convicted by a military court. (Lincoln saw to it, however, that rather than serving his sentence, Vallandigham was deported to the Confederacy.) Soon thereafter, Vallandigham went to Canada and from there campaigned for governor of Ohio. He lost the election, but Lincoln, in order to defuse negative public opinion, shrewdly allowed the Copperhead to return the following year to Ohio, where, with the end of the war in sight, the furor around him subsided.

As a congressman, Vallandigham accused Lincoln of abusing his constitutional authority by issuing a call for recruits and proclaimed that the president was a tyrant. He was especially alarmed by Lincoln's disregard for free speech and civil liberties and by his suspension of habeas corpus—an act that Lincoln himself admitted was overstepping his constitutional authority. Lincoln's view was that he had to "bend" the Constitution temporarily in order to save it.

RESPONSE TO LINCOLN'S ADDRESS TO CONGRESS, JULY 10, 1861

. . . Sir, the Constitution not only confines to Congress the right to declare war, but expressly provides that "Congress (not the President) shall have power to

---

SOURCE: Clement L. Vallandigham, *The Record of Hon. C. L. Vallandigham on Abolition, the Union, and the Civil War* (Cincinnati: J. Walter, 1863), passim.

raise and support armies;" and to "provide and maintain a navy." In pursuance of this authority, Congress, years ago, had fixed the number of officers, and of the regiments, of the different kinds of service; and also, the number of ships, officers, marines, and seamen which should compose the navy. Not only that, but Congress has repeatedly, within the last five years, refused to increase the regular army. More than that still: in February and March last, the House, upon several test votes, repeatedly and expressly refused to authorize the President to accept the service of volunteers for the very purpose of protecting the public property, enforcing the laws, and collecting the revenue. And, yet, the President, of his own mere will and authority, and without the shadow of right, has proceeded to increase, and has increased, the standing army by twenty-five thousand men; the navy by eighteen thousand; and has called for, and accepted the services of, forty regiments of volunteers for three years, numbering forty-two thousand men, and making thus a grand army, or military force, raised by executive proclamation alone, without the sanction of Congress, without warrant of law, and in direct violation of the Constitution, and of his oath of office, of eighty-five thousand soldiers enlisted for three and five years, and already in the field. And, yet, the President now asks us to support the army which he has thus raised, to ratify his usurpations by a law ex post facto, and thus to make ourselves parties to our own degradation, and to his infractions of the Constitution. Meanwhile, however, he has taken good care not only to enlist the men, organize the regiments, and muster them into service, but to provide, in advance, for a horde of forlorn, worn-out, and broken-down politicians of his own party, by appointing, either by himself, or through the Governors of the States, major-generals, brigadier-generals, colonels, lieutenant-colonels, majors, captains, lieutenants, adjutants, quarter-masters, and surgeons, without any limit as to numbers, and without so much as once saying to Congress, "By your leave, gentlemen."

Beginning with this wide breach of the Constitution, this enormous usurpation of the most dangerous of all powers—the power of the sword—other infractions and assumptions were easy; and after public liberty, private right soon fell. The privacy of the telegraph was invaded in the search after treason and traitors; although it turns out, significantly enough, that the only victim, so far, is one of the appointees and especial pets of the Administration. The telegraphic dispatches, preserved under every pledge of secrecy for the protection and safety of the telegraph companies, were seized and carried away without search-warrant, without probable cause, without oath, and without description of the places to be searched, or of the things to be seized, and in plain violation of the right of the people to be secure in their houses, persons, papers, and effects, against unreasonable searches and seizures. One step more, sir, will bring upon us search and seizure of the public mails; and, finally, as in the worst days of English oppression—as in the times of the Russells and the Sydneys of English martyrdom—of the drawers and secretaries of the private citizen; though even then tyrants had the grace to look to the forms of the law, and the execution was judicial murder, not military slaughter. But who shall say that the future Tiberius of America shall have the modesty of his Roman predecessor, in extenuation of whose character it is written by the great historian, *avertit occulos, jussitque scelera non spectavit.*

Sir, the rights of property having been thus wantonly violated, it needed but a little stretch of usurpation to invade the sanctity of the person; and a victim was not long wanting. A private citizen of Maryland, not subject to the rules and articles of war—not in a case arising in the land or naval forces, nor in the militia, when in actual service—is seized in his own house, in the dead hour of the night, not by any civil officer, nor upon any civil process, but by a band of armed soldiers, under the verbal orders of a military chief, and is ruthlessly torn from his wife and his children, and hurried off to a fortress of the United States—and that fortress, as if in mockery, the very one over whose ramparts had floated that star-spangled banner immortalized in song by the patriot prisoner, who, "by dawn's early light," saw its folds gleaming amid the wreck of battle, and invoked the blessings of heaven upon it, and prayed that it might long wave "o'er the land of the free, and the home of the brave."

And, sir, when the highest judicial officer of the land, the Chief Justice of the Supreme Court, upon whose shoulders, "when the judicial ermine fell, it touched nothing not as spotless as itself," the aged, the venerable, the gentle, and pure-minded Taney, who, but a little while before, had administered to the President the oath to support the Constitution, and to execute the laws, issued, as by law it was his sworn duty to issue, the high prerogative writ of habeas corpus— that great writ of right, that main bulwark of personal liberty, commanding the body of the accused to be brought before him, that justice and right might be done by due course of law, and without denial or delay, the gates of the fortress, its cannon turned towards, and in plain sight of the city, where the court sat, and frowning from its ramparts, were closed against the officer of the law, and the answer returned that the officer in command has, by the authority of the President, suspended the writ of habeas corpus. And thus it is, sir, that the accused has ever since been held a prisoner without due process of law; without bail; without presentment by a grand jury; without speedy, or public trial by a petit jury, of his own State or district, or any trial at all; without information of the nature and cause of the accusation; without being confronted with the witnesses against him; without compulsory process to obtain witnesses in his favor; and without the assistance of counsel for his defense. And this is our boasted American liberty? And thus it is, too, sir, that here, here in America, in the seventy-third year of the Republic, that great writ and security of personal freedom, which it cost the patriots and freemen of England six hundred years of labor and toil and blood to extort and to hold fast from venal judges and tyrant kings; written in the great charter of Runnymede by the iron barons, who made the simple Latin and uncouth words of the times, *nullus liber homo,* in the language of Chatham, worth all the classics; recovered and confirmed a hundred times afterward, as often as violated and stolen away, and finally, and firmly secured at last by the great act of Charles II, and transferred thence to our own Constitution and laws, has been wantonly and ruthlessly trampled in the dust. Ay, sir, that great writ, bearing, by a special command of Parliament, those other uncouth, but magic words, *per statutum tricessimo primo Caroli secundi regis,* which no English judge, no English minister, no king or queen of England, dare disobey; that writ, brought over by our fathers, and cherished by them, as a priceless inheritance of liberty, an American President has contemptuously set at defiance. Nay, more, he has ordered his subordinate military chiefs to suspend it at their discretion! And, yet, after all this, he cooly comes before this House and the Senate and the country, and pleads that he is only preserving and protecting the Constitution; and demands and expects of this House and of the Senate and the country their thanks for his usurpations; while, outside of this capitol, his myrmidons are clamoring for impeachment of the Chief Justice, as engaged in a conspiracy to break down the Federal Government.

Sir, however much necessity—the tyrant's plea—may be urged in extenuation of the usurpations and infractions of the President in regard to public liberty, there can be no such apology or defense for his invasions of private right. What overruling necessity required the violation of the sanctity of private property and private confidence? What great public danger demanded the arrest and imprisonment, without trial by common law, of one single private citizen, for an act done weeks before, openly, and by authority of his State? If guilty of treason, was not the judicial power ample enough and strong enough for his conviction and punishment? What, then, was needed in his case, but the precedent under which other men, in other places, might become the victims of executive suspicion and displeasure?

As to the pretense, sir, that the President has the Constitutional right to suspend the writ of habeas corpus, I will not waste time in arguing it. The case is as plain as words can make it. It is a legislative power; it is found only in the legislative article; it belongs to Congress only to do it. Subordinate officers have disobeyed it; General Wilkinson disobeyed it, but he sent his prisoners on for judicial trial; General Jackson disobeyed it, and was reprimanded by James Madison; but no President, nobody but Congress, ever before assumed the right to suspend it. And, sir, that other pretense of necessity, I repeat, can not be allowed. It had no existence in fact. The Constitution can not be preserved by violating it. It is an offense to the intelligence of this House, and of the country, to pretend that all this, and the other gross and multiplied infractions of the Constitution and usurpations of power were done by the President and his advisors out of pure love and devotion to the Constitution. But if so, sir, then they have but one step further to take, and declare, in the language of Sir Boyle Roche, in the Irish House of Commons, that such is the depth of their attachment to it, that they are prepared to give up, not merely a part, but the whole of the Constitution, to preserve the remainder. And yet, if indeed this pretext of necessity be well founded, then let me say, that a cause which demands the sacrifice of the Constitution and of the dearest securities of property, liberty, and life, can not be just; at least, it is not worth the sacrifice.

Sir, I am obliged to pass by for want of time, other grave and dangerous infractions and usurpations of the President since the 4th of March. I only allude casually to the quartering of soldiers in private houses without the consent of the owners, and without any manner having been prescribed by law; to the subversion in a part, at least, of Maryland of her own State Government and of the authorities under it; to the censorship over the telegraph, and the infringement, repeatedly, in one or more of the States, of the right of the people to keep and to bear arms for their defense. But if all these things, I ask, have been done in the first two months after the commencement of this war, and by men not military chieftains, and unused to arbitrary power, what may we not expect to see in three years, and by the successful heroes of the fight? Sir, the power and rights of the States and the people, and of their Representatives, have been usurped; the sanctity of the private house and of private property has been invaded; and the liberty of the person wantonly and wickedly stricken down; free speech, too, has been repeatedly denied; and all this under the plea of necessity. Sir, the right of petition will follow next—nay, it has already been shaken; the freedom of the press will soon fall after it; and let me whisper in your ear, that there will be few to mourn over its loss, unless, indeed, its ancient high and honorable character shall be rescued and redeemed from its present reckless mendacity and degradation. Freedom of religion will yield too, at last, amid the exultant shouts of millions, who have seen its holy temples defiled, and its white robes of a former innocency trampled now under the polluting hoofs of an ambitious and faithless or fanatical clergy. Meantime national banks, bankrupt laws, a vast and permanent public debt, high tariffs, heavy direct taxation, enormous expenditures, gigantic and stupendous peculation, anarchy first, and a strong government afterward—no more State lines, no more State governments, and a consolidated monarchy or vast centralized military despotism must all follow in the history of the future, as in the history of the past they have, centuries ago, been written. Sir, I have said nothing, and have time to say nothing now, of the immense indebtedness and the vast expenditures which have already accrued, nor of the folly and mismanagement of the war so far, nor of the atrocious and shameless peculations and frauds which have disgraced it in the State governments and the Federal Government from the beginning. The avenging hour for all these will come hereafter, and I pass by them now.

I have finished now, Mr. Chairman, what I proposed to say at this time upon the message of the President. As to my own position in regard to this most unhappy civil war, I have only to say that I stand to-day just where I stood upon the 4th of March last; where the whole Democratic party, and the whole Constitutional Union party, and a vast majority, as I believe, of the people of the United States stood too. I am for peace, speedy, immediate, honorable peace, with all its blessings. Others may have changed—I have not. I question not their motives nor quarrel with their course. It is vain and futile for them to question or to quarrel with me. My duty shall be discharged—calmly, firmly, quietly, and regardless of consequences. The approving voice of conscience void of offense, and the approving judgment which shall follow "after some time be past," these, God help me, are my trust and my support.

Sir, I have spoken freely and fearlessly to-day, as became an American Representative and an American citizen; one firmly resolved, come what may, not to lose his own Constitutional liberties, nor to surrender his own Constitutional rights in the vain effort to impose these rights and liberties upon ten millions of unwilling people. I have spoken earnestly, too, but yet not as one unmindful of the solemnity of the scenes which surround us upon every side to-day. Sir, when the Congress of the United States assembled here on the 3rd of December, 1860, just seven months ago, the Senate was composed of sixty-six Senators, representing the thirty-three States of the Union, and this House of two hundred and thirty-seven members—every State being present. It was a grand and solemn spectacle—the ambassadors of three and thirty sovereignties and thirty-one millions of people, the mightiest republic on earth, in general Congress assembled. In the Senate, too, and this House, were some of the ablest and most distinguished statesmen of the country; men whose names were familiar to the whole country—some of them destined to pass into history. The new wings of the capitol had then but just recently been finished, in all their gorgeous magnificence, and, except a hundred marines at the navy-yard, not a soldier was within forty miles of Washington.

Sir, the Congress of the United States meets here again to-day; but how changed the scene! Instead of thirty-four States, twenty-three only, one less than the number forty years ago, are here, or in the other wing of the capitol. Forty-six Senators and a hundred and seventy-three Representatives constitute the Congress of the now United States. And of these, eight Senators and twenty-four Representatives, from four States only, linger here yet as deputies from that great South which, from the beginning of the Government, contributed so much to mold its policy, to build up its greatness, and to control its destinies. All the other States of that South are gone. Twenty-two Senators and sixty-five Representatives no longer answer to their names. The vacant seats are, indeed, still here; and the escutcheons of their respective States look down now solemnly and sadly from these vaulted ceilings. But the Virginia of Washington and Henry and Madison, of Marshall and Jefferson, of Randolph and Monroe, the birthplace of Clay, the mother of States and of Presidents; the Carolinas of Pinckney and Sumter and Marion, of Calhoun and Macon; and Tennessee, the home and burial-place of Jackson; and other States, too, once most loyal and true, are no longer here. The voices and the footsteps of the great dead of the past two ages of the Republic linger still—it may be in echo—along the stately corridors of this capitol; but their descendants, from nearly one-half of the States of the Republic, will meet with us no more within these marble halls. But in the parks and lawns, and upon the broad avenues of this spacious city, seventy thousand soldiers have supplied their places; and the morning drum-beat from a score of encampments, within sight of this beleaguered capitol, give melancholy warning to the Representatives of the States and of the people, that amid arms the laws are silent.

Sir, some years hence—I would fain hope some months hence, if I dare— the present generation will demand to know the cause of all this; and, some ages hereafter, the grand and impartial tribunal of history will make solemn and diligent inquest of the authors of this terrible revolution.

William Brownlow (1805–1877)

*Although he supported the institution of slavery, Tennessee newspaper
publisher and Methodist preacher William G. ("Parson") Brownlow
became one of the most outspoken and acerbic opponents of secession in
the South. His influence in eastern Tennessee was so powerful that Union
sentiment remained very high in that part of the state throughout the
war. In May 1861, shortly before Tennessee seceded from the Union,
Parson Brownlow published a statement in his paper, the Knoxville
Whig, adamantly asserting his right to fly the American flag, even though
his view was the minority opinion in secessionist Tennessee. As a result,
his newspaper was suppressed, his press was destroyed, and he was tried
for treason against the Confederacy. Like Vallandigham in the North, he
was eventually banished behind enemy lines. In a sense, he can be
regarded as Jefferson Davis's Vallandigham.*

KNOXVILLE *WHIG* ANTISECESSION LETTERS AND EDITORIAL, MAY 1861

Albany, N.Y., May 8, 1861

W. G. BROWNLOW, Esq.:

I send you by mail the Albany *Evening Journal,* containing Hon. Benj. Nott's
speech on the crisis. Judge Nott is a life-long Democrat, of the Hard-Shell
school, and an avowed advocate of the Dred Scott decision.

I read your paper with great interest, and your course is the subject of conversation in every circle North, meeting the approval of all parties, for all parties
here are for the Union. We understand you to be a pro-Slavery man, but for the
Union, opposed to Secession—not even regarding the election of Lincoln as any
just cause for dissolving the Union. Can't you give us a leading editorial on these
points, and at the same time state the position of the Union men in the border
Slave States in the event the Administration were to interfere in any way with the
institution of slavery?

The masses of the Northern people have no feelings but the most friendly
towards their brethren of the South, and are ready to concede to them all their
rights. They are even for returning to them their slaves who have escaped, as the
law requires. This Administration would protect Southern rights, and if it

---

SOURCE: Stephen V. Ash, ed., *Secessionists and Other Scoundrels: Selections from Parson
Brownlow's Book* (Baton Rouge: Louisiana State University Press, 1999), 56–63.

would not of choice, the public would require it to be done. And, in saying this, I assure you I am no Lincoln man. But this you very well know.

Hoping that you may be sustained, and live to see the Stars and Stripes float on every hill-top, and in every valley, from the St. Lawrence to the Rio Grande, I remain, very truly,

L. M. E.

Knoxville, May 14, 1861

To L. M. E.:

I have your letter of the 8th, and also the *Evening Journal.* I have perused the speech of Judge Nott: it is able, conservative, and eminently patriotic. Had you more Notts in the North, and fewer Slavery agitators, and had we fewer Rhetts, Yanceys, and Davises, in the South, none of these troubles would now be upon the country.

You correctly interpret the Union men of the border Slave States when you pronounce them "pro-Slavery men." I think I correctly represent them in my paper, as I shall do in this brief epistle, except, perhaps, that I am more *ultra* than most of them. I am a native of Virginia, and so were my parents before me, and, together with a numerous train of relatives, they were and are slave-holders. For thirty years I have lived in Tennessee, and my wife and children are native Tennesseans. My native State did more to form the old Confederacy and to form the Constitution of the United States than any other State; her soil is now the resting-place of the honored dead, the most ultra old Unionists dead or alive—Washington, Jefferson, Madison, Monroe, Marshall, Henry, and a host of others. I am sorry to have to record that it has, in the mysterious providence of God, been reserved to Virginia to do more towards overthrowing the [old] Confederacy and the Constitution than any other State, South Carolina not even excepted. It took the Virginia [Secession] Convention of 1861 to overthrow her State Government—changing her organic political *status* contrary to the expressed direction of her people at the ballot-box when they elected the men who perpetrated the deed! Virginia, I am sorry to say, if I may be allowed to use an humble illustration, is like a *hill of potatoes*—the best part under ground: the part above ground reminds me but of *vines.* When citizens of other States are called upon to name their great statesmen, they point to *living men.* Make the call upon Virginians, and they ask you out into *a graveyard,* when they will point you to the tomb of Washington, the monument erected over Madison, or the grave of Jefferson!

I am a pro-Slavery man, and so are the Union men generally of the border Slave States. I have long since made up my mind upon the Slavery question, but not without studying it thoroughly. The result of my investigation is, that there is not a single passage in the New Testament, nor a single act in the records of the Church, during her early history even for centuries, containing any direct, professed, or *intended* censure of slavery. Christ and the apostles found the institution existing under the authority and sanction of law; and in their labors among the people, unlike *ultra* Abolitionists, *masters* and *slaves* bowed at the same altars, and were taken into the same Church, communing together around the same table—the Saviour and his apostles exhorting *owners* to treat *slaves* as became the gospel, and slaves to obedience and honesty, that their religious profession might not be evil spoken of.

The original Church of Christ not only admitted the lawfulness of slavery, but in various ways, by her teachings and discipline, expressed her *approbation* of it, enforcing the observance of "Fugitive Slave Laws" which had been enacted by the State. God intended the relation of master and slave to exist, both *in* and *out* of his Church. Hence, when Christ and his apostles found slavery *incorporated with every department of society,* they went to work and adopted rules for the government of the Church providing alike for the *rights* of slave-holders and the *wants* of slaves. Slavery in the days of the apostles had so penetrated society, and was so intimately interwoven with it, that a religion *preaching freedom to the slaves* would have arrayed against it the civil authorities, armed against it the whole power of the State, and destroyed the usefulness of its preachers.

Finally, I hold—and thirty years of observation and experience among slave-holders in the South have convinced me that I am not mistaken—that all the finer feelings of humanity may be cherished in the bosoms of slave-owners; that there are thousands of devout slave-owners and slaves in the South who are acceptable to God, through Christ. And, however much the bonds of the slaves of the South may provoke the wrath of the ultra Abolitionists of the North, the Redeemer of the world smiles alike upon the devout master and the pious slave!

Now, sir, allow me further to say that the Union men of the border Slave States are loyal to their Government, and do not regard the election of Lincoln as any just cause for dissolving this Union. We believe that slavery had very little to do with inaugurating armed secession, which commenced at Charleston, to overthrow the United States Government: it was the loss of the offices, power, and patronage of the Government by corrupt politicians and bad men in the South, who had long controlled the Government. Believing this, as we honestly do, we can never, like Mexico, inaugurate political conflicts and anarchy by armed secession. We can never agree to assist in the inauguration of a Government of conventions by armed secession. . . .

Whilst I say this, let me say, in all candor, that if we were once convinced in the border Slave States that the Administration at Washington, and the people of the North who are backing up the Administration with men and money, contemplated the *subjugation* of the South or the *abolishing* of slavery, there would not be a Union man among us in twenty-four hours. Come what might, sink or swim, survive or perish, we would fight you to the death, and we would unite our fortunes and destinies with even these demoralized seceded States, for whose leaders and laws we have no sort of respect. But we have not believed, nor do we yet believe, that the Administration has such purposes in view. Demagogues and designing men charge it here, and by this means enlist thousands under their banner who, otherwise, would never support their wicked schemes of Secession. We Union men believe that the blow was struck upon Fort Sumter to induce Virginia to go out, and to create sympathy elsewhere, and that the Administration at

Washington is seeking to repossess its forts and property and to preserve its existence; and, as long as we believe this, we are for the Union and the Administration. I, of course, speak for Union men in the general. We are sustained in this by the Mobile *Advertiser,* which glories in the fact that the seven Confederated States *"struck the first blow in the conflict,"* and *"threw down the glove of mortal combat to their powerful foe."* The Mobile organ of Secession adds, "It was plucky in the seven Confederates: it was more—it was sublimely courageous and patriotic."

Allow me to say that the curse of the country has been that, for years, north of Mason & Dixon's line, you have kept pulpits open to the abuse of Southern slavery and of the Southern people.

In like manner, the clergy of the South—without distinction of sects—men of talents, learning, and influence—have raised the howl of Secession, and it falls like an Indian war-cry upon our citizens from their prostituted pulpits every Sabbath. Many of them go so far as to petition their God, in their public prayers, to *blast* the people of the North! I have no idea that a God of peace will answer any such blasphemous supplications; but it shows the spirit of these minions of anarchy, who have sworn allegiance to the kingdom of Davis, and have been released from any further obligations to the kingdom of Jesus—at least during the war! Some of our clergy are officers in volunteer companies, with swords hung to their sides, and stripes on their pants. Others, having an eye to the loaves and fishes, are anxious to serve as chaplains.

We are in the midst of a reign of terror in Tennessee, and where it will end, and in what, I am not able to conjecture. We vote for or against the Ordinance of Secession on the 8th of June; and, although there is a majority of the voters of the State utterly and irreconcilably opposed to Secession, I can't promise you that it will not carry. Fraud and force, and all the other appliances of Secessionism, will be brought to bear in carrying the State out of the Union. When overpowered and voted down, we shall be forced to submit. When I surrender, it will be because I can no longer help myself; but it shall be under protest, claiming the right, as a Union man, to curse this whole movement in my heart of hearts! And, whether in or out of the Union, as long as I remember it was Washington who told us, *"The Constitution is sacredly obligatory upon all"*; and that it was Jackson who told us, *"The Union, it must be preserved"*—I shall offer this prayer upon the altar of my country: Mania to the brain of him who would conceive, and palsy to the arm of him who would perpetrate, the dissolution of the Union!

And, whether my humble voice is hushed in death, or my press is muzzled by foul legislation, I beg you, and all into whose hands this letter may fall, to credit no Secession falsehood which may represent me as having changed.

W. G. BROWNLOW

Editorial, May 25, 1861

It is known to this community and to the people of this county that I have had the Stars and Stripes, in the character of a small flag, floating over my dwelling, in East Knoxville, since February. This flag has become very offensive to certain leaders of the Secession party in this town, and to certain would-be leaders, and the more so as it is about the only one of the kind floating in the city. Squads of troops, from three to twenty, have come over to my house, within the last several days, cursing the flag in front of my house, and threatening to take it down, greatly to the annoyance of my wife and children. No attack has been made upon it, and consequently we have had no difficulty. It is due to the Tennessee troops to say that they have never made any such demonstrations. Other troops from the Southern States, passing on to Virginia, have been induced to do so, by certain cowardly, sneaking, white-livered scoundrels, residing here, who have not the *melt* to undertake what they urge strangers to do. One of the Louisiana squads proclaimed in front of my house, on Thursday, that they were told to take it down by citizens of Knoxville.

Now, I wish to say a few things to the public in connection with this subject. This flag is private property, upon a private dwelling, in a State that has *never voted herself out of the Union* or into the Southern Confederacy, and is therefore lawfully and constitutionally under these same Stars and Stripes I have floating over my house. Until the State, by her citizens, through the ballot-box, changes her Federal relations, her citizens have a right to fling this banner to the breeze. Those who are in rebellion against the Government represented by the Stars and Stripes have up the Rebel flag, and it is a high piece of work to deny loyal citizens of the Union the privilege of displaying their colors!

But there is one other feature of this tyranny and of these mobocratic assaults I wish to lay before the people, irrespective of parties. There are but a few of the leaders of this Secession movement in Knoxville—less than half a dozen—for whom I entertain any sort of respect, or whose good opinions I esteem. With one of these I had a free and full conversation, more than two weeks ago, in regard to this whole question. I told him that we Union men would make the best fight we could at the ballot-box, on the 8th of June, to keep the State in the Union; but that if we were overpowered, and a majority of the people of the State should say in this constitutional way that she must secede, we should have to come down, and bring our flags with us, bowing to the will of the majority with the best grace we could. I made the same statement to the colonel who got up a regiment here, and to one of his subordinate officers. I made the same statement to the president of the railroad, and I have repeatedly made the same statement through my paper. The whole Secession party here know this to be the position and purpose of the Union party; but a portion of them seek to bring about personal conflicts, and to engage strangers, under the influence of whiskey, to do a dirty and villainous work they have the meanness to do, without the courage.

If these God-forsaken scoundrels and hell-deserving assassins want satisfaction out of me for what I have said about them—and it has been no little—they can find me on these streets every day of my life but Sunday. I am at all times prepared to give them satisfaction. I take back nothing I have ever said against the corrupt and unprincipled villains, but reiterate all, cast it in their dastardly faces, and hurl down their lying throats their own infamous calumnies.

Finally, the destroying of my small flag or of my town-property is a small matter. The carrying out of the State upon the mad wave of Secession is also a small matter, compared with the great Principle involved. Sink or swim, live or die, survive or perish, I am a Union man, and owe my allegiance to the Stars and Stripes of my country. Nor can I, in any possible contingency, have any respect for the Government of the Confederated States, originating as it did with, and being controlled by, the worst men in the South. And any man saying—whether of high or low degree—that I am an Abolitionist or a Black Republican, is a Liar and a Scoundrel.

The Arkansas Peace Society

Just as there was antiwar sentiment in the North during the Civil War, a large number of Southerners resisted the war. Indeed, during the first year of the Civil War, Confederate authorities became aware of a secret antiwar organization in Arkansas. More than a thousand Unionists opposed to secession had formed the Arkansas Peace Society in 1861, vowing to resist the war effort. But Confederate authorities got wind of the society, and hundreds of people were arrested and forced either to stand trial for treason or to suffer conscription into the Confederate army. Many of those impressed into Confederate service wound up deserting to Union lines at the first opportunity.

Arkansas Peace Society Documents, 1861

SAM LESLIE TO GOVERNOR H. M. RECTOR

Wiley's Cove, Arks Oct 21 1861 H. M. Rector Gov of Ark

Dear sir

Your Letter of the 16th Inst is now before me and contents notised. You say it has been reported to the Military Board there are One Hundred Good fighting men in Cove Township, Searcy Co that has not nor will not volunteer thir servicis In behalf of the South. What would prompt aney one to attempt to cast such a stigma upon the people of this Township I am not able to comprehend, ware your informant a citizen of Searcy Co I might have some Ida of the cause, this Township (Cove) has not turned out as many volunteers as she might have don, this county has about 300 men in service of the Confederate States though

Source: Ted R. Worley, ed., "Documents Relating to the Arkansas Peace Society of 1861," *The Arkansas Historical Quarterly*, vol. 17, Spring 1958, no. 1. The original documents are located in the Kie Oldham Collection, at the Arkansas History Commission.

we are only represented by two companies the rest of our men Joined compained in the adjoining counties and those counties is receiving the credit. Cove Township has about 60 able bodied men subject to military duty all told only five out of that number single men and Eight volunteers which will leave 52 now subject to duty the Great bulk of our men now in service has been furnished by three Townships, there is other Townships in the County that has done but little better than Cove, and they pass unnoticed. I will say to you that the citizens of Cove Township is as Law abiding a people as lives and the records of out corts will bear me out in the assursion, which may account in some degree for their not being more ready to volunteer there is other causes, so many Misourians running off and leaving the state, has had its influence I know this county has had a bad name at a distance we have been called Black Republicans and Abolitionists &c but we have never had aney of thos characters amongst us. It is true that the citizens of this county war union men as long as there was aney hope of the Union and perhaps a little longer, but all Ida of the Union as it onst was is banished the time has passsed for the North and South to live to gether in pease and harmoney and we must be loyal to the government we live under this is the fealings of the people of this Co so fare as I have any knolledg and when you hear men call the pople of Searcy Co. by hard names rest assured they are willfully lying or uninformed with the character of our people. I write you this letter Gov. in order to plase the Good people of Searcy Co. write before you I feel it is a duty I owe to them to do so.

I hope Cove Township will yet give a Good account of hir self that you may have no reason to complain.

Respectfully your friend Sam Leslie. . . .

GOVERNOR H. M. RECTOR TO SAM LESLIE

Executive Office, Little Rock, Nov 28, 1861, Sam Leslie Col Commandant 45th Regt A.M.

Sir

Your letter of the 26 Inst has just reached me by couriers Melton and Griffin. I regret extremely that any of our citizens should prove disloyal to their government. But if they so conduct themselves the power of those in authority must be exercised to preserve peace, and enforce obedience to the Constitution and the Laws.

The people of the State Arkansas through their representatives in Convention have taken the State out of the Old Union and attached it to the Confederacy. And although there may be a minority against this action, yet ours is a government where a majority rules and the minority must submit.

I and my officers in the State are sworn to support and enforce the laws as they are and individuals, one or many, rebelling against those laws, must be looked after and if for the safety of the country, it becomes necessary to arrest and imprison them or to execute them for treason, that must and will be done promptly and certainly, if it is necessary to call out every man in the State to accomplish it.

Still, I deeply regret the necessity, but will not be deterred from doing my whole duty let the blow fall where it may. You will therefore proceed to arrest all men in your county who profess friendship for the Lincoln government or who harbor or support others arousing hostility to the Confederate States or the State of Arkansas. And when so arrested you will march them to this place, where they will be dealt with, as enemies of their country whose peace and safety is being endangered by their disloyal and treasonable acts.

To enable you to enforce this order you will call out such of the Militia as may be necessary and you will be careful also to afford protection to the loyal citizens and their property in your county, as occurring events may seem to require your interposition for their security.

Confiding in your intelligence and devotion to your state, and to the Confederacy of which you are a citizen, I entertain no opinion other than that you will do your whole duty, as a man and an officer.

Respectfully H. M. Rector Gov and Commander in Chief, A. M.

IZARD COUNTY COMMITTEE OF INVESTIGATION

To His Excellency H. M. Rector Govr. and Prest. Military Board of the State of Arkansas....

Some ten days ago it became a matter of publicity in this county that a secret conspiracy against the laws and liberties of the people of this state was on foot extending from Fulton county this State quite through this and perhaps Searcy and Van Buren Counties.

Immediately the citizens of this county were in arms to quell the same. Scouting parties were sent out in every direction in search of those suspected of having connections with the organization; and a committee of investigation was elected to enquire into the existence, objects, and purposes of the aforesaid secret conspiracy which committee is composed of the undersigned, who have proceeded to examine and have examined all the persons apprehended and brought before us all of whose names are hereto attached.

And after a full and fair investigation of the matter with all the lights before us, we find that the persons above named together with others we have not found, had formed themselves into a secret organization having a constitution and by laws and secret signs a copy of which constitution is herewith submitted to your excellency and marked A. and we considered that the organization is a secret thing dangerous in its operations and subversive of the rights and liberties of the people of this State, and of the Confederate States; and if not treason itself, at least treasonable, and being acquainted with most if not all of the persons examined, and many of them being young, mere boys, who were doubtless led ignorantly into the society, that is led into it not being informed of its objects and purposes, and feeling willing in our minds that they should wipe out the foul stain, by enlisting in the service of the Confederate States for and during the war, we accordingly gave them an opportunity of so enlisting, whereupon the whole of them, that is to say forty seven the same whose names are hereunto attached immediately enrolled their names as volunteers in the Confederate Service for and during the war. This we think is a matter of lenity toward them and that they may possibly do good service to our country. They leave here as soon as transportation can be had, for Genl Borland's headquarters at Pocahontas Ark. Should it appear to your Excellency that we have not taken the proper steps in this matter we have reserved the right of your Excellency to do with them as you may deem proper, and have so informed Genl Borland with regard thereto. . . .

Sylamore Ark Nov 28 1861
W. B. F. Treat, Chairman Daniel Jeffery Wm. C. Dixon Simon E. Rosson Jesse Hinkle A. W. Harris R. B. Dicksen Moses Bishop G. W. Gray Henry Cole T. W. Edmundson A. P. Mix Secy

CONSTITUTION OF THE MILL CREEK PEACE ORGANIZATION SOCIETY

We the undersigned subscribers agree to form ourselves into an association call and known by the name and style of the Mill Creek peace organization society. Self preservation being an undisputed natural right, and the right of communities to combine together for the mutual protection of themselves their families and their property being well established. This being the sole purpose for which we met for this purpose alone we do adopt the following resolutions by which we expect to be governed in all our proceedings.

Resolved 1st. That each member before entering into this society shall take an oath as follows I do solemnly swear in the presence of Almighty God and these witnesses that I will well and truly keep all the secrets of this society that I will ever hail always conceal and never reveal anything. I will on the shortest notice go to the assistance of any other brother So help me God.

2nd As it is a matter of life or death with us any member of this society who shall betray to our enemies the existence of this society he shall forfeit his life and it shall be the duty of each member of this society having received knowledge of such betrayal to forthwith inform the brethren each of whose duty it shall be to follow such traitor and take his life at the price of their own. The manner of admitting members shall be in strict accordance with the foregoing preamble and resolutions and by such members as the society may select.

A true copy from the original furnished by a member of the society.

RECOMMENDATION FOR RELEASE OF WITNESSES AGAINST PEACE SOCIETY

Head Quarters Battalion Arkansas Cavalry Vounteers Camp Culloden, Carroll Co. Arks Decr. 6th, 1861

To the Governor, Military Board and Judicial Tribunals of the State of Arkansas Whereas this day John Christy and his two sons Joseph C. Christy and

J. F. H. Christy and P. M. Hensly, Gilmore Smith and D. C. Baker Citizens of Searcy County Arkansas voluntarily came and appeared before Honbles Kelly Featherstone and William Owens associate justices sitting as a court of Enquiry and Investigation into certain secret treasonable and Insurrectionary movements believed to exist and formed into societies under various appellations held together by oaths, Signs, Tokens and pass words and made known to said court the existence of a society represented to them as a Peace Society organizations being a good thing and for the protection of their homes property and family against Robbers and thieves and that it was a neighborhood society and that the best men and oldest citizens of the County were members of it and by which representation they were induced to go into the same and took the oath as members and whereas from their testimony given before this court and to which your attention is particularly invited to, we are fully satisfied that these men were gulled and deceived into the same by false representations.

We would most respectfully Petition the Executive of the State for their release from confinement and that they may be used if necessary in behalf of the State as to what they know, that we believe them to be honest Respectable and unsuspecting men who have without design or intention of wrong to the State or Confederate States been induced by intriguing and designing men to become members of a society which they now believe had an evil design in it though so far as they were capable of judging at the time they were not capable of discovering although the said John Christy, Joseph C. Christy, J. F. H. Christy, and Gilmore Smith said from their evidence which was taken separate and apart from each other and voluntarily given that they did not like the secret signs & tokens and while the oath was being given them and objected to that part at the time and that we are satisfied from the matter in which they came before the court and testified that they were anxious to ferret out all the wrong & evil if there was one in it.

Signed

We the undersigned cheerfully join in the recommendation for release of the parties above named and all others testifying voluntarily & making confessions as done by these parties and upon pledges of Fidelity and Support to the State of Arkansas and the Confederate States of America.

Signed. . . .

COMMITMENT OF PRISONERS IN CARROLL COUNTY JUSTICE OF PEACE COURT

Head Quarters Battalion Arkansas Cavalry Volunteers Camp Culloden Carroll County, Arks Dec 9, 1861

Now on this day it is ordered by Honbles Kelly Featherston and William Owens associate justices of this county of Carroll Arkansas, siting as a Court of Enquiry & Investigation into a certain secret Treasonable and Insurrectionary Society said to exist in this and the adjoining counties of the State of Arkansas and which society is said to be held together by secret oaths signed and pass words with the penalty of Death attached if revealed.

That the following named persons be committed for further trial and that Capt Jno R. H. Scott commanding Battalion Arks Cavalry Volunteers C. S. A be requested to convey them or have them conveyed under guard to Little Rock Arkansas and surrendered there to the Governor of the State of Arkansas Namely George Long, Solomon Branum, Joshua Reeves, David Curry, James Latterel, Samuel Thompson, Patrick L. Downey, James Thompson, James E. Curry, Charles W. Price, William Brown, George Hooten, Mike Tinkle, William Dugger, Luther Phillips, Thomas Dugger, William M. Will, James Hollis, Jasper Dugger, Mayfield Addison, William C. Singletary, and John M. Carithers.

And it is further ordered by the court that the following named persons enter in Bond the sum of Five Hundred dollars each for their appearance forthwith before the Governor of the State of Arkansas to testify in regard to certain matters voluntarily acknowledged before this court and not depart the order or decree of the Governor without leave therefrom, To Wit:

John Christy, Joseph Christy, J. F. H. Christy, P. M. Hensley, Gilmore Smith, Carroll Kilburn, E. L. Osborn, Carlton Keeling, George M. Hays, J. W. Kirkham, John McEntire, and John C. McNair.

Which is accordingly here done in open court, on this 9th day of Decr. 1861. William Owens, J.P. Kelly Featherston J.P. . . . .

HEAD QUARTERS BURROWSVILLE, 11ARK. DEC 9TH, [1861]
To His Excellency H. M. Rector Gov. of Ark.

Dear Sir:

I have this day ordered the prisoners under my care at this place to take up the line of march to Little Rock under a guard of one hundred Soldiers commanded by Lt. Brevet Lieut Col A. Ham, Maj John Bradshaw, and Agt Mager Jesse Cypert. I have no testimony only the testimony of the prisoners in their own confessions. You will call on Brev. Lieut. Col. Ham, Maj Bra[d]shaw, and Adj Maj Cypert, they can point out to you such other testimony as would become necessary, the most of the prisoners came in and surrendered, acknowledging their guilt and willing to Bide by the Law of their country, there is several men implicated in this seacret order skulking about in the woods and have not been arrested. I will do all I can to have then taken and brought to Justice. It seems as if the Whole Countrey have become ingaged in this matter to some Extent, and but for the timely discovery of it there is no telling what the can cequence would have been. Men who was considered to be amongst our best citizes has acknowledged them selves to be members of this secret order, said by some to be a home guard, by others home protection. I called on Capt Scott commanding Squadron at Camp Colodn Carroll Co. Capt Scott informs me that he would give me the aid ast fer and sent a portion of his command into this and Last Week arrested several men and carrying them to his head quarters and has them in his care and informed me that he would convey them to Little Rock. So soon as I think it safe to do so I will disband the men that I ordered into service. I have been sick for the last twelve [days] not able to attend to any kind of business and am just now able to sit up and write consequently I am not prepared any report at this time. Any instructions that you think [I] should have you will please Informe by Brevet Lieut Col Ham. I also send you a list of the names of the persons I have retained three prisoners here that could [not] travle on account of their health So soon as [I can] I will send them to Little Rock unless you see proper to order some other disposition made of them.

Respectfully your Obt serv Sam Leslie Col Commanding 45th Reg Arkansas Militia

TESTIMONY OF PETER TYLER ON THE PEACE SOCIETY

Head Qrs Battalion Arks Cav Volunteers Camp Culloden Carroll Co. Arkansas Decr. 18th, 1861 The State of Arkansas Vs Knowledge of and identity with Secret Treasonable and Insurrectionary Society Peter Tyler and Isaiah Ezell

Before the Honble Kelly Featherston Justice of the Peace within and for the County of Carroll State of Arkansas

Personally came and appeared Peter A. Tyler party in the above action said to have a knowledge of and perhaps Identity with a certain secret society hold together by certain oaths signs Tokens pass word &c & the revelation of which subjected its members to the punishment of death and upon his own voluntary request makes the following acknowledgments in relations to the matter and things wherof he has knowledge.

I am a member of a certain secret society represented to me by Long and D. Jamison who initiated me into the society in company with Samuel Grinder and Josiah Lane all taking the oath & receiving the signs tokens and pass words from Jamison at one & the same time about three weeks ago more or less as a "home protection" society and that there was no harm in it but to protect our selves our families & property and that it came from the North and that it was all over the South. I told him I was no northern man what I have is here and he said it was for home protection & after he administered the oath to me & grinder & lane he then gave me and them the signs tokens and pass words, which as well as I remember are as follows. The first sign was placing the three fingers of the left hand angling across the nose the answer was carelessly feeling under the chin with one of the hands. The next sign was to place one finger in the shirt collar I believe left hand and the answer was to put the right hand on the left breast. The next was to raise the hat with one hand and place it back on the head the answer was turn the back to the person moving the hat.

A token was in meeting after night on speaking if anyone was with him you said "It was a very dark night" and the answer would be "Not so dark as it will be in the morning." One sign was to hang up in the front door of the house a piece of red ribbon, calico, or flannel. Another token was when they were separate to get together was to Hoot like and Owl, and the answer was to howl like a wolf I think. I heard somewhere after the noise commenced about it that it came from Washington City but Jamison did not tell me if I recollect right he said to me it was for protection when invaded by robbers, I gave the paper or obligation to David Curry & told him to take care of it for it might be of an advantage to them. I & Sam Grinder & Jo Lane were all sworn in by Jamison at the same time, and after that I rode around among the boys & swore in the following persons as members to wit Isaiah Ezell, David Curry, Peter Reeves, Joshua Reeves, Robert Grinder, David Barnett, John McEntire, Thomas Younger, Alexander Younger, George Hooten, John Brown, Robert Tinkle, Mike Tinkle, James Thompson, Thomas Thompson, Samuel Thompson, J. C. Mc Nair, Claiborn Maness, James Curry, Patrick L. Downly, A. J. Love, Green Adams, Spencer Adams, Joseph Adams, William Brown, Robert Grinder, Charles Price, Lindsay Price, Lindsay Bishop, John Ezell, Daniel Parks, & Austin Pierce I think is the name, then maybe some more but I do not now recollect them if there are. I told Jamison I was not no northern man all I had was here. I told him I did not like the oath he said there was nothing wrong about it & he did not want any thing said about it, wanted it secret not to tell any body of it although it was all over the South or something to this amount. All those named above & my self and Grinder & Lane all held up our right hands when the obligations recd by us and given to them by me, all of which I am ready [to] and here verify. P. A. Tyler.

Sworn and subscribed to before me this 18th day of Decr. 1861 Kelly Featherston J P

It is ordered here by this court that the said P. A. Tyler above named be committed for further trial and that he be conveyed to the city of Little Rock and surrendered to the Governor of the State of Arkansas and that he be placed in the hands of Captn Jno R. H. Scott commanding Squadron Arks Cavalry Volunteers C. S. A. with a request that he send him under guard to the City of Little Rock with such number of means he may deem sufficient to prevent his escape from custody in accordance with this order. Given under my hand and seal this 18th day of December 1861 Kelly Featherston, J. P.

TESTIMONY OF ISAIAH EZELL ON THE PEACE SOCIETY

Arks Cav Vol Camp Culoden Carroll Co Arks Decr. 18 1861
State of Arks Vs Knowledge of and Identity with Secret Treasonable and Insurrectionary Society Peter Tyler and Isaiah Ezell

Before the Honble Kelly Featherston J. P. of Carroll Co. Arkansas Personally came & appeared Isaiah Ezell one of the parties above and on oath sayeth. That he belongs to a home guard or Home protection Society of a Secret nature held together by certain oaths Signs tokens & pass words the revelation of which was punishable by death that he was initiated into the same by Peter Tyler, of Tomahawk Township Searcy County Arkansas he presented me with a paper purporting to be an obligation to which I was sworn but to which I did not affix my name. I saw no other one taken into the society nor never initiated any one into it, myself, except seeing John Ezell initiated at another time by Peter Tyler. I do not know the wording of the oath. One of the signs given was to place one of the hands about the nose the answer was perhaps rubing the hand under the chin. There was a sign to be put up somewhere about the house a piece of Ribbon or calico dont recollect the color. I dont know the meaning of this sign. There was something about an owl but I don't recollect what or how it was represented to me to be for the protection of our homes and families against robbers &c and if it was for any other purpose I was deceived in it. his Isaiah X Ezell mark Sworn and subscribed to before me this 18th day of Decr. 1861

Kelly Featherston J P

COLONEL WILLIAM C. MITCHELL TO GOVERNOR RECTOR
Camp Madison, Ark. Decr. 23 1861
Hon. H. M. Rector Governor of the State of Arkansas

Sir

Three men enlisted by the name of George M. Hays Eli L. Osborn and John W. Kirkham from the countys of Marion and Carroll and from what I understand they are bound over to appear at Little Rock on a charge of Treason to the Confederate States. They belong to Captain R. E. Trimble Company in this Regt if you wish them conveyed to Little Rock a requisition for them you can make they are in safe hands and will be safely kept, subject to your demand.

I am Yours Respectfully
Wm C Mitchell
Col. 14 Regt Arks Vol

Joseph E. Brown (1821–1894)

Not only in the North did concerned citizens protest their government's tendency to step on civil liberties during the wartime emergency. In the South, too, many people were critical of the Confederacy's disregard of civil liberties and its fondness for martial law. One of the ironies of the Civil War is that the Confederacy, in order to strengthen the war effort, which it claimed was to preserve and defend the principle of states' rights, was obliged to extend the power of the central government in Richmond. In this way, the Confederacy began to resemble the Union it was fighting against. In the first selection here, Georgia Governor Joseph E. Brown, in a letter to Alexander H. Stephens, vice-president of the Confederacy, attacks a policy that gives too much power to the military. In the second selection, an 1864 address delivered to the Georgia State Legislature, Brown takes on the issues of conscription and the suspension of the writ of habeas corpus. Brown was a Jacksonian Democrat who so staunchly defended states' rights that it could be argued that he was a hindrance to Jefferson Davis and the Confederate government, damaging the South's chances of winning the war. To Brown, martial law decreed by the Davis government infringed on both states' rights and individual rights.

LETTER TO ALEXANDER H. STEPHENS, 1862

Dear Sir:

I have the pleasure to acknowledge the receipt of your letter. . . . And am gratified that you take the view which you have expressed about the action of Genl. Bragg in his declaration of martial law over Atlanta and his appoint[ment], as the newspapers say, of a civil governor with aids, etc.

I have viewed this proceeding as I have others of our military authorities of late with painful apprehensiveness for the future. It seems military men are assuming the whole powers of government to themselves and setting at defiance constitution, laws, state rights, state sovereignty, and every other principle of civil liberty, and that our people engrossed in the struggle with the enemy are disposed to submit to these bold usurpations tending to military despotism without murmur, much less resistance. I should have called this proceeding into question before this time but I was hopeful from the indications which I had noted that Congress would take such action as would check these dangerous usurpations of power, and for the further reasons that I have already come almost into conflict with the Confederate authorities in vindication of what I have considered the rights of the State and people of Georgia, and I was fearful, as no other governor seems to raise these questions, that I might be considered by good and true men in and out of Congress too refractory for the times. I had therefore concluded to take no notice of this matter till the meeting of the legislature when I expect to ask the representatives of the people to define the bounds to which they desire the Governor to go in the defense of the rights and sovereignty of the state. I confess I have apprehensions that our present General Assembly does not properly reflect the sentiments of our people upon this great question, but if the Executive goes beyond the bounds where he is sustained by the representatives of the people he exposes himself to censure without the moral power to do service to the great principles involved. I fear we have much more to apprehend from military despotism than from subjugation by the

SOURCE: *Message of His Excellency Joseph E. Brown, to the Extra Session of the Legislature, Convened March 10th, 1864 . . .* (Milledgeville, GA: Boughton, Nisbet, Barnes & Moore, 1864), 11–21.

enemy. I trust our generals will improve well their time while we have the advantage and the enemy are organizing another army. Hoping that your health is good and begging that you will write me when your important duties are not too pressing to permit it. I am very truly your friend.

Message to the Legislature, March 10, 1864

THE NEW MILITIA ORGANIZATION AND CONSCRIPTION

Since your adjournment in December, the Adjutant and Inspector General, under my direction, has done all in his power to press forward the organization of the militia of the State, in conformity to the act passed for that purpose; and I have the pleasure to state, that the enrollments are generally made, except in a few localities, where proximity to the enemy has prevented it; and the organizations will soon be completed.

At this stage in our proceedings, we are met with formidable obstacles, thrown in our way by the late act of Congress, which subjects those between 17 and 50 to enrollment as Conscripts, for Confederate service. This act of Congress proposes to take from the State, as was done on a former occasion, her entire military force, who belong to the active list, and to leave her without a force, in the different counties, sufficient to execute her laws or suppress servile insurrection. Our Supreme Court has ruled, that the Confederate government has the power to raise armies by conscription, but it has not decided that it also has the power to enroll the whole population of the State who remain at home, so as to place the whole people under the military control of the Confederate government, and thereby take from the States all command over their own citizens, to execute their own laws, and place the internal police regulations of the States in the hands of the President. It is one thing to "raise armies," and another, and quite a different thing, to put the whole population at home under military law, and compel every man to obtain a military detail, upon such terms as the central government may dictate, and to carry a military pass in his pocket while he cultivates his farm, or attends to his other necessary avocations at home.

Neither a planter nor an overseer engaged upon the farm, nor a blacksmith making agricultural implements, nor a miller grinding for the people at home, belongs to, or constitutes any part of the armies of the Confederacy; and there is not the shadow of Constitutional power, vested in the Confederate government, for conscribing and putting these classes, and others engaged in home pursuits, under military rule, while they remain at home to discharge these duties. If conscription were constitutional as a means of raising armies by the Confederate government, it could not be constitutional to conscribe those not *actually* needed, and to be *employed* in the army, and the constitutional power to "raise armies," could never carry with it the power in Congress to conscribe the whole people, who are not needed for the armies, but are left at home, because more useful there, and place them under military government and compel them to get military details to plough in their fields, shoe their farm horses, or to go to mill.

Conscription carried to this extent, is the essence of military despotism; placing all civil rights in a state of subordination to military power, and putting the personal freedom of each individual, in civil life, at the will of the chief of the military power. But it may be said that conscription may act upon one class as legally as another, and that all classes are equally subject to it. This is undoubtedly true. If the government has a right to conscribe at all, it has a right to conscribe persons of all classes, till it has raised enough to supply its armies. But it has no right to go farther and conscribe all, who are, by its own consent, to remain at home to make supplies. If it considers supplies necessary, somebody must make them, and those who do it, being no part of the army, should be exempt from conscription, and the annoyance of military dictation, while engaged in civil, and not military pursuits.

If all between 17 and 50 are to be enrolled and placed in constant military service, we must conquer the enemy while we are consuming our present crop of provisions, or we are ruined; as it will be impossible for the old men over 50, and the boys under 17, to make supplies enough to feed our armies and people another year. I think every practical man in the Confederacy who knows anything about our agricultural interests and resources, will readily admit this. If, on the other hand, it is not the intention to put those between 17 and 18, and between 45 and 50, into service, as *soldiers,* but to leave them at home to produce supplies, and occasionally to do police and other duties, within the State, which properly belong to the militia of a State; or in other words, if it is the intention simply to take the control of them from the State, so as to deprive her of all power, and leave her without sufficient force to execute her own laws, or suppress servile insurrection, and place the whole militia of the State, not needed for constant service, in the Confederate armies, under the control of the President, while engaged in their civil pursuits, the act, is unconstitutional and oppressive, and ought not to be executed.

If the act is executed in this State, it deprives her of her whole *active* militia, as Congress has so shaped it as to include the identical persons embraced in the act passed at your late session, and to transfer the control of them all from the State to the Confederate government.

The State has already enrolled these persons under the solemn act of her Legislature, for her own defense, and it is a question for you to determine, whether the necessities of the State, her sovereignty and dignity, and justice to those who are to be affected by the act, do not forbid that she should permit her organization to be broken up, and her means of self-preservation to be taken out of her hands. If this is done, what will be our condition? I prefer to answer by adopting the language of the present able and patriotic Governor of Virginia: "A sovereign State without a soldier, and without the dignity of strength—stripped of all her men, and with only the form and pageantry of power—would indeed be nothing more than a wretched dependency, to which I should grieve to see our proud old Commonwealth reduced." . . .

CONFLICT WITH THE CONFEDERATE GOVERNMENT

But it may be said that an attempt to maintain the rights of the State will produce conflict with the Confederate Government. I am aware that there are those who, from motives not necessary to be here mentioned, are ever ready to raise the cry of *conflict*, and to criticise and condemn the action of Georgia, in every case where her constituted authorities protest against the encroachments of the central power, and seek to maintain her dignity and sovereignty as a State, and the constitutional rights and liberties of her people.

Those who are unfriendly to State sovereignty, and desire to consolidate all power in the hands of the Confederate Government, hoping to promote their undertaking by operating upon the fears of the timid, after each new aggression upon the constitutional rights of the States, fill the newspaper presses with the cry of *conflict*, and warn the people to beware of those who seek to maintain their constitutional rights, as *agitators* or *partisans* who may embarrass the Confederate Government in the prosecution of the war.

Let not the people be deceived by this false clamor. It is the same cry of *conflict* which the Lincoln Government raised against all who defended the rights of the Southern States against its tyranny. It is the cry which the usurpers of power have ever raised against those who rebuke their encroachments and refuse to yield to their aggressions. . . .

SUSPENSION OF THE HABEAS CORPUS

I cannot withhold the expression of the deep mortification I feel at the late action of Congress, in attempting to suspend the privilege of the writ of *Habeas Corpus*, and to confer upon the President powers expressly denied to him by the Constitution of the Confederate States. Under pretext of a *necessity* which our whole people know does not exist in this case whatever may have been the motives, our Congress, with the assent, and at the *request* of the Executive, has struck a fell blow at the liberties of these States.

The Constitution of the Confederate States declares that, "The privilege of the writ of *habeas corpus* shall not be suspended, unless when in cases of rebellion or invasion the public safety may require it." The power to suspend the *habeas corpus* at all, is derived, not from express and direct delegation, but from implication only, and an implication can never be raised in opposition to an express restriction. In case of any conflict between the two, an implied power must always yield to express restrictions upon its exercise. The power to suspend the privilege of the writ of *habeas corpus* derived by implication, must therefore be always limited by the *express* declaration in the Constitution that:

> "The right of the people to be secure in their *persons*, houses, papers, and effects, against unreasonable searches and seizures *shall not be violated;* and *no warrants shall issue* but upon probable cause, supported by *oath or affirmation,* and particularly describing the place to be searched, and the *persons* or things to be seized," and the further declaration that, "no person shall be deprived of life, *liberty* or property, without due process of law."

And that,

"In all *criminal prosecutions* the accused shall enjoy the right of a *speedy* and public trial by an *impartial jury* of the State or District where the crime shall have been committed, which district shall have been previously ascertained by law, and to be informed of the nature and cause of the accusation; to be confronted with the witnesses against him; to have compulsory process for obtaining witnesses in his favor; and to have the assistance of counsel for his defense."

Thus it is an express guaranty of the Constitution, that the "*persons*" of the people shall be secure, and "*no warrants* shall issue," but upon probable cause, supported by "*oath* or *affirmation*," particularly describing "the *persons* to be seized;" that, "no *person* shall be deprived of *liberty,* without due process of law," and that, in "all criminal prosecutions the accused shall enjoy the right of a *speedy* and *public* trial, by an *impartial jury.*"

The Constitution also defines the *powers* of the Executive, which, are limited to those delegated, among which there is no one, authorizing him to issue *warrants* or *order arrests* of persons not in *actual* military service; or to sit as a judge in any case, to try any person for a criminal offense, or to appoint any *court* or *tribunal* to do it, not provided for in the Constitution, as part of the judiciary. The power to *issue warrants* and try persons under criminal accusations are *judicial* powers, which belong, under the Constitution, *exclusively* to the *judiciary* and not to the *Executive.* His power to order arrests, as Commander-in-Chief, is strictly a *military* power, and is confined to the arrest of *persons subject to military power,* as to the arrest of persons in the army or navy of the Confederate States; or in the Militia, when in the *actual* service of the Confederate States, and does not extend to any persons in civil life, unless they be followers of the camp, or within the lines of the army. This is clear from that provision of the Constitution which declares, that,

"No person shall be held to answer for a capital, or otherwise infamous crime, unless on a *presentment* or *indictment* of a *grand jury,* except in cases arising *in the land or naval forces,* or *in the militia,* when in *actual service* in time of war or public danger." But even here, the power of the President as Commander-in-Chief, is not absolute, as his powers and duties, in ordering arrests of persons, in the land or naval forces, or in the militia, when in *actual* service, are clearly defined by the rules and articles of war, prescribed by Congress. *Any warrant* issued by the President, or *any arrest* made by him, or under his order, of *any person* in civil life and not subject to military command, is *illegal* and in *plain violation of the Constitution;* as it is impossible for Congress, by implication, to confer upon the President the right to exercise powers of arrest, expressly forbidden to him by the Constitution. Any effort, on the part of Congress, to do this, is but an attempt to revive the odious practice of ordering political arrests, or issuing letters *de cachet* by royal prerogative, so long since renounced by our English ancestors; and the denial of the right of the constitutional judiciary to investigate such cases, and the provision for creating a court appointed by the Executive, and changeable at his will, to take jurisdiction of the same, are in violation of the great principles of *Magna Charta*, the Bill of Rights, the *habeas corpus* act, and the Constitution of the Confederate States, upon which both English and American liberty rest; and are but an attempt to revive the odious Star-Chamber court of England, which, in the hands of wicked kings, was used for tyrannical purposes, by the crown, until it was finally abolished by act of parliament, of 16th Charles the First, which went into operation on the first of August 1641. This act has ever since been regarded as one of the great bulwarks of English liberty; and as it was passed by the English Parliament to secure our English ancestors against the very same character of arbitrary arrests which the late act of Congress is intended to authorize the President to make, I append a copy of it to this message, with the same italics and small capital letters, which are used in the printed copy in the book from which it is taken. It will be seen that the court of "Star-Chamber," which was the instrument in the hands of the English king, for *investigating* his illegal arrests and carrying out his arbitrary decrees, was much more respectable, on account of the character, learning and ability of its members, than the Confederate Star-Chamber, or court of "proper officers," which the act of Congress gives the President power to appoint, to *investigate* his illegal arrests. . . .

The only suspension of the privilege of the writ of *habeas corpus*, known to our Constitution, and compatible with the provisions already stated, goes to the simple extent of preventing the release, under it, of persons whose arrests have been ordered under constitutional warrants from judicial authority. To this extent the Constitution allows the suspension, in case of rebellion or invasion, in order that the accused may be certainly and safely held for trial; but Congress has no right, under pretext of exercising this power, to authorize the President to make *illegal arrests*, prohibited by the Constitution; and when Congress has attempted to confer such powers on the President, if he should order such illegal arrests, it would be the imperative duty of the judges, who have solemnly sworn to support the Constitution, to disregard such unconstitutional legislation, and grant relief to persons so illegally imprisoned; and it would be the duty of the Legislative and Executive departments of the States to sustain and protect the judiciary in the discharge of this obligation.

By an examination of the act of Congress, now under consideration, it will be seen that it is not an act to suspend the privilege of the writ of *habeas corpus* in case of warrants issued by *judicial authority;* but the main purpose of the act seems to be to authorize the President to issue warrants, supported by neither *oath* nor *affirmation,* and to make arrests of persons not in military service, upon charges of a nature proper for investigation in the judicial tribunals only, and to prevent the Courts from inquiring into such arrests, or granting relief against such illegal usurpations of power, which are in direct and palpable violation of the Constitution. . . .

This then is not an act to suspend the privilege of the writ of *habeas corpus*, in the manner authorized by implication by the Constitution; but it is an act to authorize the President to make *illegal and unconstitutional arrests*, in cases which the Constitution gives to the judiciary, and denies to the Executive; and to prohibit all judicial interference for the relief of the citizen, when tyranized over by illegal arrest, under letters *de cachet* issued by Executive authority.

Instead of the legality of the arrest being examined in the judicial tribunals appointed by the Constitution, it is to be examined in the Confederate Star Chamber; that is, by *officers* appointed by the President. Why say that the "*President shall cause proper officers* to investigate" the legality of arrests ordered by him? Why not permit the Judges, whose constitutional right and duty it is to do it?

We are witnessing with too much indifference assumptions of power by the Confederate Government which in ordinary times would arouse the whole country to indignant rebuke and stern resistance. History teaches us that submission to one encroachment upon constitutional liberty is always followed by another; and we should not forget that important rights, yielded to those in power, without rebuke or protest, are never recovered by the people without revolution. . . .

When such bold strides towards military despotism and absolute authority, are taken, by those in whom we have confided, and who have been placed in high official position to guard and protect constitutional and personal liberty, it is the duty of every patriotic citizen to sound the alarm, and of the State Legislatures to say, in thunder tones, to those who assume to govern us by absolute power, that there is a point beyond which freemen will not permit encroachments to go.

The Legislatures of the respective States are looked to as the guardians of the rights of those whom they represent, and it is their duty to meet such dangerous encroachments upon the liberties of the people, promptly, and express their unqualified condemnation, and to instruct their Senators, and request their Representatives to repeal this most monstrous act, or resign a trust, which, by permitting it to remain on the statute book, they abuse, to the injury of those who have honored them with their confidence in this trying period of our history. I earnestly recommend that the Legislature of this State take prompt action upon this subject, and stamp the act with the seal of their indignant rebuke. . . .

Cyrus Pringle (1838–1911)

Throughout history, dissenters have opposed war for a variety of reasons. Often the reasons are political and connected to a specific war, such as Henry David Thoreau's opposition to the Mexican War. Thoreau was not necessarily a pacifist opposed to all wars. He was opposed to the war with Mexico because of its intention to extend slavery. There are individuals, however, who for moral or religious reasons are opposed to war in general. In both cases, whether the individual is a pacifist or a political dissenter, the antiwar stance is ultimately a question of conscience.

During the Civil War, Cyrus Pringle was drafted into the Union Army but, because of his Quaker convictions, refused to serve and even refused, when the option was offered to him, to pay for a substitute. His diary, discovered and published 50 years after the war, has been a source of inspiration for pacifists objecting to the First World War, the Second World War, and the Vietnam War in the twentieth century.

THE RECORD OF A QUAKER CONSCIENCE, 1863

At Burlington, Vt., on the 13th of the seventh month, 1863, I was drafted. Pleasant are my recollections of the 14th. Much of that rainy day I spent in my chamber, as yet unaware of my fate; in writing and reading and in reflecting to compose my mind for any event. The day and the exercise, by the blessing of the Father, brought me precious reconciliation to the will of Providence.

With ardent zeal for our Faith and the cause of our peaceable principles; and almost disgusted at the lukewarmness and unfaithfulness of very many who profess these; and considering how heavily slight crosses bore upon their shoulders, I felt to say, "Here am I, Father, for thy service. As thou will." May I trust it was He who called me and sent me forth with the consolation: "My grace is sufficient for thee." Deeply have I felt many times since that I am nothing without the companionship of the Spirit.

I was to report on the 27th. Then, loyal to our country, Wm. Lindley Dean and I appeared before the Provost Marshal with a statement of our cases. We were ordered for a hearing on the 29th. On the afternoon of that day W. L. D. was rejected upon examination of the Surgeon, but my case not coming up, he remained with me, much to my strength and comfort. Sweet was his converse and long to be remembered, as we lay together that warm summer night on the straw of the barracks. By his encouragement much was my mind strengthened; my desires for a pure life, and my resolutions for good. In him and those of whom he spoke I saw the abstract beauty of Quakerism. On the next morning came Joshua M. Dean to support me and plead my case before the Board of Enrollment. On the day after, the 31st, I came before the Board. Respectfully those men listened to the exposition of our principles; and, on our representing that we looked for some relief from the President, the marshal released me for twenty days. Meanwhile appeared Lindley M. Macomber and was likewise, by the kindness of the marshal, though they had received instructions from the Provost Marshal General to show such claims no partiality, released to appear on the 20th day of the eighth month.

All these days we were urged by our acquaintances to pay our commutation money; by some through well-meant kindness and sympathy; by others through interest in the war; and by others still through a belief they entertained it was our duty. But we confess a higher duty than that to country; and, asking no military

SOURCE: Cyrus Pringle, *The Civil War Diary of Cyrus Pringle* (Wallingford, PA: Pendle Hill Pamphlet 122, 1962), 7–15, 27–39.

protection of our Government and grateful for none, deny any obligation to support so unlawful a system, as we hold a war to be even when waged in opposition to an evil and oppressive power and ostensibly in defence of liberty, virtue, and free institutions; and, though touched by the kind interest of friends, we could not relieve their distress by a means we held even more sinful than that of serving ourselves, as by supplying money to hire a substitute we would not only be responsible for the result, but be the agents in bringing others into evil. So looking to our Father alone for help, and remembering that "Whoso loseth his life for my sake shall find it; but whoso saveth it shall lose it," we presented ourselves again before the Board, as we had promised to do when released. Being offered four days more of time, we accepted it as affording opportunity to visit our friends; and moreover as there would be more probability of meeting Peter Dakin at Rutland.

Sweet was the comfort and sympathy of our friends as we visited them. There was a deep comfort, as we left them, in the thought that so many pure and pious people follow us with their love and prayers. Appearing finally before the marshal on the 24th, suits and uniforms were selected for us, and we were called upon to give receipts for them. L.M.M. was on his guard, and, being first called upon, declared he could not do so, as that would imply acceptance. Failing to come to any agreement, the matter was postponed till next morning, when we certified to the fact that the articles were "with us." Here I must make record of the kindness of the marshal, Rolla Gleason, who treated us with respect and kindness. He had spoken with respect of our Society; had given me furloughs to the amount of twenty four days, when the marshal at Rutland considered himself restricted by his oath and duty to six days; and here appeared in person to prevent any harsh treatment of us by his sergeants; and though much against his inclinations, assisted in putting on the uniform with his own hands. We bade him farewell with grateful feelings and expressions of fear that we should not fall into as tender hands again; and amid the rain in the early morning, as the town clock tolled the hour of seven, we were driven amongst the flock that was going forth to the slaughter, down the street and into the cars for Brattleboro. Dark was the day with murk and cloud and rain; and, as we rolled down through the narrow vales of eastern Vermont, somewhat of the shadow crept into our hearts and filled them with dark apprehensions of evil fortune ahead; of long, hopeless trials; of abuse from inferior officers; of contempt from common soldiers; of patient endurance (or an attempt at this), unto an end seen only by the eye of a strong faith.

Herded into a car by ourselves, we conscripts, substitutes, and the rest, through the greater part of the day, swept over the fertile meadows along the banks of the White River and the Connecticut, through pleasant scenes that had little of delight for us. At Woodstock we were joined by the conscripts from the 1st District—altogether an inferior company from those before with us, who were honest yeomen from the northern and mountainous towns, while these were many of them substitutes from the cities.

At Brattleboro we were marched up to the camp; our knapsacks and persons searched; and any articles of citizen's dress taken from us; and then shut up in a rough board building under a guard. . . .

Brattleboro, 26th, 8th month, 1863. Twenty-five or thirty caged lions roam lazily to and fro through this building hour after hour through the day. On every side without, sentries pace their slow beat, bearing loaded muskets. Men are ranging through the grounds or hanging in synods about the doors of the different buildings, apparently without a purpose. Aimless is military life, except betimes its aim is deadly. Idle life blends with violent death-struggles till the man is unmade a man; and henceforth there is little of manhood about him. Of a man he is made a soldier, which is a man-destroying machine in two senses,—a thing for the prosecuting or repelling an invasion like the block of stone in the fortress or the plate of iron on the side of the Monitor. They are alike. I have tried in vain to define a difference, and I see only this. The iron-clad with its gun is the bigger soldier: the more formidable in attack, the less liable to destruction in a given time; the block the most capable of resistance; both are equally obedient to officers. Or the more perfect is the soldier, the more nearly he approaches these in this respect.

Three times a day we are marched out to the mess houses for our rations. In our hands we carry a tin plate, whereon we bring back a piece of bread (sour and tough most likely), and a cup. Morning and noon a piece of meat, antique betimes, bears company with the bread. They who wish it receive in their cups two sorts of decoctions: in the morning burnt bread, or peas perhaps, steeped in water with some saccharine substance added (I dare not affirm it to be sugar). At night steeped tea extended by some other herbs probably and its pungency and acridity assuaged by the saccharine principle aforementioned. On this we have so far subsisted and, save some nauseating, comfortably. As we go out and return, on right and left and in front and rear go bayonets. Some substitutes heretofore have escaped and we are not to be neglected in our attendants. Hard beds are healthy, but I query cannot the result be defeated by the *degree?* Our mattresses are boards. Only the slight elasticity of our thin blankets breaks the fall of our flesh and bones thereon. Oh! now I praise the discipline I have received from uncarpeted floors through warm summer nights of my boyhood.

The building resounds with petty talk; jokes and laughter and swearing. Something more than that. Many of the caged lions are engaged with cards, and money changes hands freely. Some of the caged lions read, and some sleep, and so the weary day goes by.

L.M.M. and I addressed the following letter to Governor Holbrook and hired a corporal to forward it to him.

Brattleboro, Vt., 26th, 8th month, 1863.

Frederick Holbrook,

Governor of Vermont:—

We, the undersigned members of the Society of Friends, beg leave to represent to thee, that we were lately drafted in the 3d Dist. of Vermont, have been forced into the army and reached the camp near: this town yesterday.

That in the language of the elders of our New York Yearly Meeting, "We love our country and acknowledge with gratitude to our Heavenly Father the many blessings we have been favoured with under the government; and can feel no sympathy with any who seek its overthrow."

But that, true to well-known principles of our Society, we cannot violate our religious convictions either by complying with military requisitions or by the equivalents of this compliance, the furnishing of a substitute or payment of commutation money. That, therefore, we are brought into suffering and exposed to insult and contempt from those who have us in charge, as well as to the penalties of insubordination, though liberty of conscience is granted us by the Constitution of Vermont as well as that of the United States.

Therefore, we beg of thee as Governor of our State any assistance thou may be able to render, should it be no more than the influence of thy position interceding in our behalf.

Truly Thy Friend,
Cyrus G. Pringle.

P.S.—We are informed we are to be sent to the vicinity of Boston tomorrow.

27th. On board train to Boston. The long afternoon of yesterday passed slowly away. This morning passed by,—the time of our stay in Brattleboro, and we neither saw nor heard anything of our Governor. We suppose he could not or would not help us. So as we go down to our trial we have no arm to lean upon among all men; but why dost thou complain, oh, my Soul? Seek thou that faith that will prove a buckler to thy breast, and gain for thee the protection of an arm mightier than the arms of all men.

Camp Vermont: Long Island, Boston Harbour. 28th—In the early morning damp and cool we marched down off the heights of Brattleboro to take train for this place. Once in the car the dashing young cavalry officer, who had us in charge, gave notice he had placed men through the cars, with loaded revolvers, who had orders to shoot any person attempting to escape, or jump from the window, and that any one would be shot if he even put his head out of the window. Down the beautiful valley of the Connecticut, all through its broad intervals, heavy with its crops of corn or tobacco, or shaven smooth by the summer harvest; over the hard and stony counties of northern Massachusetts, through its suburbs and under the shadow of Bunker Hill Monument we came into the City of Boston, "the Hub of the Universe." Out through street after street we were marched double guarded to the wharves, where we took a small steamer for the island some six miles out in the harbour. A circumstance connected with this march is worth mentioning for its singularity: at the head of this company, like convicts (and feeling very much like such), through the City of Boston walked, with heavy hearts and down-cast eyes, two Quakers.

Here on this dry and pleasant island in the midst of the beautiful Massachusetts Bay, we have the liberty of the camp, the privilege of air and sunshine and hay beds to sleep upon. So we went to bed last night with somewhat of gladness elevating our depressed spirits.

Here are many troops gathering daily from all the New England States except Connecticut and Rhode Island. Their white tents are dotting the green slopes and hilltops of the island and spreading wider and wider. This is the flow of military tide here just now. The ebb went out to sea in the shape of a great shipload just as we came in, and another load will be sent before many days. All is war here. We are surrounded by the pomp and circumstance of war, and enveloped in the cloud thereof. The cloud settles down over the minds and souls of all; they cannot see beyond, nor do they try; but with the clearer eye of Christian faith I try to look beyond all this error unto Truth and Holiness immaculate: and thanks to our Father, I am favoured with glimpses that are sweet consolation amid this darkness.

This is one gratification: the men with us give us their sympathy. They seem to look upon us tenderly and pitifully, and their expressions of kind wishes are warm. Although we are relieved from duty and from drill, and may lie in our tents during rain and at night, we have heard of no complaint. This is the more worthy of note as there are so few in our little (Vermont) camp. Each man comes on guard half the days. It would probably be otherwise were their hearts in the service; but I have yet to find the man in any of these camps or at any service who does not wish himself at home. Substitutes say if they knew all they know now before leaving home they would not have enlisted; and they have been but a week from their homes and have endured no hardships. Yesterday L. M. M. and I appeared before the Captain commanding this camp with a statement of our cases. He listened to us respectfully and promised to refer us to the General commanding here, General Devens; and in the meantime released us from duty. In a short time afterward he passed us in our tent, asking our names. We have not heard from him, but do not drill or stand guard; so, we suppose, his release was confirmed. At that interview a young lieutenant sneeringly told us he thought we had better throw away our scruples and fight in the service of the country; and as we told the Captain we could not accept pay, he laughed mockingly, and said he would not stay here for $13.00 per month. He gets more than a hundred, I suppose.

How beautiful seems the world on this glorious morning here by the seaside! Eastward and toward the sun, fair green isles with outlines of pure beauty are scattered over the blue bay. Along the far line of the mainland white hamlets and towns glisten in the morning sun; countless tiny waves dance in the wind that comes off shore and sparkle sunward like myriads of gems. Up the fair vault, flecked by scarcely a cloud, rolls the sun in glory. Though fair be the earth, it has come to be tainted and marred by him who was meant to be its crowning glory. Behind me on this island are crowded vile and wicked men, the murmur of whose ribaldry riseth continually like the smoke and fumes of a lower world. Oh! Father of Mercies, forgive the hard heartlessness and blindness and scarlet sins of my fellows, my brothers. . . .

Regimental Hospital, 4th Vermont. 29th—On the evening of the 26th the Colonel came to us apologizing for the roughness with which he treated us at first, which was, as he insisted, through ignorance of our real character and position. He told us if we persisted in our course, death would probably follow; though at another time he confessed to P. D. that this would only be the extreme sentence of court-martial. He urged us to go into the hospital, stating that this course was advised by Friends about New York. We were too well aware of such a fact to make any denial, though it was a subject of surprise to us that he should be informed of it. He pleaded with us long and earnestly, urging us with many promises of indulgence and favour and attentions we found afterwards to be untrue. He gave us till the next morning to consider the question and report our decision. In our discussion of the subject among ourselves, we were very much perplexed. If all his statements concerning the ground taken by our Society were true, we seemed to be liable, if we persisted in the course which alone seemed to us to be in accordance with Truth, to be exposed to the charge of over-zeal and fanaticism even among our own brethren. Regarding the work to be done in hospital as one of mercy and benevolence, we asked if we had any right to refuse its performance; and questioned whether we could do more good by deavouring to bear to the end a clear testimony against war, than by labouring by word and deed among the needy in the hospitals and camps. We saw around us a rich field for usefulness in which there were scarce any labourers and toward whose work our hands had often started involuntarily and unbidden. At last we consented to a trial, at least till we could make inquiries concerning the Colonel's allegations, and ask the counsel of our friends, reserving the privilege of returning to our former position.

At first a great load seemed rolled away from us; we rejoiced in the prospect of life again. But soon there prevailed a feeling of condemnation, as though we had sold Our Master. And that first day was one of the bitterest I ever experienced. It was a time of stern conflict of soul. The voice that seemed to say, "Follow me," as I sought guidance the night before, kept pleading with me, convincing of sin, till I knew of a truth my feet had strayed from His path. The Scriptures, which the day before I could scarcely open without finding words of strength and comfort, seemed closed against me, till after a severe struggle alone in the wood to which I had retired, I consented to give up and retrace my steps in faith. But it was too late. L.M.M. wishing to make a fair, honest trial, we were brought here— P.D. being already here unwell. We feel we are erring; but scarce anything is required of us and we wait to hear from Friends.

Of these days of going down into sin, I wish to make little mention. I would that my record of such degradation be brief. We wish to come to an understanding with our friends and the Society before we move, but it does not seem that we can repress the up-heavings of Truth in our hearts. We are bruised by sin.

It is with pleasure I record we have just waited upon the Colonel with an explanation of our distress of mind, requesting him to proceed with court-martial. We were kindly and tenderly received. "If you want a trial I can give it to you," he answered. The brigade has just marched out to join with the division for inspection. After that we are to have attention to our case.

P.M. There is particular cause for congratulation in the consideration that we took this step this morning, when now we received a letter from H. D. charging us to faithfulness.

When lately I have seen dear L. M. M. in the thoroughness and patience of his trial to perform service in hospital, his uneasiness and the intensity of his struggle as manifested by his silence and disposition to avoid the company of his friends, and seen him fail and declare to us, "I cannot stay here," I have received a new proof, and to me a strong one, because it is from the experimental knowledge of an honest man, that no Friend, who is really such, desiring to keep himself clear of complicity with this system of war and to bear a perfect testimony against it, can lawfully perform service in the hospitals of the Army in lieu of bearing arms.

3rd, 10th month—Today dawned fair and our Camp is dry again. I was asked to clean the gun I brought, and declining, was tied some two hours upon the ground.

At Washington. 6th—At first, after being informed of our declining to serve in his hospital, Colonel Foster did not appear altered in his kind regard for us. But his spleen soon became evident. At the time we asked for a trial by court-martial, and it was his duty to place us under arrest and proceed with the preferring of his charges against us. For a while he seemed to hesitate and consult his inferior officers, and among them his Chaplain. The result of the conference was our being ordered into our companies, that, separated, and with the force of the officers of a company bearing upon us, we might the more likely be subdued. Yet the Colonel assured L.M.M., interceding in my behalf, when the lieutenant commanding my company threatened force upon me, that he should not allow any personal injury. When we marched next day I was compelled to bear a gun and equipments. My associates were more fortunate, for, being asked if they would carry their guns, declined and saw no more trouble from them. The captain of the company in which P.D. was placed told him he did not believe he was ugly about it, and that he could only put him under arrest and prefer charges against him. He accordingly was taken under guard, where he lay till we left for here.

The next morning the men were busy in burnishing their arms. When I looked toward the one I had borne, yellow with rust, I trembled in the weakness of the flesh at the trial I felt impending over me. Before the Colonel was up I knocked at his tent, but was told he was asleep, though, through the opening, I saw him lying gazing at me. Although I felt I should gain no relief from him, I applied again soon after. He admitted me and, lying on his bed, inquired with cold heartlessness what I wanted. I stated to him, that I could never consent to serve, and, being under the war-power, was resigned to suffer instead all the just penalties of the law. I begged of him release from the attempts by violence to compel my obedience and service, and a trial, though likely to be made by those having no sympathy with me, yet probably in a manner comfortable to law.

He replied that he had shown us all the favour he should; that he had, now, turned us over to the military power and was going to let that take its course; that is, henceforth we were to be at the mercy of the inferior officers, without appeal to law, justice, or mercy. He said he had placed us in a pleasant position, against which we could have no reasonable objection, and that we had failed to perform our agreement. He wished to deny that our consent was only temporary and conditional. He declared, furthermore, his belief, that a man who would not fight for his country did not deserve to live. I was glad to withdraw from his presence as soon as I could.

I went back to my tent and lay down for a season of retirement, endeavouring to gain resignation to any event. I dreaded torture and desired strength of flesh and spirit. My trial soon came. The lieutenant called me out, and pointing to the gun that lay near by, asked if I was going to clean it. I replied to him, that I could not comply with military requisitions, and felt resigned to the consequences. "I do not ask about your feelings; I want to know if you are going to clean that gun?" "I cannot do it," was my answer. He went away, saying, "Very well," and I crawled into the tent again. Two sergeants soon called for me, and taking me a little aside, bid me lie down on my back, and stretching my limbs apart tied cords to my wrists and ankles and these to four stakes driven in the ground somewhat in the form of an X.

I was very quiet in my mind as I lay there on the ground with the rain of the previous day, exposed to the heat of the sun, and suffering keenly from the cords binding my wrists and straining my muscles. And, if I dared the presumption, I should say that I caught a glimpse of heavenly pity. I wept, not so much from my own suffering as from sorrow that such things should be in our own country, where Justice and Freedom and Liberty of Conscience have been the annual boast of Fourth-of-July orators so many years. It seemed that our forefathers in the faith had wrought and suffered in vain, when the privileges they so dearly bought were so soon set aside. And I was sad, that one endeavouring to follow our dear Master should be so generally regarded as a despicable and stubborn culprit.

After something like an hour had passed, the lieutenant came with his orderly to ask me if I was ready to clean the gun. I replied to the orderly asking the question, that it could but give me pain to be asked or required to do anything I believed wrong. He repeated it to the lieutenant just behind him, who advanced and addressed me. I was favoured to improve the opportunity to say to him a few things I wished. He said little; and, when I had finished, he withdrew with the others who had gathered around. About the end of another hour his orderly came and released me.

I arose and sat on the ground. I did not rise to go away. I had not where to go, nothing to do. As I sat there my heart swelled with joy from above. The consolation and sweet fruit of tribulation patiently endured. But I also grieved, that the world was so far gone astray, so cruel and blind. It seemed as if the gospel of Christ had never been preached upon earth, and the beautiful example of his life had been utterly lost sight of.

Some of the men came about me, advising me to yield, and among them one of those who had tied me down, telling me what I had already suffered was nothing to what I must yet suffer unless I yielded; that human flesh could not endure what they would put upon me. I wondered if it, could be that they could force me to obedience by torture, and examined myself closely to see if they had advanced as yet one step toward the accomplishment of their purposes. Though weaker in body, I believed I found myself, through divine strength, as firm in my resolution to maintain my allegiance to my Master.

The relaxation of my nerves and muscles after having been so tensely strained left me that afternoon so weak that I could hardly walk or perform any mental exertion.

I had not yet eaten the mean and scanty breakfast I had prepared, when I was ordered to pack up my things and report myself at the lieutenant's tent. I was accustomed to such orders and complied, little moved.

The lieutenant received me politely with, "Good-morning, Mr. Pringle," and desiring me to be seated, proceeded with the writing with which he was engaged. I sat down in some wonderment and sought to be quiet and prepared for any event.

"You are ordered to report to Washington," said he; "I do not know what it is for." I assured him that neither did I know. We were gathered before the Major's tent for preparation for departure. The regimental officers were there manifesting surprise and chagrin; for they could not but show both as they looked upon us, whom the day before they were threatening to crush into submission, and attempting also to execute their threats that morning, standing out of their power and under orders from one superior to their Major Commanding E.M. As the bird uncaged, so were our hearts that morning. Short and uncertain at first were the flights of Hope. As the slave many times before us, leaving his yoke behind him, turned from the plantations of Virginia and set his face toward the far North, so we from out a grasp as close and as abundant in suffering and severity, and from without the line of bayonets that had so many weeks surrounded us, turned our backs upon the camp of the 4th Vermont and took our way over the turnpike that ran through the tented fields of Culpeper.

At the War Office we were soon admitted to an audience with the Adjutant General, Colonel Townsend, whom we found to be a very fine man, mild and kind. He referred our cases to the Secretary of War, Stanton, by whom we were ordered report for service to Surgeon General Hammond. Here we met Isaac Newton, Commissioner of Agriculture, waiting for our arrival, and James Austin of Nantucket, expecting his son, Charles L. Austin, and Edward W. Holway of Sandwich, Mass., conscripted Friends like ourselves, and ordered here from the 22nd Massachusetts.

We understand it is through the influence of Isaac Newton that Friends have been able to approach the heads of Government in our behalf and to prevail with them to so great an extent. He explained to us the circumstance in which we are placed. That the Secretary of War and President sympathized with Friends in their present suffering, and would grant them full release, but that they felt themselves bound by their oaths that they would execute the laws, to carry out to its full extent the Conscription Act. That there appeared but one door of relief open, that was to parole us and allow us to go home, but subjected to their call again ostensibly, though this they neither wished nor proposed to do. That the fact of Friends in the Army and refusing service had attracted public attention so that it was not expedient to parole us at present. That, therefore, we were to be sent to one of the hospitals for a short time, where it was hoped and expressly requested that we would consent to remain quiet and acquiesce, if possible, in whatever might be required of us. That our work there would be quite free from objection, being for the direct relief of the sick; and that there we would release none for active service in the field, as the nurses were hired civilians.

These requirements being so much less objectionable than we had feared, we felt relief, and consented to them. I.N. went with us himself to the Surgeon General's office, where he procured peculiar favours for us: that we should be sent to a hospital in the city, where he could see us often; and that orders should be given that nothing should interfere with our comfort, or our enjoyment of our consciences.

Thence we were sent to Medical Purveyor Abbot, who assigned us to the best hospital in the city, the Douglas Hospital.

The next day after our coming here Isaac Newton and James Austin came to add to our number E.W.H. and C.L.A., so now there are five of us instead of three. We are pleasantly situated in a room by ourselves in the upper or fourth story, and are enjoying our advantages of good quarters and tolerable food as no one can except he has been deprived of them.

8th—Today we have a pass to go out to see the city.

9th—We all went, thinking to do the whole city in a day, but before the time of our passes expired, we were glad to drag ourselves back to the rest and quiet of D.H. During the day we called upon our friend I.N. in the Patent Office. When he came to see us on the 7th, he stated he had called upon the President that afternoon to request him to release us and let us go home to our friends. The President promised to consider it over-night. Accordingly yesterday morning, as I.N. told us, he waited upon him again. He found there a woman in the greatest distress. Her son, only a boy of fifteen years and four months, having been enticed into the Army, had deserted and been sentenced to be shot the next day. As the clerks were telling her, the President was in the War Office and could not be seen, nor did they think he could attend to her case that day. I.N. found her almost wild with grief. "Do not despair, my good woman," said he, "I guess the President can be seen after a bit." He soon presented her case to the President, who exclaimed at once, "That must not be, I must look into that case, before they shoot that boy"; and telegraphed at once to have the order suspended.

I.N. judged it was not a fit time to urge our case. We feel we can afford to wait, that a life may be saved. But we long for release. We do not feel easy to remain here.

11th—Today we attended meeting held in the house of a Friend, Asa Arnold, living near here. There were but four persons beside ourselves. E.W.H. and C.L.A. showed their copy of the charges about to have been preferred against them in courtmartial before they left their regiment, to a lawyer who attended the meeting. He laughed at the Specification of Mutiny, declaring such a charge could not have been lawfully sustained against them.

The experiences of our new friends were similar to ours, except they fell among officers who usually showed them favour and rejoiced with them in their release.

13th—L.M.M. had quite an adventure yesterday. He being fireman with another was in the furnace room among three or four others, when the officer of the day, one of the surgeons, passed around on inspection. "Stand up," he ordered them, wishing to be saluted. The others arose; but by no means L. The order was repeated for his benefit, but he sat with his cap on, telling the surgeon he had supposed he was excused from such things as he was one of the Friends. Thereat the officer flew at him, exclaiming, he would take the Quaker out of him. He snatched off his cap and seizing him by the collar tried to raise him to his feet; but finding his strength insufficient and that L. was not to be frightened, he changed his purpose in his wrath and calling for the corporal of the guard had him taken to the guard-house. This was about eleven A.M. and he lay there till about six P.M., when the surgeon in charge, arriving home and hearing of it, ordered the officer of the day to go and take him out, telling him never to put another man into the guard-house while he was in charge here without consulting him. The manner of his release was very satisfactory to us, and we waited for this rather than effect it by our own efforts. We are all getting uneasy about remaining here, and if our release do not come soon, we feel we must intercede with the authorities, even if the alternative be imprisonment.

The privations I have endured since leaving home, the great tax upon my nervous strength, and my mind as well, since I have had charge of our extensive correspondence, are beginning to tell upon my health and I long for rest.

20th—We begin to feel we shall have to decline service as heretofore, unless our position is changed. I shall not say but we submit too much in not declining at once, but it has seemed most prudent at least to make suit with Government rather than provoke the hostility of their subalterns. We were ordered here with little understanding of the true state of things as they really exist here; and were advised by Friends to come and make no objections, being assured it was but for a very brief time and only a matter of form. It might not have been wrong; but as we find we do too much fill the places of soldiers (L.M.M.'s fellow fireman has just left for the field, and I am to take his place, for instance), and are clearly doing military service, we are continually oppressed by a sense of guilt, that makes our struggles earnest.

21st—I.N. has not called yet; our situation is becoming almost intolerable. I query if patience is justified under the circumstances. My distress of mind may be enhanced by my feeble condition of health, for today I am confined to my bed, almost too weak to get downstairs. This is owing to exposure after being heated over the furnaces.

26th—Though a week has gone by, and my cold has left me, I find I am no better, and that I am reduced very low in strength and flesh by the sickness and pain I am experiencing. Yet I still persist in going below once a day. The food I am able to get is not such as is proper.

5th 11th month—I spend most of my time on my bed, much of it alone. And very precious to me is the nearness unto the Master I am favoured to attain to.

Notwithstanding my situation and state, I am happy in the enjoyment of His consolations. Lately my confidence has been strong, and I think I begin to feel that our patience is soon to be rewarded with relief; insomuch that a little while ago, when dear P.D. was almost overcome With sorrow, I felt bold to comfort him with the assurance of my belief, that it would not be long so. My mind is too weak to allow of my reading much; and, though I enjoy the company of my companions a part of the time, especially in the evening, I am much alone; which affords me abundant time for meditation and waiting upon God. The fruits of this are sweet, and a recompense for affliction.

6th—Last evening E.W.H. saw I.N. particularly on my behalf, I suppose. He left at once for the President. This morning he called to inform us of his interview at the White House. The President was moved to sympathy in my behalf, when I.N. gave him a letter from one of our Friends in New York. After its perusal he exclaimed to our friend, "I want you to go and tell Stanton that it is my wish all those young men be sent home at once." He was on his way to the Secretary this morning as he called.

Later—I.N. has just called again informing us in joy that we are free. At the War Office he was urging the Secretary to consent to our paroles, when the President entered. "It is my urgent wish," said he. The Secretary yielded; the order was given; and we were released. What we had waited for so many weeks was accomplished in a few moments by a Providential ordering of circumstances.

7th—I.N. came again last evening bringing our paroles. The preliminary arrangements are being made, and we are to start this afternoon for New York.

Note. Rising from my sick-bed to undertake this journey, which lasted through the night, its fatigues overcame me, and upon my arrival, in New York I was seized with delirium from which I only recovered after many weeks, through the mercy and favour of Him, who in all this trial had been our guide and strength and comfort.

African American Soldiers of the Union Army

Because of the prevalent racist beliefs that blacks would not make good soldiers, there was considerable resistance to the idea of forming black regiments. But after more than a year of fighting and the administration's extreme frustration that the war seemed to be going nowhere, President Lincoln began to support the idea of "colored regiments." More than 200,000 African Americans served in the Union army during the Civil War. The first black regiments were mustered in the autumn of 1862, and after the Emancipation Proclamation went into effect on January 1, 1863, Lincoln authorized the formation of black regiments in Massachusetts,

African American Soldiers.   *Two musicians and two infantrymen from the Massachusetts 54th Regiment, circa 1863. The Massachusetts 54th was one of the African American regiments whose soldiers protested their unequal pay.*

Connecticut, and Rhode Island. The most famous of these was the Massachusetts 54th, which, in July 1863, led a valiant yet futile attack on Fort Wagner in South Carolina.

Although African American troops were demonstrating that they could fight as well and as heroically as any white regiment, they still faced prejudicial treatment. One of the most passionate grievances that swept through their ranks was that they received about half the pay of white troops—only $7 a month. A number of black soldiers refused their duties in an effort to gain equal pay. Some were court-martialed and shot for treason. But most protestors adopted the tactic of continuing to perform their soldierly duties while refusing any pay at all. This tactic finally achieved some success in August 1864, when blacks who were already free before enlisting were granted equal pay. Eventually, in March 1865, all black soldiers were given equal pay, backdated to their enlistment.

During their fight for equal pay, many soldiers wrote letters to newspapers, friends, and relatives to make the case for their position. In the

*first letter, George E. Stephens, a sergeant in the 54ᵗʰ Massachusetts Infantry,
several weeks after his regiment's assault on Fort Wagner, criticizes the
federal government for overruling Governor John A. Andrews's announcement that black troops would receive equal pay. In the second letter, another
soldier in the 54ᵗʰ argues that the equal pay issue is not merely an economic
issue. In the third, a soldier from the 55ᵗʰ Massachusetts Infantry demands
"liberty and equality." In the next letter, a soldier from the 6ᵗʰ Pennsylvania
Infantry regiment does press the economic issue. In the fifth letter, another
member of the 54ᵗʰ (E. W. D.) eloquently questions the justness of a
government that will keep a gallant regiment in the field without
remuneration. In the sixth letter, H. I. W. of the 54ᵗʰ argues that if they
cannot be paid equally, then they should be given an honorable discharge. In
the seventh, Sergeant John H. W. N. Collins of the 54ᵗʰ complains that,
nearly a year after the battle at Fort Wagner, their pay has still not been
forthcoming. And in the final letter, J. H. Hall of the 54ᵗʰ wants to know why
the soldiers are not recognized as lawful citizens and brave soldiers but
instead are disparaged "as an inferior sort of laborer" paid $7 a month.*

CORRESPONDENCE PROTESTING UNEQUAL PAY, 1863–1864

A LETTER FROM GEORGE E. STEPHENS

. . . The question of our pay continues to be the topic of conversation and correspondence. Numerous letters have reached us from distinguished friends in the State of
Massachusetts, all expressing the utmost confidence that we will receive all of our
pay, and have secured to us every right that other Massachusetts soldiers enjoy. His
Excellency Gov. Andrew, in a letter dated, "Executive Department, Boston, August
24th," and addressed to Mr. Frederick Johnson, an officer in the regiment, says:

"I have this day received your letter of the 10th of August, and in reply desire,
in the first place, to express to you the lively interest with which I have watched
every step of the fifty-fourth Regiment since it left Massachusetts, and the feelings of pride and admiration with which I have learned and read of the accounts
of the heroic conduct of the regiment in the attack upon Fort Wagner, when you
and your brave soldiers so well proved their manhood, and showed themselves to
be true soldiers of Massachusetts. As to the matter inquired about in your letter,
you may rest assured that I shall not rest until you have secured all of your rights,
and that I have no doubt whatever of ultimate success. I have no doubt, by law,
you are entitled to the same pay as other soldiers, and on the authority of the Secretary of War, I promised that you should be paid and treated in all respects like
other soldiers of Massachusetts. Till this is done I feel that my promise is dishon-
ored by the government. The whole difficulty arises from a misapprehension, the

SOURCE: *The Weekly Anglo African* (September 19, 1868).

correction of which will no doubt be made as soon as I can get the subject fully examined by the Secretary of War. I have the honor to be your obedient servant,

JOHN A. ANDREW, Governor of Massachusetts."

The trouble seems to be something like this: The Paymaster General, whoever that may be, has directed the paymasters to pay all negro troops of African descent, $10 per month, the pay allowed to contrabands by statute when employed in the Commissary or Quartermaster's Department. There seems to have been no provision made to pay colored soldiers. There may be some reason for making a distinction between armed and unarmed men in the service of the government, but when the nationality of a man takes away his title to pay it become another thing. Suppose a regiment of Spaniards should be mustered into the service of the United States, would Congress have to pass a special law to pay Spaniards? Or, suppose, a regiment of Sandwich Islanders should do duty as soldiers of the United States, would it be necessary to pass a law to pay Sandwich Islanders? Does not the deed of muster secure the services and even life of the man mustered into the service to the government? And does not this same deed of muster give a man title to all pay and bounties awarded to soldiers bearing arms? I believe that, "by law, we are entitled to the same pay as other soldiers," and "misapprehension arises" from this: The Paymaster General will not have the colored soldiers paid under the law which pay[s] white soldiers, and virtually creates in his own mind the necessity for the passage of a special law authorizing them to be paid. Is there a special law on the statute books of the National Legislature touching the payment of colored men employed in the naval service? . . .

A LETTER FROM A MASSACHUSETTS SOLDIER

A strange misapprehension . . . exists as to the matter of pay; and it pains us deeply. We came forward at the call of Gov. Andrew, in which call he distinctly told us that we were to be subsisted, *clothed, paid,* and treated in *all* respects the same as other Massachusetts soldiers. Again, on the presentation of flags to the regiment, at Camp Meigs, the Governor reiterated this promise, on the strength of which we marched through Boston, holding our heads high, as men and as soldiers. Nor did we grumble because we were not paid the portion of United States bounty paid to other volunteer regiments in advance.

Now that we have gained some reputation as soldiers, we claim the right to be heard.

Three times have we been mustered in for pay. Twice have we swallowed the insult offered us by the United States paymaster, contenting ourselves with a simple refusal to acknowledge ourselves, in this matter, different from other Massachusetts soldiers. Once, in the face of insult and intimidation, such as no body of men and soldiers were ever subjected to before, we quietly refused, and continued to do our duty.

SOURCE: *The Boston Journal* (c. December 15, 1863).

For four months we've been steadily working, night and day, under fire. And such work! Up to our knees in mud half the time—causing the tearing and wearing out of more than the volunteer's yearly allowance of clothing—denied time to repair and wash (what we might by that means have saved), denied time to drill and perfect ourselves in soldierly quality, denied the privilege of burying our dead decently! All this we've borne patiently, waiting for justice.

Imagine our surprise and disappointment, on the receipt by the last mail of the Governor's Address to the General Court, to find him making a proposition to them to pay this regiment the difference between what the United States Government offers us and what they are legally bound to pay us, which, in effect, advertises us to the world as holding out for *money* and not from *principle*—that we sink our manhood in consideration of a few more dollars. How has this come about? What false friend has been misrepresenting us to the Governor, to make him think that our necessities outweigh our self-respect? I am sure no representation of *ours* ever impelled him to this action.

A LETTER FROM A SOLDIER OF THE 55TH MASSACHUSETTS REGIMENT

... We don't wish you to look upon us as being inclined to be a little stubborn; we were told that we would be accepted by the U.S. Government on the same terms as her other Regiments, and do you call the same terms reducing pay, and receiving part pay from Mass., and a part from the government of the same? If you look at it in that way, you don't look at it as we do. Massachusetts has always been first to open the door to the poor colored man; was first to send two colored regiments in the field to extinguish the last spark of a most infamous rebellion—one that will figure largely in the annals of history for centuries to come. You sit at your firesides and just study a little what the poor soldier is suffering. You have no idea, and just you fight and slay the rebels that are at our backs, or we will fight them that are in front of us, or fight in Congress for our rights, and we will fight here for yours. I feel proud, and so does every other man that belongs to the 55th, to think that they stand so well upon the principles which they came here to fight for. Our pride has won us a name amongst the white regiments around us; they call us the Independent Colored Regiment, and say to us, You do the work that we ought to share in, and they don't want to pay you anything for it. Do you want to break that spirit of pride! I hope not; and as you say that we have proved ourselves worthy of approbation, don't put our principle upon the grindstone. We love this government, and will sacrifice our lives to maintain it. Just think for a moment, reflect deeply, that there is good for you to gain by it; our lives we value just as highly as you do yours; but without a stimulant, our exertions would not be worth anything. Let our faces be black, but our hearts be true, you will find us true and loyal and obedient, and all qualities pertaining to a soldier. A true and rather singular idea for a colored man to wish to be placed on equal footing with a white man! Why not? Can't we fight just as well? We showed

SOURCE: *The Christian Recorder*, Philadelphia (January 2, 1864).

our qualities at Port Gibson and Wagner. Now, if there is not pluck, just fall in some big hole, and we will guarantee to pull you out without blacking your hands; fall down and we will pick you up; we won't pass by and perhaps give you a kick or a cuff, but pick you up, carry you home to your good wife, and won't ask of you your daughter for compensation; all the compensation that we ask is to give us our rights, and don't be dodging around every corner as if you owed us something, and your conscience is getting the upper hand of you. . . . Our motto: "Liberty and Equality."

A LETTER FROM A SOLDIER OF THE 6TH PENNSYLVANIA REGIMENT

I am a soldier, or at least that is what I was drafted for in the 6th USCT; have been in the service since Aug., last. I could not afford to get a substitute, or I would not be here now and my poor wife at home almost starving. When I was at home I could make a living for her and my two little ones; but now that I am a soldier they must do the best they can or starve. It almost tempts me to desert and run a chance of getting shot, when I read her letters, hoping that I would come to her relief. But what am I to do? It is a shame the way they treat us; our officers tell me now that we are not soldiers; that if we were we would get the same pay as the white men; that the government just called us out to dig and drudge, that we are to get but $7.00 per month. Really I thought I was a soldier, and it made me feel somewhat proud to think that I had a right to fight for Uncle Sam. When I was at Chelton Hill I felt very patriotic; but my wife's letters have brought my patriotism down to the freezing point, and I don't think it will ever rise again; and it is the case all through the regiment. Men having families at home, and they looking to them for support, and they not being able to send them one penny. . . .

ARMY CORRESPONDENCE

Morris Island, S. C., June 9, 1864.

Mr. Editor:

It is with pleasure I write these few lines concerning things here at present. We have had a few shells fired from Sullivan's Island on our fleet, though no damage was done, and the old ram came down to Sumpter and was fired on by our batteries on the 7th of this month.

The Fifty-fourth Regiment Massachusetts Volunteers is still in the field without pay, and the Government shows no disposition to pay us. We have declined doing active field service, except in cases of the greatest emergency, and we are, therefore, divided into four departments, doing garrison duty, we have served our country manfully for over twelve months without receiving one cent from the Government, and all that we have for our bravery is the credit of

---

SOURCE: *The Christian Recorder*, Philadelphia (February 20, 1864).
SOURCE: *The Christian Recorder*, Philadelphia (June 25, 1864).

fighting well, but we are deprived of our wages and the rights of soldiers. We are glad to see the success of our regiment, and feel thankful that so many have escaped the soldier's grave, through the instrumentality of God, who is the giver of all good. God has fought our battles for us, and in His own good time He will avenge our wrongs. We still do the duty assigned us, and trust to God for future events; but, if our merits will not warrant our acknowledgment as men, veterans and soldiers, the hand of God may send forth His destroying angel and slay our enemies. No nation has ever risen to dignity without self-sacrifice, none has ever triumphed in victory without undergoing great hardships and long forbearance; but we still abide in faith, and look forward to the time when Ethiopia shall stretch forth her hand and rise from obscurity with healing in her wings.

If the Fifty-fourth must be as the leaders of Israel, let us suffer in the wilderness until a second Moses shall rise up and smite the rock, that we may drink of the spring of freedom, and the spring of learning.

We all cry, "Union!" and shout for the battle. It is a question whether we can call this a Union Government—a free Government—that will keep a regiment in the field fifteen or sixteen months without pay because they are black. Will you call it an honorable and just Government that gives for a reason that there has been no act passed of Congress to pay negro soldiers? If we understand the Declaration of Independence, it asserts the freedom and equality of all men. We ask nothing more. Give us equality and acknowledge us as men, and we are willing to stand by the flag of our Union and support the leaders of this great Government until every traitor shall be banished from our shore, out of the North as well as the South.

Look at our families, reduced to the necessities of the alms-house for want of the support of their wounded and bleeding husbands, who have fallen before the enemy! We hope that our liberal Government will not be guilty of such atrocious robbery. When we enlisted, it was not for a large bounty nor great salary. We thought that we could help to put down the rebellion. We anticipated future benefits. We intended to distinguish ourselves as heroes and supporters of the Government, and to share alike their rights and privileges, to have the same opportunity for promotion as our freely and ability would warrant. But our bravery is always in vain, our heroism discountenanced, our patriotism disregarded, and we are offered the paltry sum of seven dollars per month, and are given the insulting reason, that the negro is not worth as much as the white man. They cannot tell us that we do not fight as well nor die as freely as the white man, but they can tell us they are a majority, and, therefore, assume presumption of their power, and intend to compel us to involuntary servitude, or, in other words, compel us to work for half pay, which is involuntary servitude. Under such wrongs no nation can prosper. If a strong power crush the weak and deprive them of the blessings which God has ordained for them, it must fall. God's supreme power will break them into pieces that will not obey His righteous laws. Let the hand of Justice have the ruling power, and his omniscience will ever guide our path and direct us in the establishment of the most pure Government.

Let the rulers of our country consult the God of nations and reconsider His instructions with the dictates of their consciences, and every soldier will receive equal compensation according to his merits. If those at the White House were compelled to encounter what the Fifty-fourth have undergone, they would not only allow the negro his rights and acknowledge his citizenship, but, in my humble opinion, they would acknowledge the independence of the Southern Confederacy. But it is not so with many brave negro troops that are in the field. We do not allow a traitor one inch of ground. Give us our rights—acknowledge us as men and citizens—and we are willing to flood the rebellious cities with pools of our blood, and never lay down our arms until every vestige of rebellion is driven from our land.

E.W.D.,
Co. B, 54th Mass. Vols.

A LETTER FROM A SOLDIER

Morris Island, South Carolina, June 8, 1864.

Mr. Editor:

What do you think of this? We rally to the defence of our imperilled country; we freely offer our lives in its defence. The Government acknowledges the value of our services, and yet they permit our brave men to be treated in a shameful manner. When I enlisted at Boston, Mass., Feb. 21st, 1863, I enlisted on the same terms as other soldiers—clothing, rations, and pay. But all their promises are false and untrue. We have been serving nearly sixteen months, faithfully and truely, the Government of the United States, yet not received one cent of pay. No! they come with woe-stricken face and say they can pay us but $10 a month, and $3 deducted for clothing, which leaves us but $7 a month. Just let them think of Fort Wagner, James' Island, and Olustee, Florida! The men of the 54th have suffered terribly, and still they have the cheek to wrest these brave men of color out of their rights. When the 54th left Boston for the South, they left many white men at home. Therefore, if we are good enough to fill up white men's places and fight, we should be treated then, in all respects, the same as the white man. We have families as well as the white man. The State of Massachusetts has given our people nothing. We, that came out of other States to fill up her regiment, the 54th, for the sake of the service, for the sake of the country, for the sake of justice, and the rights of our gallant regiment, we call upon the authorities of Mass., in behalf of this noble regiment; and, if not, we should like to have an honorable discharge. This regiment has, for many a day, mourned the loss of their gallant Colonel Shaw. The contrabands are better off to-day than the men of the 54th. If there are any slaves, the men of the 54th are as much slaves as any. But the day will soon come when God Almighty will drop the weight on their own shoulders that they are pressing on the black man.

Your humble servant,
H. I. W.

SOURCE: *The Christian Recorder*, Philadelphia (July 23, 1864).

A LETTER FROM A SOLDIER OF THE 54TH MASSACHUSETTS REGIMENT

Black Island, South Carolina,
Co. H, 54th Regt. Mass. Vols, Inf.
July 7th, 1864.

Mr. Editor:

What a great change there has taken place since I penned my last letter to you, from this little post of duty, written on the 1st of this month. There was another Expedition left this vicinity for James Island, on which occasion the gallant 54th must have a hand in the matter, as in almost every other movement of any interest transpiring within the Department's limits.

On the second day nothing of importance was done. Everything was as still as death. The 3d comes upon us, and as the bright rosy beams break gently forth, comes the sharp and rolling reverberation of the deadly "Enfields," mingled with the loud and deep-toned booming of cannon. Once more has the 54th got her foot upon that soil which was the instigation of many of the brave members of her regiment to sink to the earth, never to rise again until the last trump of God shall sound on the dawning of the resurrection morn to call each and every one to give a true and just account of the deeds done here below in the body.

For the first time since we have been in the field, we have been allowed the pleasure of the company of our sister regiment, the 55th, who has many features noticeable in the 54th, for both regiments have stood side by side and fought, never yielding an inch of ground to the stubborn foeman.

Sir, in view of such a noble and generous display of patriotism and courage, it is a disgrace to the name of this great and glorious Union, that these brave fellows should be compelled to fight and toil without receiving their stipulated remuneration. Why is it? Is the laborer not worthy of his hire? Never was such ingratitude heard of before or since the world commenced. Here we are, toiling and sweating beneath the burning rays of the sun, for nothing. We receive nothing but our hard tack and salt pork, and a constant attendance of the blues. All that we get in return for our services are such hackneyed expressions as these: "Why, boys, you are good fighters; don't want any better; white men could not do better, should they try; your bravery cannot be excelled by any troops in the field."

Day after day we await the arrival of each mail in anxious expectancy, to see whether Congress has taken any steps to pay us off, for you know that men cannot live without something to nourish them at times. We should particularly like to have such things as little eatables for our dessert.

We still hold the Island. To-day, even as I write, the booming of the distant cannon can be plainly heard.

SOURCE: *The Christian Recorder*, Philadelphia (July 23, 1864).

Dear sir, before this letter shall have reached you, I may be called away to appear before the great Tribunal of my God. Should I fall in this fearful conflict, I trust that I may, by the assistance and grace of God, be enabled to shake hands with you and all dear friends together in my Father's kingdom, where partings and sorrows are unknown.

Yours in Christ,
JOHN H. W. N. COLLINS,
Orderly Sergeant Co. H, 54 Regt. Mass. Vols.

LETTER FROM THE 54TH MASSACHUSETTS REGIMENT

Morris Island, South Carolina, August 3, 1864.

Dear Editor:

I now, in making my first attempt at correspondence with you and your paper, write you a few lines concerning things in general that have transpired of late under my own observation in this department of military affairs.

We returned from the James Island Expedition. It was indeed a most perilous undertaking; and the prompt performance of the duty assigned us necessarily involved much hazard and difficulty, as the numerical strength of our troops was much inferior to that of the rebels; but although inferior in numbers, we were vastly superior in point of courage and discipline. We had a great advantage in acting under the guidance of brave and skilful officers, who well knew how to dispose and handle the heroic band under their command.

Our forces were advanced in a most judicious and cautious manner. Heavy lines of skirmishers were thrown forward and across the entire Island, intending to present the appearance of a strong force, and succeeded in keeping the rebs at bay until we were reinforced by seven additional regiments.

We were securely intrenched, and our boys had been anticipating an attack every hour, but the rebs failed to make a general attack on our lines. Nevertheless, General Hatch succeeded in completely surprising them on John's Island. The astonished rebels at that place were rudely awakened from their morning slumbers by a loud salute from our artillery men in the shape of a perfect shower of singeing shot and screaming shell! With true cordiality and feeling the rebs returned our warm greeting, but they were soon compelled to fall back beneath the furious assault and impetuosity of our troops. In the attack, General Hatch was most nobly supported from our right. Having effected the design of the expedition, our brave General withdrew his trusty forces.

I shall now endeavor to make a few remarks in reference to the condition of the 54th. It has been sixteen months since we were mustered in as a regiment, and fourteen months of that time have been spent in active service. We have

SOURCE: *The Christian Recorder*, Philadelphia (August 27, 1864).

been on a great many arduous and dangerous expeditions, fought three hard battles, and yet after all this, we have not received one cent of remuneration from the Government. We now would ask the Christian and law-abiding citizen, and all dignitaries in authority, if we have not performed our duty as soldiers, and maintained our dignity and honour as citizens? And have we not borne a patriotic part in every campaign, and ranked in discipline, bravery and heroism with the first regiments in the Southern department? Why, then, is it that we are not recognised as true and lawful citizens, and receive our pay as soldiers? Why are we insulted and told by the paymaster that the negro is not considered as a soldier, but rather as an inferior sort of laborer, to whom he is to pay at most not more than seven dollars per month? I would respectfully ask the question, gentlemen of the city of Boston and Commonwealth of Massachusetts, if this is fit treatment for a brave and gallant regiment of men. Will the vast city of Boston, and the generous and sympathizing State of Massachusetts stand by unmoved, and with unpitying eye permit this foul opprobrium and scorn to be cast upon them? Or will they stand in our defence, even if that derision be heaped upon them which was cast upon that stern old patriot, Andrew Jackson, when he acknowledged the negroes as soldiers, as brethren, and as fellow-citizens—to incur the same dangers and share the same glory alike with their white fellow-citizens? The city of Boston has made the same kind of promises, guarantying that every colored recruit shall have all the rights and privileges, and receive the same pay, bounty, clothing, etc., as the white troops—but, alas! like Andrew Jackson, they too have promised the negroes every thing pertaining to a citizenship, in order to get them into the field, and then they keep them there, without pay, without the stipulated bounty, and not even deigning to treat them in a Christian and civil manner. No promise has been regarded by them.

Now, Boston and Massachusetts want to shift the responsibility of this inhumanity from their door, and cast it on the shoulders of the general Government. They now say that there has been no law passed in reference to the pay of colored troops.

The educated negro does not enter into contracts without knowing what recompense he is to receive or is promised for his services. The State of Massachusetts has agents in the county of Suffolk, and some one of these parties is responsible.

We are fully satisfied that our debtors are solvent, and we are determined to get all we have enlisted for, when we get back to prosecute the matter, those of us, at least, who may live to come back.

Twenty thousand dollars, over and above our three years, will be sacrificed by this regiment, in order that we may test the law upon this matter. We will have all or nothing. We will not tamely submit to the infliction of wrongs most foul, as did our forefathers, and go back to despondency and submission without even a single struggle.

We have sacrificed our homes and comforts, and even our lives, for the frivolous promise of the unprincipled recruiting officers of Boston and vicinity that we should have all the rights of citizens.

If I had not thought that there might be some truth or veracity in owl-leaders in cities, states, &c., I would have staid in England when I last visited that place— but God will avenge the wrongs of him who is oppressed—and no Government can prosper that is deceptive and false at its very foundation and rules of doing things. The Governor of the Commonwealth of Massachusetts and the Boston authorities need not think that the negro, with his present greatly increased share of learning and wealth, will be satisfied with the easy, palm-off and shut-your-eye-up style of Andrew Jackson assurance, nor be content with any thing less than their just rights and privileges. If we fight to maintain a Republican Government, we want Republican privileges; if a monarchical Government, monarchical privileges.

If we are to be recognized as citizens, we want the rights of citizens! Have we lost ground or receded any in the advanced stage of this nineteenth century, or has our race degenerated on account of living in this enlightened and free country?

If we are less worthy as soldiers, as brothers, or as citizens, which has so nobly been set forth by Washington, Madison, Jefferson and Jackson, acknowledging our dignity, honor, bravery and love of country, if we have become so degenerated in this enlightened country that our ability is less worthy our acknowledgment as citizens than they were at the time of the Revolutionary War against Great Britain, it would be better if we had been left in the States of Barbary or on the coast of Niger. Much better would it have been.

But, gentlemen, I am gratified to know that the descendants of Africa, and the so-called adopted sons of America have more than kept pace with the Anglo-Saxon. We do not claim that we are more intelligent than our so-called superior race, but we are nearly equal in intelligence, and have acquired a knowledge of science and literature that would surprise the world, if they only knew of the difficulties we have had to encounter to acquire it for ourselves and for our children.

The Anglo-Saxon in America claims that if we are acknowledged citizens, we will covet their wives, daughters and sisters—but it is to the contrary. The respectable part of the colored race consider that their own kind would make the most affectionate companions, and in the case of the so-called aristocracy, if any were known to thus sinfully amalgamate, or should cause their race to be degenerated, the same should be cut off from his inheritance. We do not covet your wives nor your daughters, nor the position of the political orator. All we ask is the proper enjoyment of the rights of citizenship, and a free title and acknowledged share in our own noble birthplace, which we are ready and willing to defend while a single drop of blood courses through our veins.

The negro has a mind susceptible and alive to improvement, and a manly spirit that aspires to dignity and refinement, and is well competent to discern when his services or society are depreciated. These are true facts which cannot be denied.

We, as a regiment, have bound ourselves together with one accord and as one man to protect our own rights: those rights which are now denied us should be given us. There is but one course left for us to pursue. If we are still persistently held and treated as aliens, we must, as a necessary and inevitable consequence, apply to aliens for redress!

And now, Mr. Editor, in conclusion, let me say that I shall correspond with you again, with your permission.

I will give you the whole particulars in reference to matters on the Island when next I write.

We have some good news to tell you. By the exchange of prisoners the following names were brought to light that were thought killed in the assault made upon Fort Wagner some time ago. General Seymour and some others were only exchanged:

Corporal Charles Hardy, Lemuel Blakes, Geo. Conneill, George Grant, Samuel Wilson, Jesse Brown, William Rigby, Solomon Anderson, Alf. Green, Daniel States.

All these have been in the city of Charleston, and were engaged while there in waiting upon officers. They were all from the city of Philadelphia, and State of Pennsylvania. It will indeed be a joyful meeting when they all get home once more.

Yours, &c.,
J.H. HALL, Co. B.,
Fifty-fourth Mass. Col. Troops.

Frederick Douglass (1818–1895)

At the close of the Civil War, Frederick Douglass was no less restrained in his political activism on behalf of African Americans than he was when he traveled throughout the country calling for the abolition of slavery. To be sure, slavery would no longer be legal in the United States, but he was quite aware that there would still be a struggle for equal rights, economic opportunity, and suffrage. Douglass dove into this struggle with the same fervor he displayed for the abolitionist crusade. He delivered this persuasive demand for the rights and privileges of full citizenship for the freedmen at the 1865 annual meeting of the Massachusetts Anti-Slavery Society.

WHAT THE BLACK MAN WANTS, APRIL 1865

... I have had but one idea for the last three years to present to the American people, and the phraseology in which I clothe it is the old abolition phraseology.

SOURCE: Philip S. Foner, *The Life and Writings of Frederick Douglass* (New York: International Publishers, 1950), vol. 4, 157–165.

Frederick Douglass, 1870.
*"No class of men can, without
insulting their own nature, be content
with any deprivation of their rights."
After the abolition of slavery,
Frederick Douglass insisted that the
federal government guarantee the
rights (especially the right to vote)
of all African Americans.*

I am for the "immediate, unconditional, and universal" enfranchisement of the black man, in every State in the Union. Without this, his liberty is a mockery; without this, you might as well almost retain the old name of slavery for his condition; for in fact, if he is not the slave of the individual master, he is the slave of society, and holds his liberty as a privilege, not as a right. He is at the mercy of the mob, and has no means of protecting himself.

It may be objected, however, that this pressing of the Negro's right to suffrage is premature. Let us have slavery abolished, it may be said, let us have labor organized, and then, in the natural course of events, the right of suffrage will be extended to the Negro. I do not agree with this. The constitution of the human mind is such, that if it once disregards the conviction forced upon it by a revelation of truth, it requires the exercise of a higher power to produce the same conviction afterwards. The American people are now in tears. The Shenandoah has run blood—the best blood of the North. All around Richmond, the blood of New England and of the North has been shed—of your sons, your brothers and your fathers. We all feel, in the existence of this Rebellion, that judgments terrible, wide-spread, far-reaching, overwhelming, are abroad in the land; and we feel, in view of these judgments, just now, a disposition to learn righteousness. This is the hour. Our streets are in mourning, tears are falling at every fireside, and under the chastisement of this Rebellion we have almost come up to the point of conceding this great, this all-important right of suffrage. I fear that if we fail to do it now, if abolitionists fail to press it now, we may not see, for centuries to come, the same disposition that exists at this moment. Hence, I say, now is the time to press this right.

It may be asked, "Why do you want it? Some men have got along very well without it. Women have not this right." Shall we justify one wrong by another? This is the sufficient answer. Shall we at this moment justify the deprivation of the Negro of the right to vote, because some one else is deprived of that privilege? I hold that women, as well as men, have the right to vote, and my heart and voice go with the movement to extend suffrage to woman; but that question rests upon another basis than which our right rests. We may be asked, I say, why we want it. I will tell you why we want it. We want it because it is our right, first of all. No class of men can, without insulting their own nature, be content with any deprivation of their rights. We want it again, as a means for educating our race. Men are so constituted that they derive their conviction of their own possibilities largely by the estimate formed of them by others. If nothing is expected of a people, that people will find it difficult to contradict that expectation. By depriving us of suffrage, you affirm our incapacity to form an intelligent judgment respecting public men and public measures; you declare before the world that we are unfit to exercise the elective franchise, and by this means lead us to undervalue ourselves, to put a low estimate upon ourselves, and to feel that we have no possibilities like other men. Again, I want the elective franchise, for one, as a colored man, because ours is a peculiar government, based upon a peculiar idea, and that idea is universal suffrage. If I were in a monarchial government, or an autocratic or aristocratic government, where the few bore rule and the many were subject, there would be no special stigma resting upon me, because I did not exercise the elective franchise. It would do me no great violence. Mingling with the mass I should partake of the strength of the mass; I should be supported by the mass, and I should have the same incentives to endeavor with the mass of my fellow-men; it would be no particular burden, no particular deprivation; but here where universal suffrage is the rule, where that is the fundamental idea of the Government, to rule us out is to make us an exception, to brand us with the stigma of inferiority, and to invite to our heads the missiles of those about us; therefore, I want the franchise for the black man. . . .

I know that we are inferior to you in some things—virtually inferior. We walk about you like dwarfs among giants. Our heads are scarcely seen above the great sea of humanity. The Germans are superior to us; the Irish are superior to us; the Yankees are superior to us; they can do what we cannot, that is, what we have not hitherto been allowed to do. But while I make this admission, I utterly deny, that we are originally, or naturally, or practically, or in any way, or in any important sense, inferior to anybody on this globe. This charge of inferiority is an old dodge. It has been made available for oppression on many occasions. It is only about six centuries since the blue-eyed and fair-haired Anglo-Saxons were considered inferior by the haughty Normans, who once trampled upon them. If you read the history of the Norman Conquest, you will find that this proud Anglo-Saxon was once looked upon as of coarser clay than his Norman master, and might be found in the highways and byways of Old England laboring with a brass collar on his neck, and the name of his master marked upon it. You were down then! You are up now. I am glad you are up, and I want you to be glad to help us up also.

The story of our inferiority is an old dodge, as I have said; for wherever men oppress their fellows, wherever they enslave them, they will endeavor to find the needed apology for such enslavement and oppression in the character of the people oppressed and enslaved. When we wanted, a few years ago, a slice of Mexico, it was hinted that the Mexicans were an inferior race, that the old Castilian blood had become so weak that it would scarcely run down hill, and that Mexico needed the long, strong and beneficent arm of the Anglo-Saxon care extended over it. We said that it was necessary to its salvation, and a part of the "manifest destiny" of this Republic, to extend our arm over that dilapidated government. So, too, when Russia wanted to take possession of a part of the Ottoman Empire, the Turks were an "inferior race." So, too, when England wants to set the heel of her power more firmly in the quivering heart of old Ireland, the Celts are an "inferior race." So, too, the Negro, when he is to be robbed of any right which is justly his, is an "inferior man." It is said that we are ignorant; I admit it. But if we know enough to be hung, we know enough to vote. If the Negro knows enough to pay taxes to support the government, he knows enough to vote; taxation and representation should go together. If he knows enough to shoulder a musket and fight for the flag, fight for the government, he knows enough to vote. If he knows as much when he is sober as an Irishman knows when drunk, he knows enough to vote, on good American principles.

But I was saying that you needed a counterpoise in the persons of the slaves to the enmity that would exist at the South after the Rebellion is put down. I hold that the American people are bound, not only in self-defence, to extend this right to the freedmen of the South, but they are bound by their love of country, and by all their regard for the future safety of those Southern States, to do this—to do it as a measure essential to the preservation of peace there. But I will not dwell upon this. I put it to the American sense of honor. The honor of a nation is an important thing. It is said in the Scriptures, "What doth it profit a man if he gain the whole world, and lose his own soul?" It may be said, also, What doth it profit a nation if it gain the whole world, but lose its honor? I hold that the American government has taken upon itself a solemn obligation of honor, to see that this war—let it be long or short, let it cost much or let it cost little—that this war shall not cease until every freedman at the South has the right to vote. It has bound itself to it. What have you asked the black men of the South, the black men of the whole country to do? Why, you have asked them to incure the enmity of their masters, in order to befriend you and to befriend this Government. You have asked us to call down, not only upon ourselves, but upon our children's children, the deadly hate of the entire Southern people. You have called upon us to turn our backs upon our masters, to abandon their cause and espouse yours; to turn against the South and in favor of the North; to shoot down the Confederacy and uphold the flag—the American flag. You have called upon us to expose ourselves to all the subtle machinations of their malignity for all time. And now, what do you propose to do when you come to make peace? To reward your enemies, and trample in the dust your friends? Do you intend to sacrifice the very men who have come to the rescue of your banner in the South, and incurred the lasting displeasure of their masters thereby? Do you intend to sacrifice them and reward your enemies? Do you mean to give your enemies the right to vote, and take it away from your friends? Is that wise policy? Is that honorable? Could American honor withstand such a blow? I do not believe you will do it. I think you will see to it that we have the right to vote. There is something too mean in looking upon the Negro, when you are in trouble, as a citizen, and when you are free from trouble, as an alien. When this nation was in trouble, in its early struggles, it looked upon the Negro as a citizen. In 1776 he was a citizen. At the time of the formation of the Constitution the Negro had the right to vote in eleven States out of the old thirteen. In your trouble you have made us citizens. In 1812 Gen. Jackson addressed us as citizens—"fellow-citizens." He wanted us to fight. We were citizens then! And now, when you come to frame a conscription bill, the Negro is a citizen again. He has been a citizen just three times in the history of this government, and it has always been in time of trouble. In time of trouble we are citizens. Shall we be citizens in war, and aliens in peace? Would that be just?

I ask my friends who are apologizing for not insisting upon this right, where can the black man look, in this country, for the assertion of his right, if he may not look to the Massachusetts Anti-Slavery Society? Where under the whole heavens can he look for sympathy, in asserting this right, if he may not look to this platform? Have you lifted us up to a certain height to see that we are men, and then are any disposed to leave us there, without seeing that we are put in possession of all our rights? We look naturally to this platform for the assertion of all our rights, and for this one especially. I understand the anti-slavery societies of this country to be based on two principles,—first, the freedom of the blacks of this country; and, second, the elevation of them. Let me not be misunderstood here. I am not asking for sympathy at the hands of abolitionists, sympathy at the hands of any. I think the American people are disposed often to be generous rather than just. I look over this country at the present time, and I see Educational Societies, Sanitary Commissions, Freedmen's Associations, and the like,—all very good: but in regard to the colored people there is always more that is benevolent, I perceive, than just, manifested towards us. What I ask for the Negro is not benevolence, not pity, not sympathy, but simply justice. The American people have always been anxious to know what they shall do with us. Gen. Banks was distressed with solicitude as to what he should do with the Negro. Everybody has asked the question, and they learned to ask it early of the abolitionists, "What shall we do with the Negro?" I have had but one answer from the beginning. Do nothing with us! Your doing with us has already played the mischief with us. Do nothing with us! If the apples will not remain on the tree of their own strength, if they are wormeaten at the core, if they are early ripe and disposed to fall, let them fall! I am not for tying or fastening them on the tree in any way, except by nature's plan, and if they will not stay there, let them fall. And if the Negro cannot stand on his own legs, let him fall also. All I ask is, give him a chance to stand on his own legs! Let him alone! If you see him on his way to school, let him alone, don't disturb him! If you see him going to the dinner table at a hotel, let him go! If you see him going to the ballot-box, let him alone, don't disturb him! If you see him going into a work-shop, just let him alone,—your interference is doing him a positive injury. Gen. Banks' "preparation" is of a piece with this attempt to prop up the Negro. Let him fall if he cannot stand alone! If the Negro cannot live by the line of eternal justice, so beautifully pictured to you in the illustration used by Mr. Phillips, the fault will not be yours, it will be his who made the Negro, and established that line for his government. Let him live or die by that. If you will only untie his hands, and give him a chance, I think he will live. He will work as readily for himself as the white man. A great many delusions have been swept away by this war. One was, that the Negro would not work; he has proved his ability to work. Another was, that the Negro would not fight; that he possessed only the most sheepish attributes of humanity; was a perfect lamb, or an "Uncle Tom;" disposed to take off his coat whenever required, fold his hands, and be whipped by anybody who wanted to whip him. But the war has proved that there is a great deal of human nature in the Negro, and that "he will fight," as Mr. Quincy, our President, said, in earlier days than these, "when there is reasonable probability of his whipping anybody."

Zion Presbyterian Church

The African American Zion Presbyterian Church of Charleston, South Carolina, submitted a petition to Congress several months after the end of the Civil War, in which the parishioners demanded that the black people of South Carolina be accorded all the rights and privileges of U.S. citizens.

PETITION TO THE UNITED STATES CONGRESS, NOVEMBER 24, 1865

Gentlemen:

We, the colored people of the State of South Carolina, in Convention assembled, respectfully present for your attention some prominent facts in relation to our present condition, and make a modest yet earnest appeal to your considerate judgment. . . .

Conscious of the difficulties that surround our position we would ask for no rights or privileges but such as rest upon the strong basis of justice and expediency, in view of the best interests of our entire country.

SOURCE: James S. Allen, *Reconstruction: The Battle for Democracy, 1865–1876* (New York: International Publishers, 1937), 228–229.

We ask first, that the strong arm of law and order be placed alike over the entire people of this State; that life and property be secured, and the laborer free to sell his labor as the merchant his goods.

We ask that a fair and impartial instruction be given to the pledges of the government to us concerning the land question.

We ask that the three great agents of civilized society—the school, the pulpit, the press—be as secure in South Carolina as in Massachusetts or Vermont.

We ask that equal suffrage be conferred upon us, in common with the white men of this State. This we ask, because "all free governments derive their just powers from the consent of the governed"; and we are largely in the majority in this State, bearing for a long period the burden of onerous taxation, without a just representation. We ask for equal suffrage as a protection for the hostility evoked by our known faithfulness to our country and flag under all circumstances.

We ask that colored men shall not in every instance be tried by white men; and that neither by custom nor enactment shall we be excluded from the jury box.

We ask that, inasmuch as the Constitution of the United States explicitly declares that the right to keep and bear arms shall not be infringed and the Constitution is the Supreme law of the land—that the late efforts of the Legislature of this State to pass an act to deprive us of arms be forbidden, as a plain violation of the Constitution, and unjust to many of us in the highest degree, who have been soldiers, and purchased our muskets from the United States Government when mustered out of service.

We protest against any code of black laws the Legislature of this State may enact, and pray to be governed by the same laws that control other men. The right to assemble in peaceful convention, to discuss the political questions of the day; the right to enter upon all the avenues of agriculture, commerce, trade; to amass wealth by thrift and industry; the right to develop our whole being by all the appliances that belong to civilized society, cannot be questioned by any class of intelligent legislators.

We solemnly affirm and desire to live orderly and peacefully with all the people of this State; and commending this memorial to your considerate judgment.

Thus we ever pray.

Charleston, S.C. November 24, 1865
Zion Presbyterian Church

American Equal Rights Association

During congressional debates on the proposed Fifteenth Amendment, many people who had been involved in the abolitionist and feminist crusades argued fervently that the suffrage amendment should include

*women. The American Equal Rights Association (founded in 1866)
issued the following resolution arguing its position on the topic. Although
such influential people as Frederick Douglass, Susan B. Anthony, and
Elizabeth Cady Stanton signed the resolution, the amendment approved
by Congress in 1869 granted the suffrage to only African American men:
"The right of citizens of the United States to vote shall not be denied or
abridged by the United States or any State on account of race, color, or
previous condition of servitude." In a bitter aftermath, the ratification
process wound up splitting the feminist movement into those who
supported the amendment with the intention of continuing the struggle
for women's suffrage and those more radical women (and men) who
fought energetically against ratification until women were included. The
Fifteenth Amendment was ratified in 1870. It would be another 50 years
before the Nineteenth Amendment opened the suffrage to women.*

NATIONAL CONVENTION RESOLUTIONS, NEW YORK, MAY 1867

RESOLVED, That as republican institutions are based on individual rights, and
not on the rights of races or sexes, the first question for the American people to
settle in the reconstruction of the government, is the RIGHTS OF INDIVIDUALS.

RESOLVED, That the present claim for "manhood suffrage," marked with
the words "equal," "impartial," "universal," is a cruel abandonment of the slave
women of the South, a fraud on the tax paying women of the North, and an
insult to the civilization of the nineteenth century.

RESOLVED, That the [Republican Party] proposal to reconstruct our government on the basis of manhood suffrage . . . [which] has received the recent
sanction of the American Anti-Slavery Society, is but a continuation of the old
system of class and caste legislation, always cruel and proscriptive in itself, and
ending in all ages in national degradation and revolution.

MEMORIAL OF THE AMERICAN EQUAL RIGHTS ASSOCIATION TO CONGRESS

The undersigned . . . respectfully but earnestly protest against any change in the
Constitution of the United States, or legislation by Congress, which shall longer
violate the principle of Republican Government, by proscriptive distinctions in
rights of suffrage or citizenship, on account of color or sex. Your Memorialists
would respectfully represent, that neither the colored man's loyalty, bravery on

SOURCE: Retrieved on 3/11/2003 from the 19th-Century American Women Writers Web
Etext Library at http://womenshistory.about.com/gi/dynamic/offsite.htm?site=http:// www.
unl.edu/legacy/19cwww/books/elibe/documents/suffrage/PURITAN6.HTM.

the battle field and general good conduct, nor woman's heroic devotion to liberty and her country, in peace and war, have yet availed to admit them to equal citizenship. . . .

We believe that humanity is one in all those intellectual, moral and spiritual attributes, out of which grow human responsibilities. The Scripture declaration is, "so God created man in his own image: male and female created he them." And all divine legislation throughout the realm of nature recognizes the perfect equality of the two conditions. For male and female are but different conditions. neither color nor sex is ever discharged from obedience to law, natural or moral; written or unwritten. The commands, thou shalt not steal, nor kill, nor commit adultery, know nothing of sex in their demands; nothing in their penalty. And hence we believe that all human legislation which is at variance with the divine code, is essentially unrighteous and unjust. Woman and the colored man are taxed. . . . Woman has been fined, whipped, branded with red-hot irons, imprisoned and hung; but when was woman ever tried by a jury of her peers? . . .

Woman and the colored man are loyal, patriotic, property-holding, tax-paying, liberty-loving citizens; and we can not believe that sex or complexion should be any ground for civil or political degradation. In our government, one-half the citizens are disfranchised by their sex, and about one-eighth by the color of their skin; and thus a large majority have no voice in enacting or executing the laws they are taxed to support and compelled to obey. . . . Against such outrages on the very name of republican freedoms, your memorialists do and must ever protest. And is not our protest pre-eminently as just against the tyranny of "taxation without representation," as was that thundered from Bunker Hill . . . ?

And your Memorialists especially remember . . . that our country is still reeling [from] . . . a terrible civil war. . . . [I]n restoring the foundations of our nationality, [we] . . . pray that all discriminations on account of sex or race may be removed; and that our Government may be republican in fact as well as form; A GOVERNMENT BY THE PEOPLE, AND THE WHOLE PEOPLE; FOR THE PEOPLE, AND THE WHOLE PEOPLE. . . .

[Signed by Theodore Tilton, Frederick Douglass, Elizabeth Cady Stanton, Lucretia Mott, and Susan B. Anthony].

Susan B. Anthony (1820–1906)

Susan B. Anthony fought for temperance, abolition, labor reform, educational reform, and most notably women's rights. A close friend of Elizabeth Cady Stanton, she became by mid-century a driving force in nineteenth-century feminism and perhaps the most important person in the struggle for women's suffrage. At the end of the Civil War, she *cofounded with Stanton the American Equal Rights Association and campaigned vigorously for women to be included in the amendment that would give black men the vote. In 1870, after the Fifteenth Amendment was ratified, indignant that women had been excluded, Anthony stepped up her campaign. In 1872, she was arrested in Rochester, New York, when she voted in the presidential election. She was tried and fined $100 in June 1873. When she refused to pay the fine, the judge, not wanting to create more publicity for her cause, shrewdly chose not to sentence her to a jail term. It was Susan B. Anthony who wrote the women's suffrage constitutional amendment that was introduced in Congress, where it was repeatedly debated, tabled, defeated, reintroduced, rejected, and eventually, more than a decade after her death, approved and ratified as the Nineteenth Amendment to the Constitution.*

There is no accurate account of her comments at the trial. The first document here is an excerpt from one of three separate accounts reported after the event. The second document is a speech she gave on more than twenty occasions between her arrest and her trial.

From an Account of the Trial of Susan B. Anthony, July 3, 1873

As a matter of outward form the defendant was asked if she had anything to say why the sentence of the court should not be pronounced upon her.

"Yes, your honor," replied Miss Anthony, "I have many things to say. My every right, constitutional, civil, political and judicial has been tramped upon. I have not only had no jury of my peers, but I have had no jury at all."

COURT— "Sit down Miss Anthony. I cannot allow you to argue the question."

MISS ANTHONY— "I shall not sit down. I will not lose my only chance to speak."

COURT— "You have been tried, Miss Anthony, by the forms of law, and my decision has been rendered by law."

MISS ANTHONY— "Yes, but laws made by men, under a government of men, interpreted by men and for the benefit of men. The only chance women have for justice in this country is to violate the law, as I have done, and as I shall *continue* to do," and she struck her hand heavily on the table in emphasis of what she said. "Does your honor suppose that we obeyed the infamous fugitive slave law which forbade to give a cup of cold water to a slave fleeing from his master? I tell you we did not obey it; we fed him and clothed him, and sent him on his way to Canada. *So shall we trample all unjust laws* under foot. I do not ask the clemency of the court. I came into it to get justice, having failed in this, I demand the full rigors of the law."

SOURCE: Matilda Joslyn Gage to Editor, 20 June 1873, Kansas *Leavenworth Times*, 3 July 1873, SBA scrapbook 6, Rare Books, DLC.

COURT— "The sentence of the court is $100 fine and the costs of the prosecution."
MISS ANTHONY— "I have no money to pay with, but am $10,000 in debt."
COURT— "You are not ordered to stand committed till it is paid."

IS IT A CRIME FOR A U.S. CITIZEN TO VOTE?, 1873

Friends and Fellow-citizens: I stand before you to-night, under indictment for the alleged crime of having voted at the last Presidential election, without having a lawful right to vote. It shall be my work this evening to prove to you that in thus voting, I not only committed no crime, but, instead, simply exercised my citizen's right, guaranteed to me and all United States citizens by the National Constitution, beyond the power of any State to deny.

Our democratic-republican government is based on the idea of the natural right of every individual member thereof to a voice and a vote in making and executing the laws. We assert the province of government to be to secure the people in the enjoyment of their unalienable rights. We throw to the winds the old dogma that governments can give rights. Before governments were organized, no one denies that each individual possessed the right to protect his own life, liberty and property. And when 100 or 1,000,000 people enter into a free government, they do not barter away their natural rights; they simply pledge themselves to protect each other in the enjoyment of them, through prescribed judicial and legislative tribunals. They agree to abandon the methods of brute force in the adjustment of their differences, and adopt those of civilization.

Nor can you find a word in any of the grand documents left us by the fathers that assumes for government the power to create or to confer rights. The Declaration of Independence, the United States Constitution, the constitutions of the several states and the organic laws of the territories, all alike propose to protect the people in the exercise of their God-given rights. Not one of them pretends to bestow rights.

"All men are created equal, and endowed by their Creator with certain unalienable rights. Among these are life, liberty and the pursuit of happiness. That to secure these, governments are instituted among men, deriving their just powers from the consent of the governed."

Here is no shadow of government authority over rights, nor exclusion of any from their full and equal enjoyment. Here is pronounced the right of all men, and "consequently," as the Quaker preacher said, "of all women," to a voice in the government. And here, in this very first paragraph of the declaration, is the assertion of the natural right of all to the ballot; for, how can "the consent of

---

SOURCE: Retrieved on 10/19/2003 from www.pbs.org/stantonanthony/resources/index. html?body=crime_to_vote.html. For the full text of another copy of this address, see Ann D. Gordon, ed., *The Selected Papers of Elizabeth Cady Stanton and Susan B. Anthony* (New Brunswick, NJ: Rutgers University Press, 2000), vol. 2, 554–583.

the governed" be given, if the right to vote be denied? Again: "That whenever any form of government becomes destructive of these ends, it is the right of the people to alter or abolish it, and to institute a new government, laying its foundations on such principles, and organizing its powers in such forms as to them shall seem most likely to effect their safety and happiness."

Surely, the right of the whole people to vote is here clearly implied. For however destructive in their happiness this government might become, a disfranchised class could neither alter nor abolish it, nor institute a new one, except by the old brute force method of insurrection and rebellion. One-half of the people of this nation to-day are utterly powerless to blot from the statute books an unjust law, or to write there a new and a just one. The women, dissatisfied as they are with this form of government, that enforces taxation without representation, that compels them to obey laws to which they have never given their consent, that imprisons and hangs them without a trial by a jury of their peers, that robs them, in marriage, of the custody of their own persons, wages and children, are this half of the people left wholly at the mercy of the other half, in direct violation of the spirit and letter of the declarations of the framers of this government, every one of which was based on the immutable principle of equal rights to all. By those declarations, kings, priests, popes, aristocrats, were all alike dethroned, and placed on a common level politically, with the lowliest born subject or serf. By them, too, men, as such, were deprived of their divine right to rule, and placed on a political level with women. By the practice of those declarations all class and caste distinction will be abolished; and slave, serf, plebeian, wife, woman, all alike, bound from their subject position to the proud platform of equality.

The preamble of the federal constitution says: "We, the people of the United States, in order to form a more perfect union, establish justice, insure domestic tranquility, provide for the common defense, promote the general welfare and secure the blessings of liberty to ourselves and our posterity, do ordain and established this constitution for the United States of America."

It was we, the people, not we, the white male citizens, nor yet we, the male citizens; but we, the whole people, who formed this Union. And we formed it, not to give the blessings of liberty, but to secure them; not to the half of ourselves and the half of our posterity, but to the whole people—women as well as men. And it is downright mockery to talk to women of their enjoyment of the blessings of liberty while they are denied the use of the only means of securing them provided by this democratic-republican government—the ballot.

The early journals of Congress show that when the committee reported to that body the original articles of confederation, the very first article which became the subject of discussion was that respecting equality of suffrage. Article 4th said: "The better to secure and perpetuate mutual friendship and intercourse between the people of the different States of this Union, the free inhabitants of each of the States, (paupers, vagabonds and fugitives from justice excepted,) shall be entitled to all the privileges and immunities of the free citizens of the several States."

Thus, at the very beginning, did the fathers see the necessity of the universal application of the great principle of equal rights to all—in order to produce the desired result—a harmonious union and a homogeneous people. . . .

The preamble of the Constitution of the State of New York declares . . . : "We, the people of the State of New York, grateful to Almighty God for our freedom, in order to secure its blessings, do establish this Constitution."

Here is not the slightest intimation either of receiving freedom from the United States Constitution, or of the State conferring the blessings of liberty upon the people; and the same is true of every one of the thirty-six State Constitutions. Each and all, alike declare rights God-given, and that to secure the people in the enjoyment of their inalienable rights, is their one and only object in ordaining and establishing government. And all of the State Constitutions are equally emphatic in their recognition of the ballot as the means of securing the people in the enjoyment of these rights.

Article 1 of the New York State Constitution says: "No member of this State shall be disfranchised or deprived of the rights or privileges secured to any citizen thereof, unless by the law of the land, or the judgement of his peers."

And so carefully guarded is the citizen's right to vote, that the Constitution makes special mention of all who may be excluded. It says: "Laws may be passed excluding from the right of suffrage all persons who have been or may be convicted of bribery, larceny or any infamous crime."

In naming the various employments that shall not affect the residence of voters the 3d section of article 2d says "that being kept at any alms house, or other asylum, at public expense, nor being confined at any public prison, shall deprive a person of his residence," and hence his vote. Thus is the right of voting most sacredly hedged about. The only seeming permission in the New York State Constitution for the disfranchisement of women is in section 1st of article 2d, which says "Every male citizen of the age of twenty-one years, shall be entitled to vote."

But I submit that in view of the explicit assertions of the equal right of the whole people, both in the preamble and previous article of the constitution, this omission of the adjective "female" in the second, should not be construed into a denial; but, instead, counted as of no effect. Mark the direct prohibition: "No member of this State shall be disfranchised, unless by the law of the land, or the judgment of his peers." "The law of the land," is the United States Constitution: and there is no provision in that document that can be fairly construed into a permission to the States to deprive any class of their citizens of their right to vote. Hence New York can get no power from that source to disfranchise one entire half of her members. Nor has "the judgment of their peers" been pronounced against women exercising their right to vote; no disfranchised person is allowed to be judge or juror and none but disfranchised persons can be women's peers; nor has the legislature passed laws excluding them on account of idiocy of lunacy; nor yet the courts convicted them of bribery, larceny, or any infamous crime. Clearly, then, there is no constitutional ground for the exclusion of women from the ballot-box in the State of New York. No barriers whatever stand to-day between women and the exercise of their right to vote save those of precedent and prejudice. . . .

The only question left to be settled, now, is: Are women persons? And I hardly believe any of our opponents will have the hardihood to say they are not. Being persons, then, women are citizens, and no state has a right to make any new law, or to enforce any old law, that shall abridge their privileges or immunities. Hence, every discrimination against women in the constitutions and laws of the several states, is to-day null and void, precisely as is every one against negroes. Is the right to vote one of the privileges or immunities of citizens? I think the disfranchised ex-rebels, and the ex-state prisoners will agree with me, that it is not only one of them, but the one without which all the others are nothing. Seek first the kingdom of the ballot, and all things else shall be given thee, is the political injunction.

Webster, Worcester and Bouvier all define citizen to be a person, in the United States, entitled to vote and hold office.

Prior to the adoption of the thirteenth amendment, by which slavery was forever abolished, and black men transformed from property to persons, the judicial opinions of the country had always been in harmony with these definitions. To be a person was to be a citizen, and to be a citizen was to be a voter. . . .

If we once establish the false principle, that United States citizenship does not carry with it the right to vote in every state in this Union, there is no end to the petty freaks and cunning devices, that will be resorted to, to exclude one and another class of citizens from the right of suffrage. It will not always be men combining to disfranchise all women; native born men combining to abridge the rights of all naturalized citizens, as in Rhode Island. It will not always be the rich and educated who may combine to cut off the poor and ignorant; but we may live to see the poor, hardworking, uncultivated day laborers, foreign and native born, learning the power of the ballot and their vast majority of numbers, combine and amend state constitutions so as to disfranchise the Vanderbilts and A. T. Stewarts, the Conklings and Fentons. It is poor rule that won't work more ways than one. Establish this precedent, admit the right to deny suffrage to the states, and there is no power to foresee the confusion, discord and disruption that may await us. There is, and can be, but one safe principle of government—equal rights to all. And any and every discrimination against any class, whether on account of color, race, nativity, sex, property, culture, can but embitter and disaffect that class, and thereby endanger the safety of the whole people.

Clearly, then, the national government must not only define the rights of citizens, but it must stretch out its powerful hand and protect them in every state in this Union.

But if you will insist that the fifteenth amendment's emphatic interdiction against robbing United States citizens of their right to vote, "on account of race, color, or previous condition of servitude," is a recognition of the right, either of the United States, or any state, to rob citizens of that right, for any or all other reason, I will prove to you that the class of citizens for which I now plead, and to which I belong, may be, by all the principles of our government, and many of the laws of the states, included under the term "previous condition of servitude."

First.—The married women and their legal status. What is servitude? "The condition of a slave." What is a slave? "A person who is robbed of the proceeds of his labor; a person who is subject to the will of another."

By the law of Georgia, South Carolina, and all the states of the South, the negro had no right to the custody and control of his person. He belonged to his master. If he was disobedient, the master had the right to use correction. If the negro didn't like the correction, and attempted to run away, the master had a right to use coercion to bring him back.

By the law of every state in this Union to-day, North as well as South, the married woman has no right to the custody and control of her person. The wife belongs to her husband; and if she refuses obedience to his will, he may use moderate correction, and if she doesn't like his moderate correction, and attempts to leave his "bed and board," the husband may use moderate coercion to bring her back. The little word "moderate," you see, is the saving clause for the wife, and would doubtless be overstepped should offended husband administer his correction with the "cat-o'-nine-tails," or accomplish his coercion with blood-hounds.

Again, the slave had no right to the earnings of his hands, they belonged to his master; no right to the custody of his children, they belonged to his master; no right to sue or be sued, or testify in the courts. If he committed a crime, it was the master who must sue or be sued.

In many of the states there has been special legislation, giving to married women the right to property inherited, or received by bequest, or earned by the pursuit of any avocation outside of the home; also, giving her the right to sue and be sued in matters pertaining to such separate property; but not a single state of this Union has ever secured the wife in the enjoyment of her right to the joint ownership of the joint earnings of the marriage copartnership. And since, in the nature of things, the vast majority of married women never earn a dollar, by work outside of their families, nor inherit a dollar from their fathers, it follows that from the day of their marriage to the day of the death of their husbands, not one of them ever has a dollar, except it shall please her husband to let her have it.

In some of the states, also, there have been laws passed giving to the mother a joint right with the father in the guardianship of the children. But twenty years ago, when our woman's rights movement commenced, by the laws of the State of New York, and all the states, the father had the sole custody and control of the children. No matter if he were a brutal, drunken libertine, he had the legal right, without the mother's consent, to apprentice her sons to rumsellers, or her daughters to brothel keepers. He could even will away an unborn child, to some other person than the mother. And in many of the states the law still prevails, and the mothers are still utterly powerless under the common law....

There is an old saying that "a rose by any other name would smell as sweet," and I submit it the deprivation by law of the ownership of one's own person, wages, property, children, the denial of the right as an individual, to sue and be sued, and to testify in the courts, is not a condition of servitude most bitter and absolute, though under the sacred name of marriage?

Does any lawyer doubt my statement of the legal status of married women? I will remind him of the fact that the old common law of England prevails in every State in this Union, except where the Legislature has enacted special laws annulling it. And I am ashamed that not one State has yet blotted from its statute books the old common law of marriage, by which Blackstone, summed up in the fewest words possible, is made to say, "husband and wife are one, and that one is the husband."

Thus may all married women, wives and widows, by the laws of the several States, be technically included in the fifteenth amendment's specification of "condition of servitude," present or previous. And not only married women, but I will also prove to you that by all the great fundamental principles of our free government, the entire womanhood of the nation is in a "condition of servitude" as surely as were our revolutionary fathers, when they rebelled against old King George. Women are taxed without representation, governed without their consent, tried, convicted and punished without a jury of their peers. And is all this tyranny any less humiliating and degrading to women under our democratic-republican government to-day than it was to men under their aristocratic, monarchical government one hundred years ago? There is not an utterance of old John Adams, John Hancock or Patrick Henry, but finds a living response in the soul of every intelligent, patriotic woman of the nation. Bring to me a common-sense woman property holder, and I will show you one whose soul is fired with all the indignation of 1776 every time the tax-gatherer presents himself at her door. You will not find one such but feels her condition of servitude as galling as did James Otis when he said: "The very act of taxing exercised over those who are not represented appears to me to be depriving them of one of their most essential rights, and if continued, seems to be in effect an entire disfranchisement of every civil right. For, what one civil right is worth a rush after a man's property is subject to be taken from him at pleasure without his consent? If a man is not his own assessor in person, or by deputy, his liberty is gone, or he is wholly at the mercy of others." . . .

That liberty or freedom consists in having an actual share in the appointment of those who are to frame the laws, and who are to be the guardians of every man's life, property and peace. For the all of one man is as dear to him as the all of another; and the poor man has an equal right, but more need to have representatives in the Legislature than the rich one. That they who have no voice or vote in the electing of representatives, do not enjoy liberty, but are absolutely enslaved to those who have votes and their representatives; for to be enslaved is to have governors whom other men have set over us, and to be subject to laws made by the representatives of others, without having had representatives of our own to give consent in our behalf."

Suppose I read it with the feminine gender: "That women who have no voice nor vote in the electing of representatives, do not enjoy liberty, but are absolutely enslaved to men who have votes and their representatives; for to be enslaved is to have governors whom men have set over us, and to be subject to the laws made by the representatives of men, without having representatives of our own to give consent in our behalf."

And yet one more authority; that of Thomas Paine, than whom not one of the Revolutionary patriots more ably vindicated the principles upon which our government is founded: "The right of voting for representatives is the primary right by which other rights are protected. To take away this right is to reduce man to a state of slavery; for slavery consists in being subject to the will of another; and he that has not a vote in the election of representatives is in this case. The proposal, therefore, to disfranchise any class of men is as criminal as the proposal to take away property."

Is anything further needed to prove woman's condition of servitude sufficiently orthodox to entitle her to the guaranties of the fifteenth amendment?

Is there a man who will not agree with me, that to talk of freedom without the ballot, is mockery—is slavery—to the women of this Republic, precisely as New England's orator Wendell Phillips, at the close of the late war, declared it to be to the newly emancipated black men? . . .

We no longer petition Legislature or Congress to give us the right to vote. We appeal to the women everywhere to exercise their too long neglected "citizen's right to vote." We appeal to the inspectors of election everywhere to receive the votes of all United States citizens as it is their duty to do. We appeal to United States commissioners and marshals to arrest the inspectors who reject the names and votes of United States citizens, as it is their duty to do, and leave those alone who, like our eighth ward inspectors, perform their duties faithfully and well.

We ask the juries to fail to return verdicts of "guilty" against honest, law-abiding, tax-paying United States citizens for offering their votes at our elections. Or against intelligent, worthy young men, inspectors of elections, for receiving and counting such citizens votes.

We ask the judges to render true and unprejudiced opinions of the law, and wherever there is room for a doubt to give its benefit on the side of liberty and equal rights to women, remembering that "the true rule of interpretation under our national constitution, especially since its amendments, is that anything for human rights is constitutional, everything against human right unconstitutional."

And it is on this line that we propose to fight our battle for the ballot—all peaceably, but nevertheless persistently through to complete triumph, when all United States citizens shall be recognized as equals before the law.

Robert B. Elliott (1842–1884)

Born and reared in England, Robert B. Elliott moved to South Carolina in the aftermath of the Civil War, where in 1869 he became the first black commander of the state's national guard. From 1871 to 1874 he served in the U.S. House of Representatives. He became an active participant in the congressional debates on the civil rights bill that was eventually passed in 1875.

SPEECH IN CONGRESS ON THE CIVIL RIGHTS BILL, JANUARY 6, 1874

... While I am sincerely grateful for this high mark of courtesy that has been accorded to me by this House, it is a matter of regret to me that it is necessary at this day that I should rise in the presence of an American Congress to advocate a bill which simply asserts equal rights and equal public privileges for all classes of American citizens. I regret, sir, that the dark hue of my skin may lend a color to the imputation that I am controlled by motives personal to myself in my advocacy of this great measure of national justice. Sir, the motive that impels me is restricted by no such narrow boundary, but is as broad as your Constitution. I advocate it, sir, because it is right. The bill, however, not only appeals to your justice, but it demands a response from your gratitude.

In the events that led to the achievement of American Independence the negro was not an inactive or unconcerned spectator. He bore his part bravely upon many battle-fields, although uncheered by that certain hope of political elevation which victory would secure to the white man. The tall granite shaft, which a grateful State has reared above its sons who fell in defending Fort Griswold against the attack of Benedict Arnold, bears the name of Jordan, Freeman, and other brave men of the African race who there cemented with their blood the corner-stone of the Republic. In the State which I have the honor in part to represent the rifle of the black man rang out against the troops of the British crown in the darkest days of the American revolution. Said General Greene, who has been justly termed the Washington of the North, in a letter written by him to Alexander Hamilton, on the 10th day of January, 1781, from the vicinity of Camden, South Carolina: There is no such thing as national character or national sentiment. The inhabitants are numerous, but they would be rather formidable abroad than at home. There is a great spirit of enterprise among the black people, and those that come out as volunteers are not a little formidable to the enemy.

At the battle of New Orleans, under the immortal Jackson, a colored regiment held the extreme right of the American line unflinchingly, and drove back the British column that pressed upon them, at the point of the bayonet. So marked was their valor on that occasion that it evoked from their great commander the warmest encomiums, as will be seen from his dispatch announcing the brilliant victory.

SOURCE: Retrieved on 3/11/2003 from www.law.nyu.edu/davisp/neglectedvoices/ElliotJan061874.html.

As the gentleman from Kentucky, [Mr. Beck,] who seems to be the leading exponent on this floor of the party that is arrayed against the principle of this bill; has been pleased, in season and out of season, to cast odium upon the negro and to vaunt the chivalry of his state, I may be pardoned for calling attention to another portion of the same dispatch. Referring to the various regiments under his command, and their conduct on that field which terminated the second war of American Independence, General Jackson says: At the very moment when the entire discomfiture of the enemy was looked for with a confidence amounting to certainty, the Kentucky reinforcements, in whom so much reliance had been placed, ingloriously fled.

In quoting this indisputable piece of history, I do so only by way of admonition and not to question the well-attested gallantry of the true Kentuckian, and to suggest to the gentleman that it would be well that he should not flaunt his heraldry so proudly while he bears this scar—sinister on the military escutcheon of his State—a State which answered the call of the Republic in 1861, when treason thundered at the very gates of the capital by coldly declaring her neutrality in the impending struggle. The negro, true to that patriotism and love of country that have ever characterized and marked his history on this continent, came to the aid of the Government in its efforts to maintain the Constitution. To that Government he now appeals; that Constitution he now invokes for protection against outrage and unjust prejudices founded upon caste.

But, sir, we are told by the distinguished gentleman from Georgia [Mr. Stephens] that Congress has no power under the Constitution to pass such a law, and that the passage of such an act is in direct contravention of the rights of the States. I cannot assent to any such proposition. The constitution of a free government ought always to be construed in favor of human rights. Indeed, the thirteenth, fourteenth, and fifteenth amendments, in positive words, invest Congress with the power to protect the citizen in his civil and political rights. Now, sir, what are civil rights: Rights natural, modified by civil society. . . .

Is it the interest of the Government to sacrifice individual rights to the preservation of the rights of an artificial being called States? There can be no truer principle than this, that every individual of the community at large has an equal right to the protection of Government. Can this be a free Government if partial distinctions are tolerated or maintained? . . .

The process of restoring to their proper relations with the Federal Government and with the other States those which had sided with the rebellion, undertaken under the proclamation of President Johnson in 1865, and before the assembling of Congress, developed the fact that, notwithstanding the formal recognition by those states of the abolition of slavery, the condition of the slave race would, without further protection of the Federal Government, be almost as bad as it was before. Among the first acts of legislation adopted by several of the states in the legislative bodies which claimed to be in their normal relations with the Federal government, were laws which imposed upon the colored race onerous disabilities and burdens, and curtailed their rights in the pursuit of life, liberty, and property to such an extent that their freedom was of little value, while they had lost the protection which they had received from their former owners from motives both of interest and humanity.

They were in some States forbidden to appear in the towns in any other character than menial servants. They were required to reside on and cultivate the soil, without the right to purchase or own it. They were excluded from any occupations of gain, and were not permitted to give testimony in the courts in any case where a white man was a party. It was said that their lives were at the mercy of bad men, either because the laws for their protection were insufficient or were not enforced.

These circumstances, whatever of falsehood or misconception may have been mingled with their presentation forced upon the statesmen who had conducted the Federal government in safety through the crisis of the rebellion, and who supposed that by the thirteenth article of amendment they had secured the result of their labors, the conviction that something more was necessary in the way of constitutional protection to the unfortunate race who had suffered so much. They accordingly passed through Congress the proposition for the fourteenth amendment, and they declined to treat as restored to their full participation in the Government of the Union the States which had been in insurrection until they ratified that article by a formal vote of their legislative bodies.

Before we proceed to examine more critically the provisions of this amendment, on which the plaintiffs in error rely, let us complete and dismiss the history of the recent amendments, as that history relates to the general purpose which pervades them all. A few years' experience satisfied the thoughtful men who had been the authors of the other two amendments that, notwithstanding the restraints of those articles on the States and the laws passed under the additional powers granted to Congress, these were inadequate for the protection of life, liberty, and property, without which freedom to the slave was no boon. They were in all those States denied the right of suffrage. The laws were administered by the white man alone. It was urged that a race of men distinctively marked as was the negro, living in the midst of another and dominant race, could never be fully secured in their person and their property without the right of suffrage.

Hence the fifteenth amendment, which declares that "the right of a citizen of the United States to vote shall not be denied or abridged by any state on account of race, color, or previous condition of servitude." The negro having, by the fourteenth amendment, been declared to be a citizen of the United states, is thus made a voter in every State of the Union.

We repeat, then, in the light of this recapitulation of events almost too recent to be called history, but which are familiar to us all, and on the most casual examination of the language of these amendments, no one can fail to be impressed with the one pervading purpose found in them all, lying at the foundation of each, and without which none of them would have been even suggested: we mean the freedom of the slave race, the security and firm establishment of that freedom and the protection of the newly-made freeman and citizen from the oppressions of those who had formerly exercised unlimited dominion over him.

It is true that only the fifteenth amendment in terms mentions the negro by speaking of his color and his slavery. But it is just as true that each of the other articles was addressed to the grievances of that race, and designed to remedy them, as the fifteenth.

These amendments, one and all, are thus declared to have as their all-pervading design and end the security to the recently enslaved race, not only their nominal freedom, but their complete protection from those who had formerly exercised unlimited dominion over them. It is in this broad light that all these amendments must be read, the purpose to secure the perfect equality before the law of all citizens of the United states. What you give to one class you must give to all; what you deny to one class you shall deny to all, unless in the exercise of the common and universal police power of the state you find it needful to confer exclusive privileges on certain citizens, to be held and exercised still for the common good of all....

Sir, it is scarcely twelve years since that gentleman [Alexander H. Stephens] shocked the civilized world by announcing the birth of a government which rested on human slavery as its corner-stone. The progress of events has swept away that *pseudo*-government which rested on greed, pride, and tyranny; and the race whom he then ruthlessly spurned and trampled on are here to meet him in debate, and to demand that the rights which are enjoyed by their former oppressors—who vainly sought to overthrow a Government which they could not prostitute to the base uses of slavery—shall be accorded to those who even in the darkness of slavery kept their allegiance true to freedom and the Union. Sir, the gentleman from Georgia has learned much since 1861; but he is still a laggard. Let him put away entirely the false and fatal theories which have so greatly marred an otherwise enviable record. Let him accept, in its fullness and beneficence, the great doctrine that American citizenship carries with it every civil and political right which manhood can confer. Let him lend his influence, with all his masterly ability, to complete the proud structure of legislation which makes his nation worthy of the great declaration which heralded its birth, and he will have done that which will most nearly redeem his reputation in the eyes of the world, and best vindicate the wisdom of that policy which has permitted him to regain his seat upon this floor.

To the diatribe of the gentleman from Virginia, [Mr. Harris,] who spoke on yesterday, and who so far transcended the limits of decency and propriety as to announce upon this floor that his remarks were addressed to white men alone, I shall have no word of reply. Let him feel that a negro was not only too magnanimous to smite him in his weakness, but was even charitable enough to grant him the mercy of his silence. [Laughter and applause on the floor and in the galleries.] I shall, sir, leave to others less charitable the unenviable and fatiguing task of sifting out of that mass of chaff the few grains of sense that may, perchance, deserve notice. Assuring the gentleman that the negro in this country aims at a higher degree of intellect than that exhibited by him in this debate, I cheerfully commend him to the commiseration of all intelligent men the world over—black men as well as white men.

Sir, equality before the law is now the broad, universal, glorious rule and mandate of the Republic. No State can violate that. Kentucky and Georgia may crowd their statute-books with retrograde and barbarous legislation; they may rejoice in the odious eminence of their consistent hostility to all the great steps of human progress which have marked our national history since slavery tore down the stars and stripes on Fort Sumter; but, if Congress shall do its duty, if Congress shall enforce the great guarantees which the Supreme Court has declared to be the one pervading purpose of all the recent amendments, then their unwise and unenlightened conduct will fall with the same weight upon the gentlemen from those States who now lend their influence to defeat this bill, as upon the poorest slave who once had no rights which the honorable gentlemen were bound to respect.

But, sir, not only does the decision in the Slaughter-house[1] cases contain nothing which suggests a doubt of the power of Congress to pass the pending bill, but it contains an express recognition and affirmance of such power. I quote now from page 81 of the volume:

"Nor shall any State deny to any person within its jurisdiction the equal protection of the laws."

In the light of the history of these amendments, and the pervading purpose of them, which we have already discussed, it is not difficult to give a meaning to this clause. The existence of laws in the States where the newly emancipated negroes resided, which discriminated with gross injustice and hardship against them as a class, was the evil to be remedied by this clause, and by it such laws are forbidden.

If, however, the States did not conform their laws to its require-ments, then, by the fifth section of the article of amendment, Congress was authorized to enforce it by suitable legislation. We doubt very much whether any action of a State not directed by way of discrimination against the negroes as a class, or on account of their race, will ever be held to come within the purview of this provision. It is so clearly a provision for that race and that emergency, that a strong case would be necessary for its application to any other. But as it is a State that is to be dealt with, and not alone the validity of its laws, we may safely leave that matter until Congress shall have exercised its power, or some case of State oppression, by denial of equal justice in its courts shall, have claimed a decision at our hands.

---

[1] When the city of New Orleans granted a monopoly to a slaughterhouse, other slaughter-house companies sued that the monopoly was depriving them of their livelihood in violation of the 14th Amendment's due process of law clause. The Supreme Court ruled, in 1873, that the 14th Amendment was written to guarantee the rights of former slaves and did not apply to these companies' grievances. However, the court also affirmed that the amendment did not deny a state's right of jurisdiction over its citizens' civil rights.

No language could convey a more complete assertion of the power of Congress over the subject embraced in the present bill than is here expressed. If the States do not conform to the requirements of this clause, if they continue to deny to any person within their jurisdiction the equal protection of the laws, or as the Supreme Court had said, "deny equal justice in its courts," then Congress is here said to have power to enforce the constitutional guarantee by appropriate legislation. That is the power which this bill now seeks to put in exercise. It proposes to enforce the constitutional guarantee against inequality and discrimination by appropriate legislation. It does not seek to confer new rights, nor to place rights conferred by State citizenship under the protection of the United States, but simply to prevent and forbid inequality and discrimination on account of race, color, or previous condition of servitude. Never was there a bill more completely within the constitutional power of Congress. Never was there a bill which appealed for support more strongly to that sense of justice and fair-play which has been said, and in the main with justice, to be a characteristic of the Anglo-Saxon race. The Constitution warrants it; the Supreme Court sanctions it; justice demands it.

Sir, I have replied to the extent of my ability to the arguments which have been presented by the opponents of this measure. I have replied also to some of the legal propositions advanced by gentlemen on the other side; and now that I am about to conclude, I am deeply sensible of the imperfect manner in which I have preformed the task. Technically, this bill is to decide upon the civil status of the colored American citizen: a point disputed at the very formation of our present Government, when by a short-sighted policy, a policy repugnant to true republican government, one negro counted as three-fifths of a man. The logical result of this mistake of the framers of the Constitution strengthened the cancer of slavery, which finally spread its poisonous tentacles over the southern portion of the body-politic. To arrest its growth and save the nation we have passed through the harrowing operation of internecine war, dreaded at all times, resorted to at the last extremity, like the surgeon's knife, but absolutely necessary to extirpate the disease which threatened with the life of the nation the overthrow of civil and political liberty on this continent. In that dire extremity the members of the race which I have the honor in part to represent—the race which pleads for justice at your hands today, forgetful of their inhuman and brutalizing servitude at the South, their degradation and ostracism at the North—flew willingly and gallantly to the support of the national Government. Their sufferings, assistance, privations, and trials in the swamps and in the rice-fields, their valor on the land and on the sea, is a part of the ever-glorious record which makes up the history of a nation preserved, and might, should I urge the claim, incline you to respect and guarantee their rights and privileges as citizens of our common Republic. But I remember that valor, devotion, and loyalty are not always rewarded according to their just deserts, and that after the battle some who have borne the brunt of the fray may, through neglect or contempt, be assigned to a subordinate place, while the enemies in war may be preferred to the sufferers.

The results of the war, as seen in reconstruction, have settled forever the political status of my race. The passage of this bill will determine the civil status, not only of the negro, but of any other class of citizens who may feel themselves discriminated against. It will form the cap-stone of that temple of liberty, begun on this continent under discouraging circumstances, carried on in spite of the sneers of monarchists and the cavils of pretended friends of freedom, until at last it stands in all its beautiful symmetry and proportions, a building the grandest which the world has ever seen, realizing the most sanguine expectations and the highest hopes of those who, in the name of equal, impartial, and universal liberty, laid the foundation stones. . . .

PART FIVE

Industry and Reform, 1877–1912

Five Labor Activists, 1887.
August Spies, Albert Parsons, Louis Lingg, George Engel, and Adolph Fischer (from top left) were anarchists who advocated the right for workers to strike, protested the 60-hour work week, and called for an 8-hour day. During a rally at Haymarket Square in Chicago on May 4, 1886, someone threw a bomb that killed eight policemen. Several of the anarchist speakers were arrested, and these five men were tried, convicted, and condemned to death. Lingg cheated the hangman by committing suicide in his jail cell the day before the scheduled execution.

INTRODUCTION: PROGRESS AND DISCONTENT

The Gilded Age was an era of unprecedented growth, a time of seemingly unlimited expansion of American business and industry. Huge fortunes were made by such skillful entrepreneurs as Andrew Carnegie and John D. Rockefeller as they expanded their companies into monopolies and trusts that seemed more powerful than the government in Washington. It was an age of innovation and mass marketing in which department stores, professional spectator sports like baseball, and inventions like the telephone, electric streetlights, the phonograph, the motion picture camera, electric trolleys, and subways significantly altered people's daily lives. The nation transformed rapidly from a primarily agrarian and rural society into an industrial and urban society.

Such rapid growth and prosperity, however, was not without serious problems. Workers were forced to exchange their labor for subsistence wages in grueling jobs in unsafe factories. A huge influx of immigrants from eastern and southern Europe flooded into ethnic enclaves in America's cities. Factory owners knew that this vast labor force meant that wages could remain at the subsistence level and that competition among workers would act as a brake on unionization efforts. Railroad financier Jay Gould purportedly boasted that he could easily persuade half the working class to kill the other half. The federal government, in spite of the glaring need to address innumerable complex problems, was unwilling to enact any legislation that would curb business growth.

English philosopher Herbert Spencer and Yale professor William Graham Sumner applied Darwin's theory of evolution to society by arguing that just as in nature, where only the fit survive, so, too, in the social order. The rich, according to these "social Darwinists," were stronger and fitter than their workers. Their proof was that they had, in the struggle for survival, emerged at the top as the owners of businesses; if the workers had been fit, they, too, would have risen. "Millionaires," Sumner confidently declared in *What the Social Classes Owe Each Other*, "are a product of natural selection." This, of course, provided perfect justification to the likes of Rockefeller, Carnegie, Vanderbilt, and Morgan. It meant that whatever their exploitive practices, and however harshly they took advantage of workers, they were thoroughly and "scientifically" justified. Spencer and Sumner argued that any kind of governmental intervention in the economy would, in effect, be going against science and evolution. The poor should not be helped, for in doing so the government would be encouraging the proliferation of the "unfit." "Taxing the wealthy," Sumner reasoned, "would be like killing your generals in time of war." This harsh philosophy underlay many of the congressional debates over proposed social legislation. It was also used to justify the dispossession of the Plains tribes and the conquest of the frontier by "fitter" Americans, to justify the implementation of Jim Crow laws and the emergence of segregation, and to justify imperialism. President Theodore Roosevelt insisted that industrial "civilized" nations had a duty to dominate the backward "uncivilized" nations by bestowing on them the benefits of Western culture and Christianity.

Throughout the era, workers' organizing efforts advanced by fits and starts. Although it lasted only six years, in 1869 the National Labor Union was founded. Also in 1869, the Knights of Labor came into being. Under Terence Powderly's leadership, it became an effective advocate of workers' interests but began to disintegrate in the aftermath of the Haymarket bombing. In May 1886 more than 350,000 workers, in order to force industrialists to consider their demand for an eight-hour workday, declared a general strike. During a rally at Chicago's Haymarket Square, while members of the Knights of Labor were addressing the protestors, the police moved in to disperse the crowd. Someone threw a bomb that killed eight policemen, and in the ensuing melee more than seventy people were injured. Eight anarchists were arrested, and the subsequent trial and executions derailed the labor movement. To most Americans, it seemed proof that unions would lead to anarchy and undermine American values. In the summer of 1892, workers at Carnegie's steel mill in Homestead, Pennsylvania, went on strike, but when Carnegie's partner Henry Clay Frick employed Pinkertons as strikebreakers, violence broke out. After ten people were killed and more than sixty wounded, the strike was broken, and the effort to unionize the steel industry was set back more than 40 years.

Farmers, too, banded together to promote their interests. Based primarily in the Midwest and South, the Granges and the Alliances were cooperative societies that demanded the federal government reform the currency system through the free and unlimited coinage of silver, as well as regulate banks, insurance companies, railroads, and telegraph companies. In 1892, the Populist Party published a platform urging these reforms as well as women's suffrage and the direct election of senators. It nominated James B. Weaver for president, who astonished complacent Washington by winning more than a million votes.

Workers and farmers were not the only groups protesting against the hardships they faced. Minorities, especially Chinese immigrants on the West Coast, African Americans, and Indians, found that their rights were disregarded—even at times taken away. Ironically, the government treated these three minority groups in three entirely disparate ways: exclusion, assimilation, and separation. The Chinese Exclusion Act, passed in 1882, prohibited further Chinese immigration into the country and denied citizenship to those already living in the United States. The Dawes Act of 1887 was Washington's attempt to assimilate the Indian tribes into the American way of life by distributing land on the reservations to individuals and educating Native American children in such private academies as the Carlisle School in Pennsylvania, where they were immersed in white culture and the English language and compelled to forget Indian ways. The literacy tests, poll taxes, and Jim Crow laws of the Southern states that prevented African Americans from enjoying the full rights of citizenship were officially validated in 1896 by the *Plessy v. Ferguson* decision, in which the Supreme Court ruled that providing "separate but equal" facilities for blacks was constitutional. Dozens of Chinese protested against policies that discriminated against them, usually unsuccessfully, by taking the government to court. Indians struggled against assimilation and frequently attempted to escape from the reservations. However, when a band of 340 Miniconjou Sioux under Big Foot fled the Pine Ridge Reservation in December 1890, the Seventh Cavalry (Custer's old command) intercepted them a few days after Christmas at Wounded Knee. When the Indians resisted the cavalry's attempt to disarm them, the soldiers returned fire with cannon and Gatling guns. Most of the 146 killed were women and children, and the survivors were forced back onto the reservation. Wounded Knee—designated a "battle" by whites and a "massacre" by Indians—marked the end of Indian resistance. W. E. B. DuBois demanded full and immediate equality for African Americans. He was one of the founders of the Niagara Movement (forerunner of the National Association for the Advancement of Colored People), which began an organized campaign to overturn the *Plessy* decision. African American journalist Ida B. Wells-Barnett campaigned for the federal government to enact and enforce antilynching laws.

Middle-class reformers also spoke out in response to the problems of industrialization. Brown University Professor Lester Frank Ward turned Spencer and Sumner's application of the theory of evolution on its head in a forceful attack on social Darwinism. Because humans have intelligence, Ward wrote in *Mind as a Social Factor*, we are capable of having an effect on natural selection. We can, through government, create economic and social legislation that will benefit the masses, and further the evolution of the human race. In contrast to Spencer's "survival of the fittest," Ward argued for making as many people as possible "fit to survive." The ideas of what became known as reform Darwinism became part of the intellectual underpinnings of many progressive reformers. Jane Addams initiated the settlement house movement. Walter Rauschenbusch, claiming that the elimination of suffering was a moral necessity, applied Christian principles to the everyday work of making life better for the downtrodden. This Social Gospel subsequently had a significant impact in the twentieth century, most notably on Martin Luther King Jr.'s tactics in the civil rights movement.

Alcohol consumption was one of the most popular forms of entertainment in nineteenth-century America. As a result alcoholism, unemployment, spousal abuse, poverty, and crime all came to be viewed as the results of "demon rum." The impetus for reform in the antebellum period gave birth to a temperance movement that grew throughout the century, becoming, by the last quarter of the century, a formidable force. Many women viewed it as a feminist issue equal in importance to women's suffrage. Women were tired of husbands who would come home from work on payday after a stopover at the local saloon, not only inebriated but also with their weekly salaries half-consumed. Many arguments ensued, many wives were beaten, and many men became alcoholics and lost their jobs, plunging their families into poverty. The Women's Christian Temperance Union, under the leadership of Frances Willard, led the fight against alcohol abuse. Temperance was a moral as well as a feminist issue, especially for millions of conservative rural Protestants, but this morality was tightly linked with nativism and xenophobia. As millions of immigrants flocked to the United States from eastern and southern Europe, many temperance advocates believed that prohibiting alcohol would somehow penalize and maybe even discourage immigration from these Roman Catholic, Eastern Orthodox, and Jewish areas.

The census report for 1890 revealed that, for the first time in American history, there was no discernible frontier line beyond which white settlement had not penetrated. By mid-decade, industrialists and politicians, fearing that American expansion had reached a limit that would lead to a severe contraction of economic growth, began to look abroad for markets and raw materials. In 1890 Navy Captain Alfred Thayer Mahan published a widely acclaimed book, *The Influence of Seapower upon History: 1660–1783*, in which he argued that all great empires in world history had controlled the seas. The United States, with a vast coastline on both the Atlantic and Pacific oceans, was in a position to become the dominant world power if the government would expand the navy, acquire overseas bases to furnish supplies for the fleet, and construct a canal through the Isthmus of Panama. Mahan's advice was heeded. The acquisition of Hawaii and Samoa and the Spanish American War of 1898 were the first steps to a new international outlook on the part of a nation that had long remained faithful to George Washington's counsel to avoid entangling itself in international alliances. By the turn of the century, the United States had acquired Guantanamo Bay in Cuba, as well as Guam, Puerto Rico, and the Philippine Islands. There was, however, widely based and passionate protest that such exercise of imperialist power so contradicted democratic principles that the United States was in danger of negating its own highly vaunted belief in "government of the people, by the people, and for the people."

Many writers and journalists embarked on intense efforts to expose— frequently with exaggeration and sensationalism—the evils of political corruption, worker exploitation, and conning of consumers. Muckrakers like Lincoln Steffens, Frank Norris, Ida M. Tarbell, and Upton Sinclair influenced local governments to pass regulatory legislation. Indeed, Sinclair's popular novel *The Jungle* persuaded President Theodore Roosevelt to initiate the legislation that created the Food and Drug Administration.

Terence Powderly (1849–1924)

As industrialization developed during the nineteenth century, American workers, in an effort to improve their lot, formed small craft unions. By 1866, many of these small unions had combined to form the National Labor Union (NLU). Although difficulties in maintaining solidarity among NLU members caused it to collapse within seven years, one of those who was influenced by the union movement was Terence Powderly. Believing that better wages and shorter hours would enable workers to live more satisfying lives and participate more fully in the American dream, Powderly joined the Knights of Labor in 1876. As he rose to a leadership position in this national union, Powderly realized that political power was one of the keys to workers' rights. With the support of labor, he was elected mayor of Scranton, Pennsylvania, in 1878 and began serving the first of three terms as a reformer. Also in 1878, he opened up the Knights of Labor, making it a more inclusive union, and helped formulate a new constitution for the organization.

When workers around the country gathered at rallies, they often sang such songs as the one appended here, "Eight Hours," by I. G. Blanchard and Jesse Jones.

Preamble to the Constitution of the Knights of Labor, January 3, 1878

The recent alarming development and aggression of aggregated wealth, which, unless checked, will inevitably lead to the pauperization and hopeless degradation of the toiling masses, render it imperative, if we desire to enjoy the blessings of life, that a check should be placed upon its power and upon unjust accumulation, and a system adopted which will secure to the laborer the fruits of his toil; and as this much-desired object can only be accomplished by the thorough unification of labor, and the united efforts of those who obey the divine injunction that "In the sweat of thy brow shalt thou eat bread," we have formed the [Knights of Labor] with a view of securing the organization and direction, by co-operative effort, of the power of the industrial classes; and we submit to the world the objects sought to be accomplished by our organization, calling upon all who believe in securing "the greatest good to the greatest number" to aid and assist us:

I. To bring within the folds of organization every department of productive industry, making knowledge a standpoint for action, and industrial and moral worth, not wealth, the true standard of individual and national greatness.

II. To secure to the toilers a proper share of the wealth that they create; more of the leisure that rightfully belongs to them; more societary advantages; more of the benefits, privileges and emoluments of the world; in a word, all those rights and privileges necessary to make them capable of enjoying, appreciating, defending and perpetuating the blessings of good government.

III. To arrive at the true condition of the producing masses in their educational, moral and financial condition, by demanding from the various governments the establishment of Bureaus of Labor Statistics.

IV. The establishment of co-operative institutions, productive and distributive.

V. The reserving of the public lands—the heritage of the people—for the actual settler; not another acre for railroads or speculators.

VI. The abrogation of all laws that do not bear equally upon capital and labor, the removal of unjust technicalities, delays and discriminations in the administration of justice, and the adopting of measures providing for the health and safety of those engaged in mining, manufacturing or building pursuits.

VII. The enactment of laws to compel chartered corporations to pay their employe[e]s weekly, in full, for labor performed during the preceding week, in the lawful money of the country.

SOURCE: Terence V. Powderly, *Thirty Years of Labor, 1859 to 1889* (Philadelphia, 1890), 128–130.

VIII. The enactment of laws giving mechanics and laborers a first lien on their work for their full wages.

IX. The abolishment of the contract system on national, State and municipal work.

X. The substitution of arbitration for strikes, whenever and wherever employers and employe[e]s are willing to meet on equitable grounds.

XI. The prohibition of the employment of children in workshops, mines and factories before attaining their fourteenth year.

XII. To abolish the system of letting out by contract the labor of convicts in our prisons and reformatory institutions.

XIII. To secure for both sexes equal pay for equal work.

XIV. The reduction of the hours of labor to eight per day, so that the laborers may have more time for social enjoyment and intellectual improvement, and be enabled to reap the advantages conferred by the labor-saving machinery which their brains have created.

XV. To prevail upon governments to establish a purely national circulating medium, based upon the faith and resources of the nation, and issued directly to the people, without the intervention of any system of banking corporations, which money shall be a legal tender in payment of all debts, public or private.

"Eight Hours," by I. G. Blanchard and Jesse Jones, 1880s

We mean to make things over,
We are tired of toil for naught
With but bare enough to live upon
And ne'er an hour for thought.
We want to feel the sunshine
And we want to smell the flow'rs
We are sure that God has willed it
And we mean to have eight hours;
We're summoning our forces
From the shipyard, shop and mill

Eight hours for work, eight hours for rest
Eight hours for what we will;
Eight hours for work, eight hours for rest
Eight hours for what we will.

SOURCE: Margaret Bradford Boni, ed., *The Fireside Book of Favorite American Songs* (New York: Simon and Shuster, 1952)

The beasts that graze the hillside,
And the birds that wander free,
In the life that God has meted,
Have a better life than we.
Oh, hands and hearts are weary,
And homes are heavy with dole;
If our life's to be filled with drudg'ry,
What need of a human soul.
Shout, shout the lusty rally,
From shipyard, shop, and mill.

Eight hours for work, eight hours for rest
Eight hours for what we will;
Eight hours for work, eight hours for rest
Eight hours for what we will.

The voice of God within us
Is calling us to stand
Erect as is becoming
To the work of His right hand.
Should he, to whom the Maker
His glorious image gave,
The meanest of His creatures crouch,
A bread-and-butter slave?
Let the shout ring down the valleys
And echo from every hill.

Ye deem they're feeble voices
That are raised in labor's cause,
But bethink ye of the torrent,
And the wild tornado's laws.
We say not toil's uprising
In terror's shape will come,
Yet the world were wise to listen
To the monetary hum.
Soon, soon the deep toned rally
Shall all the nations thrill.

Eight hours for work, eight hours for rest
Eight hours for what we will;
Eight hours for work, eight hours for rest
Eight hours for what we will.

From factories and workshops
In long and weary lines,

From all the sweltering forges,
And from out the sunless mines,
Wherever toil is wasting
The force of life to live
There the bent and battered armies
Come to claim what God doth give
And the blazon on the banner
Doth with hope the nation fill:

Eight hours for work, eight hours for rest
Eight hours for what we will;
Eight hours for work, eight hours for rest
Eight hours for what we will.

Hurrah, hurrah for labor,
For it shall arise in might
It has filled the world with plenty,
It shall fill the world with light
Hurrah, hurrah for labor,
It is mustering all its powers
And shall march along to victory
With the banner of Eight Hours.
Shout, shout the echoing rally
Till all the welkin thrill.

Eight hours for work, eight hours for rest
Eight hours for what we will;
Eight hours for work, eight hours for rest
Eight hours for what we will.

Lyrics by I. G. Blanchard
Music by Rev. Jesse H. Jones

Chief Joseph (1840–1904)

Chief Joseph was the name whites gave Heinmot Tooyalaket (Thunder Coming from the Mountain), chief of the Nez Percé. The Nez Percé had given Lewis and Clark provisions when their expedition crossed the Continental Divide on its way to the Pacific in 1805, and the grateful explorers had promised them that the government in Washington would

always be their friend. However, in 1877 the Nez Percé were told they had to
leave their homes in the Wallowa Valley of eastern Oregon and settle on the
Lapwai reservation in Idaho. They refused to go, and when the U.S. Army
tried to force them, Chief Joseph led his tribe on an extraordinary journey
of more than a thousand miles in an effort to escape to Canada. Finally
overtaken 40 miles from the border, Joseph surrendered to Colonel Nelson B.
Miles. "I am tired of fighting," Joseph reputedly said. "Our chiefs are killed.
. . . It is cold and we have no blankets. The little children are freezing to
death. My people—some of them have run away to the hills and have no
blankets and no food. No one knows where they are—perhaps freezing to
death. I want to have time to look for my children and see how many of
them I can find. Maybe I shall find them among the dead. Hear me, my
chiefs, my heart is sick and sad. From where the sun now stands I will fight
no more forever." General Miles had promised Joseph that the tribe would be
returned to Oregon, but instead they were sent to a reservation in
Oklahoma. Within two years, many of the Nez Percé had died in the terribly
unhealthy conditions of the reservation, and Chief Joseph went to
Washington, where he made the following appeal to President Rutherford B.
Hayes, members of his cabinet, and a number of congressmen. Eventually
the Nez Percé were returned to the Pacific Northwest, but Joseph himself was
sent to a separate reservation in Washington, where, in 1904, he died, it was
commonly said, of a broken heart.

Appeal to the Hayes Administration, 1879

At last I was granted permission to come to Washington and bring my friend
Yellow Bull and our interpreter with me. I am glad I came. I have shaken hands
with a good many friends, but there are some things I want to know which no
one seems able to explain. I cannot understand how the Government sends a
man out to fight us, as it did General Miles, and then breaks his word. Such a
government has something wrong about it. I cannot understand why so many
chiefs are allowed to talk so many different ways, and promise so many different
things. I have seen the Great Father Chief [Hayes] . . . and many other law
chiefs, and they all say they are my friends, and that I shall have justice, but while
all their mouths talk right I do not understand why nothing is done for my
people.

I have heard talk and talk but nothing is done. Good words do not last long
unless they amount to something. Words do not pay for my dead people. They
do not pay for my country now overrun by white men. They do not protect my
father's grave. They do not pay for my horses and cattle.

Source: *North American Review* 128 (April 1879), 431–432.

Good words do not give me back my children. Good words will not make good the promise of your war chief, General Miles. Good words will not give my people a home where they can live in peace and take care of themselves.

I am tired of talk that comes to nothing. It makes my heart sick when I remember all the good words and all the broken promises. There has been too much talking by men who had no right to talk. Too many misinterpretations have been made; too many misunderstandings have come up between the white men and the Indians.

If the white man wants to live in peace with the Indian he can live in peace. There need be no trouble. Treat all men alike. Give them the same laws. Give them all an even chance to live and grow. All men were made by the same Great Spirit Chief. They are all brothers. The earth is the mother of all people, and all people should have equal rights upon it. You might as well expect all rivers to run backward as that any man who was born a free man should be contented penned up and denied liberty to go where he pleases. If you tie a horse to a stake, do you expect he will grow fat? If you pen an Indian up on a small spot of earth and compel him to stay there, he will not be contented nor will he grow and prosper.

I have asked some of the Great White Chiefs where they get their authority to say to the Indian that he shall stay in one place, while he sees white men going where they please. They cannot tell me.

I only ask of the Government to be treated as all other men are treated. If I cannot go to my own home, let me have a home in a country where my people will not die so fast. I would like to go to Bitter Root Valley. There my people would be happy; where they are now they are dying. Three have died since I left my camp to come to Washington. When I think of our condition, my heart is heavy. I see men of my own race treated as outlaws and driven from country to country, or shot down like animals.

I know that my race must change. We cannot hold our own with the white men as we are. We only ask an even chance to live as other men live. We ask to be recognized as men. We ask that the same law shall work alike on all men. If an Indian breaks the law, punish him by the law. If a white man breaks the law, punish him also.

Let me be a free man—free to travel, free to stop, free to work, free to trade where I choose, free to choose my own teachers, free to follow the religion of my fathers, free to talk, think and act for myself—and I will obey every law or submit to the penalty.

Whenever the white man treats the Indian as they treat each other then we shall have no more wars. We shall be all alike—brothers of one father and mother, with one sky above us and one country around us and one government for all. Then the Great Spirit Chief who rules above will smile upon this land and send rain to wash out the bloody spots made by brothers' hands upon the face of the earth. For this time the Indian race is waiting and praying. I hope no more groans of wounded men and women will ever go to the ear of the Great Spirit Chief above, and that all people may be one people.

Indian Delegation to Washington, 1874.
Just as Chief Joseph went to Washington to appeal to the president for the rights of his people, so too did other Indians like this Mandan and Arikara delegation.

Mary Elizabeth Lease (1850–1933)

Mary Elizabeth Lease was a charismatic and eloquent political agitator who traveled the country in the 1890s to make stirring inflammatory speeches against the exploitation of farmers and workers by industrialists, bankers, and railroads. She was active in the leadership of the Farmers' Alliance, the Knights of Labor, and the Populist Party, as well as an ardent suffragist who urged women to be politically engaged in anticapitalist agitation. Although it is apparently only a legend that she urged farmers in her speeches to "raise less corn and more hell," she truly was a firebrand, as this speech at a Women's Christian Temperance Union (WCTU) convention attests.

SPEECH TO THE WCTU, 1890

Madame President and Fellow Citizens:—

If God were to give me my choice to live in any age of the world that has flown, or in any age of the world yet to be, I would say, O God, let me live here and now, in this day and age of the world's history.

For we are living in a grand and wonderful time—a time when old ideas, traditions and customs have broken loose from their moorings and are hopelessly adrift on the great shoreless, boundless sea of human thought—a time when the

SOURCE: Mary Elizabeth Lease, "Speech to the Woman's Christian Temperance Union," in Joan M. Jensen, *With These Hands: Women Working on the Land* (Old Westbury, NY: Feminist Press and McGraw-Hill Book Company, 1981), 154–160.

gray old world begins to dimly comprehend that there is no difference between the brain of an intelligent woman and the brain of an intelligent man; no difference between the soul-power or brainpower that nerved the arm of Charlotte Corday [the assassin of Jean-Paul Marat during the French Revolution] to deeds of heroic patriotism and the soul-power or brain-power that swayed old John Brown behind his death dealing barricade at Ossawattomie. We are living in an age of thought. The mighty dynamite of thought is upheaving the social and political structure and stirring the hearts of men from centre to circumference. Men, women and children are in commotion, discussing the mighty problems of the day. The agricultural classes, loyal and patriotic, slow to act and slow to think, are to-day thinking for themselves; and their thought has crystallized into action. Organization is the key-note to a mighty movement among the masses which is the protest of the patient burden-bearers of the nation against years of economic and political superstition. . . .

The movement among the masses today is an echo of the life of Jesus of Nazareth, an honest endeavor on the part of the people to put into practical operation the basic principles of Christianity: "Whatsoever ye would that men should do unto you, do ye even so unto them."

In an organization founded upon the eternal principles of truth and right, based upon the broad and philanthropic principle, "Injury to one is the concern of all," having for its motto, "Exact justice to all, special privileges to none,"—the farmers and laborers could not well exclude their mothers, wives and daughters, the patient burden bearers of the home, who had been their faithful companions, their tried friends and trusted counselors through long, weary years of poverty and toil. Hence the doors of the Farmers' Alliance were thrown open wide to the women of the land. They were invited into full membership, with all the privileges of promotion; actually recognized and treated as human beings. And not only the mothers, wives and daughters, but "the sisters, the cousins and the aunts," availed themselves of their newly offered liberties, till we find at the present time upward of a half-million women in the Alliance, who, because of their loyalty to home and loved ones and their intuitive and inherent sense of justice, are investigating the condition of the country, studying the great social, economic and political problems, fully realizing that the political arena is the only place where the mighty problems of to-day and tomorrow can be satisfactorily fought and settled, and amply qualified to go hand-in-hand with fathers, husbands, sons and brothers to the polls and register their opinion against legalized robbery and corporate wrong.

George Eliot tells us that "much that we are and have is due to the unhistoric acts of those who in life were ungarlanded and in death sleep in unvisited tombs." So to the women of the Alliance, who bravely trudged twice a week to the bleak country schoolhouse, literally burning midnight oil as they studied with their loved ones the economic and political problems, and helped them devise methods by which the shackels of industrial slavery might be broken, and the authors of the nation's liberties, the creators of the nation's wealth and greatness, might be made free and prosperous—to these women, unknown and uncrowned, belongs the honor of defeating for reelection to the United

States Senate that man who for eighteen years has signally failed to represent his constituents, and who during that time has never once identified himself with any legislation for the oppressed and overburdened people.

Three years ago this man [John James] Ingalls [Republican Senator from Kansas] made a speech on woman suffrage at Abilene, Kan., in which he took occasion to speak in the most ignorant and vicious manner of women, declaring that "a woman could not and should not vote because she was a woman." Why? She was a woman, and that was enough; the subject was too delicate for further discussion.

But we treasured up these things in our hearts, and then his famous, or rather, infamous interview in a New York paper appeared, in which he declared that: "It is lawful to hire Hessians to kill, to mutilate, to destroy. Success is the object to be attained; the decalogue and the golden rule have no place in a political campaign; the world has outgrown its Christ and needs a new one." This man, said the law-abiding God fearing women, must no longer be permitted to misrepresent us. So we worked and waited for his defeat. And the cyclone, the political Johnstown, that overtook the enemies of the people's rights last November, proves what a mighty factor the women of the Alliance have been in the political affairs of the nation.

I overheard yesterday morning at the hotel breakfast table a conversation between two gentlemen in regard to Ingalls. "I consider his defeat," said the first speaker, "to be a national calamity." "Your reasons," said the second. "Why, he is such a brilliantly smart man," he replied. "True," said the other; "but he must needs be a smart man to be the consummate rascal he has proven himself to be." And I thought as I heard the remarks, "Our opinion is also shared by men." You wonder, perhaps, at the zeal and enthusiasm of the Western women in this reform movement. Let me tell you why they are interested. Turn to your old school-maps and books of a quarter of a century ago, and you will find that what is now the teeming and fruitful West was then known as the Treeless Plain, the Great American Desert. To this sterile and remote region, infested by savage beasts and still more savage men, the women of the New England States, the women of the cultured East, came with husbands, sons and brothers to help them build up a home upon the broad and vernal prairies of the West. We came with the roses of health on our cheek, the light of hope in our eyes, the fires of youth and hope burning in our hearts. We left the old familiar paths, the associations of home and the friends of childhood. We left schools and churches—all that made life dear—and turned our faces toward the setting sun. We endured hardships, dangers and privations; hours of loneliness, fear and sorrow; our little babes were born upon these wide, unsheltered prairies; and there, upon the sweeping prairies beneath the cedar trees our hands have planted to mark the sacred place, our little ones lie buried. We toiled in the cabin and in the field; we planted trees and orchards; we helped our loved ones to make the prairie blossom as the rose. The neat cottage took the place of the sod shanty, the log-cabin and the humble dug-out.

Yet, after all our years of toil and privation, dangers and hardships upon the Western frontier, monopoly is taking our homes from us by an infamous system of mortgage foreclosure, the most infamous that has ever disgraced the statutes of a civilized nation. It takes from us at the rate of five hundred a month the homes that represent the best years of our life, our toil, our hopes, our happiness. How did it happen? The government, at the bid of Wall Street, repudiated its contracts with the people; the circulating medium was contracted in the interest of Shylock from $54 per capita to less than $8 per capita; or, as Senator [Preston] Plumb [of Kansas] tells us, "Our debts were increased, while the means to pay them was decreased;" or as grand Senator [William Morris] Stewart [of Nevada] puts it, "For twenty years the market value of the dollar has gone up and the market value of labor has gone down, till today the American laborer, in bitterness and wrath, asks which is the worst—the black slavery that has gone or the white slavery that has come?"

Do you wonder the women are joining the Alliance? I wonder if there is a woman in all this broad land who can afford to stay out of the Alliance. Our loyal, white-ribbon women should be heart and hand in this Farmers' Alliance movement, for the men whom we have sent to represent us are the only men in the councils of this nation who have not been elected on a liquor platform; and I want to say here, with exultant pride, that the five farmer Congressmen and the United States Senator we have sent up from Kansas—the liquor traffic, Wall Street, "nor the gates of hell shall not prevail against them."

It would sound boastful were I to detail to you the active, earnest part the Kansas women took in the recent campaign. A Republican majority of 82,000 was reduced to less than 8,000 when we elected 97 representatives, 5 out of 7 Congressmen, and a United States Senator, for to the women of Kansas belongs the credit of defeating John J. Ingalls; he is feeling badly about it yet, too, for he said today that "women and Indians were the only class that would scalp a dead man." I rejoice that he realises that he is politically dead.

I might weary you to tell you in detail how the Alliance women found time from cares of home and children to prepare the tempting, generous viands for the Alliance picnic dinners; where hungry thousands and tens of thousands gathered in the forests and groves to listen to the words of impassioned oratory, ofttimes from woman's lips, that nerved the men of Kansas to forget their party prejudice and vote for "Mollie and the babies." And not only did they find their way to the voters' hearts, through their stomachs, but they sang their way as well. I hold here a book of Alliance songs, composed and set to music by an Alliance woman, Mrs. Florence Olmstead of Butler County, Kan., that did much toward moulding public sentiment. Alliance Glee Clubs composed of women, gave us such stirring melodies as the nation has not heard since the Tippecanoe and Tyler campaign of 1840. And while I am individualizing, let me call your attention to a book written also by an Alliance woman. I wish a copy of it could be placed in the hands of every woman in this land. "The Fate of a Fool" is written by Mrs. Emma G. Curtis of Colorado. This book in the hands of women would teach them to be just and generous toward women, and help them to forgive and condone in each other the sins so sweetly forgiven when committed by men.

Let no one for a moment believe that this uprising and federation of the people is but a passing episode in politics. It is a religious as well as a political movement, for we seek to put into practical operation the teachings and precepts of Jesus of Nazareth. We seek to enact justice and equity between man and man. We seek to bring the nation back to the constitutional liberties guaranteed us by our fore-fathers. The voice that is coming up today from the mystic chords of the American heart is the same voice that Lincoln heard blending with the guns of Fort Sumter and the Wilderness, and it is breaking into a clarion cry today that will be heard around the world.

Crowns will fall, thrones will tremble, kingdoms will disappear, the divine right of kings and the divine right of capital will fade away like the mists of the morning when the Angel of Liberty shall kindle the fires of justice in the hearts of men. "Exact justice to all, special privileges to none." No more millionaires, and no more paupers; no more gold kings, silver kings and oil kings, and no more little waifs of humanity starving for a crust of bread. No more gaunt faced, hollow-eyed girls in the factories, and no more little boys reared in poverty and crime for the penitentiaries and the gallows. But we shall have the golden age of which Isaiah sang and the prophets have so long foretold; when the farmers shall be prosperous and happy, dwelling under their own vine and fig tree; when the laborer shall have that for which he toils; when occupancy and use shall be the only title to land, and every one shall obey the divine injunction, "In the sweat of thy face shalt thou eat bread." When men shall be just and generous, little less than gods, and women shall be just and charitable toward each other, little less than angels; when we shall have not a government of the people by capitalists, but a government of the people, by the people. . . .

The People's Party

During the 1880s and 1890s, thousands of small midwestern and southern farmers formed cooperative organizations like the Grange and the Farmers' Alliance as a united front to combat the excesses of big business and demand that the federal government overcome its unwillingness to regulate industrialists, railroads, bankers, and processors. By 1892, their discontent and frustration had led them to form a new political party—the People's Party. In July they convened in Omaha, Nebraska, nominated James B. Weaver for president, and issued the Omaha Platform, in which they proclaimed their grievances and demands as well as their solidarity with exploited industrial workers. Dubbed the Populist Party by the press, their ardent campaign for Weaver made the Populists the most successful third party in the nation up to that time. Weaver received more than a million votes in the November election and won four states with 22 electoral votes, forcing Republicans and Democrats to take notice.

THE OMAHA PLATFORM, JULY 1892

Assembled upon the 116th anniversary of the Declaration of Independence, the People's Party of America, in their first national convention, invoking upon their action the blessing of Almighty God, put forth in the name and on behalf of the people of this country, the following preamble and declaration of principles:

PREAMBLE

The conditions which surround us best justify our cooperation; we meet in the midst of a nation brought to the verge of moral, political, and material ruin. Corruption dominates the ballot-box, the Legislatures, the Congress, and touches even the ermine of the bench. The people are demoralized; most of the States have been compelled to isolate the voters at the polling places to prevent universal intimidation and bribery. The newspapers are largely subsidized or muzzled, public opinion silenced, business prostrated, homes covered with mortgages, labor impoverished, and the land concentrating in the hands of capitalists. The urban workmen are denied the right to organize for self-protection, imported pauperized labor beats down their wages, a hireling standing army, unrecognized by our laws, is established to shoot them down, and they are rapidly degenerating into European conditions. The fruits of the toil of millions are badly stolen to build up colossal fortunes for a few, unprecedented in the history of mankind; and the possessors of these, in turn, despise the Republic and endanger liberty. From the same prolific womb of governmental injustice we breed the two great classes—tramps and millionaires.

The national power to create money is appropriated to enrich bond-holders; a vast public debt payable in legal-tender currency has been funded into gold-bearing bonds, thereby adding millions to the burdens of the people. Silver, which has been accepted as coin since the dawn of history, has been demonetized to add to the purchasing power of gold by decreasing the value of all forms of property as well as human labor, and the supply of currency is purposely abridged to fatten usurers, bankrupt enterprise, and enslave industry. A vast conspiracy against mankind has been organized on two continents, and it is rapidly taking possession of the world. If not met and overthrown at once it forebodes terrible social convulsions, the destruction of civilization, or the establishment of an absolute despotism.

We have witnessed for more than a quarter of a century the struggles of the two great political parties for power and plunder, while grievous wrongs have been inflicted upon the suffering people. We charge that the controlling influences dominating both these parties have permitted the existing dreadful conditions to develop without serious effort to prevent or restrain them. Neither do they now promise us any substantial reform. They have agreed together to ignore, in the coming campaign, every issue but one. They propose to drown the outcries of a

---

SOURCE: "People's Party Platform," *Omaha Morning World-Herald.* July 5, 1892.

plundered people with the uproar of a sham battle over the tariff, so that capitalists, corporations, national banks, rings, trusts, watered stock, the demonetization of silver and the oppressions of the usurers may all be lost sight of. They propose to sacrifice our homes, lives, and children on the altar of mammon; to destroy the multitude in order to secure corruption funds from the millionaires.

Assembled on the anniversary of the birthday of the nation, and filled with the spirit of the grand general and chief who established our independence, we seek to restore the government of the Republic to the hands of "the plain people," with which class it originated. We assert our purposes to be identical with the purposes of the National Constitution; "to form a more perfect union and establish justice, insure domestic tranquillity, provide for the common defense, promote the general welfare, and secure the blessings of liberty for ourselves and our posterity." We declare that this republic can only endure as a free government while built upon the love to the whole people for each other and for the nation; that it cannot be pinned together by bayonets; that the civil war is over, and that every passion and resentment which grew out of it must die with it; and that we must be in fact, as we are in name, one united brotherhood of freemen.

Our country finds itself confronted by conditions for which there is not precedent in the history of the world; our annual agricultural productions amount to billions of dollars in value, which must, within a few weeks or months, be exchanged for billions of dollars' worth of commodities consumed in their production; the existing currency supply is wholly inadequate to make this exchange; the results are falling prices, the formation of combines and rings, the impoverishment of the producing class. We pledge ourselves that if given power we will labor to correct these evils by wise and reasonable legislation, in accordance with the terms of our platform. We believe that the power of government—in other words, of the people—should be expanded (as in the case of the postal service) as rapidly and as far as the good sense of an intelligent people and the teaching of experience shall justify, to the end that oppression, injustice, and poverty shall eventually cease in the land. . . .

PLATFORM

We declare, therefore—

First.—That the union of the labor forces of the United States this day consummated shall be permanent and perpetual; may its spirit enter into all hearts for the salvation of the republic and the uplifting of mankind!

Second.—Wealth belongs to him who creates it, and every dollar taken from industry without an equivalent is robbery. "If any will not work, neither shall he eat." The interests of rural and civil labor are the same; their enemies are identical.

Third.—We believe that the time has come when the railroad corporations will either own the people or the people must own the railroads; and should the government enter upon the work of owning and managing all railroads, we should favor an amendment to the constitution by which all persons engaged in the government service shall be placed under a civil-service regulation of the most rigid character, so as to prevent the increase of the power of the national administration by the use of such additional government employees.

FIRST, *Money*—We demand a national currency, safe, sound, and flexible issued by the general government only, a full legal tender for all debts, public and private, and that without the use of banking corporations; a just, equitable, and efficient means of distribution direct to the people, at a tax not to exceed 2 percent, per annum, to be provided as set forth in the sub-treasury plan of the Farmers' Alliance, or a better system; also by payments in discharge of its obligations for public improvements.

   a. We demand free and unlimited coinage of silver and gold at the present legal ratio of 16 to 1.
   b. We demand that the amount of circulating medium be speedily increased to not less than $50 per capita.
   c. We demand a graduated income tax.
   d. We believe that the money of the country should be kept as much as possible in the hands of the people, and hence we demand that all State and national revenues shall be limited to the necessary expenses of the government, economically and honestly administered.
   e. We demand that postal savings banks be established by the government for the safe deposit of the earnings of the people and to facilitate exchange.

SECOND, *Transportation*—Transportation being a means of exchange and a public necessity, the government should own and operate the railroads in the interest of the people.

   a. The telegraph and telephone, like the post-office system, being a necessity for the transmission of news, should be owned and operated by the government in the interest of the people.

THIRD, *Land*—The land, including all the natural sources of wealth, is the heritage of the people, and should not be monopolized for speculative purposes, and alien ownership of land should be prohibited. All land now held by railroads and other corporations in excess of their actual needs, and all lands now owned by aliens should be reclaimed by the government and held for actual settlers only.

EXPRESSIONS OF SENTIMENTS

Your Committee on Platform and Resolutions beg leave unanimously to report the following: Whereas, Other questions have been presented for our consideration, we hereby submit the following, not as a part of the Platform of the People's Party, but as resolutions expressive of the sentiment of this Convention.

RESOLVED, That we demand a free ballot and a fair count in all elections and pledge ourselves to secure it to every legal voter without Federal Intervention, through the adoption by the States of the unperverted Australian or secret ballot system.

RESOLVED, That the revenue derived from a graduated income tax should be applied to the reduction of the burden of taxation now levied upon the domestic industries of this country.

RESOLVED, That we pledge our support to fair and liberal pensions to ex-Union soldiers and sailors.

RESOLVED, That we condemn the fallacy of protecting American labor under the present system, which opens our ports to the pauper and criminal classes of the world and crowds out our wage-earners; and we denounce the present ineffective laws against contract labor, and demand the further restriction of undesirable emigration.

RESOLVED, That we cordially sympathize with the efforts of organized workingmen to shorten the hours of labor, and demand a rigid enforcement of the existing eight-hour law on Government work, and ask that a penalty clause be added to the said law.

RESOLVED, That we regard the maintenance of a large standing army of mercenaries, known as the Pinkerton system, as a menace to our liberties, and we demand its abolition. . . .

RESOLVED, That we commend to the favorable consideration of the people and the reform press the legislative system known as the initiative and referendum.

RESOLVED, That we favor a constitutional provision limiting the office of President and Vice-President to one term, and providing for the election of Senators of the United States by a direct vote of the people.

RESOLVED, That we oppose any subsidy or national aid to any private corporation for any purpose.

RESOLVED, That this convention sympathizes with the Knights of Labor and their righteous contest with the tyrannical combine of clothing manufacturers of Rochester, and declare it to be a duty of all who hate tyranny and oppression to refuse to purchase the goods made by the said manufacturers, or to patronize any merchants who sell such goods.

Jane Addams (1860–1935)

In 1889, Jane Addams founded Hull House in Chicago. Hull House was part of the settlement house movement, which provided a place for

*immigrant women and children to stay while they were trying to adapt to
life in the United States. Settlement houses offered English and hygiene
lessons, after-school programs for children, and often training in job
skills, like sewing and bookbinding. Addams, like many other reformers of
her time, believed that philanthropic endeavors, such as Hull House,
would ease immigrants into American life and therefore serve as a
counterbalance to radical or anarchistic tendencies. Hull House was
founded only three years after the Haymarket Riots frightened many
middle-class Americans into believing that the influx of foreigners would
inevitably lead to violent revolution. Lightening the burdens and
hardships immigrants faced would give them reason to believe that they
could become part of American society. Reform defuses revolution.*

*Addams, of course, was not only operating from this conservative
view to thwart radical tendencies; she truly believed in helping people for
purely humanitarian purposes. Places like Hull House also provided job
opportunities for many women, and these reform-minded women later
became significant players in the suffrage movement. Jane Addams herself
was involved in both the women's suffrage and early civil rights
movements. She was one of the cofounders of the National Association for
the Advancement of Colored People (NAACP). In 1931, she was awarded
the Nobel Peace Prize. The following excerpts are from an address Jane
Addams delivered in 1892 that was later published in her book* Twenty
Years at Hull House.

The Subjective Necessity of Social Settlements, 1892

In a thousand voices singing the Hallelujah Chorus in Handel's "Messiah," it is
possible to distinguish the leading voices, but the differences of training and
cultivation between them and the voices of the chorus, are lost in the unity of
purpose and in the fact that they are all human voices lifted by a high motive.
This is a weak illustration of what a Settlement attempts to do. It aims, in a
measure, to develop whatever of social life its neighborhood may afford, to
focus and give form to that life, to bring to bear upon it the results of cultivation
and training; but it receives in exchange for the music of isolated voices the
volume and strength of the chorus. It is quite impossible for me to say in what
proportion or degree the subjective necessity which led to the opening of Hull-
House combined the three trends: first, the desire to interpret democracy in
social terms; secondly, the impulse beating at the very source of our lives, urging
us to aid in the race progress; and; thirdly, the Christian movement toward
humanitarianism. . . .

SOURCE: Jane Addams, *Twenty Years at Hull House* (New York: Macmillan, 1910), 99–100.

The Settlement then, is an experimental effort to aid in the solution of the social and industrial problems which are engendered by the modern conditions of life in a great city. It insists that these problems are not confined to any one portion of a city. It is an attempt to relieve, at the same time, the overaccumulation at one end of society and the destitution at the other; but it assumes that this overaccumulation and destitution is most sorely felt in the things that pertain to social and educational privileges. From its very nature it can stand for no political or social propaganda. It must, in a sense, give the warm welcome of an inn to all such propaganda, if perchance one of them be found an angel. The only thing to be dreaded in the Settlement is that it lose its flexibility, its power of quick adaptation, its readiness to change its methods as its environment may demand. It must be open to conviction and must have a deep and abiding sense of tolerance. It must be hospitable and ready for experiment. It should demand from its residents a scientific patience in the accumulation of facts and the steady holding of their sympathies as one of the best instruments for that accumulation. It must be grounded in a philosophy whose foundation is on the solidarity of the human race, a philosophy which will not waver when the race happens to be represented by a drunken woman or an idiot boy. Its residents must be emptied of all conceit of opinion and all self-assertion, and ready to arouse and interpret the public opinion of their neighborhood. They must be content to live quietly side by side with their neighbors, until they grow into a sense of relationship and mutual interests. Their neighbors are held apart by differences of race and language which the residents can more easily overcome. They are bound to see the needs of their neighborhood as a whole, to furnish data for legislation, and to use their influence to secure it. In short, residents are pledged to devote themselves to the duties of good citizenship and to the arousing of the social energies which too largely lie dormant in every neighborhood given over to industrialism. They are bound to regard the entire life of their city as organic, to make an effort to unify it, and to protest against its over-differentiation.

It is always easy to make all philosophy point one particular moral and all history adorn one particular tale; but I may be forgiven the reminder that the best speculative philosophy sets forth the solidarity of the human race; that the highest moralists have taught that without the advance and improvement of the whole, no man can hope for any lasting improvement in his own moral or material individual condition; and that the subjective necessity for Social Settlements is therefore identical with that necessity, which urges us on toward social and individual salvation.

Frances E. Willard (1839–1898)

After graduating from Northwestern Female College in 1859, Frances E. Willard taught for several years, traveled abroad, and eventually was offered the presidency of Evanston College for Ladies. When the college

*was absorbed by Northwestern University, Willard became dean of
women. In 1874, however, she gave up her academic career to devote
herself to the temperance crusade. As corresponding secretary for
the Woman's Christian Temperance Union (WCTU), she became
increasingly radical, eventually splitting with the organization's first
president, Annie Wittenmeyr, over the issue of women's suffrage. Against
Wittenmeyr's opposition, Willard argued that other reforms, especially
women's suffrage, should be linked to the temperance issue and therefore
be a central plank in the WCTU's platform. By 1879, her political
struggle with Wittenmeyr ended triumphantly for Willard, when she was
elected the organization's second president. In 1883, Willard founded the
World's Woman's Christian Temperance Union, which was the first
international women's organization. She also was one of the founders of
the Prohibition Party and the National Council of Women. She served as
the latter's first president from 1888 to 1890. Her attempt in 1892 to form
a coalition with the Populist Party failed, however. Through persistent
mobilization, political activism, lobbying of Congress, and putting
political pressure on senators and other influential politicians, the WCTU
was eventually instrumental in the passage and ratification in 1919 of the
Eighteenth Amendment, which prohibited the sale of alcohol in the
United States as of January 1, 1920. (The Twenty-first Amendment, in
1933, repealed prohibition.)*

*Willard's motto, "Do everything," which she refers to in this excerpt
from her 1893 presidential address to the WCTU, reflects her belief that
all reforms were interrelated. Throughout her activist career, she was as
ardent an advocate of women's suffrage, equal pay for equal work, and
other reforms as she was a champion of temperance.*

SPEECH TO THE WORLD'S WOMAN'S CHRISTIAN TEMPERANCE UNION, 1893

Beloved Comrades of the White Ribbon Army:

When we began the delicate, difficult, and dangerous operation of dissecting out
the alcohol nerve from the body politic, we did not realize the intricacy of the
undertaking nor the distances that must be traversed by the scalpel of investigation and research. In about seventy days from now, twenty years will have elapsed
since the call of battle sounded its bugle note among the homes and hearts of
Hillsboro, Ohio. We have all been refreshing our knowledge of those days by
reading the "Crusade Sketches" of its heroic leader, Mrs. Eliza J. Thompson, "the

SOURCE: Frances E. Willard, in *Women's Speeches Around the World*, "Gifts of Speech,"
Sweet Briar College, retrieved 3/14/2003 from http://gos.sbc.edu/.

mother of us all," and we know that but one thought, sentiment and purpose animated those saintly "Praying Bands" whose name will never die out from human history. "Brothers, we beg you not to drink and not to sell!" This was the one wailing note of these moral Paganinis, playing on one string. It caught the universal ear and set the key of that mighty orchestra, organised with so much toil and hardship, in which the tender and exalted strain of the Crusade violin still soars aloft, but upborne now by the clanging cornets of science, the deep trombones of legislation, and the thunderous drums of politics and parties. The "Do-Everything-Policy" was not of our choosing, but is an evolution as inevitable as any traced by the naturalist or described by the historian. Woman's genius for details, and her patient steadfastness in following the enemies of those she loves "through every lane of life," have led her to antagonise the alcohol habit and the liquor traffic just where they are, wherever that may be. If she does this, since they are everywhere, her policy will be "Do Everything."

A one-sided movement makes one-sided advocates. Virtues, like hounds, hunt in packs. Total abstinence is not the crucial virtue in life that excuses financial crookedness, defamation of character, or habits of impurity. The fact that one's father was, and one's self is, a bright and shining light in the total abstinence galaxy, does not give one a vantage ground for high-handed behaviour toward those who have not been trained to the special virtue that forms the central idea of the Temperance Movement. We have known persons who, because they had "never touched a drop of liquor," set themselves up as if they belonged to a royal line, but whose tongues were as biting as alcohol itself, and whose narrowness had no competitor save a straight line. An all-round movement can only be carried forward by all-round advocates; a scientific age requires the study of every subject in its correlations. It was once supposed that light, heat, and electricity were wholly separate entities; it is now believed and practically proved that they are but different modes of motion. Standing in the valley we look up and think we see an isolated mountain; climbing to its top we see that it is but one member of a range of mountains many of them of well-nigh equal altitude. . . .

Joseph Cook, that devoted friend of every good cause has wisely said: "If England were at war with Russia, and the latter were to have several allies, it would obviously be necessary for England to attack the allies as well as the principal enemy. Not to do this would be foolishness, and might be suicide. In the conflict with the liquor traffic, the policy of the W.C.T.U. is to attack not only the chief foe, but also its notorious and open allies. This is the course dictated not only by common sense, but by absolute necessity. If the home is to be protected, not only must the dram-shop be made an outlaw, but its allies, the gambling hells, the houses of unreportable infamy, the ignorance of the general population as to alcoholics and other narcotics, the timidity of trade, the venality of portions of the press, and especially the subserviency of political parties to the liquor traffic, must be assailed as confederates of the chief enemy of the home. . . . It is certain that the broad and progressive policy of the W.C.T.U. in the United States makes the whiskey rings and time-serving politicians greatly dread its influence. They honour the Union by frequent and bitter attacks. It is a recognised power in international affairs. If its policy were made narrow and non-partisan, its influence would immensely wane in practical matters of great importance. . . .

Let us not be disconcerted, but stand bravely by that blessed trinity of movements, Prohibition, Woman's Liberation and Labour's uplift.

Everything is not in the Temperance Reform, but the Temperance Reform should be in everything.

There is no better motto for the "Do-Everything-Policy," than this which we are saying by our deeds: "Make a chain, for the land is full of bloody crimes and the city of violence."

If we can remember this simple rule, it will do much to unravel the mystery of the much controverted "Do-Everything-Policy," viz: that every question of practical philanthropy or reform has its temperance aspect, and with that we are to deal. . . .

The Temperance cause started out . . . alone, but mighty forces have joined us in the long march. We are now in the midst of the Waterloo battle, and in the providence of God the Temperance army will not have to fight that out all by itself. For Science has come up with its glittering contingent, political economy deploys its legions, the woman question brings an Amazonian army upon the field, and the stout ranks of labor stretch away far as the eye can reach. As in the old Waterloo against Napoleon, so now against the Napoleon of the liquor traffic, no force is adequate except the allied forces. . . .

The three requisites for success are ability, availability, and responsibility. The first is native, the second acquired, the last conferred. In every White Ribboner, whose work is worth the name, these three must meet, and the greatest outcome of the crusade in its original and organic form was that it gave to women of ability the schooling in which they acquired availability, and helped them to the positions in which, through responsibility, they grew from what they were to what they had the power to be. . . .

The history of the reformer, whether man or woman, on any line of action is but this: when he sees it all alone he is a fanatic; when a good many see it with him they are enthusiasts; when all see it he is a hero. The gradations are as clearly marked by which he ascends from zero to hero, as the lines of latitude from the North Pole to the Equator. . . .

Concerning the Temperance Movement in our land and throughout the world to-day, the pessimist says—and says truly— "There was never so much liquor manufactured in any one year since time began as in the year 1893, and as a consequence never did so much liquor flow down the people's throats as in this same year of grace." "But," says the optimist, "There is each year a larger acreage from which the brewer and distiller may gather the golden grain and luscious fruits, there are more people to imbibe the exhilarating poison; but, per contra, there was never so much intelligent thinking in any one year as to the drink delusion, there were never so many children studying in the schools the laws written in their members, there were never such gatherings together of temperance people to consult on the two great questions what to do and what not to do as in this year; there was never such a volume of experience and expert testimony and knowledge so varied, so complete, as we have had this year at the International Congress; there were never so many total abstainers in proportion to the population, never so many intelligent people who could render a reason scientific, ethical, aesthetic, for their total abstinence faith as now; there were never so many pulpits from which to bombard the liquor traffic and the drink habit; there were never so many journalists who had a friendly word to say for the Temperance Reform; there was never such a stirring up of temperance politics; for the foremost historic nation of the world, Great Britain, has this year, for the first time, adopted as a plank in the platform of the dominant party the principle that the people shall themselves decide whether or not they want the public house; and as a natural consequence of this political action there was never a public sentiment so respectful toward the Temperance Reform. The great world-brain is becoming saturated with the idea that it is reasonable and kind to let strong drink alone. The vastness of these changes can only be measured by the remembrance that a few generations ago these same drinks were the accredited emblems in cot and palace alike, of hospitality, kindness, and good-will.

So far as the White Ribbon movement is concerned, this has been its best and brightest year from the outlook of the World's W.C.T.U., and that is the only point of view that is adequate. How little did they dream, those devoted women of the praying bands, who with their patient footsteps bridged the distance between home and saloon, and in their little despised groups poured out their souls to God, and their pitiful plea into the ears of men, that the "Movement" would be systematized twenty years later into an organization known and loved by the best men and women in every civilized nation on the earth; and that its heroic missionaries would be obliged to circumnavigate the globe in order to visit the outposts of the Society. How little did they dream that in the year of the World's Columbian Exposition well nigh half a million of children would send their autographs on the triple pledge cards of our Loyal Temperance Legions, and Sunday School Department; that we should have a publishing house, owned and conducted by the Society itself, from which more than a hundred million pages of the literature of light and leading should go forth this year; how little could they have conceived of the significance that is wrapt up in the lengthening folds of the Polyglot Petition, signed and circulated in fifty languages, and containing the signatures and attestations of between three and four million of the best people that live, praying for the abolition of the alcohol traffic, the opium traffic, and the licensed traffic in degraded women. How little they dreamed of that great movement by which the study of physiology and hygiene were to bring the arrest of thought to millions of young minds concerning the true inwardness of all narcotic poisons in their effects on the body and the brain. How "far beyond their thought" the enfranchisement of women in New Zealand and Wyoming, Kansas and "Michigan, my Michigan!" How inconceivable to them the vision of our House Beautiful reared in the heart of the world's most electric city, and sending forth its influence to the furthest corner of the globe. How little did they dream that the echo of their hymns should yet be heard and heeded by a woman whose lineage, and the prowess of whose historic name may be traced through centuries, and that not alone from the cottage and the homestead, but from the emblazoned walls of splendid castles, should be driven the cup that seems to cheer, but at the last inebriates. But we must remember that, after all, these are but the days of small beginnings compared with what 20 more years shall show. Doubtless if we could see the power to which this movement of women's hearts for the protection of their hearthstones shall attain in the next generation, the inspiration of that knowledge would exhilarate us beyond that which is good for such steady patient workers as we have been, are, and wish to be; but I dare prophesy that twenty years from now woman will be fully panoplied in the politics and government of all English-speaking nations; she will find her glad footsteps impeded by no artificial barriers, but whatever she can do well she will be free to do in the enlightened age of worship, helpfulness and brotherhood, toward which we move with steps accelerated far beyond our ken. The momentum of the centuries is in the widening, deepening current of 19th century reform; the 20th century's dawn shall witness our compensations and reprisals, and as these increase humanity shall pay back into the mother-heart of woman its unmeasured penitence and unfathomed regret for all that she has missed (and through her, every son and daughter that she has brought into the world), by reason of the awful mistake by which, in the age of force, man substituted his "thus far and no farther," in place of the "thus far and no farther" of God; one founded in a selfish and ignorant view of woman's powers, the other giving her what every sentient being ought to have—a fair field and a free course to run and be glorified.

The Prohibition agitation in America has not been as great in the past year as formerly, and the reasons are not far to seek. A presidential campaign always lowers the moral atmosphere for a year before it begins and a year after it is over. Legislators become timid, politicians proceed to "hedge," journalists, with an eye to the loaves and fishes, furl their sails concerning issues that have at best only a fighting chance; the world, the flesh, and the devil get their innings, and the time is not yet. In the past year the attention of the nation has been focused on the World's Fair and the endless difficulties to which that has given birth. There has been an incalculable amount of ill-will set in motion as the result of personal financial interest and ignoble ambition. All this savours not the things of God or of humanity. The re-adjustment of political parties is still inchoate; men's hearts are failing them for fear; leaders in the traditional party of moral ideas have thrown off all disguises and grounded any weapons of rebellion they may once have lifted against the liquor traffic. The financial panic has riveted the attention of the public on their own dangers and disasters, and the spirit of money-making has lamentably invaded the ranks of the temperance army itself; but prohibition is as lively an issue to-day as emancipation was in 1856; an issue that stirs such deadly hatred is by no means dead. It is still quick with fighting blood, and its enemies know this even better than its friends. . . .

The economic view of prohibition is one that appeals to the largest number of our people, and none will deny that more and more they are separating into two camps, the industrious and thrifty favouring prohibition, the idle and spendthrift class opposing it. This is no doubt the most helpful report that can be made upon the present situation. The general drift, or as a great statesman in England has said, "The flowing tide's with us." Those who let strong drink alone must always be the most forceful and in the long run successful and potential portion of the country. Our fathers were as good as we, but they took no stand against the drink habit or the liquor traffic. There is hardly a woman here upon the side-board of whose grandfather's home would not have been found a decanter if not a demijohn. The same influences that have brought us out of the passive into the active voice may be trusted steadily to swell the number of recruits who shall join their intelligence, energy, talents, and sobriety with ours. The Temperance cause has everything to gain and nothing to lose from free discussion, from experimental study of its results, whether physical or financial, moral or mercantile, ethical or aesthetic. . . .

A Bill has been for many years before Congress for the appointment of a commission on the investigation of the liquor traffic. . . . The vast importance of this measure is demonstrated by the ceaseless efforts of the whiskey power to defeat its passage, in which they have thus far been successful, and are likely to be for many years to come. The power of the saloon is nowhere more conspicuously manifested than in the annual defeat of this great measure. Congress has appointed commissions on well-nigh every conceivable subject,—the investigation of the slums of our cities, of sweating establishments, of agricultural interests, of farm mortgages, of immigration, quarantine, railroads, monetary problems, cattle diseases, fisheries, and I know not what besides; but to investigate the liquor monopoly is to touch the very ark of the covenant with hell, and agreement with damnation to which the American people has been sworn by their political leaders. In spite of all this, we have gained an intelligent idea of the business from the internal revenue reports and from state and police records; but what we want is the attestation of the national government to the truth of these figures of perdition. If Congress persists in its refusal, why shall not the W.C.T.U. make a sweeping, and thorough investigation of the liquor traffic? Undoubtedly the political machinery of state and nation would place all possible obstacles in our way; but we have a personnel in every community throughout the republic, than which none that exists is more intelligent and devoted. Such a commission would be absolutely reliable so far as information could be obtained, and unless Congress in creating such a commission would agree to place upon it two or three prohibitionists or White Ribbon women the returns would be unreliable; for no politicians of the two leading parties would dare to weaken their great stronghold—the saloon. . . .

Mrs. Frances Belford of Denver, Colorado, has tabulated the following suggestive specifications. . . .

COMMISSION TO INVESTIGATE THE LIQUOR TRAFFIC

In relation:

- to Crime.
- to Divorce.
- to Education.
- to Alms houses.
- to Asylums.
- to Charitable Institutions and organized Charities.
- to Adulteration.
- to Society or the status of social drinking.
- to Police expenses.
- to Revenue—Municipal, State, Nation.
- to Disease—Heredity. Acquired.
- to Attitude of the Church by denomination.
- to Number of Professors of Religion who are actual Prohibitionists.
- to Number who are not.
- to Statistics of homes ruined.
- to Children at work who ought to be in school, where whiskey is the direct cause of absence.
- to Mortgages.
- to Number of women impoverished and self-supporting.
- to Ownership of Property by professed Christians, who lease it for saloon and other immoral purposes.
- to Hindrances to Prohibition.
- to Home Missions.
- to Sunday Schools.

Booker T. Washington (1856–1915)

Booker T. Washington was one of the leading spokesmen for African Americans in the late nineteenth and early twentieth centuries. Born a slave, Washington believed deeply in the indispensable importance of education for the advancement of freedmen. In 1881, he became the first principal of the Normal School for Negroes in Tuskegee, Alabama. Over the next several years, as Washington presided over the transformation of this school into the Tuskegee Institute, he became one of the most influential voices promoting African American education.

Washington believed, however, that blacks should not seek education for education's sake, and that they should not bother learning Latin,

Greek, philosophy, or other esoteric subjects. Rather, they should concern themselves with technical education, so that they could become more productive members of society and enter occupations that would advance them economically. The Tuskegee Institute emphasized mechanics and agricultural economics—subjects that were practical.

In his famous "Atlanta Compromise" speech of 1895 at the Cotton States Exposition, Washington urged blacks to accept the Jim Crow laws and acquiesce in segregation, and he urged whites to encourage black economic opportunity. This would be the surest path to achieving equality in the United States. By concentrating on economic betterment, the former slaves would rise up the ladder to such a degree that whites would eventually bestow political and civil rights upon them. "No race that has anything to contribute to the markets of the world is long in any degree ostracized." This pragmatic, compliant philosophy endeared him to whites but also earned him the opprobrium of many of his African American contemporaries. Black leaders such as Ida B. Wells-Barnett and W. E. B. DuBois, concerned with white racism and the rise in lynchings, believed that Washington's accommodationist philosophy made things worse.

Cast Down Your Bucket Where You Are, 1895

. . . .One-third of the population of the South is of the Negro race. No enterprise seeking the material, civil, or moral welfare of this section can disregard this element of our population and reach the highest success. I but convey to you, Mr. President and Directors, the sentiment of the masses of my race when I say that in no way have the value and manhood of the American Negro been more fittingly and generously recognized than by the managers of this magnificent Exposition at every stage of its progress. It is a recognition that will do more to cement the friendship of the two races than any occurrence since the dawn of our freedom.

Not only this, but the opportunity here afforded will awaken among us a new era of industrial progress. Ignorant and inexperienced, it is not strange that in the first years of our new life we began at the top instead of at the bottom; that a seat in Congress or the state legislature was more sought than real estate or industrial skill; that the political convention or stump speaking had more attractions than starting a dairy farm or truck garden.

A ship lost at sea for many days suddenly sighted a friendly vessel. From the mast of the unfortunate vessel was seen a signal, "Water, water; we die of thirst!" The answer from the friendly vessel at once came back, "Cast down your bucket where you are." A second time the signal, "Water, water; send us water!" ran up from the distressed vessel, and was answered, "Cast down your bucket where you

SOURCE: Louis R. Harlan, ed., *The Booker T. Washington Papers*, vol. 3 (Urbana: University of Illinois Press, 1974), 583–587.

are." And a third and fourth signal for water was answered, "Cast down your bucket where you are." The captain of the distressed vessel, at last heeding the injunction, cast down his bucket, and it came up full of fresh, sparkling water from the mouth of the Amazon River. To those of my race who depend on bettering their condition in a foreign land or who underestimate the importance of cultivating friendly relations with the Southern white man, who is their next-door neighbor, I would say: "Cast down your bucket where you are"— cast it down in making friends in every manly way of the people of all races by whom we are surrounded.

Cast it down in agriculture, mechanics, in commerce, in domestic service, and in the professions. And in this connection it is well to bear in mind that whatever other sins the South may be called to bear, when it comes to business, pure and simple, it is in the South that the Negro is given a man's chance in the commercial world, and in nothing is this Exposition more eloquent than in emphasizing this chance. Our greatest danger is that in the great leap from slavery to freedom we may overlook the fact that the masses of us are to live by the productions of our hands, and fail to keep in mind that we shall prosper in proportion as we learn to dignify and glorify common labour, and put brains and skill into the common occupations of life; shall prosper in proportion as we learn to draw the line between the superficial and the substantial, the ornamental gewgaws of life and the useful. No race can prosper till it learns that there is as much dignity in tilling a field as in writing a poem. It is at the bottom of life we must begin, and not at the top. Nor should we permit our grievances to overshadow our opportunities.

To those of the white race who look to the incoming of those of foreign birth and strange tongue and habits for the prosperity of the South, were I permitted I would repeat what I say to my own race, "Cast down your bucket where you are." Cast it down among the eight millions of Negroes whose habits you know, whose fidelity and love you have tested in days when to have proved treacherous meant the ruin of your firesides. Cast down your bucket among these people who have, without strikes and labour wars, tilled your fields, cleared your forests, builded your railroads and cities, and brought forth treasures from the bowels of the earth, and helped make possible this magnificent representation of the progress of the South. Casting down your bucket among my people, helping and encouraging them as you are doing on these grounds, and to education of head, hand, and heart, you will find that they will buy your surplus land, make blossom the waste places in your fields, and run your factories. While doing this, you can be sure in the future, as in the past, that you and your families will be surrounded by the most patient, faithful, law-abiding, and unresentful people that the world has seen. As we have proved our loyalty to you in the past, in nursing your children, watching by the sick-bed of your mothers and fathers, and often following them with tear-dimmed eyes to their graves, so in the future, in our humble way, we shall stand by you with a devotion that no foreigner can approach, ready to lay down our lives, if need be, in defense of yours, interlacing our industrial, commercial, civil, and religious life with yours in a way that shall make the interests of both races one. In all things that are purely social we can be as separate as the fingers, yet one as the hand in all things essential to mutual progress. . . .

The wisest among my race understand that the agitation of questions of social equality is the extremest folly, and that progress in the enjoyment of all the privileges that will come to us must be the result of severe and constant struggle rather than of artificial forcing. No race that has anything to contribute to the markets of the world is long in any degree ostracized. It is important and right that all privileges of the law be ours, but it is vastly more important that we be prepared for the exercise of these privileges. The opportunity to earn a dollar in a factory just now is worth infinitely more than the opportunity to spend a dollar in an opera-house.

In conclusion, may I repeat that nothing in thirty years has given us more hope and encouragement, and drawn us so near to you of the white race, as this opportunity offered by the Exposition; and here bending, as it were, over the altar that represents the results of the struggles of your race and mine, both starting practically empty-handed three decades ago, I pledge that in your effort to work out the great and intricate problem which God has laid at the doors of the South, you shall have at all times the patient, sympathetic help of my race; only let this be constantly in mind, that, while from representations in these buildings of the product of field, of forest, of mine, of factory, letters, and art, much good will come, yet far above and beyond material benefits will be that higher good, that, let us pray God, will come, in a blotting out of sectional differences and racial animosities and suspicions, in a determination to administer absolute justice, in a willing obedience among all classes to the mandates of law. This, coupled with our material prosperity, will bring into our beloved South a new heaven and a new earth.

W. E. B. DuBois (1868–1963)

The first African American to earn a PhD from Harvard, W. E. B. DuBois was one of the most influential figures in the fight for African American rights. Throughout his long life, DuBois fought incessantly against racism and passionately argued that blacks should demand full and immediate political, social, and civil rights. He was a harsh critic of Booker T. Washington's accommodationist philosophy and was instrumental in the founding of the Niagara Movement, out of which the National Association for the Advancement of Colored People (NAACP) was formed in 1909. In his 1903 book, The Souls of Black Folk, *DuBois called on the "talented tenth" of African Americans not to settle for anything less than a full academic education and to demand what is theirs by right. For*

25 years, DuBois was the editor-in-chief of the NAACP publication The
Crisis, *in which his stinging editorials frequently caused division within
the organization. DuBois had no objections to whites being active
members of the NAACP, but he believed they should be in subordinate,
not leadership, roles. As time went by, DuBois felt increasingly alienated
in the United States, and toward the end of his life he moved to Ghana,
became a Ghanaian citizen, and joined the Communist Party. He died on
the eve of the March on Washington in August 1963, and as news of his
death spread amid the marchers gathering at the Lincoln Memorial to
listen to Martin Luther King Jr.'s "I Have A Dream" speech, there was a
sense that the "torch had been passed."*

"Of Mr. Booker T. Washington and Others," 1903

. . . .Easily the most striking thing in the history of the American Negro since 1876
is the ascendancy of Mr. Booker T. Washington. It began at the time when war
memories and ideals were rapidly passing; a day of astonishing commercial development was dawning; a sense of doubt and hesitation overtook the freedmen's
sons,—then it was that his leading began. Mr. Washington came, with a single definite programme, at the psychological moment when the nation was a little
ashamed of having bestowed so much sentiment on Negroes, and was concentrating its energies on Dollars. His programme of industrial education, conciliation
of the South, and submission and silence as to civil and political rights, was not
wholly original; the Free Negroes from 1830 up to wartime had striven to build
industrial schools, and the American Missionary Association had from the first
taught various trades; and Price and others had sought a way of honorable
alliance with the best of the Southerners. But Mr. Washington first indissolubly
linked these things; he put enthusiasm, unlimited energy, and perfect faith into
this programme, and changed it from a by-path into a veritable Way of Life. And
the tale of the methods by which he did this is a fascinating study of human life.

It startled the nation to hear a Negro advocating such a programme after
many decades of bitter complaint; it startled and won the applause of the South,
it interested and won the admiration of the North; and after a confused murmur of protest, it silenced if it did not convert the Negroes themselves.

To gain the sympathy and cooperation of the various elements comprising
the white South was Mr. Washington's first task; and this, at the time Tuskegee
was founded, seemed, for a black man, well-nigh impossible. And yet ten years
later it was done in the word spoken at Atlanta: "In all things purely social we

SOURCE: W. E. B. DuBois, *The Souls of Black Folk*, ed. David W. Blight and Robert Gooding-
Williams (Boston: Bedford, 1977), 62–72.

can be as separate as the five fingers, and yet one as the hand in all things essential to mutual progress." This "Atlanta Compromise" is by all odds the most notable thing in Mr. Washington's career. The South interpreted it in different ways: the radicals received it as a complete surrender of the demand for civil and political equality; the conservatives, as a generously conceived working basis for mutual understanding. So both approved it, and today its author is certainly the most distinguished Southerner since Jefferson Davis, and the one with the largest personal following.

Next to this achievement comes Mr. Washington's work in gaining place and consideration in the North. Others less shrewd and tactful had formerly essayed to sit on these two stools and had fallen between them; but as Mr. Washington knew the heart of the South from birth and training, so by singular insight he intuitively grasped the spirit of the age which was dominating the North. And so thoroughly did he learn the speech and thought of triumphant commercialism, and the ideals of material prosperity that the picture of a lone black boy poring over a French grammar amid the weeds and dirt of a neglected home soon seemed to him the acme of absurdities. One wonders what Socrates and St. Francis of Assisi would say to this.

And yet this very singleness of vision and thorough oneness with his age is a mark of the successful man. It is as though Nature must needs make men narrow in order to give them force. So Mr. Washington's cult has gained unquestioning followers, his work has wonderfully prospered, his friends are legion, and his enemies are confounded. To-day he stands as the one recognized spokesman of his ten million fellows, and one of the most notable figures in a nation of seventy millions. One hesitates, therefore, to criticise a life which, beginning with so little has done so much. And yet the time is come when one may speak in all sincerity and utter courtesy of the mistakes and shortcomings of Mr. Washington's career, as well as of his triumphs, without being thought captious or envious, and without forgetting that it is easier to do ill than well in the world. . . .

Among his own people . . . Mr. Washington has encountered the strongest and most lasting opposition, amounting at times to bitterness, and even to-day continuing strong and insistent even though largely silenced in outward expression by the public opinion of the nation. Some of this opposition is, of course, mere envy; the disappointment of displaced demagogues and the spite of narrow minds. But aside from this, there is among educated and thoughtful colored men in all parts of the land a feeling of deep regret, sorrow, and apprehension at the wide currency and ascendancy which some of Mr. Washington's theories have gained. These same men admire his sincerity of purpose, and are willing to forgive much to honest endeavor which is doing something worth the doing. They cooperate with Mr. Washington as far as they conscientiously can; and, indeed, it is no ordinary tribute to this man's tact and power that, steering as he must between so many diverse interests and opinions, he so largely retains the respect of all.

But the hushing of the criticism of honest opponents is a dangerous thing. It leads some of the best of the critics to unfortunate silence and paralysis of effort, and others to burst into speech so passionately and intemperately as to lose listeners. Honest and earnest criticism from those whose interests are most nearly touched,—criticism of writers by readers, of government by those governed, of leaders by those led, —this is the soul of democracy and the safeguard of modern society. If the best of the American Negroes receive by outer pressure a leader whom they had not recognized before, manifestly there is here a certain palpable gain. Yet there is also irreparable loss,—a loss of that peculiarly valuable education which a group receives when by search and criticism it finds and commissions its own leaders. The way in which this is done is at once the most elementary and the nicest problem of social growth. History is but the record of such group-leadership; and yet how infinitely changeful is its type and character! And of all types and kinds, what can be more instructive than the leadership of a group within a group?—that curious double movement where real progress may be negative and actual advance be relative retrogression. All this is the social student's inspiration and despair.

Now in the past the American Negro has had instructive experience in the choosing of group leaders, founding thus a peculiar dynasty which in the light of present conditions is worth while studying. When sticks and stones and beasts form the sole environment of a people, their attitude is largely one of determined opposition to and conquest of natural forces. But when to earth and brute is added an environment of men and ideas, then the attitude of the imprisoned group may take three main forms,—a feeling of revolt and revenge; an attempt to adjust all thought and action to the will of the greater group; or, finally, a determined effort at self-realization and self-development despite environing opinion. The influence of all of these attitudes at various times can be traced in the history of the American Negro, and in the evolution of his successive leaders.

Before 1750, while the fire of African freedom still burned in the veins of the slaves, there was in all leadership or attempted leadership but the one motive of revolt and revenge,—typified in the terrible Maroons, the Danish blacks, and Cato of Stono, and veiling all the Americas in fear of insurrection. The liberalizing tendencies of the latter half of the eighteenth century brought, along with kindlier relations between black and white, thoughts of ultimate adjustment and assimilation. Such aspiration was especially voiced in the earnest songs of Phyllis [Wheatley], in the martyrdom of Attucks, the fighting of Salem and Poor, the intellectual accomplishments of Banneker and Derham, and the political demands of the Cuffes.

Stern financial and social stress after the war cooled much of the previous humanitarian ardor. The disappointment and impatience of the Negroes at the persistence of slavery and serfdom voiced itself in two movements. The slaves in the South, aroused undoubtedly by vague rumors of the Haitian revolt, made three fierce attempts at insurrection,—in 1800 under Gabriel in Virginia, in 1822 under Vesey in Carolina, and in 1831 again in Virginia under the terrible Nat Turner. In the Free States, on the other hand, a new and curious attempt at self-development was made. In Philadelphia and New York color-prescription led to a withdrawal of Negro communicants from white churches and the formation of a peculiar socio-religious institution among the Negroes known as the African Church,—an organization still living and controlling in its various branches over a million of men.

Walker's wild appeal against the trend of the times showed how the world was changing after the coming of the cotton-gin. By 1830 slavery seemed hopelessly fastened on the South, and the slaves thoroughly cowed into submission. The free Negroes of the North, inspired by the mulatto immigrants from the West Indies, began to change the basis of their demands; they recognized the slavery of slaves, but insisted that they themselves were freemen, and sought assimilation and amalgamation with the nation on the same terms with other men. Thus, Forten and Purvis of Philadelphia, Shad of Wilmington, Du Bois of New Haven, Barbadoes of Boston, and others, strove singly and together as men, they said, not as slaves; as "people of color," not as "Negroes." The trend of the times, however, refused them recognition save in individual and exceptional cases, considered them as one with all the despised blacks, and they soon found themselves striving to keep even the rights they formerly had of voting and working and moving as freemen. Schemers of migration and colonization arose among them; but these they refused to entertain, and they eventually turned to the Abolition movement as a final refuge.

Here, led by Remond, Nell, Wells-Brown, and Douglass, a new period of self-assertion and self-development dawned. To be sure, ultimate freedom and assimilation was the ideal before the leaders, but the assertion of the manhood rights of the Negro by himself was the main reliance, and John Brown's raid was the extreme of its logic. After the war and emancipation, the great form of Frederick Douglass, the greatest of American Negro leaders, still led the host. Self-assertion, especially in political lines, was the main programme, and behind Douglass came Elliot, Bruce, and Langston, and the Reconstruction politicians, and, less conspicuous but of greater social significance Alexander Crummell and Bishop Daniel Payne.

Then came the Revolution of 1876, the suppression of the Negro votes, the changing and shifting of ideals, and the seeking of new lights in the great night. Douglass, in his old age, still bravely stood for the ideals of his early manhood,— ultimate assimilation through self-assertion, and no other terms. For a time Price arose as a new leader, destined, it seemed, not to give up, but to re-state the old ideals in a form less repugnant to the white South. But he passed away in his prime. Then came the new leader. Nearly all the former ones had become leaders by the silent suffrage of their fellows, had sought to lead their own people alone, and were usually, save Douglass, little known outside their race. But Booker T. Washington arose as essentially the leader not of one race but of two,—a compromiser between the South, the North, and the Negro. Naturally the Negroes resented, at first bitterly, signs of compromise which surrendered their civil and political rights, even though this was to be exchanged for larger chances of economic development. The rich and dominating North, however, was not only weary of the race problem, but was investing largely in Southern enterprises, and welcomed any method of peaceful cooperation. Thus, by national opinion, the Negroes began to recognize Mr. Washington's leadership; and the voice of criticism was hushed.

Mr. Washington represents in Negro thought the old attitude of adjustment and submission; but adjustment at such a peculiar time as to make his programme unique. This is an age of unusual economic development, and Mr. Washington's programme naturally takes an economic cast, becoming a gospel of Work and Money to such an extent as apparently almost completely to overshadow the higher aims of life. Moreover, this is an age when the more advanced races are coming in closer contact with the less developed races, and the race-feeling is therefore intensified; and Mr. Washington's programme practically accepts the alleged inferiority of the Negro races. Again, in our own land, the reaction from the sentiment of war time has given impetus to race-prejudice against Negroes, and Mr. Washington withdraws many of the high demands of Negroes as men and American citizens. In other periods of intensified prejudice all the Negro's tendency to self-assertion has been called forth; at this period a policy of submission is advocated. In the history of nearly all other races and peoples the doctrine preached at such crises has been that manly self-respect is worth more than lands and houses, and that a people who voluntarily surrender such respect, or cease striving for it, are not worth civilizing.

In answer to this, it has been claimed that the Negro can survive only through submission. Mr. Washington distinctly asks that black people give up, at least for the present, three things,—

First, political power,
Second, insistence on civil rights,
Third, higher education of Negro youth,

—and concentrate all their energies on industrial education, the accumulation of wealth, and the conciliation of the South. This policy has been courageously and insistently advocated for over fifteen years, and has been triumphant for perhaps ten years. As a result of this tender of the palm-branch, what has been the return? In these years there have occurred:

1. The disfranchisement of the Negro.
2. The legal creation of a distinct status of civil inferiority for the Negro.
3. The steady withdrawal of aid from institutions for the higher training of the Negro.

These movements are not, to be sure, direct results of Mr. Washington's teachings; but his propaganda has, without a shadow of doubt, helped their speedier accomplishment. The question then comes: Is it possible, and probable, that nine millions of men can make effective progress in economic lines if they are deprived of political rights, made a servile caste, and allowed only the most meagre chance for developing their exceptional men? If history and reason give any distinct answer to these questions, it is an emphatic No. And Mr. Washington thus faces the triple paradox of his career:

1. He is striving nobly to make Negro artisans business men and property-owners; but it is utterly impossible, under modern competitive methods, for

workingmen and property-owners to defend their rights and exist without the right of suffrage.

2. He insists on thrift and self-respect, but at the same time counsels a silent submission to civic inferiority such as is bound to sap the manhood of any race in the long run.

3. He advocates common-school and industrial training, and depreciates institutions of higher learning; but neither the Negro common-schools, nor Tuskegee itself, could remain open a day were it not for teachers trained in Negro colleges, or trained by their graduates.

This triple paradox in Mr. Washington's position is the object of criticism by two classes of colored Americans. One class is spiritually descended from Toussaint the Savior, through Gabriel, Vesey, and Turner, and they represent the attitude of revolt and revenge; they hate the white South blindly and distrust the white race generally, and so far as they agree on definite action, think that the Negro's only hope lies in emigration beyond the borders of the United States. And yet, by the irony of fate, nothing has more effectually made this programme seem hopeless than the recent course of the United States toward weaker and darker peoples in the West Indies, Hawaii, and the Philippines,—for where in the world may we go and be safe from lying and brute Force?

The other class of Negroes who cannot agree with Mr. Washington has hitherto said little aloud. They deprecate the sight of scattered counsels, of internal disagreement; and especially they dislike making their just criticism of a useful and earnest man an excuse for a general discharge of venom from small-minded opponents. Nevertheless, the questions involved are so fundamental and serious that it is difficult to see how men like the Grimkes, Kelly Miller, J. W. E. Bowen, and other representatives of this group, can much longer be silent. Such men feel in conscience bound to ask of this nation three things.

1. The right to vote.
2. Civic equality.
3. The education of youth according to ability.

They acknowledge Mr. Washington's invaluable service in counselling patience and courtesy in such demands; they do not ask that ignorant black men vote when ignorant whites are debarred, or that any reasonable restrictions in the suffrage should not be applied; they know that the low social level or the mass of the race is responsible for much discrimination against it, but they also know, and the nation knows, that relentless color-prejudice is more often a cause than a result of the Negro's degradation; they seek the abatement of this relic or barbarism, and not its systematic encouragement and pampering by all agencies of social power from the Associated Press to the Church of Christ. They advocate, with Mr. Washington, a broad system of Negro common schools supplemented by thorough industrial training; but they are surprised that a man of Mr. Washington's insight cannot see that no such educational system ever has rested or can rest on any other basis than that of the well-equipped college and university, and they insist that there is a demand for a few such institutions throughout the South to train the best of the Negro youth as teachers, professional men, and leaders.

This group of men honor Mr. Washington for his attitude of conciliation toward the white South; they accept the "Atlanta Compromise" in its broadest interpretation; they recognize, with him, many signs of promise, many men of high purpose and fair judgment, in this section; they know that no easy task has been laid upon a region already tottering under heavy burdens. But, nevertheless, they insist that the way to truth and right lies in straightforward honesty, not in indiscriminate flattery; in praising those of the South who do well and criticising uncompromisingly those who do ill; in taking advantage of the opportunities at hand and urging their fellows to do the same, but at the same time in remembering that only a firm adherence to their higher ideals and aspirations will ever keep those ideals within the realm of possibility. They do not expect that the free right to vote, to enjoy civic rights, and to be educated, will come in a moment; they do not expect to see the bias and prejudices of years disappear at the blast of a trumpet; but they are absolutely certain that the way for a people to gain their reasonable rights is not by voluntarily throwing them away and insisting that they do not want them; that the way for a people to gain respect is not by continually belittling and ridiculing themselves; that, on the contrary, Negroes must insist continually, in season and out of season, that voting is necessary to modern manhood, that color discrimination is barbarism, and that black boys need education as well as white boys.

In failing thus to state plainly and unequivocally the legitimate demands of their people, even at the cost of opposing an honored leader, the thinking classes of American Negroes would shirk a heavy responsibility,—a responsibility to themselves, a responsibility to the struggling masses, a responsibility to the darker races of men whose future depends so largely on this American experiment, but especially a responsibility to this nation,—this common Fatherland. It is wrong to encourage a man or a people in evil-doing; it is wrong to aid and abet a national crime simply because it is unpopular not to do so. The growing spirit of kindliness and reconciliation between the North and South after the frightful difference of a generation ago ought to be a source of deep congratulation to all, and especially to those whose mistreatment caused the war; but if that reconciliation is to be marked by the industrial slavery and civic death of those same black men, with permanent legislation into a position of inferiority, then those black men, if they are really men, are called upon by every consideration of patriotism and loyalty to oppose such a course by all civilized methods, even though such opposition involves disagreement with Mr. Booker T. Washington. We have no right to sit silently by while the inevitable seeds are sown for a harvest of disaster to our children, black and white.

First, it is the duty of black men to judge the South discriminatingly. The present generation of Southerners are not responsible for the past, and they should not be blindly hated or blamed for it. Furthermore, to no class is the indiscriminate endorsement of the recent course of the South toward Negroes more nauseating than to the best thought of the South. The South is not "solid";

it is a land in the ferment of social change, wherein forces of all kinds are fighting for supremacy; and to praise the ill the South is to-day perpetrating is just as wrong as to condemn the good. Discriminating and broad-minded criticism is what the South needs,—needs it for the sake of her own white sons and daughters, and for the insurance of robust, healthy mental and moral development.

To-day even the attitude of the Southern whites toward the blacks is not, as so many assume, in all cases the same; the ignorant Southerner hates the Negro, the workingmen fear his competition, the money-makers wish to use him as a laborer, some of the educated see a menace in his upward development, while others—usually the sons of the masters—wish to help him to rise. National opinion has enabled this last class to maintain the Negro common schools, and to protect the Negro partially in property, life, and limb. Through the pressure of the money-makers, the Negro is in danger of being reduced to semi-slavery, especially in the country districts; the workingmen, and those of the educated who fear the Negro, have united to disfranchise him, and some have urged his deportation; while the passions of the ignorant are easily aroused to lynch and abuse any black man. To praise this intricate whirl of thought and prejudice is nonsense; to inveigh indiscriminately against "the South" is unjust; but to use the same breath in praising Governor Aycock, exposing Senator Morgan, arguing with Mr. Thomas Nelson Page, and denouncing Senator Ben Tillman, is not only sane, but the imperative duty of thinking black men.

It would be unjust to Mr. Washington not to acknowledge that in several instances he has opposed movements in the South which were unjust to the Negro; he sent memorials to the Louisiana and Alabama constitutional conventions, he has spoken against lynching, and in other ways has openly or silently set his influence against sinister schemes and unfortunate happenings. Notwithstanding this, it is equally true to assert that on the whole the distinct impression left by Mr. Washington's propaganda is, first, that the South is justified in its present attitude toward the Negro because of the Negro's degradation; secondly, that the prime cause of the Negro's failure to rise more quickly is his wrong education in the past; and, thirdly, that his future rise depends primarily on his own efforts. Each of these propositions is a dangerous half-truth. The supplementary truths must never be lost sight of: first, slavery and race-prejudice are potent if not sufficient causes of the Negro's position; second, industrial and common-school training were necessarily slow in planting because they had to await the black teachers trained by higher institutions,—it being extremely doubtful if any essentially different development was possible, and certainly a Tuskegee was unthinkable before 1880; and, third, while it is a great truth to say that the Negro must strive and strive mightily to help himself, it is equally true that unless his striving be not simply seconded, but rather aroused and encouraged, by the initiative of the richer and wiser environing group, he cannot hope for great success.

In his failure to realize and impress this last point, Mr. Washington is especially to be criticised. His doctrine has tended to make the whites, North and

South, shift the burden of the Negro problem to the Negro's shoulders and stand aside as critical and rather pessimistic spectators; when in fact the burden belongs to the nation, and the hands of none of us are clean if we bend not our energies to righting these great wrongs.

The South ought to be led, by candid and honest criticism, to assert her better self and do her full duty to the race she has cruelly wronged and is still wronging. The North—her co-partner in guilt—cannot salve her conscience by plastering it with gold. We cannot settle this problem by diplomacy and suaveness, by "policy" alone. If worse comes to worst, can the moral fibre of this country survive the slow throttling and murder of nine millions of men?

The black men of America have a duty to perform, a duty stern and delicate,—a forward movement to oppose a part of the work of their greatest leader. So far as Mr. Washington preaches Thrift, Patience, and Industrial Training for the masses, we must hold up his hands and strive with him, rejoicing in his honors and glorying in the strength of this Joshua called of God and of man to lead the headless host. But so far as Mr. Washington apologizes for injustice, North or South, does not rightly value the privilege and duty of voting, belittles the emasculating effects of caste distinctions, and opposes the higher training and ambition of our brighter minds,—so far as he, the South, or the Nation, does this,—we must unceasingly and firmly oppose them. By every civilized and peaceful method we must strive for the rights which the world accords to men, clinging unwaveringly to those great words which the sons of the Fathers would fain forget: "We hold these truths to be self-evident: That all men are created equal; that they are endowed by their Creater with certain unalienable rights; that among these are life, liberty, and the pursuit of happiness."

Address to the Niagara Conference, Harpers Ferry, West Virginia, 1906

. . . . In the past year the work of the Negro-hater has flourished in the land. Step by step the defenders of the rights of American citizens have retreated. The work of stealing the black man's ballot has progressed and the fifty and more representatives of stolen votes still sit in the nation's capital. Discrimination in travel and public accommodation has so spread that some of our weaker brethren are actually afraid to thunder against color discrimination as such and are simply whispering for ordinary decencies.

Against this the Niagara Movement eternally protests. We will not be satisfied to take one jot or tittle less than our full manhood rights. . . . [We] claim for ourselves every single right that belongs to a freeborn American, political, civil and social; and until we get these rights we will never cease to protest and assail

SOURCE: W. E. B. DuBois, "Niagara Address of 1906," W. E. B. DuBois Manuscripts, University of Massachusetts, Amherst, Massachusetts.

the ears of America. The battle we wage is not for ourselves alone but for all true Americans. It is a fight for ideals, lest this, our common fatherland, false to its founding, become in truth, the land of the thief and the home of the slave, a byword and a hissing among the nations for its sounding pretensions and pitiful accomplishments.

Never before in the modern age has a great and civilized folk threatened to adopt so cowardly a creed in the treatment of its fellow citizens born and bred on its soil. Stripped of verbiage and subterfuge and in its naked nastiness, the new American creed says: "Fear to let black men even try to rise lest they become the equals of the white." And this is the land that professes to follow Jesus Christ! The blasphemy of such a course is only matched by its cowardice.

In detail, our demands are clear and unequivocal. First, we would vote; with the right to vote goes everything: freedom, manhood, the honor of your wives, the chastity of your daughters, the right to work, and the chance to rise, and let no man listen to those who deny this.

We want full manhood suffrage, and we want it now, henceforth and forever!

Second. We want discrimination in public accommodation to cease. Separation in railway and street cars, based simply on race and color, is un-American, undemocratic, and silly. We protest against all such discrimination.

Third. We claim the right of freemen to walk, talk, and be with them that wish to be with us. No man has a right to choose another man's friends, and to attempt to do so is an impudent interference with the most fundamental human privilege.

Fourth. We want the laws enforced against rich as well as poor; against capitalist as well as laborer; against white as well as black. We are not more lawless than the white race: We are more often arrested, convicted and mobbed. We want Congress to take charge of Congressional elections. We want the Fourteenth Amendment carried out to the letter and every state disfranchised in Congress which attempts to disfranchise its rightful voters. We want the Fifteenth Amendment enforced and no state allowed to base its franchise simply on color. . . .

Fifth. We want our children educated. The school system in the country districts of the South is a disgrace, and in few towns and cities are the Negro schools what they ought to be. We want the national government to step in and wipe out illiteracy in the South. Either the United States will destroy ignorance, or ignorance will destroy the United States.

And when we call for education we mean real education. We believe in work. We ourselves are workers, but work is not necessarily education. Education is the development of power and ideal. We want our children trained as intelligent human beings should be, and we will fight for all time against any proposal to educate black boys and girls simply as servants and underlings, or simply for the use of other people. They have a right to know, to think, to aspire.

These are some of the chief things which we want. How shall we get them? By voting where we may vote, by persistent, unceasing agitation, by hammering at the truth, by sacrifice and work.

We do not believe in violence, neither in the despised violence of the raid nor the lauded violence of the soldier, nor the barbarous violence of the mob, but we do believe in John Brown, in that incarnate spirit of justice, that hatred of a lie, that willingness to sacrifice money, reputation, and life itself on the altar of right. And here on the scene of John Brown's martyrdom, we reconsecrate ourselves, our honor, our property to the final emancipation of the race which John Brown died to make free.

Our enemies, triumphant for the present, are fighting the stars in their courses. Justice and humanity must prevail. We live to tell these dark brothers of ours—scattered in counsel, wavering, and weak—that no bribe of money or notoriety, no promise of wealth or fame, is worth the surrender of a people's manhood or the loss of a man's self-respect. We refuse to surrender the leadership of this race to cowards and trucklers. We are men; we will be treated as men. On this rock we have planted our banners. We will never give up, though the trump of doom finds us still fighting.

And we shall win! The past promised it. The present foretells it. Thank God for John Brown. Thank God for Garrison and Douglass, Sumner and Phillips, Nat Turner and Robert Gould Shaw, and all the hallowed dead who died for freedom. Thank God for all those today, few though their voices be, who have not forgotten the divine brotherhood of all men, white and black, rich and poor, fortunate and unfortunate.

We appeal to the young men and women of this nation, to those whose nostrils are not yet befouled by greed and snobbery and racial narrowness: Stand up for the right, prove yourselves worthy of your heritage and, whether born North or South, dare to treat men as men. Cannot the nation that has absorbed ten-million foreigners into its political life without catastrophe absorb ten-million Negro Americans into that same political life at less cost than their unjust and illegal exclusion will involve?

Courage, brothers! The battle for humanity is not lost or losing. All across the skies sit signs of promise! The Slav is rising in his might, the yellow millions are tasting liberty, the black Africans are writhing toward the light, and everywhere the laborer, with ballot in his hand, is voting open the gates of opportunity and peace.

The morning breaks over blood-stained hills. We must not falter, we may not shrink. Above are the everlasting stars.

Ida B. Wells-Barnett (1862–1931)

Ida B. Wells-Barnett was born a slave in Mississippi during the Civil War. She attended Rust University in Mississippi and later Fisk University in Memphis. After she earned her college degree, she became first a teacher

*and, by the end of the 1880s, a journalist. In 1889, she began working as
an editor of the* Memphis Free Speech, *a weekly newspaper, for which
she contributed many articles on education and self-help for African
Americans. Living in the South, she was, of course, afflicted by the Jim
Crow laws. Once in 1884, she refused to sit in the black car of a train and
was consequently physically ejected from the train. She sued the railroad
and eventually lost her case.*

*Segregation laws were hardly the only evils African Americans had to
endure. In 1892, three of Wells-Barnett's friends who owned a small,
prosperous grocery store were lynched. Booker T. Washington had argued
that if blacks would achieve economic success, they would be respected by
whites and eventually achieve civil and political equality. The lynching of
small business owners was an appalling and indisputable refutation of this
notion. This event had a powerful impact on Wells-Barnett, and from this
point on, she began using her position as a writer to denounce lynching and
expose the truth behind the racial stereotypes that whites used to subjugate
blacks. She contended that whites' reliance on the charge of rape as a
justification for lynching black men was a lie. It was merely a subterfuge,
both an excuse to murder African Americans who were becoming an
economic threat for whites and a very effective way to keep them down. Her
editorials in the* Free Speech *antagonized the white community so
thoroughly that the offices and presses of the newspaper were destroyed and
Wells-Barnett driven out of town. She moved to New York, where she began
writing primarily investigative articles on lynching for the* New York Age.
*By the end of 1892, she had published a pamphlet, "Southern Horrors," and
had begun giving speeches in both the United States and Europe in which
she militantly protested against lynching and advocated that the federal
government enact strong laws against the practice. In 1895, she published* A
Red Record *and in 1899,* Lynch Law in Georgia. *Through her determined
antilynching campaign Ida B. Wells-Barnett became a prominent and
effective figure in the early civil rights movement.*

Lynch Law in Georgia, June 20, 1899

Consider The Facts.

During six weeks of the months of March and April just past, twelve colored
men were lynched in Georgia, the reign of outlawry culminating in the torture

SOURCE: Ida B. Wells-Barnett, *Lynch Law in Georgia: A Six-Weeks' Record in the Center of
Southern Civilization, As Faithfully Chronicled by the "Atlanta Journal" and the "Atlanta Constitution." Also the Full Report of Louis P. Le Vin, The Chicago Detective Sent to Investigate the
Burning of Samuel Hose, the Torture and Hanging of Elijah Strickland, the Colored Preacher, and
the Lynching of Nine Men for Alleged Arson* (Chicago: Chicago Colored Citizens, 1899), 1–11.

and hanging of the colored preacher, Elijah Strickland, and the burning alive of Samuel Wilkes, alias Hose, Sunday, April 23, 1899.

The real purpose of these savage demonstrations is to teach the Negro that in the South he has no rights that the law will enforce. Samuel Hose was burned to teach the Negroes that no matter what a white man does to them, they must not resist. Hose, a servant, had killed Cranford, his employer. An example must be made. Ordinary punishment was deemed inadequate. This Negro must be burned alive. To make the burning a certainty the charge of outrage was invented, and added to the charge of murder. The daily press offered reward for the capture of Hose and then openly incited the people to burn him as soon as caught. The mob carried out the plan in every savage detail.

Of the twelve men lynched during that reign of unspeakable barbarism, only one was even charged with an assault upon a woman. Yet Southern apologists justify their savagery on the ground that Negroes are lynched only because of their crimes against women.

The Southern press champions burning men alive, and says, "Consider the facts." The colored people join issue and also say, "Consider the fact." The colored people of Chicago employed a detective to go to Georgia, and his report in this pamphlet gives the facts. We give here the details of the lynching as they were reported in the Southern papers, then follows the report of the true facts as to the cause of the lynchings, as learned by the investigation. We submit all to the sober judgment of the Nation, confident that, in this cause, as well as all others, "Truth is mighty and will prevail."

Ida B. Wells-Barnett
2939 Princeton Avenue, Chicago, June 20, 1899

"Tortured and Burned Alive," 1899

.... The burning of Samuel Hose, or, to give his right name, Samuel Wilkes, gave to the United States the distinction of having burned alive seven human beings during the past ten years. The details of this deed of unspeakable barbarism have shocked the civilized world, for it is conceded universally that no other nation on earth, civilized or savage, has put to death any human being with such atrocious cruelty as that inflicted upon Samuel Hose by the Christian white people of Georgia.

The charge is generally made that lynch law is condemned by the best white people of the South, and that lynching is the work of the lowest and lawless class. Those who seek the truth know the fact to be, that all classes are equally guilty, for what the one class does the other encourages, excuses and condones.

This was clearly shown in the burning of Hose. This awful deed was suggested, encouraged and made possible by the daily press of Atlanta, Georgia, until the burning actually occurred, and then it immediately condoned the burning by a hysterical plea to "consider the facts."

Samuel Hose killed Alfred Cranford Wednesday afternoon, April 12, 1899, in a dispute over the wages due Hose. The dispatch which announced the killing of Cranford stated that Hose had assaulted Mrs. Cranford and that bloodhounds had been put on his track.

The next day the Atlanta Constitution, in glaring double headlines, predicted a lynching and suggested burning at the stake. This it repeated in the body of the dispatch in the following language: "When Hose is caught he will either be lynched and his body riddled with bullets or he will be burned at the stake." And further in the same issue the Constitution suggests torture in these words: "There have been whisperings of burning at the stake and of torturing the fellow, and so great is the excitement, and so high the indignation, that this is among the possibilities."

In the issue of the 15th, in another double-column display heading, the Constitution announces: "Negro will probably be burned," and in the body of the dispatch burning and torture is confidently predicted in these words: "Several modes of death have been suggested for him, but it seems to be the universal opinion that he will be burned at the stake and probably tortured before burned."

The next day, April 16th, the double-column head still does its inflammatory work. Never a word for law and order, but daily encouragement for burning. The headlines read: "Excitement still continues intense, and it is openly declared that if Sam Hose is brought in alive he will be burned," and in the dispatch it is said: "The residents have shown no disposition to abandon the search in the immediate neighborhood of Palmetto; their ardor has in no degree cooled, and if Sam Hose is brought here by his captors he will be publicly burned at the stake as an example to members of his race who are said to have been causing the residents of this vicinity trouble for some time."

On the 19th the Constitution assures the public that interest in the pursuit of Hose does not lag, and in proof of the zeal of the pursuers said: "'If Hose is on earth I'll never rest easy until he's caught and burned alive. And that's the way all of us feel,' said one of them last night."

Clark Howell, editor, and W. A. Hemphill, business manager, of the Constitution, had offered through their paper a reward of five hundred dollars for the arrest of the fugitive. This reward, together with the persistent suggestion that the Negro be burned as soon as caught, make it plain as day that the purpose to burn Hose at the stake was formed by the leading citizens of Georgia. The Constitution offered the reward to capture him, and then day after day suggested and predicted that he be burned when caught. The Chicago anarchists [at Haymarket Square] were hanged, not because they threw the bomb, but because they incited to that act the unknown man who did throw it. Pity that the same law cannot be carried into force in Georgia!

Hose was caught Saturday night, April 23, and let the Constitution tell the story of his torture and death.

From the issue of April 24th the following account is condensed: Newman, Ga., April 23.—(Special.)—Sam Hose, the Negro murderer of Alfred Cranford and the assailant of Cranford's wife, was burned at the stake one mile and a quarter from this place this afternoon at 2:30 o'clock. Fully 2,000 people surrounded the small sapling to which he was fastened and watched the flames eat away his flesh, saw his body mutilated by knives and witnessed the contortions of his body in his extreme agony.

Such suffering has seldom been witnessed, and through it all the Negro uttered hardly a cry. During the contortions of his body several blood vessels bursted. The spot selected was an ideal one for such an affair, and the stake was in full view of those who stood about and with unfeigned satisfaction saw the Negro meet his death and saw him tortured before the flames killed him.

A few smoldering ashes scattered about the place, a blackened stake, are all that is left to tell the story. Not even the bones of the Negro were left in the place, but were eagerly snatched by a crowd of people drawn here from all directions, who almost fought over the burning body of the man, carving it with knives and seeking souvenirs of the occurrence.

Preparations for the execution were not necessarily elaborate, and it required only a few minutes to arrange to make Sam Hose pay the penalty of his crime. To the sapling Sam Hose was tied, and he watched the cool, determined men who went about arranging to burn him.

First he was made to remove his clothing, and when the flames began to eat into his body it was almost nude. Before the fire was lighted his left ear was severed from his body. Then his right ear was cut away. During this proceeding he uttered not a groan. Other portions of his body were mutilated by the knives of those who gathered about him, but he was not wounded to such an extent that he was not fully conscious and could feel the excruciating pain. Oil was poured over the wood that was placed about him and this was ignited.

The scene that followed is one that never will be forgotten by those who saw it, and while Sam Hose writhed and performed contortions in his agony, many of those present turned away from the sickening sight, and others could hardly look at it. Not a sound but the crackling of the flames broke the stillness of the place, and the situation grew more sickening as it proceeded.

The stake bent under the strains of the Negro in his agony and his sufferings cannot be described, although he uttered not a sound. After his ears had been cut off he was asked about the crime, and then it was he made a full confession. At one juncture, before the flames had begun to get in their work well, the fastenings that held him to the stake broke and he fell forward partially out of the fire.

He writhed in agony and his sufferings can be imagined when it is said that several blood vessels burst during the contortions of his body. When he fell from the stake he was kicked back and the flames renewed. Then it was that the flames consumed his body and in a few minutes only a few bones and a small part of the body was all that was left of Sam Hose.

One of the most sickening sights of the day was the eagerness with which the people grabbed after souvenirs, and they almost fought over the ashes of the dead criminal. Large pieces of his flesh were carried away, and persons were seen walking through the streets carrying bones in their hands.

When all the larger bones, together with the flesh, had been carried away by the early comers, others scraped in the ashes, and for a great length of time a crowd was about the place scraping in the ashes. Not even the stake to which the Negro was tied when burned was left, but it was promptly chopped down and carried away as the largest souvenir of the burning.

Carl Schurz (1829–1906)

Carl Schurz was a German immigrant who served as a brigadier general during the Civil War, Republican senator from Missouri during Reconstruction, and secretary of the interior during the Hayes administration. He later moved to New York, where he helped found the New York Evening Post *and wrote extensive political columns for* Harper's Weekly. *At the turn of the century, just as the United States was beginning to redefine its notion of manifest destiny, Schurz became an outspoken critic of American expansionism. "My Country!" he once wrote, "when right keep it right; when wrong, set it right!" In June 1898, believing that the war with Spain was wrong, he became very active (along with such diverse celebrated individuals as Jane Addams, Andrew Carnegie, William James, and Mark Twain) in the Anti-Imperialist League. Early in 1899, he delivered a speech at the University of Chicago in which he emphatically denounced the acquisition of the Philippines and Puerto Rico as a result of the Spanish-American War.*

ADDRESS AT THE UNIVERSITY OF CHICAGO DENOUNCING U.S. IMPERIALISM, JANUARY 4, 1899

It is proposed to embark this republic in a course of imperialistic policy by permanently annexing to it certain islands taken, or partly taken, from Spain in the late war. The matter is near its decision, but not yet ratified by the Senate; but even if it were, the question whether those islands, although ceded by Spain, shall be permanently incorporated in the territory of the United States would still be open for final determination by Congress. As an open question therefore I shall discuss it.

If ever, it behooves the American people to think and act with calm deliberation, for the character and future of the republic and the welfare of its people now living and yet to be born are in unprecedented jeopardy....

SOURCE: *Speeches, Correspondence, and Political Papers of Carl Schurz*, ed. by Frederic Bancroft, vol.6 (New York: G. P. Putnam's Sons, 1913), 2, 4, 6, 8,10–11, 14–15, 26–29.

According to the solemn proclamation of our government, [the Spanish-American War] had been undertaken solely for the liberation of Cuba, as a war of humanity and not of conquest. But our easy victories had put conquest within our reach, and when our arms occupied foreign territory, a loud demand arose that, pledge or no pledge to the contrary, the conquests should be kept, even the Philippines on the other side of the globe, and that as to Cuba herself, independence would only be a provisional formality. Why not? was the cry. Has not the career of the republic almost from its very beginning been one of territorial expansion? . . .

Compare now with our old acquisitions as to all these important points those at present in view.

They are not continental, not contiguous to our present domain, but beyond seas, the Philippines many thousand miles distant from our coast. They are all situated in the tropics, where people of the northern races, such as Anglo-Saxons, or generally speaking, people of Germanic blood, have never migrated in mass to stay; and they are more or less densely populated, parts of them as densely as Massachusetts—their populations consisting almost exclusively of races to whom the tropical climate is congenial—Spanish creoles mixed with negroes in the West Indies, and Malays, Tagals, Filipinos, Chinese, Japanese, Negritos, and various more or less barbarous tribes in the Philippines. . . .

Whatever we may do for their improvement the people of the Spanish Antilles will remain in overwhelming numerical predominance . . . , some of them quite clever in their way, but the vast majority utterly alien to us not only in origin and language, but in habits, traditional ways of thinking, principles, ambitions—in short, in most things that are of the greatest importance in human intercourse and especially in political cooperation. And under the influences of their tropical climate they will prove incapable of becoming assimilated to the Anglo-Saxon. They would, therefore, remain in the population of this republic a hopelessly heterogeneous element—in some respects more hopeless even than the colored people now living among us. . . .

If we [become an imperialist power], we shall transform the government of the people, for the people, and by the people, for which Abraham Lincoln lived, into a government of one part of the people, the strong, over another part, the weak. Such an abandonment of a fundamental principle as a permanent policy may at first seem to bear only upon more or less distant dependencies, but it can hardly fail in its ultimate effects to disturb the rule of the same principle in the conduct of democratic government at home. And I warn the American people that a democracy cannot so deny its faith as to the vital conditions of its being—it cannot long play the king over subject populations without creating within itself ways of thinking and habits of action most dangerous to its own vitality. . . .

Conservative citizens will tell [us] that thus the homogeneousness of the people of the republic, so essential to the working of our democratic institutions, will be irretrievably lost; that our race troubles, already dangerous, will be infinitely aggravated, and that the government of, by, and for the people will be in imminent danger of fatal demoralization. . . . The American people will be driven on and on by the force of events as Napoleon was when started on his career of limitless conquest. This is imperialism as now advocated. Do we wish to prevent its excesses? Then we must stop at the beginning, before taking Porto Rico. If we take that island, not even to speak of the Philippines, we shall have placed ourselves on the inclined plane, and roll on and on, no longer masters of our own will, until we have reached the bottom. And where will that bottom be? Who knows? . . .

What can there be to justify a change of policy fraught with such direful consequences? Let us pass the arguments of the advocates of such imperialism candidly in review.

The cry suddenly raised that this great country has become too small for us is too ridiculous to demand an answer, in view of the fact that our present population may be tripled and still have ample elbow-room, with resources to support many more. But we are told that our industries are gasping for breath; that we are suffering from over production; that our products must have new outlets, and that we need colonies and dependencies the world over to give us more markets. More markets? Certainly. But do we, civilized beings, indulge in the absurd and barbarous notion that we must own the countries with which we wish to trade? . . .

"But the Pacific Ocean," we are mysteriously told, "will be the great commercial battlefield of the future, and we must quickly use the present opportunity to secure our position on it. The visible presence of great power is necessary for us to get our share of the trade of China. Therefore, we must have the Philippines." Well, the China trade is worth having, although for a time out of sight the Atlantic Ocean will be an infinitely more important battlefield of commerce. . . . But does the trade of China really require that we should have the Philippines and make a great display of power to get our share? . . .

"But we must have coaling stations for our navy!" Well, can we not get as many coaling stations as we need without owning populous countries behind them that would entangle us in dangerous political responsibilities and complications? Must Great Britain own the whole of Spain in order to hold Gibraltar?

"But we must civilize those poor people!" Are we not ingenious and charitable enough to do much for their civilization without subjugating and ruling them by criminal aggression?

The rest of the pleas for imperialism consist mostly of those high-sounding catch-words of which a free people when about to decide a great question should be especially suspicious. We are admonished that it is time for us to become a "world power." Well, we are a world power now, and have been for many years. What is a world power? A power strong enough to make its voice listened to with deference by the world whenever it chooses to speak. Is it necessary for a world power, in order to be such, to have its finger in every pie? Must we have the Philippines in order to become a world power? To ask the question is to answer it.

The American flag, we are told, whenever once raised, must never be hauled down. Certainly, every patriotic citizen will always be ready, if need be, to fight and to die under his flag wherever it may wave in justice and for the best interests of the country. But I say to you, woe to the republic if it should ever be without citizens patriotic and brave enough to defy the demagogues' cry and to haul down the flag wherever it may be raised not in justice and not for the best interests of the country. Such a republic would not last long. . . .

William Jennings Bryan (1860–1925)

The 1900 presidential election was a rematch between Democrat William Jennings Bryan and the incumbent president, William McKinley. Both elections were hard-fought campaigns, and both saw Bryan narrowly defeated by the Republicans. In 1896, the primary issue was silver. In 1900, however, a new issue had arisen: imperialism. The United States had just acquired Guam, Puerto Rico, and the Philippines from Spain, and although a great deal of pride had swept the country as a result of American expansion, a significant minority believed the United States was turning its back on its own democratic values by emulating European imperialism.

As soon as the United States began exerting authority in the Philippines, Filipino nationalist Emilio Aguinaldo resumed his guerrilla activity. This time, instead of fighting the Spanish, Aguinaldo led the fight against the American occupying forces. As the Filipino insurrection picked up steam, Bryan and the Democratic Party took up the anti-imperialist cause. Bryan believed that the American attempt to conquer the Philippines and impose American principles and democracy on an unwilling people was contrary to the values of the founding fathers and the very principles on which this nation was founded.

The Paralyzing Influence of Imperialism, July 1900

. . . Someone has said that a truth once spoken can never be recalled. It goes on and on, and no one can set a limit to its ever widening influence. But if it were possible to obliterate every word written or spoken in defense of the principles set forth in the Declaration of Independence, a war of conquest would still leave its legacy of perpetual hatred, for it was God Himself who placed in every

---

SOURCE: *Official Proceedings of the Democratic National Convention Held in Kansas City, MO., July 4, 5 and 6, 1900* (Chicago, 1900), 205–227.

human heart the love of liberty. He never made a race of people so low in the scale of civilization or intelligence that it would welcome a foreign master.

Those who would have this nation enter upon a career of empire must consider not only the effect of imperialism on the Filipinos but they must also calculate its effects upon our own nation. We cannot repudiate the principle of self-government in the Philippines without weakening that principle here.

Lincoln said that the safety of this nation was not in its fleets, its armies, its forts, but in the spirit which prizes liberty as the heritage of all men, in all lands, everywhere, and he warned his countrymen that they could not destroy this spirit without planting the seeds of despotism at their own doors.

Even now we are beginning to see the paralyzing influence of imperialism. Heretofore this nation has been prompt to express its sympathy with those who were fighting for civil liberty. While our sphere of activity has been limited to the Western Hemisphere, our sympathies have not been bounded by the seas. We have felt it due to ourselves and to the world, as well as to those who were struggling for the right to govern themselves, to proclaim the interest which our people have, from the date of their own independence, felt in every contest between human rights and arbitrary power. . . .

A colonial policy means that we shall send to the Philippine Islands a few traders, a few taskmasters, and a few officeholders, and an army large enough to support the authority of a small fraction of the people while they rule the natives.

If we have an imperial policy we must have a great standing army as its natural and necessary complement. The spirit which will justify the forcible annexation of the Philippine Islands will justify the seizure of other islands and the domination of other people, and with wars of conquest we can expect a certain, if not rapid, growth of our military establishment.

That a large permanent increase in our regular army is intended by Republican leaders is not a matter of conjecture but a matter of fact. In his message of Dec. 5, 1898, the President asked for authority to increase the standing army to 100,000. In 1896 the army contained about 25,000. Within two years the President asked for four times that many, and a Republican House of Representatives complied with the request after the Spanish treaty had been signed, and when no country was at war with the United States.

If such an army is demanded when an imperial policy is contemplated but not openly avowed, what may be expected if the people encourage the Republican Party by endorsing its policy at the polls?

A large standing army is not only a pecuniary burden to the people and, if accompanied by compulsory service, a constant source of irritation but it is even a menace to a republican form of government. The army is the personification of force, and militarism will inevitably change the ideals of the people and turn the thoughts of our young men from the arts of peace to the science of war. The government which relies for its defense upon its citizens is more likely to be just than one which has at call a large body of professional soldiers.

A small standing army and a well-equipped and well-disciplined state militia are sufficient at ordinary times, and in an emergency the nation should in the future as in the past place its dependence upon the volunteers who come from all occupations at their country's call and return to productive labor when their services are no longer required—men who fight when the country needs fighters and work when the country needs workers. . . .

The Republican platform promises that some measure of self-government is to be given the Filipinos by law; but even this pledge is not fulfilled. Nearly sixteen months elapsed after the ratification of the treaty before the adjournment of Congress last June and yet no law was passed dealing with the Philippine situation. The will of the President has been the only law in the Philippine Islands wherever the American authority extends.

Why does the Republican Party hesitate to legislate upon the Philippine question? Because a law would disclose the radical departure from history and precedent contemplated by those who control the Republican Party. The storm of protest which greeted the Puerto Rican bill was an indication of what may be expected when the American people are brought face to face with legislation upon this subject.

If the Puerto Ricans, who welcomed annexation, are to be denied the guarantees of our Constitution, what is to be the lot of the Filipinos, who resisted our authority? If secret influences could compel a disregard of our plain duty toward friendly people living near our shores, what treatment will those same influences provide for unfriendly people 7,000 miles away? If, in this country where the people have a right to vote, Republican leaders dare not take the side of the people against the great monopolies which have grown up within the last few years, how can they be trusted to protect the Filipinos from the corporations which are waiting to exploit the islands?

Is the sunlight of full citizenship to be enjoyed by the people of the United States and the twilight of semi-citizenship endured by the people of Puerto Rico, while the thick darkness of perpetual vassalage covers the Philippines? The Puerto Rico tariff law asserts the doctrine that the operation of the Constitution is confined to the forty-five states.

The Democratic Party disputes this doctrine and denounces it as repugnant to both the letter and spirit of our organic law. There is no place in our system of government for the deposit of arbitrary and irresistible power. That the leaders of a great party should claim for any President or Congress the right to treat millions of people as mere "possessions" and deal with them unrestrained by the Constitution or the Bill of Rights shows how far we have already departed from the ancient landmarks and indicates what may be expected if this nation deliberately enters upon a career of empire.

The territorial form of government is temporary and preparatory, and the chief security a citizen of a territory has is found in the fact that he enjoys the same constitutional guarantees and is subject to the same general laws as the citizen of a state. Take away this security and his rights will be violated and his interests sacrificed at the demand of those who have political influence. This is the evil of the colonial system, no matter by what nation it is applied.

What is our title to the Philippine Islands? Do we hold them by treaty or by conquest? Did we buy them or did we take them? Did we purchase the people? If not, how did we secure title to them? Were they thrown in with the land? Will the Republicans say that inanimate earth has value but that when that earth is molded by the Divine Hand and stamped with the likeness of the Creator it becomes a fixture and passes with the soil? If governments derive their just powers from the consent of the governed, it is impossible to secure title to people, either by force or by purchase.

We could extinguish Spain's title by treaty, but if we hold title we must hold it by some method consistent with our ideas of government. When we made allies of the Filipinos and armed them to fight against Spain, we disputed Spain's title. If we buy Spain's title, we are not innocent purchasers. There can be no doubt that we accepted and utilized the services of the Filipinos and that when we did so we had full knowledge that they were fighting for their own independence; and I submit that history furnishes no example of turpitude baser than ours if we now substitute our yoke for the Spanish yoke. . . .

Some argue that American rule in the Philippine Islands will result in the better education of the Filipinos. Be not deceived. If we expect to maintain a colonial policy, we shall not find it to our advantage to educate the people. The educated Filipinos are now in revolt against us, and the most ignorant ones have made the least resistance to our domination. If we are to govern them without their consent and give them no voice in determining the taxes which they must pay, we dare not educate them lest they learn to read the Declaration of Independence and the Constitution of the United States and mock us for our inconsistency.

The principal arguments, however, advanced by those who enter upon a defense of imperialism are:

First, that we must improve the present opportunity to become a world power and enter into international politics.

Second, that our commercial interests in the Philippine Islands and in the Orient make it necessary for us to hold the islands permanently.

Third, that the spread of the Christian religion will be facilitated by a colonial policy.

Fourth, that there is no honorable retreat from the position which the nation has taken.

The first argument is addressed to the nation's pride and the second to the nation's pocketbook. The third is intended for the church member and the fourth for the partisan.

It is sufficient answer to the first argument to say that for more than a century this nation has been a world power. For ten decades it has been the most potent influence in the world. Not only has it been a world power but it has done more to affect the policies of the human race than all the other nations of the world combined. Because our Declaration of Independence was promulgated, others have been promulgated. Because the patriots of 1776 fought for liberty, others have fought for it. Because our Constitution was adopted, other constitutions have been adopted.

The growth of the principle of self-government, planted on American soil, has been the overshadowing political fact of the 19th century. It has made this nation conspicuous among the nations and given it a place in history, such as no other nation has ever enjoyed. Nothing has been able to check the onward march of this idea. I am not willing that this nation shall cast aside the omnipotent weapon of truth to seize again the weapons of physical warfare. I would not exchange the glory of this republic for the glory of all the empires that have risen and fallen since time began.

The permanent chairman of the last Republican National Convention presented the pecuniary argument in all its baldness when he said:

> We make no hypocritical pretense of being interested in the Philippines solely on account of others. While we regard the welfare of those people as a sacred trust, we regard the welfare of the American people first. We see our duty to ourselves as well as to others. We believe in trade expansion. By every legitimate means within the province of government and constitution we mean to stimulate the expansion of our trade and open new markets.

This is the commercial argument. It is based upon the theory that war can be rightly waged for pecuniary advantage and that it is profitable to purchase trade by force and violence. Franklin denied both of these propositions. When Lord Howe asserted that the acts of Parliament which brought on the Revolution were necessary to prevent American trade from passing into foreign channels, Franklin replied:

> To me it seems that neither the obtaining nor retaining of any trade, howsoever valuable, is an object for which men may justly spill each other's blood; that the true and sure means of extending and securing commerce are the goodness and cheapness of commodities, and that the profits of no trade can ever be equal to the expense of compelling it and holding it by fleets and armies. I consider this war against us, therefore, as both unjust and unwise.

I place the philosophy of Franklin against the sordid doctrine of those who would put a price upon the head of an American soldier and justify a war of conquest upon the ground that it will pay. The Democratic Party is in favor of the expansion of trade. It would extend our trade by every legitimate and peaceful means; but it is not willing to make merchandise of human blood.

But a war of conquest is as unwise as it is unrighteous. A harbor and coaling station in the Philippines would answer every trade and military necessity and such a concession could have been secured at any time without difficulty. It is not necessary to own people in order to trade with them. We carry on trade today with every part of the world, and our commerce has expanded more rapidly than the commerce of any European empire. We do not own Japan or China, but we trade with their people. We have not absorbed the republics of Central and South America, but we trade with them. Trade cannot be permanently profitable unless it is voluntary.

When trade is secured by force, the cost of securing it and retaining it must be taken out of the profits, and the profits are never large enough to cover the expense. Such a system would never be defended but for the fact that the expense is borne by all the people while the profits are enjoyed by a few.

Imperialism would be profitable to the Army contractors; it would be profitable to the shipowners, who would carry live soldiers to the Philippines and bring dead soldiers back; it would be profitable to those who would seize upon the franchises, and it would be profitable to the officials whose salaries would be fixed here and paid over there; but to the farmer, to the laboring man, and to the vast majority of those engaged in other occupations, it would bring expenditure without return and risk without reward.

Farmers and laboring men have, as a rule, small incomes, and, under systems which place the tax upon consumption, pay much more than their fair share of the expenses of government. Thus the very people who receive least benefit from imperialism will be injured most by the military burdens which accompany it.

In addition to the evils which he and the former share in common, the laboring man will be the first to suffer if Oriental subjects seek work in the United States; the first to suffer if American capital leaves our shores to employ Oriental labor in the Philippines to supply the trade of China and Japan; the first to suffer from the violence which the military spirit arouses, and the first to suffer when the methods of imperialism are applied to our own government. . . .

The religious argument varies in positiveness from a passive belief that Providence delivered the Filipinos into our hands for their good and our glory to the exultation of the minister who said that we ought to "thrash the natives (Filipinos)" until they understand who we are," and that "every bullet sent, every cannon shot, and every flag waved means righteousness."

We cannot approve of this doctrine in one place unless we are willing to apply it everywhere. If there is poison in the blood of the hand, it will ultimately reach the heart. It is equally true that forcible Christianity, if planted under the American flag in the far-away Orient, will sooner or later be transplanted upon American soil. . . .

If true Christianity consists of carrying out in our daily lives the teachings of Christ, who will say that we are commanded to civilize with dynamite and proselyte with the sword? . . .

There is an easy, honest, honorable solution of the Philippine question . . . first, to establish a stable form of government in the Philippine Islands, just as we are now establishing a stable form of government in Cuba; second, to give independence to the Filipinos as we have promised to give independence to the Cubans; third, to protect the Filipinos from outside interference while they work out their destiny, just as we have protected the republics of Central and South America, and are, by the Monroe Doctrine, pledged to protect Cuba.

A European protectorate often results in the plundering of the ward by the guardian. An American protectorate gives to the nation protected the advantage of our strength without making it the victim of our greed. For three-quarters of a century the Monroe Doctrine has been a shield to neighboring republics and yet it has imposed no pecuniary burden upon us. After the Filipinos had aided us in the war against Spain, we could not honorably turn them over to their former masters; we could not leave them to be the victims of the ambitious designs of European nations, and since we do not desire to make them a part of us or to hold them as subjects, we propose the only alternative, namely, to give them independence and guard them against molestation from without.

When our opponents are unable to defend their position by argument, they fall back upon the assertion that it is destiny and insist that we must submit to it no matter how much it violates our moral precepts and our principles of government. This is a complacent philosophy. It obliterates the distinction between right and wrong and makes individuals and nations the helpless victims of circumstances.

Destiny is the subterfuge of the invertebrate, who, lacking the courage to oppose error, seeks some plausible excuse for supporting it. Washington said that the destiny of the republican form of government was deeply, if not finally, staked on the experiment entrusted to the American people. How different Washington's definition of destiny from the Republican definition! . . .

The Republicans say that this nation is in the hands of destiny; Washington believed that not only the destiny of our own nation but the destiny of the republican form of government throughout the world was entrusted to American hands. Immeasurable responsibility!

The destiny of this republic is in the hands of its own people, and upon the success of the experiment here rests the hope of humanity. No exterior force can disturb this republic, and no foreign influence should be permitted to change its course. What the future has in store for this nation no one has authority to declare, but each individual has his own idea of the nation's mission, and he owes it to his country as well as to himself to contribute as best he may to the fulfillment of that mission. . . .

Mother Jones (1830–1930)

Throughout her long life, Mary Harris (Mother) Jones was a leading activist in the labor movement. When she was 37, her husband and four children died in a yellow fever epidemic. Soon thereafter, she involved herself in the union cause and became active as a strike organizer with the Knights of Labor and the United Mine Workers. By the twentieth century,

she had joined the Socialist Party, and was one of the founders of the
Industrial Workers of the World. Even in her nineties, she was still active in
helping to organize strikes. As she strove to alleviate the hardships faced by
all victims of industrialization, she became especially dedicated to the
abolition of child labor. In 1903, at the age of 73, she led a march of more
than a hundred miles from Philadelphia to Sagamore Hill to confront
President Theodore Roosevelt with the harsh realities of the exploitation of
children, which she describes in this chapter from her autobiography.

"THE MARCH OF THE MILL CHILDREN," 1903

In the spring of 1903 I went to Kensington, Pennsylvania, where seventy-five thousand textile workers were on strike. Of this number at least ten thousand were little children. The workers were striking for more pay and shorter hours. Every day little children came into Union Headquarters, some with their hands off, some with the thumb missing, some with their fingers off at the knuckle. They were stooped things, round shouldered and skinny. Many of them were not over ten years of age, the state law prohibited their working before they were twelve years of age.

The law was poorly enforced and the mothers of these children often swore falsely as to their children's age. In a single block in Kensington, fourteen women, mothers of twenty-two children all under twelve, explained it was a question of starvation or perjury. That the fathers had been killed or maimed at the mines.

I asked the newspaper men why they didn't publish the facts about child labor in Pennsylvania. They said they couldn't because the mill owners had stock in the papers.

"Well, I've got stock in these little children," said I, "and I'll arrange a little publicity."

We assembled a number of boys and girls one morning in Independence Park and from there we arranged to parade with banners to the court house where we would hold a meeting. A great crowd gathered in the public square in front of the city hall. I put the little boys with their fingers off and hands crushed and maimed on a platform. I held up their mutilated hands and showed them to the crowd and made the statement that Philadelphia's mansions were built on the broken bones, the quivering hearts and drooping heads of these children. That their little lives went out to make wealth for others. That neither state or city officials paid any attention to these wrongs. That they did not care that these children were to be the future citizens of the nation.

SOURCE: *The Autobiography of Mother Jones,* 4th ed. (Chicago: Charles H. Kerr, 1990), chapter 10.

The officials of the city hall were standing in the open windows. I held the little ones of the mills high up above the heads of the crowd and pointed to their puny arms and legs and hollow chests. They were light to lift.

I called upon the millionaire manufactures to cease their moral murders, and I cried to the officials in the open windows opposite, "Some day the workers will take possession of your city hall, and when we do, no child will be sacrificed on the altar of profit."

The officials quickly closed the windows, as they had closed their eyes and hearts.

The reporters quoted my statement that Philadelphia mansions were built on the broken bones and quivering hearts of children. The Philadelphia papers and the New York papers got into a squabble with each other over the question. The universities discussed it. Preachers began talking. That was what I wanted. Public attention on the subject of child labor.

The matter quieted down for a while and I concluded the people needed stirring up again. The Liberty Bell that a century ago rang out for freedom against tyranny was touring the country and crowds were coming to see it everywhere. That gave me an idea. These little children were striking for some of the freedom that childhood ought to have, and I decided that the children and I would go on a tour.

I asked some of the parents if they would let me have their little boys and girls for a week or ten days, promising to bring them back safe and sound. They consented. A man named Sweeny was marshal for our "army." A few men and women went with me to help with the children. They were on strike and I thought, they might well have a little recreation.

The children carried knapsacks on their backs which had a knife and fork, a tin cup and plate. We took along a wash boiler in which to cook the food on the road. One little fellow had drum and another had a fife. That was our band. We carried banners that said, "We want more schools and less hospitals." "We want time to play." "Prosperity is here. Where is ours?"

We started from Philadelphia where we held a great mass meeting. I decided to go with the children to see President Roosevelt to ask him to have Congress pass a law prohibiting the exploitation of childhood. I thought that President Roosevelt might see these mill children and compare them with his own little ones who were spending the summer on the seashore at Oyster Bay. I thought too, out of politeness, we might call on Morgan in Wall Street who owned the mines where many of these children's fathers worked.

The children were very happy, having plenty to eat, taking baths in the brooks and rivers every day. I thought when the strike is over and they go back to the mills, they will never have another holiday like this. All along the line of march the farmers drove out to meet us with wagon loads of fruit and vegetables. Their wives brought the children clothes and money. The interurban train-men would stop their trains and give us free rides.

Marshal Sweeny and I would go ahead to the towns and arrange sleeping quarters for the children, and secure meeting halls. As we marched on, it grew terribly hot. There was no rain and the roads were heavy with dust. From time to time we had to send some of the children back to their homes. They were too weak to stand the march.

We were on the outskirts of New Trenton, New Jersey, cooking our lunch in the wash boiler, when the conductor on the interurban car stopped and told us the police were coming down to notify us that we could not enter the town. There were mills in the town and the mill owners didn't like our coming.

I said, "All right, the police will be just in time for lunch."

Sure enough, the police came and we invited them to dine with us. They looked at the little gathering of children with their tin plates and cups around the wash boiler. They just smiled and spoke kindly to the children, and said nothing at all about not going into the city.

We went in, held our meeting, and it was the wives of the police who took the little children and cared for them that night, sending them back in the morning with a nice lunch rolled up in paper napkins.

Everywhere we had meetings, showing up with living children, the horrors of child labor. . . .

I called on the mayor of Princeton and asked for permission to speak opposite the campus of the University. I said I wanted to speak on higher education. The mayor gave me permission. A great crowd gathered, professors and students and the people; and I told them that the rich robbed these little children of any education of the lowest order that they might send their sons and daughters to places of higher education. That they used the hands and feet of little children that they might buy automobiles for their wives and police dogs for their daughters to talk French to. I said the mill owners take babies almost from the cradle. And I showed those professors children in our army who could scarcely read or write because they were working ten hours a day in the silk mills of Pennsylvania.

"Here's a text book on economics," I said pointing to a little chap, James Ashworth, who was ten years old and who was stooped over like an old man from carrying bundles of yarn that weighed seventy-five pounds. "He gets three dollars a week and his sister who is fourteen gets six dollars. They work in a carpet factory ten hours a day while the children of the rich are getting their higher education." . . .

I sent a committee over to the New York Chief of Police, Ebstein, asking for permission to march up Fourth Avenue to Madison Square where I wanted to hold a meeting. The chief refused and forbade our entrance to the city.

I went over myself to New York and saw Mayor Seth Low. The mayor was most courteous but he said he would have to support the police commissioner. I asked him what the reason was for refusing us entrance to the city and he said that we were not citizens of New York.

"Oh, I think we will clear that up, Mr. Mayor," I said. "Permit me to call your attention to an incident which took place in this nation just a year ago. A piece of rotten royalty came over here from Germany, called Price Henry. The Congress of the United States voted $45,000 to fill that fellow's stomach three weeks and to entertain him. His highness was getting $4,000,000 dividends out of the blood of the workers in this country. Was he a citizen of this land?"

"And it was reported, Mr. Mayor, that you and all the officials of New York and the University Club entertained that chap." And repeated, "Was he a citizen of New York!"

"No, Mother," said the mayor, "he was not." . . .

"Well, Mr. Mayor, these are the little citizens of the nation and they also produce its wealth. Aren't we entitled to enter your city?" . . .

We marched to Twentieth Street. I told an immense crowd of the horrors of child labor in the mills around the anthracite region and I showed them some of the children. I showed them Eddie Dunphy, a little fellow of twelve, whose job it was to sit all day on a high stool, handing in the right thread to another worker. Eleven hours a day he sat on the high stool with dangerous machinery all about him. All day long, winter and summer, spring and fall, for three dollars a week.

And then I showed them Gussie Rangnew, a little girl from whom all the childhood had gone. Her face was like an old woman's. Gussie packed stockings in a factory, eleven hours a day for a few cents a day.

We raised a lot of money for the strikers and hundreds of friends offered their homes to the little ones while we were in the city.

The next day we went to Coney Island at the invitation of Mr. Bostick who owned the wild animal show The children had a wonderful day such as they never had in all their lives. After the exhibition of the trained animals, Mr. Bostick let me speak to the audience. . . . Right in front of the emperors were the empty iron cages of the animals. I put my little children in the cages and they clung to the iron bars while I talked.

I told the crowd that the scene was typical of the aristocracy of employers with their thumb down to the little ones of the mills and factories, and people sitting dumbly by.

"We want President Roosevelt to hear the wail of the children who never have a chance to go to school but work eleven and twelve hours a day in the textile mills of Pennsylvania; who weave the carpets that he and you walk upon and the lace curtains in your windows, and the clothes of the people. Fifty years ago there was a cry against slavery and men gave up their lives to stop the selling of black children on the block. Today the white child is sold for two dollars a week to the manufacturers. Fifty years ago the black babies were sold C.O.D. Today the white baby is sold on the installment plan.

"In Georgia where children work day and night in the cotton mills they have just passed a bill to protect song birds. What about little children from whom all song is gone?

"I shall ask the president in the name of the aching hearts of these little ones that he emancipate them from slavery. I will tell the president that the prosperity he boasts of is the prosperity of the rich wrung from the poor and the helpless.

"The trouble is that no one in Washington cares. I saw our legislators in one hour pass three bills for the relief of the railways but when labor cries for aid for the children they will not listen.

"I asked a man in prison once how he happened to be there and he said he had stolen a pair of shoes. I told him if he had stolen a railroad he would be a United States Senator.

"We are told that every American boy has the chance of being president. I tell you that these little boys in the iron cages would sell their chance any day for good square meals and a chance to play. These little toilers whom I have taken from the mills—deformed, dwarfed in body and soul, with nothing but toil before them—have never heard that they have a chance, the chance of every American male citizen, to become the president.

"You see those monkeys in those cages over there." I pointed to a side cage. "The professors are trying to teach them to talk. The monkeys are too wise for they fear that the manufacturers would buy them for slaves in their factories." . . .

The next day we left Coney Island for Manhattan Beach to visit Senator Platt, who had made an appointment to see me at nine o'clock in the morning. The children got stuck in the sand banks and I had a time cleaning the sand off the littlest ones. So we started to walk on the railroad track. I was told it was private property and we had to get off. Finally a saloon keeper showed us a short cut into the sacred grounds of the hotel and suddenly the army appeared in the lobby. The little fellows played "Hail, hail, the gang's all here" their fifes and drums, and Senator Platt when he saw the little army ran away through the back door to New York.

I asked the manager if he would give children breakfast and charge it up to Senator as we had an invitation to breakfast that morning with him. He gave us a private room and he gave those children such a breakfast as they had never had in all their lives. I had breakfast too, and a reporter from of the Hearst papers and I charged it all to Senator Platt.

We marched down to Oyster Bay but the president refused to see us and he would not answer my letters. But our march had done its work. We had drawn the attention of the nation to the crime of child labor. And while the strike of the textile workers in Kensington was lost and the children driven back to work, not long afterward the Pennsylvania legislature passed a child labor law that sent thousands of children home from the mills, and kept thousands of others from entering the factory until they were fourteen years of age.

John Muir (1838–1914)

Born in Scotland and reared in Wisconsin, John Muir became one of the leading exponents and founders of the ecological movement. As a young man, he traveled extensively around the United States, and after his first visit to the Hetch Hetchy Valley in 1868, he made up his mind to settle in California. Concerned that loggers, miners, cattlemen, and sheepherders were despoiling the meadows and mountainsides of the Sierra Nevada, he begin writing articles extolling the beauties of nature and advocating the preservation of the wilderness. By the end of the 1870s, his reputation had spread, not only throughout the United States but also around the world. In 1890, along with Century *magazine editor Robert Underwood Johnson and several other supporters, Muir convinced Congress to preserve the Hetch Hetchy Valley and the surrounding area by passing an act establishing Yosemite National Park. Later he was influential in the creation of the Sequoia and Grand Canyon national parks, which earned him the nickname of "Father" of the national park system.*

Determined to prevent ranchers from encroaching on the new park, Muir founded the Sierra Club in 1892 to protect the Sierras and the redwoods. In 1903, President Theodore Roosevelt camped out with Muir in Yosemite and began to shape his own conservation and preservation policy. Claiming that "everybody needs beauty as well as bread, places to play in and pray in, where nature may heal and give strength to body and soul alike," Muir campaigned ardently, until his death in 1914, against business interests and politicians who would destroy the natural beauty of the forests and wilderness. The year before his death, he fought a losing and disheartening battle against the proposal to dam the Hetch Hetchy Valley to create a reservoir for San Francisco. Still, his efforts to preserve the redwoods and create a national park system bore fruit. One of the most beautiful state parks in California, in Marin County just north of the Golden Gate Bridge, is Muir Woods, and nearby is Muir Beach. Participants in the environmental movement that emerged from 1960s activism still regard Muir's writings to be as relevant and applicable today as they were a century ago.

"The Hetch Hetchy Valley," January 1908

It is impossible to overestimate the value of wild mountains and mountain temples as places for people to grow in, recreation grounds for soul and body. They are the greatest of our natural resources, God's best gifts, but none, however high and holy, is beyond reach of the spoiler. In these ravaging money-mad days monopolizing San Francisco capitalists are now doing their best to destroy the Yosemite Park, the most wonderful of all our great mountain national parks. Beginning on the Tuolumne side, they are trying with a lot of sinful ingenuity to get the Government's permission to dam and destroy the Hetch-Hetchy Valley for a reservoir, simply that comparatively private gain may be made out of universal public loss, while of course the Sierra Club is doing all it can to save the valley. The Honorable Secretary of the Interior has not yet announced his decision in the

SOURCE: *Sierra Club Bulletin*, vol. 6, no. 4, January 1908.

case, but in all that has come and gone nothing discouraging is yet in sight on our side of the fight.

As long as the busy public in general knew little or nothing about the Hetch-Hetchy Valley, the few cunning drivers of the damming scheme, working in darkness like moles in a low-lying meadow, seemed confident of success; but when light was turned on and the truth became manifest that next to Yosemite, Hetch-Hetchy is the most wonderful and most important feature of the great park, that damming it would destroy it, render it inaccessible, and block the way through the wonderful Tuolumne Cañon to the grand central campground in the upper Tuolumne Valley, thousands from near and far came to our help,— mountaineers, nature-lovers, naturalists. Most of our thousand club members wrote to the President or Secretary protesting against the destructive reservoir scheme while other sources of city water as pure or purer than the Hetch-Hetchy were available; so also did the Oregon and Washington mountaineering clubs and the Appalachian of Boston and public-spirited citizens everywhere. And the President, recognizing the need of beauty as well as bread and water in the life of the nation, far from favoring the destruction of any of our country's natural wonder parks and temples, is trying amid a host of other cares to save them all. Within a very short time he has saved the petrified forests of Arizona and the Grand Cañon, and in our own State the jagged peaks of San Benito county known as "The Pinnacles," making them national monuments or parks to be preserved for the people forever. None, therefore, need doubt that everything possible will be done to save Hetch-Hetchy.

After my first visit, in the autumn of 1871, I have always called it the Tuolumne Yosemite, for it is a wonderfully exact counterpart of the great Yosemite, not only in its crystal river and sublime rocks and waterfalls, but in the gardens, groves, and meadows of its flower park-like floor. The floor of Yosemite is about 4000 feet above the sea, the Hetch-Hetchy floor about 3700; the walls of both are of gray granite, rise abruptly out of the flowery grass and groves are sculptured in the same style, and in both every rock is a glacial monument.

Standing boldly out from the south wall is a strikingly picturesque rock called "Kolana" by the Indians, the outermost of a group 2300 feet high, corresponding with the Cathedral Rocks of Yosemite both in relative position and form. On the opposite side of the Valley, facing Kolana, there is a counterpart of the El Capitan of Yosemite rising sheer and plain to a height of 1800 feet, and over its massive brow flows a stream which makes the most graceful fall I have ever seen. From the edge of the cliff it is perfectly free in the air for a thousand feet, then breaks up into a ragged sheet of cascades among the boulders of an earthquake talus. It is in all its glory in June, when the snow is melting fast, but fades and vanishes toward the end of summer. The only fall I know with which it may fairly be compared is the Yosemite Bridal Veil; but it excels even that favorite fall both in height and fineness of fairy-airy beauty and behavior. Lowlanders are apt to suppose that mountain streams in their wild career over cliffs lose control of themselves and tumble in a noisy chaos of mist and spray. On the contrary, on no part of their travels are they more harmonious and self-controlled. Imagine yourself in Hetch Hetchy on a sunny day in June, standing waist-deep in grass and flowers (as I have oftentimes stood), while the great pines sway dreamily with scarce perceptible motion. Looking northward across the Valley you see a plain, gray granite cliff rising abruptly out of the gardens and groves to a height of 1800 feet, and in front of it Tueeulala's silvery scarf burning with irised sun-fire in every fiber. In the first white outburst of the stream at the head of the fall there is abundance of visible energy, but it is speedily hushed and concealed in divine repose, and its tranquil progress to the base of the cliff is like that of downy feathers in a still room. Now observe the fineness and marvelous distinct-ness of the various sun-illumined fabrics into which the water is woven; they sift and float from form to form down the face of that grand gray rock in so leisurely and unconfused a manner that you can examine their texture, and patterns and tones of color as you would a piece of embroidery held in the hand. Near the head of the fall you see groups of booming, comet-like masses, their solid, white heads separate, their tails like combed silk interlacing among delicate shadows, ever forming and dissolving, worn out by friction in their rush through the air. Most of these vanish a few hundred feet below the summit, changing to the var-ied forms of cloud-like drapery. Near the bottom the width of the fall has increased from about twenty-five to a hundred feet. Here it is composed of yet finer tissues, and is still without a trace of disorder—air, water and sunlight woven into stuff that spirits might wear.

So fine a fall might well seem sufficient to glorify any valley; but here, as in Yosemite, Nature seems in nowise moderate, for a short distance to the eastward of Tueeulala booms and thunders the great Hetch Hetchy Fall, Wapama, so near that you have both of them in full view from the same standpoint. It is the coun-terpart of the Yosemite Fall, but has a much greater volume of water, is about 1700 feet in height, and appears to be nearly vertical, though considerably inclined, and is dashed into huge outbounding bosses of foam on the projecting shelves and knobs of its jagged gorge. No two falls could be more unlike—Tueeulala out in the open sunshine descending like thistledown; Wapama in a jagged, shadowy gorge roaring and plundering, pounding its way with the weight and energy of an avalanche. Besides this glorious pair there is a broad, massive fall on the main river a short distance above the head of the Valley. Its position is something like that of the Vernal in Yosemite, and its roar as it plunges into a surging trout-pool may be heard a long way, though it is only about twenty feet high. There is also a chain of magnificent cascades at the head of the valley on a stream that comes in from the northeast, mostly silvery plumes, like the one between the Vernal and Nevada falls of Yosemite, half-sliding, half-leaping on bare glacier polished granite, covered with crisp clashing spray into which the sunbeams pour with glorious effect. And besides all these a few small streams come over the walls here and there, leaping from ledge to ledge with birdlike song and watering many a hidden cliff-garden and fernery, but they are too unshowy to be noticed in so grand a place.

The correspondence between the Hetch Hetchy walls in their trends, sculp-ture, physical structure, and general arrangement of the main rock-masses has excited the wondering admiration of every observer. We have seen that the El Capitan and Cathedral rocks occupy the same relative positions in both valleys; so also do their Yosemite Points and North Domes. Again that part of the Yosemite north wall immediately to the east of the Yosemite Fall has two horizontal benches timbered with golden-cup oak about 500 and 1500 feet above the floor. Two benches similarly situated and timbered occur on the same relative portion of the Hetch Hetchy north wall, to the east of Wapama Fall, and on no other. The Yosemite is bounded at the head by the great Half Dome. Hetch Hetchy is bounded in the same way though its head rock is far less wonderful and sublime in form.

The floor of the Valley is about three and a half miles long and from a fourth to half a mile wide. The lower portion is mostly a level meadow about a mile long, with the trees restricted to the sides, and partially separated from the upper forested portion by a low bar of glacier-polished granite across which the river breaks in rapids.

The principal trees are the yellow and sugar pines, Sabine pine, incense cedar, Douglas spruce, silver fir, the California and gold-cup oaks, balm of Gilead poplar, Nuttall's flowering dogwood, alder, maple, laurel, tumion, etc. The most abundant and influential are the great yellow pines, the tallest over two hundred feet in height, and the oaks with massive rugged trunks four to six or seven feet in diameter, and broad arching heads, assembled in magnificent groves. The shrubs forming conspicuous flowery clumps and tangles are manzanita, azalea, spiraea, brier-rose, ceanothus, calycanthus, philadelphus, wild cherry, etc.; with abundance of showy and fragrant herbaceous plants growing about them or out in the open in beds by themselves—lilies, Mariposa tulips, brodiaeas, orchids—several species of each,—iris, spraguea, draperia, collomia, collinsia, castilleia, nemophila, larkspur, columbine, goldenrods, sunflowers, and mints of many species, honeysuckle, etc. etc. Many fine ferns dwell here also, especially the beautiful and interesting rock-ferns—pellaea, and cheilanthes of several species—fringing and rosetting dry rock-piles and ledges; woodwardia and asplenium on damp spots with fronds six or seven feet high; the delicate maidenhair in mossy nooks by the falls, and the sturdy, broad-shouldered pteris beneath the oaks and pines.

It appears therefore that Hetch-Hetchy Valley, far from being a plain, common, rock-bound meadow, as many who have not seen it seem to suppose, is a grand landscape garden, one of Nature's rarest and most precious mountain mansions. As in Yosemite, the sublime rocks of its walls seem to the nature-lover to glow with life, whether leaning back in repose or standing erect in thoughtful attitudes, giving welcome to storms and calms alike. And how softly these mountain rocks are adorned, and how fine and reassuring the company they keep—their brows in the sky, their feet set in groves and gay emerald meadows, a thousand flowers leaning confidingly against their adamantine bosses, while birds, bees, and butterflies help the river and waterfalls to stir all the air into music—things frail and fleeting and types of permanence meeting here and blending, as if into this glorious mountain temple Nature had gathered here choicest treasures, whether great or small, to draw her lovers into close confiding communion with her.

Strange to say, this is the mountain temple that is now in danger of being dammed and made into a reservoir to help supply San Francisco with water and light. This use of the valley, so destructive and foreign to its proper park use, has long been planned and prayed for, and is still being prayed for by the San Francisco board of supervisors, not because water as pure and abundant cannot be got from adjacent sources outside the park—for it can,—but seemingly only because of the comparative cheapness of the dam required.

Garden- and park-making goes on everywhere with civilization, for everybody needs beauty as well as bread, places to play in and pray in, where Nature may heal and cheer and give strength to body and soul. This natural beauty-hunger is displayed in poor folks' window-gardens made up of a few geranium slips in broken cups, as well as in the costly lily gardens of the rich, the thousands of spacious city parks and botanical gardens, and in our magnificent National parks—the Yellowstone, Yosemite, Sequoia, etc.—Nature's own wonderlands, the admiration and joy of the world. Nevertheless, like everything else worth while, however sacred and precious and well-guarded, they have always been subject to attack, mostly by despoiling gainseekers,—mischief-makers of every degree from Satan to supervisors, lumbermen, cattlemen, farmers, etc., eagerly trying to make everything dollarable, often thinly disguised in smiling philanthropy, calling pocket-filling plunder "Utilization of beneficent natural resources, that man and beast may be fed and the dear Nation grow great." Thus long ago a lot of enterprising merchants made part of the Jerusalem temple into a place of business instead of a place of prayer, changing money, buying and selling cattle and sheep and doves. And earlier still, the Lord's garden in Eden, and the first forest reservation, including only one tree, was spoiled. And so to some extent have all our reservations and parks. Ever since the establishment of the Yosemite National Park by act of Congress, October 8, 1890, constant strife has been going on around its borders and I suppose this will go on as part of the universal battle between right and wrong, however its boundaries may be shorn or its wild beauty destroyed. The first application to the Government by the San Francisco Supervisors for the use of Lake Eleanor and the Hetch Hetchy Valley was made in 1903, and denied December 22nd of that year by the Secretary of the Interior. In his report on this case he well says: "Presumably the Yosemite National Park was created such by law because of the natural objects, of varying degrees of scenic importance, located within its boundaries, inclusive alike of its beautiful small lakes, like Eleanor, and its majestic wonders, like Hetch-Hetchy and Yosemite Valley. It is the aggregation of such natural scenic features that makes the Yosemite Park a wonderland which the Congress of the United States sought by law to preserve for all coming time as nearly as practicable in the condition fashioned by the hand of the Creator—a worthy object of national pride and a source of healthful pleasure and rest for the thousands of people who may annually sojourn there during the heated months."

The most delightful and wonderful campgrounds in the Park are the three great valleys—Yosemite, Hetch-Hetchy, and Upper Tuolumne; and they are also the most important places with reference to their positions relative to the other great features—the Merced and Tuolumne Cañons, and the High Sierra peaks and glaciers, etc., at the head of the rivers. The main part of the Tuolumne Valley is a beautiful spacious flowery lawn four or five miles long, surrounded by magnificent snowy mountains. It is about 8500 feet above the sea, and forms the grand central High Sierra camp ground from which excursions are made to the noble mountains, domes, glaciers, etc.; across the Range to the Mono Lake and volcanoes and down the Tuolumne Cañon to Hetch Hetchy. But should Hetch Hetchy be submerged, as proposed, not only would it be made utterly inaccessible, but the sublime cañon way to the heart of the High Sierra would be hopelessly blocked. None, as far as I have learned, of all the thousands who have seen the park is in favor of this destructive water scheme.

My last visit to the Valley was made in the autumn of last year, with William Keith, the artist. The leaf-colors were then ripe, and the great godlike rocks in repose seemed to glow with life. The artist, under their spell, wandered day after day along the beautiful river and through the groves and gardens, studying the wonderful scenery; and, after making about forty sketches, declared with enthusiasm that in picturesque beauty and charm Hetch Hetchy surpassed even Yosemite.

That any one would try to destroy such a place seemed impossible; but sad experience shows that there are people good enough and bad enough for anything. The proponents of the dam scheme bring forward a lot of bad arguments to prove that the only righteous thing for Hetch-Hetchy is its destruction. These arguments are curiously like those of the devil devised for the destruction of the first garden—so much of the very best Eden fruit going to waste; so much of the best Tuolumne water. Very few of their statements are even partly true, and all are misleading. Thus, Hetch Hetchy, they say, is a "low-lying meadow."

On the contrary, it is a high-lying natural landscape garden.

"It is a common minor feature, like thousands of others."

On the contrary, it is a very uncommon feature; after Yosemite, the rarest and in many ways the most important in the park.

"Damming and submerging it 175 feet deep would enhance its beauty by forming a crystal-clear lake."

Landscape gardens, places of recreation and worship, are never made beautiful by destroying and burying them. The beautiful lake, forsooth, should be only an eyesore, a dismal blot on the landscape, like many others to be seen in the Sierra. For, instead of keeping it at the same level all the year, allowing Nature to make new shores, it would, of course, be full only a month or two in the spring, when the snow is melting fast; then it would be gradually drained, exposing the slimy sides of the basin and shallower parts of the bottom, with the gathered drift and waste, death and decay of the upper basins, caught here instead of being swept on to decent natural burial along the banks of the river or in the sea. Thus the Hetch Hetchy dam-lake would be only a rough imitation of a natural lake for a few of the spring months, an open mountain sepulcher for the others.

"Hetch Hetchy water is the purest, wholly unpolluted, and forever unpollutable."

On the contrary, excepting that of the Merced below Yosemite, it is less pure than that of most of the other Sierra streams, because of the sewerage of campgrounds draining into it, especially of the Big Tuolumne Meadows campgrounds, where hundreds of tourists and mountaineers, with their animals, are encamped for months every summer, soon to be followed by thousands of travelers from all the world.

These temple destroyers, devotees of ravaging commercialism, seem to have a perfect contempt for Nature, and, instead of lifting their eyes to the mountains, lift them to dams and town skyscrapers.

Dam Hetch-Hetchy! As well dam for water-tanks the people's cathedrals and churches, for no holier temple has ever been consecrated by the heart of man.

"SAVE THE REDWOODS," JANUARY 1920

We are often told that the world is going from bad to worse, sacrificing everything to mammon. But this righteous uprising in defense of God's trees in the midst of exciting politics and wars is telling a different story, and every Sequoia, I fancy, has heard the good news and is waving its branches for joy. The wrongs done to trees, wrongs of every sort, are done in the darkness of ignorance and unbelief, for when light comes the heart of the people is always right. Forty-seven years ago one of these Calaveras King Sequoias was laboriously cut down, that the stump might be had for a dancing-floor. Another, one of the finest in the grove, more than three hundred feet high, was skinned alive to a height of one hundred and sixteen feet from the ground and the bark sent to London to show how fine and big that Calaveras tree was—as sensible a scheme as skinning our great men would be to prove their greatness. This grand tree is of course dead, a ghastly disfigured ruin, but it still stands erect and holds forth its majestic arms as if alive and saying, "Forgive them; they know not what they do." Now some millmen want to cut all the Calaveras trees into lumber and money. But we have found a better use for them. No doubt these trees would make good lumber after passing through a sawmill, as George Washington after passing through the hands of a French cook would have made good food. But both for Washington and the tree that bears his name higher uses have been found.

Could one of these Sequoia Kings come to town in all its godlike majesty so as to be strikingly seen and allowed to plead its own cause, there would never again be any lack of defenders. And the same may be said of all the other Sequoia groves and forests of the Sierra with their companions and the noble *Sequoia sempervirens*, or redwood, of the coast mountains.

In a general view we find that the *Sequoia gigantea*, or Big Tree, is distributed in a widely interrupted belt along the west flank of the Sierra, from a small grove on the middle fork of the American River to the head of Deer Creek, a distance of about two hundred and sixty miles, at an elevation of about five thousand to a little over eight thousand feet above the sea. From the American River grove to the forest on Kings River the species occurs only in comparatively small isolated patches or groves so sparsely distributed along the belt that three of the gaps in it are from forty to sixty miles wide. From Kings River southward the Sequoia is not restricted to mere groves, but extends across the broad rugged basins of the Kaweah and Tule rivers in majestic forests a distance of nearly seventy miles, the continuity of this portion of the belt being but slightly broken save by the deep cañons.

In these noble groves and forests to the southward of the Calaveras Grove the axe and saw have long been busy, and thousands of the finest Sequoias have been felled, blasted into manageable dimensions, and sawed into lumber by methods destructive almost beyond belief, while fires have spread still wider and more lamentable ruin. In the course of my explorations twenty-five years ago, I found five sawmills located on or near the lower margin of the Sequoia belt, all of which were cutting more or less Big Tree lumber, which looks like the redwood of the coast, and was sold as redwood. One of the smallest of these mills in the season of 1874 sawed two million feet of Sequoia lumber. Since that time other mills have been built among the Sequoias, notably the large ones on Kings River and the head of the Fresno. The destruction of these grand trees is still going on.

On the other hand, the Calaveras Grove for forty years has been faithfully protected by Mr. Sperry, and with the exception of the two trees mentioned above is still in primeval beauty. The Tuolumne and Merced groves near Yosemite, the Dinky Creek grove, those of the General Grant National Park and the Sequoia National Park, with several outstanding groves that are nameless on the Kings, Kaweah, and Tule river basins, and included in the Sierra forest reservation, have of late years been partially protected by the Federal Government; while the well-known Mariposa Grove has long been guarded by the State.

For the thousands of acres of Sequoia forest outside of the reservation and national parks, and in the hands of lumbermen, no help is in sight. Probably more than three times as many Sequoias as are contained in the whole Calaveras Grove have been cut into lumber every year for the last twenty-six years without let or hindrance, and with scarce a word of protest on the part of the public, while at the first whisper of the bonding of the Calaveras Grove to lumbermen most everybody rose in alarm. This righteous and lively indignation on the part of Californians after the long period of deathlike apathy, in which they have witnessed the destruction of other groves unmoved, seems strange until the rapid growth that right public opinion has made during the last few years is considered and the peculiar interest that attaches to the Calaveras giants. They were the first discovered and are best known. Thousands of travelers from every country have come to pay them tribute of admiration and praise, their reputation is world-wide, and the names of great men have long been associated with them—Washington, Humboldt, Torrey and Gray, Sir Joseph Hooker, and others. These kings of the forest, the noblest of a noble race, rightly belong to the world, but as they are in California we cannot escape responsibility as their guardians. Fortunately the American people are equal to this trust, or any other that may arise, as soon as they see it and understand it.

Any fool can destroy trees. They cannot defend themselves or run away. And few destroyers of trees ever plant any; nor can planting avail much toward restoring our grand aboriginal giants. It took more than three thousand years to make some of the oldest of the Sequoias, trees that are still standing in perfect strength and beauty, waving and singing in the mighty forests of the Sierra. Through all the eventful centuries since Christ's time, and long before that, God has cared for these trees, saved them from drought, disease, avalanches, and a thousand storms; but he cannot save them from sawmills and fools; this is left to the American people. . . .

Emma Goldman. Emma Goldman, an outspoken advocate of socialism, workers' rights, birth control, full equality of the sexes, and sexual liberation, speaking for birth control at Union Square, New York City, May 20, 1916. "If the world is ever to give birth to true companionship and oneness," she once wrote, "not marriage, but love, will be the parent."

Emma Goldman (1869–1940)

Emma Goldman, a Lithuanian Jew, spent much of her youth in St. Petersburg, Russia, at a time when Jews were persecuted and the political philosophy of anarchism was having a huge impact on revolutionary students. In 1881, revolutionary factions had become so sure of the righteousness of their cause that they assassinated Czar Alexander III. In the aftermath of the authoritarian crackdown on anarchists, 16-year-old Emma Goldman emigrated to the United States in 1885. She must have had a sense that she would find a golden land of opportunity in the New World—at least that there would be more opportunities for a young woman than there were in czarist Russia. But it did not take her long to realize that life in her new home was not exactly a bed of roses. She took a low-paying job in a factory in Rochester, New York, and began to engage in political activities. Influenced by newspaper accounts of the trial, conviction, and execution of the anarchists who had been accused of killing several police officers at Haymarket Square in Chicago, Goldman left her job in 1889, moved to New York City, and joined an anarchist association. Within a few short years, she became one of the most outspoken and notorious anarchist-feminists in the nation. Believing that a society could be created in which there would be no private property or repression and in which absolute freedom would exist for all individuals, she became an activist campaigning for women's rights to birth control, full equality, and sexual liberation, as well as the rights of workers to unionize. In 1892, she went so far as to aid and abet her lover (and fellow anarchist) Alexander Berkman in his unsuccessful attempt to assassinate the chairman of the Carnegie Steel Company, Henry Clay Frick, during the Homestead Strike. During the First World War, her protests against conscription and her speeches praising the Bolshevik revolution in Russia led to her arrest and, after two years in jail, her eventual deportation in 1919.

The institution of marriage, Goldman believed, was nothing but legalized prostitution. In a patriarchic society that deprived them of social and economic equality, women were forced to "sell themselves" into marriage to survive. The only way women would ever achieve equality was not through gaining political power or the right to vote but through abolishing the institution of marriage altogether and securing absolute control over their own bodies. "True emancipation," she declared, "begins neither at the polls nor in court. It begins in a woman's soul." The goal was complete and total emotional and sexual liberation.

In her writings, Emma Goldman argues persuasively for the creation of a society in which democracy and freedom are truly realized and in which distinctions of gender and race have been obliterated.

"Marriage and Love," 1911

The popular notion about marriage and love is that they are synonymous, that they spring from the same motives, and cover the same human needs. Like most popular notions this also rests not on actual facts, but on superstition.

Marriage and love have nothing in common; they are as far apart as the poles; are, in fact, antagonistic to each other. No doubt some marriages have been the result of love. Not, however, because love could assert itself only in marriage; much rather is it because few people can completely outgrow a convention.

SOURCE: Emma Goldman, *Anarchism and Other Essays*, 2nd ed. (New York & London: Mother Earth Publishing Association, 1911), 233–245.

There are to-day large numbers of men and women to whom marriage is naught but a farce, but who submit to it for the sake of public opinion. At any rate, while it is true that some marriages are based on love, and while it is equally true that in some cases love continues in married life, I maintain that it does so regardless of marriage, and not because of it.

On the other hand, it is utterly false that love results from marriage. On rare occasions one does hear of a miraculous case of a married couple falling in love after marriage, but on close examination it will be found that it is a mere adjustment to the inevitable. Certainly the growing used to each other is far away from the spontaneity, the intensity, and beauty of love, without which the intimacy of marriage must prove degrading to both the woman and the man.

Marriage is primarily an economic arrangement, an insurance pact. It differs from the ordinary life insurance agreement only in that it is more binding, more exacting. Its returns are insignificantly small compared with the investments. In taking out an insurance policy one pays for it in dollars and cents, always at liberty to discontinue payments. If, however, woman's premium is a husband, she pays for it with her name, her privacy, her self-respect, her very life, "until death doth part." Moreover, the marriage insurance condemns her to life-long dependency, to parasitism, to complete uselessness, individual as well as social. Man, too, pays his toll, but as his sphere is wider, marriage does not limit him as much as woman. He feels his chains more in an economic sense.

Thus Dante's motto over Inferno applies with equal force to marriage: "Ye who enter here leave all hope behind."

That marriage is a failure none but the very stupid will deny. One has but to glance over the statistics of divorce to realize how bitter a failure marriage really is. ... [S]cores of ... writers are discussing the barrenness, the monotony, the sordidness, the inadequacy of marriage as a factor for harmony and understanding.

The thoughtful social student will not content himself with the popular superficial excuse for this phenomenon. He will have to dig down deeper into the very life of the sexes to know why marriage proves so disastrous.

Edward Carpenter says that behind every marriage stands the life-long environment of the two sexes; an environment so different from each other that man and woman must remain strangers. Separated by an insurmountable wall of superstition, custom, and habit, marriage has not the potentiality of developing knowledge of, and respect for, each other, without which every union is doomed to failure.

Henrik Ibsen, the hater of all social shams, was probably the first to realize this great truth. Nora leaves her husband, not—as the stupid critic would have it—because she is tired of her responsibilities or feels the need of woman's rights, but because she has come to know that for eight years she had lived with a stranger and borne him children. Can there be any thing more humiliating, more degrading than a life-long proximity between two strangers? No need for the woman to know anything of the man, save his income. As to the knowledge of the woman—what is there to know except that she has a pleasing appearance? We have not yet outgrown the theologic myth that woman has no soul, that she is a mere appendix to man, made out of his rib just for the convenience of the gentleman who was so strong that he was afraid of his own shadow.

Perchance the poor quality of the material whence woman comes is responsible for her inferiority. At any rate, woman has no soul—what is there to know about her? Besides, the less soul a woman has the greater her asset as a wife, the more readily will she absorb herself in her husband. It is this slavish acquiescence to man's superiority that has kept the marriage institution seemingly intact for so long a period. Now that woman is coming into her own, now that she is actually growing aware of herself as a being outside of the master's grace, the sacred institution of marriage is gradually being undermined, and no amount of sentimental lamentation can stay it.

From infancy, almost, the average girl is told that marriage is her ultimate goal; therefore her training and education must be directed towards that end. Like the mute beast fattened for slaughter, she is prepared for that. Yet, strange to say, she is allowed to know much less about her function as wife and mother than the ordinary artisan of his trade. It is indecent and filthy for a respectable girl to know anything of the marital relation. Oh, for the inconsistency of respectability, that needs the marriage vow to turn something which is filthy into the purest and most sacred arrangement that none dare question or criticize. Yet that is exactly the attitude of the average upholder of marriage. The prospective wife and mother is kept in complete ignorance of her only asset in the competitive field—sex. Thus she enters into life-long relations with a man only to find herself shocked, repelled, outraged beyond measure by the most natural and healthy instinct, sex. It is safe to say that a large percentage of the unhappiness, misery, distress, and physical suffering of matrimony is due to the criminal ignorance in sex matters that is being extolled as a great virtue. Nor is it at all an exaggeration when I say that more than one home has been broken up because of this deplorable fact.

If, however, woman is free and big enough to learn the mystery of sex without the sanction of State or Church, she will stand condemned as utterly unfit to become the wife of a "good" man, his goodness consisting of an empty head and plenty of money. Can there be anything more outrageous than the idea that a healthy, grown woman, full of life and passion, must deny nature's demand, must subdue her most intense craving, undermine her health and break her spirit, must stunt her vision, abstain from the depth and glory of sex experience until a "good" man comes along to take her unto himself as a wife? That is precisely what marriage means. How can such an arrangement end except in failure? This is one, though not the least important, factor of marriage, which differentiates it from love.

Ours is a practical age. . . . If, on rare occasions young people allow themselves the luxury of romance they are taken in care by the elders, drilled and pounded until they become "sensible."

The moral lesson instilled in the girl is not whether the man has aroused her love, but rather is it, "How much?" The important and only God of practical American life: Can the man make a living? Can he support a wife? That is the only thing that justifies marriage. Gradually this saturates every thought of the girl; her dreams are not of moonlight and kisses, of laughter and tears; she dreams of shopping tours and bargain counters. This soul-poverty and sordidness are the elements inherent in the marriage institution. The State and the Church approve of no other ideal, simply because it is the one that necessitates the State and Church control of men and women.

Doubtless there are people who continue to consider love above dollars and cents. Particularly is this true of that class whom economic necessity has forced to become self-supporting. The tremendous change in woman's position, wrought by that mighty factor, is indeed phenomenal when we reflect that it is but a short time since she has entered the industrial arena. Six million women wage-earners; six million women, who have the equal right with men to be exploited, to be robbed, to go on strike; aye, to starve even. Anything more, my lord? Yes, six million wage-workers in every walk of life, from the highest brain work to the most difficult menial labor in the mines and on the railroad tracks; yes, even detectives and policemen. Surely the emancipation is complete.

Yet with all that, but a very small number of the vast army of women wage-workers look upon work as a permanent issue, in the same light as does man. No matter how decrepit the latter, he has been taught to be independent, self-supporting. Oh, I know that no one is really independent in our economic tread mill; still, the poorest specimen of a man hates to be a parasite; to be known as such, at any rate.

The woman considers her position as worker transitory, to be thrown aside for the first bidder. That is why it is infinitely harder to organize women than men. "Why should I join a union? I am going to get married, to have a home." Has she not been taught from infancy to look upon that as her ultimate calling? She learns soon enough that the home, though not so large a prison as the factory, has more solid doors and bars. It has a keeper so faithful that naught can escape him. The most tragic part, however, is that the home no longer frees her from wage slavery; it only increases her task.

According to the latest statistics submitted before a Committee "on labor and wages, and congestion of Population," ten per cent. of the wage workers in New York City alone are married, yet they must continue to work at the most poorly paid labor in the world. Add to this horrible aspect the drudgery of house work, and what remains of the protection and glory of the home? As a matter of fact, even the middle class girl in marriage can not speak of her home, since it is the man who creates her sphere. It is not important whether the husband is a brute or a darling. What I wish to prove is that marriage guarantees woman a home only by the grace of her husband. There she moves about in *his* home, year after year until her aspect of life and human affairs becomes as flat, narrow, and drab as her surroundings. Small wonder if she becomes a nag, petty, quarrelsome, gossipy, unbearable, thus driving the man from the house. She could not go, if she wanted to; there is no place to go. Besides, a short period of married life, of complete surrender of all faculties, absolutely incapacitates the average woman for the outside world. She becomes reckless in appearance, clumsy in her movements, dependent in her decisions, cowardly in her judgment, a weight and a bore, which most men grow to hate and despise. Wonderfully inspiring atmosphere for the bearing of life, is it not?

But the child, how is it to be protected, if not for marriage? After all, is not that the most important consideration? The sham, the hypocrisy of it! Marriage protecting the child, yet thousands of children destitute and homeless. Marriage protecting the child, yet orphan asylums and reformatories over crowded, the Society for the Prevention of Cruelty to Children keeping busy in rescuing the little victims from "loving" parents, to place them under more loving care, the Gerry Society. Oh, the mockery of it! . . .

As to the protection of the woman,—therein lies the curse of marriage. Not that it really protects her, but the very idea is so revolting, such an outrage and insult on life, so degrading to human dignity, as to forever condemn this parasitic institution.

It is like that other paternal arrangement—capitalism. It robs man of his birthright, stunts his growth, poisons his body, keeps him in ignorance, in poverty and dependence, and then institutes charities that thrive on the last vestige of man's self-respect.

The institution of marriage makes a parasite of woman, an absolute dependent. It incapacitates her for life's struggle, annihilates her social consciousness, paralyzes her imagination, and then imposes its gracious protection, which is in reality a snare, a travesty on human character.

If motherhood is the highest fulfillment of woman's nature, what other protection does it need save love and freedom? Marriage but defiles, outrages, and corrupts her fulfillment. Does it not say to woman, Only when you follow me shall you bring forth life? Does it not condemn her to the block, does it not degrade and shame her if she refuses to buy her right to motherhood by selling herself? Does not marriage only sanction motherhood, even though conceived in hatred, in compulsion? Yet, if motherhood be of free choice, of love, of ecstasy, of defiant passion, does it not place a crown of thorns upon an innocent head and carve in letters of blood the hideous epithet, Bastard? Were marriage to contain all the virtues claimed for it, its crimes against motherhood would exclude it forever from the realm of love.

Love, the strongest and deepest element in all life, the harbinger of hope, of joy, of ecstasy; love, the defier of all laws, of all conventions; love, the freest, the most powerful moulder of human destiny; how can such an all-compelling force be synonymous with that poor little State and Church-begotten weed, marriage?

Free love? As if love is anything but free! Man has bought brains, but all the millions in the world have failed to buy love. Man has subdued bodies, but all the power on earth has been unable to subdue love. Man has conquered whole nations, but all his armies could not conquer love. Man has chained and fettered the spirit, but he has been utterly helpless before love. High on a throne, with all the splendor and pomp his gold can command, man is yet poor and desolate, if love passes him by. And if it stays, the poorest hovel is radiant with warmth, with life and color. Thus love has the magic power to make of a beggar a king. Yes, love is free; it can dwell in no other atmosphere. In freedom it gives itself unreservedly, abundantly, completely. All the laws on the statutes, all the courts in the universe, cannot tear it from the soil, once love has taken root. If, however, the soil is sterile, how can marriage make it bear fruit? It is like the last desperate struggle of fleeting life against death.

Love needs no protection; it is its own protection. So long as love begets life no child is deserted, or hungry, or famished for the want of affection. I know this to be true. I know women who became mothers in freedom by the men they loved. Few children in wedlock enjoy the care, the protection, the devotion free motherhood is capable of bestowing.

The defenders of authority dread the advent of a free motherhood, lest it will rob them of their prey. Who would fight wars? Who would create wealth? Who would make the policeman, the jailer, if woman were to refuse the indiscriminate breeding of children? The race, the race! shouts the king, the president, the capitalist, the priest. The race must be preserved, though woman be degraded to a mere machine,—and the marriage institution is our only safety valve against the pernicious sex-awakening of woman. But in vain these frantic efforts to maintain a state of bondage. In vain, too, the edicts of the Church, the mad attacks of rulers, in vain even the arm of the law. Woman no longer wants to be a party to the production of a race of sickly, feeble, decrepit, wretched human beings, who have neither the strength nor moral courage to throw off the yoke of poverty and slavery. Instead she desires fewer and better children, begotten and reared in love and through free choice; not by compulsion, as marriage imposes. Our pseudo-moralists have yet to learn the deep sense of responsibility toward the child, that love in freedom has awakened in the breast of woman. Rather would she forego forever the glory of motherhood than bring forth life in an atmosphere that breathes only destruction and death. And if she does become a mother, it is to give to the child the deepest and best her being can yield. To grow with the child is her motto; she knows that in that manner alone can she help build true manhood and womanhood. . . .

In our present pygmy state love is indeed a stranger to most people. Misunderstood and shunned, it rarely takes root; or if it does, it soon withers and dies. Its delicate fiber can not endure the stress and strain of the daily grind. Its soul is too complex to adjust itself to the slimy woof of our social fabric. It weeps and moans and suffers with those who have need of it, yet lack the capacity to rise to love's summit.

Some day, some day men and women will rise, they will reach the mountain peak, they will meet big and strong and free, ready to receive, to partake, and to bask in the golden rays of love. What fancy, what imagination, what poetic genius can foresee even approximately the potentialities of such a force in the life of men and women. If the world is ever to give birth to true companionship and oneness, not marriage, but love will be the parent.

Walter Rauschenbusch (1861–1918)

Throughout history, when the destitute sought solace and relief from hardship from their clergy, they were usually advised to pray and look forward to their reward in the next life. Walter Rauschenbusch, however, believed that it was as important to address people's needs in this life as it was to minister to their spiritual needs. After studying in Germany and England, where he was influenced by the Fabian socialist movement, he returned to the United States and became pastor of the Second German Baptist Church in New York City. While ministering to the German immigrants in the Hell's Kitchen section of the city, he began to develop the Social Gospel. By applying Christian principles to his critique of capitalism and Spencer and Sumner's social Darwinism, he, in effect, brought a moral dimension to the progressive movement. It was not enough to approach the problems of society from a political or social standpoint, for the problems were also, in Rauschenbusch's eyes, moral ones. By bringing morality into the discussion, he had a profound impact on many other reformers at the beginning of the twentieth century. His Social Gospel's appeal to Christian ethics brought many people who had previously been apathetic to the plight of the poor into the progressive movement. One of Rauschenbusch's contemporaries, Charles Sheldon, wrote a popular and influential book, In His Steps, *in which he urged businessmen and politicians, whenever they were confronted with a decision that would affect the lives of workers, always to ask themselves one simple question before making that decision: "What would Jesus do?" Later in the century, another clergyman, Martin Luther King Jr., would apply a moral dimension to the civil rights movement.*

CHRISTIANIZING THE SOCIAL ORDER, 1912

The chief purpose of the Christian Church in the past has been the salvation of individuals. But the most pressing task of the present is not individualistic. Our business is to make over an antiquated and immoral economic system: to get rid of laws, customs, maxims, and philosophies inherited from an evil and despotic

---

SOURCE: Walter Rauschenbusch, *Christianizing the Social Order* (New York: Macmillan, 1912), 41–44.

past; to create just and brotherly relations between great groups and classes of society; and thus to lay a social foundation on which modern men individually can live and work in a fashion that will not outrage all the better elements in them. . . .

The Christian Church in the past has taught us to work with our eyes fixed on another world and a life to come. But the business before us is concerned with refashioning the present world, making this earth clean and sweet and habitable. . . .

Twenty-five years ago the social wealth of the Bible was almost undiscovered to most of us. . . . Even Jesus talked like an individualist in those days and seemed to repudiate the social interest when we interrogated him. He said his kingdom was not of this world; the things of God had nothing to do with the things of Caesar; the poor we would always have with us; and his ministers must not be judges and dividers when Labor argued with Capital about the division of the inheritance. Today he has resumed the spiritual leadership of social Christianity, of which he was the founder. It is a new tribute to his mastership that the social message of Jesus was the first great possession which social Christianity rediscovered. . . .

With true Christian instinct men have turned to the Christian law of love as the key to the situation. If we all loved our neighbor, we should "treat him right," pay him a living wage, give sixteen ounces to the pound, and not charge so much for beef. But this appeal assumes that we are still living in the simple personal relations of the good old times, and that every man can do the right thing when he wants to do it. But suppose a business man would be glad indeed to pay his young women the $12 a week which they need for a decent living, but all his competitors are paying from $7 down to $5. Shall he love himself into bankruptcy? . . . The old advice of love breaks down before the hugeness of modern relations. . . . It is indeed love that we want, but it is socialized love. Blessed be the love that holds a cup of water to thirsty lips. . . . What we most need today is not the love that will break its back drawing water for a growing factory town from a well that was meant to supply a village, but a love so large and intelligent that it will persuade an ignorant people to build a system of waterworks up in the hills, and that will get after the thoughtless farmers who contaminate the brooks with typhoid bacilli, and after the lumber concern that is denuding the watershed of its forests. We want a new avatar of love. . . .

The Socialist Party

In 1912, the Socialist Party's presidential candidate, Eugene V. Debs, received a remarkable 6 percent of the popular vote. Democrats, Republicans, industrial leaders, and bankers were shocked that nearly a

million men voted for a party that wanted to abolish capitalism and turn
the United States into a socialist society. In the ensuing years, especially
after the Bolshevik revolution in Russia in 1917, opposition to socialism
increased dramatically, as politicians and businessmen did everything in
their power to discredit the Socialist Party, as well as all other left-wing
political organizations.

SOCIALIST PARTY PLATFORM, MAY 12, 1912

The Socialist party declares that the capitalist system has outgrown its historical function, and has become utterly incapable of meeting the problems now confronting society. We denounce this outgrown system as incompetent and corrupt and the source of unspeakable misery and suffering to the whole working class.

Under this system the industrial equipment of the nation has passed into the absolute control of a plutocracy which exacts an annual tribute of hundreds of millions of dollars from the producers. Unafraid of any organized resistance, it stretches out its greedy hands over the still undeveloped resources of the nation— the land, the mines, the forests and the water powers of every State of the Union.

In spite of the multiplication of laborsaving machines and improved methods in industry which cheapen the cost of production, the share of the producers grows ever less, and the prices of all the necessities of life steadily increase. The boasted prosperity of this nation is for the owning class alone. To the rest it means only greater hardship and misery. The high cost of living is felt in every home. Millions of wage-workers have seen the purchasing power of their wages decrease until life has become a desperate battle for mere existence.

Multitudes of unemployed walk the streets of our cities or trudge from State to State awaiting the will of the masters to move the wheels of industry.

The farmers in every state are plundered by the increasing prices exacted for tools and machinery and by extortionate rents, freight rates and storage charges.

Capitalist concentration is mercilessly crushing the class of small business men and driving its members into the ranks of propertyless wage-workers. The overwhelming majority of the people of America are being forced under a yoke of bondage by this soulless industrial despotism.

It is this capitalist system that is responsible for the increasing burden of armaments, the poverty, slums, child labor, most of the insanity, crime and prostitution, and much of the disease that afflicts mankind.

Under this system the working class is exposed to poisonous conditions, to frightful and needless perils to life and limb, is walled around with court decisions, injunctions and unjust laws, and is preyed upon incessantly for the benefit of the controlling oligarchy of wealth. Under it also, the children of the working class are doomed to ignorance, drudging toil and darkened lives.

SOURCE: Retrieved on 12/22/2003 from www.utdallas.edu/~pryan/4378%20Readings/ socialist.html.

In the face of these evils, so manifest that all thoughtful observers are appalled at them, the legislative representatives of the Republican and Democratic parties remain the faithful servants of the oppressors. Measures designed to secure to the wage-earners of this Nation as humane and just treatment as is already enjoyed by the wage-earners of all other civilized nations have been smothered in committee without debate, the laws ostensibly designed to bring relief to the farmers and general consumers are juggled and transformed into instruments for the exaction of further tribute. The growing unrest under oppression has driven these two old parties to the enactment of a variety of regulative measures, none of which has limited in any appreciable degree the power of the plutocracy, and some of which have been perverted into means of increasing that power. Anti-trust laws, railroad restrictions and regulations, with the prosecutions, indictments and investigations based upon such legislation, have proved to be utterly futile and ridiculous.

Nor has this plutocracy been seriously restrained or even threatened by any Republican or Democratic executive. It has continued to grow in power and insolence alike under the administration of Cleveland, McKinley, Roosevelt and Taft.

We declare, therefore, that the longer sufferance of these conditions is impossible, and we purpose to end them all. We declare them to be the product of the present system in which industry is carried on for private greed, instead of for the welfare of society. We declare, furthermore, that for these evils there will be and can be no remedy and no substantial relief except through Socialism under which industry will be carried on for the common good and every worker receive the full social value of the wealth he creates.

Society is divided into warring groups and classes, based upon material interests. Fundamentally, this struggle is a conflict between the two main classes, one of which, the capitalist class, owns the means of production, and the other, the working class, must use these means of production, on terms dictated by the owners.

The capitalist class, though few in numbers, absolutely controls the government, legislative, executive and judicial. This class owns the machinery of gathering and disseminating news through its organized press. It subsidizes seats of learning—the colleges and schools—and even religious and moral agencies. It has also the added prestige which established customs give to any order of society, right or wrong.

The working class, which includes all those who are forced to work for a living whether by hand or brain, in shop, mine or on the soil, vastly outnumbers the capitalist class. Lacking effective organization and class solidarity, this class is unable to enforce its will. Given such a class solidarity and effective organization, the workers will have the power to make all laws and control all industry in their own interest. All political parties are the expression of economic class interests. All other parties than the Socialist party represent one or another group of the ruling capitalist class. Their political conflicts reflect merely superficial rivalries between competing capitalist groups. However they result, these conflicts have no issue of real value to the workers. Whether the Democrats or Republicans win politically, it is the capitalist class that is victorious economically.

The Socialist party is the political expression of the economic interests of the workers. Its defeats have been their defeats and its victories their victories. It is a party founded on the science and laws of social development. It proposes that, since all social necessities to-day are socially produced, the means of their production and distribution shall be socially owned and democratically controlled.

In the face of the economic and political aggressions of the capitalist class the only reliance left the workers is that of their economic organizations and their political power. By the intelligent and class conscious use of these, they may resist successfully the capitalist class, break the fetters of wage slavery, and fit themselves for the future society, which is to displace the capitalist system. The Socialist party appreciates the full significance of class organization and urges the wage-earners, the working farmers and all other useful workers to organize for economic and political action, and we pledge ourselves to support the toilers of the fields as well as those in the shops, factories and mines of the nation in their struggles for economic justice.

In the defeat or victory of the working class party in this new struggle for freedom lies the defeat or triumph of the common people of all economic groups, as well as the failure or triumph of popular government. Thus the Socialist party is the party of the present day revolution which makes the transition from economic individualism to socialism, from wage slavery to free co-operation, from capitalist oligarchy to industrial democracy.

WORKING PROGRAM

As measures calculated to strengthen the working class in its fight for the realization of its ultimate aim, the co-operative commonwealth, and to increase its power against capitalist oppression, we advocate and pledge ourselves and our elected officers to the following program:

COLLECTIVE OWNERSHIP

1. The collective ownership and democratic management of railroads, wire and wireless telegraphs and telephones, express service, steamboat lines, and all other social means of transportation and communication and of all large scale industries.
2. The immediate acquirement by the municipalities, the states or the federal government of all grain elevators, stock yards, storage warehouses, and other distributing agencies, in order to reduce the present extortionate cost of living.
3. The extension of the public domain to include mines, quarries, oil wells, forests and water power.
4. The further conservation and development of natural resources for the use and benefit of all the people . . .

5. The collective ownership of land wherever practicable, and in cases where such ownership is impracticable, the appropriation by taxation of the annual rental value of all the land held for speculation and exploitation.
6. The collective ownership and democratic management of the banking and currency system.

UNEMPLOYMENT

The immediate government relief of the unemployed by the extension of all useful public works. All persons employed on such works to be engaged directly by the government under a work day of not more than eight hours and at not less than the prevailing union wages. The government also to establish employment bureaus; to lend money to states and municipalities without interest for the purpose of carrying on public works, and to take such other measures within its power as will lessen the widespread misery of the workers caused by the misrule of the capitalist class.

INDUSTRIAL DEMANDS

The conservation of human resources, particularly of the lives and well-being of the workers and their families:

1. By shortening the work day in keeping with the increased productiveness of machinery.
2. By securing for every worker a rest period of not less than a day and a half in each week.
3. By securing a more effective inspection of workshops, factories and mines.
4. By forbidding the employment of children under sixteen years of age.
5. By the co-operative organization of the industries in the federal penitentiaries for the benefit of the convicts and their dependents.
6. By forbidding the interstate transportation of the products of child labor, of convict labor and of all uninspected factories and mines.
7. By abolishing the profit system in government work and substituting either the direct hire of labor or the awarding of contracts to co-operative groups of workers.
8. By establishing minimum wage scales.
9. By abolishing official charity and substituting a non-contributory system of old age pensions, a general system of insurance by the State of all its members against unemployment and invalidism and a system of compulsory insurance by employers of their workers, without cost to the latter, against industrial diseases, accidents and death.

POLITICAL DEMANDS

1. The absolute freedom of press, speech and assemblage.
2. The adoption of a graduated income tax and the extension of inheritance

taxes, graduated in proportion to the value of the estate and to nearness of kin—the proceeds of these taxes to be employed in the socialization of industry.

3. The abolition of the monopoly ownership of patents and the substitution of collective ownership, with direct rewards to inventors by premiums or royalties.

4. Unrestricted and equal suffrage for men and women.

5. The adoption of the initiative, referendum and recall and of proportional representation, nationally as well as locally.

6. The abolition of the Senate and of the veto power of the President.

7. The election of the President and Vice-President by direct vote of the people.

8. The abolition of the power usurped by the Supreme Court of the United States to pass upon the constitutionality of the legislation enacted by Congress. National laws to be repealed only by act of Congress or by a referendum vote of the whole people.

9. Abolition of the present restrictions upon the amendment of the constitution, so that instrument may be made amendable by a majority of the voters in a majority of the States.

10. The granting of the right of suffrage in the District of Columbia with representation in Congress and a democratic form of municipal government for purely local affairs.

11. The extension of democratic government to all United States territory.

12. The enactment of further measures for the conservation of health. The creation of an independent bureau of health, with such restrictions as will secure full liberty to all schools of practice.

13. The enactment of further measures for general education and particularly for vocational education in useful pursuits. The Bureau of Education to be made a department.

14. The separation of the present Bureau of Labor from the Department of Commerce and Labor and its elevation to the rank of a department.

15. Abolition of all federal district courts and the United States circuit court of appeals. State courts to have jurisdiction in all cases arising between citizens of several states and foreign corporations. The election of all judges for short terms.

16. The immediate curbing of the power of the courts to issue injunctions.

17. The free administration of the law.

18. The calling of a convention for the revision of the constitution of the U.S.

Such measures of relief as we may be able to force from capitalism are but a preparation of the workers to seize the whole powers of government, in order that they may thereby lay hold of the whole system of socialized industry and thus come to their rightful inheritance.

PART SIX

Conflict and Depression, 1912–1945

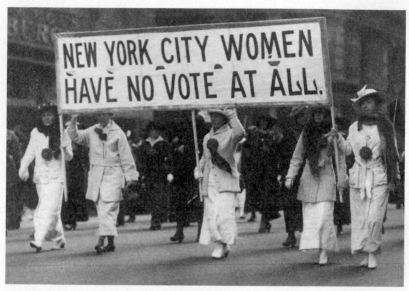

Women Demanding the Right to Vote in New York City, circa 1917. *During Woodrow Wilson's presidency women stepped up their campaign for suffrage. After several years of protests and marches they were finally successful when the Nineteenth Amendment was ratified in 1920.*

INTRODUCTION: BECOMING A WORLD POWER

During the first two decades of the twentieth century, women were ever more insistently demanding suffrage. Woodrow Wilson's inauguration as president raised hopes that a Democrat would now, finally, support the suffragist cause. It was soon apparent, however, that Wilson had no intention to fight for women's suffrage, and so militants, led by Alice Paul, increased their pressure by picketing the White House six days a week. Their signs displayed passages from Wilson's speeches justifying America's entry into the Great War as part of the nation's mission to spread democracy to people who had no say in their government; suffragists demanded to know why the president was blind to the fact that 50 percent of America's citizens were denied a say in their own government. By

1918, Wilson gave in and began to urge congressional Democrats to vote for the suffrage amendment. With the ratification of the Nineteenth Amendment in 1920, women had finally won the right to vote, 144 years after Abigail Adams had exhorted her husband "not to forget the ladies" and 72 years after Lucretia Mott and Elizabeth Cady Stanton had written the "Declaration of Sentiments" at Seneca Falls. Still, the vote did not bring equality for women, and in 1923 Alice Paul launched a new campaign for an equal rights amendment that would give women full economic and social rights.

Simultaneous with the battle for political rights, Margaret Sanger led the feminist movement into new territory by championing a woman's right to have complete control over her body. Sanger's successful assault on the Comstock Law, which equated the promotion of birth control with pornography, resulted in the repeal of the law and the opening of the first clinics that would later become known as Planned Parenthood.

Women were not the only people fighting the status quo. A growing number of radical dissenters were also agitating for reform and, in some cases, for outright revolution. Radicals like Joe Hill, Big Bill Haywood, and Eugene V. Debs condemned capitalism itself and argued for a new economic system based on socialism. Hill and Haywood were major forces in the socialist Industrial Workers of the World union (the Wobblies), which demanded worker ownership of the means of production. In 1915, because of his ties to the Wobblies, Joe Hill was tried, convicted, and executed for murder on dubious circumstantial evidence. Eugene V. Debs, the Socialist Party's presidential candidate in 1920, had to run his campaign from a jail cell because of his outspoken criticism of the U.S. entry into the war. As we have seen, anarchist Emma Goldman spoke out for many radical causes, especially complete sexual freedom for women and the right to birth control, and she continued to do so even after she was deported to the Soviet Union in the 1920s.

Theodore Roosevelt had set the United States on a course of increasing international involvement well before the war. By 1917, Washington was exerting more and more influence in Latin America, but it was the First World War that finally gave rise to the United States as a world power. But entering the war was not easy for the Wilson administration because antiwar sentiment ran high. German Americans, Irish Americans, Quakers, intellectuals like Randolph Bourne, politicians like Robert M. LaFollette, and radicals like Eugene V. Debs all spoke out strongly against the war. As a result, Congress enacted the Espionage and Sedition Acts in an attempt to stifle dissent and authorized the Committee on Public Information to implement a full-scale propaganda campaign to convince skeptical Americans of the necessity to unite against the barbaric "Huns." Somes states outlawed the teaching of the German language and banned German books (in some instances, books were even burned), frankfurters became hot dogs, hamburgers became Salisbury steak, sauerkraut became "liberty cabbage," and people who publicly expressed opposition to the war were summarily arrested.

While escalating class and gender tensions were causing alarm in the United States, the level of anxiety increased exponentially in the wake of the Russian revolution. Fear of communism, socialism, and anarchy led Attorney General

A. Mitchell Palmer to initiate a campaign of wholesale arrests of thousands of left-wing sympathizers around the country. This "Red Scare" lasted well into the 1920s and resulted in innumerable civil liberties violations. As was the case when Lincoln suspended habeas corpus during the Civil War, hundreds of Americans and aliens were held without charges filed against them. The most notorious civil liberties violation was the murder trial of Nicola Sacco and Bartolomeo Vanzetti, two Italian immigrants who were convicted and executed because of their anarchist philosophy and not because of incontestable evidence proving their guilt. Tied in with the Red Scare was a surge of xenophobia and nativism that reached fever pitch in the 1920s. A second incarnation of the Ku Klux Klan (KKK) appealed to a far wider audience than the Reconstruction era Klan. This KKK, whose membership was just as extensive in the North and Midwest as it was in the South, added foreigners, Jews, Catholics, communists, modernists, divorcees, and feminists to their list of those who were not "100% pure American" and who therefore should not be tolerated. Congress, responding to these concerns, passed immigration acts that set strict quotas which drastically reduced the number of immigrants from Eastern Europe, Asia, and Latin America.

As young men were sent off to fight in Europe, industry in the northern United States needed more workers, so industrialists began actively to entice southern blacks to move north and fill the laboring ranks. The lure of economic improvement, combined with the indignities suffered in the Jim Crow South, led many impoverished African Americans to move north. This Great Migration, which continued for the next several decades, created a demographic shift that raised racial tensions in many northern cities. At the conclusion of the war, as one contemporary observed, "Americans stopped hating the Germans and started hating each other," and in this climate, racial violence, brutal lynchings, and rioting occurred in Omaha, Tulsa, Washington, Chicago, and in many other cities. Despite the violence, there were many positive developments for African Americans. The Harlem Renaissance brought black writers, artists, and musicians great acclaim in the 1920s. The popular enthusiasm for jazz and the blues created an awareness on the part of whites of the vibrancy and originality of African American culture and, at the same time, created a deeper sense of racial pride, racial awareness, and racial solidarity in blacks. Marcus Garvey inspired many African Americans with his view that "black is beautiful" and his admonition that social and economic advancement would only come through "black power."

Before the war, there had been a nearly universal belief in progress. The nineteenth century had witnessed so many scientific advances that people assumed that society itself was evolving toward a bright future. The dawn of the twentieth century was hailed as the beginning of an era of peace, progress, and prosperity. However, the war shook this conviction, and it suddenly seemed to many people that so much of what had been taken for granted was no longer certain. Freud's theories of the unconscious and his contention that "man is wolf to man" seemed confirmed by the terrible slaughter of a war in which science and technology were employed to increase human killing. Heisenberg's principle of uncertainty and Einstein's theory of relativity raised doubts about the inviolability of science itself. Darwin's theory of evolution cast doubt on the existence of God. Was nothing certain? In a sense, the 1920s can be best understood as a clash between the emergence of this new modern skepticism and the traditionalists who fought desperately to restore the old ways. The rise of Protestant fundamentalism attempted to restore God to a central place in the American ideology, the John Scopes "Monkey Trial" in mid-decade was a battle between science and old-time religion, the strict new immigration laws that limited the number of non-Western European immigrants were an attempt to turn the United States back to a purer, more Anglo-Saxon time, and the Ku Klux Klan fought to return to an all-white America that had never really existed.

President Calvin Coolidge said, "The business of America is business." In the great financial boom of the Roaring Twenties, mass consumption became central to the American way of life, but it was based on an insufficiently well-rounded economy. There was a maldistribution of purchasing power and not enough diversification. Most discretionary income was in the hands of the wealthy, and too much of the economy was dependent on the success of Henry Ford's Model T. In 1929 the boom crashed, and within three years the nation, as well as much of the Western world, was mired in the Great Depression. The inauguration of Franklin Delano Roosevelt in March 1933 helped to restore confidence to a desperate people, but all of the resourcefulness and ingenuity of the new president's New Deal programs were not enough to turn the economy around. It was the Second World War that would end the Depression. Nevertheless, despite the intense criticism of an antagonistic business community, the New Deal was ultimately successful in saving capitalism from itself. But the New Deal's essentially pro-capitalist stance gave rise to left-wing critics who vigorously attacked the Roosevelt administration for not going far enough to reform society. Membership in the Communist Party of the USA rose dramatically during the Depression, making it the bastion of the Old Left in its call for a Marxist revision of American society. Retired physician Francis Townsend strongly criticized the administration and called for a national pension plan for all citizens over age 65 (Roosevelt later used a modified version of Townsend's plan as the springboard for Social Security.) Senator Huey Long of Louisiana demanded a redistribution of wealth by which taxation of the rich would guarantee an annual income of $2500 to each citizen. And Father Charles Coughlin condemned the president for not cracking down hard enough on the excessive influence and power of unscrupulous eastern industrial and banking elites.

While most Americans suffered terribly during the Depression, minority groups were especially hard hit. If a job was to be had at a time when the unemployment rate soared to 25 percent, an African American, for example, had little chance of being hired. Still, even while enduring such circumstances, African Americans were heartened to see that First Lady Eleanor Roosevelt was very much on their side. The president's wife was an influential advocate for equal treatment and helped raise African American expectations that the future would bring better times. Her promotion of equal rights was dramatically spotlighted when she organized African American opera singer Marian Anderson's historic recital on the steps of the Lincoln Memorial in 1939, an event that prefigured the modern civil rights movement that would emerge after World War II. As the United States entered the war, there were other signs that the times were changing. African American leader A. Philip Randolph convinced President Roosevelt to sign executive orders opening up defense contract jobs to all people on an equal opportunity basis. More than 750,000 black men and women served in the armed forces during World War II, an experience that increased their self-esteem and opened up a wider world of possibilities.

Although the Second World War is frequently referred to as the "good war," and few people today doubt that the defeat of Hitler and Tojo was a positive undertaking, there was nevertheless significant antiwar sentiment throughout the conflict. Even before the war, the America First Committee and its most famous spokesman, Charles Lindbergh, denounced policies that most people correctly sensed would inevitably draw the United States into the war. In fact, antiwar sentiment was so strong that, had the Japanese not attacked Pearl Harbor, it is highly doubtful that even 50 percent of the American people would have united behind the war effort. Of course, the Japanese did attack, and a high level of unity was achieved. Still, many conscientious objectors—both religious and political—protested and refused to fight, and for many of these people (as well as for Japanese Americans, who would discover that American citizenship was not sufficient protection for their civil liberties), the war was a particularly traumatic time. When the long-awaited peace finally arrived in the summer of 1945, a new crisis emerged from the ashes of the old, and the world entered a new, and seemingly more dangerous era.

Joe Hill (1879–1915)

Born Joel Haggland in Sweden, Joe Hill emigrated to the United States in 1902. A great deal of mythologizing surrounds him, for little is known about his adventures in America during the first years after his arrival, other than that his expectations of finding the streets paved with gold were, as they were with so many other immigrants, quickly dashed. For several years, he traveled around the country, trying to make a living at various odd jobs and, perhaps, engaging in petty thievery. Sometime during these years, he changed his name—perhaps to keep one step ahead of the law—to Joseph Hillstrom. He is known to have joined the Industrial Workers of the World (IWW) in San Pedro, California, in 1910. Popularly known as the Wobblies, the IWW was part of the early socialist movement in the United States that called for a radical transformation of the capitalist system. Soon after joining the Wobblies, he changed his name again (to Joe Hill) and quickly became an important recruiter, organizer, and agitator for this radical union.

One of the most effective means Hill used to spread the Wobbly gospel was through song. He wrote dozens of pro-union, anticapitalist songs that were eventually published in the IWW's Little Red Song Book. In 1913, Hill went to Utah, a notoriously conservative and antiunion state, in order to organize mine workers. Early in 1914, Hill was arrested for murdering two men during a grocery store holdup. Although he claimed his innocence, Hill was tried, convicted, and sentenced to death. Big Bill Haywood, the leader of the IWW, immediately denounced the verdict and declared that business interests were out to destroy Hill and the Wobblies. For several months, workers around the world, as well as such national figures as Elizabeth Gurley Flynn, Helen Keller, and even President Woodrow Wilson, appealed to the governor of Utah to free Joe Hill. Despite the public outcry, Hill was executed by firing squad in November 1915. Just before his execution, he sent a telegram to Haywood exhorting the IWW and his supporters worldwide not to mourn his death: "Don't waste time mourning, organize!" Joe Hill has, in subsequent years, become semideified in the pantheon of the labor movement's heroes.

"We Will Sing One Song" is one of many songs Hill wrote to urge workers to organize. "The Preacher and the Slave Girl," is Hill's denunciation of the role organized religion plays in supporting big business. During the struggle to unionize, music played a significant role, as it did later in the century in the civil rights movement and in antiwar protests.

"We Will Sing One Song," 1913

We will sing one song of the meek and humble slave,
The horn-handed son of the soil,
He's toiling hard from the cradle to the grave,
But his master reaps the profits from his toil.
Then we'll sing one song of the greedy master class,
They're vagrants in broadcloth, indeed,
They live by robbing the ever-toiling mass,
Human blood they spill to satisfy their greed.

Organize! Oh, toilers, come organize your might;
Then we'll sing one song of the workers' commonwealth,
Full of beauty, full of love and health.

We will sing one song of the politician sly,
He's talking of changing the laws;
Election day all the drinks and smokes he'll buy,
While he's living from the sweat of your brow.
Then we'll sing one song of the girl below the line,

SOURCE: The Industrial Workers of the World, Little Red Songbook (I.W.W., March 6, 1913).

She's scorned and despised everywhere,
While in their mansions the "keepers" wine and dine
From the profits that immoral traffic bear.
Organize! Oh, toilers, come organize your might;
Then we'll sing one song of the workers' commonwealth,
Full of beauty, full of love and health.

We will sing one song of the preacher, fat and sleek,
He tells you of homes in the sky.
He says, "Be generous, be lowly, and be meek,
If you don't you'll sure get roasted when you die."
Then we'll sing one song of the poor and ragged tramp,
He carries his home on his back;
Too old to work, he's not wanted 'round the camp,
So he wanders without aim along the track.

Organize! Oh, toilers, come organize your might;
Then we'll sing one song of the workers' commonwealth,
Full of beauty, full of love and health.

We will sing one song of the children in the mills,
They're taken from playgrounds and schools,
In tender years made to go the pace that kills,
In the sweatshops, 'mong the looms and the spools.
Then we'll sing one song of the One Big Union Grand,
The hope of the toiler and slave,
It's coming fast; it is sweeping sea and land,
To the terror of the grafter and the knave.

Organize! Oh, toilers, come organize your might;
Then we'll sing one song of the workers' commonwealth,
Full of beauty, full of love and health.

"THE PREACHER AND THE SLAVE GIRL," 1913

Long haired preachers come out ev'ry night,
Try to tell you what's wrong and what's right;
But when asked, how 'bout something to eat, (Let us eat)
They will answer with voices so sweet; (Oh so sweet)

You will eat, (You will eat)
Bye and bye, (Bye and bye) in that glorious land above the sky;
(way up high)
work and pray, (work and pray) live on hay, (Live on hay)
you'll get pie in the sky when you die. (That's a lie)

And the starvation army they play,
And they sing and they clap and they pray.

Till they get all your coin on the drum,
Then they'll tell you when you're on the bum:
You will eat, (You will eat)
Bye and bye, (Bye and bye) in that glorious land above the sky;
  (way up high)
work and pray, (work and pray) live on hay, (Live on hay)
you'll get pie in the sky when you die. (That's a lie)

Holy Rollers and Jumpers come out,
And they holler, they jump and they shout
"Give your money to Jesus," they say,
"He will cure all diseases today."

You will eat, (You will eat)
Bye and bye, (Bye and bye) in that glorious land above the sky;
  (way up high)
work and pray, (work and pray) live on hay, (Live on hay)
you'll get pie in the sky when you die. (That's a lie)

If you fight hard for children and wife—
Try to get something good in this life—
You're a sinner and bad man, they tell,
When you die you will sure go to hell.

You will eat, (You will eat)
Bye and bye, (Bye and bye) in that glorious land above the sky;
  (way up high)
work and pray, (work and pray) live on hay, (Live on hay)
you'll get pie in the sky when you die. (That's a lie)

Workingmen of all countries unite,
Side by side we for freedom will fight!
When the world and its wealth we have gained,
To the grafters we'll sing this refrain:

You will eat, bye and bye,
When you've learned how to cook and to fry.
Chop some wood, 'twill do you good,
And you'll eat in the sweet bye and bye.

Robert M. LaFollette (1855–1925)

Wisconsin Republican Robert M. LaFollette served his state first as governor
and later as U.S. senator. Claiming that his role as a politician was to
"protect the people" from exploitive industrialists and businessmen, LaFollete

*gained prominence as one of the most progressive and reform-minded
politicians of the early twentieth century. He championed such radical causes
as racial equality, women's suffrage, and the right of workers to organize
unions. He supported the Democratic presidential candidate, Woodrow
Wilson, in 1912 because of Wilson's program of social reform and regulation
of big business. However, he parted ways with Wilson in 1917 when the
president asked Congress for a declaration of war. He became even more
critical when the Conscription Act was passed. The administration's attempt
to stifle dissent with the passage of the Espionage and Sedition Acts, which
made even questioning the government's war policy a federal crime, drew
LaFollette's most scathing criticism and led to accusations of treason against
him. After he voted against the declaration of war, which the Senate
overwhelmingly approved, someone handed him a coil of rope as he was
leaving the chamber, presumably so he could save the country the cost of a
trial for treason.*

Antiwar Speech, April 4, 1917

The poor, sir, who are the ones called upon to rot in the trenches, have no organized power, have no press to voice their will upon this question of peace or war;
but, oh, Mr. President, at some time they will be heard. I hope and I believe they
will be heard in an orderly and a peaceful way. I think they may be heard from
before long. I think, sir, if we take this step, when the people to-day who are staggering under the burden of supporting families at the present prices of the necessaries of life find those prices multiplied, when they are raised a hundred
percent, or 200 percent, as they will be quickly, aye, sir, when beyond that those
who pay taxes come to have their taxes doubled and again doubled to pay the
interest on the nontaxable bonds held by Morgan and his combinations, which
have been issued to meet this war, there will come an awakening; they will have
their day and they will be heard. It will be as certain and as inevitable as the
return of the tides, and as resistless. . . .

If we are to enter upon this war in the manner the President demands, let us
throw pretense to the winds, let us be honest, let us admit that this is a ruthless
war against not only Germany's Army and her Navy but against her civilian
population as well, and frankly state that the purpose of Germany's hereditary
European enemies has become our purpose.

Again, the President says "we are about to accept the gauge of battle with
this natural foe of liberty and shall, if necessary, spend the whole force of the
nation to check and nullify its pretensions and its power." That much, at least, is
clear; that program is definite. The whole force and power of this nation, if necessary, is to be used to bring victory to the Entente Allies, and to us as their ally

---

SOURCE: Ronald F. Reid, *American Rhetorical Discourse*, 2nd ed. (Prospect Heights,
IL: Waveland Press, 1994), 702–705.

in this war. Remember, that not yet has the "whole force" of one of the warring nations been used.

Countless millions are suffering from want and privation; countless other millions are dead and rotting on foreign battlefields; countless other millions are crippled and maimed, blinded, and dismembered; upon all and upon their children's children for generations to come has been laid a burden of debt which must be worked out in poverty and suffering, but the "whole force" of no one of the warring nations has yet been expended; but our "whole force" shall be expended, so says the President. We are pledged by the President, so far as he can pledge us, to make this fair, free, and happy land of ours the same shambles and bottomless pit of horror that we see in Europe today.

Just a word of comment more upon one of the points in the President's address. He says that this is a war "for the things which we have always carried nearest to our hearts—for democracy, for the right of those who submit to authority to have a voice in their own government." In many places throughout the address is this exalted sentiment given expression.

It is a sentiment peculiarly calculated to appeal to American hearts and, when accompanied by acts consistent with it, is certain to receive our support; but in this same connection, and strangely enough, the President says that we have become convinced that the German government as it now exists—"Prussian autocracy" he calls it—can never again maintain friendly relations with us. His expression is that "Prussian autocracy was not and could never be our friend," and repeatedly throughout the address the suggestion is made that if the German people would overturn their government, it would probably be the way to peace. So true is this that the dispatches from London all hailed the message of the President as sounding the death knell of Germany's government.

But the President proposes alliance with Great Britain, which, however liberty-loving its people, is a hereditary monarchy, with a hereditary ruler, with a hereditary House of Lords, with a hereditary landed system, with a limited and restricted suffrage for one class and a multiplied suffrage power for another, and with grinding industrial conditions for all the wageworkers. The President has not suggested that we make our support of Great Britain conditional to her granting home rule to Ireland, or Egypt, or India. We rejoice in the establishment of a democracy in Russia, but it will hardly be contended that if Russia was still an autocratic government, we would not be asked to enter this alliance with her just the same. . . .

Is it not a remarkable democracy which leagues itself with allies already far overmatching in strength the German nation and holds out to such beleaguered nation the hope of peace only at the price of giving up their Government? I am not talking now of the merits or demerits of any government, but I am speaking of a profession of democracy that is linked in action with the most brutal and domineering use of autocratic power. Are the people of this country being so well represented in this war movement that we need to go abroad to give other people control of their governments? Will the President and the supporters of this war bill submit it to a vote of the people before the declaration of war goes into effect? Until we are willing to do that, it ill becomes us to offer as an excuse for our entry into the war the unsupported claim that this war was forced upon the German people by their Government "without their previous knowledge or approval."

Who has registered the knowledge or approval of the American people of the course this Congress is called upon in declaring war upon Germany? Submit the question to the people, you who support it. You who support it dare not do it, for you know that by a vote of more than ten to one the American people as a body would register their declaration against it.

In the sense that this war is being forced upon our people without their knowing why and without their approval, and that wars are usually forced upon all peoples in the same way, there is some truth in the statement; but I venture to say that the response which the German people have made to the demands of this war shows that it has a degree of popular support which the war upon which we are entering has not and never will have among our people. The espionage bills, the conscription bills, and other forcible military measures which we understand are being ground out of the war machine in this country is the complete proof that those responsible for this war fear that it has no popular support and that armies sufficient to satisfy the demand of the entente allies can not be recruited by voluntary enlistments.

Defense of Free Speech, October 6, 1917

Mr. President:

. . . Six Members of the Senate and fifty Members of the House voted against the declaration of war. Immediately there was let loose upon those Senators and Representatives a flood of invective and abuse from newspapers and individuals who had been clamoring for war, unequalled, I believe, in the history of civilized society.

Prior to the declaration of war every man who had ventured to oppose our entrance into it had been condemned as a coward or worse, and even the President had by no means been immune from these attacks.

Since the declaration of war, the triumphant war press has pursued those Senators and Representatives who voted against war with malicious falsehood and recklessly libelous attacks, going to the extreme limit of charging them with treason against their country.

This campaign of libel and character assassination directed against the Members of Congress who opposed our entrance into the war has . . . continued. . . . One of these newspaper reports most widely circulated represents a Federal judge in the State of Texas as saying, in a charge of a grand jury—I read the article as it appeared in the newspaper. . . .

Houston, Texas, October 1, 1917. Judge Waller T. Burns, of the United States district court, in charging a Federal grand jury at the beginning of the October term today, after calling by name Senators Stone of Missouri,

Hardwick of Georgia, Vardaman of Mississippi, Gronna of North Dakota, Gore of Oklahoma, and LaFollette of Wisconsin, said: "If I had a wish, I would wish that you men had jurisdiction to return bills of indictment against these men. They ought to be tried promptly and fairly, and I believe this court could administer the law fairly; but I have a conviction, as strong as life, that this country should stand them up against an adobe wall tomorrow and give them what they deserve. If any man deserves death, it is a traitor. I wish that I could pay for the ammunition. I would like to attend the execution, and if I were in the firing squad I would not want to be the marksman who had the blank shell.". . .

If this newspaper clipping were a single or exceptional instance of lawless defamation, I should not trouble the Senate with a reference to it. But, Mr. President, it is not.

In this mass of newspaper clippings which I have here upon my desk, and which I shall not trouble the Senate to read unless it is desired, and which represent but a small part of the accumulation clipped from the daily press of the country in the last three months, I find other Senators, as well as myself, accused of the highest crimes of which any man can be guilty—treason and disloyalty—and, sir, accused not only with no evidence to support the accusation, but without the suggestion that such evidence anywhere exists. . . .

I am aware, Mr. President, that in pursuance of this campaign of vilification and attempted intimidation, requests from various individuals and certain organizations have been submitted to the Senate for my expulsion from this body, and that such requests have been referred to and considered by one of the committees of the Senate.

If I alone had been made the victim of these attacks, I should not take one moment of the Senate's time for their consideration, and I believe that other Senators who have been unjustly and unfairly assailed, as I have been, hold the same attitude upon this that I do. Neither the clamor of the mob nor the voice of power will ever turn me by the breadth of a hair from the course I mark out for myself, guided by such knowledge as I can obtain and controlled and directed by a solemn conviction of right and duty.

But, sir, it is not alone Members of Congress that the war party in this country has sought to intimidate. The mandate seems to have gone forth to the sovereign people of this country that they must be silent while those things are being done by their Government which most vitally concern their well-being, their happiness, and their lives.

Today, and for weeks past, honest and law-abiding citizens of this country are being terrorized and outraged in their rights by those sworn to uphold the laws and protect the rights of the people. I have in my possession numerous affidavits establishing the fact that people are being unlawfully arrested, thrown into jail, held incommunicado for days, only to be eventually discharged without ever having been taken into court, because they have committed no crime. Private residences are being invaded, loyal citizens of undoubted integrity and probity arrested, cross-examined, and the most sacred constitutional rights guaranteed to every American citizen are being violated.

It appears to be the purpose of those conducting this campaign to throw the country into a state of terror, to coerce public opinion, to stifle criticism, and suppress discussion of the great issues involved in this war.

I think all men recognize that in time of war the citizen must surrender some rights for the common good which he is entitled to enjoy in time of peace. *But, sir, the right to control their own Government according to constitutional forms is not one of the rights that the citizens of this country are called upon to surrender in time of war.*

Rather, in time of war, the citizen must be more alert to the preservation of his right to control his Government. He must be most watchful of the encroachment of the military upon the civil power. He must beware of those precedents in support of arbitrary action by administration officials which, excused on the pleas of necessity in war time, become the fixed rule when the necessity has passed and normal conditions have been restored.

More than all, the citizen and his representative in Congress in time of war must maintain his right of free speech. More than in times of peace it is necessary that the channels for free public discussion of governmental policies shall be open and unclogged.

I believe, Mr. President, that I am now touching upon the most important question in this country today—and that is the right of the citizens of this country and their representatives in Congress to discuss in an orderly way, frankly and publicly and without fear, from the platform and through the press, every important phase of this war; its causes, and manner in which it should be conducted, and the terms upon which peace should be made.

The belief which is becoming widespread in this land that this most fundamental right is being denied to the citizens of this country is a fact, the tremendous significance of which those in authority have not yet begun to appreciate. I am contending, Mr. President, for the great fundamental right of the sovereign people of this country to make their voice heard and have that voice heeded upon the great questions arising out of this war, including not only how the war shall be prosecuted but the conditions upon which it may be terminated with a due regard for the rights and the honor of this Nation and the interests of humanity.

I am contending for this right because the exercise of it is necessary to the welfare, to the existence of this Government, to the successful conduct of this war, and to a peace which shall be enduring and for the best interests of this country.

Suppose success attends the attempt to stifle all discussion of the issues of this war, all discussions of the terms upon which it should be concluded, all discussion of the objects and purposes to be accomplished by it, and concede the demand of the war-mad press and war extremists that they monopolize the right of public utterance upon these questions unchallenged. What think you would be the consequences to this country not only during the war but after the war?

Mr. President, our Government, above all others, is founded on the right of the people freely to discuss all matters pertaining to their Government, in war not less than in peace. . . . How can that popular will express itself between elections except by meetings, by speeches, by publications, by petitions, and by addresses to the representatives of the people?

Any man who seeks to set a limit upon those rights, whether in war or peace, aims a blow at the most vital part of our Government. And then, as the time for election approaches and the official is called to account for his stewardship—not a day, not a week, not a month, before the election, but a year or more before it, if the people choose—they must have the right to the freest possible discussion of every question upon which their representative has acted, of the merits of every measure he has supported or opposed, of every vote he has cast, and every speech that he has made. And before this great fundamental right every other must, if necessary, give way. For in no other manner can representative government be preserved.

Eugene V. Debs (1855–1926)

As a young man, Eugene V. Debs worked in the railroad industry and became active in the Brotherhood of Locomotive Firemen. In 1893 he organized the American Railway Union and in 1894 helped lead the Pullman strike. For his part in this strike, he was imprisoned for six months, during which time he became a socialist. After his release, he was instrumental in founding the American Socialist Party. He also was involved with organizing the Industrial Workers of the World and associated with other radical activists such as Emma Goldman and Margaret Sanger. For the remainder of his life, he worked hard for the workingman and for socialist principles. In 1900, 1904, 1908, 1912, and 1920, he was the Socialist Party's candidate for president, and as the United States moved ever closer to entering the Great War, he became an articulate antiwar critic. A few months after the United States declared war on Germany, Debs was arrested under the Sedition and Espionage Acts for delivering an antiwar speech and for hindering the draft. These acts of Congress, in addition to singling out actions that would aid the enemy, interfere with conscription, or encourage soldiers to desert, also condemned anyone who would "willfully utter, print, write, or publish any disloyal, profane, scurrilous, or abusive language about the form of government of the United States, or the Constitution of the United States, or the military or naval forces of the United States, or the flag of the United States . . . or shall willfully utter, print, write, or publish any language intended to incite, provoke, or encourage resistance to the United States, or . . . willfully advocate, teach, defend, or suggest the doing of any of the acts or things in this section enumerated." Debs was convicted, sentenced to ten years in prison, and stripped of his American citizenship. He served nearly three years of this sentence and, despite losing his American citizenship, he was nominated as the Socialist Party's candidate for President; he conducted his

*entire 1920 campaign from behind bars. He was released on Christmas in
1921, when President Warren G. Harding commuted his sentence, and
eventually, in 1976 (50 years after his death), his citizenship was restored.
Though his health had deteriorated in prison, he spent the remaining five
years of his life continuing to fight to make life better for American workers.
"While there is a lower class," Debs proclaimed, "I am in it; while there is a
criminal element, I am of it; while there is a soul in prison, I am not free!"*

Antiwar Speech, Canton, Ohio, June 1918

Comrades, friends and fellow-workers, for this very cordial greeting, this very
hearty reception, I thank you all with the fullest appreciation of your interest in
and your devotion to the cause for which I am to speak to you this afternoon.

To speak for labor; to plead the cause of the men and women and children
who toil; to serve the working class, has always been to me a high privilege; a
duty of love.

I have just returned from a visit over yonder, where three of our most loyal
comrades are paying the penalty for their devotion to the cause of the working
class. They have come to realize, as many of us have, that it is extremely dangerous to exercise the constitutional right of free speech in a country fighting to
make democracy safe in the world.

I realize that, in speaking to you this afternoon, there are certain limitations
placed upon the right of free speech. I must be exceedingly careful, prudent, as to
what I say, and even more careful and prudent as to how I say it. I may not be able
to say all I think; but I am not going to say anything that I do not think. I would
rather a thousand times be a free soul in jail than to be a sycophant and coward in
the streets. They may put those boys in jail—and some of the rest of us in jail—
but they cannot put the Socialist movement in jail. Those prison bars separate
their bodies from ours, but their souls are here this afternoon. They are simply
paying the penalty that all men have paid in all the ages of history for standing
erect, and for seeking to pave the way to better conditions for mankind.

If it had not been for the men and women who, in the past, have had the
moral courage to go to jail, we would still be in the jungles. . . .

There is but one thing you have to be concerned about, and that is that you
keep foursquare with the principles of the international Socialist movement. It is
only when you begin to compromise that trouble begins. So far as I am
concerned, it does not matter what others may say, or think, or do, as long as I am
sure that I am right with myself and the cause. There are so many who seek refuge
in the popular side of a great question. As a Socialist, I have long since learned how
to stand alone. For the last month I have been traveling over the Hoosier State;
and, let me say to you, that, in all my connection with the Socialist movement, I

SOURCE: *The Call*, 1918, online version: E. V. Debs Internet Archive, 2001. Retrieved on
8/11/2003 from www.marxists.org/archive/debs/works/1918/canton.htm.

have never seen such meetings, such enthusiasm, such unity of purpose; never have I seen such a promising outlook as there is today, notwithstanding the statement published repeatedly that our leaders have deserted us. Well, for myself, I never had much faith in leaders. I am willing to be charged with almost anything, rather than to be charged with being a leader. I am suspicious of leaders, and especially of the intellectual variety. Give me the rank and file every day in the week. If you go to the city of Washington, and you examine the pages of the Congressional Directory, you will find that almost all of those corporation lawyers and cowardly politicians, members of Congress, and misrepresentatives of the masses—you will find that almost all of them claim, in glowing terms, that they have risen from the ranks to places of eminence and distinction. I am very glad I cannot make that claim for myself. I would be ashamed to admit that I had risen from the ranks. When I rise it will be with the ranks, and not from the ranks. . . .

Why should a Socialist be discouraged on the eve of the greatest triumph in all the history of the Socialist movement? It is true that these are anxious, trying days for us all—testing days for the women and men who are upholding the banner of labor in the struggle of the working class of all the world against the exploiters of all the world; a time in which the weak and cowardly will falter and fail and desert. They lack the fiber to endure the revolutionary test; they fall away; they disappear as if they had never been. On the other hand, they who are animated by the unconquerable spirit of the social revolution; they who have the moral courage to stand erect and assert their convictions; stand by them; fight for them; go to jail or to hell for them, if need be—they are writing their names, in this crucial hour—they are writing their names in faceless letters in the history of mankind.

Those boys over yonder—those comrades of ours—and how I love them! Aye, they are my younger brothers; their very names throb in my heart, thrill in my veins, and surge in my soul. I am proud of them; they are there for us; and we are here for them. Their lips, though temporarily mute, are more eloquent than ever before; and their voice, though silent, is heard around the world.

Are we opposed to Prussian militarism? Why, we have been fighting it since the day the Socialist movement was born; and we are going to continue to fight it, day and night, until it is wiped from the face of the earth. Between us there is no truce—no compromise. . . .

To whom do the Wall Street Junkers [aristocrats] in our country marry their daughters? After they have wrung their countless millions from your sweat, your agony and your life's blood, in a time of war as in a time of peace, they invest these untold millions in the purchase of titles of broken-down aristocrats, such as princes, dukes, counts and other parasites and no-accounts. Would they be satisfied to wed their daughters to honest workingmen? To real democrats? Oh, no! They scour the markets of Europe for vampires who are titled and nothing else. And they swap their millions for the titles, so that matrimony with them becomes literally a matter of money.

These are the gentry who are today wrapped up in the American flag, who shout their claim from the housetops that they are the only patriots, and who have their magnifying glasses in hand, scanning the country for evidence of disloyalty, eager to apply the brand of treason to the men who dare to even whisper their opposition to Junker rule in the United Sates. No wonder Sam Johnson declared that "patriotism is the last refuge of the scoundrel." He must have had this Wall Street gentry in mind, or at least their prototypes, for in every age it has been the tyrant, the oppressor and the exploiter who has wrapped himself in the cloak of patriotism, or religion, or both to deceive and overawe the people.

They would have you believe that the Socialist Party consists in the main of disloyalists and traitors. It is true in a sense not at all to their discredit. We frankly admit that we are disloyalists and traitors to the real traitors of this nation. . . .

How stupid and shortsighted the ruling class really is! Cupidity is stone blind. It has no vision. The greedy, profit-seeking exploiter cannot see beyond the end of his nose. He can see a chance for an "opening"; he is cunning enough to know what graft is and where it is, and how it can be secured, but vision he has none—not the slightest. He knows nothing of the great throbbing world that spreads out in all directions. He has no capacity for literature; no appreciation of art; no soul for beauty. That is the penalty the parasites pay for the violation of the laws of life. The Rockefellers are blind. Every move they make in their game of greed but hastens their own doom. Every blow they strike at the Socialist movement reacts upon themselves. Every time they strike at us they hit themselves. It never fails. Every time they strangle a Socialist paper they add a thousand voices proclaiming the truth of the principles of socialism and the ideals of the Socialist movement. They help us in spite of themselves.

Socialism is a growing idea; an expanding philosophy. It is spreading over the entire face of the earth: It is as vain to resist it as it would be to arrest the sunrise on the morrow. It is coming, coming, coming all along the line. Can you not see it? If not, I advise you to consult an oculist. There is certainly something the matter with your vision. It is the mightiest movement in the history of mankind. What a privilege to serve it! I have regretted a thousand times that I can do so little for the movement that has done so much for me. The little that I am, the little that I am hoping to be, I owe to the Socialist movement. It has given me my ideas and ideals; my principles and convictions, and I would not exchange one of them for all of Rockefeller's bloodstained dollars. It has taught me how to serve—a lesson to me of priceless value. It has taught me the ecstasy in the handclasp of a comrade. It has enabled me to hold high communion with you, and made it possible for me to take my place side by side with you in the great struggle for the better day; to multiply myself over and over again, to thrill with a fresh-born manhood; to feel life truly worthwhile; to open new avenues of vision; to spread out glorious vistas; to know that I am kin to all that throbs; to be class-conscious, and to realize that, regardless of nationality, race, creed, color or sex, every man, every woman who toils, who renders useful service, every member of the working class without an exception, is my comrade, my brother and sister—and that to serve them and their cause is the highest duty of my life.

And in their service I can feel myself expand; I can rise to the stature of a man and claim the right to a place on earth—a place where I can stand and strive to speed the day of industrial freedom and social justice.

Wars throughout history have been waged for conquest and plunder. In the Middle Ages when the feudal lords who inhabited the castles whose towers may still be seen along the Rhine concluded to enlarge their domains, to increase their power, their prestige and their wealth they declared war upon one another. But they themselves did not go to war any more than the modern feudal lords, the barons of Wall Street go to war. The feudal barons of the Middle Ages, the economic predecessors of the capitalists of our day, declared all wars. And their miserable serfs fought all the battles. The poor, ignorant serfs had been taught to revere their masters; to believe that when their masters declared war upon one another, it was their patriotic duty to fall upon one another and to cut one another's throats for the profit and glory of the lords and barons who held them in contempt. And that is war in a nutshell. The master class has always declared the wars; the subject class has always fought the battles. The master class has had all to gain and nothing to lose, while the subject class has had nothing to gain and all to lose—especially their lives.

They have always taught and trained you to believe it to be your patriotic duty to go to war and to have yourselves slaughtered at their command. But in all the history of the world you, the people, have never had a voice in declaring war, and strange as it certainly appears, no war by any nation in any age has ever been declared by the people.

And here let me emphasize the fact—and it cannot be repeated too often—that the working class who fight all the battles, the working class who make the supreme sacrifices, the working class who freely shed their blood and furnish the corpses, have never yet had a voice in either declaring war or making peace. It is the ruling class that invariably does both. They alone declare war and they alone make peace.

Yours not to reason why;
Yours but to do and die.

That is their motto and we object on the part of the awakening workers of this nation.

If war is right let it be declared by the people. You who have your lives to lose, you certainly above all others have the right to decide the momentous issue of war or peace. . . .

What a compliment it is to the Socialist movement to be. . . persecuted for the sake of the truth! The truth alone will make the people free. And for this reason the truth must not be permitted to reach the people. The truth has always been dangerous to the rule of the rogue, the exploiter, the robber. So the truth must be ruthlessly suppressed. That is why they are trying to destroy the Socialist movement; and every time they strike a blow they add a thousand new voices to the hosts proclaiming that socialism is the hope of humanity and has come to emancipate the people from their final form of servitude. . . .

It is the minorities who have made the history of this world. It is the few who have had the courage to take their places at the front; who have been true enough to themselves to speak the truth that was in them; who have dared oppose the established order of things; who have espoused the cause of the suffering, struggling poor; who have upheld without regard to personal consequences the cause of freedom and righteousness. It is they, the heroic, self-sacrificing few who have made the history of the race and who have paved the way from barbarism to civilization. The many prefer to remain upon the popular side. They lack the courage and vision to join a despised minority that stands for a principle; they have not the moral fiber that withstands, endures and finally conquers. They are to be pitied and not treated with contempt for they cannot help their cowardice. But, thank God, in every age and in every nation there have been the brave and self-reliant few, and they have been sufficient to their historic task; and we, who are here today, are under infinite obligations to them because they suffered, they sacrificed, they went to jail, they had their bones broken upon the wheel, they were burned at the stake and their ashes scattered to the winds by the hands of hate and revenge in their struggle to leave the world better for us than they found it for themselves. We are under eternal obligations to them because of what they did and what they suffered for us and the only way we can discharge that obligation is by doing the best we can for those who are to come after us. And this is the high purpose of every Socialist on earth. Everywhere they are animated by the same lofty principles; everywhere they have the same noble ideals; everywhere they are clasping hands across national boundary lines; everywhere they are calling one another Comrade, the blessed word that springs from the heart of unity and bursts into blossom upon the lips. Each passing day they are getting into closer touch all along the battle line, waging the holy war of the working class of the world against the ruling and exploiting class of the world. They make many mistakes and they profit by them all. They encounter numerous defeats, and grow stronger through them all. They never take a backward step.

The heart of the international Socialist never beats a retreat. . . .

Do you wish to hasten the day of victory? Join the Socialist Party! Don't wait for the morrow. Join now! Enroll your name without fear and take your place where you belong. You cannot do your duty by proxy. You have got to do it yourself and do it squarely and then as you look yourself in the face you will have no occasion to blush. You will know what it is to be a real man or woman. You will lose nothing; you will gain everything. Not only will you lose nothing but you will find something of infinite value, and that something will be yourself. And that is your supreme need—to find yourself—to really know yourself and your purpose in life.

You need at this time especially to know that you are fit for something better than slavery and cannon fodder. You need to know that you were not created to work and produce and impoverish yourself to enrich an idle exploiter. You need to know that you have a mind to improve, a soul to develop, and a manhood to sustain. . . .

Anybody can be nobody; but it takes a man to be somebody.

To turn your back on the corrupt Republican Party and the still more corrupt Democratic Party—the gold-dust lackeys of the ruling class counts for still more after you have stepped out of those popular and corrupt capitalist parties to join a minority party that has an ideal, that stands for a principle, and fights for a cause. This will be the most important change you have ever made and the time will come when you will thank me for having made the suggestion. . . .

Randolph Bourne (1886–1918)

A man of extraordinary intellect, Randolph Bourne's life was problematic from the beginning. His face was misshapen at birth by a botched forceps delivery, and before the age of five, he had contracted spinal tuberculosis, which dwarfed him and gave him a hunchbacked appearance. Growing up very much an outsider in suburban Bloomfield, New Jersey, he suffered inordinately from his physical disability and from his awareness of being a social outcast. But his remarkable intellect blossomed when he entered Columbia University in 1909. There he became editor of the Columbia Monthly *and wrote numerous articles on radical politics. After graduation, he became an articulate and influential spokesman for his generation. He contributed articles to* The Atlantic, The New Republic, The Dial, *and* Seven Arts, *in which he encouraged the nation's youth to question conventional social roles, personal relationships, and American values. He also angrily criticized corporate capitalism and condemned the Wilson administration's policy of suppressing dissent. His strident opposition to U.S. entry into the First World War went so far against the grain of his more complacent contemporaries that he was fired from* The New Republic *and put under surveillance by the Wilson administration. Bourne could never accept President Wilson's conviction that the war would be the "war to end wars" or that it would "make the world safe for democracy," nor could he accept the intellectuals who supported and condoned the war, especially those who wrote propaganda for the Committee on Public Information. To Bourne, American participation in the Great War revealed that the United States, despite its deeply held belief in the virtues of democracy, was no different from any other nation. The state, Bourne declared, is simply "the organization of the herd to act offensively or defensively against another herd similarly organized."*

"War Is the Health of the State," an unfinished essay published after Bourne's death in the 1918 flu epidemic at the age of 32, is a provocative and compelling indictment of the First World War that seems applicable to any war.

"War Is the Health of the State," 1918

To most Americans of the classes which consider themselves significant the war brought a sense of the sanctity of the State which, if they had had time to think about it, would have seemed a sudden and surprising alteration in their habits of thought. In times of peace, we usually ignore the State in favor of partisan political controversies, or personal struggles for office, or the pursuit of party policies. It is the Government rather than the State with which the politically minded are concerned. The State is reduced to a shadowy emblem which comes to consciousness only on occasions of patriotic holiday.

Government is obviously composed of common and unsanctified men, and is thus a legitimate object of criticism and even contempt. If your own party is in power, things may be assumed to be moving safely enough; but if the opposition is in, then clearly all safety and honor have fled the State. Yet you do not put it to yourself in quite that way. What you think is only that there are rascals to be turned out of a very practical machinery of offices and functions which you take for granted. When we say that Americans are lawless, we usually mean that they are less conscious than other peoples of the august majesty of the institution of the State as it stands behind the objective government of men and laws which we see. In a republic the men who hold office are indistinguishable from the mass. Very few of them possess the slightest personal dignity with which they could endow their political role; even if they ever thought of such a thing. And they have no class distinction to give them glamour. In a republic the Government is obeyed grumblingly, because it has no bedazzlements or sanctities to gild it. If you are a good old-fashioned democrat, you rejoice at this fact, you glory in the plainness of a system where every citizen has become a king. If you are more sophisticated you bemoan the passing of dignity and honor from affairs of State. But in practice, the democrat does not in the least treat his elected citizen with the respect due to a king, nor does the sophisticated citizen pay tribute to the dignity even when he finds it. The republican State has almost no trappings to appeal to the common man's emotions. What it has are of military origin, and in an unmilitary era such as we have passed through since the Civil War, even military trappings have been scarcely seen. In such an era the sense of the State almost fades out of the consciousness of men.

With the shock of war, however, the State comes into its own again. The Government, with no mandate from the people, without consultation of the people, conducts all the negotiations, the backing and filling, the menaces and explanations, which slowly bring it into collision with some other Government, and gently and irresistibly slides the country into war. For the benefit of proud

Source: Bourne's unfinished essay, "War Is the Health of the State." The original manuscript is in the Bourne MSS, Columbia University Libraries.

and haughty citizens, it is fortified with a list of the intolerable insults which have been hurled toward us by the other nations; for the benefit of the liberal and beneficent, it has a convincing set of moral purposes which our going to war will achieve; for the ambitious and aggressive classes, it can gently whisper of a bigger role in the destiny of the world. The result is that, even in those countries where the business of declaring war is theoretically in the hands of representatives of the people, no legislature has ever been known to decline the request of an Executive, which has conducted all foreign affairs in utter privacy and irresponsibility, that it order the nation into battle. Good democrats are wont to feel the crucial difference between a State in which the popular Parliament or Congress declares war, and the State in which an absolute monarch or ruling class declares war. But, put to the stern pragmatic test, the difference is not striking. In the freest of republics as well as in the most tyrannical of empires, all foreign policy, the diplomatic negotiations which produce or forestall war, are equally the private property of the Executive part of the Government, and are equally exposed to no check whatever from popular bodies, or the people voting as a mass themselves.

The moment war is declared, however, the mass of the people, through some spiritual alchemy, become convinced that they have willed and executed the deed themselves. They then, with the exception of a few malcontents, proceed to allow themselves to be regimented, coerced, deranged in all the environments of their lives, and turned into a solid manufactory of destruction toward whatever other people may have, in the appointed scheme of things, come within the range of the Government's disapprobation. The citizen throws off his contempt and indifference to Government, identifies himself with its purposes, revives all his military memories and symbols, and the State once more walks, an august presence, through the imaginations of men. Patriotism becomes the dominant feeling, and produces immediately that intense and hopeless confusion between the relations which the individual bears and should bear toward the society of which he is a part.

The patriot loses all sense of the distinction between State, nation, and government. In our quieter moments, the Nation or Country forms the basic idea of society. We think vaguely of a loose population spreading over a certain geographical portion of the earth's surface, speaking a common language, and living in a homogeneous civilization. Our idea of Country concerns itself with the non-political aspects of a people, its ways of living, its personal traits, its literature and art, its characteristic attitudes toward life. We are Americans because we live in a certain bounded territory, because our ancestors have carried on a great enterprise of pioneering and colonization, because we live in certain kinds of communities which have a certain look and express their aspirations in certain ways. We can see that our civilization is different from contiguous civilizations like the Indian and Mexican. The institutions of our country form a certain network which affects us vitally and intrigues our thoughts in a way that these other civilizations do not. We are a part of Country, for better or for worse. We have arrived in it through the operation of physiological laws, and not in any way through our own choice. By the time we have reached what are called years of discretion, its influences have molded our habits, our values, our ways of thinking, so that however aware we may become, we never really lose the stamp of our civilization, or could be mistaken for the child of any other country. Our feeling for our fellow countrymen is one of similarity or of mere acquaintance. We may be intensely proud of and congenial to our particular network of civilization, or we may detest most of its qualities and rage at its defects. This does not alter the fact that we are inextricably bound up in it. The Country, as an inescapable group into which we are born, and which makes us its particular kind of a citizen of the world, seems to be a fundamental fact of our consciousness, an irreducible minimum of social feeling.

Now this feeling for country is essentially noncompetitive; we think of our own people merely as living on the earth's surface along with other groups, pleasant or objectionable as they may be, but fundamentally as sharing the earth with them. In our simple conception of country there is no more feeling of rivalry with other peoples than there is in our feeling for our family. Our interest turns within rather than without, is intensive and not belligerent. We grow up and our imaginations gradually stake out the world we live in, they need no greater conscious satisfaction for their gregarious impulses than this sense of a great mass of people to whom we are more or less attuned, and in whose institutions we are functioning. The feeling for country would be an uninflatable maximum were it not for the ideas of State and Government which are associated with it. Country is a concept of peace, of tolerance, of living and letting live. But State is essentially a concept of power, of competition: it signifies a group in its aggressive aspects. And we have the misfortune of being born not only into a country but into a State, and as we grow up we learn to mingle the two feelings into a hopeless confusion.

The State is the country acting as a political unit, it is the group acting as a repository of force, determiner of law, arbiter of justice. International politics is a "power politics" because it is a relation of States and that is what States infallibly and calamitously are, huge aggregations of human and industrial force that may be hurled against each other in war. When a country acts as a whole in relation to another country, or in imposing laws on its own inhabitants, or in coercing or punishing individuals or minorities, it is acting as a State. The history of America as a country is quite different from that of America as a State. In one case it is the drama of the pioneering conquest of the land, of the growth of wealth and the ways in which it was used, of the enterprise of education, and the carrying out of spiritual ideals, of the struggle of economic classes. But as a State, its history is that of playing a part in the world, making war, obstructing international trade, preventing itself from being split to pieces, punishing those citizens whom society agrees are offensive, and collecting money to pay for all.

Government on the other hand is synonymous with neither State nor Nation. It is the machinery by which the nation, organized as a State, carries out its State functions. Government is a framework of the administration of laws, and the carrying out of the public force. Government is the idea of the State put into practical operation in the hands of definite, concrete, fallible men. It is the visible sign of the invisible grace. It is the word made flesh. And it has necessarily the limitations inherent in all practicality. Government is the only form in which we can envisage the State, but it is by no means identical with it. That the State is a mystical conception is something that must never be forgotten. Its glamour and its significance linger behind the framework of Government and direct its activities.

Wartime brings the ideal of the State out into very clear relief, and reveals attitudes and tendencies that were hidden. In times of peace the sense of the State flags in a republic that is not militarized. For war is essentially the health of the State. The ideal of the State is that within its territory its power and influence should be universal. As the Church is the medium for the spiritual salvation of man, so the State is thought of as the medium for his political salvation. Its idealism is a rich blood flowing to all the members of the body politic. And it is precisely in war that the urgency for union seems greatest, and the necessity for universality seems most unquestioned. The State is the organization of the herd to act offensively or defensively against another herd similarly organized. The more terrifying the occasion for defense, the closer will become the organization and the more coercive the influence upon each member of the herd. War sends the current of purpose and activity flowing down to the lowest level of the herd, and to its most remote branches. All the activities of society are linked together as fast as possible to this central purpose of making a military offensive or a military defense, and the State becomes what in peacetimes it has vainly struggled to become—the inexorable arbiter and determinant of men's business and attitudes and opinions. The slack is taken up, the cross-currents fade out, and the nation moves lumberingly and slowly, but with ever accelerated speed and integration, toward the great end, toward the "peacefulness of being at war . . . "

The classes which are able to play an active and not merely a passive role in the organization for war get a tremendous liberation of activity and energy. Individuals are jolted out of their old routine, many of them are given new positions of responsibility, new techniques must be learned. Wearing home ties are broken and women who would have remained attached with infantile bonds are liberated for service overseas. A vast sense of rejuvenescence pervades the significant classes, a sense of new importance in the world. Old national ideals are taken out, re-adapted to the purpose and used as universal touchstones, or molds into which all thought is poured. Every individual citizen who in peacetimes had no function to perform by which he could imagine himself an expression or living fragment of the State becomes an active amateur agent of the Government in reporting spies and disloyalists, in raising Government funds, or in propagating such measures as are considered necessary by officialdom. Minority opinion, which in times of peace, was only irritating and could not be dealt with by law unless it was conjoined with actual crime, becomes, with the outbreak of war, a case for outlawry. Criticism of the State, objections to war, lukewarm opinions concerning the necessity or the beauty of conscription, are made subject to ferocious penalties, far exceeding in severity those affixed to actual pragmatic crimes. Public opinion, as expressed in the newspapers, and the pulpits and the schools, becomes one solid block. "Loyalty," or rather war orthodoxy, becomes the sole test for all professions, techniques, occupations. Particularly is this true in the sphere of the intellectual life. There the smallest taint is held to spread over the whole soul, so that a professor of physics is *ipso facto* disqualified to teach physics or to hold honorable place in a university—the republic of learning—if he is at all unsound on the war. Even mere association with persons thus tainted is considered to disqualify a teacher. Anything pertaining to the enemy becomes taboo. His books are suppressed wherever possible, his language is forbidden. His artistic products are considered to convey in the subtlest spiritual way taints of vast poison to the soul that permits itself to enjoy them. So enemy music is suppressed, and energetic measures of opprobrium taken against those whose artistic consciences are not ready to perform such an act of self-sacrifice. The rage for loyal conformity works impartially, and often in diametric opposition to other orthodoxies and traditional conformities, or even ideals. The triumphant orthodoxy of the State is shown at its apex perhaps when Christian preachers lose their pulpits for taking in more or less literal terms the Sermon on the Mount, and Christian zealots are sent to prison for twenty years for distributing tracts which argue that war is unscriptural.

War is the health of the State. It automatically sets in motion throughout society those irresistible forces for uniformity, for passionate cooperation with the Government in coercing into obedience the minority groups and individuals which lack the larger herd sense. The machinery of government sets and enforces the drastic penalties; the minorities are either intimidated into silence, or brought slowly around by a subtle process of persuasion which may seem to them really to be converting them. Of course, the ideal of perfect loyalty, perfect uniformity is never really attained. The classes upon whom the amateur work of coercion falls are unwearied in their zeal, but often their agitation instead of converting, merely serves to stiffen their resistance. Minorities are rendered sullen, and some intellectual opinion bitter and satirical. But in general, the nation in wartime attains a uniformity of feeling, a hierarchy of values culminating at the undisputed apex of the State ideal, which could not possibly be produced through any other agency than war. Loyalty—or mystic devotion to the State—becomes the major imagined human value. Other values, such as artistic creation, knowledge, reason, beauty, the enhancement of life, are instantly and almost unanimously sacrificed, and the significant classes who have constituted themselves the amateur agents of the State are engaged not only in sacrificing these values for themselves but in coercing all other persons into sacrificing them.

War—or at least modern war waged by a democratic republic against a powerful enemy—seems to achieve for a nation almost all that the most inflamed political idealist could desire. Citizens are no longer indifferent to their Government, but each cell of the body politic is brimming with life and activity. We are at last on the way to full realization of that collective community in which each individual somehow contains the virtue of the whole. In a nation at war, every citizen identifies himself with the whole, and feels immensely strengthened in that identification. The purpose and desire of the collective community live in each person who throws himself wholeheartedly into the cause of war. The impeding distinction between society and the individual is almost blotted out. At war, the individual becomes almost identical with his society. He achieves a superb self-assurance, an intuition of the rightness of all his ideas and emotions, so that in the suppression of opponents or heretics he is invincibly strong; he feels behind him all the power of the collective community. The individual as social being in war seems to have achieved almost his apotheosis. Not for any religious impulse could the American nation have been expected to show such devotion *en masse,* such sacrifice and labor. Certainly not for any secular good, such as universal education or the subjugation of nature, would it have poured forth its treasure and its life, or would it have permitted such stern coercive measures to be taken against it, such as conscripting its money and its men. But for the sake of a war of offensive self-defense, undertaken to support a difficult cause to the slogan of "democracy," it would reach the highest level ever known of collective effort.

For these secular goods, connected with the enhancement of life, the education of man and the use of the intelligence to realize reason and beauty in the nation's communal living, are alien to our traditional ideal of the State. The State is intimately connected with war, for it is the organization of the collective community when it acts in a political manner, and to act in a political manner towards a rival group has meant, throughout all history—war.

There is nothing invidious in the use of the term "herd" in connection with the State. It is merely an attempt to reduce closer to first principles the nature of this institution in the shadow of which we all live, move, and have our being. Ethnologists are generally agreed that human society made its first appearance as the human pack and not as a collection of individuals or of couples. The herd is in fact the original unit, and only as it was differentiated did personal individuality develop. All the most primitive surviving tribes of men are shown to live in a very complex but very rigid social organization where opportunity for individuation is scarcely given. These tribes remain strictly organized herds, and the difference between them and the modern State is one of degree of sophistication and variety of organization, and not of kind.

Psychologists recognize the gregarious impulse as one of the strongest primitive pulls which keeps together the herds of the different species of higher animals. Mankind is no exception. Our pugnacious evolutionary history has prevented the impulse from ever dying out. This gregarious impulse is the tendency to imitate, to conform, to coalesce together, and is most powerful when the herd believes itself threatened with attack. Animals crowd together for protection, and men become most conscious of their collectivity at the threat of war. Consciousness of collectivity brings confidence and a feeling of massed strength, which in turn arouses pugnacity and the battle is on. In civilized man, the gregarious impulse acts not only to produce concerted action for defense, but also to produce identity of opinion. Since thought is a form of behavior, the gregarious impulse floods up into its realms and demands that sense of uniform thought which wartime produces so successfully. And it is in this flooding of the conscious life of society that gregariousness works its havoc.

For just as in modern societies the sex instinct is enormously oversupplied for the requirements of human propagation, so the gregarious impulse is enormously oversupplied for the work of protection which it is called upon to perform. It would be quite enough if we were gregarious enough to enjoy the companionship of others, to be able to cooperate with them, and to feel a slight malaise at solitude. Unfortunately, however, this impulse is not content with these reasonable and healthful demands, but insists that like-mindedness shall prevail everywhere, in all departments of life. So that all human progress, all novelty, and nonconformity, must be carried against the resistance of this tyrannical herd instinct which drives the individual into obedience and conformity with the majority. Even in the most modern and enlightened societies this impulse shows little sign of abating. As it is driven by inexorable economic demand out of the sphere of utility, it seems to fasten itself ever more fiercely in the realm of feeling and opinion, so that conformity comes to be a thing aggressively desired and demanded.

The gregarious impulse keeps its hold all the more virulently because when the group is in motion or is taking any positive action, this feeling of being with and supported by the collective herd very greatly feeds that will to power, the nourishment of which the individual organism so constantly demands. You feel powerful by conforming, and you feel forlorn and helpless if you are out of the crowd. While even if you do not get any access of power by thinking and feeling just as everybody else in your group does, you get at least the warm feeling of obedience, the soothing irresponsibility of protection.

Joining as it does to these very vigorous tendencies of the individual—the pleasure in power and the pleasure in obedience—this gregarious impulse becomes irresistible in society. War stimulates it to the highest possible degree, sending the influences of its mysterious herd-current with its inflations of power and obedience to the farthest reaches of the society, to every individual and little group that can possibly be affected. And it is these impulses which the State—the organization of the entire herd, the entire collectivity—is founded on and makes use of.

There is, of course, in the feeling toward the State a large element of pure filial mysticism. The sense of insecurity, the desire for protection, sends one's desire back to the father and mother, with whom is associated the earliest feelings of protection. It is not for nothing that one's State is still thought of as Father or Motherland, that one's relation toward it is conceived in terms of family affection. The war has shown that nowhere under the shock of danger have these primitive childlike attitudes failed to assert themselves again, as much in this country as anywhere. If we have not the intense Father-sense of the German who worships his Vaterland, at least in Uncle Sam we have a symbol of protecting, kindly authority, and in the many Mother-posters of the Red Cross, we see how easily in the more tender functions of war service, the ruling organization is conceived in family terms. A people at war have become in the most literal sense obedient, respectful, trustful children again, full of that naïve faith in the all-wisdom and all-power of the adult who takes care of them, imposes his mild but necessary rule upon them and in whom they lose their responsibility and anxieties. In this recrudescence of the child, there is great comfort, and a certain influx of power....

In this great herd machinery, dissent is like sand in the bearings. The State ideal is primarily a sort of blind animal push toward military unity. Any difference with that unity turns the whole vast impulse toward crushing it. Dissent is speedily outlawed, and the Government, backed by the significant classes and those who in every locality, however small, identify themselves with them, proceeds against the outlaws, regardless of their value to the other institutions of the nation, or to the effect their persecution may have on public opinion. The herd becomes divided into the hunters and the hunted, and war enterprise becomes not only a technical game but a sport as well.

It must never be forgotten that nations do not declare war on each other, nor in the strictest sense is it nations that fight each other. Much has been said to the effect that modern wars are wars of whole peoples and not of dynasties. Because the entire nation is regimented and the whole resources of the country are levied on for war, this does not mean that it is the country qua country which is fighting. It is the country organized as a State that is fighting, and only as a State would it possibly fight. So literally it is States which make war on each other and not peoples. Governments are the agents of States, and it is Governments which declare war on each other, acting truest to form in the interests of the great State ideal they represent. There is no case known in modern times of the people being consulted in the initiation of a war. The present demand for "democratic control" of foreign policy indicates how completely, even in the most democratic of modern nations, foreign policy has been the secret private possession of the executive branch of the Government.

However representative of the people Parliaments and Congresses may be in all that concerns the internal administration of a country's political affairs, in international relations it has never been possible to maintain that the popular body acted except as a wholly mechanical ratifier of the Executive's will. The formality by which Parliaments and Congresses declare war is the merest technicality. Before such a declaration can take place, the country will have been brought to the very brink of war by the foreign policy of the Executive. A long series of steps on the downward path, each one more fatally committing the unsuspecting country to a warlike course of action, will have been taken without either the people or its representatives being consulted or expressing its feeling. When the declaration of war is finally demanded by the Executive, the Parliament or Congress could not refuse it without reversing the course of history, without repudiating what has been representing itself in the eyes of the other States as the symbol and interpreter of the nation's will and animus. To repudiate an Executive at that time would be to publish to the entire world the evidence that the country had been grossly deceived by its own Government, that the country with an almost criminal carelessness had allowed its Government to commit it to gigantic national enterprises in which it had no heart. In such a crisis, even a Parliament which in the most democratic States represents the common man and not the significant classes who most strongly cherish the State ideal, will cheerfully sustain the foreign policy which it understands even less than it would care for if it understood, and will vote almost unanimously for an incalculable war, in which the nation may be brought well nigh to ruin. That is why the referendum which was advocated by some people as a test of American sentiment in entering the war was considered even by thoughtful democrats to be something subtly improper. The die had been cast. Popular whim could only derange and bungle monstrously the majestic march of State policy in its new crusade for the peace of the world. The irresistible State ideal got hold of the bowels of men. Whereas up to this time, it had been irreproachable to be neutral in word and deed, for the foreign policy of the State had so decided it, henceforth it became the most arrant crime to remain neutral. The Middle West, which had been soddenly pacifistic in our days of neutrality, became in a few months just as soddenly bellicose, and in its zeal for witch-burnings and its scent for enemies within gave precedence to no section of the country. The herd-mind followed faithfully the State-mind and, the agitation for a referendum being soon forgotten, the country fell into the universal conclusion that, since its Congress had formally declared the war, the nation itself had in the most solemn and universal way devised and brought on the entire affair. Oppression of minorities became justified on the plea that the latter were perversely resisting the rationally constructed and solemnly declared will of a majority of the nation. The herd coalescence of opinion which became inevitable the moment the State had set flowing the war attitudes became interpreted as a prewar popular decision, and disinclination to bow to the herd was treated as a monstrously antisocial act. So that the State, which had vigorously resisted the idea of a referendum and clung tenaciously and, of course, with entire success to its autocratic and absolute control of foreign policy, had the pleasure of seeing the country, within a few months, given over to the retrospective impression that a genuine referendum had taken place. When once a country has lapped up these State attitudes, its memory fades; it conceives itself not as merely accepting, but of having itself willed, the whole policy and technique of war. The significant classes, with their trailing satellites, identify themselves with the State, so that what the State, through the agency of the Government, has willed, this majority conceives itself to have willed.

All of which goes to show that the State represents all the autocratic, arbitrary, coercive, belligerent forces within a social group, it is a sort of complexus of everything most distasteful to the modern free creative spirit, the feeling for life, liberty, and the pursuit of happiness. War is the health of the State. Only when the State is at war does the modern society function with that unity of sentiment, simple uncritical patriotic devotion, cooperation of services, which have always been the ideal of the State lover. With the ravages of democratic ideas, however, the modern republic cannot go to war under the old conceptions of autocracy and death-dealing belligerency. If a successful animus for war requires a renaissance of State ideals, they can only come back under democratic forms, under this retrospective conviction of democratic control of foreign policy, democratic desire for war, and particularly of this identification of the democracy with the State. How unregenerate the ancient State may be, however, is indicated by the laws against sedition, and by the Government's unreformed attitude on foreign policy. One of the first demands of the more farseeing democrats in the democracies of the Alliance was that secret diplomacy must go. The war was seen to have been made possible by a web of secret agreements between States, alliances that were made by Governments without the shadow of popular support or even popular knowledge, and vague, half-understood commitments that scarcely reached the stage of a treaty or agreement, but which proved binding in the event. Certainly, said these democratic thinkers, war can scarcely be avoided unless this poisonous underground system of secret diplomacy is destroyed, this system by which a nation's power, wealth, and manhood may be signed away like a blank check to an allied nation to be cashed in at some future crisis. Agreements which are to affect the lives of whole peoples must be made between peoples and not by Governments, or at least by their representatives in the full glare of publicity and criticism.

Such a demand for "democratic control of foreign policy" seemed axiomatic. Even if the country had been swung into war by steps taken secretly and announced to the public only after they had been consummated, it was felt that the attitude of the American State toward foreign policy was only a relic of the bad old days and must be superseded in the new order. The American President himself, the liberal hope of the world, had demanded, in the eyes of the world, open diplomacy, agreements freely and openly arrived at. Did this mean a genuine transference of power in this most crucial of State functions from Government to people? Not at all. When the question recently came to a challenge in Congress, and the implications of open discussion were somewhat specifically discussed, and the desirabilities frankly commended, the President let his disapproval be known in no uncertain way. No one ever accused Mr. Wilson of not being a State idealist, and whenever democratic aspirations swung ideals too far out of the State orbit, he could be counted on to react vigorously. Here was a clear case of conflict between democratic idealism and the very crux of the concept of the State. However unthinkingly he might have been led on to encourage open diplomacy in his liberalizing program, when its implication was made vivid to him, he betrayed how mere a tool the idea had been in his mind to accentuate America's redeeming role. Not in any sense as a serious pragmatic technique had he thought of a genuinely open diplomacy. And how could he? For the last stronghold of State power is foreign policy. It is in foreign policy that the State acts most concentratedly as the organized herd, acts with fullest sense of aggressive-power, acts with freest arbitrariness. In foreign policy, the State is most itself. States, with reference to each other, may be said to be in a continual state of latent war. The "armed truce," a phrase so familiar before 1914, was an accurate description of the normal relation of States when they are not at war. Indeed, it is not too much to say that the normal relation of States is war. Diplomacy is a disguised war, in which States seek to gain by barter and intrigue, by the cleverness of wits, the objectives which they would have to gain more clumsily by means of war. Diplomacy is used while the States are recuperating from conflicts in which they have exhausted themselves. It is the wheedling and the bargaining of the worn-out bullies as they rise from the ground and slowly restore their strength to begin fighting again. If diplomacy had been a moral equivalent for war, a higher stage in human progress, an inestimable means of making words prevail instead of blows, militarism would have broken down and given place to it. But since it is a mere temporary substitute, a mere appearance of war's energy under another form, a surrogate effect is almost exactly proportioned to the armed force behind it. When it fails, the recourse is immediate to the military technique whose thinly veiled arm it has been. A diplomacy that was the agency of popular democratic forces in their non-State manifestations would be no diplomacy at all. It would be no better than the Railway or Education commissions that are sent from one country to another with rational constructive purpose. The State, acting as a diplomatic-military ideal, is eternally at war. Just as it must act arbitrarily and autocratically in time of war, it must act in time of peace in this particular role where it acts as a unit. Unified control is necessarily autocratic control. Democratic control of foreign policy is therefore a contradiction in terms. Open discussion destroys swiftness and certainty of action. The giant State is paralyzed. Mr. Wilson retains his full ideal of the State at the same time that he desires to eliminate war. He wishes to make the world safe for democracy as well as safe for diplomacy. When the two are in conflict, his clear political insight, his idealism of the State, tells him that it is the naïver democratic values that must be sacrificed. The world must primarily be made safe for diplomacy. The State must not be diminished.

What is the State essentially? The more closely we examine it, the more mystical and personal it becomes. On the Nation we can put our hand as a definite social group, with attitudes and qualities exact enough to mean something. On the Government we can put our hand as a certain organization of ruling functions, the machinery of lawmaking and law-enforcing. The Administration is a recognizable group of political functionaries, temporarily in charge of the government. But the State stands as an idea behind them all, eternal, sanctified, and from it Government and Administration conceive themselves to have the breath of life. Even the nation, especially in times of war—or at least, its significant classes—considers that it derives its authority and its purpose from the idea of the State. Nation and State are scarcely differentiated, and the concrete, practical, apparent facts are sunk in the symbol. We reverence not our country but the flag. We may criticize ever so severely our country, but we are disrespectful to the flag at our peril. It is the flag and the uniform that make men's heart beat high and fill them with noble emotions, not the thought of and pious hopes for America as a free and enlightened nation.

It cannot be said that the object of emotion is the same, because the flag is the symbol of the nation, so that in reverencing the American flag we are reverencing the nation. For the flag is not a symbol of the country as a cultural group, following certain ideals of life, but solely a symbol of the political State, inseparable from its prestige and expansion. The flag is most intimately connected with military achievement, military memory. It represents the country not in its intensive life, but in its far-flung challenge to the world. The flag is primarily the banner of war; it is allied with patriotic anthem and holiday. It recalls old martial memories. A nation's patriotic history is solely the history of its wars, that is, of the State in its health and glorious functioning. So in responding to the appeal of the flag, we are responding to the appeal of the State, to the symbol of the herd organized as an offensive and defensive body, conscious of its prowess and its mystical herd strength.

Even those authorities in the present Administration, to whom has been granted autocratic control over opinion, feel, though they are scarcely able to philosophize over, this distinction. It has been authoritatively declared that the horrid penalties against seditious opinion must not be construed as inhibiting legitimate, that is, partisan criticism of the Administration. A distinction is made between the Administration and the Government. It is quite accurately suggested by this attitude that the Administration is a temporary band of partisan politicians in charge of the machinery of Government, carrying out the mystical policies of State. The manner in which they operate this machinery may be freely discussed and objected to by their political opponents. The Governmental machinery may also be legitimately altered, in case of necessity. What may not be discussed or criticized is the mystical policy itself or the motives of the State in inaugurating such a policy. The President, it is true, has made certain partisan distinctions between candidates for office on the ground of support or nonsupport of the Administration, but what he means was really support or nonsupport of the State policy as faithfully carried out by the Administration. Certain of the Administration measures were devised directly to increase the health of the State, such as the Conscription and the Espionage laws. Others were concerned merely with the machinery. To oppose the first was to oppose the State and was therefore not tolerable. To oppose the second was to oppose fallible human judgment, and was therefore, though to be depreciated, not to be wholly interpreted as political suicide.

The distinction between Government and State, however, has not been so carefully observed. In time of war it is natural that Government as the seat of authority should be confused with the State or the mystic source of authority. You cannot very well injure a mystical idea which is the State, but you can very well interfere with the processes of Government. So that the two become identified in the public mind, and any contempt for or opposition to the workings of the machinery of Government is considered equivalent to contempt for the sacred State. The State, it is felt, is being injured in its faithful surrogate, and public emotion rallies passionately to defend it. It even makes any criticism of the form of Government a crime. . . .

Such attitudes are inevitable as arising from the devotees of the State. For the State is a personal as well as a mystical symbol, and it can only be understood by tracing its historical origin. The modern State is not the rational and intelligent product of modern men desiring to live harmoniously together with security of life, property, and opinion. It is not an organization which has been devised as pragmatic means to a desired social end. All the idealism with which we have been instructed to endow the State is the fruit of our retrospective imaginations. What it does for us in the way of security and benefit of life, it does incidentally as a by-product and development of its original functions, and not because at any time men or classes in the full possession of their insight and intelligence have desired that it be so. It is very important that we should occasionally lift the incorrigible veil of that *ex post facto* idealism by which we throw a glamour of rationalization over what is, and pretend in the ecstasies of social conceit that we have personally invented and set up for the glory of God and man the hoary institutions which we see around us. Things are what they are, and come down to us with all their thick encrustations of error and malevolence. Political philosophy can delight us with fantasy and convince us who need illusion to live that the actual is a fair and approximate copy—full of failings, of course, but approximately sound and sincere—of that ideal society which we can imagine ourselves as creating. From this it is a step to the tacit assumption that we have somehow had a hand in its creation and are responsible for its maintenance and sanctity.

Nothing is more obvious, however, than that every one of us comes into society as into something in whose creation we had not the slightest hand. . . . By the time we find ourselves here we are caught in a network of customs and attitudes, the major directions of our desires and interests have been stamped on our minds, and by the time we have emerged from tutelage and reached the years of discretion when we might conceivably throw our influence to the reshaping of social institutions, most of us have been so molded into the society and class we live in that we are scarcely aware of any distinction between ourselves as judging, desiring individuals and our social environment. We have been kneaded so successfully that we approve of what our society approves, desire what our society desires, and add to the group our own passionate inertia against change, against the effort of reason, and the adventure of beauty.

Every one of us, without exception, is born into a society that is given, just as the fauna and flora of our environment are given. Society and its institutions are, to the individual who enters it, as much naturalistic phenomena as is the weather itself. There is, therefore, no natural sanctity in the State any more than there is in the weather. We may bow down before it, just as our ancestors bowed before the sun and moon, but it is only because something in us unregenerate finds satisfaction in such an attitude, not because there is anything inherently reverential in the institution worshiped. Once the State has begun to function, and a large class finds its interest and its expression of power in maintaining the State, this ruling class may compel obedience from any uninterested minority. The State thus becomes an instrument by which the power of the whole herd is wielded for the benefit of a class. The rulers soon learn to capitalize the reverence which the State produces in the majority, and turn it into a general resistance toward a lessening of their privileges. The sanctity of the State becomes identified with the sanctity of the ruling class, and the latter are permitted to remain in power under the impression that in obeying and serving them, we are obeying and serving society, the nation, the great collectivity of all of us. . . .

A. Philip Randolph (1889–1979)

Suffering from the injustices of living in the Jim Crow South, Asa Philip Randolph moved to New York City in 1911. The vibrant culture of the

Harlem Renaissance was liberating for Randolph, and soon he became involved in class and race issues. Impressed by the efforts of the socialist Industrial Workers of the World to free all workers from "wage slavery," Randolph began promoting the union cause and, in 1916, joined the Socialist Party. Socialism, he believed, was the solution to the inequities and exploitation inherent in the capitalist system. Through socialism, a society would be created that would provide full equality to all citizens, including African Americans. In 1917, in collaboration with Chandler Owen, Randolph began publishing The Messenger, *a radical magazine urging blacks to join unions and convert to socialism if they wanted economic, social, and political equality.*

Although he later moderated his socialist views, Randolph worked throughout his life as a civil rights activist. In 1925, he founded the Brotherhood of Sleeping Car Porters, which, after 12 years of effort, finally achieved the Pullman company's recognition and improved job security and higher wages for its members. This success augmented his reputation as an African American leader and gained him an audience with President Franklin D. Roosevelt in 1941. At this meeting, Randolph threatened that he and his union would lead a march on Washington if the president did not do something about racial discrimination in the defense industry. Not wishing to expose to the rest of the world the inequality that existed in the United States at a time when the nation was being drawn into a war against fascism and racism, Roosevelt signed an executive order stipulating that federally-funded defense jobs must be made available on an equal-opportunity basis. When Roosevelt signed the executive order, Randolph called off the march. After the war, he continued to press for civil rights and, in 1963, proposed a march on Washington to pressure Congress to pass President Kennedy's Civil Rights Bill. And so it was that, at age 74, he was the first speaker on the steps of the Lincoln Memorial on August 28, 1963. And it was A. Philip Randolph who introduced Martin Luther King Jr.

"On Socialism," 1919

Socialism would deprive individuals of the power to make fortunes out of the labor of other individuals by virtue of their ownership of the machinery which the worker must use in order to live. When an individual or class may make profits out of the labor of black and white workers, it is to his or to the interest of the class to use any means to keep them (the workers) from combining in order to raise wages, to lower their hours of work or to demand better working conditions. This is the only reason why prejudice is fostered in the South. Of course, it may not be possible to trace every lynching or act of prejudice to a direct economic cause, but

---

SOURCE: *The Messenger*, March 1919.

the case may be explained by the law of habit. When social practices are once set they act or recur with a dangerous accuracy. So that it is now a social habit to lynch Negroes. But when the motive for promoting race prejudice is removed, viz., profits, by the social ownership, control and operation of the machinery and sources of production through the government, the government being controlled by the workers; the effects of prejudice, race riots, lynching, etc., will also be removed.

For instance, if railroads were owned and democratically managed by the government, its collective and social service function would not be prostituted to jim-crow cars in order to pander and cater to race prejudice. No individuals would be making profits out of them and consequently there would be no interest in promoting race antagonisms. Lynchings, the product of capitalism, would pass as the burning of heretics and the Spanish Inquisition, the product of religious intolerance, passed.

Besides Socialism would arm every man and woman with the ballot. Education would be compulsory and universal. The vagrancy law, child labor and peonage would no longer exist. Tenant-farming and the crop-lien system would be discarded. And every worker would receive the full product of his toil.

This is the goal of Socialism. This is why every Negro should be a Socialist.

Marcus Garvey (1887–1940)

In 1914, Marcus Garvey founded the Universal Negro Improvement Association (UNIA) in his native Jamaica. Garvey believed that blacks around the world would only ever rise up out of oppression by uniting in a powerful worldwide movement. Much like Booker T. Washington's Tuskegee Institute, UNIA's mission was to promote education in practical skills so that blacks could advance themselves economically. But, significantly, Garvey was a vocal champion of racial pride. In 1916, seeking to create an international movement, Garvey went to New York and began promoting the UNIA in Harlem. Claiming that America was a white man's country that would never fully accept blacks, he urged African Americans not to cooperate with whites but to work only for their own power. Coining the phrase "black power," he advocated the creation of a separate nation for blacks in Africa. He also argued that, in their efforts to achieve black power, blacks should abandon the effort to fit into white society and recognize instead the beauty and uniqueness of their racial heritage. "Black," Garvey proclaimed, "is beautiful," and African Americans should proudly accentuate their Africanness. He composed an anthem and designed a red, green, and white flag that would symbolize the Pan-Africa movement, and he organized and sold shares in a steamship company, the Black Star Line (a play on England's White Star Line), that would be an example of a successful black business venture.

*The scheme, however, failed in 1922, and in 1927, after being convicted of
and serving time for mail fraud, he was deported. Although he had been
vehemently disparaged as a charlatan by A. Philip Randolph and W. E. B.
DuBois, among others, and although many of his followers deserted him
in the end, he had awakened African American racial pride and helped to
create a deep sense of racial solidarity that would have an enormous
impact during the civil rights movement.*

Speech to the Universal Negro Improvement Association, Philadelphia, 1919

We have lived upon the farce of brotherhood for hundreds of years, and if there
is anybody who has suffered from that farce it is the Negro. The white man goes
forth with the Bible and tells us that we are all brothers, but it is against the
world to believe, against all humanity to believe, that really there is but one
brotherhood. And if there are six brothers in any family, at least those six brothers from natural ties ought to be honest in their dealings with each other to the
extent of not seeing any of the six starve. If one has not a job, naturally the
others would see to it that the one that is out of a job gets something to eat and a
place to sleep so as to prevent him from starving and dying. This is brotherhood. Now there is one brother with all the wealth; he has more than he wants
and there is the other brother. What is he doing to the other brother? He is murdering the other brother. He is lynching the other brother, and still they are
brothers. Now, if I have any brother in my family who has no better love for me
than to starve me, to whip me and to burn me, I say, brother, I do not want your
relationship at all. To hell with it. . . .

Tonight the Universal Negro Improvement Association is endeavoring to
teach Negroes that the time has come for them to help themselves. We have
helped the white man in this Western Hemisphere for over three hundred years
until he has become so almighty that he respects not even God himself. The
white man believes that there is only one God, and that is the white man. We
have a different idea about God. We believe that there is but one God, and he is
in a place called heaven. There is a heaven, we believe, and a God presides over
that heaven, and as far as the Negro is concerned that God is the only being in
the world whom we respect. We believe with Theodore Roosevelt, "Fear God
and know no other fear." And if every Negro in Philadelphia could just get that
one thought into his or her mind, to fear God and him alone and let the world
take care of itself, the better it would be for each and every one.

The white man comes before you in his imperial and majestic pomp and
tries to impress upon you the idea that he is your superior. Who made him your

---

Source: *Negro World*, November 1, 1919.

superior? You stick his face with a pin and blood runs out. Starve the white man and he dies. Starve the black man and he dies. What difference is there, therefore, in black and white. If you stick the white man, blood comes out. If you starve the white man he dies. The same applies to the black man. They said the white man was the superior being and the black man was the inferior being. That is the old time notion, but today the world knows that all men were created equal. We were created equal and were put into this world to possess equal rights and equal privileges, and the time has come for the black man to get his share. . . .

[T]he Universal Negro Improvement Association is no joke. It is a serious movement. It is as serious a movement as the movement of the Irish today to have a free Ireland; as the determination of the Jew to recover Palestine. The Negro peoples of the world should be so determined to reclaim Africa and found a government there, so that if any black man in any part of the world is abused we can call the mighty power of Africa to come to our aid. Men, a Negro government we had once, and a Negro government we must have again. Tell me that I must live everlastingly under the domination of a white man, that I must bequeath to my children white overlordship, then I say, let me die now, Almighty God. If there is no better future in the world for me than to be the slave of a white man, I say, take the life you gave me. I do not want it. You would not be my God if you created me to be a slave to other men; but you are my God and will continue to be my God if you created me an equal of all men. . . .

Again I want you to understand that economically we are flirting with our graves if we do not start out to make ourselves economically independent. This war brought about new conditions in America and all over the world. America sent hundreds of thousands of colored soldiers to fight the white man's battles, during which time she opened the doors of industry to millions of white American men and women and created a new problem in the industrial market. And now the war is over and those millions who took the places of the soldiers who have returned home say: "We are not going to give up our jobs. We are going to remain in the industrial life of the world." This makes it difficult for returned soldiers to get work now. There will be sufficient jobs now for returned soldiers and for white men, because abnormal conditions are still in existence, but in the next two years these abnormal conditions will pass away and the industries will not be opened up for so long. It means that millions are going to starve. Do you think the white industrial captains are going to allow the white men and the white women to starve and give you bread? To the white man blood is thicker than water.

Therefore, in the next two years there is going to be an industrial boomerang in this country, and if the Negroes do not organize now to open up economic and industrial opportunities for themselves there will be starvation among all Negroes. It is because we want to save the situation when this good time shall have passed by and the white man calls you, "My dear John, I haven't any job for you today," and you can leave the white man's job as a porter and go into the Negro factory as a clerk, you can leave the white man's kitchen and go into your home as the wife of a big Negro banker or a corporation manager.

APPEAL TO THE SOUL OF WHITE AMERICA, 1923

The Negro needs a nation and a country of his own, where he can best show evidence of his own ability in the art of human progress. Scattering him as an unmixed and unrecognized part of alien nations and civilizations is but to demonstrate his imbecility, and point him out as an unworthy derelict, fit neither for the society of Greek, Jew nor Gentile. It is unfortunate that we should so drift apart, as a race, as not to see that we are but perpetuating our own sorrow and disgrace in failing to appreciate the first requisite of all peoples—organization. . . .

No Negro, let him be American, European, West Indian or African, shall be truly respected until his race as a whole has emancipated itself, through self-achievement and progress, from universal prejudice. The Negro will have to build his own government, industry, art, science, literature and culture, before the world will stop to consider him. Until then, we are but wards of a superior race and civilization, and the outcasts of a standard social system. The race needs workers at this time, not plagiarists, copyists and mere imitators, but men and women who are able to create, to originate and improve, and thus make an independent racial contribution to the world and civilization.

The unfortunate thing about it is that we take the monkey apings of our so-called "leading men" for progress. There is no real progress in Negroes aping white people and telling us that they represent the best in the race, for in that respect any dressed monkey would represent the best of its species, irrespective of the creative matter of the monkey instinct. The best in a race is not reflected through or by the action of its apes, but by its ability to create of and by itself. It is such creation that our organization seeks. Let us not try to be the best or worst of others, but let us make the effort to be the best of ourselves. Our own racial critics criticize us as dreamers and fanatics, and call us benighted and ignorant, because they lack backbone. They are unable to see themselves creators of their own needs. The slave instinct has not yet departed from them. They still believe that they can only live or exist through the good graces of their "masters." The good slaves have not yet thrown off their shackles; thus to them, the U.N.I.A. is an "impossibility." . . .

Margaret Sanger (1879–1966)

While the battle for women's suffrage was being waged, Margaret Sanger fought a different fight, but one that was just as important for women in the United States. Living in New York City and associating with such intellectuals as John Reed, Emma Goldman, and Max Eastman, she began participating in Socialist Party and Industrial Workers of the

---

SOURCE: *Negro World*, October 2, 1923.

World activities. Becoming especially concerned with the plight of
women, in 1912 she launched a column, "What Every Girl Should
Know," in the New York Call. *Although one of her articles on venereal*
disease was suppressed by the censors, giving her her first run-in with
authorities, she was in no way discouraged from continuing to educate
women about their sexual health. She also worked in a clinic in the lower
East Side, where she was confronted daily with the plight of poor women
suffering from the results of illegal and often self-induced abortions.
Sanger later wrote in her autobiography that one of her patients, Sadie
Sachs, asked the doctor, as she was about to return home, how she could
avoid pregnancy. The doctor flippantly advised the woman to tell her
husband to "sleep on the roof." When Mrs. Sachs returned a year later,
dying from a botched abortion, Sanger decided she had no alternative but
to act. Claiming this event changed her life, Sanger committed herself to
fight for contraception for women. In 1914, she began publication of The
Woman Rebel, *a radical feminist magazine (its masthead proclaiming*
"No Gods, No Masters") that advocated women's rights, especially the
right to birth control, and provided explicit information on contracep-
tion. She was arrested for violating the Comstock Law and for breaking
postal obscenity laws. Unwilling to go to prison, she jumped bail and
went to England for a year.

When she returned, charges against her were dropped, and she
continued to agitate for birth control by going on a national speaking tour.
In 1916, she opened a clinic in Brooklyn where women could be advised on
contraception, but the clinic was raided and Sanger spent a month in jail.
In 1921, Sanger founded the American Birth Control League, and
eventually enough people supported her position that Congress finally
acceded to the idea that physicians, if medical reasons warranted, could
disseminate birth control information. This led Sanger to open a legal
clinic staffed with female doctors in 1923. In 1939, she founded the Birth
Control Federation of America, later renamed the Planned Parenthood
Federation of America. In the 1950s, Sanger was instrumental in the
development of the birth control pill. Among Margaret Sanger's many
publications, Woman and the New Race *(1920) puts forth many cogent*
arguments supporting women's reproductive rights.

"Legislating Woman's Morals," 1920

One of the important duties before those women who are demanding birth
control as a means to a New Race is the changing of our so-called obscenity
laws. This will be no easy undertaking; it is usually much easier to enact statutes

SOURCE: Margaret Sanger, *Woman and the New Race* (New York: Brentano's, 1920), chapters 15 and 18.

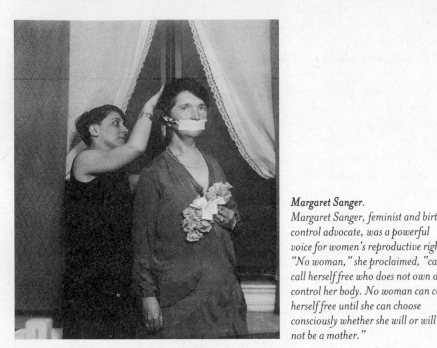

Margaret Sanger.
Margaret Sanger, feminist and birth
control advocate, was a powerful
voice for women's reproductive rights.
"No woman," she proclaimed, "can
call herself free who does not own and
control her body. No woman can call
herself free until she can choose
consciously whether she will or will
not be a mother."

than to revise them. Laws are seldom exactly what they seem, rarely what their advocates claim for them. The "obscenity" statutes are particularly deceptive.

Enacted, avowedly, to protect society against the obscene and the lewd, they make no distinction between the scientific works of human emancipators like Forel and Ellis and printed matter such as they are ostensibly aimed at. Naturally enough, then, detectives and narrow-minded judges and prosecutors who would chuckle over pictures that would make a clean-minded woman shudder, unite to suppress the scientific works and the birth-control treatises which would enable men and women to attain higher physical, mental, moral and spiritual standards.

Woman, bent upon her freedom and seeking to make a better world, will not permit the indecent and unclean forces of reaction to mask themselves forever behind the plea that it is necessary to keep her in ignorance to preserve her purity. In the birth-control movement, she has already begun to fight for her right to have, without legal interference, all knowledge pertaining to her sex nature. This is the third and most important of the epoch-making battles for general liberty upon American soil. It is most important because it is to purify the very fountain of the race and make the race completely free.

The first and most dramatic of the three great struggles for liberty reached its apex, as we know, in the American Revolution. It had for its object the right to hold such political beliefs as one might choose, and to act in accordance with those beliefs. If this political freedom is now lost to us, it is because we did not hold strongly enough to those liberties fought for by our forefathers.

Nearly a hundred years after the Revolution the battle for religious liberty came to a climax in the career of Robert G. Ingersoll. His championship of the much vaunted and little exercised freedom of religious opinion swept the blasphemy laws into the lumber room of outworn tyrannies. Those yet remaining upon the statute books are invoked but rarely, and then the effort to enforce them is ridiculous.

Within a few years the tragic combination of false moral standards and infamous obscenity laws will be as ridiculous in the public mind as are the now all but forgotten blasphemy laws. If the obscenity laws are not radically revised or repealed, few reactionaries will dare to face the public derision that will greet their attempts to use them to stay woman's progress.

The French have a saying concerning "mort main"—the dead hand. This hand of the past reaches up into the present to smother the rising flame of modern ideals, to reforge our chains when we have broken them, to arrest progress. It is the hand of such as have lived on earth but have not loved humanity. At the call of those who fear progress and freedom, it rises from the gloom of forgotten things to oppress the living.

It is the dead hand that holds imprisoned within the obscenity laws all direct information concerning birth control. It is the dead hand that thus compels millions of American women to remain in the bondage of maternity.

Previous to the year 1868, the obscenity laws of the various states in the Union contained no specific prohibition of information concerning contraceptives. In that year, however, the General Assembly of New York passed an act which specifically included the subject of contraceptives. The act made it exactly as great an offense to give such information as to exhibit the sort of pictures and writings at which the legislation was ostensibly aimed.

In 1873, the late Anthony Comstock, who with a list of contributors, most of whom did not realize the real effects of his work, constituted the so-called Society for the Suppression of Vice, succeeded in obtaining the passage of the federal obscenity act. This act was presented as one to prevent the circulation of pornographic literature and pictures among school children. As such, it was rushed through with two hundred sixty other acts in the closing hours of the Congress. This act made it a crime to use the mails to convey contraceptives or information concerning contraceptives. Other acts later made the original law applicable to express companies and other common carriers, as well as to the mails.

With this precedent established—a precedent which a majority of the congressmen could hardly have understood because of the hasty passage of the act—Comstock secured the enactment of state laws to the same effect. Meanwhile, the provisions regarding contraceptives had been dropped from the amended New York State law of 1872. In 1873, however, a new section, said to have been drafted by Comstock himself, was substituted for the one enacted in 1872, and that section is essentially the substance of the present law. None of these acts made it an offense to prevent conception—all of them provided punishment for anyone disseminating information concerning the prevention of conception. In the federal statutes, the maximum penalties were fixed at a fine of $5,000 or five years imprisonment, or both. The usual maximum penalty under a state law is a fine of $1,000 or one year's imprisonment, or both.

Comstock has passed out of public notice. His body has been entombed but the evil that he did lives after him. His dead hand still reaches forth to keep the subject of prevention of conception where he placed it—in the same legal category with things unclean and vile. Forty years ago the laws were changed and the chief work of Comstock's life accomplished. Those laws still live, legal monuments to ignorance and to oppression. Through those laws reaches the dead hand to bring to the operating table each year hundreds of thousands of women who undergo the agony of abortion. Each year this hand reaches out to compel the birth of hundreds of thousands of infants who must die before they are twelve months old.

Like many laws upon our statute books, these are being persistently and intelligently violated. Few members of the well-to-do and wealthy classes think for a single moment of obeying them. They limit their families to one, two or three well-cared-for children Usually the prosecutor who presents the case against a birth-control advocate, trapped by a detective hired by the Comstock Society, has no children at all or a small family. The family of the judge who passes upon the case is likely to be smaller still. The words "It is the law" sums it all up for these officials when they pass sentence in court. But these words, so magical to the official mind, have no weight when these same officials are adjusting their own private lives. They then obey the higher laws of their own beings—they break the obsolete statutes for themselves while enforcing them for others.

This is not the situation with the poorer people of the United States, however. Millions of them know nothing of reliable contraceptives. When women of the impoverished strata of society do not break these laws against contraceptives, they violate those laws of their inner beings which tell them not to bring children into the world to live in want, disease and general misery. They break the first law of nature, which is that of self preservation. Bound by false morals, enchained by false conceptions of religion, hindered by false laws, they endure until the pressure becomes so great that morals, religion and laws alike fail to restrain them. Then they for a brief respite resort to the surgeon's instruments.

For many years the semi-official witch hunting of the Comstock organization had a remarkable and a deadly effect. Everyone, whether it was novelist, essayist, publicist, propagandist or artist, who sought to throw definite light upon the forbidden subject of sex, or upon family limitation, was prosecuted if detected. Among the many books suppressed were works by physicians designed to warn young men and women away from the pitfalls of venereal diseases and sexual errors. The darkness that surrounded the whole field of sex was made as complete as possible.

Since then the feeling of the awakened women of America has intensified. The rapidity with which women are going into industry, the increasing hardship and poverty of the lower strata of society, the arousing of public conscience, have all operated to give force and volume to the demand for woman's right to control her own body that she may work out her own salvation.

Those who believe in strictly legal measures, as well as those who believe both in legal measures and in open defiance of these brutal and unjust laws, are demanding amendments to the obscenity statutes, which shall remove information concerning contraceptives from its present classification among things filthy and obscene.

An amendment typical of those offered is that drawn up for the New York statutes under the direction of Samuel McClure Lindsey, of Columbia University. The words and sentences in italics are those which it proposed to add:

> (Section 1145.) Physicians' instruments *and information*. An article or instrument used or applied by physicians lawfully practicing, or by their direction or prescription, for the cure or prevention of disease, is not an article of indecent or immoral nature or use, within this article. The supplying of such articles to such physicians or by their direction or prescription, is not an offense under this article. *The giving by a duly licensed physician or registered nurse lawfully practicing, of information or advice in regard to, or the supplying to any person of any article or medicine for the prevention of, conception is not a violation of any provision of this article.*

This proposed amendment should without doubt include midwives as well as nurses. There are thousands of women who never see a nurse or a physician. Under this section, even as it now stands, physicians have a right to prescribe contraceptives, but few of them have claimed that right or have even known that it has existed. It does exist, however, and was specifically declared by the New York State Court of Appeals, as we shall see when we consider that court's opinion in the Sanger case, farther on in the book. It can do no harm to make the intent of the law as regards physicians plainer, and it would be an immense step forward to include nurses and midwives in the section. With this addition it would remove one of the most serious obstacles to the freedom and advancement of American womanhood. Every woman interested in the welfare of women in general should make it her business to agitate for such a change in the obscenity laws.

The above provision would take care of the case of the woman who is ill, or who is plainly about to become ill, but it does not take care of the vast body of women who have not yet ruined their health by childbearing and who are not yet suffering from diseases complicated by pregnancy. If this amendment had been attached to the laws in all the states, there would still remain much to be done.

Shall we go on indefinitely driving the now healthy mother of two children into the hands of the abortionist, where she goes in preference to constant ill health, overwork and the witnessing of dying and starving babies? It is each woman's duty to herself and to society to hasten the repeal of all laws against the communication of birth-control information. Now that she has the vote, she should use her political influence to strike, first of all, at these restrictive statutes. It is not to her credit that a district attorney, arguing against a birth control advocate, is able to show that women have made no effort to wipe out such laws in states where they have had the ballot for years.

It is time that women assert themselves upon this fundamental right, and the first and best use they can make of the ballot is in this direction. These laws were made by men and have been instruments of martyrdom and death for unnumbered thousands of women. Women now have the opportunity to sweep them into the trash heap. They will do it at once unless, like men, they use the ballot for those political honors which many years of experience have taught men to be hollow.

It is only a question of how long it will take women to make up their minds to this result. The law of woman's being is stronger than any statute, and the man-made law must sooner or later give way to it. Man has not protected woman in matters most vital to her—but she is awaking and will sooner or later realize this and assert herself. If she acts in mass now, it will be another cheering evidence that she is moving consciously toward her goal.

"The Goal," 1920

What is the goal of woman's upward struggle? Is it voluntary motherhood? Is it general freedom? Or is it the birth of a new race? For freedom is not fruitless, but prolific of higher things. Being the most sacred aspect of woman's freedom, voluntary motherhood is motherhood in its highest and holiest form. It is motherhood unchained—motherhood ready to obey its own urge to remake the world.

Voluntary motherhood implies a new morality—a vigorous, constructive, liberated morality. That morality will, first of all, prevent the submergence of womanhood into motherhood. It will set its face against the conversion of women into mechanical maternity and toward the creation of a new race.

Woman's role has been that of an incubator and little more. She has given birth to an incubated race. She has given to her children what little she was permitted to give, but of herself, of her personality, almost nothing. In the mass, she has brought forth quantity, not quality. The requirement of a male dominated civilization has been numbers. She has met that requirement.

It is the essential function of voluntary motherhood to choose its own mate, to determine the time of childbearing and to regulate strictly the number of offspring. Natural affection upon her part, instead of selection dictated by social or economic advantage, will give her a better fatherhood for her children. The exercise of her right to decide how many children she will have and when she shall have them will procure for her the time necessary to the development of other faculties than that of reproduction. She will give play to her tastes, her talents and her ambitions. She will become a full-rounded human being.

Thus and only thus will woman be able to transmit to her offspring those qualities which make for a greater race.

The importance of developing these qualities in the mothers for transmission to the children is apparent when we recall certain well-established principles of biology. In all of the animal species below the human, motherhood has a clearly discernible superiority over fatherhood. It is the first pulse of organic life. Fatherhood is the fertilizing element. Its development, compared to that of the mother cell, is comparatively new. Likewise, its influence upon the progeny is comparatively small. There are weighty authorities who assert that through the female alone comes those modifications of form, capacity and ability which constitute evolutionary progress. It was the mothers who first developed cunning in chase, ingenuity in escaping enemies, skill in obtaining food, and adaptability. It was they also who attained unfailing discretion in leadership, adaptation to environment and boldness in attack. When the animal kingdom as a whole is surveyed, these stand out as distinctly feminine traits. They stand out also as the characteristics by which the progress of species is measured.

Why is all this true of the lower species yet not true of human beings? The secret is revealed by one significant fact—the female's functions in these animal species are not limited to motherhood alone. Every organ and faculty is fully employed and perfected. Through the development of the individual mother, better and higher types of animals are produced and carried forward. In a word, natural law makes the female the expression and the conveyor of racial efficiency.

Birth control itself, often denounced as a violation of natural law, is nothing more or less than the facilitation of the process of weeding out the unfit, of preventing the birth of defectives or of those who will become defectives. So, in compliance with nature's working plan, we must permit womanhood its full development before we can expect of it efficient motherhood. If we are to make racial progress, this development of womanhood must precede motherhood in every individual woman. Then and then only can the mother cease to be an incubator and be a mother indeed. Then only can she transmit to her sons and daughters the qualities which make strong individuals and, collectively, a strong race.

Voluntary motherhood also implies the right of marriage without maternity. Two utterly different functions are developed in the two relationships. In order to give the mate relationship its full and free play, it is necessary that no woman should be a mother against her will. There are other reasons, of course—reasons more frequently emphasized—but the reason just mentioned should never be overlooked. It is as important to the race as to the woman, for through it is developed that high love impulse which, conveyed to the child, attunes and perfects its being.

Marriage, quite aside from parentage, also gives two people invaluable experience. When parentage follows in its proper time, it is a better parentage because of the mutual adjustment and development—because of the knowledge thus gained. Few couples are fitted to understand the sacred mystery of child life until they have solved some of the problems arising out of their own love lives.

Maternal love, which usually follows upon a happy, satisfying mate love, becomes a strong and urgent craving. It then exists for two powerful, creative functions. First, for its own sake, and then for the sake of further enriching the conjugal relationship. It is from such soil that the new life should spring. It is the inherent right of the new life to have its inception in such physical ground, in such spiritual atmosphere. The child thus born is indeed a flower of love and tremendous joy. It has within it the seeds of courage and of power. This child will have the greatest strength to surmount hardships, to withstand tyrannies, to set still higher the mark of human achievement.

Shall we pause here to speak again of the rights of womanhood, in itself and of itself, to be absolutely free? We have talked of this right so much in these pages, only to learn that in the end, a free womanhood turns of its own desire to a free and happy motherhood, a motherhood which does not submerge the woman, but which is enriched because she is unsubmerged. When we voice, then, the necessity of setting the feminine spirit utterly and absolutely free, thought turns naturally not to rights of the woman, nor indeed of the mother, but to the rights of the child—of all children in the world. For this is the miracle of free womanhood, that in its freedom it becomes the race mother and opens its heart in fruitful affection for humanity.

How narrow, how pitifully puny has become motherhood in its chains! The modern motherhood enfolds one or two adoring children of its own blood, and cherishes, protects and loves them. It does not reach out to all children. When motherhood is a high privilege, not a sordid, slavish requirement, it will encircle all. Its deep, passionate intensity will overflow the limits of blood relationship. Its beauty will shine upon all, for its beauty is of the soul, whose power of enfoldment is unbounded.

When motherhood becomes the fruit of a deep yearning, not the result of ignorance or accident, its children will become the foundation of a new race. There will be no killing of babies in the womb by abortion, nor through neglect in foundling homes, nor will there be infanticide. Neither will children die by inches in mills and factories. No man will dare to break a child's life upon the wheel of toil.

Voluntary motherhood will not be passive, resigned, or weak. Out of its craving will come forth a fierceness of love for its fruits that will make such men as remain unawakened stand aghast at its fury when offended. The tigress is less terrible in defense of her offspring than will be the human mother. The daughters of such women will not be given over to injustice and to prostitution; the sons will not perish in industry nor upon the battle field. Nor could they meet these all too common fates if an undaunted motherhood were there to defend. Childhood and youth will be too valuable in the eyes of society to waste them in the murderous mills of blind greed and hate.

This is the dawn. Womanhood shakes off its bondage. It asserts its right to be free. In its freedom, its thoughts turn to the race. Like begets like. We gather perfect fruit from perfect trees. The race is but the amplification of its mother body, the multiplication of flesh habitations—beautified and perfected for souls akin to the mother soul.

The relentless efforts of reactionary authority to suppress the message of birth control and of voluntary motherhood are futile. The powers of reaction cannot now prevent the feminine spirit from breaking its bonds. When the last fetter falls the evils that have resulted from the suppression of woman's will to freedom will pass. Child slavery, prostitution, feeblemindedness, physical deterioration, hunger, oppression and war will disappear from the earth.

In their subjection women have not been brave enough, strong enough, pure enough to bring forth great sons and daughters. Abused soil brings forth stunted growths. An abused motherhood has brought forth a low order of humanity.

Great beings come forth at the call of high desire. Fearless motherhood goes out in love and passion for justice to all mankind. It brings forth fruits after its own kind. When the womb becomes fruitful through the desire of an aspiring love, another Newton will come forth to unlock further the secrets of the earth and the stars. There will come a Plato who will be understood, a Socrates who will drink no hemlock, and a Jesus who will not die upon the cross. These and the race that is to be in America await upon a motherhood that is to be sacred because it is free.

H. L. Mencken (1880–1956)

Baltimore journalist Henry Louis Mencken's dissenting voice was laced with vitriol. A master of withering sarcasm and mocking satire, Mencken was perhaps the most perceptive, humorous, and outrageous critic of all aspects of American society in the first half of the twentieth century. Nothing, with the exception of free speech, was too sacred to escape his derision. Republicans, Democrats, Socialists, presidents, Congress, the common man, women, democracy, religion, Victorian morality, politicos, the American South, prohibition—all fell victim to the finely honed scalpel of his ridicule. He paid tribute to intelligence and critical thinking for the simple reason that "the most dangerous man, to any government, is the man who is able to think things out for himself, without regard to the prevailing superstitions and taboos. Almost inevitably he comes to the conclusion that the government he lives under is dishonest, insane and intolerable."

Mencken wrote thousands of articles for newspapers, including the Baltimore Sun *and the* Baltimore Herald Tribune, *and his own magazine,* The American Mercury. *Frequently his articles oozed with such impudence that it was difficult to distinguish between a facetious tongue-in-cheek commentary and a thought-provoking appraisal of the subject at hand. Claiming that Americans (the "Booboisie") were uncivilized idiots, the most gullible people in the world who readily believed everything advertisers and politicians told them, he argued that this was the natural consequence of democracy. "We live in a land of abounding quackeries," Mencken wrote, "and if we do not learn how to laugh we succumb to the melancholy disease which afflicts the race of viewers-with-alarm.... I do not believe in democracy, but I am perfectly willing to admit that it provides the only really amusing form of government ever endured by mankind." By today's standards, his disparaging comments about blacks and Jews have raised the accusation that he was a bigot, but no group was spared Mencken's satire, especially white males. A detractor once demanded to know why, if he was so disenchanted with the United States, he did not move to some other country. Mencken's response: "Why do people like to visit the zoo?"*

H. L. Mencken.   *In April 1926, after an issue of his* American Mercury *magazine was banned in Boston, Mencken defied the ban and proceeded to sell copies of the magazine in Boston Common. "I enjoy democracy immensely," Mencken once observed, "it is incomparably idiotic, and hence incomparably amusing."*

"On Being an American," 1922

All the while I have been forgetting the third of my reasons for remaining so faithful a citizen of the Federation, despite all the lascivious inducements from expatriates to follow them beyond the seas, and all the surly suggestions from patriots that I succumb. It is the reason which grows out of my mediaeval but unashamed taste for the bizarre and indelicate, my congenital weakness for comedy of the grosser varieties. The United States, to my eye, is incomparably the greatest show on earth. It is a show which avoids diligently all the kinds of clowning which tire me most quickly—for example, royal ceremonials, the tedious hocus-pocus of haut politique, the taking of politics seriously—and lays chief stress upon the kinds which delight me unceasingly—for example, the ribald combats of demagogues, the exquisitely ingenious operations of master rogues, the pursuit of witches and heretics, the desperate struggles of inferior men to claw their way into Heaven. We have clowns in constant practice among us who are as far above the clowns of any other great state as a Jack Dempsey is above a paralytic—and not a few dozen or score of them, but whole droves and herds. Human enterprises which, in all other Christian countries, are resigned despairingly to an incurable dullness—things that seem devoid of exhilarating amusement, by their very nature—are here lifted to such vast heights of buffoonery that contemplating them strains the midriff almost to breaking. I cite an example: the worship of God. Everywhere else on earth it is carried on in a solemn and dispiriting manner; in England, of course, the bishops are obscene, but the average man seldom gets a fair chance to laugh at them and enjoy them. Now come home. Here we not only have bishops who are enormously more

SOURCE: H. L. Mencken, *Prejudices, Third Series* (New York: Knopf, 1922), 57–64.

obscene than even the most gifted of the English bishops; we have also a huge force of lesser specialists in ecclesiastical mountebankery—tin-horn Loyolas, Savonarolas and Xaviers of a hundred fantastic rites, each performing untiringly and each full of a grotesque and illimitable whimsicality. Every American town, however small, has one of its own: a holy clerk with so fine a talent for introducing the arts of jazz into the salvation of the damned that his performance takes on all the gaudiness of a four-ring circus, and the bald announcement that he will raid Hell on such and such a night is enough to empty all the town blind-pigs and bordellos and pack his sanctuary to the doors. And to aid him and inspire him there are travelling experts to whom he stands in the relation of a wart to the Matterhorn—stupendous masters of theological imbecility, contrivers of doctrines utterly preposterous, heirs to the Joseph Smith, Mother Eddy and John Alexander Dowie tradition—[William Jennings] Bryan, [Billy] Sunday, and their like. These are the eminences of the American Sacred College. I delight in them. Their proceedings make me a happier American.

Turn, now, to politics. Consider, for example, a campaign for the Presidency. Would it be possible to imagine anything more uproariously idiotic—a deafening, nerve-wracking battle to the death between Tweedledum and Tweedledee . . . — the unspeakable, with fearful snorts, gradually swallowing the inconceivable? I defy any one to match it elsewhere on this earth. In other lands, at worst, there are at least intelligible issues, coherent ideas, salient personalities. Somebody says something, and somebody replies. But what did Harding say in 1920, and what did Cox reply? Who was Harding, anyhow, and who was Cox? Here, having perfected democracy, we lift the whole combat to symbolism, to transcendentalism, to metaphysics. Here we load a pair of palpably tin cannon with blank cartridges charged with talcum power, and so let fly. Here one may howl over the show without any uneasy reminder that it is serious, and that some one may be hurt. I hold that this elevation of politics to the plane of undiluted comedy is peculiarly American, that no-where else on this disreputable ball has the art of the sham-battle been developed to such fineness. . . .

Here politics is purged of all menace, all sinister quality, all genuine significance, and stuffed with such gorgeous humors, such inordinate farce that one comes to the end of a campaign with one's ribs loose, and ready for "King Lear," or a hanging, or a course of medical journals.

But feeling better for the laugh. *Ridi si sapis,* said Martial. Mirth is necessary to wisdom, to comfort, above all to happiness. Well, here is the land of mirth, as Germany is the land of metaphysics and France is the land of fornication. Here the buffoonery never stops. What could be more delightful than the endless struggle of the Puritan to make the joy of the minority unlawful and impossible? The effort is itself a greater joy to one standing on the side-lines than any or all of the carnal joys it combats. Always, when I contemplate an uplifter at his hopeless business, I recall a scene in an old-time burlesque show, witnessed for hire in my days as a dramatic critic. A chorus girl executed a fall upon the stage, and Rudolph Krausemeyer, the Swiss comedian, rushed to her aid. As he stooped painfully to succor her, Irving Rabinovitz, the Zionist comedian, fetched him a fearful clout across the cofferdam with a slap-stick. So the uplifter, the soul-saver, the Americanizer, striving to make the Republic fit for Y.M.C.A. secretaries. He is the eternal American, ever moved by the best of intentions, ever running a la Krausemeyer to the rescue of virtue, and ever getting his pantaloons fanned by the Devil. I am naturally sinful, and such spectacles caress me. If the slap-stick were a sash-weight, the show would be cruel, and I'd probably complain to the Polizei. As it is, I know that the uplifter is not really hurt, but simply shocked. The blow, in fact, does him good, for it helps get him into Heaven, as exegetes prove from Matthew v, 11: *Hereux serez-vous, lorsqu'on vous outragera, qu'on vous persecutera,* and so on. As for me, it makes me a more contented man, and hence a better citizen. One man prefers the Republic because it pays better wages than Bulgaria. Another because it has laws to keep him sober and his daughter chaste. Another because the Woolworth Building is higher than the cathedral at Chartres. Another because, living here, he can read the New York Evening Journal. Another because there is a warrant out for him somewhere else. Me, I like it because it amuses me to my taste. I never get tired of the show. It is worth every cent it costs.

That cost, it seems to me is very moderate. Taxes in the United States are not actually high. I figure, for example, that my private share of the expense of maintaining the Hon. Mr. Harding in the White House this year will work out to less than 80 cents. Try to think of better sport for the money: in New York it has been estimated that it costs $8 to get comfortably tight, and $17.50, on an average, to pinch a girl's arm. The United States Senate will cost me perhaps $11 for the year, but against that expense set the subscription price of the Congressional Record, about $15, which, as a journalist, I receive for nothing. For $4 less than nothing I am thus entertained as Solomon never was by his hooch dancers. Col. George Brinton McClellan Harvey costs me but 25 cents a year; I get Nicholas Murray Butler free. Finally, there is young Teddy Roosevelt, the naval expert. Teddy costs me, as I work it out, about 11 cents a year, or less than a cent a month. More, he entertains me doubly for the money, first as a naval expert, and secondly as a walking attentat upon democracy, a devastating proof that there is nothing, after all, in that superstition. We Americans subscribe to the doctrine of human equality—and the *Rooseveltii* reduce it to an absurdity as brilliantly as the sons of Veit Bach. Where is your equal opportunity now? Here in this Eden of clowns, with the highest rewards of clowning theoretically open to every poor boy—here in the very citadel of democracy we found and cherish a clown dynasty!

"Last Words," 1926

I have alluded somewhat vaguely to the merits of democracy. One of them is quite obvious: it is, perhaps, the most charming form of government ever

Source: H. L. Mencken, *Last Words* (1926). Retrieved on 3/11/2004 from www.bigeye.com/mencken.htm.

devised by man. The reason is not far to seek. It is based upon propositions that are palpably not true and what is not true, as everyone knows, is always immensely more fascinating and satisfying to the vast majority of men than what is true. Truth has a harshness that alarms them, and an air of finality that collides with their incurable romanticism. They turn, in all the great emergencies of life, to the ancient promises, transparently false but immensely comforting, and of all those ancient promises there is none more comforting than the one to the effect that the lowly shall inherit the earth. It is at the bottom of the dominant religious system of the modern world, and it is at the bottom of the dominant political system. The latter, which is democracy, gives it an even higher credit and authority than the former, which is Christianity. More, democracy gives it a certain appearance of objective and demonstrable truth. The mob man, functioning as citizen, gets a feeling that he is really important to the world—that he is genuinely running things. Out of his maudlin herding after rogues and mountebanks there comes to him a sense of vast and mysterious power—which is what makes archbishops, police sergeants, the grand goblins of the Ku Klux and other such magnificoes happy. And out of it there comes, too, a conviction that he is somehow wise, that his views are taken seriously by his betters—which is what makes United States Senators, fortune tellers and Young Intellectuals happy. Finally, there comes out of it a glowing consciousness of a high duty triumphantly done which is what makes hangmen and husbands happy.

All these forms of happiness, of course, are illusory. They don't last. The democrat, leaping into the air to flap his wings and praise God, is for ever coming down with a thump. The seeds of his disaster, as I have shown, lie in his own stupidity: he can never get rid of the naive delusion—so beautifully Christian—that happiness is something to be got by taking it away from the other fellow. But there are seeds, too, in the very nature of things: a promise, after all, is only a promise, even when it is supported by divine revelation, and the chances against its fulfillment may be put into a depressing mathematical formula. Here the irony that lies under all human aspiration shows itself: the quest for happiness, as always, brings only unhappiness in the end. But saying that is merely saying that the true charm of democracy is not for the democrat but for the spectator. That spectator, it seems to me, is favoured with a show of the first cut and calibre. Try to imagine anything more heroically absurd! What grotesque false pretenses! What a parade of obvious imbecilities! What a welter of fraud! But is fraud unamusing? Then I retire forthwith as a psychologist. The fraud of democracy, I contend, is more amusing than any other, more amusing even, and by miles, than the fraud of religion. Go into your praying-chamber and give sober thought to any of the more characteristic democratic inventions: say, Law Enforcement. Or to any of the typical democratic prophets: say, the late Archangel [William Jennings] Bryan. If you don't come out paled and palsied by mirth then you will not laugh on the Last Day itself, when Presbyterians step out of the grave like chicks from the egg, and wings blossom from their scapulae, and they leap into interstellar space with roars of joy.

I have spoken hitherto of the possibility that democracy may be a self-limiting disease, like measles. It is, perhaps, something more: it is self-devouring. One cannot observe it objectively without being impressed by its curious distrust of itself—its apparently ineradicable tendency to abandon its whole philosophy at the first sign of strain. I need not point to what happens invariably in democratic states when the national safety is menaced. All the great tribunes of democracy, on such occasions, convert themselves, by a process as simple as taking a deep breath, into despots of an almost fabulous ferocity. Lincoln, Roosevelt and Wilson come instantly to mind: Jackson and Cleveland are in the background, waiting to be recalled. Nor is this process confined to times of alarm and terror: it is going on day in and day out. Democracy always seems bent upon killing the thing it theoretically loves. I have rehearsed some of its operations against liberty, the very cornerstone of its political metaphysic. It not only wars upon the thing itself; it even wars upon mere academic advocacy of it. I offer the spectacle of Americans jailed for reading the Bill of Rights as perhaps the most gaudily humorous ever witnessed in the modern world. Try to imagine monarchy jailing subjects for maintaining the divine right of Kings! Or Christianity damning a believer for arguing that Jesus Christ was the Son of God! This last, perhaps, has been done: anything is possible in that direction. But under democracy the remotest and most fantastic possibility is a common-place of every day. All the axioms resolve themselves into thundering paradoxes, many amounting to downright contradictions in terms. The mob is competent to rule the rest of us—but it must be rigorously policed itself. There is a government, not of men, but of laws—but men are set upon benches to decide finally what the law is and may be. The highest function of the citizen is to serve the state—but the first assumption that meets him, when he essays to discharge it, is an assumption of his disingenuousness and dishonour. Is that assumption commonly sound? Then the farce only grows the more glorious.

I confess, for my part, that it greatly delights me. I enjoy democracy immensely. It is incomparably idiotic, and hence incomparably amusing. Does it exalt dunderheads, cowards, trimmers, frauds, cads? Then the pain of seeing them go up is balanced and obliterated by the joy of seeing them come down. Is it inordinately wasteful, extravagant, dishonest? Then so is every other form of government: all alike are enemies to laborious and virtuous men. Is rascality at the very heart of it? Well, we have borne that rascality since 1776, and continue to survive. In the long run, it may turn out that rascality is necessary to human government, and even to civilization itself—that civilization, at bottom, is nothing but a colossal swindle. I do not know: I report only that when the suckers are running well the spectacle is infinitely exhilarating. But I am, it may be, a somewhat malicious man: my sympathies, when it comes to suckers, tend to be coy. What I can't make out is how any man can believe in democracy who feels for and with them, and is pained when they are debauched and made a show of. How can any man be a democrat who is sincerely a democrat?

"Mencken's Creed"

I believe that religion, generally speaking, has been a curse to mankind—that its modest and greatly overestimated services on the ethical side have been more than overcome by the damage it has done to clear and honest thinking.

I believe that no discovery of fact, however trivial, can be wholly useless to the race, and that no trumpeting of falsehood, however virtuous in intent, can be anything but vicious.

I believe that all government is evil, in that all government must necessarily make war upon liberty. . . .

I believe that the evidence for immortality is no better than the evidence of witches, and deserves no more respect.

I believe in the complete freedom of thought and speech. . . .

I believe in the capacity of man to conquer his world, and to find out what it is made of, and how it is run.

I believe in the reality of progress. . . .

I believe that it is better to tell the truth than to lie. I believe that it is better to be free than to be a slave. And I believe that it is better to know than be ignorant.

Langston Hughes (1902–1967)

One of the seminal figures in the Harlem Renaissance of the 1920s, Langston Hughes has had a significant impact on American literature, as well as influence in the civil rights movement. His essays, poems, short stories, novels, and plays sensitively portrayed the experience of being black in white America. He wrote for The Nation, *the NAACP's* Crisis Magazine, *and many other publications. His first book of poetry,* The Weary Blues, *was published in 1926 and his first novel,* Not Without Laughter, *in 1930. He claimed that in his effort to write of the real experiences of real black people, he approached his writing as the blues and jazz musician approaches music.*

In a 1926 essay, "The Negro Artist and the Racial Mountain," he revealed that he, just like any other serious writer, was not worried about bringing himself into his writing. The key to great writing is to write fearlessly and above all to be honest, he said. "We younger Negro artists," he wrote, "now intend to express our individual dark-skinned selves without fear or shame. If white people are pleased we are glad. If they aren't, it doesn't matter. We know we are beautiful. And ugly too. . . . If colored

SOURCE: Retrieved on 3/11/2004 from www.crispinsartwell.com/mencken.htm.

*people are pleased we are glad. If they are not, their displeasure doesn't
matter either. We build our temples for tomorrow, as strong as we know
how and we stand on the top of the mountain, free within ourselves."*

"I, Too, Sing America," 1925

I, too, sing America.
I am the darker brother.
They send me to eat in the kitchen
When company comes,
But I laugh,
And eat well,
And grow strong.

Tomorrow,
I'll be at the table
When company comes.
Nobody'll dare
Say to me,
"Eat in the kitchen,"
Then.

Besides,
They'll see how beautiful I am
And be ashamed—

I, too, am America.

Father Charles Coughlin (1891–1979)

*Father Charles Coughlin, a Catholic priest in Detroit, Michigan, emerged
during the 1930s as an important and notorious radical demagogue. The
"Radio Priest's" weekly radio broadcasts attracted an estimated
30 million listeners around the nation who believed that he was fighting
for the interests of the common man against the power of Wall Street.
Coughlin was against capitalism, socialism, and communism—all, in his
eyes, were equally evil. He attacked business leaders, but he was so
suspicious of bureaucratic elites and politicians that he had no respect for
Roosevelt or the Democratic administration, even though he had at first
supported Roosevelt in 1932. He founded the National Union for Social*

SOURCE: Langston Hughes, *The Collected Poems of Langston Hughes*, ed. by Arnold Rampersad (New York: Knopf, 1994), 46.

Justice in 1934 to promote his ideas about reforming the economy. By the late 1930s, Coughlin's comments were taking on an increasingly bigoted and anti-Semitic tone, as he regularly condemned the New Deal as the "Jew Deal" and scorned the president for being a mere puppet dancing to the tunes of international Jewish bankers and industrialists. Eventually, when he began praising Hitler and Mussolini, the archbishop of Detroit forbade him to continue his radio broadcasts. Along with his undoubted impact on millions of Americans, his rabble-rousing diatribes also had an influence on Roosevelt, goading the president into a more combative stance against powerful business leaders.

Father Charles Coughlin, the "Radio Priest."   *Coughlin founded the National Union for Social Justice to promote his plan for reforming the economy and redistributing wealth. Here he addresses a throng of 20,000 people at Cleveland's Municipal Stadium in 1936.*

National Radio Address, November 1934

"Increase and multiply" was the command of God—a command that has been sterilized in the heart of every thinking young man who dares not marry because he dares not inflict poverty upon his children.

And this in a nation where the birth rate and the death rate are sparring for supremacy; this in a nation that dares not invite the immigrant to enter because already there is too much unemployment!

Yes, "increase and multiply" was the command which echoed over the flowering fields and the towering forests. It was heard in the sheep-folds and on the pasture-lands. It broke forth in holy emotions as lovers clasped in fond embrace.

"Increase and multiply and I shall kiss your fields with the lips of the sun and water them with the fountains of rain. I will unfold to you the secrets of

SOURCE: Retrieved on 8/11/2003 from www.ssa.gov/history/fcspeech.html.

nature. And I shall teach your nimble fingers to work and labor as I do the wings of a bird to fly."

Oh! how this Sacred Scripture has become perverted as, in the midst of plenty, we struggle to create want—we struggle to create profits—all for the purpose of perpetuating a slavery which has been so often described as the concentration of wealth in the hands of a few!

My friends, the outworn creed of capitalism is done for. The clarion call of communism has been sounded. I can support one as easily as the other. They are both rotten! But it is not necessary to suffer any longer the slings and arrows of modern capitalism any more than it is to surrender our rights to life, to liberty and to the cherished bonds of family to communism.

The high priests of capitalism bid us beware of the radical and call upon us to expel him from our midst. There will be no expulsion of radicals until the causes which breed radicals will first be destroyed!

The apostles of Lenin and Trotsky bid us forsake all rights to private ownership and ask us to surrender our liberty for that mess of pottage labeled "prosperity," while it summons us to worship at the altar where a dictator of flesh and blood is enthroned as our god and the citizens are branded as his slaves.

Away with both of them! But never into the discard with the liberties which we have already won and the economic liberty which we are about to win—or die in the attempt!

My friends, I have spent many hours during these past two weeks—hours, far into the night, reading thousands of letters which have come to my office from the young folks and the old folks of this nation. I believe that in them I possess the greatest human document written within our times.

I am not boasting when I say to you that I know the pulse of the people. I know it better than all your newspaper men. I know it better than do all your industrialists with your paid-for advice. I am not exaggerating when I tell you of their demand for social justice which, like a tidal wave, is sweeping over this nation.

Nor am I happy to think that, through my broadcasts, I have placed myself today in a position to accept the challenge which these letters carry to me—a challenge for me to organize these men and women of all classes not for the protection of property rights as does the American Liberty League; not for the protection of political spoils as do the henchmen of the Republican or Democratic parties. Away with them too!

But, happy or unhappy as I am in my position, I accept the challenge to organize for obtaining, for securing and for protecting the principles of social justice.

To organize for action, if you will! To organize for social united action which will be founded on God-given social truths which belong to Catholic and Protestant, to Jew and Gentile, to black and white, to rich and poor, to industrialist and to laborer.

I realize that I am more or less a voice crying in the wilderness. I realize that the doctrine which I preach is disliked and condemned by the princes of wealth. What care I for that! And, more than all else, I deeply appreciate how limited are my qualifications to launch this organization which shall be known as the NATIONAL UNION FOR SOCIAL JUSTICE.

But the die is cast! The word has been spoken! And by it I am prepared either to stand or to fall; to fall, if needs be, and thus, to be remembered as an arrant upstart who succeeded in doing nothing more than stirring up the people.

National Radio Address, June 1936

Ladies and gentlemen:

In the Autumn of 1932, it was my privilege to address the American people on the causes of the so-called depression and upon the obvious remedies required to bring about a permanent recovery.

Those were days which witnessed a complete breakdown of the financial system under which our Western civilization had been developed. It was also evident that under this financial system there resulted a concentration of wealth and a multiplication of impoverished families. Unjust wages and unreasonable idleness were universally recognized as contradictions in an age of plenty.

To my mind it was inconceivable that irrational and needless want should exist in an age of plenty. Were there not plenty of raw materials in America? Were not our citizens and our countryside inhabited by plenty of skilled inventors, engineers, executives, workmen and farmers? At no time in the history of civilization was it possible for man to produce such an abundant supply, thanks to the benedictions of mass production machinery. At no time within the last two centuries was there such a demand on the part of our population for the thousands of good things capable of being produced in our fields and in our factories.

What was the basic cause which closed factories, which created idleness, which permitted weeds to overrun our golden fields and plowshares to rust? There was and is but one answer. Some call it lack of purchasing power. Others, viewing the problem in a more philosophic light, recognize that the financial system which was able to function in an age of scarcity was totally inadequate to operate successfully in an age of plenty.

Let me explain this statement briefly: Before the nineteenth century, the ox-cart, the spade and the crude instruments of production were handicaps to the rapid creation of real wealth.

By 1932, a new era of production had come into full bloom. It was represented by the motor car, the tractor and the power lathe, which enabled the laborer to produce wealth ten times more rapidly than was possible for his ancestors. Within the short expanse of 150 years, the problem of production had been solved, due to the ingenuity of men like Arkwright and his loom, Fulton and his steam engine, and Edison and his dynamo. These and a thousand

SOURCE: Retrieved on 8/11/2003 from www.pbs.org/greatspeeches/timeline/c_cough-lin_s2. html.

other benefactors of mankind made it possible for the teeming millions of people throughout the world to transfer speedily the raw materials into the thousand necessities and conveniences which fall under the common name of wealth.

Thus, with the advent of our scientific era, with its far-flung fields, its spacious factories, its humming motors, its thundering locomotives, its highly trained mechanics, it is inconceivable how such a thing as a so-called depression should blight the lives of an entire nation when there was a plenitude of everything surrounding us, only to be withheld from us because the so-called leaders of high finance persisted in clinging to an outworn theory of privately issued money, the medium through which wealth is distributed. . . .

Before the year 1932, very few persons fully realized the existence of this financial bondage. Millions of citizens began asking the obvious questions: "Why should the farmer be forced to follow his plow at a loss?" "Why should the citizens—at least 90 per cent of them—be imprisoned behind the cruel bars of want when, within their grasp, there are plenty of shoes, of clothing, of motor cars, of refrigerators, to which they are entitled?" At last, when the most brilliant minds amongst the industrialists, bankers and their kept politicians had failed to solve the cause of the needless depression, there appeared upon the scene of our national life a new champion of the people, Franklin Delano Roosevelt! He spoke golden words of hope. He intimated to the American people that the system of permitting a group of private citizens to create money, then to issue it to the government as if it were real money, then to exact payment from the entire nation through a system of taxation earned by real labor and service, was immoral. With the whip of his scorn he castigated these usurers who exploited the poor. With his eloquent tongue he lashed their financial system which devoured the homes of widows and orphans. No man in modern times received such plaudits from the poor as did Franklin Roosevelt when he promised to drive the money-changers from the temple—the money-changers who had clipped the coins of wages, who had manufactured spurious money, and who had brought proud America to her knees.

March 4, 1933! I shall never forget the inaugural address, which seemed to re-echo the very words employed by Christ Himself as He actually drove the money-changers from the temple. The thrill that was mine was yours. Through dim clouds of the depression, this man Roosevelt was, as it were, a new savior of his people! Oh, just a little longer shall there be needless poverty! Just another year shall there be naked backs! Just another moment shall there be dark thoughts of revolution! Never again will the chains of economic poverty bite into the hearts of simple folks, as they did in the past days of the Old Deal! Such were our hopes in the springtime of 1933. It is not pleasant for me who coined the phrase "Roosevelt *or* ruin"—a phrase fashioned upon promises—to voice such passionate words. But I am constrained to admit that "Roosevelt *and* ruin" is the order of the day, because the money-changers have not been driven from the temple.

My friends, I come before you tonight not to ask you to return to . . . the Hoovers, to the Old Deal exploiters, who honestly defended the dishonest system of gold standardism and rugged individualism. Their sun has set never to rise again. America has turned its back definitely upon the platitudinous platforms of "rugged individualism." These Punch and Judy Republicans, whose actions and words were dominated by the ventriloquists of Wall Street, are so blind that they do not recognize, even in this perilous hour, that their gold basis and their private coinage of money have bred more radicals than did Karl Marx or Lenin. To their system or ox-cart financialism we must never return!

On the other hand, the Democratic platform is discredited before it is published. Was there not a 1932 platform? By Mr. Roosevelt and his colleagues, was it not regarded as a solemn pledge to the people? Certainly! [But] it was plowed under like the cotton, slaughtered like the pigs. . . . Therefore, the veracity of the future upstage pledges must be judged by the echoings of the golden voice of a lost leader.

Said he, when the flag of hope was proudly unfurled on March 4, 1933: "Plenty is at our doorsteps, but the generous use of it languished in the very sight of the supply. Primarily, this is because the rulers of the exchange of mankind's goods have failed through their own stubbornness and their own incompetence—have admitted their failure and abdicated. Practices of the unscrupulous money-changers stand indicted in the court of public opinion, rejected by the hearts and minds of men. . . . "

These words, my friends, are not mine. These are the caustic, devastating words uttered by Franklin Delano Roosevelt on March 4, 1933, condemning Franklin Delano Roosevelt in November of 1936.

Alas! The temple still remains the private property of the money-changers. The golden key has been handed over to them for safekeeping—the key which now is fashioned in the shape of a double cross!

Huey Long (1893–1935)

Democrat Huey ("Kingfish") Long was one of the most controversial and colorful figures of the 1920s and 1930s. Elected governor of Louisiana in 1928 (his campaign slogan was "every man a king, but no one wears a crown"), Long's populist policies—his reform efforts in education, road construction and internal improvements in the state, and notions of taxing big business more heavily—earned him a national reputation. Although he was extraordinarily popular with his constituents, his dictatorial rule and questionable morals (he was known to extort bribes and pay graft) created formidable enemies. People either loved or hated Huey Long. In 1930, he was elected to the U.S. Senate but still controlled Louisiana politics through his hand-picked successor. Within two years of the election of Franklin Delano Roosevelt, Long, although he was a

Democrat, became one of the president's most vocal critics. Gearing
himself for a run at the presidency in 1936, Long criticized the New Deal
as not going far enough to alleviate poverty and injustice and devised a
"Share Our Wealth" program. This program, guaranteeing an annual
income of $2500 for every citizen in the nation, went down well with
voters, especially those who were unemployed or otherwise experiencing
the hardships of the Depression. Before the "Kingfish" could challenge
FDR for the Democratic nomination or make a run for the presidency on a
third-party ticket, however, one of his enemies caught up with him in the
state capitol building in September 1935 and assassinated him.

The first document is the 1934 Senate speech in which Huey Long
proposes his Share Our Wealth program. The second is a 1935 national
radio address in which Long criticizes Roosevelt and reiterates his own
plan.

Speech in the U.S. Senate, February 5, 1934

People of America: In every community get together at once and organize a
share-our-wealth society—Motto: Every man a king.

Principles and platform:

1. To limit poverty by providing that every deserving family shall share in
the wealth of America for not less than one third of the average wealth, thereby
to possess not less than $5,000 free of debt.

2. To limit fortunes to such a few million dollars as will allow the balance of
the American people to share in the wealth and profits of the land.

3. Old-age pensions of $30 per month to persons over 60 years of age who
do not earn as much as $1,000 per year or who possess less than $10,000 in cash
or property, thereby to remove from the field of labor in times of unemployment those who have contributed their share to the public service.

4. To limit the hours of work to such an extent as to prevent overproduction and to give the workers of America some share in the recreations, conveniences, and luxuries of life.

5. To balance agricultural production with what can be sold and consumed
according to the laws of God, which have never failed.

6. To care for the veterans of our wars.

7. Taxation to run the Government to be supported, first, by reducing big
fortunes from the top, thereby to improve the country and provide employment
in public works whenever agricultural surplus is such as to render unnecessary,
in whole or in part, any particular crop.

Source: Retrieved on 8/14/2003 from www.ssa.gov/history/longsen.html.

SIMPLE AND CONCRETE—NOT AN EXPERIMENT

To share our wealth by providing for every deserving family to have one third of the average wealth would mean that, at the worst, such a family could have a fairly comfortable home, an automobile, and a radio, with other reasonable home conveniences, and a place to educate their children. Through sharing the work, that is, by limiting the hours of toil so that all would share in what is made and produced in the land, every family would have enough coming in every year to feed, clothe, and provide a fair share of the luxuries of life to its members. Such is the result to a family, at the worst.

From the worst to the best there would be no limit to opportunity. One might become a millionaire or more. There would be a chance for talent to make a man big, because enough would be floating in the land to give brains its chance to be used. As it is, no matter how smart a man may be, everything is tied up in so few hands that no amount of energy or talent has a chance to gain any of it.

Would it break up big concerns? No. It would simply mean that, instead of one man getting all the one concern made, that there might be 1,000 or 10,000 persons sharing in such excess fortune, any one of whom, or all of whom, might be millionaires and over.

I ask somebody in every city, town, village, and farm community of America to take this as my personal request to call a meeting of as many neighbors and friends as will come to it to start a share-our-wealth society. Elect a president and a secretary and charge no dues. The meeting can be held at a courthouse, in some town hall or public building, or in the home of someone.

It does not matter how many will come to the first meeting. Get a society organized, if it has only two members.

Then let us get to work quick, quick, quick to put an end by law to people starving and going naked in this land of too much to eat and too much to wear. The case is all with us. It is the word and work of the Lord. The Gideons had but two men when they organized. Three tailors of Tooley Street drew the Magna Carta of England.

The Lord says: "For where two or three are gathered together in My name, there am I in the midst of them."

We propose to help our people into the place where the Lord said was their rightful own and no more.

We have waited long enough for these financial masters to do these things. They have promised and promised.

Now we find our country $10 billion further in debt on account of the depression, and big lenders even propose to get 90 percent of that out of the hides of the common people in the form of a sales tax.

There is nothing wrong with the United States. We have more food than we can eat. We have more clothes and things out of which to make clothes than we can wear. We have more houses and lands than the whole 120 million can use if they all had good homes. So what is the trouble? Nothing except that a handful of men have everything and the balance of the people have nothing if their debts were paid. There should be every man a king in this land flowing with milk and honey instead of the lords of finance at the top and slaves and peasants at the bottom.

Now be prepared for the slurs and snickers of some high-ups when you start your local spread-our-wealth society. Also when you call your meeting be on your guard for some smart-aleck tool of the interests to come in and ask questions. Refer such to me for an answer to any question, and I will send you a copy. Spend your time getting the people to work to save their children and to save their homes, or to get a home for those who have already lost their own.

To explain the title, motto, and principles of such a society I give the full information, viz:

Title: Share-our-wealth society is simply to mean that God's creatures on this lovely American continent have a right to share in the wealth they have created in this country. They have the right to a living, with the conveniences and some of the luxuries of this life, so long as there are too many or enough for all. They have a right to raise their children in a healthy, wholesome atmosphere and to educate them, rather than to face the dread of their under-nourishment and sadness by being denied a real life.

Motto: "Every man a king" conveys the great plan of God and of the Declaration of Independence, which said: "All men are created equal." It conveys that no one man is the lord of another, but that from the head to the foot of every man is carried his sovereignty.

Now to cover the principles of the share-our-wealth society, I give them in order:

1. To limit poverty: We propose that a deserving family shall share in our wealth of America at least for one third the average. An average family is slightly less than five persons. The number has become less during depression. The United States total wealth in normal times is about $400 billion or about $15,000 to a family. If there were fair distribution of our things in America, our national wealth would be three or four or five times the $400 billion, because a free, circulating wealth is worth many times more than wealth congested and frozen into a few hands as is America's wealth. But, figuring only on the basis of wealth as valued when frozen into a few hands, there is the average of $15,000 to the family. We say that we will limit poverty of the deserving people. One third of the average wealth to the family, or $5,000, is a fair limit to the depths we will allow any one man's family to fall. None too poor, none too rich.

2. To limit fortunes: The wealth of this land is tied up in a few hands. It makes no difference how many years the laborer has worked, nor does it make any difference how many dreary rows the farmer has plowed, the wealth he has created is in the hands of manipulators. They have not worked any more than many other people who have nothing. Now we do not propose to hurt these very rich persons. We simply say that when they reach the place of millionaires they have everything they can use and they ought to let somebody else have

something. As it is, 0.1 of 1 percent of the bank depositors nearly half of the money in the banks, leaving 99.9 of bank depositors owning the balance. Then two thirds of the people do not even have a bank account. The lowest estimate is that 4 percent of the people own 85 percent of our wealth. The people cannot ever come to light unless we share our wealth, hence the society to do it.

3. Old-age pensions: Everyone has begun to realize something must be done for our old people who work out their lives, feed and clothe children and are left penniless in their declining years. They should be made to look forward to their mature years for comfort rather than fear. We propose that, at the age of 60, every person should begin to draw a pension from our Government of $30 per month, unless the person of 60 or over has an income of over $1,000 per year or is worth $10,000, which is two thirds of the average wealth in America, even figured on a basis of it being frozen into a few hands. Such a pension would retire from labor those persons who keep the rising generations from finding employment.

4. To limit the hours of work: This applies to all industry. The longer hours the human family can rest from work, the more it can consume. It makes no difference how many labor-saving devices we may invent, just as long as we keep cutting down the hours and sharing what those machines produce, the better we become. Machines can never produce too much if everybody is allowed his share, and if it ever got to the point that the human family could work only 15 hours per week and still produce enough for everybody, then praised be the name of the Lord. Heaven would be coming nearer to earth. All of us could return to school a few months every year to learn some things they have found out since we were there: All could be gentlemen: Every man a king.

5. To balance agricultural production with consumption: About the easiest of all things to do when financial masters and market manipulators step aside and let work the law of the Lord. When we have a supply of anything that is more than we can use for a year or two, just stop planting that particular crop for a year either in all the country or in a part of it. Let the Government take over and store the surplus for the next year. If there is not something else for the farmers to plant or some other work for them to do to live on for the year when the crop is banned, then let that be the year for the public works to be done in the section where the farmers need work. There is plenty of it to do and taxes of the big fortunes at the top will supply plenty of money without hurting anybody. In time we would have the people not struggling to raise so much when all were well fed and clothed. Distribution of wealth almost solves the whole problem without further trouble.

6. To care for the veterans of our wars: A restoration of all rights taken from them by recent laws and further, a complete care of any disabled veteran for any ailment, who has no means of support.

7. Taxation: Taxation is to be levied first at the top for the Government's support and expenses. Swollen fortunes should be reduced principally through taxation. The Government should be run through revenues it derives after allowing persons to become well above millionaires and no more. In this

manner the fortunes will be kept down to reasonable size and at the same time all the works of the Government kept on a sound basis, without debts.

Things cannot continue as they now are. America must take one of three choices, viz:

1. A monarchy ruled by financial masters—a modern feudalism.
2. Communism.
3. Sharing of the wealth and income of the land among all the people by limiting the hours of toil and limiting the size of fortunes.

The Lord prescribed the last form. It would preserve all our gains, share them among our population, guarantee a greater country and a happy people.

The need for such share-our-wealth society is to spread the truth among the people and to convey their sentiment to their Members of Congress.

Whenever such a local society has been organized, please send me notice of the same, so that I may send statistics and data which such local society can give out in their community, either through word of mouth in meetings, by circulars, or, when possible, in local newspapers.

Please understand that the Wall Street controlled public press will give you as little mention as possible and will condemn and ridicule your efforts. Such makes necessary the organizations to share the wealth of this land among the people, which the financial masters are determined they will not allow to be done. Where possible, I hope those organizing a society in one community will get in touch with their friends in other communities and get them to organize societies in them. Anyone can have copies of this article reprinted in circular form to distribute wherever they may desire, or, if they want me to have them printed for them, I can do so and mail them to any address for 60 cents per hundred or $4 per thousand copies.

I introduced in Congress and supported other measures to bring about the sharing of our wealth when I first reached the United States Senate in January 1932. The main efforts to that effect polled about six votes in the Senate at first. Last spring my plan polled the votes of nearly twenty United States Senators, becoming dangerous in proportions to the financial lords. Since then I have been abused in the newspapers and over the radio for everything under the sun. Now that I am pressing this program, the lies and abuse in the big newspapers and over the radio are a matter of daily occurrence. It will all become greater with this effort. Expect that. Meantime go ahead with the work to organize a share-our-wealth society.

Sincerely,
Huey P. Long,
United States Senator.

Radio Address, January 1935

President Roosevelt was elected on November 8, 1932. People look upon an elected President as the President. This is January 1935. We are in our third year of the Roosevelt depression, with the conditions growing worse. . . .

We must now become awakened! We must know the truth and speak the truth. There is no use to wait three more years. It is not Roosevelt or ruin; it is Roosevelt's ruin.

Now, my friends, it makes no difference who is President or who is senator. America is for 125 million people and the unborn to come. We ran Mr. Roosevelt for the presidency of the United States because he promised to us by word of mouth and in writing:

That the size of the big man's fortune would be reduced so as to give the masses at the bottom enough to wipe out all poverty; and

That the hours of labor would be so reduced that all would share in the work to be done and in consuming the abundance mankind produced.

Hundreds of words were used by Mr. Roosevelt to make these promises to the people, but they were made over and over again. He reiterated these pledges even after he took his oath as President. Summed up, what these promises meant was: "Share our wealth."

When I saw him spending all his time of ease and recreation with the business partners of Mr. John D. Rockefeller, Jr., with such men as the Astors, etc., maybe I ought to have had better sense than to have believed he would ever break down their big fortunes to give enough to the masses to end poverty—maybe some will think me weak for ever believing it all, but millions of other people were fooled the same as myself. I was like a drowning man grabbing at a straw, I guess. The face and eyes, the hungry forms of mothers and children, the aching hearts of students denied education were before our eyes, and when Roosevelt promised, we jumped for that ray of hope.

So therefore I call upon the men and women of America to immediately join in our work and movement to share our wealth.

There are thousands of share-our-wealth societies organized in the United States now. We want 100,000 such societies formed for every nook and corner of this country—societies that will meet, talk, and work, all for the purpose that the great wealth and abundance of this great land that belongs to us may be shared and enjoyed by all of us.

We have nothing more for which we should ask the Lord. He has allowed this land to have too much of everything that humanity needs.

SOURCE: Retrieved on 8/14/2003 from www.americanrhetoric.com/speeches/hueyplong share.htm.

So in this land of God's abundance we propose laws, viz.:

1. The fortunes of the multimillionaires and billionaires shall be reduced so that no one person shall own more than a few million dollars to the person. We would do this by a capital levy tax. On the first million that a man was worth, we would not impose any tax. We would say, "All right for your first million dollars, but after you get that rich you will have to start helping the balance of us." So we would not levy any capital levy tax on the first million one owned. But on the second million a man owns, we would tax that 1 percent, so that every year the man owned the second million dollars he would be taxed $10,000. On the third million we would impose a tax of 2 percent. On the fourth million we would impose a tax of 4 percent. On the fifth million we would impose a tax of 8 percent. On the sixth million we would impose a tax of 16 percent. On the seventh million we would impose a tax of 32 percent. On the eighth million we would impose a tax of 64 percent; and on all over the eighth million we would impose a tax of 100 percent.

What this would mean is that the annual tax would bring the biggest fortune down to $3 or $4 million to the person because no one could pay taxes very long in the higher brackets. But $3 to $4 million is enough for any one person and his children and his children's children. We cannot allow one to have more than that because it would not leave enough for the balance to have something.

2. We propose to limit the amount any one man can earn in one year or inherit to $1 million to the person.

3. Now, by limiting the size of the fortunes and incomes of the big men, we will throw into the government Treasury the money and property from which we will care for the millions of people who have nothing; and with this money we will provide a home and the comforts of home, with such common conveniences as radio and automobile, for every family in America, free of debt.

4. We guarantee food and clothing and employment for everyone who should work by shortening the hours of labor to thirty hours per week, maybe less, and to eleven months per year, maybe less. We would have the hours shortened just so much as would give work to everybody to produce enough for everybody; and if we were to get them down to where they were too short, then we would lengthen them again. As long as all the people working can produce enough of automobiles, radios, homes, schools, and theaters for everyone to have that kind of comfort and convenience, then let us all have work to do and have that much of heaven on earth.

5. We would provide education at the expense of the states and the United States for every child, not only through grammar school and high school but through to a college and vocational education. We would simply extend the Louisiana plan to apply to colleges and all people. Yes; we would have to build thousands of more colleges and employ 100,000 more teachers; but we have materials, men, and women who are ready and available for the work. Why have the right to a college education depend upon whether the father or mother is so well-to-do as to send a boy or girl to college? We would give every child the right to education and a living at birth.

6. We would give a pension to all persons above sixty years of age in an amount sufficient to support them in comfortable circumstances, excepting those who earn $1,000 per year or who are worth $10,000.

7. Until we could straighten things out—and we can straighten things out in two months under our program—we would grant a moratorium on all debts which people owe that they cannot pay.

And now you have our program, none too big, none too little, but every man a king.

We owe debts in America today, public and private, amounting to $252 billion. That means that every child is born with a $2,000 debt tied around his neck to hold him down before he gets started. Then, on top of that, the wealth is locked in a vise owned by a few people. We propose that children shall be born in a land of opportunity, guaranteed a home, food, clothes, and the other things that make for living, including the right to education.

Our plan would injure no one. It would not stop us from having millionaires—it would increase them tenfold, because so many more people could make $1 million if they had the chance our plan gives them. Our plan would not break up big concerns.

The only difference would be that maybe 10,000 people would own a concern instead of 10 people owning it.

But, my friends, unless we do share our wealth, unless we limit the size of the big man so as to give something to the little man, we can never have a happy or free people. God said so! He ordered it.

We have everything our people need. Too much of food, clothes, and houses—why not let all have their fill and lie down in the ease and comfort God has given us? Why not? Because a few own everything—the masses own nothing.

I wonder if any of you people who are listening to me were ever at a barbecue! We used to go there—sometimes 1,000 people or more. If there were 1,000 people, we would put enough meat and bread and everything else on the table for 1,000 people. Then everybody would be called and everyone would eat all they wanted. But suppose at one of these barbecues for 1,000 people that one man took 90 percent of the food and ran off with it and ate until he got sick and let the balance rot. Then 999 people would have only enough for 100 to eat and there would be many to starve because of the greed of just one person for something he couldn't eat himself.

Well, ladies and gentlemen, America, all the people of America, have been invited to a barbecue. God invited us all to come and eat and drink all we wanted. He smiled on our land and we grew crops of plenty to eat and wear. He showed us in the earth the iron and other things to make everything we wanted. He unfolded to us the secrets of science so that our work might be easy. God called: "Come to my feast."

Then what happened? Rockefeller, Morgan, and their crowd stepped up and took enough for 120 million people and left only enough for 5 million for all the other 125 million to eat. And so many millions must go hungry and without these good things God gave us unless we call on them to put some of it back.

Emma Goldman (1869–1940)

Emma Goldman (see also Part Five, pp. 383–390) published a pamphlet in 1936, The Individual, Society, and the State, *in which she explicitly outlines her anarchistic views.*

The Individual, Society, and the State, 1936

The minds of men are in confusion, for the very foundations of our civilization seem to be tottering. People are losing faith in the existing institutions, and the more intelligent realize that capitalist industrialism is defeating the very purpose it is supposed to serve.

The world is at a loss for a way out. Parliamentarism and democracy are on the decline. Salvation is being sought in Fascism and other forms of "strong" government.

The struggle of opposing ideas now going on in the world involves social problems urgently demanding a solution. The welfare of the individual and the fate of human society depend on the right answer to those questions The crisis, unemployment, war, disarmament, international relations, etc., are among those problems.

The State, government with its functions and powers, is now the subject of vital interest to every thinking man. Political developments in all civilized countries have brought the questions home. Shall we have a strong government? Are democracy and parliamentary government to be preferred, or is Fascism of one kind or another, dictatorship—monarchical, bourgeois or proletarian—the solution of the ills and difficulties that beset society today?

In other words, shall we cure the evils of democracy by more democracy, or shall we cut the Gordian knot of popular government with the sword of dictatorship?

My answer is neither the one nor the other. I am against dictatorship and Fascism as I am opposed to parliamentary regimes and so-called political democracy.

Nazism has been justly called an attack on civilization. This characterization applies with equal force to every form of dictatorship; indeed, to every kind of

SOURCE: Emma Goldman, *The Individual, Society, and the State* (Chicago: Free Society Forum Pamphlet, 1936).

suppression and coercive authority. For what is civilization in the true sense? All progress has been essentially an enlargement of the liberties of the individual with a corresponding decrease of the authority wielded over him by external forces. This holds good in the realm of physical as well as of political and economic existence. In the physical world man has progressed to the extent in which he has subdued the forces of nature and made them useful to himself. Primitive man made a step on the road to progress when he first produced fire and thus triumphed over darkness, when he chained the wind or harnessed water.

What role did authority or government play in human endeavor for betterment, in invention and discovery? None whatever, or at least none that was helpful. It has always been the individual that has accomplished every miracle in that sphere, usually in spite of the prohibition, persecution and interference by authority, human and divine.

Similarly, in the political sphere, the road of progress lay in getting away more and more from the authority of the tribal chief or of the clan, of prince and king, of government, of the State. Economically, progress has meant greater well-being of ever larger numbers. Culturally, it has signified the result of all the other achievements—greater independence, political, mental and psychic.

Regarded from this angle, the problems of man's relation to the State assumes an entirely different significance. It is no more a question of whether dictatorship is preferable to democracy, or Italian Fascism superior to Hitlerism. A larger and far more vital question poses itself: Is political government, is the State beneficial to mankind, and how does it affect the individual in the social scheme of things?

The individual is the true reality in life. A cosmos in himself, he does not exist for the State, nor for that abstraction called "society," or the "nation," which is only a collection of individuals. Man, the individual, has always been and, necessarily is the sole source and motive power of evolution and progress. Civilization has been a continuous struggle of the individual or of groups of individuals against the State and even against "society," that is, against the majority subdued and hypnotized by the State and State worship. Man's greatest battles have been waged against man-made obstacles and artificial handicaps imposed upon him to paralyze his growth and development. Human thought has always been falsified by tradition and custom, and perverted false education in the interests of those who held power and enjoyed privileges. In other words, by the State and the ruling classes. This constant incessant conflict has been the history of mankind.

Individuality may be described as the consciousness of the individual as to what he is and how he lives. It is inherent in every human being and is a thing of growth. The State and social institutions come and go, but individuality remains and persists. The very essence of individuality is expression; the sense of dignity and independence is the soil wherein it thrives. Individuality is not the impersonal and mechanistic thing that the State treats as an "individual." The individual is not merely the result of heredity and environment, of cause and effect. He is that and a great deal more, a great deal else. The living man cannot be defined; he is the fountain-head of all life and all values; he is not a part of this or of that; he is a whole, an individual whole, a growing, changing, yet always constant whole.

Individuality is not to be confused with the various ideas and concepts of Individualism; much less with that "rugged individualism" which is only a masked attempt to repress and defeat the individual and his individuality. So-called Individualism is the social and economic *laissez faire:* the exploitation of the masses by the classes by means of legal trickery, spiritual debasement and systematic indoctrination of the servile spirit, which process is known as "education." That corrupt and perverse "individualism" is the strait-jacket of individuality. It has converted life into a degrading race for externals, for possession, for social prestige and supremacy. Its highest wisdom is "the devil take the hindmost."

This "rugged individualism" has inevitably resulted in the greatest modern slavery, the crassest class distinctions, driving millions to the breadline. "Rugged individualism" has meant all the "individualism" for the masters, while the people are regimented into a slave caste to serve a handful of self-seeking "supermen." America is perhaps the best representative of this kind of individualism, in whose name political tyranny and social oppression are defended and held up as virtues; while every aspiration and attempt of man to gain freedom and social opportunity to live is denounced as "unAmerican" and evil in the name of that same individualism.

There was a time when the State was unknown. In his natural condition man existed without any State or organized government. People lived as families in small communities; they tilled the soil and practiced the arts and crafts. The individual, and later the family, was the unit of social life where each was free and the equal of his neighbor. Human society then was not a State but an *association;* a *voluntary* association for mutual protection and benefit. The elders and more experienced members were the guides and advisers of the people. They helped to manage the affairs of life, not to rule and dominate the individual.

Political government and the State were a much later development, growing out of the desire of the stronger to take advantage of the weaker, of the few against the many. The State, ecclesiastical and secular, served to give an appearance of legality and right to the wrong done by the few to the many. That appearance of right was necessary the easier to rule the people, because no government can exist without the consent of the people, consent open, tacit or assumed. Constitutionalism and democracy are the modern forms of that alleged consent; the consent being inoculated and indoctrinated by what is called "education," at home, in the church, and in every other phase of life.

That consent is the belief in authority, in the necessity for it. At its base is the doctrine that man is evil, vicious, and too incompetent to know what is good for him. On this all government and oppression is built. God and the State exist and are supported by this dogma.

Yet the State is nothing but a name. It is an abstraction. Like other similar conceptions—nation, race, humanity—it has no organic reality. To call the State an organism shows a diseased tendency to make a fetish of words.

The State is a term for the legislative and administrative machinery whereby certain business of the people is transacted, and badly so. There is nothing sacred, holy or mysterious about it. The State has no more conscience or moral mission than a commercial company for working a coal mine or running a railroad.

The State has no more existence than gods and devils have. They are equally the reflex and creation of man, for man, the individual, is the only reality. The State is but the shadow of man, the shadow of his opaqueness of his ignorance and fear.

Life begins and ends with man, the individual. Without him there is no race, no humanity, no State. No, not even "society" is possible without man. It is the individual who lives, breathes and suffers. His development, his advance, has been a continuous struggle against the fetishes of his own creation and particularly so against the "State."

In former days religious authority fashioned political life in the image of the Church. The authority of the State, the "rights" of rulers came from on high; power, like faith, was divine. Philosophers have written thick volumes to prove the sanctity of the State; some have even clad it with infallibility and with godlike attributes. Some have talked themselves into the insane notion that the State is "superhuman," the supreme reality, "the absolute."

Enquiry was condemned as blasphemy. Servitude was the highest virtue. By such precepts and training certain things came to be regarded as self-evident, as sacred of their truth, but because of constant and persistent repetition.

All progress has been essentially an unmasking of "divinity" and "mystery," of alleged sacred, eternal "truth"; it has been a gradual elimination of the abstract and the substitution in its place of the real, the concrete. In short, of facts against fancy, of knowledge against ignorance, of light against darkness.

That slow and arduous liberation of the individual was not accomplished by the aid of the State. On the contrary, it was by continuous conflict, by a life-and-death struggle with the State, that even the smallest vestige of independence and freedom has been won. It has cost mankind much time and blood to secure what little it has gained so far from kings, tsars and governments.

The great heroic figure of that long Golgotha has been Man. It has always been the individual, often alone and singly, at other times in unity and co-operation with others of his kind, who has fought and bled in the age-long battle against suppression and oppression, against the powers that enslave and degrade him.

More than that and more significant: It was man, the individual, whose soul first rebelled against injustice and degradation; it was the individual who first conceived the idea of resistance to the conditions under which he chafed. In short, it is always the individual who is the parent of the liberating thought as well as of the deed.

This refers not only to political struggles, but to the entire gamut of human life and effort, in all ages and climes. It has always been the individual, the man of strong mind and will to liberty, who paved the way for every human advance, for every step toward a freer and better world; in science, philosophy and art, as well as in industry, whose genius rose to the heights, conceiving the "impossible," visualizing its realization and imbuing others with his enthusiasm to work and strive for it. Socially speaking, it was always the prophet, the seer, the idealist, who dreamed of a world more to his heart's desire and who served as the beacon light on the road to greater achievement.

The State, every government whatever its form, character or color—be it absolute or constitutional, monarchy or republic, Fascist, Nazi or Bolshevik—is by its very nature conservative, static, intolerant of change and opposed to it. Whatever changes it undergoes are always the result of pressure exerted upon it, pressure strong enough to compel the ruling powers to submit peaceably or otherwise, generally "otherwise"—that is, by revolution. Moreover, the inherent conservatism of government, of authority of any kind, unavoidably becomes reactionary. For two reasons: first, because it is in the nature of government not only to retain the power it has, but also to strengthen, widen and perpetuate it, nationally as well as internationally. The stronger authority grows, the greater the State and its power, the less it can tolerate a similar authority or political power along side of itself. The psychology of government demands that its influence and prestige constantly grow, at home and abroad, and it exploits every opportunity to increase it. This tendency is motivated by the financial and commercial interests back of the government, represented and served by it. The fundamental *raison d'etre* of every government to which, incidentally, historians of former days wilfully shut their eyes, has become too obvious now even for professors to ignore.

The other factor which impels governments to become even more conservative and reactionary is their inherent distrust of the individual and fear of individuality. Our political and social scheme cannot afford to tolerate the individual and his constant quest for innovation. In "self-defense" the State therefore suppresses, persecutes, punishes and even deprives the individual of life. It is aided in this by every institution that stands for the preservation of the existing order. It resorts to every form of violence and force, and its efforts are supported by the "moral indignation" of the majority against the heretic, the social dissenter and the political rebel—the majority for centuries drilled in State worship, trained in discipline and obedience and subdued by the awe of authority in the home, the school, the church and the press.

The strongest bulwark of authority is uniformity; the least divergence from it is the greatest crime. The wholesale mechanisation of modern life has increased uniformity a thousandfold. It is everywhere present, in habits, tastes, dress, thoughts and ideas. Its most concentrated dullness is "public opinion." Few have the courage to stand out against it. He who refuses to submit is at once labelled "queer," "different," and decried as a disturbing element in the comfortable stagnancy of modern life.

Perhaps even more than constituted authority, it is social uniformity and sameness that harass the individual most. His very "uniqueness," "separateness" and "differentiation" make him an alien, not only in his native place, but even in his own home. Often more so than the foreign born who generally falls in with the established.

In the true sense one's native land, with its back ground of tradition, early impressions, reminiscences and other things dear to one, is not enough to make sensitive human beings feel at home. A certain atmosphere of "belonging," the consciousness of being "at one" with the people and environment, is more essential to one's feeling of home. This holds good in relation to one's family, the smaller local circle, as well as the larger phase of the life and activities commonly called one's country. The individual whose vision encompasses the whole world often feels nowhere so hedged in and out of touch with his surroundings than in his native land.

In pre-war time the individual could at least escape national and family boredom. The whole world was open to his longings and his quests. Now the world has become a prison, and life continual solitary confinement. Especially is this true since the advent of dictatorship, right and left.

Friedrich Nietzsche called the State a cold monster. What would he have called the hideous beast in the garb of modern dictatorship? Not that government had ever allowed much scope to the individual; but the champions of the new State ideology do not grant even that much. "The individual is nothing," they declare, "it is the collectivity which counts." Nothing less than the complete surrender of the individual will satisfy the insatiable appetite of the new deity.

Strangely enough, the loudest advocates of this new gospel are to be found among the British and American intelligentsia. Just now they are enamored with the "dictatorship of the proletariat." In theory only, to be sure. In practice, they still prefer the few liberties in their own respective countries. They go to Russia for a short visit or as salesmen of the "revolution," but they feel safer and more comfortable at home.

Perhaps it is not only lack of courage which keeps these good Britishers and Americans in their native lands rather than in the millenium come. Subconsciously there may lurk the feeling that individuality remains the most fundamental fact of all human association, suppressed and persecuted yet never defeated, and in the long run the victor.

The "genius of man," which is but another name for personality and individuality, bores its way through all the caverns of dogma, through the thick walls of tradition and custom, defying all taboos, setting authority at naught, facing contumely and the scaffold—ultimately to be blessed as prophet and martyr by succeeding generations. But for the "genius of man," that inherent, persistent quality of individuality, we would be still roaming the primeval forests.

Peter Kropotkin has shown what wonderful results this unique force of man's individuality has achieved when strengthened by *co-operation* with other individualities. The one-sided and entirely inadequate Darwinian theory of the struggle for existence received its biological and sociological completion from the great Anarchist scientist and thinker. In his profound work, *Mutual Aid*, Kropotkin shows that in the animal kingdom, as well as in human society, co-operation—as opposed to internecine strife and struggle—has worked for the survival and evolution of the species. He demonstrated that only mutual aid and voluntary co-operation—not the omnipotent, all-devastating State—can create the basis for a free individual and associational life.

At present the individual is the pawn of the zealots of dictatorship and the equally obsessed zealots of "rugged individualism." The excuse of the former is its claim of a new objective. The latter does not even make a pretense of anything new. As a matter of fact "rugged individualism" has learned nothing and forgotten nothing. Under its guidance the brute struggle for physical existence is still kept up. Strange as it may seem, and utterly absurd as it is, the struggle for physical survival goes merrily on though the necessity for it has entirely disappeared. Indeed, the struggle is being continued apparently because there is no necessity for it. Does not so-called overproduction prove it? Is not the world-wide economic crisis an eloquent demonstration that the struggle for existence is being maintained by the blindness of "rugged individualism" at the risk of its own destruction?

One of the insane characteristics of this struggle is the complete negation of the relation of the producer to the things he produces. The average worker has no inner point of contact with the industry he is employed in, and he is a stranger to the process of production of which he is a mechanical part. Like any other cog of the machine, he is replaceable at any time by other similar depersonalized human beings.

The intellectual proletarian, though he foolishly thinks himself a free agent, is not much better off. He, too, has a little choice or self-direction, in his particular metier as his brother who works with his hands. Material considerations and desire for greater social prestige are usually the deciding factors in the vocation of the intellectual. Added to it is the tendency to follow in the footsteps of family tradition, and become doctors, lawyers, teachers, engineers, etc. The groove requires less effort and personality. In consequence nearly everybody is out of place in our present scheme of things. The masses plod on, partly because their senses have been dulled by the deadly routine of work and because they must eke out an existence. This applies with even greater force to the political fabric of today. There is no place in its texture for free choice of independent thought and activity. There is a place only for voting and tax-paying puppets.

The interests of the State and those of the individual differ fundamentally and are antagonistic. The State and the political and economic institutions it supports can exist only by fashioning the individual to their particular purpose; training him to respect "law and order"; teaching him obedience, submission and unquestioning faith in the wisdom and justice of government; above all, loyal service and complete self-sacrifice when the State commands it, as in war. The State puts itself and its interests even above the claims of religion and of God. It punishes religious or conscientious scruples against individuality because there is no individuality without liberty, and liberty is the greatest menace to authority.

The struggle of the individual against these tremendous odds is the more difficult—too often dangerous to life and limb—because it is not truth or falsehood which serves as the criterion of the opposition he meets. It is not the validity or usefulness of his thought or activity which rouses against him the forces of the State and of "public opinion." The persecution of the innovator and protestant has always been inspired by fear on the part of constituted authority of having its infallibility questioned and its power undermined.

Man's true liberation, individual and collective, lies in his emancipation from authority and from the belief in it. All human evolution has been a struggle in that direction and for that object. It is not invention and mechanics which constitute development. The ability to travel at the rate of 100 miles an hour is no evidence of being civilized. True civilization is to be measured by the individual, the unit of all social life; by his individuality and the extent to which it is free to have its being to grow and expand unhindered by invasive and coercive authority.

Socially speaking, the criterion of civilization and culture is the degree of liberty and economic opportunity which the individual enjoys; of social and international unity and co-operation unrestricted by man-made laws and other artificial obstacles; by the absence of privileged castes and by the reality of liberty and human dignity; in short, by the true emancipation of the individual.

Political absolutism has been abolished because men have realized in the course of time that absolute power is evil and destructive. But the same thing is true of all power, whether it be the power of privilege, of money, of the priest, of the politician or of so-called democracy. In its effect on individuality it matters little what the particular character of coercion is—whether it be as black as Fascism, as yellow as Nazism or as pretentiously red as Bolshevism. It is power that corrupts and degrades both master and slave and it makes no difference whether the power is wielded by an autocrat, by parliament or Soviets. More pernicious than the power of a dictator is that of a class; the most terrible—the tyranny of a majority.

The long process of history has taught man that division and strife mean death, and that unity and cooperation advance his cause, multiply his strength and further his welfare. The spirit of government has always worked against the social application of this vital lesson, except where it served the State and aided its own particular interests. It is this anti-progressive and anti-social spirit of the State and of the privileged castes back of it which has been responsible for the bitter struggle between man and man. The individual and ever larger groups of individuals are beginning to see beneath the surface of the established order of things. No longer are they so blinded as in the past by the glare and tinsel of the State idea, and of the "blessings" of "rugged individualism." Man is reaching out for the wider scope of human relations which liberty alone can give. For true liberty is not a mere scrap of paper called "constitution," "legal right" or "law." It is not an abstraction derived from the non-reality known as "the State." It is not the *negative* thing of being free *from* something, because with such freedom you may starve to death. Real freedom, true liberty *is positive*: it is freedom *to* something; it is the liberty to be, to do; in short, the liberty of actual and active opportunity.

That sort of liberty is not a gift: it is the natural right of man, of every human being. It cannot be given: it cannot be conferred by any law or government. The need of it, the longing for it, is inherent in the individual. Disobedience to every form of coercion is the instinctive expression of it. Rebellion and revolution are the more or less conscious attempt to achieve it. Those manifestations, individual and social, are fundamentally expressions of the values of man. That those values may be nurtured, the community must realize that its greatest and most lasting asset is the unit—the individual.

In religion, as in politics, people speak of abstractions and believe they are dealing with realities. But when it does come to the real and the concrete, most people seem to lose vital touch with it. It may well be because reality alone is too matter-of-fact, too cold to enthuse the human soul. It can be aroused to enthusiasm only by things out of the commonplace, out of the ordinary. In other words, the Ideal is the spark that fires the imagination and hearts of men. Some ideal is needed to rouse man out of the inertia and humdrum of his existence and turn the abject slave into an heroic figure.

Right here, of course, comes the Marxist objector who has outmarxed Marx himself. To such a one, man is a mere puppet in the hands of that metaphysical Almighty called economic determinism or, more vulgarly, the class struggle. Man's will, individual and collective, his psychic life and mental orientation count for almost nothing with our Marxist and do not affect his conception of human history.

No intelligent student will deny the importance of the economic factor in the social growth and development of mankind. But only narrow and wilful dogmatism can persist in remaining blind to the important role played by an idea as conceived by the imagination and aspirations of the individual.

It were vain and unprofitable to attempt to balance one factor as against another in human experience. No one single factor in the complex of individual or social behavior can be designated as the factor of decisive quality. We know too little, and may never know enough, of human psychology to weigh and measure the relative values of this or that factor in determining man's conduct. To form such dogmas in their social connotation is nothing short of bigotry; yet, perhaps, it has its uses, for the very attempt to do so proved the persistence of the human will and confutes the Marxists.

Fortunately even some Marxists are beginning to see that all is not well with the Marxian creed. After all, Marx was but human—all too human—hence by no means infallible. The practical application of economic determinism in Russia is helping to clear the minds of the more intelligent Marxists. This can be seen in the transvaluation of Marxian values going on in Socialist and even Communist ranks in some European countries. They are slowly realising that their theory has overlooked the human element, *den Menschen*, as a Socialist paper put it. Important as the economic factor is, it is not enough. The rejuvenation of mankind needs the inspiration and energising force of an ideal.

Such an ideal I see in Anarchism. To be sure, not in the popular misrepresentations of Anarchism spread by the worshippers of the State and authority. I mean the philosophy of a new social order based on the released energies of the individual and the free association of liberated individuals.

Of all social theories Anarchism alone steadfastly proclaims that society exists for man, not man for society. The sole legitimate purpose of society is to serve the needs and advance the aspiration of the individual. Only by doing so can it justify its existence and be an aid to progress and culture.

The political parties and men savagely scrambling for power will scorn me as hopelessly out of tune with our time. I cheerfully admit the charge. I find comfort in the assurance that their hysteria lacks enduring quality. Their hosanna is but of the hour.

Man's yearning for liberation from all authority and power will never be soothed by their cracked song. Man's quest for freedom from every shackle is eternal. It must and will go on.

Woody Guthrie.
Political activist and social commentator Woody Guthrie wrote hundreds of protest songs and influenced many subsequent musicians from Pete Seeger to Bruce Springsteen, Bob Dylan to Bono. His most famous song, "This Land Is Your Land," was Guthrie's acerbic response to Irving Berlin's "God Bless America."

Woody Guthrie (1912–1967)

Woodrow Wilson Guthrie, born in Oklahoma the year of his namesake's election to the presidency, was a rambler, a musician, a critical observer of American society, a union organizer, and a radical, who, through hundreds of protest songs, left behind an exceptional legacy of dissent that is still felt today. At the age of 23, he left his wife and three children and, along with thousands of other Okies fleeing the dust bowl of Oklahoma, bummed his way to the "promised land" of California. There he ran head-on into the anti-Okie discrimination and hatred that greeted all desperate migrant workers during the dislocation of the Great Depression. Although he was living on the outside of society, he was able to make a living singing songs of social protest on the radio. "Goin' Down the Road Feelin' Bad," "Hard Travelin'," and many of the other songs he called his dust bowl ballads virtually became anthems for those who, like Guthrie, also felt like outcasts. He wrote union songs like "Union Maid," antiestablishment songs like "Philadelphia Lawyer," children's songs like

"Car, Car," and droll songs like "Do Re Me." Frequently, he visited the government camps and Hoovervilles in California to sing to migrant workers. His most famous song, "This Land is Your Land," was Guthrie's response to Irving Berlin's "God Bless America," a song which Guthrie loathed as the epitome of American self-righteousness. In the original draft, Guthrie penned several radical verses (later eliminated) that revealed his belief that America was for the common people, the ordinary people, and that it belonged to everyone, not just the wealthy, or the pious, or the powerful. In one verse he wonders, while observing his fellow Americans standing on line at the relief office, "if God blessed America for me." In another verse he sings about "a sign that says 'private property,'" on one side while on the other side it says nothing. He felt the implication was clear: "that side was made for you and me."

At the end of the decade, he was living in New York, where he teamed up with Pete Seeger, Lee Hayes, Leadbelly, Cisco Houston, and other leftist musicians and songwriters and, with the outbreak of the Second World War, added antifascist songs to his repertoire. He was against "Hitlerism and fascism homemade and imported," he wrote in his autobiography, "and made up songs to pay honor and tribute to the story of the trade union workers around the world." In 1943 he joined the merchant marine and in 1945 was drafted into the army.

Though he had inscribed on the front of his guitar "this machine kills fascists," many critics detested his radical lyrics and questioned his patriotism. Once, when asked if he was a "Red," he replied that he did not know if he would call himself a "Red," although he had to admit that he had always been "in the red" all his life.

Guthrie did a number of recordings for the Library of Congress and also performed and recorded with the Almanac Singers, a group that was the forerunner of the Weavers. In 1943, he published Bound for Glory, *an autobiographical account of his life. Although he continued to travel about the country writing, performing, and recording, his health began to fail on account of a debilitating hereditary nerve disease, Huntington's chorea. In the last 13 years of his life, he was unable to sing, and he spent most of his time in and out of hospitals as the disease gradually consumed him. In 1961, a young musician-songwriter who had grown up listening to Woody Guthrie's records and who had begun to model his own approach to music on Guthrie's example made a pilgrimage to New York to pay homage to his hero. During his visits Robert Zimmerman of Hibbing, Minnesota, would sit with Woody while reading some of his own poetry and playing both his and Woody's songs to the invalid. It was during this time that Zimmerman began to perform at a Manhattan folk club, Gerde's Folk City, going by the name of Bob Dylan.*

"The Ballad of Pretty Boy Floyd" turns a notorious bank robber who was hunted down by the FBI into a modern-day Robin Hood. In "Jesus Christ," Guthrie portrays Jesus Christ as an activist.

"The Ballad of Pretty Boy Floyd," 1939

If you'll gather 'round me, children,
A story I will tell
'Bout Pretty Boy Floyd, an outlaw,
Oklahoma knew him well.

It was in the town of Shawnee,
A Saturday afternoon,
His wife beside him in his wagon
As into town they rode.

There a deputy sheriff approached him
In a manner rather rude,
Vulgar words of anger,
An' his wife she overheard.

Pretty Boy grabbed a log chain,
And the deputy grabbed his gun;
In the fight that followed
He laid that deputy down.

Then he took to the trees and timber
To live a life of shame;
Every crime in Oklahoma
Was added to his name.

There's many a starving farmer
The same old story told
How the outlaw paid their mortgage
And saved their little home.

Others tell you of a stranger
That came to beg a meal,
Underneath his napkin
Left a thousand dollar bill.

It was in Oklahoma City,
It was on a Christmas Day,
There was a whole car load of groceries
Come with a note to say:

"Well, you say that I'm an outlaw,
You say that I'm a thief.
Here's a Christmas dinner
For the families on relief."

Source: Harold Leventhal and Marjorie Guthrie, eds., *The Woody Guthrie Songbook* (New York: Grosset and Dunlap, 1976), 186–187.

Now as through this world I ramble
I see lots of funny men;
Some will rob you with a six-gun,
And some with a fountain pen.

And as through your life you travel,
Yes, as through your life you roam,
You won't never see an outlaw
Drive a family from their home.

"Jesus Christ," 1940

Jesus Christ was a man who traveled through the land,
A hard working man and brave.
He said to the rich "Give your goods to the poor."
But they laid Jesus Christ in His grave.

Jesus was a man, a carpenter by hand,
His followers true and brave,
One dirty little coward called Judas Iscariot
Has laid Jesus Christ in His grave.

He went to the preacher, He went to the sheriff,
He told them all the same,
"Sell all of your jewelry and give it to the poor,"
And they laid Jesus Christ in his grave.

When Jesus come to town, all the working folks around
Believed what He did say,
But bankers and the preachers they nailed Him on a cross.
And they laid Jesus Christ in His grave.

The poor workin' people, they followed Him around,
They sung and they shouted gay,
The cops and the soldiers, they nailed Him in the air,
And they laid Jesus Christ in His grave.

And the people held their breath when they heard about His death,
Everybody wondered why.
It was the big landlord and the soldiers that they hired
To nail Jesus Christ in the sky.

SOURCE: Harold Leventhal and Marjorie Guthrie, eds., *The Woody Guthrie Songbook* (New York: Grosset and Dunlap 1976), 153–155. JESUS CHRIST, words and music by Woody Guthrie. TRO— © 1961 (renewed) 1963 (renewed) Ludlow Music, Inc., New York, NY. Used by permission.

This song it was wrote in New York City,
Of rich man, preacher and slave,
If Jesus was to preach what He preached in Galilee,
They would lay poor Jesus Christ in His grave.

J. Saunders Redding (1906–1988)and Charles F. Wilson (Unknown)

The First World War was a bitterly disillusioning experience for African Americans. Many had joined the army in hopes that their patriotism and gallantry in battle would guarantee equal treatment for them after the war. But racism was in no way diminished following the war—in fact, there were a number of bloody race riots in several cities—and African Americans were still treated as second-class citizens. When the Second World War broke out, there was concern that this time there should be a different outcome. The first selection here is J. Saunders Redding's attempt to analyze the meaning of the war for African Americans. The second selection, by Charles F. Wilson, an African American private in the Army Air Corps, is a letter to President Roosevelt in which he protests the undemocratic nature of the segregated U.S. Army.

J. SAUNDERS REDDING, "A NEGRO LOOKS AT THIS WAR," 1942

War had no heroic traditions for me. Wars were white folks'. All wars in historical memory. The last war, and the Spanish-American War before that, and the Civil War. I had been brought up in a way that admitted of no heroics. I think my parents were right. Life for them was a fierce, bitter, soul-searching war of spiritual and economic attrition; they fought it without heroics, but with stubborn heroism. Their heroism was screwed up to a pitch of idealism so intense that it found a safety valve in cynicism about the heroics of white folks' war. This cynicism went back at least as far as my paternal grandmother, whose fierce eyes used to lash the faces of her five grandchildren as she said, "An' he done som'pin big an' brave away down dere to Chickymorgy an' dey made a iron image of him 'cause he got his head blowed off an' his stomick blowed out fightin' to keep his slaves." I cannot convey the scorn and the cynicism she put into her picture of that hero-son of her slave-master, but I have never forgotten.

SOURCE: J. Saunders Redding, "A Negro Looks at This War," *American Mercury* 55 (November 1942): 585–592.

I was nearly ten when we entered the last war in 1917. The European fighting, and the sinking of the Lusitania, had seemed as remote, as distantly meaningless to us, as the Battle of Hastings. Then we went in and suddenly the city was flag-draped, slogan-plastered, and as riotously gay as on circus half-holidays. I remember one fine Sunday we came upon an immense new billboard with a new slogan: GIVE! TO MAKE THE WORLD SAFE FOR DEMOCRACY. My brother, who was the oldest of us, asked what making the world safe for democracy meant. My father frowned, but before he could answer, my mother broke in.

"It's just something to say, like . . . "—and then she was stuck until she hit upon one of the family's old jokes—"like 'Let's make a million dollars.'" We all laughed, but the bitter core of her meaning lay revealed, even for the youngest of us, like the stone in a halved peach. . . .

And so, since I have reached maturity and thought a man's thoughts and had a man's—a Negro man's—experiences, I have thought that I could never believe in war again. Yet I believe in this one.

There are many things about this war that I do not like, just as there are many things about "practical" Christianity that I do not like. But I believe in Christianity, and if I accept the shoddy and unfulfilling in the conduct of this war, I do it as voluntarily and as purposefully as I accept the trash in the workings of "practical" Christianity. I do not like the odor of political pandering that arises from some groups. I do not like these "race incidents" in the camps. I do not like the world's not knowing officially that there were Negro soldiers on Bataan with General Wainwright. I do not like the constant references to the Japs as "yellow bastards," "yellow bellies," and "yellow monkeys," as if color had something to do with treachery, as if color were the issue and the thing we are fighting rather than oppression, slavery, and a way of life hateful and nauseating. These and other things I do not like, yet I believe in the war. . . .

This is a war to keep men free. The struggle to broaden and lengthen the road of freedom—our own private and important war to enlarge freedom here in America—will come later. That this private, intra-American war will be carried on and won is the only real reason we Negroes have to fight. We must keep the road open. Did we not believe in a victory in that intra-American war, we could not believe in nor stomach the compulsion of this. If we could not believe in the realization of democratic freedom for ourselves, certainly no one could ask us to die for the preservation of that ideal for others. But to broaden and lengthen the road of freedom is different from preserving it. And our first duty is to keep the road of freedom open. It must be done continuously. It is the duty of the whole people to do this. Our next duty (and this, too, is the whole people's) is to broaden the road so that more people can travel it without snarling traffic. To die in these duties is to die for something. . . .

I believe in this war, finally, because I believe in the ultimate vindication of the wisdom of the brotherhood of man. This is not foggy idealism. I think that the growing manifestations of the interdependence of all men is an argument for the wisdom of brotherhood. I think that the shrunk compass of the world is an argument. I think that the talk of united nations and of planned interdependence is an argument.

More immediately, I believe in this war because I believe in America. I believe in what America professes to stand for. Nor is this, I think, whistling in the dark. There are a great many things wrong here. There are only a few men of good will. I do not lose sight of that. I know the inequalities, the outraged hopes and faith, the inbred hate; and I know that there are people who wish merely to lay these by in the closet of the national mind until the crisis is over. But it would be equally foolish for me to lose sight of the advances that are made, the barriers that are leveled, the privileges that grow. Foolish, too, to remain blind to the distinction that exists between simple race prejudice, already growing moribund under the impact of this war, and theories of racial superiority as a basic tenet of a societal system—theories that at bottom are the avowed justification for suppression, defilement and murder.

I will take this that I have here. I will take the democratic theory. The bit of road of freedom that stretches through America is worth fighting to preserve. The very fact that I, a Negro in America, can fight against the evils in America is worth fighting for. This open fighting against the wrongs one hates is the mark and the hope of democratic freedom. I do not underestimate the struggle. I know the learning that must take place, the evils that must be broken, the depths that must be climbed. But I am free to help in doing these things. I count. I am free (though only a little as yet) to pound blows at the huge body of my American world until, like a chastened mother, she gives me nurture with the rest.

CHARLES F. WILSON, LETTER TO PRESIDENT ROOSEVELT, 1944

Dear President Roosevelt:

It was with extreme pride that I, a soldier in the Armed Forces of our country, read the following affirmation of our war aims, pronounced by you at a recent press conference:

> "The United Nations are fighting to make a world in which tyranny, and aggression cannot exist; a world based upon freedom, equality, and justice; a world in which all persons, regardless of race, color and creed, may live in peace, honor and dignity." . . .

But the picture in our country is marred by one of the strangest paradoxes in our whole fight against world fascism. The United States Armed Forces, to

---

SOURCE: Phillip McGuire, ed. *Taps for a Jim Crow Army: Letters from Black Soldiers in World War II* (Santa Barbara, CA: ABC-CLIO, 1983), 134–139.

fight for World Democracy, is within itself undemocratic. The undemocratic policy of Jim Crow and segregation is practiced by our Armed Forces against its Negro members. Totally inadequate opportunities are given to the Negro members of our Armed Forces, nearly one tenth of the whole, to participate with "equality". . . "regardless of race and color" in the fight for our war aims. In fact it appears that the army intends to follow the very policy that the FEPC [Fair Employment Practices Committee] is battling against in civilian life, the pattern of assigning Negroes to the lowest types of work.

Let me give you an example of the lack of democracy in our Field, where I am now stationed. Negro soldiers are completely segregated from the white soldiers on the base. And to make doubly sure that no mistake is made about this, the barracks and other housing facilities (supply room, mess hall, etc.) of the Negro section C are covered with black tar paper, while all other barracks and housing facilities on the base are painted white.

It is the stated policy of the Second Air Force that "every potential fighting man must be used as a fighting man. If you have such a man in a base job, you have no choice. His job must be eliminated or be filled by a limited service man, WAC, or civilian." And yet, leaving out the Negro soldiers working with the Medical Section, fully 50% of the Negro soldiers are working in base jobs, such as, for example, at the Resident Officers' Mess, Bachelor Officers' Quarters, and Officers' Club, as mess personnel, BOQ orderlies, and bar tenders. Leaving out the medical men again, based on the section C average only 4% of this 50% would not be "potential fighting men." . . .

How can we convince nearly one tenth of the Armed Forces, the Negro members, that your pronouncement of the war aims of the United Nations means what it says, when their experience with one of the United Nations, the United States of America, is just the opposite? . . .

With your issuance of Executive Order 8802, and the setting up of the Fair Employment Practices Committee, you established the foundation for fighting for democracy in the industrial forces of our country, in the interest of victory for the United Nations. In the interest of victory for the United Nations, another Executive Order is now needed. An Executive Order which will lay the base for fighting for democracy in the Armed Forces of our country. An Executive Order which would bring about the result here at Davis-Monthan Field whereby the Negro soldiers would be integrated into all of the Sections on the base, as fighting men, instead of in the segregated Section C as housekeepers.

Then and only then can your pronouncement of the war aims of the United Nations mean to all that we "are fighting to make a world in which tyranny, and aggression cannot exist; a world based upon freedom, equality and justice; a world in which all persons, regardless of race, color and creed, may live in peace, honor and dignity."

Respectfully yours,
Charles F. Wilson, 36794590
Private, Air Corps

David Dellinger (1915–2004)

A year before the United States entered the Second World War, Congress passed the Selective Training and Service Act, establishing the first peacetime draft in the nation's history. A person given the 1-A classification was at the top of the conscription list; 4-F meant the person was physically unable to enter the military. The act also assigned two classifications for those opposed to the war: 1-AO, for people who would be willing to work in the medical corps, and 4-E, for those who would not accept any assignment connected to the military but who would agree to do alternative civilian work. Selective Service records show that about 12,000 men refused to fight in the "good war" and were classified as conscientious objectors. Another 6000 men refused to participate in any way in the war effort and wound up serving prison terms. They came from all backgrounds: Quakers, Jehovah's Witnesses, Seventh Day Adventists, Buddhists, pacifists, and others.

David Dellinger, who later was prominent in the 1960s antiwar movement and was tried as one of the Chicago Seven for his role in the demonstrations at the 1968 Democratic convention, believed deeply that the only viable method of fighting evil was through nonviolence. Inspired by the example of Mahatma Gandhi and disgusted with U.S. bankers and industrialists' complicity in the rise of Adolf Hitler, Dellinger was sent to prison for his refusal to register for the draft. The following document is Dellinger's firsthand account of his experience.

WHY I REFUSED TO REGISTER IN THE OCTOBER 1940 DRAFT AND A LITTLE OF WHAT IT LED TO

I believe that there are mysterious spiritual factors that influence who we are and what we do. For me, beginning in early childhood, these were the solitary experiences of the ecstasies of Nature and having to deal with the racism and classism of many of the well-to-do adults in the suburb of Boston where I grew up (even as I saw indications that they were not as happy as they would have been had they lived a more egalitarian and sharing life-style). I can think of four other influences that led me to become an objector to World War II long before the United States officially entered.

First, I was influenced by my exposure to the lies and failures of World War I and the examples of persons who fought in that war or went to prison for resisting it. A second influence included my visits to Nazi Germany in 1936 and 1937 when

SOURCE: Larry Gara and Lenna Mae Gara, eds., *A Few Small Candles: War Resisters of World War II Tell Their Stories* (Kent, OH: Kent State University Press, 1999), 20–37.

I was anti-Nazi and the U.S. government, banks, and major corporations were supporting Hitler. A third was my experience, after returning from Europe, going "on the road," penniless, riding the rails, and staying at missions and hobo jungles. The fourth influence was the inspiring example of grass-roots practitioners of nonviolent resistance to oppression and injustice. The practitioners included radical Christians, Jews, Buddhists, atheists, anarchists, Native Americans, African Americans, the labor organizers with whom I worked in the thirties, and Gandhians in India. I mention Buddhists, anarchists, and Native Americans, even though I knew none of them personally. But I read widely, and all the major influences I have listed were broadened and deepened by this.

One of my most vivid memories is of the widespread rejoicing I observed— and felt—when World War I came to an end in November 1918, about three months after my third birthday. "Now no one will have to kill other people," is the way my father put it at the time. When I was thirteen, a German officer from that war was invited to speak in our Wakefield, Massachusetts, town hall in a celebration of the tenth anniversary of the ending of the war. Many people spoke out against allowing an "enemy" to speak, but my father and I went to hear him. I was profoundly moved by the German's appeal for the people of the world to work across national boundaries to solve their differences rather than going to war and doing the terrible things that he had done. And it was an early lesson on the gains to be made by following one's own common sense and conscience, rather than being intimidated by self-styled patriots.

Sometime during college I read a book that contained a moving account of something that happened during the Christmas season among soldiers in rival trenches. One night the Germans, as I remember it, started singing Christmas carols. After a while the British also began singing carols. Soon a few soldiers started climbing out of their trenches and singing on the strip of land that separated them. Others joined in and together they shared the Christmas spirit. When dawn came they climbed back into their trenches. I don't remember if the story relates whether or when they resumed shooting at one another. But soldiers in many wars often shoot over the heads of their enemies when they receive orders to fire. My guess is that that's what most of those soldiers did.

Harry Rudin, a history teacher at Yale, participated in that war. He was the first person who told me that quite a few disillusioned soldiers made a point of firing over the heads of opponents rather than trying to kill them. He didn't do this at first, but he soon became horrified enough by the senseless slaughter to start doing so. Though I had no courses with Rudin, we became good friends and he strengthened my determination never to support war. He also had a historical perspective that supported my early antinazism.

An even more inspiring example to me than Gandhi (who offered military support to the British during World War I) was Eugene Victor Debs, the charismatic labor leader who was sentenced to ten years in federal prison for his antiwar speeches. In the end he served only three years because the country had begun to realize that entering the war had been a terrible mistake. Even Woodrow Wilson, the president who had demanded U.S. participation in "A War to Make the World Safe for Democracy," reached a point of utter disillusionment when he said, "Is there any man, woman or child in America—let me repeat, is there any child—who does not know that this was an industrial and commercial war?"

I knew those words by heart long before the United States came close to entering what is known as the Second World War. And I also knew the words of Debs which told me that going to prison could have desirable spiritual consequences. At the time of his sentencing he said, "While there is a lower class I am in it; while there is a criminal element I am of it; while there is a soul in prison I am not free." Debs also said something that encouraged me long before World War II to develop my own conscience and to follow it rather than becoming a follower of role models; "I would not be a Moses to lead you into the Promised Land, because if I could lead you into it someone else could lead you out of it." This became especially relevant when most of the peace leaders from whom I had learned valuable lessons tried to persuade me to register for the 1940 draft.

Even Roger Baldwin, the head of the American Civil Liberties Union who had been jailed in the earlier war, appealed to me to register. Otherwise, he said, I would embarrass the peace organizations that had secured passage of a special nonmilitary assignment for draftees whose religious training forbade them to kill. Primarily the exemption was for Quakers, Mennonites, and Brethren, the so-called "peace churches." And indeed, the head of the American Friends Service Committee, whom I had long admired, tried to persuade me to register so that I could become the director of one of the camps for such draftees. Under my leadership, he argued, it could become a worldwide example of the importance of nonviolence. But I was working with youth gangs in a racially conflicted inner city, and to leave that to supervise nonviolent religionists raking leaves in an isolated geographical area wasn't the kind of nonviolence I believed in. To make it even worse, the rules were set by Gen. Lewis B. Hershey, and he forbade the residents to use their weekends or other spare time to go where other people lived and speak against the war. For a final example, Reinhold Niebuhr, who had inspired me at Yale with his brilliant, deeply religious, anti-imperialist pacifist sermons, went through a subsequent spiritual crisis. He became obsessed with the sinfulness of human beings, including himself, and condemned sinful "addiction" to nonviolent soul force as "arrogant utopianism." The day that I and seven other students at Union were carted off to prison, he preached a sermon in the chapel saying that his greatest failure as a Christian had been his inability to educate us as to the true nature of Christianity.

Shortly after Hitler came to power, I became an anti-Nazi. One of my favorite poets at the time was Archibald MacLeish, who expressed his condemnation of fascism in 1933, both verbally and in his "frescoes for Mr. Rockefeller's City." But there were other influences as well: Jewish friends; E. Fay Campbell, an adult adviser at the University Christian Association; and other radicals I have mentioned. And opposition to nazism flowed naturally from my early opposition to lynching and other racial oppressions. This had developed as a result of the "mistake" I made in junior high school of falling in love with a poor Irish girl and having a poor Italian boy for my best friend. That was in the twenties, when there were no Negroes in town; but in my neighborhood the Irish and Italians were treated as if they were inherently inferior members of worthless races.

When I graduated from Yale in 1936, I had won a graduate fellowship to study at Oxford University for two or three years. Before I entered Oxford, I made two trips to Nazi Germany, with a visit to Spain and Italy in between. In Spain I was so impressed with the grass-roots soldiers who had been attending the People's University in Madrid, where I stayed for a time, that I seriously considered joining them in fighting Franco. This is how I put it in my book *From Yale to Jail:* "If my friends were going to die I was ready to die with them, and who knows, maybe we'll win. But by then I knew that the Communists were shooting the Trotskyists, both were shooting the anarchists, and the anarchists had shot at the car in which I had been riding in Barcelona when it made a wrong turn into their sector. Whoever won that way it wouldn't be the people. I knew that I had to find a better way of fighting, a nonviolent way."

Earlier that summer I had read the book *The Conquest of Violence*, which gave historic examples of how even idealists who pick up the gun for a just cause tend to become corrupted, much as some of the Communists, Trotskyists, and anarchists had. The book was written by a Dutch anarchist named Bart de Ligt, who advocated the kind of nonviolent anarchism I soon became attracted to.

Between Spain and Germany I spent a week or more tracing one of the routes of Francis of Assisi through southern Italy, stopping to spend solitary time in each of the little chapels identified with him. Like me, Francis was the son of a rich man but became committed to nonviolence, justice, and sharing. Of course, he went much further than I have in sharing worldly goods with the poor. But after Spain, and from what I had already learned about the challenges of being an anti-Nazi in Germany, I wanted to absorb as much as I could of Francis's spirit before going back for a second visit.

Before my first trip to Germany, I knew that the U.S. government and banks were supporting and arming Adolf Hitler, much as in later years they armed and supported Saddam Hussein before waging war against Iraq. As Thomas Mann wrote in his diary in 1934, "Russian socialism has a powerful opponent in the West, Hitler, and this is more important to Britain's ruling class than the moral . . . climate of the continent . . . the governor of the Bank of England was sent to the United States to obtain credits for war materials for Germany, armament credits."

I also knew that a number of major U.S. corporations had set up plants in Nazi Germany for reasons similar to those that more recently have led corporations to set up plants in dictatorships supported by the United States in Central and South America. General Motors, ITT, and Ford come most readily to mind as having plants protected by Hitler, but there were others. In all my visits the pro-Nazis used these activities by the United States as an example of why I should support the Nazis, while the anti-Nazis cited them as an example of what they were up against in their efforts to get rid of Hitler. Some middle-of-the-roaders agreed with some of my complaints about the Nazis, but said that if Hitler was as dangerous as I claimed, the United States would not support him as strongly as it did. Others argued that Hitler's main purpose was to get rid of the Versailles Treaty, which extorted German reparations long after the end of World War I, imposed repressive restrictions on the German economy and armed forces, and robbed Germany of some of its traditional territories.

When I first entered Germany, I went to bookstores and asked for the works of Heinrich Heine, one of my favorite poets, whose works were banned because he was Jewish. This led to some fascinating discussions. One was with a Jewish manager who, after getting the book from the store's cellar, suggested that I stay in a bed-and-breakfast near his home in the ghetto. After that I often stayed in similar places in other cities. Especially in the ghettoes, but elsewhere as well, I was asked why the United States had a limited quota on German immigrants and was turning away Jewish refugees and other anti-Nazis, except for well-known individuals like Thomas Mann and Albert Einstein. Many times I was urged to go back to the United States to work against this and other evil practices that supported the Nazis. Later I canceled the last two years at Oxford in order to do some of these things while also working against lynching. Lynching was on the increase during that period, and the pro-Nazis frequently cited it as the American equivalent of their country's occasional mistreatment of Jews.

When I finally got to Oxford, I learned that Jobst von der Gröben, a German Rhodes scholar, was a member of my residential college, New College. Since the Nazis had not vetoed his selection, I assumed that he was pro-Nazi. But when we met, I found that Jobst was strongly anti-Nazi. Apparently he came from a leading family and had a brilliant record. So, for public relations reasons, the Nazis decided not to oppose his selection. We became good friends, discussing, among other things, what we could do to strengthen the anti-Nazi movement inside Germany, which was far stronger than most Americans realized, then or to this day. Also, what we could do to get the United States to work with the anti-Nazi movement rather than the Nazis. When I went back to Germany in the spring and summer of 1937, Jobst felt that because of his publicized anti-Nazi activities in England it was not safe for him to return to Germany. He did give me the names and addresses of a number of anti-Nazis, and I was able to carry a few messages from those in one city to those in another. He also told me that a number of anti-Nazis worked in the German Foreign Ministry, and he gave me the names of two or three who were apt to be sent to the United States from time to time, in case I could help them in any way. The only one I ever saw in the United States said that the U.S. officials he talked with liked the similarities between German fascism and the U.S. system, so they didn't want to hear any of his criticisms of the Nazis.

It was clear to me during this period that England, France, and the United States were working with Hitler not only for the profits to be gained by U.S. banks and corporations, but also with the major aim of influencing the Nazis to expand militarily to the east, destroying, or at least crippling, the Communist enemy. On the other hand, the Soviet Union was wooing the Nazis in the hope that they would expand westward and engage in a war with its capitalist enemies. When the Nazi-Soviet Pact was signed in August 1939, the United States knew that it had lost this diplomatic war and for the first time Roosevelt and other top capitalists began to prepare for war against their German ally. . . .

The thirties was a time when the nonviolent Gandhian movement against the British occupation and rule in India was heavily publicized in the U.S. media. In part this was because the revolt was against the British rather than against U.S. imperialism in Cuba, Puerto Rico, Central America, and the Philippines. Also, the rulers of the United States were already aiming to replace British colonialism in much of the world by "more enlightened, more democratic" American imperialism, which was the underlying reason they entered both world wars. In any event, I got more extensive details of the spirit, methods, defeats, and triumphs of the Gandhian campaigns than today's media ever prints about nonviolent campaigns for justice within the United States or its territories. In addition, there were radical visitors from the United States to India who supplied additional information that I savored. Primary among them were Richard Gregg and a number of nonviolent activists who, as teaching missionaries, became a part of the Gandhian movement. These included Ralph Templin and Jay Holmes Smith, who were expelled from India when they refused to sign the oath of allegiance that the British rulers required of all foreigners in 1939. When they returned to this country, I learned from them of a number of books by Indian nonviolent activists that had a profound influence on me. I particularly remember *War Without Violence* by Krishnalal Shridharani. So, whereas U.S. Communist party members were thrilled to "know" (despite evidence to the contrary) that the Soviet Union was a shining example of Leninist successes, I was thrilled to know that a creative and powerful nonviolent movement for justice and equality existed in India, even if it had not yet achieved most of its objectives. And soon the radical intentional pacifist community that I was a part of in the inner city of Newark was sharing experiences with the Nonviolent Ashram that Smith had helped start in Harlem and with the communitarians in Yellow Springs, Ohio, with whom Templin was working....

... During every April since 1934, there was a day whose growing list of sponsors called for a National Student Strike Against War. Originally it was in response to the Oxford Pledge, in which a large number of students at Oxford pledged that they would never take part in an international war. Soon the pledge and the day of observance grew in this country and became very powerful. I can't remember whether I began to observe this strike in my sophomore year at Yale or slightly later. But for many years before the draft law was passed, many of my friends and I stayed away from classes on that day, holding a variety of public vigils, rallies, and demonstrations. And of course we did this in prison in April 1940, with the ultimately exciting results noted by George Houser.

We eight Union Seminary students spent the first week of our imprisonment in New York City's West Street Jail. There we mingled with Leo Lepke, the head of the Mafia, and several of his adjutants. To our surprise, they were friendly to us while saying to me such things as "I am in jail for killing people but you are here for refusing to kill anyone. It doesn't make sense." Or, "I just gave my lawyer a few thousand dollars to give to the judge to lessen my sentence, but all you guys had to do was to sign a paper that wouldn't have required you to do anything, and yet you refused. WOW!" Later, after one of my arrests, I stepped between another Mafioso and a guard who was roughing him up. He thanked me and said something like this: "Like us, you know that the system is based on stealing as much as you can from anyone you can, but unlike us you are trying to work out a better way of living." That was before I temporarily shared a cell with a bank robber, who told me that with the right pieces of paper (stocks, bonds, property deeds) he wouldn't have had to use guns, knives, and jimmies. Instead of becoming a bank robber, he could have been a banker who robbed people legally.

After West Street, we were transferred to the Federal Correctional Institution at Danbury, Connecticut. None of the top officials there showed any interest in making it a genuine correctional institution. I walked into the first Saturday night movie with a black man with whom I had been talking. The guard pointed to the white section for me and the black section for him, but I sat next to my friend in the black section. It was not a planned protest, just the instinctive, natural thing to do. Soon I was carried out and placed in a solitary cell in the maximum security "troublemakers" cell block. Later, war objectors organized a number of protests against racial segregation, both at Danbury and in other prisons, including Lewisburg Penitentiary, where I did two years. When we took such actions, or did other things that I thought were in accord with the best teachings of Jesus and the Jewish prophets, we never received any support or understanding from the Christian chaplains at either Danbury or Lewisburg. But I developed a fruitful relationship with the rabbi at Danbury, who stimulated me spiritually and encouraged me to be true to what I saw as the prophetic heritage.

One aspect of my working with John L. Lewis was that Eleanor Roosevelt proposed that I be included in the list of organizers of the biggest antiwar demonstration where Lewis would speak. After the event she invited me into the White House and we had a friendly talk in which she expressed her support for my nonviolent efforts for justice and equality and for changing from a greedy, selfishly competitive society to a more communal one. After I had been in Danbury a short while, I got a letter from my brother, who was a student at Swarthmore College. He had been part of a committee that had lunch with Mrs. Roosevelt when she came to the college to speak. When she heard his name she asked if I were his brother and pumped him for prison news about me. She also said, "When you write Dave, tell him that I admire him. Tell him that I think he is right in the stand he had taken." Knowing the attacks she was under for attitudes and practices that differed from those of her opportunistic husband, I decided to view this as a personal message that I would not publicize because of the difficulties it might cause her. I did this because of my belief that true nonviolence requires special sensitivities not only toward one's opponents but also toward persons with whom one shares many convictions but who have to decide for themselves when they will go public about some of them. I don't know if my decision was a correct one, but looking back now I wonder if she might have sent the message both personally and with the hope that I would release it and put her antiwar sentiments in the context that she associated with me, instead of the selfish isolationism of those who wanted to let the Europeans fight while the United States profited. Perhaps I lacked the faith in Mrs. Roosevelt that I should have had.

The other reason I mention the message is that the censors had decreed that I should not see the letter in which my younger brother wrote the words that Mrs. Roosevelt had asked him to send me. When his letter arrived, I was in solitary confinement, but a lieutenant with whom I had become friends showed it to me, saying that I should read it but never tell anyone that he had shown it to me. If I did, he would be in dire trouble, perhaps discharged or worse. His willingness to show me the letter came out of a friendship that we had gradually developed as he and I each tried to live up to our best selves. For the lieutenant that meant not blindly accepting the prison system's condemnation of criminals as evil subhumans who could never be trusted. For me it meant trying to treat each prison guard as an individual with a potential humanity that lay beneath the surface but was usually frustrated by the routine cruelties he was supposed to inflict on prisoners. I understood why so many prisoners called the guards "hacks" and why they would not consider being friends with any of them, except as a way to obtain dope or other forbidden items. But, in addition to my understanding of the need to treat every person, in or out of prison, as a potential friend, I also realized that most of the guards were working-class people who had taken the job as the only way they could earn a living and support their families, especially during the depression. So sometimes I tried to get into a discussion about that aspect of their employment, hoping that later I would be able to suggest that even as they were sometimes forced to do terrible things that the prison system required, similarly many of the prisoners were there because they had done terrible things that society required in order for them to feed their families or provide them with other forms of security. This led to several good friendships with guards who did their best to be as decent as possible with their "fellow prisoners."

My belief in the submerged humanity of prisoners who had committed the most heinous crimes was strengthened in a Hudson County, New Jersey, jail shortly before I landed at Lewisburg's maximum security prison. I was in the jail because I had refused to pay bail during the period between my arraignment and trial. I do this as often as I can because I don't believe that the inability to raise money for bail should force people to spend weeks, months, sometimes a year or more in jail before they have even been tried. This time my wife, Elizabeth, called the judge after a week or two and explained why I had refused bail. He responded by releasing me on my own recognizance. And when he sentenced me to two years, which was less time than the court sentenced most war objectors at that time, he suggested that I spend the evening at home with my wife and voluntarily return to the federal building the next morning to meet a sheriff who would drive me to Lewisburg.

But at my arrival at the New Jersey jail, the officials had concluded that I must be "yellow," since I was refusing to defend my country militarily. Saying this to my face and to the prisoners in my assigned cell, they asked the prisoners to "take care of this unpatriotic guy." The men they said this to were in a small, overcrowded cell where the most violent prisoners were kept. Later, when I was leaving on my own recognizance, a slightly nicer guard said that he hadn't approved of where I had been put but hoped that I had learned how evil prisoners and Nazis can be and had given up my ideas that nonviolence is a practical way of combating them. Despite all this, I was clearly saved from what might have happened to me—not by my own efforts, but because this was the prison where, on my arrival, I had intervened when a Mafioso was being roughed up by a guard. Word of what had happened came rather quickly to the "worthless, evil" prisoners in the cell where I had been assigned and, step by step, several of them became my friends.

Not long after I arrived at Lewisburg, five of us conducted a long hunger strike for abolishing "the Hole" and eliminating the censorship of mail, books, and magazines. Winning the issue on censorship and feeling that the issue of the Hole had reached a fairly wide audience on the outside through prison visitors and progressive publicity, we stopped the strike on the sixty-fifth day (after a month of force feeding). The next day I was put in the "fuck-up dorm," which had a high percentage of southern military prisoners who had committed violent crimes. One of the two guards who took me there addressed the prisoners as follows: "This guy is one of those phonies who says he's too good to be in regular prison with you." This was a total lie. Unlike a few war objectors, I had always opposed special classification and treatment as a political prisoner. "He's a nigger-lover who says that you guys should eat and sleep with the niggers and use the same toilets and showers as niggers do." True. "And he's a Nazi who spits on the flag and refuses to fight for our country." And, after a pause, as if to let his words sink in, "We're leaving now so that you guys can take care of him." Just before they closed the door, the other guard spoke for the first time: "When we come back, we hope you give him to us with his head in his hands."

Here I will have to paraphrase what I said because I don't remember it word for word the way I remember what the guards had said; but this was the general line of attack, using street language and drawing on things I had learned from my earlier prison experiences: "You guys know enough not to believe those hacks. That's a lot of bullshit they're trying to shove down your throats and you know it. It's the hacks who act like Nazis, not me. You know how they treat you. I've been up there in solitary fightin' for you guys. Five of us have been up there fightin' to get rid of the goddam Hole. We're fightin' for the cons and the hacks don't like it. I know a lot of you guys have been in the Hole, so I don't have to tell you what it's like. I don't have to tell you why we've been on hunger strike demanding that they stop acting like Nazis and do away with the Hole once and for all. You want to know why they're tellin' all those lies about me? To get you and me fightin' amongst ourselves instead of stickin' together against them. Anyone who has been doin' time like you guys have won't fall for that shit. You know the score. And so do I."

I survived, though there were times, especially that night after the lights went out, when I didn't expect to. But it was more than a month before I made a request to be transferred to a cellblock, where I desperately needed the relative quiet of a cell after that noisy "fuck-up dorm." I waited that long because the one thing you can't do as a serious nonviolent activist, especially in prison, is to run away from threats or danger. If you do, the wrong reputation will follow you wherever you go or are moved.

This was only one of several times in Lewisburg when prisoners were asked to "take care of Dellinger," sometimes with the offer of parole if they did. But this was the most difficult occasion for me to handle because of my exhaustion from the long hunger strike. A few years later I wasn't surprised at something Dorothy Day, the cofounder of the Catholic Worker movement, said when she visited me and Elizabeth at our intentional pacifist community. It was the day after William Remington, a former commerce department official who was a victim of the McCarthy era, had been killed at Lewisburg. "You don't believe the official version, do you?" she asked. "That he was killed by a prisoner who was stealing his cigarettes when Remington came back to his cell and caught him?" Based on our similar prison experiences, we agreed that the officials had asked some prisoners to kill him, probably saying something like, "He's a dirty Communist, so why don't you get rid of him. If you do, we'll reward you with parole, or time off your long sentence."

Is it any wonder that in my resume I included under "Education" the following: "Three years' imprisonment at Danbury, Connecticut, Federal Correctional Institution (1940–41) and Lewisburg, Pennsylvania, Federal Penitentiary (1942–45). . . . "

Minoru Yasui (1916–1986)

In the panic following Pearl Harbor, anti-Japanese sentiment in the United States rose to a fever pitch. Washington's first reaction, in Public Proclamation Number 3, was to establish a curfew for all people of Japanese ethnic origin living on the West Coast. Subsequently, in February 1942, President Roosevelt signed Executive Order 9066, which authorized Secretary of War Henry Stimson to delegate to a responsible military authority the discretionary right to exclude or remove anybody from certain designated "military areas." Lieutenant General John L. DeWitt, commanding general of the Western Defense Command and of the Fourth Army, promptly did so. All people of one-sixteenth Japanese descent or more were evacuated and removed to internment camps. Thus, not only were the Issei (those who were born in Japan) subject to incarceration in the camps but so too were the Nisei (those who were born in the United States and were American citizens). In 1943 and 1944, Japanese Americans protested the order by taking cases to the Supreme Court. The constitutionality of the order was upheld in three cases: Hirabayashi v. United States (1943), Yasui v. United States (1943), and Korematsu v. United States (1944). Minoru Yasui, who was born in the United States in 1916 and earned his law degree from the University of Oregon in 1939, broke the curfew law and refused to report for evacuation. He served nine months in solitary confinement and, in 1943, took his case to the Supreme Court. The Supreme Court upheld the evacuation order, and Yasui lost his case. Although wartime hysteria cost so many Japanese Americans their homes, occupations, and self-esteem, not one case of espionage or sabotage was brought against any of them.

Fred Korematsu, Minoru Yasui, and Gordon Hirabayashi.   In three separate court cases in 1943 and 1944, the Supreme Court ruled against these men when they challenged the constitutionality of Executive Order 9066 evacuating 120,000 Japanese Americans from the west coast and relocating them to internment camps during World War II. This photograph was taken in 1983 when Korematsu, Yasui, and Hirabayashi filed a petition demanding the reopening of their cases.

Reflections on Executive Order 9066

The evacuation came out of Executive Order 9066. The thing that struck me immediately was that the military was ordering the civilian to do something. In my opinion, that's the way dictatorships are formed. And if I, as an American citizen stood still for this, I would be derogating the rights of all citizens. By God, I had to stand up and say, "That's wrong." I refused to report for evacuation. Sure enough, within the week, I got a telephone call from the military police saying, "We're coming to get you." I was thrown into the North Portland Livestock Pavilion where Japanese Americans had been put. In September, they started moving us into the desert camps. You were surrounded with barbed-wire fences. There were armed guards, search lights, and machine-gun nests. We wondered how long we were going to be there. What was going to happen? No one knew. By then, we had heard rumors of forced labor camps in Germany. Were they, indeed, as Westbrook Pegler and others were suggesting, going to castrate the men and ship them back to Japan? These things were in the paper constantly: Make them suffer. Make them hurt. *And you keep thinking, "What did I do?"*

SOURCE: Retrieved on 7/26/2003 from www.hrcr.org/ccr/yasui.html.
SOURCE: John Tateishi, ed. *And Justice for All* (New York: Random House, 1984). Retrieved on 7/26/2003 from www.geocities.com/Athens/8420/memories.html.

RESISTANCE

In mid-December, 1941, I received official orders to report for active duty with the United States Army at Camp Vancouver, Washington. I held a reserve commission as a second lieutenant in the U.S. Army. The instructions ordered me to report for duty on January 19, 1942. So I went down to the Union Pacific Railroad station to purchase a ticket back to Portland, Oregon. But the ticket agent wanted to know if I were a "Jap." When I foolishly answered truthfully that I was of Japanese ancestry, he responded that he could not sell transportation to a "Jap." Despite my showing him travel orders from the U.S. Army, I could not persuade him to issue me a railroad ticket. I finally had to make an appointment to see one of the attorneys in the general counsel's office for the Union Pacific Railroad in Chicago to obtain authorization for me to buy a ticket to report for active duty with the U.S. Army. I had to point to the Fourteenth Amendment to the Constitution of the United States to persuade that lawyer that I was a citizen of the United States, on the basis of my birth certificate alone.

. . . at 8:00 P.M., March 28, 1942, after having asked Rae Shimojima, my assistant, to notify the FBI and the local Portland police, I started to walk the streets of Portland in deliberate violation of Military Proclamation No. 3. The principle involved was whether the military could single out a specific group of U.S. citizens on the basis of ancestry and require them to do something not required of other U.S. citizens. As a lawyer, I knew that unless legal protest is made at the time of injury, the doctrine of laches or indeed the statute of limitations would forever bar a remedy. . . .

So on March 28, 1942, I began to walk the streets of Portland, up and down Third Avenue until about 11:00 P.M., and I was getting tired of walking. I stopped a Portland police officer, and I showed him a copy of Military Proclamation No. 3, prohibiting persons of Japanese ancestry from being away from their homes after 8:00 P.M.; and I pulled out my birth certificate to show him that I was a person of Japanese ancestry. When I asked him to arrest me, he replied, "Run along home, sonny boy, or you'll get in trouble." So I had to go on down to the Second Avenue police station and argue myself into jail. I pulled this thing on a Saturday and didn't get bailed out until the following Monday.

. . . At the end of April 1942, military orders were posted for all residents of Japanese ancestry, aliens and nonaliens (a euphemism for citizens), calling for them to report for evacuation and processing at the North Portland Livestock Pavilion.

. . . So before the deadline to report to the North Portland Livestock Pavilion, I packed my files and my few belongings and left for Hood River. I had given the military my address and invited them to arrest me. . . . After I was home for a few days, I received a call from the military offices in Portland saying that the MPs would be coming to get me on May 12, 1942, and that they would escort me to the North Portland Livestock Pavilion. I indicated that I would cooperate but would go under coercion only. Sure enough, on May 12, 1942, a sedan with a second lieutenant, a driver, and a jeep with four MPs came to our home in Hood

River at the appointed time. The lieutenant said, "Let's go," and I complied in my 1935 Chevy.

. . . At the North Portland Assembly Center I . . . remember Benny Higashi's and Don Sugai's families. Both men were married to local Chinese American women, and both had two children. The wives, LaLun Higashi and Pil Sugai, endured camp with us. Even though they themselves would have been exempt, their children would not, because they were half Japanese. The children, in each case, were two and four years old.

. . . Judge [James Alger] Fee sentenced me to one year in jail and a five-thousand dollar fine. . . . I wanted my attorneys to apply for an appeal bond so I could be free pending appeal. (They subsequently did, and it was refused.)

. . . At first the guards would not let me out long enough to take a bath or to get a haircut or shave. At the end of several months I was stinking dirty, although I tried to wash myself in the washbasin with rags. My hair was growing long and shaggy, unkempt and tangled. My facial hair was growing in all directions, untrimmed. And my nails were growing so long that they began to curl over on themselves, both on my hands and feet. I found I could chew off my fingernails, but the nails on my toes gave me trouble. It was not until after Christmas that I was given permission to take a bath and get a haircut and shave, and that seemed like such a luxury then. Thereafter, they permitted me monthly baths and monthly hair trims.

. . . I learned that during my absence the military draft had been reopened for Nisei, and further volunteers were being sought for both the 442nd Infantry Combat Team and for the Camp Savage military intelligence school in Minnesota. Because of my infantry training, I immediately volunteered for the infantry, and many months later was advised that I had been rejected.

. . . I had not seen my father since February 1942, nor my mother and younger brother since May 1942, or my younger sister since Christmas of 1939. . . . I applied for a temporary leave from Minidoka for thirty days to visit them.

My official records at the Minidoka WRA [War Relocation Authority] administration evidently indicated I was not a very desirable individual. . . . A charade of a hearing was held for me, and the result was mixed, with the civilian hearing officer recommending that temporary leave be granted and the two military officials recommending that I be kept in custody. I offered to test this matter by a habeas corpus proceeding, and the project director relented by issuing me a thirty-day temporary leave in October 1943.

. . . I remember going with Joe Grant to the FCI [Federal Correctional Institution] and meeting a young Nisei who had just turned eighteen years of age, who had refused to register and refused to conform to draft-board orders. He had been indicted, arrested, and was being held, pending trial.

We said to him, "Son, you're ruining your life. You're still a young man, and you'll have a criminal record that will hold you back for the rest of your life. Please reconsider and cooperate with your draft board."

He replied, "Why should I when the government has taken away our rights and locked us up like a bunch of criminals anyway?"

We responded, "But, you've got to fulfill your obligations to the government. When you fulfill your responsibilities, you'll be in a much stronger position to demand your rights."

To which he said, "Look, the government took my father away, and interned him someplace. My mother is alone at the Granada camp with my younger sister who is only fourteen. If the government would take care of them here in America, I'd feel like going out to fight for my country, but this country is treating us worse than shit!"

STATEMENT UPON SENTENCING, 1942

Your Honor—if the Court please, I should like to say a few words. There is no intent to plead for leniency for myself or to request a mitigation of the punishment that is about to be inflicted upon me.

Despite the circumstances, I am compelled to pay tribute and give my unreserved respect to this honorable court for its clear-cut and courageous reaffirmation of the inviolability of the fundamental civil rights and liberties of an American citizen.

As an American citizen, it was for a clarification and the preservation of those rights that I undertook this case, confident that the American judiciary would zealously defend those rights, war or no war, in order to preserve the fundamental democratic doctrines of our nation and to perpetuate the eternal truths of America.

My confidence has been justified and I feel the greatest satisfaction and patriotic uplift in the decision of this honorable court, for it is full of significance for every American, be he humble or mighty.

I say that I am glad, regardless of the personal consequences to me, because I believe in the future and in the ultimate destiny of America. Ever since I was a child, I have been inculcated in the basic concepts and the traditions of those great patriots who founded our nation.

I have lived, believed, worked and aspired as an American. With due respect to this honorable court, in all good conscience, I can say that I have never, and will never, voluntarily relinquish my American citizenship.

The decision of this honorable court to the contrary notwithstanding, I am confident that I can establish in law and in fact that I am an American citizen, who is not only proud of that fact, but who is willing to defend that right.

When I attained majority, I swore allegiance to the United States of America, renouncing any and all other allegiances that I may have unknowingly owed. That solemn obligation to my native land has motivated me during the past 12 months upon three separate and distinct occasions to volunteer for

SOURCE: Gordon B. Dodds, ed., *Varieties of Hope—An Anthology of Oregon Prose* (Corvallis: Oregon State University Press, 1993), 117–119. Retrieved on 7/26/2003 from www.minoruyasui. com/history_4.htm.

active service in the United States army, wheresoever it may be fighting to preserve the American way of life.

For I would a thousand times prefer to die on a battlefront as an American soldier in defense of freedom and democracy, for the principles which I believe, rather than to live in relative comfort as an interned alien Jap.

The treacherous attack on Pearl Harbor, the bombing of Manila, the aggressor policies of the warlords of Japan are just as reprehensible to me as to any American citizen.

If America were invaded today, I and 70,000 other loyal American citizens of Japanese ancestry would be willing, eager, to lay down our lives in the streets, down in the gutters, to defend our homes, our country, and our liberties!

Be that as it may; I reiterate, regardless of the personal consequences, even though it entail the sacrifice of my American citizenship which I regard as sacred and more dear than life itself I pay homage and salute this honorable court and my country, the United States of America, for the gallant stand that has been taken for the preservation of the fundamental principles of democracy and freedom!

Letters from Jail to His Sister Yuka Yasui, 1942–1943

Min (to Yuka, in Denver)
Multnomah County Jail

April 5, 1942

. . . Anyway, I'm sure that the case is now in good hands. I've been re-reading "The Federalist" written by Alexander Hamilton, John Jay and James Madison in 1787–1788, and I find much which is encouraging, so far as the theories of government are concerned. And too, I'm particularly thankful for Jefferson's democratic principles and safeguards that were included in the first 10 amendments. The more I think about the fundamental issues involved, the more sure I feel that the principles advanced in my case are *RIGHT,* and the more confident I am that the Supreme Court will re-affirm my beliefs.

It seems funny that a Nihonjin should be the instrument for bringing about a supreme judicial declaration of Americanism. I guess that's only possible in America. . . .

Min (to Yuka, in Denver)
Multnomah County Jail

November 30, 1942

. . . I am glad to read Mom's concept of America. I realize all that she and Dad has [*sic*] done for our country, and particularly for Hood River. It is my

SOURCE: Letters in Yuka Yasui Fujikura's private collection. Used with permission.

proud boast that Dad is a better American than I am, and I consider myself a pretty fine American too! I know too that both Dad and Mom raised us to be good American citizens, and I felt that as an American, I should personally do something to prevent the deterioration of the fundamental principles which made America great. I felt that I was compelled to do so if I were to be a worthy son of a worthy father.

The insidious danger of creating a precedent of confining American citizens behind barbed wire fences and machine guns when they have committed no crime seemed reprehensible to me. Perhaps the analogy is far fetched, but surely as the attack on Pearl Harbor endangered our democracy, evacuation of American citizens on the basis of race is just as dangerous a threat to democracy!

I have always contended, and shall continue to maintain, that if it be repugnant to the Constitution of the United States of America, then it is tyrannical, dictatorial and unreasonable to impose restrictive and discriminatory measures upon the basis of race, and moreover, it is just as shameful and disgraceful for proud and loyal American citizens to submit to such dictatorial measures without a legal reservation [?] of their rights!

I feel and I know that Caucasian Americans are no better nor worse than I, for we are all human beings. It is only the principles of liberty, democracy and justice, and the adherence to these principles that made America great, and as a loyal American who can suffer his native land to do no wrong, I must hold true to those principles.

Obviously, we are regarded with suspicion and distrust, but can we call ourselves worthy Americans if we tolerate the destruction of those eternal truths of America without an effort to preserve them?

But, all of this you know and fully appreciate. I only wish that 130,000,000 [other] Americans would too!. . .

Min (to Yuka, in Denver)
Multnomah County Jail

March 5, 1943

. . . Nope, I've been here in the Multnomah County "College for Criminals" as per usual. Suma Tsuboi was mistaken about my going to San Francisco. All of my hopes and prayers were there though! [This was in reference to a hoped-for appeal to the U.S. Ninth Circuit Court of Appeals.] Gee, I wish I could have gone to argue my case! But no such luck, I'm still sitting here like a canary in a bird cage only I can't sing.

Because my attorney went back East on another case, I'm probably going to be here for some little time yet. Aw, if I left now, the cockroaches might miss me! But, I'm still hoping for some type of conditional release, either on bail, or by parole to the relocation center. After all, I'm not going to run away anywhere! Besides, instead of sitting here like bump on a log (and twice as useless) I could be doing something worthwhile elsewhere. As for the Circuit Court decision,

I'm afraid that it will be a long time before they will come to any conclusion. Probably, it will be some 3 or 4 months. But, cheer up, if I lose there, it will be about a year before the U.S. Supreme Court will get around to it. Meanwhile, I'd hate to be sitting in jail. I'd rather be packing a rifle for Uncle Sam, somewhere out in the deserts of the Sahara, just to prove to Judge Fee that, by golly, I'm a man! And not only that, an American that has a stake in America too! This case, I hope, will secure legal recognition of that fact. Yep, and it's for you too, Punkus, as well as for every American, white, yellow, or black, that these principles *must* be recognized. I think that they will be.

But, my ideas aren't very interesting. I generate them looking at the same 4 walls every day. . . . Anyway, Yuka, when you're going to school, learn well the lessons of democracy; learn them well so that you will love them too, and be prepared to defend them. After going through Pinedale, and Tule Lake, you might be inclined to think that all the idealistic principles of democracy are hooey, but that isn't so! Some of those principles in practice have been distorted by men who have not thought deeply enough, who have failed to appreciate their full significance; but those principles, I believe, are true. At least, that is what I'm trying to establish by my case.

Henry Miller (1891–1980)

Because of his sexually explicit autobiographical novels Tropic of Cancer, Tropic of Capricorn, Sexus, *and* Quiet Days in Clichy, *Henry Miller's name has become almost synonymous with the sexual revolution. However, these few novels have created an aura of notoriety that obfuscates the true nature of Miller's contribution to American literature. While he was labeled as a writer of obscenity, Miller was an inward-looking man whose numerous essays explored such matters as art, spirituality, creativity, psychology, Buddhism, politics, and, above all, his never-ending and agonizing struggle to be true to himself and to find his own way to express that truth. Life, to Miller, in spite of its hardships, was to be lived fully and joyously each moment of the day. He spent his first 42 years trying to "find his voice," as he put it, and struggling to become a writer. In 1930 he went to Paris—the gathering place for between-the-wars American literati— because he felt that the atmosphere in America stifled creativity. After several failed attempts, he finally gave up the effort to be "literary" and wrote an autobiographical novel,* Tropic of Cancer, *which was published in Paris in 1934. In 1939, after ten years in Paris, he traveled to Corfu to visit his friend, the English writer Lawrence Durrell. While Miller was in Greece, Hitler's army invaded Poland, and the Second World War began. In December, the American embassy in Athens ordered all Americans to return to the United States because of the war. Reluctantly, Miller set sail for New York. With Pearl Harbor, the United States was brought into the war, but despite the fact that American forces were fighting against the Axis powers in the Pacific and in Europe, Miller took the unpopular stance of opposing what most Americans believed was a "just" war. "Murder the Murderer" is a lengthy letter that Miller wrote to an Austrian friend, Alfred Perles, whom he had met in Paris. It is a vitriolic, sarcastic, Milleresque diatribe on the follies of those who believe that war is a viable means to bring about peace.*

Miller writes: "Nations make war upon one another on the assumption that the views of the people and those who govern them are one. The moment war is declared it is impossible to dissent. . . . Nor is there ever the remotest possibility of establishing a situation whereby those in favor of war go to war and those not in favor remain passive. The unanimity of a nation, in times of war, is brought about by coercion pure and simple." Notice the similarity of Miller's view with that of Randolph Bourne's 1918 essay "War Is the Health of the State."

Murder the Murderer, 1944

June 25, 1944.

A period of darkness has set in. The world seems determined to resolve its problems by force. No single individual can stem the tide of hate. We are in the grip of cosmic forces and each one does what he can, or must.

To each man the conflict assumes a different face. Millions of men and women will sacrifice their lives; millions more will be maimed and mutilated. The innocent will suffer with the guilty, the wise with the foolish. It is beyond control now; we are in the hands of Fate.

Useless to say now that it need not have happened. It is not for us to question what happens; it is for us to accept. But there are a thousand ways of accepting the inevitable. In the way we accept lies our ability to transform a situation. No disaster is irremediable. The whole meaning of life is contained in the word suffering. That all the world can be suffering at one time is a fact of tremendous significance. (Not quite the whole world!—the "civilized" peoples mostly.) It never has happened before. It is an opportunity which we can reject or use to advantage.

Since I am having my say, I want to reveal what I sincerely believe this opportunity may be. We, the American people, having resisted war to the very last, have now thrown ourselves into the universal conflict. Whether we admit it to ourselves or not, whether or not we have lived up to that faith which the other peoples of the world have in us, *we are the hope of the world*. That is the rock on which America was founded. Let it be our rock now!

SOURCE: Henry Miller, "Murder the Murderer," in *Remember to Remember* (New York: New Directions, 1947), 164–169, 191–196, 198–199, 204–216.

Are we at war to extend our empire, to increase our possessions, to gain ascendancy over the other nations of this earth? I believe the great body of American people would answer NO! Like other peoples, we have been misguided. Above all, we had grown callous and indifferent. That was our crime. To-day we are ready to accept our share of suffering, along with the righteous and the unrighteous. Moreover, we are determined to endure what we have never endured before. That was evident the day war was declared.

What can we as a people do beyond anything our allies may expect of us? We can be magnanimous and far-sighted, we can be patient and full of understanding; we can be hard as steel, yet wise and full of tenderness when the time is ripe. We can be all these things because we are the favored people of the earth. Our forefathers, when first they came to this country, were hailed as gods. To our disgrace they behaved as demons. They asked for gold instead of grace. To-day their sins are visited upon us. We are paying now for the crimes committed by our ancestors. They fled their self-imposed prisons because they had a vision of Paradise. Had they acted as the gods they were mistaken for by the aborigines of this continent they could have realized the Paradise which they were seeking. But they were only men and they were weak, and because they were weak the dream of Paradise was forgotten. Dreams are hard to kill; they linger on even when the memory of them is faded. The dream of golden opportunity still clings to the name America no matter what part of the world you may go to. It is regrettable that we, the American people, have fostered a false interpretation of that dream and thereby helped to further poison the world. We have given the impression that America was a place in which to grow rich. We have emphasized gold instead of opportunity. Out of greed we killed the goose that laid the golden egg. Yet, despite the tragic error, we all know that there *was* a golden goose. We are now at the point where we are obliged to interpret the fable intelligently.

What *was* the golden opportunity which was offered the American pilgrim? The opportunity to serve the world, the opportunity to bring about enlightenment and justice. Since the inception of this republic we had no enemies save the mother country, England. We were surrounded by friends. The only great struggle we had was an internal one. Then, in the last war, we were dragged into a world-wide conflict whose significance we only partially understood. The war over, we tried to take refuge again in our comfortable shell, unwilling to accept the responsibilities we had assumed as participants of that great conflict. We refused to sit at the Hague Tribunal and assist in the first crude attempt to establish some kind of international law and order. We refused for years to recognize the one government which had taken the lesson of the war to heart and was endeavoring to bring about a more intelligent and equitable order of human society. With the emergence of the dictators we sat by and watched one little nation after the other swallowed up and enslaved. When France fell we were full of bitterness. We cried "Shame!" though we hadn't lifted a finger to help her. We would have suffered England to undergo the same fate, but the English were made of different stuff. Until the treacherous attack by Japan, which we should have anticipated, considering all the lessons we had been given, we were undecided what course to pursue. Now suddenly we are united and, as in the last war, we are pretending that we are fighting to free the world. The newspapers are doing their best to make the American people believe this beautiful legend, knowing well that the psychology of the American people is based on a sense of utter unreality, that only when we visualize ourselves as saviours and crusaders can we kill with fury and efficiency. . . .

It is unthinkable that we shall lose. But what do we hope to win? Or better, what do we hope to win to? That is the question which the editorial gentry cleverly evade by grandiloquent phrases such as "ridding the world forever of the Nazi pestilence," and so on. Are we microbe hunters and bug exterminators? Are we merely going to preserve the *tomb* of Christ from the desecrating paw of the infidel? For two thousand years the world has been squabbling over the dead body of Christ. The Christians themselves will admit that God sent his son, a *living* Christ, to redeem the world. He didn't send us a corpse to fight over. In effect, however, that is what the Christian world has done: it has welcomed every excuse to fight in the name of Christ who came to bring peace on earth. There can be no end to this repetitious pattern until each and every one of us become as Christ, until belief and devotion transform our words into deeds and thus make of myth reality.

. . . We are all interested in what lies beyond the war. Nobody is any longer interested in war for the sake of war. But what comes after the war depends altogether on the spirit in which we wage war. We will accomplish exactly what we aim to accomplish, and no more. In this respect war is no different from peace. The fact that we are desperate instead of lethargic means nothing, if we are not clear as to what we wish to attain. To defeat Hitler and his gang is not a particularly brilliant goal to set oneself. Hitler and his gang could have been defeated without war had we possessed the intelligence, the will, and the purity to undertake the task. Wherever there is indecision, confusion, dalliance and an atmosphere of unreality, you have Hitler. Just as Judas was necessary in order for Christ to enact the drama which was ordained, so Hitler was necessary for this age in order that the world might enact the drama of unification and regeneration. Christ chose Judas to betray him; we have chosen Hitler. All the intermediary figures, the supernumeraries, so to speak, good, honest gentlemen though they be, are dwarfed by this Satanic figure which looms across the horizon. Churchill, Roosevelt, Stalin, none of these is big enough to cope with the monster alone. It is fortunate that they are not, for now it devolves upon the little men, the poor anonymous figures who make up the great mass of humanity, to answer the challenge. Christ chose twelve little men to do his work—not great world figures.

I come back to that idea which America has always inspired in the minds of other peoples, the idea that the lowest man may rise and "make his place" in the world. (It would have been better had we inspired the idea of "finding one's place" in the world.) I repeat that the behavior of the American people has brought about a distortion of that idea. We have shown in ways too numerous to specify that we have reduced the conception of freedom and service to mankind to a poverty-stricken notion of power and riches. Power and riches, not for *all* Americans—that would be bad enough!—but for the few. Our democracy has been the worst democracy that has ever been tried out. It has never had anything to do with freedom, has never been anything more than a name. . . .

Nobody can deny that we're the most philanthropic-minded people in the world. A few months ago there were eight or nine million people unemployed in this wonder-working land. Now it's down to about a million, an irreducible minimum, I believe it's called. We work fast, I'll say. And all because that half-witted Hirohito stabbed us in the back. Some say we had no right to be taken by surprise—criminal negligence they call it. Others seem pleased that it turned out so—it proved that we were angels, that we had no intention of going to war with Japan, that our fleet and our fortifications were created only to *frighten* the enemy away. It's six one way and a half dozen the other. I was always of the opinion that if you make cannon you've got to use them some time or other. I'm never surprised when a gun goes off unexpectedly. I expect the unexpected. What does surprise me is that people who believe in making cannon should be aggrieved to see them used so effectively. "In time of peace prepare for war," said the Father of this beloved country. He was a realist, just as Stalin is to-day. He didn't get himself elected a third time by promising to keep his people out of war. He was no half-wit. No sir, he was an aristocrat, a great land-holder with slaves and port and sherry in the cellar. The people were so grateful to him for making this country a democracy that they almost made him a king. About seventy years later there appeared in the State of Massachusetts, noted even then for its hypocrisy, repression and iniquity, a troublesome character who sensed that all was not well with the government of these United States. What's more, he had the courage to say so. He wrote a paper called "Civil Disobedience" which we look upon to-day as a monument to the democratic spirit. Here is a citation from this beautifully embalmed document:

"The progress from an absolute to a limited monarchy, from a limited monarchy to a democracy, is a progress towards a true respect for the individual. Even the Chinese philosopher was wise enough to regard the individual as the basis of the empire. Is a democracy, such as we know it, the last improvement possible in government? Is it not possible to take a step further towards recognizing and organizing the rights of man? There will never be a really free and enlightened State until the State comes to recognize the individual as a higher and independent power, from which all its own power and authority are derived, and treats him accordingly. I please myself with imagining a State at last which can afford to be just to all men, and to treat the individual with respect as a neighbor; which even would not think it inconsistent with its own repose if a few were to live aloof from it, not meddling with it, nor embraced by it, who fulfilled all the duties of neighbors and fellowmen. A State which bore this kind of fruit, and suffered it to drop off as fast as it ripened, would prepare the way for a still more perfect and glorious State, which also I have imagined, but not yet anywhere seen."

That was Henry David Thoreau, author of *Walden* and defender of John Brown, speaking. No doubt the only excuse we can make to-day for such a treasonable anarchistic utterance is to palm him off as a half-witted graduate of the then Transcendentalist School of Philosophy. About the only person I can think of who would have dared to defend him, in our time, had he openly expressed his desire to live a life apart from the most holy and sacrosanct State, is the recently defunct Justice of the Supreme Court, Louis D. Brandeis. In the case of Whitney versus the State of California, Brandeis, whose vote was overruled, wrote a brief in which there appeared these words:

"Those who won our independence by revolution were not cowards. They did not fear political change. They did not exalt order at the cost of liberty. To courageous, self-reliant men, with confidence in the power of free and fearless reasoning applied through the processes of popular government, no danger flowing from speech can be deemed clear and present, unless the incidence of evil apprehended is so imminent that it may befall before there is opportunity for full discussion. If there be time to expose through discussion the falsehood and fallacies, to avert the evil by the processes of education, the remedy to be applied is more speech, not enforced silence. Only an emergency can justify repression. Such must be the rule if authority is to be reconciled with freedom. Such, in my opinion, is the command of the Constitution. It is, therefore, always open to Americans to challenge a law abridging free speech and assembly by showing that there was no emergency justifying it."

Nevertheless, when the good shoe-maker and the poor fish-peddler found themselves at the bar of justice in the benighted State of Massachusetts some few years ago, they were unable to get a fair, honest hearing. Despite all the noble words handed down by the upstanding members of the judiciary, and they are the wordiest people on God's green earth, Sacco and Vanzetti were foully murdered. But just before he went to the chair Vanzetti gave birth to a few lines which are destined to be as immortal as any of Lincoln's or Jefferson's . . .

"If it had not been for these thing, I might have live out my life talking at street corners to scorning men. I might have died, unmarked, unknown, a failure. Now we are not a failure. This is our career and our triumph. Never in our full life could we hope to do such work for tolerance, for justice, for man's understanding of man as now we do by accident. Our words—our lives—our pains—nothing! The taking of our lives—lives of a good shoemaker and a poor fish-peddler—all. That last moment belongs to us—that agony is our triumph."

A few days ago, moved by the President's declaration of war the newspapers gave some space to the remarks made by John Haynes Holmes, Minister of the Community Church, N. Y., in tendering his resignation. He had just finished a sermon, it seems, on the 150th anniversary of the Bill of Rights. Mr. Holmes is quoted as saying that "neither as clergyman nor as citizen would he participate in the war," adding however that "neither would he oppose, obstruct or interfere with officials, soldiers or citizens in the performance of what they regard as their patriotic duty."

Then he threw this bombshell:

"I will be loyal and obedient to my government, and loyal and obedient to my God; and when these loyalties conflict, I will choose, as did the Apostles, to 'obey God rather than men.'"

I wait to see if Mr. Holmes will be condemned to prison. In the last world war there were three great figures who, because they openly announced their opposition to war, suffered dire persecution. They were Romain Rolland, Bertrand Russell and Eugene V. Debs. Unimpeachable characters, all three. I'm going to give you Debs' speech on being condemned to prison, but before I do so I want to mention the Very Reverend Dean Inge's statement about a German theologian named Harnack. "War," writes the gloomy Dean, "is a very horrible thing, an unmixed evil, a reversion to barbarism no less than cannibalism, human sacrifice and judicial torture. Most of us think that we were obliged to resist German agression, which threatens to extinguish liberty, and with liberty all that makes life worth living, over the whole continent of Europe. But no good can ever come out of war. It is a flat negation of Christianity. Even Harnack, a Prussian and the most learned theologian in Europe, said that it is futile to deny that Christ condemned war absolutely." He adds that the Quakers believe they are the only consistent Christians. And what is the history of the Quaker movement? According to recent authority on the subject, the Quaker movement was met with terrific persecution, first from mob violence and later from organized legal procedure. George Fox himself endured eight imprisonments, and more than fifteen thousand Quakers were imprisoned in England before the period of toleration, of whom three hundred and sixty-six died under their sufferings. Four Quakers were hanged on Boston Common and a great number in the American Colonies endured beatings and mutilation.

To-day the Quakers are exempt from military service, in these United States. But what a battle! A man who is not a Quaker, like Eugene V. Debs for example, gets it in the neck. Yet no Quaker could have made a more simple, honest, dignified statement of his views than did Eugene V. Debs. Here are his beautiful, moving words:

"Gentleman of the Jury, I am accused of having obstructed the war. I admit it. Gentlemen, I abhor war. I would oppose the war if I stood alone. When I think of a cold, glittering steel bayonet being plunged in the white, quivering flesh of a human being, I recoil with horror.

"Men talk about holy wars. There are none. War is the trade of unholy savages and barbarians. . . .

"Gentlemen of the Jury, I am accused of being unpatriotic. I object to that accusation. It is not true. I believe in patriotism. I have never uttered a word against the flag. I love the flag as a symbol of freedom. . . .

"I believe, however, in a wider patriotism. Thomas Paine said, 'My country is the world. To do good is my religion.' That is the sort of patriotism I believe in. I am an Internationalist. I believe that nations have been pitted against nations long enough in hatred, in strife, in warfare. I believe there ought to be a bond of unity between all of these nations. I believe that the human race consists of one great family. I love the people of this country, but I don't hate a human being because he happens to be born in some other country. Why should I? Like myself, he is the image of his Creator. I would infinitely rather serve him and love him than to hate him and kill him. . . .

"Yes, I am opposed to killing him. I am opposed to war. I am perfectly willing on that account to be branded as a traitor. And if it is a crime under the American law to be opposed to human bloodshed, I am perfectly willing to be branded as a criminal and to end my days in a prison cell. . . .

"And now, Gentlemen of the Jury, I am prepared for the sentence. I will accept your verdict. What you will do to me does not matter much. Years ago I recognized my kinship with all living beings, and I made up my mind that I was not one whit better than the meanest of earth. I said then, and I say now, that while there is a lower class, I am in it; while there is a criminal element, I am of it; while there is a soul in prison, I am not free."

. . . War now means just as it did in the past, "blood, sweat and tears"— oodles of it. Not blood, sweat and tears for those who launch it, but for those who have to go through with it. And that means practically everybody, except, as I said before, the favored few who direct the show. The latter are just as eager to give their lives as the little fellows, don't make any mistake about that. Only, because of the peculiar set-up involved in these fracases, they are somehow never privileged to enjoy this supreme sacrifice. They must be protected in order that the others can be most efficiently sacrificed. You can understand what anguish this causes the political and military leaders of any war. (Yet few of them ever pine away because of it. On the contrary, they seem to grow tough as steel.) However, if it were possible to take them by surprise, assure them that nothing they said would be held against them, it's just possible you'd discover that they were fed up with it too. A moment later, to be sure, they would be ready to deny such weak sentiments. "What would the people think?" they'd say. Always that to fall back on. *The people!* It was the people who wanted the war. Of course. Yes, when they're stabbed in the back the people may cry for war, *but*— how does it happen that they get stabbed in the back, and at just the right moment? And so, right or wrong, willing or unwilling, "the war must be fought to a just and victorious conclusion!" From time immemorial every leader has proclaimed that high and mighty truth. That's why the future is always so full of death. Right or wrong, the war must be continued, always. No looking back. No looking forward. *Head down and charge!* That's the order of the day. Victory? Just around the corner. And if not victory, death. Death, death, death. Always death. Or, if you're lucky, your old job back in the mines. The future? It never begins. You had your future yesterday, don't you remember? There is only the present, and the present is never pleasant. Only the future is bright. But then, the future never takes place. The future always recedes, that's the law. When the original Fascists have been vanquished, or exterminated, we'll all be Fascists— that's what the future, if there is to be any future, promises. And that means more death, more blood, sweat and tears, more Churchills, more Roosevelts, more Hitlers, more Stalins. . . .

With the conclusion of this war it is not even probable that we shall see the dissolution of national boundaries. To eliminate race prejudice no one can say how many more wars it will require. There are thousands of problems for which men will find no solution but war. No system of government now in vogue offers the slightest hope of a future free of war. The remedy for dissent is still, as it was in the past, subjugation or extirpation. The government has never existed which recognizes the freedom and equality of all men. As for freedom of thought, freedom to express one's ideas—not to speak of living them out— where is the government which ever permitted this? Conformity is the rule, and conformity will be the rule as long as men believe in governing one another.

Men of good-will need no government to regulate their affairs. In every age there is a very small minority which lives without thought of, or desire for, government. These men never brought about a war. So long as civilization lasts it is quite possible that this minority will never be substantially increased. Such men are not the products of our religious organizations or our educational systems; they live outside the cultural pattern of the times. The most we can say, in explanation of their appearance and existence, is that they are evolved beings. And here we must needs touch on the drawback to all schemes, Utopian or otherwise, for the improvement of human society: the failure inherent in all of them to recognize that the human race does not evolve at the same speed nor with the same rhythm. Where there is dream and wish fulfillment merely—and what else can there be if one focuses on society instead of the individual?—there is confusion and disillusionment. Even with redhot bayonets up their rear, men cannot be prodded all at the same time into Paradise. It is this fact, of course, which the so-called realists, who are always defeatists, seize upon with grim relish in order to excuse and perpetuate the business of murder. With each war they pretend that they are preserving society from a dire fate, or that they are protecting the weak and the helpless. The men of wisdom, who are really the men of good-will, and who are found in every stratum of society and not in any particular class, never make such pretences. They are often accused of being aloof, remote, out of touch with the world. Yet it is to them that all men turn for comfort and guidance in their hour of need. For, even the clod seems to sense that genuine disinterestedness is a source of strength.

If any particular set of men were destined to rule the world it would seem logical that it should be ruled by the men of wisdom. But that is not the case, and there is good reason for it. No one man, no set of men, is capable of ruling the world. The world is ruled by its own inner, mysterious laws. It evolves according to a logic which defies our man-made logic. The higher the type of man, moreover, the less inclined he feels to rule others; he lives in harmony with the world despite the fact that he is in total disagreement with the vast majority, as well as with the leaders of the world. Were there good reason to kill, he could find a thousand justifications to the ordinary man's one. The principal reason, however, for his failure to become embroiled in world conflicts is his absence of fear.

Accustomed as he is to live habitually in the world of ideas, he is not frightened when he learns that his neighbor thinks differently from him. Indeed, he might really become alarmed if he found that his neighbors were in agreement with him. The average man, on the contrary, is more frightened of alien ideas than of cold steel or flame throwers. He has spent most of his empty life getting adjusted to the few simple ideas which were thrust on him by his elders or superiors. Anything which menaces this precarious adjustment, which he calls his liberty, throws him into a panic. Let an alien idea become active, and the transition from fear to hate proceeds like clock-work. Trot out the word "enemy," and the whole bloody race behaves as if it had the blind staggers. The nit-wits who never showed the least ability to govern themselves suddenly get the idea that their last mission on earth is to teach the enemy good government. It makes no difference whether this nit-wit be a Communist, Fascist, or Democrat: the reaction is always the same. Just tell him that the other fellow is threatening his liberty, and he reaches for his gun—*automatically*.

And what is the little bundle of ideas around which this precious notion of liberty is formed? Private property, the sanctity of the home, the church he belongs to, the preservation of the political party, or the system, which gives him the privilege of being a drudge all his life. If he could but take one sweeping view of the planet, see what different things the same words mean everywhere, see how all men, including the primitives, believe that whatever they believe is right and just, and of course supremely intelligent, would he be so quick to reach for the sword or the gun? Yes, he would, because he has been educated to understand with his head but not with the rest of his being. As a civilized creature, a man can study and know the ways and customs of a thousand different peoples, yet insist on defending the ways of his own, even though he knows them to be stupid, inadequate or wrong. He will describe with irony and subtle discrimination the reasons why other peoples make war, but he will go to war himself when the time comes, even though he does not believe in killing. He will kill rather than be humiliated by his own people.

In how many wars have people killed who had no desire to kill? Many who killed one another had more in common than with their own compatriots. Were men to seek their real enemies they would have only to turn round and examine the ranks behind them. If men were to realize who their true enemies were, what a scrimmage would ensue! But again, one of the disadvantages of living under civilized rule is that only those may be considered as enemies, and therefore killed or enslaved, whom the governments designate as such. To kill your commanding officer, for example, even though he be the bitterest enemy you have, is strictly taboo. So it goes . . . scholars killing scholars, poets killing poets, workers killing workers, teachers killing teachers, and no one killing the munitions makers, the politicians, the priests, the military idiots or any of the other criminals who sanction war and egg one on to kill one another off.

Just to take one element, the munitions makers, for example: who could be more international-minded than they? Come war and they will sell to any side that has the money to buy. Strictly neutral, these birds, until they see which way the wind blows. No amount of taxation impoverishes them; the longer the war lasts, the more the dead pile up, the fatter they grow. Imagine the colossal absurdity of supporting a body of men whose mission in life it is to supply us with the means of self-destruction. (Whereas it is a crime to attempt to take one's own life by one's own means, no matter how unbearable life becomes!) Nobody considers the munitions maker—not even the Communist, mind you—as an enemy. Yet he is the greatest enemy man has. He sits like a vulture and waits and prays for the day to come when we shall lose our reason and beg him to furnish us with his most expensive lethal products. Instead of being looked upon as a leper he is given a place of honor in human society; often he is knighted for his indubitably dubious services. On the other hand, Monsieur le Paris [the executioner], who really performs a service for society, albeit a most disagreeable one, is shunned like a pariah. Strange paradox. If there is any logic to it it is thus: the man who by our own sanction justly removes a murderer from the ranks of society is a worthless wretch, whereas the man who provides the means of killing en masse, for no matter what reason good or bad, deserves a place of honor in our midst. Corollary logic: murder on a wholesale scale is always justifiable, as well as profitable and honorable, but ordinary murder, whether for passion or greed, is so disgraceful that even the man whose duty it is to make way with the culprit appears to us as tainted.

And what of all the plans fond parents make for their children's sake? Why bother to make plans when we know for a certainty that in each generation there will be one or more wars? Why not plan to make no plans at all, to just veg-etate until the bugle calls? What a waste of time, money and effort to prepare your son for the ministry or the law, or any other pursuit, when you know that the army or navy will get him, and if not the army or navy, then the marines. Why think of training your boy to go into business when the only important business of every new generation is to make war? Talk about common sense . . . what sense is there in pretending that one will engage in peaceful pursuits when the only pursuit we ever enter whole-heartedly, and with vim and vigor, is the pursuit of war? Why not train your son from the beginning to be a killer, an expert killer? Why delude yourself and him too? Sooner or later your boy must learn to kill; the quicker he learns the less pain and disillusionment he will suf-fer. Don't teach him how to live, teach him how to die! Prepare him not for the pleasures of this world, for the chances are he will never taste them; prepare him for the pleasures of the afterworld. If you find that he is hypersensitive, kill him while he is still young. Better to kill him with your own hands than to let him die at the hands of a ruthless enemy. Kill off all the males, if possible, and let only the females survive. And if the females begin warring with one another, kill them off at birth too. In any case, believe no one who promises you peace and prosperity unless all the munitions makers have been killed off and the machines they employ destroyed.

If the idea that your son must become a killer as well as a provider is abhor-rent to you, if you believe that death-dealing weapons should not continue to be manufactured, even if never used, then make a new world in which killing will be unnecessary. Concentrate all your energies upon that, and that alone. If you had a home which you were fond of, and it were suddenly invaded by rats, would you not set everything aside to eliminate the pest? War is the greatest plague that civilized man has had to contend with. And what has he done in all these thousands of years to grapple with the problem? Nothing, really. With the passage of time he has devoted increasing effort, ingenuity and money towards aggrandizing the horrors of war, as though pretending to himself that if war became too horrible it might cease of itself. The greatest nations have ruined themselves in preparing for and making war. Nevertheless the whole civilized world deludes itself into believing (by what amazing self-hypnosis!) that men are becoming better, more humane, more intelligent, more considerate of one another. The truth is that the farther along the path of civilization we go the more diabolical men seem to become. The torture inflicted upon one another by savages is nothing compared to the torture which civilized beings inflict upon one another. (This is true even in times of peace.) Add to this, that in taking over the so-called inferior peoples of the earth, in adapting them to our ways, the price we demand of them is that they become good auxiliary fighters. When there is a particularly dirty job of butchering to be done, we throw in the colonial troops. Progress! Progress!

Moreover, and above all, and to add to the illogical, the inconsistent and the paradoxical—does any serious-minded person believe for one moment that a victorious China, Russia, America, England will not become more militant, more ready and prepared for war, more suited to find fresh problems to quarrel over? Germany and Japan *may* be put out of harm's way. Agreed. But what then? Are they the only enemies man will ever have or could have? Since when have Big Powers agreed with one another, or laid down their arms and become as lambs? Since when have the Big Powers treated Little Powers with equal tact and consideration? And what of the Little Powers, when we have liberated them by our victorious but ruinous campaigns? Will they be grateful and ready to fall in line with our way of life when their people return to the desolate, ruined lands which we turned into a stupendous proving ground? Will they perhaps differ with us as to how life and liberty is to be maintained in the future?

Who will rule the coming world? The strong ones. And who are the strong? America, Russia, England, China. . . .

The great question, to be sure, which will come up as soon as the war ends, is: who will buy whose goods and how? As for the debt problem, that is easily solved. The people will pay off the debts. The people always pay. Though the people never start a war, nor even a revolution, the government somehow always convinces the people that they must pay for these adventures, both before and after. A war is fought for the benefit of the people. By the time the war is over, however, there are no benefits, just debts, death and desolation. All of which has to be paid for.

This time the peoples who make up the victorious nations won't mind the cost because they will have the Four Freedoms [freedom of speech, freedom of worship, freedom from want, freedom from fear]. They will also have all sorts of new machines, new labor-saving devices, which will make work a pleasure. (And the harder they work the faster the debts will be paid off; the more ready they will be, too, for the next war.) Yes, there will be all sorts of new inventions, which, if they are not used destructively, will bring untold bliss. There will be, among other things, new airplanes capable of taking us back and forth to China in twenty-four hours—and for a song! Week-ends the workers of the world will be flying around the globe greeting their fellow-workers in Java, Borneo, Mozambique, Saskatchewan, Tierra del Fuego and such places. No need to go to Coney Island any more, or Deauville, or Brighton—there will be far more interesting places at which to spend the week-end. There will be television, too, don't forget. If you don't care to fly around the world in your spare time you can sit quietly by the hearth and watch the Eskimos climbing up and down the slippery icebergs, or look at the primitive peoples in the jungle busy gathering rice, ivory, coffee, tea, rubber, chicle and other useful commodities for our delectation. Every one will be working blissfully, even the Chinese coolies. For, by that time the vast and all-powerful Chiang Kai-shek dynasty will be operating with the smoothness of a highpowered dynamo. The opium traffic will be wiped out, and the heretofore ignorant coolies will be able to understand and appreciate American movies, which are an excellent substitute for opium. We will probably make special Grade D pictures for them at a figure so absurd that even the lowest coolie will be able to afford the price of admission. We will have Grade K or J pictures for "our little brown brothers" too. We will make chewing gum in greater quantities, and Eskimo pies, and malted milk shakes, to say nothing of can openers and other gadgets, so that the little people everywhere may enjoy some of the luxuries of our economic millennium.

The thing to guard against, however, is that the little peoples of the world should not be infected with Communism. Russia will have to be content to communize Siberia, Mongolia, and possibly Japan. But not China! And not the Malay archipelago, nor Africa, nor South America. South America will be somewhat of a problem, especially as miscegenation assumes increasing proportions. It won't do for the peoples of North America, "the melting pot," to begin intermarrying with the black, brown and yellow races. Marrying red-skins is quite another matter; the Indian, it seems, is a hundred percent American, and we don't mind any more if they have a touch of color. But don't let any one think, especially south of the Mason-Dixon line, that the Four Freedoms means freedom for blacks and whites to intermarry! That belongs to the fifth or sixth freedom, and will probably demand another war.

With a plethora of new labor-saving devices flooding the market there will no longer be any question of who is to do the dirty work of the world. *The machine will do it!* No one will need to soil his hands. The machines will work with such efficiency, in fact, that there may be danger of the workers growing bored. Unless the master minds introduce new forms of creative activity. It is quite possible that in the next few hundred years we shall see everybody turning artist. An hour or two at the machine each day, and the rest of the day for art! Perhaps that will be the new order in the world to come. How glorious! *The joy of creation:* something man has never known before, at least not the civilized races. Suddenly, thanks to the ubiquity and the domination of the machine, we will become again as the primitives, only wiser, happier, conscious at last of our blessedness. Everybody dancing, singing, painting, carying, fiddling, drumming, strumming . . . so marvelous! All due to the machine. How simple!

Finally, when every one has become a genius, when genius becomes the norm, there will be no room for envy or rivalry. Art will be truly universal. There will be no need for critics or interpreters; the dealers and middle men will perish, and with them the publishers and editors, the lawyers, the bookkeepers, the politicians, perhaps even the police. Every one will have the kind of home he chooses to live in, and with it a frigidaire, a radio, a telephone, a vacuum cleaner, a washing machine, an automobile, an airplane, a parachute, *and*—a full set of Dr. Cowen's light-weight platinum teeth. The cripples will all have the most wonderful, the most extraordinary, light-weight artificial limbs, which will enable them to run, skip, dance, jump or walk with perfect ease. The insane will have better lunatic asylums, and more humane, more intelligent keepers. The prisons will be more spacious, more sanitary, more comfortable in every way. There will be hospitals in abundance, on every street, and ambulances fitted up like Pullmans. There will be such a variety of pain removers that no one need ever suffer any more, not even the throes of death. Add to this, that when all the world learns English, which will happen inevitably, there won't be the least possibility of a misunderstanding any more. One language, one flag, one way of life. The machine doing all the dirty work, the master minds doing all the thinking: an Entente Cordiale with a vengeance.

That's how it looks for the next five hundred years or so. *Or doesn't it?* Anyway, that's how it *could* look, you must admit. And what's to hinder? Well, we don't know yet, but undoubtedly there will arise some idiot, some fanatic, who will have a better idea to foist upon us. And that will cause trouble. Trouble always starts with "a better idea." It's too soon to predict the nature of the monkey wrench which will wreck the Utopian machine we have just described, but that there will be such a joy-killer we have no doubt. It's in the cards.

So, just to play safe, hold on to your battle-ships and battle wagons, your tanks, your flame-throwers, your bombing machines and everything super-duper in the way of destructive devices—we may have need for them again. One day, out of a clear sky—always a clear sky, mind you!—some fanatic will make an issue of some unforeseeable little incident, magnify it to the proportions of a calamity, and then a fresh catastrophe will be at our door. But if we are armed to the teeth, if we are better prepared than we were this last time, perhaps we shall get it over with more quickly. We must never relinquish the Four Freedoms, remember that! If possible, we must pave the way for a fifth and sixth freedom. Because, the more freedoms we pile up, the nearer we will be to freedom in the abstract.

Each new freedom, to be sure, will entail a few million deaths, as well as the destruction of our principal cities. But, if we achieve ten or twelve freedoms, we won't mind how many millions of lives are sacrificed, nor will we care how many cities are destroyed. After all, we can always make babies, and we can always build new cities—better babies, better cities. If we were able to discover a way to homogenize and irradiate cow's milk we surely will find the way to homogenize and irradiate the minds of our children. If we have to destroy everything now standing, including the Vatican, it will be worth it. What we want is a world in which war will be unthinkable. And, by God, if we have to wipe out the human race in order to achieve it, we will. *Mieux vaut revenir en fantôme que jamais,* as the French say.

So, until that blessed day looms upon the horizon, do please go on murdering one another. Murder as you have never murdered before. Murder the murderers, murder murder, but murder! murder! murder! Murder for God and country! Murder for peace! Murder for sweet murder's sake! Don't stop murdering ever! Murder! Murder! Murder! Murder your mother! Murder your brother! Murder the animals of the field, murder the insects, the birds, the flowers, the grass! Murder the microbes! Murder the molecule and the atom! Murder the electron! Murder the stars, and the sun and moon, if you can get at them! Murder everything off, so that we shall have at last a bright, pure, clean world in which to live in peace, bliss and security until the end of time!

PART SEVEN

The Affluent Society, 1945–1966

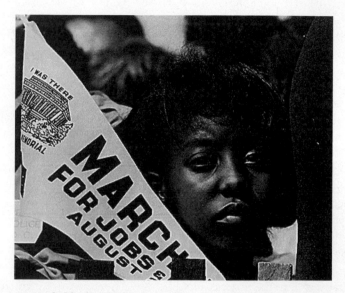

Young Demonstrator at the March on Washington, 1963.   *One of the more than 250,000 civil rights demonstrators at the historic March on Washington.*

INTRODUCTION: THE CRACK IN THE PICTURE WINDOW

As GIs came back from Europe and the Pacific to the euphoric welcome of an exultant nation, there was already a sense that "returning home" would be anything but normal. With the defeat of Germany and Japan, the division of Europe, and the dawn of the Atomic Age, the world had irrevocably changed. Uncertainty was in the air. The Soviet Union, its massive armies occupying Eastern Europe, loomed as a menace.

Even during the war, much of President Roosevelt (FDR) and Prime Minister Churchill's military strategy and diplomatic policy was determined by their recognition that the war would result in the emergence of the United States and the Soviet Union as the two major super powers. Although he did not fully trust

Stalin, at Tehran and again at Yalta FDR was convinced he could work out an adequate understanding with the Soviet leader. However, Roosevelt's successor, Harry Truman, did not trust Stalin at all and was adamant about holding the line against what was perceived as Soviet imperialism. Stalin's actions fed these suspicions. Not only were the Soviets in control of Eastern Europe but also Stalin presented an ultimatum to Turkey and attempted to carve a sphere of influence in Iran. In 1946, Churchill gave his famous "iron curtain" speech, which seemed to draw the line in the sand, dividing West from East. And so, less than a year after the war's end, the cold war was a reality.

Historians have debated at length the question "who started the cold war?" Some have argued that it was the result of Soviet expansion and U.S. resistance to that expansion. Others have contended that it was the U.S. wish to expand capitalism and control markets and raw materials around the world that was the cause. Still others have claimed that the cold war was simply a result of misunderstanding on the part of the two great powers: If only the United States had realized that the Soviet grip on Eastern Europe had less to do with imperialism and expansion and was more a matter of Russia's attempt to create a secure buffer zone on its western flank to guard against the possibility of yet another German invasion. (Millions of people in the Soviet Union had experienced two German invasions, and millions had died as a result—approximately 27 million in World War II alone!) However one interprets its origins, the cold war was the determining factor presiding over international relations for the next 46 years.

Because it was not possible to unseat the Soviets from the positions they already occupied, Truman's response was the policy of "containment." Communism must not be allowed to spread; it must be contained. After 1947, the Marshall Plan, channeling billions of dollars into the rebuilding of Europe, became one of the more successful devices for containing communism. In 1948, the United States set the wheels in motion to unify the three allied occupied sectors of Germany into the Federal Republic of Germany (which came into being in 1949). In response, the Soviets initiated the Berlin blockade to force the allies out of West Berlin. The Americans and British reacted with the Berlin airlift.

In 1949, the North Atlantic Treaty Organization (NATO) was founded to defend Western Europe from Soviet aggression. Even earlier, the Soviet Union created its own bloc through a system of separate military-political alliances with Eastern European countries. (Later, in 1955, the Soviets initiated the Warsaw Pact, uniting the Soviet Union with East Germany, Hungary, Czechoslovakia, Poland, Romania, and Bulgaria in a defense pact against capitalist aggression.) Also in 1949, the Soviets successfully tested their first atomic bomb, and in October the Chinese communist revolution became a victorious reality. The North Korean invasion of South Korea followed closely in June 1950, bringing a wave of anxiety across the United States. Just five years after having won the biggest war in history, how could we suddenly be living in such a perilous, uncertain world, in which our mortal enemies seemed to be building in strength? Fear of Soviet expansion abroad was accompanied by an equally deep fear of communism at home. The Alger Hiss case, which brought national attention to a young, previously unknown congressman from California—Richard Nixon—and the trial of the Communist Party in 1948–1949 was part of the spy mania that beset the nation after the war. The House Committee on UnAmerican Activities (HUAC) held scores of hearings in an effort to unmask Americans working to spread communist propaganda within the United States. Because Hollywood had a powerful influence on American attitudes, HUAC concentrated much of its efforts on the "Hollywood Ten" and others in the entertainment industry. Unions and other "left-wing" organizations were also targeted. In 1950, Senator Joseph McCarthy, proclaiming there were 205 card-carrying members of the Communist Party employed by the State Department, began his infamous witch hunt that would last for the next four years. This Red Scare reached such proportions that it stifled legitimate political discourse and debate, even within the Capitol. Senators and congressmen were afraid to voice criticism of American policy, lest they be labeled "soft on communism" or "pinko." As those investigated by HUAC and McCarthy quickly discovered, such allegations destroyed reputations and careers. There were many, however, who did take a stand against the hysteria. Senator Margaret Chase Smith of Maine issued a "declaration of conscience" to warn about the destruction of civil liberties. Even though it got them blacklisted, Paul Robeson, Pete Seeger, John Howard Lawson, and others being investigated stood up for the Bill of Rights and condemned the committee itself for being un-American.

With the American and Soviet development of the hydrogen bomb (a thousand times more powerful than the atomic bomb dropped on Hiroshima), the nuclear arms race took a more alarming, more terrifying turn. Fears rose that a simple miscalculation, a failure of the United States and Soviet Union to communicate, could lead to Armageddon—the destruction of the world. The fact that the Eisenhower administration was relying more on the development of nuclear weapons than on stockpiling conventional weapons made the situation more unsettling. Secretary of State John Foster Dulles's diplomatic strategy was "brinkmanship." When negotiating with the Soviets over a crisis, let them know that if a compromise could not be reached, we would be prepared to launch an attack. The policy at the negotiating table was therefore to force the issue to the brink of catastrophe and then wait for someone to pull back. In this way, it seemed, every confrontation could lead to the end of the world. Every school in America began instituting regular air raid drills (along with the customary fire drills). National air raid drills were also introduced, with members of Congress and even the president participating. Underground areas in every city were designated as fallout shelters. Many citizens built their own private fallout shelters in backyards or basements and stockpiled water, canned food, and weapons so that, if the worst happened, they could fend off those who would try to seize their shelter. Anxiety was on the rise.

Cold war reality, along with anticommunist hysteria, was one fundamental development that shaped 1950s America. The other was the booming economy. After 15 years of depression and war, Americans were, at first, nervous that the wartime economy would collapse and the nation would sink once again into depression. Indeed, strikes and labor unrest for the first three years after the war were ominous warnings that a recession could ensue. However, the return of GIs eager to start families (leading to the baby boom), the burgeoning housing industry (to accommodate growing families), the production of consumer goods (especially automobiles), and the nuclear arms race all led to a soaring economy, creating such a sense of progress and affluence that it became a widely accepted belief that the American dream was within the reach of every citizen. With an attitude bordering on arrogance, Americans were convinced that the United States was the greatest country on earth. Part of this patriotic pride, of course, was in reaction to the Soviet threat. Patriotic Americans, viewing the two sides through somewhat distorted lenses, compared the free, democratic United States with the atheistic, totalitarian Soviet Union and saw obvious, unacceptable differences. Anticommunist attitudes combined with the postwar economic miracle to encourage conformity. The cultural mantra became: Everyone should be prosperous, everyone should have a good job, everyone should have a nice house in the suburbs with a nice picture window, everyone should value the American way of life, and everyone should oppose communism. Television, the new technological innovation that burst on the scene in the 1950s, underscored and enabled this ideology. Every night, people were glued to their television sets watching *Gunsmoke, Have Gun Will Travel,* and *The Rifleman* extolling the virtues of the rugged individuals who made America great. Or they were watching *Leave It to Beaver, The Donna Reed Show, Father Knows Best,* or *Ozzie and Harriet* extolling the virtues of white, middle-class, male-dominated America. The message was clear. This is the way it ought to be for every American.

But, as writer John Keats observed, there was a "crack in the picture window" of suburbia. Not everyone was happy with the American dream. Not everyone, indeed, was able to participate in that dream. Vance Packard passed judgment on the advertising industry and the urge so many Americans had to achieve status in his widely read books *The Hidden Persuaders* and *The Status Seekers.* Sociologists David Riesman, in *The Lonely Crowd,* and William Whyte, in *The Organization Man,* critically analyzed the conformity that seemed so attractive to so many people. Americans, Whyte maintained, were no longer concerned with standing out, thinking for themselves, and being innovative; rather, they were more inclined to "fit in" to become part of the corporate team. Riesman argued that Americans were no longer "inner-directed" individuals, guided by inner principles and morality, but were becoming "other directed," more concerned with what others thought of them and with pleasing others than with being faithful to their own principles.

To be sure, there were many who did not conform to conventional standards. In art, there was the abstract expressionism of Jackson Pollock, Robert Motherwell, and Mark Rothko that mystified and bewildered critics. In music, there was bebop, an unwaveringly individualistic, improvisational style of jazz performed by Charlie Parker, Thelonious Monk, Dizzy Gillespie, and others. In literature, J. D. Salinger's *Catcher in the Rye* criticized the shallowness and phoniness of American society, and Arthur Miller's *The Crucible* compared the McCarthy hearings to the Salem witchcraft trials. Thus in some ways it can be argued that the conformity of the 1950s was not so widespread and deeply ingrained as some historians and sociologists have maintained—otherwise, how does one explain the rebellion of the 1960s? The rise of the Beat Movement and the sudden popularity of rock and roll are two developments often viewed as seeds of the sixties. William Burroughs, Allen Ginsberg, Jack Kerouac, and others attacked pervasive conformist values in their books. Teenagers devoured the music of Chuck Berry, Little Richard, Elvis Presley, Jerry Lee Lewis, Fats Domino, and many others with such enthusiasm that their parents began to worry that rock and roll was part of the international communist conspiracy to corrupt America's youth and eventually destroy the United States. The fact that the nation's youth took to rock and roll so quickly and passionately suggested that there was an indefinable hunger for something else, something that the material comforts of the affluent 1950s were not providing.

The most obvious indication of the crack in the American picture window—in fact, a development that significantly challenged the fundamental assumption that the United States was a democracy—was the emergence of the civil rights movement. After the 1954 *Brown v. Board of Education* decision outlawing segregation in public schools, African Americans began to hope that nearly a century of discrimination and second-class citizenship would finally come to an end. However, southern states and school districts resisted implementation of the decision and in some cases delayed school integration, for many years. Blacks understood that achieving parity with whites would involve more than the long struggle to change racist laws; they understood that the rights of American citizenship were not simply going to be given to them; they would have to struggle to claim them. In 1955, Rosa Parks refused to give up her seat on a Montgomery, Alabama, bus, thus leading to the year-long Montgomery bus boycott and the rise of Dr. Martin Luther King Jr. to national prominence. In 1957, Governor Orval Faubus ordered the Arkansas National Guard to prevent nine black students from entering Little Rock Central High School. After a tense confrontation, a reluctant President Eisenhower was eventually forced to send in the U.S. Army to enforce compliance with the *Brown* decision. (Ironically he sent in the 101st Airborne Division, the elite division that parachuted into Normandy in the predawn hours of June 6, 1944. Some thought it appropriate that the 101st, which helped restore freedom to France in 1944, would also facilitate bringing freedom to Arkansas in 1957.) These events, broadcast on national television, awakened many people to the reality that the United States had not yet lived up to its ideal that "all men are created equal." In 1960 black students in Greensboro, North Carolina, and Nashville, Tennessee, began a new campaign of sit-ins at segregated lunch counters, and in 1961 Congress of Racial Equality (CORE) and Student Nonviolent Coordinating Committee (SNCC) activists launched the Freedom Rides to push the new Kennedy administration to enforce the Supreme Court's decision outlawing bus segregation. A pivotal year for the civil rights movement was 1963. In April and May, Martin Luther King Jr. initiated a series of demonstrations in Birmingham, Alabama, during which the police and fire departments attacked the demonstrators with dogs and fire hoses. The shock of this violent reaction to nonviolent protest generated so much positive publicity for the civil rights movement that Kennedy finally threw the weight of the Oval Office behind the movement, calling civil rights a "moral issue" and forwarding a bill to Congress that would outlaw segregation in workplaces, public housing, and public accommodation. In August, the Freedom Now movement sponsored the historic March on Washington, where King delivered his celebrated "I Have a Dream" speech to an orderly crowd of more than 250,000 people. King, although the most famous of the civil rights leaders, was only one of hundreds of deeply dedicated individuals who risked their lives for the cause. Though they had differing points of view on how best to achieve their rights as American citizens, Robert Moses, John Lewis, Ella Baker, Malcolm X, Anne Moody, Stokely Carmichael, Floyd McKissick, and countless others were profoundly committed to transforming race relations in the United States.

In 1964, when the Civil Rights Act became law, hundreds of white and black students participated in Freedom Summer—a voter registration drive for Mississippi blacks. Although three civil rights workers were killed during the first week of the campaign, volunteers kept arriving in Mississippi. In 1965, the Voting Rights Bill, providing for federal overseers to monitor voter registration to make sure no citizen was prevented from registering, was signed into law by President Johnson. As the civil rights movement moved north, however, it began to splinter between advocates of King's nonviolent resistance and supporters of Black Power.

When Democrat John F. Kennedy became president, it was not only civil rights activists who had high hopes for the country. Young people generally were idealistic and hopeful, especially after Kennedy exhorted them, in his inaugural address, to "ask not what your country can do for you, ask what you can do for your country!" Thousands joined the Peace Corps or involved themselves in the civil rights movement. At the University of Michigan, a group of students formed Students for a Democratic Society and, in 1962, issued the Port Huron Statement, in which they questioned cold war assumptions, analyzed American capitalism from a Marxist perspective, criticized racial bigotry, and called for a "participatory democracy" in which all Americans would work for bringing about a more just society. In 1963, in *The Feminine Mystique,* Betty Friedan wrote that for American women, being trapped in the only accepted role—of homemaker—was frustrating and unfulfilling. This "problem that has no name," she insisted, needed to be addressed. That same year, the President's Commission on the Status of Women (which Kennedy had set up in 1961) reported that there was indeed pervasive discrimination against women in education, in jobs, and in salaries. As a result, Kennedy backed the Equal Pay Act of 1963 and signed an executive order that civil service hiring must be done "without regard to sex." A feeling of change was in the air.

The idealism that Kennedy and the civil rights struggle had generated in the nation's young baby boomers, however, was dealt a severe blow on

November 22, 1963. As news of Kennedy's assassination in Dallas flashed over the airwaves, the country ground to a halt. For four days, the sense of grief was overwhelming. For those young idealists Kennedy had inspired, the assassination was especially devastating. Many sensed, just as those in the current generation did on September 11, 2001, that somehow their lives would unfold differently because of this event. The historical and the personal had come together in a way that no one could have imagined.

In the aftermath of the assassination, great numbers of young people, no longer quite so naive, tried to work out how they might carry on what was perceived as Kennedy's legacy. Even though Kennedy himself had been very slow to endorse civil rights, the fact that he had finally done so during his last months convinced many that he would have become a major force in accomplishing the movement's goals. Over the next few years, many young men, also beguiled by Kennedy's inaugural injunction to "pay any price, bear any burden," eagerly enlisted in the Armed Forces in order to fight communists in Vietnam. Ironically, in the end, Vietnam became the final spark igniting the student movement.

John Howard Lawson (1894–1977)

John Howard Lawson, a Hollywood screenwriter and president of the Screen Writers Guild, was brought before the House Committee on Un-American Activities (HUAC) in 1947 to respond to questions about his communist activity and his efforts to put communist propaganda into his film scripts. HUAC was convinced that there was an international communist conspiracy to overthrow the American government and that the media and Hollywood had a particularly powerful influence on public thinking. If communists infiltrated the film industry or the media, they could "brainwash" Americans with insidious, subversive pro-leftist ideas. The committee therefore singled out Hollywood for investigation. During the hearings, Lawson, who had joined the Communist Party in 1934, attempted to read a statement into the record that accused the committee of undermining the Bill of Rights. Lawson's strategy was to get the Supreme Court to rule that HUAC was violating the free speech amendment of the Constitution and therefore overturn the committee's rulings. In 1949, however, the court refused to hear the appeal, and Lawson (along with the other nine members of the Hollywood Ten, Herbert Biberman, Albert Maltz, Lester Cole, Dalton Trumbo, Alvah Bessie, Samuel Ornitz, Edward Dmytryk, Adrian Scott, and Ring Lardner Jr.) was blacklisted and imprisoned.

The first document here is Lawson's HUAC testimony, during which he tried to read his statement into the record. The second document is the disallowed statement.

Testimony Before the House Committee on Un-American Activities, 1947

Mr. Lawson: Mr. Chairman, I have a statement here which I wish to make—

The Chairman: Well, all right, let me see your statement.

(Statement handed to the chairman.)

The Chairman: I don't care to read any more of the statement. The statement will not be read. I read the first line.

Mr. Lawson: You have spent one week vilifying me before the American public—

The Chairman: Just a minute—

Mr. Lawson: And you refuse to allow me to make a statement on my rights as an American citizen.

The Chairman: I refuse you to make the statement, because of the first sentence in your statement. That statement is not pertinent to the inquiry. Now, this is a congressional committee— a congressional committee set up by law. We must have orderly procedure, and we are going to have orderly procedure.

Mr. Stripling, identify the witness.

Mr. Lawson: The rights of American citizens are important in this room here, and I intend to stand up for those rights, Congressman Thomas.

Mr. Stripling: Mr. Lawson, will you state your full name, please?

Mr. Lawson: I wish to protest against the unwillingness of this committee to read a statement, when you permitted Mr. Warner, Mr. Mayer, and others to read statements in this room.

My name is John Howard Lawson. . . .

Mr. Stripling: What is your occupation, Mr. Lawson?

Mr. Lawson: I am a writer.

Mr. Stripling: How long have you been a writer?

Mr. Lawson: All my life—at least 35 years—my adult life.

Mr. Stripling: Are you a member of the Screen Writers Guild?

Source: From Congress, House, Committee on Un-American Activities, *Hearings Regarding the Communist Infiltration of the Motion Picture Industry*, 80th Congress, 1st Session, October 1947 (Washington: Government Printing Office, 1947); "A Statement by John Howard Lawson," in Gordon Kahn, ed., *Hollywood on Trial* (New York, 1948); quoted in *Thirty Years of Treason: Excerpts from Hearings before the House Committee on Un-American Activities, 1938–1968*, Eric Bentley, ed. (New York: Viking Press, 1971), 161–165.

MR. LAWSON: The raising of any question here in regard to membership, political beliefs, or affiliation—

MR. STRIPLING: Mr. Chairman—

MR. LAWSON: Is absolutely beyond the powers of this committee.

MR. STRIPLING: Mr. Chairman—

MR. LAWSON: But—

(The chairman pounding gavel.)

MR. LAWSON: It is a matter of public record that I am a member of the Screen Writers Guild.

MR. STRIPLING: I ask—

(Applause.)

THE CHAIRMAN: I want to caution the people in the audience: You are the guests of this committee and you will have to maintain order at all times. I do not care for any applause or any demonstrations of one kind or another.

MR. STRIPLING: Now, Mr. Chairman, I am also going to request that you instruct the witness to be responsive to the questions.

THE CHAIRMAN: I think the witness will be more responsive to the questions.

MR. LAWSON: Mr. Chairman, you permitted—

THE CHAIRMAN (POUNDING GAVEL): Never mind—

MR. LAWSON (CONTINUING): Witnesses in this room to make answers of three or four or five hundred words to questions here.

THE CHAIRMAN: Mr. Lawson, you will please be responsive to these questions and not continue to try to disrupt these hearings.

MR. LAWSON: I am not on trial here, Mr. Chairman. This committee is on trial here before the American people. Let us get that straight.

THE CHAIRMAN: We don't want you to be on trial.

MR. STRIPLING: Mr. Lawson, how long have you been a member of the Screen Writers Guild?

MR. LAWSON: Since it was founded in its present form, in 1933.

MR. STRIPLING: Have you ever held any office in the guild?

MR. LAWSON: The question of whether I have held office is also a question which is beyond the purview of this Committee.

(The chairman pounding gavel.)

MR. LAWSON: It is an invasion of the right of association under the Bill of Rights of this country.

THE CHAIRMAN: Please be responsive to the question.

MR. LAWSON: It is also a matter—

(The chairman pounding gavel.)

MR. LAWSON: Of public record—

THE CHAIRMAN: You asked to be heard. Through your attorney, you asked to be heard. And we want you to be heard. And if you don't care to be heard, then we will excuse you and we will put the record in without your answers.

MR. LAWSON: I wish to frame my own answers to your questions, Mr. Chairman, and I intend to do so.

. . .

MR. LAWSON: It is absolutely beyond the power of this committee to inquire into my association in any organization.

THE CHAIRMAN: Mr. Lawson, you will have to stop or you will leave the witness stand. And you will leave the witness stand because you are in contempt. That is why you will leave the witness stand. And if you are just trying to force me to put you in contempt, you won't have to try much harder. You know what has happened to a lot of people that have been in contempt of this committee this year, don't you?

MR. LAWSON: I am glad you have made it perfectly clear that you are going to threaten and intimidate the witnesses, Mr. Chairman.

(The chairman pounding gavel.)

MR. LAWSON: I am an American and I am not at all easy to intimidate, and don't think I am.

(The chairman pounding gavel.) . . .

THE CHAIRMAN (POUNDING GAVEL): Mr. Lawson, just quiet down again.

Mr. Lawson, the most pertinent question that we can ask is whether or not you have ever been a member of the Communist Party. Now, do you care to answer that question?

MR. LAWSON: You are using the old technique, which was used in Hitler Germany in order to create a scare here—

THE CHAIRMAN (POUNDING GAVEL): Oh—

MR. LAWSON: In order to create an entirely false atmosphere in which this hearing is conducted—

(The chairman pounding gavel.)

THE CHAIRMAN (POUNDING GAVEL): Excuse the witness—

MR. LAWSON: As they do from what I have written.

THE CHAIRMAN (POUNDING GAVEL): Stand away from the stand—

MR. LAWSON: I have written Americanism for many years, and I shall continue to fight for the Bill of Rights, which you are trying to destroy.

THE CHAIRMAN: Officers, take this man away from the stand—

(Applause and boos.)

THE CHAIRMAN (POUNDING GAVEL): There will be no demonstrations. No demonstrations, for or against. Everyone will please be seated. . . .

LAWSON'S STATEMENT THAT WAS EXCLUDED
FROM THE PUBLIC RECORD, 1947

For a week, this Committee has conducted an illegal and indecent trial of American citizens, whom the Committee has selected to be publicly pilloried and smeared. I am not here to defend myself, or to answer the agglomeration of falsehoods that has been heaped upon me, I believe lawyers describe this material, rather mildly, as "hearsay evidence." To the American public, it has a shorter name: dirt. Rational people don't argue with dirt. I feel like a man who has had truckloads of filth heaped upon him; I am now asked to struggle to my feet and talk while more truckloads pour more filth around my head.

No, you don't argue with dirt. But you try to find out where it comes from. And to stop the evil deluge before it buries you—and others. The immediate source is obvious. The so-called "evidence" comes from a parade of stool-pigeons, neurotics, publicity-seeking clowns, Gestapo agents, paid informers, and a few ignorant and frightened Hollywood artists. I am not going to discuss this perjured testimony. Let these people live with their consciences, with the knowledge that they have violated their country's most sacred principles.

These individuals are not important. As an individual, I am not important. The obvious fact that the Committee is trying to destroy me personally and professionally, to deprive me of my livelihood and what is far dearer to me—my honor as an American—gains significance only because it opens the way to similar destruction of any citizen whom the Committee selects for annihilation.

I am not going to touch on the gross violation of the Constitution of the United States, and especially of its First and Fifth Amendments, that is taking place here. The proof is so overwhelming that it needs no elaboration. The Un-American Activities Committee stands convicted in the court of public opinion.

I want to speak here as a writer and a citizen. . . .

My political and social views are well known. My deep faith in the motion picture as a popular art is also well known. I don't "sneak ideas" into pictures. I never make a contract to write a picture unless I am convinced that it serves democracy and the interests of the American people. I will never permit what I write and think to be subject to the orders of self-appointed dictators, ambitious politicians, thought-control gestapos, or any other form of censorship this Un-American Committee may attempt to devise. My freedom to speak and write is not for sale in return for a card signed by J. Parnell Thomas saying "O.K. for employment until further notice."

Pictures written by me have been seen and approved by millions of Americans. A subpoena for me is a subpoena for all those who have enjoyed these pictures and recognized them as an honest portrayal of our American life.

Thus, my integrity as a writer is obviously an integral part of my integrity as a citizen. As a citizen I am not alone here. I am not only one of nineteen men who have been subpoenaed. I am forced to appear here as a representative of one hundred and thirty million Americans because the illegal conduct of this Committee has linked me with every citizen. If I can be destroyed no American is safe. You can subpoena a farmer in a field, a lumberjack in the woods, a worker at a machine, a doctor in his office—you can deprive them of a livelihood, deprive them of their honor as Americans.

Let no one think that this is an idle or thoughtless statement. This is the course that the Un-American Activities Committee has charted. Millions of Americans who may as yet be unconscious of what may be in store for them will find that the warning I speak today is literally fulfilled. No American will be safe if the Committee is not stopped in its illegal enterprise.

I am like most Americans in resenting interference with my conscience and belief. I am like most Americans in insisting on my right to serve my country in the way that seems to me most helpful and effective. I am like most Americans in feeling that loyalty to the United States and pride in its traditions is the guiding principle of my life. I am like most Americans in believing that divided loyalty—which is another word for treason—is the most despicable crime of which any man or woman can be accused.

It is my profound conviction that it is precisely because I hold these beliefs that I have been hailed before this illegal court. These are the beliefs that the so-called Un-American Activities Committee is seeking to root out in order to subvert orderly government and establish an autocratic dictatorship.

I am not suggesting that J. Parnell Thomas aspires to be the man on horseback. He is a petty politician, serving more powerful forces. Those forces are trying to introduce fascism in this country. They know that the only way to trick the American people into abandoning their rights and liberties is to manufacture an imaginary danger, to frighten the people into accepting repressive laws which are supposedly for their protection.

. . . Today, we face a serious crisis in the determination of national policy. The only way to solve that crisis is by free discussion. Americans must know the facts. The only plot against American safety is the plot to conceal facts. I am plastered with mud because I happen to be an American who expresses opinions that the House Un-American Activities Committee does not like. But my opinions are not an issue in this case. The issue is my right to have opinions. The Committee's logic is obviously: Lawson's opinions are properly subject to censorship; he writes for the motion picture industry, so the industry is properly subject to censorship; the industry makes pictures for the American people, so the minds of the people must be censored and controlled.

Why? What are J. Parnell Thomas and the Un-American interests he serves, afraid of? They're afraid of the American people. They don't want to muzzle me. They want to muzzle public opinion. They want to muzzle the great Voice of democracy. Because they're conspiring against the American way of life. They want to cut living standards, introduce an economy of poverty, wipe out labor's rights, attack Negroes, Jews, and other minorities, drive us into a disastrous and unnecessary war.

The struggle between thought-control and freedom of expression is the struggle between the people and a greedy unpatriotic minority which hates and fears the people. I wish to present as an integral part of this statement, a paper which I read at a Conference on Thought Control in the United States held in Hollywood on July 9th to 13th. The paper presents the historical background of the threatening situation that we face today, and shows that the attack on freedom of communication is, and has always been, an attack on the American people.

The American people will know how to answer that attack. They will rally, as they have always rallied, to protect their birthright.

Margaret Chase Smith (1897–1995)

Maine's Margaret Chase Smith was the first woman to be elected to both houses of Congress. She was a representative from 1940 to 1949 and U. S. senator from 1949 to 1973. In 1963 she declared her candidacy for the Republican presidential nomination and was thus the first woman to have her name put forth at a national convention. She came to prominence during the height of Senator Joseph McCarthy's anticommunist crusade and in 1950 was the first senator to speak out against him. Her "Declaration of Conscience" speech denouncing McCarthy's smear campaign and his recklessness in trying to uncover communists in the federal government is a classic statement of the constitutionally guaranteed right to dissent and protest. Senator Smith claimed that McCarthy's campaign was endangering the central principle of American democracy: freedom of conscience. As a result, Smith's "Declaration of Conscience" can be viewed as an early seed of the more radical dissent of the 1960s.

DECLARATION OF CONSCIENCE, 1950

For Release upon Delivery

Statement of Senator Margaret Chase Smith

June 1, 1950

Mr. President:

I would like to speak briefly and simply about a serious national condition. It is a national feeling of fear and frustration that could result in national suicide and the end of everything that we Americans hold dear. It is a condition that comes from the lack of effective leadership in either the Legislative Branch or the Executive Branch of our Government.

That leadership is so lacking that serious and responsible proposals are being made that national advisory commissions be appointed to provide such critically needed leadership.

I speak as briefly as possible because too much harm has already been done with irresponsible words of bitterness and selfish political opportunism. I speak as simply as possible because the issue is too great to be obscured by eloquence. I speak simply and briefly in the hope that my words will be taken to heart.

SOURCE: "Declaration of Conscience" by Senator Margaret Chase Smith and "Statement of Seven Senators," June 1, 1950, *Congressional Record*, 82nd Congress. 1st Session, in Arthur M. Schlesinger Jr. and Roger Burns, *Congress Investigates: A Documented History, 1792–1974* (New York: Chelsea House, 1963), 84–88.

I speak as a Republican, I speak as a woman. I speak as a United States Senator. I speak as an American.

The United States Senate has long enjoyed worldwide respect as the greatest deliberative body in the world. But recently that deliberative character has too often been debased to the level of a forum of hate and character assassination sheltered by the shield of congressional immunity.

It is ironical that we Senators can in debate in the Senate directly or indirectly, by any form of words impute to any American, who is not a Senator, any conduct or motive unworthy or unbecoming an American—and without that non-Senator American having any legal redress against us—yet if we say the same thing in the Senate about our colleagues we can be stopped on the grounds of being out of order.

It is strange that we can verbally attack anyone else without restraint and with full protection and yet we hold ourselves above the same type of criticism here on the Senate Floor. Surely the United States Senate is big enough to take self-criticism and self-appraisal. Surely we should be able to take the same kind of character attacks that we dish out to outsiders.

I think that it is high time for the United States Senate and its members to do some soul searching—for us to weigh our consciences—on the manner in which we are performing our duty to the people of America—on the manner in which we are using or abusing our individual powers and privileges.

I think that it is high time that we remembered that we have sworn to uphold and defend the Constitution. I think that it is high time that we remembered; that the Constitution, as amended, speaks not only of the freedom of speech but also of trial by jury instead of trial by accusation.

Whether it be a criminal prosecution in court or a character prosecution in the Senate, there is little practical distinction when the life of a person has been ruined.

Those of us who shout the loudest about Americanism in making character assassinations are all too frequently those who, by our own words and acts, ignore some of the basic principles of Americanism—

The right to criticize;
The right to hold unpopular beliefs;
The right to protest;
The right of independent thought.

The exercise of these rights should not cost one single American citizen his reputation or his right to a livelihood nor should he be in danger of losing his reputation or livelihood merely because he happens to know some one who holds unpopular beliefs. Who of us doesn't? Otherwise none of us could call our souls our own. Otherwise thought control would have set in.

The American people are sick and tired of being afraid to speak their minds lest they be politically smeared as "Communists" or "Fascists" by their opponents. Freedom of speech is not what it used to be in America. It has been so abused by some that it is not exercised by others. The American people are sick and tired of seeing innocent people smeared and guilty people whitewashed. But there have been enough proved cases to cause nationwide distrust and strong suspicion that there may be something to the unproved, sensational accusations.

As a Republican, I say to my colleagues on this side of the aisle that the Republican Party faces a challenge today that is not unlike the challenge that it faced back in Lincoln's day. The Republican Party so successfully met that challenge that it emerged from the Civil War as the champion of a united nation—in addition to being a Party that unrelentingly fought loose spending and loose programs.

Today our country is being psychologically divided by the confusion and the suspicions that are bred in the United States Senate to spread like cancerous tentacles of "know nothing, suspect everything" attitudes. Today we have a Democratic Administration that has developed a mania for loose spending and loose programs. History is repeating itself—and the Republican Party again has the opportunity to emerge as the champion of unity and prudence.

The record of the present Democratic Administration has provided us with sufficient campaign issues without the necessity of resorting to political smears. America is rapidly losing its position as leader of the world simply because the Democratic Administration has pitifully failed to provide effective leadership.

The Democratic Administration has completely confused the American people by its daily contradictory grave warnings and optimistic assurances— that show the people that our Democratic Administration has no idea of where it is going.

The Democratic Administration has greatly lost the confidence of the American people by its complacency to the threat of communism here at home and the leak of vital secrets to Russia through key officials of the Democratic Administration. There are enough proved cases to make this point without diluting our criticism with unproved charges.

Surely these are sufficient reasons to make it clear to the American people that it is time for a change and that a Republican victory is necessary to the security of this country. Surely it is clear that this nation will continue to suffer as long as it is governed by the present ineffective Democratic Administration.

Yet to displace it with a Republican regime embracing a philosophy that lacks political integrity or intellectual honesty would prove equally disastrous to this nation. The nation sorely needs a Republican victory. But I don't want to see the Republican Party ride to political victory on the Four Horsemen of Calumny—Fear, Ignorance, Bigotry and Smear.

I doubt if the Republican Party could—simply because I don't believe the American people will uphold any political party that puts political exploitation above national interest. Surely we Republicans aren't that desperate for victory.

I don't want to see the Republican Party win that way. While it might be a fleeting victory for the Republican Party, it would be a more lasting defeat for the American people. Surely it would ultimately be suicide for the Republican Party and the two-party system that has protected our American liberties from the dictatorship of a one party system.

As members of the Minority Party, we do not have the primary authority to formulate the policy of our Government. But we do have the responsibility of rendering constructive criticism, of clarifying issues, of allaying fears by acting as responsible citizens.

As a woman, I wonder how the mothers, wives, sisters and daughters feel about the way in which members of their families have been politically mangled in Senate debate—and I use the word "debate" advisedly.

As a United States Senator, I am not proud of the way in which the Senate has been made a publicity platform for irresponsible sensationalism. I am not proud of the reckless abandon in which unproved charges have been hurled from this side of the aisle. I am not proud of the obviously staged, undignified countercharges that have been attempted in retaliation from the other side of the aisle.

I don't like the way the Senate has been made a rendezvous for vilification, for selfish political gain at the sacrifice of individual reputations and national unity. I am not proud of the way we smear outsiders from the Floor of the Senate and hide behind the cloak of congressional immunity and still place ourselves beyond criticism on the Floor of the Senate.

As an American, I am shocked at the way Republicans and Democrats alike are playing directly into the Communist design of "confuse, divide and conquer." As an American, I don't want a Democratic Administration "white wash" or "cover up" any more than I want a Republican smear or witch hunt.

As an American, I condemn a Republican "Fascist" just as much as I condemn a Democrat "Communist." I condemn a Democrat "Fascist" just as much as I condemn a Republican "Communist." They are equally dangerous to you and me and to our country. As an American, I want to see our nation recapture the strength and unity it once had when we fought the enemy instead of ourselves.

It is with these thoughts I have drafted what I call a "Declaration of Conscience." I am gratified that Senator Tobey, Senator Aiken, Senator Morse, Senator Ives, Senator Thye and Senator Hendrickson, have concurred in that declaration and have authorized me to announce their concurrence.

STATEMENT OF THE SEVEN REPUBLICAN SENATORS; 1950

1. We are Republicans. But we are Americans first. It is as Americans that we express our concern with the growing confusion that threatens the security and stability of our country. Democrats and Republicans alike have contributed to that confusion.

2. The Democratic administration has initially created the confusion by its lack of effective leadership, by its contradictory grave warnings and optimistic assurances, by its complacency to the threat of communism here at home, by its oversensitiveness to rightful criticism, by its petty bitterness against its critics.

3. Certain elements of the Republican Party have materially added to this confusion in the hopes of riding the Republican party to victory through the selfish political exploitation of fear, bigotry, ignorance, and intolerance. There are enough mistakes of the Democrats for Republicans to criticize constructively without resorting to political smears.

4. To this extent, Democrats and Republicans alike have unwittingly, but undeniably, played directly into the Communist design of "confuse, divide and conquer."

5. It is high time that we stopped thinking politically as Republicans and Democrats about elections and started thinking patriotically as Americans about national security based on individual freedom. It is high time that we all stopped being tools and victims of totalitarian techniques—techniques that, if continued here unchecked, will surely end what we have come to cherish as the American way of life.

Singer and actor Paul Robeson testifying before the House Committee on Un-American Activities, June 13, 1956.   "You ought to be ashamed of yourselves," he exclaimed when he accused members of the Committee of being un-American and unpatriotic.

Paul Robeson (1898–1976)

When the distinguished African American actor and concert singer Paul Robeson visited the Soviet Union in the 1930s, he was so impressed by the unprejudiced treatment he received that he became convinced that a communist society was more egalitarian and less racist than the democratic society of the United States. By the time he returned home, he had embraced communist ideology and had begun promoting communism as well as actively protesting against racism. In 1949, he advised African

Americans not to fight in an "imperialist war" if the United States should go to war against the Soviet Union. As a result, Robeson was investigated by the House Committee on Un-American Activities, and his passport was revoked. Members of the committee browbeat Robeson in an effort to get him to admit that he was a member of the Communist Party, but Robeson repeatedly invoked the Fifth Amendment.

Testimony Before the House Committee on Un-American Activities, June 12, 1956

THE CHAIRMAN: The Committee will be in order. This morning the Committee resumes its series of hearings on the vital issue of the use of American passports as travel documents in furtherance of the objectives of the Communist conspiracy. . . .

MR. ARENS: Now, during the course of the process in which you were applying for this passport, in July of 1954, were you requested to submit a non-Communist affidavit?

MR. ROBESON: We had a long discussion—with my counsel, who is in the room, Mr. [Leonard B.] Boudin—with the State Department, about just such an affidavit and I was very precise not only in the application but with the State Department, headed by Mr. Henderson and Mr. McLeod, that under no conditions would I think of signing any such affidavit, that it is a complete contradiction of the rights of American citizens.

MR. ARENS: Did you comply with the requests?

MR. ROBESON: I certainly did not and I will not.

MR. ARENS: Are you now a member of the Communist Party?

MR. ROBESON: Oh please, please, please.

MR. SCHERER: Please answer, will you, Mr. Robeson?

MR. ROBESON: What is the Communist Party? What do you mean by that?

MR. SCHERER: I ask that you direct the witness to answer the question.

MR. ROBESON: What do you mean by the Communist Party? As far as I know it is a legal party like the Republican Party and the Democratic Party. Do you mean a party of people who have sacrificed for my people, and for all Americans and workers, that they can live in dignity? Do you mean that party?

MR. ARENS: Are you now a member of the Communist Party?

MR. ROBESON: Would you like to come to the ballot box when I vote and take out the ballot and see?

MR. ARENS: Mr. Chairman, I respectfully suggest that the witness be ordered and directed to answer that question.

SOURCE: Congress, House, Committee on Un-American Activities, *Investigation of the Unauthorized Use of U.S. Passports*, 84th Congress, Part 3, June 12, 1956; in *Thirty Years of Treason: Excerpts from Hearings Before the House Committee on Un-American Activities, 1938–1968*, Eric Bentley, ed. (New York: Viking Press, 1971), 770.

THE CHAIRMAN: You are directed to answer the question.

(*The witness consulted with his counsel.*)

MR. ROBESON: I stand upon the Fifth Amendment of the American Constitution.

MR. ARENS: Do you mean you invoke the Fifth Amendment?

MR. ROBESON: I invoke the Fifth Amendment.

MR. ARENS: Do you honestly apprehend that if you told this Committee truthfully—

MR. ROBESON: I have no desire to consider anything. I invoke the Fifth Amendment, and it is none of your business what I would like to do, and I invoke the Fifth Amendment. And forget it.

THE CHAIRMAN: You are directed to answer that question.

MR. ROBESON: I invoke the Fifth Amendment, and so I am answering it, am I not?

MR. ARENS: I respectfully suggest the witness be ordered and directed to answer the question as to whether or not he honestly apprehends, that if he gave us a truthful answer to this last principal question, he would be supplying information which might be used against him in a criminal proceeding.

(*The witness consulted with his counsel.*)

THE CHAIRMAN: You are directed to answer that question, Mr. Robeson.

MR. ROBESON: Gentlemen, in the first place, wherever I have been in the world, Scandinavia, England, and many places, the first to die in the struggle against Fascism were the Communists and I laid many wreaths upon graves of Communists. It is not criminal, and the Fifth Amendment has nothing to do with criminality. The Chief Justice of the Supreme Court, Warren, has been very clear on that in many speeches, that the Fifth Amendment does not have anything to do with the inference of criminality. I invoke the Fifth Amendment.

MR. ARENS: Have you ever been known under the name of "John Thomas"?

MR. ROBESON: Oh, please, does somebody here want—are you suggesting—do you want me to be put up for perjury some place? "John Thomas"! My name is Paul Robeson, and anything I have to say, or stand for, I have said in public all over the world, and that is why I am here today.

MR. SCHERER: I ask that you direct the witness to answer the question. He is making a speech.

MR. FRIEDMAN: Excuse me, Mr. Arens, may we have the photographers take their pictures, and then desist, because it is rather nerve-racking for them to be there.

THE CHAIRMAN: They will take the pictures.

MR. ROBESON: I am used to it and I have been in moving pictures. Do you want me to pose for it good? Do you want me to smile? I cannot smile when I am talking to him.

MR. ARENS: I put it to you as a fact, and ask you to affirm or deny the fact, that your Communist Party name was "John Thomas."

MR. ROBESON: I invoke the Fifth Amendment. This is really ridiculous.

MR. ARENS: Now, tell this Committee whether or not you know Nathan Gregory Silvermaster.

MR. SCHERER: Mr. Chairman, this is not a laughing matter.

MR. ROBESON: It is a laughing matter to me, this is really complete nonsense.

MR. ARENS: Have you ever known Nathan Gregory Silvermaster?

(*The witness consulted with his counsel.*)

MR. ROBESON: I invoke the Fifth Amendment.

MR. ARENS: Do you honestly apprehend that if you told whether you know Nathan Gregory Silvermaster you would be supplying information that could be used against you in a criminal proceeding?

MR. ROBESON: I have not the slightest idea what you are talking about. I invoke the Fifth—

MR. ARENS: I suggest, Mr. Chairman, that the witness be directed to answer that question.

THE CHAIRMAN: You are directed to answer the question.

MR. ROBESON: I invoke the Fifth.

MR. SCHERER: The witness talks very loud when he makes a speech, but when he invokes the Fifth Amendment I cannot hear him.

MR. ROBESON: I invoked the Fifth Amendment very loudly. You know I am an actor, and I have medals for diction.

. . .

MR. ROBESON: Oh, gentlemen, I thought I was here about some passports.

MR. ARENS: We will get into that in just a few moments.

MR. ROBESON: This is complete nonsense.

. . .

THE CHAIRMAN: This is legal. This is not only legal but usual. By a unanimous vote, this Committee has been instructed to perform this very distasteful task.

MR. ROBESON: To whom am I talking?

THE CHAIRMAN: You are speaking to the Chairman of this Committee.

MR. ROBESON: Mr. Walter?

THE CHAIRMAN: Yes.

MR. ROBESON: The Pennsylvania Walter?

THE CHAIRMAN: That is right.

MR. ROBESON: Representative of the steelworkers?

THE CHAIRMAN: That is right.

MR. ROBESON: Of the coal-mining workers and not United States Steel, by any chance? A great patriot.

THE CHAIRMAN: That is right.

MR. ROBESON: You are the author of all of the bills that are going to keep all kinds of decent people out of the country.

THE CHAIRMAN: No, only your kind.

MR. ROBESON: Colored people like myself, from the West Indies and all kinds. And just the Teutonic Anglo-Saxon stock that you would let come in.

THE CHAIRMAN: We are trying to make it easier to get rid of your kind, too.

MR. ROBESON: You do not want any colored people to come in?

THE CHAIRMAN: Proceed. . . .

MR. ROBESON: Could I say that the reason that I am here today, you know, from the mouth of the State Department itself, is: I should not be allowed to travel because I have struggled for years for the independence of the colonial peoples of Africa. For many years I have so labored and I can say modestly that my name is very much honored all over Africa, in my struggles for their independence. That is the kind of independence like Sukarno got in Indonesia. Unless we are double-talking, then these efforts in the interest of Africa would be in the same context. The other reason that I am here today, again from the State Department and from the court record of the court of appeals, is that when I am abroad I speak out against the injustices against the Negro people of this land. I sent a message to the Bandung Conference and so forth. That is why I am here. This is the basis, and I am not being tried for whether I am a Communist, I am being tried for fighting for the rights of my people, who are still second-class citizens in this United States of America. My mother was born in your state, Mr. Walter, and my mother was a Quaker, and my ancestors in the time of Washington baked bread for George Washington's troops when they crossed the Delaware, and my own father was a slave. I stand here struggling for the rights of my people to be full citizens in this country. And they are not. They are not in Mississippi. And they are not in Montgomery, Alabama. And they are not in Washington. They are nowhere, and that is why I am here today. You want to shut up every Negro who has the courage to stand up and fight for the rights of his people, for the rights of workers, and I have been on many a picket line for the steelworkers too. And that is why I am here today. . . .

MR. ARENS: Did you make a trip to Europe in 1949 and to the Soviet Union?

MR. ROBESON: Yes, I made a trip. To England. And I sang.

MR. ARENS: Where did you go?

MR. ROBESON: I went first to England, where I was with the Philadelphia Orchestra, one of two American groups which was invited to England. I did a long concert tour in England and Denmark and Sweden, and I also sang for the Soviet people, one of the finest musical audiences in the world. Will you read what the *Porgy and Bess* people said? They never heard such applause in their lives. One of the most musical peoples in the world, and the great composers and great musicians, very cultured people, and Tolstoy, and—

THE CHAIRMAN: We know all of that.

MR. ROBESON: They have helped our culture and we can learn a lot.

MR. ARENS: Did you go to Paris on that trip?

MR. ROBESON: I went to Paris.

MR. ARENS: And while you were in Paris, did you tell an audience there that the American Negro would never go to war against the Soviet government?

MR. ROBESON: May I say that is slightly out of context? May I explain to you what I did say? I remember the speech very well, and the night before, in London, and do not take the newspaper, take me: I made the speech, gentlemen, Mr. So-and-So. It happened that the night before, in London, before I went to Paris . . . and will you please listen?

Mr. Arens: We are listening.

Mr. Robeson: Two thousand students from various parts of the colonial world, students who since then have become very important in their governments, in places like Indonesia and India, and in many parts of Africa, two thousand students asked me and Mr. [Dr. Y. M.] Dadoo, a leader of the Indian people in South Africa, when we addressed this conference, and remember I was speaking to a peace conference, they asked me and Mr. Dadoo to say there that they were struggling for peace, that they did not want war against anybody. Two thousand students who came from populations that would range to six or seven hundred million people.

Mr. Kearney: Do you know anybody who wants war?

Mr. Robeson: They asked me to say in their name that they did not want war. That is what I said. No part of my speech made in Paris says fifteen million American Negroes would do anything. I said it was my feeling that the American people would struggle for peace, and that has since been underscored by the President of these United States. Now, in passing, I said—

Mr. Kearney: Do you know of any people who want war?

Mr. Robeson: Listen to me. I said it was unthinkable to me that any people would take up arms, in the name of an Eastland, to go against anybody. Gentlemen, I still say that. This United States Government should go down to Mississippi and protect my people. That is what should happen.

The Chairman: Did you say what was attributed to you?

Mr. Robeson: I did not say it in that context.

Mr. Arens: I lay before you a document containing an article, "I Am Looking for Full Freedom," by Paul Robeson, in a publication called the *Worker*, dated July 3, 1949. "At the Paris Conference I said it was unthinkable that the Negro people of America or elsewhere in the world could be drawn into war with the Soviet Union."

Mr. Robeson: Is that saying the Negro people would *do* anything? I said it is unthinkable. I did not say that there [in Paris]: I said that in the *Worker*.

Mr. Arens: "I repeat it with hundredfold emphasis: they will not." Did you say that?

Mr. Robeson: I did not say that in Paris, I said that in America. And, gentlemen, they have not yet done so, and it is quite clear that no Americans, no people in the world probably, are going to war with the Soviet Union. So I was rather prophetic, was I not?

Mr. Arens: On that trip to Europe, did you go to Stockholm?

Mr. Robeson: I certainly did, and I understand that some people in the American Embassy tried to break up my concert. They were not successful.

Mr. Arens: While you were in Stockholm, did you make a little speech?

Mr. Robeson: I made all kinds of speeches, yes.

Mr. Arens: Let me read you a quotation.

Mr. Robeson: Let me listen.

Mr. Arens: Do so, please.

MR. ROBESON: I am a lawyer.

MR. KEARNEY: It would be a revelation if you would listen to counsel.

MR. ROBESON: In good company, I usually listen, but you know people wander around in such fancy places. Would you please let me read my statement at some point?

THE CHAIRMAN: We will consider your statement.

MR. ARENS: "I do not hesitate one second to state clearly and unmistakably: I belong to the American resistance movement which fights against American imperialism, just as the resistance movement fought against Hitler."

MR. ROBESON: Just like Frederick Douglass and Harriet Tubman were underground railroaders, and fighting for our freedom, you bet your life.

THE CHAIRMAN: I am going to have to insist that you listen to these questions.

MR. ROBESON: I am listening.

MR. ARENS: "If the American warmongers fancy that they could win America's millions of Negroes for a war against those countries (i.e., the Soviet Union and the peoples' democracies) then they ought to understand that this will never be the case. Why should the Negroes ever fight against the only nations of the world where racial discrimination is prohibited, and where the people can live freely? Never! I can assure you, they will never fight against either the Soviet Union or the peoples' democracies." Did you make that statement?

MR. ROBESON: I do not remember that. But what is perfectly clear today is that nine hundred million other colored people have told you that *they* will not. Four hundred million in India, and millions everywhere, have told you, precisely, that the colored people are not going to die for anybody: they are going to die for their independence. We are dealing not with fifteen million colored people, we are dealing with hundreds of millions.

MR. KEARNEY: The witness has answered the question and he does not have to make a speech. . . .

MR. ROBESON: In Russia I felt for the first time like a full human being. No color prejudice like in Mississippi, no color prejudice like in Washington. It was the first time I felt like a human being. Where I did not feel the pressure of color as I feel [it] in this Committee today.

MR. SCHERER: Why do you not stay in Russia?

MR. ROBESON: Because my father was a slave, and my people died to build this country, and I am going to stay here, and have a part of it just like you. And no Fascist-minded people will drive me from it. Is that clear? I am for peace with the Soviet Union, and I am for peace with China, and I am not for peace or friendship with the Fascist Franco, and I am not for peace with Fascist Nazi Germans. I am for peace with decent people.

MR. SCHERER: You are here because you are promoting the Communist cause.

MR. ROBESON: I am here because I am opposing the neo-Fascist cause which I see arising in these committees. You are like the Alien [and] Sedition Act, and Jefferson could be sitting here, and Frederick Douglass could be sitting here, and Eugene Debs could be here.

. . .

THE CHAIRMAN: Now, what prejudice are you talking about? You were graduated from Rutgers and you were graduated from the University of Pennsylvania. I remember seeing you play football at Lehigh.

MR. ROBESON: We beat Lehigh.

THE CHAIRMAN: And we had a lot of trouble with you.

MR. ROBESON: That is right. DeWysocki was playing in my team.

THE CHAIRMAN: There was no prejudice against you. Why did you not send your son to Rutgers?

MR. ROBESON: Just a moment. This is something that I challenge very deeply, and very sincerely: that the success of a few Negroes, including myself or Jackie Robinson can make up—and here is a study from Columbia University—for seven hundred dollars a year for thousands of Negro families in the South. My father was a slave, and I have cousins who are sharecroppers, and I do not see my success in terms of myself. That is the reason my own success has not meant what it should mean: I have sacrificed literally hundreds of thousands, if not millions, of dollars for what I believe in.

MR. ARENS: While you were in Moscow, did you make a speech lauding Stalin?

MR. ROBESON: I do not know.

MR. ARENS: Did you say, in effect, that Stalin was a great man, and Stalin had done much for the Russian people, for all of the nations of the world, for all working people of the earth? Did you say something to that effect about Stalin when you were in Moscow?

MR. ROBESON: I cannot remember.

MR. ARENS: Do you have a recollection of praising Stalin?

MR. ROBESON: I said a lot about Soviet people, fighting for the peoples of the earth.

MR. ARENS: Did you praise Stalin?

MR. ROBESON: I do not remember.

MR. ARENS: Have you recently changed your mind about Stalin?

MR. ROBESON: Whatever has happened to Stalin, gentlemen, is a question for the Soviet Union, and I would not argue with a representative of the people who, in building America, wasted sixty to a hundred million lives of my people, black people drawn from Africa on the plantations. You are responsible, and your forebears, for sixty million to one hundred million black people dying in the slave ships and on the plantations, and don't ask me about anybody, please.

MR. ARENS: I am glad you called our attention to that slave problem. While you were in Soviet Russia, did you ask them there to show you the slave labor camps?

THE CHAIRMAN: You have been so greatly interested in slaves, I should think that you would want to see that.

MR. ROBESON: The slaves I see are still in a kind of semiserfdom. I am interested in the place I am, and in the country that can do something about it. As far as I know, about the slave camps, they were Fascist prisoners who had murdered millions of the Jewish people, and who would have wiped out millions of the Negro people, could they have gotten a hold of them. That is all I know about that.

MR. ARENS: Tell us whether or not you have changed your opinion in the recent past about Stalin.

MR. ROBESON: I have told you, mister, that I would not discuss anything with the people who have murdered sixty million of my people, and I will not discuss Stalin with you.

MR. ARENS: You would not, of course, discuss with us the slave labor camps in Soviet Russia.

MR. ROBESON: I will discuss Stalin when I may be among the Russian people some day, singing for them, I will discuss it there. It is their problem. . . .

MR. ARENS: Now I would invite your attention, if you please, to the *Daily Worker* of June 29, 1949, with reference to a get-together with you and Ben Davis. Do you know Ben Davis?

MR. ROBESON: One of my dearest friends, one of the finest Americans you can imagine, born of a fine family, who went to Amherst and was a great man.

THE CHAIRMAN: The answer is yes?

MR. ROBESON: Nothing could make me prouder than to know him.

THE CHAIRMAN: That answers the question.

MR. ARENS: Did I understand you to laud his patriotism?

MR. ROBESON: I say that he is as patriotic an American as there can be, and you gentlemen belong with the Alien and Sedition Acts, and you are the nonpatriots, and you are the un-Americans, and you ought to be ashamed of yourselves.

THE CHAIRMAN: Just a minute, the hearing is now adjourned.

MR. ROBESON: I should think it would be.

THE CHAIRMAN: I have endured all of this that I can.

MR. ROBESON: Can I read my statement?

THE CHAIRMAN: No, you cannot read it. The meeting is adjourned.

MR. ROBESON: I think it should be, and you should adjourn this forever, that is what I would say. . . .

Harry Hay (1912–2002)

Harry Hay is considered by many to be the founder of the modern gay movement in the United States. He was active in progressive politics for many years, promoted trade unionism in the 1930s and 1940s, was associated with radical songwriters Woody Guthrie and Pete Seeger, and joined the Communist Party (which resulted in his being interrogated by the House Committee on Un-American Activities in 1955). Calling for others of the "androgynous minority" to form a political organization,

*he founded Bachelors Anonymous primarily to promote the 1948
presidential campaign of Progressive Party candidate Henry Wallace. In
1950, he founded the Mattachine Society in California, which was the
first state organization designed to promote gay rights. Although the
oppressive homophobia of the 1950s compelled the Mattachine Society
to be a secret organization, it rapidly expanded by forming chapters
in many cities throughout the nation. Because of his communist
affiliation, however, Hay became a liability to the Mattachine Society,
and he wound up leaving the organization. Ironically, because of his
homosexuality, he was also booted out of the Communist Party. In 1969,
when the Stonewall riots spawned the more radical gay civil rights
movement of the 1970s, it was Hay's Mattachine Society and its sister
organization, the lesbian Daughters of Bilitis (founded in San Francisco
in 1955), that provided examples on which other gay organizations could
model themselves. In 1979, he was a founder of the Radical Faeries, which
advocated that gays should stress the differences between themselves and
heterosexuals because, as Hay believed, the alternative gay perception of
the world enabled them to offer a new range of insights and responses that
could help solve society's problems. Hay opposed the view that many other
gay rights activists held, that gays were just like everyone else and should
therefore be assimilated into American society. Instead, he proclaimed
that gays and lesbians were a distinct minority and should be treated as
such. He believed that gay activists should not be merely concerned with
electing gay politicians to office but should be more concerned about
changing the basic structure of a consumerist society that systematically
treated all people as objects and as a result demeaned the human spirit.
He did not want gays to be assimilated into such a society but instead
aimed to create a more humane society that was not controlled by
corporate industrialism. In 1990, Hay reflected on the historical
background of the gay movement in a speech he gave at the Gay Spirit
Visions Conference in Highlands, North Carolina.*

Speech at the Gay Spirit Visions Conference, Highlands, North Carolina, November 1990

"Where have we been and where are we now?" is an interesting topic because it is
one of the places where my head is at the moment. One of the places in my
Consciousness where my preparations for the two addresses I made at the university this week took me, has made me realize that we—as a distinct biologically

Source: Retrieved on 12/18/2003 from www.geocities.com/WestHollywood/Heights/5347/
gsv.html. For more on Hay, see Harry Hay and Will Roscoe, *Radically Gay: Gay Liberation in
the Words of Its Founder* (Boston: Beacon Press, 1997).

determined human variant—have been developing our own collection of Gay Consciousness (by inventing it as we went along) for a long, long, long time. Maybe for as far back as when Species Homo began to emerge as hominids.

Taking the liberty of citing Sir Julian Huxley, the great biologist of the century, who said, "No negative trait" (and as you know, a negative trait in biology is one which does not reproduce itself) "appears in a given species millennia after millennia after millennia unless it in some way insures the survival of that species." (Parenthetically, we should hardly be expecting that the heteros have been hastening to discover how we Queers are about to insure THEIR survival. If anyone's going to discover it, it obviously is going to have to be US!). . . .

One of the most obvious observations might be how often, at not only previous Faerie gatherings but even at the planning sessions for this one, that it is our Faerie collective inclination to be functioning by consensus—to reflect on how it really is, for us, rather distasteful to engage in the endless bickering and to placate ego-posturings in the give-and-take of so-called democratic procedures. Recognizing—in a rush—those of us here tonight who were at the First Radical Faerie gathering eleven years ago in 1979, that the galvanizing revelation that overtook us all on that occasion was the instant centrifugal rush by which we all realized how we had been longing (maybe all our lives hitherto) to connect in a circular celebration of our Faerie inclination to loving, sharing, consensual interaction with one another. For me, this has always been intensely interesting and important, because that was exactly the way it was with the first discussion groups first coming together in my first Mattachine Society 40 years ago. That same breathless, nameless excitement, as though it was something we'd always known, something that must have happened long ago of which we were a part. And now it was about to happen again. . . .

[P]erhaps the most important thing encompassed by my Mattachine Society was that for the first time in American homosexual experience our guild brotherhoods developed BEING GAY into a POSITIVE SELF-LOVING identity. Up until then, we had been only perverted heteros—EVEN IN OUR OWN EYES. According to every known social REFERENT, we were heteros who occasionally degraded ourselves through degenerate behavior. The best that I would hear in the 1930s was that maybe I, someday, would discover words which could explain to heteros just how beautiful our deviant voices and visions really were. But that we might be a different people altogether wouldn't be a concept until the 1970s. Although sometimes I'd wonder if, in the ballads of Thomas the Rhymer, I wasn't hearing of the Faerie People as being a different race.

In 1969, the Stonewall Rebellion exploded. The powder-train which my Mattachine . . . had been laying across the country in the 60's took off like a barrage of Roman candles. The "I" in the positive Gay identity changed to "WE," and suddenly from everywhere Gay Brothers and Sisters were on the march, making the first lap of that social and political change which had always been implicit in the original dream of Mattachine—the vision of a social, minority who had contributions to share. At this point I need to point out the huge difference between the American Gay Movement and all the movements that came previously in

Europe, as well as those which still exist in Europe. The Mattachine Society, as I conceived it, and all the others who have developed subsequently, have been perceived as politically-based, so that we all have continually perceived ourselves as being on the cutting edge of change. The European groups, of both the 19th and 20th centuries, have perceived themselves as "social" in orientation and therefore were and are concerned, not with political and social change, but with "accommodations" just as our middle-class "sell-out" assimilationists are now.

In the early '70s, the Gay and Lesbian Brothers and Sisters, exploding out of the Stonewall rage, screamed and hollered and zapped their way into the public media in ways never before experienced by the Gay Movement. But for all its rhetoric and thunder, and the political friends it was making in high places, the Movement remained essentially lily-white and middle-class. And hetero-imitative like you wouldn't believe. By 1978, the steam which had impelled the earlier zapping fury had mostly dissipated—apathy was everywhere in Gay and Lesbian land. The first Radical Faerie Gathering was a call to the Radical Brothers to see what all we might have developed and experienced since Stonewall. Also, I had this wonderful vision about a new type of consciousness which I felt we had been carrying with us down through the millennia, waiting for that time when the hetero "subject-object" way of growing and developing would be obsolete, and new directions would have to be taken if the race were to survive. The murderous nuclear competition between U.S. Imperialism and Soviet Imperialism had become so lethal that the fate of the planet seemed at stake. I felt that those Gay Brothers who could share my new vision of what I was calling "subject-subject" consciousness, might be able to begin to learn to turn the tide.

This is what we've been experimenting with for these last ten years. Radical Faerie experience has spread across this country and Canada. It has made its way to Australia and New Zealand, and in the last several years it has spread into England, Scotland and Ireland, with occasional echoes in Scandinavia. The most immediate result of our work has been in the conscious encouragement of the use of the loving-sharing consensus. Our occasional impatiences that our subject-subject way of perceiving, and our work in the loving-sharing consensus, does not spread as fast and as far as our impatience does is political naïveté. The hetero-male subject-object mind set is supported by the hierarchical dominant-male competition by which men developed the incentives needed to spur themselves to achievement. It was, of course, the social process par excellence whereby the hominid strain, having devised as yet ONLY an oral culture was able to train all its offspring and so remember EVERYTHING discovered by the ancestors because anything forgotten is lost forever. . . .

In the two million years during which our hominid ancestors were slowly evolving, our planet was also evolving in terms of its spherically volcanic nature. When cracks and crevices in the walls of a given social climate permitted, when a given culture required new solutions which the hetero ice-age originating MIND-SET couldn't assess, the phylogenetically inherited potentials to perceive and invent (what we today recognize as Gay Consciousness) have indeed appeared. They appeared briefly and brilliantly at given junctures in history: in Ancient

Imperial China for three or four hundred years; in the great Songhai educational center of the Western Sudan for a century; or on a Chimu village pot whose myth stretches back into the mist. Each of these episodes is, in turn, followed by long ages of blank—ages not so much of silence as of VOID! And yet, WE WERE THERE! Silenced, muzzled, driven out of villages and towns again and again and again in myth and story; burned at stakes and in wicker baskets, and giggling at some hysterical absurdity even as the flames began to leap; drowned face down in bogs; obliterated by being thrown off cliffs. Yet we continued to appear in this generation or that, as though to assure the cosmos we were still a viable syndrome in the hominid biological make-up. Remember my earlier quotation from Sir Julian Huxley, "No negative trait appears in a given species millennia after millennia after millennia unless it in some way contributes to the survival or that species?"

... John (Burnside) and I felt in the late '70s that the obsession of the Harvard sociobiologists to find THE gene which makes us all Queer was much too simplistic. We felt that the ongoing discoveries on the brain's several hemispheres, and its mysterious intercameral connections, were marking not only new territories to be perceived, but new dimensions of territoriality to be perceived. We felt that all the new and exciting discoveries in Ethnology—the recognitions of Lorenz and Tinberggen and Fox and Morris and others—indicated that in our own phylogenetic inheritances we would have received many of the traits we would need for survival, and for learning to adapt to what had earlier been threatening and alien. We would have acquired that which—in the course of evolutionary development, reassembled in consciousness—would be the one new dimension Humans had evolved through natural selection. It would be only natural to call upon the newer disciplines—Ethnology or Sociobiology—to supply new models by which to encompass it.

We proposed Gay Consciousness needed to be perceived as a syndrome, a sheaf of hundreds of traits inherited from ancestors weaving together in hominid psychosexual natures so as to develop, in a small percentage of humans, what is known in physics and chemistry as "the critical mass." This biologically inherited, as well as phylogenetically inherited, "critical mass" in turn precipitates out a separate strain of people, a mutant strain of people psychically as well as emotionally different enough from their Parent Society. A strain that could devise ways of being totally self-reliant in situations where the Parent Society—as presently constituted—couldn't survive. The psychic and emotional differences of these Separate People had combined to create a spiritual difference and the key to their new dimensions of vision was their lovely deviant sexuality. . . .

Meantime, for us Radical Faeries here and now, I would like to suggest that in our last eleven years we have, through our Country Gatherings and City Circles, been devising ways and means to cut through the many layers of guilt and shame our Parent Society has forced us to disguise our Separate and Deviant lives within. And now many of us are experiencing even newer pressures to begin releasing visions of memories of ancient discoveries in physical and spirit hearings which we were forced to silence and subvert and bury and pretend to forget in order for us to survive. Some of us feel we are occasionally visited by spatial blurs, things that seem to have sought crevices in past times and perhaps, were partially or even wholly denied. Last summer, for example, John and I began a sex magic ritual, brain storming workshop, (a week-long session as we envisioned it) that has been pressing on me to explore for many years. . . .

In these next few days, here at Highlands, a number of us have brought new Faerie Spirit Visions to share. I fervently pray that what we bring is pure Faerie in Spirit, and not reworked or warmed-over Hetero material garnished with a little glitter here and there. The Radical Faeries, and all Gay spirit-seeking groups, need to attempt to keep as pure and as untrammeled as possible those channels from our precious secrets that have been long guarded at the cost of lives if they are to now be brought into service as powerfully and as brilliantly as they have long deserved.

Allen Ginsberg.
Beat poet and social and political
critic Allen Ginsberg championed civil
rights; criticized the "split-level
American dream"; demonstrated
against the Vietnam War, nuclear
proliferation, and President Reagan's
Latin American policy; and protested
against a society that sought to
marginalize free spirits. "Are you
going to let your emotional life," he
asked drolly in his poem "America,"
"be run by Time *magazine?"*

Allen Ginsberg (1926–1997)

Allen Ginsberg was one of the most gifted and influential American poets
of the twentieth century. His influence, however, was not limited to poetry
and literature, for he was a deeply engaged social, cultural, and political
activist. He, along with Jack Kerouac, William Burroughs, Lawrence
Ferlinghetti, Gregory Corso, and others, were the focal points of the Beat
Movement that emerged in the 1950s in response to the stultifying,
suffocating conformity of the times. Decrying the "split-level American

dream," Beats called for a more honest, introspective morality. Ginsberg once declared in an interview that the Beats' response to the pervasive American values and morality of the 1950s was to discard the old morality and build a new one from scratch. "The generation that was responsible for the Holocaust and Hiroshima had no right to tell us what was moral. So we threw it all out." Ginsberg first achieved national prominence in 1955, when he performed his iconoclastic poem "Howl" at the Six Gallery in San Francisco. After City Lights Press published "Howl," the book was promptly banned and confiscated as obscene. The resulting court case wound up a publicity bonanza, and when the court ruled that "Howl" was indeed constitutionally protected "literature," everyone, it seemed, wanted to read it. Ginsberg's notoriety was assured, and his influence continued to be felt for the remainder of the 1950s, and in the early 1960s, he in a sense became the godfather of the emerging counterculture. Ginsberg's use of words and imagery had an influence on Bob Dylan's song lyrics; Ginsberg's advocacy of marijuana and peyote and his LSD experiments with Timothy Leary influenced millions of people to explore drugs as a means to self-discovery; Ginsberg's sojourn in India and his espousal of Buddhism offered an alternative philosophy to those Americans who were beginning to question the validity and relevance of Christianity and Judaism; Ginsberg's unconventional appearance and his unashamed open homosexuality encouraged many others to "do their own thing." Throughout the 1960s and 1970s Ginsberg, in his beard, long hair, and black-framed glasses was a highly visible figure at antiwar demonstrations in San Francisco, New York, Chicago, London, Prague, and many other cities.

In the 1970s, Ginsberg founded the Jack Kerouac School of Disembodied Poetics at the Naropa Institute in Boulder, Colorado. By the 1980s and 1990s he was an antinuclear protestor and unwaveringly continued his social activism right up to his death in 1997. "I want to be known," Ginsberg wrote in Ego Confessions in 1974, "as the most brilliant man in America . . . [As the man who] Prepared the way for Dharma in America without mentioning Dharma . . . distributed monies to poor poets & nourished imaginative genius of the land. Sat silent in jazz roar writing poetry with an ink pen—wasn't afraid of God or Death after his 48th year." In his 1956 poem "America," Ginsberg, with characteristic humor, takes on consumerism and the superficiality of American values.

"AMERICA," 1956

America I've given you all and now I'm nothing.
America two dollars and twenty-seven cents January 17, 1956.

SOURCE: Allen Ginsberg, *Howl and Other Poems* (San Francisco: City Lights Press, 1956), 31–34.

I can't stand my own mind.
America when will we end the human war?
Go fuck yourself with your atom bomb
I don't feel good don't bother me.
I won't write my poem till I'm in my right mind.
America when will you be angelic?
When will you take off your clothes?
When will you look at yourself through the grave?
When will you be worthy of your million Trotskyites?
America why are your libraries full of tears?
America when will you send your eggs to India?
I'm sick of your insane demands.
When can I go into the supermarket and buy what I need with my good looks?
America after all it is you and I who are perfect not the next world.
Your machinery is too much for me.
You made me want to be a saint.
There must be some other way to settle this argument.
Burroughs is in Tangiers I don't think he'll come back it's sinister.
Are you being sinister or is this some form of practical joke?
I'm trying to come to the point.
I refuse to give up my obsession.
America stop pushing I know what I'm doing.
America the plum blossoms are falling.
I haven't read the newspapers for months, everyday somebody goes on trial for
  murder.
America I feel sentimental about the Wobblies.
America I used to be a communist when I was a kid and I'm not sorry.
I smoke marijuana every chance I get.
I sit in my house for days on end and stare at the roses in the closet.
When I go to Chinatown I get drunk and never get laid.
My mind is made up there's going to be trouble.
You should have seen me reading Marx.
My psychoanalyst thinks I'm perfectly right.
I won't say the Lord's Prayer.
I have mystical visions and cosmic vibrations.
America I still haven't told you what you did to Uncle Max after he came over
  from Russia.
I'm addressing you.
Are you going to let your emotional life be run by Time *magazine?*
I'm obsessed by Time *magazine.*
I read it every week.
Its cover stares at me every time I slink past the corner candystore.
I read it in the basement of the Berkeley Public Library.
It's always telling me about responsibility. Businessmen are serious. Movie
  producers are serious. Everybody's serious but me.

It occurs to me that I am America.
I am talking to myself again.
Asia is rising against me.
I haven't got a chinaman's chance.
I'd better consider my national resources.
My national resources consist of two joints of marijuana millions of genitals
    an unpublishable private literature that goes 1400 miles an hour and
    twentyfivethousand mental institutions.
I say nothing about my prisons nor the millions of underpriviliged who live in
    my flowerpots under the light of five hundred suns.
I have abolished the whorehouses of France, Tangiers is the next to go.
My ambition is to be President despite the fact that I'm a Catholic.
America how can I write a holy litany in your silly mood?
I will continue like Henry Ford my strophes are as individual as his
    automobiles more so they're all different sexes
America I will sell you strophes $2500 apiece $500 down on your old strophe
America free Tom Mooney
America save the Spanish Loyalists
America Sacco & Vanzetti must not die
America I am the Scottsboro boys.
America when I was seven momma took me to Communist Cell meetings they
    sold us garbanzos a handful per ticket a ticket costs a nickel and the
    speeches were free everybody was angelic and sentimental about the
    workers it was all so sincere you have no idea what a good thing the party
    was in 1935 Scott Nearing was a grand old man a real mensch Mother
    Bloor made me cry I once saw Israel Amter plain. Everybody must have
    been a spy.
America you don't really want to go to war.
America it's them bad Russians.
Them Russians them Russians and them Chinamen. And them Russians.
The Russia wants to eat us alive. The Russia's power mad. She wants to take
    our cars from out our garages.
Her wants to grab Chicago. Her needs a Red Reader's Digest. Her wants
    our auto plants in Siberia. Him big bureaucracy running our
    fillingstations.
That no good. Ugh. Him makes Indians learn read. Him need big black
    niggers.
Hah. Her make us all work sixteen hours a day. Help.
America this is quite serious.
America this is the impression I get from looking in the television set.
America is this correct?
I'd better get right down to the job.
It's true I don't want to join the Army or turn lathes in precision parts
    factories, I'm nearsighted and psychopathic anyway.
America I'm putting my queer shoulder to the wheel.

Songs of the Civil Rights Movement

Songs that grow out of protests and demonstrations have a significant impact in two main ways. First, they get a message across, not only to those in power but also to those who are either unaware of the issue or have not yet made up their minds where they stand on it. A second and equally important effect the songs have is that they create a level of consciousness and solidarity among the demonstrators themselves. This was particularly true in the civil rights movement. A song like "We Shall Overcome," as sung by thousands of marchers during a demonstration, was a powerful galvanizer of unity and resolve. Daniel Wood was a student from Beloit College when he participated in the third Selma march in 1965. He remembers that as the demonstrators were crossing the Edmund Pettis Bridge leading out of Selma, they were singing "We Shall Overcome." When they noticed that the policemen lining the roadway were all armed with semiautomatic weapons trained on the marchers, the activists sang the "we are not afraid" verse of the song. As Wood puts it, "we were scared shitless, but still we sang it anyway!" Fortunately, no weapons were discharged, and the march proceeded toward Montgomery.

The civil rights movement embraced hundreds of songs. Some were adaptations of old slave songs; some were made up on the spot with lyrics referring to a town or a governor or a sheriff opposing the demonstrators; some were carefully crafted by popular musicians like Bob Dylan or Phil Ochs. There are rich resources on the Internet where you can read protest lyrics and even hear these songs.

The first two songs here emerged from civil rights demonstrations. "I Ain't Scared of Your Jail," as Pete Seeger explained during his June 1963 Carnegie Hall concert, was a spontaneous ditty that grew out of the Birmingham protests of the previous month. As the young people were beginning to march, Reverend King had told them that it was to be a silent demonstration that day, and that singing could begin only if arrests were made. This, indeed, did happen, and as the police moved in and began making arrests, the marchers all begin singing, "I ain't scared of your jail." The second song, "If You Miss Me at the Back of the Bus," refers to several events: the Montgomery bus boycott, the Freedom Rides, and voter registration drives. The last song is Bob Dylan's response to the assassination of Medgar Evers.

During an interview on German radio in 1988, Pete Seeger was asked: "Mr. Seeger can you change the world with a song?" "No," Seeger responded, "I can't change the world with a song. But if I write a song, and someone else designs a poster, and someone else gives a speech, and someone else organizes a teach-in, and someone else leads a demonstration, together we can change the world."

Pete Seeger, "I Ain't Scared of Your Jail," 1963

I ain't scared of your jail
Because I want my freedom,
I want my freedom,
I want my freedom.
I ain't scared of your jail
Because I want my freedom,
I want my freedom,
Now!

Carver Neblett, "If You Miss Me at the Back of the Bus," 1960

If you miss me at the back of the bus
You can't find me nowhere
Oh come on over to the front of the bus
I'll be riding up there
I'll be riding up there, I'll be riding up there
Oh come on over to the front of the bus
Because I'll be riding up there

If you miss me on the picket line
You can't find me nowhere
Come on over to the city jail
Because I'll be rooming over there
I'll be rooming over there
I'll be rooming over there oh
Come on over to the city jail
Because I'll be rooming over there

If you miss me at the Mississippi river
You can't find me nowhere
Come on over to the swimming pool
Because I'll be swimming over there
I'll be swimming over there, over there
I'll be swimming right there
Come on over to the swimming pool
Because I'll be swimming over there

If you miss me in the cotton fields
You can't find me nowhere

SOURCE: Pete Seeger, *We Shall Overcome: The Carnegie Hall Concert*, Columbia 1963.

Come on over to the voting booth
Because I'll be a voting right there
I'll be voting right there, right there
I'll be voting right there
Well come on over to the voting booth
Because I'll be voting right there

Bob Dylan, "Only a Pawn in Their Game," 1963

A bullet from the back of a bush took Medgar Evers' blood.
A finger fired the trigger to his name.
A handle hid out in the dark
A hand set the spark
Two eyes took the aim
Behind a man's brain
But he can't be blamed
He's only a pawn in their game.

A South politician preaches to the poor white man,
"You got more than the blacks, don't complain.
You're better than them, you been born with white skin," they explain.
And the Negro's name
Is used it is plain
For the politician's gain
As he rises to fame
And the poor white remains
On the caboose of the train
But it ain't him to blame
He's only a pawn in their game.

The deputy sheriffs, the soldiers, the governors get paid,
And the marshals and cops get the same,
But the poor white man's used in the hands of them all like a tool.
He's taught in his school
From the start by the rule
That the laws are with him
To protect his white skin
To keep up his hate
So he never thinks straight
'Bout the shape that he's in
But it ain't him to blame
He's only a pawn in their game.

Source: Bob Dylan, *The Times They Are A-Changin',* Columbia 1964.

From the poverty shacks, he looks from the cracks to the tracks,
And the hoof beats pound in his brain.
And he's taught how to walk in a pack
Shoot in the back
With his fist in a clinch
To hang and to lynch
To hide 'neath the hood
To kill with no pain
Like a dog on a chain
He ain't got no name
But it ain't him to blame
He's only a pawn in their game.

Today, Medgar Evers was buried from the bullet he caught.
They lowered him down as a king.
But when the shadowy sun sets on the one
That fired the gun
He'll see by his grave
On the stone that remains
Carved next to his name
His epitaph plain:
Only a pawn in their game.

Martin Luther King Jr. (1929–1968)

This icon of American history, recognized as one of the most influential and significant figures of the twentieth century, had a career on the public stage—from the beginning of the Montgomery bus boycott in December 1955 to his assassination in April 1968—that spanned less than 13 years.

Developing his own weltanschauung as he studied for the ministry, Martin Luther King Jr. drew his inspiration from many sources—from the teachings of Christ and the Social Gospel, from Locke, Jefferson, and Lincoln, from Henry David Thoreau, Mahatma Gandhi, Walter Rauschenbusch, and Reinhold Niebuhr. He first came to public attention during the 11-month Montgomery bus boycott. In 1957 he founded the Southern Christian Leadership Conference (SCLC), a grassroots civil rights organization whose membership consisted primarily of members of black congregations, as distinct from the earlier National Association for the Advancement of Colored People (NAACP), which had been founded by intellectuals and lawyers in order to overturn segregation through the legal system. After less than a decade of political activism, by 1963 (the centennial year of Lincoln's Emancipation Proclamation) King was

widely understood to be the leader of the civil rights movement. That year
he urged President Kennedy to issue a new emancipation proclamation
and to come out forcefully for civil rights, and he was deeply disappointed
when Kennedy, at first, did nothing.

In April 1963, King brought the movement to Birmingham—the
most segregated city in the South. The events that followed proved the
catalyst for finally convincing the president to use the power of the Oval
Office to guarantee civil rights for all Americans. Newsreel footage coming
out of Birmingham—of Police Chief Bull Connor's men loosing dogs on
the demonstrators, of the city's fire department hosing protestors with
enough force to roll them down the street—convinced many that
segregation had to go. These disturbing images made civil rights
supporters of people who had known virtually nothing about the plight of
African Americans. In a nationally televised address, President Kennedy
called civil rights a "moral issue as old as the scriptures" and declared
"race has no place in American society." He announced that he would
send a sweeping civil rights bill to Congress that would outlaw
segregation. This, of course, is what King and the movement had been
hoping to accomplish throughout their long campaign.

At one point during the Birmingham demonstrations, King was
arrested and jailed for eight days. Meanwhile, a group of white Alabama
ministers put an ad in the New York Times *condemning King as an*
"outside agitator" whose poorly timed campaign was itself the cause of
violence. King's eloquent reply, written in the margins of a newspaper and
on scraps of paper, is a persuasive statement of the necessity of nonviolent
direct action. Like Thoreau more than a century earlier, he argues that
while just laws must be obeyed, unjust laws must be broken.

LETTER FROM A BIRMINGHAM JAIL, APRIL 16, 1963

My Dear Fellow Clergymen:

While confined here in the Birmingham City Jail, I came across your recent
statement calling our present activities "unwise and untimely." Seldom, if ever,
do I pause to answer criticism of my work and ideas. If I sought to answer all the
criticisms that cross my desk, my secretaries would be engaged in little else in
the course of the day, and I would have no time for constructive work. But since
I feel that you are men of genuine goodwill and your criticisms are sincerely set
forth, I would like to answer your statement in what I hope will be patient and
reasonable terms.

I think I should give the reason for my being in Birmingham, since you have
been influenced by the argument of "outsiders coming in." I have the honor of

---

SOURCE: Martin Luther King Jr., *Why We Can't Wait* (New York: Mentor, 1963), 76–95.

Martin Luther King Jr.
"We have waited for more than three hundred and forty years," King wrote while incarcerated in Birmingham Jail in 1963, "for our constitutional and God-given rights. The nations of Asia and Africa are moving with jet-like speed toward the goal of political independence, and we still creep at horse and buggy pace toward the gaining of a cup of coffee at a lunch counter."

serving as president of the Southern Christian Leadership Conference, an organization operating in every Southern state, with headquarters in Atlanta, Georgia. We have some eighty-five affiliate organizations all across the South—one being the Alabama Christian Movement for Human Rights. Whenever necessary and possible we share staff, educational and financial resources with our affiliates. Several months ago our local affiliate here in Birmingham invited us to be on call to engage in a nonviolent direct action program if such were deemed necessary. We readily consented and when the hour came we lived up to our promises. So I am here, along with several members of my staff, because I have basic organizational ties here.

Beyond this, I am in Birmingham because injustice is here. Just as the eighth century prophets left their little villages and carried their "thus saith the Lord" far beyond the boundaries of their home towns; and just as the Apostle Paul left his little village of Tarsus and carried the gospel of Jesus Christ to practically every hamlet and city of the Graeco-Roman world, I too am compelled to carry the gospel of freedom beyond my particular home town. Like Paul, I must constantly respond to the Macedonian call for aid.

Moreover, I am cognizant of the interrelatedness of all communities and states. I cannot sit idly by in Atlanta and not be concerned about what happens in Birmingham. Injustice anywhere is a threat to justice everywhere. We are caught in an inescapable network of mutuality, tied in a single garment of destiny.

Whatever affects one directly affects all indirectly. Never again can we afford to live with the narrow, provincial "outside agitator" idea. Anyone who lives inside the United States can never be considered an outsider anywhere in this country.

You deplore the demonstrations that are presently taking place in Birmingham. But I am sorry that your statement did not express a similar concern for the conditions that brought the demonstrations into being. I am sure that each of you would want to go beyond the superficial social analyst who looks merely at effects, and does not grapple with underlying causes. I would not hesitate to say that it is unfortunate that so-called demonstrations are taking place in Birmingham at this time, but I would say in more emphatic terms that it is even more unfortunate that the white power structure of this city left the Negro community with no other alternative.

In any nonviolent campaign there are four basic steps: 1) Collection of the facts to determine whether injustices are alive. 2) Negotiation. 3) Self-purification and 4) Direct action. We have gone through all of these steps in Birmingham. There can be no gainsaying of the fact that racial injustice engulfs this community.

Birmingham is probably the most thoroughly segregated city in the United States. Its ugly record of police brutality is known in every section of this country. Its unjust treatment of Negroes in the courts is a notorious reality. There have been more unsolved bombings of Negro homes and churches in Birmingham than any city in this nation. These are the hard, brutal and unbelievable facts. On the basis of these conditions, Negro leaders sought to negotiate with the city fathers. But the political leaders consistently refused to engage in good faith negotiation.

Then came the opportunity last September to talk with some of the leaders of the economic community. In these negotiating sessions certain promises were made by the merchants—such as the promise to remove the humiliating racial signs from the stores. On the basis of these promises Rev. Shuttlesworth and the leaders of the Alabama Christian Movement for Human Rights agreed to call a moratorium on any type of demonstrations. As the weeks and months unfolded we realized that we were the victims of a broken promise. The signs remained. Like so many experiences of the past we were confronted with blasted hopes, and the dark shadow of a deep disappointment settled upon us. So we had no alternative except that of preparing for direct action, whereby we would present our very bodies as a means of laying our case before the conscience of the local and national community. We were not unmindful of the difficulties involved. So we decided to go through a process of self-purification. We started having workshops on nonviolence and repeatedly asked ourselves the questions: "Are you able to accept blows without retaliating?" "Are you able to endure the ordeals of jail?" We decided to set our direct-action program around the Easter season, realizing that with the exception of Christmas, this was the largest shopping period of the year. Knowing that a strong economic withdrawal program would be the by-product of direct action, we felt that this was the best time to bring pressure on the merchants for the needed changes. Then it occurred to us that the March election was ahead and so we speedily decided to postpone action until after election day. When we discovered that Mr. Connor was in the run-off, we decided again to postpone action so that the demonstrations could not be used to cloud the issues. At this time we agreed to begin our nonviolent witness the day after the run-off.

This reveals that we did not move irresponsibly into direct action. We too wanted to see Mr. Connor defeated; so we went through postponement after postponement to aid in this community need. After this we felt that direct action could be delayed no longer.

You may well ask: "Why direct action? Why sit-ins, marches, etc.? Isn't negotiation a better path?" You are exactly right in your call for negotiation. Indeed, this is the purpose of direct action. Nonviolent direct action seeks to create such a crisis and establish such creative tension that a community that has constantly refused to negotiate is forced to confront the issue. It seeks so to dramatize the issue that it can no longer be ignored. I just referred to the creation of tension as a part of the work of the nonviolent resister. This may sound rather shocking. But I must confess that I am not afraid of the word tension. I have earnestly worked and preached against violent tension, but there is a type of constructive nonviolent tension that is necessary for growth. Just as Socrates felt that it was necessary to create a tension in the mind so that individuals could rise from the bondage of myths and half-truths to the unfettered realm of creative analysis and objective appraisal, we must see the need of having nonviolent gadflies to create the kind of tension in society that will help men to rise from the dark depths of prejudice and racism to the majestic heights of understanding and brotherhood. So the purpose of the direct action is to create a situation so crisis-packed that it will inevitably open the door to negotiation. We, therefore, concur with you in your call for negotiation. Too long has our beloved Southland been bogged down in the tragic attempt to live in monologue rather than dialogue.

One of the basic points in your statement is that our acts are untimely. Some have asked, "Why didn't you give the new administration time to act?" The only answer that I can give to this inquiry is that the new Birmingham administration must be prodded about as much as the outgoing one before it acts. We will be sadly mistaken if we feel that the election of Mr. Boutwell will bring the millennium to Birmingham. While Mr. Boutwell is much more articulate and gentle than Mr. Connor, they are both segregationists, dedicated to the task of maintaining the status quo. The hope I see in Mr. Boutwell is that he will be reasonable enough to see the futility of massive resistance to desegregation. But he will not see this without pressure from the devotees of civil rights. My friends, I must say to you that we have not made a single gain in civil rights without determined legal and nonviolent pressure. History is the long and tragic story of the fact that privileged groups seldom give up their privileges voluntarily. Individuals may see the moral light and voluntarily give up their unjust posture; but as Reinhold Niebuhr has reminded us, groups are more immoral than individuals.

We know through painful experience that freedom is never voluntarily given by the oppressor; it must be demanded by the oppressed. Frankly, I have never yet engaged in a direct action movement that was "well timed," according to the timetable of those who have not suffered unduly from the disease of segregation. For years now I have heard the words [sic] "Wait!" It rings in the ear of every Negro with a piercing familiarity. This "Wait" has almost always meant "Never." We must come to see with the distinguished jurist of yesterday that "justice too long delayed is justice denied."

We have waited for more than three hundred and forty years for our constitutional and God-given rights. The nations of Asia and Africa are moving with jet-like speed toward the goal of political independence, and we still creep at horse and buggy pace toward the gaining of a cup of coffee at a lunch counter. I guess it is easy for those who have never felt the stinging darts of segregation to say, "Wait." But when you have seen vicious mobs lynch your mothers and fathers at will and drown your sisters and brothers at whim; when you have seen hate filled policemen curse, kick, brutalize and even kill your black brothers and sisters with impunity; when you see the vast majority of your twenty million Negro brothers smothering in an airtight cage of poverty in the midst of an affluent society; when you suddenly find your tongue twisted and your speech stammering as you seek to explain to your six-year-old daughter why she can't go to the public amusement park that has just been advertised on television, and see tears welling up in her eyes when she is told that Funtown is closed to colored children, and see the depressing clouds of inferiority begin to form in her little mental sky, and see her begin to distort her little personality by unconsciously developing a bitterness toward white people; when you have to concoct an answer for a five-year-old son asking in agonizing pathos: "Daddy, why do white people treat colored people so mean?"; when you take a cross-country drive and find it necessary to sleep night after night in the uncomfortable corners of your automobile because no motel will accept you; when you are humiliated day in and day out by nagging signs reading "white" and "colored"; when your first name becomes "nigger," your middle name becomes "boy" (however old you are) and your last name becomes "John," and your wife and mother are never given the respected title "Mrs."; when you are harried by day and haunted by night by the fact that you are a Negro, living constantly at tip-toe stance never quite knowing what to expect next, and plagued with inner fears and outer resentments; when you are forever fighting a degenerating sense of "nobodiness"; then you will understand why we find it difficult to wait. There comes a time when the cup of endurance runs over, and men are no longer willing to be plunged into an abyss of despair. I hope, sirs, you can understand our legitimate and unavoidable impatience.

You express a great deal of anxiety over our willingness to break laws. This is certainly a legitimate concern. Since we so diligently urge people to obey the Supreme Court's decision of 1954 outlawing segregation in the public schools, it is rather strange and paradoxical to find us consciously breaking laws. One may well ask: "How can you advocate breaking some laws and obeying others?" The answer is found in the fact that there are two types of laws: There are *just* and there are *unjust* laws. I would agree with Saint Augustine that "An unjust law is no law at all."

Now, what is the difference between the two? How does one determine when a law is just or unjust? A just law is a man-made code that squares with the moral law or the law of God. An unjust law is a code that is out of harmony with the moral law. To put it in the terms of Saint Thomas Aquinas, an unjust law is a human law that is not rooted in eternal and natural law. Any law that uplifts human personality is just. Any law that degrades human personality is unjust. All segregation statutes are unjust because segregation distorts the soul and damages the personality. It gives the segregator a false sense of superiority, and the segregated a false sense of inferiority. To use the words of Martin Buber, the Jewish philosopher, segregation substitutes an "I-it" relationship for an "I-thou" relationship, and ends up relegating persons to the status of things. So segregation is not only politically, economically and sociologically unsound, but it is morally wrong and sinful. Paul Tillich has said that sin is separation. Isn't segregation an existential expression of man's tragic separation, an expression of his awful estrangement, his terrible sinfulness? So I can urge men to disobey segregation ordinances because they are morally wrong.

Let us turn to a more concrete example of just and unjust laws. An unjust law is a code that a majority inflicts on a minority that is not binding on itself. This is difference made legal. On the other hand a just law is a code that a majority compels a minority to follow that it is willing to follow itself. This is sameness made legal.

Let me give another explanation. An unjust law is a code inflicted upon a minority which that minority had no part in enacting or creating because they did not have the unhampered right to vote. Who can say that the legislature of Alabama which set up the segregation laws was democratically elected? Throughout the state of Alabama all types of conniving methods are used to prevent Negroes from becoming registered voters and there are some counties without a single Negro registered to vote despite the fact that the Negro constitutes a majority of the population. Can any law set up in such a state be considered democratically structured?

These are just a few examples of unjust and just laws. There are some instances when a law is just on its face and unjust in its application. For instance, I was arrested Friday on a charge of parading without a permit. Now there is nothing wrong with an ordinance which requires a permit for a parade, but when the ordinance is used to preserve segregation and to deny citizens the First-Amendment privilege of peaceful assembly and peaceful protest, then it becomes unjust.

I hope you can see the distinction I am trying to point out. In no sense do I advocate evading or defying the law as the rabid segregationist would do. This would lead to anarchy. One who breaks an unjust law must do it *openly, lovingly* (not hatefully as the white mothers did in New Orleans when they were seen on television screaming "nigger, nigger, nigger") and with a willingness to accept the penalty. I submit that an individual who breaks a law that conscience tells him is unjust, and willingly accepts the penalty by staying in jail to arouse the conscience of the community over its injustice, is in reality expressing the very highest respect for law.

Of course, there is nothing new about this kind of civil disobedience. It was seen sublimely in the refusal of Shadrach, Meshach and Abednego to obey the laws of Nebuchadnezzar because a higher moral law was involved. It was practiced superbly by the early Christians who were willing to face hungry lions and the excruciating pain of chopping blocks, before submitting to certain unjust laws of the Roman empire. To a degree academic freedom is a reality today because Socrates practiced civil disobedience.

We can never forget that everything Hitler did in Germany was "legal" and everything the Hungarian freedom fighters did in Hungary was "illegal." It was "illegal" to aid and comfort a Jew in Hitler's Germany. But I am sure that if I had lived in Germany during that time I would have aided and comforted my Jewish brothers even though it was illegal. If I lived in a Communist country today where certain principles dear to the Christian faith are suppressed, I believe I would openly advocate disobeying these anti-religious laws. I must make two honest confessions to you, my Christian and Jewish brothers. First, I must confess that over the last few years I have been gravely disappointed with the white moderate. I have almost reached the regrettable conclusion that the Negro's great stumbling block in the stride toward freedom is not the White Citizen's Counciler or the Ku Klux Klanner, but the white moderate who is more devoted to "order" than to justice; who prefers a negative peace which is the absence of tension to a positive peace which is the presence of justice; who constantly says "I agree with you in the goal you seek, but I can't agree with your methods of direct action"; who paternalistically feels he can set the timetable for another man's freedom; who lives by the myth of time and who constantly advises the Negro to wait until a "more convenient season." Shallow understanding from people of goodwill is more frustrating than absolute misunderstanding from people of ill will. Lukewarm acceptance is much more bewildering than outright rejection.

I had hoped that the white moderate would understand that law and order exist for the purpose of establishing justice, and that when they fail to do this they become dangerously structured dams that block the flow of social progress. I had hoped that the white moderate would understand that the present tension in the South is merely a necessary phase of the transition from an obnoxious negative peace, where the Negro passively accepted his unjust plight, to a substance-filled positive peace, where all men will respect the dignity and worth of human personality. Actually, we who engage in nonviolent direct action are not the creators of tension. We merely bring to the surface the hidden tension that is already alive. We bring it out in the open where it can be seen and dealt with. Like a boil that can never be cured as long as it is covered up but must be opened with all its pus-flowing ugliness to the natural medicines of air and light, injustice must likewise be exposed, with all of the tension its exposing creates, to the light of human conscience and the air of national opinion before it can be cured.

In your statement you asserted that our actions, even though peaceful, must be condemned because they precipitate violence. But can this assertion be logically made? Isn't this like condemning the robbed man because his possession of money precipitated the evil act of robbery? Isn't this like condemning Socrates because his unswerving commitment to truth and his philosophical delvings precipitated the misguided popular mind to make him drink the hemlock? Isn't this like condemning Jesus because His unique God-Consciousness and never-ceasing devotion to His will precipitated the evil act of crucifixion? We must come to see, as the federal courts have consistently affirmed, that it is immoral to urge an individual to withdraw his efforts to gain his basic constitutional rights because the quest precipitates violence. Society must protect the robbed and punish the robber.

I had also hoped that the white moderate would reject the myth of time. I received a letter this morning from a white brother in Texas which said: "All Christians know that the colored people will receive equal rights eventually, but it is possible that you are in too great of a religious hurry. It has taken Christianity almost 2000 years to accomplish what it has. The teachings of Christ take time to come to earth." All that is said here grows out of a tragic misconception of time. It is the strangely irrational notion that there is something in the very flow of time that will inevitably cure all ills. Actually time is neutral. It can be used either destructively or constructively. I am coming to feel that the people of ill-will have used time much more effectively than the people of good will. We will have to repent in this generation not merely for the vitriolic words and actions of the bad people, but for the appalling silence of the good people. We must come to see that human progress never rolls in on wheels of inevitability. It comes through the tireless efforts and persistent work of men willing to be co-workers with God, and without this hard work time itself becomes an ally of the forces of social stagnation. We must use time creatively, and forever realize that the time is always ripe to do right. Now is the time to make real the promise of democracy, and transform our pending national elegy into a creative psalm of brotherhood. Now is the time to lift our national policy from the quicksand of racial injustice to the solid rock of human dignity.

You spoke of our activity in Birmingham as extreme. At first I was rather disappointed that fellow clergymen would see my nonviolent efforts as those of the extremist. I started thinking about the fact that I stand in the middle of two opposing forces in the Negro community. One is a force of complacency made up of Negroes who, as a result of long years of oppression, have been so completely drained of self-respect and a sense of "somebodiness" that they have adjusted to segregation, and, of a few Negroes in the middle class who, because of a degree of academic and economic security, and because at points they profit by segregation, have unconsciously become insensitive to the problems of the masses. The other force is one of bitterness, and hatred comes perilously close to advocating violence. It is expressed in the various black nationalist groups that are springing up over the nation, the largest and best-known being Elijah Muhammad's Muslim movement. This movement is nourished by the contemporary frustration over the continued existence of racial discrimination. It is made up of people who have lost faith in America, who have absolutely repudiated Christianity, and who have concluded that the white man is an incurable "devil." I have tried to stand between these two forces saying that we need not follow the "do-nothingism" of the complacent or the hatred and despair of the black nationalist. There is the more excellent way of love and nonviolent protest. I'm grateful to God that, through the Negro church, the dimension of nonviolence entered our struggle. If this philosophy had not emerged, I am convinced that by now many streets of the South would be flowing with floods of blood. And I am further convinced that if our white brothers dismiss as "rabble rousers" and "outside agitators" those of us who are working through the channels of nonviolent direct action and refuse to support our nonviolent efforts, millions of Negroes, out of frustration and despair, will seek solace and security in black-nationalist ideologies, a development that will lead inevitably to a frightening racial nightmare.

Oppressed people cannot remain oppressed forever. The urge for freedom will eventually come. This is what happened to the American Negro. Something within has reminded him of his birthright of freedom; something without has reminded him that he can gain it. Consciously and unconsciously, he has been swept in by what the Germans call the *Zeitgeist,* and with his black brothers of Africa, and his brown and yellow brothers of Asia, South America and the Caribbean, he is moving with a sense of cosmic urgency toward the promised land of racial justice. Recognizing this vital urge that has engulfed the Negro community, one should readily understand public demonstrations. The Negro has many pent up resentments and latent frustrations. He has to get them out. So let him march sometime; let him have his prayer pilgrimages to the city hall; understand why he must have sit-ins and freedom rides. If his repressed emotions do not come out in these nonviolent ways, they will come out in ominous expressions of violence. This is not a threat; it is a fact of history. So I have not said to my people "get rid of your discontent." But I have tried to say that this normal and healthy discontent can be channelized through the creative outlet of nonviolent direct action. Now this approach is being dismissed as extremist. I must admit that I was initially disappointed in being so categorized.

But as I continued to think about the matter I gradually gained a bit of satisfaction from being considered an extremist. Was not Jesus an extremist for love—"Love your enemies, bless them that curse you, pray for them that despitefully use you." Was not Amos an extremist for justice—"Let justice roll down like waters and righteousness like a mighty stream." Was not Paul an extremist for the gospel of Jesus Christ—"I bear in my body the marks of the Lord Jesus." Was not Martin Luther an extremist—"Here I stand; I can do none other so help me God." Was not John Bunyan an extremist —"I will stay in jail to the end of my days before I make a butchery of my conscience." Was not Abraham Lincoln an extremist—"This nation cannot survive half slave and half free." Was not Thomas Jefferson an extremist—"We hold these truths to be self-evident, that all men are created equal." So the question is not whether we will be extremist but what kind of extremist will we be. Will we be extremists for hate or will we be extremists for love? Will we be extremists for the preservation of injustice—or will we be extremists for the cause of justice? In that dramatic scene on Calvary's hill, three men were crucified. We must not forget that all three were crucified for the same crime—the crime of extremism. Two were extremists for immorality, and thusly fell below their environment. The other, Jesus Christ, was an extremist for love, truth and goodness, and thereby rose above his environment. So, after all, maybe the South, the nation and the world are in dire need of creative extremists.

I had hoped that the white moderate would see this. Maybe I was too optimistic. Maybe I expected too much. I guess I should have realized that few members of a race that has oppressed another race can understand or appreciate the deep groans and passionate yearnings of those that have been oppressed and still fewer have the vision to see that injustice must be rooted out by strong, persistent and determined action. I am thankful, however, that some of our white brothers have grasped the meaning of this social revolution and committed themselves to it. They are still all too small in quantity, but they are big in quality. Some like Ralph McGill, Lillian Smith, Harry Golden and James Dabbs have written about our struggle in eloquent, prophetic and understanding terms. Others have marched with us down nameless streets of the South. They have languished in filthy roach-infested jails, suffering the abuse and brutality of angry policemen who see them as "dirty nigger lovers." They, unlike so many of their moderate brothers and sisters, have recognized the urgency of the moment and sensed the need for powerful "action" antidotes to combat the disease of segregation.

Let me rush on to mention my other disappointment. I have been so greatly disappointed with the white church and its leadership. Of course, there are some notable exceptions. I am not unmindful of the fact that each of you has taken some significant stands on this issue. I commend you, Rev. Stallings, for your Christian stand on this past Sunday, in welcoming Negroes to your worship service on a non-segregated basis. I commend the Catholic leaders of this state for integrating Spring Hill College several years ago.

But despite these notable exceptions I must honestly reiterate that I have been disappointed with the church. I do not say that as one of those negative critics who can always find something wrong with the church. I say it as a minister of the gospel, who loves the church; who was nurtured in its bosom; who has been sustained by its spiritual blessings and who will remain true to it as long as the cord of life shall lengthen.

I had the strange feeling when I was suddenly catapulted into the leadership of the bus protest in Montgomery several years ago, that we would have the support of the white church. I felt that the white ministers, priests and rabbis of the South would be some of our strongest allies. Instead, some have been outright opponents, refusing to understand the freedom movement and misrepresenting its leaders; all too many others have been more cautious than courageous and have remained silent behind the anesthetizing security of the stained-glass windows.

In spite of my shattered dreams of the past, I came to Birmingham with the hope that the white religious leadership of this community would see the justice of our cause, and with deep moral concern, serve as the channel through which our just grievances would get to the power structure. I had hoped that each of you would understand. But again I have been disappointed. I have heard numerous religious leaders of the South call upon their worshippers to comply with a desegregation decision because it is the *law,* but I have longed to hear white ministers say, "follow this decree because integration is morally *right* and the Negro is your brother." In the midst of blatant injustices inflicted upon the Negro, I have watched white churches stand on the sideline and merely mouth pious irrelevancies and sanctimonious trivialities. In the midst of a mighty struggle to rid our nation of racial and economic injustice, I have heard so many ministers say, "Those are social issues with which the gospel has no real concern." And I have watched so many churches commit themselves to a completely other-worldly religion which made a strange distinction between body and soul, the sacred and the secular.

So here we are moving toward the exit of the twentieth century with a religious community largely adjusted to the status quo, standing as a tail-light behind other community agencies rather than a headlight leading men to higher levels of justice.

I have traveled the length and breadth of Alabama, Mississippi and all the other southern states. On sweltering summer days and crisp autumn mornings I have looked at her beautiful churches with their lofty spires pointing heavenward. I have beheld the impressive outlay of her massive religious education buildings. Over and over again I have found myself asking: "What kind of people worship here? Who is their God? Where were their voices when the lips of Governor Barnett dripped with words of interposition and nullification? Where were they when Governor Wallace gave the clarion call for defiance and hatred? Where were their voices of support when tired, bruised and weary Negro men and women decided to rise from the dark dungeons of complacency to the bright hills of creative protest?"

Yes, these questions are still in my mind. In deep disappointment, I have wept over the laxity of the church. But be assured that my tears have been tears of love. There can be no deep disappointment where there is not deep love. Yes, I love the church; I love her sacred walls. How could I do otherwise? I am in the rather unique position of being the son, the grandson and the great-grandson of preachers. Yes, I see the church as the body of Christ. But, oh! How we have blemished and scarred that body through social neglect and fear of being nonconformists.

There was a time when the church was very powerful. It was during that period when the early Christians rejoiced when they were deemed worthy to suffer for what they believed. In those days the church was not merely a thermometer that recorded the ideas and principles of popular opinion; it was a thermostat that transformed the mores of society. Whenever the early Christians entered a town the power structure got disturbed and immediately sought to convict them for being "disturbers of the peace" and "outside agitators." But they went on with the conviction that they were "a colony of heaven," and had to obey God rather than man. They were small in number but big in commitment.

They were too God-intoxicated to be "astronomically intimidated." They brought an end to such ancient evils as infanticide and gladiatorial contest.

Things are different now. The contemporary church is often a weak, ineffectual voice with an uncertain sound. It is so often the arch supporter of the status quo. Far from being disturbed by the presence of the church, the power structure of the average community is consoled by the church's silent and often vocal sanction of things as they are.

But the judgement of God is upon the church as never before. If the church of today does not recapture the sacrificial spirit of the early church, it will lose its authentic ring, forfeit the loyalty of millions, and be dismissed as an irrelevant social club with no meaning for the twentieth century. I am meeting young people every day whose disappointment with the church has risen to outright disgust.

Maybe again, I have been too optimistic. Is organized religion too inextricably bound to the status quo to save our nation and the world? Maybe I must turn my faith to the inner spiritual church, the church within the church, as the true *ecclesia* and the hope of the world. But again I am thankful to God that some noble souls from the ranks of organized religion have broken loose from the paralyzing chains of conformity and joined us as active partners in the struggle for freedom. They have left their secure congregations and walked the streets of Albany, Georgia, with us. They have gone through the highways of the South on tortuous rides for freedom. Yes, they have gone to jail with us. Some have been kicked out of their churches, and lost support of their bishops and fellow ministers. But they have gone with the faith that right defeated is stronger than evil triumphant. These men have been the leaven in the lump of the race. Their witness has been the spiritual salt that has preserved the true meaning of the Gospel in these troubled times. They have carved a tunnel of hope though the dark mountain of disappointment.

I hope the church as a whole will meet the challenge of this decisive hour. But even if the church does not come to the aid of justice, I have no despair about the future. I have no fear about the outcome of our struggle in Birmingham, even if our motives are presently misunderstood. We will reach the goal of freedom in Birmingham and all over the nation, because the goal of America is freedom. Abused and scorned though we may be, our destiny is tied up with the destiny of America. Before the pilgrims landed at Plymouth we were here. Before the pen of Jefferson etched across the pages of history the majestic words of the Declaration of Independence, we were here. For more than two centuries our fore-parents labored in this country without wages; they made cotton king; and they built the homes of their masters in the midst of brutal injustice and shameful humiliation— and yet out of a bottomless vitality they continued to thrive and develop. If the inexpressible cruelties of slavery could not stop us, the opposition we now face will surely fail. We will win our freedom because the sacred heritage of our nation and the eternal will of God are embodied in our echoing demands.

I must close now. But before closing I am impelled to mention one other point in your statement that troubled me profoundly. You warmly commended the Birmingham police force for keeping "order" and "preventing violence."

I don't believe you would have so warmly commended the police force if you had seen its angry violent dogs literally biting six unarmed, nonviolent Negroes. I don't believe you would so quickly commend the policemen if you would observe their ugly and inhuman treatment of Negroes here in the city jail; if you would watch them push and curse old Negro women and young Negro girls; if you would see them slap and kick old Negro men and young boys; if you will observe them, as they did on two occasions, refuse to give us food because we wanted to sing our grace together. I'm sorry that I can't join you in your praise for the police department.

It is true that they have been rather disciplined in their public handling of the demonstrators. In this sense they have been rather publicly "nonviolent." But for what purpose? To preserve the evil system of segregation. Over the last few years I have consistently preached that nonviolence demands that the means we use must be as pure as the ends we seek. So I have tried to make it clear that it is wrong to use immoral means to attain moral ends. But now I must affirm that it is just as wrong, or even more so, to use moral means to preserve immoral ends. Maybe Mr. Connor and his policemen have been rather publicly nonviolent, as Chief Pritchett was in Albany, Georgia, but they have used the moral means of nonviolence to maintain the immoral end of flagrant racial injustice. T. S. Eliot has said that there is no greater treason than to do the right deed for the wrong reason.

I wish you had commended the Negro sit-inners and demonstrators of Birmingham for their sublime courage, their willingness to suffer and their amazing discipline in the midst of the most inhuman provocation. One day the South will recognize its real heroes. They will be the James Merediths, courageously and with a majestic sense of purpose, facing jeering and hostile mobs and with the agonizing loneliness that characterizes the life of the pioneer. They will be old oppressed, battered Negro women, symbolized in a seventy-two year old woman of Montgomery, Alabama, who rose up with a sense of dignity and with her people decided not to ride the segregated buses, and responded to one who inquired about her tiredness with ungrammatical profundity: "my feet is tired, but my soul is rested." They will be the young high school and college students, young ministers of the gospel and a host of their elders courageously and nonviolently sitting-in at lunch counters and willingly going to jail for conscience's sake. One day the South will know that when these disinherited children of God sat down at lunch counters they were in reality standing up for the best in the American dream and the most sacred values in our Judaeo-Christian heritage, and thusly, carrying our whole nation back to those great wells of democracy which were dug deep by the founding fathers in the formulation of the Constitution and the Declaration of Independence.

Never before have I written a letter this long (or should I say a book?). I'm afraid it is much too long to take your precious time. I can assure you that it would have been much shorter if I had been writing from a comfortable desk, but what else is there to do when you are alone for days in the dull monotony of a narrow jail cell other than write long letters, think strange thoughts, and pray long prayers?

If I have said anything in this letter that is an overstatement of the truth and is indicative of an unreasonable impatience, I beg you to forgive me. If I have said anything in this letter that is an understatement of the truth and is indicative of my having a patience that makes me patient with anything less than brotherhood, I beg God to forgive me.

I hope this letter finds you strong in the faith. I also hope that circumstances will soon make it possible for me to meet each of you, not as an integrationist or a civil rights leader, but as a fellow clergyman and a Christian brother. Let us all hope that the dark clouds of racial prejudice will soon pass away and the deep fog of misunderstanding will be lifted from our fear-drenched communities and in some not too distant tomorrow the radiant stars of love and brotherhood will shine over our great nation with all their scintillating beauty.

Yours for the cause of Peace and Brotherhood,

Martin Luther King, Jr.

Fannie Lou Hamer (1917–1977)

Black and white civil rights activists spent the summer of 1964 in Mississippi registering African Americans to vote. Three civil rights volunteers, James Chaney, Andrew Goodman, and Michael Schwerner, were murdered during that "Freedom Summer." The Mississippi Freedom Democratic Party (MFDP) sent a delegation to the Democratic National Convention in Atlantic City in August, hoping that liberals in the party who supported the civil rights movement would seat them rather than the regular, all-white Mississippi delegation. Student Nonviolent Coordinating Committee (SNCC) worker Fannie Lou Hamer, granddaughter of a slave, was a member of the delegation. The credentials committee held a televised hearing, and while Fannie Lou Hamer's gripping testimony was being aired, President Johnson, angry that the issue would divide the Democratic Party, deliberately preempted the proceedings by holding a spur-of-the-moment press conference. Hamer's testimony was aired later that evening by the networks, and although it was no longer prime time, millions of viewers around the country then heard of the injustices faced by blacks in Mississippi. Johnson and the Democratic leadership still refused to seat the MFDP, although they offered a compromise: admitting two MFDP members as delegates-at-large and agreeing that at the next convention in 1968 delegations from states that denied citizens suffrage would not be seated. The MFDP rejected the compromise: "We didn't come all this way for no two seats," Fannie Lou Hamer indignantly announced. An important result of this episode was that many African Americans began losing faith in the political process. Over the next few years, the civil rights movement itself fragmented as advocates of Black Power became critical of the moderate approach of such leaders as Martin Luther King Jr. and Roy Wilkins of the NAACP.

TESTIMONY BEFORE THE CREDENTIALS COMMITTEE OF THE DEMOCRATIC NATIONAL CONVENTION, 1964

Mr. Chairman, and the Credentials Committee, my name is Mrs. Fanny Lou Hamer, and I live at 626 East Lafayette Street, Ruleville, Mississippi, Sunflower County, the home of Senator James O. Eastland, and Senator Stennis.

It was the 31st of August in 1962 that 18 of us traveled 26 miles to the county courthouse in Indianola to try to register to try to become first-class citizens. We was met in Indianola by Mississippi men, Highway Patrolmens and they only allowed two of us in to take the literacy test at the time. After we had taken this test and started back to Ruleville, we was held up by the City Police and the State Highway Patrolmen and carried back to Indianola where the bus driver was charged that day with driving a bus the wrong color.

After we paid the fine among us, we continued on to Ruleville, and Reverend Jeff Sunny carried me four miles in the rural area where I had worked as a time-keeper and sharecropper for 18 years. I was met there by my children, who told me that the plantation owner was angry because I had gone down to try to register. After they told me, my husband came, and said that the plantation owner was raising cain because I had tried to register, and before he quit talking the plantation owner came, and said, "Fanny Lou, do you know—did Pap tell you what I said?"

And I said, "yes, sir."

He said, "I mean that," he said, "If you don't go down and withdraw your registration, you will have to leave," said, "Then if you go down and withdraw," he said, "You will—you [still] might have to go because we are not ready for that in Mississippi."

And I addressed him and told him and said, "I didn't try to register for you. I tried to register for myself." I had to leave that same night.

On the 10th of September 1962, 16 bullets was fired into the home of Mr. and Mrs. Robert Tucker for me. That same night two girls were shot in Ruleville, Mississippi. Also Mr. Joe McDonald's house was shot in.

And in June the 9th, 1963, I had attended a voter registration workshop, was returning back to Mississippi. Ten of us was traveling by the Continental Trailway bus. When we got to Winona, Mississippi, which is in Montgomery County, four of the people got off to use the washroom, and two of the people—to use the restaurant—two of the people wanted to use the washroom. The four people that had gone in to use the restaurant was ordered out. During this time I was on the

SOURCE: Reprinted in Peter B. Levy, ed., *Documentary History of the Modern Civil Rights Movement* (New York: Greenwood Press, 1992), 139–141.

bus. But when I looked through the window and saw they had rushed out I got off of the bus to see what had happened, and one of the ladies said, "It was a State Highway Patrolman and a Chief of Police ordered us out."

I got back on the bus and one of the persons had used the washroom got back on the bus, too. As soon as I was seated on the bus, I saw when they began to get the four people in a highway patrolman's car, I stepped off of the bus to see what was happening and somebody screamed from the car that the four workers was in and said, "Get that one there," and when I went to get in the car, when the man told me I was under arrest, he kicked me.

I was carried to the county jail, and put in the booking room. They left some of the people in the booking room and began to place us in cells. I was placed in a cell with a young woman called Miss Ivesta Simpson. After I was placed in the cell I began to hear the sound of kicks and horrible screams, and I could hear somebody say, "Can you say, yes, sir, nigger? Can you say yes, sir?"

And they would say other horrible names. She would say, "Yes, I can say yes, sir."

"So say it."

She says, "I don't know you well enough."

They beat her, I don't know how long, and after a while she began to pray, and asked God to have mercy on those people.

And it wasn't too long before three white men came to my cell. One of these men was a State Highway Patrolman and he asked me where I was from, and I told him Ruleville, he said, "We are going to check this." And they left my cell and it wasn't too long before they came back. He said, "You are from Ruleville all right," and he used a curse word, and he said, "We are going to make you wish you was dead."

I was carried out of that cell into another cell where they had two Negro prisoners. The State Highway Patrolmen ordered the first Negro to take the blackjack. The first Negro prisoner ordered me, by orders from the State Highway Patrolman for me, to lay down on a bunk bed on my face, and I laid on my face. The first Negro began to beat, and I was beat by the first Negro until he was exhausted, and I was holding my hands behind me at that time on my left side because I suffered from polio when I was six years old. After the first Negro had beat until he was exhausted the State Highway Patrolman ordered the second Negro to take the blackjack.

The second Negro began to beat and I began to work my feet, and the State Highway Patrolman ordered the first Negro who had beat me to sit upon my feet to keep me from working my feet. I began to scream and one white man got up and began to beat me my head and told me to hush. One white man—since my dress had worked up high, walked over and pulled my dress down and he pulled my dress back, back up. . . .

All of this is on account of us wanting to register, to become first-class citizens, and if the freedom Democratic Party is not seated now, I question America, is this America, the land of the free and the home of the brave where we have to sleep with our telephones off of the hooks because our lives be threatened daily because we want to live as decent human beings, in America?

Malcolm X (1925–1965)

By the time Malcolm Little was a teenager, he was involved in drugs, pimping, and burglary. He was finally arrested and sent to prison. While incarcerated, he began reading avidly and converted to Elijah Muhammad's Nation of Islam. Having learned that all African Americans had lost their original African names when they were forced into slavery, he dropped his own surname upon his release in 1952. He called himself Malcolm X—the X representing his lost African name.

During the next several years, his eloquence and personal charisma brought Malcolm X to the fore in the Nation of Islam, and he spent most of his time giving speeches that condemned white America and urged blacks to convert to Islam. His message contrasted sharply with Martin Luther King Jr.'s advocacy of nonviolent direct action as a means to achieve integration. Malcolm X believed that all whites were racists and that there was no way white America would ever respect black America's rights; rejecting integration as a goal, he called instead for black separatism. In 1964, however, after his hajj to Mecca, where he met many white Muslims who were not racist, he began to believe that there was some hope of working together with whites to eradicate racism. By this time, he had had a falling out with Elijah Muhammad and founded his own Organization of Afro-American Unity. In February 1965, Nation of Islam gunmen assassinated him while he was addressing supporters in the Avalon Ballroom in Harlem.

THE BLACK REVOLUTION, 1964

Friends and enemies, tonight I hope that we can have a little fireside chat with as few sparks as possible being tossed around. . . . I hope that this little conversation tonight about the black revolution won't cause many of you to accuse us of igniting it when you find it at your doorstep. . . . I'm still a Muslim but I'm also a nationalist, meaning that my political philosophy is black nationalism, my economic philosophy is black nationalism, my social philosophy is black nationalism. And when I say that this philosophy is black nationalism, to me this means that the political philosophy of black nationalism is that which is designed to encourage our people, the black people, to gain complete control over the politics and the politicians of our own community.

Our economic philosophy is that we should gain economic control over the economy of our own community, the businesses and the other things which

SOURCE: Malcolm X, "The Black Revolution," in *Two Speeches by Malcolm X* (New York: Merit, 1965), 5, 14.

create employment so that we can provide jobs for our own people instead of having to picket and boycott and beg someone else for a job. And, in short, our social philosophy means that we feel that it is time to get together among our own kind and eliminate the evils that are destroying the moral fiber of our society, like drug addiction, drunkenness, adultery that leads to an abundance of bastard children, welfare problems. We believe that we should lift the level or the standard of our own society to a higher level wherein we will be satisfied and then not inclined toward pushing ourselves into other societies where we are not wanted.

Why is America in a position to bring about a bloodless revolution? Because the Negro in this country holds the balance of power and if the Negro in this country were given what the Constitution says he is supposed to have, the added power of the Negro in this country would sweep all of the racists and the segregationists out of office. It would change the entire political structure of the country. It would wipe out the Southern segregationism that now controls America's foreign policy, as well as America's domestic policy.

And the only way without bloodshed that this can be brought about is that the black man has to be given full use of the ballot in every one of the 50 states. But if the black man doesn't get the ballot, then you are going to be faced with another man who forgets the ballot and starts using the bullet.

Revolutions are fought to get control of land, to remove the absentee landlord and gain control of the land and the institutions that flow from that land. The black man has been in a very low condition because he has had no control whatsoever over any land. He has been a beggar economically, a beggar politically, a beggar socially, a beggar even when it comes to trying to get some education. So that in the past the type of mentality that was developed in this colonial system among our people, today is being overcome. And as the young ones come up they know what they want. And as they listen to your beautiful preaching about democracy and all those other flowery words, they know what they're supposed to have.

So you have a people today who not only know what they want, but also know what they are supposed to have. And they themselves are clearing another generation that is coming up that not only will know what it wants and know what it should have, but also will be ready and willing to do whatever is necessary to see that what they should have materializes immediately. Thank you.

Stokely Carmichael (1941–1998)

By 1965, the civil rights movement was entering the final stages of overturning segregation in the Jim Crow South. There had been boycotts, freedom rides, and sit-ins. The Civil Rights Bill became law in 1964. Jim Crow was dying. In the aftermath of the Selma march, in March 1965,

President Johnson submitted the Voting Rights Bill to Congress, which, when it was passed, sent federal examiners into the South to make sure that all citizens, regardless of race, would be permitted to register to vote. Over the next few years, political power in the South began to shift away from white segregationists, and all politicians were forced, if they hoped to be elected, to address the needs of all their constituents. However, there were many civil rights activists who believed the federal government had not responded to the campaign quickly or effectively enough and that many important issues still needed to be tackled.

African Americans living in the North had also been closely watching the fight for equality in the South, and although many successes could be claimed, those in the ghettos of Detroit, Chicago, New York, and other cities did not perceive that their lives had in any way changed or improved. Civil rights activists like Stokely Carmichael of the Student Nonviolent Coordinating Committee (SNCC), Floyd McKissick of the Congress of Racial Equality (CORE), and many others grew impatient with Reverend King's nonviolent passive resistance and began advocating that blacks no longer turn the other cheek. African Americans, they proclaimed, should and must fight back. Recovering Marcus Garvey's phrase from the 1920s, Stokely Carmichael called for black power. Equality was not going to be handed to African Americans by benevolent whites. It had to be seized. Black power "is a call for black people in this country to unite," Carmichael and Charles Hamilton wrote in their book, Black Power, "to recognize their heritage, to build a sense of community. It is a call for black people to define their own goals, to lead their own organizations." These radicals also questioned the basic premise of Martin Luther King Jr.'s assumption that integration was a worthy goal. White society had nothing to offer blacks, so why, then, should they want to be integrated into it? Rejecting both segregation and integration, black power militants demanded separation. After he became chairman of SNCC in 1966, Carmichael began a speaking tour at universities around the country, urging blacks to build their own "independent political, economic, and cultural institutions."

Berkeley Speech, October 1966

It's a privilege and an honor to be in the white intellectual ghetto of the West. This is a student conference, as it should be, held on a campus, and we'll never be caught up in intellectual masturbation on the question of Black Power. That's the function of the people who are advertisers but call themselves reporters.

Source: Stokely Carmichael, "Berkeley Speech," in Contemporary American Voices, ed. James R. Andrews and David Zarefsky (White Plains, NY: Longman, 1992), 100–107.

Incidentally, for my friends and members of the press, my self-appointed white critics, I was reading Mr. Bernard Shaw two days ago, and I came across a very important quote that I think is most apropos to you. He says, "All criticism is an autobiography." Dig yourself. Ok.

The philosophers Camus and Sartre raise the question of whether or not a man can condemn himself. The black existentialist philosopher who is pragmatic, Frantz Fanon, answered the question. He said that man could not. Camus and Sartre don't answer the question. We in SNCC tend to agree with Fanon—a man cannot condemn himself. If he did, he would then have to inflict punishment upon himself. An example is the Nazis. Any of the Nazi prisoners who, after he was caught and incarcerated, admitted that he committed crimes, that he killed all the many people he killed, had to commit suicide. The only ones able to stay alive were the ones who never admitted that they committed a crime against people—that is, the ones who rationalized that Jews were not human beings and deserved to be killed, or that they were only following orders. There's another, more recent example provided by the officials and the population—the white population—of Neshoba County, Mississippi (that's where Philadelphia is). They could not condemn Sheriff Rainey, his deputies, and the other fourteen men who killed three human beings. They could not because they elected Mr. Rainey to do precisely what he did; and condemning him would be condemning themselves.

In a much larger view, SNCC says that white America cannot condemn herself for her criminal acts against black America. So black people have done it—you stand condemned. The institutions that function in this country are clearly racist; they're built upon racism. The questions to be dealt with then are: how can black people inside this country move? How can white people who say they're not part of those institutions begin to move? And how then do we begin to clear away the obstacles that we have in this society, to make us live like human beings?

Several people have been upset because we've said that integration was irrelevant when initiated by blacks, and that in fact it was an insidious subterfuge for the maintenance of white supremacy. In the past six years or so, this country has been feeding us a "thalidomide drug of integration," and some negroes have been walking down a dream street talking about sitting next to white people. That does not begin to solve the problem. We didn't go to Mississippi to sit next to Ross Barnett [former governor of Mississippi], we did not go to sit next to Jim Clark [sheriff of Selma, Alabama], we went to get them out of our way. People ought to understand that; we were never fighting for the right to integrate, we were fighting against white supremacy. In order to understand white supremacy we must dismiss the fallacious notion that white people can give anybody his freedom. A man is born free. You may enslave a man after he is born free, and that is in fact what this country does. It enslaves blacks after they're born. The only thing white people can do is stop denying black people their freedom.

I maintain that every civil rights bill in this country was passed for white people, not for black people. For example, I am black. I know that. I also know that while I am black I am a human being. Therefore I have the right to go into any public place. White people don't know that. Every time I tried to go into a public place they stopped me. So some boys had to write a bill to tell that white man, "He's a human being; don't stop him." That bill was for the white man, not for me. I knew I could vote all the time and that it wasn't a privilege but my right. Every time I tried I was shot, killed or jailed, beaten or economically deprived. So somebody had to write a bill to tell white people, "When a black man comes to vote, don't bother him." That bill was for white people. I know I can live anyplace I want to live. It is white people across this country who are incapable of allowing me to live where I want. You need a civil rights bill, not me. The failure of the civil rights bill isn't because of Black Power or because of the Student Nonviolent Coordinating Committee or because of the rebellions that are occurring in the major cities. That failure is due to the white's incapacity to deal with their own problems inside their own communities.

And so in a sense we must ask, How is it that black people move? And what do we do? But the question in a much greater sense is, How can white people who are the majority, and who are responsible for making democracy work, make it work? They have never made democracy work, be it inside the United States, Vietnam, South Africa, the Philippines, South America, Puerto Rico, or wherever America has been. We not only condemn the country for what it has done internally, but we must condemn it for what it does externally. We see this country trying to rule the world, and someone must stand up and start articulating that this country is not God, and that it cannot rule the world.

The white supremacist attitude, which you have either consciously or subconsciously, is running rampant through society today. For example, missionaries were sent to Africa with the attitude that blacks were automatically inferior. As a matter of fact, the first act the missionaries did when they got to Africa was to make us cover up our bodies, because they said it got them excited. We couldn't go bare-breasted any more because they got excited! When the missionaries came to civilize us because we were uncivilized, to educate us because we were uneducated, and to give us some literate studies because we were illiterate, they charged a price. The missionaries came with the Bible, and we had the land: When they left, they had the land, and we still have the Bible. That's been the rationalization for Western civilization as it moves across the world—stealing, plundering, and raping everybody in its path. Their one rationalization is that the rest of the world is uncivilized and they are in fact civilized. But the West is un-civ-i-lized. And that still runs on today, you see, because now we have "modern-day missionaries," and they come into our ghettos—they Head Start, Upward Lift, Bootstrap, and Upward Bound us into white society. They don't want to face the real problem. A man is poor for one reason and one reason only—he does not have money. If you want to get rid of poverty, you give people money. And you ought not tell me about people who don't work, and that you can't give people money if they don't work, because if that were true, you'd have to start stopping Rockefeller, Kennedy, Lyndon Baines Johnson, Lady Bird Johnson, the whole of Standard

Oil, the Gulf Corporation, all of them, including probably a large number of the board of trustees of this university. The question, then, is not whether or not one can work; it's Who has power to make his or her acts legitimate? That is all. In this country that power is invested in the hands of white people, and it makes their acts legitimate.

We are now engaged in a psychological struggle in this country about whether or not black people have the right to use the words they want to use without white people giving their sanction. We maintain the use of the words Black Power—let them address themselves to that. We are not going to wait for white people to sanction Black Power. We're tired of waiting; every time black people try to move in this country, they're forced to defend their position beforehand. It's time that white people do that. They ought to start defending themselves as to why they have oppressed and exploited us. A man was picked as a slave for one reason—the color of his skin. Black was automatically inferior, inhuman. And therefore fit for slavery, so the question of whether or not we are individually suppressed is nonsensical, and it's a downright lie. We are oppressed as a group because we are black, not because we are lazy or apathetic, not because we're stupid or we stink, not because we eat watermelon or have good rhythm. We are oppressed because we are black.

In order to escape that oppression we must wield the group power we have, not the individual power that this country sets as the criterion under which a man may come into it. That's what is called integration. "You do what I tell you to do and we'll let you sit at the table with us." Well, if you believe in integration, you can come live in Watts, send your children to the ghetto schools. Let's talk about that. If you believe in integration, then we're going to start adopting us some white people to live in our neighborhoods. So it is clear that this question is not one of integration or segregation. We cannot afford to be concerned about the 6 percent black children in this country whom you allow to enter white schools. We are going to be concerned about the 94 percent. You ought to be concerned about them too. But are we willing to be concerned about the black people who will never get to Berkeley, never get to Harvard, and cannot get an education, the ones you'll never get a chance to rub shoulders with and say, "Why, he's almost as good as we are; he's not like the others"? The question is, How can white society begin to move to see black people as human beings? I am black, therefore I am. Not I am black and I must go to college to prove myself. I am black, therefore I am. And don't deprive me of anything and say to me that you must go to college before you gain access to X, Y, and Z. That's only a rationalization for suppression.

The political parties of this country do not meet the needs of the people on a day-to-day basis. How can we build new political institutions that will become the political expressions of people? How can you build political institutions that will begin to meet the needs of Oakland, California? The need of Oakland, California, is not 1,000 policemen with submachine guns. They need that least of all. How can we build institutions that will allow those people to function on a day-to-day basis, so that they can get decent jobs and have decent houses, and they can begin to participate in the policy and make the decisions that affect their lives? That's what they need, not Gestapo troops, because this is not 1942, and if you play like Nazis, we're not going to play Jew this time around. Get hip to that. Can white people move inside their own community and start tearing down racism where in fact it exists? It is you who live in Cicero and stopped us from living there. White people stopped us from moving into Grenada, Mississippi. White people make sure that we live in the ghettos of this country. White institutions do that. They must change. In order for America to really live on a basic principle of human relationships, a new society must be born. Racism must die. The economic exploitation by this country of non-white people around the world must also die.

There are several programs in the South where whites are trying to organize poor whites so they can begin to move around the question of economic exploitation and political disfranchisement. We've all heard the theory several times. But few people are willing to go into it. The question is, Can the white activist stop trying to be a Pepsi generation who comes alive in the black community, and be a man who's willing to move into the white community and start organizing where the organization is needed? Can he do that? Can the white activist disassociate himself from the clowns who waste time parrying with each other and start talking about the problems that are facing people in this state? You must start inside the white community. Our political position is that we don't think the Democratic Party represents the needs of black people. We know that it does not. If, in fact, white people believe that they're going to move inside that structure, how are they going to organize around a concept of whiteness based on true brotherhood and on stopping economic exploitation in order to form a coalition base for black people to hook up with? You cannot build a coalition based on national sentiment. If you want a coalition to address itself to real changes in this country, white people must start building those institutions inside the white community. And that's the real question facing the white activists today. Can they tear down the institutions that have put us all in the trick bag we've been into for the last hundreds of years? Frederick Douglass said that the youth should fight to be leaders today. God knows we need to be leaders today, because the men who run this country are sick. We must begin to start building those institutions and to fight to articulate our position, to fight to be able to control our universities (we need to be able to do that), to fight to control the basic institutions that perpetuate racism by destroying them and building new ones. That's the real question that faces us today, and it is a dilemma because most of us don't know how to work.

Most white activists run into the black community as an excuse. We cannot have white people working in the black community—on psychological grounds. The fact is that all black people question whether or not they are equal to whites, since every time they start to do something, white people are around showing them how to do it. If we are going to eliminate that for the generation that comes after us, then black people must be in positions of power, doing and articulating for themselves. That's not reverse racism; it is moving onto healthy ground; it is becoming what the philosopher Sartre says, an "antiracist racist."

And this country can't understand that. If everybody who's white sees himself as racist and sees us against him, he's speaking from his own guilt.

We do not have the power in our hands to change the institution of war in this country—to begin to recreate it so that they can learn to leave the Vietnamese people alone. The only power we have is the power to say, "Hell, no!" to the draft.

The war in Vietnam is illegal and immoral. The question is, What can we do to stop that war? What can we do to stop the people who, in the name of America, are killing babies, women, and children? We have to say to ourselves that there's a higher law than the law of a fool named Rusk; there's a higher law than the law of a buffoon named Johnson. It's the law of each of us. We will not murder anybody who they say kill, and if we decide to kill, "we're" going to decide who it shall be. This country will only stop the war in Vietnam when the young men who are made to fight it begin to say, "Hell, no, we aren't going."

The peace movement has been a failure because it hasn't gotten off the college campuses where everybody has a 2S and is not afraid of being drafted anyway. The problem is how you can move out of that into the white ghettos of this country and articulate a position for those white youth who do not want to go. You cannot do that. It is sometimes ironic that many of the peace groups have begun to call SNCC violent and they say they can no longer support us, when we are in fact the most militant organization for peace or civil rights or human rights against the war in Vietnam in this country today. There isn't one organization that has begun to meet our stand on the war in Vietnam. We not only say we are against the war in Vietnam; we are against the draft. No man has the right to take a man for two years and train him to be a killer. Any black man fighting in the war in Vietnam is nothing but a black mercenary. Any time a black man leaves the country where he can't vote to supposedly deliver the vote to somebody else, he's a black mercenary. Any time a black man leaves this country, gets shot in Vietnam on foreign ground, and returns home and you won't give him a burial place in his own homeland, he's a black mercenary. Even if I believed the lies of Johnson, that we're fighting to give democracy to the people of Vietnam, as a black man living in this country I wouldn't fight to give this to anybody. We have to use our bodies and our minds in the only way that we see fit. We must begin, as the philosopher Camus says, to come alive by saying "no." This country is a nation of thieves. It stole everything it has, beginning with black people. The U.S. cannot justify its existence as the policeman of the world any longer. The marines are at ready disposal to bring democracy, and if the Vietnamese don't want democracy, well then, "We'll just wipe them out, because they don't deserve to live if they won't have our way of life."

There is a more immediate question: What do you do on your campus? Do you raise questions about the hundred black students who were kicked off campus a couple of weeks ago? Eight hundred? And how does that question begin to move? Do you begin to relate to people outside the ivory tower and university walls? Do you think you're capable of building those human relationships based on humanity when the country is the way it is, when the institutions are clearly against us.

We have found all the myths of the country to be nothing but downright lies. We were told that if we worked hard we would succeed, and if that were true we would own this country lock, stock, and barrel. We have picked the cotton for nothing; we are the maids in the kitchens of liberal white people; we are the janitors, the porters, the elevator men; we sweep up your college floors. We are the hardest workers and the lowest paid. It is nonsensical for people to talk about human relationships until they are willing to build new institutions. Black people are economically insecure. White liberals are economically secure. Can you begin to build an economic coalition? Are the liberals willing to share their salaries with the economically insecure black people they so much love? Then if you're not, are you willing to start building new institutions that will provide economic security for black people? That's the question we want to deal with!

American students are perhaps the most politically unsophisticated students in the world. Across every country of the world, while we were growing up, students were leading the major revolutions of their countries. We have not been able to do that. They have been politically aware of their existence. In South America our neighbors have one every 24 hours just to remind us that they are politically aware. But we have been unable to grasp it because we've always moved in the field of morality and love while people have been politically jiving with our lives. You can't move morally against men like Brown and Reagan. You can't move morally against Lyndon Baines Johnson because he is an immoral man. He doesn't know what it's all about. So you've got to move politically. We have to develop a political sophistication that doesn't parrot "the two-party system is the best system in the world." We have to raise questions about whether we need new types of political institutions in this country, and we in SNCC maintain that we need them now. Any time Lyndon Baines Johnson can head a party that has in it Bobby Kennedy, Wayne Morse, Eastland, Wallace, and all those other supposed-to-be-liberal cats, there's something wrong with that party. They're moving politically, not morally. If that party refuses to seat black people from Mississippi and goes ahead and seats racists like Eastland and his clique, it's clear to me that they're moving politically, and that one cannot begin to talk morality to people like that.

We must question the values of this society, and I maintain that black people are the best people to do that since we have been excluded from that society. We ought to think whether or not we want to become a part of that society. That's precisely what the Student Nonviolent Coordinating Committee is doing. We are raising questions about this country. I do not want to be a part of the American pie. The American pie means raping South Africa, beating Vietnam, beating South America, raping the Philippines, raping every country you've been in. I don't want any of your blood money. I don't want to be part of that system. We are the generation who has found this country to be a world power and the wealthiest country in the world. We must question whether or not we want this country to continue being the wealthiest country in the world at the price of raping everybody else. And because black people are saying we do not now want to become a part of you, we are called reverse racists. Ain't that a gas?

White society has caused the failure of nonviolence. I was always surprised at Quakers who came to Alabama and counseled me to be nonviolent, but didn't have the guts to tell James Clark to be nonviolent. That's where nonviolence needs to be preached—to Jim Clark, not to black people. White people should conduct their nonviolent schools in Cicero where they are needed, not among black people in Mississippi. Six-foot-two men kick little black children in Grenada—can you conduct nonviolent schools there? Can you name one black man today who has killed anybody white and is still alive? Even after a rebellion, when some black brothers throw bricks and bottles, ten thousand of them have to pay the price. When the white policeman comes in, anybody who's black is arrested because we all look alike.

The youth of this country must begin to raise those questions. We are going to have to change the foreign policy of this country. One of the problems with the peace movement is that it is too caught up in Vietnam, and if America pulled out the troops from Vietnam this week, next week you'd have to get another peace movement for Santo Domingo. We have to hook up with black people around the world; and that hookup must not only be psychological, but real. If South America were to rebel today, and black people were to shoot the hell out of all the white people there, as they should, Standard Oil would crumble tomorrow. If South Africa were to go today, Chase Manhattan Bank would crumble tomorrow. If Zimbabwe, which is called Rhodesia by white people, were to go tomorrow, General Electric would cave in on the East Coast. How do we stop those institutions that are so willing to fight against "Communist aggression" but close their eyes against racist oppression? We're not talking about a policy of aid or sending Peace Corps people in to teach people how to read and write and build houses while we steal their raw materials from them. Because that's all this country does. What underdeveloped countries need is information about how to become industrialized, so they can keep their raw materials where they have them, produce goods, sell them to this country for the price it's supposed to pay. Instead, America keeps selling goods back to them for a profit and keeps sending our modern day missionaries there, calling them the sons of Kennedy. And if the youth are going to participate in that program, how do you begin to control the Peace Corps.

This country assumes that if someone is poor, they are poor because of their own individual blight, or because they weren't born on the right side of town, or they had too many children, or went in the army too early, or because their father was a drunk, or they didn't care about school—they made a mistake. That's a lot of nonsense. Poverty is well calculated in this country, and the reason why the poverty program won't work is because the calculators of poverty are administering it.

How can you, as the youth in this country, move to start carrying those things out? Move into the white community. We have developed a movement in the black community. The white activist has miserably failed to develop the movement inside of his community. Will white people have the courage to go into the white communities and start organizing them? That's the question for the white activist. We won't get caught up in questions about power. This country knows what power is. It knows what Black Power is because it deprived black people of it for over four hundred years. White people associate Black Power with violence because of their own inability to deal with blackness. If we had said "Negro power" nobody would get scared. Everybody would support it. If we said power for colored people, everybody'd be for that, but it is the word "black" that bothers people in this country, and that's their problem, not mine. That's the lie that says anything black is bad.

You're all a college and university crowd. You've taken your basic logic course. You know about major premise, minor premise. People have been telling you anything all black is bad. Let's make that our major premise.

Major premise: Anything all black is bad. Minor premise or particular premise: I am all black. Therefore . . . I'm never going to be put in that bag; I'm all black and I'm all good. Anything all black is not necessarily bad. Anything all black is only bad when you use force to keep whites out. Now that's what white people have done in this country, and they're projecting their same fears and guilt on us, and we won't have it. Let them handle their own affairs and their own guilt. Let them find their own psychologists. We refuse to be the therapy for white society any longer. We have gone stark, raving mad trying to do it.

I look at Dr. King on television every single day, and I say to myself: "Now there is a man who's desperately needed in this country. There is a man full of love. There is a man full of mercy. There is a man full of compassion." But every time I see Lyndon on television, I say, "Martin, baby, you got a long way to go."

If we were to be real and honest, we would have to admit that most people in this country see things black and white. We live in a country that's geared that way. White people would have to admit that they are afraid to go into a black ghetto at night. They're afraid because they'd be "beat up," "lynched," "looted," "cut up," etc. It happens to black people inside the ghetto every day, incidentally. Since white people are afraid of that, they get a man to do it for them—a policeman. Figure his mentality. The first time a black man jumps, that white man's going to shoot him. Police brutality is going to exist on that level. The only time I hear people talk about nonviolence is when black people move to defend themselves against white people. Black people cut themselves every night in the ghetto—nobody talks about nonviolence. White people beat up black people every day—nobody talks about nonviolence. But as soon as black people start to move, the double standard comes into being. You can't defend yourself. You show me a black man who advocates aggressive violence who would be able to live in this country. Show him to me. Isn't it hypocritical for Lyndon to talk about how you can't accomplish anything by looting and you must accomplish it by the legal ways? What does he know about legality? Ask Ho Chi Minh.

We must wage a psychological battle on the right for black people to define themselves as they see fit, and organize themselves as they see fit. We don't know whether the white community will allow for that organizing, because once they do they must also allow for the organizing inside their own community.

It doesn't make a difference, though—we're going to organize our way. The question is how we're going to organize our way. The question is how we're going to facilitate those matters, whether it's going to be done with a thousand policemen with submachine guns, or whether it's going to be done in a context where it's allowed by white people warding off those policemen. Are white people who call themselves activists ready to move into the white communities on two counts, on building new political institutions to destroy the old ones that we have, and to move around the concept of white youth refusing to go into the army? If so, then we can start to build a new world. We must urge you to fight now to be the leaders of today, not tomorrow. This country is a nation of thieves. It stands on the brink of becoming a nation of murderers. We must stop it. We must stop it.

We are on the move for our liberation. We're tired of trying to prove things to white people. We are tired of trying to explain to white people that we're not going to hurt them. We are concerned with getting the things we want, the things we have to have to be able to function. The question is, Will white people overcome their racism and allow for that to happen in this country? If not, we have no choice but to say very clearly, "Move on over, or we're going to move over you."

The Black Panther Party

As the civil rights movement entered the Black Power phase, Bobby Seale and Huey Newton founded the Black Panther Party in Oakland, California. The Panthers attempted to apply Marxist principles to the idea of black nationalism and called for black autonomy in the United States. Spurning Martin Luther King Jr.'s nonviolent approach and proclaiming that all black people should be allowed to defend themselves against the establishment, they patrolled the streets of Oakland in black berets and leather jackets while openly carrying arms. If police officers stopped an African American on the street and questioned him, within minutes a group of armed Black Panthers would appear to guarantee that the police refrained from any sort of brutality or provocative action.

White Americans reacted strongly, afraid of the violent message the Panthers seemed to be advocating. Armed Panthers, to be sure, were very intimidating, but they seldom provoked violence. In spite of this, the FBI and police forces around the country targeted them, and by the early 1970s there had been a number of shootouts (mostly provoked by the FBI and the police), during which many Black Panther leaders were killed. As a result the party disintegrated in the early 1970s.

Black Panther Party Platform, 1966

1. We want freedom. We want power to determine the destiny of our Black Community. We believe that black people will not be free until we are able to determine our destiny.

2. We want full employment for our people. We believe that the federal government is responsible and obligated to give every man employment or a guaranteed income. We believe that if the white American businessmen will not give full employment, then the means of production should be taken from the businessmen and placed in the community so that the people of the community can organize and employ all of its people and give a high standard of living.

3. We want an end to the robbery by the white man of our Black Community. We believe that this racist government has robbed us and now we are demanding the overdue debt of forty acres and two mules. Forty acres and two mules was promised 100 years ago as restitution for slave labor and mass murder of black people. We will accept the payment as currency which will be distributed to our many communities. The Germans are now aiding the Jews in Israel for the genocide of the Jewish people. The Germans murdered six million Jews. The American racist has taken part in the slaughter of over twenty million black people; therefore, we feel that this is a modest demand that we make.

4. We want decent housing, fit for shelter of human beings. We believe that if the white landlords will not give decent housing to our black community, then the housing and the land should be made into cooperatives so that our community, with government aid, can build and make decent housing for its people.

5. We want education for our people that exposes the true nature of this decadent American society. We want education that teaches us our true history and our role in the present-day society. We believe in an educational system that will give to our people a knowledge of self. If a man does not have knowledge of himself and his position in society and the world, then he has little chance to relate to anything else.

6. We want all black men to be exempt from military service. We believe that Black people should not be forced to fight in the military service to defend a racist government that does not protect us. We will not fight and kill other people of color in the world who, like black people, are being victimized by the white racist government of America. We will protect ourselves from the force and violence of the racist police and the racist military, by whatever means necessary.

7. We want an immediate end to POLICE BRUTALITY and MURDER of black people. We believe we can end police brutality in our black community by

---

SOURCE: The Black Panther Party, "Platform and Program of the Black Panther Party" (October 1966). Retrieved on 3/7/2004 from www.stanford.edu/group/blackpanthers/history. shtml.

organizing black self-defense groups that are dedicated to defending our black community from racist police oppression and brutality. The Second Amendment to the Constitution of the United States gives a right to bear arms. We therefore believe that all black people should arm themselves for self defense.

8. We want freedom for all black men held in federal, state, county and city prisons and jails. We believe that all black people should be released from the many jails and prisons because they have not received a fair and impartial trial.

9. We want all black people when brought to trial to be tried in court by a jury of their peer group or people from their black communities, as defined by the Constitution of the United States. We believe that the courts should follow the United States Constitution so that black people will receive fair trials. The 14th Amendment of the U.S. Constitution gives a man a right to be tried by his peer group. A peer is a person from a similar economic, social, religious, geographical, environmental, historical and racial background. To do this the court will be forced to select a jury from the black community from which the black defendant came. We have been, and are being tried by all-white juries that have no understanding of the "average reasoning man" of the black community.

10. We want land, bread, housing, education, clothing, justice and peace. And as our major political objective, a United Nations–supervised plebiscite to be held throughout the black colony in which only black colonial subjects will be allowed to participate for the purpose of determining the will of black people as to their national destiny.

When in the course of human events, it becomes necessary for one people to dissolve the political bands which have connected them with another, and to assume, among the powers of the earth, the separate and equal station to which the laws of nature and nature's God entitle them, a decent respect to the opinions of mankind requires that they should declare the causes which impel them to the separation.

We hold these truths to be self-evident, that all men are created equal; that they are endowed by their Creator with certain unalienable rights; that among these are life, liberty, and the pursuit of happiness. That, to secure these rights, governments are instituted among men, deriving their just powers from the consent of the governed; that, whenever any form of government becomes destructive of these ends, it is the right of the people to alter or to abolish it, and to institute a new government, laying its foundation on such principles, and organizing its powers in such form, as to them shall seem most likely to effect their safety and happiness. Prudence, indeed, will dictate that governments long established should not be changed for light and transient causes; and accordingly, all experience hath shown, that mankind are more disposed to suffer, while evils are sufferable, than to right themselves by abolishing the forms to which they are accustomed. But, when a long train of abuses and usurpations, pursuing invariable the same object, evinces a design to reduce them under absolute despotism, it is their right, it is their duty, to throw off such government, and to provide new guards for their future security.

Students for a Democratic Society

Robert Haber, Tom Hayden, Sharon Jeffrey, Robert Ross, and other students at the University of Michigan formed Students for a Democratic Society (SDS) in 1960. Influenced by the civil rights movement and specifically by sit-ins organized by black students in Greensboro, North Carolina, SDS sought to address many diverse issues that the United States was confronting at the end of the complacent 1950s. Basing much of their thinking on the writings of Marx, Lenin, Fanon, Marcuse, and other left-wing philosophers, SDS wanted the United States to live up to its lofty ideals of equality and freedom for all. In 1962, at a convention in Port Huron, Michigan, they released the following statement, written primarily by Tom Hayden, in which they called for a participatory democracy. For the rest of the decade, as the civil rights movement progressed and the Vietnam War eventually took center stage, SDS grew rapidly and had a huge impact on radicals. Unlike the Old Left, this New Left organization was not content merely to change the power structure but urged people to change their values, to change their consciousness. Only in this way could a true revolution come to fruition. SDS provided much of the intellectual foundation for the emerging student movement.

The Port Huron Statement, 1962

We are people of this generation, bred in at least modest comfort, housed now in universities, looking uncomfortably to the world we inherit.

When we were kids the United States was the wealthiest and strongest country in the world; the only one with the atom bomb, the least scarred by modern war, an initiator of the United Nations that we thought would distribute Western influence throughout the world. Freedom and equality for each individual, government of, by, and for the people—these American values we found good, principles by which we could live as men. Many of us began maturing in complacency.

As we grew, however, our comfort was penetrated by events too troubling to dismiss. First, the permeating and victimizing fact of human degradation, symbolized by the Southern struggle against racial bigotry, compelled most of us from silence to activism. Second, the enclosing fact of the Cold War, symbolized by the presence of the Bomb, brought awareness that we ourselves, and our friends, and millions of abstract "others" we knew more directly because of our common peril, might die at any time. We might deliberately ignore, or avoid, or fail to feel all other human problems, but not these two, for these were too

SOURCE: James Miller, *"Democracy Is In the Streets:" From Port Huron to the Siege of Chicago* (Cambridge, MA: Harvard University Press, 1987), 329–345.

immediate and crushing in their impact, too challenging in the demand that we as individuals take the responsibility for encounter and resolution.

While these and other problems either directly oppressed us or rankled our consciences and became our own subjective concerns, we began to see complicated and disturbing paradoxes in our surrounding America. The declaration "all men are created equal . . . " rang hollow before the facts of Negro life in the South and the big cities of the North. The proclaimed peaceful intentions of the United States contradicted its economic and military investments in the Cold War status quo.

We witnessed, and continue to witness, other paradoxes. With nuclear energy whole cities can easily be powered, yet the dominant nation-states seem more likely to unleash destruction greater than that incurred in all wars of human history. Although our own technology is destroying old and creating new forms of social organization, men still tolerate meaningless work and idleness. While two-thirds of mankind suffers undernourishment, our own upper classes revel amidst superfluous abundance. Although world population is expected to double in forty years, the nations still tolerate anarchy as a major principle of international conduct and uncontrolled exploitation governs the sapping of the earth's physical resources. Although mankind desperately needs revolutionary leadership, America rests in national stalemate, its goals ambiguous and tradition-bound instead of informed and clear, its democratic system apathetic and manipulated rather than "of, by, and for the people."

Not only did tarnish appear on our image of American virtue, not only did disillusion occur when the hypocrisy of American ideals was discovered, but we began to sense that what we had originally seen as the American Golden Age was actually the decline of an era. The worldwide outbreak of revolution against colonialism and imperialism, the entrenchment of totalitarian states, the menace of war, overpopulation, international disorder, supertechnology—these trends were testing the tenacity of our own commitment to democracy and freedom and our abilities to visualize their application to a world in upheaval.

Our work is guided by the sense that we may be the last generation in the experiment with living. But we are a minority—the vast majority of our people regard the temporary equilibriums of our society and world as eternally functional parts. In this is perhaps the outstanding paradox; we ourselves are imbued with urgency, yet the message of our society is that there is no viable alternative to the present. Beneath the reassuring tones of the politicians, beneath the common opinion that America will "muddle through," beneath the stagnation of those who have closed their minds to the future, is the pervading feeling that there simply are no alternatives, that our times have witnessed the exhaustion not only of Utopias, but of any new departures as well.

Feeling the press of complexity upon the emptiness of life, people are fearful of the thought that at any moment things might be thrust out of control. They fear change itself, since change might smash whatever invisible framework seems to hold back chaos for them now.

For most Americans, all crusades are suspect, threatening. The fact that each individual sees apathy in his fellows perpetuates the common reluctance to organize for change. The dominant institutions are complex enough to blunt the minds of their potential critics, and entrenched enough to swiftly dissipate or entirely repel the energies of protest and reform, thus limiting human expectancies. Then, too, we are a materially improved society, and by our own improvements we seem to have weakened the case for further change.

Some would have us believe that Americans feel contentment amidst prosperity—but might it not better be called a glaze above deeply felt anxieties about their role in the new world? And if these anxieties produce a developed indifference to human affairs, do they not as well produce a yearning to believe that there is an alternative to the present, that something can be done to change circumstances in the school, the workplaces, the bureaucracies, the government?

It is to this latter yearning, at once the spark and engine of change, that we direct our present appeal. The search for truly democratic alternatives to the present, and a commitment to social experimentation with them, is a worthy and fulfilling human enterprise, one which moves us and, we hope, others today.

On such a basis do we offer this document of our convictions and analysis: as an effort in understanding and changing the conditions of humanity in the late twentieth century, an effort rooted in the ancient, still unfulfilled conception of man attaining determining influence over his circumstances of life. . . .

Making values explicit—an initial task in establishing alternatives—is an activity that has been devalued and corrupted. The conventional moral terms of the age, the politician moralities—"free world," "people's democracies"—reflect realities poorly, if at all, and seem to function more as ruling myths than as descriptive principles. But neither has our experience in the universities brought us moral enlightenment. Our professors and administrators sacrifice controversy to public relations; their curriculums change more slowly than the living events of the world; their skills and silence are purchased by investors in the arms race; passion is called unscholastic. The questions we might want raised—what is really important? can we live in a different and better way? if we wanted to change society, how would we do it?—are not thought to be questions of a "fruitful, empirical nature," and thus are brushed aside. . . .

Theoretic chaos has replaced the idealistic thinking of old—and, unable to reconstitute theoretic order, men have condemned idealism itself. Doubt has replaced hopefulness—and men act out a defeatism that is labeled realistic. The decline of utopia and hope is in fact one of the defining features of social life today. The reasons are various: the dreams of the older left were perverted by Stalinism and never re-created; the congressional stalemate makes men narrow their view of the possible; the specialization of human activity leaves little room for sweeping thought; the horrors of the twentieth century symbolized in the gas ovens and concentration camps and atom bombs, have blasted hopefulness. To be idealistic is to be considered apocalyptic, deluded. To have no serious aspirations, on the contrary, is to be "tough-minded."

In suggesting social goals and values, therefore, we are aware of entering a sphere of some disrepute. Perhaps matured by the past, we have no formulas, no closed theories—but that does not mean values are beyond discussion and tentative determination. A first task of any social movement is to convince people that the search for orienting theories and the creation of human values is complex but worthwhile. We are aware that to avoid platitudes we must analyze the concrete conditions of social order. But to direct such an analysis we must use the guideposts of basic principles. Our own social values involve conceptions of human beings, human relationships, and social systems.

We regard men as infinitely precious and possessed of unfulfilled capacities for reason, freedom, and love. In affirming these principles we are aware of countering perhaps the dominant conceptions of man in the twentieth century: that he is a thing to be manipulated, and that he is inherently incapable of directing his own affairs. We oppose the depersonalization that reduces human being to the status of things—if anything, the brutalities of the twentieth century teach that means and ends are intimately related, that vague appeals to "posterity" cannot justify the mutilations of the present. We oppose, too, the doctrine of human incompetence because it rests essentially on the modern fact that men have been "competently" manipulated into incompetence—we see little reason why men cannot meet with increasing the skill the complexities and responsibilities of their situation, if society is organized not for minority, but for majority, participation in decision-making.

Men have unrealized potential for self-cultivation, self-direction, self-understanding, and creativity. It is this potential that we regard as crucial and to which we appeal, not to the human potentiality for violence, unreason, and submission to authority. The goal of man and society should be human independence: a concern not with image of popularity but with finding a meaning in life that is personally authentic; a quality of mind not compulsively driven by a sense of powerlessness, nor one which unthinkingly adopts status values, nor one which represses all threats to its habits, but one which has full, spontaneous access to present and past experiences, one which easily unites the fragmented parts of personal history, one which openly faces problems which are troubling and unresolved; one with an intuitive awareness of possibilities, an active sense of curiosity, an ability and willingness to learn.

This kind of independence does not mean egotistic individualism—the object is not to have one's way so much as it is to have a way that is one's own. Nor do we deify man—we merely have faith in his potential.

Human relationships should involve fraternity and honesty. Human interdependence is contemporary fact; human brotherhood must be willed, however, as a condition of future survival and as the most appropriate form of social relations. Personal links between man and man are needed, especially to go beyond the partial and fragmentary bonds of function that bind men only as worker to worker, employer to employee, teacher to student, American to Russian.

Loneliness, estrangement, isolation describe the vast distance between man and man today. These dominant tendencies cannot be overcome by better personnel management, nor by improved gadgets, but only when a love of man overcomes the idolatrous worship of things by man. As the individualism we affirm is not egoism, the selflessness we affirm is not self-elimination. On the contrary, we believe in generosity of a kind that imprints one's unique individual qualities in the relation to other men, and to all human activity. Further, to dislike isolation is not to favor the abolition of privacy; the latter differs from isolation in that it occurs or is abolished according to individual will.

Finally, we would replace power rooted in possession, privilege, or circumstance by power and uniqueness rooted in love, reflectiveness, reason, and creativity. As a *social system* we seek the establishment of a democracy of individual participation, governed by two central aims: that the individual share in those social decisions determining the quality and direction of his life; that society be organized to encourage independence in men and provide the media for their common participation.

In a participatory democracy, the political life would be based in several root principles: that decision-making of basic social consequence be carried on by public groupings; that politics be seen positively, as the art of collectively creating an acceptable pattern of social relations; that politics has the function of bringing people out of isolation and into community, thus being a necessary, though not sufficient, means of finding meaning in personal life; that the political order should serve to clarify problems in a way instrumental to their solution; it should provide outlets for the expression of personal grievance and aspiration; opposing views should be organized so as to illuminate choices and facilitate the attainment of goals; channels should be commonly available to relate men to knowledge and to power so that private problems—from bad recreation facilities to personal alienation—are formulated as general issues.

The economic sphere would have as its basis the principles: that work should involve incentives worthier than money or survival. It should be educative, not stultifying; creative, not mechanical; self-directed, not manipulated, encouraging independence, a respect for others, a sense of dignity, and a willingness to accept social responsibility, since it is this experience that has crucial influence on habits, perceptions and individual ethics; that the economic experience is so personally decisive that the individual must share in its full determination; that the economy itself is of such social importance that its major resources and means of production should be open to democratic participation and subject to democratic social regulation.

Like the political and economic ones, major social institutions—cultural, educational, rehabilitative, and others—should be generally organized with the well-being and dignity of man as the essential measure of success.

In social change or interchange, we find violence to be abhorrent because it requires generally the transformation of the target, be it a human being or a community of people, into a depersonalized object of hate. It is imperative that the means of violence be abolished and the institutions—local, national, international—that encourage non-violence as a condition of conflict be developed. These are our central values, in skeletal form. It remains vital to understand their denial or attainment in the context of the modern world. . . .

Betty Friedan (1921–2006)

Freelance writer Betty Friedan, a 1942 graduate of Smith College, sent out a questionnaire on the occasion of her fifteenth class reunion to her fellow alumna to evaluate how successful they had become. The replies suggested that though most of them were doing quite well materially, a substantial number felt deeply discontented with how their lives had turned out. This prompted Friedan to do extensive research and a series of in-depth interviews to write about what she called the "problem that has no name." When she had finished, she submitted the article to McCall's *and* Ladies' Home Journal. *Both magazines rejected it. Though frustrated about the rejections, she continued and expanded her research, and in 1963 the article was finally published as a book.* The Feminine Mystique *was an immediate best seller and a significant factor in launching the modern feminist movement. It was foolish, Friedan wrote, for people to believe in the feminine mystique—the assumption that women could achieve happiness only by waxing the kitchen floor, scrubbing the bathtub, and taking care of husband and children. Many of her classmates from Smith were living in nice suburbs, with nice husbands, and nice children. To Friedan, however, these suburbs were nothing more than "comfortable concentration camps" in which women's creativity was stifled. The time had now come, she claimed, for women to cast off the false ideology and values that stultified their ambitions and opportunities.*

Though Friedan had been active, before she wrote The Feminine Mystique, *in the labor movement, left-wing politics, and the civil rights movement, she was criticized for concentrating mostly on middle-class white women in her analysis. In 1966 she founded the National Organization for Women (NOW), dedicated "to the proposition that women, first and foremost, are human beings who, like all other people in our society, must have the chance to develop their fullest human potential." From its founding to the present, NOW continues to campaign for equal opportunities for women in the workplace and in education and is committed to changing "the false image of women now prevalent in the mass media, and in the texts, ceremonies, laws, and practices of our major social institutions."*

THE FEMININE MYSTIQUE, 1963

The problem lay buried, unspoken, for many years in the minds of American women. It was a strange stirring, a sense of dissatisfaction, a yearning that

SOURCE: Betty Friedan, *The Feminine Mystique* (New York: Norton, 1963), 15–20.

women suffered in the middle of the twentieth century in the United States. Each suburban wife struggled with it alone. As she made the beds, shopped for groceries, matched slipcover material, ate peanut butter sandwiches with her children, chauffeured Cub Scouts and Brownies, lay beside her husband at night—she was afraid to ask even of herself the silent question—"Is this all?"

For over fifteen years there was no word of this yearning in the millions of words written about women, for women, in all the columns, books and articles by experts telling women their role was to seek fulfillment as wives and mothers. Over and over women heard in voices of tradition and of Freudian sophistication that they could desire no greater destiny than to glory in their own femininity. Experts told them how to catch a man and keep him, how to breastfeed children and handle their toilet training, how to cope with sibling rivalry and adolescent rebellion; how to buy a dishwasher, bake bread, cook gourmet snails, and build a swimming pool with their own hands; how to dress, look, and act more feminine and make marriage more exciting; how to keep their husbands from dying young and their sons from growing into delinquents. They were taught to pity the neurotic, unfeminine, unhappy women who wanted to be poets or physicists or presidents. They learned that truly feminine women do not want careers, higher education, political rights—the independence and the opportunities that the old-fashioned feminists fought for. Some women, in their forties and fifties, still remembered painfully giving up those dreams, but most of the younger women no longer even thought about them. A thousand expert voices applauded their femininity, their adjustment, their new maturity. All they had to do was devote their lives from earliest girlhood to finding a husband and bearing children.

By the end of the nineteen-fifties, the average marriage age of women in America dropped to 20, and was still dropping, into the teens. Fourteen million girls were engaged by 17. The proportion of women attending college in comparison with men dropped from 47 percent in 1920 to 35 percent in 1958. A century earlier, women had fought for higher education; now girls went to college to get a husband. By the mid-fifties, 60 percent dropped out of college to marry, or because they were afraid too much education would be a marriage bar. Colleges built dormitories for "married students," but the students were almost always the husbands. A new degree was instituted for the wives—"Ph.T." (Putting Husband Through).

Then American girls began getting married in high school. And the women's magazines, deploring the unhappy statistics about these young marriages, urged that courses on marriage, and marriage counselors, be installed in the high schools. Girls started going steady at twelve and thirteen, in junior high. Manufacturers put out brassieres with false bosoms or foam rubber for little girls of ten. And an advertisement for a child's dress, size 3–6s, in the *New York Times* in the fall of 1960, said: "She Too Can Join the Man-Trap Set."

By the end of the fifties, the United States birthrate was overtaking India's. The birth-control movement, renamed Planned Parenthood, was asked to find a method whereby women who had been advised that a third or fourth baby would be born dead or defective might have it anyhow. Statisticians were especially astounded at the fantastic increase in the number of babies among college women. Where once they had two children, now they had four, five, six. Women who had once wanted careers were now making careers out of having babies. So rejoiced *Life* magazine in a 1956 paean to the movement of American women back to the home.

In a New York hospital, a woman had a nervous breakdown when she found she could not breastfeed her baby. In other hospitals, women dying of cancer refused a drug which research had proved might save their lives: its side effects were said to be unfeminine. "If I have only one life, let me live it as a blonde," a larger-than-life-sized picture of a pretty, vacuous woman proclaimed from newspaper, magazine, and drugstores ads. And across America, three out of every ten women dyed their hair blonde. They ate a chalk called Metrecal, instead of food, to shrink to the size of the thin young models. Department-store buyers reported that American women, since 1939, had become three and four sizes smaller, "Women are out to fit the clothes, instead of vice-versa," one buyer said.

Interior decorators were designing kitchens with mosaic murals and original paintings, for kitchens were once again the center of women's lives. Home sewing became a million-dollar industry. Many women no longer left their homes, except to shop, chauffeur their children, or attend a social engagement with their husbands. Girls were growing up in America without ever having jobs outside the home. In the late fifties, a sociological phenomenon was suddenly remarked: a third of American women now worked, but most were no longer young and very few were pursuing careers. They were married women who held part-time jobs, selling or secretarial, to put their husbands through school, their sons through college, or to help pay the mortgage. Or they were widows supporting families. Fewer and fewer women were entering professional work. The shortages in the nursing, social work, and teaching professions caused crises in almost every American city. Concerned over the Soviet Union's lead in the space race, scientists noted the America's greatest source of unused brainpower was women. But girls would not study physics: it was "unfeminine." A girl refused a science fellowship at Johns Hopkins to take a job in a real-estate office. All she wanted, she said, was what every other American girl wanted—to get married, have four children and live in a nice house in a nice suburb.

The suburban housewife—she was the dream image of the young American women and the envy, it was said, of women all over the world. The American housewife—freed by science and labor-saving appliances from the drudgery, the angers of childbirth and the illnesses of her grandmother. She was healthy, beautiful, educated, concerned only about her husband, her children, her home. She had found true feminine fulfillment. As a housewife and mother, she was respected as a full and equal partner to man in his world. She was free to choose automobiles, clothes, appliances, supermarkets; she had everything that women ever dreamed of.

In the fifteen years after World War II, this mystique of feminine fulfillment became the cherished and self-perpetuating core of contemporary American culture. Millions of women lived their lives in the image of those pretty pictures of the American suburban housewife, kissing their husbands goodbye in front of the picture window, depositing their station wagons full of children at school, and smiling as they ran the new electric waxer over the spotless kitchen floor. They baked their own bread, sewed their own and their children's clothes, kept their new washing machines and dryers running all day. They changed the sheets on the beds twice a week instead of once, took the rug-hooking class in adult education, and pitied their poor frustrated mothers, who had dreamed of having a career. Their only dream was to be perfect wives and mothers; their highest ambition to have five children and a beautiful house, their only fight to get and keep their husbands. They had no thought for the unfeminine problems of the world outside the home; they wanted the men to make the major decisions. They gloried in their role as women, and wrote proudly on the census blank: "Occupation: housewife."

For over fifteen years, the words written for women, and the words women used when they talked to each other, while their husbands sat on the other side of the room and talked shop or politics or septic tanks, were about problems with their children, or how to keep their husbands happy, or improve their children's school or cook chicken or make slipcovers. Nobody argued whether women were inferior or superior to men; they were simply different. Words like "emancipation" and "career" sounded strange and embarrassing; no one had used them for years. When a Frenchwoman named Simone de Beauvoir wrote a book called *The Second Sex*, an American critic commented that she obviously "didn't know what life was all about," and besides, she was talking about French women. The "woman problem" in America no longer existed.

If a woman had a problem in the 1950's and 1960's she knew that something must be wrong with her marriage, or with herself. Other women were satisfied with their lives, she thought. What kind of woman was she if she did not feel this mysterious fulfillment waxing the kitchen floor? She was so ashamed to admit her dissatisfaction that she never knew how many other women shared it. If she tried to tell her husband, he didn't understand what she was talking about. She did not really understand it herself. For over fifteen years women in America found it harder to talk about this problem than about sex. Even the psychoanalysts had no name for it. When a woman went to a psychiatrist for help, as many women did, she would say, "I'm so ashamed," or "I must be hopelessly neurotic." "I don't know what's wrong with women today," a suburban psychiatrist said uneasily. "I only know something is wrong because most of my patients happen to be women. And their problem isn't sexual." Most women with this problem did not go to see a psychoanalyst, however. "There's nothing wrong really," they kept telling themselves. "There isn't any problem."

But on an April morning in 1959, I heard a mother of four, having coffee with four other mothers in a suburban development fifteen miles from New York, say in a tone of quiet desperation, "the problem." And the others knew, without words, that she was not talking about a problem with her husband, or her children, or her home. Suddenly they realized they all shared the same problem, the problem that has no name. They began, hesitantly, to talk about it. Later, after they had picked up their children at nursery school and taken them home to nap, two of the women cried, in sheer relief, just to know they were not alone.

Gradually I came to realize that the problem that has no name was shared by countless women in America. As a magazine writer I often interviewed women about problems with their children, or their marriages, or their houses, or their communities. But after a while I began to recognize the telltale signs of this other problem. I saw the same signs in suburban ranch houses and split-levels on Long Island and in New Jersey and Westchester County; in colonial houses in the small Massachusetts town; on patios in Memphis; in suburban and city apartments; in living rooms in the Midwest. Sometimes I sensed the problem, not as a reporter, but as a suburban housewife, for during this time I was also bringing up my own three children in Rockland County, New York. I heard echoes of the problem in college dormitories and semi-private maternity wards, at PTA meetings and luncheons of the League of Women Voters, at suburban cocktail parities, in station wagons waiting for trains, and in snatches of conversation overheard at Schrafft's. The groping words I heard from other women, on quiet afternoons when children were at school or on quiet evenings when husbands worked late, I think I understood first as a woman long before I understood their larger social and psychological implications.

Protest Music I

During the latter half of the 1950s a number of coffee houses and folk clubs opened in New York and San Francisco. This was partly an outgrowth of the popularity of the Weavers folk group as well as the growing Beat Movement. Beat poets (and would-be poets) often gathered in these smoke-filled clubs to exchange ideas, denounce the conformist social atmosphere of the 1950s, read their poetry, and, in some cases, sing their songs. The result was the folk music revival. In 1958, when the Kingston Trio's "Tom Dooley" raced to the top of the charts, folk music became a force in popular culture. By the early 1960s, numerous performers such as Peter, Paul, and Mary, Joan Baez, Phil Ochs, and Bob Dylan were appealing to a rapidly growing audience of baby boomers. At first these musicians recorded and performed traditional songs; the songs of Woody Guthrie, Leadbelly, and Pete Seeger; or songs from 1920s blues artists like Mississippi John Hurt or Robert Johnson. Soon, however, many folk artists began writing their own songs. This was especially true of Bob Dylan and Phil Ochs, who had such an influence that by 1965 it was almost a requirement for any would-be folksingers to be writing their own songs.

Folk songs tell a story. A story can be political. Many of the songs performed at the clubs (and later at larger venues like Carnegie Hall) were critical and probing explorations of the problems facing the nation: civil rights, the cold war, the uptight conformity of crew-cut, gray-flannel-suit America, and the arms race that seemed to be pushing the world to the brink of Armageddon.

Phil Ochs presents his version of history here in his antiwar "I Ain't Marchin' Anymore," and Malvina Reynolds takes on conventionality and "fitting in" in "Little Boxes." Bob Dylan's "The Times They Are A-Changin' " has become one of the anthems of the 1960s and in "It's Alright Ma (I'm Only Bleeding)" Dylan seems to take on everything.

Phil Ochs, "I Ain't Marching Anymore," 1965

Oh I marched to the battle of New Orleans
At the end of the early British war
The young land started growing
The young blood started flowing
But I ain't marching anymore

For I've killed my share of Indians
In a thousand different fights
I was there at the Little Big Horn
I heard many men lying
I saw many more dying
But I ain't marching anymore

It's always the old to lead us to the war
It's always the young to fall
Now look at all we've won with the sabre and the gun
Tell me is it worth it all

For I stole California from the Mexican land
Fought in the bloody Civil War
Yes I even killed my brother
And so many others
And I ain't marching anymore

For I marched to the battles of the German trench
In a war that was bound to end all wars
Oh I must have killed a million men
And now they want me back again
But I ain't marching anymore

SOURCE: Phil Ochs, *I Ain't Marching Anymore*, Hannibal 1965.

For I flew the final mission in the Japanese sky
Set off the mighty mushroom roar
When I saw the cities burning
I knew that I was learning
That I ain't marching anymore

Now the labor leader's screamin' when they close the missile plants,
United Fruit screams at the Cuban shore,
Call it "Peace" or call it "Treason,"
Call it "Love" or call it "Reason,"
But I ain't marching any more.

MALVINA REYNOLDS, "LITTLE BOXES," 1962

Little boxes on the hillside,
Little boxes made of ticky tacky
Little boxes on the hillside,
Little boxes all the same,
There's a green one and a pink one
And a blue one and a yellow one
And they're all made out of ticky tacky
And they all look just the same.

And the people in the houses
All went to the university
Where they were put in boxes
And they came out all the same
And there's doctors and lawyers
And business executives
And they're all made out of ticky tacky
And they all look just the same.

And they all play on the golf course
And drink their martinis dry
And they all have pretty children
And the children go to school,
And the children go to summer camp
And then to the university
Where they are put in boxes
And they come out all the same.

And the boys go into business
And marry and raise a family

SOURCE: Pete Seeger, *We Shall Overcome: The Carnegie Hall Concert,* Columbia 1963.

In boxes made of ticky tacky
And they all look just the same,
There's a green one and a pink one
And a blue one and a yellow one
And they're all made out of ticky tacky
And they all look just the same.

Bob Dylan, "The Times They Are A-Changin'," 1963

Come gather 'round people
Wherever you roam
And admit that the waters
Around you have grown
And accept it that soon
You'll be drenched to the bone.
If your time to you
Is worth savin'
Then you better start swimmin'
Or you'll sink like a stone
For the times they are a-changin'.

Come writers and critics
Who prophesize with your pen
And keep your eyes wide
The chance won't come again
And don't speak too soon
For the wheel's still in spin
And there's no tellin' who
That it's namin'.
For the loser now
Will be later to win
For the times they are a-changin'.

Come senators, congressmen
Please heed the call
Don't stand in the doorway
Don't block up the hall
For he that gets hurt
Will be he who has stalled
There's a battle outside
And it is ragin'.

SOURCE: Bob Dylan, *The Times They are A-Changin'*, Columbia 1964.

It'll soon shake your windows
And rattle your walls
For the times they are a-changin'.

Come mothers and fathers
Throughout the land
And don't criticize
What you can't understand
Your sons and your daughters
Are beyond your command
Your old road is
Rapidly agin'.
Please get out of the new one
If you can't lend your hand
For the times they are a-changin'.

The line it is drawn
The curse it is cast
The slow one now
Will later be fast
As the present now
Will later be past
The order is
Rapidly fadin'.
And the first one now
Will later be last
For the times they are a-changin'.

Bob Dylan, "It's Alright Ma (I'm Only Bleeding)," 1965

Darkness at the break of noon
Shadows even the silver spoon
The handmade blade, the child's balloon
Eclipses both the sun and moon
To understand you know too soon
There is no sense in trying.

Pointed threats, they bluff with scorn
Suicide remarks are torn
From the fool's gold mouthpiece
The hollow horn plays wasted words
Proves to warn

Source: Bob Dylan. *Bringing It All Back Home*, Columbia 1965.

That he not busy being born
Is busy dying.

Temptation's page flies out the door
You follow, find yourself at war
Watch waterfalls of pity roar
You feel to moan but unlike before
You discover
That you'd just be
One more person crying.

So don't fear if you hear
A foreign sound to your ear
It's alright, Ma, I'm only sighing.

As some warn victory, some downfall
Private reasons great or small
Can be seen in the eyes of those that call
To make all that should be killed to crawl
While others say don't hate nothing at all
Except hatred.

Disillusioned words like bullets bark
As human gods aim for their mark
Made everything from toy guns that spark
To flesh-colored Christs that glow in the dark
It's easy to see without looking too far
That not much
Is really sacred.

While preachers preach of evil fates
Teachers teach that knowledge waits
Can lead to hundred-dollar plates
Goodness hides behind its gates
But even the president of the United States
Sometimes must have
To stand naked.

An' though the rules of the road have been lodged
It's only people's games that you got to dodge
And it's alright, Ma, I can make it.

Advertising signs that con you
Into thinking you're the one
That can do what's never been done
That can win what's never been won
Meantime life outside goes on
All around you.

You lose yourself, you reappear
You suddenly find you got nothing to fear
Alone you stand with nobody near
When a trembling distant voice, unclear
Startles your sleeping ears to hear
That somebody thinks
They really found you.

A question in your nerves is lit
Yet you know there is no answer fit to satisfy
Insure you not to quit
To keep it in your mind and not fergit
That it is not he or she or them or it
That you belong to.

Although the masters make the rules
For the wise men and the fools
I got nothing, Ma, to live up to.

For them that must obey authority
That they do not respect in any degree
Who despise their jobs, their destinies
Speak jealously of them that are free
Cultivate their flowers to be
Nothing more than something
They invest in.

While some on principles baptized
To strict party platform ties
Social clubs in drag disguise
Outsiders they can freely criticize
Tell nothing except who to idolize
And then say God bless him.

While one who sings with his tongue on fire
Gargles in the rat race choir
Bent out of shape from society's pliers
Cares not to come up any higher
But rather get you down in the hole
That he's in.

But I mean no harm nor put fault
On anyone that lives in a vault
But it's alright, Ma, if I can't please him.

Old lady judges watch people in pairs
Limited in sex, they dare
To push fake morals, insult and stare

While money doesn't talk, it swears
Obscenity, who really cares
Propaganda, all is phony.

While them that defend what they cannot see
With a killer's pride, security
It blows the minds most bitterly
For them that think death's honesty
Won't fall upon them naturally
Life sometimes
Must get lonely.

My eyes collide head-on with stuffed graveyards
False gods, I scuff
At pettiness which plays so rough
Walk upside-down inside handcuffs
Kick my legs to crash it off
Say okay, I have had enough
What else can you show me?

And if my thought-dreams could be seen
They'd probably put my head in a guillotine
But it's alright, Ma, it's life, and life only.

PART EIGHT

Mobilization: Vietnam and the Counterculture, 1964–1975

March on the Pentagon, October 21, 1967. *Anti–Vietnam War demonstrators, led by activist Dr. Benjamin Spock, leaving the Lincoln Memorial on their way to the Pentagon.*

INTRODUCTION: THE MOVEMENT

The radical 1960s was not a period confined to the boundaries of the actual decade. The seeds were sown in the 1950s and early 1960s, but the era of "doing your own thing," believing "we can change the world," and demanding an end to the Vietnam War and the draft really did not begin until the mid-1960s, and it did not suddenly end on January 1, 1970. Indeed the second wave of the movement, according to historian Terry Anderson, the most radical phase, took place primarily in the early 1970s.

In 1964 and 1965, in the aftermath of the Kennedy assassination, the fight against segregation in the South peaked. The culmination of the civil rights movement overlapped the emerging issue of Vietnam, and as discussion of the war heated up and took center stage by 1967, many of the civil disobedience tactics of the civil rights movement were adopted by antiwar activists. Although it appeared on the surface to American foreign policy experts that Vietnam was simply another front line of the cold war in which the United States was committed to containing the spread of communism, the fact remains that Vietnam was a far thornier and more complex issue. Vietnamese nationalist Ho Chi Minh had been agitating for Vietnamese independence from France throughout most of the twentieth century. In Paris at the end of the First World War, Ho Chi Minh had tried to gain an audience with President Woodrow Wilson in an effort to win the U.S. president's support for an independent Vietnam. Ignored in 1919, Ho Chi Minh refused to give up. Throughout the 1920s and 1930s, he lived in the Soviet Union and China, during which time he helped found the Indochinese Communist Party. In 1941, after the Japanese overran the French colony of Indochina (Vietnam, Laos, and Cambodia), Ho founded a new Vietnamese communist party dedicated to Vietnamese independence, the Vietminh. During the war, as the Vietminh fought against the Japanese occupiers, their efforts were supported by U.S. aid. When the Japanese surrendered, Ho declared the new independent Democratic Republic of Vietnam and hoped that now, surely, the United States would support Vietnamese independence. Indeed, he had taken to heart many of President Roosevelt's comments about the ending of colonialism and imperialism in the postwar world. However, Roosevelt did not survive to see the postwar world, and his successor, Harry S Truman, believed that France's wishes were far more important to the security of Europe and the United States than the hopes of the Vietnamese. The French regained control in Vietnam, and war with Ho Chi Minh's forces ensued. In 1954, after the French defeat at Dien Bien Phu, France decided to abandon the colony.

An agreement was reached in Geneva that Vietnam would be split at the 17th parallel into North and South Vietnam. Ho would head a communist government in the north, and, after a brief interval with Emperor Bao Dai, Ngo Dinh Diem, an ardent anticommunist nationalist, would lead the south. The agreement also called for elections two years hence, in which the Vietnamese people could vote to reunite the country under one government. In 1956, however, the election was canceled because South Vietnamese leaders and the United States realized that the very popular Ho Chi Minh would easily win the election. It was from this point on that the United States began to be drawn ever more deeply into what was to become a quagmire.

With the clarity of hindsight, we can see that central to the problem was that the United States was never able to see Ho Chi Minh for what he was—a nationalist first and foremost, whose primary goal was a free and independent Vietnam. When we looked at him, we only saw red, so to speak; we saw him only as a communist and that meant, according to the cold war paradigm, that he was a pawn of Soviet and Chinese communist expansionists. Under Eisenhower, the United States poured billions of dollars in aid to support the anticommunist Diem in South Vietnam. When Eisenhower left office, there were approximately 900 U.S. military advisors in South Vietnam. Under Kennedy, this number jumped to 16,000. The plot thickened when, in the summer of 1963, the Kennedy administration, embarrassed by Diem's brutal oppression of Buddhists after several monks protested Diem's policies through the shocking tactic of self-immolation, gave tacit approval to a cadre of South Vietnamese generals who were plotting a coup against Diem. The coup took place at the beginning of November, Diem was assassinated and replaced by the generals, Kennedy was distraught that Diem had been murdered (he had, perhaps naively, expected that Diem would be sent into exile), and the United States found itself morally bound up with the outcome.

This was the situation Lyndon Johnson inherited three weeks later, when Kennedy was assassinated. In the atmosphere of grief that engulfed the nation in the aftermath of November 22, Johnson felt bound to carry on Kennedy's policies exactly as Kennedy would have carried them on. "Let us continue," Johnson had said in a speech to the joint houses of Congress the day after Kennedy's funeral. The two most visible legacies Kennedy left behind were civil rights and the commitment in Vietnam. Johnson urged a quick and swift passage to the Civil Rights Bill for which the slain president had so long worked (certainly a stretch, in that JFK finally introduced the bill in June 1963). As far as Vietnam was concerned, Johnson believed that withdrawing the U.S. military advisors would be seen as a rejection of Kennedy's policy, even though Kennedy's ambiguous comments in a September 1963 interview with Walter Cronkite indicated that he himself was undecided as to whether to strengthen or reduce our commitment in Vietnam. Furthermore, Johnson's policy in Vietnam was entirely consistent with 25 years of the policy of containment. Like so many others, Johnson accepted as true the "domino principle," that if one nation would fall to communism, then, like a row of toppling dominoes, the neighboring nations would fall, too. In August 1964, after the U.S. destroyer the *Maddox* was fired on in the Gulf of Tonkin, Johnson asked for, and Congress passed, the Gulf of Tonkin Resolution, which gave the president the necessary authority to protect American interests in Vietnam. This resolution, based, it turns out, on a somewhat fictionalized incident, was the authority on which the "war" was fought. Vietnam was not a declared war. This was the beginning of the escalation. Step by step, the United States was inexorably drawn into a conflict that it could not back out of without appearing weak or unreliable to its allies.

The late summer of 1964 was a pivotal moment for the United States. Not only did the Gulf of Tonkin Resolution signal the beginning of a deeper involvement in Vietnam but also it coincided with the end of one of the most significant civil rights operations, Freedom Summer. As many of the student volunteers who had worked in Mississippi that summer, registering African Americans to vote, returned to their campuses, they brought with them an extraordinarily high level of idealism and commitment to making the United States a better place. Setting up tables on campuses and distributing brochures and leaflets urging other students to get involved in the southern struggle for civil rights, young activists spread the word that "the times were a-changin.'" At the University of California at Berkeley, students were dismayed when the university told them they could *not* disseminate political information on campus. The resulting uproar led to the Berkeley Free Speech Movement, which rather quickly spread to other campuses around the country. The student movement was born. At first, students demonstrated for free speech, for civil rights, and against the university policy of *in loco parentis*, in which university officials attempted to control student behavior and morals. Vietnam became part of the mix in March 1965, when the University of Michigan inaugurated the first teach-in, in which professors and students examined, discussed, and debated the historical background of Vietnam. Also in 1965, the New Left group, Students for a Democratic Society, which had been founded in 1960, issued a statement condemning "American imperialism" in Vietnam. Within a year, Vietnam became the focus of most student activism. And activism gained noteworthy credibility as many Christian clergymen, such as Father Daniel Berrigan and the Reverend William Sloane Coffin, joined with the protesters. Bringing Christian precepts to protest added a deeply moral element reminiscent of the Social Gospel movement of the early twentieth century.

Simultaneously with the rise of a left-wing political consciousness, many young people also developed a concern with inner values. If, as it was perceived, the older generation was responsible for policies that led the nation into a questionable war in Southeast Asia and a policy of racial discrimination at home, and if these policies were all being severely condemned, then, it was reasoned, the moral values decreed by society should also be called into question. Perhaps the origin of the so-called counterculture can be traced to an event that, at the time, did not seem historically significant—the Beatles' appearance on the *Ed Sullivan Show*. "Beatlemania" had a profound influence on the youth of America and eventually influenced popular culture to such an extent that rock and roll and folk rock, along with the lifestyles and fashions of popular musicians, became central features in a rapidly evolving counterculture. Within days of the Beatles' February 1964 television appearance, teenage boys around the nation began to let their hair down, literally. The "mop top" hairstyle was here to stay—at least for a while. It was only a foretaste of things to come. The arrival of the Beatles on the American cultural scene coincided with the height of the civil rights movement, the aftermath of the Kennedy assassination, the launch of the student movement, and the first hints at the escalation of the Vietnam War. During a 1965 tour in the United States, the Beatles met Bob Dylan, and there seems little doubt that the English rock group and the American folk singer influenced each other. In the summer of that year, at the Newport Folk Festival, Bob Dylan made his historic appearance on stage with an electric guitar and a backing group rather than his trademark acoustic guitar and harmonica. Singing the surrealistic "Like a Rolling Stone," Dylan seemed to be abandoning the political protest songs that had brought him to national prominence. Many diehard folk purists felt betrayed and accused their idol of having sold out to pop culture. But from this point on, Dylan began paving a new way for himself and for other musicians. Folk rock was born. Also in 1965, the Beatles began writing and recording rock and roll songs with meaningful political and social lyrics, like "Eleanor Rigby" and "Nowhere Man." Within two years the Beatles recorded *Sergeant Pepper's Lonely Hearts Club Band*—arguably the most influential rock album ever—which contained "A Day in the Life," "She's Leaving Home," "Lucy in the Sky with Diamonds," and other songs of social meaning. By the late 1960s, rock and roll in the United States and England had been so radically transformed that it little resembled the teenybopper, bubble-gum music that had been popular earlier in the decade. The Fugs, The Mothers of Invention, The Doors, The Grateful Dead, Jimi Hendrix, Janis Joplin, Jefferson Airplane, and The Rolling Stones all began releasing songs filled with meaningful content. Some songs were thought pro-voking, some extolled drugs and free love, some were humorous parodies of the establishment, and others were filled with scathing, sarcastic comments on the state of the world. To be sure, many folk singers such as Pete Seeger, Phil Ochs, and Arlo Guthrie still performed protest songs without significantly changing their style, but popular music in America would never be the same.

While music was taking on a political character and heightening a sense of generational solidarity, other ideas became part of the evolving counterculture. Timothy Leary and others began to argue for the mind-expanding benefits of such drugs as LSD; drugs were a path to self-discovery and self-fulfillment. Sex, too, was being touted as a path to self-fulfillment. Many thinkers, taking the the-ories of Freud about sexual repression as a departure point, urged people to be conscious of their sexual repression and then through this awareness develop a healthier attitude about sex that would help them lead a more fulfilled life. These ideas, along with the invention of the birth control pill in 1960, triggered the "sexual revolution." Other trends developed. The 1950s Beat Movement's interest in Zen and Eastern thought also spread among members of the counterculture, who were very willing to experiment and try out any idea that might lead toward self-realization and spiritual growth. Alan Watts, Maharishi Mahesh Yogi, and Ram Dass among others espoused meditation as the way to enlightenment. In this way, the spiritual, the erotic, the intellectual, and the emotional faculties of the individual began to be viewed as political. All facets of life, all relationships, were political. The old set of values, the ideas about fitting in and being respectable, were jettisoned in favor of the view that it was what was inside each person that mattered. And since the inner person was what counted, it became central to the "hippie" mind-set that people should look like they did not care what they looked like. Thus long hair and beards, unshaven legs and armpits, thrift shop clothing and tie-dye expressed a new set of values.

The United States that emerged at the end of the watershed year of 1968 had drastically changed from the United States of a year earlier. The Tet Offen-sive in Vietnam, although it was a defeat for the communists, revealed that much of what the media and the administration was reporting about the war was overly optimistic and that the "light at the end of the tunnel" was nowhere in sight. (One pundit commented that the "light at the end of the tunnel" was the headlight of an oncoming, speeding locomotive.) As a result many ordinary middle-class citizens began to join with student activists in opposing the war. When Senator Eugene McCarthy of Minnesota, running in the Democratic primaries as an antiwar candidate, won more than 40 percent of the vote in the New Hampshire primary, many of the party faithful were shocked that in a conservative state like New Hampshire such a large minority would vote against Johnson's policy. Shortly after the primary, Senator Robert F. Kennedy threw his hat into the ring, declared his candidacy, and vowed to end the war in Vietnam. On March 31, President Johnson, painfully aware of Robert Kennedy's appeal to liberals, African Americans, Latinos, students, and labor, announced during a nationally televised address that he would neither seek nor accept his party's nomination for president. Antiwar activists around the nation were overjoyed, believing as they did that their antiwar posture had convinced the president to abdicate. But their joy perished four days later, on April 4, when an assassin gunned down Martin Luther King Jr. Grief and fear swept over much of the nation. Blacks rioted in many urban centers, extra security was implemented in Washington to protect the Capitol and the White House from violence, and dozens were killed. Robert Kennedy, in a speech the evening of King's assassination, urged restraint and invited blacks and whites to come together. "It is not the end of violence," he said, but we can, and we must, stand for what King stood for and go beyond violence to cultivate love for each other as a people.

In May, students at Columbia University in New York City took over the university and forced it to close down for the academic year. A wave of demonstrations swept around the world—Berlin, London, Paris. In France, students from the Sorbonne united with workers and forced the DeGaulle government to call for elections. The youth movement and the impetus for change spread behind the Iron Curtain as Czechoslovakia celebrated its Prague Spring—featuring an awakening of free speech and a critical reassessment of communism after the freeze of Stalinism.

In early June, moments after winning the California Democratic primary, Senator Kennedy, the man who had said only two months before that it was not the end of violence, was himself assassinated. By the time the Democratic convention met in Chicago, with demonstrators on the street being clubbed by police all the while chanting "the whole world is watching," it seemed that the United States was on the verge of revolution or maybe self-destruction. The United States did not self-destruct, but the Democratic Party did. The Republican candidate Richard Nixon won the November election, the war in Vietnam would continue for another six years, and many of the student activists who had, as recently as March, believed they could change the world had given up on the political process. By 1969, many had opted out and gone off to live on communes to explore alternative peaceful lifestyles, while others became more radical, like the Weathermen, who broke off from the disintegrating SDS and set out on a campaign of bombing and violence against the establishment.

Although 1968 was a dividing point, the movement continued on until the mid-1970s. In 1969, there were the rock festivals at Woodstock and at Altamont, and there were international moratorium days against the war in October and November—two of the largest antiwar demonstrations of the entire era. In 1970, when the *New York Times* reported on the Nixon administration's secret bombing of Cambodia, another huge wave of demonstrations swept the country. At Kent State University in Ohio, the National Guard fired on students, killing four and wounding several others. Though students were appalled, many Americans applauded the killings, boldly declaring the students deserved what they got. As Nixon stepped up the process of withdrawing American troops ("Vietnamization"), the antiwar demonstrations did begin to subside. As the antiwar movement declined, activists got more involved in local issues and the problems of specific minority groups. The lesson many people had learned from the 1960s is that activism led to empowerment, and empowerment gave groups and individuals some influence in forcing local governments to confront important local issues. In some places, for example, demonstrations were held and petitions signed against building interstate highways through inner-city neighborhoods, forcing local ruling bodies to comply with the public will. In 1969 gays in New York City took to the streets to demand the end of police raids on gay bars and nightclubs. The Gay Liberation Front was born. César Chávez led Chicano migrant workers in California to unionize and demand fair treatment. The American Indian Movement formed and, demanding Red Power, occupied Alcatraz Island and the town of Wounded Knee, South Dakota. Hundreds of thousands of citizens, troubled by industrial pollution and the harm being done to the environment, joined together to compel the government to deal with environmental concerns. In the late 1960s and early 1970s, women, who can hardly be called a "minority," campaigned to raise consciousness and awareness of the inequality of women in American society and pushed the women's movement in a more radical direction. The 1973 *Roe v. Wade* decision finally won for women the right to have control over their own bodies. Even conservatives learned from the protestors by employing the same tactics in marches supporting U.S. troops in Vietnam, in massive demonstrations against federally mandated busing, and at antiabortion rallies at Planned Parenthood clinics around the nation.

When Nixon became president, many observers believed his victory was the result of the Democratic Party having splintered between the doves and the hawks, between its peace faction and its war faction. However, in retrospect, recent historians have viewed Nixon's election as the beginning of a deeply conservative trend in the United States, a trend signifying that the middle class was fed up with the radical excesses of the 1960s. In some ways this view is accurate, but the legacy of the 1960s, the idea that people can and should stand up for issues and concerns that they believe are important, still survives. Whether conservative or liberal, reactionary or radical, people have no qualms about participating in demonstrations or signing petitions for redress of grievances. Though most dissenters have criticized the American mainstream from the left, it is not principally a left-wing phenomenon. Dissent encompasses all political persuasions because the essence of dissent is that it is beyond politics. Dissent is neither Democratic nor Republican. From the end of the Vietnam War in 1975 to the present, even during quiescent times, dissent continues to flourish. The triumph of conservatism did not and does not mean the silencing of dissent.

Mario Savio (1942–1996)

The Berkeley Free Speech Movement grew out of the aftermath of Freedom Summer. When a number of students from the University of California at Berkeley returned home after working for SNCC and CORE in Mississippi, they were understandably very enthusiastic about their experiences there. With evangelical fervor, they began spreading news about the voter registration drive and began recruiting other students for future activities in the South. The University of California announced that they could not set up tables on university property to promote civil rights. To students who believed that civil rights was the most important issue confronting the nation in 1964, this was unacceptable. When they refused to move, security staff were sent in to remove them. Believing that the university was stifling First Amendment freedom of speech, student organizations of every political persuasion, from the radical left to the radical right, began demonstrating against the university policy. Events escalated. During the fall of 1964, the demonstrations grew, many students were arrested, and daily university operations were greatly impaired. In December, one of the Free Speech Movement student leaders, Mario Savio, in an impassioned speech at a demonstration on the steps of Sproul Hall, urged the students to occupy it. The students occupied the building all night, brought the administration of the university to a halt, and remained until the police arrested 800 of them the following day.

SPEECH AT THE UNIVERSITY OF CALIFORNIA AT BERKELEY, DECEMBER 2, 1964

Now there are at least two ways in which sit-ins and civil disobedience, and whatever, at least two major ways in which it can occur. One when a law exists, is promulgated, which is totally unacceptable to people and they violate it again and again and again until it is rescinded, repealed. All right. But there is another way, . . . Sometimes the pull of the law is such as to render impossible its effective violation as a method to have it repealed. Sometimes the grievances of people **are more**, extend **more**, to more than just the law, extend to a whole mode of arbitrary power, a whole mode of arbitrary exercise of arbitrary power. And that's what we have here.

We have an autocracy which runs, . . . this university. It's managed. We were told the following: if President Kerr actually tried to get something more

---

SOURCE: From a copy in Lynne Hollander Savio's private collection.

liberal out of the regents in his telephone conversation why didn't he make some public statement to that effect? And the answer we received from a well-meaning liberal was the following: He said, "Would you ever imagine the manager of a firm making a statement publicly in opposition to his board of directors? That's the answer! Well I ask you to consider: If this is a firm and if the board of regents are the board of directors and if President Kerr in fact is the manager, then I'll tell you something: the faculty are a bunch of employees and we're the raw materials. But we're a bunch of raw materials that don't mean to **be**, have any process upon us, don't mean to be made into any product, don't mean . . . to end up being bought by some clients of the university, be they the government, be they industry, be they organized labor, be they anyone! We're human beings!

And that . . . brings me to the second mode of civil disobedience. There's a time when the operation of the machine becomes so odious, makes you so sick at heart that you can't take part. You can't even passively take part. And you've got to put your bodies upon the gears and upon the wheels, upon the levers, upon all apparatus, and you've got to make it stop. And you've got to indicate to the people who run it, to the people who own it, that unless you're free the machine will be prevented from working at all!

That doesn't mean—and it will be interpreted to mean unfortunately by the bigots who run The [San Francisco] Examiner for example—that doesn't mean that you have to break anything. One thousand people sitting down someplace not letting anybody by, not letting anything happen can stop any machine, including this machine, and it will stop! We're going to do the following and the greater the number of people the safer they'll be and the more effective it will be. We're going once again to march up to the second floor of Sproul Hall. And we're going to conduct our lives for a while in the second floor of Sproul Hall. We'll show movies for example. We tried to get Une Chante d'Amour. Unfortunately that's tied up in the courts because of a lot of squeamish moral mothers for a moral America and other people on the outside. The same people who get all their ideas out of The San Francisco Examiner. Sad. Sad. But Mr. Landau, . . . has gotten us some other films. Likewise we'll do something . . . which hasn't occurred at this university in a good long time. We're going to have *real classes* up there. There are going to be freedom schools conducted up there. We're going to have classes on [the] First and Fourteenth Amendments. We're going to spend our time learning about the things this university is afraid that we know. We're going to learn about freedom up there. And we're going to learn by doing.

Now we've had some good long rallies. Just one moment. **We've had some good long rallies**. And I think I'm sicker of rallies than anyone else here. It's not going to be long. I'd like to introduce one last person . . . before we enter Sproul Hall. And the person is Joan Baez.

. . . We're going to march in singing "We Shall Overcome." Slowly, there are a lot of us. . . .

Carl Oglesby (1935–)

Students for a Democratic Society (SDS)(see pages 580–584), founded at
the beginning of the decade, was by the mid-1960s the leading New Left
organization of the student movement. During a major antiwar march
on Washington on November 27, 1965, newly-elected SDS president
Carl Oglesby delivered a well-received speech denouncing the war and
analyzing the dichotomy between U.S. policy in Vietnam and America's
revolutionary heritage.

Speech Denouncing the War in Vietnam, Washington, DC, November 27, 1965

Seven months ago at the April March on Washington, Paul Potter, then President of Students for a Democratic Society, stood in approximately this spot and said that we must name the system that creates and sustains the war in Vietnam—name it, describe it, analyze it, understand it, and change it.

Today I will try to name it—to suggest an analysis which, to be quite frank, may disturb some of you—and to suggest what changing it may require of us.

We are here again to protest a growing war. Since it is a very bad war, we acquire the habit of thinking it must be caused by very bad men. But we only conceal reality, I think, to denounce on such grounds the menacing coalition of industrial and military power, or the brutality of the blitzkrieg we are waging against Vietnam, or the ominous signs around us that heresy may soon no longer be permitted. We must simply observe, and quite plainly say, that this coalition, this blitzkrieg, and this demand for acquiescence are creatures, all of them, of a government that since 1932 has considered itself to be fundamentally *liberal.*

The original commitment in Vietnam was made by President Truman, a mainstream liberal. It was seconded by President Eisenhower, a moderate liberal. It was intensified by the late President Kennedy, a flaming liberal. Think of the men who now engineer that war—those who study the maps, give the commands, push the buttons, and tally the dead: Bundy, McNamara, Rusk, Lodge, Goldberg, the President himself.

They are not moral monsters.
They are all honorable men.
They are all liberals.

But so, I'm sure, are many of us who are here today in protest. To understand the war, then, it seems necessary to take a closer look at this American liberalism.

Source: Retrieved 3/9/2004 from http://sdsrebels.com/oglesby.htm.

Maybe we are in for some surprises. Maybe we have here two quite different liberalisms: one authentically humanist; the other not so humane at all.

Not long ago I considered myself a liberal and if, someone had asked me what I meant by that, I'd perhaps have quoted Thomas Jefferson or Thomas Paine, who first made plain our nation's unprovisional commitment to human rights. But what do you think would happen if these two heroes could sit down now for a chat with President Johnson and McGeorge Bundy?

They would surely talk of the Vietnam war. Our dead revolutionaries would soon wonder why their country was fighting against what appeared to be a revolution. The living liberals would hotly deny that it is one: there are troops coming in from outside, the rebels get arms from other countries, most of the people are not on their side, and they practice terror against their own. Therefore: *not* a revolution.

What would our dead revolutionaries answer? They might say: "What fools and bandits, sirs, you make then of us. Outside help? Do you remember Lafayette? Or the three thousand British freighters the French navy sank for our side? Or the arms and men, we got from France and Spain? And what's this about terror? Did you never hear what we did to our own Loyalists? Or about the thousands of rich American Tories who fled for their lives to Canada? And as for popular support, do you not know that we had less than one-third of our people with us? That, in fact, the colony of New York recruited more troops for the British than for the revolution? Should we give it all back?"

Revolutions do not take place in velvet boxes. They never have. It is only the poets who make them lovely. What the National Liberation Front is fighting in Vietnam is a complex and vicious war. This war is also a revolution, as honest a revolution as you can find anywhere in history. And this is a fact which all our intricate official denials will never change.

But it doesn't make any difference to our leaders anyway. Their aim in Vietnam is really much simpler than this implies. It is to safeguard what they take to be American interests around the world against revolution or revolutionary change, which they always call communism—as if that were that. In the case of Vietnam, this interest is, first, the principle that revolution shall not be tolerated anywhere, and second, that South Vietnam shall never sell its rice to China—or even to North Vietnam.

There is simply no such thing now, for us, as a just revolution—never mind that for two-thirds of the world's people the Twentieth Century might as well be the Stone Age; never mind the melting poverty and hopelessness that are the basic facts of life for most modern men; and never mind that for these millions there is now an increasingly perceptible relationship between their sorrow and our contentment.

Can we understand why the Negroes of Watts rebelled? Then why do we need a devil theory to explain the rebellion of the South Vietnamese? Can we understand the oppression in Mississippi, or the anguish that our Northern ghettoes makes epidemic? Then why can't we see that our proper human struggle is not with communism or revolutionaries, but with the social desperation that drives good men to violence, both here and abroad?

To be sure, we have been most generous with our aid, and in Western Europe, a mature industrial society, that aid worked. But there are always political and financial strings. And we have never shown ourselves capable of allowing others to make those traumatic institutional changes that are often the prerequisites of progress in colonial societies. For all our official feeling for the millions who are enslaved to what we so self-righteously call the yoke of communist tyranny, we make no real effort at all to crack through the much more vicious right-wing tyrannies that our businessmen traffic with and our nation profits from every day. And for all our cries about the international Red conspiracy to take over the world, we take only pride in the fact of our six thousand military bases on foreign soil.

We gave Rhodesia a grave look just now—but we keep on buying her chromium, which is cheap because black slave labor mines it.

We deplore the racism of Verwoert's fascist South Africa—but our banks make big loans to that country and our private technology makes it a nuclear power....

This country, with its thirty-some years of liberalism, can send 200,000 young men to Vietnam to kill and die in the most dubious of wars, but it cannot get 100 voter registrars to go into Mississippi.

What do you make of it?

The financial burden of the war obliges us to cut millions from an already pathetic War on Poverty budget. But in almost the same breath, Congress appropriates one hundred forty million dollars for the Lockheed and Boeing companies to compete with each other on the supersonic transport project—that Disneyland creation that will cost us all about two billion dollars before it's done.

What do you make of it? ...

In 1953 our Central Intelligence Agency managed to overthrow Mossadegh in Iran, the complaint being his neutralism in the Cold War and his plans to nationalize the country's oil resources to improve his people's lives. Most evil aims, most evil man. In his place we put in General Zahedi, a World War II Nazi collaborator. New arrangements on Iran's oil gave twenty-five year leases on forty percent of it to three U.S. firms, one of which was Gulf Oil. The C.I.A.'s leader for this coup was Kermit Roosevelt. In 1960, Kermit Roosevelt became a vice president of Gulf Oil.

In 1954, the democratically elected Arbenz of Guatemala wanted to nationalize a portion of United Fruit Company's plantations in his country, land he needed badly for a modest program of agrarian reform. His government was overthrown in a C.I.A.-supported rightwing coup. The following year, Gen. Walter Bedell Smith, director of the C.I.A. when the Guatemala venture was being planned, joined the board of directors of the United Fruit Company.

Comes 1960 and Castro cries we are about to invade Cuba. The Administration sneers, "poppycock," and we Americans believe it. Comes 1961 and the invasion. Comes with it the awful realization that the United States Government had lied.

Comes 1962 and the missile crisis, and our Administration stands prepared to fight global atomic war on the curious principle that another state does not have the right to its own foreign policy.

Comes 1963 and British Guiana where Cheddi Jagan wants independence from England and a labor law modeled on the Wagner Act. And Jay Lovestone, the AFL-CIO foreign policy chief, acting, as always, quite independently of labor's rank and file, arranges with our Government to finance an eleven-week dock strike that brings Jagan down, ensuring that the state will remain *British* Guiana, and that any workingman who wants a wage better than fifty cents a day is a dupe of communism.

Comes 1964. Two weeks after Undersecretary Thomas Mann announces that we have abandoned the Alianza's principle of no aid to tyrants, Brazil's Goulart is overthrown by the vicious right-winger Ademar Barros, supported by a show of American gunboats at Rio de Janeiro. Within twenty-four hours, the new head of state, Mazzilli, receives a congratulatory wire from our President.

Comes 1965. The Dominican Republic. Rebellion in the streets. We scurry to the spot with twenty thousand neutral Marines and our neutral peacemakers— like Ellsworth Bunker Jr., Ambassador to the Organization of American States. Most of us know that our neutral Marines fought openly on the side of the junta, a fact that the Administration still denies. But how many also know that what was at stake was our new Caribbean Sugar Bowl? That this same neutral peacemaking Bunker is a board member and stock owner of the National Sugar Refining Company, a firm his father founded in the good old days, and one which has a major interest in maintaining the status quo in the Dominican Republic? Or that the President's close personal friend and advisor, our new Supreme Court Justice Abe Fortas, has sat for the past 19 years on the board of the Sucrest Company, which imports blackstrap molasses from the Dominican Republic? Or that the rhetorician of corporate liberalism and the late President Kennedy's close friend Adolf Berle, was chairman of that same board? Or that our roving ambassador Averill Harriman's brother Roland is on the board of National Sugar? Or that our former ambassador to the Dominican Republic, Joseph Farland, is a board member of the South Puerto Rico Sugar Co., which owns two hundred and seventy-five thousand acres of rich land in the Dominican Republic and is the largest employer on the island—at about one dollar a day?

Neutralists! God save the hungry people of the world from such neutralists!

We do not say these men are evil. We say, rather, that good men can be divided from their compassion by the institutional system that inherits us all. Generation in and out, we are put to use. People become instruments. Generals do not hear the screams of the bombed; sugar executives do not see the misery of the cane cutters: for to do so is to be that much less the general, that much less the executive.

The foregoing facts of recent history describe one main aspect of the estate of Western liberalism. Where is our American humanism here? What went wrong?

Let's stare our situation coldly in the face. All of us are born to the colossus of history, our American corporate system—in many ways an awesome organism.

There is one fact that describes it: With about five percent of the world's people, we consume about half the world's goods. We take a richness that is in good part not our own, and we put it in our pockets, our garages, our split-levels, our bellies, and our futures.

On the *face* of it, it is a crime that so few should have so much at the expense of so many. Where is the moral imagination so abused as to call this just? Perhaps many of us feel a bit uneasy in our sleep. We are not, after all, a cruel people. And perhaps we don't really need this super-dominance that deforms others. But what can we do? The investments are made. The financial ties are established. The plants abroad are built. Our system exists. One is swept up into it. How intolerable—to be born moral, but addicted to a stolen and maybe surplus luxury. Our goodness threatens to become counterfeit before our eyes—unless we change. But change threatens us with uncertainty—at least.

Our problem, then, is to justify this system and give its theft another name—to make kind and moral what is neither, to perform some alchemy with language that will make this injustice seem a most magnanimous gift.

A hard problem. But the Western democracies, in the heyday of their colonial expansionism, produced a hero worthy of the task.

Its name was free enterprise, and its partner was an *illiberal liberalism* that said to the poor and the dispossessed: What we acquire of your resources we repay in civilization: the white man's burden. But this was too poetic. So a much more hard-headed theory was produced. This theory said that colonial status is in fact a *boon* to the colonized. We give them technology and bring them into modern times.

But this deceived no one but ourselves. We were delighted with this new theory. The poor saw in it merely an admission that their claims were irrefutable. They stood up to us, without gratitude. We were shocked—but also confused, for the poor seemed again to be right. How long is it going to be the case, we wondered, that the poor will be right and the rich will be wrong?

Liberalism faced a crisis. In the face of the collapse of the European empires, how could it continue, to hold together, our twin need for richness and righteousness? How can we continue to sack the ports of Asia and still dream of Jesus?

The challenge was met with a most ingenious solution: the ideology of anti-Communism. This was the bind: we cannot call revolution bad, because we started that way ourselves, and because it is all too easy to see why the dispossessed should rebel. So we will call revolution Communism. And we will reserve for ourselves the right to say what Communism means. We take note of revolution's enormities, wrenching them where necessary from their historical context and often exaggerating them, and say: Behold, Communism is a bloodbath. We take note of those reactionaries who stole the revolution, and say: Behold, Communism is a betrayal of the people. We take note of the revolution's need to consolidate itself, and say: Behold, Communism is a tyranny.

It has been all these things, and it will be these things again, and we will never be at a loss for those tales of atrocity that comfort us so in our self-righteousness. Nuns will be raped and bureaucrats will be disemboweled. Indeed, revolution is a *fury.* For it is a letting loose of outrages pent up sometimes over centuries. But the more brutal and longer-lasting the suppression of this energy, all the more ferocious will be its explosive release.

Far from helping Americans deal with this truth, the anti-Communist ideology merely tries to disguise it so that things may stay the way they are. Thus, it depicts our presence in other lands not as a coercion, but a protection. It allows us even to say that the napalm in Vietnam is only another aspect of our humanitarian love—like those exorcisms in the Middle Ages that so often killed the patient. So we say to the Vietnamese peasant, the Cuban intellectual, the Peruvian worker: "You are better dead than Red. If it hurts or if you don't understand why—sorry about that."

This is the action of *corporate liberalism.* It performs for the corporate state a function quite like what the Church once performed for the feudal state. It seeks to justify its burdens and protect it from change. As the Church exaggerated this office in the Inquisition, so with liberalism in the McCarthy time— which, if it was a reactionary phenomenon, was still made possible by our anti-communist corporate liberalism.

Let me then speak directly to humanist liberals. If my facts are wrong, I will soon be corrected. But if they are right, then you may face a crisis of conscience. Corporatism or humanism: which? For it has come to that. Will you let your dreams be used? Will you be a grudging apologist for the corporate state? Or will you help try to change it—not in the name of this or that blueprint or ism, but in the name of simple human decency and democracy and the vision that wise and brave men saw in the time of our own Revolution?

And if your commitment to human values is unconditional, then disabuse yourselves of the notion that statements will bring change, if only the right statements can be written, or that interviews with the mighty will bring change if only the mighty can be reached, or that marches will bring change if only we can make them massive enough, or that policy proposals will bring change if only we can make them responsible enough.

We are dealing now with a colossus that does not want to be changed. It will not change itself. It will not cooperate with those who want to change it. Those allies of ours in the Government—are they *really* our allies? If they *are*, then they don't need advice, they need *constituencies*; they don't need study groups, they need a *movement*. And if they are *not*, then all the more reason for building that movement with the most relentless conviction.

There are people in this country today who are trying to build that movement, who aim at nothing less than a humanist reformation. And the humanist liberals must understand that it is this movement with which their own best hopes are most in tune. We radicals know the same history that you liberals know, and we can understand your occasional cynicism, exasperation, and even distrust. But we ask you to put these aside and help us risk a leap. Help us find enough time for the enormous work that needs doing here. Help us build. Help us shape the future in the name of plain human hope.

National Guard Troops and Antiwar Demonstrators in Chicago August 28, 1968.   During the
*Democratic National Convention demonstrators flocked to Chicago to protest the Vietnam War policy of
the Johnson administration. The protests became violent when Mayor Richard Daley ordered the
Chicago police and the National Guard to curtail the demonstrations and prevent the protestors from
spending the night in the city's parks.*

The Weather Underground

*In 1968, after the assassinations of Martin Luther King Jr. and Robert F.
Kennedy and the events in Chicago at the Democratic National
Convention, many activists began to give up hope in the political process.
Some protestors became more radicalized; others began to "drop out" and
to form communes in an effort to achieve personal growth. The idea was
to concentrate on reforming oneself and not society—the inner revolution
rather than the outer. Students for a Democratic Society itself, the leading
New Left student organization, disintegrated.*

*A splinter group, the Weathermen (taking their name from a line in
Bob Dylan's "Subterranean Homesick Blues"), organized itself in 1969
and advocated violent confrontation with the "police state." The
Weathermen, (later the gender-neutral "Weather Underground"), of
course, did not have much chance for success in bringing down the U.S.
government, and their membership was never more than two or three
hundred, but police forces and the FBI targeted them after their "Days
of Rage" campaign in Chicago in October 1969 when they rampaged
through the streets breaking store windows and damaging automobiles.*

You Don't Need a Weatherman to Know Which Way the Wind Blows, 1969

People ask, what is the nature of the revolution that we talk about? Who will it be made by, and for, and what are its goals and strategy?

The overriding consideration in answering these questions is that the main struggle going on in the world today is between U.S. imperialism and the national liberation struggles against it. This is essential in defining political matters in the whole world: because it is by far the most powerful, every other empire and petty dictator is in the long run dependent on U.S. imperialism, which has unified, allied with, and defended all of the reactionary forces of the whole world. Thus, in considering every other force or phenomenon, from Soviet imperialism or Israeli imperialism to "workers struggle" in France or Czechoslovakia, we determine who are our friends and who are our enemies according to whether they help U.S. imperialism or fight to defeat it.

So the very first question people in this country must ask in considering the question of revolution is where they stand in relation to the United States as an oppressor nation, and where they stand in relation to the masses of people throughout the world whom U.S. imperialism is oppressing.

The primary task of revolutionary struggle is to solve this principal contradiction on the side of the people of the world. It is the oppressed peoples of the world who have created the wealth of this empire and it is to them that it belongs; the goal of the revolutionary struggle must be the control and use of this wealth in the interests of the oppressed peoples of the world.

It is in this context that we must examine the revolutionary struggles in the United States. We are within the heartland of a world-wide monster, a country so rich from its world-wide plunder that even the crumbs doled out to the enslaved masses within its borders provide for material existence very much above the conditions of the masses of people of the world. The U.S. empire, as a world-wide system, channels wealth, based upon the labor and resources of the rest of the world, into the United States. The relative affluence existing in the United States is directly dependent upon the labor and natural resources of the Vietnamese, the Angolans, the Bolivians, and the rest of the peoples of the Third World. All of the United Airlines Astrojets, all of the Holiday Inns, all of Hertz's automobiles, your television set, car, and wardrobe already belong, to a large degree to the people of the rest of the world.

Therefore, any conception of "socialist revolution" simply in terms of the working people of the United States, failing to recognize the full scope of interests of the most oppressed peoples of the world, is a conception of a fight for a particular privileged interest, and is a very dangerous ideology. While the control

SOURCE: From *New Left Notes*, June 18, 1969, in Harold Jacobs, *Weatherman* (Berkeley, CA: Ramparts Press, 1970), 51–53.

and use of the wealth of the Empire for the people of the whole world is also in the interests of the vast majority of the people in this country, if the goal is not clear from the start we will further the preservation of class society, oppression, war, genocide, and the complete emiseration of everyone, including the people of the U.S.

The goal is the destruction of U.S. imperialism and the achievement of a classless world: world communism. Winning state power in the U.S. will occur as a result of the military forces of the U.S. overextending themselves around the world and being defeated piecemeal; struggle within the U.S. will be a vital part of this process, but when the revolution triumphs in the U.S. it will have been made by the people of the whole world. For socialism to be defined in national terms within so extreme and historical an oppressor nation as this is only imperialist national chauvinism on the part of the "movement."

John Kerry (1943–)

When John Kerry served in Vietnam, he was awarded the Combat Action Ribbon, the Silver Star, the Bronze Star, the Republic of Vietnam Campaign Medal, the National Defense Service Medal, and three Purple Hearts. By the time he returned to the United States, however, he was a firm opponent of the war and became one of the founders of Vietnam Veterans Against the War. His 1971 testimony before the Senate Foreign Relations Committee was a sobering appraisal of the war in Vietnam. In 1984 Kerry won election to the U.S. Senate from Massachusetts, and in 2004 he was the Democratic Party's candidate for president.

STATEMENT TO THE SENATE COMMITTEE ON FOREIGN RELATIONS, APRIL 23, 1971

... I would like to say for the record, and also for the men behind me who are also wearing the uniform and their medals, that my sitting here is really symbolic, I am not here as John Kerry. I am here as one member of the group of 1,000 which is a small representation of a very much larger group of veterans in this country, and were it possible for all of them to sit at this table they would be here and have the same kind of testimony. . . .

SOURCE: "Legislative Proposals Relating to the War in Southeast Asia," *Hearings before the Committee on Foreign Relations, United States Senate, Ninety-Second Congress, First Session, April–May 1971,* (Washington, DC: Government Printing Office, 1971), 180–208 passim.

I would like to talk on behalf of all those veterans and say that several months ago in Detroit we had an investigation at which over 150 honorably discharged, and many very highly decorated, veterans testified to war crimes committed in Southeast Asia. These were not isolated incidents but crimes committed on a day-to-day basis with the full awareness of officers at all levels of command.

It is impossible to describe to you exactly what did happen in Detroit—the emotions in the room and the feelings of the men who were reliving their experiences in Vietnam. They relived the absolute horror of what this country, in a sense, made them do.

They told stories that at times they had personally raped, cut off ears, cut off heads, taped wires from portable telephones to human genitals and turned up the power, cut off limbs, blown up bodies, randomly shot at civilians, razed villages in fashion reminiscent of Genghis Khan, shot cattle and dogs for fun, poisoned food stocks, and generally ravaged the countryside of South Vietnam in addition to the normal ravage of war and the normal and very particular ravaging which is done by the applied bombing power of this country.

We call this investigation the Winter Soldier Investigation. The term Winter Soldier is a play on words of Thomas Paine's in 1776 when he spoke of the Sunshine Patriots and summertime soldiers who deserted at Valley Forge because the going was rough.

We who have come here to Washington have come here because we feel we have to be winter soldiers now. We could come back to this country, we could be quiet, we could hold our silence, we could not tell what went on in Vietnam, but we feel because of what threatens this country, not the reds, but the crimes which we are committing that threaten it, that we have to speak out. . . .

In our opinion and from our experience, there is nothing in South Vietnam which could happen that realistically threatens the United States of America. And to attempt to justify the loss of one American life in Vietnam, Cambodia or Laos by linking such loss to the preservation of freedom, which those misfits supposedly abuse, is to us the height of criminal hypocrisy, and it is that kind of hypocrisy which we feel has torn this country apart. . . .

We found that not only was it a civil war, an effort by a people who had for years been seeking their liberation from any colonial influence whatsoever, but also we found that the Vietnamese whom we had enthusiastically molded after our own image were hard put to take up the fight against the threat we were supposedly saving them from.

We found most people didn't even know the difference between communism and democracy. They only wanted to work in rice paddies without helicopters strafing them and bombs with napalm burning their villages and tearing their country apart. They wanted everything to do with the war, particularly with this foreign presence of the United States of America, to leave them alone in peace, and they practiced the art of survival by siding with whichever military force was present at a particular time, be it Viet Cong, North Vietnamese or American.

We found also that all too often American men were dying in those rice paddies for want of support from their allies. We saw first hand how monies from American taxes were used for a corrupt dictatorial regime. We saw that many people in this country had a one-sided idea of who was kept free by the flag, and blacks provided the highest percentage of casualties. We saw Vietnam ravaged equally by American bombs and search and destroy missions, as well as by Viet Cong terrorism—and yet we listened while this country tried to blame all of the havoc on the Viet Cong.

We rationalized destroying villages in order to save them. We saw America lose her sense of morality as she accepted very coolly a My Lai and refused to give up the image of American soldiers who hand out chocolate bars and chewing gum.

We learned the meaning of free fire zones, shooting anything that moves, and we watched while America placed a cheapness on the lives of orientals.

We watched the United States falsification of body counts, in fact the glorification of body counts. We listened while month after month we were told the back of the enemy was about to break. We fought using weapons against "oriental human beings." We fought using weapons against those people which I do not believe this country would dream of using were we fighting in the European theater. We watched while men charged up hills because a general said that hill has to be taken, and after losing one platoon or two platoons they marched away to leave the hill for reoccupation by the North Vietnamese. We watched pride allow the most unimportant battles to be blown into extravaganzas, because we couldn't lose, and we couldn't retreat, and because it didn't matter how many American bodies were lost to prove that point, and so there were Hamburger Hills and Khe Sanhs and Hill 81s and Fire Base 6s, and so many others.

Now we are told that the men who fought there must watch quietly while American lives are lost so that we can exercise the incredible arrogance of Vietnamizing the Vietnamese.

Each day to facilitate the process by which the United States washes her hands of Vietnam someone has to give up his life so that the United States doesn't have to admit something that the entire world already knows, so that we can't say that we have made a mistake. Someone has to die so that President Nixon won't be, and these are his words, "the first President to lose a war."

We are asking Americans to think about that because how do you ask a man to be the last man to die in Vietnam? How do you ask a man to be the last man to die for a mistake? . . . We are here in Washington to say that the problem of this war is not just a question of war and diplomacy. It is part and parcel of everything that we are trying as human beings to communicate to people in this country—the question of racism which is rampant in the military, and so many other questions such as the use of weapons; the hypocrisy in our taking umbrage at the Geneva Conventions and using that as justification for a continuation of this war when we are more guilty than any other body of violations of those Geneva Conventions; in the use of free fire zones, harassment interdiction fire, search and destroy missions, the bombings, the torture of prisoners, all accepted policy by many units in South Vietnam. That is what we are trying to say. It is part and parcel of everything.

An American Indian friend of mine who lives in the Indian Nation of Alcatraz put it to me very succinctly. He told me how as a boy on an Indian reservation he had watched television and he used to cheer the cowboys when they came in and shot the Indians, and then suddenly one day he stopped in Vietnam and he said, "my God, I am doing to these people the very same thing that was done to my people," and he stopped. And that is what we are trying to say, that we think this thing has to end.

We are here to ask, and we are here to ask vehemently, where are the leaders of our country? Where is the leadership? We're here to ask where are McNamara, Rostow, Bundy, Gilpatrick, and so many others? Where are they now that we, the men they sent off to war, have returned? These are the commanders who have deserted their troops. And there is no more serious crime in the laws of war. The Army says they never leave their wounded. The marines say they never even leave their dead. These men have left all the casualties and retreated behind a pious shield of public rectitude. They've left the real stuff of their reputations bleaching behind them in the sun in this country. . . .

We wish that a merciful God could wipe away our own memories of that service as easily as this administration has wiped away their memories of us. But all that they have done and all that they can do by this denial is to make more clear than ever our own determination to undertake one last mission—to search out and destroy the last vestige of this barbaric war, to pacify our own hearts, to conquer the hate and fear that have driven this country these last ten years and more. And more. And so when thirty years from now our brothers go down the street without a leg, without an arm, or a face, and small boys ask why, we will be able to say "Vietnam" and not mean a desert, not a filthy obscene memory, but mean instead where America finally turned and where soldiers like us helped it in the turning.

Timothy Leary (1920–1996)

Harvard psychologist Timothy Leary, fired in 1963 for controversial experimentation with the effects of LSD (lysergic acid diethylamide) on the human nervous system (famously, his own and his students'), became a central figure in the counterculture of the 1960s. Many well-known figures—Aldous Huxley, Allen Ginsberg, Alan Watts—were also extolling the mind-expanding benefits of LSD, but Leary became the chief apostle. Traveling around the country, Leary urged audiences to "tune in, turn on, and drop out" with LSD. Tuning in to your inner spirit, he declared, and then turning on with one dose of LSD, would inevitably lead to a more meaningful, more evolved relationship to life. After such an experience, individuals would more than likely drop out of the competitive, hollow, materialistic world of shopping malls and suburban developments. Acid, Leary proclaimed, expanded the consciousness to such an extent that it was a spiritual experience not unlike that of Tibetan Buddhist monks.

To young people who were already questioning the suffocating conformity of the "square" 1950s and who were listening to songs like "Little Boxes," Leary's message resonated, and millions wound up taking him seriously. Leary's guide books to the psychedelic experience—The Psychedelic Experience, (with co-authors Ralph Meltzer and Richard Alpert), and The Politics of Ecstasy, Confessions of a Hope Fiend, and High Priest—were popular with hippies seeking to expand their minds. Drugs were not to be "abused" as an escape from reality but "used" as a vehicle for self-discovery. "Acid is not for every brain," Leary stressed, "only the healthy, happy, wholesome, handsome, hopeful, humorous, high-velocity should seek these experiences. This elitism is totally self-determined. Unless you are self-confident, self-directed, self-selected, please abstain." In the following essay, Leary outlines useful tips on how to have a safe and successful LSD experience rather than a "bad trip."

Using LSD to Imprint the Tibetan–Buddhist Experience, 1964

A GUIDE TO SUCCESSFUL PSYCHEDELIC EXPERIENCE

Having read this preparatory manual one can immediately recognize symptoms and experiences that might otherwise be terrifying, only because of lack of understanding. Recognition is the key word. Recognizing and locating the level of consciousness. This guidebook may also be used to avoid paranoid trips or to regain transcendence if it has been lost. If the experience starts with light, peace, mystic unity, understanding, and continues along this path, then there is no need to remember the manual or have it reread to you. Like a road map, consult it only when lost, or when you wish to change course.

PLANNING A SESSION

What is the goal? Classic Hinduism suggests four possibilities:

> Increased personal power, intellectual understanding, sharpened insight into self and culture, improvement of life situation, accelerated learning, professional growth.
> Duty, help of others, providing care, rehabilitation, rebirth for fellow men.

Fun, sensuous enjoyment, esthetic pleasure, interpersonal closeness, pure experience.

Trancendence, liberation from ego and space-time limits; attainment of mystical union.

The manual's primary emphasis on the last goal does not preclude other goals—in fact, it guarantees their attainment because illumination requires that the person be able to step out beyond problems of personality, role, and professional status. The initiate can decide beforehand to devote their psychedelic experience to any of the four goals.

In the extroverted transcendent experience, the self is ecstatically fused with external objects (e.g., flowers, other people). In the introverted state, the self is ecstatically fused with internal life processes (lights, energy waves, bodily events, biological forms, etc.). Either state may be negative rather than positive, depending on the voyager's set and setting. For the extroverted mystic experience, one would bring to the session candles, pictures, books, incense, music, or recorded passages to guide the awareness in the desired direction. An introverted experience requires eliminating all stimulation: no light, no sound, no smell, no movement.

The mode of communication with other participants should also be agreed on beforehand, to avoid misinterpretations during the heightened sensitivity of ego transcendence.

If several people are having a session together, they should at least be aware of each other's goals. Unexpected or undesired manipulations can easily "trap" the other voyagers into paranoid delusions.

PREPARATION

Psychedelic chemicals are not drugs in the usual sense of the word. There is no specific somatic or psychological reaction. The better the preparation, the more ecstatic and revelatory the session. In initial sessions with unprepared persons, set and setting—particularly the actions of others—are most important. Long-range set refers to personal history, enduring personality, the kind of person you are. Your fears, desires, conflicts, guilts, secret passions, determine how you interpret and manage any psychedelic session. Perhaps more important are the reflex mechanisms, defenses, protective maneuvers, typically employed when dealing with anxiety. Flexibility, basic trust, philosophic faith, human openness, courage, interpersonal warmth, creativity, allow for fun and easy learning. Rigidity, desire to control, distrust, cynicism, narrowness, cowardice, coldness, make any new situation threatening. Most important is insight. The person who has some understanding of his own machinery, who can recognize when he is not functioning as he would wish, is better able to adapt to any challenge—even the sudden collapse of his ego.

Immediate set refers to expectations about the session itself. People naturally tend to impose personal and social perspectives on any new situation. For example, some ill-prepared subjects unconsciously impose a medical model on the experience. They look for symptoms, interpret each new sensation in terms of sickness/health, and, if anxiety develops, demand tranquilizers. Occasionally, ill-planned sessions end in the subject demanding to see a doctor.

Rebellion against convention may motivate some people who take the drug. The naive idea of doing something "far out" or vaguely naughty can cloud the experience.

LSD offers vast possibilities of accelerated learning and scientific-scholarly research, but for initial sessions, intellectual reactions can become traps. "Turn your mind off" is the best advice for novitiates. After you have learned how to move your consciousness around—into ego loss and back, at will—then intellectual exercises can be incorporated into the psychedelic experience. The objective is to free you from your verbal mind for as long as possible.

Religious expectations invite the same advice. Again, the subject in early sessions is best advised to float with the stream, stay "up" as long as possible, and postpone theological interpretations.

Recreational and esthetic expectations are natural. The psychedelic experience provides ecstatic moments that dwarf any personal or cultural game. Pure sensation can capture awareness. Interpersonal intimacy reaches Himalayan heights. Esthetic delights—musical, artistic, botanical, natural—are raised to the millionth power. But ego-game reactions—"I am having this ecstasy. How lucky I am!"—can prevent the subject from reaching pure ego loss.

SOME PRACTICAL RECOMMENDATIONS

The subject should set aside at least three days: a day before the experience, the session day, and a follow-up day. This scheduling guarantees a reduction in external pressure and a more sober commitment. Talking to others who have taken the voyage is excellent preparation, although the hallucinatory quality of all descriptions should be recognized. Observing a session is another valuable preliminary.

Reading books about mystical experience and of others' experiences is another possibility (Aldous Huxley, Alan Watts, and Gordon Wasson have written powerful accounts). Meditation is probably the best preparation. Those who have spent time in a solitary attempt to manage the mind, to eliminate thought and reach higher stages of concentration, are the best candidates for a psychedelic session. When the ego loss occurs, they recognize the process as an eagerly awaited end.

THE SETTING

First and most important, provide a setting removed from one's usual interpersonal games, and as free as possible from unforeseen distractions and intrusions. The voyager should make sure that he will not be disturbed; visitors or a phone call will often jar him into hallucinatory activity. Trust in the surroundings and privacy are necessary.

The day after the session should be set aside to let the experience run its natural course and allow time for reflection and meditation. A too-hasty return to game involvements will blur the clarity and reduce the potential for learning. It is very useful for a group to stay together after the session to share and exchange experiences.

Many people are more comfortable in the evening, and consequently their experiences are deeper and richer. The person should choose the time of day that seems right. Later, he may wish to experience the difference between night and day sessions. Similarly, gardens, beaches, forests, and open country have specific influences that one may or may not wish. The essential thing is to feel as comfortable as possible, whether in one's living room or under the night sky. Familiar surroundings may help one feel confident in hallucinatory periods. If the session is held indoors, music, lighting, the availability of food and drink, should be considered beforehand. Most people report no hunger during the height of the experience, then later on prefer simple ancient foods like bread, cheese, wine, and fresh fruit. The senses are wide open, and the taste and smell of a fresh orange are unforgettable.

In group sessions, people usually will not feel like walking or moving very much for long periods, and either beds or mattresses should be provided. One suggestion is to place the heads of the beds together to form a star pattern. Perhaps one may want to place a few beds together and keep one or two some distance apart for anyone who wishes to remain aside for some time. The availability of an extra room is desirable for someone who wishes to be in seclusion.

THE PSYCHEDELIC GUIDE

With the cognitive mind suspended, the subject is in a heightened state of suggestibility. For initial sessions, the guide possesses enormous power to move consciousness with the slightest gesture or reaction.

The key here is the guide's ability to turn off his own ego and social games, power needs, and fears—to be there, relaxed, solid, accepting, secure, to sense all and do nothing except let the subject know his wise presence.

A psychedelic session lasts up to twelve hours and produces moments of intense, intense, INTENSE reactivity. The guide must never be bored, talkative, intellectualizing. He must remain calm during long periods of swirling mindlessness. He is the ground control, always there to receive messages and queries from high-flying aircraft, ready to help negotiate their course and reach their destination. The guide does not impose his own games on the voyager. Pilots who have their own flight plan, their own goals, are reassured to know that an expert is down there, available for help. But if ground control is harboring his own motives, manipulating the plane towards selfish goals, the bond of security and confidence crumbles.

To administer psychedelics without personal experience is unethical and dangerous. Our studies concluded that almost every negative LSD reaction has been caused by the guide's fear, which augmented the transient fear of the subject. When the guide acts to protect himself, he communicates his concern. If momentary discomfort or confusion happens, others present should not be sympathetic or show alarm but stay calm and restrain their "helping games." In particular, the "doctor" role should be avoided.

The guide must remain passively sensitive and intuitively relaxed for several hours—a difficult assignment for most Westerners. The most certain way to maintain a state of alert quietism, poised in ready flexibility, is for the guide to take a low dose of the psychedelic with the subject. Routine procedure is to have one trained person participating in the experience, and one staff member present without psychedelic aid. The knowledge that one experienced guide is "up" and keeping the subject company is of inestimable value: the security of a trained pilot flying at your wingtip; the scuba diver's security in the presence of an expert companion.

The less experienced subject will more likely impose hallucinations. The guide, likely to be in a state of mindless, blissful flow, is then pulled into the subject's hallucinatory field and may have difficulty orienting himself. There are no familiar fixed landmarks, no place to put your foot, no solid concept upon which to base your thinking. All is flux. Decisive action by the subject can structure the guide's flow if he has taken a heavy dose.

The psychedelic guide is literally a neurological liberator, who provides illumination, who frees men from their lifelong internal bondage. To be present at the moment of awakening, to share the ecstatic revelation when the voyager discovers the wonder and awe of the divine life-process, far outstrips earthly game ambitions. Awe and gratitude—rather than pride—are the rewards of this new profession.

THE PERIOD OF EGO LOSS OR NON-GAME ECSTASY

Success implies very unusual preparation in consciousness expansion, as well as much calm, compassionate game playing (good karma) on the part of the participant. If the participant can see and grasp the idea of the empty mind as soon as the guide reveals it—that is to say, if he has the power to die consciously— and, at the supreme moment of quitting the ego, can recognize the ecstasy that will dawn upon him and become one with it, then all bonds of illusion are broken asunder immediately: the dreamer is awakened into reality simultaneously with the mighty achievement of recognition.

It is best if the guru from whom the participant received guiding instructions is present. But if the guru cannot be present, then another experienced person, or a person the participant trusts, should be available to read this manual without imposing any of his own games. Thereby the participant will be put in mind of what he had previously heard of the experience.

Liberation is the nervous system devoid of mental-conceptual redundancy. The mind in its conditioned state, limited to words and ego games, is continuously in thought-formation activity. The nervous system in a state of quiescence, alert, awake but not active, is comparable to what Buddhists call the highest state of *dhyana* (deep meditation). The conscious recognition of the Clear Light induces an ecstatic condition of consciousness such as saints and mystics of the West have called illumination.

The first sign is the glimpsing of the "Clear Light of Reality, the infallible mind of the pure mystic state"—an awareness of energy transformations with no imposition of mental categories.

The duration of this state varies, depending on the individual's experience, security, trust, preparation, and the surroundings. In those who have a little practical experience of the tranquil state of non-game awareness, this state can last from 30 minutes to several hours. Realization of what mystics call the "Ultimate Truth" is possible, provided that the person has made sufficient preparation beforehand. Otherwise he cannot benefit now, and must wander into lower and lower conditions of hallucinations until he drops back to routine reality.

It is important to remember that the consciousness-expansion is the reverse of the birth process, the ego-loss experience being a temporary ending of game life, a passing from one state of consciousness into another. Just as an infant must wake up and learn from experience the nature of this world, so a person must wake up in this new brilliant world of consciousness expansion and become familiar with its own peculiar conditions.

In those heavily dependant on ego games, who dread giving up control, the illuminated state endures only for a split second. In some, it lasts as long as the time taken for eating a meal. If the subject is prepared to diagnose the symptoms of ego-loss, he needs no outside help at this point. The person about to give up his ego should be able to recognize the Clear Light. If the person fails to recognize the onset of ego-loss, he may complain of strange bodily symptoms that show he has not reached a liberated state:

Bodily pressure
Clammy coldness followed by feverish heat
Body disintegrating or blown to atoms
Pressure on head and ears
Tingling in extremities
Feelings of body melting or flowing like wax
Nausea
Trembling or shaking, beginning in pelvic region and spreading up torso.

The guide or friend should explain that the symptoms indicate the onset of ego-loss. These physical reactions are signs heralding transcendence: avoid treating them as symptoms of illness. The subject should hail stomach messages as a sign that consciousness is moving around in the body. Experience the sensation fully, and let consciousness flow on to the next phase. It is usually more natural to let the subject's attention move from the stomach and concentrate on breathing and heartbeat. If this does not free him from nausea, the guide should move the consciousness to external events—music, walking in the garden, etc. As a last resort, heave.

The physical symptoms of ego-loss, recognized and understood, should result in peaceful attainment of illumination. The simile of a needle balanced and set rolling on a thread is used by the lamas to elucidate this condition. So long as the needle retains its balance, it remains on the thread. Eventually, however, the pull of the ego or external stimulation affects it, and it falls. In the realm of the Clear Light, similarly, a person in the ego-transcendent state momentarily enjoys a condition of perfect equilibrium and oneness. Unfamiliar with such an ecstatic non-ego state, the average consciousness lacks the power to function in it. Thoughts of personality, individualized being, dualism, prevent the realization of nirvana (the "blowing out of the flame" of fear or selfishness). When the voyager is clearly in a profound ego-transcendent ecstasy, the wise guide remains silent.

Herbert Marcuse (1898–1979)

Philosopher Herbert Marcuse studied under Martin Heidigger at Freiburg University in Germany and later worked at the Frankfurt Institute for Social Research. After Hitler came to power in 1933, he emigrated to the United States, became a citizen in 1940, and worked for the Office of Strategic Services. After the war, he taught at Columbia, Harvard, Brandeis, and the University of California at San Diego. His research led him to combine Freud and Marx in his analysis of capitalist society, taking ideas from Civilization and Its Discontents, *in which Freud argues that civilization itself is the result of the sublimation of sexual desire. All societies, according to Marcuse, need a level of repression in order to maintain control. In a totalitarian society, the repression is physical terror. You criticized Hitler; you were shot. In capitalist society, however, repression is primarily sexual. By putting restrictions on sexuality, those in control ensure that the people sublimate their libidinal energy into feelings of patriotism and nationalism, and thus control is preserved.*

In the United States, Marcuse contends, there is too much sexual repression, and this "surplus repression" is manipulated by the government and business leaders to fuel consumer capitalism. People must cope with the inexplicable emptiness they feel, and they do so through consumerism—drinking, smoking, overeating, buying goods that are unnecessary, gathering possessions, traveling, attending sporting events. In One-Dimensional Man *and in* Eros and Civilization, *Marcuse argues that being aware of and coping with sexual repression and then developing a healthy attitude about sex is not only a way to find erotic self-fulfillment, but is also an act of revolution against capitalism. If sexual repression is overcome, you consume less. For some people,*

Marcuse's theory became the intellectual foundation for the so-called sexual revolution that emerged in the 1960s. Sex is political. Relationships are political. "Make love, not war" is both a social statement and a political statement. In the 1966 preface to Eros and Civilization, *Marcuse comments on the student movement and its attempt to address these issues.*

POLITICAL PREFACE, *EROS AND CIVILIZATION*, 1966

. . . As the affluence of society depends increasingly on the uninterrupted production and consumption of waste, gadgets, planned obsolescence, and means of destruction, the individuals have to be adapted to these requirements in more than the traditional ways. The "economic whip," even in its most refined forms, seems no longer adequate to insure the continuation of the struggle for existence in today's outdated organization, nor do the laws and patriotism seem adequate to insure active popular support for the ever more dangerous expansion of the system. Scientific management of instinctual needs has long since become a vital factor in the reproduction of the system: merchandise which has to be bought and used is made into objects of the libido; and the national Enemy who has to be fought and hated is distorted and inflated to such an extent that he can activate and satisfy aggressiveness in the depth dimension of the unconscious. Mass democracy provides the political paraphernalia for effectuating this introjection of the Reality Principle; it not only permits the people (up to a point) to choose their own masters and to participate (up to a point) in the government which governs them—it also allows the masters to disappear behind the technological veil of the productive and destructive apparatus which they control, and it conceals the human (and material) costs of the benefits and comforts which it bestows upon those who collaborate. The people, efficiently manipulated and organized, are free; ignorance and impotence, introjected heteronomy is the price of their freedom.

It makes no sense to talk about liberation to free men—and we are free if we do not belong to the oppressed minority. And it makes no sense to talk about surplus repression when men and women enjoy more sexual liberty than ever before. But the truth is that this freedom and satisfaction are transforming the earth into hell. The inferno is still concentrated in certain far away places: Vietnam, the Congo, South Africa, and in the ghettos of the "affluent society": in Mississippi and Alabama, in Harlem. . . .

I hesitate to use the word—freedom—because it is precisely in the name of freedom that crimes against humanity are being perpetrated. The situation

SOURCE: Herbert Marcuse, *Eros and Civilization: A Philosophical Inquiry into Freud* (Boston: Beacon Press, 1955, 1966), xii–xiii, xx–xxii, xxiv–xxv.

is certainly not new in history: poverty and exploitation were products of economic freedom; time and again, people were liberated all over the globe by their lords and masters, and their new liberty turned out to be submission, not to the rule of law but to the rule of the law of the others. . . . [T]he general presumption is that aggressiveness in defense of life is less detrimental to the life Instincts than aggressiveness in aggression.

In defense of life: the phrase has explosive meaning in the affluent society. It involves not only the protest against neo-colonial war and slaughter, the burning of draft cards at the risk of prison, the fight for civil rights, but also the refusal to speak the dead language of affluence, to wear the clean clothes, to enjoy the gadgets of affluence, to go through the education for affluence. The new bohéme, the beatniks and hipsters, the peace creeps—all these "decadents" now have become what decadence probably always was: poor refuge of defamed humanity.

Can we speak of a juncture between the erotic and political dimension?

In and against the deadly efficient organization of the affluent society, not only radical protest, but even the attempt to formulate, to articulate, to give word to protest assume a childlike, ridiculous immaturity. Thus it is ridiculous and perhaps "logical" that the Free Speech Movement at Berkeley terminated in the row caused by the appearance of a sign with the four-letter word. It is perhaps equally ridiculous and right to see deeper significance in the buttons worn by some of the demonstrators (among them infants) against the slaughter in Vietnam: MAKE LOVE, NOT WAR. On the other side, against the new youth who refuse and rebel, are the representatives of the old order who can no longer protect its life without sacrificing it in the work of destruction and waste and pollution. They now include the representatives of organized labor—correctly so to the extent to which employment within the capitalist prosperity depends on the continued defense of the established social system.

Can the outcome, for the near future, be in doubt? The people, the majority of the people in the affluent society, are on the side of that which is—not that which can and ought to be. And the established order is strong enough and efficient enough to justify this adherence and to assume its continuation. However, the very strength and efficiency of this order may become factors of disintegration. Perpetuation of the obsolescent need for full-time labor (even in a very reduced form) will require the increasing waste of resources, the creation of ever more unnecessary jobs and services, and the growth of the military or destructive sector. Escalated wars, permanent preparation for war, and total administration may well suffice to keep the people under control, but at the cost of altering the morality on which the society still depends. . . .

In the meantime, there are things to be done. The system has its weakest point where it shows its most brutal strength: in the escalation of its military potential (which seems to press for periodic actualization with ever shorter interruptions of peace and preparedness). This tendency seems reversible only under strongest pressure, and its reversal would open the danger spots in the social structure: its conversion into a "normal" capitalist system is hardly imaginable without a serious crisis and sweeping economic and political changes. Today, the opposition to war and military intervention strikes at the roots: it revels against those whose economic and political dominion depends on the continued (and enlarged) reproduction of the military establishment, its "multipliers," and the policies which necessitate this reproduction. These interests are not hard to identify, and the war against them does not require missiles, bombs, and napalm. But it does require something that is much harder to produce—the spread of uncensored and unmanipulated knowledge, consciousness, and above all, the organized refusal to continue work on the material and *intellectual* instruments which are now being used against man—for the defense of the liberty and prosperity of those who dominate the rest.

To the degree to which organized labor operates in defense of the status quo, and to the degree to which the share of labor in the material process of production declines, *intellectual* skills and capabilities become social and political factors. Today, the organized refusal to cooperate of the scientists, mathematicians, technicians, industrial psychologists and public opinion pollsters may well accomplish what a strike, even a large-scale strike, can no longer accomplish but once accomplished, namely, the beginning of the reversal, the preparation of the ground for political action. That the idea appears utterly unrealistic does not reduce the political responsibility involved in the position and function of the intellectual in contemporary industrial society. The intellectual refusal may find support in another catalyst, the instinctual refusal among the youth in protest. It is their lives which are at stake, and if not their lives, their mental health and their capacity to function as unmutilated humans. Their protest will continue because it is a biological necessity. "By nature," the young are in the forefront of those who live and fight for Eros against Death, and against a civilization which strives to shorten the "detour to death" while controlling the means for lengthening the detour. But in the administered society, the biological necessity does not immediately issue in action; organization demands counter-organization. Today the fight for life, the fight for Eros, is the *political* fight.

Abbie Hoffman (1936–1989)

Abbie Hoffman was one of the most visible and colorful figures of the counterculture. He brought his Youth International Party (Yippies) to Chicago in 1968 to confound and confuse the authorities and the American public during the Democratic National Convention. He was as much a showman and comedian as a political activist; most "straight" people (as opposed to "hippies") usually had no idea what he was talking about. He claimed the Yippies were going to put LSD into Chicago's reservoirs in order to turn on the whole city and, astonishingly, many people believed him! He and Jerry Rubin nominated a pig for president in an alternative convention. In 1969, Hoffman went onstage at Woodstock to advise the audience which pills to take and which ones not to take. He published a number of books, notably Woodstock Nation *and* Steal This Book.

In the aftermath of the chaotic and violent Chicago Democratic convention, he was one of the "Chicago Seven" who were brought to trial for causing the riots. Hoffman's testimony at the trial was a tour de force. When asked to identify himself, he said he was "an orphan of America." When asked where he lived, he said, "Woodstock Nation." When asked where that was, he replied: "It is a nation of alienated young people. We carry it around with us as a state of mind in the same way as the Sioux Indians carried the Sioux nation around with them. It is a nation dedicated to cooperation versus competition, to the idea that people should have better means of exchange than property or money."

What Hoffman understood very well was how to confuse, hoodwink, and bamboozle. He and the Yippies generated an enormous amount of publicity—far more than their numbers would warrant. As a result, many Americans were convinced that the counterculture was on the verge of causing a revolution in America, never realizing that the Yippie plot was not much more than street theater.

The following introduction to Steal This Book *provides some insight into Abbie Hoffman's outrageous mind.*

INTRODUCTION, *STEAL THIS BOOK*, 1970

It's perhaps fitting that I write this introduction in jail—that graduate school of survival. Here you learn how to use toothpaste as glue, fashion a shiv out of a spoon and build intricate communication networks. Here too, you learn the only rehabilitation possible—hatred of oppression.

Steal This Book is, in a way, a manual of survival in the prison that is Amerika. It preaches jailbreak. It shows you where exactly to place the dynamite that will destroy the walls. The first section—SURVIVE!—lays out a potential action program for our new Nation. The chapter headings spell out the demands for a free society. A community where the technology produces goods and services for whoever needs them, come who may. It calls on the Robin Hoods of Santa Barbara Forest to steal from the robber barons who own the castles of capitalism. It implies that the reader already is "ideologically set," in that he understands corporate feudalism as the only robbery worthy of being called "crime," for it is committed against the people as a whole. Whether the ways it describes to rip-off shit are legal or illegal is irrelevant. The dictionary of

SOURCE: Abbie Hoffman, *Steal This Book* (New York: Pirate Editions, 1971), iii–viii.

law is written by the bosses of order. Our moral dictionary says no heisting from each other. To steal from a brother or sister is evil. To not steal from the institutions that are the pillars of the Pig Empire is equally immoral.

Community within our Nation, chaos in theirs; that is the message of SURVIVE!

We cannot survive without learning to fight and that is the lesson in the second section. FIGHT! separates revolutionaries from outlaws. The purpose of part two is not to fuck the system, but destroy it. The weapons are carefully chosen. They are "home-made," in that they are designed for use in our unique electronic jungle. Here the uptown reviewer will find ample proof of our "violent" nature. But again, the dictionary of law fails us. Murder in a uniform is heroic, in a costume it is a crime. False advertisements win awards, forgers end up in jail. Inflated prices guarantee large profits while shoplifters are punished. Politicians conspire to create police riots and the victims are convicted in the courts. Students are gunned down and then indicted by suburban grand juries as the trouble-makers. A modern, highly mechanized army travels 9,000 miles to commit genocide against a small nation of great vision and then accuses its people of aggression. Slumlords allow rats to maim children and then complain of violence in the streets. Everything is topsy-turvy. If we internalize the language and imagery of the pigs, we will forever be fucked. Let me illustrate the point. Amerika was built on the slaughter of a people. That is its history. For years we watched movie after movie that demonstrated the white man's benevolence. Jimmy Stewart, the epitome of fairness, puts his arm around Cochise and tells how the Indians and the whites can live in peace if only both sides will be reasonable, responsible and rational (the three R's imperialists always teach the "natives"). "You will find good grazing land on the other side of the mountain," drawls the public relations man. "Take your people and go in peace." Cochise as well as millions of youngsters in the balcony of learning, were being dealt off the bottom of the deck. The Indians should have offed Jimmy Stewart in every picture and we should have cheered ourselves hoarse. Until we understand the nature of institutional violence and how it manipulates values and mores to maintain the power of the few, we will forever be imprisoned in the caves of ignorance. When we conclude that bank robbers rather than bankers should be the trustees of the universities, then we begin to think clearly. When we see the Army Mathematics Research and Development Center and the Bank of Amerika as cesspools of violence, filling the minds of our young with hatred, turning one against another, then we begin to think revolutionary.

Be clever using section two; clever as a snake. Dig the spirit of the struggle. Don't get hung up on a sacrifice trip. Revolution is not about suicide, it is about life. With your fingers probe the holiness of your body and see that it was meant to live. Your body is just one in a mass of cuddly humanity. Become an internationalist and learn to respect all life. Make war on machines, and in particular the sterile machines of corporate death and the robots that guard them. The duty of a revolutionary is to make love and that means staying alive and free. That doesn't allow for cop-outs. Smoking dope and hanging up Che's picture is no more a commitment than drinking milk and collecting postage stamps. A revolution in consciousness is an empty high without a revolution in the distribution of power. We are not interested in the greening of Amerika except for the grass that will cover its grave.

Section three—LIBERATE!—concerns itself with efforts to free stuff (or at least make it cheap) in four cities. Sort of a quick U.S. on no dollars a day. It begins to scratch the potential for a national effort in this area. Since we are a nation of gypsies, dope on how to move around and dig in anywhere is always needed. Together we can expand this section. It is far from complete, as is the entire project. Incomplete chapters on how to identify police agents, steal a car, run day-care centers, conduct your own trial, organize a G.I. coffee house, start a rock and roll band and make neat clothes, are scattered all over the floor of the cell. The book as it now stands was completed in the late summer of 1970. For three months manuscripts made the rounds of every major publisher. In all, over 30 rejections occurred before the decision to publish the book ourselves was made, or rather made for us. Perhaps no other book in modern times presented such a dilemma. Everyone agreed the book would be a commercial success. But even greed had its limits, and the IRS and FBI following the manuscript with their little jive rap had a telling effect. Thirty "yeses" become thirty "noes" after "thinking it over." Liberals, who supposedly led the fight against censorship, talked of how the book "will end free speech."

Finally the day we were bringing the proofs to the printer, Grove consented to act as distributor. To pull a total solo trip, including distribution, would have been neat, but such an effort would be doomed from the start. We had tried it before and blew it. In fact, if anyone is interested in 4,000 1969 Yippie calendars, they've got a deal. Even with a distributor joining the fight, the battle will only begin when the books come off the press. There is a saying that "Freedom of the press belongs to those who own one." In past eras, this was probably the case, but now, high speed methods of typesetting, offset printing and a host of other developments have made substantial reductions in printing costs. Literally anyone is free to print their own works. In even the most repressive society imaginable, you can get away with some form of private publishing. Because Amerika allows this, does not make it the democracy Jefferson envisioned. Repressive tolerance is a real phenomenon. To talk of true freedom of the press, we must talk of the availability of the channels of communication that are designed to reach the entire population, or at least that segment of the population that might participate in such a dialogue. Freedom of the press belongs to those that own the distribution system. Perhaps that has always been the case, but in a mass society where nearly everyone is instantaneously plugged into a variety of national communications systems, wide-spread dissemination of the information is the crux of the matter. To make the claim that the right to print your own book means freedom of the press is to completely misunderstand the nature of a mass society. It is like making the claim that anyone with a pushcart can challenge Safeway supermarkets, or that any child can grow up to be president.

State legislators, librarians, PTA members, FBI agents, church-goers, and parents: a veritable legion of decency and order already is on the march. To get the book to you might be the biggest challenge we face. The next few months should prove really exciting. . . .

If you have comments, law suits, suggestions or death threats, please send them to: Dear Abbie P.O. Box 213, Cooper Station, New York, NY 10003. Many of the tips might not work in your area, some might be obsolete by the time you get to try them out, and many addresses and phone numbers might be changed. If the reader becomes a participating researcher then we will have achieved our purpose.

Watch for a special edition called Steal This White House, complete with blueprints of underground passages, methods of jamming the communications network and a detailed map of the celebrated room where according to Tricia Nixon, "Daddy loves to listen to Mantovanni records, turn up the air conditioner full blast, sit by the fireplace, gaze out the window to the Washington Monument and meditate on those difficult problems that face all the peoples of this world."

December, 1970
Cook County Jail, Chicago

> "Free speech is the right to shout 'theater' in a crowded fire."

A yippie proverb

Ram Dass (1931–)

One of Timothy Leary's colleagues at Harvard and the coauthor of
The Psychedelic Experience *was Richard Alpert. Along with Leary, Alpert experimented with LSD and other hallucinogens as a path to self-discovery. However, after a number of years of "tripping" and searching, during which time he became increasingly dissatisfied with the drug experience, Alpert went to India in 1967. He studied in the Himalayas with Neem Karoli Baba, and in 1968, after a profound spiritual awakening, he returned to the United States renamed Ram Dass ("Servant of God"). Since then, he has lectured to hundreds of thousands of people around the world on such topics as meditation, karma yoga, aging, and death and dying. This extract from* Be Here Now *details part of the journey of his spiritual awakening and turning his back on drugs.*

Be Here Now, 1971

At one point in the evening I was looking in my shoulder bag and came across the bottle of LSD.

"Wow! I've finally met a guy who is going to Know! He will definitely know what LSD is. I'll have to ask him. That's what I'll do. I'll ask him." Then I forgot about it.

The next morning, at 8 o'clock a messenger comes. Maharaji wants to see you immediately. We went in the Land Rover. The 12 miles to the other temple. When I'm approaching him, he yells out at me, "Have you got a question?"

And I take one look at him, and it's like looking at the sun. I suddenly feel all warm.

And he's very impatient with all of this nonsense, and he says, "Where's the medicine?"

I got a translation of this. He said medicine. I said, "Medicine?" I never thought of LSD as medicine! And somebody said, he must mean the LSD. "LSD?" He said, "Ah-cha—bring the LSD."

So I went to the car and got the little bottle of LSD and I came back.

"Let me see?"

So I poured it out in my hand—"What's that?"

"That's STP. . . . That's librium and that's. . . . " A little of everything. Sort of a little traveling kit.

He says, "Gives you siddhis?"

I had never heard the word "siddhi" before. So I asked for a translation and siddhi was translated as "power." From where I was at in relation to these concepts, I thought he was like a little old man, asking for power. Perhaps he was losing his vitality and wanted Vitamin B 12. That was one thing I didn't have and I felt terribly apologetic because I would have given him anything. If he wanted the Land Rover, he could have it. And I said, "Oh, no, I'm sorry." I really felt bad I didn't have any and put it back in the bottle.

He looked at me and extended his hand. So I put into his hand what's called a "White Lightning." This is an LSD pill and this one was from a special batch that had been made specially for me for traveling. And each pill was 305 micrograms, and very pure. Very good acid. Usually you start a man over 60, maybe with 50 to 75 micrograms, very gently, so you won't upset him. 300 of pure acid is a very solid dose.

He looks at the pill and extends his hand further. So I put a second pill—that's 610 micrograms—then a third pill—that's 915 micrograms—into his palm.

That is sizeable for a first dose for anyone!

"Ah-cha."

And he swallows them! I see them go down. There's no doubt. And that little scientist in me says, "This is going to be very interesting!"

SOURCE: Ram Dass, *Be Here Now* (New York: Crown, 1971), from the unpaginated preface.

All day long I'm there, and every now and then he twinkles at me and nothing—nothing happens! That was his answer to my question. Now you have the data I have.

I was taken back to the temple. It was interesting. At no time was I asked, do you want to stay? Do you want to study? Everything was understood. There were no contracts. There were no promises. There were no vows. There was nothing. The next day Maharaji instructed them to take me out and buy me clothes. They gave me a room. Nobody ever asked me for a nickel. Nobody ever asked me to spread the word. Nobody ever did anything. There was no commitment whatsoever required. It was all done internally. And that day I met a man who was to become my teacher, Hari Dass Baba.

Hari Dass Baba is quite an incredible fellow, as I found out. I spent five months under his tutelage. He is 48 years old. He weighs 90 pounds. He is a jungle saddhu. He went into the jungle when he was 8 years old. He is silent (mauna). He has been mauna for 15 years. He writes with a chalkboard. He only uses his voice to sing holy songs. He reads and writes six or eight different languages, including Chinese, English, French, Hindi. He taught me always in beautiful English.

This guru—Maharaji—has only his blanket. You see, he's in a place called SAHAJ SAMADHI and he's not identified with this world as most of us identify with it. If you didn't watch him, he'd just disappear altogether into the jungle or leave his body, but his devotees are always protecting him and watching him so they can keep him around. They've got an entourage around him and people come and bring gifts to the holy man because that's part of the way in which you gain holy merit in India. And money piles up, and so they build temples, or they build schools. He will walk to a place and there will be a saint who has lived in that place or cave and he'll say, "There will be a temple here," and then they build a temple. And they do all this around Maharaji. He does nothing.

Hari Dass Baba—this little 90 pound fellow—architecturally designed all of the temples and schools, supervised all the buildings and grounds, had many followers of his own, slept two hours a night. His food intake for the last 15 years had been 2 glasses of milk a day. That's it. His feces are like two small marbles each day. His arms are about this big around, tiny, but when the workmen can't lift a particularly heavy rock, they call for 'Chota Maharaji'—the little great king. As in a comic strip, he goes over and lifts the rock, just with one-pointedness of mind. He had met Maharaji in the jungle 15 years before, and he had become a disciple of Maharaji.

As an example of Maharaji's style, I was once going through my address book and I came to Lama Govinda's name (he wrote *Foundations of Tibetan Mysticism* and *Way of the White Cloud*) and I thought, "Gee, I ought to go visit him. I'm here in the Himalayas and it wouldn't be a long trip and I could go and pay my respects. I must do that some time before I leave."

And the next day there is a message from Maharaji saying, "You are to go immediately to see Lama Govinda."

Another time, I had to go to Delhi to work on my visa and I took a bus. This was the first time after four months that they let me out alone. They were so protective of me. I don't know what they were afraid would happen to me, but they were always sending somebody with me. . . . They weren't giving me elopement privileges, as they say in mental hospitals.

But they allowed me to go alone to Delhi and I took a 12 hour bus trip. I went to Delhi and I was so high. I went through Connaught Place, which is the western hustle part of New Delhi. It's mostly BOAC and American Express and restaurants that serve ice cream sodas. The whole scene, which is right in the middle of India, has nothing to do with India particularly and all the Indians who hustle westerners walk around in this block. And I went through that barefoot, silent with my chalkboard—I was silent all the time. At American Express, writing my words it was so high that not at one moment was there even a qualm or a doubt. I got so high that I went into some stores to buy things—right in Connaught Place, which is designed to hustle westerners. . . . And everybody knew I was a westerner, and yet they insisted on giving me the stuff free!

"You are a saddhu—it's a blessing to me that you'll take my goods." That's how powerful the thing was that I was into at that time.

So after all day long of doing my dramas with the Health Department and so on, it came time for lunch. I had been on this very fierce austere diet and I had lost 60 lbs. I was feeling great—very light and very beautiful—but there was enough orality still left in me to want to have a feast. I'll have a vegetarian feast. I thought. So I went to a fancy vegetarian restaurant and I got a table over in a corner and ordered their special deluxe vegetarian dinner, from nuts to nuts, and I had the whole thing and the last thing they served was vegetarian ice cream with 2 english biscuits stuck into it. And those biscuits . . . the sweet thing has always been a big part of my life, but I knew somehow, maybe I shouldn't be eating those. They're so far out from my diet. It's not vegetables—it's not rice. And so I was almost secretly eating the cookies in this dark corner. I was feeling very guilty about eating these cookies. But nobody was watching me. And then I went to a Buddhist monastary for the night and the next day took the bus back up to the mountain.

Two days later, we heard Maharaji was back—he had been up in the mountains in another little village. He travels around a lot, moves from place to place. I hadn't seen him in about a month and a half—I didn't see much of him at all. We all went rushing to see Maharaji and I got a bag of oranges to bring to him and I came and took one look at him, and the oranges went flying and I started to cry and I fell down and they were patting me. Maharaji was eating oranges as fast as he could, manifesting through eating food the process of taking on the karma of someone else.

Women bring him food all day long. He just opens his mouth and they feed him and he's taking on karma that way. And he ate eight oranges right before my eyes. I had never seen anything like that. And the principal of the school was feeding me oranges and I was crying and the whole thing was very maudlin, and he pulls me by the hair, and I look up and he says to me, "How did you like the biscuits?"

I'd be at my temple. And I'd think about arranging for a beautiful lama in America to get some money, or something like that. Then I'd go to bed and pull the covers over my head and perhaps have a very worldly thought; I would think about what I'd do with all my powers when I got them; perhaps a sexual thought. Then when next I saw Maharaji he would tell me something like, "You want to give money to a lama in America." And I'd feel like I was such a beautiful guy. Then suddenly I'd be horrified with the realization that if he knew that thought, then he must know that one, too ... ohhhhh ... and that one, too! Then I'd look at the ground. And when I'd finally steal a glance at him, he'd be looking at me with such total love.

Now the impact of these experiences was very profound. As they say in the Sikh religion—Once you realize God knows everything, you're free. I had been through many years of psychoanalysis and still I had managed to keep private places in my head—I wouldn't say they were big, labeled categories, but they were certain attitudes or feelings that were still very private. And suddenly I realized that he knew everything that was going on in my head, all the time, and that he still loved me. Because who we are is behind all that.

I said to Hari Dass Baba, "Why is it that Maharaji never tells me the bad things I think?" and he says, "It does not help your sadhana—your spiritual work. He knows it all, but he just does the things that help you."

The sculptor had said he loved Maharaji so much, we should keep the Land Rover up there. The Land Rover was just sitting around and so Maharaji got the Land Rover after all, for that time. And then one day, I was told we were going on an outing up in the Himalayas for the day. This was very exciting, because I never left my room in the temple. Now in the temple, or around Maharaji, there were eight or nine people. Bhagwan Dass and I were the only westerners. In fact, at no time that I was there did I see any other westerners. This is clearly not a western scene, and in fact, I was specifically told when returning to the United States that I was not to mention Maharaji's name or where he was, or anything.

The few people that have slipped by this net and figured out from clues in my speech and their knowledge of India where he was and have gone to see him, were thrown out immediately ... very summarily dismissed, which is very strange. All I can do is pass that information on to you. I think the message is that you don't need to go to anywhere else to find what you are seeking.

So there were eight or nine people and whenever there was a scene, I walked last. I was the lowest man on the totem pole. They all loved me and honored me and I was the novice, like in a karate or judo class, where you stand at the back until you learn more. I was always in the back and they were always teaching me.

So we went in the Land Rover. Maharaji was up in the front—Bhagwan Dass was driving. Bhagwan Dass turned out to be very high in this scene. He was very very highly thought of and honored. He had started playing the sitar; he was a fantastic musician and the Hindu people loved him. He would do bhajan—holy music—so high they would go out on it. So Bhagwan Dass was driving and I was way in the back of the Land Rover camper with the women and some luggage.

And we went up into the hills and came to a place where we stopped and were given apples, in an orchard and we looked at a beautiful view. We stayed about 10 minutes, and then Maharaji says, "We've got to go on."

We got in the car, went further up the hill and came to a Forestry camp. Some of his devotees are people in the Forestry department so they make this available to him.

So we got to this place and there was a building waiting and a caretaker— "Oh, Maharaji, you've graced us with your presence." He went inside with the man that is there to take care of him or be with him all the time—and we all sat on the lawn.

After a little while, a message came out, "Maharaji wants to see you." And I got up and went in, and sat down in front of him. He looked at me and said.

"You make many people laugh in America?"

I said, "Yes, I like to do that."

"Good . . . You like to feed children?"

"Yes. Sure."

"Good."

He asked a few more questions like that, which seemed to be nice questions, but . . . ? Then he smiled and he reached forward and he tapped me right on the forehead, just three times. That's all.

Then the other fellow came along and lifted me and walked me out the door. I was completely confused. I didn't know what had happened to me—why he had done it—what it was about.

When I walked out, the people out in the yard said that I looked as if I were in a very high state. They said tears were streaming down my face. But all I felt inside was confusion. I have never felt any further understanding of it since then. I don't know what it was all about. It was not an idle movement, because the minute that was over, we all got back in the car and went home.

I pass that on to you. You know now, what I know about that. Just an interesting thing. I don't know what it means, yet.

Hari Dass Baba was my teacher. I was taught by this man with a chalkboard in the most terse way possible. I would get up early, take my bath in the river or out of a pail with a lota (a bowl). I would go in and do my breathing exercises, my pranayam and my hatha yoga, meditate, study, and around 11:30 in the morning, this man would arrive and with chalkboard he would write something down:

"If a pickpocket meets a saint, he sees only his pockets."

Then he'd get up and leave. Or he'd write,

"If you wear shoeleather, the whole earth is covered with leather."

These were his ways of teaching me about how motivation affects perception. His teaching seemed to be no teaching because he always taught from within . . . that is, his lessons aroused in me just affirmation . . . as if I knew it all already.

When starting to teach me about what it meant to be "ahimsa" or non-violent, and the effect on the environment around you of the vibrations—when he started to teach me about energy and vibrations, his opening statement was "Snakes Know Heart." "Yogis in jungle need not fear." Because if you're pure enough, cool it, don't worry. But you've got to be very pure.

So his teaching was of this nature. And it was not until a number of months later that I got hold of Vivekananda's book "Raja Yoga" and I realized that he had been teaching me Raja Yoga, very systematically—an exquisite scientific system that had been originally enunciated somewhere between 500 BC and 500 AD by Patanjali, in a set of sutras, or phrases, and it's called Ashtanga Yoga, or 8-limbed yoga—and also known as Raja or Kingly yoga. And this beautiful yogi was teaching me this wisdom with simple metaphor and brief phrase.

Now, though I am a beginner on the path, I have returned to the West for a time to work out karma or unfulfilled commitment. Part of this commitment is to share what I have learned with those of you who are on a similar journey. One can share a message through telling "our-story" as I have just done, or through teaching methods of yoga, or singing, or making love. Each of us finds his unique vehicle for sharing with others his bit of wisdom.

For me, this story is but a vehicle for sharing with you the true message . . . the living faith in what is possible.

Protest Music II

By mid-decade folk music had begun to have an impact on popular music. Many rock and roll musicians, in the aftermath of the Beatles invasion and Bob Dylan's going electric at Newport in the summer of 1965, began to write songs with political content. As these songs proliferated on the airways and young people flocked to record stores to buy the latest albums, the effect was to unify student activists around the country. Students from New York or Chicago or San Francisco—when they arrived in Washington for an antiwar demonstration—all shared familiarity with the songs of The Doors, Bob Dylan, Country Joe and the Fish, Simon and Garfunkel, Jefferson Airplane, and the Beatles. And, as in the civil rights movement, many songs would be sung during the demonstrations, adding further to a sense of unity and common purpose. Along with "We Shall Overcome" and "Where Have All the Flowers Gone," protestors sang John Lennon's "All We Are Saying, Is Give Peace a Chance" and Country Joe McDonald's "I-Feel-Like-I'm-Fixin'-to-Die Rag."

In addition to antiwar compositions, rock bands also explored social and cultural themes. The Mothers of Invention's "Plastic People," for example, ridicules middle-class consumerist values. The Doors' "The End"—Jim Morrison's surrealistic, primal outburst—seemed so suited to the disintegration of a society consumed by the madness in Vietnam that Francis Ford Coppola featured it in his 1978 film Apocalypse Now. *More conventional protest songs were still being written. Pete Seeger's "Waist*

Deep in the Big Muddy" is his comment on Johnson's escalation of the Vietnam War. Seeger sang this on the Smothers Brothers Comedy Hour in 1968, and it was so controversial that CBS eventually canceled the popular show. Country Joe McDonald's "I-Feel-Like-I'm-Fixin'-to-Die Rag"—the most famous Vietnam War protest song—electrified the crowd at Woodstock in 1969. Creedence Clearwater Revival's "Fortunate Son" highlights the age-old historical truism that the poor fight and die in wars for the rich. As dissent and protest took center stage during the civil rights movement, other groups were encouraged to demand their rights. Buffy Sainte-Marie, a Cree Indian, for example, compellingly sang of the plight of Native Americans in "My Country 'Tis of Thy People You're Dying."

PETE SEEGER, "WAIST DEEP IN THE BIG MUDDY," 1967

It was back in nineteen forty-two,
I was a member of a good platoon.
We were on maneuvers in Loozianna,
one night by the light of the moon.
The Captain told us to ford a river,
That's how it all begun.
We were—knee deep in the Big Muddy
But the big fool said to push on.

The Sergeant said, "Sir, are you sure
This is the best way back to the base?"
"Sergeant, go on, I forded this river
'Bout a mile above this place.
It'll be a little soggy but just keep slogging.
We'll soon be on dry ground."
We were—waist deep in the Big Muddy
but the big fool said to push on.

The Sergeant said, "Sir, with all this equipment
No man will be able to swim."
"Sergeant, don't be a nervous Nellie,"
The Captain said to him.
"All we need is a little determination;
Men, follow me, I'll lead on."
We were—neck deep in the Big Muddy
but the big fool said to push on.

SOURCE: *Waist Deep in the Big Muddy (The Big Muddy)*, words and music by Pete Seeger. TRO—© copyright 1967(renewed) Melody Trails, Inc., New York, NY. Used by permission.

All at once, the moon clouded over,
We heard a gurgling cry.
A few seconds later, the captain's helmet
Was all that floated by.
The Sergeant said, "Turn around men!
I'm in charge from now on."
And we just made it out of the Big Muddy
With the captain dead and gone.

We stripped and dived and found his body
Stuck in the old quicksand.
I guess he didn't know that the water was deeper
Than the place he'd once before been.
Another stream had joined the Big Muddy
'Bout a half mile from where we'd gone.
We were lucky to escape from the Big Muddy
When the big fool said to push on.

Well, I'm not going to point any moral;
I'll leave that for yourself
Maybe you're still walking, you're still talking
You'd like to keep your health.
But every time I read the papers
That old feeling comes on;
We're—waist deep in the Big Muddy
And the big fool says to push on.

Waist deep in the Big Muddy
And the big fool says to push on.
Waist deep in the Big Muddy
And the big fool says to push on.
Waist deep! Neck deep! Soon even a
Tall man'll be over his head, we're
Waist deep in the Big Muddy!
And the big fool says to push on!

COUNTRY JOE MCDONALD, "I-FEEL-LIKE-I'M-FIXIN'-TO-DIE RAG," 1965

Yeah, come on all of you, big strong men,
Uncle Sam needs your help again.
He's got himself in a terrible jam

SOURCE: Country Joe and The Fish, *I Feel Like I'm Fixin' to Die*, Vanguard Records 1967.

Way down yonder in Vietnam
So put down your books and pick up a gun,
We're gonna have a whole lotta fun.
And it's one, two, three,
What are we fighting for?
Don't ask me, I don't give a damn,
Next stop is Vietnam;
And it's five, six, seven,
Open up the pearly gates,
Well there ain't no time to wonder why,
Whoopee! we're all gonna die.

Well, come on Wall Street, don't move slow,
Why man, this is war au-go-go.
There's plenty good money to be made
By supplying the Army with the tools of the trade,
Just hope and pray that if they drop the bomb,
They drop it on the Viet Cong.
And it's one, two, three,
What are we fighting for?
Don't ask me, I don't give a damn,
Next stop is Vietnam.
And it's five, six, seven,
Open up the pearly gates,
Well there ain't no time to wonder why
Whoopee! we're all gonna die.

Well, come on generals, let's move fast;
Your big chance has come at last.
Gotta go out and get those reds—
The only good commie is the one who's dead
And you know that peace can only be won
When we've blown 'em all to kingdom come.
And it's one, two, three,
What are we fighting for?
Don't ask me, I don't give a damn,
Next stop is Vietnam;
And it's five, six, seven,
Open up the pearly gates,
Well there ain't no time to wonder why
Whoopee! we're all gonna die.

Well, come on mothers throughout the land,
Pack your boys off to Vietnam.
Come on fathers, don't hesitate,
Send 'em off before it's too late.

Be the first one on your block
To have your boy come home in a box.
And it's one, two, three
What are we fighting for?
Don't ask me, I don't give a damn,
Next stop is Vietnam.
And it's five, six, seven,
Open up the pearly gates,
Well there ain't no time to wonder why,
Whoopee! we're all gonna die.

Buffy Sainte-Marie, "My Country 'Tis of Thy People You're Dying," 1965

Now that your big eyes have finally opened
Now that you're wondering how must they feel,
Meaning them that you've chased across America's movie screens.
Now that you're wondering how can it be real
That the ones you've called colorful, noble and proud
In your school propaganda
They starve in their splendor?
You've asked for my comment I simply will render:
My country 'tis of thy people you're dying.

Now that the longhouses breed superstition
You force us to send our toddlers away
To your schools where they're taught to despise their traditions.
You forbid them their languages, then further say
That American history really began
When Columbus set sail out of Europe, then stress
That the nation of leeches that conquered this land
Are the biggest and bravest and boldest and best.
And yet where in your history books is the tale
Of the genocide basic to this country's birth,
Of the preachers who lied, how the Bill of Rights failed,
How a nation of patriots returned to their earth?
And where will it tell of the Liberty Bell
As it rang with a thud
O'er Kinzua mud,

SOURCE: Buffy Sainte-Marie, *Little Wheel Spin and Spin*, Vanguard Records 1966.

And of brave Uncle Sam in Alaska this year?
My country 'tis of thy people you're dying.

Hear how the bargain was made for the West:
With her shivering children in zero degrees,
Blankets for your land, so the treaties attest,
Oh well, blankets for land is a bargain indeed,
And the blankets were those Uncle Sam had collected
From smallpox-diseased dying soldiers that day.
And the tribes were wiped out and the history books censored,
A hundred years of your statesmen have felt it's better this way.
And yet a few of the conquered have somehow survived,
Their blood runs the redder though genes have paled.
From the Grand Canyon's caverns to Craven's sad hills
The wounded, the losers, the robbed sing their tale.
From Los Angeles County to upstate New York
The white nation fattens while others grow lean;
Oh the tricked and evicted they know what I mean.
My country 'tis of thy people you're dying.

The past it just crumbled, the future just threatens;
Our life blood's shut up in your chemical tanks.
And now here you come, bill of sale in your hands
And surprise in your eyes that we're lacking in thanks
For the blessings of civilization you've brought us,
The lessons you've taught us, the ruin you've wrought us—
Oh see what our trust in America's brought us.
My country 'tis of thy people you're dying.

Now that the pride of the sires receives charity,
Now that we're harmless and safe behind laws,
Now that my life's to be known as your "heritage,"
Now that even the graves have been robbed,
Now that our own chosen way is a novelty—
Hands on our hearts we salute you your victory,
Choke on your blue white and scarlet hypocrisy
Pitying the blindness that you've never seen
That the eagles of war whose wings lent you glory
They were never no more than carrion crows,
Pushed the wrens from their nest, stole their eggs, changed their story;
The mockingbird sings it, it's all that he knows.
"Ah what can I do?" say a powerless few
With a lump in your throat and a tear in your eye—
Can't you see that their poverty's profiting you.
My country 'tis of thy people you're dying.

John Fogerty, Creedence Clearwater Revival, "Fortunate Son," 1969

Some folks are born to wave the flag,
Ooh, they're red, white and blue.
And when the band plays "Hail to the chief,"
Ooh, they point the cannon at you, Lord,

It ain't me, it ain't me, I ain't no senator's son, son.
It ain't me, it ain't me; I ain't no fortunate one, no,
Yeah!

Some folks are born silver spoon in hand,
Lord, don't they help themselves, oh.
But when the taxman comes to the door,
Lord, the house looks like a rummage sale, yes,

It ain't me, it ain't me, I ain't no millionaire's son, no.
It ain't me, it ain't me; I ain't no fortunate one, no.

Some folks inherit star spangled eyes,
Ooh, they send you down to war, Lord,
And when you ask them, "How much should we give?"
Ooh, they only answer More! more! more! yoh,

It ain't me, it ain't me, I ain't no military son, son.
It ain't me, it ain't me; I ain't no fortunate one, one.
It ain't me, it ain't me, I ain't no fortunate one, no no no,
It ain't me, it ain't me, I ain't no fortunate son, no no no,

Redstockings

After women got the vote in 1920, many people assumed that there was
no further need for women to agitate for their rights. Alice Paul
introduced the Equal Rights Amendment in 1923, but by the 1960s most
people had forgotten about it. Betty Friedan's The Feminine Mystique
and the founding of the National Organization of Women, in conjunction
with women's experience participating in civil rights and antiwar
activism, reawakened the feminist movement. As a result, by the late
1960s, many women were becoming committed to change.

SOURCE: Creedence Clearwater Revival. *Willy and the Poor Boys,* Fantasy 1969.

The earlier movement had concentrated on political and, to some extent, on economic rights. The second wave of feminism now began to emphasize attitudes and consciousness. It was not enough for women to be able to vote; they needed also to be viewed and treated as equal members of society. Ironically, one of the forces that radicalized the women's movement was the counterculture and New Left itself. Women who attended Students for a Democratic Society (SDS) meetings found that after an evening of discussing Marx and Marcuse or analyzing race and class issues in the United States or examining the historical background of the war in Vietnam, they were usually expected to make sandwiches and coffee for their male comrades. One woman observed at the 1965 national SDS convention that "women only made peanut butter sandwiches, waited on tables, cleaned up and got laid. That was their role." Being treated as objects by left-wing men, who should have known better, was a wake-up call that radicalized many women. Feminists began setting up caucuses and workshops where they gathered to discuss women's problems in a classist, racist, sexist society. Before the decade was out, many radical women's groups had formed. Some believed that women should completely separate from male-dominated society; others believed that women would only achieve liberation if the entire class structure of society was first eliminated.

Redstockings was a group formed by Ellen Willis and Shulamith Firestone (the name is a left-wing play on "Blue Stockings," a pejorative term for intelligent women) that called for consciousness-raising sessions to enable women to see through the artificial roles that had been forced on them by men. They asked: Are women really more nurturing than men and consequently more suited to be the caregiver in a family? Is this biologically determined or a social construct? Redstockings also participated in demonstrations along with many other more radical feminist groups. Some picketed the Miss America contest in Atlantic City in 1968. Another group, W.I.T.C.H. (Women's International Terrorist Conspiracy from Hell) held a witches' dance on Wall Street in October 1968 and put a hex on the Stock Exchange. (The Dow Jones Industrial Average declined the next day!)

THE REDSTOCKINGS MANIFESTO, 1969

I. After centuries of individual and preliminary political struggle, women are uniting to achieve their final liberation from male supremacy. Redstockings is dedicated to building this unity and winning our freedom.

II. Women are an oppressed class. Our oppression is total, affecting every facet of our lives. We are exploited as sex objects, breeders, domestic servants, and cheap

---

SOURCE: "Redstockings Manifesto" (Notes from the Second Year, 1970), reprinted in full in *Feminism in Our Time: The Essential Writings, World War II to the Present*, Miriam Schneir, Ed. (New York: Vintage Books, 1994), 125–129.

labor. We are considered inferior beings, whose only purpose is to enhance men's lives. Our humanity is denied. Our prescribed behavior is enforced by the threat of violence.

Because we have lived so intimately with our oppressors, in isolation from each other, we have been kept from seeing our personal suffering as a political condition. This creates the illusion that a woman's relationship with her man is a matter of interplay between two unique personalities, and can be worked out individually. In reality, every such relationship is a "class" relationship, and the conflicts between individual men and women are political conflicts that can only be solved collectively.

III. We identify the agents of our oppression as men. Male supremacy is the oldest, most basic form of domination. All other forms of exploitation and oppression (racism, capitalism, imperialism, etc.) are extensions of male supremacy; men dominate women, a few men dominate the rest. All power structures throughout history have been male-dominated and male-oriented. Men have controlled all political, economic, and cultural institutions and backed up this control with physical force. They have used their power to keep women in an inferior position. All men receive economic, sexual, and psychological benefits from male supremacy. All men have oppressed women.

IV. Attempts have been made to shift the burden of responsibility from men to institutions or to women themselves. We condemn these arguments as evasions. Institutions alone do not oppress; they are merely tools of the oppressor. To blame institutions implies that men and women are equally victimized, obscures the fact that men benefit from the subordination of women, and gives men the excuse that they are forced to be oppressors. On the contrary, any man is free to renounce his superior position provided he is willing to be treated like a woman by other men.

We also reject the idea that women consent to or are to blame for their oppression. Women's submission is not the result of brainwashing, stupidity, or mental illness but of continual, daily pressure from men. We do not need to change ourselves, but to change men.

The most slanderous evasion of all is that women can oppress men. The basis for this illusion is the isolation of individual relationships from their political context and the tendency of men to see any legitimate challenge to their privileges as persecutions.

V. We regard our personal experience, and our feelings about that experience, as the basis for an analysis of our common situation. We cannot rely on existing ideologies as they are all products of male supremacist culture. We question every generalization and accept none that are not confirmed by our experience.

Our chief task at present is to develop female class consciousness through sharing experience and publicly exposing the sexist foundation of all our institutions. Consciousness-raising is not "therapy," which implies the existence of individual solutions and falsely assumes that the male-female relationship is purely personal, but the only method by which we can ensure that our program for liberation is based on the concrete realities of our lives.

The first requirement for raising class consciousness is honesty, in private and in public, with ourselves and other women.

VI. We identify with all women. We define our best interest as that of the poorest, most brutally exploited woman. We repudiate all economic, racial, educational, or status privileges that divide us from other women. We are determined to recognize and eliminate any prejudices we may hold against other women. We are committed to achieving internal democracy. We will do whatever is necessary to ensure that every woman in our movement has an equal chance to participate, assume responsibility, and develop her political potential.

VII. We call on all our sisters to unite with us in struggle. We call on all men to give up their male privileges and support women's liberation in the interest of our humanity and their own. In fighting for our liberation, we will always take the side of women against their oppressors. We will not ask what is "revolutionary" or "reformist," only what is good for women.

The time for individual skirmishes is passed. This time we are going all the way.

S.C.U.M. Society for Cutting Up Men

Valerie Solanas was an intriguing figure. She was abused as a child, went to live in New York, made a living as a prostitute, appeared in a couple of Andy Warhol films, and put a lot of effort into a script she wrote, "Up Your Ass," that she hoped Warhol would produce. Warhol, however, after praising her typing (!), misplaced the script and, affronted, she walked into his studio in June 1968 and shot him. The year before, she founded S.C.U.M., the Society for Cutting Up Men, and wrote a manifesto in which she claimed that the male was a biological accident, a mistake of nature. Her notoriety after she shot Warhol and was sent to prison led to the publication of the manifesto, which was avidly read by many feminists (although most did not take her statements seriously). It remains, however, an excellent example of extreme dissent.

S.C.U.M. MANIFESTO, 1968

Life in this society being, at best, an utter bore and no aspect of society being at all relevant to women, there remains to civic-minded, responsible, thrill-seeking

Source: Valerie Solanas, *S.C.U.M. Manifesto*, (Oakland, CA: AK Press, 1968), passim.

females only to overthrow the government, eliminate the money system, institute complete automation and destroy the male sex.

It is now technically feasible to reproduce without the aid of males (or, for that matter, females) and to produce only females. We must begin immediately to do so. Retaining the male has not even the dubious purpose of reproduction. The male is a biological accident: the Y (male) gene is an incomplete X (female) gene, that is, it has an incomplete set of chromosomes. In other words, the male is an incomplete female, a walking abortion, aborted at the gene stage. To be male is to be deficient, emotionally limited; maleness is a deficiency disease and males are emotional cripples.

The male is completely egocentric, trapped inside himself, incapable of empathizing or identifying with others, or love, friendship, affection or tenderness. He is a completely isolated unit, incapable of rapport with anyone. His responses are entirely visceral, not cerebral; his intelligence is a mere tool in the services of his drives and needs; he is incapable of mental passion, mental interaction; he can't relate to anything other than his own physical sensations. He is a half-dead, unresponsive lump, incapable of giving or receiving pleasure or happiness; consequently, he is at best an utter bore, an inoffensive blob, since only those capable of absorption in others can be charming. He is trapped in a twilight zone halfway between humans and apes, and is far worse off than the apes because, unlike the apes, he is capable of a large array of negative feelings—hate, jealousy, contempt, disgust, guilt, shame, doubt—and moreover, he is *aware* of what he is and what he isn't.

Although completely physical, the male is unfit even for stud service. Even assuming mechanical proficiency, which few men have, he is, first of all, incapable of zestfully, lustfully, tearing off a piece, but instead is eaten up with guilt, shame, fear and insecurity, feelings rooted in male nature, which the most enlightened training can only minimize; second, the physical feeling he attains is next to nothing; and third, he is not empathizing with his partner, but is obsessed with how he's doing, turning in an A performance, doing a good plumbing job. To call a man an animal is to flatter him; he's a machine, a walking dildo. It's often said that men use women. Use them for what? Surely not pleasure.

Eaten up with guilt, shame, fears and insecurities and obtaining, if he's lucky, a barely perceptible physical feeling, the male is, nonetheless, obsessed with screwing; he'll swim through a river of snot, wade nostril-deep through a mile of vomit, if he thinks there'll be a friendly pussy awaiting him. He'll screw a woman he despises, any snaggle-toothed hag, and furthermore, pay for the opportunity. Why? Relieving physical tension isn't the answer, as masturbation suffices for that. It's not ego satisfaction; that doesn't explain screwing corpses and babies.

Completely egocentric, unable to relate, empathize or identify, and filled with a vast, pervasive, diffuse sexuality, the male is psychically passive. He hates his passivity, so he projects it onto women, defines the male as active, then sets out to prove that he is ("prove that he is a Man"). His main means of attempting to prove it is screwing (Big Man with a Big Dick tearing off a Big Piece). Since he's attempting to prove an error, he must "prove" it again and again. Screwing, then, is a desperate compulsive attempt to prove he's not passive, not a woman; but he *is* passive and *does* want to be a woman.

Being an incomplete female, the male spends his life attempting to complete himself, to become female. He attempts to do this by constantly seeking out, fraternizing with and trying to live through and fuse with the female, and by claiming as his own all female characteristics—emotional strength and independence, forcefulness, dynamism, decisiveness, coolness, objectivity, assertiveness, courage, integrity, vitality, intensity, depth of character, grooviness, etc.—and projecting onto women all male traits—vanity, frivolity, triviality, weakness, etc. It should be said, though, that the male has one glaring area of superiority over the female—public relations. (He has done a brilliant job of convincing millions of women that men are women and women are men). The male claim that females find fulfillment through motherhood and sexuality reflects what males think they'd find fulfilling if they were female.

Women, in other words, don't have penis envy; men have pussy envy. When the male accepts his passivity, defines himself as a women (males as well as females think men are women and women are men), and becomes a transvestite he loses his desire to screw (or to do anything else, for that matter; he fulfills himself as a drag queen) and gets his cock chopped off. He then achieves a continuous diffuse sexual feeling from "being a woman." Screwing is, for a man, a defense against his desire to be female. Sex is itself a sublimation. . . .

He is responsible for:

War: The male's normal compensation for not being female, namely, getting his Big Gun off, is grossly inadequate, as he can get it off only a very limited number of times; so he gets it off on a really massive scale, and proves to the entire world that he's a "Man." Since he has no compassion or ability to empathize or identify, proving his manhood is worth an endless amount of mutilation and suffering and an endless number of lives, including his own—his own life being worthless, he would rather go out in a blaze of glory than to plod grimly on for fifty more years.

Niceness, Politeness, and "Dignity": Every man, deep down, knows he's a worthless piece of shit. Overwhelmed by a sense of animalism and deeply ashamed of it; wanting, not to express himself, but to hide from others his total physicality, total egocentricity, the hate and contempt he feels for other men, and to hide from himself the hate and contempt he suspects other men feel for him; having a crudely constructed nervous system that is easily upset by the least display of emotion or feeling, the male tries to enforce a "social" code that ensures perfect blandness, unsullied by the slightest trace or feeling or upsetting opinion. He uses terms like "copulate," "sexual congress," "have relations with" (to men sexual relations is a redundancy), overlaid with stilted manners; the suit on the chimp. . . .

Gloria Steinem (1934–)

Gloria Steinem has had a critical influence on the feminist movement. In 1963 she wrote an article about her experience working in a Playboy Club, "I Was a Playboy Bunny," and by the late 1960s she was a regular columnist for New York *magazine. Her influence became more significant in 1971, when, with Betty Friedan, Shirley Chisholm, and Bella Abzug, she cofounded the National Woman's Caucus. Before the year was over, she had published the first issue of* Ms. Magazine, *which became a leading instrument in raising women's consciousness about feminist issues. Steinem, more radical than feminist Betty Friedan, is famous for her comment that "a woman needs a man like a fish needs a bicycle."*

In this article, which first appeared in the Washington Post *in 1970 and was later reprinted several times in different versions, Steinem presents the case for feminism.*

"'WOMEN'S LIBERATION' AIMS TO FREE MEN, TOO," JUNE 7, 1970

This is the year of Women's Liberation. Or at least, it's the year the press has discovered a movement that has been strong for several years now, and reported it as a small, privileged, rather lunatic event instead of the major revolution in consciousness—in everyone's consciousness, male or female—that I believe it truly is.

It is a movement that some call "feminist" but should more accurately be called humanist; a movement that is an integral part of rescuing this country from its old, expensive patterns of elitism, racism and violence.

The first problem for all of us, men and women, is not to learn, but to unlearn. We are filled with the popular wisdom of several centuries just past, and we are terrified to give it up. Patriotism means obedience, age means wisdom, woman means submission, black means inferior: these are preconceptions imbedded so deeply in our thinking that we honestly may not know that they are there.

Unfortunately, authorities who write textbooks are sometimes subject to the same popular wisdom as the rest of us. They gather their proof around it, and end by becoming the theoreticians of the status quo. Using the most respectable of scholarly methods, for instance, English scientists proved definitively that the English were descended from the angels while the Irish were descended from the apes.

Source: Gloria Steinem, "'Women's Liberation' Aims to Free Men, Too." *Washington Post,* Sunday, June 7, 1970.

It was beautifully done, complete with comparative skull measurements, and it was a rationale for the English domination of the Irish for more than 100 years. I try to remember that when I'm reading Arthur Jensen's current and very impressive work on the limitations of black intelligence, or when I'm reading Lionel Tiger on the inability of women to act in groups.

It wasn't easy for the English to give up their mythic superiority. Indeed, there are quite a few Irish who doubt that they have done it yet. Clearing our minds and government policies of outdated myths is proving to be at least as difficult, but it is also inevitable. Whether it's woman's secondary role in society or the paternalistic role of the United States in the world, the old assumptions just don't work any more.

Part of living this revolution is having the scales fall from our eyes. Every day we see small obvious truths that we had missed before. Our histories, for instance, have generally been written for and about white men. Inhabited countries were "discovered" when the first white male set foot there, and most of us learned more about any one European country than we did about Africa and Asia combined.

I confess that, before some consciousness-changing of my own, I would have thought that the women's history courses springing up around the country belonged in the same cultural ghetto as home economics. The truth is that we need Women's Studies almost as much as we need Black Studies, and for exactly the same reason: too many of us have completed a "good" education believing that everything from political power to scientific discovery was the province of white males.

We believed, for instance, that the vote had been "given" to women in some whimsical, benevolent fashion. We never learned about the long desperation of the women's struggle, or about the strength and wisdom of the women who led it. We knew a great deal more about the outdated, male supremacist theories of Sigmund Freud than we did about societies where women had equal responsibility, or even ruled.

"Anonymous," Virginia Woolf once said sadly, "was a woman."

A BLACK PARALLEL

I don't mean to equate our problems of identity with those that flowed from slavery. But, as Gunnar Myrdal pointed out in his classic study *An American Dilemma*, "In drawing a parallel between the position of, and feeling toward, women and Negroes, we are uncovering a fundamental basis of our culture."

Blacks and women suffer from the same myths of childlike natures; smaller brains; inability to govern themselves, much less white men; limited job skills; identity as sex objects, and so on. Ever since slaves arrived on these shores and were given the legal status of wives—that is, chattel—our legal reforms have followed on each other's heels—with women, I might add, still lagging considerably behind.

President Nixon's Commission on women concluded that the Supreme Court sanctions discrimination against women—discrimination that it long ago ruled unconstitutional in the case of blacks—but the commission report remains mysteriously unreleased by the White House. An equal rights amendment now up again before the Senate has been delayed by a male-chauvinist Congress for 47 years. Neither blacks nor women have role-models in history: models of individuals who have been honored in authority outside the home.

As Margaret Mead has noted, the only women allowed to be dominant and respectable at the same time are widows. You have to do what society wants you to do, have a husband who dies, and then have power thrust upon you through no fault of your own. The whole thing seems very hard on the men.

Before we go on to other reasons why Women's Liberation Is Men's Liberation, too—and why this incarnation of the women's movement is inseparable from the larger revolution—perhaps we should clear the air of a few more myths—the myth that women are biologically inferior, for instance. In fact, an equally good case could be made for the reverse.

Women live longer then men. That's when the groups being studied are always being cited as proof that we work them to death, but the truth is that women live longer than men even when the groups being studied are monks and nuns. We survived Nazi concentration camps better, are protected against heart attacks by our female hormones, are less subject to many diseases, withstand surgery better and are so much more durable at every stage of life that nature conceives 20 to 50 percent more males just to keep the balance going.

The Auto Safety Committee of the American Medical Association has come to the conclusion that women are better drivers because they're less emotional than men. I never thought I would hear myself quoting the AMA, but that one was too good to resist.

I don't want to prove the superiority of one sex to another: that would only be repeating a male mistake. The truth is that we're just not sure how many of our differences are biological and how many are societal. What we do know is that the differences between the two sexes, like the differences between races, are much less great than the differences to be found within each group.

CHAINS OF MINK

A second myth is that women are already being treated equally in this society. We ourselves have been guilty of perpetuating this myth, especially at upper economic levels where women have grown fond of being lavishly maintained as ornaments and children. The chains may be made of mink and wall-to-wall carpeting, but they are still chains.

The truth is that a woman with a college degree working full time makes less than a black man with a high school degree working full time. And black women make least of all. In many parts of the country—New York City, for instance—a woman has no legally guaranteed right to rent an apartment, buy a house, get accommodations in a hotel or be served in a public restaurant. She can be refused simply because of her sex.

In some states, women get longer jail sentences for the same crime. Women on welfare must routinely answer humiliating personal questions; male welfare recipients do not. A woman is the last to be hired, the first to be fired. Equal pay for equal work is the exception. Equal chance for advancement, especially at upper levels or at any level with authority over men, is rare enough to be displayed in a museum.

As for our much-touted economic power, *we* make up only 5 percent of the Americans receiving $10,000 a year or more, and that includes all the famous rich widows. We are 51 per cent of all stockholders, a dubious honor these days, but we hold only 18 per cent of the stock—and that is generally controlled by men.

In fact, the myth of economic matriarchy in this country is less testimony to our power than to resentment of the little power we do have.

You may wonder why we have submitted to such humiliations all these years; why, indeed, women will sometimes deny that they are second-class citizens at all. The answer lies in the psychology of second-classness. Like all such groups, we come to accept what society says about us. We believe that we can make it in the world only by "Uncle Tom-ing," by a real or pretended subservience to white males.

Even when we come to understand that we, as individuals, are not second class, we still accept society's assessment of our group—a phenomenon psychologists refer to as internalized aggression. From this stems the desire to be the only woman in an office, an academic department or any other part of the man's world. From this also stems women who put down their sisters—and my own profession of journalism has some of them.

INHUMANITY TO MAN

I don't want to give the impression, though, that we want to join society exactly as it is. I don't think most women want to pick up briefcases and march off to meaningless, depersonalized jobs. Nor do we want to be drafted—and women certainly should be drafted; even the readers of Seventeen magazine were recently polled as being overwhelmingly in favor of women in national service—to serve in a war like the one in Indochina.

We want to liberate men from those inhuman roles as well. We want to share the work and responsibility, and to have men share equal responsibility for the children. Probably the ultimate myth is that children must have fulltime mothers, and that liberated women make bad ones. The truth is that most American children seem to be suffering from too much mother and too little father.

Women now spend more time with their homes and families than in any other past or present society we know about. To get back to the sanity of the agrarian or joint family system, we need free universal day care. With that aid, as in Scandinavian countries, and with laws that permit women equal work and equal pay, man will be relieved of his role as sole breadwinner and stranger to his own children.

No more alimony. Fewer boring wives. Fewer childlike wives. No more so-called "Jewish mothers," who are simply normally ambitious human beings with all their ambitiousness confined to the house. No more wives who fall apart with the first wrinkle because they've been taught that their total identity depends on their outsides. No more responsibility for another adult human being who has never been told she is responsible for her own life, and who sooner or later says some version of, "If I hadn't married you, I could have been a star." Women's Liberation really is Men's Liberation, too.

The family system that will emerge is a great subject of anxiety. Probably there will be a variety of choices. Colleague marriages, such as young people have now, with both partners going to law-school or the Peace Corps together, is one alternative. At least they share more than the kitchen and the bedroom. Communes; marriages that are valid for the child-rearing years only—there are many possibilities.

The point is that Women's Liberation is not destroying the American family. It is trying to build a human compassionate alternative out of its ruins.

SIMPLY INCORRUPTIBLE

One final myth that women are more moral than men. We are not more moral; we are only uncorrupted by power. But until the old generation of male chauvinists is out of office women in positions of power can increase our chances of peace a great deal.

I personally would rather have had Margaret Mead as President during the past six years of Vietnam than either Lyndon Johnson or Richard Nixon. At least she wouldn't have had her masculinity to prove. Much of the trouble this country is in has to do with the masculine mystique: The idea that manhood somehow depends on the subjugation of other people. It's a bipartisan problem.

The challenge to all of us is to live a revolution, not to die for one. There has been too much killing, and the weapons are now far too terrible. This revolution has to change consciousness, to upset the injustice of our current hierarchy by refusing to honor it. And it must be a life that enforces a new social justice.

Because the truth is that none of us can be liberated if other groups are not. Women's Liberation is a bridge between black and white women, but also between the construction workers and the suburbanites, between Mr. Nixon's Silent Majority and the young people it fears. Indeed, there's much more injustice and rage among working-class women than among the much publicized white radicals.

Women are sisters; they have many of the same problems, and they can communicate with each other. "You only get radicalized," as black activists always told us, "on your own thing." Then we make the connection to other injustices in society. The women's movement is an important revolutionary bridge, and we are building It.

Stonewall

The Movement of the 1960s led to the mobilization of minorities around the country. Chicanos, Native Americans, homosexuals, lesbians, and many others were inspired to stand up for their rights. In June 1969, the dissenting impulse spawned the gay rights movement. After one of the routine police raids at the Stonewall Inn in Greenwich Village (a bar frequented by gays), a succession of demonstrations broke out. Many gay men decided they were no longer going to take the harassment, and by the end of the summer the Gay Liberation Front was born. The following flyers were distributed during the summer of 1969 to spread the word and encourage more people to join the movement.

STONEWALL DOCUMENTS, 1969

FLYER 1

Get the mafia and the cops out of gay bars.

The nights of Friday, June 27, 1969 and Saturday, June 28, 1969 will go down in history as the first time that thousands of Homosexual men and women went out into the streets to protest the intolerable situation which has existed in New York City for many years—namely, the Mafia (or syndicate) control of this city's Gay bars in collusion with certain elements in the Police Dept. of the City of New York. The demonstrations were triggered by a Police raid on the Stonewall Inn late Friday night, June 27th. The purported reason for the raid was the Stonewall's lack of a liquor license. Who's kidding whom here? Can anybody really believe that an operation as big as the Stonewall could continue for almost three years just a few blocks from the 6th Precinct house without having a liquor license? No! The Police have known about the Stonewall operation all along. What's happened is the presence of new "brass" in 6th Precinct which has vowed to "drive the fags out of the Village."

SOURCE: Donn Teal, *The Gay Militants* (New York: St. Martin's Press, 1971), 24–25, 36, 37.

Many of you have noticed one of the signs which the "management" of the Stonewall has placed outside stating "Legalize Gay bars and lick the problem." Judge Kenneth Keating (a former US Senator) ruled in January 1968 that even close dancing between Homosexuals is legal. Since that date there has been nothing illegal, per se, about a Gay bar. What is illegal about New York City's Gay bars today is the Mafia (or syndicate) stranglehold on them. Legitimate Gay businessmen are afraid to open decent Gay bars with a healthy social atmosphere (as opposed to the hell-hole atmosphere of places typified by the Stonewall) because of fear of pressure from the unholy alliance of the Mafia and elements in the Police Dept. who accept payoffs and protect the Mafia monopoly.

We at the Homophile Youth Movement (HYMN) believe that the only way this monopoly can be broken is through the action of Homosexual men and women themselves. We obviously cannot rely on the various agencies of government who for years have known about this situation but who have refused to do anything about it. Therefore we urge the following:

1. That Gay businessmen step forward and open Gay bars that will be run legally with competitive pricing and a healthy social atmosphere.

2. That Homosexual men and women boycott places like the Stonewall. The only way, it seems, that we can get the criminal elements out of gay bars is simply to make it unprofitable for them.

3. That the Homosexual citizens of New York City, and concerned Heterosexuals, write to mayor Lindsay demanding a thorough investigation and effective action to correct this intolerable situation.

FLYER 2

July 24th
Do you think homosexuals are revolting?
You bet your sweet ass we are.

We're going to make a place for ourselves in the revolutionary movement. We challenge the myths that are screwing up this society. MEETING: Thursday, July 24th, 6:30 PM at Alternate U, 69 West 14th Street at Sixth Avenue.

FLYER 3

Homosexuals are coming.
Together at last.

To examine how we are oppressed and how we oppress ourselves. To fight for gay control of gay businesses. To publish our own newspaper. To these and other radical ends. . . .

César Chávez (1927–1993)

*César Chávez spent most of his early life traveling around the southwest
as a migrant farm worker with other Chicanos (Americans of Mexican
heritage), eking out a subsistence living by going from farm to farm
during harvest season. In the early 1960s, inspired by the civil rights
movement and Martin Luther King Jr.'s leadership, he began to organize
the first farm workers' union in America. "If you're outraged at
conditions, then you can't possibly be free or happy until you devote all
your time to changing them and do nothing but that," he said. In 1965 his
union, the National Farm Workers Association, with about 1200
members, joined with another union in a grape strike in Delano. The
strike (La Huelga) wound up lasting five years, during which time
millions of supporters and sympathizers around the country showed their
solidarity by boycotting California grapes. From the beginning, the
NFWA (United Farm Workers after 1966), under Chávez's direction,
adhered to the principles of nonviolence espoused by Gandhi and King. In
fact, Chávez, emulating Gandhi, went on a hunger strike in 1968 for
25 days. Robert Kennedy, who by that time had thrown his full support
behind Chávez, flew to California to be the one to give Chávez bread
when he broke the fast. Economic pressure finally forced the growers to
negotiate with the UFW in 1970, and Chávez's long campaign finally
achieved its goal.*

*Chávez's efforts were not the only ones to promote the rights of
Chicanos and Latinos. In 1969, a new organization, La Raza Unida (the
United Race), influenced by Chávez's struggle and the optimistic activism
of the 1960s, spread throughout the southwest. In Texas, Colorado, New
Mexico, and California, chapters of La Raza Unida opened, each
emphasizing the issues of its locality, each working to elect their own
representatives in their own districts, and each working to overturn
anti-Chicano/Latino discrimination.*

Interview with César Chávez, Apostle of Non-Violence, May 1970

OBSERVER: *Why do you insist on non-violent means in this struggle?*
CHÁVEZ: Our conviction is that human life and limb are a very special possession given by God to man and that no one has the right to take that away, in
any cause, however just. We also find that violence is contagious; it is

---

SOURCE: *The Observer*, May 1970.

uncontrollable. If we use it, then the opposition is going to respond in kind and it is going to be escalated.

Also we are convinced that non-violence is more powerful than violence. We are convinced that non-violence supports you if you have a just and moral cause. Non-violence gives the opportunity to stay on the offensive, which is of vital importance to win any contest. Suppose we are striking and the opponent appears to be getting the best of us and we resort to violence. Then he will bring in other forces and one of two things happens: violence has to be escalated, or there is total demoralization of the workers. Non-violence works in exactly the opposite manner: when for every violent action committed against us, we respond with non-violence, we tend to attract people's support; we have a chance of attracting other people who are not involved because they are workers, but are involved because they have a conscience and because they would rather see a non-violent solution to things.

OBSERVER: *So it is a good strategy.*

CHÁVEZ: Yes, but that alone is not reason enough. If you have no basis for non-violence other than a strategy, a tactic, then when it fails your only alternative is completely the reverse and that's violence. So you have to balance the strategy with a clear understanding of what you are doing. However important the struggle is and however much misery and poverty and degradation exist, we know that it cannot be more important than one human life. That's basic. Second, we operate on the theory that men who are involved and truly concerned about people are not by nature violent. If they were violent they couldn't have that love and that concern for people. That sort of man becomes violent when that deep concern he has for people is frustrated, when he's faced with overwhelming odds against what he is trying to do. Then sometimes he feels that violence is really a short-cut or a sort of miracle to end everything and bring about a solution. We don't want to get into that trap.

OBSERVER: *What if violence is a short-cut?*

CHÁVEZ: It isn't. It has never been proved in the history of mankind that it is a short-cut.

OBSERVER: *You're using a very broad perspective.*

CHÁVEZ: Well, let me tell you—if I were to tell the workers: "All right, we're going to be violent; we're going to burn the sheds and we're going to dynamite the grower's homes and we're going to burn the vineyards," provided we could get away with it, the growers would sign a contract. But you see that that victory came at the expense of violence; it came at the expense of injuring. I think that once that happens it would have a tremendous impact on us. We would lose our perspective and we would lose the regard we have for human beings—and then the struggle would become a mechanical thing.

OBSERVER: *If you lose a sense of justice in your cause, you lose a lot of strength....*

CHÁVEZ: Nothing can replace that strength. And the victory is not total. If you use violence, you have to sell part of yourself for that violence, either because of your own self-guilt or because you have to incorporate people who are extremists and violent or whatever it might be. Then you are no longer the master of your own struggle, and the important thing is that for poor people to be able to get a clean victory is something you don't often see. If we get it through violence, then the employers will just wait long enough until they can get even with you—and then the workers will respond, and then—

OBSERVER: *So a violent resolution to a problem is never a resolution, just a cessation?*

CHÁVEZ: Let me give you an example: the armed revolutions we have. What happens? Once you set up an army or militia to gain independence you have to maintain that army. You know against whom? Against your own people.

OBSERVER: *All violence is necessarily an oppression then?*

CHÁVEZ: That's right. If we were to become violent and we won the strike, as an example, then what would prevent us from turning violence against opponents in the movement who wanted to displace us? Say they felt they had more leadership and they wanted to be the leaders. What would prevent us from turning violence against them? Nothing. Because we had already experienced that violence awarded us victory. If we are concerned about human beings and if we are concerned about respecting man, then we have to be concerned about the consequences.

Another thing is that people think non-violence is really weak and non-militant. These are misconceptions that people have because they don't understand what non-violence means. Non-violence takes more guts, if I can put it bluntly, than violence. Most violent acts are accomplished by getting the opponent off guard, and it doesn't take that much character, I think, if one wants to do it. I am confronted frequently by people who say, "So-and-so tried non-violence and it didn't work." That's not really so. Non-violence is very weak in the theoretical sense; it cannot defend itself. But it is most powerful in the action situation where people are using non-violence because they want desperately to bring about some change. Non-violence in action is a very potent force and it can't be stopped. The people who are struggling have the complete say-so. No man-made law, no human ruler, no army can destroy this. There is no way it can be destroyed, except by those within the non-violent struggle. And so, if we have the capacity to endure, if we have the patience, things will change.

OBSERVER: *What do you say to the honest activist who feels that so many of the channels to change in this society are closed that he has no choice but to take up arms? I'm thinking of people like Camillo Torres in Columbia.*

CHÁVEZ: There is no question that they have tremendous love for people and they want to bring about change. In the case of Torres, we see very clearly how he went from a life of priesthood to the extreme of using violence. And I'm sure he felt he had no other way of doing it. But I'm sure that if we examine the development of this man, and if we examine the reasons for which he worked, we would find that he probably was a failure as an organizer, an organizer of masses of people. . . .

OBSERVER: *Then for you non-violence is a universal approach regardless of the degree of oppression?*

CHÁVEZ: The greater the oppression, the more leverage you have. What I'm trying to say is violence didn't work and it's not going to work, and if it works it replaces, as in Latin America, one violent government with another that is more violent. People are abused with violence. In Latin America, who gets killed in case of a revolution? The poor people, the workers. Who gets nothing but crumbs when another force comes into power? Take the Mexican revolution, take any revolution—the people of the land are the ones who give their bodies, who get killed, and they really don't gain that much from it. I think it's too big a price to pay for not getting anything. They are being exploited as much by the ones who "help" them as by the others. To call men to arms with a lot of promises and to ask them to give their lives for a cause, and then not produce for them afterward is the most vicious sort of oppression. And we've seen it happen.

OBSERVER: *Has Christianity affected your philosophy of non-violence?*

CHÁVEZ: Very definitely. Christianity is not the only religion, but it is the one that I am a believer in. It has taught us the message of Christ with regard to loving our neighbor and with regard to respecting one another and exhorting us to be able to forgive. Now these are very difficult things and, of course, we are not even approaching that. But we have seen very little action in a dramatic form by Christians in our world. There is a lot of good will, and they talk a lot about that—but people sacrificing themselves—very little.

Gandhi is an example. He was not a Christian but in my estimation he probably personifies a Christian more than most men. He showed us not by talking, not by what he wrote as much as by his actions, his own willingness to live by truth and by respect for mankind and accepting the sacrifices. You see non-violence exacts a very high price from one who practices it. But once you are able to meet that demand then you can do most things, provided you have the time. Gandhi showed how a whole nation could be liberated without an army. This is the first time in the history of the world when a huge nation, occupied for over a century, achieved independence by non-violence. It was a long struggle and it takes time.

OBSERVER: *You speak of patience and determination as a necessary part of non-violent politics. The grape workers' strike is one of the longest in American history. What keeps you going?*

CHÁVEZ: I think that it is a conviction in what we are doing—that we are involved in a just cause. We know that most likely we are not going to do anything else in the rest of our life except this. We know that if we weren't doing this we wouldn't be doing anything we would like to do more than this. We know really there is nowhere else to go and although we would like to see victory come soon we are willing to wait. Non-violence calls for hard-nosed organizing, for a minimum of dramatics and a great deal of understanding of what the situation is—being able to assess the opposition, being able to win by winning small victories constantly, and by not letting yourself be locked into a position where you can't move because you're cornered.

OBSERVER: *Do you see your struggle as having historical significance?*

CHÁVEZ: All successful struggles tend to set precedents, but I think more important than that, perhaps for the first time in the history of the richest nation in the world, it would give those people who work at producing food some food for themselves. . . . And also it would point out very concretely that this came about because of the determination of the people in the struggle, and more important because of the way the people conducted themselves through the struggle.

The American Indian Movement

In the aftermath of the civil rights movement's call for black power, red power became the rallying cry of American Indians. A new organization, the American Indian Movement (AIM), was founded in 1968. From November 1969 to June 1971, approximately a hundred Indians from several different tribes joined AIM in reclaiming and occupying Alcatraz Island. Wanting to call attention to the plight of Native Americans, they occupied the island in the name of Indians of All Tribes, demanded the deed for the island, and insisted that they be allowed to set up an Indian university, a museum, and a cultural center. After fruitless negotiations between the Indians and the federal government, President Nixon ordered the island retaken. On June 11, 1971, a force of FBI agents and federal marshals forcibly removed them.

In 1972, AIM sponsored a march on Washington billed as the Trail of Broken Treaties. AIM members occupied the Bureau of Indian Affairs (BIA) headquarters and issued a 20-point proposal for President Richard Nixon to consider. The following year, elders from the Lakota Sioux nation requested AIM's assistance in dealing with BIA and tribal council corruption in South Dakota. This led to AIM's occupation of Wounded Knee (site of the last armed Indian resistance in 1890) and an infamous 71-day standoff between armed Indians and federal marshals. The Indians demanded that the 1868 Fort Laramie Treaty guaranteeing the Black Hills to the Lakota be honored. They also wanted an end to the strip mining at the Pine Ridge Reservation. At the end of the siege, however, the federal government made no concessions, and the Indians were removed.

A Proclamation: To the Great White Father and All His People, 1969

We, the Native Americans, reclaim the land known as Alcatraz Island in the name of all American Indians by right of discovery.

We wish to be fair and honorable in our dealings with the Caucasian inhabitants of this land, and hereby offer the following treaty:

We will purchase said Alcatraz Island for $24 in glass beads and red cloth, a precedent set by the white man's purchase of a similar island about 300 years ago. We know that $24 in trade goods for these 16 acres is more than was paid when Manhattan Island was sold, but we know that land values have risen over the years.

Our offer of $1.24 per acre is greater than the 47 cents per acre that the white men are now paying the California Indians for their land. We will give to the inhabitants of this land a portion of that land for their own, to be held in trust by the American Indian Affairs and by the bureau of Caucasian affairs to hold in perpetuity—for as long as the sun shall rise and the rivers go down to the sea.

We will further guide the inhabitants in the proper way of living. We will offer them our religion, our education, our lifeways, in order to help them achieve our level of civilization and thus raise them and all their white brothers up from their savage and unhappy state.

We offer this treaty in good faith and wish to be fair and honorable in our dealings with all white men.

We feel that this so-called Alcatraz Island is more than suitable for an Indian Reservation, as determined by the white man's own standards. By this we mean that this place resembles most Indian reservations in that:

1. It is isolated from modern facilities, and without adequate means of transportation.
2. It has no fresh running water.
3. It has inadequate sanitation facilities.
4. There are no oil or mineral rights.
5. There is no industry and so unemployment is very great.
6. There are no health care facilities.
7. The soil is rocky and non-productive; and the land does not support game.
8. There are no educational facilities.
9. The population has always exceeded the land base.
10. The population has always been held as prisoners and kept dependent upon others.

Further, it would be fitting and symbolic that ships from all over the world, entering the Golden Gate, would first see Indian land, and thus be reminded of

---

Source: Retrieved on 5/10/2004 from http://cwis.org/fwdp/Americas/alcatraz.txt.

the true history of this nation. This tiny island would be a symbol of the great lands once ruled by free and noble Indians.

What use will we make of this land?

Since the San Francisco Indian Center burned down, there is no place for Indians to assemble and carry on tribal life here in the white man's city. Therefore, we plan to develop on this island several Indian institutions:

1. A Center for Native American Studies will be developed which will educate them to the skills and knowledge relevant to improve the lives and spirits of all Indian peoples. Attached to this center will be travelling universities, managed by Indians, which will go to the Indian Reservations, learning those necessary and relevant materials now about.

2. An American Indian Spiritual Center, which will practice our ancient tribal religious and sacred healing ceremonies. Our cultural arts will be featured and our young people trained in music, dance, and healing rituals.

3. An Indian Center of Ecology, which will train and support our young people in scientific research and practice to restore our lands and waters to their pure and natural state. We will work to de-pollute the air and waters of the Bay Area. We will seek to restore fish and animal life to the area and to revitalize sealife which has been threatened by the white man's way. We will set up facilities to desalt sea water for human benefit.

4. A Great Indian Training School will be developed to teach our people how to make a living in the world, improve our standard of living, and to end hunger and unemployment among all our people. This training school will include a center for Indian arts and crafts, and an Indian restaurant serving native foods, which will restore Indian culinary arts. This center will display Indian arts and offer Indian foods to the public, so that all may know of the beauty and spirit of the traditional Indian ways.

Some of the present buildings will be taken over to develop an American Indian Museum which will depict our native food and other cultural contributions we have given to the world. Another part of the museum will present some of the things the white man has given to the Indians in return for the land and life he took: disease, alcohol, poverty, and cultural decimation (as symbolized by old tin cans, barbed wire, rubber tires, plastic containers, etc.). Part of the museum will remain a dungeon to symbolize both those Indian captives who were incarcerated for challenging white authority and those who were imprisoned on reservations. The museum will show the noble and tragic events of Indian history, including the broken treaties, the documentary of the Trail of Tears, the Massacre of Wounded Knee, as well as the victory over Yellow-Hair Custer and his army.

In the name of all Indians, therefore, we reclaim this island for our Indian nations, for all these reasons. We feel this claim is just and proper, and that this land should rightfully be granted to us for as long as the rivers run and the sun shall shine.

We hold the rock!

American Indian Movement 20 Point Proposal, October 1972, Minneapolis, Minnesota

"TRAIL OF BROKEN TREATIES": FOR RENEWAL OF CONTRACTS, RECONSTRUCTION OF INDIAN COMMUNITIES & SECURING AN INDIAN FUTURE IN AMERICA!

RESTORATION OF CONSTITUTIONAL TREATY-MAKING AUTHORITY: The U.S. President should propose by executive message, and the Congress should consider and enact legislation, to repeal the provision in the 1871 Indian Appropriations Act which withdrew federal recognition from Indian Tribes and Nations as political entities, which could be contracted by treaties with the United States, in order that the President may resume the exercise of his full constitutional authority for acting in the matters of Indian Affairs—and in order that Indian Nations may represent their own interests in the manner and method envisioned and provided in the Federal Constitution.

ESTABLISHMENT OF TREATY COMMISSION TO MAKE NEW TREATIES: The President should impanel and the Congress establish, within the next year, a Treaty Commission to contract a security and assistance treaty of treaties, with Indian people to negotiate a national commitment to the future of Indian people for the last quarter of the Twentieth Century. Authority should be granted to allow tribes to contract by separate and individual treaty, multitribal or regional groupings or national collective, respecting general or limited subject matter . . . and provide that no provisions of existing treaty agreements may be withdrawn or in any manner affected without the explicit consent and agreement of any particularly related Indian Nation.

AN ADDRESS TO THE AMERICAN PEOPLE & JOINT SESSIONS OF CONGRESS: The President and the leadership of Congress should make a commitment now and next January to request and arrange for four Native Americans—selected by Indian people at a future date—and the President of the United States and any designated U.S. Senators and Representatives to address a joint session of Congress and the American people through national communications media regarding the Indian future within the American Nation, and relationships between the Federal Government and Indian Nations—on or before June 2, 1974, the first half century anniversary of the 1924 "Indian Citizenship Act."

COMMISSION TO REVIEW TREATY COMMITMENTS & VIOLATIONS: The President should immediately create a multi-lateral, Indian and non-Indian Commission to review domestic treaty commitments and complaints of chronic violations and to recommend or act for corrective actions including

SOURCE: Retrieved on 10/3/2002 from www.aimovement.org/archives/index.html

the imposition of mandatory sanctions or interim restraints upon violative activities, and including formulation of legislation designed to protect the jeopardized Indian rights and eliminate the unending patterns of prohibitively complex lawsuits and legal defenses—which habitually have produced indecisive and interment results, only too frequently forming guidelines for more court battles, or additional challenges and attacks against Indian rights. (Indians have paid attorneys and lawyers more than $40,000,000 since 1962. Yet many Indian people are virtually imprisoned in the nation's courtrooms in being forced constantly to defend their rights, while many tribes are forced to maintain a multitude of suits in numerous jurisdictions relating to the same or a single issue, or a few similar issues. There is less need for more attorney assurances than there is for institution of protections that reduce violations and minimize the possibilities for attacks upon Indian rights.)

RESUBMISSION OF UNRATIFIED TREATIES TO THE SENATE: The President should resubmit to the U.S. Senate of the next Congress those treaties negotiated with Indian nations or their representatives, but never heretofore ratified nor rendered moot by subsequent treaty contract with such Indians not having ratified treaties with the United States. . . .

ALL INDIANS TO BE GOVERNED BY TREATY RELATIONS: The Congress should enact a Joint Resolution declaring that as a matter of public policy and good faith, all Indian people in the United States shall be considered to be in treaty relations with the Federal Government and governed by doctrines of such relationship.

MANDATORY RELIEF AGAINST TREATY RIGHTS VIOLATIONS: The Congress should add a new section to Title 28 of the United States Code to provide for the judicial enforcement and protection of Indian Treaty Rights. Such section should direct that upon petition of any Indian Tribe or prescribed Indian groups and Individuals claiming substantial injury to, or interference in the equitable and good faith exercise of any rights, governing authority or utilization and preservation of resources, secured by Treaty, mandatorily the Federal District courts shall grant immediate enjoinder or injunctive relief against any non-Indian party or defendants, including State governments and their subdivisions or officers, alleged to be engaged in such injurious actions, until such time as the District U.S. Court may be reasonably satisfied that a Treaty Violation is not being committed, or otherwise satisfied that the Indians' interests and rights, in equity and in law, are preserved and protected from jeopardy and secure from harm.

JUDICIAL RECOGNITION OF INDIAN RIGHT TO INTERPRET TREATIES: The Congress should by law provide for a new system of federal court jurisdiction and procedure, when Indian treaty or governmental rights are at issue, and when there are non-Indian parties involved in the controversy, whereby an Indian Tribe or Indian party may by motion advance the case from a federal District Court for hearing, and decision by the related U.S. Circuit Court of Appeals. . . .

CREATION OF CONGRESSIONAL JOINT COMMITTEE ON RECON-
STRUCTION OF INDIAN RELATIONS: The next Congress of the United
States, and its respective houses, should agree at its outset and in its organization to withdraw jurisdiction over Indian Affairs and Indian-related program authorizations from all existing Committees except Appropriations
of the House and Senate, and create a Joint House-Senate "Committee on
Reconstruction of Indian Relations and Programs" to assume such jurisdiction and responsibilities for recommending new legislation and program
authorizations to both houses of Congress—including consideration and
action upon all proposals presented herewith by the "Trail of Broken
Treaties Caravan," as well as matters from other sources. The Joint Committee membership should consist of Senators and Representatives who would
be willing to commit considerable amounts of time and labors and conscientious thought to an exhaustive review and examining evaluation of past
and present policies, program and practices of the Federal Government
relating to Indian people, to the development of a comprehensive broadly-
inclusive "American Indian Community Reconstruction Act," which shall
provide for certain of the measures herein proposed, repeal numerous laws
which have oppressively disallowed the existence of a viable "Indian Life" in
this country, and affect the purposes while constructing the provisions
which shall allow and ensure a secure Indian future in America.

LAND REFORM AND RESTORATION OF A 110-MILLION ACRE NATIVE
LAND BASE: The next Congress and Administration should commit themselves and effect a national commitment implemented by statutes or executive
and administrative actions, to restore a permanent non-diminishing Native
American land base of not less than 110-million acres by July 4, 1976....

REVISION OF 25 U.S.C. 163; RESTORATION OF RIGHTS TO INDIANS
TERMINATED BY ENROLLMENT AND REVOCATION OF PROHIBI-
TIONS AGAINST "DUAL BENEFITS": The Congress should enact measures fully in support of the doctrine that an Indian Nation has complete
power to govern and control its own membership—but eradicating the
extortive and coercive devices in federal policy and programming which
have subverted and denied the natural human relationships and natural
development of Indian communities, and committed countless injuries
upon Indian families and individuals....

REPEAL OF STATE LAWS ENACTED UNDER PUBLIC LAW 280 (1953): State
enactment's under the authority conferred by the Congress in Public Law
280 has posed the most serious threat to Indian sovereignty and local self-
government of any measure in recent decades. Congress must now nullify
those State statutes....

RESUME FEDERAL PROTECTIVE JURISDICTION FOR OFFENSES
AGAINST INDIANS: The Congress should enact, the Administration support and seek passage of, new provisions under Titles 18 and 25 of the U.S.
Code, which shall extend the protective jurisdiction of the United States
over Indian persons wherever situated in its territory and the territory of

the several States, outside of Indian Reservations or Country, and provide the prescribed offenses of violence against Indian persons shall be federal crimes, punishable by prescribed penalties through prosecutions in the federal judiciary, and enforced in arrest actions by the Federal Bureau of Investigation. . . .

ABOLITION OF THE BUREAU OF INDIAN AFFAIRS BY 1976: A New Structure: The Congress working through the proposed Senate-House "Joint Committee on Reconstruction of Indian Relations and Programs," in formulation of an Indian Community Reconstruction Act should direct that the Bureau of Indian Affairs shall be abolished as an agency on or before July 4, 1976. . . .

CREATION OF AN "OFFICE OF FEDERAL INDIAN RELATIONS AND COMMUNITY RECONSTRUCTION": The Bureau of Indian Affairs should be replaced by a new unit in the federal government which represents an equality of responsibility among and between the President, the Congress, and the Governments of the separate Indian Nations (or their respective people collectively), and equal standing in the control of relations between the Federal Government and the Indian Nations. . . .

PRIORITIES AND PURPOSE OF THE PROPOSED NEW OFFICE: The central purpose of the proposed "Office of Federal Indian Relations and Community Reconstruction" is to remedy the break-down in constitutionally-prescribed relationships between the United States and Indian Nations and people and to alleviate the destructive impact that distortion in those relationships has rendered upon the lives of Indian people. . . .

INDIAN COMMERCE AND TAX IMMUNITIES: The Congress should enact a statute or Joint Resolution certifying that trade, commerce, and transportation of Indians remain wholly outside the authority, control, and regulation of the several States. Congressional acts should provide that complete taxing authority upon properties, use of properties and incomes derived therefrom, and business activities within the exterior boundaries of Indian reservations, as well as commerce between reservations and Indian Nations, shall be vested with the respective or related tribal governments, or their appropriate subdivisions—or certify that consistent with the Fourteenth Amendment, Section 2 statehood enabling acts, prevailing treaty commitments, and the general policy of the United States, that total Indian immunity to taxing authority of states is reaffirmed and extended with uniformity to all Indian Nations as a matter of established or vested right. . . .

PROTECTION OF INDIANS' RELIGIOUS FREEDOM AND CULTURAL INTEGRITY: The Congress shall proclaim its insistence that the religious freedom and cultural integrity of Indian people shall be respected and protected throughout the United States, and provide that Indian religion and culture, even in regenerating or renaissance or developing stages, or when manifested in the personal character and treatment of one's own body, shall not be interfered with, disrespected, or denied. (No Indian shall be forced to cut their hair by any institution or public agency or official, including military authorities or prison regulation, for example.) . . .

NATIONAL REFERENDUMS, LOCAL OPTIONS, AND FORMS OF INDIAN
ORGANIZATION: The Indian population is small enough to be amenable
to voting and elective processes of national referendums, local option referendums, and other elections for rendering decisions, approvals, or disapproval on many issues and matters. The steady proliferation of Indian and
Indian-interest organizations and Indian advisory boards and the like, the
multiplication of Indian officials and the emergence of countless Indian
"leaders," represent a less preferable form for decision-making a state of
disorganization, and a clear reflection of deterioration in the relations
between the United States and Indian people as contracting sovereigns
holding a high standard of accountability and responsibility. Some Indians
seem to stand by to ratify any viewpoints relating to any or all Indians;
others conditioned to accept any viewpoint or proposal from official
sources. Whereas Indian people were to be secure from political manipula-
tion and the general political system in the service of Indian needs, political
favor, and cutthroat competition for funds with grants made among limited alliances of agency-Indian friends have become the rule—while
responsibilities and accountability to Indian people and Indian communities have been forgotten. While the treaty relationship allows that we should
not be deprived by power what we are possessed of by right—little personal
power and political games are being played by a few Indians while we are
being deprived our rights. This dissipation of strength, energies, and commitment should end. We should consolidate our resources and purpose to
restore relations born of sovereignty and to resume command of our communities, our rights, our resources, and our destiny. (The National Council
on Indian Opportunity Association on American Indian Affairs, and the
National Tribal Chairman's Association are examples of government, non-
Indian directed, and Indian organizations which are among many which
could and should be eliminated). (At least none should be funded from federal sources.)

HEALTH, HOUSING, EMPLOYMENT, ECONOMIC DEVELOPMENT, AND
EDUCATION: The Congress and Administration and proposed Indian
Community Reconstruction Office must allow for the most creative, if
demanding and disciplined forms of community development and pur-
poseful initiatives. . . . Death remains a standard cure for environmentally
induced diseases afflicting many Indian children without adequate housing
facilities, heating systems, and pure water sources. Their delicate bodies
provide their only defense and protection—and too often their own body
processes become allies to the quickening of their deaths as with numerous
cases of dysentery and diarrhea. Still, more has been spent on hotel bills for
Indian-related problem-solving meetings, conferences, and conventions,
than has been spent on needed housing in recent years. More is being spent
from federal and tribal fund sources on such decision-making activities
that is being committed to assist but two-thirds of Indian college students
having desperate financial need. Rather, few decisions are made, and less

problems solved, because there has developed an insensitivity to conscience which has eliminated basic standards of accountability. Indian communities have been fragmented in governmental, social, and constitutional functions as they have become restructured or de-structured to accommodate the fragmentation in governmental programming and contradictions in federal policies. There is a need to reintegrate these functions into the life and fabric of the communities. Of treaty provisions standard to most treaties, none has been breached more viciously and often as those dealing with education—first by withdrawing education processes from jurisdiction and responsibility of Indian communities, and from the power of Indian self-government—and failing yet to restore authority to our people, except through increased funding of old advisory and contract-delegation laws, or through control to conduct school in the conditioned forms and systems devised by non-Indians, or otherwise commended by current popularity. At minimum, Indian Nations have to reclaim community education authority to allow creative education processes in forms of their free choice, in a system of federally-sanctioned units or consolidated Indian districts, supported by a mandatory recognition of accreditation in all other systems in this land.

PART NINE

Contemporary Dissent, 1975–Present

Julia Butterfly Hill.
To protest the Pacific Lumber
Company's plan to cut down a
1000-year-old giant redwood in a
forest in Humboldt County,
California, Julia Butterfly Hill lived
in the tree for two years. Hill
passionately believes that
environmental issues are deeply
entwined with social justice issues.
"The destroyer and the hero lies
within the hearts of each and every
one of us," she said. "Who are you
going to choose to be?"

INTRODUCTION: CROSSING THE THRESHOLD INTO THE NEW MILLENNIUM—GLOBALIZATION VS. JIHAD

Throughout the nation's history, there was always the assumption that politicians were corruptible, but generally speaking people tended to have faith in the president and in his pronouncements. When FDR, Ike, or JFK spoke to the public, people believed them. The Johnson administration's deceptions, however, revealed by the publication of the Pentagon Papers in the *New York Times,* began to change that. When Richard Nixon was forced to resign over the Watergate scandal, what remaining faith the majority had in the integrity of Washington evaporated. Ford and Carter were honest men and did help to restore some confidence in the political process, but ever since the 1970s, the American people are far more cynical about government.

After the excitement of the 1960s and Watergate, many people simply wanted to have a breather and return to some sense of business as usual. Dissent and protest did continue, but with the big issues apparently solved, activists concentrated on specific local concerns. Ecology, of course, is a global issue, but environmentalists generally acted locally by demonstrating against industrial polluters, such as General Electric in New York, in an effort to get laws passed that would restrict the amount of toxic waste companies were allowed to dump in rivers and streams or release into the atmosphere. Pete Seeger, whose activism spans several decades and multiple causes, organized the Clearwater Hudson River Revival, an annual folk festival dedicated to putting pressure on the industries that were polluting the Hudson River. The success of this local movement was quite apparent by the 1980s, when sturgeon appeared again in the cleaner waters of the Hudson after an absence of a century. Greenpeace, founded in the early 1970s, concentrated its activities on specific incidents perpetrated by companies and countries that were damaging the environment. Environmentalists also were opposed to the proliferation of nuclear power plants, and many thousands of people participated in anti-nuke demonstrations, especially after the near meltdown at Three Mile Island in 1979.

Later, in the 1990s, environmentalist Julia Butterfly Hill performed an unusual act of civil disobedience in order to save a thousand-year-old giant redwood tree from the Pacific Lumber Company—she climbed 180 feet up into the tree and proceeded to live in its branches for the next 738 days until the lumber company finally agreed not to cut it down. "I gave my word," she said, "to this tree, the forest, and all the people, that my feet would not touch the ground until I had done everything in my power to make the world aware of this problem and to stop the destruction." Unlike the Earth Liberation Front, which does not shrink from using violence to preserve the environment, "tree hugger" Julia Butterfly Hill called on people to unite together in love for all living things.

When Reagan became president, there was hope that the economy, which had stagnated as a result of Vietnam and the OPEC oil embargoes of 1973 and 1978, would rebound. Tax cuts and the revenue poured into defense spending and the Strategic Defense Initiative, the "Star Wars" program designed to create an antimissile defense system, did create more wealth for many industries, but the predicted "trickle down" effect, whereby prosperity would trickle down to the working class through more job opportunities, did not take place.

As far as foreign policy was concerned, Reagan was determined to fight communism around the globe. The United States must stand firm against the Soviet Union, which he referred to as the "evil empire." This strategy in effect reversed the détente process that Nixon had begun to relieve tensions between the United States and the Soviet Union and the People's Republic of China. After the Soviet Union invaded Afghanistan, President Jimmy Carter and National Security

Advisor Zbigniew Brzezinski began to provide assistance to the mujahedin. As the Soviets became more embroiled in the war, it became Reagan's policy to do everything possible to thwart and frustrate them and to make Afghanistan into the Soviet Union's Vietnam. With congressional approval, Reagan expanded this effort by authorizing the CIA to aid, equip, and train Muslim fundamentalists in their fight against the Soviets. The training, the supplies, the money, and the Stinger missiles were highly effective in frustrating the Soviet attempt to subdue Afghanistan, prolonged the war until 1989, and eventually led to the Soviet withdrawal. The U.S. involvement also gave rise to the Taliban and the career of Osama bin Laden. Later the CIA would refer to bin Laden's subsequent terrorist campaign against the U.S. as "blowback," a term signifying unexpected consequences of CIA operations. Reagan was also concerned about communist inroads in Central America, especially in Nicaragua and El Salvador. American efforts to undermine the left-wing Sandinista regime in Nicaragua, primarily by training counterrevolutionaries to overthrow the Sandinistas, raised concerns that the United States might get entangled in another Vietnam. There were some scattered protests, but they did not become widespread because Congress passed legislation forbidding the CIA to train the "Contras."

In 1988, the last full year of his term, Reagan began to moderate his anticommunist rhetoric, mostly because of the influence of Mikhail Gorbachev. Gorbachev had come to power in the Soviet Union in 1985, and his policies of *glasnost* and *perestroika* began opening up Soviet society and paving the way for the end of the cold war. In one of the ironies of history, the Soviet Union's anti-American propaganda efforts in the 1960s helped bring this about. During the 1960s, the Soviet press had a field day with the antiwar and civil rights protests in America, which were depicted as proof of the "anti-imperialist struggle under capitalism." According to cold war scholar Vladislav Zubok, this was a serious miscalculation on the part of the Soviet propaganda machine. One of the reasons communism failed in the Soviet Union and Eastern Europe is that people living under communism became painfully aware that the American people could at least march, protest, and dissent. This proved that the United States was indeed a freer society than the Soviet Union. As a result, many Soviet citizens began to overcome their distrust of the United States. When they saw protestors and demonstrators in the streets, they saw democracy at work and therefore realized that the United States, despite its faults, was a democratic society. In this way the United States as early as the 1960s unwittingly motivated a minority of dissidents and educated youth in the eastern bloc countries to strive for democracy. "We knew," a Soviet citizen once told Zubok, "*we* had to create democracy when we saw American protestors take to the streets."

In November 1989, one of the most memorable events of the twentieth century took place. The East German government, after months of unrest and economic crisis, opened the Berlin Wall. It was the moment the cold war disintegrated. Thousands of Germans flocked to Berlin. From east and west, they came, and they brought their sledgehammers and chisels, and the wall came down. Within months, each of the Soviet satellite nations abandoned communism and voted in new democratic regimes. The Soviet Union itself, in December 1991, was dissolved. Mikhail Gorbachev, who had intended to allow dissent and discussion to build "socialism with a human face" along the model of the Prague Spring of 1968, had instead opened a Pandora's box that wound up being far more momentous than anyone could have imagined, and by doing away with the Soviet Union, Gorbachev no longer had a job.

At first Americans were jubilant, believing, as many did, that "we won the cold war," and that now the terrible threat of a nuclear confrontation that could potentially destroy civilization was gone. The world, it was assumed, was a safer place. Indeed, when Saddam Hussein invaded neighboring Kuwait, the unity of the coalition that fought the Persian Gulf War to remove the Iraqis from Kuwait boosted this optimistic view. But within a few years a new reality emerged, and grave doubts began to creep in.

The Clinton administration concentrated on the economy, which did indeed rebound during his two terms in office. In fact, the economy soared so high that most Americans considered that Clinton was doing such an excellent job of running the country that they were able to overlook the Monica Lewinsky scandal that swamped his administration. The domestic issue that proved controversial enough to arouse dissenters was globalization. Clinton had backed the North American Free Trade Agreement and the General Agreement on Tariffs and Trade. Antiglobalists were vehemently opposed to this spreading of free enterprise, claiming that it was merely an updated version of capitalist imperialism. A wide variety of diverse groups came together to oppose the World Trade Organization: Labor unions were concerned that more American jobs would disappear; environmentalists were alarmed that moving industrial plants and factories to third world nations, where environmental standards were laxer than they were in the United States, would exacerbate the problems of global warming and the destruction of the environment; human rights activists were troubled about the exploitation of children and poor people in third world sweatshops. Criticizing the pro-business collaboration of both Republicans and Democrats, Ralph Nader ran for president in 1996 and in 2000 as the standard-bearer of the Green Party.

Other dissenters made their voices heard in the 1990s. Along with the continuation of pro-life activists picketing abortion clinics and pro-choice advocates demanding the safeguarding of a woman's right to choose, various right-wing groups protested what they viewed as too much government intrusion into their lives. The Michigan Militia, the Freemen in Montana, and other groups called for individuals to arm themselves and be ready to resist any attempt by the government in Washington to undermine the Bill of Rights. Timothy McVeigh was responsible for the single most devastating act of domestic terrorism in American history when he detonated a bomb at the Alfred P. Murrah Federal Building in Oklahoma City that killed 168 people. Theodore Kaczynski, the Unabomber, killed people with letter bombs because he believed technology, and those promoting it, was a disaster for the human race. There was also a proliferation of right-wing talk-show hosts like Rush Limbaugh, who protested zealously and effectively against the Clinton administration. Such critics, although they might appear on the surface to be part of the dissenting tradition, are not actually genuine protestors advocating social change but instead the cutting edge of a well-organized, well-funded, and ultimately successful Republican offensive to regain power.

In the post–cold war world, Clinton's foreign policy had to feel its way along as diplomats were forced to learn the new rules of engagement. Confrontation between two superpowers was a thing of the past, but new, more complex realities surfaced. The United States continued to maintain a military presence in Saudi Arabia after the Persian Gulf War had come to an end. This fact, along with U.S. support of Israel, angered many Arabs. The inexorable spread of American mass culture and consumerist values around the world also created resistance from people who believed their own values and culture would be subverted and eventually destroyed. Political Scientist Benjamin R. Barber has called this confrontation between traditional societies and American globalism "Jihad vs. McWorld."

Terrorism has been around for centuries, but in the 1970s and 1980s it began to be employed more frequently by disempowered groups who felt there was no other alternative for them to get their point across. Palestinians in particular, knowing the most powerful nation in the world supported Israel, felt helpless. Regularly, members of the Palestinian Liberation Organization (PLO) or the Popular Front for the Liberation of Palestine (PFLP) would hijack a commercial jet, make their demands (perhaps the release of other terrorists who were serving prison sentences), and, after the demands were met, escape. By the 1990s, however, terrorism had begun to have a new, more terrifying face. Increasingly, terrorists used suicide missions. As early as 1983, suicide bombers struck in Lebanon, when a truck filled with explosives rammed into the U.S. Marine barracks in Beirut, killing 241 Marines. During Clinton's presidency, in 1996, suicide bombers struck at the American embassies in Tanzania and Kenya, killing 224 people. The terrorists behind this were not Palestinians but Saudis linked to Osama bin Laden's al-Qaeda network. Clinton's response was to order a missile attack on reputed al-Qaeda training camps in Afghanistan and a chemical plant in Somalia. Some observers believe this retribution only exacerbated the problem. Chalmers Johnson, for instance, in his book *Blowback,* published a year before September 11, suggests that the appropriate response would have been to remove American military personnel from Saudi Arabia. If bin Laden was behind the embassy bombings, Johnson wrote, then we still do not know what the blowback will be from Clinton's missile attack in Afghanistan. Perhaps the response occurred in 2000, when al-Qaeda suicide bombers blew a hole in the side of the U.S. destroyer *Cole* in Yemen, killing 17 sailors.

At first, after George W. Bush was declared the winner of the contested 2000 election, the new president concentrated on resurrecting the defense projects of the Reagan administration, specifically the missile defense shield. But on September 11, 2001, it became devastatingly apparent that such highly sophisticated methods of national security were helpless in the face of a relatively low-tech type of attack. The terrorists who hijacked four jetliners—turning them into highly explosive missiles that brought down the twin towers of the World Trade Center, ripped open the Pentagon, and killed nearly 3000 innocent people—were able to accomplish their feat using box cutters.

In the aftermath of the attacks, the United States has been forced to face a different truth. It is not simply that the "world changed" on September 11. The world was pretty much the same on the twelfth as it was on the tenth. What had changed is that Americans had lost their innocence (or perhaps we should say naiveté). They awoke to the fact that the perception many others around the world, including our allies, have about America does not match the way we see ourselves. The aftermath of September 11 saw the advent of the war on terrorism. For many people, this has meant fighting back and making our nation more secure against such threats. For some people, it has also meant a time of self-reflection and reevaluation of America's priorities. Dissent, which had seemed subdued in the 1990s with the exception of the World Trade Organization demonstrations, once again reared its head. As the United States bombed Afghanistan, thousands of protestors took to the streets. When the PATRIOT Act was passed, many more feared that in our quest for security we were eroding the basic constitutional principles that has made this country great. Even before the United States invaded Iraq in 2003, millions of people took to the streets to demonstrate against such a war.

We cannot know what lies in store. We *do* know that as long as the United States is the United States, there will always be differences of opinion on social, political, diplomatic, and military issues and that people from all walks of life, from all political persuasions, Republicans, Democrats, Socialists, Libertarians, will speak their minds. In a time of war, however, when national security itself is threatened, is it unpatriotic to dissent? Have those who protest given up on the American dream? Are dissenters undermining the very society that guarantees the right to dissent? What takes precedence, national security or civil liberties? Or is dissent itself an expression of patriotism?

Edward Abbey (1927–1989)

In 1948 Edward Abbey hitchhiked through the American West. He felt himself irresistibly attracted to the desert and finally settled in Arizona. He wrote several novels about loners and would-be anarchists, as well as nonfiction works that have since become classics of the environmental movement. For a time he worked as a park ranger in Utah at Arches National Monument. His journal of his two years of solitude in the wilderness, Desert Solitaire, *was published in 1968 and is considered by many a twentieth-century* Walden. *His most celebrated book is* The Monkey Wrench Gang, *a tongue-in-cheek, wildly funny novel about a gang of misfit environmental terrorists who travel about the American Southwest blowing up dams and bridges, sabotaging road construction sites, and otherwise wreaking havoc in an attempt to save the wilderness from the developers. Writer Larry McMurtry called Abbey the "Thoreau of the West," a title that Abbey himself belittled. However, like Thoreau, Abbey was a champion of nonconformity and a sworn enemy of hypocrisy, sanctimoniousness, and smug intellectualism. "I hate intellectual discussion," he once said. "When I hear the words 'phenomenology' or 'structuralism,' I reach for my buck knife."*

Along with the mobilization of minority groups, environmentalism was another outgrowth of the 1960s. Greenpeace, one of the most effective and visible organizations, was founded in 1971 and dedicated to save the forests, protect the oceans, stop global warming, and oppose nuclear power. During the Reagan years, when Secretary of the Interior James Watt opened up millions of acres of public land for development, the environmental movement and such organizations as Greenpeace expanded and strengthened. Realizing that the future of humanity was dependent on a sane ecological policy millions of Americans, regardless of political affiliation, vowed to "save the planet."

Though Abbey is known as one of the heroes of the environmental movement, ranking alongside John Muir, John Burroughs, and Rachel Carson, it would not be accurate to look at a man so irreverently original and anarchistic as Abbey as a product of the activism that emerged from the 1960s. He had no tolerance for anyone who belonged to any movement. Like H. L. Mencken, nothing escaped his withering sarcasm regardless of political orientation. Reaganites, feminists, television evangelists, hippies, corporate executives, Indians, lumberjacks, tree-huggers, tourists, and Sierra Clubbers all were targets of his scorn. He hated seeing the wilderness being developed, but part of his reasoning had nothing to do with environmentalism; it was because he still believed in the frontier myth that open spaces had created the American character and American democracy—a myth that has largely been discredited by historians. The settlement of the American West depended on federal grants and subsidies for railroads in the nineteenth century and irrigation projects in the twentieth, as well as federal land grants to homesteaders and stationing the U.S. army to protect settlers from the Indians. Abbey also hated the fact that national parks enticed so many tourists to drive through them in their campers and Winnebagos. In Desert Solitaire he demanded that cars be prohibited from national parks.

Let the people walk. Or ride horses, bicycles, mules, wild pigs—anything—but keep the automobiles and the motorcycles and all their motorized relatives out. We have agreed not to drive our automobiles into cathedrals, concert halls, art museums,

legislative assemblies, private bedrooms and the other sanctums
of our culture; we should treat our national parks with the same
deference, for they, too, are holy places. . . . [T]he forests and
mountains and desert canyons are holier than our churches. Let
us behave accordingly.

The fictional ecoterrorists in The Monkey Wrench Gang *subsequently
inspired acts of sabotage and vandalism against ski lodges, tourist enclaves,
lumber companies, and power companies by a group calling themselves
Earth First! Abbey, while not actually endorsing such actions, had
proclaimed that ecoterrorism was "illegal but ethically imperative."*

In this excerpt from Desert Solitaire, *Abbey extols the virtues of the
wilderness. Abbey always insisted that development for the benefit of the
growing urban centers of the West (what he called "Californication") was
detrimental to human freedom. In fact, in his view, it was simply one of
the government's methods of maintaining control and keeping Americans
subjugated.*

DESERT SOLITAIRE, 1968

Once upon a time there was a continent covered with beautiful pristine wilderness, where giant trees towered over lush mountainsides and rivers ran wild and
free through deserts, where raptors soared and beavers labored at their pursuits
and people lived in harmony with wild nature, accomplishing every task they
needed to accomplish on a daily basis using only stones, bones and wood, walking gently on the Earth. Then came the explorers, conquerors, missionaries, soldiers, merchants and immigrants with their advanced technology, guns, and
government. The wild life that had existed for millennia started dying, killed by
a disease brought by alien versions of progress, arrogant visions of manifest destiny and a runaway utilitarian science.

In just 500 years, almost all the giant trees have been clear-cut and chemicals now poison the rivers; the eagle has faced extinction and the beaver's work
has been supplanted by the Army Corps of Engineers. And how have the people
fared? What one concludes is most likely dependent on how well one is faring
economically, emotionally and physically in this competitive technological
world and the level of privilege one is afforded by the system. But for those who
feel a deep connection to, a love and longing for, the wilderness and the wildness
that once was, for the millions now crowded in cities, poor and oppressed,
unable to find a clear target for their rage because the system is virtually
omnipotent, these people are not faring well. All around us, as a result of human

SOURCE: Edward Abbey, *Desert Solitaire* (New York: Simon & Schuster, 1968), 155–156.

greed and a lack of respect for all life, wild nature and Mother Earth's creatures are suffering. These beings are the victims of industrial society. . . .

Cutting the bloody cord, that's what we feel, the delirious exhilaration of independence, a rebirth backward in time and into primeval liberty, into freedom in the most simple, literal, primitive meaning of the word, the only meaning that really counts. The freedom, for example, to commit murder and get away with it scot-free, with no other burden than the jaunty halo of conscience.

(My God! I'm thinking, what incredible shit we put up with most of our lives—the *domestic* routine, (same old wife *every* night), the stupid and useless and degrading *jobs,* the *insufferable* arrogance of elected officials, the crafty *cheating* and the *slimy* advertising of the businessmen, the tedious wars in which we kill our buddies instead of our *real* enemies back home in the capital, the foul, diseased and *hideous* cities and towns we live in, the constant *petty* tyranny of the automatic washers, the automobiles and TV machines and telephones! ah Christ! . . . what *intolerable* garbage and what utterly *useless crap* we bury ourselves in day by day, while patiently enduring at the same time the creeping strangulation of the clean white *collar* and the rich but *modest* four-in-hand garrote!)

Such are my thoughts—you wouldn't call them thoughts would you?—such are my feelings, a mixture of revulsion and delight, as we float away on the river, leaving behind for a while all that we most heartily and joyfully detest. That's what the first taste of the wild does to a man, after having been penned up for too long in the city. No wonder the Authorities are so anxious to smother the wilderness under asphalt and reservoirs. They know what they are doing. Play safe. Ski only in a clockwise direction. Let's all have fun together.

Paul Weyrich (1941–)

Paul Weyrich, founder of the American Legislative Exchange Council, chairman and CEO of the Free Congress Foundation, and founder (with Joseph Coors) of the Heritage Foundation, is a persuasive, passionate conservative. An advocate of free trade and family values and the coiner of the term "moral majority," he has been called "one of the conservative movement's more vigorous thinkers." He has written perceptive policy reports and numerous articles, all espousing a conservative, religious viewpoint. In 1987, in response to the Iran-Contra affair, he wrote "A Conservative's Lament," condemning the manner in which the Reagan administration was contravening the Constitution in the way it was conducting its covert foreign policy. Weyrich believes that the United States must live up to its ideals of preserving freedom.

"A Conservative's Lament: After Iran, We Need to Change Our System and Grand Strategy," March 8, 1987

As proponents of a strong foreign policy and defense, conservatives have a special responsibility. Our advocacy brings with it the burden of doing the job competently. We must be leaders in thinking deeply and carefully about America's role in the world, about relating goals to means and about our national strengths and weaknesses and the opportunities and constraints they impose. If we fail to do this, we lose our legitimacy as advocates.

In the Iran-contra mess, conservatives have failed. Obviously, they failed in the way the matter was handled. But the failure is really much more profound than that. The scandal is not a disease, but a symptom. It is a symptom of some underlying contradictions in our national strategy and national institutions.

Conservatives should have identified and addressed these long ago, but we did not. Now, conservative leaders seem to be looking little if at all beyond the details of the scandal—and how to distance themselves from it. That merely compounds the failure.

Instead, as conservatives, we should be taking the lead in looking for the roots of the crisis. There are three.

First, our national strategy is outdated, dysfunctional and insupportable. Essentially it is still containment, a strategy developed in the late 1940s. It was an arguable strategy even then. But at least we had the power to carry it out. We had only one rival: the Soviet Union. Europe and Asia were both power vacuums. We moved to fill those vacuums, lest the Soviets do so.

Today, the situation is vastly different. Europe, Asia and the Middle East are power centers, not vacuums. The concept of a superpower is waning rapidly. The world includes many other forces—China, Islamic nationalism, Polish Catholicism— which are more powerful locally than either the United States or the Soviet Union.

In pursuit of containment, we still thrust ourself into everything that happens around the world. But what we put forward, increasingly, is weakness, not strength. In a world where we control far less of the total sum of power than we did forty years ago, we cannot do otherwise. The real strength is no longer there. We are propping up a hollow facade, vast commitments unsupported by either capabilities or popular will. So we stumble from failure to failure; in Southeast Asia, in Iran, in Lebanon and now in the Iran-contra mess.

It is time for a new national grand strategy. Nothing less will address the real problem. Conservatives have a responsibility to take the lead in developing one.

Second, there is a basic contradiction between the structure of our government and our role as a great power. Our government was designed not to play great-power politics but to preserve domestic liberty. To that end—at which it has

SOURCE: Paul M. Weyrich, "A Conservative's Lament: After Iran, we Need to Change Our System and Grand Strategy," in the *Washington Post*, March 8, 1987, B-5.

been remarkably successful—it was structured so as to make decisions difficult. Separation of powers, congressional checks on executive authority, the primacy of law over *raison d'tat*—all of these were intentionally built into our system. The Founding Fathers knew a nation, with such a government could not play the role of great power. They had no such ambition for us—quite the contrary.

For about 20 years after World War II, we were able to act as a great power without running into this contradiction. We could do so because we had only one serious rival, and even over that rival, our superiority was immense. Now, we have to play on a much more crowded and competitive field. Our institutions are not adequate to the game. If the executive does what it must in the international arena, it violates the domestic rules. If the Congress enforces those rules, as it is supposed to do, it cripples us internationally.

Since Watergate, some 140 measures have been passed by Congress to restrict the president's power to conduct foreign policy.

Third, our current system institutionalizes amateurism. Unlike European parliamentary democracies, we have no "shadow cabinet," no group of experts who are groomed by their party for decades before they take high office. Our presidents can be peanut farmers or Hollywood actors. They can choose their top advisors either from among "professionals" who may not share their goals or supporters who often have no background or expertise in policy. Either way, they lose, and so does the country.

The current crisis could not make the point better; our foreign policy was set by an admiral and a Marine lieutenant colonel, neither of whom had any background in the field. The resulting failure is not their fault. The system by which they were chosen is defective.

If we are going to be a serious nation, we need a serious system for selecting our leaders and advisors. We need some type of shadow government, in which leaders and top advisors can be identified and developed, and through which our politics can be better focused on policy choices. The world is a professional league, and we cannot win fielding amateur teams.

If the crisis leads us to get at the systemic problems it manifests, it will, on the whole, have been a good thing. But that is not what we are doing. We are letting ourselves be captured by the symptoms and ignoring the disease.

We—especially conservatives—owe the country something better. On foreign policy and the institutions that make it, it is a time for us to show some leadership—or give it over to someone who can do a better job.

ACT UP

In 1987, when the AIDS crisis was exploding across the nation, many gays and lesbians were outraged that the Reagan administration was doing nothing to deal with the epidemic. AIDS was viewed by Washington as a problem that concerned only homosexuals and intravenous drug users, not the white, middle-class, heterosexual majority. Politicians often conveyed an attitude that such people deserved what they got. In response to this cavalier indifference, the AIDS Coalition to Unleash Power (ACT UP) was formed as an in-your-face, direct-action organization that would coordinate protests in an effort to force the do-nothing federal government to do something about the epidemic. Although ACT UP was formed by gay men, the organization, from the beginning, welcomed others who were affected by AIDS (e.g., drug users, hemophiliacs), as well as anyone else who felt that all people should be treated with fairness and respect. Adopting the tactics of the civil rights and antiwar movements, ACT UP held its first demonstration on March 24, 1987, on Wall Street, where they singled out the pharmaceutical companies that were withholding vital AIDS drugs in order to increase profits, as well as the homophobia that lay behind the government's unwillingness to act. Within a few months, ACT UP demonstrations were attracting hundreds and even thousands of participants, whose pressure eventually induced the Food and Drug Administration to grant approval for the release of the controversial AIDS drugs.

The documents included here are the flyer for the first demonstration, one demonstrator's reasoning for participating in a civil disobedience action, and a speech delivered by Vito Russo at a 1988 demonstration.

ACT UP Protest, 1992.   Gay rights protestors from the AIDS Coalition to Unleash Power demanding an increase of federal funding for AIDS treatment and research outside the Republican National Convention in Houston, Texas.

ACT UP Activist Aldyn McKean Explains Civil Disobedience, 1987

I have an arrest record for civil disobedience that spans 23 years and covers seven states, the District of Columbia, and one foreign country. However, I never go to a demonstration to get arrested; I go to demonstrations to bring about change, and am willing to risk arrest to produce that desired change.

Any group that wishes to use civil disobedience or direct action to achieve change must:

1. make absolutely clear what change is desired, usually by listing specific demands;
2. target a group or individual with the power to bring about the desired change;
3. design actions so that the cost of resisting change is perceived by the person/group in power to be greater than the cost of giving in.

The classic type of civil disobedience advocated by Gandhi and Martin Luther King Jr. is one in which an unjust law is deliberately and openly violated. Most of the demands of AIDS activists do not lend themselves to the classic Gandhi/King style of civil disobedience. Nevertheless, the same basic principles apply: Make it more costly for those in power to resist than to give in.

This is done in one of two ways:

1. create problems for those in power that will not go away until they give in (for example, occupy their offices or zap their phone lines), and/or
2. educate the public in ways that both cause embarrassment to those in power and cause them to be fearful that the popular movement for change may grow strong enough to threaten their power (for example, interrupt news broadcasts or hang banners).

We should be thinking and talking about what we do much more carefully. For example, when we sat down and blockaded the entrance to the New York State Senate last year in Albany, we were very clear about what we were doing. We did not say we were there to get arrested. We said we had a set of demands and that if Ralph Marino (the Senate Majority Leader) and Governor Cuomo would agree to our demands, we would go home because we were there to pursue a specific set of demands; those demands were picked up and publicized by the media covering the arrests. That helped to educate people, embarrassed Cuomo and Marino, and contributed to the building of our movement and the achievement of change. Other ACT UP members who were in Albany that same day apparently told a

---

Source: Retrieved on 5/4/2006 from www.actupny.org/documents.

NO MORE BUSINESS AS USUAL!

Come to Wall Street in front of Trinity Church
at 7AM Tuesday March 24 for a

MASSIVE AIDS DEMONSTRATION

To demand the following

1. Immediate release by the Federal Food & Drug Administration of drugs that might help save our lives.
   These drugs include: Ribavirin (ICN Pharmaceuticals); Ampligen (HMR Research Co.);
   Glucan (Tulane University School of Medicine);
   DTC (Merieux); DDC (Hoffman-LaRoche); AS 101
   (National Patent Development Corp.); MTP-PE
   (Ciba-Geigy); AL 721 (Praxis Pharmaceuticals).
2. Immediate abolishment of cruel double-blind studies wherein some get the new drugs and some don't.
3. Immediate release of these drugs to everyone with AIDS or ARC.
4. Immediate availability of these drugs at affordable prices. Curb your greed!
5. Immediate massive public education to stop the spread of AIDS.
6. Immediate policy to prohibit discrimination in AIDS treatment, insurance, employment, housing.
7. Immediate establishment of a coordinated, comprehensive, and compassionate national policy on AIDS.

President Reagan, nobody is in charge!

AIDS IS THE BIGGEST KILLER IN NEW YORK CITY OF YOUNG MEN AND WOMEN.

Tell your friends. Spread the
word. Come protest together.

7 AM . . . March 24 . . . You must be
on time!

AIDS IS EVERYBODY'S BUSINESS NOW.

The AIDS Network is an ad hoc and broad-based community of AIDS-related organizations and individuals.

SOURCE: Retrieved on 1/3/2004 from www.actupny.org/documents/1stFlyer. html.

local newspaper reporter that they were "going to get arrested." That reporter then wrote a column that described people who were intent on getting arrested, as if getting arrested were an end in itself. There was no mention in this column of the specific issues that drove people to commit civil disobedience.

If these individuals had instead told the reporter that they were willing to risk arrest in order to bring about X, Y and Z, the action might have been more powerful. My point is simply this: When we engage in civil disobedience, we do so to achieve change, not to get arrested. Getting arrested is of little significance in and of itself. We're not out to accumulate arrests like merit badges. Arrests result from our commitment to achieve change; they are the means to an end, not the end in themselves.

Aldyn Mckean (d. 1994)

Vito Russo, "Why We Fight," 1988

A friend of mine in New York City has a half-fare transit card, which means that you get on buses and subways for half price. And the other day, when he showed his card to the token attendant, the attendant asked what his disability was and he said, I have AIDS. And the attendant said, no you don't, if you had AIDS, you'd be home dying. And so, I wanted to speak out today as a person with AIDS who is not dying.

You know, for the last three years, since I was diagnosed, my family thinks two things about my situation. One, they think I'm going to die, and two, they think that my government is doing absolutely everything in their power to stop that. And they're wrong, on both counts.

So, if I'm dying from anything, I'm dying from homophobia. If I'm dying from anything, I'm dying from racism. If I'm dying from anything, it's from indifference and red tape, because these are the things that are preventing an end to this crisis. If I'm dying from anything, I'm dying from Jesse Helms. If I'm dying from anything, I'm dying from the President of the United States. And, especially, if I'm dying from anything, I'm dying from the sensationalism of newspapers and magazines and television shows, which are interested in me, as a human interest story—only as long as I'm willing to be a helpless victim, but not if I'm fighting for my life.

If I'm dying from anything—I'm dying from the fact that not enough rich, white, heterosexual men have gotten AIDS for anybody to give a shit. You know, living with AIDS in this country is like living in the twilight zone. Living with AIDS is like living through a war which is happening only for those people who happen to be in the trenches. Every time a shell explodes, you look around and you discover that you've lost more of your friends, but nobody else notices. It

SOURCE: Video transcript of speech delivered at the ACT UP Demonstration, Albany, NY, May 9, 1988, and the ACT UP Demonstration at the Department of Health and Human Services, Washington, DC, October 10, 1988. Retrieved on 5/4/2006 from www.actupny.org/documents/whfight.html.

isn't happening to them. They're walking the streets as though we weren't living through some sort of nightmare. And only you can hear the screams of the people who are dying and their cries for help. No one else seems to be noticing.

And it's worse than a war, because during a war people are united in a shared experience. This war has not united us, it's divided us. It's separated those of us with AIDS and those of us who fight for people with AIDS from the rest of the population.

Two and a half years ago, I picked up *Life* magazine, and I read an editorial which said, "it's time to pay attention, because this disease is now beginning to strike the rest of us." It was as if I wasn't the one holding the magazine in my hand. And since then, nothing has changed to alter the perception that AIDS is not happening to the real people in this country.

It's not happening to us in the United States, it's happening to them—to the disposable populations of fags and junkies who deserve what they get. The media tells them that they don't have to care, because the people who really matter are not in danger. Twice, three times, four times—*The New York Times* has published editorials saying, don't panic yet, over AIDS—it still hasn't entered the general population, and until it does, we don't have to give a shit.

And the days, and the months, and the years pass by, and they don't spend those days and nights and months and years trying to figure out how to get hold of the latest experimental drug, and which dose to take it at, and in what combination with other drugs, and from what source? And, how are you going to pay for it? And where are you going to get it? Because it isn't happening to them, so they don't give a shit.

And they don't sit in television studios, surrounded by technicians who are wearing rubber gloves, who won't put a microphone on you, because it isn't happening to them, so they don't give a shit.

And they don't have their houses burned down by bigots and morons. They watch it on the news and they have dinner and they go to bed, because it isn't happening to them, and they don't give a shit.

And they don't spend their waking hours going from hospital room to hospital room, and watching the people that they love die slowly—of neglect and bigotry, because it isn't happening to them and they don't have to give a shit. They haven't been to two funerals a week for the last three or four or five years— so they don't give a shit, because it's not happening to them.

And we read on the front page of *The New York Times* last Saturday that Anthony Fauci now says that all sorts of promising drugs for treatment haven't even been tested in the last two years because he can't afford to hire the people to test them. We're supposed to be grateful that this story has appeared in the newspaper after two years. Nobody wonders why some reporter didn't dig up that story and print it 18 months ago, before Fauci got dragged before a Congressional hearing.

How many people are dead in the last two years, who might be alive today, if those drugs had been tested more quickly? Reporters all over the country are busy printing government press releases.

They don't give a shit, it isn't happening to them—meaning that it isn't happening to people like them—the real people, the world-famous general public we all keep hearing about.

Legionnaire's Disease was happening to them because it hit people who looked like them, who sounded like them, who were the same color as them. And that fucking story about a couple of dozen people hit the front page of every newspaper and magazine in this country, and it stayed there until that mystery got solved.

All I read in the newspapers tells me that the mainstream, white heterosexual population is not at risk for this disease. All the newspapers I read tell me that IV drug users and homosexuals still account for the overwhelming majority of cases, and a majority of those people at risk.

And can somebody please tell me why every single penny allocated for education and prevention gets spent on ad campaigns that are directed almost exclusively to white, heterosexual teenagers—who they keep telling us are not at risk!

Can somebody tell me why the only television movie ever produced by a major network in this country, about the impact of this disease, is not about the impact of this disease on the man who has AIDS, but of the impact of AIDS on his white, straight, nuclear family? Why, for eight years, every newspaper and magazine in this country has done cover stories on AIDS only when the threat of heterosexual transmission is raised?

Why, for eight years, every single educational film designed for use in high schools has eliminated any gay positive material, before being approved by the Board of Education? Why, for eight years, every single public information pamphlet and videotape distributed by establishment sources has ignored specific homosexual content?

Why is every bus and subway ad I read and every advertisement and every billboard I see in this country specifically not directed at gay men? Don't believe the lie that the gay community has done its job and done it well and educated its people. The gay community and IV drug users are not all politicized people living in New York and San Francisco. Members of minority populations, including so called sophisticated gay men are abysmally ignorant about AIDS.

If it is true that gay men and IV drug users are the populations at risk for this disease, then we have a right to demand that education and prevention be targeted specifically to these people. And it is not happening. We are being allowed to die, while low risk populations are being panicked—not educated, panicked—into believing that we deserve to die.

Why are we here together today? We're here because it is happening to us, and we do give a shit. And if there were more of us AIDS wouldn't be what it is at this moment in history. It's more than just a disease, which ignorant people have turned into an excuse to exercise the bigotry they have always felt.

It is more than a horror story, exploited by the tabloids. AIDS is really a test of us, as a people. When future generations ask what we did in this crisis, we're going to have to tell them that we were out here today. And we have to leave the legacy to those generations of people who will come after us.

Someday, the AIDS crisis will be over. Remember that. And when that day comes—when that day has come and gone, there'll be people alive on this earth—gay people and straight people, men and women, black and white, who will hear the story that once there was a terrible disease in this country and all over the world, and that a brave group of people stood up and fought and, in some cases, gave their lives, so that other people might live and be free.

So, I'm proud to be with my friends today and the people I love, because I think you're all heroes, and I'm glad to be part of this fight. But, to borrow a phrase from Michael Callen's song: all we have is love right now, what we don't have is time.

In a lot of ways, AIDS activists are like those doctors out there—they're so busy putting out fires and taking care of people on respirators, that they don't have the time to take care of all the sick people. We're so busy putting out fires right now, that we don't have the time to talk to each other and strategize and plan for the next wave, and the next day, and next month and the next week and the next year.

And, we're going to have to find the time to do that in the next few months. And, we have to commit ourselves to doing that. And then, after we kick the shit out of this disease, we're all going to be alive to kick the shit out of this system, so that this never happens again.

Vito Russo, 1988

Jeff Paterson (1968–)

There has not been a war in American history that has not seen opposition, even from within the military. Operation Desert Storm, the first Gulf War in 1991, although enthusiastically supported by the American people was no exception. In August 1990, Marine Corps Corporal Jeff Paterson refused to board the troop transport that would take him to Saudi Arabia. He was the first of many military resisters during the Gulf War and has recently been very active in the antiwar demonstrations protesting the 2003 Iraq War. Marine Glen Motil and West Point graduate Dave Wiggins also opposed the first Gulf War while serving, and Andrew McGuffin, Charles Sheehan-Miles, and Alan Gunderson have claimed that their service in Desert Storm irrevocably changed them and convinced them to become antiwar activists.

In January 2001, the tenth anniversary of the commencement of Operation Desert Storm, the Revolutionary Worker *(a fiercely anticapitalist weekly that supports radical causes and worldwide communist revolution) interviewed Mr. Paterson.*

Interview with Jeff Paterson, January 2001

UP AGAINST THE WAR MACHINE

RW: January 2001 is the 10th anniversary of the start of the U.S. war in the Persian Gulf. Many long-time readers of the RW remember the stand you took in 1990, as the first GI to refuse orders to fight in the war. But newer readers may not have heard about this. Could you run down what happened to you?

JP: Ten years ago the U.S. launched a protracted bombing campaign against Iraq, but for me the war began four months before that. In the days following the Iraqi invasion of Kuwait a small number of troops were already being prepared for deployment and I was part of that deployment force of Marines. At that point I had been in the Marine Corps for almost four years of my four-year enlistment. I only had a couple of weeks left, and I was looking forward to getting out in a couple of weeks and signing up for community college and getting on with my life.

I came from a small rural town in northern California. I lived on a ranch outside of town. My mom could barely make ends meet. We had one car. There was no bus to get into town. The only real option was being a ranch hand, and the Marine Corps seemed like a good alternative to that. I liked punk music, I thought it was kind of in your face. At the same time I thought the Marine Corps mystique was kind of in your face too.

I found myself stationed in Okinawa, Japan, isolated on a small island, where, for reasons unknown to me, the local population despised us. Many of my so-called friends, their main thing in life was getting drunk and purchasing prostitutes. I was really feeling down. I couldn't relate to anybody or anything.

About that time I decided to check out the base library. On a dusty bottom shelf there were books about El Salvador and Nicaragua. During this time I was in an artillery unit and Central America was headline news. We were mainly training and preparing to help overthrow the Sandinista government in Nicaragua, or to "save" El Salvador from the FMLN rebels. I started checking out those books and reading about the armed struggles taking place in those countries and the peasants organizing and standing up against U.S. intervention. I didn't understand all the politics at the time of those particular groups but I dug what they were doing—fighting U.S. intervention. I came to have more sympathy for them than the organization I was a part of.

The U.S. military, particularly the Marine Corps, tells you there's no point in talking to anyone about what you've been through because they could just never understand. What are they talking about? About how we fucked over all the people in the countries that we were in. How it's perfectly acceptable to purchase a woman for a week or give their parents a

SOURCE: *The Revolutionary Worker Online*. Retrieved on 5/4/2006 from http://rwor.org.

dishwasher in exchange for a servant and a sex slave. How it is perfectly fine to blow up somebody's house with a 155 mm Howitzer artillery—which we did a couple of times—and then pay off these peasants with canned foods from our mess hall. They told us that people on the outside wouldn't understand all this. They're right.

All this really laid the basis for a couple of years later when I was ordered to pack my bags for Saudi Arabia. I put all of the pieces together: what I saw in Okinawa, Japan, how we treated people and how we were looked at by the local people as an occupying force, being stationed briefly near Subic Bay in the Philippines, in South Korea. I started to see that all of these things are not the exception but the rule. Although I had never been to the Middle East, I was rather certain that what we were going to do there would not be in the interests of the people there, but more of the same—controlling the resources of these countries for U.S. interests.

I was serving out the last months of my enlistment in Hawaii when I checked out the scene around the university to better understand what was really happening in Central America, and the bigger picture of what the U.S. was up to in all of these places around the world. I soon hooked up with activists around the university—Refuse & Resist!, CISPES, and others—who turned me on to the struggle of the Hawaiian people against the destruction of their homeland. While I was in Hawaii I was ordered to be part of a bombing campaign against one of the islands there called Kahoolawe, similar to what's going on in Puerto Rico right now in Vieques. Connecting all these experiences with the activist scene around the university gave me the strength to take a stand against this war.

RW: On August 16, 1990, you had a press conference where you said, "I will not be a pawn in America's power plays for profit and oil in the Middle East." You said you would refuse to board the plane and if dragged out to the Saudi desert you would refuse to fight. What was happening at that point and what was the response of the authorities to that?

JP: All this happened very quickly. In early August Iraq invaded Kuwait and 48 hours later Bush was on TV saying we couldn't let this stand. Forty-eight hours after that I was told to pack my bags and be ready to catch a plane within 48 hours. I was not sure what to do. I asked friends. Most of them said the situation sucks but what can you do, you have to go. But there were a handful of friends, one in particular from Refuse & Resist!, who said, "Just do what's right." That's what made me seriously consider what I was going to do. For four years I had followed orders, done what I was told to do. But now for the first time I was being challenged to do what was right and that was something very new to me.

Once I knew that I had a small core of people who were going to take up my case, help me, or at least visit me while I was in jail, that gave me strength to do what was right. Once I decided to do what was right, all my feelings for the last three or four years—all the stuff that I had seen that was so fucked up came to the surface. I decided I wasn't going to go. What I said at that first press conference was those four years of pent-up frustration and anger—to make amends for all the things I participated in as part of the military.

One night I was introduced to a well-known activist lawyer, Eric Seitz, who, during the Vietnam War, had defended many GI resisters. The next day, instead of reporting for regular duty, I wrote a statement and held a press conference in his office. I returned to the base that evening and ran into a guard who was watching the barracks. He told me that everybody had seen me on TV and the officers had a big meeting and they were saying that they needed to make an example out of me so other people won't have crazy ideas.

I came back the next morning to my unit—160 Marines. The commanding officer was giving a speech and saying that he could understand why people might want to kick my ass and rip off my head but that would be illegal and technically people shouldn't do that but if anybody did do that he could understand that too.

After that day there was a whole month of back and forth with the military. The military was telling people on the outside, in response to my support committee, that I wasn't going to Saudi Arabia, they would never make anybody go, that I was a coward, that I was bad, that I would be thrown in jail or whatever. But all the while the military was telling me that there was no way they could let me not go. If other Marines got the idea that they could choose what's right and wrong, that was something they couldn't stand for. They told me they were going to make me go, even if I was just going to dig ditches or peel potatoes.

And all during that time there were at least two sides—officers and what we called lifers, people who actually believed all the propaganda vs. the huge number of people in the military who joined just like me, confused 18-year-olds who didn't know what they wanted to do with their lives, young Black men escaping the inner cities of Chicago or Compton, poor white people from Louisiana who didn't want to live their father's life on the farm. Most of them didn't understand what I was saying politically about the situation in the Middle East but I struck a chord with them. They looked at me as someone who was going up against the military. For years we sat around drinking beers and talking about how everything was fucked up. They saw me as going up against all the stuff that we'd talk about over beers, bringing it out into the open.

RW: What was your situation after the press conference? Did they throw you in the brig?

JP: Not yet. They were undecided about what they wanted to do with me. There was a train of thought that the best thing that could happen was that I would just go along with the program. They thought that even if people saw me on TV saying that I would not go, they could turn that around if they had movie footage showing that I went after all.

There was a three week period of dealing back and forth. I filed to be discharged as a conscientious objector. I stated that there was no conceivable war that this military would fight that would serve any good for mankind.

On questioning, I refused to put down those people around the world who were resisting the same war machine. They used my refusal to condemn those just armed struggles as the basis to deny my discharge.

During those three weeks I went on a hunger strike. The military was telling the whole world that I was not going to be forced to go to Saudi Arabia but I knew the opposite was true. So I stopped eating as a way of saying that even if they forced me to go I would be more of a burden than an asset.

During this time my case gained more publicity. Some of the rebellious Black Marines kind of took me under their wing and gave me some cover. There were a couple of rednecks—goons—they came to get me and said something like "Your n****r friends ain't going to help you." And that made things a lot easier for me because the battle lines were clearly drawn.

During this time I was under room arrest so I wouldn't "infect" other people with my ideas. One night, in the middle of the night, these four guys climbed through the window and woke me up poking me with broomsticks and one guy was playing with his bayonet. I was half asleep and I heard them say something like "We're going to kill you, mother-fucker." And my response was, "Why? What's the reasoning behind that?" Their response was, "You're a chicken shit coward, motherfucking faggot, that's why."

I thought that I better wake up quickly and engage these guys. I ran down all the things that I had read about. I asked them if they knew about how Iraq had gassed the Kurdish people, while the U.S. continued to supply them with arms, how the U.S. played off Iraq and Iran during their war. What exactly was this dictatorship in Kuwait that we were protecting? Their response was like, "Nobody had ever told us what was really going on." After a couple of hours of this, at least it seemed like a couple of hours, they declared that they were not going to kick my ass because I was doing this for a reason and I wasn't a coward after all.

Two days later one of the same guys came up to me in the hallway and he snuck me this funky looking leaflet that he had done on his office computer. He had taken my photograph from the newspaper and scribbled "Free Jeff Paterson." He told me that he made a few copies and that he spread them around the PX and the commissary. I asked him why he did this and his reply was that he wanted to "blow their minds." He said, "The general will shit when he sees this."

I thought that incident was pretty amazing. I think at first they thought they were rebelling against the stated official policy of "hands off the coward," but they saw that there was something bigger to rebel against and they dug that even more.

Almost every day something like that happened. One of the charges brought against me was "giving away classified information to potential enemies." This was supposedly my statement that I was going to be deployed to the Middle East because I had a classified security clearance due to my train-

ing in nuclear weapons. For some reason they dropped that charge. Later I
learned from a clerk in the general's office that he shredded my clearance
files to get back at the fucking general who made his life miserable.

RW: The picture of you sitting on the tarmac, refusing to fight in the Gulf War,
made national headlines. Did you have a sense of the kind of impact your
case was having more broadly outside the military?

JP: At the time I didn't really have a sense of how things would develop. I
thought there would be a headline in the local paper that said 10,000
troops deployed and at the bottom it would say one guy says no. I thought
that would be a great success. People would know that one guy protested.

All this was in August, four months before the actual bombing began.
But from where I was at the bombing was imminent, it was going to happen, all the talk about negotiated settlement that was not real. We were
loading our cannons onto the boats and we weren't doing it for a show. We
were doing it to kill a lot of people. One of the things that really moved me
was when the colonel gathered our battalion on the base. People were worried; they wanted to be home by Christmas. And his reassurance was that if
anything goes wrong we're going to let loose the "silver bullet"—which was
what I was trained to work with, artillery fired nuclear warheads—and
"nuke those fucking rag heads." And just hearing that pushed me a long
way toward refusing to have any part of that war.

RW: Then you were ordered to go to the Middle East. How did that come down?

JP: A week into my hunger strike on August 30 my unit was gathered and my
commanding officer said we need a dozen volunteers that would be leaving immediately. About a third of the lifers and others raised their hands. A
lot more people volunteered than they needed but the CO made a point of
"volunteering" me. We were told to pack our bags, that we would be leaving immediately.

They let me leave the base to store my car off the base. And the person
they had to escort me was a close friend of mine who let me contact my
supporters and set up a press conference. So, upon returning to the base, I
participated in a large press conference at the gates to the air station. The
press asked me what I was going to do. I hadn't thought about what I was
going to do if they actually tried to put me on a plane. I said I would have
to sit down or something. And a few hours later, that's exactly what happened. I was ordered onto the transport plane and I sat down on the runway and watched people that I knew get on the plane.

While I was sitting there on the runway, various lifers—my master sergeant, CO, and a naval investigator—jumped around me yelling shit about
me being chicken shit, that they would hunt me down when they got back
from the war. I just sat there, ignoring them, looking straight ahead. That
just pissed them off more.

RW: After they removed you from the runway what happened next?

JP: I was taken to the military brig at Pearl Harbor to await my court-martial
trial which began in late November. The prosecution was asking for five

years in Leavenworth. I was thinking about what people around the world go up against to oppose the U.S., and what the people of Iraq were facing. My personal sacrifice didn't seem that big in comparison.

As the trial started we took every opportunity to publicize my case and use it as an organizing means, not just to challenge the charges against me but to also mobilize against the war. Every day my trial went on people protested outside the gates, people chained themselves to the gate, people hung banners over freeways leading into the base. One day the judge was an hour late and he was joking about how there was a "Free Jeff Paterson" banner blocking the freeway and he had to sit in the tunnel for a half-hour choking on fumes because of that.

My case was becoming such an issue and point of debate that eventually the military decided that they had a war to fight and it was in their interest to get rid of me as quickly as possible. So they just discharged me. One day I was facing five years. Then, because of our strategy of mobilizing as many people as possible around my case and against the war, 48 hours later I was back in California. And a few days after that I was part of the mobilization of hundreds of thousands of people in the SF Bay Area and the bigger movement to stop the war.

During a so-called "victory parade" in San Francisco I was arrested for climbing on a five-ton truck while others disrupted the parade. A week later I was arrested for trying to chain myself to the turret of a tank during the Oakland parade. I shared a cell that day with dozens of activists who unmasked that parade of shame.

RW: Can you talk about other GI resisters during the Persian Gulf War?

JP: People told me of the legacy of resistance among GI's during the Vietnam War—organizations like Vietnam Veterans Against the War. I got calls from Vietnam veterans like Brian Willson who had his legs cut off by a train during a protest against U.S. intervention in Central America. So I had some frame of reference. I was able to get some strength from feeling a part of that legacy.

After my initial press conference, my support committee began receiving calls from other people around the country who were reservists in the Army or Marine Corps, active duty Air Force. People put me in touch with dozens and later hundreds of people who were going through the same decision that I had gone through regarding what to do and what was right. There was a committee set up in New York City that defended dozens of people, most of them from just one military reserve unit based there. There were news articles, hidden in the press, about two or three people refusing to fight and being put in the brig in Arizona. Here in the SF Bay Area there were local reservists who refused to fight, held press conferences and were imprisoned by the Marine Corps for two years each. The Marine Corps took a lesson from my case. They saw I was able to get support in the surrounding community, which made them uneasy. They began identifying resisters and sending them to places where they thought they could isolate them from their community, from their base of support, or from lawyers who might take up their cases.

After the war I spent two years publishing a newsletter called *The Anti-Warrior*. It gave voice to these resisters. It was a way they could have their stories and poems published so people knew what was going on.

One hundred fifty people in the military publicly made statements against the war. Over 100 of those were sentenced and did some time in prison. Several did a year or more at Leavenworth prison. The military released numbers indicating 7,500 GIs officially filed for discharge as conscientious objectors during the Gulf War. Beyond that, I heard numerous accounts of commanding officers tearing up these petitions in front of a GI.

RW: For 10 years the war against the people of Iraq has continued. Could you talk about that?

JP: There's no doubt that the war has never ended against the people of Iraq. UN studies show that 1.5 million Iraqi people have died, not mainly from the war, but from the U.S. sanctions, from malnutrition and preventable diseases. They are dying from contaminated water supplies after the U.S. deliberately and systematically destroyed Iraq's water treatment facilities. The U.S. continues to pound Iraq, during some periods averaging a bombing every other day. And this hardly makes the news.

A couple of years ago the U.S. was again threatening a large scale bombing of Iraq. I had just spoken at a protest rally when a Marine Corps vet, Andrew McGuffin, told me about some of the shit he was a part of in Iraq during the war—the burned bodies, miles and miles of smoldering cars, flesh cooking. He said, back then, I thought people like you were a big wuss—but those smells have changed me forever. I pushed him up to the microphone at that rally and we did a radio show together in Berkeley that night. Tens of thousands of Gulf War vets are now suffering from Gulf War Syndrome, and the reality that they are disposable is setting in. One in seven Gulf War vets have already filed for disability. That's twice the rate of the Vietnam War or World War II!

Recently I signed on to "A Call from Veterans: End the U.S./UN Sanctions—Stop the U.S. War Against the People of Iraq!" petition which is being circulated by Vietnam Veterans Against the War Anti-Imperialist.

Ten years later, the U.S. war machine continues to pound the people of Iraq. The same things that jarred me awake while I was in the military are still happening. But people around the world are seeing what this U.S. new world order-globalization is all about and people are fighting back, like the Seattle WTO meeting being shut down. Like in the Philippines, where I was stationed, there is an armed struggle and the New People's Army is fighting against U.S. imperialism. In Peru, the People's War is continuing. I've been reading about the Maoist revolution in Nepal, like the great series that Li Onesto did in the *RW*. All of this can't help but give people hope for the future. Many of us who have been in the military, especially Vietnam vets, know better than anyone else that the U.S. war machine can be defeated.

Gay Liberation

During the 1980s and 1990s, many gays and lesbians demonstrated
passionately for their rights, and the gay liberation movement became far
more visible. In 1994 the House of Representatives held hearings, during
which a number of gay activists testified to urge Congress to pass
legislation that would end discrimination against gays in the workforce.

STATEMENT OF ERNEST DILLON, 1994

I would like to thank the panel for inviting me to this hearing. I would like to
thank you for inviting me to this affair. I am just here to tell a story. I wish I
didn't have a story to tell, and I wish panels like this were not necessary. But they
are necessary because people in the workplace are being discriminated against
because of sexual orientation.

My story started in 1980. I began working for the Post Office in 1980, and I
was a pretty good postal employee. I was a teamworker and I worked hard. And
I worked with other individuals when my work was done. I worked in that kind
of environment for about four years. Then an individual, a coworker of mine,
began to verbally shout sexual epithets about my sexual orientation towards me
and to verbally harass me.

I apprised my supervisors of this situation, and I also apprised my union of
the situation. My supervisors told me that nothing could be done to this individual until he did something to me. The union, on the other hand, told me that I
should keep notes about the things that had been written about me and the things
that they were saying about me. People heard those things, and so I did that.

Then in 1985, in May of 1985, I walked into the restroom during the washup
period to get washed up to go to lunch and this individual was in the restroom.
And he—as I washed my hands and turned to dry them at the paper towel rack,
he assaulted me. He knocked me out, knocked me unconscious. When I came to,
there was blood all over the floor. I sustained several injuries, a bruised sternum
and two black eyes and I required several stitches in my forehead.

I was off from work for a period of three weeks because of those injuries.
And when I returned to work, I learned that that individual had been fired but
there were two other individuals in the same work area who kind of picked up
the ball and started rolling with it again. And I again began to apprise my supervisors and other management personnel of what was going on and that I was
afraid that another assault was going to ensue. They told me the same thing.
There was nothing they could do about it.

SOURCE: Congress, House, Committee on Education and Labor, *Employment Discrimination
Against Gay Men and Lesbians*, 103d Congress, 2d Session, June 20, 1994 (Washington, D.C.:
U.S. Government Printing Office, 1994). Retrieved on 12/27/2003 from http://historymatters.
gmu.edu/d/6463/.

That was in 1985. I dealt with that for three years, until 1988, and finally an individual came over into my work area and made another violent, threatening remark to me. I asked to be sent to the nurse's office and I asked to be sent home. She saw that I was pretty upset and so she sent me home.

That was on a Friday and on that following Monday, I made an appointment to see a mental health consultant. I saw a therapist and explained my situation. He took down what was going on with me on the job. He immediately took me off the job and advised me to file an equal opportunity claim and a worker's compensation claim. So I did both of those things. Eventually, the worker's compensation claim was accepted and EEOC began to investigate and we went through the channels and the procedures necessary.

I won the case at the initial level but when we got out of the internal system and into the court system, I lost on every level. I lost because there was no law that protected people from such a harassment because of sexual orientation.

I am now back with the Post Office after being off of work for four years. I returned to the Post Office in 1992, but at a different postal installation. So far everything there is okay.

I just think that a law needs to be passed so that people will not have to go through the kind of thing that I had to go through. . . .

STATEMENT OF DANIEL MILLER, 1994

My name is Dan Miller. I am a Certified Public Accountant living in Harrisburg, Pennsylvania. I operate my own CPA firm. I am an employer, homeowner, landlord, and church member. I derive much enjoyment from close family relationships with my parents, siblings, and my personal partner, Carl, and his two young children.

In most respects I am a typical middle-class American. Unlike most Americans, I am a victim of blatant discrimination and the experience has radically changed my life.

Prior to owning my own CPA firm, I was employed by Donald L. DeMuth Professional Management Consultants. It was Mr. Donald DeMuth's firm that irrationally discriminated against me on the basis of my sexual orientation. . . .

My story begins late in the summer of 1990. Several incidents of anti-gay violence occurred in Harrisburg and I was one of several community leaders informing city council and requesting action. Eventually, I appeared on several local TV news programs asking for increased police protection for gay and lesbian residents.

On Wednesday, October 17, 1990, at 10 a.m., my boss, Donald L. DeMuth, called me into his office. I was fired effective immediately. I sat in his office in stunned silence. "You are fired" kept ringing over and over in my mind. I was devastated. DeMuth continued: I would receive no severance pay or vacation pay, no benefits. Nothing.

And then he went for the final and most severe blow, asking, "What do you want me to tell our clients?" He assumed that I was humiliated and embarrassed at being gay. Apparently DeMuth expected me to leave his firm and hang my head in shame.

I was enraged. I told him, "Tell them the truth: Tell them you fired me because I'm gay." In front of the entire office staff, I cleaned out my desk and left the office of DeMuth Professional Management Consultants for the last time.

At home I didn't know what to do next. I didn't know how being fired would affect future job prospects. My life was in turmoil. How was I going to pay my bills, my mortgage, my taxes? I signed up for unemployment compensation, but DeMuth contested benefit payment. He claimed firing me for homosexuality was just cause. I was forced to return to the unemployment office for several additional interviews before benefits were approved. It was humiliating.

At home, I became depressed. I couldn't eat and I just barely slept. My life was collapsing and it had all happened because I am gay and not willing to deny it.

In fact, I had never publicly acknowledged that I was gay. I had only exercised my freedom of speech and spoke in support of increased protection from anti-gay violence. Speaking on this issue cost me my job. My boss automatically assumed I was gay and fired me without even knowing the facts.

The following trial testimony displays the pure bigotry espoused by Donald DeMuth when questioned by my attorney Daniel Sullivan.

"Now, as of October 17, 1990, Mr. Miller was properly discharging his duties?"

DeMuth responds: "I consider homosexuality as cause that incapacitated him from properly discharging his duties."

"Was he properly discharging his duties with respect to his services as a professional financial consultant as of October 17, 1990?"

DeMuth: "Not if he is a homosexual." . . .

I then went to the Pennsylvania Human Relations Commission. I was even more disappointed. The law didn't include the term "sexual orientation" and there was nothing they could do. They even refused to record my case for use as a statistical reference. I was forced to accept the fact that with no legal protection, I had to move on as best I could.

Six weeks passed and on December 1, 1990, I opened my own CPA office in downtown Harrisburg. Approximately one-third of DeMuth's former clients engaged me as their accountant. Although the future looked promising, my troubles with DeMuth were not over. In some ways they were just beginning.

At the end of my first tax season, I began receiving letters from DeMuth and his attorney demanding compensation for his former clients that had hired me. It wasn't enough that he fired me solely for being gay. Now he wanted to be compensated for his costly business decision.

DeMuth based this claim on a contract I was required to sign six months after I began working with him. The contract in effect punished me for being gay. It stated that if I was fired for just cause and I opened a competing CPA firm, I was required to pay DeMuth for former clients that retained my services. It further defined homosexuality as just cause.

Appalled at this clause, I sought legal advice. Believing that the contract was illegal and unenforceable, I signed the contract.

One year after opening my firm, in November 1991, DeMuth filed suit against me for $124,000. He claimed that I had breached our contract and sought to have the courts enforce his personal prejudice. In June 1993, our case was heard before a jury in Cumberland County presided by Judge Kevin Hess.

Lacking a specific law prohibiting employment discrimination on the basis of sexual orientation, Judge Hess refused to let us argue that the firing was unconstitutional or against public policy, and subsequently the jury awarded DeMuth a total judgment plus interest of $130,000. The entire experience has cost me a considerable amount of emotional turmoil and just under $200,000 in judgment, interest, appeal costs and attorney's fees.

Later, juror Mary Warner wrote in the Harrisburg *Patriot News*, "DeMuth took the witness stand, thrust out his jaw and said unapologetically that he had fired a good employee for being gay." She goes on to say, "It was outrageous to hear intolerance like that in a court of law where people come to seek protection from intolerance. But the law was silent."

In a separate editorial, the paper wrote, "Until the civil rights of all Americans, homosexual and heterosexual, are given equal authority under the law, discrimination shall infect the Land of the Free." . . .

I ask you, as leaders of this country, to stop this injustice. You have the power to help stop anti-gay discrimination by passing civil rights legislation. Unless such legislation is passed, anti-gay employment discrimination will continue to occur in America and the law will be silent. . . .

Statement of Nancy McDonald, 1994

I am Nancy McDonald and I am a retired educator, school administrator, and educational consultant from Tulsa, Oklahoma. My husband and I have four children. Our youngest daughter is a lesbian.

We are copresidents of the Tulsa Chapter of Parents, Friends and Families of Lesbians and Gays, and I also serve as a regional director and a member of the national board of directors.

I am here today to speak to you about workplace discrimination against our gay, lesbian and bisexual children.

Our lesbian daughter is a teacher and she specializes in bilingual education, and as any parent, we would love to have her return to Oklahoma to teach. But in Oklahoma, if a teacher is perceived to be gay, by a parent, a coworker or an administrator, the charge can be used to initiate an investigation or dismissal.

I do not want to subject her to that. This is included in the State of Oklahoma's school reform passed by the State legislature in 1990. Gay, lesbian or bisexual educators must remain in the closet. And yet I know from my experience that they are the most creative, talented and dedicated educators any school system could employ, and it is unfortunate that they must hide their sexual orientation.

On the other hand, there are no role models, gay or lesbian role models, in our schools for our gay, lesbian and bisexual children. They have no one to turn to for factual information.

This produces very low self-esteem and puts our children at risk for suicide. Consequently 30 percent—30 percent—of all suicides committed by youth are by our gay and lesbian children. This was reported in the study on youth suicide conducted by the Federal Government.

Gay educators are employed in our public schools, in our colleges, in our universities, and they are victims of discrimination. As in most cases, grounds for dismissal are contrived. Many of them are minor infractions of the rules, subjective opinions, not adequately validated. Gay, lesbian, or bisexual teachers find it extremely difficult to combat these allegations because they will have to identify themselves, and when they do, they can be dismissed. It is a Catch-22 situation.

I would like to share with you some additional examples that I know of personally in Tulsa, Okalahoma. . . .

I know a lesbian who was employed as a caregiver in a community home for the retarded. She was dismissed because there was concern that she would molest the persons residing in the home. She has an excellent work record and was never, ever, given any negative evaluations. She is very fearful of being identified and not being able to get another job. . . .

A young woman, a lesbian, was dismissed from a fast food restaurant. Here coworkers had told the owners that she was a lesbian, and he was concerned that she would keep customers away from the store. She had worked at this fast food restaurant for 18 months. . . .

A minister of a mainline Christian denominational church is dismissed because he performed a commitment ceremony for two gay men. The ceremony took place away from the church. The denomination declares that it is accepting of gays and lesbians. This minister has served this church for over 20 years, and only now accusations of his inability to serve that congregation have come forth. The church board of directors does not want to be perceived as a congregation encouraging gays and lesbians to attend this particular church. He is terribly concerned about losing his retirement benefits.

A social worker with outstanding credentials in working with families and child abuse was dismissed because the board of directors of the agency, after learning that she is a lesbian, was concerned about her working with children. The reason that they gave in her dismissal: She had poor work habits. . . .

I want you to know that our children live with fear, fear that if they are honest about their sexual orientation they will be dismissed. For the most part, sexual orientation will not be identified as the main reason for dismissal. They will be dismissed because of trumped-up, minor infractions of the rules.

They are trapped. If they are honest, as we have taught them to be as parents, they are dismissed. If they remain in the closet, they live with the fear, the stress, that every day someone will snitch on them.

Discrimination on the basis of sexual orientation is prohibited by statute in only eight States and the District of Columbia. While a growing number of cities are enacting local nondiscrimination codes, there is also a growing movement to repeal or prohibit State or municipal nondiscrimination provisions.

We have just gone through this in Tulsa. It is not a pleasant experience. Only a Federal law will ensure that all individuals are protected from discrimination on the basis of sexual orientation. . . .

STATEMENT OF PHILL WILSON, DIRECTOR OF PUBLIC POLICY, AIDS PROJECT, LOS ANGELES, 1994

Thank you, and good afternoon. My name is Phill Wilson. I am Director of Public Policy for AIDS Project Los Angeles, one of the largest AIDS service organizations in the country. I am also the founder of the Black Gay and Lesbian Leadership Forum.

A national climate of fear and discrimination has thrust APLA into the role of having to preserve and protect the dignity and self-respect of persons affected by HIV and AIDS. We provide critically needed education to the public, health care providers, educators, business and religious leaders, the media, public officials and other opinion leaders.

It is within this framework that I address this panel today. I thank you for this invitation. I am honored to speak to you on an issue of paramount importance to me personally as a black gay man who is living with AIDS. That issue is the elimination of discrimination against gay and lesbians in general, and particularly the eradication of prejudice faced by people of color in this country.

Too often I am faced with young black men who carry with them the promise and the dreams of their family. Often they are the first ones in their families to go to college. I meet them when they have their first bout of pneumocystis or they find a Kaposi's sarcoma lesion. I always ask them, "Why didn't you come forward sooner? Why didn't you find out your HIV status? Why didn't you exercise the possibility of accessing treatment?" All too often the response is, "I didn't want anyone to know that I way gay. I was afraid to lose my job." All too often this fear around losing their job has cost them their lives.

We have a crisis in America that affects all our communities, not just African Americans and other people of color, not just lesbians and gay men, but every person who has ever come to the table in search of justice, but was met with discrimination. . . .

A recent court ruling in the State of Arizona attests to this fact. In the case of *Blaine vs. Golden State Container Company*, the Arizona Court of Appeals held that gays and lesbians are not protected from discrimination by private employers.

In addition to this ruling, a proposed amendment to the Nevada State constitution says that objection to homosexuality based upon one's convictions is a liberty and right of conscience and shall not be considered discrimination related to civil rights.

Both of these examples highlight a troubling situation in this country. States categorically deny basic civil rights to a group of their own law-abiding, tax-paying residents. Basic civil rights such as protection from harassment in the workplace and wrongful termination, granted as a matter of course to the majority of citizens, are legally denied to lesbians and gay men in most States.

A widespread misconception is that lesbians and gay men have legal recourse when discrimination occurs in the workplace. We do not. There is no Federal law against discrimination based on sexual orientation.

We need a Federal bill enacted that explicitly protects gays and lesbians from discrimination in all aspects of life, especially in the workplace. . . .

This country is a special place. It is special because at our core is the ideal of equality. At our core is the understanding that equality, equal rights, are not special.

Special rights is the banner under which opponents to a Federal bill will rally. There is nothing special about the right to a job for which you are qualified. There is nothing special about the right to perform your job free of harassment and fear. There is nothing special about the right to life, liberty, and the pursuit of happiness.

In 1968, an act of violence took the life of Dr. Martin Luther King, Jr. I was 11 years old, but I remember the day clearly. More importantly, I remember Dr. King's words as he told of his dream.

"I have a dream today," he said, and when he spoke about the sons of former slaves and the sons of former slave owners, he made no distinction between the gay ones and the straight ones. When Dr. King sang, "Free at last, free at last, thank God almighty, we are free at last," he included all of us.

I am the great-grandson of a slave. I was a part of that dream, as all of us are. From the floor of the Democratic national convention, I quote Mel Boozer: "I have been called a nigger and I have been called a faggot and I can describe for you the difference in the marrow of my soul. I can describe difference in one word: None."

Many people compare the discrimination based on sexual orientation to the discrimination based on race. I do not believe they are the same. I do not think it is important that they be the same. The tragedies that happen in Mogadishu are not the tragedies that are happening in Sarajevo, and yet we understand that the tragedies in Mogadishu and the tragedies in Sarajevo are both wrong.

When you deny someone a job because they are gay or you deny someone a job because they are a woman or you deny someone a job because they are black, when you deny someone a home because they are gay or lesbian, or you deny someone a home because they are black or you deny someone a home because they are a woman, in the end, you have people who are jobless, you have people who are homeless. . . .

Statement of Letitia Gomez, Executive Director, Latino/a Lesbian and Gay Organization, 1994

Good afternoon. I want to start by thanking you, Congressman Owens, and the other members of the committee for attending. My name is Letitia Gomez and I am Executive Director of the National Latino Lesbian and Gay Organization, LLEGO. LLEGO is committed to educating the public, in general, as well as the gay and lesbian Latino community, in particular, about the contributions of gay and lesbian Latinos in the U.S.

Our mission is to work toward providing resources to the gay and lesbian Latino community that will facilitate self-empowerment and enable gay and lesbian Latinos to deal effectively with the issues of civil rights, health and culture. . . .

I am glad to testify before you today about employment discrimination against gay men, lesbians and bisexual people who are Latinos. Unlike gays, lesbians and bisexual people who are white or African American, lesbians and gay Latinos are viewed as foreigners, although a majority of Latinos in the United States are U.S. born. The gay and lesbian Latino community is a mirror of the larger Latino community in that we are young and growing in population and in the work force.

Gay, lesbian and bisexual Latinos work in the government and private sector as professionals, technicians, and administrative staff in many service jobs. We are unlike the larger Latino community in that many times it is difficult for us to separate discrimination against us based on sexual orientation from racial discrimination, because when you are a person of multiple oppressions you have to wonder if the discrimination is about your race, gender, if you are a woman, or sexual orientation.

Discrimination forces some gay, lesbian and bisexual Latinos to live in a climate of fear that their livelihood could be jeopardized and therefore perpetuates self-hatred that has an adverse impact on their psychological, economic and social well-being. I would like to provide you with a specific example of what I am talking about.

In 1986 Angela Romero, a veteran of the Denver police department and a member of the Denver police department's School Resource Program was called out of a lecture at one of her assigned schools and told to report to her supervisor's office immediately. When she arrived at his office, her supervisor told her that her division chief and sergeant had information that would damage her work integrity. While they did not say so in the meeting, the implication was that her lesbianism made her a threat to children. She would later learn that the session was raised because she had stopped one day to buy a book at a lesbian book store. Her supervisor asked Angela if she had anything to say to him about this.

Angela didn't know quite what to make of her supervisor's inquiry. Up to this point in her career, she received outstanding reviews from all the schools; however, she and her sergeant had had a difficult relationship during the previous year. Angela thought his behavior towards her was because she was a Mexican. Her supervisor's inquiries started her to think about the damaging information that her sergeant purported to have.

Alcohol and drugs were not a part of her life and she had never discussed her sexual orientation with any of her fellow police officers. When she confronted her supervisor with the nature of the information, he refused to say what it was.

The next thing Angela knew, she was asked to transfer out of the School Resource Program to the ID unit. She refused, even though she was guaranteed that she could keep her recent promotion. After she protested her transfer, Angela was relieved of her duties with the schools and was assigned to street patrol. Sometime later, she learned that the underlying reason for the personnel action was because she was suspected of being a lesbian.

Angela decided to come out to protect her job so that she could do the work she most wanted to do. Angela spent more than four years fighting the system, virtually alone. She had nowhere to turn inside of the police department that would offer her protection or support. She consulted outside agencies.

One equal employment opportunity specialist told her that it was too bad her case was not based on the fact that she was Hispanic, because it would be a lot tougher to get support for discrimination against her based on sexual orientation. The local American Civil Liberties Union would not take her case. The Denver gay and lesbian community was not in a position to support or help her.

When she finally found a private practice lawyer who specialized in employment discrimination, this lawyer told her that the statute of limitations for a case based on sexism or racism had expired. She was determined not to quit her job, but make the State change its sexual harassment policy.

During this process, Angela continued to work. And as I stated earlier, she was assigned to work street patrol. There were several occasions when her fellow officers would not respond to her calls for backup. She began to fear for her life.

During roll call, disparaging remarks were made about homosexuals and lesbians in her presence and about her. She found herself calling her superiors on their homophobia and sexism and she documented all the retaliation. One aspect of her superior's response was to place unmarked cars in front of her house and the houses of the friends she visited in off-duty hours.

Just when the system seems to be shutting down on her, the City of Denver passed its civil rights ordinance. Shortly afterwards, the Denver Police Department amended its sexual harassment policies to include sexual orientation. Today, Angela is still an officer for the Denver Police Department, but the memory of this series of events is still difficult for her to talk about. However, she is proud of the fact that she decided not to compromise who she is as a Latino lesbian for the job she loves, being a police officer.

I have to emphasize, however, that this discrimination did exact a price on Angela that she could almost not pay. She paid a high personal price for the emotional and mental torment that she endured as a result of the unprofessional behavior of her fellow police officers. She also came close to losing her life or risking severe injury several times because of the failure to get backup on high risk calls. This failure also resulted in dangerous criminals staying on the street longer than they should have because her only recourse at times was to retreat. . . .

Therefore, I ask this committee to seriously consider the merit of legislation that will protect the rights of gay men, lesbians and bisexual people and our friends to work regardless of their sexual orientation. And please do not be led into the discussion that we, lesbians, gay men and bisexual people, want special rights. This is about the equal right to work in the U.S. As we are all painfully aware in this day and time, we need to be about keeping people employed and providing safe workplace environments so that they can carry out their jobs. . . .

The Michigan Militia

After the destruction of the Alfred P. Murrah Federal Building in Oklahoma City, many newspaper articles were written about the Michigan Militia and other right-wing organizations and militias. Timothy McVeigh, who set off the bomb that killed 168 people, had had some ties with the militia, as did his partner, Terry Nichols. The Michigan Militia denied having any involvement with the bombing, but concern heightened about the climate of hate and distrust that such extralegal militias were breeding around the country. Militias are particularly angry about heavy-handed, violent federal responses to groups that have set themselves apart from American society, especially the 1992 FBI shootout with members of a white supremacist group at Ruby Ridge, Idaho, and the 1993 ATF confrontation with David Koresh's Branch Davidians in Waco, Texas. But even if armed confrontations between the government and such groups did not occur, many militias, especially in the western states, remain adamantly opposed to any governmental interference in their lives. American citizens, they believe, should be allowed to free themselves of the constraints of the federal government and return to the days of "rugged individualism." Their argument, however, overlooks the fact that much of the land that was supposedly settled by pioneering rugged individualists was given to the settlers at nominal prices by the federal government, that the railroads that took settlers west were built with federal subsidies, that the irrigation projects that made much of the land arable were constructed with federal funds, and that even the interstate highway system was built by the federal government. To be sure, only a very small minority of people want to return to a (largely mythical) simpler existence, but the fact that they have armed themselves in an effort to protect the Constitution has caused some concern—especially in the aftermath of the Oklahoma City bombing. Some observers claim that the militia ideology is just a smokescreen for racism and that their objection to the federal government derives more from their perception that the government, through welfare legislation and entitlements, favors minorities, primarily African Americans. The "Statement of Purpose" and "In Defense of Liberty II" are posted on the Michigan Militia Web site.

Statement of Purpose and Mission, 1995

As it becomes increasingly obvious that the Constitution of the State of Michigan and the Constitution of the United States are being ignored, violated, and trampled on, we find it necessary to establish the Southern Michigan Regional Militia.

It shall be the sworn duty of this Militia to protect, defend, support, uphold and obey the Constitutions of the State of Michigan and the United States of America. Notice is hereby given that violations of either the State or National Constitution, by any alliance, nation, power, state, organization, agency, office, or individual shall be met with a fierce and determined resistance.

It shall also be the duty of this Militia to provide each member with a thorough working knowledge of Constitutional rights and a good understanding of State, Local, and Federal Government. The Militia shall at all times assist members who wish to contact their elected representatives. The command staff of the brigade shall inform the unit of any pending legislative action that may be of concern to the Militia.

It shall also be the duty of the Militia to continually strive for a high state of preparedness for a number of situations that may arise. These situations include, but are not limited to: invasion by a foreign power, invasion by foreign soldiers under multinational command, suspension of Constitutional rule, natural and man-made disasters, support of Constitutionally legitimate State and Local Government agencies, search and rescue situations, and any other number of emergencies.

The Militia shall, at all times, act with the highest standards of decency and honor.

In Defense of Liberty II, 1995

The concept of "In Defense of Liberty" was originated by Dave Franey in response to the Oklahoma City bombing. This updated edition has been put together on account of the changes that have occurred over the years. We have not softened any of the questions; they are presented in the same manner in which they were asked. We hope this will assist you in understanding a little more about the militia, and what we represent. Many thanks to all the dedicated patriots who helped!

1. What is the militia?
The militia is: all able-bodied citizens who are capable of bearing arms; the absolute last line of defense against any threat to the State or Country, whether that threat is natural or man made, foreign or domestic.

Our motivation is patriotism and a sincere desire to defend the Constitution. Our goal is to encourage all citizens to achieve a high level of preparedness for a wide variety of possible emergencies.

SOURCE: Retrieved on 5/4/2006 from www.michiganmilitia.com/literature/in_defense_of_liberty.htm.

We support a Constitutionally limited government and defend the American ideals of Life, Liberty and the pursuit of Happiness. We are open to all citizens regardless of race, sex, religion, or political affiliation. Groups not open to public membership and/or which are organized for any other purposes are not militias. The militia, as an organization, has no religious theme; is not racial in nature; nor does it advocate terrorism or violence.

2. Why would you want to join an extremist organization like the militia?
The militia as an organization, represents beliefs in: the inalienable right to keep and bear arms; the American ideals of Life, Liberty, and the pursuit of Happiness; freedom and love of country. If being a patriot has become so unfashionable with the general populace as to be considered extreme, then so be it. We joined because these qualities, whether popular or not, are honorable.

3. Is militia activity legal?
Yes, we all have the inalienable rights of self-defense; to keep and bear arms; freedom of speech; and to peaceably assemble. These cover the majority of militia activities. The Constitution of the United States prohibits government, at any level, from interfering or infringing on these rights. Additionally, the Geneva Convention, Hague Protocols, International Law, Laws of Land Warfare, as well as Michigan State Law and Federal Law, all specifically provide for citizen militias, with or without state recognition.

4. Is the government going to target me if I join the militia?
If you are asking this question there is obviously something enormously wrong; it places emphasis on the fact that people are fearful of government reprisal for engaging in legal activities. Law-abiding American citizens participating in legal activities are afraid of their government! Unfortunately, we cannot answer this question for you, we can only speculate. You will have to ask the government, as we do not speak for them. However, the fear behind this question should compel you to at least look into the patriot movement. . . .

5. Are you racists?
No, we welcome Americans of all races, cultures, and beliefs; we gain nothing from turning anyone away, regardless of the hue of their skin. We do not side ourselves with, advocate, or discriminate against any one particular race or culture; the militia is as diverse as the general population.
     There are, however, individuals or groups that claim to be militias that say they are of a superior race fighting the "great race war . . . to annihilate the mud people." These individuals or groups are not militias—they are racists.

6. Are you militant?
No, the nature and purpose of a citizen militia is defensive and concerns itself with the preservation of Life, Liberty and the pursuit of Happiness. We may be regarded as serious and ever vigilant, but we are not militant.

However, there are individuals or groups that claim to be militias that are determined to be engaged in combat and are aggressively active. These individuals or groups are not militias—they are militant. . . .

7. The members of the Army, Navy, Air Force, Marines, Coast Guard and the state and local police are all sworn to protect and uphold the Constitution. Why do we need militias or even armed citizens?
As Americans, it is "everyone's" responsibility to uphold and defend the Constitution; this is a requirement of a free people.

The militia is needed as the absolute last line of defense against any threat, whether natural or man-made, foreign or domestic; it is everyone's responsibility to be prepared to protect and defend state and country.

As to the need for armed citizens, as a human being you have the right to live for your own sake, and while living, you are responsible for defending the life of you and yours.

It is irresponsible, unwise, cowardly, and just plain un-American to deny these responsibilities. "If a people expect to be ignorant and free, they expect what never was and never will be."

8. Are you terrorists?
No, the militia does not advocate terrorism or violence. Only lunatics, including those in government, destroy buildings full of men, women, and children. The militia is a dedicated group of citizen patriots who volunteer their time and energy to further the cause of freedom. The only thing we blow to pieces are bowling pins; and if we are ever attacked by them, we will win! (Bowling pins are commonly used for target practice at militia training.)

9. What good does the militia do? What is your contribution to society?
The militia fulfills a long established American tradition as the ultimate and final guarantor of freedom; it establishes that as a free people we are ready, willing and able to defend our lives and country.

We hold informative monthly meetings, update those in attendance on topics such as: pending legislation, civic activities, current events, safety bulletins; and we offer training opportunities in the areas of: weapons safety, CPR, first aid, land navigation, and other useful field techniques. We strongly encourage everyone to vote and become involved in the safeguarding of rights within their local communities. We believe that the educated, responsible citizen is the best possible guarantee of all our freedoms. . . .

Theodore Kaczynski (1942–)

Harvard graduate Theodore Kaczynski, better known as the Unabomber, was a brilliant mathematician who, after teaching briefly at the University of California at Berkeley, left academia in 1971 and began his reclusive life in Montana. Kaczynski can be viewed as a twentieth-century Luddite, but instead of breaking factory machines, as did the eighteenth-century British Luddites opposing the industrial revolution, he began mailing letter bombs to universities and research laboratories. In 1978 he sent off his first letter bomb (to a professor at the University of Chicago), which, when it was opened, injured a police officer. For the next 18 years, he sent more sophisticated, more lethal bombs to academics who specialized in technological subjects at universities and to research and development people at high-tech companies. The FBI doggedly pursued him without much success. The break came when he insisted that his "Manifesto" denouncing technology and progress be published in several mainstream newspapers (like the New York Times*). When his younger brother read the manifesto, he immediately recognized the style and phrasing, as well as many of the ideas, as his brother's. He tipped off the FBI, and in 1996 Kaczynski was arrested in his cabin in the Montana woods. Here are a few passages from his long, rambling manifesto, along with an excerpt from an interview Kaczynski gave to a reporter from* Earth First! Journal.

Theodore Kaczynski.   Mathematician Theodore Kaczynski led a one-man revolution from 1978 to 1996 against technology by sending letter bombs to academics and research-and-development scientists in order "to overthrow not governments but the economic and technological basis of the present society." Here the "Unabomber" is taken into custody.

The Unabomber Manifesto, 1996

INTRODUCTION

1. The Industrial Revolution and its consequences have been a disaster for the human race. They have greatly increased the life-expectancy of those of us who live in "advanced" countries, but they have destabilized society, have made life

SOURCE: Retrieved on 8/11/2003 from www.panix.com/~clays/Una/.

unfulfilling, have subjected human beings to indignities, have led to widespread psychological suffering (in the Third World to physical suffering as well) and have inflicted severe damage on the natural world. The continued development of technology will worsen the situation. It will certainly subject human beings to greater indignities and inflict greater damage on the natural world, it will probably lead to greater social disruption and psychological suffering, and it may lead to increased physical suffering even in "advanced" countries.

2. The industrial-technological system may survive or it may break down. If it survives, it MAY eventually achieve a low level of physical and psychological suffering, but only after passing through a long and very painful period of adjustment and only at the cost of permanently reducing human beings and many other living organisms to engineered products and mere cogs in the social machine. Furthermore, if the system survives, the consequences will be inevitable: There is no way of reforming or modifying the system so as to prevent it from depriving people of dignity and autonomy.

3. If the system breaks down the consequences will still be very painful. But the bigger the system grows the more disastrous the results of its breakdown will be, so if it is to break down it had best break down sooner rather than later.

4. We therefore advocate a revolution against the industrial system. This revolution may or may not make use of violence: it may be sudden or it may be a relatively gradual process spanning a few decades. We can't predict any of that. But we do outline in a very general way the measures that those who hate the industrial system should take in order to prepare the way for a revolution against that form of society. This is not to be a POLITICAL revolution. Its object will be to overthrow not governments but the economic and technological basis of the present society.

5. In this article we give attention to only some of the negative developments that have grown out of the industrial-technological system. Other such developments we mention only briefly or ignore altogether. This does not mean that we regard these other developments as unimportant. For practical reasons we have to confine our discussion to areas that have received insufficient public attention or in which we have something new to say. For example, since there are well developed environmental and wilderness movements, we have written very little about environmental degradation or the destruction of wild nature, even though we consider these to be highly important. . . .

207. An argument likely to be raised against our proposed revolution is that it is bound to fail, because (it is claimed) throughout history technology has always progressed, never regressed, hence technological regression is impossible. But this claim is false.

208. We distinguish between two kinds of technology, which we will call small-scale technology and organization-dependent technology. Small-scale technology is technology that can be used by small-scale communities without outside assistance. Organization-dependent technology is technology that depends on large-scale social organization. We are aware of no significant cases of regression in small-scale technology. But organization-dependent technology DOES regress when the social organization on which it depends breaks down. Example: When

the Roman Empire fell apart the Romans' small-scale technology survived because any clever village craftsman could build, for instance, a water wheel, any skilled smith could make steel by Roman methods, and so forth. But the Romans' organization-dependent technology DID regress. Their aqueducts fell into disrepair and were never rebuilt. Their techniques of road construction were lost. The Roman system of urban sanitation was forgotten, so that until rather recent times did the sanitation of European cities equal that of Ancient Rome.

209. The reason why technology has seemed always to progress is that, until perhaps a century or two before the Industrial Revolution, most technology was small-scale technology. But most of the technology developed since the Industrial Revolution is organization-dependent technology. Take the refrigerator for example. Without factory-made parts or the facilities of a post-industrial machine shop it would be virtually impossible for a handful of local craftsmen to build a refrigerator. If by some miracle they did succeed in building one it would be useless to them without a reliable source of electric power. So they would have to dam a stream and build a generator. Generators require large amounts of copper wire. Imagine trying to make that wire without modern machinery. And where would they get a gas suitable for refrigeration? It would be much easier to build an icehouse or preserve food by drying or picking, as was done before the invention of the refrigerator.

210. So it is clear that if the industrial system were once thoroughly broken down, refrigeration technology would quickly be lost. The same is true of other organization-dependent technology. And once this technology had been lost for a generation or so it would take centuries to rebuild it, just as it took centuries to build it the first time around. Surviving technical books would be few and scattered. An industrial society, if built from scratch without outside help, can only be built in a series of stages: You need tools to make tools to make tools to make tools. . . . A long process of economic development and progress in social organization is required. And, even in the absence of an ideology opposed to technology, there is no reason to believe that anyone would be interested in rebuilding industrial society. The enthusiasm for "progress" is a phenomenon particular to the modern form of society, and it seems not to have existed prior to the 17th century or thereabouts. . . .

INTERVIEW WITH THEODORE KACZYNSKI, JUNE 1999

TK: . . . I read Edward Abbey in mid-eighties and that was one of the things that gave me the idea that, 'yeah, there are other people out there that have the same attitudes that I do.' I read *The Monkey Wrench Gang*, I think it was. But what first motivated me wasn't anything I read. I just got mad seeing the machines ripping up the woods and so forth. . . .

SOURCE: Dr. Theodore Kaczynski, in an interview with the *Earth First! Journal*, Administrative Maximum Facility Prison, Florence, Colorado, USA, June 1999. Retrieved on 5/10/2004 from http://www.primitivism.com/Kaczynski.htm. Also see www.earthfirstjournal.org.

EF: Why, I asked, did he personally come to be against technology? His immediate response was,

TK: Why do you think? It reduces people to gears in a machine, it takes away our autonomy and our freedom. . . . The honest truth is that I am not really politically oriented. I would have really rather just be living out in the woods. If nobody had started cutting roads through there and cutting the trees down and come buzzing around in helicopters and snowmobiles I would still just be living there and the rest of the world could just take care of itself. I got involved in political issues because I was driven to it, so to speak. I'm not really inclined in that direction. . . .

Unquestionably there is no doubt that the reason I dropped out of the technological system is because I had read about other ways of life, in particular that of primitive peoples. When I was about eleven I remember going to the little local library in Evergreen Park, Illinois. They had a series of books published by the Smithsonian Institute that addressed various areas of science. Among other things, I read about anthropology in a book on human prehistory. I found it fascinating. After reading a few more books on the subject of Neanderthal man and so forth, I had this itch to read more. I started asking myself why and I came to the realization that what I really wanted was not to read another book, but that I just wanted to live that way. . . .

I don't think it [fixing the system] can be done. In part because of the human tendency, for most people, there are exceptions, to take the path of least resistance. They'll take the easy way out, and giving up your car, your television set, your electricity, is not the path of least resistance for most people. As I see it, I don't think there is any controlled or planned way in which we can dismantle the industrial system. I think that the only way we will get rid of it is if it breaks down and collapses. That's why I think the consequences will be something like the Russian Revolution, or circumstances like we see in other places in the world today like the Balkans, Afghanistan, Rwanda. This does, I think, pose a dilemma for radicals who take a non-violent point of view. When things break down, there is going to be violence and this does raise a question, I don't know if I exactly want to call it a moral question, but the point is that for those who realize the need to do away with the techno-industrial system, if you work for its collapse, in effect you are killing a lot of people. If it collapses, there is going to be social disorder, there is going to be starvation, there aren't going to be any more spare parts or fuel for farm equipment, there won't be any more pesticide or fertilizer on which modern agriculture is dependent. So there isn't going to be enough food to go around, so then what happens? This is something that, as far as I've read, I haven't seen any radicals facing up to. . . .

The big problem is that people don't believe a revolution is possible, and it is not possible precisely because they do not believe it is possible. To a large extent I think the eco-anarchist movement is accomplishing a great deal, but I think they could do it better. . . . The real revolutionaries should separate themselves from the reformers. . . . And I think that it would be good if a conscious effort was being made to get as many people as possible introduced to the wilderness. In a general way, I think what has to be done is not to try and convince or persuade the majority of people that we are right, as much as try to increase tensions in society to the point where things start to break down. To create a situation where people get uncomfortable enough that they're going to rebel. So the question is how do you increase those tensions? I don't know. . . .

Ralph Nader (1934–)

In the year 2000, the Green Party nominated Ralph Nader for president. Nader and his followers believed that the Democratic and Republican parties no longer responded to the needs of the people, but instead only answered to corporate interests that were the single biggest threat to American democracy. The United States, as Nader often put it, was a government "of the Exxons, by the General Motors and for the DuPonts." In 1965 his book Unsafe at Any Speed *took on General Motors and launched the Princeton- and Harvard-educated lawyer's long career as the nation's leading consumer advocate. Nader's book detailed how the quest for profit led to faulty automobile design, especially in GM's Corvair, which frequently had lethal results. Like Upton Sinclair's* The Jungle, *which swayed Congress to pass the Pure Food and Drug Act 60 years earlier, the uproar over the book resulted in the passage of the Traffic and Motor Vehicle Safety Act, shifting the power to determine motor vehicle safety from the automobile manufacturers to the federal government. Over the subsequent decades, Nader and the activist attorneys he employed, Nader's Raiders, put pressure on the government to pass protective legislation and create several watchdog agencies: the Environmental Protection Agency, the Occupational Safety and Health Administration, the Consumer Product Safety Commission, and others. However, in the 1980s, President Reagan cut the funding for many of these regulatory agencies, and as a result corporations had more leeway to exploit the environment and workers. Profits soared, the gap between the rich and the poor widened, and Nader found much of what he had worked for slipping away.*

In the 1990s, Nader shifted his focus away from congressional regulation to the growing issue of globalization, which he believed was endangering democracy by concentrating wealth and power in the hands of a few multinational corporations. When the Clinton administration sponsored the North Atlantic Free Trade Agreement (NAFTA), creating a

free-trade zone linking the United States with Canada and Mexico, and
the General Agreement on Tariffs and Trade (GATT), establishing the
World Trade Organization, Nader became convinced that the Democrats
were just as much a tool of big business as the Republicans and that
therefore the time had come to create a third party that would look after
the interests of the people. He ran for president in 1996 and again in
2000, but never got more than 2.7 percent of the popular vote. The impact
in 2000, however, had long-range consequences that are still unfolding.
Because many of Nader's supporters were disillusioned Democrats, the
Greens drew enough votes away from Al Gore in Florida that George W.
Bush wound up winning the election, even though Gore had won the
popular vote nationally. Many people therefore believed that the Green
Party was culpable for the Republican victory.

The first document here is Nader's attack on "corporate welfare"; the
second is the preamble and key values of the Green Party platform.

It's Time to End Corporate Welfare As We Know It, 1996

The issue of concentration of power and the growing conflict between the civil society and the corporate society is not a conflict that you read about or see on television. So unfortunately, most of us grow up corporate; we don't grow up civic.

If I utter the following words, what images come to mind: crime, violence, welfare and addictors? What comes to mind is street crime; people lining up to get their welfare checks; violence in the streets; and drug dealers—the addictors.

And yet, by any yardstick, there is far more crime, and far more violence, and far more welfare disbursement (and there are far more addictors) in the corporate world than in the impoverished street arena. The federal government's corporate welfare programs number over 120. They are so varied and embedded that we actually grow up thinking that the government interferes with the free enterprise system, rather than subsidizing it.

It's hard to find a major industry today whose principal investments were not first made by the government—in aerospace, telecommunications, biotechnology and agribusiness. Government research and development money funds the drug and pharmaceutical industry. Government research and development funds are given freely to corporations, but they don't announce it in ads the next day.

Corporate welfare has never been viewed as debilitating. Nobody talks about imposing workfare requirements on corporate welfare recipients or putting them on a program of "two years and you're out." Nobody talks about aid to dependent corporations. It's all talked about in terms of "incentives."

Source: Ralph Nader, *The Ralph Nader Reader* (New York: Seven Stories Press, 2000), 154–158.

At the local community level, in cities that can't even refurbish their crumbling schools—where children are without enough desks or books—local governments are anteing up three, four, five hundred million dollars to lure very profitable baseball, football and basketball sports moguls who don't want to share the profits. Corporate sports are being subsidized by cities.

Corporations have perfected socializing their losses while they capitalize on their profits. There was the savings-and-loan debacle—and you'll be paying for that until the year 2020. In terms of principal and interest, it was a half-trillion-dollar bailout of 1,000 savings-and-loans banks. Their executives looted, speculated and defrauded people of their savings—and then turned to Washington for a bailout.

Foreign and domestic corporations can go on our land out West. If they discover gold, they can buy the acreage over the gold for no more than $5 an acre. That's been the going rate since the Mining Act of 1872 was enacted. That is taking inflation-fighting too far.

There's new drug called Taxol to fight ovarian cancer. That drug was produced by a grant of $31 million of taxpayer money through the National Institutes of Health, right through the clinical testing process. The formula was then given away to the Bristol-Myers Squibb company. No royalties were paid to the taxpayer. There was no restraint on the price. Charges now run $10,000 to $15,000 per patient for a series of treatments. If the patients can't pay, they go on Medicaid, and the taxpayer pays at the other end of the cycle, too.

Yet what is the big issue in this country and in Washington when the word "welfare" is spoken? It is the $300 monthly check given a welfare mother, most of which is spent immediately in the consumer economy. But federal corporate welfare is far bigger in dollars. At the federal, state and local levels there is no comparison between the corporate welfare and poverty welfare programs.

We have 179 law schools and probably only 15 of them (and only recently) offer a single course or seminar on corporate crime. You think that's an accident? Law school curricula are pretty much shaped by the job market, and if the job market has slots in commercial law, bankruptcy law, securities and exchange law, tax law or estate planning law, the law schools will oblige with courses and seminars.

One professor studying corporate crime believes that it costs the country $200 billion a year. And yet you don't see many congressional hearings on corporate crime. You see very few newspapers focusing on corporate crime. Yet 50,000 lives a year are lost due to air pollution, 100,000 are lost due to toxics and trauma in the workplace, and 420,000 lives are lost due to tobacco smoking. The corporate addictor has a very important role here, since it has been shown in recent months that the tobacco companies try to hook youngsters into a lifetime of smoking from age 10 to 15.

When you grow up corporate, you don't learn about the reality of corporate welfare. The programs that shovel huge amounts of taxpayer dollars to corporations through inflated government contracts via the Pentagon, or through subsidies, loan guarantees, giveaways and a variety of clever transfers of taxpayer assets get very little attention.

We grow up never learning what we own together, as a commonwealth. If somebody asks you what you and your parents own, you'd say: homes, cars and artifacts. Most of you would not say that you are owners of the one-third of America that is public land or that you are part owners of the public airwaves.

When you ask students today who owns the public airwaves you get the same reply—"the networks," or maybe "the government." We own the public airwaves and the Federal Communications Commission is our real estate agent. The radio and TV stations are the tenants who are given licenses to dominate their part of the spectrum 24 hours a day, and for four hours a day they decide who says what.

You pay more for your auto license than the biggest TV station pays for its broadcast license. But if you, the landlord, want in on its property, the radio and TV stations say, "Sorry, you're not going to come in." These companies say they've got to air trash TV—sensual TV, home shopping and rerun movies.

We have the greatest communications system in the world and we have the most demeaning subject matter and the most curtailed airing of public voices (known in the trade as the "sound bite"). The sound bite is down to about five seconds now.

You and your parents also may be part owners of $4 trillion in pension funds invested in corporations. The reason this doesn't get much attention is that although we own it, corporations control it. Corporations, banks and insurance companies invest our pension money. Workers have no voting mechanism regarding this money. If they did, they'd have a tremendous influence over corporations that have major pension trust investments.

Not controlling what we own should be a public issue, because if we begin to develop control of what we own, we will marshal vast existing assets that are legally ours for the betterment of our society. That will not happen unless we talk about why people don't control what they own.

All of the reforms require a rearrangement of how we spend our time. The women who launched the women's right-to-vote movement decided to spend time—in the face of incredible opposition. The people who fought to abolish slavery also decided to spend time. The workers who formed trade unions gave time.

Historically, how have we curbed corporate power? By child labor prohibition, by occupational health and safety rules, by motor vehicle standards and food and drug safety standards. But the regulatory agencies in these areas are now on their knees. Their budgets are very small—far less than 1 percent of the federal budget.

Their job is to put the federal cop on the corporate beat against the illegal dumping of toxics. But these laws do not get high compliance by corporations, and the application of regulatory law and order against corporate crime, fraud, abuse and violence is at its lowest ebb. I've never seen some of these agencies as weak as they are now. President Ronald Reagan started it and President George Bush extended it. And now we have "George Ronald Clinton" making the transition very easy.

The dismantling of democracy is perhaps now the most urgent aspect of the corporatization of our society. And notice, if you will, two pillars of our legal system—tort law and contract law.

The principle of tort law is that if you are wrongfully injured, you have a remedy against the perpetrator. That's well over 200 years old. And now, in state legislatures and in Congress, laws have been passed, or are about to be passed, that protect the perpetrators, the harm-doers—that immunize them from their liability.

When the physicians at the Harvard School of Public Health testify that about 80,000 people die in hospitals every year from medical malpractice—a total larger than the combined fatalities in motor vehicle accidents, homicides and death by fire each year in the U.S.—it raises the issue of why our elected representatives are vigorously trying to make it more difficult for victims of medical malpractice to have their day in court.

As in the Middle Ages, 1 percent of the richest people in this country own 90 percent of the wealth. The unemployment rate doesn't take into account the people who looked for a job for six months and gave up, and it doesn't take into account the underemployed who work 20 hours a week. Part of growing up corporate is that we let corporations develop the yardsticks by which we measure the economy's progress.

Democracy is the best mechanism ever devised to solve problems. That means the more we refine it—the more people practice it, the more people use its tools—the more likely it is we will not only solve our problems or at least diminish them, we also will foresee and forestall risk levels. When you see corporations dismantling democracy, you have to take it very seriously and turn it into a public political issue.

Among the five roles that we play, one is voter-citizen, another is taxpayer, another is worker, another is consumer and another is shareholder through worker pension trusts. These are critical roles in our political economy. Yet they have become weaker and weaker as the concentration of corporate power over our political and cultural and economic institutions has increased year by year.

We're supposed to have a government of, by and for the people. Instead we have a government of the Exxons, by the General Motors and for the DuPonts. We have a government that recognizes the rights and liabilities and privileges of corporations, which are artificial entities created by state charters, against the rights and privileges of ordinary people.

Jefferson warned us that the purpose of representative government is to counteract "the excesses of the monied interests"—then the merchant class; now the corporations. Beware of the government that doesn't do that.

GREEN PARTY PLATFORM, 2000

PLATFORM PREAMBLE

As the new century dawns, we look back with somber reflection at how we have been as a people and as a nation. Realizing our actions will be judged by future

SOURCE: Retrieved on 8/11/2003 from www.gp.org.

generations, we ask how with foresight and wisdom, we can renew the best of our past, calling forth a spirit of change and participation that speaks for a free and democratic society.

We submit a bold vision of our future, a PLATFORM on which we stand:

An ethic of KEY VALUES leading to a POLITICS OF ACTION.
A hopeful, challenging plan for A PROSPERING, SUSTAINABLE ECONOMY.
A call to CREATE and CONSERVE a rich, DIVERSE environment character-
ized by a sense of COMMUNITY.

What we are proposing is a vision of our common good that goes beyond special interests and the business of politics.

What we are proposing is an INDEPENDENT POLITICS, a democratic vision that empowers and reaches beyond background and political loyalty to bring together our combined strengths as a people.

We, the GREEN PARTY, see our political and economic progress, and our individual lives, within the context of an evolving, challenging world.

As in nature, where adaptation and diversity provide key strategies of sur-vival, a successful political strategy is one that is diverse, adaptable to changing needs, and strong and resilient in its core values:

Democracy, practiced most effectively at the grassroots level and in local
communities.
SOCIAL JUSTICE and EQUAL OPPORTUNITY, emphasizing personal and
social responsibility, accountability, and non-violence.
ENVIRONMENTAL and ECONOMIC SUSTAINABILITY, balancing the
interests of market- and value-driven business, of the community and
land, of living and future generations.

Looking to the future with hope and optimism, we believe we can truly change history—that together we can make a real difference in the quality of our lives and environment. Our common destiny brings us together across our nation and around the globe. It is for us to choose how we will be remembered. It is for us to choose the future we are creating today.

GREEN KEY VALUES

1. Grassroots democracy: Every human being deserves a say in the deci-sions that affect their lives and not be subject to the will of another. Therefore, we will work to increase public participation at every level of government and to ensure that our public representatives are fully accountable to the people who elect them. We will also work to create new types of political organizations which expand the process of participatory democracy by directly including citi-zens in the decision-making process.

2. Social justice and equal opportunity: All persons should have the rights and opportunity to benefit equally from the resources afforded us by society and the environment. We must consciously confront in ourselves, our organizations, and society at large, barriers such as racism and class oppression, sexism and homophobia, ageism and disability, which act to deny fair treatment and equal justice under the law.

3. Ecological wisdom: Human societies must operate with the understanding that we are part of nature, not separate from nature.

We must maintain an ecological balance and live within the ecological and resource limits of our communities and our planet. We support a sustainable society which utilizes resources in such a way that future generations will benefit and not suffer from the practices of our generation. To this end we must practice agriculture which replenishes the soil; move to an energy efficient economy; and live in ways that respect the integrity of natural systems.

4. Non-violence:
It is essential that we develop effective alternatives to society's current patterns of violence. We will work to demilitarize, and eliminate weapons of mass destruction, without being naive about the intentions of other governments.

We recognize the need for self-defense and the defense of others who are in helpless situations. We promote non-violent methods to oppose practices and policies with which we disagree, and will guide our actions toward lasting personal, community and global peace.

5. Decentralization:
Centralization of wealth and power contributes to social and economic injustice, environmental destruction, and militarization. Therefore, we support a restructuring of social, political and economic institutions away from a system which is controlled by and mostly benefits the powerful few, to a democratic, less bureaucratic system. Decision-making should, as much as possible, remain at the individual and local level, while assuring that civil rights are protected for all citizens.

6. Community-based economics and economic justice: We recognize it is essential to create a vibrant and sustainable economic system, one that can create jobs and provide a decent standard of living for all people while maintaining a healthy ecological balance. A successful economic system will offer meaningful work with dignity, while paying a "living wage" which reflects the real value of a person's work.

Local communities must look to economic development that assures protection of the environment and workers' rights; broad citizen participation in planning; and enhancement of our "quality of life." We support independently owned and operated companies which are socially responsible, as well as cooperatives and public enterprises that distribute resources and control to more people through democratic participation.

7. Feminism and gender equity: We have inherited a social system based on male domination of politics and economics. We call for the replacement of the cultural ethics of domination and control with more cooperative ways of interacting that respect differences of opinion and gender. Human values such as

equity between the sexes, interpersonal responsibility, and honesty must be developed with moral conscience. We should remember that the process that determines our decisions and actions is just as important as achieving the outcome we want.

8. Respect for diversity: We believe it is important to value cultural, ethnic, racial, sexual, religious and spiritual diversity, and to promote the development of respectful relationships across these lines. We believe that the many diverse elements of society should be reflected in our organizations and decision-making bodies, and we support the leadership of people who have been traditionally closed out of leadership roles. We acknowledge and encourage respect for other life forms than our own and the preservation of biodiversity.

9. Personal and global responsibility: We encourage individuals to act to improve their personal well-being and, at the same time, to enhance ecological balance and social harmony. We seek to join with people and organizations around the world to foster peace, economic justice, and the health of the planet.

10. Future focus and sustainability: Our actions and policies should be motivated by long-term goals. We seek to protect valuable natural resources, safely disposing of or "unmaking" all waste we create, while developing a sustainable economics that does not depend on continual expansion for survival. We must counterbalance the drive for short-term profits by assuring that economic development, new technologies, and fiscal policies are responsible to future generations who will inherit the results of our actions.

QUALITY OF LIFE

Our overall goal is not merely to survive, but to share lives that are truly worth living. We believe the quality of our individual lives is enriched by the quality of all of our lives. We encourage everyone to see the dignity and intrinsic worth in all of life, and to take the time to understand and appreciate themselves, their community and the magnificent beauty of this world.

Michael Moore (1953–)

With his Academy Award–winning film Bowling for Columbine *(which examines the issue of school violence in the United States) and the Cannes Award–winning film* Fahrenheit 9/11 *(which critically explores the methods used by the Bush administration to make the case for invading Iraq), Michael Moore has become an international phenomenon—a "celebrity dissenter." Like many dissenters, such as the nineteenth-century abolitionists who became intensely contentious and blatantly disruptive, he has used hyperbole and selected factual evidence to advance his case.*

Similarly, Moore has relied on humor as an effective tool of political dissent just as medieval court jesters, H. L. Mencken, and Jon Stewart with his Daily Show *all have. However, Moore's use of black comedy and his uncompromising contempt for those he targets have lifted him to an even higher level of popularity and notoriety.*

Despite his distinction, it is difficult for some people to regard a person who has found such a spectacularly lucrative way to express dissent as a representative of the poor, the disenfranchised, or the disempowered. Furthermore, many feel that Moore's message sometimes goes over the top and loses its effectiveness. In his 2004 film Fahrenheit 9/11, *for example, these people claim that if Moore's sermonizing had been toned down, the film would have been much more effective—less would have been more. The message of* Fahrenheit 9/11 *is considered valid by most people, especially in its critique of the rationale for invading Iraq, but Moore hammers the message so hard that he winds up preaching only to the choir while offending and alienating the people he seeks to convince.*

The following extract is the Introduction to Moore's book Stupid White Men *that was published just prior to the September 11 terrorist attacks and illustrates his use of hyperbole and humor to get his point across to the reader.*

Introduction, *Stupid White Men*, 2001

There are those who say it all started to unravel the night of November 7, 2000, when Jeb Bush gave his brother George Jr. an early Christmas present—the state of Florida.

For others, those upon whom a decade's fortune had smiled, the turning point came when the Dow had its biggest annual loss in almost twenty years.

For most, though, the day the music died came the night we were told Pluto was no longer a planet, and life as we knew it was as distant as the look in the new "President"'s eyes.

Wherever you choose to pinpoint the *exact* moment when it all crumbled before your eyes, it matters not. The only thing that matters is that we, collectively, as Americans, all know that someone has pulled the plug on our all-night binge. The American Century? That's over. Welcome to your Century 21 Nightmare!

A man no one elected sits in the White House.

California can't find enough electricity to operate its juicers, or execute its inmates.

SOURCE: Michael Moore, *Stupid White Men* (Regan Books: New York, 2001), Introduction, xi–xx.

It's cheaper to FedEx yourself across town than to drive there.

Russia and China have signed a new pact—just when we'd dismantled the last of the fallout shelters.

Dot-coms have turned into Not-coms, making the NASDAQ as safe a bet as a backroom craps game in Reno.

The past two years have seen the most layoffs since the worst years of the Reagan Renaissance devastated the country.

You stand a better chance of dating Katherine Harris or Tom DeLay than of making your Northwest connection in Detroit on a sunny day.

What's that you say? You want to talk to a real human being in "customer service"? HA HA HA! Press "4" and kiss the rest of your day good-bye.

Oh, and aren't you lucky! You're working two jobs, and so is your wife, and you've got little Jimmy working down at McDonald's, too, so you can afford that new home on the tree-lined street with neatly trimmed lawns and little white picket fences, and—*look, there goes Spot to greet Grandpa as he pulls into the driveway!*—and next month you're going to make the last payment on that student loan you've had for the past twenty years, but then . . . SUDDENLY, your company has announced it's moving to Mexico—without you! Your wife's employer has decided she's no longer needed because the new "human resources" consultant believes that one person can easily do the jobs of three, and little Jimmy has come down with an unknown illness from something he ate out of the McNugget fryer, and your HMO says they won't cover little Jimmy's operation but they'll be happy to treat him as an outpatient if you're willing to drive to Tijuana twice a week because, well, they've built a new outpatient clinic just across the border, thanks to free trade, which may or may not be responsible for the worm found in Jimmy's half-eaten McNugget—oh, sorry, the collection agency just called and they'd like your new Celica back because you've *missed a payment!* Hey, maybe when you go to Tijuana and drop Jimmy off you can head down the street and reapply for your old job, where all the "associates" are given their own outhouse and fed a free breakfast burrito when they arrive at work at five o'clock every morning.

Pardon me if I was dreaming, but weren't things looking *up* just a year or so ago? Weren't we supposed to be living through the "largest economic expansion in history"? Hadn't the government ended fifty-five years of operating in the red and finally boasted a "cash surplus" large enough to fix every road, bridge, and tooth in America? Air and water pollution were at their lowest levels in decades, crime was at a record low, teen pregnancies had dropped out of sight, and more kids were graduating from high school and college than ever before. Old people lived longer, you could call Katmandu for 12 cents a minute, and the Internet was bringing all the world (save the two billion or so who live without electricity) closer together. Palestinians broke bread with Israelis, Catholics shared a pint with Protestants in Northern Ireland. Yes, life was getting a whole lot better—and we all felt it. People were friendlier, strangers on the street would give you the time of day, and Regis made the questions easier so we could have more millionaires.

Then something happened.

Investors lost millions in the stock market. Crime went up for the first time in a decade. Job losses skyrocketed. American icons like Montgomery Ward and TWA vanished. Suddenly we were 2.5 million barrels short of oil—*every day!* Israelis started killing Palestinians again, and Palestinians returned the favor. By mid-2001, thirty-seven countries were at war around the world. China became our new enemy—again. The United Nations kicked us off their Human Rights Commission, and the European Union attacked us for unilaterally violating the ABM treaty by reintroducing "Star Wars." It was hard, damn hard, to find a good movie; millions stopped watching network television; and every radio station you tuned in sounded the same—like crap.

In short, all of a sudden everything sucked. Whether it's the shaky economy, depleted energy supplies, elusive world peace, no job security, no health care, or the simple unusable ballot we were given to pick a President, it has become maddeningly clear to most Americans that nothing seems to work. Firestone tires don't work, and the Ford Explorers that ride atop them don't work either—which means *you* don't work at all because you're dead and decapitated and lying in a ditch outside the Dunkin' Donuts.

911 doesn't work. 411 doesn't work. Cell phones don't work, and when they do, it's some asshole having an argument with his broker at the table next to you while you're trying to eat dinner.

Freedom of choice is a thing of the past. We're down to six media companies, six airlines, two and a half carmakers, and one radio conglomerate. Everything you will ever need is at Wal-Mart. You can choose between two political parties that sound alike, vote alike, and are funded alike by the same exact wealthy donors. You can choose to wear nondescript pastels and keep your mouth shut, or you can choose to wear a Marilyn Manson T-shirt and get kicked out of school. Britney or Christina, WB or UPN, Florida or Texas—there ain't no friggin' difference, folks, it's all the same, it's all the same, it's all the same. . . .

How did all this happen? Three little words:

Stupid White Men.

Think about it: the Bush boys, who took the slender inheritance of Poppy's political mind (not to mention charisma) and spread it even thinner among themselves. Dick Cheney, Donald Rumsfeld, Spencer Abraham, and the other old shills Bush revived to prop him up. The CEOs of the Fortune 500; the wizards behind Hollywood and five-hundred-channel TV; hell, the average Joe who sees 15 mpg on his new-car sticker and thinks "not bad!" as the ozone clouds part above his head.

That's right, the whole planet is being overrun—and I'm convinced it's starting to fight back. One day last February in Chicago the temperature hit 70 degrees, and what happened? Everyone was, like, *Wow, this is great!* People were walking around in shorts, and the beach along Lake Michigan was filled with sunbathers. "Boy, I love this weather," said one lady to me on the street.

You love this? Let me ask you—if the sun suddenly rose at midnight tonight, would you say, "Oh, wow, this is beautiful! I love it! More daylight!"

No, of course you wouldn't. You'd be freaking out on a level that has never been measured. You would be screaming bloody murder that the Earth was spinning out of control, heading toward the sun at a million miles a second. I doubt anyone would be running to the beach to catch any of those bonus rays. Of course, maybe it's not that bad: maybe someone just launched a thousand warheads on Milwaukee, and *that's* the bright light you're seeing to the north as nuclear fission interacts with vacant boarded-up breweries. Either way, you'd be ripping through so many Hail Marys and God Have Mercies you might just knock ten years off your sentence to purgatory.

So why on earth do we think a 70-degree day in the coldest month of the year, in one of the coldest cities in America, is something to crow about? We ought to be demanding action from our representatives, and swift retribution against those responsible for these climate changes. This isn't *right*, folks: something is terribly wrong. And if you don't believe me, ask that dead infected cow you're drowning in A-1. He knew the answer, but we killed him before we could moo it out of him.

But let's not worry about Mother Earth—she's lasted through much worse. Let the tree-huggers lose *their* sleep over it—we're too damn busy trying to make money!

Ah, money. The sweet stench of success. A couple years ago I was talking to a guy in a bar who happened to be a stockbroker. He asked me about my "investments." I told him I didn't have any, that I don't own a single share of stock. He was stunned.

"You mean you don't have a portfolio where you keep your money?"

"I don't think it's a good idea to keep your money in portfolios," I replied, "or in a briefcase, or even under the futon. I save what little I can in a place called a 'bank,' where I have what the old-timers call a 'savings account.'"

He was not amused. "You're just screwing yourself," he said. "And you're being irresponsible. I remember reading you made a lot of money from your first film, right? Do you know how much you'd have today if you'd invested it in the stock market ten years ago? Probably about thirty mil."

Thirty million? *Dollars?* Coulda been mine? Agggghhhh!!! What was I thinking?

Suddenly I got very queasy, and it felt like all my principles and beliefs were about to end up on my shoes. I excused myself and went outside.

Some time after this event, the stockbroker guy got hold of my home address and started sending me weekly "market updates" and other propaganda in the hope that I'd give him my kid's college fund to gamble with on the Strip known as Wall Street.

Well, the "Investment Opportunities" flyers have stopped coming. In the past eighteen months, Microsoft has gone from $120 to $40, Dell from $50 to $16, and Pets.com and its cute little sock puppet have gone to puppy heaven. The NASDAQ has lost nearly 40 percent of its value, and average Americans, snookered into the madness of playing the market with their meager savings, have lost billions. Any thoughts of "early retirement" we may have entertained are out the window; we'll be lucky if they let us cut back to forty hours a week when we're eighty-two, or incontinent, whichever comes first.

Actually, not all of us. There are almost fifty-six thousand new millionaires in the country—and they've made out like bandits. They made their money because they already had a goodly sum to begin with and then invested it in companies that got rich by throwing people out of work, exploiting children and the poor in other countries, and receiving big reductions in their taxes. For them greed wasn't good, it was mandatory. In fact, they were so good at creating a climate of greed that the word itself went out of style. Now it's called SUCCESS! and, yes, it comes with its own punctuation. Soon virtually no one questioned all this gluttony as wrong or obscene; it became such a part of our daily life that when this character from Texas got greedy and took an election he didn't win, we stood back and gave it to him—he wasn't being greedy, after all, just being *smart*. Just as corporate agriculture's dicey schemes to corrupt the genetic makeup of your corn flakes aren't insane or greedy—that's *progress*. Just as the guy next door who wants the biggest SUV ever built isn't being greedy—he just wants more torque, baby!

This Stupid White Virus is so powerful it has even infected ringers like Colin Powell, Interior Secretary Gale Norton, and National Security Adviser Condoleeza Rice. And it's created a deep funk—a grand, national funk you can feel wherever you go. It has permeated us so profoundly I wonder if we'll ever recover.

Of course, we're all trying hard to forget about the moment when this ugly cultural shift hit critical mass and the Forces of Evil took over. I know what it is, you know what it is, even an idiot like Brit Hume knows what it is. It's that damn stolen election. Stolen, hijacked, abducted, and ripped from the very hands and hearts of the American people. There is absolutely NO DISPUTE over who got the most votes, and there's little question now about the shenanigans that took place in Florida; yet he who won is not the man we see playing Wiffle ball on the South Lawn this afternoon.

Yes, we're all telling ourselves nothing all that bad really happened—*get over it*, we've been told—but the events of those thirty-six days shook us hard, knocked the wind out of us, and wedged something deep in our national craw. Nothing short of one big national Heimlich maneuver can save us now. We're stumbling around blue in the face, wondering if relief will come in time. Will I have my job next year? What will happen to my retirement fund? Do ice cubes count as a food group?

YOU DO NOT COUNT! It's a tough lesson to learn. And tougher still to discover that all the stuff you've always been told to do—vote, obey the law, recycle your wine-cooler bottles—doesn't really matter, either. You might as well pull the shades and take the phone off the hook, because you and your fellow Americans have just been declared irrelevant. *Your services as a citizen, we regret to inform you, are no longer required*.

So confusion reigns, and the seismic tremors of national frustration are starting to rumble beneath our feet. The grumbling isn't subsiding, it's growing each day. Eight months after the election, deep into 2001, a Fox News poll announced that nearly 60 percent of the American public had NOT gotten over how Bush took the White House—that we're still "angry." That's a long time to harbor aggressive ill will toward our Leader. A mood that swings out of control like this—with no prompting from refined sugar or Oprah—is a mood that can alter history. Millions of Americans, from all points on the political spectrum, are feeling off-balance, unsure, upset, unglued. The rest are in prison.

The common view in the heartland is that the ship of state is running on fumes, and no one's at the wheel; after all, the designated driver wasn't designated by anyone—and he's a self-confessed drunk driver to boot.

Hard-core Republicans are desperately hoping that Big Dick Cheney can survive half a dozen more heart attacks and last long enough to oversee the raping and pillaging of everything west of Wichita. What they don't realize is that he's already put the rest of the country into cardiac arrest. Meanwhile, he and his gang are double-timing it to dismantle as much of the environment, the Constitution, and the evidence in Tallahassee as they can before the EMS unit called Election 2002 arrives.

And if there's one thing I'm certain of, there's a triage a-comin'. The American public will be turning off the life support system on this administration faster than you can say "Jack Splat Kevorkian."

So hack away, Ms. Norton—last I heard, trees grow back! Bombs away, Mr. Rumsfeld and General Powell—we're all out of Sergeant McVeighs for you to pin medals on! Drill away, Mr. Abraham—we'll have you parking those big gas hogs at the Grosse Pointe Yacht Club before you know it!

Soon, like good Saint Jeffords of Vermont, the elephants will be jumping from the sinking ship. The rest of us will just sit back and enjoy the show while contemplating how to make next month's house payment, and where to take cover as the remains of Antonin Scalia rain down upon us like a cold shower in January. Hey, dammit—wait! IT'S NOT SUPPOSED TO RAIN IN JANUARY!

So the panic builds. The media can turn and look the other way if they want, and the pundits can keep trying to sell their lies by repeating them so often that they start seeming true. But we millions of Americans aren't going to fall for the deception. The stock market isn't just going through a "natural cycle." There's nothing beneficial about "genetically enhanced beef." The bank doesn't want to "work with you" to help you catch up. And the cable guy isn't coming "between 8 A.M. and 5 P.M."—or any other time, for that matter. It's all a bunch of hooey, from top to bottom, and as soon as they recognize we're onto them, the sooner we'll get our country back.

Today I took my year-old car, with less than 4,000 miles on it, into the repair shop at the dealership where I bought it. Why? Seems that every other time I go to start the car, it won't start. I've replaced the starter, the battery, the fuse, the computer chip. But none of that has solved the problem.

When I told the service manager all this, he looked at me with a witheringly vacant stare. "Oh, these new Beetles—they don't start unless you drive them every day."

I thought for sure I must have heard him wrong—after all, he was speaking perfect English. So I asked him again what the problem was.

"You see," he said, shaking his head in pity, "these VWs are run by a computer system, and if the computer hasn't read any activity—namely, you turning it on and driving it every day or so—then the computer assumes the battery is dead or something, and just shuts down the whole car. Is there any way you or someone you know can go down to the garage and start it once a day?"

I didn't know what to say. "If you don't start the car every day, it will die"— what is this, 1901? Am I being arrogant to expect that a car I spent $20,000 on is supposed to start *whenever I put the key in the ignition*? There aren't many sure things left in the world these days: the sun still sets in the west, the Pope still says Midnight Mass on Christmas Eve, Strom Thurmond still comes back to life whenever there's an ex-First Lady around to grope. I would have thought I could cling to at least this one last article of faith: *a brand-new car always starts—period!*

"Like ninety-five percent of the customers you've sold these new Beetles to," I said, "I live in Manhattan. Do you know *anybody* in Manhattan who drives their car every day?"

"Yes, sir, we understand. Nobody in the city drives a car every day. They use the subways! I don't know why they even sell these cars in the city. It's really a shame. Have you tried writing to Volkswagen? Is there a kid on your block you can get to start it for a few minutes every day or so?"

So I'm stuck with a car that doesn't run, in a country where nothing works, everything sucks, and it's every man, woman, and state-tested child for themselves. Survival of the richest—no more lifeboats for you, or you, or *you!*

There's got to be a better way. . . .

Ani DiFranco (1970–)

Ani DiFranco, self-described feminist, bisexual, and "righteous babe," is one of the most creative and electrifying voices on the contemporary singer-songwriter-poet scene. She has performed in numerous venues all over the world, from the Hudson River Clearwater Revival and Carnegie Hall in New York to the Fuji Rock Festival in Japan. Her recordings are all self-produced so that she can maintain complete autonomy over her work. In spite of not being signed by a major label (she has turned down offers), she has achieved astonishing success over the past decade. Her songs and poetry deal with feminist, political, and social issues.

Shortly after September 11, 2001, she posted the following poem on her Web site. Although she specifically blasts President George W. Bush, the poem is not merely a partisan anti-Republican diatribe. DiFranco, in looking for the cause of the September 11 terrorist attacks, lays blame on American energy policy and foreign policy in general, and therefore just as much of the culpability can be assigned to the Clinton administration as well as those of George H. W. Bush, Ronald Reagan, and every administration since the onset of the cold war.

The March for Women's Lives, 2004.   *Hundreds of thousands of demonstrators marched for women's health and reproductive rights in Washington, D.C., in April 2004, including such celebrities as Ashley Judd, Cybil Shepherd, Susan Sarandon, Julianne Moore, and Ani DiFranco.*

"SELF EVIDENT," 2001

yes,
us people are just poems
we're 90% metaphor
with a leanness of meaning
approaching hyper-distillation
and once upon a time
we were moonshine
rushing down the throat of a giraffe
yes, rushing down the long hallway
despite what the p.a. announcement says
yes, rushing down the long stairs
with the whiskey of eternity
fermented and distilled
to eighteen minutes
burning down our throats
down the hall
down the stairs
in a building so tall
that it will always be there
yes, it's part of a pair
there on the bow of noah's ark

SOURCE: Retrieved on 9/12/2002 from www.righteousbabe.com/ani/l_self_evident.html.

the most prestigious couple
just kickin back parked
against a perfectly blue sky
on a morning beatific
in its indian summer breeze
on the day that america
fell to its knees
after strutting around for a century
without saying thank you
or please

and the shock was subsonic
and the smoke was deafening
between the setup and the punch line
cuz we were all on time for work that day
we all boarded that plane for to fly
and then while the fires were raging
we all climbed up on the windowsill
and then we all held hands
and jumped into the sky

and every borough looked up when it heard the first blast
and then every dumb action movie was summarily surpassed
and the exodus uptown by foot and motorcar
looked more like war than anything i've seen so far
so far
so far
so fierce and ingenious
a poetic specter so far gone
that every jackass newscaster was struck dumb and stumbling
over 'oh my god' and 'this is unbelievable' and on and on
and i'll tell you what, while we're at it
you can keep the pentagon
keep the propaganda
keep each and every tv
that's been trying to convince me
to participate
in some prep school punk's plan to perpetuate retribution
perpetuate retribution
even as the blue toxic smoke of our lesson in retribution
is still hanging in the air
and there's ash on our shoes
and there's ash in our hair
and there's a fine silt on every mantle
from hell's kitchen to brooklyn

and the streets are full of stories
sudden twists and near misses
and soon every open bar is crammed to the rafters
with tales of narrowly averted disasters
and the whiskey is flowin
like never before
as all over the country
folks just shake their heads
and pour

so here's a toast to all the folks who live in palestine
afghanistan
iraq

el salvador

here's a toast to the folks living on the pine ridge reservation
under the stone cold gaze of mt. rushmore

here's a toast to all those nurses and doctors
who daily provide women with a choice
who stand down a threat the size of oklahoma city
just to listen to a young woman's voice

here's a toast to all the folks on death row right now
awaiting the executioner's guillotine
who are shackled there with dread and can only escape into their heads
to find peace in the form of a dream

cuz take away our playstations
and we are a third world nation
under the thumb of some blue blood royal son
who stole the oval office and that phony election
i mean
it don't take a weatherman
to look around and see the weather
jeb said he'd deliver florida, folks
and boy did he ever

and we hold these truths to be self evident:
#1 george w. bush is not president
#2 america is not a true democracy
#3 the media is not fooling me
cuz i am a poem heeding hyper-distillation
i've got no room for a lie so verbose
i'm looking out over my whole human family

and i'm raising my glass in a toast
here's to our last drink of fossil fuels
let us vow to get off of this sauce
shoo away the swarms of commuter planes
and find that train ticket we lost
cuz once upon a time the line followed the river
and peeked into all the backyards
and the laundry was waving
the graffiti was teasing us
from brick walls and bridges
we were rolling over ridges
through valleys
under stars
i dream of touring like duke ellington
in my own railroad car
i dream of waiting on the tall blonde wooden benches
in a grand station aglow with grace
and then standing out on the platform
and feeling the air on my face

give back the night its distant whistle
give the darkness back its soul
give the big oil companies the finger finally
and relearn how to rock-n-roll
yes, the lessons are all around us and a change is waiting there
so it's time to pick through the rubble, clean the streets
and clear the air
get our government to pull its big dick out of the sand
of someone else's desert
put it back in its pants
and quit the hypocritical chants of
freedom forever

cuz when one lone phone rang
in two thousand and one
at ten after nine
on nine one one
which is the number we all called
when that lone phone rang right off the wall
right off our desk and down the long hall
down the long stairs
in a building so tall
that the whole world turned
just to watch it fall
and while we're at it

remember the first time around?
the bomb?
the ryder truck?
the parking garage?
the princess that didn't even feel the pea?
remember joking around in our apartment on avenue D?

can you imagine how many paper coffee cups would have to change their design
following a fantastical reversal of the new york skyline?!

it was a joke, of course
it was a joke
at the time
and that was just a few years ago
so let the record show
that the FBI was all over that case
that the plot was obvious and in everybody's face
and scoping that scene
religiously
the CIA
or is it KGB?
committing countless crimes against humanity
with this kind of eventuality
as its excuse
for abuse after expensive abuse
and it didn't have a clue
look, another window to see through
way up here
on the 104th floor
look
another key
another door
10% literal
90% metaphor
3000 some poems disguised as people
on an almost too perfect day
should be more than pawns
in some asshole's passion play
so now it's your job
and it's my job
to make it that way
to make sure they didn't die in vain
sshhhhhh. . . .
baby listen
hear the train?

Protest Music III

By the mid 1970s, the innovative and political aspect of popular music had succumbed to commercialism. Songs were losing their power. With the Vietnam War coming to an end, songwriters were no longer writing antiwar songs. Disco came on the scene, and rock and roll seemed stale. Punk and later grunge were efforts to inject some life into music, but the jaded messages that were being put across lacked the passion and freshness of earlier protest music. African American rap music and hip hop, and artists like Talib Kweli, The Coup, and Public Enemy, however, brought more fervor and excitement in their lyrical condemnation of life in a racist society. Recently, many performers have begun to take on broader issues, such as globalization and American diplomacy. This is most notably seen in Mos Def's "New World Water," which departs from the racial theme and touches on the issues of globalization and the "new world order," and in Immortal Technique's "The 4th Branch," which contemptuously condemns American foreign policy. Still, there are many songwriters, such as Steve Earle, Dan Bern, and Ani DiFranco, who continue to write songs along the more traditional lines of 1960s songwriters. It is clear, at the beginning of the twenty-first century, that protest songs still reach a wide audience and still have the power to raise important questions and impact people's lives.

RAGE AGAINST THE MACHINE, "KNOW YOUR ENEMY," 1992

Huh
Yeah, we're comin' back then with another bombtrack
Think ya know what it's all about
Huh
Hey yo, so check this out
Yeah
Know your enemy

Come on

Born with insight and a raised fist
A witness to the slit wrist, that's with
As we move into '92

SOURCE: Rage Against the Machine, *Rage Against the Machine*, Sony Records 1992.

Still in a room without a view
Ya got to know
Ya got to know
That when I say go, go, go
Amp up and amplify
Defy
I'm a brother with a furious mind
Action must be taken
We don't need the key
We'll break in

Something must be done
About vengeance, a badge and a gun
'Cause I'll rip the mike, rip the stage, rip the system
I was born to rage against 'em

Fist in ya face, in the place
And I'll drop the style clearly
Know your enemy . . . Know your enemy

Yeah

Hey yo, and dick with this . . . uggh
Word is born
Fight the war, fuck the norm
Now I got no patience
So sick of complacence
With the D the E the F the I the A the N the C the E
Mind of a revolutionary
So clear the lane
The finger to the land of the chains
What? The land of the free?
Whoever told you that is your enemy?

Now something must be done
About vengeance, a badge and a gun
'Cause I'll rip the mike, rip the stage, rip the system
I was born to rage against 'em

Now action must be taken
We don't need the key
We'll break in

I've got no patience now
So sick of complacence now

I've got no patience now
So sick of complacence now
Sick of sick of sick of sick of you
Time has come to pay . . .
Know your enemy

Come on
Yes I know my enemies
They're the teachers who taught me to fight me
Compromise, conformity, assimilation, submission
Ignorance, hypocrisy, brutality, the elite
All of which are American dreams

Mos Def, "Mathematics," 1999

[Mos Def]
Booka booka booka booka booka booka
Ha hah
You know the deal
It's just me yo
Beats by Su Primo for all of my peoples negroes and latinos
and even the gringos

Yo check it one for Charlie Hustle two for Steady Rock
Three for the fourth comin live future shock
It's five dimensions six senses
Seven firmaments of heaven to hell 8 Million Stories to tell
Nine planets faithfully keep in orbit
with the probable tenth, the universe expands length
The body of my text posess extra strength
Power-liftin powerless up, out of this, towerin inferno
My ink so hot it burn through the journal
I'm blacker than midnight on Broadway and Myrtle
Hip-Hop past all your tall social hurdles
like the nationwide projects, prison-industry complex
Broken glass wall better keep your alarm set
Streets too loud to ever hear freedom sing
Say evacuate your sleep, it's dangerous to dream
but you chain cats get they CHA-POW, who dead now
Killin fields need blood to graze the cash cow
It's a number game, but shit don't add up somehow

SOURCE: Mos Def, *Black on Both Sides*, Priority Records, 1999.

Like I got, sixteen to thirty-two bars to rock it
but only 15% of profits, ever see my pockets like
sixty-nine billion in the last twenty years
spent on national defense but folks still live in fear like
nearly half of America's largest cities is one-quarter black
That's why they gave Ricky Ross all the crack
Sixteen ounces to a pound, twenty more to a ki
A five minute sentence hearing and you no longer free
40% of Americans own a cell phone
so they can hear, everything that you say when you ain't home
I guess, Michael Jackson was right, "You Are Not Alone"
Rock your hardhat black cause you in the Terrordome
full of hard niggaz, large niggaz, dice tumblers
Young teens and prison greens facin life numbers
Crack mothers, crack babies and AIDS patients
Young bloods can't spell but they could rock you in PlayStation
This new math is whippin motherfuckers ass
You wanna know how to rhyme you better learn how to add
It's mathematics

Chorus: scratched by DJ Premier(repeat 2X)

"The Mighty Mos Def.."
"It's simple mathematics" -> Fat Joe
"Check it out!"
"I revolve around science.."
"What are we talking about here?"

.. "Do your math" -> Erykah Badu (2X) ..
.. "One.. t-t-two.. three, four" -> James Brown ..
.. "What are we talking about here?" ..

[Mos Def]
Yo, it's one universal law but two sides to every story
Three strikes and you be in for life, manditory
Four MC's murdered in the last four years
I ain't tryin to be the fifth one, the millenium is here
Yo it's 6 Million Ways to Die, from the seven deadly thrills
Eight heroes gettin found with 9 mill's
It's 10 P.M., where your seeds at? What's the deal
He on the hill puffin krill to keep they belly filled
Light in the ass with heavy steel, sights on the pretty shit in life
Young soldiers tryin to earn they next stripe
When the average minimum wage is $5.15

You best believe you gotta find a new ground to get cream
The white unemployment rate, is nearly more than triple for black
so frontliners got they gun in your back
Bubblin crack, jewel theft and robbery to combat poverty
and end up in the global jail economy
Stiffer stipulations attached to each sentence
Budget cutbacks but increased police presence
And even if you get out of prison still livin
join the other five million under state supervision
This is business, no faces just lines and statistics
from your phone, your zip code, to S-S-I digits
The system break man child and women into figures
Two columns for who is, and who ain't niggaz
Numbers is hardly real and they never have feelings
but you push too hard, even numbers got limits
Why did one straw break the camel's back? Here's the secret:
the million other straws underneath it—it's all mathematics

Chorus

{closing scratch} "Mathematics."

MOS DEF, "NEW WORLD WATER," 1999

[Mos Def]
There's nothing more refreshing (that cool refreshing drink)
Than a cool crisp clean glass of water
On a warm summer's day (That cool refreshing drink)
Try it with your friends

New World Water make the tide rise high
Come in and it'll make your house go "Bye" (My house!)
Fools done upset the Old Man River
Made him carry slave ships and fed him dead nigga
Now his belly full and he about to flood somethin
So I'ma throw a rope that ain't tied to nothin
til your crew use the H2 in wise amounts since
it's the New World Water; and every drop counts
You can laugh and take it as a joke if you wanna
But it don't rain for four weeks some summers

SOURCE: Mos Def, *Black on Both Sides*, Priority Records, 1999.

And it's about to get real wild in the half
You be buying Evian just to take a fuckin bath
Heads is acting wild, sippin poor, puffin dank
Competin with the next man, but how your playa rank?
See I ain't got time try to be Big Hank,
Fuck a bank; I need a twenty-year water tank
Cause while these knuckleheads is out here sweatin they goods
The sun is sitting in the treetops burnin the woods
And as the flames from the blaze get higher and higher
They say, "Don't drink the water! We need it for the fire!"
New York is drinkin it (New World Water)
Now all of California is drinkin it (New World Water)
Way up north and down south is drinkin it (New World Water)
Used to have minerals and zinc in it (New World Water)
Now they say it got lead and stink in it (New World Water)
Four carbons and monoxide
Push the water table lopside
Used to be free now it cost you a fee
Cause all things fully loaded they roam cross the sea
Man, you gotta cook with it, bathe and clean with it (That's right)
When it's hot, summertime you fiend for it (Let em know)
You gotta put it in the iron you steamin with (That's right)
It's what they dress wounds and treat diseases with (Shout it out)
The rich and poor, black and white got need for it (That's right)
And everybody in the world can agree with this (Let em know)
Assumption promotes health and easiness (That's right)
Go too long without it on this earth and you leavin it (Shout it out)
Americans wastin it on some leisure shit (Say word?)
And other nations be desperately seekin it (Let em know)
Bacteria washing up on they beaches (Say word?)
Don't drink the water, son they can't wash they feet with it (Let em know)
Young babies and professional neediness (Say word?)
Epidemics hoppin up off the petri dish (Let em know)
Control centers try to play it all secretive (Say word?)
To avoid public panic and freakiness (Let em know)
There are places where TB is common as TV
Cause foreign-based companies go and get greedy
The type of cats who pollute the whole shore line
Have it purified, sell it for a dollar twenty-five
Now the world is drinkin it
Your moms, wife, and baby girl is drinkin it
Up north and down south is drinkin it
You just have to go to your sink for it
The cash registers is goin to chink for it
Four carbons and monoxide

Got the fish lookin cockeyed
Used to be free now it cost you a fee
Cause it's all about gettin that cash (Money)

Said it's all about gettin that cash (Money)(x9)
Johny cash (Money)
Roseland cash (Money)
Give me cash (Money)
Cold cash (Money)
(Repeat to fade)

Cash rules everything around me,
Move!

PUBLIC ENEMY, "SON OF A BUSH," 2002

oh no
struck by greased lightning
F'd by the same last name, you know what?
China ain't never givin back that gottdamn plane
must got this ol nation trained
on some kennel ration
refrain
the same train
fulla cocaine
froze the brain
have you forgotten
i been thru the first term of rotten
the father, the son
and the holy Bush-it we all in
dont look at me
i aint callin for no assassination
im just sayin who voted for this asshole of the nation

deja Bush
crushed by the head rush
15 years back
when i wrote the first bum rush
saw you salute
to the then
vice prez

SOURCE: Public Enemy, *Revolverlution*, Koch Records, 2002.

who did what Raygun said
and then became prez
himself went for delf
knee deep in his damn self
stuck in a 3 headed bucket
of trilateral Bush-it
sorry ain't no better way of puttin it
no you cannot freestyle this
cause yo ass still ain't free
if fight for yall
and they get me
how many of yall is comin to get me?
none
cause its easier to forget me

ain't that a Bush
son of a Bush is here
all up in your zone
you aint never heard so much soul to the bone
i told y'all when the first Bush was tappin my phone
spy vs spy
can't truss em
as you salute to the Illuminati
take your ass to your 1 millionth party
now here's the pitch
high and inside
certified genocide
ain't that a Bush repeat ain't that a Bush
out of nowhere
headed to the hothouse?
killed 135 at the last count . . . Texas bounce
cats in the cage
got a ghost of a chance
of comin back
from your whack ass killin machine

son of a Bush ain't that a son of a Bush
cats doin bids
for doin the same Bush shit that you did
serial killer kid uh serial killer kid
Coke its the real thing
used to make you swing
used to be your thing
daddy had you under his wing
bringin kilos to fill up silos

you probably sniffed piles
got inmates in Texas scrubbin tiles
that shit is wild
CIA child
that shit is wild
CIA child

IMMORTAL TECHNIQUE, "THE 4TH BRANCH," 2003

[Talking]
The new age is upon us
And yet the past refuses to rest in its shallow grave
For those who hide behind the false image of the son of man
shall stand before God!!! It has begun
The beginning of the end
Yeah . .
Yeah . . . yeah, yeah

[Verse 1]
The voice of racism preaching the gospel is devilish
A fake church called the prophet Muhammad a terrorist
Forgetting God is not a religion, but a spiritual bond
And Jesus is the most quoted prophet in the Qu'ran
They bombed innocent people, tryin' to murder Saddam
When you gave him those chemical weapons to go to war with Iran
This is the information that they hold back from Peter Jennings
Cause Condoleeza Rice is just a new age Sally Hemmings
I break it down with critical language and spiritual anguish
The Judas I hang with, the guilt of betraying Christ
You murdered and stole his religion, and painting him white
Translated in psychologically tainted philosophy
Conservative political right wing, ideology
Glued together sloppily, the blasphemy of a nation
Got my back to the wall, cause I'm facin' assassination
Guantanamo Bay, federal incarceration
How could this be, the land of the free, home of the brave?
Indigeneous holocaust, and the home of the slaves
Corporate America, dancin' offbeat to the rhythm
You really think this country, never sponsored terrorism?
Human rights violations, we continue the saga
El Savador and the contras in Nicaragua

SOURCE: Immortal Technique, *Revolutionary, Vol. 2,* Viper Records, 2003.

And on top of that, you still wanna take me to prison
Just cause I won't trade humanity for patriotism

[Hook]
It's like MK-ULTRA, controlling your brain
Suggestive thinking, causing your perspective to change
They wanna rearrange the whole point of view of the ghetto
The fourth branch of the government, want us to settle
A bandana full of glittering, generality
Fighting for freedom and fighting terror, but what's reality?
Read about the history of the place that we live in
And stop letting corporate news tell lies to your children

[Verse 2]
Flow like the blood of Abraham through the Jews and the Arabs
Broken apart like a woman's heart, abused in a marriage
The brink of holy war, bottled up, like a miscarriage
Embedded correspondents don't tell the source of the tension
And they refuse to even mention, European intervention
Or the massacres in Jenin, the innocent screams
U.S. manufactured missles, and M-16's
Weapon contracts and corrupted American dreams
Media censorship, blocking out the video screens
A continent of oil kingdoms, bought for a bargain
Democracy is just a word, when the people are starvin'
The average citizen, made to be, blind to the reason
A desert full of genocide, where the bodies are freezin'
And the world doesn't believe that you fightin' for freedom
Cause you fucked the Middle East, and gave birth to a demon
It's open season with the CIA, bugging my crib
Trapped in a ghetto region like a Palestinian kid
Where nobody gives a fuck whether you die or you live
I'm tryin' to give the truth, and I know the price is my life
But when I'm gone they'll sing a song about Immortal Technique
Who beheaded the President, and the princes and sheiks
You don't give a fuck about us, I can see through your facade
Like a fallen angel standing in the presence of God
Bitch niggaz scared of the truth, when it looks at you hard

[Hook]
It's like MK-ULTRA, controlling your brain
Suggestive thinking, causing your perspective to change
They wanna rearrange the whole point of view in the ghetto
The fourth branch of the government, want us to settle
A bandana full of glittering, generality

Fighting for freedom and fighting terror, but what's reality?
Martial law is coming soon to the hood, to kill you
While you hanging your flag out your project window

[Talking]
Yeah ..
The fourth branch of the government AKA the media
Seems to now have a retirement plan for ex-military officials
As if their opinion was at all unbiased
A machine shouldn't speak for men
So shut the fuck up you mindless drone!
And you know it's serious
When these same media outfits are spending millions of dollars on a PR
    campaign
To try to convince you they're fair and balanced
When they're some of the most ignorant, and racist people
Giving that type of mentality a safe haven
We act like we share in the spoils of war that they do
We die in wars, we don't get the contracts to make money off 'em afterwards!
We don't get weapons contracts, nigga!
We don't get cheap labor for our companies, nigga!
We are cheap labor, nigga!
Turn off the news and read, nigga!
Read . . . read . . . read . . .

Steve Earle, "Rich Man's War," 2004

Jimmy joined the army 'cause he had no place to go
There ain't nobody hirin'
'round here since all the jobs went
down to Mexico
Reckoned that he'd learn himself a trade maybe see the world
Move to the city someday and marry a black haired girl
Somebody somewhere had another plan
Now he's got a rifle in his hand
Rollin' into Baghdad wonderin' how he got this far
Just another poor boy off to fight a rich man's war

Bobby had an eagle and a flag tattooed on his arm
Red white and blue to the bone when he landed in Kandahar
Left behind a pretty young wife and a baby girl

Source: Steve Earle, *The Revolution Starts Now*, Artemis Records, 2004.

A stack of overdue bills and went off to save the world
Been a year now and he's still there
Chasin' ghosts in the thin dry air
Meanwhile back at home the finance company took his car
Just another poor boy off to fight a rich man's war

When will we ever learn
When will we ever see
We stand up and take our turn
And keep tellin' ourselves we're free

Ali was the second son of a second son
Grew up in Gaza throwing bottles and rocks when the tanks would come
Ain't nothin' else to do around here just a game children play
Somethin' 'bout livin' in fear all your life makes you hard that way
He answered when he got the call
Wrapped himself in death and praised Allah
A fat man in a new Mercedes drove him to the door
Just another poor boy off to fight a rich man's war

Amnesty International

As would be expected in the aftermath of the September 11 terrorist
attacks, many people were detained and questioned. Amnesty
International (AI), founded in London in 1961, is an international
organization that investigates alleged human rights abuses around the
globe. In the weeks and months following the attacks, AI received
testimony from many sources that rights abuses were occurring in the
United States. AI issued a report, which is here excerpted.

AMNESTY INTERNATIONAL'S CONCERNS REGARDING POST–SEPTEMBER 11 DETENTIONS IN THE U.S.A., MARCH 14, 2002

. . . In the two months following the September 11 attacks on the World Trade Center and Pentagon, more than 1,200 non-U.S. nationals were taken into custody in the USA, in nationwide sweeps for possible suspects. Partial data

SOURCE: Retrieved on 8/11/2003 from www.amnestyusa.org/waronterror/9.11.detentions 2. rtf. 1–2, 43–44.

released by the government last November revealed that most were men of Arab or South Asian origin detained for immigration violations. Another 100 or so were charged with criminal offences, none directly relating to the events of 11 September.

Six months on, some 300 people arrested in the post September 11 (post 9.11) sweeps are believed to remain in the custody of the Immigration and Naturalization Service (INS); an unknown number of others have been deported or released on bail, sometimes after months in custody. . . .

There continues to be a disturbing level of secrecy surrounding the detentions, which has made it difficult to monitor the situation. To date, the government has provided only limited data, which includes neither the names nor the places of detention of those held in post 9.11 INS custody, and immigration proceedings in many such cases have been ordered closed to public scrutiny. However, AI has gathered information from various sources, including a recent visit to two jails identified as housing detainees and extensive interviews with attorneys, detainees, relatives and former detainees.

Amnesty International's findings confirm many of the organization's earlier concerns and suggest that a significant number of detainees continue to be deprived of certain basic rights guaranteed under international law. These include the right to humane treatment, as well as rights which are essential to protection from arbitrary detention, such as the right of anyone deprived of their liberty to be informed of the reasons for the detention; to be able to challenge the lawfulness of the detention; to have prompt access to and assistance from a lawyer; and to the presumption of innocence.

According to immigration attorneys, many post 9.11 detainees have been charged with routine visa violations for which they would not normally be detained. While technically in INS custody, some have been held for weeks or months pending security "clearance" by the Federal Bureau of Investigation (FBI), a process shrouded in secrecy. Lack of information given to detainees or their attorneys as to why they are being held has made it difficult for them effectively to challenge their detention.

Amnesty International recognizes that governments need to be vigilant in investigating potential "terrorist" links. However, the secrecy surrounding the current proceedings creates the potential for abuse. There is also concern that the immigration system is being used to hold non-nationals on flimsy evidence pending broad criminal probes, without the safeguards which are present in the criminal justice system.

For example, unlike people detained in the context of criminal procedures, INS detainees have no right to court-appointed attorneys. Contrary to assertions made by Attorney General Ashcroft in November 2001 that all INS detainees had the opportunity to seek legal assistance through probono legal service providers if necessary, AI has learned that many detainees have been without access to lawyers for far longer than was initially reported. This is of particular concern given that some are being simultaneously investigated by the FBI and subjected to lengthy—and possibly indefinite—detention. . . .

Amnesty International also remains deeply concerned that, although they are not charged with crimes, many post 9.11 detainees are held in punitive conditions in jails, sometimes alongside people charged or convicted of criminal offences. AI has received reports of cruel treatment, including prolonged solitary confinement, heavy shackling of detainees (including use of chains and leg shackles) during visits or court appearances and lack of adequate outdoor exercise. There have also been allegations of physical and verbal abuse.

. . . Amnesty International fully recognizes the government's obligation to take all necessary measures to protect its borders and investigate crimes and potential threats to national security. However, the organization is concerned that the government has used its expanded powers to detain non-nationals in the wake of September 11 without the necessary safeguards under international law. AI is concerned that the detentions in some cases may amount to arbitrary deprivation of liberty in violation of Article 9(1) of the ICCPR [International Covenant on Civil and Political Rights]. The secrecy surrounding the detention process has, further, created a serious lack of public accountability. Transparency in the process is necessary to ensure that all persons deprived of their liberty can fully exercise their rights under US and international law. Amnesty International urges the U.S. Government to:

Provide in full the information requested under the FOIA [Freedom of Information Act]; make public information on the number and nationalities of those still detained; the reasons for their detention; the date and place of arrest; date and charges; and place of detention; provide information on the numbers and nationalities of those deported or removed under voluntary departure arrangements and the countries to which they have been returned.

Ensure that all persons in federal custody, including those held in local or county jails, are treated humanely in accordance with international standards and that no-one is subjected to torture or other cruel, inhuman or degrading treatment. The Department of Justice should fully investigate all allegations of ill-treatment of detainees or prisoners and take appropriate action in the case of those found guilty of misconduct.

Ensure respect for the rights of everyone arrested or detained as set out under international standards, including Article 9 of the ICCPR and the Body of Principles. Such rights include the right to be informed of the reasons for arrest and to be given prompt access to attorneys and relatives and consular officials or representatives of relevant international organizations as requested. Ensure that all detained persons are provided with written notification of their rights as guaranteed by international standards and U.S. law, in a language they understand.

Ensure that all arrested or detained persons are brought promptly before a judge and have access to the courts and a procedure in which they may challenge the lawfulness of their detention.

Ensure that no-one is detained on national security grounds unless charged
    with a recognizable offence or action is being taken to deport within a
    reasonable period. There must be a realistic possibility of deportation
    being effected.

Ensure that no-one is removed or deported to a country where they risk being
    subjected to serious human rights abuses.

Ensure that asylum seekers are not generally detained and that anyone claiming
    asylum is allowed a full and fair hearing of their claim as provided under
    the 1951 Refugee Convention and the 1967 Protocol.

The UN High Commissioner for Refugees should be granted access to all
    asylum seekers and refugees in detention.

Ensure that restraints are applied only when strictly necessary as a precaution
    against escape, on medical grounds or to prevent damage or injury, in
    accordance with international standards. Under no circumstances should
    detainees be shackled when appearing before immigration judges. . . .

Earth Liberation Front

*According to the FBI, the radical Earth Liberation Front (ELF), which
preaches a policy of "ecoterrorism," is one of the top domestic terrorist
organizations in the United States. ELF has taken credit for many acts of
sabotage and arson against lumber companies, ski lodges, and even the
U.S. Forestry Service in an effort to thwart industrial and tourist
encroachment into the natural habitat of endangered species. ELF
claimed, for example, that the reason it torched a Vail, Colorado, ski lodge
in 1998 was to prevent the ski company from expanding into 885 acres of
forest that was the habitat for the Canada lynx. Though little is known
about the origins of ELF, which is said to be an offshoot of Earth First!, it
does issue press releases taking responsibility for its members' actions.
One of the people associated with ELF is "spokesperson" Craig
Rosebraugh. Rosebraugh claims that he is merely an "intermediary"
between the organization and the media who reports information that
was passed on to him about ELF activities. In 2002, while the United
States was stepping up its antiterrorism campaign, domestic terrorism,
too, became a significant target of federal law enforcement agencies and
congressional investigations. The following testimony was submitted by
Rosebraugh to a congressional hearing on ecoterrorism. Also reprinted
here is one of the Earth Liberation Front's press releases. This one is from
September 2002, after a fire severely damaged a U.S. Forestry Service
facility in Irvine, Pennsylvania.*

Written Testimony Supplied to the U.S. House of Representatives for the February 12, 2002, Hearing on "Ecoterrorism"

Submitted to the House on February 7, 2002

> *When a long train of abuses and usurpations, pursuing invariably the same object, evinces a design to reduce [the people] under absolute despotism, it is their right, it is their duty, to throw off such government, and to provide new guards for their future security.*

> *The oppressed should rebel, and they will continue to rebel and raise disturbance until their civil rights are fully restored to them and all partial distinctions, exclusions and incapacitations are removed.*

Thomas Jefferson, 1776

. . . Throughout my childhood and adolescent years, the education I received from my parents, schools, popular media and culture instilled in me a pride for my country, for my government, and everything the United States represented. I was taught about the great American history, our Constitution, Bill of Rights, and our legacy of being at the forefront of democracy and freedom. I considered myself to be just an average boy taking an active part in the popular American pastimes of competitive sports, consumer culture, and existing within a classic representation of the standard, middle-class suburban lifestyle. . . .

Particularly, with the advent of the industrial revolution in the United States, the destruction of the natural world took a sharp turn for the worse. The attitude, more so than ever, turned to one of profits at any cost and a major shift from sustainable living to stockpiling for economic benefit. This focus on stockpiling and industrial productivity caused hardship on communities, forcing local crafters and laborers to be driven out of business by overly competitive industries. Additionally, with this new focus on sacrificing sustainable living for financial gain, natural resources were in greater demand than ever. Semi-automatic to automatic machinery, production lines, the automobile, the roadway system, suburbs, and the breakup of small, fairly self-sufficient communities all came about, at least in part, due to the industrial revolution. This unhealthy and deadly transgression of course was supported and promoted by the U.S. government, always eager to see growth in the domestic economy.

All of this set the stage for the threatening shortage of natural resources and the massive environmental pollution and destruction present today in the United States. In cities such as Los Angeles, Detroit, and Houston, the air and soil pollution levels are so extreme people have suffered and continue to face deadly health

---

SOURCE: Retrieved on 8/29/2003 from www.earthliberationfront.com.

problems. Waterways throughout the country, including the Columbia Slough in my backyard, are so polluted from industries it is recommended that humans don't even expose themselves to the moisture let alone drink unfiltered, unbottled water. The necessary and crucial forests of the Pacific Northwestern region of the country have been systematically destroyed by corporations such as Boise Cascade, Willamette Industries, and others within the timber industry whose sole motive is profits regardless of the expense to the health of an ecosystem. In Northern California, the sacred old growths, dreamlike in appearance, taking your breath away at first glance, have been continuously threatened and cut by greedy corporations such as Pacific Lumber/Maxxam. The same has occurred and still is a reality in states including Washington, Oregon, Idaho, and Colorado.

The first National Forests were established in the United States more than a century ago. One hundred fifty-five of them exist today spread across 191 million acres. Over the years, the forest products industry has decimated publicly owned National Forests in this country, leaving a horrendous trail of clearcuts and logging roads. Commercial logging has been responsible for annihilating nearly all of the nation's old growth forests, draining nutrients from the soil, washing topsoil into streams, destroying wildlife habitat, and creating an increase in the incidence and severity of forest fires. Only an estimated 4 percent of old growth forests in the United States are remaining.

The National Forests in the United States contain far more than just trees. In fact, more than 3,000 species of fish and wildlife, in addition to 10,000 plant species, have their habitat within the National Forests. This includes at least 230 endangered plant and animal species. All of these life forms co-exist symbiotically to naturally create the rich and healthy ecosystems needed for life to exist on this planet.

The benefits of a healthy forest cannot be overrated. Healthy forests purify drinking water, provide fresh clean air to breathe, stabilize hillsides, and prevent floods. Hillsides clearcut or destroyed by logging roads lose their ability to absorb heavy rainfall. If no trees exist to soak up moisture with roots to hold the soil, water flows freely down slopes, creating muddy streams, polluting drinking water, strengthening floods, and causing dangerous mudslides. Instead of valuing trees and forests for being necessary providers of life, the U.S. Forest Service and commercial logging interests have decimated these precious ecosystems.

The timber corporations argue that today in the United States more forests exist than perhaps at any time in the last century or more. It doesn't take a forestry specialist to realize that monoculture tree farms—in which one species of tree, often times non-native to the area, is grown in mass in a small area for maximum production—do not equate to a healthy forest. Healthy forests are made up of diverse ecosystems consisting of many native plant and animal species. These healthy ecosystems are what grant humans and all other life forms on the planet with the ability to live. Without clean air, clean water, and healthy soil, life on this planet will cease to exist. There is an overwhelming battery of evidence that conclusively shows that we are already well on our path toward massive planetary destruction.

The popular environmental movement in the United States, which arguably began in the 1960s, has failed to produce the necessary protection needed to ensure that life on this planet will continue to survive. This is largely due to the fact that the movement has primarily consisted of tactics sanctioned by the very power structure that is benefiting economically from the destruction of the natural world. While a few minor successes in this country should be noted, the overwhelming constant trend has been the increasingly speedy liquidation of natural resources and annihilation of the environment.

The state sanctioned tactics, that is, those approved by the U.S. government and the status quo and predominantly legal in nature, rarely, if ever, actually challenge or positively change the very entities that are responsible for oppression, exploitation, and, in this case, environmental destruction. Throughout the history of the United States, a striking amount of evidence indicates that it wasn't until efforts strayed beyond the state sanctioned that social change ever progressed. In the abolitionist movement, the Underground Railroad, public educational campaigns, in addition to slave revolts, forced the federal government to act. With the Suffragettes in the United States, individuals such as Alice Paul acting with various forms of civil disobedience added to the more mainstream efforts to successfully demand the vote for women. Any labor historian will assert that in addition to the organizing of the workplace, strikes, riots, and protests dramatically assisted in producing more tolerable work standards. The progress of the civil rights movement was primarily founded upon the massive illegal civil disobedience campaigns against segregation and disenfranchisement. Likewise, the true pressure from the Vietnam anti-war movement in this country only came after illegal activities such as civil disobedience and beyond were implemented. Perhaps the most obvious, yet often overlooked, historical example of this notion supporting the importance of illegal activity as a tool for positive, lasting change, came just prior to our war for independence. Our educational systems in the United States glorify the Boston Tea Party while simultaneously failing to recognize and admit that the dumping of tea was perhaps one of the most famous early examples of politically motivated property destruction.

In the mid-1990s, individuals angry and disillusioned with the failing efforts to protect the natural environment through state sanctioned means, began taking illegal action. At first, nonviolent civil disobedience was implemented, followed by sporadic cases of nonviolent property destruction. In November 1997, an anonymous communiqué was issued by a group called the Earth Liberation Front claiming responsibility for their first-ever action in North America.

Immediately, the label of *ecoterrorism* appeared in news stories describing the actions of the Earth Liberation Front. Where exactly this label originated is open for debate, but all indications point to the federal government of the United States in coordination with industry and sympathetic mass media. Whatever the truth may be regarding the source of this term, one thing is for certain—the decision to attach this label to illegal actions taken for environmental protection was very conscious and deliberate. Why? The need for the U.S. federal government to control and mold public opinion through the power of propaganda to ensure an absence of threat is crucial. If information about illegal actions taken to protect the natural environment were presented openly to the public without biased interpretation, the opportunity would exist for citizens to make up their *own* minds about the legitimacy of the tactic, target, and movement. By attaching a label such as "terrorism" to the activities of groups such as the Earth Liberation Front, the public is left with little choice but to give in to their preconceived notions negatively associated with that term. For many in this country, including myself, information about terrorism came from schools and popular culture. Most often times, the definition of terrorism was overtly racist associated frequently in movies and on television shows with Arabs and the *others* our government told us were threatening. Terrorism usually is connected with violence, with politically motivated physical harm to humans.

Yet, in the history of the Earth Liberation Front, both in North America and abroad in Europe, no one has ever been injured by the group's many actions. This is not a mere coincidence, but rather a deliberate decision that illustrates the true motivation behind the covert organization. Simply put and most fundamentally, the goal of the Earth Liberation Front is to save life. The group takes actions directly against the property of those who are engaged in massive planetary destruction in order for all of us to survive. This noble pursuit does not constitute terrorism, but rather seeks to abolish it.

A major hypocrisy exists when the U.S. government labels an organization such as the Earth Liberation Front a terrorist group while simultaneously failing to acknowledge its own terrorist history. In fact, the U.S. government by far has been the most extreme terrorist organization in planetary history. Some, but nowhere near all, of the examples of domestic terrorism were discussed earlier in this writing. Yet, further proof can be found by taking a glimpse at the foreign policy record of the United States even as recently as from the 1950s. In Guatemala (1953–1990s) the CIA organized a coup that overthrew the democratically elected government led by Jacobo Arbenz. This began some 40 years of death squads, torture, disappearances, mass executions, totaling well over 100,000 victims. The U.S. government apparently didn't want Guatemala's social democracy spreading to other countries in Latin America.

In the Middle East (1956–1958) the United States twice tried to overthrow the Syrian government. Additionally, the U.S. government landed 14,000 troops to purportedly keep the peace in Lebanon and to stop any opposition to the U.S. supported Lebanese government. The U.S. government also conspired to overthrow or assassinate Nasser of Egypt. . . .

Here in the United States, the growth of the empire, of capitalism, and of industry, has meant greater discrepancies between the wealthy and poor, a continued rise in the number of those considered to be a threat to the system, as well as irreversible harm done to the environment and life on the planet. Corporations in the United States literally get away with murder, facing little or no repercussions due to their legal structures. The U.S. government, which sleeps in the same bed as U.S. corporations, serves to ensure that the "business as usual" policies of imperialism can continue with as little friction as possible. Anyone questioning the mere logic of this genocidal culture and governing policy is considered a dissident and, more often than not, shipped off to one of the fastest growing industries of all, the prison industrial complex....

U.S. imperialism is a disease, one that continues to grow and become more powerful and dangerous. It needs to be stopped. One of the chief weapons used by those protecting the imperialist policies of the United States is a slick, believable propaganda campaign designed to ensure U.S. citizens do not question or threaten the "American way of life." Perhaps the strongest factor in this campaign is the phenomenon of capitalism. By creating a consumer demand for products, corporations, greatly aided by the U.S. government, can effectively influence people's dreams, desires, wants, and life plans. The very American Dream promoted throughout the world is that anyone can come to the United States, work hard, and become happy and financially secure. Through the use of the propaganda campaign designed, promoted, and transmitted by the U.S. ruling class, people are nearly coerced into adopting unhealthy desires for, often times, unreachable, unneeded, and dangerous consumer goods. Through impressive societal mind control, the belief that obtaining consumer products will equal security and happiness has spread across the United States, and much of the planet at this point, like some extreme plague. The fact that the policies of the United States murder people on a daily basis is unseen, forgotten, or ignored, as every effort is made by people to fit into the artificial model life manufactured by the ruling elite....

I was asked originally if I would voluntarily testify before the House Subcommittee on Forests and Forest Health at a hearing focused on "ecoterrorism." I declined in a written statement. U.S. Marshals then subpoenaed me on October 31, 2001 to testify at this hearing on February 12, 2002, against my will. Is this hearing a forum to discuss the threats facing the health of the natural environment, specifically the forests? No, clearly there is not even the remotest interest in this subject from the U.S. government or industry. The goal of this hearing is to discuss methodologies to improve the failed attempts law enforcement have made since the mid-1990s in catching and prosecuting individuals and organizations who take nonviolent, illegal direct action to stop the destruction of the natural environment. I have no interest in this cause or this hearing. In fact, I consider it a farce.

Since 1997, the U.S. government has issued me seven grand jury subpoenas, raided my home and work twice, stealing hundreds of items of property, and, on many occasions, sent federal agents to follow and question me. After this effort, which has lasted nearly five years, federal agents have yet to obtain any information from me to aid their investigations. As I have never been charged with one crime related to these so-called ecoterrorist organizations or their activities, the constant harassment by the federal government constitutes a serious infringement on my Constitutional right to freedom of speech. This Congressional Subcommittee hearing appears to be no different, harassing and targeting me for simply voicing my ideological support for those involved in environmental protection.

I fully praise those individuals who take direct action, by any means necessary, to stop the destruction of the natural world and threats to all life. They are the heroes, risking their freedom and lives so that we as a species as well as all life forms can continue to exist on the planet. In a country so fixated on monetary wealth and power, these brave environmental advocates are engaging in some of the most selfless activities possible.

It is my sincere desire that organizations such as the Earth Liberation Front continue to grow and prosper in the United States. In fact, more organizations, using similar tactics and strategies, need to be established to directly focus on U.S. imperialism and the U.S. government itself. For, as long as the quest for monetary gain continues to be the predominant value within U.S. society, human, animal, and environmental exploitation, destruction, and murder will continue to be a reality. This drive for profits at any cost needs to be fiercely targeted, and those responsible for the massive injustices punished. If there is any real concern for justice, freedom, and, at least, a resemblance of a true democracy, this revolutionary ideal must become a reality.

All power to the people. Long live the earth liberation front. Long live the animal liberation front. Long live all the sparks attempting to ignite the revolution. Sooner or later the sparks *will* turn into a flame!

Press Release, September 3, 2002

The ELF Press Office received the following communique September 1, 2002:

The Earth Liberation Front is claiming responsibility for the 8/11/02 arson attack on the United States Forest Service Northeast Research Station in Irvine, Pennsylvania.

The laboratory was set ablaze during the early morning hours, causing over $700,000 damage, and destroying part of 70 years worth of research. This lesson in "prescribed fire" was a natural, necessary response to the threats posed to life in the Allegheny Forest by proposed timber sales, oil drilling, and greed driven manipulation of Nature.

This facility was strategically targeted, and if rebuilt, will be targeted again for complete destruction. Furthermore, all other U.S. Forest Service administration and research facilities, as well as all DCNR buildings nationwide should now be considered likely targets.

These agencies continue to ignore and mislead the public, at the bidding of their corporate masters, leaving us with no alternative to underground direct action. Their blatant disregard for the sanctity of life and its perfect Natural balance, indifference to strong public opposition, and the irrevocable acts of extreme violence they perpetrate against the Earth daily are all inexcusable, and will not be tolerated. If they persist in their crimes against life, they will be met with maximum retaliation.

In pursuance of justice, freedom, and equal consideration for all innocent life across the board, segments of this global revolutionary movement are no longer limiting their revolutionary potential by adhering to a flawed, inconsistent "non-violent" ideology. While innocent life will never be harmed in any action we undertake, where it is necessary, we will no longer hesitate to pick up the gun to implement justice, and provide the needed protection for our planet that decades of legal battles, pleading, protest, and economic sabotage have failed so drastically to achieve.

The diverse efforts of this revolutionary force cannot be contained, and will only continue to intensify as we are brought face to face with the oppressor in inevitable, violent confrontation. We will stand up and fight for our lives against this iniquitous civilization until its reign of TERROR is forced to an end—by any means necessary.

In defense of all life,
Pacific E.L.F.

Not in Our Name

As the United States prepared for war with Iraq in the winter of 2003, despite overwhelming popular support for the administration, a wave of dissent swept across the nation. One group, Not in Our Name, NION, circulated an antiwar petition on the Internet. A remarkable thing about the antiwar movement in 2003 was that a large minority of American citizens were opposed to a war that had not even begun. It took four years of fighting in Vietnam before the antiwar movement began to attract such numbers in the late 1960s.

The NION Statement of Conscience is the petition that was signed by more than 65,000 people. However, it had no effect on deterring the administration's decision to go to war.

STATEMENT OF CONSCIENCE, 2003

Let it not be said that people in the United States did nothing when their government declared a war without limit and instituted stark new measures of repression.

The signers of this statement call on the people of the U.S. to resist the policies and overall political direction that have emerged since September 11, 2001, and which pose grave dangers to the people of the world.

We believe that peoples and nations have the right to determine their own destiny, free from military coercion by great powers. We believe that all persons detained or prosecuted by the United States government should have the same

SOURCE: Retrieved on 5/4/2006 from www.nion.us/NION.HTM. Used by permission.

rights of due process. We believe that questioning, criticism, and dissent must be valued and protected. We understand that such rights and values are always contested and must be fought for.

We believe that people of conscience must take responsibility for what their own governments do—we must first of all oppose the injustice that is done in our own name. Thus we call on all Americans to RESIST the war and repression that has been loosed on the world by the Bush administration. It is unjust, immoral, and illegitimate. We choose to make common cause with the people of the world.

We too watched with shock the horrific events of September 11, 2001. We too mourned the thousands of innocent dead and shook our heads at the terrible scenes of carnage—even as we recalled similar scenes in Baghdad, Panama City, and, a generation ago, Vietnam. We too joined the anguished questioning of millions of Americans who asked why such a thing could happen.

But the mourning had barely begun, when the highest leaders of the land unleashed a spirit of revenge. They put out a simplistic script of "good vs. evil" that was taken up by a pliant and intimidated media. They told us that asking why these terrible events had happened verged on treason. There was to be no debate. There were by definition no valid political or moral questions. The only possible answer was to be war abroad and repression at home.

In our name, the Bush administration, with near unanimity from Congress, not only attacked Afghanistan but abrogated to itself and its allies the right to rain down military force anywhere and anytime. The brutal repercussions have been felt from the Philippines to Palestine, where Israeli tanks and bulldozers have left a terrible trail of death and destruction. The government has waged an all-out war on and occupied Iraq—a country which has no connection to the horror of September 11. What kind of world will this become if the U.S. government has a blank check to drop commandos, assassins, and bombs wherever it wants?

In our name, within the U.S., the government has created two classes of people: those to whom the basic rights of the U.S. legal system are at least promised, and those who now seem to have no rights at all. The government rounded up over 1,000 immigrants and detained them in secret and indefinitely. Hundreds have been deported and hundreds of others still languish today in prison. This smacks of the infamous concentration camps for Japanese-Americans in World War 2. For the first time in decades, immigration procedures single out certain nationalities for unequal treatment.

In our name, the government has brought down a pall of repression over society. The President's spokesperson warns people to "watch what they say." Dissident artists, intellectuals, and professors find their views distorted, attacked, and suppressed. The so-called Patriot Act—along with a host of similar measures on the state level—gives police sweeping new powers of search and seizure, supervised if at all by secret proceedings before secret courts.

In our name, the executive has steadily usurped the roles and functions of the other branches of government. Military tribunals with lax rules of evidence and no right to appeal to the regular courts are put in place by executive order. Groups are declared "terrorist" at the stroke of a presidential pen.

We must take the highest officers of the land seriously when they talk of a war that will last a generation and when they speak of a new domestic order. We are confronting a new openly imperial policy towards the world and a domestic policy that manufactures and manipulates fear to curtail rights.

There is a deadly trajectory to the events of the past months that must be seen for what it is and resisted. Too many times in history people have waited until it was too late to resist.

President Bush has declared: "you're either with us or against us." Here is our answer: We refuse to allow you to speak for all the American people. We will not give up our right to question. We will not hand over our consciences in return for a hollow promise of safety. We say NOT IN OUR NAME. We refuse to be party to these wars and we repudiate any inference that they are being waged in our name or for our welfare. We extend a hand to those around the world suffering from these policies; we will show our solidarity in word and deed.

We who sign this statement call on all Americans to join together to rise to this challenge. We applaud and support the questioning and protest now going on, even as we recognize the need for much, much more to actually stop this juggernaut. We draw inspiration from the Israeli reservists who, at great personal risk, declare "there IS a limit" and refuse to serve in the occupation of the West Bank and Gaza.

We also draw on the many examples of resistance and conscience from the past of the United States: from those who fought slavery with rebellions and the underground railroad, to those who defied the Vietnam war by refusing orders, resisting the draft, and standing in solidarity with resisters.

Let us not allow the watching world today to despair of our silence and our failure to act. Instead, let the world hear our pledge: we will resist the machinery of war and repression and rally others to do everything possible to stop it.

THE OVER 65,000 SIGNERS INCLUDE . . .

Robert Altman	Rev. Jesse Jackson
Edward Asner	Jim Jarmusch
Kevin Bacon	Spike Lee
Noam Chomsky	Toni Morrison
Deepak Chopra	Graham Nash
Jill Clayburgh	Claes Oldenburg
John Cusack	Yoko Ono
Angela Davis	Grace Paley
Ossie Davis	Bonnie Raitt
Mos Def	John Sayles
Ani Di Franco	Kyra Sedgwick
Diane DiPrima	Pete and Toshi Seeger
Steve Earle	Martin Sheen
Barbara Ehrenreich	Gloria Steinem

Daniel Ellsberg
Brian Eno
Fifty-three Maryknoll
priests and brothers
Jane Fonda
Tom Hayden

Oliver Stone
Gore Vidal
Alice Walker
Howard Zinn

(*partial list as of 4/15/03*)

Veterans Against the Iraq War

Of the many thousands of Vietnam veterans who were against the Vietnam War, many have resurfaced to oppose the Iraq War. A smaller number of Desert Storm veterans also came out strongly against the latest war.

Within weeks of the invasion, there were documented cases of soldiers resisting the war. Marine Corps Reservist Stephen Funk, for example, refused to serve and turned himself in to military authorities on April 1, 2003.

A nonpartisan group of U.S. veterans issued the Call to Conscience from Veterans to Active Duty Troops and Reservists, urging all current military personnel to examine their consciences and reevaluate their stance on war with Iraq. The other two selections reprinted here are from West Point graduate David Wiggins. Wiggins, a conscientious objector during the First Gulf War (Operation Desert Storm), is a physician who has been writing and publishing antiwar articles on the Internet aimed at the military. The first is an open letter asking troops to examine whose interests would be served by a war in Iraq; the second is his ruminations about defending freedom.

CALL TO CONSCIENCE FROM VETERANS TO ACTIVE DUTY TROOPS AND RESERVISTS, 2003

We are veterans of the United States armed forces. We stand with the majority of humanity, including millions in our own country, in opposition to the United States' all-out war on Iraq. We span many wars and eras, have many political views and we all agree that this war is wrong.

Many of us believed serving in the military was our duty, and our job was to defend this country. Our experiences in the military caused us to question much of what we were taught. Now we see our REAL duty is to encourage you as members of the U.S. armed forces to find out what you are being sent to fight

---

SOURCE: Retrieved on 5/4/2006 from www.calltoconscience.net/.

and die for and what the consequences of your actions will be for humanity. We call upon you, the active duty and reservists, to follow your conscience and do the right thing.

In the last Gulf War, as troops, we were ordered to murder from a safe distance. We destroyed much of Iraq from the air, killing hundreds of thousands, including civilians. We remember the road to Basra—the Highway of Death—where we were ordered to kill fleeing Iraqis. We bulldozed trenches, burying people alive. The use of depleted uranium weapons left the battlefields radioactive. Massive use of pesticides, experimental drugs, burning chemical weapons depots and oil fires combined to create a toxic cocktail affecting both the Iraqi people and Gulf War veterans today. One in four Gulf War veterans is disabled.

During the Vietnam War we were ordered to destroy Vietnam from the air and on the ground. At My Lai we massacred over 500 women, children and old men. This was not an aberration, it's how we fought the war. We used Agent Orange on the *enemy* and then experienced first hand its effects. We know what Post Traumatic Stress Disorder looks, feels and tastes like because the ghosts of over two million men, women and children still haunt our dreams. More of us took our own lives after returning home than died in battle.

If you choose to participate in the invasion of Iraq you will be part of an occupying army. Do you know what it is like to look into the eyes of a people that hate you to your core? You should think about what your "mission" really is. You are being sent to invade and occupy a people who, like you and me, are only trying to live their lives and raise their kids. They pose no threat to the United States even though they have a brutal dictator as their leader. Who is the U.S. to tell the Iraqi people how to run their country when many in the U.S. don't even believe their own President was legally elected?

Saddam is being vilified for gassing his own people and trying to develop weapons of mass destruction. However, when Saddam committed his worst crimes the U.S. was supporting him. This support included providing the means to produce chemical and biological weapons. Contrast this with the horrendous results of the U.S.-led economic sanctions. More than a million Iraqis, mainly children and infants, have died because of these sanctions. After having destroyed the entire infrastructure of their country including hospitals, electricity generators, and water treatment plants, the U.S. then, with the sanctions, stopped the import of goods, medicines, parts, and chemicals necessary to restore even the most basic necessities of life.

There is no honor in murder. This war is murder by another name. When, in an unjust war, an errant bomb dropped kills a mother and her child it is not "collateral damage," it is murder. When, in an unjust war, a child dies of dysentery because a bomb damaged a sewage treatment plant, it is not "destroying enemy infrastructure," it is murder. When, in an unjust war, a father dies of a heart attack because a bomb disrupted the phone lines so he could not call an ambulance, it is not "neutralizing command and control facilities," it is murder. When, in an unjust war, a thousand poor farmer conscripts die in a trench defending a town they have lived in their whole lives, it is not victory, it is murder.

There will be veterans leading protests against this war on Iraq and your participation in it. During the Vietnam War thousands in Vietnam and in the U.S. refused to follow orders. Many resisted and rebelled. Many became conscientious objectors and others went to prison rather than bear arms against the so-called enemy. During the last Gulf War many GIs resisted in various ways and for many different reasons. Many of us came out of these wars and joined with the antiwar movement.

If the people of the world are ever to be free, there must come a time when being a citizen of the world takes precedence over being the soldier of a nation. Now is that time. When orders come to ship out, your response will profoundly impact the lives of millions of people in the Middle East and here at home. Your response will help set the course of our future. You will have choices all along the way. Your commanders want you to obey. We urge you to think. We urge you to make your choices based on your conscience. If you choose to resist, we will support you and stand with you because we have come to understand that our REAL duty is to the people of the world and to our common future.

Message to the Troops: Resist!, October 11, 2002

Dear Soldier of the U.S. Military:

Considering the common practice of talking about "supporting the troops" in times of hostilities, I should let you know how I feel.

With all due respect, I want you to know that if you participate in this conflict, you are not serving me, and I don't support you. Speaking for myself, I feel those who participate will be damaging my reputation as an American, and further endangering me and my children by creating hatred that will someday be returned to us—perhaps someday soon. Your actions will not lead to a safer world, but a more dangerous world of pre-emption and unilateral decisions to commit mayhem. I don't support that.

This talk of "supporting the troops" is just another method our government uses to manipulate and control us. I don't support the troops, but I certainly fear for the lives of the troops. I would support the troops staying home. I regret that our so-called leaders have involved the troops in such a foolish, misguided undertaking. I would support the troops disobeying orders. I feel sorry for the troops' families. I would support the troops if they realized that the best way to defend their families would be to stay alive and healthy and resist this war.

The only people the troops are possibly serving are those who agree with this act of military aggression. Perhaps you are not even serving them if they end up suffering retribution for your actions.

Source: Retrieved on 3/10/2004 from www.strike-the-root.com/archive/wiggins.html.

Oh yes, and you are serving the President, of course—the man who avoided combat duty and deserted his National Guard unit. You are serving the man who enriched himself through crony capitalism, shady accounting practices and insider trading while running multiple corporations into bankruptcy. You will be serving the man who lost the popular vote for president, but was handed the presidency by a Supreme Court influenced by his father and through voting irregularities in a state governed by his brother. You will be serving the man who, as President, turned the budget surplus into a deficit and presided over the largest stock market decline since the great depression. You will be serving the man who unilaterally withdrew from the Anti-Ballistic Missile Treaty, ignored the Nuclear Non-Proliferation Treaty and rejected the International Criminal Court and Kyoto Protocol on Global Warming.

If you are involved in an invasion of Iraq, you will be faced with some difficult ethical decisions. Are the Iraqi foot soldiers really the guilty party here? Is it reasonable to expect them to refuse orders to defend themselves against an invading force (you)? Is this conflict really necessary at all? If not, why kill these people? If it is, are there other means our Commander-in-Chief and others are not exploring that might prevent you from having to kill these people and possibly civilians too, and possibly die yourself or contribute to your friend's death? I'm glad I don't have to make those decisions.

I feel for you and the difficult decisions you must make. I hope this note frees you of any sense of obligation to serve me you must feel, and helps you make a conscientious decision that you will be proud to accept complete responsibility for making. Please pass the sentiments I expressed in this letter on to your fellow soldiers.

David Wiggins

DEFENDING MY FREEDOM, MARCH 21, 2003

I am sitting here defending my freedom. By that, I mean exercising my freedom. By that, I mean opposing this naked aggression on Iraq. In agreement, freedom is moot. I revel in defiance because defiance makes me free. I defy this Government. I defy this President. I defy these soldiers. I defy; therefore I am free.

It has been said, "Give me liberty or give me death." We will all have death. The question remains; will I live in freedom or in fear? No soldier gives me the ability to think, the ability to express my thoughts, or the ability to act. A soldier may take my arms, my legs, my voice, or my life; but a soldier cannot take me. At best, a soldier is a baby's blanket for freedom that diminishes fear but offers no substantial protection. How can a soldier protect that which he does not possess? No soldier invading Iraq will make me free.

By what twisted logic do soldiers tell me they defend my freedom? First, soldiers "give up their freedom so that they may defend the freedom of others." This is impossible. By giving up their freedom, soldiers might be used to threaten freedom or to defend freedom. The soldiers follow orders in either case. Attacking and destroying a nation and killing its people "preemptively" on flimsy pretenses and unproven assertions is not defending my freedom.

By voluntarily giving up their own freedom, soldiers damage the cause of freedom for all. To defend freedom, soldiers should refuse to give up their freedom. Soldiers should obey their conscience without question, not their orders without question. Let us, without orders, try to convince the soldiers to leave their families and their lives to fly across an ocean for the purpose of attacking a people that has not attacked us and poses us no palpable threat. Let us, without half-truths, mistruths, propaganda and lies; convince the soldiers to do this. This would be freedom. This would be the end of soldiers and the end of war. This would be the end of the preemptive attack on Iraq.

Soldiers fly and sail and drive and march and intimidate and destroy and kill. In this way, it is said, they prevent others from causing me fear and harm. Perhaps this makes some feel safer, but those that need to feel safe to feel free are neither safe nor free. Defeating Iraq is but a distraction. Defeat your fears and you will be free.

Consider the soldiers' victims. Are they not encouraged to fly and sail and drive and march and intimidate and destroy and kill in response? Will not the sons and daughters and family and friends and countrymen and all the descendants of those killed, and crippled, and destitute, and diseased cry for revenge? How does this improve my safety? When was the war to end all wars? I must have missed it. This war in Iraq will certainly make me less safe for the rest of my life. I oppose this government that demands my money, and this President who uses it to violate the peace. I oppose this President who assaults those who have not assaulted me. I oppose this President who invades, bombs, kills, assassinates, destroys, and sows fear and death. For every action, there is an equal and opposite reaction. I oppose this President who, by his aggression invites aggression; who by his violence, invites violence; who by causing death, invites death. I declare my independence from this self-destructive system. I wash my hands of this invasion of Iraq.

Why should I rally behind the United States Commander in Chief? Because I am free, I resist. My conscience is my Commander in Chief. Peace, Truth, Justice and Freedom are my generals. This is my land, I was born here. I have no other land. The government of the United States of America, a co-inhabitant of this land, claims sovereignty over me. By claiming me as its own, it purports to make me free. This Government demands the results of my labor so that it might live and act. Though I do not give permission, though I resist, this government uses the fruits of my labor to send soldiers to destroy, to maim, and to kill in my name. By this, it purports to defend my freedom. If I resist, this government may follow me, eavesdrop on my conversations, and keep me under video surveillance, strip search me at airports, keep secret files on my past and present activities, and similarly treat my family and friends. If my peaceful expressions of my freedom make this Government insecure, or if I refuse its demands, this Government will send police and eventually soldiers to my door. Though I resist peacefully and am a danger to no person, though I seek only to act conscientiously and defend my freedom, this Government will place me in handcuffs and imprison me. If I resist, if I protest, this Government, this President, these soldiers promise "serious consequences" and will use "all necessary force" to subdue me. This Government, this President, these soldiers may force me to the ground, kick me and beat me with sticks until I am unconscious, or sodomize me with a broomstick. This Government, this President, these soldiers may shoot and kill me for demonstrating on campus, or they may pump poison gas into my house to choke me, and ignite it to burn me to death. This is how the Government of the United States, the President, and the soldiers defend my freedom. God Bless America.

The American Civil Liberties Union

The mission of the American Civil Liberties Union (ACLU), founded in 1920 during the Red Scare that followed the First World War, is to safeguard the Bill of Rights. Throughout the years, the nonpartisan ACLU has taken on many controversial issues on all sides of the political spectrum. The central concern for the ACLU, though, always comes down to whether it is guaranteed in the Bill of Rights. The ACLU has battled for the right of free speech for everyone, from antiwar protestors and civil rights demonstrators to the Ku Klux Klan.

In May 2003, the ACLU issued a report, Freedom Under Fire: Dissent in Post-9/11 America (a portion of which is here excerpted), detailing some of the civil liberties infractions that have occurred in the aftermath of the terrorist attacks. According to the ACLU, the government, in its efforts to create unanimity of opinion backing the decision to go to war with Iraq, is stifling free speech and dissent and is therefore overstepping its bounds.

FREEDOM UNDER FIRE: DISSENT IN POST-9/11 AMERICA, MAY 2003

INTRODUCTION

There is a pall over our country. In separate but related attempts to squelch dissent, the government has attacked the patriotism of its critics, police have barricaded and jailed protesters, and the New York Stock Exchange has revoked the press credentials of the most widely watched television network in the Arab world. A chilling message has gone out across America: Dissent if you must, but proceed at your own risk.

SOURCE: Retrieved on 8/11/2003 from www.aclu.org/SafeandFree/SafeandFree.cfm?ID= 12666&c=206, i–ii, 1–3, 5, 7, 10.

Government-sanctioned intolerance has even trickled into our private lives. People brandishing anti-war signs or slogans have been turned away from commuter trains in Seattle and suburban shopping malls in upstate New York. Cafeterias are serving "freedom fries." Country music stations stopped playing Dixie Chicks songs, and the Baseball Hall of Fame cancelled an event featuring "Bull Durham" stars Tim Robbins and Susan Sarandon, after they spoke out against the war on Iraq.

Compounding the offense is the silence from many lawmakers. There is palpable fear even in the halls of Congress of expressing an unpopular view.

Why should this disturb us? Because democracy is not a quiet business. Its lifeblood is the free and vibrant exchange of ideas. As *New York Times* columnist and author Thomas L. Friedman has pointed out, the war on terror is also a war of ideas. How are we going to convince holdouts in other countries about the importance of free speech and civil liberties if we show so little faith in our own?

With U.S. forces deployed overseas, and concerns about safety and freedom at home, we ought to be having as robust a debate as possible. . . .

Yes, some government officials, including local police, have come down hard on protesters, as this report makes clear. But in most of the cases that have come to light, protesters have stood firm. Lawsuits alleging excessive force, wrongful arrest and denial of due process have been filed on behalf of hundreds of protesters in New York and Washington alone. Undaunted by suspensions, arrests or other actions taken against them, a high school student in Michigan, a pair of college students in Iowa, a shopkeeper in Colorado and two grandmothers in Tampa are among those stepping forward to challenge those who would violate their First Amendment rights.

These democratic stirrings encourage us. We recall that although some of the greatest names in American liberalism (President Franklin D. Roosevelt and Supreme Court Justices Earl Warren and Hugo Black) supported the Japanese internments after Pearl Harbor, history has exonerated the people of good hearts and minds who opposed them.

Dissenters who take unpopular positions in their own times are often seen as heroes later on. We believe that when future generations look at what was done to our core freedoms and values after 9/11, the voices of dissent will stand out as the true defenders of democracy.

Anthony D. Romero
Executive Director, ACLU

FREEDOM UNDER FIRE: DISSENT IN POST-9/11 AMERICA

In the tense time following the Sept. 11, 2001, terrorist attacks on New York and Washington, Attorney General John Ashcroft mocked government critics and assailed their patriotism, calling their concerns "phantoms of lost liberty." And the American Civil Liberties Union shot back with a national ad campaign asserting our right to be "safe and free."

"The nation's highest ranking law enforcement officer is using his bully pulpit to shut down dissent and debate," ACLU Executive Director Anthony D. Romero charged, declaring that free and robust debate is the engine of social and political justice.

But Ashcroft's words were just the opening volley in a war of intimidation. White House spokesman Ari Fleischer also warned Americans to "watch what they say." Conservative commentators like Bill O'Reilly suggested prosecuting war protesters as "enemies of the state." Since 2001, hundreds have been arrested for exercising their constitutionally protected freedoms, and some have lost their jobs or been suspended from school. Many have called on the ACLU for assistance.

We need to stop and consider the direction in which we are going, for we are in danger of allowing ourselves to be governed by our fears rather than our values. We are not the first generation to face this challenge.

Since the administration of President John Adams, who feared that sympathy with the radical ideas of the French Revolution would throw America into upheaval, there have been attempts to silence dissent. The Alien Act of 1798, which gave Adams the power to deport any non-citizen he judged dangerous, was never enforced, but his Sedition Act was used to suppress freedom of the press. President Abraham Lincoln suspended the writ of habeas corpus during the Civil War. And President Woodrow Wilson used the Espionage Act of 1917 not to catch spies but to mount a full-scale assault on free speech.

Faced with strong domestic opposition to the First World War from citizens who believed he was less interested in "making the world safe for democracy" than in protecting the investments of the wealthy, Wilson encouraged "patriotic citizens" to report on neighbors they suspected of disloyalty. His Justice Department prosecuted more than 2,000 critics of the war and judges were quick to hand down harsh punishments. In 1918, Congress also enacted a Sedition Act, restricting criticism of the government, the Constitution, the flag and the military.

The decades that followed ushered in some of the most shameful chapters in American history: the World War II internments of Japanese Americans; the McCarthy hearings; the Pentagon Papers, Watergate and FBI spy scandals. All involved government restrictions on speech, the press and freedom of movement. All were popular at the time, and are now seen as abhorrent to the national interest. . . .

Dissent since 9/11 has taken three principal forms: mass protests and rallies, messages on signs or clothing, and other acts of defiance by communities and individuals. These have ranged from silent vigils in parks to the passage of resolutions by dozens of local governments protesting federal measures that threaten fundamental freedoms.

Some government officials, including local police, have gone to extraordinary lengths to squelch dissent wherever it has sprung up, drawing on a breathtaking array of tactics—from censorship and surveillance to detention, denial of due process and excessive force. Police have beaten and maced protesters in

Missouri, spied on law-abiding activists in Colorado and fired on demonstrators in California, and campus police have helped FBI agents to spy on professors and students in Massachusetts. Ashcroft's Justice Department has further asserted the right to seize protesters' assets and deport immigrants under anti-terrorism statutes rushed through Congress after the attacks, and debated whether to revoke U.S. citizenship in some cases....

MASS MOVEMENT IN WASHINGTON

In a class-action lawsuit filed March 27, 2003, the ACLU of the National Capital Area charged police with deliberately violating the constitutional rights of more than 400 peaceful anti-war demonstrators and bystanders by directing them into a police trap and then arresting them—though they had not violated any law.

"In this country, the government is not supposed to arrest you unless you break the law," said local ACLU Legal Director Arthur Spitzer. "But the evidence will show that the police deliberately rounded up hundreds of people who had not broken any law, many of whom were not even involved in the demonstration. No one in the neighborhood was safe from the lawless conduct of the D.C. police."

The arrests occurred on Sept. 27, 2002, in Pershing Park, two blocks from the White House. Arrestees were charged with failing to obey a police order—though no order to disperse was ever given; in fact, people who tried to leave were physically prevented from doing so, according to the ACLU complaint. One demonstrator suffered broken ribs after being knocked down by the police. The true purpose of the mass arrests, the ACLU contends, was to disrupt and prevent peaceful political demonstrations scheduled for that weekend....

DISTRESS SIGNAL AT GRINNELL

The Iowa Civil Liberties Union in December 2002 sued two police officers and a county attorney who threatened to arrest a pair of Grinnell College students for hanging a U.S. flag upside-down from their dormitory window. "People tell me it offends them to see the flag upside-down, but sometimes I tell them it offends me to see one right-side up," said Juan Diaz, 18, who with John Bohman hung the flag Sept. 26, 2002, as a sign of their "displeasure with the policies of the United States Government" toward Iraq.

Flag etiquette says that a flag should be flown upside-down only as a sign of distress. And after the lawsuit was filed in U.S. District Court in Des Moines, authorities agreed that hanging it upside-down was protected under the First Amendment. But officials defended other restrictions in their flag ordinance, which the suit says is unconstitutional in its entirety. The students also seek damages for willful violation of their speech rights.

"Police use this (flag etiquette) law for no other purpose than to silence government critics," ICLU executive director Ben Stone said, citing a 30-year-old

Iowa Supreme Court ruling (State v. Kool, 212 N. W. 2d 518 (Iowa 1973), that displaying an American flag upside-down was protected speech and could not be prosecuted. In 1989, the U.S. Supreme Court threw out the conviction of a protester who was arrested for actually burning a flag during a demonstration (Texas v. Johnson, 491 U.S. 397), declaring that the right of free speech protected symbolic use of the flag. . . .

PEACE OFFENSE IN NEW YORK

Oddly, a T-shirt promoting "Peace" brought out the cavalry at a mall in upstate Guilderland, N.Y., where Stephen Downs, a 61-year-old lawyer, was arrested for refusing to leave or remove a shirt he'd bought there. The New York Civil Liberties Union on March 11, 2003, wrote the operators of the Crossgates Mall after Downs was led away in handcuffs on a trespassing charge. "Give Peace a Chance," his shirt said on one side, and "Peace On Earth" on the other. Downs was accompanied by his 31-year-old son Roger, who also wore an anti-war T-shirt, but was allowed to leave after removing it.

The mall operators later asked the Guilderland Police Department to drop the trespassing charge but the news coverage made Downs a local hero and the NYCLU erected a billboard in protest near the entrance. "Welcome to the mall, you have the right to remain silent," it said. The security officer who called police was way out of line, NYCLU Executive Director Donna Lieberman said; decades earlier, at the height of the Vietnam War, the Supreme Court had even upheld the right of a protester (in *Cohen v. California*) to wear a jacket emblazoned with "Fuck the Draft" in a county courthouse.

"While the issue of free speech in shopping malls came to a head with Mr. Downs' arrest at Crossgates, it remains an issue at malls across the country," Lieberman said. "When, as here, the mall replaces Main Street as a center of commercial and social activity, the censorship of expression has a devastating effect on the freedom and diversity that is at the heart of a free society." . . .

FULL EXPOSURE IN FLORIDA

A U.S. District Court judge in West Palm Beach, Fla. prohibited officials from blocking a nude anti-war demonstration in a state park. The ACLU of Florida went to court on behalf of T. A. Wayner, a Fort Pierce naturist who planned to choreograph the creation of a peace symbol on Singer Island using nude bodies, and videographer George T. Simon, who planned to observe. Randall Marshall, legal director for the ACLU of Florida, said the intent was "not mere nudity, but political protest against the government's plans for war." For these demonstrators, he said, "nudity is an essential part of their political expression."

Judge Donald M. Middlebrook agreed, calling it "well within the ambit of the First Amendment." (He added that the state was free to put up signs notifying the public that the Feb. 14 demonstration would be taking place, or to erect screens around it.) . . .

MoveOn.org

By September 1998, Californians Joan Blades and Wes Boyd had had enough. They were exasperated that Congress was enmeshed in a political fight over the impeachment of President Bill Clinton while far more significant issues, like health care reform, were left to languish. As a result, Blades and Boyd set up an online petition to "Censure President Clinton and Move On to Pressing Issues Facing the Nation." Within days, thousands of people had signed up, and the MoveOn.org organization was born.

As a political action committee, MoveOn.org seeks to motivate all Americans to involve themselves in the political process, to overcome their apathy and take responsibility for forcing politicians to respond to the people's wishes. Like the 1960s organization Students for a Democratic Society, MoveOn.org advocates participatory democracy not only within the nation but within its own organizational structure. "Every member has a voice in choosing the direction for both MoveOn.org Political Action and MoveOn.org Civic Action." Every member is encouraged to propose tactics and strategies to influence elections and make politicians accountable. On its Web site MoveOn.org states that it "provides individuals, who normally have little political power, an opportunity to aggregate their contributions with others to gain a greater voice in the political process, and brings people together to take important stands on the most important issues facing our country."

After September 11, 2001, MoveOn.org, along with peace activist Eli Pariser, expanded its mission and began mounting a vigorous antiwar campaign. As the United States went to war against Iraq, MoveOn produced a documentary film, Uncovered: The Whole Truth About the Iraq War, which investigated convincing evidence that Saddam Hussein had not been stockpiling or producing weapons of mass destruction and that the Bush administration had knowingly "cherry picked" intelligence in order to convince the American people to back the decision to go to war. Truth, MoveOn.org claimed, was the first casualty of the war.

The organization continues to produce films and commercials aimed at informing and awakening Americans about the issues it feels are most pressing: campaign finance reform, ecological awareness, opposition to the repeal of the estate tax, and the effort to explore viable ways for America to overcome its addiction to oil. MoveOn also pushes for a more discerning and scrupulous media that will cease cheerleading for the administration and return to its original purpose of being the fourth branch of government whose duty it is to challenge, criticize, and prod public officials. In 2006, MoveOn's stated purpose is to continue conducting a drive to protect "the Supreme Court from a hard-right justice" and to go all-out in an effort "to *defeat the right wing and elect moderates and progressives in 2006. But in contrast to most PACs, which funnel industry contributions to candidates in exchange for access, MoveOn.org Political Action brings hundreds of thousands of small donors together to elect candidates who will represent the American people."*

In 2004, MoveOn published a book, MoveOn's 50 Ways to Love Your Country, *in which fifty members contributed personal vignettes on how they were working to effect change.*

Two of these vignettes are reprinted here.

The Many Faces of the Media, 2004

"READ MORE, WATCH TV NEWS LESS"

by Kate Cox, 27, Astoria, Queens, New York

My father is a journalist. He has written for the same newspaper for 30 years. The children in my family were bred with a healthy respect for freedom of the press, as well as freedom of speech and expression. My parents taught us to view every issue with a critical eye and to analyze any given situation for truthful content, not merely sentiment. I have taken those lessons with me into the workplace, the community, and the voting booth.

On September 11, 2001, my critical eye was tested. While the mass media have always bombarded us with images of human suffering and injustice, for me, this was different. This was my city on fire. These were my friends and neighbors running for their lives. Any amount of desensitization I might have developed in the past was shattered in an instant. Like many people in this country, I was glued to my television set for weeks on end, watching images of the attacks on the World Trade Center and the Pentagon play over and over, while commentators tried to make sense of the events for us. I went to bed every night with a deeper and deeper sense of foreboding about what our world was quickly evolving into.

In nightly phone conversations with my father, I ran down the list of things I'd heard and seen on television that day that I found sad or terrifying. The nation was entering a very scary time, and I was firmly in the grip of intense fear and anxiety. Each night as I ended the conversations with my father, he said, "Remember, read more than you watch." In daily emails, he also urged me to start the day with a newspaper, instead of the morning news programs. He told me that limiting myself to a half hour of coverage per night would help me sleep better. My father reminded me that we are all incredibly susceptible to images and pictures, especially those set to softly touching music. If we allow ourselves to take all of our information from the footage we see on the nightly news, we lose sight of the truth in any given situation. We lose our ability to relate. We become uninformed. He told me that pictures tell only part of the story.

My father was right. I started to read everything I could get my hands on, from newspapers and magazines to social and historical commentary. I read articles and essays written by theologians, teachers, and scientists. I became a subscriber to several publications to ensure that I would always have information first, before images. Each time I sat down to read, my critical eye became more able to focus. I found a sense of perspective and learned to put world events into a historical context. For every essay that said the world was ending, there was one that said it was being rebuilt.

I slowly began to sleep better. I began to feel I had power in a situation that had previously made me feel powerless. I read about opportunities for participation and service, and I started to see myself as a vessel of peace and a force for change.

I am still deeply moved by the images of profound suffering and injustice I see in every corner of the world. I am still brought to tears each time I see footage of the collapse of the World Trade Center. I have learned, however, always to read what's behind the picture. There, I find hope, truth, and details. For me, there is healing in those details. Information is power.

MoveOn Tips

In your search for information, include types of written material that you have not previously explored, such as published sermons, speeches, and essays.
Read material featuring viewpoints that differ from yours politically, spiritually, or emotionally. This will help you see all sides of an issue.
Limit your television viewing. Before tuning in, thoughtfully consider which programs will be most valuable to you in your personal search for information.

Kate Cox is an actress and co–artistic director of the not-for-profit theatre company This Woman's Work Theatre.

The Power of Connecting, 2004

"CREATE AN EFFECTIVE ONLINE PETITION"
by Dorothy Keeler, 51, Anchorage, Alaska

The wolves of Denali National Park were in danger, and we had to spread the word fast.

As wildlife photographers, my husband and I have worked with the Toklat wolves in Denali since 1990. The Toklat and Sanctuary wolves had been seen and enjoyed by tens of thousands of visitors each year inside the park. They were remarkably accepting of humans at close distances, making them unique among

Source: From MoveOn's *50 Ways to Love Your Country: How to Find Your Political Voice and Become a Catalyst for Change* (Inner Ocean Publishing: Makawao, Maui, 2004); "Read More, Watch TV News Less" was retrieved on 4/6/2006 from http://civic.moveon.org/book// media.html; and "Create an Effective Online Petition" was retrieved on 4/6/2006 from http:// civic.moveon.org/book//connecting.html.

wild wolves. However, during the winter, both packs would leave the safety of the park on hunting forays, where they were routinely trapped and killed. Near the park entrance, the entire Sanctuary pack was killed by trappers. The Toklat family dropped from a high of 18 members in the early 1990s to just 2 in 1998. Luckily, the 2 were an alpha male and alpha female, which are the leaders of the pack, who mated and had pups the next year. When the Sanctuary pack was killed off, a nearby group, the Margaret pack, moved into their territory.

In 2001, our friends at the Alaska Wildlife Alliance submitted a proposal to the Alaska Board of Game (the wildlife-policy decision maker) to create a no-kill "buffer zone" adjacent to the park, covering the areas the remaining packs were known to frequent. The Board of Game would decide the fate of the buffer zone at an upcoming meeting, and the hunting lobby was already using heavy-handed political pressure. Though more than 80 percent of Alaskans were wildlife viewers, the Board of Game was composed entirely of hunters and trappers, who were dead set against additional hunting restrictions.

Facing such odds, we had to show massive support for protecting the packs. With the Board of Game meeting just a week away, I created a simple website that included a summary of the issue and photos showing why the wolves deserved special protection. I then established a petition on www.thepetitionsite.com, asking signers to answer questions in order to personalize the petition.

With only a week's time, I had to jump-start the word-of-mouth process. First I sent the e-card to everyone in my address book. Then I sent it to the leaders of every environmental group I could find in Alaska. Next I wrote a short press release. Finally I composed a letter to the editor that summarized the issue and included the URL of the website, and I sent that to every newspaper in Alaska.

Almost 1,000 people signed our petition, from every state in the union and more than 36 countries. I called the local newsrooms to say I'd be wheeling boxes of signed petitions into the Board of Game meeting on a hand truck. We made the six o'clock news, and the petition helped convince the Board of Game to create the buffer zone. At the moment, the wolves are protected by the buffer zone, thanks in part to all those wonderful people who signed the petition. However, there are still pressures against wolves and the environment in Alaska, and we're standing by.

MoveOn Tips

Make a targeted website the center of your campaign. Make certain everything on the site relates to the action you want visitors to take.

Create a petition at www.thepetitionsite.com.

Spread your message through emails and electronic postcards, which are similar to the electronic birthday cards many people send online. Dorothy Keeler used http://mypostcards.com, a site that offers several postcard web hosting services, including a free service.

Write a letter to the editor that gives a reference to your website. This improves the odds that locals will sign the petition, and it saves the cost of buying an expensive ad.

Dorothy Keeler is a professional wildlife photographer/activist who lives with her husband, Leo. The Keelers have appeared on CBS News *in regard to their conservation efforts, and they're now moving their entire business to www.akwildlife.com so they'll have more time for activism.*

Michael Berg (1945–)

Nicholas Berg was a 26-year-old telecommunications contractor working in Iraq in April 2004 when he was kidnapped by Muntada al-Ansar, an Al Qaeda–linked terrorist group led by Jordanian Abu Musa'b al-Zarqawi. To the horror of millions of people worldwide, Nick's gruesome beheading on May 7th was videotaped and shown over the Internet. In the aftermath of the murder, the young man's father, Michael Berg, a retired schoolteacher and peace activist who had earlier opposed both the Vietnam War and the first Gulf War, began a nationwide campaign denouncing the Bush administration. Berg traveled the country leading protests, marches, and peace vigils calling for an end to the war in Iraq. In 2006, he campaigned as the Green Party candidate for the United States Congressional seat for the state of Delaware.

Shortly after his son's execution in May 2004, Michael Berg wrote the following article for the British newspaper The Guardian. *In 2005, he delivered a speech at Oklahoma City's St. Paul's Cathedral, marking the tenth anniversary of the Oklahoma City bombing. In both of these pieces, he expresses his feelings about the war in Iraq and the policies of the Bush administration in no uncertain terms.*

"GEORGE BUSH NEVER LOOKED INTO NICK'S EYES," MAY 21, 2004

My son, Nick, was my teacher and my hero. He was the kindest, gentlest man I know; no, the kindest, gentlest human being I have ever known. He quit the Boy Scouts of America because they wanted to teach him to fire a handgun. Nick, too, poured into me the strength I needed, and still need, to tell the world about him.

People ask me why I focus on putting the blame for my son's tragic and atrocious end on the Bush administration. They ask: "Don't you blame the five men who killed him?" I have answered that I blame them no more or less than

---

SOURCE: Retrieved on 2/28/2006 from http://www.guardian.co.uk/Iraq/Story/0,2763, 1221644,00.html.

the Bush administration, but I am wrong: I am sure, knowing my son, that somewhere during their association with him these men became aware of what an extraordinary man my son was. I take comfort that when they did the awful thing they did, they weren't quite as in to it as they might have been. I am sure that they came to admire him.

I am sure that the one who wielded the knife felt Nick's breath on his hand and knew that he had a real human being there. I am sure that the others looked into my son's eyes and got at least a glimmer of what the rest of the world sees. And I am sure that these murderers, for just a brief moment, did not like what they were doing.

George Bush never looked into my son's eyes. George Bush doesn't know my son, and he is the worse for it. George Bush, though a father himself, cannot feel my pain, or that of my family, or of the world that grieves for Nick, because he is a policymaker, and he doesn't have to bear the consequences of his acts. George Bush can see neither the heart of Nick nor that of the American people, let alone that of the Iraqi people his policies are killing daily.

Donald Rumsfeld said that he took responsibility for the sexual abuse of Iraqi prisoners. How could he take that responsibility when there was no consequence? Nick took the consequences.

Even more than those murderers who took my son's life, I can't stand those who sit and make policies to end lives and break the lives of the still living.

Nick was not in the military, but he had the discipline and dedication of a soldier. Nick Berg was in Iraq to help the people without any expectation of personal gain. He was only one man, but through his death he has become many. The truly unselfish spirit of giving your all to do what you know in your own heart is right even when you know it may be dangerous; this spirit has spread among the people who knew Nick, and that group has spread and is spreading all over the world.

So what were we to do when we in America were attacked on September 11, that infamous day? I say we should have done then what we never did before: stop speaking to the people we labelled our enemies and start listening to them. Stop giving preconditions to our peaceful coexistence on this small planet, and start honouring and respecting every human's need to live free and autonomously, to truly respect the sovereignty of every state. To stop making up rules by which others must live and then separate rules for ourselves.

George Bush's ineffective leadership is a weapon of mass destruction, and it has allowed a chain reaction of events that led to the unlawful detention of my son which immersed him in a world of escalated violence. Were it not for Nick's detention, I would have had him in my arms again. That detention held him in Iraq not only until the atrocities that led to the siege of Fallujah, but also the revelation of the atrocities committed in the jails in Iraq, in retaliation for which my son's wonderful life was put to an end.

My son's work still goes on. Where there was one peacemaker before, I now see and have heard from thousands of peacemakers. Nick was a man who acted on his beliefs. We, the people of this world, now need to act on our beliefs. We need to let the evildoers on both sides of the Atlantic know that we are fed up with war. We are fed up with the killing and bombing and maiming of innocent people. We are fed up with the lies. Yes, we are fed up with the suicide bombers, and with the failure of the Israelis and Palestinians to find a way to stop killing each other. We are fed up with negotiations and peace conferences that are entered into on both sides with preset conditions that preclude the outcome of peace. We want world peace now.

Many have offered to pray for Nick and my family. I appreciate their thoughts, but I ask them to include in their prayers a prayer for peace. And I ask them to do more than pray. I ask them to demand peace now.

Transcript of Oklahoma City Speech (Given at a Church), May 5, 2005

Whenever some tragedy befalls an American, or a group of Americans, I feel guilty for not hating those who are responsible for it. It seems like I'm being disloyal, that it's my patriotic duty as an American to hate America's enemies.

During the Vietnam War, I found it impossible to blame the people of either North Vietnam or South Vietnam for being host to a war between two giant military machines.

When airplanes struck the Twin Towers in New York City on Sept. 11, 2001, my high school students wanted to know why. I didn't tell them what I think most wanted to hear, that evil people from far away attacked us for no reason at all. Instead, I told them that communication broke down, or never was given a chance to exist, between two sides. And that when communication ceases, or fails to exist, violence begins.

I think at the very moment I heard of my son Nick's brutal death in Iraq last May, I at once thought of vengeance, and simultaneously thought that were I to wish for immediate and equal retribution against my son's killers, and feel justified in doing so, I would be in fact justifying his death, a retaliation for wrongs done by Americans in Iraq. And to that justification, I can never agree.

And what of their parents? Would I not then be justifying their vengeance against me?

I had a little more difficulty understanding the men who murdered so many innocent people here in Oklahoma ten years ago. But still, hating them, seeking vengeance against them, only seemed to keep the cycle of hate and escalated violence going.

In a course that I took at a nearby university to my house, in Immaculata, Pa., the course's title was "Forgiveness: the way to love in a wounded world."

In it, I learned that when we seek to even the score, we rarely do. Mostly what we do is a little more than even it, at least in the mind of the one who withstood

Source: Retrieved on 2/28/2006 from http://www.peacefultomorrows.org/article.php? id=544.

the evening. And so that person's response is to even the score against us. And so it goes.

Crusades, the Moorish invasion, Charlemagne, the western occupation of the Middle East, terrorism and 9/11, the holocaust, the disenfranchisement of the Palestinian people, a suicide bomber, a bulldozed house and a young woman standing in front of it.

Where does it all stop? When does it all stop? How do we stop it? We stop it by being first to stop.

So I have stopped blaming and getting even. I have come to realize that all human beings, no matter where they live, are basically the same in what they want, what they fear, and in that they love and laugh and cry, and they value their family and their community, in whatever terms they define them.

I have learned that the line between good and evil crosses not between groups of people or even between individual people, but it crosses through the heart of each individual. We all have free will and are responsible for our actions. And because we have free will, we are capable of good and evil.

The men who killed my son are capable of good. And I, were I exposed to what they were exposed to, would be capable of the same evil.

It's true that people react differently to the same circumstances, some with good and some with evil, but it remains that we all have the same capabilities. If we did not, then we would have built a fail-proof argument for the insanity plea: They had no choice.

The only thing that really matters is how I react, how you react.

So yes, I forgive the men who killed my son.

And I forgive George Bush, who stabilized Iraq, so they could enter and do their killing. And I forgive him for listening to the legal advice of Alberto Gonzales, who redefined torture. And forgiving Donald Rumsfeld the wink and the nod that torture is okay, on down the chain of command, until it reached the Abu Ghraib prison, and where it motivated retaliation against my son Nick.

And yes, I forgive Alberto Gonzales and Donald Rumsfeld, too.

Let me tell you what forgiveness does not mean to me.

It does not mean that I am not angry with all of those people that I just mentioned, whom I hold responsible for my son's death. I am angry at their actions, but not at them as human beings. And I suppose I will always be angry at their actions.

It does not mean that I do not wish for those responsible to feel and express their condition, their . . . heart sorrow, over what they have done.

And for them to be open to reconciliation.

That I want more than anything short of having my son back, and I always will.

And it does not mean that I do not still seek justice.

Up until last night, I would have said that for the men who killed my son I wanted separation from society.

But last night, I heard some things that have made me think. And maybe I've grown a little since then. I don't know. I'm still trying the ideas out.

But at least, restorative justice. At least I would like to see the man who wielded the knife spend the rest of his life working in a hospital, as Father Michael said, maybe with amputees, maybe helping them throughout the rest of their life.

And the American politicians who are responsible, I would like to see deprived of their power. And the American military and FBI who illegally detained my son and thrust him into a part of the war he was unaware of, they need to be corrected, too.

Now hear what I believe forgiveness does mean.

It means that I do not, when I forgive, desire to see harm—physical, psychological or emotional—come to any of these people.

It means that I restore them to the position in my life that they played before their evil acts. If I loved them then, then I still love them. If I valued their lives and well-being as human beings like myself, then I still value them.

And I learned that forgiveness is like quitting smoking cigarettes.

Sometimes, the evil gets to you, and you have to quit all over again.

Sometimes, you have to forgive over and over again.

I started out on my quest for forgiveness for two reasons. One was to confirm my lack of hatred for some of those responsible, and the other was to give up my hatred for those with whom it still haunted me.

I no longer feel guilty because I don't hate. And I am well on my way most days to giving up the hate that occasionally lingers.

I am a man of peace. I beseech others at every opportunity to be the same. I cannot accomplish my goal with hatred in my heart.

Peace is forgiveness. Forgiveness is peace. They both are love.

And love, I've learned, is the only hope of healing this wounded world.

Cindy Sheehan (1957–)

On April 4, 2004, U.S. Army Specialist Casey Austin Sheehan was killed by small arms fire and a rocket-propelled grenade in Iraq. Two months later, President George W. Bush met with parents of soldiers killed in Iraq and expressed his condolences to Casey's mother, Cindy Sheehan, saying, "Mom, I don't think I can understand your pain." Ms. Sheehan felt outraged at what she considered the President's blasé indifference and pledged that she would do everything she could to protest the war in Iraq. She cofounded Gold Star Families for Peace, an organization of families who lost a son or daughter in Iraq, dedicated to ending the war, and in August 2005, Sheehan led a vigil near President Bush's ranch in Crawford, Texas. Accompanied by a handful of antiwar activists, she vowed to camp out there until the President met with her to explain why her son was killed and why U.S. troops were still in Iraq even after the administration acknowledged that the rationale for the invasion, the weapons of mass destruction, was a pretense.

*When the President refused to meet with her, hundreds of antiwar
demonstrators went to Texas to join Sheehan's vigil. As the days went by,
more and more supporters showed up, and Cindy Sheehan became an
international cause celebre and the focus of media attention. "People are
dying every day for lies," Sheehan told one reporter. "The only way we can
support our troops at this point is to bring them home."*

*Sheehan wrote Not Worth My Son's Sacrifice shortly after her
appearance on a television show was preempted for a story about pop
singer Michael Jackson's sexual abuse trial; she wrote A Lie of Historic
Proportions during her vigil in Texas; and the third piece, Carly's Poem,
is a commentary on a poem her daughter composed a few days after
Casey's death.*

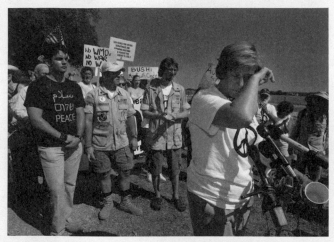

Cindy Sheehan.   Speaking to the press during her vigil in Crawford, Texas, on August 17, 2005.

Not Worth My Son's Sacrifice,
February 7, 2005

I was supposed to be on the *Larry King Live* show last week. I was asked to be on
the show to offer my opinion on the election in Iraq from the perspective of a
mom whose son was killed in the war prior to the elections. One of the questions I was going to be asked was: Do I think my son's sacrifice was "worth it?"
Well, I didn't get a chance to be on the show, because I was bumped for something that is really important: the Michael Jackson Trial.

If I had been allowed to go on *Larry King Live* last night and give my opinion about the elections and about my son's sacrifice, this is what I would have
told Mr. King and his viewers:

SOURCE: Retrieved on 2/28/2006 from http://www.gsfp.org/article.php?id=80.

My son, Specialist Casey Austin Sheehan (KIA, Sadr City, 04/04/04), enlisted in the Army to protect America and give something back to our country. He didn't enlist to be used and misused by a reckless Commander-in-Chief who sent his troops to preemptively attack and occupy a country that was no imminent threat (or any threat) to our country. Casey was sent to die in a war that was based on the imagination of some Neo-Cons who love to fill our lives with fear.

Casey didn't agree with the "Mission," but being the courageous and honorable man that he was, he knew he had to go to this mistake of a war to support his buddies. Casey also wondered aloud many times why precious troops and resources were being diverted from the real war on terror.

Casey was told that he would be welcomed to Iraq as a liberator with chocolates and rose petals strewn in front of his unarmored Humvee. He was in Iraq for two short weeks when the Shi'ite rebel "welcome wagon" welcomed him to Baghdad with bullets and RPG's, which took his young and beautiful life. I think my son's helmet and Viet Nam era flak jacket would have protected him better from the chocolates and flower petals.

Casey was killed after George Bush proclaimed "Mission Accomplished" on May 1, 2003—he was also killed after Saddam was captured in December of that same year. Casey was killed before the transfer of power in June of 2004 and before these elections. Four marines were tragically killed after the election. By my count, about five dozen Iraqis and coalition troops were killed on Election Day—is that the definition of "Catastrophic Success?" But is that a good day in Iraq? Hundreds of our young people and thousands of Iraqis have been needlessly and senselessly murdered since George Bush triumphantly announced an end to "major combat" almost 2 years ago now. All of the above events have been heralded by this administration as "turning points" in the "war on terror"—or as wonderful events in the "march of democracy." Really? I don't think, judging by very recent history, that the elections will stop the bloodshed and destruction.

I would have asked Mr. King if he would want to sacrifice one of his children for sham elections in Iraq. Would he or George Bush send their children to be killed, or maimed for life, for a series of lies, mistakes and miscalculations? Now that every lie has been exposed to the light for the invasion and occupation of Iraq—why are our sons and daughters still there? NOT ONE MORE DROP OF BLOOD SHOULD BE SPILLED FOR THIS PACK OF LIES.

This war was sold to the American people by a slimy leadership with a maniacal zeal and phony sincerity that would have impressed snake oil salesmen a century ago. The average American needs to hear from people who have been devastated by the arrogance and ignorance of an administration that doesn't even have the decency or compassion to sign our "death" letters.

In the interest of being "fair and balanced" (oops, wrong network), I would have been pitted against a parent who still agrees with the "Mission" and the President. Although I grieve for that parent's loss and I respect that parent's opinion, I would have defied Mr. King or that parent to explain the "Mission" to me. I don't think anyone can do it with a straight face. The President has also stated that we need to keep our troops in Iraq to honor our sacrifices by completing this elusive and ever-changing "Mission." My response to him is "Just because it is too late for Casey and the Sheehan family, why would we want another innocent life taken, in the name of this chameleon of a 'Mission'?"

Well, I was bumped from the show anyway. Now that Scott Peterson has been convicted and sentenced for his crimes and Laci and Connor's families have the justice they deserve, we have the new "trial of the century" to keep our minds off of the nasty and annoying fact that we are waging an immoral war in Iraq. We can fill our TV screens and homes with the glorified images of the Michael Jackson molestation trial. We can fill our lives with outrage over MJ's victims and hope they get justice, not even questioning the fact that George Bush, his dishonest cabinet, and their misguided policies aren't even brought to the court of public opinion. We won't have to confront ourselves with the fact that the leaders of our country and their lies are responsible for the deaths of 1438 brave Americans—tens of thousands of innocent Iraqis—and the loss of our Nation's credibility throughout the world. That might mean we would have to turn off our television sets and do something about it.

Oh yeah. In answer to the original question Larry: No it wasn't worth it!!

A Lie of Historic Proportions, August 8, 2005

Iraq has been the tragic Lie of Historic Proportions of Washington, DC, since before the first gulf war. For years, Saddam was one of our government's propped up and militarily supported puppets. Many people have seen the famous footage of Donald Rumsfeld shaking hands with Saddam. I suppose the two are smiling so big for the cameras because they are kindred spirits. After all of the hand-shaking and weapon brokering, when did Saddam become such a bad guy to Bush, Cheney, Halliburton and Co.? (Insert your favorite reason here).

During the Clinton regime, the US-UN led sanctions against Iraq and the weekly bombing raids killed tens of thousands of innocent people in Iraq. Many of them were children, but since one of her children didn't have to be sacrificed to the homicidal war machine, Madeline Albright thinks the slaughter during the "halcyon" Clinton years was "worth it." More lies.

Anyone with even a rudimentary understanding of current events understands that this invasion/occupation of Iraq was not about Saddam being a "bad guy." If that logic is used, then how many innocent Iraqi people have to die before the citizens of America wake up and know that our government is a "bad guy"? We also know that Iraq was not about WMD's. They weren't there and they weren't going to be there for at least a decade, by all reports. Another reason, so wispy and more difficult to disprove, is that America invaded Iraq to bring freedom and democracy to the Iraqi people. When one tries to dispute

SOURCE: Retrieved on 3/1/2006 from http://www.gsfp.org/article.php?id=43.

this particular deception, one is accused of being unpatriotic or hating freedom. Even though correct, the statement "Freedom isn't Free" is very insulting to me. False freedom is very expensive. Fake freedom costs over one billion of our tax dollars a week; phony freedom has cost the Iraqi people tens of thousands of innocent lives; fanciful freedom has meant the destruction of a country and its infrastructure. Tragically, this fabricated notion of freedom and democracy cost me far more than I was willing to pay: the life of my son, Casey. The Lie of Historic Proportions also cost me my peace of mind, I do not feel free and I do not feel like I live in a democracy.

One of the other great deceits that is being perpetuated on the American public and the world is that this occupation is to fight terrorism: If we don't fight terrorism in Iraq, then we will have to fight it "on our streets." In fact, terrorist attacks have skyrocketed in Iraq and all over the world. So much so that the State Department has stopped compiling the statistics and quit issuing the yearly terrorism report. I guess if one doesn't write a report, then terrorism doesn't exist? All of Casey's commendations say that he was killed in the "GWOT," the Global War on Terrorism. I agree with most of GWOT, except that Casey was killed in the Global War Of Terrorism waged on the world and its own citizens by the biggest terrorist outfit in the world: George and his destructive Neo-Con cabal.

The evidence is overwhelming, compelling, and alarming that George and his indecent bandits traitorously had intelligence fabricated to fit their goal of invading Iraq. The criminals foisted a Lie of Historic Proportions on the world. It was clear to many of us more aware people that George, Condi, Rummy, the two Dicks: Cheney and Perle, Wolfie, and most effectively and treacherously, Colin Powell, lied their brains out before the invasion. The world was even shown where the WMD'S were on the map. We were told that the "smoking gun" could come at any time in the form of a "mushroom cloud" or a cloud of toxic biological or chemical weapons. Does anyone remember duct tape and plastic sheeting?

Finally, the side of peace, truth, and justice has our own smoking gun and it is burning our hands. It is the so-called Downing Street Memo dated 23, July 2002 (almost 8 months before the invasion) that states that military action (against Iraq) is now seen as "inevitable." The memo further states that: "Bush wanted to remove Saddam through military action," justified by the conjunction of "terrorism and WMD's." The most damning thing to George in the memo is where the British intelligence officer who wrote the memo claims that the intelligence to base Great Britain and the US staging a devastating invasion on Iraq was being "fixed around the policy." Now, after over three years of relentless propaganda, it is difficult to distinguish the proven lies from the new "truth": that this occupation is bringing freedom and democracy to the people of Iraq.

Casey took an oath to protect the US from all enemies "foreign and domestic." He was sent to occupy and die in a foreign country that was no threat to the USA. However, the biggest threat to our safety, humanity, and our way of life in America [is] George and his cronies. Congress made a Mistake of Historic

Proportions and waived its Constitutional responsibility to declare war. It is time for the House to make up for that mistake and introduce Articles of Impeachment against the murderous thugs who have caused so much mindless mayhem. It is time for Congress to re-validate itself by holding a hearing about the Downing Street Memo. . . .

It is time to put partisan politics behind us to do what is correct for once and reclaim America's humanity. It is time for Congress and the American people to work together in peace and justice to rid our country of the stench of greed, hypocrisy, and unnecessary suffering that permeates our White House and our halls of Congress. It is time to hold someone accountable for the carnage and devastation that has been caused. As a matter of fact, it is past time, but it is not too late.

Cindy Sheehan
Mother of needlessly slain soldier, Casey Sheehan

CARLY'S POEM—A NATION ROCKED TO SLEEP, AUGUST 15, 2005

"A NATION ROCKED TO SLEEP"

by Carly Sheehan

Have you ever heard the sound of a mother screaming for her son?
The torrential rains of a mother's weeping will never be done
They call him a hero, you should be glad that he's one, but
Have you ever heard the sound of a mother screaming for her son?

Have you ever heard the sound of a father holding back his cries?
He must be brave because his boy died for another man's lies
The only grief he allows himself are long, deep sighs
Have you ever heard the sound of a father holding back his cries?

Have you ever heard the sound of taps played at your brother's grave?
They say that he died so that the flag will continue to wave
But I believe he died because they had oil to save
Have you ever heard the sound of taps played at your brother's grave?

Have you ever heard the sound of a nation being rocked to sleep?
The leaders want to keep you numb so the pain won't be so deep
But if we the people let them continue another mother will weep
Have you ever heard the sound of a nation being rocked to sleep?

SOURCE: Retrieved on 3/1/2006 from http://www.gsfp.org/article.php?id=44.

The sounds my daughter wrote about in her inspired poem, so poignantly and amazingly a few weeks after her brother, my son, was killed in Iraq, have been repeated over and over again too many times since the criminal invasion/occupation of Iraq began in March of 2003.

These sounds are imprinted in my DNA. I will never, ever forget the night of April 4, 2004, when I found out that Casey had been killed. After what seemed an eternity, I finally began to wonder who or what was making those horrible screaming noises. Then I realized it was me. It couldn't have been Casey's father, because he was paralyzed in stunned silence holding the pair of pants he had been folding when the deliverers of death news arrived.

I will also never forget the day when we buried my sweet boy, my oldest son. I'll never forget the playing of taps, or the violent, and in hindsight, thoughtless, volley of the 21-gun salute. If I live to be a very old lady and forget everything else, I will never forget when the general handed me the folded flag that had lain on Casey's coffin, as his brother and sisters, standing behind me, sobbed.

The saddest thing about the obscene sounds of violence is that they never should have been heard in the first place. From Maine to California, and from Baghdad to Falluja, these dirges were unnecessary. In my travels, and from hundreds of emails, phone calls, and cards and letters, I am discovering that people who formerly supported the invasion of Iraq are withdrawing their support. I even believe that many of our fellow citizens who still support the ignominy of Iraq are doing so because they are clinging to the deceptions so desperately, because they want the deceptions to so be the truth. It will be painful to come to terms with supporting the lies of this administration. It will be painful to know that wholesale killing of innocent people occurred because you and so many others believed the betrayals, but acknowledging the mistake is the first step to correcting it. And believe me, acknowledging the mistake is not as painful as hearing those devastating sounds.

Rep. Walter Jones (R-NC) has realized that he had been duped into supporting the invasion. I have spoken to him about his change of heart, and he is so sad that his wholehearted support of the administration helped cause so many good people to hear those gut-wrenching sounds of grief. But he is going forward to do what he can to end this occupation as soon as possible. He has co-sponsored a bipartisan bill (HRJ 55) with other Congressional leaders like Dennis Kucinich (D-OH) and Ron Paul (R-TX) to force our administration into a troop withdrawal beginning October 1, 2006. The bill is a good first step to ensuring that families here in America and all over the world do not have to suffer needless death in war. However, I would like the withdrawal to begin tomorrow, because I don't even want to try and imagine the sounds Casey heard before he died. I don't want to imagine the sound of the bullet strong enough to pierce the Kevlar coating on his helmet to rip through his skull. I don't want to know the sounds of a mother in Iraq wailing for her entire family. These sounds need to stop immediately. It is time to bring our troops home.

The sound I do want to hear is the sound of a Nation Waking Up. I will rejoice to hear the sounds of the collective Mea Culpa and the beating of breasts.

I want to hear the deafening clicks as the steady stream of news-o-tainment is turned off, propaganda that is turning us into zombies who are numb to the truth. I want to hear the sound of our children getting off planes and boats from Iraq to the joyful squealing of their children and the deep sighs of relief from their spouses, parents, and other loved ones. I want to hear our citizenry lifting up their voices in chorus and singing, "We will never let this happen again."

AUTHOR'S NOTE

If a man does not keep pace with his companions, perhaps it is because
he hears a different drummer. Let him step to the music which he hears,
however measured or far away.

—Henry David Thoreau

. . . .I'd like to make a promise and I'd like to make a vow
That when I've got something to say, sir, I'm gonna say it now.

—Phil Ochs

Between 1955 and 1975, the United States underwent a profound change: from a nation that (somewhat naively and arrogantly) believed in its own myths to a nation that (somewhat naively and angrily) began to question those very myths.

For some citizens the 1960s and the five years on either side of the decade were profoundly disturbing. For others they were a breath of fresh air. For everyone, no matter what their perspective, it seemed that protest and dissent had reached a high-water mark. But the years that brought the Montgomery bus boycott, the lunch counter sit-ins, the Freedom Rides, the March on Washington, the Berkeley Free Speech Movement, the March on the Pentagon, Woodstock, Altamont, and Kent State; the years that brought Allen Ginsberg, Malvina Reynolds, Joan Baez, Bob Dylan, Phil Ochs, Timothy Leary, Abbie Hoffman, Ella Baker, Malcolm X, Bobby Seale, Angela Davis, Betty Friedan, and Elizabeth Martinez; the years that brought SDS, AIM, NOW, and the GLF—those years were in no way an aberration; in no way were they contrary to American ideals and American principles. In fact, the political, cultural, and social upheavals of the 1960s were simply a culmination of the very spirit upon which this country was founded—the spirit of dissent.

All of a sudden, or so it seemed, Civil Rights activists, antiwar liberals, and songwriters took seriously the injunctions of John Locke and Thomas Jefferson that all men were endowed with unalienable natural rights. They took seriously the lesson taught to every primary school pupil that the United States was the greatest country in the world because it stood for the inherent equality of *all* people. And yet when these same pupils, growing into adolescence and young adulthood, saw televised images of soldiers of the 101st Airborne (one of the first divisions to parachute into Normandy on June 6, 1944) protecting black teenagers as they entered Little Rock Central High School in 1957, it suddenly dawned on many of them that the grand American values that they had been taught were simply not realized. It was this blatant discrepancy between ideal and reality that had a huge impact on the escalation of dissent in the sixties.

781

Between 1965 and 1967, while studying Puritanism as a graduate student at Michigan State University, I attended speeches by Martin Luther King Jr., Stokely Carmichael, Timothy Leary, and (of all people) the Führer of the American Nazi Party George Lincoln Rockwell, during their whirlwind visits to the campus. All four of these men, in their own way, dissented against the norms of American society and, to varying extents, the values of the "American way of life." Yet each man's convictions had historical antecedents. Martin Luther King adopted the words and ideas of Henry David Thoreau and Mahatma Gandhi, Reinhold Niebuhr and Walter Rauschenbusch, as well as the Bible and the Declaration of Independence, and applied them to America in the 1950s and 1960s. Stokely Carmichael took Marcus Garvey's expressions of "black power" and "black is beautiful" and applied them to the African American experience as the Civil Rights movement was entering a more cynical phase in the late 1960s. Timothy Leary harked back to the visionaries and mystics of India and Tibet, to European Romanticism, and to the psychedelic experiences of North American Indian shamanism. George Lincoln Rockwell repeated the anti-Semitic, xenophobic sentiments that have persisted in America ever since the founding of the Grand Order of the Star Spangled Banner and the Know-Nothing Party in the nineteenth century.

What I heard in those speeches at Michigan State University was nothing new. Those who espouse radical (or reactionary) revolutionary (or counterrevolutionary) ideas are carrying on a tradition that began during the earliest days of settlement in the New World. In fact, theirs is a tradition that originated even before the foundation of the permanent English colonies that would eventually become the United States. For four centuries, dissent has played a central role in the American experience.

ACKNOWLEDGMENTS

A number of my colleagues at Temple University graciously took time from their busy schedules to read and criticize portions of this book as it evolved. Gregory Urwin, Susan Klepp, Ruth Ost, James Hilty, Kenneth Kusmer, Richard Immerman, Vladislav Zubok, Herbert Ershkowitz, Howard Ohline, David Waldstreicher, and Liz Varon gave advice and pointed me in the direction of many important and neglected documents of dissent. Lively discussions with Beth Bailey, David Farber, Jay Lockenour, Arthur Schmidt, Howard Spodek, Kathy Walker, Barbara Day-Hickman, Phil Evanson, Bryant Simon, Petra Goedde, Drew Isenberg, Will Hitchcock, Peter Gran, David Watt, Wilbert Jenkins, and Craig Eisendrath helped hone my views about dissent.

Phyllis Cole of the Pennsylvania State University gave me important insights into the Transcendentalist movement. Barbara Winslow of Brooklyn College clarified many aspects of early feminism. David Wrobel of the University of Nevada, Las Vegas, was instrumental in my thinking about this book from its inception and his advice has greatly improved the finished product.

Homer Yasui graciously offered expert advice on the Japanese-American experience during World War II and furnished me with his brother Minoru's letters.

My students have, of course, influenced my thinking and my approach to dissent and protest. Justin Chapman, Julia Foley, Zachary Hanson-Hart, Evan Hoffman, Xandra Kanoff, Courtney Mendillo, Barbara Saba, Adam Squire, Regina Szeszniak, Stefanie Woolridge, and the rest of the students in Dissent in America are just a few of those I've taught over the years who have challenged me, inspired me, encouraged me, and made the classroom experience a sheer joy. Jonas Oesterle and Ismael Jimenez were especially helpful in expanding my insights into contemporary protest music.

Terry Halbert's close reading of the manuscript, enthusiasm for the project, and advice greatly added to whatever value this book has. Even while in Helsinki, she went through the manuscript with the proverbial fine-tooth comb, tearing it apart and putting it back together again.

Without Ashley Dodge, my original editor at Longman, this book would not exist. It was she who first recognized the importance of such a book and the significance of dissent in American history. Without her insights, assistance, challenging criticism, and valued friendship, this book would have never gotten off the ground. *Dissent in America* is as much Ashley's book as it is mine. Also at Longman I am indebted to Priscilla McGeehon for her confidence in me and to Michael Boezi and Stephanie Ricotta, who accomplished miracles in preparing this edition for publication.

Many others, in their own small way, have contributed to this project. Thanks to Rafe for his special Italian tuna salad, tiramisu, and total zest for life; Norbert for his Vega banjo and Dutch bicycle; Istvan for the story about that stormy night in Fairmount Park; the Radziwill clan of Dangast, Germany, for "adopting" me; Vlad for his special horseradish vodka; the Taubmans for the birthday cake on the banks of the Volga; Chris for being bothered enough to make all those telephone calls from Australia; Rachael for telling me to "go for it"; Tara Nevins for "No Place Like the Right Time"; Bruno et Marie-Camille for the fromage lessons; Annie for those quirky short stories; Tom for proving I really wasn't a computer Luddite; Sean for always caring for those who are in need; Cara for her choreographed Latin American geography lesson; Don for all those all-night Michigan talkathons; Peter for the never-ending supply of books and Jerry Garcia ties; Rich for the pesto and squash; Leif for his bullet-proof vest; Beverly and Clare for that fiddle session; Len and Veronika for taking me under their collective wing; Gudrun for the seventeenth of January; Riley and Musette for their meditation lessons; Ann and Jessie for questioning my sanity; and Allen Ginsberg for playing his harmonium and singing Blake's "Tyger, Tyger Burning Bright" to me in my VW that day we were stuck in a traffic jam in the shadow of the Walt Whitman Bridge.

Finally there is Patricia Rosemary Flavin, who is my inspiration, my muse, my love. From the moment we met, *she knew.* Her love and faith in me have given me more than I can ever express. This book is dedicated to her.

ABOUT THE DOCUMENTS

In tracing the theme of dissent as it weaves its way through the fabric of American history, the foremost difficulty is picking and choosing satisfactory samples that construct an accurate picture of American dissent. Many of the documents are influential groundbreaking sources of dissent. Paine's pamphlet, Garrison's editorial, Stanton's declaration, Thoreau's essay, and Martin Luther King's letter are all major documents that influenced the course of American history, and their authors were chief spokespersons for their cause. Also included in this book are lesser known documents that have had an impact on our country, such as the Native American speeches and petitions, Woolman's essay, Pringle's diary, the African American soldiers' letters to the editor, Schurz's speech, Bourne's essay, Yasui's letters, Smith's declaration, Reynolds' song, Weyrich's lament, and DiFranco's poem. Many of these people are unfamiliar to most contemporary Americans—indeed many of them were unknown to their own contemporaries—yet they spoke out eloquently about the issues and events of their day and are exemplars for all of us that even ordinary people have had an impact on history. Keep in mind that for every one of these documents, scores of others are accessible for anyone wishing to learn more about dissent and protest.

Some of the documents here are speeches, petitions, broadsides, posters, and songs that deal with various injustices. Others are interviews, articles, recollections, and memoirs of events by the people involved, in which they retell their experiences in jail or on a protest march, or simply their personal agonizing over how far to take their protest. Some of the documents were published at the time of the event; others were published years later. It is important with the early Native American documents to remember that many of the documents are speeches that were translated and transcribed by an English-speaking white Christian European who was not a neutral observer and therefore might not accurately reflect the sentiments of the speaker. Some of these transcriptions and memoirs were written years and even decades after the event and were therefore clouded by the passage of time.

It is my modest hope that this book serves to illustrate that dissent, in all its forms, has been a powerful and defining force throughout American history. Religious, political, cultural, and social dissenters have helped shaped the United States. There is little doubt that dissent will continue to have an impact on the direction this nation takes in the twenty-first century.

TEXT CREDITS

Page 450: From *The Collected Poems of Langston Hughes* by Langston Hughes. Copyright © 1994 by the Estate of Langston Hughes. Used by permission of Alfred A. Knopf, a division of Random House, Inc. and Harold Ober Associates Incorporated.

Page 475: "Pretty Boy Floyd" by Woody Guthrie. Copyright © 1958 (renewed) by Sanga Music, Inc. All rights reserved. Used by permission.

Page 476: "Jesus Christ," words and music by Woody Guthrie. TRO—© Copyright 1961 (renewed) 1963 (renewed) Ludlow Music, Inc., New York, NY. Used by permission.

Page 477: J. Saunders Redding, "The Meaning of World War Two for a Negro, 1942" from J. Saunders Redding, "A Negro Looks at This War," *American Mercury 55* (November 1942). Reprinted with permission.

Page 481: David Dellinger, from Larry Gara & Lenna Mae Gara, eds., *A Few Small Candles: War Resisters of World War II Tell Their Stories*. Published by Kent State University Press, 1999. Used with permission of The Kent State University Press.

Page 492: From John Tateishi and Roger Daniels, *And Justice for All*. Copyright © 1999 The University of Washington Press. Used with permission.

Page 495: From Minoru Yasui's letters, 1942 and 1943. Obtained from letters in Yuka Yasui Fujikura's Private Collection. Reprinted by permission.

Page 498: By Henry Miller, from *Remember to Remember*, copyright © 1961 (renewed) by Henry Miller. Reprinted by permission of New Directions Publishing Corp.

Page 538: Harry Hay, "Keynote Speech" at the Gay Spirit Visions Conference in Highlands, North Carolina, 1990. Copyright © by the estate of Harry Hay. Reprinted by permission of the estate of Harry Hay and Gay Spirit Visions (www.gayspiritvisions.org).

Page 543: Allen Ginsberg, "America" from *Collected Poems 1947–1980* by Allen Ginsberg. Copyright © 1956, 1959 by Allen Ginsberg. Reprinted by permission of HarperCollins Publishers Inc.

Page 547: "I Ain't Scared of Your Jail" by Lester Cobb. Copyright 1963 (renewed) by Sanga Music, Inc. All rights reserved. Used by permission.

Page 547: Pete Seeger, "If You Miss Me at the Back of the Bus" by Carver Neblett. Copyright © 1963 (renewed) by Sanga Music, Inc. All rights reserved. Used by permission.

Page 548: "Only a Pawn in Their Game" by Bob Dylan. Copyright © 1963 by Warner Bros, Inc. Copyright renewed 1991 by Special Rider Music. All rights reserved. International copyright secured. Reprinted by permission.

Page 550: Copyright 1963 Martin Luther King Jr., "Letter From a Birmingham Jail," copyright renewed 1991 Coretta Scott King. Reprinted by arrangement with the Estate of Martin Luther King Jr., c/o Writers House as agent for the proprietor New York, NY.

Page 564: Fanny Lou Hamer, "Testimony" from the records of the Democratic National Committee, Series II, Box 102 , Folder: DNC Credentials 1964—Mississippi Credentials Committee, Atlantic City, NJ, August 22, 1964. Used by permission.

Page 566: From Malcolm X, *Two Speeches by Malcolm X*. Copyright © 1965, 1990 by Betty Shabazz and Pathfinder Press. Reprinted by permission.

Page 568: Stokely Carmichael, "Berkeley Speech," October 1966. Used by permission of the Foundation Kwame Ture, Inc.

Page 578: The Black Panther Party, "Platform and Program of The Black Panther Party," October 1966 by Bobby Seale and Huey Newton. Reprinted with permission.

Page 585: Betty Friedan, "The Problem That Has No Name" from *The Feminine Mystique*. Copyright © 1983, 1974, 1973, 1963 by Betty Friedan. Used by permission of W. W. Norton and Company, Inc. and Victor Gollancz, a division of The Orion Publishing Group.

Page 590: "I Ain't Marchin' Anymore" by Phil Ochs. Copyright © 1964, renewed 1992 Barricade Music Inc. All rights administered by Almo Music Corp./ASCAP. All rights reserved. Used by permission.

Page 712: Ralph Nader, "It's Time to End Corporate Welfare as We Know It, 1996," reprinted in Ralph Nader, *The Ralph Nader Reader* (New York: Seven Stories Press, 2000), copyright © 2000 Seven Stories Press. Originally from *Earth Island Journal*, Fall 1996. Used by permission.

Page 715: Green Party Platform, 2000 from http://www.gp.org. Reprinted by permission.

Page 719: Michael Moore, Introduction from pages xi–xx, from *Stupid White Men . . . and Other Sorry Excuses for the State of the Nation*. Copyright © 2002 by Michael Moore. Reprinted by permission of HarperCollins Publishers.

Page 726: Ani DiFranco, "self evident," 2001 from http://www.righteousbabe.com/ ani/l_self_evident. html. Used by permission.

Page 731: "Know Your Enemy," (Zack de la Rocha, Tom Morello, Tim Commerford, Brad Wilk), copyright © 1992 Retribution Music. Reprinted by permission.

Page 733: "Mathematics," Words and Music by Dante Beze and Christopher Martin. Copyright © 1999 EMI Blackwood Music Inc., Empire International, Medina Sound Music, EMI April Music Inc. and Gifted Pearl Music. All rights for Empire International and Medina Sound Music controlled and administered by EMI Blackwood Music Inc. All rights for Gifted Pearl Music controlled and administered by EMI April Music Inc. All rights reserved. International copyright secured. Used by permission.

Page 735: "New World Water," Words and Music by Dante Smith and Lester Fernandez. Copyright © 1999 EMI Blackwood Music Inc., Empire International, Medina Sound Music and Psycho Les Publishing. All rights for Empire International and Medina Sound Music controlled and administered by EMI Blackwood Music Inc. All rights reserved. International copyright secured. Used by permission.

Page 737: "Son of a Bush" written by Carlton Ridehour, Kavon Shah & Lord Aswod. Copyright © 2002. Published by Terrordome Music Publishing LLC. (BMI) and Taqiyyah Music (BMI), administered by Reach Global Songs (BMI). Used by permission. All rights reserved.

Page 739: Song lyrics from Immortal Technique, "The 4th Branch," *Revolutionary*, Vol. 2, Viper Records, 2003. Reprinted by permission.

Page 741: Steve Earle, "Rich Man's War" from *The Revolution Starts Now*, Artemis Records, 2004. Reprinted by permission.

Page 742: "USA: Amnesty International Concerns Regarding Post-September 11 Detentions in the USA", An Amnesty International Report, March 14, 2002. Copyright © Amnesty International. Reprinted by permission.

Page 746: Earth Liberation Front, "Written Testimony Supplied to The U.S. House Subcommittee on Forests and Forests Health for the February 12, 2002 Hearing on 'Ecoterrorism,'" from North American Earth Liberation Front Press Office. Used by permission.

Page 751: Earth Liberation Front Press Office sample press release, Sept. 2002 from http://www.earthliberationfront.com. Used by permission.

Page 752: Not In Our Name, "Statement of Conscience" from www.nion.us. Used by permission.

Page 755: Veterans Call to Conscience, "Call to Conscience from Veterans to Active Duty Troops and Reservists: Statement to the Troops." Used with permission.

Page 757: David Wiggins, "Message to the Troops: Resist!" October 11, 2002 and "Defending My Freedom," March 21, 2003. Used by permission.

Page 760: From "Freedom Under Fire: Dissent in Post-9/11 America" report by the American Civil Liberties Union, May 2003. Used by permission.

Page 766: From *50 Ways to Love Your Country: How to Find Your Political Voice and Become a Catalyst for Change* published by Inner Ocean Publishing: Makawao, Maui, 2004. Reprinted by permission.

Page 769: Michael Berg, "George Bush Never Looked into Nick's Eyes," May 21, 2004. Reprinted with permission.

Page 771: Michael Berg, "Transcript of Oklahoma City Speech" (given at St. Paul's Cathedral, Oklahoma City, OK) on May 5, 2005. Reprinted with permission.

Page 774: Cindy Sheehan "Not Worth My Son's Sacrifice," Feb. 7, 2005. Reprinted by permission of the author.

Page 776: Cindy Sheehan "A Lie of Historic Proportions," August 8, 2005. Reprinted by permission.

Page 778: Carly Sheehan "Carly's Poem—A Nation Rocked to Sleep," Aug. 15, 2005. Reprinted by permission.

PHOTO CREDITS

Page 1: Anne Hutchinson, photograph courtesy of Bettmann/Corbis.

Page 28: Bacon's Rebellion, photograph courtesy of Bettmann/Corbis.

Page 51: Boston Massacre, photograph courtesy of Bettmann/Corbis.

Page 80: Abigail Adams, photograph courtesy of Bettmann/Corbis.

Page 107: Judith Sargent Murray, photograph courtesy of Terra Foundation for American Art, Chicago/Art Resource, NY.

Page 129: Henry David Thoreau, photograph courtesy of Thoreau Society at the Thoreau Institute.

Page 135: Chief John Ross, photograph courtesy of Corbis.

Page 187: Margaret Fuller, photograph courtesy of Bettmann/Corbis.

Page 192: Lowell Mill Girls, photograph courtesy of American Textile History Museum, Lowell, Massachusetts.

Page 204: Sojourner Truth, photograph courtesy of Bettmann/Corbis.

Page 235: New York Draft Riots, photograph courtesy of The Granger Collection.

Page 278: African American Soldiers, photograph courtesy of the State Archives of Florida.

Page 290: Frederick Douglass, photograph courtesy of Bettmann/Corbis.

Page 313: The Five Anarchists, photograph courtesy of Corbis.

Page 324: Indian Delegation to Washington, photograph courtesy of Bettmann/Corbis.

Page 383: Emma Goldman, photograph courtesy of Bettmann/Corbis.

Page 397: Women Demanding Right to Vote, photograph courtesy of Bettmann/Corbis.

Page 436: Margaret Sanger, photograph courtesy of Bettmann/Corbis.

Page 444: H. L. Mencken, photograph courtesy of Bettmann/Corbis.

Page 451: Father Charles Coughlin, photograph courtesy of Bettmann/Corbis.

Page 473: Woody Guthrie, photograph courtesy of Bettmann/Corbis.

Page 491: Fred Korematsu, Minoru Yasui, and Gordon Hirabayashi, photograph courtesy of Bettmann/Corbis.

Page 513: Young Civil Rights Demonstrator, photograph courtesy of National Archives and Records Administration, Records of the U.S. Information Agency.

Page 529: Paul Robeson, photograph courtesy of Bettmann/Corbis.

Page 542: Allen Ginsberg, photograph courtesy of Associated Press.

Page 551: Martin Luther King Jr., photograph courtesy of Bettmann/Corbis.

Page 597: March on the Pentagon, photograph courtesy of Bettmann/Corbis.

Page 612: National Guard Troops and Antiwar Demonstrators, photograph courtesy of Bettmann/Corbis.

Page 669: Julia Butterfly Hill, photograph courtesy of Associated Press.

Page 680: Act Up Protest, photograph courtesy of Greg Smith/Corbis.

Page 707: Theodore Kaczynski, photograph courtesy of Seanna O'Sullivan/Corbis Sygma.

Page 726: March for Women's Lives, photograph courtesy of Krista Kennell/Zuma/Corbis.

Page 774: Cindy Sheehan, photograph courtesy of Jason Reed/Reuters/Corbis.

INDEX

Contributors to the readings in this book are indicated in bold.

A

Abbey, Edward, 674–677, 709
Abzug, Bella, 649
ACT UP, 679–686
Adams, Abigail, 79–83, 397
Adams, John, 79–83, 173, 304, 762
Adams, Samuel, 59–64
Addams, Jane, 316, 332–334, 360
African American Civil War Soldiers, 237, 277–289, 784
Alien and Sedition Acts, 53, 117–120, 537
American Anti-Slavery Society, 131, 151, 296
American Civil Liberties Union (ACLU), 483, 702, 760–764
American Colonization Society, 53, 127
American Equal Rights Association, 295–298
American Indian Movement, 603, 660–668
American Woman's Suffrage Association, 237
Amnesty International, 742–745
Anonymous Slaves, 33–34, 95–96
Anthony, Susan B., xxi, xxii, 198, 237, 296–305
Apess, William, 153–158
Arkansas Peace Society, The, 250–258
Atiwaneto, 42–43

B

Bacon, Nathaniel, 27–30
Bacon's Rebellion, 4, 27–30
Baez, Joan, 589, 605, 781
Bagley, Sarah, 192–194
Baker, Ella, 518, 781
Beatles, 600, 637
Benezet, Anthony, 53
Berg, Michael, 769–773
Bern, Dan, 731
Berrigan, Father Daniel, 600
Black Panther Party, 577–579

Blackwell, Henry B., 228–229
Blanchard, I.G., 317, 319–321
Boston Massacre, 51, 52, 60, 83
Boston Tea Party, 52, 64, 83, 748
Bourne, Randolph, 398, 416–429, 498, 784
Brant, Joseph, 96–98
Brooke Farm, 131
Brown, John, xxiii, 132, 141, 231–233, 355
Brown, Joseph E., 258–265
Brownlow, William, 245–250
Bryan, William Jennings, 363–369, 445, 447
Burroughs, John, 675
Burroughs, William, 517, 542

C

Carmichael, Stokely, 518, 567–577, 782
Carnegie, Andrew, 313, 314, 315, 360, 384
Carson, Rachel, 675
Chávez, César, 603, 656–660
Chisholm, Shirley, 649
Christian Coalition of America, xxii
Coffin, William Sloane, 600
Copperheads, 236, 239
Coughlin, Father Charles, xxiii, 400, 450–455
Crazy Horse, 238
Creedence Clearwater Revival, 638, 643

D

Dass, Ram (Richard Alpert), xxii, 601, 618, 631–637
Davis, Angela, 754, 781
Davis, Jefferson, 236, 245, 259
Debs, Eugene V., 391, 398, 410–416, 482, 483, 503, 535
Declaration of Independence, 72, 84, 86–95, 131, 152, 198, 208, 211, 283, 299, 329, 363, 366, 367, 458, 561, 562, 782
Def, Mos, 731, 733–737, 754
Dellinger, David, 481–490

DiFranco, Ani, 725–730, 731, 784
Dillon, Ernest, 694–695
Doors, The, 601, 637
Douglass, Frederick, xxii, 141, 205–211, 289–294, 296, 297, 348, 355, 535, 572
Dred Scott Decision, 132, 245
Dubois, Sylvia, 137–141
DuBois, W.E.B., 315, 342, 344–355, 432
Dyer, Mary, 4, 21–27
Dyer, William, 21–27
Dylan, Bob, 473, 474, 543, 546, 548–549, 589, 590, 592–596, 600, 612, 637, 781

E
Earle, Steve, 731, 741–742, 754
Earth First!, 676, 709–711, 745
Earth Liberation Front, 670, 745–752
Elliott, Robert B., 305–312
Emerson, Ralph Waldo, 176–187, 212

F
Falwell, Jerry, xxii
Fanon, Franz, 569, 580
Firestone, Shulamith, 644
Fogerty, John, 643
Free Blacks of Philadelphia, 127–128
Frelinghuysen, Theodore, 132–135
Friedan, Betty, 518, 585–589, 643, 649, 781
Fugitive Slave Law, 132, 177, 185–186, 247, 298,
Fugs, The, 601
Fuller, Margaret, 176, 187–191

G
Gandhi, Mohandas K., 212–213, 481, 482, 549, 656, 659, 681, 782
Garangula, 35–37
Garrison, William Lloyd, 131, 141, 150–153, 161, 205, 212, 231, 232, 355, 784
Garvey, Marcus, 399, 431–434, 568, 782
Gay Liberation Documents, 694–703
Gay Liberation Front, 603, 654
George III, 52, 77, 96
Ginsberg, Allen, xxii, 517, 542–545, 617, 781, 783
Goldman, Emma, xxiii, 383–390, 398, 410, 434, 464–473
Gomez, Letitia, 700–703
Grateful Dead, The, 601
Green Party, 672, 711–712, 715–718, 769

Greenpeace, 670, 675
Griffiths, Hannah, 64–65
Grimké, Angelina, 161–169, 188, 189, 350
Grimké, Sarah, 161–162, 169–172, 350
Guthrie, Arlo, 601
Guthrie, Woody, 473–477, 537, 589, 594

H
Haber, Robert, 580
Hamer, Fannie Lou, xxii, 563–565
Hartford Convention, 125–127
Hay, Harry, xxii, 537–542
Hayden, Tom, 580, 755
Haymarket, 313, 314, 333, 358, 384
Haywood, "Big Bill", 398, 402
Hendrix, Jimi, 601
Henry VIII, 2–3
Hill, Joe (Joe Hillstrom), 398, 401–404
Hill, Julia Butterfly, 669, 670
Hirabayashi, Gordon, 490, 491
Hoffman, Abbie, 627–631, 781
Hughes, Langston, 449–450
Hutchinson, Anne, xxiii, 1, 4, 12–17, 21
Hutchinson, Thomas, 83–94

I
Immortal Technique, 731, 739–741

J
Jackson, Andrew, 125, 131, 135, 136, 158, 242, 244, 287, 288, 293, 306
James, William, 360
Jefferson Airplane, 601, 637
Jefferson, Thomas, 52, 53, 103, 117–120, 147–149, 495, 502, 549, 558, 561, 607, 630, 715, 746, 781
Jeffrey, Sharon, 580
Jones, Jesse, 317, 319–321
Jones, Mother Mary Harris, xxii, 369–374
Joplin, Janis, 601
Joseph, Chief (Nez Percé), 321–324

K
Kaczynski, Theodore (The Unabomber), 672, 706–711
Kennedy, John F., 430, 518–519, 550, 575, 597, 599, 600, 606, 609, 610, 613
Kennedy, Robert F., 570, 574, 602, 612, 656
Kerouac, Jack, 517, 542, 543
Kerry, John, 614–617
Killbuck, John, 58–59

King, Jr., Martin Luther, xxi, xxiii, 213, 316, 345, 390, 430, 517–518, 546, 549–563, 564, 566, 568, 576, 577, 602, 612, 656, 681, 700, 782, 784
Know Nothings, The (American Party), xxiii, 229–231
Korematsu, Fred, 490, 491

L
Laborers of Boston, 158–161
Ladies of Edenton, 64, 66
LaFollette, Robert M., 398, 404–410
Lawson, John Howard, 515, 519–524
Leary, Timothy, xxii, 543, 601, 617–624, 631, 781, 782
Lease, Mary Elizabeth, 324–328
Lenni Lenape Indians, 40–42
Lennon, John, 637
Liberator, The, 131, 141, 151–153, 161, 167
Limbaugh, Rush, 672
Lincoln, Abraham, 212, 235–236, 239, 277, 398, 549, 558, 762
Locke, John, 45, 52, 61, 549, 781
Long, Huey, 400, 455–464
Lovejoy, Elijah P., 141, 172–176
Lowell Mill Girls, 159, 192–197
Luther, Martin, 1–3, 180, 219

M
Madison, James, 117–120, 124, 125
Malcolm X, 518, 566–567, 781
Marcuse, Herbert, 580, 624–627, 644
Martinez, Elizabeth, 781
Mashpee Indians, 43–44
Mason, George, 104–106
McDonald, Country Joe, 637, 638, 639–641
McDonald, Nancy, 697–699
McGillivray, Alexander, 98–100
McKean, Aldyn, 681–683
McVeigh, Timothy, xxii, 672, 703, 724
Mencken, H.L., 443–449, 675, 719
Mexican War, xxii, 131, 212, 213, 265
Michigan Militia, 672, 703–706
Miller, Daniel, 695–697
Miller, Henry, xxii, 497–511
Missouri Compromise, 130, 132, 231
Moore, Michael, 718–725
Morrison, Jim, 637
Mothers of Invention, The, 601, 637
Mott, Lucretia, 197–198, 297, 397
MoveOn.org, 765–769

Muckrakers, 317
Muir, John, 374–383, 675
Murray, Judith Sargent, 106–115

N
Nader, Ralph, 672, 711–718
Nat Turner's Rebellion, 131, 141, 347, 355
National Organization for Women, 585
National Woman's Suffrage Association, 237
Neblett, Carter, 547–548
New England Anti-Slavery Society, 151
New Harmony, 131
New York Draft Riots, 235, 236
Newton, Huey, 577
Niebuhr, Reinhold, 483, 549, 553, 782
Not in Our Name, 752–755

O
Ochs, Phil, 546, 589–591, 601, 781
Oglesby, Carl, 606–611
Oneida Community, 131

P
Paine, Thomas, 72–79, 305, 503, 607, 615, 784
Parker, Theodore, 212
Paterson, Jeff, 686–693
Paul, Alice, 397–398, 643, 748
Penn, William, 5, 40
People's Party, The (Populist Party), 315, 324, 328–332, 335
Phillips, Wendell, 172–176, 305, 355
Powderly, Terence, 314, 317–319
Powhatan, 34–35
Pringle, Cyrus, 237, 265–277, 784
Public Enemy, 731, 737–739

Q
Quakers (Society of Friends), 5, 21–27, 30–33, 53, 141, 151, 161, 237, 265–277, 299, 398, 481, 483, 503, 533, 575

R
Rage Against the Machine, 731–733
Randolph, A. Philip, 400, 429–431, 432
Rauschenbusch, Walter, xxii, 316, 390–391, 549, 782
Redding, J. Saunders, 477–479
Redstockings, 643–646
Reynolds, Malvina, 590, 591–592, 781, 784

Robertson, Pat, xxiii
Robeson, Paul, 515, 529–537
Rockefeller, John D., 313, 314
Rockwell, George Lincoln, 782
Rolling Stones, The, 601
Rosebraugh, Craig, 745–751
Ross, John, 135–137
Ross, Robert, 580
Runaway Women, 48–50
Russo, Vito, 680, 683–686

S
Sainte-Marie, Buffy, 638, 641–642
Sanger, Margaret, xxii, 18, 398, 410,
    434–443
Sauguaarum, Loron, 38–40
Savio, Mario, 604–605
Schurz, Carl, 360–363, 784
S.C.U.M. (Society for Cutting Up Men),
    646–648
Seale, Bobby, 577, 781
Second Continental Congress, 67–72, 79
Seeger, Pete, 473, 474, 515, 537, 546, 547,
    589, 591, 601, 637–639, 670, 754
Seneca Falls, 197–203, 205, 206, 397
Shays, Daniel, 53, 103–104
Shays's Rebellion, 53, 103–104
Sheehan, Carly, 774, 778
Sheehan, Cindy, 773–780
Simon and Garfunkel, 637
Sinclair, Upton, 317, 711
Sitting Bull, 238
Smith, Margaret Chase, xxiii, 515,
    525–529, 784
Socialist Party, 370, 391–396, 398, 401,
    410–416, 430, 431, 435, 443, 472, 674
Solanas, Valerie, 646–648
Sons of Liberty, 51, 52, 60
Spencer, Herbert, 314, 316, 390
Spock, Dr. Benjamin, 597
"Spot Resolution", 212
Stanton, Elizabeth Cady, xxii, 197–203,
    237, 296, 297, 298, 397, 784
Steinem, Gloria, 549–654, 754
Stewart, Jon, 719
Stone, Lucy, 198, 228–229, 237
Stonewall, 538, 539, 540, 654–655
Stowe, Harriet Beecher, 132
Students for a Democratic Society, 518,
    580–584, 600, 602, 606, 612, 644,
    765, 781

Stung Serpent, 37–38
Sumner, Charles, 132
Sumner, William Graham, 314, 316, 390

T
Tecumseh, 120–124
Thoreau, Henry David, 129, 176, 187,
    211–228, 265, 502, 549, 551, 675,
    781, 782, 784
Tilly, Alice, 18–21
Trail of Tears, 131, 133, 135, 136, 662
Truth, Sojourner, 204–205
Twain, Mark, 360

U
Uncle Tom's Cabin, 132
United Indian Nations, 100–103, 120

V
Vallandigham, Clement L., 236, 238–245
Veterans Against the Iraq War, 755–760

W
Walker, David, 141–150, 348,
Ward, Lester Frank, 316
Washington, Booker T., 341–353, 356, 431
Washington, George, 52, 81, 115, 120,
    129, 183, 188, 216, 219, 244,
    246–248, 288, 317, 369, 533
Watts, Alan, 601, 617, 620
**Weather Underground, The (The
    Weathermen)**, 602, 612–614
Wells-Barnett, Ida B., 316, 342, 355–360
Weyrich, Paul, 677–679, 784
Wiggins, David, 686, 755, 757–760
Willard, Frances E., xxii, 316, 334–341
Williams, Roger, 4, 5–11
Willis, Ellen, 644
Wilson, Charles F., 477, 479–480
Wilson, Phill, 699–700
Winthrop, John, 4, 5, 12, 18
W.I.T.C.H. (Women's International
    Terrorist Conspiracy from Hell), 644
Wollstonecraft, Mary, 106
Woolman, John, 53–58, 784

Y
Yasui, Minoru, 490–497, 784

Z
Zenger, John Peter, 44–48
Zion Presbyterian Church, 294–295